고1 — 영어

기출의
바이블

Bible of English

특별
부록

기출 EXTRACT

1강 글의 목적 파악

01

- [ ] professor 교수
- [ ] chemistry 화학
- [ ] fair 박람회
- [ ] encourage 장려하다
- [ ] experiment 실험
- [ ] recommend 추천하다
- [ ] department 부서, 학과
- [ ] participant 참가자
- [ ] experience 경험

02

- [ ] travel agency 여행사
- [ ] customer 고객
- [ ] reality 현실
- [ ] include 포함하다
- [ ] meditation 명상
- [ ] relax 쉬다
- [ ] provide 제공하다
- [ ] experienced 숙련된
- [ ] instructor 강사
- [ ] book 예약하다
- [ ] reasonable 합리적인
- [ ] unforgettable 잊지 못할, 잊을 수 없는
- [ ] detail 세부 사항

03

- [ ] concern ~에 관계하다
- [ ] resident 거주자
- [ ] recently 최근에
- [ ] observe 보고 알다, 목격하다
- [ ] repair 수리; 수리하다
- [ ] equipment 설비
- [ ] damage 손상시키다, 훼손하다
- [ ] fall off 떨어져 나가다
- [ ] facility 시설
- [ ] terrible 형편없는
- [ ] appreciate 감사하다
- [ ] immediate 즉각적인
- [ ] matter 문제

04

- [ ] loyal 충실한, 충성스러운
- [ ] essential 필수적인
- [ ] develop 개발하다
- [ ] innovative 혁신적인, 획기적인
- [ ] contribute 기여하다
- [ ] major 주요한, 중대한
- [ ] client 고객
- [ ] voluntarily 자발적으로
- [ ] request 요청하다
- [ ] raise 인상하다
- [ ] reflect 반영하다
- [ ] performance 실적, 성과
- [ ] industry 산업, ~업

05

- [ ] guardian 보호자
- [ ] hold 열다, 개최하다
- [ ] sweets 사탕
- [ ] crisp 포테이토 칩
- [ ] request 요청하다
- [ ] prepared 조리된
- [ ] sealed 밀봉된
- [ ] packet 꾸러미
- [ ] ingredient 성분
- [ ] list 목록을 작성하다
- [ ] pack 포장하다
- [ ] contain 포함하다
- [ ] nut 견과류
- [ ] severe 심각한
- [ ] support 지원
- [ ] cooperation 협조
- [ ] headteacher 교장

06

- [ ] return 돌아오다
- [ ] lap 무릎
- [ ] floor 바닥
- [ ] take off ~을 떼어내다
- [ ] inside 안쪽, 내부
- [ ] appreciate 감사히 여기다

07

- [ ] choir 합창단
- [ ] announce 알리다, 발표하다

□ compete 겨루다, 경쟁하다
□ international 국제적인
□ competition 대회, 경쟁
□ participate in ~에 참가하다
□ necessary 필요한
□ fund 자금, 기금
□ support 후원하다; 후원
□ fundraising 모금
□ passion 열정

08

□ president 회장
□ increase 늘리다, 증가시키다
□ aim 목표
□ news media 언론 매체
□ printed newspaper 인쇄 신문
□ access 이용하다, 접근하다
□ humble 겸허한, 겸손한
□ appreciate 고마워하다
□ grant (허가 등을) 주다, 부여하다
□ permission 허락

09

□ be honored 영광스럽다
□ be delighted to ~하게 되어 기쁘다
□ annual 일 년마다의
□ offer 제공하다
□ showcase 소개하다, 전시하다
□ gifted 재능 있는
□ grateful 고마워하는, 감사한
□ occasion 행사, 때
□ celebration 기념[축하] 행사

10

□ PR director 홍보부 이사(= Public Relations)
□ corporation 기업
□ identity 정체성
□ launch 새로 시작하다
□ celebrate 축하하다
□ anniversary 기념일
□ request A to B A가 B할 것을 요청[의뢰]하다
□ suit 잘 맞다
□ inspire 고무하다, 영감을 주다
□ humanity 인류(애)
□ convey 전달하다, 알리다

□ capture 포착하다
□ value 가치
□ proposal 제안서

11

□ successfully 성공적으로
□ raise (자금 등을) 모으다
□ remodel 리모델링하다, 개축하다
□ local 지역의
□ builder 건축업자
□ volunteer 자원하다
□ assistance 도움, 지원
□ grab 쥐다
□ donate 기부[기증]하다
□ construction 공사

12

□ scenic 경치 좋은
□ proposed 제안된
□ walking trail 산책길, 산책로
□ wildlife 야생 동물
□ face 직면하다, 맞닥뜨리다
□ pressure 압력
□ access 접근하다; 접근
□ appreciate 감상하다
□ destroy 파괴하다
□ habitat 서식지
□ excess 지나친, 과잉의
□ reconsider 재고하다

2강 심경, 분위기 파악

01

□ definitely 확실히, 틀림없이
□ persuade 설득하다
□ pinned 꼼짝 못하는
□ deceptively 믿을 수 없게도
□ handhold (손으로) 잡을 수 있는 부분
□ clumsily 서투르게
□ cliff 절벽
□ reach 손이 닿는 거리
□ tremble 떨리다
□ exhaustion 극도의 피로
□ fright 공포

□ tie 묶다

02

□ midnight 자정
□ nowhere 어디에도 ~없다
□ nearby 근처의, 가까이에
□ approach 다가가다
□ familiar 친숙한, 익숙한
□ disappear 사라지다

03

□ grizzly bear 회색곰
□ habitat 서식지
□ sniff 코를 킁킁거리다
□ realize 깨닫다
□ giant 거대한
□ freeze 얼어붙다, 등골이 오싹하다
□ experience 경험
□ issue 문제
□ survival 생존
□ motivation 동기

04

□ mute 소리를 줄이다, 무음으로 하다
□ disconnect 접속을 끊다, 연결을 끊다
□ comfortable 편안한
□ immediately 즉시, 즉각
□ injured 다친, 부상을 입은
□ seat 앉히다
□ concerned 걱정하는
□ recover 회복되다
□ surgery 수술
□ rush 급히 움직이다

05

□ submission 제출
□ deadline 마감 시간
□ article 기사
□ typewriter 타자기
□ work 작동하다
□ lever 레버
□ strike 두드리다
□ desperately 필사적으로
□ rest 놓다
□ lap 무릎

□ manage (무기 · 도구를) 잘 쓰다[사용하다]
□ paper clip 클립, 종이 집게
□ press 누르다
□ pull 당기다
□ smoothly 매끄럽게
□ breathe 숨을 내쉬다

06

□ quickly 서둘러, 빨리
□ swing 그네
□ explain 설명하다
□ slide 미끄럼틀
□ available 이용 가능한
□ broken 부서진
□ sink 내려앉다, 가라앉다

07

□ principal 교장
□ academic 학업의
□ placing 순위
□ row 열, 줄
□ finalist 최종 후보, 결선 진출자
□ sweaty 땀에 젖은
□ glance 힐끗 보다
□ uneasy 불안한
□ rank 평가하다, 순위를 매기다
□ confidence 자신감
□ declare 공표하다
□ applause 박수갈채

08

□ absolutely 완전히
□ thrilled 신이 난, 흥분한
□ communicate 소통하다
□ daydream 공상하다
□ cool 멋진
□ hand 건네다
□ hide 숨기다
□ inside 안에

09

□ awaken 잠에서 깨다; 깨우다
□ glance 힐끗 쳐다보다
□ instant 순간, 아주 짧은 동안
□ wonder 궁금해하다

□ rub 문지르다
□ assure 안심시키다
□ rhythmic 규칙적으로 순환하는, 리드미컬한
□ scratchy 긁는 듯한 소리가 나는
□ lie 누워 있다, 눕다(-lay-lain)

10
□ used 사용된
□ awe 경외심
□ throw away 던지다, 버리다
□ stop 말리다, 멈추다
□ reply 응답하다
□ at a loss 어쩔 줄을 모르는
□ still 가만히

11
□ notice 알아차리다
□ neighbor 이웃
□ joyfully 기쁘게
□ playmate 놀이 친구
□ nearly 거의
□ drop 떨어뜨리다
□ pray 기도하다

12
□ leash (개 등을 매어 두는) 가죽 끈
□ fur 털
□ adorable 귀여운, 사랑스러운
□ tail 꼬리
□ get out of ~ 밖으로 나가다
□ backyard 뒤뜰
□ for hours 몇 시간 동안
□ exhausted 기진맥진한
□ grief 슬픔, 비애
□ loss 상실, 잃음

3강 필자의 주장 파악

01
□ overhear 우연히 듣다
□ priority 우선순위
□ principle (도덕적) 원칙, 원리
□ behavior 행동
□ tempting 유혹적인, 구미가 당기는

□ uphold 수호하다, 옹호하다
□ compassion 연민
□ concern 걱정
□ self-discipline 자기 훈련, 자제력

02
□ sensible 현명한, 분별 있는, 합리적인
□ separate 분리된, 별도의
□ distraction 주의 산만, 정신이 흐트러짐
□ missing 없어진, 빠진[누락된], 실종된
□ to-do list 해야 할 일 목록
□ multiple 많은, 다수의
□ organize 정리하다
□ matter 중요하다
□ professional 직업의, 전문적인
□ divide 나누다

03
□ maintain 유지하다
□ constant 일정한
□ attention 주의 (집중)
□ throughout 내내
□ characterise 특징짓다(= characterize)
□ peak 정점, 최고조
□ valley 저점, 골짜기
□ demanding 힘든, 부담이 큰
□ observe 관찰하다
□ note 알아차리다, 주의하다

04
□ launch 시작하다, 착수하다
□ product 생산물, 상품, 제품
□ mind 정신, 마음
□ promote 홍보하다
□ strictly 엄격하게
□ shamelessly 뻔뻔스럽게, 부끄러움 없이
□ give ~ away ~을 그냥 주다
□ entertaining 재미있는, 즐거움을 주는

05
□ expert 전문가
□ adequately 적절하게
□ elaborate (더) 자세히 말[설명]하다, 상술하다
□ equipped with ~을 갖춘
□ distract (마음·주의 등을) 흩뜨리다

WORD EXTRACT

☐ crucial 중요한

06
☐ encourage 촉진하다, 장려하다
☐ participant 참석자
☐ consider 여기다, 고려하다
☐ unproductive 비생산적인
☐ participate 참석하다, 참여하다

07
☐ instructor 교관
☐ inspect 검사하다
☐ task 일, 과업
☐ require 요구하다
☐ perfection 완벽
☐ ridiculous 우스꽝스러운
☐ prove 증명하다
☐ accomplish 성취하다, 해내다
☐ pride 자존감
☐ encourage 장려하다, 용기를 주다
☐ complete 완료하다
☐ turn into ~로 변하다

08
☐ estimate 추정하다
☐ nonverbal 비언어적인
☐ make a difference 변화를 가져오다
☐ significant 상당한
☐ initial 처음의
☐ empowering 힘을 주는
☐ climate 분위기

09
☐ remind 상기시키다
☐ a point of view 관점
☐ argument 주장
☐ involved 몰입한, 몰두한
☐ committed 열성적인, 헌신적인
☐ insight 통찰, 간파
☐ expose 드러내다, 노출하다
☐ passivity 수동성, 소극성

10
☐ avoid 피하다
☐ discomfort 불편(함)

☐ extra 추가의
☐ shut out 차단하다
☐ instinct 본능
☐ essential 필수적인
☐ comfort 안락, 편안
☐ formula 공식, 방식

11
☐ publishing house 출판사
☐ end up 결국 ~이 되다
☐ misspelling 틀린 철자
☐ comment 지적, 비판
☐ obvious 명백한
☐ matter 중요하다, 문제되다
☐ attractive 매력적인
☐ command 명령
☐ document 문서, 서류

12
☐ distracted (정신이) 산만해진
☐ seek 찾다, 얻다(-sought-sought)
☐ distraction 집중에 방해가 되는 것
☐ tackle 맞붙다, 대결하다
☐ ensure 보장하다

4강 밑줄 함의 추론

01
☐ no doubt 틀림없이 (~일 것이다)
☐ pressure waves 압력파
☐ similarly 비슷하게, 마찬가지로
☐ perceive 감지하다, 인지하다
☐ understand 이해하다(-understood-understood)
☐ intended 의도된, 계획된
☐ audience 청중, 관객
☐ restate 재진술하다, 다시 이야기하다
☐ complete 완성된

02
☐ post-purchase 구매 후
☐ influence 영향력
☐ likelihood 가능성
☐ repurchase 재구매하다
☐ determine 알아내다, 밝히다

□ encourage 장려하다, 권장하다
□ satisfied 만족한
□ unpaid 무급의, 무보수의
□ ambassador 대사
□ to-do list 할 일 목록
□ continually 계속해서
□ avoid 피하다
□ negative 부정적인
□ word-of-mouth 구두의, 입소문의

03

□ adopt 받아들이다, 채택하다
□ livelihood 생계 수단
□ progress 발전, 전진
□ remove 없애다
□ produce 생산하다, 제작하다
□ physical 육체의, 신체의
□ pain 고통, 통증
□ disability 장애
□ disease 질환, 질병
□ mass 대중(의)
□ education 교육
□ train 훈련시키다
□ avoid 피하다
□ seek 찾다, 구하다
□ divorce 단절, 이혼
□ stress 부담, 긴장
□ indeed 실제로, 참으로
□ risk 위험 (요소)

04

□ reveal 드러내다
□ assumption 전제, 추정, 상정
□ phrase 구절, 관용구
□ accomplish 성취하다
□ tear 눈물
□ achievement 업적, 성취한 것
□ earn 얻다
□ imply 넌지시 나타내다
□ obtain 얻다
□ means 수단, 방법
□ criticism 비판, 비난
□ inevitably 필연적으로, 반드시
□ challenge 이의를 제기하다
□ sacred 신성시되는

□ pause (잠시) 멈추다
□ valuable 소중한, 귀중한
□ effort 노력, 수고

05

□ customer 고객
□ return 반품하다, 돌리다
□ broken 고장 난
□ fixture 설비(물)
□ replacement 대체품
□ maintain 유지하다
□ relation 관계
□ warranty (품질 · 안정성 등의) 보증(서)
□ undamaged 멀쩡한, 완전한
□ abuse 남용하다
□ entrepreneur 기업가
□ own 소유하다
□ e-commerce 전자 상거래
□ fire 해고하다
□ resolve 해결하다
□ complaint 불만
□ dissatisfy 불만을 느끼게 하다
□ reason 비결, 이유, 동기

06

□ psychology 심리학
□ raise 들어 올리다
□ management 관리
□ principle 원칙
□ absolute 절대적인
□ matter 중요하다
□ severe 심각한
□ agreement 동의
□ sign 신호

07

□ job search 구직 활동
□ passive 수동적인
□ browse 대강 훑어보다
□ effective 효과적인
□ claim 주장하다
□ purpose 목적
□ direct 직접적인
□ focused 집중하는
□ rest 나머지

WORD EXTRACT

☐ herd 무리
☐ proactive 상황을 앞서서 주도하는
☐ logically 논리적으로
☐ occasional 가끔의
☐ resume 이력서
☐ sheep 양, 어리석은 사람

08

☐ fossil fuel 화석 연료
☐ agricultural 농업의
☐ rainforest 열대 우림
☐ excessive 과도한, 지나친
☐ drive ~하게 만들다, 몰아가다
☐ industrial 산업의
☐ consumption 소비
☐ sum 합계하다
☐ drill (드릴로) 구멍을 뚫다
☐ incentive 동기, 유인
☐ crude oil 원유
☐ slap (손바닥으로) 철썩 때리기

09

☐ by nature 본래부터
☐ anthropologist 인류학자
☐ analyze 해석하다, 분석하다
☐ matter 상황, 문제
☐ relative 상대적인
☐ emphasize 강조하다
☐ sort 분류하다
☐ systematic 체계적인
☐ classify 분류하다
☐ eliminate 제거하다

10

☐ tendency 경향
☐ interpret 해석하다
☐ selectively 선택적으로
☐ stack 쌓다
☐ viewpoint 관점
☐ perception 지각, 인식
☐ stand out 두드러지다, 눈에 띄다
☐ expectation 기대, 예상
☐ current 현재의
☐ quote 인용(문)
☐ highlight 강조하다

☐ phenomenon 현상

11

☐ reaction 반응
☐ disappointment 실망
☐ impress 인상을 남기다
☐ entirely 전적으로
☐ approach 접근법
☐ pay-off 보상, 이득
☐ significant 중요한
☐ virtual 가상의, 허상의
☐ work out ~을 해결하다

12

☐ lack 부족
☐ issue 문제
☐ organization 조직
☐ pop 튀어나오다
☐ competitor 경쟁자
☐ distribution 유통, 배분
☐ truthfulness 진실성
☐ forum 포럼, 토론회
☐ instantly 즉시, 즉각

5강 요지 추론

01

☐ negotiate 협상하다
☐ realise 인식하다, 알고 있다
☐ traditional 전통적인
☐ approach 접근법
☐ win-win 모두에게 이익이 되는
☐ agreement 합의
☐ old-school 옛 방식의, 구식의
☐ one-off 일회성의
☐ transaction 거래
☐ increasingly 더욱 더
☐ rare 드문, 희귀한
☐ repeatedly 반복해서, 거듭
☐ spouse 배우자

☐ essential 필수적인
☐ successful 성공적인
☐ maintain 유지하다
☐ relationship 관계
☐ interdependent 상호 의존적인
☐ outcome 결과
☐ acceptable 받아들일 수 있는

02

☐ repetitive 반복적인
☐ pursue 추구하다
☐ purpose 목적
☐ leisure 여가
☐ consumer 소비자
☐ value-added 부가 가치의
☐ complete 완료하다, 완수하다
☐ reservation 예약
☐ employee 직원
☐ agent 대행사
☐ bag 봉지[가방]에 넣다
☐ purchase 구매

03

☐ approach 접근하다
☐ rubber-stamp 고무도장
☐ funeral 장례식
☐ bathing suit 수영복
☐ religious 종교적인
☐ service 예식
☐ probably 아마
☐ appropriate 적합한, 알맞은
☐ occasion 행사
☐ setting 상황, 장소
☐ skillful 숙련된, 능숙한
☐ flexible 유연한
☐ strategy 전략
☐ multiple-choice test 선다형 시험
☐ essay test 논술 시험

04

☐ threatening 위협적인
☐ suggest 시사하다, 암시하다
☐ exact 정확한, 정밀한
☐ opposite 반대
☐ rob 빼앗다, 강탈하다

☐ present 제시하다
☐ pessimistic 비관적인
☐ intend 의도하다, 생각하다
☐ rate 비율, ~율
☐ screen 검진하다
☐ terrified 두려워하는
☐ doom 파멸
☐ gloom 암울
☐ depressed 우울한
☐ ecological 생태계의
☐ collapse 붕괴

05

☐ indicate 시사하다, 보여 주다
☐ decoration 장식
☐ distraction 주의 산만
☐ directly 직접적으로
☐ cognitive 인지적인
☐ performance 수행, 성과
☐ visually 시각적으로
☐ overstimulate 지나치게[과도하게] 자극시키다
☐ concentrate 집중하다
☐ academic 학업의
☐ distracted 산만해진
☐ attention 집중
☐ excessive 지나친, 과도한
☐ complete 완전한
☐ absence 없는 것, 부재

06

☐ attention 주목, 관심
☐ unreliable 신뢰할 수 없는
☐ inaccurate 부정확한
☐ source 원천
☐ reflection 반영
☐ conclude 결론을 내리다
☐ reflect 나타내다, 반영하다
☐ depressed 우울한
☐ mislead 속이다, 잘못 이끌다
☐ support 뒷받침하다

07

☐ down time 가동되지 않는 시간
☐ shut off 멈추다
☐ responsibility 책임

□ cut back on ~을 줄이다
□ reveal 밝히다, 드러내다
□ vital 필수적인
□ maintain 유지하다
□ enable 가능하게 하다
□ evidence 증거

08

□ worthless 가치가 없는
□ ensure 보장하다
□ accessible 접근 가능한
□ appropriate 적절한
□ frequently 자주
□ indication 표시, 암시
□ recognize 알아보다, 인식하다
□ prime 최상의, 주요한
□ utilize 활용하다
□ loyalty 충성(도)
□ delightful 즐거운, 유쾌한

09

□ independently 독자적으로
□ trustworthy 신뢰할 수 있는
□ extremely 매우, 극히
□ ultimately 궁극적으로, 결국
□ conclusion 결론
□ blind ~을 못 보는, 눈이 먼
□ evidence 증거
□ incredibly 믿을 수 없을 정도로
□ encounter 접하다, 마주치다
□ bet 틀림없다, 분명하다

10

□ punish 벌주다
□ motivate 동기 부여를 하다
□ additional 추가적인, 추가의
□ performance (과제) 수행
□ up to ~까지
□ acceptable 받아들일 수 있는
□ policy 방침, 방책
□ submit 제출하다
□ reason 판단하다, 생각하다
□ substandard 수준 미달의, 저질의
□ appropriate 적절한
□ satisfactory 만족스러운

11

□ pressure 압박, 압력
□ normal 정상적인, 일반적인
□ doubt 의심하다; 의심
□ self-worth 자아 존중감
□ suffer 상처를 입다, 괴로워하다
□ uniquely 특유의 방식으로
□ activate 활성화하다
□ bother 괴롭히다
□ neutral 중립적인
□ genuinely 진짜로, 정말로
□ reflection 반영
□ shortcoming 단점
□ objectively 객관적으로

12

□ option 선택(지), 선택권
□ anxiety 불안(감), 염려
□ undesirable 달갑지 않은
□ abundance 풍요, 풍부
□ assess 평가하다
□ move on ~으로 나아가다[이동하다]
□ inevitable 꼭 해야 할 것, 필연적인 것
□ snooze button 스누즈 버튼(아침에 잠이 깬 뒤 조금 더 자기 위해 누르는 알람시계나 라디오의 타이머 버튼)
□ ruin 망치다
□ ultimately 결국
□ demand a price 대가를 요구하다

6강 주제 추론

01

□ spillover 파급
□ degree 정도, 수준
□ variety 다양성
□ excessive 과도한
□ transaction cost 거래 비용
□ diversity 다양성
□ impact 영향을 미치다
□ affect 영향을 미치다
□ tolerant 관대한, 아량 있는
□ region 지역
□ range 범위

□ available 이용할 수 있는
□ perceive 인식하다
□ unattractive 매력적이지 않은
□ distortion 왜곡
□ discriminate 차별하다
□ ethnic 인종의, 민족의
□ conflict 갈등
□ import 유입되다, 수입하다

02

□ possess 소유하다
□ a host of 많은, 다수의 ∼
□ desirable 바람직한
□ intelligent 지적인
□ fair-minded 공정한
□ prejudiced 편견이 있는
□ average 보통의, 평균의
□ phenomenon 현상
□ reliable 믿을[신뢰할] 수 있는
□ fictional 허구적인
□ in terms of ∼의 면에서, ∼에 관하여

03

□ economic 경제의
□ situation 상황
□ wage 임금, 급료
□ level 수준
□ improve 개선되다, 향상되다
□ gradually 점차
□ form 형태
□ transport 운송, 수송
□ industrial 산업의
□ revolution 혁명
□ coast-to-coast 대륙 횡단의
□ arrival 출현, 도래
□ growth 성장, 발전

04

□ remarkable 놀라운
□ consequence 결과
□ melt 녹다
□ alter 바꾸다, 고치다
□ duration (지속) 기간
□ work 작동되다
□ glacier 빙하

□ gravity 중력
□ force 억지로 밀어 넣다, 강요하다
□ equator 적도
□ slightly 약간, 조금
□ rotation 회전, 자전
□ spread out ∼을 뻗다, 펼치다
□ barely 간신히
□ noticeable 뚜렷한
□ last 지속되다, 계속되다

05

□ evolution 진화
□ survival 생존
□ reproduction 번식
□ criterion 기준, 규준(pl. criteria)
□ resource 자원
□ predator 포식자
□ efficiency 효율성
□ prevail 승리하다, 이기다
□ competition 경쟁
□ likewise 마찬가지로
□ potential 잠재적인
□ caregiver (아이나 병자를) 돌보는 사람

06

□ construct 구성하다
□ object 사물, 물체
□ calculate 계산하다
□ fit 알맞다, 적합하다
□ notion 개념
□ quantity 양
□ reveal 밝히다, 드러내다
□ investigate 조사하다, 연구하다
□ sort 분류하다

07

□ operate 운영되다
□ monsoon 몬순(특히 인도양에서 여름은 남서, 겨울은 북동에서 부는 계절풍)
□ crop 작물
□ harvest 수확
□ predict 예측하다
□ influence 영향을 미치다
□ railway 철도
□ design 설계하다

- □ climate 기후
- □ central heating 중앙난방
- □ temperature 기온
- □ air-conditioning 냉방(기)
- □ opposite 정반대

08

- □ neuroscientist 신경과학자
- □ circuit 회로
- □ fundamentally 근본적으로
- □ gratitude 감사
- □ neuron 뉴런, 신경 세포
- □ activate 활성화시키다
- □ encouraging 고무적인, 용기를 주는
- □ bottom line 요점, 핵심
- □ intentionally 의도적으로

09

- □ vegetarian 채식의
- □ mainstream 주류
- □ approximately 거의 정확하게, 가까이
- □ nutritionally 영양학적으로
- □ adequate 적당한
- □ prevention 예방
- □ treatment 치료
- □ statistics 통계자료
- □ confinement 갇힘, 가둠
- □ vegetarianism 채식주의
- □ animal waste 가축 배설물
- □ resulting 결과로 초래된

10

- □ motivate 동기를 부여하다
- □ threat 위협
- □ approach 접근법, 접근
- □ defensive 방어적인
- □ aggression 공격성, 공격
- □ irritation 짜증, 화

11

- □ flow 흐름
- □ exchange 이야기를 나눔, 대화
- □ response 반응
- □ process 처리하다
- □ invention 꾸며낸 이야기, 창작

- □ recall 기억해 내다
- □ stored 저장된
- □ disbelieve 믿지 않다, 의심하다
- □ pause 잠시 멈추다

12

- □ renewable 재생 가능한
- □ secure 확보하다
- □ objective 목적
- □ consequence 결과
- □ consideration 생각, 숙고
- □ hydropower 수력 발전
- □ aquatic 수생의
- □ identify 확인하다
- □ significant 주요한, 중요한
- □ intensive 집중적인, 집약적인
- □ occupation 점유
- □ population 개체군

7강 제목 추론

01

- □ development 개발
- □ construction 건축물
- □ carve 조각하다
- □ ancestor 조상, 선조
- □ erect 세우다
- □ erection 건설
- □ successive 연이은, 잇따른
- □ generation 세대
- □ innovator 혁신가
- □ process 과정
- □ radically 완전히, 근본적으로
- □ remake 다시 만들다, 탈바꿈하다

02

- □ poverty 가난
- □ journal 저널, 학술지
- □ note 언급하다
- □ socioeconomic 사회 경제적
- □ status 지위
- □ economy (경제 주체로서의) 국가

□ distinct 뚜렷한
□ pressure 압박
□ psychologist 심리학자
□ industrialized 산업화된
□ standard 수준
□ constant 지속적인
□ urgency 촉박, 긴급성
□ productivity 생산력
□ lack 부족하다
□ relax 긴장을 풀다, 쉬다

03

□ intend 의도하다
□ path 길
□ comfortable 편안한
□ reward 보상을 주다; 보상
□ realize 깨닫다
□ breathe 호흡하다, 숨 쉬다
□ slippery 미끄러운
□ superhuman 초인적인
□ effort 노력
□ effectively 사실상, 실질적으로
□ situation 상황
□ employment 고용
□ locked 갇힌
□ secure 안정적인
□ ultimately 궁극적으로

04

□ suggestion 제안, 의견
□ immediately 즉시, 바로
□ possibility 가능성
□ viewpoint 관점, 시각
□ opportunity 기회
□ period 마침표
□ particular 특정한
□ consider 고려하다
□ option 선택, 선택지
□ beneficial 이로운, 유익한
□ experience 경험하다
□ eliminate 없애다, 제거하다

05

□ operate 움직이다, 가동되다

□ process 과정
□ achieve 성취하다, 달성하다
□ returns 보상, 수익
□ derive 끌어내다
□ overcautious 지나치게 조심하는
□ attain 이루다, 달성하다
□ potential 잠재력
□ bold 용감한

06

□ generation 세대
□ mention 언급하다
□ algorithm 알고리즘
□ draw a blank 아무 반응을 얻지 못하다
□ civilization 문명
□ everyday 일상의, 매일의
□ appliances 가전제품
□ switch 스위치
□ trade 거래하다
□ goods 상품
□ keep records 기록 문서를 보관하다

07

□ accurately 정확하게
□ recognize 인식하다
□ label 이름을 붙이다
□ psychologist 심리학자
□ absolutely 전적으로
□ transformative (사람을) 변화시키는
□ communicate 전달하다
□ distinguish 구별하다
□ a range of 다양한 ~
□ ups and downs 좋은 일과 나쁜 일
□ ordinary 평범한
□ existence 존재
□ regulation 조절
□ psychosocial 심리 사회적인
□ well-being 행복

08

□ dynamic 역동적인
□ mobility 이동성
□ exercise (권력 등을) 행사하다
□ regarding ~에 관하여
□ profession 직업

WORD EXTRACT

□ pose 제기하다
□ evident 분명한
□ alternative 대안
□ desired 바람직한
□ identity 정체성
□ ready-made 이미 주어진
□ prescribe 규정하다
□ underneath 아래에

09

□ diversity 다양성
□ challenge 어려움, 도전
□ conflict 갈등
□ comfort zone 안락 지대(편안함을 느끼는 구역)
□ medical insurance 의료보험
□ sufficient 충분한
□ finance 재정
□ capability 능력, 역량
□ navigate 운전하다, 항해하다
□ trial 시련
□ occasional 가끔의
□ hang out 서성대다, 시간을 보내다
□ pose (문제 등을) 제기하다

10

□ development 발전
□ rarely 좀처럼 ~하지 않는
□ critical 대단히 중요한
□ vertical 수직의, 종적인
□ transportation 운송, 수송
□ journey 이동, 여행
□ efficient 효율적인
□ skyscraper 고층 건물, 마천루
□ architecture 건축
□ advance 발전, 진전
□ record 기록

11

□ electronic equipment 전자 기기
□ estimate 추산하다
□ billion 10억
□ approximately 약, 대략
□ goods 물건, 제품, 상품
□ government 정부
□ household 가구, 세대

□ dust 먼지
□ waste 낭비, 쓰레기
□ pure 순전한, 순수한
□ rubbish 쓸모없는 물건, 쓰레기
□ observe (발언·의견을) 말하다
□ stuff 물건

12

□ chewing 씹기
□ exposed 노출된
□ digestive 소화의
□ extraction 추출
□ raw material 원료
□ mammal 포유류
□ cover (언급된 거리를) 가다[이동하다]
□ predator 포식자, 천적
□ capture 포획하다
□ prey 먹이
□ incredible 믿을 수 없는, 엄청난
□ Arctic 북극의
□ tundra 툰드라
□ pack ice 유빙, 총빙
□ high-altitude 고도가 높은

8강 도표의 이해

01

□ percentage 백분율, 비율
□ report 보고하다
□ decrease 감소, 저하

02

□ share 점유율
□ region 지역
□ decline 감소하다
□ gap 차이

03

□ decrease 감소하다
□ throughout ~ 동안 쭉, 내내
□ period 기간
□ gap 차이
□ slightly 약간
□ increase 증가하다

□ steadily 꾸준히
□ except ~을 제외하고

04

□ survey 설문 조사
□ reason 이유
□ motivator 동기 (부여 요소)
□ welfare 복지
□ whereas 반면에, ~임에 반하여
□ cite 언급하다, 말하다
□ reduce 줄이다
□ consumption 섭취, 소비
□ management 관리

05

□ share 점유율, 몫
□ urban 도시의
□ continent 대륙
□ reverse 역전
□ rank (순위를) 차지하다

06

□ household 가정
□ ownership 소유
□ increase 증가하다
□ additional 추가의
□ rate 비율

07

□ course 강의
□ learning material 학습 자료
□ age group 연령 집단
□ graph 도표
□ aged (나이가) ~살의
□ gap 차이, 격차

08

□ homeschool 홈스쿨링을 하다
□ public school 공립 학교
□ cultural 문화의
□ performance 공연
□ sporting event 스포츠 경기
□ gallery 미술관
□ aquarium 수족관
□ respectively 각각

09

□ consumer 소비자
□ trust 신뢰
□ source 출처, 정보원
□ distrust 불신
□ outweigh ~보다 크다[우세하다]
□ influencer 영향력 있는 사람

10

□ spending 지출, 소비
□ share 점유율
□ GDP 국내 총생산(= gross domestic product)
□ select 선별하다, 선택하다
□ average 평균
□ estimate 추정하다
□ difference 차이, 구분

11

□ device 기기, 장치
□ access 접속하다, 접근하다
□ laptop 노트북 (컴퓨터)
□ e-reader 전자책 단말기
□ kindergarten 유치원
□ a third 3분의 1
□ rank 순위를 차지하다

12

□ quit 중단하다
□ regularly 정기적으로
□ participation 참여
□ survey (설문) 조사
□ meanwhile 한편, 반면

9강 내용 일치 파악

01

□ classical music 클래식 음악
□ bachelor 학사 학위 소지자
□ education 교육
□ composition 작곡, 작품
□ composer 작곡가
□ admire 감탄하다, 높이 평가하다
□ hire 고용하다
□ expressive 표현력이 뛰어난

- □ harmonic 화성의, 화음의
- □ inspire 영감을 주다
- □ generation 세대

02
- □ educated 교육을 받은, 교양 있는
- □ financial 금융의, 재정의
- □ political 정치의
- □ economics 경제학
- □ handle 다루다
- □ degree 학위
- □ doctoral 박사학위의
- □ committee 위원회
- □ contribution 기여
- □ regular 정기적인, 정규의
- □ analysis 분석
- □ economic science 경제학

03
- □ trousers 바지
- □ adventurous 모험적인
- □ career 경력
- □ photographer 사진작가
- □ airplane 비행기
- □ persuade 설득하다
- □ slightly 약간
- □ car dealer 자동차 판매원
- □ nonetheless 그럴더라도

04
- □ exceptionally 특별히, 유난히
- □ journalist 기자, 언론인
- □ occasionally 이따금, 가끔
- □ witness 목격하다
- □ faulty 결함이 있는
- □ equipment 장비
- □ invention 발명품
- □ fold 접다
- □ glue (접착제로) 붙이다
- □ flat-bottomed 바닥이 평평한
- □ eliminate 제거하다
- □ assemble 조립하다, 모으다

05
- □ journalist 언론인

- □ supportive of ~을 지지하는
- □ force A to B A가 B하도록 강요하다
- □ tax accountant 세무사
- □ rejection 거절
- □ publish 출간하다
- □ producer 제작자
- □ film right 영화 판권
- □ result (결과로서) 생기다, 발생하다
- □ worldwide 전 세계적으로

06
- □ composer 작곡가
- □ classical music 클래식 음악
- □ excellent 훌륭한
- □ win 수상하다
- □ prize 상
- □ amateur 아마추어
- □ successful 성공적인
- □ collaborate 협업하다
- □ publish 발매하다
- □ well-known 잘 알려진

07
- □ Dutch 네덜란드어
- □ unusual 드문
- □ endless 끝없는
- □ come in handy 도움이 되다
- □ microscope 현미경
- □ tiny 아주 작은

08
- □ soar 날아오르다
- □ save (돈을) 모으다
- □ flight 비행
- □ admit (단체·학교 등에서) 받아들이다, 입학을 허락하다
- □ international 국제적인
- □ license 면허
- □ appearance 출현, 나타남
- □ pioneer 개척자
- □ inspire 영감을 주다
- □ generation 세대
- □ pursue 추구하다

09
- □ publish 발표하다

- fine 훌륭한
- financially 재정적으로
- operator (기계) 기사, 조작자
- expense 비용
- recognition 인정, 인식
- dialect 방언, 사투리
- outnumber ~보다 많다
- attention 주목, 관심

10
- on account of ~ 때문에
- unique 독특한
- appearance (겉)모습, 외모
- native 토종의, 토박이의
- nursery 묘목장, 종묘장
- compacted 빽빽한, 꽉 찬
- resemble 닮다, 유사하다
- stem (식물의) 줄기
- conserving 보존하는
- moisture 수분

11
- slave 노예
- disallow 허가하지 않다, 금하다
- entrance 입학
- fine arts 순수 미술
- represent 대변하다, 대표하다
- injustice 불평등
- recognize 인정하다
- honor 훈장
- citizenship 시민권

12
- orphan (아이를) 고아로 만들다
- mark 특징짓다
- hardship 어려움
- washerwoman 세탁부
- backbreaking 매우 힘든, 등골 빠지는
- maid 가정부, 하녀
- chemist 화학자
- recruit 모집하다
- agent 대리인
- share 몫, 지분
- profit 이익, 수익
- self-made 자수성가한

- financial 재정의, 금융의

10강 안내문의 이해

01
- offer 제공하다
- fine 정교한, 우아한
- registration 등록
- available 이용할 수 있는, 효력이 있는
- fee 비용, 요금
- include 포함하다
- tool 도구
- material 재료
- participant 참가자
- refund 환불
- cancellation 취소

02
- annual 연례의
- knowledge 지식
- marine 해양의, 바다에 사는
- conservation 보호, 보존
- theme 주제
- pollution 오염
- participant 참가자
- submission 제출
- entry 출품작, 응모작
- announce 발표하다

03
- opportunity 기회
- prove 증명하다
- requirement 필요조건
- award 수여하다
- participant 참가자
- souvenir 기념품
- detail 세부 사항

04
- beginner 초보자
- underwater 수중의
- explorer 탐험가
- rent 빌리다
- equipment 장비

☐ register 등록하다

05
☐ article 기사
☐ publish 출간하다
☐ include 포함하다
☐ high-quality 고화질의
☐ per ~당

06
☐ fee 요금
☐ session 기간, 시간
☐ admission 입장
☐ first-come, first-served 선착순
☐ reservation 예약
☐ accompany 동행하다
☐ adult 어른, 성인
☐ contact 연락하다

07
☐ annual 연례의, 연간의
☐ electronics 전자 제품
☐ accept 허용하다
☐ light bulb 전구
☐ microwave 전자레인지
☐ wipe out 삭제하다
☐ resident 주민, 거주자

08
☐ fascinating 매력적인, 매혹적인
☐ witness 보다, 목격하다
☐ marine 해양의
☐ requirement 요건, 조건
☐ insurance fee 보험료
☐ experienced 숙련된, 능숙한
☐ accompany 동행하다, 동반하다
☐ reservation 예약
☐ on-site 현장의, 현지의

09
☐ host 열다, 개최하다
☐ online 온라인으로
☐ registration 등록
☐ room 공간
☐ cancel 취소하다

☐ unfavorable 좋지 않은, 불리한

10
☐ propose 제안하다
☐ measure 대책, 조치
☐ water pollution 수질 오염
☐ submission 제출
☐ proposal 제안서
☐ participant 참가자
☐ gift certificate 상품권

11
☐ participant 참가자
☐ self-defense 자기 방어
☐ develop 개발하다
☐ participation fee 참가비
☐ per ~당, ~마다
☐ include 포함하다

12
☐ operating hours 운영 시간
☐ process 과정
☐ taste 시식하다
☐ allow 허용하다

13
☐ flower arrangement 꽃꽂이
☐ material 재료
☐ sign up for ~을 등록하다
☐ refund 환불
☐ cancellation 취소
☐ contact 연락하다

14
☐ palace 궁궐
☐ booking 예약
☐ traditional 전통의, 전통적인
☐ extra charge 추가 비용

15
☐ amazing 놀라운, 멋진
☐ maximum 최대
☐ deadline 마감 기한
☐ winner 수상작, 수상자

□ post 게시하다
□ exhibit 전시하다
□ further 추가의, 더 이상의

16
□ hot air balloon 열기구
□ ride 놀이 기구
□ capacity 수용 인원
□ duration 지속 시간
□ insurance 보험
□ reservation 예약
□ full refund 전액 환불
□ in advance 사전에, 미리

17
□ premier 최고의, 제1의
□ inspire 불어넣다, 격려하다
□ bookmark 책갈피

18
□ howl (개 등의) 울음소리; 울다
□ pack 무리, 떼
□ location 장소, 위치
□ resident 거주자

19
□ conserve 보호하다, 보존하다
□ participant 참가자
□ entry 출품작, (개별) 항목
□ announce 발표하다

20
□ virtual (컴퓨터를 이용한) 가상의
□ connect 접속하다
□ upcoming 다가오는
□ theme 테마, 주제
□ budget 예산
□ access 입장, 접근

21
□ hands-on 직접 해 보는
□ participation 참가, 참여

22
□ aquarium 수족관

□ entry 입장
□ holder 보유자, 소지자
□ up to ~까지

23
□ competition 대회, 경기
□ compete 경쟁하다
□ livable 살기에 좋은
□ on site 현장의
□ assistance 도움
□ sign up 등록하다
□ registration 등록

24
□ fireworks 불꽃놀이
□ display 전시, 보여 주는 것
□ location 위치, 장소
□ maze 미로
□ accompany 동행하다
□ reserve 예약하다
□ beforehand 사전에, ~ 전에 미리

11강 어법

01
□ exist 존재하다
□ discuss 토론하다
□ field 경기장; 분야, 영역
□ professional 전문가
□ specialized 전문의, 전문화된
□ degree 학위
□ expertise 전문 지식
□ executive 중역
□ decade 10년
□ experience 경험
□ respective 각각의, 각자의
□ face 직면하다
□ criticism 비판, 비난
□ accountant 회계사
□ tax 세금
□ organization 조직

WORD EXTRACT

02
- □ praise 칭찬
- □ improve 개선하다
- □ equally 똑같이, 동등하게
- □ self-esteem 자존감
- □ preschooler 미취학 아동
- □ cognitive 인지적인
- □ reason 추론하다
- □ analytically 분석적으로
- □ reject 거절하다
- □ consistently 지속적으로, 일관성 있게
- □ incorporate 통합시키다
- □ endure 지속하다
- □ effort 노력
- □ confidence 자신감
- □ similarly 유사하게

03
- □ noticeable 눈에 띄는
- □ characteristic 특징, 특성
- □ project 투영하다
- □ made after ~을 본떠 만들어진
- □ resemble 닮다
- □ achieve 달성하다, 이루다
- □ feature 특징, 특색
- □ trend 경향, 추세
- □ lift 들어 올리다
- □ object 물체
- □ appropriate 적절한, 적당한
- □ expression 표정
- □ strategy 전략
- □ emotionally 감정적으로
- □ appealing 매력적인
- □ enlarge 확대하다

04
- □ power 동력을 공급하다, 작동시키다
- □ consider 고려하다
- □ perform 수행하다
- □ quite 꽤
- □ mind-blowing 놀라운, 경이로운
- □ feature 특징
- □ require 필요로 하다
- □ specific to ~에게 특화된, 고유한
- □ core 핵심의, 가장 중요한

(우측 상단)
- □ self-improve 스스로 개선하다
- □ virtual 가상의
- □ assistant 비서, 조수
- □ exactly 정확히
- □ recognize 인식하다
- □ implication 영향, 결과

05
- □ shrink 줄어들다
- □ peak 절정에 달하다
- □ predator 포식자
- □ wit 기지, 재치
- □ domesticate 길들이다
- □ immediate 즉각적인
- □ shelter 은신처
- □ outsource 외부에 위탁하다
- □ characteristic 특징
- □ domestic animal 가축
- □ dumb 멍청한, 어리석은
- □ indicator 지표

06
- □ high-tech 첨단 기술의
- □ double 두 배가 되다
- □ consume 소비하다
- □ globally 전 세계적으로
- □ resource 자원
- □ advance 발전, 진보
- □ promise 가능성, 약속
- □ material 재료
- □ industrial 산업의
- □ mineral 광물
- □ rare metal 희귀 금속
- □ individually 개인적으로

07
- □ seek ~ out (특히 많은 노력을 기울여) ~을 찾아내다
- □ religion 종교
- □ value 가치관
- □ feather 깃털
- □ flock 모이다, 무리 짓다
- □ tendency 성향, 경향
- □ be conditioned to ~에 조건화되어 있다
- □ unfamiliar 익숙하지 않은
- □ foreign 낯선

□ likelihood 가능성
□ similarity 유사성
□ relate 마음이 통하다, 잘 어울리다

08

□ reduction 감소
□ fertilizer 비료
□ beneficial 이로운
□ essential 필수의
□ nutrient 영양소
□ in the first place 우선, 첫째로
□ uptake 흡수
□ fertilize 비료를 주다
□ decline 감소
□ on average 평균적으로
□ acidic 산성의
□ overall 전반적인
□ characteristic 특징
□ accumulation 축적

09

□ economic 경제의
□ theory 이론
□ produce 생산하다
□ firm 회사
□ dismiss 해고하다
□ factory 공장
□ recession 경기 후퇴, 불경기
□ unemployment 실업, 실업 상태
□ earnings 소득, 수입
□ leakage 누수, 누출

10

□ occasion 경우, 기회
□ observe 관찰하다
□ genuine 진짜의, 참된
□ obvious 분명한, 명백한
□ insincere 진실되지 못한
□ fake 가짜의
□ primarily 주로
□ involved 관련이 있는
□ manufacture 짓다, 제조하다
□ noticeably 눈에 띄게
□ slightly 살짝, 약간

11

□ instruction 가르침, 지도
□ look after ~을 관리하다, ~을 돌보다
□ explore 탐구하다, 탐험하다
□ handle 다루다
□ produce 만들어 내다, 생산하다
□ stage 단계
□ desire 욕구, 욕망
□ appropriate 알맞은
□ quality 질, 품질
□ comfortable 편안한
□ complex 복잡한
□ relevant 유의미한, 관련된

12

□ species 종
□ detect 감지하다
□ odour[odor] 냄새, 향기
□ molecule 분자
□ present 존재하는
□ soapy 비누 냄새가 나는
□ unpleasant 유쾌하지 않은
□ underlying 내재하는
□ component 구성 성분
□ perceive 감지하다
□ depend upon[on] ~에 의지[의존]하다
□ ecology 생태(학)

12강 어휘

01

□ particularly 특히
□ security 안도(감)
□ disoriented 갈피를 못 잡는, 혼란스러운
□ disrupt 방해하다, 지장을 주다
□ affect 영향을 미치다
□ literal 고지식한, 상상력이 부족한
□ beforehand 미리, 사전에
□ establish 형성하다, 확립하다
□ balance 균형
□ validate 헤아리다, 존중하다
□ past 과거(의)
□ opportunity 기회

☐ background 배경
☐ respect 존중하다

02

☐ display 보여 주다
☐ considerable 상당한
☐ facility 능력
☐ adapt A to B A를 B에 맞게 바꾸다
☐ ingredient 재료
☐ consumer 소비자
☐ demand 수요
☐ decline 감소하다
☐ hire 고용하다
☐ agency 대행사
☐ strategy 전략
☐ boost 촉진하다
☐ soul 정수, 핵심
☐ significant 상당한
☐ benefit 혜택
☐ reposition (제품의) 이미지 전환을 꾀하다

03

☐ philosophical 철학적인
☐ shift 변화
☐ competitive 경쟁적인
☐ geographically 지리적으로
☐ spread out 퍼져 나가다
☐ relation 관계
☐ quality 양질의, 질 좋은
☐ reasonable 합리적인
☐ equally 마찬가지로
☐ essential 매우 중요한
☐ modernization 현대화
☐ revolution 혁명
☐ demand 수요
☐ meet 충족시키다
☐ diverse 다양한
☐ complex 복잡한
☐ focus 초점, 중점

04

☐ tip 끝
☐ stem 줄기
☐ root 뿌리

☐ accumulate 축적되다
☐ accordingly 따라서
☐ shade 그늘, 그늘지게 하다
☐ face ~을 마주하다
☐ phenomenon 현상
☐ appear to ~하게 보이다
☐ opposite 반대의, 상반하는
☐ horizontal 수평의
☐ interfere 방해하다
☐ development 발달
☐ lower 아래의
☐ upper 위쪽의
☐ downwards 아래로

05

☐ somehow 어떻게든
☐ magically 마법처럼, 마법으로
☐ organ 기관, 장기
☐ specific 특정한
☐ groundless 근거 없는
☐ circulation 순환
☐ aggressive 공격적인
☐ eliminate 제거하다
☐ temporary 일시적인
☐ intelligence 지능, 지성
☐ intelligently 영리하게, 총명하게
☐ fix 고치다, 해결하다

06

☐ influence 영향을 미치다
☐ expectation 기대
☐ social pressure 사회적 압력
☐ deceiving 현혹시키는, 속이는
☐ impact 영향을 주다
☐ notice 알아차리다
☐ ownership 소유권
☐ end up 결국 ~하게 되다
☐ regain 되찾다
☐ passion 열정
☐ recover 회복하다
☐ room 여지

07

☐ rejection 거절
☐ handle 감당하다, 다루다

□ painful 고통스러운
□ risk 위험을 무릅쓰다
□ affect 영향을 미치다
□ aspect 측면
□ tough 강한
□ therapy 요법, 치료
□ discount 할인
□ unfavorable 호의적이지 않은
□ circumstance 상황

08

□ establish 수립하다
□ coordinate 통합하다
□ conservationist 환경 보호 활동가
□ authorities 당국
□ diminish 감소하다
□ extinction 멸종
□ release 풀어주다
□ supplement 보충하다
□ population 개체 수
□ adulthood 성년
□ capture 포획하다
□ hatchling 부화한 유생

09

□ primates 영장류
□ extensive 광범위한
□ decade 10년
□ game 사냥감
□ exceed 초과하다
□ immediate family 직계 가족
□ consume 소비하다, 먹다
□ variable 가변적인
□ leftover 남은 음식
□ spoil 상하다
□ return 보답하다, 갚다
□ generous 관대한
□ extra 여분의, 추가의

10

□ decade 10년
□ straighten 직선으로 하다, 곧게 하다
□ cross-section 횡단면
□ disastrous 재앙의, 비참한
□ spill 넘치다

□ floodplain 범람원
□ leak 새다
□ wetland 습지
□ ever-changing 늘 변화하는
□ shoreline 강가
□ square mile 제곱마일

11

□ fundamental 기본적인
□ drop 하락하다
□ consider 생각하다, 고려하다
□ artificial light 인공조명
□ cost ~의 비용이 들다; 비용
□ amount 양
□ light up (빛 등으로) ~을 환하게 만들다
□ turn A into B A를 B로 바꾸다

12

□ evolve 진화하다
□ relationship 관계
□ species 종
□ domestication 사육, 길들이기
□ reduction 감소
□ no longer 더 이상 ~ 않다
□ function 기능
□ ancestor 조상
□ firmly 확고하게
□ establish 확립하다, 규정하다

13강 빈칸 추론 1 (31~32번)

01

□ fear 두려움, 공포
□ a lack of ~의 부족함
□ potential 잠재적인
□ solely 오직, 오로지
□ statistically 통계적으로
□ odds 확률
□ crash 사고, 충돌
□ involve 포함하다

02

□ downplay 경시하다

WORD EXTRACT

□ imaginary 상상의
□ offender 범죄자, 위반자
□ employ 쓰다, 이용하다
□ technical 기술적인, 전문적인
□ contact 접촉
□ primates 영장류
□ qualitatively 질적으로
□ cognitive 인지의
□ precise 정확한
□ term 일컫다, 칭하다; 용어
□ linguistic 언어의
□ castration 거세
□ disempower ~로부터 힘을 빼앗다

03

□ perform 수행하다
□ instant 즉각적인
□ credibility 신뢰(성)
□ admire 존경하다
□ area 분야
□ endorse 보증하다, 선전하다
□ expertise 전문 지식
□ talent 재능
□ excellence 탁월함
□ connect 관련이 있다
□ possess 소유하다

04

□ interaction 상호 작용
□ element 요소
□ merchant 상인
□ operation 작동
□ spot 장소
□ material 재료
□ process 처리하다
□ raw 가공되지 않은, 날것의
□ sensory 감각의
□ organ 기관
□ transport 전달하다
□ superhighway 초고속도로
□ neuron 뉴런, 신경
□ undergo 겪다
□ transformation 변형
□ conscious 의식적인

05

□ biological clock 체내 시계
□ overcome 극복하다
□ recovery 회복
□ lengthen 연장하다
□ shorten 단축하다
□ sizable 큰
□ impact 영향
□ performance 경기력, 성과
□ perform 행하다, 수행하다
□ significantly 상당히
□ professional 프로의, 전문적인
□ recent 최근의
□ additional 추가적인
□ evidence 증거
□ tough 힘든, 거친

06

□ confidence 자신감, 확신
□ achieve 성취하다
□ set out ~에 착수하다
□ over-optimism 지나친 낙관주의
□ make a practice of ~을 습관화하다
□ estimate 추산하다, 어림잡다
□ amount 양
□ expect 기대하다
□ attention 주의
□ fit 맞추다
□ available 이용 가능한
□ significant 상당한
□ period 시간, 기간
□ schedule 일정을 잡다
□ spare 남는, 여분의

07

□ demonstrate 설명하다, 입증하다
□ defeat 무너뜨리다, 극복하다
□ delay 지연시키다
□ psychology 심리학
□ behavioral 행동의
□ economics 경제학
□ perform 수행하다
□ assign 할당하다, 과제를 부여하다
□ semester 학기
□ due 예정된

- [ ] for oneself 자신 스스로
- [ ] submit 제출하다
- [ ] conclude 결론짓다
- [ ] recognize 인식하다, 인지하다
- [ ] improve 향상시키다
- [ ] self-control 자기 통제
- [ ] performance 성과

08

- [ ] innovation 혁신
- [ ] steadily 꾸준히
- [ ] specialized in ~에 전문화된
- [ ] diversified 다양화된
- [ ] consume 소비하다
- [ ] unstable 불안정한
- [ ] self-sufficiency 자급자족
- [ ] mutual 서로 간의
- [ ] interdependence 상호 의존
- [ ] concentrate on ~에 집중하다
- [ ] rely on ~에 의존하다
- [ ] provide A to B A를 B에 제공하다
- [ ] afford ~할 여유가 있다
- [ ] electric 전기의
- [ ] quantity 양
- [ ] require 요구하다
- [ ] sesame 참깨
- [ ] fat 지방

09

- [ ] common 흔한
- [ ] warehouse 창고
- [ ] grab 잡다
- [ ] headpiece 헤드폰
- [ ] detail 세부 사항
- [ ] instruction 지시 사항
- [ ] minimise 최소화하다
- [ ] maximise 최대화하다
- [ ] productivity 생산성
- [ ] flesh 살, 피부
- [ ] adapt 적응하다
- [ ] inexpensive 값싼, 비싸지 않은
- [ ] processing 처리
- [ ] opposable 마주 볼 수 있는

10

- [ ] prevailing 지배적인
- [ ] developmental 발달의
- [ ] contributor 기여자, 기부자
- [ ] influence 영향을 주다
- [ ] interact with ~와 상호 작용하다
- [ ] context 환경, 정황
- [ ] infant 유아
- [ ] construct 구성하다
- [ ] interaction 상호 작용
- [ ] in response 이에 응하여
- [ ] one-on-one 일대일의
- [ ] individual 개인
- [ ] manufacturer 제조자

11

- [ ] innovation 혁신
- [ ] entirely 완전히
- [ ] virtually 가상으로
- [ ] overall 대체로
- [ ] constraint 제한
- [ ] collaboration 협업
- [ ] setting 환경
- [ ] enforce 강요하다
- [ ] nonverbal 비언어적인
- [ ] arrangement 배정, 배치
- [ ] assign 배정하다, 할당하다
- [ ] boost 신장시키다

12

- [ ] demand 수요; 필요로 하다
- [ ] giffen goods 기펜재(가격이 내릴수록 오히려 수요가 적어지는 재화)
- [ ] traditional 전통적인
- [ ] apply 적용되다
- [ ] switch 바꾸다, 전환하다
- [ ] replacement 대체품
- [ ] consumer 소비자
- [ ] tend to ~하는 경향이 있다
- [ ] purchase 구입하다
- [ ] dairy 유제품

13

- [ ] generalization 일반화
- [ ] specific 구체적인

WORD EXTRACT

☐ humanize 인간미 있게 하다
☐ finest 가장 훌륭한
☐ humanitarian 인도주의적인
☐ describe 기술하다, 묘사하다
☐ main character 주인공
☐ up front 대놓고
☐ heroic 대담한, 영웅적인
☐ tragic 비극적인
☐ detailed 세부적인, 상세한
☐ engaging 마음을 끄는

14

☐ face-to-face 대면의
☐ interaction 상호 작용
☐ uniquely 유례없이
☐ complex 복잡한
☐ stimulate 자극하다
☐ shoelace 신발끈
☐ psychologist 심리학자
☐ achiever (~한) 성취도를 보이는 사람
☐ winner 수상자
☐ access 접근
☐ crucial 결정적인, 매우 중요한
☐ professional 전문적인

15

☐ telegraph 전보; 전보를 보내다
☐ communicate 통신하다, 연락하다
☐ metaphor 비유
☐ advance notice 사전 통보
☐ inform A of B A에게 B를 알리다
☐ upcoming 다가오는
☐ convey 전달하다
☐ empower ~할 수 있게 하다
☐ circumstance 상황

16

☐ underlie ~의 기저가 되다
☐ define 규정하다
☐ preserve 보존하다
☐ suffer from ~을 앓다
☐ heart failure 심부전(心不全)
☐ depend upon ~에 의존하다
☐ replace 교체하다
☐ artificial 인공의

☐ essentially 본질적으로
☐ other than ~을 제외하고
☐ advanced (병의 발달 단계 등이) 후기의, 많이 진행된
☐ fade 희미해지다

17

☐ competitive 경쟁적인
☐ advantage 이점, 장점
☐ fixed-gear 고정식 기어의
☐ minimal 최소한의, 아주 적은
☐ feature 특징, 특색
☐ profitability 수익성
☐ complexity 복잡함, 복잡성
☐ competitor 경쟁자, 경쟁 업체
☐ pressure 압력, 압박
☐ product 제품, 상품
☐ consumer 소비자
☐ loyalty 충실, 충성심

18

☐ evolutionary 진화의
☐ biologist 생물학자
☐ argue 주장하다, 다투다
☐ trade 거래하다; 거래, 교역
☐ deal 거래, (사업상의) 합의
☐ confusing 헷갈리게 하는
☐ term 조건
☐ bond 유대, 결속
☐ specific 구체적인
☐ role 역할

19

☐ belief 믿음
☐ truly 진심으로
☐ maintain 유지하다
☐ consideration 고려 사항
☐ unburden 벗어나게 하다
☐ duty 의무
☐ sort out ~을 가려내다
☐ negotiate 협상하다
☐ external 외적인
☐ pressure 부담

20

☐ research 연구, 조사; 연구하다

□ confirm 확인하다
□ participate 참여하다
□ unacceptable 받아들여질 수 없는
□ decline 감소하다
□ progress 진전을 보이다
□ competitive 경쟁적인
□ emphasis 강조
□ resist 저항하다
□ systematically 체계적으로

21

□ aspect 측면
□ make sure 확실히 하다
□ consistently 일관되게
□ predictably 예측 가능하게
□ sense 느낌
□ distress 고통, 괴로움
□ ensure ~을 보장하다
□ get up 일어나다
□ hold ~ in ~을 참다
□ discomfort 불편함
□ companion 친구, 동반자
□ display 보이다, 나타내다
□ emotional 정서적인
□ confident 자신감이 있는, 자신만만한

22

□ calm ~ down ~을 진정시키다
□ act as ~으로 작용하다
□ distraction 주의를 돌리는 것
□ shift 옮기다, 이동시키다
□ attention 주의
□ treat 특별한 먹거리; (특별하게) 대접하다
□ effective 효과적인
□ harmful 해로운

23

□ fundamental 기본적인, 근본적인
□ human spirit 인간 정신
□ intuitive 직관적인
□ spark 촉발시키다, 자극하다
□ pathway 통로
□ public transportation 대중교통
□ progress 진보, 진전
□ destination 목적지

□ access 접근
□ strengthen 강화하다
□ expand 확대[확장]하다

24

□ consultant 고문, 상담가
□ describe 설명하다
□ emergence 출현, 발생
□ discipline 지식 분야, 학과목
□ be derived from ~에서 유래하다
□ bring together ~을 함께 모으다
□ arguably 거의 틀림없이
□ combine 결합하다
□ notion 이념, 개념
□ recommend 권유하다
□ utilize 활용하다
□ perspective 관점, 시각
□ innovation 혁신, 획기적인 것

14강 빈칸 추론 2 (33~34번)

01

□ engagement 참여
□ scholarly 학문적인
□ physicist 물리학자
□ biochemist 생화학자
□ bypass 우회하다; 우회 도로
□ compensate 상쇄하다, 보완하다
□ opposite 정반대
□ enthusiastic 열성적인, 열렬한
□ seek out ~을 찾아내다
□ passionate 열정적인

02

□ intellectual 지적의, 지능의
□ competence 능력
□ legal 법률의
□ brief (짧은) 보고서, 발표
□ elegant 명쾌한, 정연한
□ exceptionally 비범하게
□ witty 재치 있는
□ define 정의하다
□ gadget 기기
□ outstanding 뛰어난

□ average 평균의

03

□ affect ~에 영향을 주다
□ emotional 감정적인
□ echo 반향
□ accordingly 그에 따라
□ copy 모방하다, 따라하다
□ transmit 전송하다
□ via ~을 통해
□ theory 이론
□ state 진술하다
□ arise from ~로부터 발생하다
□ improve 향상시키다
□ bite 물다
□ force 억지로 ~하게 하다
□ primacy 우선함, 제1지위
□ summarize 요약하다
□ phrase 문구

04

□ restrict 제한하다
□ boost 밀어 올리다
□ investigate 조사하다
□ effectiveness 효과적임
□ persuade 설득하다
□ discount 할인; 할인하다
□ control 대조군, 통제 집단
□ limit 제한; 제한하다
□ purchase 구매
□ scarce 희소한
□ scarcity 희소성
□ particularly 특히
□ genuine 진짜의
□ rely on ~에 의존하다
□ laboratory 실험실
□ consumer 소비자
□ behave 행동하다

05

□ discover 발견하다
□ still 여전히
□ biologist 생물학자
□ effect 효과, 영향, 결과
□ evolutionary 진화의

□ principle 원리
□ evolve 진화하다
□ generation 세대
□ bunny 토끼
□ gene 유전자
□ species 종

06

□ clothing 옷
□ perfect 완성하다
□ nail 못
□ drive (못·말뚝 등을) 박다
□ cloth 천, 직물
□ physical 물리적인
□ reality 실체
□ product 제품
□ process 과정
□ period 기간
□ vision 비전
□ decision 결정
□ activity 활동

07

□ trick 속이다
□ contract 계약서
□ myth 신화
□ tribe 부족
□ victim 희생자
□ irresistible 저항할 수 없는
□ resist 저항하다
□ instruct 지시하다
□ stuff A with B A를 B로 채우다
□ work for ~에게 효과가 있다
□ stay off ~을 멀리하다
□ concentrate on ~에 집중하다
□ delete 삭제하다
□ app 앱(= application)
□ distract 산만하게 하다

08

□ ecosystem 생태계
□ unique 독특한
□ host 수용하다
□ evolution 진화
□ microbe 미생물

- rat 쥐
- resistance 내성, 저항성
- antibacterial 항균제
- insecticide 살충제
- cockroach 바퀴벌레
- distaste 혐오
- trap 덫
- opportunity 기회
- counterpart 상대방
- ecologist 생태학자
- urban 도시적인
- represent 나타내다

09

- year-round 연중 계속되는
- produce 농산물
- exotic 외국의
- widespread 광범위한
- hot house 온실
- climate 기후
- reliance on ~에 대한 의존
- wastage 낭비
- institutional 제도적인
- campaigner 운동가
- retail sector 소매 산업 분야
- exceed 초과하다

10

- participant 참가자
- determine 알아내다, 밝히다
- contain 포함하다
- repeat 반복하다
- trick 속임수
- totally 완전히
- cleverly 영리하게
- process 처리하다
- accurate 정확한

11

- intellectually 지적으로
- superior 우월한; 상급자
- modify 변형하다
- receptor 수용체
- chemical 화학 물질
- genetically 유전적으로

- inferior 열등한
- standard 표준의
- interaction 상호 작용
- handicapped 장애가 있는
- triumph 승리
- nurture 양육
- nature 천성

12

- coastal 해안의
- assessment 평가
- climate change 기후 변화
- common 일반적인
- for decades 수십 년 동안
- prediction 예측
- tense 시제
- crisis 위기
- ongoing 진행 중인
- region 지역
- West Antarctic Ice Sheet 서남극 빙상
- physically 물리적으로
- remote 멀리 떨어진

13

- foreign language 외국어
- translate 통역하다, 번역하다
- viewer 관객, 시청자
- occasion 경우
- target audience 주요 대상 관객
- mainly 주로
- viewpoint 관점, 시각
- particular 특정한
- character 등장인물
- absence 부재
- incomprehension 몰이해

14

- dynamic 역학
- dramatically 극적으로
- concept 개념
- home-field advantage 홈구장 이점
- demand 부담, 요구
- resource 자원
- circumstance 상황
- competitive 경쟁력 있는

□ perception 인식
□ struggling 고전하는
□ reduce 줄이다
□ pressure 압박

15
□ construct 만들다, 구성하다
□ hold ~ in memory ~을 기억하다
□ on a regular basis 규칙적으로, 정기적으로
□ hypothesis 가설(pl. hypotheses)
□ conclude 결론을 내리다
□ systematic 체계적인
□ interval 간격
□ pitch 음조
□ store 저장소
□ neural circuit 신경 회로
□ frequency 빈도

16
□ organism 생물
□ prey 먹이
□ glow 빛; 빛나다
□ firefly 반딧불이
□ attractant 유인 물질
□ evolutionary 진화의
□ fascinating 매력적인
□ molecule 분자
□ creature 생물
□ sparkle 반짝거림
□ reflection 반사
□ scattered 분산된
□ invisibility 보이지 않음

17
□ hide 숨기다
□ show off ~을 자랑스럽게 내보이다
□ reflect on 되돌아보다, 깊게 생각하다
□ trial and error 시행착오

18
□ conclusively 확정적으로, 결정적으로
□ teaching method 교수법
□ physics 물리학
□ lecture 강의하다
□ require 요구하다

□ eventually 결국
□ concept 개념

19
□ technological 기술의
□ innovation 혁신
□ availability 이용 가능성
□ unheard-of 전례가 없는, 아주 유별난
□ confront 직면하게 하다
□ countless 셀 수 없이 많은
□ genre 장르
□ orient (새로운 상황에) 적응하다[익숙해지다]
□ filter out ~을 걸러내다
□ restrict 한정[제한]하다
□ distributor 배급업자
□ considerable 상당한

20
□ assume 가정하다
□ creativity 창조성
□ concern 관련되다
□ relation 관계
□ sociocultural 사회 문화적
□ standpoint 관점
□ distantiation 거리 두기
□ interaction 상호 작용
□ confront 마주하다
□ blend 혼합하다, 섞다
□ perspective 관점

21
□ ancestor 조상
□ water-dwelling 물에 사는
□ relative 동족, 동류
□ opportunity 기회, 가능성
□ shelter 거처, 은신처
□ lung 폐
□ take a dip (몸을) 잠깐 담그다, 잠깐 수영을 하다
□ dry out 건조해지다
□ lay (알을) 낳다
□ creature 생물
□ land-dwelling 육지에 사는
□ adult 성체

22

- □ distinguish 구별하다
- □ legally 법적으로
- □ effective 실질적인, 효과적인
- □ freedom 자유
- □ physically 물리적으로
- □ incapable 할 수 없는
- □ minimum 최소한
- □ maximum 최대한
- □ possibility 가능성
- □ restrain 저지하다, 억제하다
- □ depend on ~에 달려 있다, ~에 의존하다

23

- □ fossil 화석
- □ fossilize 화석화하다
- □ insect 곤충
- □ diverse 다양한
- □ entirely 전적으로, 완전히
- □ occasionally 때때로, 가끔

24

- □ be faced with ~에 직면하다, ~과 마주치다
- □ beg 부탁하다, 청하다
- □ serve (서비스를) 제공하다, 봉사하다
- □ turn down 거절하다
- □ tremendous 엄청난, 대단한
- □ executive 경영진, 중역
- □ sustain 유지하다
- □ margin 여유, 차이, 수익
- □ thrive 번창하다, 성장하다

15강 무관한 문장 찾기

01

- □ sensory 감각의
- □ nerve 신경
- □ tissue (세포들로 이뤄진) 조직
- □ sensation 감각, 느낌
- □ transmit 전달하다, 보내다
- □ protective 보호하는
- □ capacity 능력
- □ contract 수축하다
- □ function 기능

- □ movement 움직임

02

- □ potential 잠재력
- □ productivity 생산성
- □ environment 환경
- □ personal 개인적인
- □ productive 생산적인
- □ introduce 도입하다
- □ production 생산
- □ process 공정(工程)
- □ require 요구하다
- □ time consuming 시간이 많이 걸리는
- □ decline 감소

03

- □ affect 영향을 미치다
- □ main character 주인공
- □ focus 초점
- □ event 사건
- □ character 등장인물
- □ interpret 해석하다
- □ conflict 갈등
- □ arise 발생하다
- □ outcome 결과
- □ consider 생각해 보다
- □ tale 이야기
- □ shift 바꾸다
- □ viewpoint 관점
- □ evil 사악한
- □ stepsister 의붓자매
- □ kingdom 왕국
- □ exist 존재하다
- □ willingly 기꺼이

04

- □ engagement 관여, 관계 맺기
- □ individual 개인
- □ capacity 능력
- □ expressive 표현적인
- □ improve 향상시키다
- □ immune 면역의
- □ function 기능
- □ diminish 감소시키다
- □ psychological 심리적인

☐ distress 고통
☐ enhance 강화하다
☐ aid 지원하다
☐ empathy 공감 (능력)
☐ effective 효과적인
☐ development 발달
☐ opportunity 기회

05

☐ fast-paced 빠른 속도의
☐ evolution 진화
☐ radically 급격하게
☐ transform 변화시키다
☐ dynamics 역동성
☐ competitiveness 경쟁
☐ satisfaction 만족감
☐ loyalty 충성도
☐ boost 상승
☐ promote 증진시키다
☐ empower ~에게 권한을 주다
☐ reservation 예약
☐ recommendation 추천
☐ attractions 관광지
☐ generate 만들어 내다
☐ considerable 상당한
☐ profit 수익, 이익

06

☐ medium 매개체
☐ exhibit 드러내다, 나타내다
☐ virtue 미덕, 덕목
☐ innovative 혁신적인
☐ self-respect 자기 존중
☐ concern 관심
☐ highly 매우
☐ globalize 세계화하다
☐ sociable 사교적인

07

☐ stay awake 깨어 있다
☐ mild 가벼운
☐ soda 탄산음료
☐ attentive 주의 깊은
☐ memory 기억력
☐ beneficial 이로운

☐ improve 향상하다
☐ performance 수행
☐ ideal 이상적인
☐ currently 현재
☐ stimulation 자극
☐ indeed 실제로
☐ suffer 악화되다, 더 나빠지다

08

☐ algorithm 알고리즘
☐ tendency 성향, 경향
☐ grab hold of ~을 움켜잡다
☐ confirm (사실임을) 확인해 주다
☐ so-called 이른바
☐ constantly 끊임없이
☐ challenge 이의를 제기하다
☐ acknowledge 인정하다
☐ diversity 다양성
☐ sheltered 보호를 받는
☐ extreme 극단의
☐ disastrous 처참한
☐ isolation 고립

09

☐ be referred to as ~라고 언급되다[불리다]
☐ commonly 흔히
☐ tendency 경향, 성향, 기질
☐ subconscious 잠재적인
☐ task 과업, 과제
☐ incomplete 끝나지 않은, 미완성의
☐ psychologist 심리학자
☐ complicated 복잡한
☐ interrupt 방해하다
☐ cooperation 협동

10

☐ spread 확산, 전파
☐ operate 기능하다, 작동하다
☐ incredibly 믿기 힘들 정도로
☐ epidemic 전염병
☐ advance 발전하다
☐ destructive 파괴적인
☐ outbreak 창궐, 발생
☐ typhoid 장티푸스
☐ overcrowding 인구 과밀

□ sanitation 위생
□ recognition 인식, 인정
□ pioneering 선구적인

11

□ gatekeeper 문지기, 정보 관리[통제]자
□ label 음반사
□ spotlight 주목
□ permission 허락, 허가
□ fanbase 팬층
□ concern 우려, 염려
□ deliver 전달하다, 배달하다
□ directly 직접, 곧장
□ exposure (언론) 노출, 매스컴 출연

12

□ phenomenon 현상
□ apply 적용하다
□ statement 진술, 서술
□ seek 찾다
□ exist 존재하다
□ imagination 상상
□ principle 원리
□ countless 무수한, 셀 수 없이 많은
□ beneficial 유익한
□ prediction 예측, 예견

16강 글의 순서

01

□ atom 원자
□ block 덩어리, (모양을 만들기 위한) 형
□ rock 암석
□ hexagon 육각형
□ steady 변함없는, 안정적인
□ crystal lattice 결정격자(결정을 구성하는 원자와 이온의 규칙적인 배열)

02

□ string 줄, 끈
□ blur 흐릿해지다
□ outline 윤곽; 개요

□ vibrate 진동하다
□ hardly 거의 ~없다
□ attach 달다, 붙이다
□ hollow (속이) 빈
□ note 음, 음표
□ wooden 나무로 된, 목재의
□ panel 판(넓은 직사각형의 합판)
□ eardrum 고막
□ flex 구부리다, 굽히다

03

□ livestock 가축
□ sunrise 일출
□ sunset 일몰
□ gradually 점점
□ settlement 정착지
□ priest 성직자
□ carry out ~을 수행하다
□ religious 종교적인
□ ceremony 의식
□ device 장치
□ measure 측정하다
□ incorrect 부정확한
□ aeroplane 비행기
□ land 착륙하다

04

□ productivity 생산성
□ output 생산량
□ production 생산
□ manufacture 제조; 제조하다
□ industry 산업
□ describe 설명하다
□ efficient 효율적인
□ division of labor 노동 분업
□ involve 포함하다
□ process 과정
□ straighten 곧게 펴다
□ sharpen 뾰족하게 하다
□ polish 다듬다
□ separate 별개의
□ specialize in ~을 전문으로 하다
□ huge 거대한

WORD EXTRACT

05

- □ Old Stone Age 구석기 시대
- □ band 무리
- □ wander (걸어서) 돌아다니다
- □ settle down 정착하다
- □ community 공동체
- □ organize 조직하다
- □ efficiently 효율적으로
- □ produce 생산하다
- □ crop 농작물
- □ toolmaker 도구 제작자
- □ share 함께 하다, 공유하다
- □ ax 도끼

06

- □ mineral 광물
- □ melt 녹이다, 녹다
- □ material 물질
- □ surface 표면
- □ trap 가두다
- □ atom 원자
- □ combine 결합하다
- □ arrange 배열하다
- □ orderly 질서 있는
- □ element 원소
- □ partly 부분적으로
- □ determine 결정하다
- □ crystal 결정, 결정체
- □ rapidly 빨리
- □ individual 개별의

07

- □ be in danger 위험에 처해 있다
- □ advance 진보
- □ automation 자동화
- □ a bit 약간
- □ unrealistic 비현실적인
- □ threat 위협
- □ flip 뒤집다
- □ replace 대체하다
- □ suggest 제안하다
- □ available 이용 가능한
- □ treatment 치료법
- □ draw on ~에 의지하다, ~을 이용하다
- □ the body of 상당한 양의 ~

- □ disease 질병
- □ irreplaceable 대체할 수 없는
- □ individual 개인

08

- □ beech 너도밤나무
- □ particular 특별한
- □ vary 다양하다
- □ nutrient 영양분
- □ accordingly 이에 따라
- □ species (동식물의) 종
- □ per ~당
- □ equalize 균등하게 하다
- □ transfer 전달하다
- □ take place 일어나다
- □ an abundance of 풍부한 ~
- □ hand over 건네주다
- □ run short 부족해지다
- □ fall behind 뒤처지다

09

- □ billion 10억
- □ obviously 분명히
- □ poverty 가난
- □ product 생산물, 산물
- □ local 현지의
- □ starve 굶주리다, 굶어 죽다
- □ grand 거대한, 웅장한
- □ trend 추세, 경향
- □ lower 낮추다

10

- □ owl 올빼미
- □ organize (어떤 일을) 계획하다, 준비하다
- □ divide 나누다
- □ face 직면하다
- □ tackle (힘든 문제를) 다루다, 씨름하다
- □ attack 착수하다, 덤벼들다
- □ alert (정신이) 초롱초롱한, 기민한
- □ peak 정점(의), 한창(인)
- □ muse 영감, (영감을 주는) 뮤즈
- □ awaken 깨다
- □ loose 느슨하게 풀린, 헐거워진

11

- [ ] first grader 1학년 학생
- [ ] turkey 칠면조
- [ ] Thanksgiving 추수감사절
- [ ] softly 조용히, 부드럽게
- [ ] image 그림, 이미지
- [ ] immediately 즉시
- [ ] attract 끌어들이다
- [ ] protect 보호하다
- [ ] responsive 호응하는

12

- [ ] legend 전설
- [ ] vampire 흡혈귀
- [ ] prove 증명하다
- [ ] creature 존재
- [ ] myth 미신, 사회적 통념
- [ ] suppose 가정하다
- [ ] come into existence 생기다, 나타나다
- [ ] original 원래의
- [ ] population 인구

13

- [ ] architectural 건축학의
- [ ] attitude 사고방식
- [ ] emerge 출현하다, 나타나다
- [ ] industrial 산업의
- [ ] argument 주장
- [ ] inhuman 비인간적인
- [ ] ordinary 평범한
- [ ] generation 세대
- [ ] mastery 숙달한 기술
- [ ] simplicity 단순함
- [ ] plain 평범한
- [ ] supply (필요를) 충족시키다
- [ ] craftsman 장인
- [ ] rootedness 뿌리내림
- [ ] locality 지역

14

- [ ] moral 도덕의
- [ ] tragic 비극적인
- [ ] in nature 사실상
- [ ] somehow 어떻게든지
- [ ] uplift 높이다, (~을) 감정적으로 고양하다

- [ ] performance 연주
- [ ] accomplished 숙달된
- [ ] doubtful 미덥지 못한
- [ ] composer 작곡가
- [ ] communicate 전달하다
- [ ] honestly 정직하게

15

- [ ] electronic commerce 전자 상거래
- [ ] fundamentally 근본적으로
- [ ] perception 인식
- [ ] obvious 분명한, 확실한
- [ ] physical 물리적인
- [ ] title 서적
- [ ] virtual 가상의
- [ ] aggressive 공격적인
- [ ] operating cost 운영비
- [ ] combination 결합
- [ ] snowball 눈덩이처럼 커지다
- [ ] enormous 거대한

16

- [ ] literary work 문학 작품
- [ ] nature 본질
- [ ] imply 함축하다
- [ ] generalization 일반화
- [ ] literature 문학
- [ ] statement 진술
- [ ] implication 함축
- [ ] proportion 비율
- [ ] interpret 해석하다
- [ ] analytical 분석적인
- [ ] practice 기량, 연습

17

- [ ] respect 존중
- [ ] reexamine 재점검하다
- [ ] golden rule 황금률
- [ ] treat 대접하다
- [ ] monocultural 단일 문화의
- [ ] framework 틀, 체제
- [ ] multicultural 다문화의
- [ ] unintended 의도하지 않은
- [ ] frustrating 불만스러운
- [ ] interpret 해석하다

WORD EXTRACT

□ miscommunication 의사소통 오류

18
□ pretend ~인 척하다
□ survey 설문조사하다
□ resident 주민
□ display 전시하다
□ participant 참가자
□ naturally 당연히, 물론
□ incredible 믿을 수 없는
□ approve 승낙하다
□ commitment 약속
□ request 요청
□ astonishing 놀라운
□ initial 처음의
□ willingness 기꺼이 하려는 의향[마음]

19
□ attract 끌다
□ measure 측정하다, 판단하다
□ eyesight 시력
□ evolution 진화
□ involve 수반하다, 관련시키다
□ organism 유기체
□ generation 세대
□ alert 경계하는
□ recognize 알아보다
□ afar 멀리, 아득히

20
□ interact 상호 작용하다, 소통하다
□ critical 중요한
□ analyze 분석하다
□ demonstrate 보여 주다, 증명하다
□ weakness 약점
□ raise 제기하다
□ certainly 분명히, 확실히
□ responsibility 책임
□ combat 싸우다
□ information literate 정보를 이용할 줄 아는

21
□ include 포함하다
□ certain 어느 정도의
□ hollow 속이 빈

□ light 가벼운
□ foam rubber 발포 고무
□ bounce 튀다
□ properly 적절히
□ solid 순수한(다른 물질이 섞이지 않은), 고체의
□ rubber 고무
□ clay 점토

22
□ equation 등식, 방정식
□ chemistry 화학
□ chemist 화학자
□ list 나열하다, 열거하다
□ element 원소, 요소
□ form 구성하다, 형성하다
□ bottom 아래(의)
□ atom 원자
□ hydrogen 수소
□ oxygen 산소

23
□ grab 잡다, 움켜쥐다
□ point 초점을 맞추다
□ shoot 사진을 찍다, 촬영하다
□ available 이용할 수 있는
□ exposure 노출
□ common 흔한
□ reflect 반사시키다
□ present 있는, 존재하는
□ noticeable 두드러진, 현저한

24
□ causal 인과 관계의
□ merely 단지
□ sociologist 사회학자
□ misleading 오해의 소지가 있는
□ classic 전형적인
□ apparent 명백한
□ association 연관성, 관련성
□ ability 능력
□ independent 독립의
□ improvement 향상, 개선
□ dependent 종속의
□ factor 요인
□ hence 이런 이유로

□ claim 주장

17강 주어진 문장 넣기

01

□ boundary 경계
□ portable 휴대용의
□ differ 다르다
□ segment 분할하다, 나누다
□ minimize 최소화하다
□ account 계정
□ conduct 수행하다
□ matter 일, 사안, 문제
□ flexible 유연한
□ distinction 구별, 차별
□ integrate 통합하다
□ constantly 지속적으로

02

□ complementary 보완적인
□ consume 소비하다, 소모하다
□ alongside ~와 함께
□ pillow 베개
□ produce 생산하다
□ ensure 보장하다, 반드시 ~하게 하다
□ stream 흐름
□ demand 수요
□ status 상태
□ purchase 구매하다; 구매

03

□ pace 속도
□ reflect 비추다
□ stare 빤히 쳐다보다
□ proof 증거
□ snapshot 스냅사진
□ reflection (거울에 비친) 모습
□ interval 기간
□ recognize 알아보다
□ basic 기본적인

04

□ psychologist 심리학자
□ decrease 줄다, 줄어들다
□ disinterested 흥미 없는
□ decline 감소
□ trace 추적하다
□ infant 유아의
□ contain ~을 가지고 있다
□ neural 신경의
□ connection 연결
□ efficient 효율적인
□ perception 인식
□ consequently 결과적으로
□ intensely 대단히, 매우
□ disordered 무질서한
□ absorb 흡수하다
□ harden 굳어지다
□ regularly 주기적으로, 정기적으로

05

□ complex 복합의, 복잡한
□ break down ~을 분해하다, 분해되다
□ trap 가두다
□ nutrient 영양소
□ release 방출하다
□ fuel 연료
□ a number of 많은 ~
□ structure 구조
□ hold 가지고 있다
□ rather 상당히
□ store 저장하다

06

□ commonly 흔히
□ mistaken 잘못된
□ assumption 가정
□ characteristic 특성
□ automatically 자동적으로
□ description 설명, 묘사
□ contain 포함하다
□ impression 인상
□ original 최초의, 원래의
□ interact 소통하다, 상호 작용을 하다
□ expectation 기대
□ affect 영향을 미치다

- [ ] form 형성하다
- [ ] relationship 관계

07

- [ ] analytic 분석적인
- [ ] cognitive 인지의
- [ ] fundamental 근본적인
- [ ] countless 수많은
- [ ] navigate 항해하다
- [ ] preserve 보존하다
- [ ] assume 가정하다
- [ ] operation 작용
- [ ] enormously 매우, 엄청나게, 대단히
- [ ] contribute 기여하다
- [ ] astonishingly 놀랍게도
- [ ] depend on ~에 의존하다
- [ ] in part 부분적으로
- [ ] effective 효과적인
- [ ] contributor 기여 요소
- [ ] collaborative 협력적인

08

- [ ] essentially 본질적으로
- [ ] completely 완전히
- [ ] chemical 화학적인
- [ ] makeup 성질
- [ ] contain 들어 있다
- [ ] temperature 온도
- [ ] remove 없애다
- [ ] mix 섞이다
- [ ] perhaps 아마도, 어쩌면
- [ ] remain 여전히 ~이다, 남다, 남아 있다
- [ ] separate 분리된
- [ ] float 떠다니다, 뜨다
- [ ] surface 표면
- [ ] salt content 염분

09

- [ ] consume 소비하다
- [ ] evidence 증거
- [ ] motivate 동기를 부여하다
- [ ] sustainable 지속적인, 지속 가능한
- [ ] volunteer 할애하다, (자발적으로) 제공하다

10

- [ ] associate 연관 짓다
- [ ] concept 개념
- [ ] object 물건, 물체
- [ ] qualitative 정성적인
- [ ] indication 지표, 표시
- [ ] unreliable 신뢰할 수 없는
- [ ] mislead 잘못 인도하다, 호도하다
- [ ] transfer 전달, 이동
- [ ] reliable 신뢰할 수 있는
- [ ] reproducible 재현 가능한
- [ ] relative 상대적인
- [ ] quantitative 정량적인

11

- [ ] friction 마찰력
- [ ] force (물리적으로 나타나는) 힘
- [ ] surface 표면
- [ ] slide 미끄러지다
- [ ] opposite 반대편의
- [ ] material 물질, 재료
- [ ] produce 발생시키다
- [ ] rub 비비다
- [ ] prevent 막다, 예방하다
- [ ] grip 붙잡다

12

- [ ] sight 시력
- [ ] visual 시각적인
- [ ] collection 수집
- [ ] imaginative 상상력이 풍부한
- [ ] unique 독특한, 특별한
- [ ] construct 구성하다
- [ ] familiar 친한, 친숙한
- [ ] lighting 조명
- [ ] associate 연상하다
- [ ] combination 조합
- [ ] represent 표현하다, 나타내다
- [ ] overall 전반적인

13

- [ ] ecosystem 생태계
- [ ] wildlife 야생 생물
- [ ] opportunity 기회
- [ ] shelter 서식지

□ react 작용하다
□ respond 반응하다
□ completely 완전히
□ prey 먹이로 삼다
□ dramatic 극적인
□ drought 가뭄
□ survive 살아남다

14

□ inspire 영감을 주다
□ dawn 시작, 새벽
□ civilization 문명
□ ancestor 선조
□ myth 신화
□ legendary 전설의
□ element 요소
□ identity 정체성
□ practical 실용적인
□ aid 보조 도구
□ seasonal 계절에 따른
□ gathering 수확
□ navigation 항해
□ remote 외딴, 멀리 떨어진

15

□ nutrition 영양
□ nutrient 영양분, 영양소
□ absorb 흡수하다
□ consume 섭취하다
□ attempt 시도
□ artificial 인공적인, 인위적인
□ completely 완전히
□ substance 물질
□ ingredient 성분
□ investigative 조사의
□ regulation 규제
□ costly 대가가 큰

16

□ kinetic energy 운동 에너지
□ be associated with ~와 관련되다
□ potential energy 위치 에너지
□ conserve 보존하다
□ swing 흔들리다
□ back and forth 앞뒤로

□ sweep 쓸어내리다
□ slow down 속도가 줄어들다
□ completely 완전히
□ brief 짧은
□ constantly 끊임없이

17

□ consistently 일관적으로, 일관되게
□ effective 효율적인
□ pain reliever 진통제
□ treat 치료하다
□ positive 긍정적인
□ correlation 상관관계
□ intake 섭취(량)
□ stay alert 깨어 있는[각성된] 상태로 있다
□ reaction 반응, 반작용
□ additionally 추가로
□ adequate 적절한, 충분한

18

□ reward 보상하다
□ material 물질적인
□ recognize 인정하다
□ settle 해결하다, 합의를 보다
□ interrupt 방해하다
□ happen 일어나다, 발생하다
□ unbelievably 믿을 수 없을 정도로
□ amazingly 놀랄 만큼
□ positive 긍정적인
□ impact 영향, 충격
□ peer 동료, 또래
□ recognition 인정, 인식

19

□ wave 파동, 파장
□ surface 표면
□ still 고요한, 잔잔한
□ outwards 바깥쪽으로
□ impact 충격
□ sound source 음원
□ disturbance 방해, 교란
□ bang 쾅 하고 치다
□ compress 압축하다
□ release 방출하다
□ density 밀도

☐ displace 바꾸다

20

☐ transfer 이동; 옮기다, 이동하다
☐ source 원천, 근원
☐ organism 유기체
☐ grassland 초원, 목초지
☐ imply 의미하다
☐ sequence 연속적인 사건
☐ proportion 부분, 비율
☐ potential 잠재적인
☐ intake 섭취량

21

☐ overestimate 과대평가하다
☐ defining 결정적인, 정의하는
☐ underestimate 과소평가하다
☐ convince 확신시키다, 굳게 믿게 하다
☐ massive 거대한
☐ championship 선수권, 우승
☐ achieve 달성하다, 성취하다
☐ pressure 압력
☐ earthshaking 세상을 떠들썩하게 하는
☐ meanwhile 한편
☐ notable 눈에 띄는
☐ meaningful 의미 있는
☐ tiny 작은, 사소한
☐ end up 결국 ~하게 되다
☐ conversely 역으로
☐ decline 떨어지다, 하락하다
☐ minor 사소한
☐ failure 패배

22

☐ human race 인류
☐ adapt 적응하다
☐ ancient 고대의
☐ ancestor 조상
☐ gap 간극, 격차
☐ rely on ~에 의존하다
☐ heavily 크게, 몹시
☐ modern 현대의
☐ head off ~로 향하다
☐ wilderness 미지의 땅
☐ native 토착의, 지방 고유의

☐ gear 장비
☐ crucial 중요한
☐ arise 발생하다, 일어나다
☐ avoid 피하다

23

☐ daylight 햇빛
☐ signal 신호
☐ purpose 목적
☐ biological clock 생체 시계
☐ reset 재설정하다
☐ principal 주요한
☐ preferential 우선하는
☐ external 외부의
☐ cue 신호
☐ precise 정확한
☐ phenomenon 현상(*pl*. phenomena)
☐ zeitgeber 자연 시계(생물 시계의 주기에 영향을 미치는 외적 요소)
☐ synchronizer 동기화 장치

24

☐ agricultural 농업의
☐ integrate 통합하다
☐ co-evolve 함께 진화하다
☐ myth 신화
☐ tradition 전통
☐ crop 농작물
☐ obtain 얻다, 획득하다
☐ stable 안정적인
☐ maintain 유지하다
☐ non-destructive 비파괴적인
☐ incorporate 통합하다, 포함하다
☐ commodity 상품, 물품
☐ divert 전환하다

18강 요약문 완성

01

☐ judge 판단하다
☐ investigate 조사하다
☐ surgeon 외과 의사
☐ scrubs (외과 의사의) 수술복
☐ notable 주목할 만한, 눈에 띄는

□ exception 예외
□ observer 관찰자
□ establish 확립하다
□ norm 규범
□ competence 능력
□ deviation 일탈

02

□ spoiled stew 상한 스튜
□ poison mushroom 독버섯
□ combination 조합
□ raw 날것의
□ tofu 두부
□ nutrient-dense 영양이 풍부한
□ supply 공급하다
□ nutrient 영양소
□ occasionally 가끔
□ otherwise 그렇지 않으면
□ load up on ~로 배를 가득 채우다
□ supersized 초대형의

03

□ risky 위험한
□ trustworthy 신뢰할 수 있는
□ evidence 증거
□ evolutionary 진화의
□ positive 긍정적인
□ prospect 전망
□ survival 생존
□ psychologist 심리학자
□ frequently 자주, 빈번하게
□ product review 상품 평
□ cue 신호
□ signal 나타내다
□ in demand 수요가 많은
□ adopt 따르다, 채택하다
□ practice 행동, 관행

04

□ reflective 반성[숙고]하는
□ journaling 일기 쓰기
□ think back on ~을 되돌아보다
□ researcher 연구인
□ value 가치
□ undergraduate student 학부생

□ confident 자신 있는
□ handle 다루다
□ reflect on ~을 되돌아보다
□ support 뒷받침하다
□ perspective 관점
□ demonstration 드러냄, 입증
□ reframe 재구성하다

05

□ colleague (직장) 동료
□ experiment 실험
□ convince 납득시키다, 설득하다
□ resistant 저항하는
□ emphasize 강조하다
□ donate 기부하다
□ benefit ~에게 이익[이득]이 되다
□ faculty 교직원
□ donor 기부자
□ glow 온기, 만족감
□ unwilling 마음이 내키지 않는, 마지못해 하는
□ combine 합치다, 결합하다
□ drop 떨어지다
□ trigger 유발하다
□ awareness 인식, 인지
□ shield 보호하다

06

□ adolescent 청소년
□ academic 학문적인
□ challenge 어려움, 도전
□ authoritative 권위가 있는
□ parenting 양육
□ helpless 무기력한
□ involvement 관여, 개입
□ perform 수행하다
□ praise 칭찬하다
□ excellence 탁월함

07

□ layer 층
□ concentration 농도
□ damaging 해로운
□ redistribute 재분배하다
□ shallow 얕은
□ absorb 흡수하다

□ concentrate 농축시키다
□ decay 썩다
□ poison (독성 물질로) 오염시키다, 중독시키다
□ immune 면역성이 있는
□ toxic 유독한
□ eliminate 제거하다
□ competition 경쟁자
□ surrounding 주변의

08

□ uncertainty 불확실성
□ realm 영역
□ informed 정보에 근거한
□ in particular 특히
□ fantastically 엄청나게
□ complex 복잡한
□ black-or-white 흑백 양자택일의
□ oversimplify 지나치게 단순화하다
□ definitive 확정적인

09

□ conduct 실시하다, 실행하다
□ assign 배치하다
□ interact 상호 작용하다
□ agreement 합의, 동의
□ additional 추가적인
□ noticeable 뚜렷한, 분명한
□ reveal 나타나다
□ thirst 갈망, 열망
□ differ 의견이 다르다

10

□ classic 전형적인
□ tragedy-of-the-commons 공유지의 비극
□ share 몫, 할당
□ destroy 파괴시키다
□ behavior 행동
□ remove 없애다
□ share 함께 쓰다, 공유하다
□ satisfaction 만족
□ following 다음의

11

□ nearby 근처의
□ present 있는, 존재하는

□ participant 참가자
□ quality 질
□ relationship 관계
□ check 확인하다
□ hurt 해치다, 상하게 하다
□ connection 관계, 연결

12

□ colleague 동료
□ tendency 경향
□ infancy 유아기
□ innate 선천적인
□ measure 척도
□ attention 주의집중, 주목
□ apparently 분명히, 명백히
□ stare 쳐다보다, 응시하다
□ routinely 일상적으로, 판에 박힌 듯이
□ cite 인용하다
□ evidence 증거
□ evolutionary 진화론적인
□ favorable 호의적인

19강 장문의 이해

01~02

□ claim 주장
□ production 생산
□ greenhouse gas 온실가스
□ emission 배출
□ fuel 연료
□ wasteful 낭비되는
□ field-grown 밭에서 재배된
□ ship 수송하다
□ carbon footprint 탄소 발자국(개인 또는 단체가 발생시키는 온실가스의 총량)
□ generate 발생시키다
□ one-quarter 4분의 1
□ pastureland 목초지
□ bulk 대량의
□ halfway 절반

03~04

□ chief 추장

□ surplus 잉여, 흑자
□ vital 필수적인
□ sufficient 충분한
□ council 의회
□ agriculture 농업
□ grain 곡물
□ support 지원하다; 지원
□ practice 개업하다
□ priest 성직자
□ warrior 전사
□ in return 그 대가로
□ yield 생산량
□ consistent 지속적인
□ concentrate 집중하다
□ carpenter 목수
□ blacksmith 대장장이
□ merchant 상인
□ trader 무역업자
□ efficient 효율적인
□ quality 질
□ stability 안정성

05~06
□ piece (장기, 체스의) 말, 조각
□ reproduce 재현하다
□ position 위치
□ place 기억해 내다, 놓다
□ randomly 무작위로
□ reduce 줄어들다, 줄이다
□ expert 전문가
□ advantage 유리함
□ previously 이전에
□ face 직면하다
□ involve ~와 관련 있다
□ domain 분야
□ disappear 사라지다
□ beneficial 유익한
□ observe 관찰하다
□ including ~을 포함하여
□ accurately 정확하게
□ note 음표
□ order 배열하다
□ range 범위
□ increase 증가하다, 늘어나다

□ recognize 인식하다

07~08
□ adapt 적응하다
□ cultivate 쌓다, 구축하다
□ compensate 보충되다
□ restore 회복하다
□ perception 인식
□ disrupt 방해하다
□ overload 과부하가 걸리게 하다
□ stimuli 자극(stimulus의 복수형)
□ frightening 무서운
□ overwhelming 압도적인
□ stimulation 자극
□ confusion 혼란
□ assume 가정하다
□ neuroscientific 신경 과학의
□ collaborative 협력적인
□ disturb 방해하다
□ alter 바꾸다
□ primarily 주로
□ anticipate 예상하다

09~10
□ reject 거부하다
□ consumption 섭취
□ individual 개개인
□ overcome 극복하다
□ rejection 거부
□ attitude 태도
□ convince 납득시키다
□ lobster 바닷가재
□ luxury 고급진; 호사
□ servant 하인
□ prisoner 죄수
□ rural 시골의
□ consume 섭취하다
□ population 인구
□ poverty 가난
□ shame 수치심
□ categorize 분류하다
□ uncivilized 미개한
□ anthropologist 인류학자
□ promote 장려하다
□ educate 교육하다

11~12

- [ ] bedtime 취침 시간
- [ ] lower 낮추다
- [ ] heart disease 심장 질환
- [ ] volunteer 자원자
- [ ] monitor 추적 관찰하다
- [ ] ideal 이상적인
- [ ] comment 언급하다, 논평하다
- [ ] body clock 체내 시계
- [ ] consequence 결과
- [ ] likelihood 가능성
- [ ] reset 재설정하다
- [ ] risk 위험을 무릅쓰다
- [ ] properly 적절하게

13~14

- [ ] journey 여정, 여행
- [ ] shorten 줄이다
- [ ] misery 불행, 비참함
- [ ] impatience 조급함
- [ ] judgment 비난, 비판
- [ ] frustration 좌절
- [ ] shift 바뀌다
- [ ] unknowingly 무심코
- [ ] in traffic 차량 흐름에서
- [ ] splash 튀기다, 끼얹다
- [ ] pen (글을) 쓰다
- [ ] miserable 비참한
- [ ] statement 진술
- [ ] deny 부정하다

15~16

- [ ] diagnosis 진단(pl. diagnoses)
- [ ] genetic determinism 유전자 결정론
- [ ] subsequent 이후의
- [ ] destined ~할 운명인
- [ ] inherit 물려받다
- [ ] dynamic 역학
- [ ] predetermine 미리 결정하다
- [ ] racially 인종적으로
- [ ] simplistic 지나치게 단순화한
- [ ] remarkable 놀랄 만한

17~18

- [ ] harsh 가혹한

- [ ] complaint 불평
- [ ] handle 다루다
- [ ] cosmetics 화장품
- [ ] sticky 끈적거리는
- [ ] sunblock lotion 자외선 차단 로션
- [ ] risk 위험
- [ ] capture 점유하다, 차지하다
- [ ] opposite 반대의
- [ ] stick 달라붙다
- [ ] envelope 봉투
- [ ] moisten 적시다, 축이다
- [ ] conclusion 결론
- [ ] wet 적시다
- [ ] glue 접착제, 풀
- [ ] occur 일어나다, 발생하다
- [ ] dissatisfied 불만족스러운

19~20

- [ ] socializing 사교
- [ ] tricky 까다로운
- [ ] inanimate 무생물의
- [ ] interact 상호 작용을 하다, 소통하다
- [ ] response 반응
- [ ] unpredictable 예측할 수 없는
- [ ] complex 복잡한
- [ ] self-esteem 자존감
- [ ] confidence 자신감
- [ ] tidy 잘 정돈된, 깔끔한
- [ ] unavoidable 피할 수 없는
- [ ] experiment 실험하다
- [ ] pointless 무의미한
- [ ] exposure 노출
- [ ] messy 복잡한, 엉망진창인

21~22

- [ ] fall off 넘어지다
- [ ] attempt 시도
- [ ] judge 판단하다, 판정하다
- [ ] awkward 어색한
- [ ] shame 애석한 일, 수치
- [ ] repetition 반복
- [ ] central 핵심적인
- [ ] rewire 재연결하다, 전선을 다시 배치하다
- [ ] neuron 뉴런, 신경 세포
- [ ] reliable 신뢰할 만한

□ hit-and-miss 마구잡이의, 되는대로 하는
□ involve 연관시키다

23~24
□ primitive 원시 사회의, 원시적 단계의
□ random 무작위의
□ interpret 해석하다
□ utter (입으로 어떤 소리를) 내다, (말을) 하다
□ component (구성) 요소, 부품
□ aspiration 열망, 포부, 염원
□ ultimately 궁극적으로, 결국
□ crucial 중대한, 결정적인
□ core 핵심
□ offend 기분 상하게[불쾌하게] 하다

20강 복합 문단의 이해

01~03
□ grand 큰, 웅장한
□ temple 사원
□ worship 예배를 드리러 가다, 예배하다
□ accommodation 숙소
□ notice 공고문, 안내문
□ applicant 지원자
□ qualified 자격이 있는
□ offer 제안; 제안하다
□ educated 교육받은, 학식 있는
□ confused 당황스러운
□ bury 묻다
□ path 길
□ trip over 발이 걸려 넘어지다
□ dig up ~을 땅에서 파내다
□ duty 의무

04~06
□ anxious 불안해하는
□ severe 극심한
□ heart disease 심장병
□ barely 간신히
□ wrap (감)싸다
□ support 지지, 후원
□ suggest 제안하다
□ dawn 동틀 녘, 새벽
□ release 놓아주다

□ hesitate 머뭇거리다

07~09
□ approach 접근하다
□ guard 경비병
□ freeze 얼어붙다, 얼다
□ demand 요구하다
□ eventually 결국, 마침내
□ whole 전체(의)
□ return 돌아오다
□ immediately 즉시
□ continue 계속하다
□ gesture 행동
□ massage 마사지, 안마
□ relaxing 편안한
□ tiny 매우 작은
□ disappear 사라지다

10~12
□ present 선물
□ chat 담소를 나누다
□ mention 언급하다
□ attentive 세심한
□ for free 무료로
□ unexpectedly 갑자기
□ stuck 갇힌
□ get better 회복하다, 낫다
□ moved 감동받은
□ generosity 관대함
□ empathy 공감
□ unforgettable 잊을 수 없는
□ experience 경험

13~15
□ surround 둘러싸다
□ pair 한 쌍
□ firmly 꽉
□ gate 문
□ brilliant 굉장한, 화려한
□ exclaim 외치다
□ spot 발견하다
□ break time 쉬는 시간
□ completely 완전히
□ ignore 무시하다
□ lean 기대다(-leant-leant)

WORD EXTRACT

□ fence 울타리
□ exhausted 지친, 기진맥진한
□ crowd 무리
□ voice 목소리
□ greet ~에게 인사하다
□ mistaken 잘못된
□ argue 논쟁하다
□ arrangements 준비
□ join ~에 들다, ~의 회원이 되다
□ pupil 학생

16~18
□ precious 귀중한
□ ordinary 평범한
□ exhausted 지쳐버린, 기진맥진한
□ reward 보상; 보상을 하다
□ hay 건초(마른 풀)
□ decrease 줄어들다, 감소하다
□ chance 기회; 가능성
□ succeed 성공하다
□ direction 방향
□ delighted 기뻐하는

19~21
□ village 마을
□ notice 알아차리다
□ field 들판
□ reply 대답하다
□ valley 골짜기
□ unwelcoming 불친절한
□ lower 내리다, 낮추다
□ helplessly 힘없이
□ middle-aged 중년의
□ come upon ~을 만나다
□ wonderful 멋진
□ generous 너그러운

22~24
□ afford ~할 여유가 있다
□ beam 빛나다
□ offer 권하다, 제공하다
□ expectantly 기대하며
□ sour (맛이) 신
□ distaste 불쾌감
□ cheerfully 기꺼이, 기분 좋게

□ please 기쁘게 하다
□ move 감동시키다
□ thoughtfulness 사려 깊음

25~27
□ merchant 상인
□ pretend ~인 척하다
□ goods 물건, 물품
□ valuable 귀중품
□ gather 모으다
□ luxurious 호화로운
□ replace 바꾸다, 교체하다
□ lift 들어 올리다
□ tear apart ~을 찢다
□ say under one's breath 숨죽이며 말하다
□ skillful 능숙한
□ core 속, 중심

28~30
□ organize 정리하다
□ paper clip 종이 클립[집게]
□ rust 녹; 녹슬다
□ dust 먼지투성이로 만들다
□ equality 평등, 균등
□ marvel 놀라다, 경탄하다
□ separate 분리하다, 나누다
□ deliver (연설을) 하다
□ hand 건네주다
□ permission 허락, 허가
□ scared 겁먹은, 무서워하는
□ face 직면하다, 마주보다
□ generation 세대, (비슷한 연령의) 사람들
□ immediately 즉시

31~33
□ passion 열정
□ kingdom 왕국
□ locate 위치시키다
□ foot ~의 맨 아래 부분
□ nearby 인근의, 가까운 곳의
□ preparation 준비
□ spot 발견하다
□ pass by 지나가다
□ deerskin 사슴 가죽
□ fearlessly 두려움 없이

- ☐ lick 핥다
- ☐ servant 부하, 하인
- ☐ loss 상실, 죽음

34~36
- ☐ renowned 유명한
- ☐ tradition 전통
- ☐ demonstrate 보여 주다, 설명하다
- ☐ exhibit 전시하다, 보이다
- ☐ speechless 말을 못하는
- ☐ death wish 죽음에 대한 동경
- ☐ whisper 속삭이다
- ☐ starve 굶주리다
- ☐ distress 고통, 괴로움
- ☐ suspect 의심하다
- ☐ victorious 승리한

◆ 괄호에서 알맞은 것을 고르거나, 빈칸에 주어진 단어를 올바른 형태로 쓰시오.

01 This travel package includes special trips to Lake Madison as well as massage and meditation [helps / to help] you relax.

02 We are sure [what / that] it will be an unforgettable experience for you.

03 The facilities [have been / are being] in this terrible condition since we moved here.

04 Would you please have the facilities _____(repair)_____?

05 Moreover, in the last year alone, I have brought in two new major clients to the company, [increased / increasing] the company's total sales by 5%.

06 The case must [fall / have fallen] off my lap and onto the floor when I took it off my phone to clean it.

07 [Despite / Though] we wish to participate in the event, we do not have the necessary funds to travel to London.

08 One of the aims of these activities [is / are] to make us aware of various types of news media and the language used in printed newspaper articles.

09 It is, therefore, my humble request to you [allow / to allow] us to use old newspapers that have been stored in the school library.

10 We request you to create a logo that best _____(suit)_____ our company's core vision, 'To inspire humanity.'

11 Thanks to the Friends of Literature group, we've successfully raised enough money (remodel) the library building.

12 By grabbing a hammer or a paint brush and [donate / donating] your time, you can help with the construction.

13 Wildlife faces pressure from development, and these animals need space [which / where] they can hide from human activity.

◆ 괄호 안에 주어진 단어를 바르게 배열하시오.

14 The goal of the fair is to [to / them / encourage / be interested in] science through guided experiments.

15 I want [to / to / you / pay attention] the poor condition of the playground equipment in the zone.

16 The land [the / which / through / proposed / Pine Hill walking trail] would cut is home to a variety of species.

◆ 괄호에서 알맞은 것을 고르거나, 빈칸에 주어진 단어를 올바른 형태로 쓰시오.

01 I called them, but I heard their phones [rang / ringing] in the room.

02 He was following the scent of something, and slowly I began to realize [that / which] this giant animal was smelling me!

03 I arrived at the nail salon, and muted my cellphone [in / so] that I would be disconnected for the hour and feel calm and peaceful.

04 The swing set was his favorite thing to do at the park. But the swings were all [using / being used].

05 Zoe felt as if she [are / were] in heaven.

06 When my mom came home from the mall with a special present for me I was pretty [sure / surely] I knew what it was.

07 I flipped through the pages, figuring that maybe she _____(hide)_____ my new phone inside.

08 But I slowly realized that my mom had not got [me / for me] a phone and my present was just a little book, which was so different from what I had wanted.

09 _____ (Be) at a loss, she stood still rooted to the ground.

10 Yes, and there's one thing that may be [interesting / interested] to you.

11 It was exactly [which / what] I had always dreamed of.

12 I sat on my bed and cried for hours [during / while] my mother watched me silently from the doorway of my room.

◆ 괄호 안에 주어진 단어를 바르게 배열하시오.

13 I knew immediately that [bad / something / coming / was].

14 Zoe and one of the other finalists had won first placing in four subjects so it came down to [ranked / how / teachers] hard work and confidence.

◆ 괄호에서 알맞은 것을 고르거나, 빈칸에 주어진 단어를 올바른 형태로 쓰시오.

01 Research shows that people who work [have / to have] two calendars: one for work and one for their personal lives.

02 This will allow you _____(make)_____ informed decisions about which tasks are most important.

03 If you haven't thought about energy peaks before, take a few days to observe [you / yourself].

04 Most people believe that [having / to have] a successful business blog promoting a product, they have to stay strictly 'on the topic.'

05 You should create a list of items to be discussed and [share / shared] your list with other participants before a meeting.

06 When I was in the army, my instructors would show up in my barracks room, and the first thing they would inspect _____(be)_____ our bed.

07 If you [make / will make] your bed every morning, you will have accomplished the first task of the day.

08 [Pay / Paying] attention to the nonverbal messages you send can make a significant difference in your relationship with students.

09 Think about [how / what] encouraging and empowering it is for a student when that teacher has a friendly greeting and a welcoming smile.

10 You are [active / actively] shutting out success because you want to avoid being uncomfortable.

11 Change is always uncomfortable, but it is key to [doing / done] things differently in order to find that magical formula for success.

12 But before you hit the Send key, make sure [that / what] you read your document carefully one last time.

13 When I was in high school, we had students who could study in the coffee shop and not get distracted by the noise or everything happening around [it / them].

◆ 괄호 안에 주어진 단어를 바르게 배열하시오.

14 It is [for / maintain / difficult / to / any of us] a constant level of attention throughout our working day.

15 Only by doing this [create / can / you] an interested audience that you will then be able to sell to.

16 These students were victims of distractions who [it / to / very / found / study / difficult] anywhere except in their private bedrooms.

◆ 괄호에서 알맞은 것을 고르거나, 빈칸에 주어진 단어를 올바른 형태로 쓰시오.

01 You'll also determine [what / whether] the buyer will encourage others to purchase the product from you.

02 Satisfied customers can become [unpaid / unpaying] ambassadors for your business, so customer satisfaction should be on the top of your to-do list.

03 Thousands of traditional livelihoods have [pushed / been pushed] aside by progress, and the lifestyles around those jobs removed.

04 The divorce of the hands from the head [puts / are put] a stress on the human mind.

05 What if the biggest thing keeping us from doing what matters is the false assumption [that / what] it has to take huge effort?

06 If I hold it for a day straight, it will cause severe pain in my arm, forcing me _____ (drop) _____ the glass to the floor.

07 In each case, the weight of the glass is the same, but the longer I hold it, the _____ (heavy) _____ it feels to me.

08 When you are searching, you are not browsing, nor [you are / are you] "just looking".

09 Regardless of how long it may take you to find and get the job you want, being proactive will logically get you results faster than if you rely only on browsing online job boards and [email / emailing] an occasional resume.

10 Some people use and throw away plastic products ____(derive)____ from crude oil every day.

11 No longer [being / were] there any controlled communications or even business systems.

12 Consumers could generally learn through the Web [whatever / whenever] they wanted to know about a company, its products, its competitors, its distribution systems, and, most of all, its truthfulness when talking about its products and services.

◆ 괄호 안에 주어진 단어를 바르게 배열하시오.

13 We use the phrase "That's [to / for / easy / say / you]" as a criticism, usually when we are seeking to invalidate someone's opinion.

14 However, what seems to us to be standing out [be / may / very / to / well / related] our goals, interests, expectations, past experiences, or current demands of the situation — "with a hammer in hand, everything looks like a nail."

15 The only value of '[I / I / done / that / wish / hadn't]!' is that you'll know better what to do next time.

GRAMMAR EXTRACT

◆ 괄호에서 알맞은 것을 고르거나, 빈칸에 주어진 단어를 올바른 형태로 쓰시오.

01 The promise of a computerized society was that it would pass to machines all of the repetitive drudgery of work, _____(allow)_____ us humans to pursue higher purposes and to have more leisure time.

02 Things that [used to / are used to] be done for us, as part of the value-added service of working with a company, we are now expected to do ourselves.

03 At the grocery store, we're expected to bag our own groceries and, in some supermarkets, [scanning / to scan] our own purchases.

04 When students are starting their college life, they may approach every course, test, or learning task the same way, using [that / what] we like to call "the rubber-stamp approach."

05 Frightening news can actually rob people of their inner sense of control, making them less likely to take care of [them / themselves] and other people.

06 You may feel depressed and decide that you did [poor / poorly] in an interview when you did just fine.

07 Research reveals that a number of vital tasks carried out during sleep _____(help)_____ to maintain good health and enable people to function at their best.

08 [During / While] you sleep, your brain is hard at work forming the pathways necessary for learning and creating memories and new insights.

09 In a rush to meet work, school, family, or household responsibilities, people cut back on their sleep, thinking [it / they] won't be a problem, because all of these other activities seem much more important.

10 Far too often, companies collect valuable customer information that ends up [burying / buried] and never used.

11 [That / Whether] they have ten customers, ten thousand, or even ten million, the goal is the same: create a delightful customer experience that encourages loyalty.

12 This policy is based on the belief [that / which] students perform at a failure level or submit failing work in large part because teachers accept it.

13 Situations are uniquely stressful for each of us based on [if / whether] or not they activate our doubt.

14 It's not unlike hitting the snooze button on your alarm clock only _____(pull)_____ the covers over your head and fall back asleep.

◆ 괄호 안에 주어진 단어를 바르게 배열하시오.

15 And they [know / do / not / to / what / only], but they also know how to do it.

16 A news article that's intended to warn people about increasing cancer rates can result in [the disease / choosing to get screened for / fewer people].

◆ 괄호에서 알맞은 것을 고르거나, 빈칸에 주어진 단어를 올바른 형태로 쓰시오.

01 We tend to believe that we possess a host of socially desirable characteristics, and [that / what] we are free of most of those that are socially undesirable.

02 This phenomenon is [as / so] reliable and ubiquitous that it has come to be known as the "Lake Wobegon effect."

03 At the same time, forms of transport improved and [it / they] became faster and cheaper to get to places.

04 The most remarkable and unbelievable consequence of melting ice and rising seas [is / are] that together they are a kind of time machine, so real that they are altering the duration of our day.

05 Children reveal and investigate mathematical concepts through their own activities or experiences, such as figuring out how many crackers [take / to take] at snack time or sorting shells into piles.

06 Farmers in India know when the monsoon rains [come / will come] next year and so they know when to plant the crops.

07 Well-being is fundamentally no different than [learn / learning] to play the cello.

08 The more neurons fire as they are activated by repeated thoughts and activities, the _____(fast)_____ they develop into neural pathways, which cause lasting changes in the brain.

09 This is [so / such] an encouraging premise: bottom line — we can intentionally create the habits for the brain to be happier.

10 Health concerns are not the only reason [that / which] young adults give for changing their diets.

11 Curiosity makes us much more likely to view a tough problem as an interesting challenge _____(take)_____ on.

12 When one person lies, their responses will come [most / more] slowly because the brain needs more time to process the details of a new invention than to recall stored facts.

13 The use of renewable sources of energy to produce electricity has increasingly been ___(encourage)___ as a way to harmonize the need to secure electricity supply with environmental protection objectives.

14 Hydropower dams, for example, have an impact on aquatic ecosystems and, more recently, have been ____(identify)____ as significant sources of greenhouse emissions.

◆ 괄호 안에 주어진 단어를 바르게 배열하시오.

15 With the railways [many large hotels / came].

16 In general, curiosity motivates us [challenges / view / stressful situations / to / as] rather than threats, to talk about difficulties more openly, and to try new approaches to solving problems.

◆ 괄호에서 알맞은 것을 고르거나, 빈칸에 주어진 단어를 올바른 형태로 쓰시오.

01 Few people will be surprised to hear [that / whose] poverty tends to create stress.

02 In effect, fast-paced productivity creates wealth, but it also leads people _____(feel)_____ time-poor when they lack the time to relax and enjoy themselves.

03 If you are good at something and are well rewarded for doing it, you may want to keep doing it even if you stop [enjoying / to enjoy] it.

04 The poor employment market has left them feeling locked in [that / what] may be a secure, or even well-paying — but ultimately unsatisfying — job.

05 [Be / Being] right about something means that "it is the way it is, period."

06 If you see their side, you will see something new or, at worse, _____(learn)_____ something about how the other person looks at life.

07 Only a generation or two ago, mentioning the word *algorithms* would [draw / have drawn] a blank from most people.

08 Your bank is a huge web of algorithms, with humans [turning / turned] the switches here and there.

09 Our ability to accurately recognize and label emotions [is / are] often referred to as *emotional granularity*.

10 Traditional role identities prescribed by society began to appear as masks imposed on people [which / whose] real self was to be found somewhere underneath.

11 David explains that if we don't have a rich emotional vocabulary, it is difficult to communicate our needs and [getting / to get] the support that we need from others.

12 Antony Wood, a Professor of Architecture at the Illinois Institute of Technology, explains that advances in elevators over the past 20 years are probably the _____(great)_____ advances we have seen in tall buildings.

13 It is estimated [that / what] Australians alone spend on average $10.8 billion AUD (approximately $9.99 billion USD) every year on goods they do not use — more than the total government spending on universities and roads.

14 Chewing gives mammals the energy _____(need)_____ to be active not only during the day but also the cool night, and to live in colder climates or places with changing temperatures.

◆ 괄호 안에 주어진 단어를 바르게 배열하시오.

15 Besides [that / would be / how boring], it would eliminate all new opportunities, ideas, invention, and creativity.

16 When people think about the development of cities, rarely [do / consider / they] the critical role of vertical transportation.

◆ 괄호에서 알맞은 것을 고르거나, 빈칸에 주어진 단어를 올바른 형태로 쓰시오.

01 In 2019, the share of forest area in Europe was _____(large)_____ among the five regions, more than three times that in Asia in the same year.

02 In 2019, the gap between the number of births and deaths was the smallest, with the number of births [slightly larger / was slightly larger] than that of deaths.

03 The graph above shows the survey results on reasons for people interested in eating less meat and those [eat / eating] no meat in the UK in 2018.

04 In 2015, the rate of U.S. households with pets [was / were] 3 percentage points lower than in 2020.

05 Those aged 65 and older were the _____(little)_____ likely to use online courses among the six age groups.

06 The graph above shows the percentage of U.S. homeschooled and public school students [participated / participating] in cultural activities in 2016.

07 The percent of U.S. households with pets in 2013 was the same as that in 2017, [which / where] was 68 percent.

08 Belgium's health spending as a share of GDP sat between [that / those] of France and the UK.

09 The above graph shows the percentage of students from kindergarten to 12th grade [who / which] used devices to access digital educational content in 2016 and in 2019.

◆ 괄호 안에 주어진 단어를 바르게 배열하시오.

10 The share of forest area in America was 42.6% in 1990, which [that / than / was larger / in 2019].

11 Skateboarding was a sport children quit at the average age of 12, and the average length of participation [same / golf / was / the / as].

◆ 괄호에서 알맞은 것을 고르거나, 빈칸에 주어진 단어를 올바른 형태로 쓰시오.

01 After graduating from high school, Becker went to Princeton University, [which / where] he majored in economics.

02 [During / Since] 1985, Becker had written a regular economics column in *Business Week*, explaining economic analysis and ideas to the general public.

03 Unlike most other girls at the time she wore trousers and spent her time [to enjoy / enjoying] adventurous activities like horse riding and hunting.

04 Knight left school in 1850, at age 12, to earn money for her family at a nearby textile factory, [which / where] she witnessed a fellow worker injured by faulty equipment.

05 He [introduced / was introduced] to the world of jazz by a schoolmate.

06 [Since / Though] he couldn't draw well, he hired an artist to draw pictures of what he described.

07 As a female pioneer of flight, she inspired the next generation ____(pursue)____ their dreams of flying.

08 Lithops are small plants, rarely ____(get)____ more than an inch above the soil surface and usually with only two leaves.

09 After ____(disallow)____ entrance from the Carnegie Institute of Technology because she was black, Catlett studied design and drawing at Howard University.

10 In 1888, she moved to St. Louis, [which / where] she worked as a washerwoman for more than a decade, earning barely more than a dollar a day.

◆ 괄호 안에 주어진 단어를 바르게 배열하시오.

11 [her / to try / persuade / in order to] a slightly safer activity, Lilian's dad bought her a car.

12 [sell / only / she / not / did], she also recruited and trained lots of women as sales agents for a share of the profits.

◆ 괄호에서 알맞은 것을 고르거나, 빈칸에 주어진 단어를 올바른 형태로 쓰시오.

01 $500 and a medal will ____(award)____ to the winner.

02 Do you want to get your stories [to publish / published]?

03 All personal data on the devices must [be wiped / have wiped] out in advance.

04 You can sign up for classes either online [or / nor] by phone.

05 Bookings will [accept / be accepted] up to 2 hours before the tour starts.

06 Take this special tour and have a chance ____(enjoy)____ our most popular chocolate bars.

07 You can show the beauty of nature in Camptonville by sharing your most [amazing / amazed] photos!

08 The winners will ___(announce)___ only on the website on July 15th, 2021.

09 Get the access link by text message 10 minutes before the meeting and click [it / them].

10 Students in every grade will compete to build the most creative and livable structure ___(make)___ out of blocks!

◆ 괄호 안에 주어진 단어를 바르게 배열하시오.

11 You [your phone number / us / should send] together with your writing.

◆ 괄호에서 알맞은 것을 고르거나, 빈칸에 주어진 단어를 올바른 형태로 쓰시오.

01 Thinking of himself as a boy who is smart and knows how to do things is likely to make him endure longer in problem-solving efforts and [increase / increasing] his confidence in trying new and difficult tasks.

02 The most noticeable human characteristic projected onto animals [is / are] that they can talk in human language.

03 A general strategy that is used to make the animal characters more emotionally appealing, both to children and adults, _____(be)_____ to give them enlarged and deformed childlike features.

04 However, if you _____(be)_____ to consider all the tasks that AI-powered machines could actually perform, it would be quite mind-blowing!

05 These kinds of changes are exactly why [it / that] is so important to recognize the implications that new technologies will have for our world.

06 This is a very common human tendency that is rooted in [which / how] our species developed.

07 Similarities make us [relate / to relate] better to other people because we think they'll understand us on a deeper level than other people.

08 Fertilizing crops with nitrogen and potassium [has / have] led to declines in magnesium, zinc, iron and iodine.

09 Indeed, nowadays our soil is less healthy and so [is / are] the plants grown on it.

10 What happens if people don't spend all their money, saving some of [it / them] instead?

11 A genuine smile will impact on the muscles and wrinkles around the eyes and less [noticeable / noticeably], the skin between the eyebrow and upper eyelid is lowered slightly with true enjoyment.

12 Although there is usually a correct way of holding and playing musical instruments, the most important instruction to begin with is [that / what] they are not toys and that they must be looked after.

13 Correct playing comes from the desire to find the most appropriate sound quality and [find / finds] the most comfortable playing position so that one can play with control over time.

14 There are also differences between individuals, relating to the ability _____(smell)_____ an odour, or how pleasant it seems.

◆ 괄호 안에 주어진 단어를 바르게 배열하시오.

15 Preschoolers believe [their parents / tell / what] them in a very profound way.

16 No species can detect all the molecules that are present in [the environment / which / lives / in / it] — there are some things that we cannot smell but which some other animals can, and vice versa.

◆ 괄호에서 알맞은 것을 고르거나, 빈칸에 주어진 단어를 올바른 형태로 쓰시오.

01 Advertisers often displayed considerable facility in ___(adapt)___ their claims to the market status of the goods they promoted.

02 The producer of Fleischmann's yeast hired the J. Walter Thompson advertising agency ___(come)___ up with a different marketing strategy to boost sales.

03 This forced business ___(develop)___ closer relations with buyers and clients, which in turn made business realize that it was not enough to produce a quality product at a reasonable price.

04 In fact, [it / that] was equally essential to deliver products that customers actually wanted.

05 Plant growth is controlled by a group of hormones called auxins [finding / found] at the tips of stems and roots of plants.

06 Auxins produced at the tips of stems tend to accumulate on the side of the stem that [is / are] in the shade.

07 This phenomenon causes the stem to bend and [appear / appears] to be growing towards the light.

08 The first step to getting rid of expectations is [treated / to treat] yourself kindly.

09 For many, it's so painful that they'd rather not ask for something at all than ask and [risk / risks] rejection.

10 By deliberately getting yourself [rejecting / rejected] you'll grow a thicker skin that will allow you to take on much more in life, thus making you more successful at dealing with unfavorable circumstances.

11 The attempt to straighten rivers and give [it / them] regular cross-sections is perhaps the most disastrous example of this form-and-function relationship.

12 At that price, you would notice the cost and would think twice before _____(use)_____ artificial light to read a book.

13 About 10,000 years ago, [when / which] the role of dogs was firmly established in most human societies, the human brain also shrank by about 10 percent.

◆ 괄호 안에 주어진 단어를 바르게 배열하시오.

14 This is most successful in situations [are / where / at greatest threat / individuals] during a particular life stage.

15 [turn / only / not / did / it] night into day, but it allowed us to live and work in big buildings that natural light could not enter.

◆ 괄호에서 알맞은 것을 고르거나, 빈칸에 주어진 단어를 올바른 형태로 쓰시오.

01 Individuals who perform at a high level in their profession often [has / have] instant credibility with others.

02 He has made more money from endorsements than he ever [was / did] playing basketball.

03 In brains and in cities, everything [emerge / emerges] from the interaction between residents, at all scales, locally and distantly.

04 Generally, it's easier to fly westward and lengthen your day than it [is / does] to fly eastward and shorten it.

05 A more recent study of more than 46,000 Major League Baseball games found additional evidence [that / which] eastward travel is tougher than westward travel.

06 Ariely concludes that [restrict / restricting] freedom — whether by the professor or by students who recognize their own tendencies to delay things — improves self-control and performance.

07 Generalization without specific examples that [humanize / humanizing] writing is boring to the listener and to the reader.

08 The reason they have trouble making choices _____(be)_____ they believe that what they may want is not related to what they are supposed to do.

09 Research has confirmed that athletes are less likely to participate in unacceptable behavior than [do / are] non-athletes.

10 Character is a ____(learn)____ behavior, and a sense of fair play develops only if coaches plan to teach those lessons systematically.

11 This acts as a distraction from the feelings they are having, gives them something to do with their hands and mouth and shifts their attention from [whatever / whenever] was upsetting them.

12 In so doing, it grows communities, creates jobs, strengthens the economy, expands social and commercial networks, saves time and energy, and helps millions of people [achieve / achieving] a better life.

◆ 괄호 안에 주어진 단어를 바르게 배열하시오.

13 If you want the confidence that comes from achieving what you set out to do each day, then it's important to understand [take / things / are going to / how long].

14 The best way in which innovation changes our lives is by [people / work / to / for / enabling] each other.

15 [does / not / memory / underlie / only] our ability to think at all, it defines the content of our experiences and how we preserve them for years to come.

◆ 괄호에서 알맞은 것을 고르거나, 빈칸에 주어진 단어를 올바른 형태로 쓰시오.

01 [Strange / Strangely] as it may sound, this theory states that emotions arise from our bodies.

02 They run and they run, but then Alice discovers that they're still under the same tree [that / where] they started from.

03 For example, if you want to stay off your cellphone and concentrate on your work, [delete / deleting] the apps that distract you or ask a friend to change your password!

04 One group was made [intellectual / intellectually] superior by modifying the gene for the glutamate receptor.

05 This memory store allows them to track, within the neural circuits of their brains, the frequency of sound patterns and [uses / to use] this knowledge to make predictions about the meaning in patterns of sounds.

06 Without being restricted to the limited collection of music-distributors, nor [be / being] guided by the local radio program as a 'preselector' of the latest hits, the individual actively has to choose and determine his or her musical preferences.

07 However, from a sociocultural standpoint, the creative act is never "complete" in the absence of a second position — [that / those] of an audience.

08 Frogs must also lay their eggs in water, as their fishlike ancestors [were / did].

09 That would not, however, increase their *effective* freedom, because, although [allowing / allowed] to do so, they are physically incapable of it.

10 But in the real world most people will never have the opportunity either ___(become)___ all that they are allowed to become, or to need to be restrained from doing everything that is possible for them to do.

11 Modern insect communities are highly diverse in tropical forests, but the recent fossil record captures [few / little] of that diversity.

12 Sometimes you get very clear pictures of the past, while at [other / another] times there are big gaps, and you need to notice what they are.

◆ 괄호 안에 주어진 단어를 바르게 배열하시오.

13 It didn't rely on claimed data, nor [it / held / was] in a laboratory where consumers might behave differently.

14 We begin with an idea about [how / will be / the future].

15 Some indoor insects, which have fewer opportunities to feed than their outdoor counterparts, [the ability / seem to / developed / have] to survive when food is limited.

◆ 괄호에서 알맞은 것을 고르거나, 빈칸에 주어진 단어를 올바른 형태로 쓰시오.

01 Introducing new technology can also have a negative impact on production when it causes a change to the production process or [require / requires] workers to learn a new system.

02 In short, poetry has a lot to offer, if you give [it / them] the opportunity to do so.

03 And in dressing with taste and care, we represent both self-respect [and / or] a concern for the pleasure of others.

04 Although the fashion industry developed first in Europe and America, today it is an international and [high / highly] globalized industry.

05 Indeed, if you have too much of a stimulant, you will become nervous, find [it / that] difficult to sleep, and your memory performance will suffer.

06 Mild stimulants commonly found in tea, coffee, or sodas possibly [make / making] you more attentive and, thus, better able to remember.

07 We set up a so-called "filter-bubble" around ourselves, where we are constantly exposed only to that material that we [agree / agree with].

08 [Create / Creating] a difference that others don't have is a way to succeed in your field, leading to the creation of innovations.

09 Human psychology allows us to want to believe things that we can identify with on a personal level and even seek information [which / where] it doesn't necessarily exist, filling in the blanks with our imagination for the rest.

10 The Barnum Effect is the phenomenon where someone reads or hears something very [general / generally] but believes that it applies to them.

◆ 괄호 안에 주어진 단어를 바르게 배열하시오.

11 This can [doing / them / from / stop] their work and make them less productive.

12 [it / whose / is / story] affects what the story is.

13 Gone [of / are / musicians / the days] waiting for a gatekeeper (someone who holds power and prevents you from being let in) at a label or TV show to say they are worthy of the spotlight.

14 In today's music business, you don't need [to / a fanbase / for / permission / to / ask / build] and you no longer need to pay thousands of dollars to a company to do it.

◆ 괄호에서 알맞은 것을 고르거나, 빈칸에 주어진 단어를 올바른 형태로 쓰시오.

01 For example, priests wanted to know when [carrying / to carry] out religious ceremonies.

02 Living in communities allowed people to organize [them / themselves] more efficiently.

03 As magma cools, its atoms lose heat energy, [move / moved] closer together, and begin to combine into compounds.

04 You might say that the numbers seem a bit [unrealistic / unrealistically], but the threat is real.

05 Past styles had [much / more] to do with pretension than what people needed in their homes.

06 Those materials were local, and used with simplicity — houses [built / was built] this way had plain wooden floors and whitewashed walls inside.

07 What the great man is saying here is [that / what] there is good music and bad music.

08 The performer's basic task is to try [understanding / to understand] the meaning of the music, and then to communicate it honestly to others.

09 But whatever the proportion of a work's showing to [tell / telling], there is always something for readers to interpret.

10 By being able to recognize faces from afar or in the dark, humans were able to know someone was coming and protect [them / themselves] from possible danger.

11 One well-known study from Stanford University in 2016 demonstrated that youth [is / are] easily fooled by misinformation, especially when it comes through social media channels.

12 The rules of the game always include rules about the type of ball that is allowed, _____(start)_____ with the size and weight of the ball.

13 It is caused because the light from the flash penetrates the eyes through the pupils, and then [gets / getting] reflected to the camera from the back of the eyes where a large amount of blood is present.

14 Hence, when researchers attempt to make causal claims about the relationship between an independent and a dependent variable, they must control for — or rule out — other variables [that / what] may be creating a spurious relationship.

◆ 괄호 안에 주어진 단어를 바르게 배열하시오.

15 Whoever has an abundance of sugar hands some over; [gets help / is running short / whoever].

16 [when / depending / were / they / written / on] and by whom, literary works may contain large amounts of direct telling and lesser amounts of suggestion and implication.

◆ 괄호에서 알맞은 것을 고르거나, 빈칸에 주어진 단어를 올바른 형태로 쓰시오.

01   Sometimes the pace of change is [far / very] slower.

02   The neural pathways that enable those beliefs become faster and more automatic, while the ones that the child doesn't use regularly [is / are] pruned away.

03   Because their structure is not complex, they are easy to break down and hold few nutrients for your body other than the sugars [which / from which] they are made.

04   Half the students received a description containing the word 'warm', the other half _____(tell)_____ the speaker was 'cold'.

05   Modern cognitive science, however, rightly judges that language is just one aspect of mind of great importance in human beings but not [fundamental / fundamentally] to all kinds of thinking.

06   If we could magically remove the glasses, we [will / would] find the two water bodies would not mix well.

07   Friction can be a useful force because it prevents our shoes [to slip / slipping] on the floor when we walk and stops car tires skidding on the road.

08   A person with normal vision will dream about a familiar friend [uses / using] visual memories of shape, lighting, and colour.

09 On a practical level, the night sky helped past generations [to keep / keeping] track of time and create calendars — essential to developing societies as aids to farming and seasonal gathering.

10 We hope these [will / would] give us more energy, prevent us from catching a cold in the winter, or improve our skin and hair.

11 While the total energy remains [unchange / unchanged], the kinetic and potential parts of the total energy can change all the time.

12 [Whether / Although] it is losing weight, winning a championship, or achieving any other goal, we put pressure on ourselves to make some earthshaking improvement that everyone will talk about.

13 Daylight isn't the only signal that the brain can use for the purpose of biological clock resetting, though it is the principal and preferential signal, [when / that] present.

14 Generally, people planted a variety of crops in different areas, in the hope of obtaining a [reasonable / reasonably] stable food supply.

◆ 괄호 안에 주어진 단어를 바르게 배열하시오.

15 [surface / is / rougher / the / the], the more friction is produced.

16 This is crucial because most survival situations arise as a result of a series of events [avoided / could / that / have / been].

◆ 괄호에서 알맞은 것을 고르거나, 빈칸에 주어진 단어를 올바른 형태로 쓰시오.

01 Or take the case of the teenager who occasionally eats fried chicken, but otherwise ____(stay)____ away from fried foods.

02 But the person who eats fried foods every day, with few vegetables or fruits, and loads up on supersized soft drinks, candy, and chips for snacks [has / have] a bad diet.

03 [To help / Helping] decide what's risky and what's safe, who's trustworthy and who's not, we look for *social evidence*.

04 Three weeks later, the students who had written about their values were happier, healthier, and more confident about their ability to handle stress than the [ones / some] who had only focused on the good stuff.

05 The study reports that when [facing / faced] difficulties, adolescents exposed to an authoritative parenting style are less likely to be passive, helpless, and afraid to fail.

06 Finally, authoritative parents praise academic excellence and the importance of working hard more than other parents [do / did].

07 The common blackberry (Rubus allegheniensis) has an amazing ability to move manganese from one layer of soil to [other / another] using its roots.

08 This may seem like a funny talent for a plant [has / to have], but it all becomes clear when you realize the effect it has on nearby plants.

09 There is often a lot of uncertainty in the realm of science, [that / which] the general public finds uncomfortable.

10 A perfect example of this is [how / what] people want definitive answers as to which foods are "good" and "bad."

11 Kinzler and her team took a bunch of five-month-olds [who / whose] families only spoke English and showed the babies two videos.

◆ 괄호 안에 주어진 단어를 바르게 배열하시오.

12 And [they / to / had / do / all] was reflect and write about it — positively reframing their experiences with their personal values.

13 You might have felt good about yourself because you [it / up / pick / didn't] to check your messages, but your unchecked messages were still hurting your connection with the person sitting across from you.

14 After reading a research paper about behavior change, Rhonda put a note in one of the bathrooms [not / people / to / asking / remove] the toilet paper, as it was a shared item.

◆ 괄호에서 알맞은 것을 고르거나, 빈칸에 주어진 단어를 올바른 형태로 쓰시오.

01 In return, the nonfarmers provided leadership and security for the farming population, enabling [it / them] to continue to increase food/energy yields and provide ever larger surpluses.

02 Experienced ballet dancers are able to repeat longer sequences of steps than less experienced dancers, and they can repeat a sequence of steps [made / making] up a routine better than steps ordered randomly.

03 After he'd learned to know his family through touch and smell, he found that he couldn't recognize his children with his eyes, and this left him [puzzling / puzzled].

04 The volunteers had to wear a special watch for seven days so the researchers could collect data on [their / whose] sleeping and waking times.

05 He said that it was important for our body to wake up to the morning light, and that the worst time to go to bed [is / was] after midnight because it may reduce the likelihood of seeing morning light which resets the body clock.

06 What if we [are / were] able to love everything that gets in our way?

07 Every person who makes us miserable is like us — a human being, most likely [to do / doing] the best they can, deeply loved by their parents, a child, or a friend.

08 We are not merely expressions of coding [and / but] products of a remarkable variety of interactions that are both within and outside of our control.

09 The social situations you need to expose yourself to may not be available when you want them, or they may not go well enough [of / for] you to sense that things are under control.

10 That means the more times you try using that new feedback technique, the more [easy / easily] it will come to you when you need it.

11 But when we try something new in our adult lives we'll usually make just one attempt before judging [which / whether] it's worked.

12 These are some of the reasons why the origins of human language cannot be effectively discussed [unless / if] conversation is placed at the top of the list of things to understand.

13 Other components of language — things like grammar and stories — _____(be)_____ secondary to conversation.

◆ 괄호 안에 주어진 단어를 바르게 배열하시오.

14 And because other areas of May's brain had adapted to process information primarily through his other senses, the process of learning [was more difficult / than he'd anticipated / how to see].

15 [that / this / say / not / to / is] facing your fears is pointless when socializing.

◆ 괄호에서 알맞은 것을 고르거나, 빈칸에 주어진 단어를 올바른 형태로 쓰시오.

01 Suffering from the severe pain because of heart disease, he barely saw the young uniformed soldier [stood / standing] next to him.

02 The monster was [so / such] ugly and smelly that the guards froze in shock.

03 The server said that she had never had anyone [doing / done] anything like that for her family before.

04 It may [appear / have appeared] to be an ordinary watch to others, but it brought a lot of happy childhood memories to him.

05 The number of children [looking / looked] for the watch slowly decreased and only a few tired children were left.

06 Just when the farmer was closing the barn door, a little boy came up to him and asked the farmer to give [him / himself] another chance.

07 As he walked he noticed a monk [working / to work] in the fields.

08 I felt as though I [am / was] a member of the family in the village.

09 I am traveling from the village in the mountains to the village in the valley and I was wondering if you knew [that / what] it is like in the village in the valley.

10 I marvelled, proud of him, and wondered how, in 1920, so young, so white, and in the deep South, [where / which] the law still separated black from white, he had had the courage to deliver it.

11 The deerskin used to [make / making] this drum belonged to her mate, the deer who we hunted last year.

12 Everyone burst out laughing _____(think)_____ that it was a joke.

13 The leader announced one day that James would exhibit his skills as a wrestler and asked the people [if / through] there was anyone to challenge him for the prize money.

◆ 괄호 안에 주어진 단어를 바르게 배열하시오.

14 After she [what / told / was / happened], she went back to the room with him.

15 He [was / given / offer / whatever / them / he / would] and they would eat it together.

기출의 바이블

고1 영어

GRAMMAR
EXTRACT

정답 및
해설

01 to help　　02 that　　03 have been

04 repaired　　05 increasing　　06 have fallen

07 Though　　08 is　　09 to allow　　10 suits

11 to remodel　　12 donating　　13 where

14 encourage them to be interested in

15 you to pay attention to

16 through which the proposed Pine Hill walking trail

---

01 이 패키지 여행 상품은 당신이 편히 쉴 수 있도록 돕는 마사지와 명상뿐만 아니라 Lake Madison으로의 특별한 여행을 포함합니다.
▶ massage and meditation을 꾸며 주는 형용사 용법의 to부정사를 써야 한다. 이 문장의 동사는 includes이고, 목적어로 special trips (to Lake Madison)와 massage and meditation (to help you relax)이 as well as로 연결된 구조이다.

02 우리는 그것이 당신에게 잊지 못할 경험이 될 것을 확신합니다.
▶ 문맥상 '~라고 확신하다'라는 의미가 되어야 하므로, 「be+sure+(that절)」의 형태로 sure 뒤에 완전한 절을 이끄는 접속사 that을 써야 한다. 이때 that은 생략할 수 있다.

03 시설은 우리가 이곳으로 이사 온 이후로 이렇게 형편없는 상태였습니다.
▶ 우리가 이사 온(과거) 이후, 시설은 지금까지 계속 이렇게 형편없는 상태였다(현재 완료)는 내용이므로, 현재 진행형이 아닌 현재 완료 have been을 써야 한다.

04 그 시설들을 수리해 주시겠습니까?
▶ 사역동사 have는 「have+목적어+목적격보어」의 형태로 쓰는데, have의 목적어와 목적격보어가 능동 관계일 때는 목적격보어로 동사원형을, 수동 관계일 때는 과거분사를 쓴다. 여기서 the facilities는 '수리되는' 대상이므로, 수동 관계를 나타내는 과거분사 repaired로 써야 한다.

05 더욱이, 저는 작년 한 해에만 두 개의 주요 고객사를 회사에 새로 유치하여, 회사의 총매출을 5% 증가시켰습니다.
▶ 쉼표 뒤는 분사구문으로, 주절의 주어인 'I'가 회사의 총매출을 '증가시킨' 주체이므로 능동의 의미를 지닌 현재분사 increasing을 써야 한다.

06 케이스를 닦으려고 휴대전화에서 분리했을 때 케이스가 제 무릎에서 바닥으로 떨어졌던 게 틀림없습니다.
▶ 문장 전체가 과거 시제이므로 과거의 확실한 추측을 나타내는 (must) have fallen으로 써야 한다.

07 저희는 대회에 참가하기를 바라지만, 런던에 가기 위해 필요한 자금이 없습니다.
▶ 다음에 「주어+동사」로 이루어진 절이 왔으므로 접속사 Though를 써야 한다.

08 이 활동들의 목표 가운데 하나는 저희가 언론 매체의 다양한 유형 및 인쇄된 신문 기사에 사용된 언어를 알게 하는 것입니다.
▶ 「one of the+복수 명사」가 주어로 쓰이면 one이 주어의 핵심이므로 단수 취급한다. 따라서 단수 동사 is를 써야 한다.

09 따라서 선생님께 드리는 저의 겸허한 요청은 학교 도서관에 보관되어 온 오래된 신문을 저희가 사용하도록 허락해 달라는 것입니다.
▶ It이 가주어이고 진주어에 해당하는 to부정사가 와야 하는 자리이므로, to allow를 써야 한다.

10 당사의 가장 중요한 비전인 '인류애를 고취하자'를 가장 잘 반영한 로고를 제작해 주실 것을 요청합니다.
▶ that은 관계대명사로, 관계사절 내의 동사는 선행사에 일치해야 한다. 따라서 a logo에 맞추어 단수 동사 suits를 써야 한다.

11 Friends of Literature 동호회 덕분에, 우리는 도서관 건물을 개조하기에 충분한 자금을 성공적으로 마련했습니다.
▶ '~하기에 충분한'의 의미를 나타내고 있으므로 「enough+to부정사」의 표현을 써야 한다.

12 망치나 그림 그리는 붓을 잡고 여러분의 시간을 기부함으로써, 여러분은 공사를 도울 수 있습니다.
▶ 「by+-ing(~함으로써)」 구문이 사용된 문장으로 grabbing과 and로 대등하게 연결되므로 동명사 donating을 써야 한다.

13 야생 동물은 개발 압력에 직면해 있는데, 이 동물들은 사람들의 활동으로부터 숨을 수 있는 곳이 필요합니다.
▶ 선행사가 장소를 나타내는 space이고, 관계사절 이하가 문장 필수 요소의 결핍이 없는 완전한 문장이므로 관계부사 where를 써야 한다.

14 이 박람회의 목적은 방향을 이끌어 주는 실험을 통해 그들이 과학에 흥미를 느끼도록 장려하려는 것입니다.
▶ 동사 is의 보어로 to부정사가 온 문장이다. encourage는 「encourage+목적어+목적격보어(to부정사)」의 형태로 쓰여, '~가 …하기를 장려하다'라는 의미를 나타낸다. 목적어로 them, 목적격보어로 to be interested in을 써야 한다.

15 저는 귀하께서 그 구역 놀이터 설비의 열악한 상태에 관심을 기울여 주시기를 바랍니다.
▶ 「want+목적어+목적격보어(to부정사)」의 형태로 쓰여 '~가 …하기를 원하다'라는 의미를 나타낸다. 목적어로 you, 목적격보어로 to pay attention to 이하를 써야 한다.

16 제안된 Pine Hill 산책로가 통과하게 될 그 땅은 다양한 종의 서식지입니다.
▶ The land를 수식하는 관계절이며, the proposed Pine Hill walking trail이 관계절의 주어이고, 관계절의 동사구 would cut에 연결되려면 전치사 through가 관계사 앞에 위치하여야 한다.

01 ringing	**02** that	**03** so	**04** being used
05 were	**06** sure	**07** had hidden	
08 me	**09** Being	**10** interesting	**11** what
12 while	**13** something bad was coming		
14 how teachers ranked			

01 나는 그들에게 전화를 걸었지만, 나는 그들의 전화가 방에서 울리는 것을 들었다.
▶ '…가 ~하는 것을 듣다'라는 의미로 「지각동사 hear+목적어+목적격보어」의 형태로 쓰며, 목적어(their phones)와 목적격보어가 능동의 관계일 때 목적격보어로 동사원형 또는 현재분사를 쓴다. 따라서 목적격보어로는 자동사 ring(울리다)의 현재분사 ringing을 써야 한다.

02 그(곰)는 무언가의 냄새를 따라가고 있었고, 나는 서서히 거대한 이 동물이 내 냄새를 맡고 있다는 것을 깨닫기 시작했다!
▶ realize의 목적어인 명사절을 유도해야 하는데, this giant animal was smelling me가 완전한 절이다. 그러므로 명사절 접속사 that을 써야 한다.

03 나는 네일샵에 도착해서 그 시간 동안 단절되어 차분하고 평화롭게 느낄 수 있도록 나의 휴대폰의 음을 소거했다.
▶ in that ~은 '~라는 점에서'라는 의미를 가진 표현이고, so that은 '~하기 위해서'라는 의미이다. 문맥상 '~하기 위해서'가 적절하므로 so를 써야 한다.

04 그 그네는 그가 공원에서 하는 가장 좋아하는 것이었다. 하지만 그네는 이미 모두 이용 중이었다.
▶ 주어인 그네가 '이용되고 있는' 것이므로 수동태 진행형 being used를 써야 한다.

05 Zoe는 마치 천국에 있는 것처럼 느꼈다.
▶ '마치 ~인 것처럼'이라는 의미의 as if 다음에는 동사의 과거형 were가 와서 현재와 반대되는 사실을 나타낸다.

06 엄마가 나를 위한 특별한 선물을 가지고 쇼핑몰에서 집에 왔을 때 나는 그것이 무엇인지 알고 있다고 상당히 확신했다.
▶ 동사 was의 보어 역할을 하는 형용사가 필요한 자리이므로 sure를 써야 한다. pretty는 '매우, 상당히'라는 뜻으로 쓰인 부사이다.

07 나는 아마도 엄마가 내 새로운 휴대전화를 안에 숨겨 두었을 것이라 생각하면서 책장을 넘겨보았다.
▶ 주절의 동사의 시제가 과거(flipped)이고, 과거보다 더 이전에 물건을 숨겨 두었으므로 대과거(과거완료)인 had hidden을 써야 한다.

08 그러나 나는 엄마가 나에게 휴대전화를 사 주지 않았고 내 선물이 겨우 작은 책이라는 것을 서서히 깨달았는데, 그것은 내가 원했던 것과는 너무 달랐다.
▶ 「get+간접목적어+직접목적어」 구문이므로 me를 써야 한다.

09 그녀는 당황해서 그 자리에 가만히 서 있었다.

▶ she를 의미상의 주어로 하는 분사구문으로, 문맥상 능동의 의미이므로 현재분사 Being을 써야 한다.

10 그럼, 그리고 너에게 흥미 있을 만한 것이 하나 있지.
▶ interest는 '~의 흥미를 끌다'라는 뜻의 동사로, 문맥상 주어 that(= one thing)과 interest의 관계가 능동이다. 따라서 현재분사 interesting을 써야 한다.

11 그것은 바로 내가 언제나 꿈꿨던 것이었다.
▶ 문장 전체의 동사 was의 보어절을 이끌면서 I had 이하의 절에서 전치사 of의 목적어 역할을 하는 관계대명사가 필요한데, 선행사가 없으므로 which는 적절하지 않다. 따라서 선행사를 포함한 관계대명사 what을 써야 한다.

12 엄마가 내 방 입구에서 말없이 나를 바라보는 동안 나는 침대에 앉아 몇 시간 동안 울었다.
▶ my mother 이하가 주어와 동사를 포함한 완전한 절이므로 접속사 while을 써야 한다.

13 나는 나쁜 어떤 일이 생겼다는 것을 즉시 알게 되었다.
▶ knew의 목적어로 that절이 오는 경우이다. that 이하는 완전한 절이 되어야 하는데, something이 주어, was coming이 동사이다. bad는 something을 꾸미는데, -thing을 꾸미는 형용사는 -thing 뒤에 오므로 something bad was coming으로 써야 한다.

14 Zoe와 나머지 다른 최종 후보 중 한 명이 네 과목에서 1위를 차지했으므로, 그들의 노력과 자신감을 선생님들이 어떻게 평가하느냐로 좁혀졌다.
▶ 전치사 to의 목적어로 쓰인 간접의문문이 와야 하므로 「의문사+주어+동사」의 어순인 how teachers ranked로 써야 한다.

01 have	**02** to make	**03** yourself	**04** to have
05 share	**06** was	**07** make	
08 Paying	**09** how	**10** actively	**11** doing
12 that	**13** them		
14 difficult for any of us to maintain			
15 can you create	**16** found it very difficult to study		

01 연구는 일하는 사람들이 두 개의 달력을 가지고 있다는 것을 보여 준다: 하나는 업무를 위한 달력이고 하나는 개인적인 삶을 위한 달력이다.
▶ shows는 문장 전체의 동사이며, work는 people을 수식하는 주격 관계대명사 who절의 동사이다. 따라서 that절의 주어 people에 대한 동사가 필요한 상황이므로 to부정사가 아닌 동사의 현재형 have를 써야 한다.

02 이것은 어떤 일이 가장 중요한지에 대한 정보에 입각한 결정을 내리게 해 줄 것이다.
▶ 「allow+목적어+목적격보어(to부정사)」의 형태로 쓰여 '~가 …하는 것을 허락하다'라는 의미를 나타낸다. 그러므로 목적격보어로 to make를 써야 한다.

03 만약 이전에 에너지 정점에 관해 생각해 본 적이 없다면, 며칠 동안 스스로를 관찰하라.
▶ 명령문에서 주어 you가 생략된 상황으로, 스스로를 관찰하기 위해 며칠을 보내라는 내용이므로, observe의 목적어로는 재귀대명사 yourself를 써야 한다.

04 대부분의 사람들은 제품을 홍보하는 성공적인 상업용 블로그를 가지기 위해서 그들이 엄격하게 '그 주제에' 머물러야 한다고 믿는다.
▶ 문맥상 '~하기 위해서'라는 목적의 의미를 가진 표현이 나와야 하므로 to부정사 to have를 써야 한다.

05 여러분은 논의될 사항들의 목록을 만들고 회의 전에 다른 회의 참석자들과 여러분의 목록을 공유해야 한다.
▶ You should 뒤에 create와 share가 병렬로 연결되는 구조이므로 동사 원형 share를 써야 한다.

06 내가 군대에 있을 때, 교관들은 나의 병영 생활관에 모습을 드러내곤 했는데, 그들이 가장 먼저 검사하곤 했던 것은 우리의 침대였다.
▶ 주어 the first thing에 이어지는 동사 자리이고, 과거 시제 문장이므로 과거 시제 단수형 was로 써야 한다. they would inspect는 주어를 수식하는 관계사절이다.

07 여러분이 매일 아침 침대를 정돈한다면, 여러분은 하루의 첫 번째 과업을 성취한 것이 될 것이다.
▶ 시간과 조건을 나타내는 부사절에서는 현재 시제로 미래를 나타내므로 make를 써야 한다.

08 여러분이 보내는 비언어적인 메시지에 주목하는 것은 학생들과 여러분의 관계에 상당한 변화를 가져올 수 있다.
▶ 문장의 동사는 can make이므로 주어 역할을 하는 동명사 Paying을 써야 한다.

09 그 선생님이 친근한 인사를 하고 환영의 미소를 지을 때 그것이 학생에게 얼마나 격려가 되고 힘을 주는지 생각해 보라.
▶ about의 목적어로 쓰인 간접의문문으로, 다음에 형용사가 나오므로 how를 써야 한다.

10 불편한 상태를 피하고 싶어서 당신은 적극적으로 성공을 차단하고 있다.
▶ 동사 are shutting out을 수식할 수 있는 부사 actively를 써야 한다.

11 변화는 항상 불편하지만, 성공을 위한 마법의 공식을 찾기 위해 일을 색다르게 하려면 그것이 핵심이다.
▶ key to ~는 '~로 이르는 핵심 열쇠'라는 뜻으로, 이때의 to는 전치사이다. 따라서 목적어로 동명사 doing을 써야 한다.

12 하지만 당신이 '보내기' 키를 누르기 전에 반드시 마지막으로 한 번 문서를 주의 깊게 읽도록 하라.
▶ make sure의 목적어절을 이끌어야 하며 you read 이하의 절이 문장 필수 구성 요소의 결핍이 없는 완전한 문장이므로, 명사절 접속사 that을 써야 한다.

13 내가 고등학생이었을 때, 커피숍에서 공부하면서 주변의 소음이나 일어나는 모든 일에 방해받지 않을 수 있는 학생들이 있었다.
▶ 문맥상 앞에 나온 명사 students를 받으므로 복수 대명사 them을 써야 한다.

14 우리 중 누구라도 근무일 종일 일정한 수준의 주의 집중을 유지하기는 어렵다.
▶ '~하는 것은 …하다'라는 의미의 가주어-진주어 구조의 문장이다. It is 뒤에 「형용사+to부정사」의 순서로 써야 하는데, to부정사의 의미상 주어인 for any of us는 to부정사 앞에 써야 한다.

15 이렇게 함으로써만 여러분은 여러분이 그 다음에 판매를 할 수 있게 될 관심 있는 독자를 만들어 낼 수 있다.
▶ 준부정어구인 전치사구 Only by doing this를 강조하기 위해 문장의 맨 앞으로 가져온 경우이므로, 주어와 동사의 순서가 도치되어야 한다. 조동사인 can을 주어 you의 앞으로 도치시켜 can you create로 써야 한다.

16 이 학생들은 개인 침실을 제외하고 어디에서도 공부하기가 어렵다는 것을 알게 된, 집중에 방해가 되는 것들의 피해자였다.
▶ 동사 find를 사용하여 '~하는 것이 …하다는 것을 알게 되다'의 문장을 만들 때 목적어로 to부정사가 쓰이는 경우, 이 목적어 자리에 가목적어 it을 두어 「find it+형용사+to부정사」의 형태로 쓴다. 이때, to부정사(구)가 진목적어가 된다.

4강 밑줄 함의 추론   본문 p.54

01 whether   **02** unpaid   **03** been pushed

04 puts   **05** that   **06** to drop   **07** heavier

08 are you   **09** emailing   **10** derived   **11** were

12 whatever   **13** easy for you to say

14 may very well be related to

15 I wish I hadn't done that

---

01 당신은 구매자가 다른 사람들에게 당신으로부터 제품을 구매하도록 권장할지의 여부도 또한 알아낼 것이다.
▶ determine의 목적어로 명사절이 이어지는 문장으로 명사절이 the product가 빠진, 즉 to purchase의 목적어가 없는 불완전한 절이라면 선행사를 포함하는 관계대명사 what을 쓸 수 있지만, 여기서는 완전한 절이 이어지므로 '~인지 (아닌지)'의 의미를 가지는 명사절 접속사 whether[if]를 쓰는 것이 어법상 알맞다.

02 만족한 고객은 당신의 사업을 위한 보수를 받지 않는 대사가 될 수 있으므로, 고객 만족이 할 일 목록의 최상단에 있어야 한다.

▶ ambassadors를 꾸며 주는 형용사로, '보수를 지불하지 않는' 대사가 아니라 '보수를 받지 않는' 대사가 될 수 있다고 해야 하므로, unpaid를 써야 한다.

03 수천 가지의 전통적인 생계 수단이 발전에 의해 밀려났으며, 그 직업과 관련된 생활 방식이 없어졌다.
▶ 주어 Thousands of traditional livelihoods는 '밀려난' 대상으로 동사 push와 수동의 관계이며, 과거의 일이 현재까지 영향을 미치고 있음을 나타내야 하므로 현재완료 수동태인 have been pushed로 써야 한다. 뒤의 removed 앞에 have been이 생략되어 있다고 볼 수 있다.

04 머리로부터 손이 단절되는 것은 인간의 정신에 부담을 준다.
▶ 주어가 The divorce of the hands from the head이며, 주어의 핵은 divorce(단수 주어)이므로 단수 동사 puts를 써야 한다. 뒤에 목적어 a stress가 있으므로 수동태는 올 수 없다.

05 만약 우리가 중요한 일을 하지 못하게 하는 가장 큰 것이 그것이 엄청난 노력을 필요로 한다는 잘못된 전제라면 어떨까?
▶ the false assumption(잘못된 전제)과 it has to take huge effort(그것이 엄청난 노력을 필요로 한다)는 동격의 관계에 있으므로, 동격의 that을 써야 한다.

06 만약 제가 이것을 하루 종일 들고 있다면 이것은 제 팔에 심각한 고통을 일으키고 제가 잔을 바닥에 떨어뜨리게 할 것입니다.
▶ force는 to부정사를 목적격보어로 취하므로 to drop을 써야 한다.

07 각 경우에 잔의 무게는 같지만, 제가 오래 들고 있을수록 그것은 저에게 더 무겁게 느껴집니다.
▶ 「the+비교급 ~, the+비교급 …」(~하면 할수록 더 …하다) 구문이므로 비교급 heavier를 써야 한다.

08 일자리를 찾고 있을 때, 여러분은 대강 훑어보는 것이 아니며 '그냥 구경만 하고' 있는 것도 아니다.
▶ nor 뒤에 절이 이어져 '~도 또한 아니다'의 의미를 나타낼 때는, 「(조)동사+주어」의 어순이 되어야 한다.

09 원하는 직업을 찾아서 얻는 데에 시간이 얼마나 오래 걸리는지에 상관없이, 온라인 취업 게시판을 대충 훑어보고 가끔 이력서를 이메일로 보내는 것에만 의존하는 것보다는 능동적으로 행동하는 것이 논리적으로 여러분에게 더 빨리 결과를 가져다줄 것이다.
▶ rely on에 이어지는 동명사 browsing과 병렬 관계를 이루어야 하므로 동명사 emailing을 써야 한다.

10 어떤 사람들은 원유에서 얻은 플라스틱 제품을 매일 사용하고 버린다.
▶ 동사는 use and throw away이므로 목적어 plastic products를 수식하는 분사구여야 한다. 목적어와의 관계가 '얻게 된' 수동이므로 과거분사 derived를 써야 한다.

11 더 이상 통제된 의사소통이나 사업 시스템도 없었다.
▶ 문두에 부정어 No longer가 사용되었으므로 주어와 동사가 도치되어야 한

다. 이 문장은 「there+be동사」의 유도부사 구문이 사용된 문장으로, be동사가 there 앞으로 도치되었다. 실제 주어는 any ~ systems이므로 이에 맞추어 복수 동사 were를 써야 한다.

12 제품과 서비스에 대해 이야기할 때 소비자들은 일반적으로 웹을 통해서 그들이 회사, 제품, 경쟁업체, 유통 시스템, 그리고 무엇보다도 회사의 진실성에 대해 알고 싶어 하는 모든 것을 배울 수 있었다.
▶ learn의 목적어절을 이끄는 동시에 they wanted 이하에서 know의 목적어 역할을 해야 하므로 관계대명사가 필요한데, 선행사가 없다. 따라서 관계대명사와 선행사의 역할을 동시에 할 수 있는 복합관계대명사 whatever를 써야 한다.

13 우리는 보통 누군가의 의견이 틀렸음을 입증하고자 할 때, 우리는 "말은 쉽지"라는 문구를 비판으로 사용한다.
▶ That's 뒤에는 '~하기 쉬운'이라는 의미의 「형용사+to부정사」로 써야 한다. 그런데 for you는 to부정사의 의미상 주어이므로 to부정사 앞에 써서 「형용사+의미상 주어+to부정사」의 순서로 써야 한다.

14 그러나 우리에게 두드러져 보이고 있는 것은 우리의 목표, 관심사, 기대, 과거의 경험 또는 상황에 대한 현재의 요구와 매우 관련 있을지도 모른다. 즉, "망치를 손에 들고 있으면, 모든 것이 못처럼 보인다"와 같다.
▶ 조동사 may가 포함된 「may well+동사원형(아마 ~일 것이다/~하는 것은 당연하다)」의 구문이 사용된 문장으로 부사 very가 well을 수식하여 의미를 보다 강조하고 있다. '~와 관련이 있다'는 의미의 be related to를 may well 뒤에 연결하여 써야 한다.

15 '내가 그것을 하지 않았으면 좋을 텐데!'의 유일한 가치는 다음번에 무엇을 해야 할지 더 잘 알게 된다는 것이다.
▶ 주어로 쓰이는 I가 두 번 나왔으므로 두 개의 절이 연결되었음을, wish와 과거완료를 나타내는 표현을 통해 가정법이 쓰였다는 것을 알 수 있다. 따라서 I wish 이하에 「had+p.p.」가 사용된 문장을 연결한 형태로 써야 한다.

5강 요지 추론 본문 p. 56

01 allowing **02** used to **03** to scan **04** what
05 themselves **06** poorly **07** help **08** While
09 it **10** buried **11** Whether **12** that
13 whether **14** to pull
15 not only know what to do
16 fewer people choosing to get screened for the disease

01 컴퓨터화된 사회의 약속은 그것이 모든 반복적인 고된 일을 기계에 넘겨, 우리 인간들이 더 높은 목적을 추구하고 더 많은 여가 시간을 가질 수 있게 해 준다는 것이었다.
▶ '컴퓨터화된 사회의 약속은 그것이 모든 반복적인 고된 일을 기계에 넘기고' '그리고 그것이 ~하게 해 준다(and it would allow ~)'는 의미의 분사구문

이므로 allowing으로 써야 한다.

02 회사에 맡겨 해결되던 부가 가치 서비스의 일환으로 우리를 위해 행해지던 것들이, 이제 우리 스스로가 하도록 기대된다.
▶ '우리를 위해 행해지던 것들'이라는 의미가 되어야 하므로, '~하곤 했다, 과거 한때는[예전에는] ~이었다[했다]'라는 의미의 조동사 used to를 써야 한다. be used to는 '~하기 위해 사용되다'라는 의미이다.

03 식료품점에서는, 우리가 우리 자신의 식료품을 직접 봉지에 넣도록, 그리고 일부 슈퍼마켓에서는, 우리 자신이 구매한 물건을 스캔하도록 기대된다.
▶ '~하도록 기대되다'라는 의미를 가지는 「be expected+to부정사」의 형태이며, be expected 뒤에 and로 to부정사 2개(to bag과 to scan)가 병렬을 이루는 구조이다. 따라서 to scan을 써야 한다.

04 대학 생활을 시작할 때 학생들은 우리가 "고무도장 방식"이라고 부르고 싶은 방법을 이용하여, 모든 과목, 시험, 학습 과제를 똑같은 방식으로 접근할지도 모른다.
▶ 현재분사 using의 목적어이면서, 동시에 call의 목적어 역할을 할 수 있는 what을 써야 한다.

05 두려움을 주는 뉴스는 실제로 사람들로부터 내면의 통제력을 빼앗을 수 있어서, 그들이 스스로나 다른 사람들을 돌볼 가능성을 더 낮게 만든다.
▶ take care of를 하는 주체가 앞에 나오는 them(people)이므로 재귀대명사인 themselves를 써야 한다.

06 여러분은 기분이 우울해서 면접에서 잘했을 때도 못했다고 판단할지도 모른다.
▶ do는 자동사로 부사의 수식을 받으므로 poorly를 써야 한다.

07 수면 중에 수행되는 많은 매우 중요한 과업이 건강을 유지하는 것을 도와주고 사람들이 최상의 수준으로 기능할 수 있게 해 준다는 것을 연구는 밝히고 있다.
▶ a number of는 '수많은'이라는 의미로 주어로 쓰이면 복수 취급하여 뒤에 복수 동사가 온다. 따라서 help를 써야 한다.

08 잠을 자는 동안, 여러분의 뇌는 학습하고 기억과 새로운 통찰력을 만드는 데 필요한 경로를 형성하느라 열심히 일하고 있다.
▶ 다음에 「주어+동사」의 절이 왔으므로 접속사 While을 써야 한다.

09 일, 학교, 가족, 또는 가정의 책임을 다하기 위해 서두르는 가운데, 사람들은 수면을 줄이고, 그것이 문제가 되지 않을 것으로 생각하는데, 그 이유는 이러한 모든 다른 활동들이 훨씬 더 중요해 보이기 때문이다.
▶ 지시대명사가 가리키는 것이 앞 문장 전체를 가리키므로 단수형 it을 써야 한다.

10 너무나 자주 기업들은 결국 묻히고 결코 사용되지 않는 귀중한 고객 정보를 수집한다.
▶ end up(결국 ~하게 되다) 다음에 나오는 말이 '묻히게 된다'는 수동의 의미이므로 과거분사 buried를 써야 한다.

11 그들이 열 명, 만 명 내지 심지어 천만 명의 고객을 가지고 있든 목표는 동일하다. 즉, 그것은 충성도를 북돋우는 즐거운 고객 경험을 만들어 내는 것이다.
▶ 문맥상 '~이든 (아니든)'이라는 의미의 양보 부사절을 이끄는 접속사가 필요하므로 Whether를 써야 한다. That은 명사절을 이끈다.

12 이런 방침은, 학생이 낙제 수준으로 과제를 수행하거나 낙제 과제를 제출하는 것은 교사들이 대부분 그것을 받아들이기 때문이라는 믿음에 근거한다.
▶ students perform 이하의 절이 문장 필수 요소의 결핍이 없는 완전한 문장으로 the belief와 동격을 이루므로, 동격의 접속사 that을 써야 한다.

13 상황이 우리의 의심을 활성화하는지 여부에 따라 그것은 우리 각각에게 특유의 방식으로 스트레스를 준다.
▶ 전치사 on의 목적어절을 이끄는 접속사가 필요하며, or not과 호응하여 '~인지 아닌지'의 의미를 나타내는 whether를 써야 한다. if는 or not과 함께 쓸 수 없다.

14 그것은 알람시계의 스누즈 버튼을 누르고는 결국 이불을 머리 위로 뒤집어쓴 채 다시 잠들어 버리는 것과 다르지 않다.
▶ 전치사 unlike의 목적어로 쓰인 동명사구에 포함된 표현으로 only와 호응하여 '결국 ~하다'의 의미를 나타내며 부사적으로 쓰일 수 있는 to부정사 to pull을 써야 한다. 뒤에 이어지는 and 이하의 fall 앞에 to가 생략되었다고 볼 수 있다.

15 그리고 그들은 무엇을 해야 하는지 알고 있을 뿐만 아니라, 그것을 어떻게 해야 하는지도 알고 있다.
▶ 상관접속사 not only A but also B(A뿐만 아니라 B도)가 있는 문장으로, also know와 병렬이 되도록 동사 know 앞에 not only를 써야 한다. 그리고 동사 know의 목적어로 '무엇을 ~할지'라는 의미로 「what+to부정사」의 순서로 써야 한다.

16 증가하는 암 발생률에 대해 사람들에게 경고하려 의도된 뉴스 기사는 더 적은 사람들이 그 병에 대해 검사받는 것을 선택하는 결과를 가져올 수 있다.
▶ result in의 목적어로 동명사 choosing to get screened for 뒤에 the disease가 오면 된다. 그런데 choosing ~의 의미상 주어인 fewer people를 choosing 앞에 써야 한다.

6강 **주제 추론** 본문 p. 58

01 that **02** so **03** it **04** is **05** to take
06 will come **07** learning **08** faster **09** such
10 that **11** to take **12** more **13** encouraged
14 identified **15** came many large hotels
16 to view stressful situations as challenges

01 우리는 우리가 사회적으로 바람직한 특성들을 많이 지니고 있고, 그리고 우리는 사회적으로 바람직하지 않은 특성들의 대부분은 지니고 있지 않다고 믿는 경향이 있다.
▶ believe의 목적어로 2개의 명사절이 접속사 and로 묶인 병렬 구조를 가지는 문장으로, 첫 번째 that절(명사절)은 완전한 절이며, and 뒤의 절 또한

완전한 절이므로 명사절 접속사 that을 써야 한다. 선행사를 포함하는 관계대명사 what을 쓰기 위해서는 절이 most of ~ 이하가 없는 불완전한 절이어야 한다.

02 이 현상은 너무 신뢰할 수 있고 어디서나 볼 수 있기 때문에 "와비건 호수 효과"라고 알려지게 되었다.
▶ '너무 ~해서 …하다'를 나타내는 구문은 so ~ that 구문이다. 따라서 so를 써야 한다.

03 동시에, 운송 형태가 개선되었고 장소를 이동하는 것이 더 빠르고 더 저렴해졌다.
▶ 문맥상 and 뒤에는 forms of transport를 대신하는 대명사(they)가 아닌, 진주어 to get to places를 대신하는 가주어 it을 써야 한다.

04 녹고 있는 얼음과 해수면 상승의 가장 놀랍고 믿을 수 없는 결과는 그것들이 합쳐져 일종의 타임머신이라는 것이고, 이것은 너무나 현실적이어서 그것들이 우리 하루의 기간을 바꾸고 있다는 것이다.
▶ The most ~ rising seas가 문장의 주어이고, 주어의 핵은 consequence이다. 주어가 단수 주어이므로 문장의 동사는 주어와 수일치하여 is를 써야 한다.

05 아이들은 간식 시간에 몇 개의 크래커를 가져갈지 파악하는 것 또는 조개껍질들을 더미로 분류하는 것과 같은, 자신만의 활동이나 경험을 통해 수학적 개념을 밝히고 연구한다.
▶ how many crackers 다음에 주어가 없으므로 동사가 올 수 없고 명사구 형태가 와야 한다. 따라서 「의문사+to부정사」 구문으로 to take를 써야 한다.

06 인도의 농부들은 내년에 몬순 장마가 언제 올 것인지 알고 따라서 그들은 언제 작물을 심어야 하는지 안다.
▶ when이 이끄는 절은 시간을 나타내는 부사절이 아니라 의문사 when이 이끄는 명사절이다. 따라서 문장의 시제에 맞게 미래 시제 will come을 써야 한다.

07 행복은 첼로를 연주하는 것을 배우는 것과 근본적으로 다르지 않다.
▶ 비교 대상이 Well-being이므로 동명사 learning을 써야 한다.

08 뉴런은 그것이 반복된 생각과 활동에 의해 활성화됨에 따라 더 많이 점화할수록, 그것은 신경 경로로 더 빠르게 발달하게 되고, 이것은 뇌에 지속적인 변화를 일으킨다.
▶ 「the+비교급 ~, the+비교급 …」 구문이므로 비교급 형태인 faster를 써야 한다.

09 이는 대단히 고무적인 전제인데, 즉 요점은 뇌가 더 행복해지도록 우리가 습관을 의도적으로 만들어 낼 수 있다는 것이다.
▶ 「such+관사+형용사+명사」 또는 「so+형용사+관사+명사」의 어순으로 쓰이는데, 뒤에 「관사+형용사+명사」의 어순이 왔으므로 such를 써야 한다.

10 건강에 대한 염려가 젊은이들이 그들의 식단을 바꾸려고 하는 유일한 이유는 아니다.
▶ 선행사에 the only가 포함되어 있으므로 관계대명사 that을 써야 한다.

11 호기심은 우리로 하여금 어떤 힘든 문제를 떠맡아야 할 재미난 도전이라고 여기도록 할 가능성을 더 크게 만든다.
▶ 문맥상 an interesting challenge를 수식하여 '~할 재미난 도전'의 의미를 나타내는 것이 적절하므로 형용사적 용법의 to부정사 to take로 써야 한다.

12 한 사람이 거짓말을 하면, 그들의 반응은 더 느리게 나올 것인데, 왜냐하면 뇌는 저장된 사실을 기억해 내는 데 비해 새로 꾸며낸 이야기의 세부 사항을 처리하는 데 더 많은 시간이 필요하기 때문이다.
▶ 부사 slowly의 비교급이므로 more를 써야 한다.

13 전기를 생산하기 위한 재생 가능 에너지원의 사용은 전기 공급 확보의 필요성과 환경 보호의 목적이 조화를 이루는 방법으로 점점 더 장려되어 왔다.
▶ 문맥상 '~의 사용이 장려되어 왔다'의 의미가 되어야 하므로 수동태 문장이 되어야 한다. 따라서 앞에 쓰인 has been과 호응하여 현재완료 수동태인 (has been) encouraged로 써야 한다.

14 예를 들어, 수력 발전 댐은 수생 생태계에 영향을 끼치고, 더 최근에는 온실가스 배출의 주요 원인으로 확인되었다.
▶ 문맥상 '~으로 확인되었다'의 의미가 되어야 하므로 수동태 문장이 되어야 한다. 따라서 앞에 쓰인 have been과 호응하여 현재완료 수동태인 (have been) identified로 써야 한다.

15 철도가 생기면서 많은 대형 호텔이 생겨났다.
▶ With the railways라는 부사구를 강조하기 위해 문두에 둔 구조이므로, 뒤에는 주어와 동사의 도치가 일어난다. 그러므로, 동사 came을 먼저 쓰고 주어 many large hotels를 뒤에 써야 한다.

16 일반적으로, 호기심은 우리가 스트레스 가득한 상황을 위협보다는 도전으로 여기도록 하고, 좀 더 터놓고 어려움에 대해 말하게 하며, 문제 해결에 대한 새로운 접근법을 시도하도록 동기 부여를 해 준다.
▶ 「motivate+목적어+to부정사」 형태로 쓰여 '~에게 …하도록 동기 부여를 해 주다'라는 의미를 나타낸다. 따라서 목적어 us 다음에 to view가 와야 하고, view는 「view A as B」의 형태로 쓰여 'A를 B로 여기다'라는 의미이다. 문맥상 A에 해당하는 것은 stressful situations, B에 해당하는 것은 challenges이다. 따라서 to view stressful situations as challenges로 써야 한다.

7강	**제목 추론**	본문 p. 60

01 that　　**02** to feel　　**03** enjoying　　**04** what
05 Being　　**06** learn　　**07** have drawn
08 turning　　**09** is　　**10** whose　　**11** to get
12 greatest　　**13** that　　**14** needed
15 how boring that would be　　**16** do they consider

01 가난이 스트레스를 유발하는 경향이 있다는 것을 듣고 놀랄 사람은 거의 없을 것이다.
- ▶ hear의 목적어를 이끄는 that절이 와야 하므로 that을 써야 한다.

02 사실, 빠른 속도의 생산력은 부를 창출하지만, 그것은 또한 사람들이 긴장을 풀고 즐겁게 지낼 시간이 모자랄 때 시간에 쪼들린다고 느끼게 한다.
- ▶ 「lead+목적어+목적격보어」는 '…가 ~하게 하다[유도하다]'라는 의미를 가진다. 이때 목적격보어로는 to부정사가 와야 하므로 to feel로 써야 한다.

03 여러분이 어떤 일을 잘하고 그것을 하는 것에 대한 보상을 잘 받는다면, 그것을 즐기지 않게 되더라도 계속 그것을 하고 싶을 수도 있다.
- ▶ 문맥상 「stop+to부정사」(즐기기 위해 멈추다)가 아니라, 「stop+동명사」(즐기는 것을 멈추다)의 의미가 되어야 하므로 동명사 enjoying을 써야 한다.

04 열악한 고용 시장이 그들을 안정적이거나 심지어 보수가 좋을 수도 있지만, 궁극적으로는 만족스럽지 못한 일자리에 갇혀 있다고 느끼게 해 놓았다.
- ▶ 전치사 in의 목적어이면서 may be의 주어 역할을 동시에 할 수 있는 what을 써야 한다.

05 어떤 일에 대해 옳다는 것은 "그것은 원래 그런 거야, 끝."이라고 하는 것을 의미한다.
- ▶ means가 이 문장의 동사이고, that절이 목적어절로, means 앞이 이 문장의 주어가 되어야 한다. 주어 자리에는 Be가 아니라 동명사 Being을 써야 한다.

06 만약 여러분이 그들의 관점을 안다면, 여러분은 새로운 무언가를 보게 되거나, 그것보다는 더 안 좋게는 다른 사람이 삶을 바라보는 방식에 대한 무언가를 배우게 될 것이다.
- ▶ will 뒤에 접속사 or로 묶인 병렬구조로, see와 같은 형태인 동사원형 learn으로 써야 한다.

07 한 세대 내지 두 세대 전만 해도 '알고리즘'이라는 단어를 언급하는 것은 대부분의 사람들로부터 아무 반응을 얻지 못했을 것이다.
- ▶ '~했을 것이다'라는 과거의 추측을 나타내는 표현이므로 would have p.p.의 형태를 써야 한다.

08 여러분의 은행은 인간들이 여기저기서 스위치를 전환하고 있는 알고리즘의 거대한 망이다.
- ▶ 「with+목적어+분사」 구문에서 목적어 humans와 분사의 관계가 능동(인간이 스위치를 전환하는 것)이므로 현재분사 turning을 써야 한다.

09 감정을 정확히 인식하고 감정에 이름을 붙일 수 있는 우리의 능력은 흔히 '감정 입자도'라고 불린다.
- ▶ 주어가 Our ability이고 이를 수식하는 to부정사구 to accurately ~ emotions가 이어진 구조이므로 단수 동사 is를 써야 한다.

10 사회에 의해 규정된 전통적인 역할 정체성은 아래 어딘가에서 자신의 진정한 자아가 발견되어야 할 사람들에게 부여된 가면처럼 나타나기 시작했다.
- ▶ 관계사절이 이끄는 절에서 완전한 절이 왔고, 문맥상 선행사의 소유격 people's real self의 의미이므로 소유격 관계대명사 whose를 써야 한다.

11 David는 우리가 풍부한 감정적인 어휘를 갖고 있지 않으면, 우리의 욕구를 전달하고 우리가 필요로 하는 지지를 다른 사람들로부터 얻는 것이 어렵다고 설명한다.
- ▶ it이 가주어, to communicate ~가 진주어이며, get ~은 and로 이어져 진주어와 병렬 구조를 이루어야 하므로 to get을 써야 한다.

12 Illinois 공과 대학의 건축학과 교수인 Antony Wood는 지난 20년간의 엘리베이터의 발전은 아마도 우리가 높은 건물에서 봐 왔던 가장 큰 발전일 것이라고 설명한다.
- ▶ 문맥상 「the+최상급」 형태로 명사인 advances를 수식하는 것이 적절하므로 -est를 붙인 greatest로 써야 한다.

13 사용하지 않는 물건에 호주인들만 따져도 매년 평균 108억 호주 달러(약 99억 9천 미국 달러)를 쓰는 것으로 추산되는데, 이는 대학과 도로에 사용하는 정부 지출 총액을 넘어서는 금액이다.
- ▶ 문맥상 Australians alone 이하가 주어의 역할을 하므로 명사절을 이끄는 접속사 that을 써야 한다. 이 문장은 that절이 목적어로 쓰인 능동태 문장을 수동태로 전환한 것으로, 이러한 경우 주어로 가주어 it을 두고 진주어인 that절을 문장의 뒤에 위치시킨다.

14 씹기는 포유류에게 낮은 물론 서늘한 밤 동안에도 활동하고, 더 추운 기후나 기온이 변하는 곳에서 사는 데 필요한 에너지를 준다.
- ▶ 명사 energy와 need의 관계가 수동이므로 과거분사 needed를 써야 한다.

15 그것이 얼마나 지루할지는 제외하고라도, 그것은 모든 새로운 기회, 아이디어, 발명, 그리고 창의성을 없애게 될 것이다.
- ▶ 전치사 Besides의 목적어가 와야 하는 자리이다. how boring ~이 이끄는 명사절이 되어야 하므로 how boring 다음에 주어 that과 동사 would be를 써야 한다.

16 사람들은 도시 발전에 대해 생각할 때, 좀처럼 수직 운송 수단의 중요한 역할을 고려하지 않는다.
- ▶ 부정어인 rarely가 주절의 문두에 왔으므로 주어와 동사가 도치되어야 하는데, 일반동사일 경우 조동사 do[does]가 앞에 나와 「do[does]+주어+동사원형」의 어순으로 써야 한다.

8강 **도표의 이해** 본문 p. 62

01 the largest **02** slightly larger **03** eating
04 was **05** least **06** participating **07** which
08 that **09** who **10** was larger than that in 2019
11 was the same as golf

01 2019년 유럽의 산림 면적 점유율은 다섯 개 지역 중 가장 컸고, 같은 해 아시아의 그것의 세 배가 넘었다.

▶ 전치사 among으로 보아 형용사 large는 비교급이 아닌 최상급으로 써야 하므로 정관사와 함께 the largest로 써야 한다.

02 2019년에는 출생자 수와 사망자 수 사이의 차이가 가장 작았는데, 출생자 수가 사망자 수보다 약간 더 컸다.
▶ '~한 채', '~하면서'라는 의미의 「with+명사(구)+수식어」의 형태이므로, 명사 the number of births 뒤에 동사(was) 없이 slightly larger를 써야 한다.

03 위의 그래프는 고기를 덜 먹는 것에 관심 있는 사람들과 고기를 먹지 않는 사람들의 이유에 대한 2018년 영국에서의 조사 결과를 보여 준다.
▶ 전치사 for의 목적어로 people과 those가 and로 묶인 병렬구조로, people 뒤에는 수동의 의미로 과거분사 interested in ~이 수식을 하고 있다. those(=people) 뒤에는 those가 '먹는' 능동이므로 현재분사 eating을 써야 한다.

04 2015년에는 반려동물을 보유한 미국 가정의 비율이 2020년보다 3퍼센트포인트 더 낮았다.
▶ 주어는 the rate of U.S. households with pets이고, 주어의 핵은 the rate로 단수이므로 단수 동사 was를 써야 한다.

05 65세 이상의 사람들은 여섯 개의 연령 집단 중에서 온라인 강의를 이용할 가능성이 가장 낮았다.
▶ 앞에 the가 있으므로 최상급 표현인 least를 써야 한다.

06 위 도표는 2016년에 문화 활동에 참여하는 미국의 홈스쿨링을 받는 학생들 및 공립학교 학생들의 비율을 보여 준다.
▶ 학생들이 문화 활동에 '참여하는' 능동의 의미이므로 현재분사 participating을 써야 한다.

07 2013년의 반려동물을 보유한 미국 가정의 비율은 2017년의 비율과 같았고, 그것은 68퍼센트였다.
▶ was 68 percent가 주어가 없는 불완전한 문장이고 앞 문장 전체를 받고 있으므로 which를 써야 한다.

08 GDP 점유율로서 벨기에의 건강 관련 지출은 프랑스와 영국 사이였다.
▶ 문맥상 반복되는 명사구 health spending as a share of GDP를 대신하므로 단수 대명사 that을 써야 한다.

09 위 도표는 2016년과 2019년에 교육용 디지털 콘텐츠에 접속하기 위해 기기를 사용한 유치원에서 12학년까지의 학생들의 비율을 보여 준다.
▶ 선행사가 전치사구 from kindergarten to 12th grade의 수식을 받는 students이므로, 관계대명사 who를 써야 한다.

10 1990년 아메리카의 산림 면적 점유율은 42.6%였고, 이는 2019년의 그것보다 더 컸다.
▶ 우선 1990년의 점유율과 2019년의 점유율을 비교하는 내용이므로, The share of forest area를 that으로 바꾸어 that in 2019이라고 쓸 수 있어야 한다. 앞의 내용을 설명하는 which 뒤에는 동사와 비교하는 표현이 와야 하므로, was larger 다음에 than that in 2019을 써야 한다.

11 스케이트보드는 어린이들이 평균 12세에 중단한 스포츠였고, 그 평균 참여 기간은 골프와 같았다.
▶ 주어에 연결되는 be동사 was 뒤로 '~과 같다'는 의미가 되도록 the same as golf가 이어져야 한다. 여기서 same은 대명사로 쓰여 '동일한 것'의 의미를 나타내며, 앞에서 언급한 특정한 것을 가리키므로 정관사 the를 항상 동반한다.

<table>
<tr><td>**9강**</td><td>**내용 일치 파악**</td><td>본문 p.64</td></tr>
</table>

01 where **02** Since **03** enjoying **04** where
05 was introduced **06** Since **07** to pursue
08 getting **09** (being) disallowed **10** where
11 In order to persuade her to try
12 Not only did she sell

01 고등학교를 졸업한 후, Becker는 Princeton University로 진학했고, 거기서 그는 경제학을 전공했다.
▶ 콤마 뒤에 계속적 용법의 관계사절이 이어지는 문장으로, 관계사 뒤에 완전한 절이 이어지므로 관계대명사 which가 아닌, 관계부사 where(그리고 거기에서)를 써야 한다.

02 1985년 이후, Becker는 경제학적 분석과 아이디어를 일반 대중에게 설명하며 'Business Week'에 경제학 칼럼을 정기적으로 기고했다.
▶ 문장의 동사 had written으로 보아, 1985년 이후 칼럼을 정기적으로 계속 써 왔음을 알 수 있다. 그러므로 '~ 동안'을 나타내는 During 1985가 아니라 Since 1985로 써야 한다.

03 그 당시 대부분의 다른 여자아이와 달리 그녀는 바지를 입었고, 승마와 사냥 같은 모험적인 활동을 즐기며 시간을 보냈다.
▶ '~하는 데 (시간)을 보내다'라는 표현은 「spend+시간+-ing」의 형태로 써야 하므로 동명사 enjoying을 써야 한다.

04 Knight는 1850년 12세의 나이에 학교를 그만두었는데, 근처에 있는 직물 공장에서 가족을 위해 돈을 벌기 위해서였고, 그곳에서 그녀는 동료 노동자가 결함이 있는 장비에 의해 부상을 당하는 것을 목격했다.
▶ 선행사 a nearby textile factory 뒤에 완전한 절이 이어지고 있으므로 관계대명사 which가 아닌 관계부사 where를 써야 한다. 콤마 뒤에 관계부사 where는 계속적 용법으로 '그리고 거기서'와 같이 해석한다.

05 그는 학교 친구에 의해 재즈의 세계를 소개받았다.
▶ 주어인 He가 '소개를 받은' 수동태 문장이므로 was introduced를 써야 한다. 능동태로 바꾸면 A schoolmate introduced him to the world of jazz.이다.

06 그는 그림을 잘 그릴 수 없었기 때문에, 화가를 고용하여 자신이 설명하는 것을 그림으로 그리게 했다.
▶ 주절의 내용이 화가를 고용하여 자신이 설명하는 것을 그리게 했다고 했으므로 그림을 잘 그릴 수 없기 '때문에'라는 의미의 접속사 Since를 써야 한다.

07 여성 비행의 개척자로서 그녀는 다음 세대가 그들의 비행의 꿈을 추구하도록 영감을 주었다.
▶ 「inspire+목적어+목적격보어」 구문으로 쓰여 '~에게 …하도록 영감을 주다'라는 의미인데, 이때 목적격보어는 to부정사가 온다. 따라서 to pursue를 써야 한다.

08 Lithops는 작은 식물이고, 토양 표면 위로 거의 1인치 이상 자라지 않고 보통 두 개의 잎만 있다.
▶ 주절에 추가적 서술을 덧붙이는 분사구문으로, 문맥상 주어 Lithops와 get의 관계가 능동이므로 현재분사 getting을 써야 한다.

09 그녀가 흑인이었기 때문에 Carnegie Institute of Technology로부터 입학이 허락되지 않고 나서, Catlett은 Howard 대학교에서 디자인과 소묘를 공부했다.
▶ 접속사(After)가 생략되지 않은 분사구문으로, 주어인 Catlett과 disallow의 관계가 수동이므로 수동형 분사 (being) disallowed를 써야 한다.

10 1888년에 그녀는 St. Louis로 이주했고, 그곳에서 그녀는 10년 이상 세탁부로 일하며 간신히 하루에 1달러가 넘는 돈을 벌었다.
▶ St. Louis라는 장소를 부연 설명하는 절을 이끌며 she worked 이하가 문장 필수 성분을 모두 갖춘 완전한 절이므로, 관계부사 where를 써야 한다.

11 약간이라도 더 안전한 활동을 하도록 그녀를 설득하기 위해, Lilian의 아버지는 그녀에게 자동차를 사 주었다.
▶ in order to는 '~하기 위해서'라는 표현이므로, Lilian의 아버지가 그녀에게 자동차를 사 준 이유는 Lilian이 조금이라도 더 안전한 활동을 해 보게 하기 위해서임을 알 수 있다. persuade는 목적어 뒤에 목적격보어로 to부정사를 써야 한다. 그러므로 In order to 뒤에 동사 persuade, 그 뒤에 목적어 her, 그 뒤에 목적격보어 to try를 써야 한다.

12 그녀는 판매했을 뿐만 아니라 이익을 나누기 위하여 많은 여성들을 판매 대리인으로 모집하고 훈련시켰다.
▶ 부정어인 Not only가 문두에 사용되면 도치구문이 이어져야 하는데, 동사가 일반동사일 때는 「조동사 do[does]+주어+동사원형」의 어순으로 써야 한다. 여기서는 과거 시제이므로 Not only did she sell로 써야 한다.

10강	**안내문의 이해**	본문 p. 66

01 be awarded　　**02** published　　**03** be wiped

04 or　　**05** be accepted　　**06** to enjoy

07 amazing　　**08** be announced　　**09** it

10 made　　**11** should send us your phone number

---

01 500달러와 메달이 우승자에게 수여될 것입니다.
▶ 주어 $500 and a medal과 동사 award는 수동의 관계이므로 수동태로 써야 하며, 조동사 will이 있으므로 be는 원형으로 하여 be awarded로 써야 한다.

02 여러분의 이야기가 출간되기를 원하시나요?
▶ 「get+목적어+목적격보어」의 형태로, 목적어와 목적격보어가 능동의 관계이면 목적격보어는 to부정사를 쓰지만, 여기는 수동의 관계이므로 과거분사 published를 써야 한다.

03 기기 속 모든 개인 정보는 미리 삭제되어야 합니다.
▶ 주어 All personal data와 동사 wipe는 수동의 관계이므로 수동태인 be wiped를 써야 한다.

04 온라인이나 전화로 수업을 등록할 수 있습니다.
▶ 「either A or B」의 형태로 쓰는 상관접속사이므로 or를 써야 한다.

05 예약은 투어가 시작하기 2시간 전까지 접수될 예정입니다.
▶ 예약이 '접수될' 것이므로 수동태인 be accepted를 써야 한다.

06 이 특별한 투어에 참여하여 우리의 가장 인기 있는 초콜릿 바를 즐길 기회를 가지세요.
▶ 문맥상 초콜릿 바를 '즐길 기회'라는 의미이므로 앞의 a chance를 수식하는 to부정사 to enjoy를 써야 한다.

07 여러분은 여러분의 가장 놀라운 사진을 공유함으로써 Camptonville의 자연의 아름다움을 보여 줄 수 있습니다!
▶ '놀라운' 사진이라는 의미이므로 현재분사 amazing을 써야 한다.

08 수상자는 2021년 7월 15일에 웹 사이트에서만 공지될 것입니다.
▶ 문맥상 주어인 The winners와 announce(공지하다)의 관계가 수동이므로 수동태로 표현되어야 한다. 이때 미래를 나타내는 조동사 will이 쓰일 경우 「will be+p.p.」의 형태가 된다.

09 회의 10분 전에 문자 메시지로 접속 링크를 받아 클릭하세요.
▶ 문맥상 앞에서 언급한 명사구 the access link를 대신하므로 단수 대명사 it을 써야 한다.

10 모든 학년의 학생들은 블록으로 가장 창의적이고 살기 좋은 건축물을 만들기 위해 경쟁할 것입니다!
▶ the most creative and livable structure를 수식하는 분사구로 문맥상 수식하는 명사구와 make는 수동의 관계이므로 과거분사 made를 써야 한다.

11 원고와 함께 여러분의 전화번호를 보내야 합니다.
▶ 주어 You 뒤에는 동사 should send가 와야 하며, send는 수여동사로 「send+간접목적어+직접목적어」로 쓸 수 있다. 그러므로 간접목적어 us를 먼저 쓰고, 직접목적어 your phone number를 써야 한다. 전치사 to가 있으면, should send your phone number to us로도 쓸 수 있다.

11강 어법

01 increase	**02** is	**03** is	**04** were
05 it	**06** how	**07** relate	**08** has	**09** are
10 it	**11** noticeably	**12** that	**13** find
14 to smell	**15** what their parents tell
16 the environment in which it lives

01 스스로를 똑똑하고 일을 어떻게 하는지 아는 소년으로 생각하는 것은 그가 문제 해결 노력에 있어 더 오래 지속하도록 하고 새롭고 어려운 일을 시도하는 것에 있어 그의 자신감을 증가시킬 가능성이 높다.
▶ Thinking ~ things가 주어이고, 동사 is likely to 뒤에 make와 increase가 and로 연결되는 구조의 문장이다. 그러므로 동사원형인 increase를 써야 한다.

02 동물에게 투영된 가장 눈에 띄는 인간의 특징은 동물이 인간의 언어로 대화할 수 있다는 점이다.
▶ 문장의 주어의 핵은 characteristic이며, projected는 문장의 동사가 아닌 과거분사로 앞의 characteristic을 수식하고 있다. 문장의 동사는 be동사로 단수 주어에 일치하는 단수 동사 is를 써야 한다.

03 동물 캐릭터를 아이와 어른 모두에게 더 감정적으로 매력적이게 만들기 위해 이용하는 일반적인 전략은 그것들에 확대되고 변형된 어린이 같은 특징을 부여하는 것이다.
▶ 주어의 핵은 A general strategy이고, 바로 뒤의 that절은 A general strategy를 꾸며 주는 주격 관계대명사절이다. 그리므로 that 뒤에는 단수 동사 is를 썼다. 또한 빈칸의 be는 이 문장의 동사이므로, 여기 또한 단수 동사 is를 써야 한다. 참고로, 이 다음의 to ~ features는 이 문장의 보어이다.

04 하지만, AI로 구동되는 기계가 실제로 수행할 수 있는 모든 작업을 고려한다면, 그것은 꽤 놀라울 것이다!
▶ 뒤의 주절 동사 would be로 보아 가정법 과거 문장임을 알 수 있다. 그러므로 가정의 부사절의 동사는 과거 동사 were로 써야 한다.

05 이러한 종류의 변화들은 새로운 기술들이 우리 세계에 미칠 영향을 인식하는 것이 왜 그렇게 중요한가에 대한 정확한 이유이다.
▶ 이 문장의 주어는 These kinds of changes이고, 동사는 are, why 이하가 보어이다. to recognize ~ for our world까지 why절의 진주어이기 때문에 why 뒤에는 가주어 it을 써야 한다.

06 이것은 우리 종이 발전한 방식에 깊게 뿌리박혀 있는 매우 흔한 인간의 성향이다.
▶ 문맥상 전치사 in의 목적어는 '우리 종이 발전한 방식'이라는 의미가 되어야 하므로 선행사 the way가 생략된 형태로 쓰이는 관계부사 how를 써야 한다.

07 유사성은 우리가 다른 사람들과 마음이 더 잘 통하게 해 주는데, 그들이 우리를 다른 사람들보다 더 깊은 수준으로 이해할 거라고 생각하기 때문이다.
▶ make의 목적격보어이므로 동사원형 relate를 써야 한다.

08 농작물에 질소와 포타슘으로 비료를 주는 것은 마그네슘, 아연, 철 그리고 요오드의 감소로 이어져 왔다.
▶ 주어가 동명사구 Fertilizing ~ potassium이므로 동사는 단수형 has를 써야 한다.

09 실제로 오늘날 우리의 토양은 덜 건강하고 그 위에서 길러진 식물도 그러하다.
▶ '(주어) 또한 그렇다'라는 의미의 「so+(조)동사+주어」 구문으로 주어 the plants가 복수이므로 동사도 복수형 are를 써야 한다.

10 만약 사람들이 자신들의 돈을 모두 사용하는 대신, 돈의 일부를 저축한다면 어떤 일이 일어날까?
▶ 앞에 나온 money를 가리키는 대명사이므로 it을 써야 한다.

11 참된 미소는 눈가 근육과 주름에 영향을 주며, 티가 덜 나게 눈썹과 윗눈꺼풀 사이의 피부가 진정한 즐거움으로 살짝 내려오는 것이다.
▶ and 이하의 절에서 문장 전체를 수식하는 역할을 하므로 부사 noticeably를 써야 한다.

12 대개 악기를 잡고 연주하는 정확한 방법이 있다고 해도, 무엇보다 가장 중요한 가르침은 악기가 장난감이 아니라는 것과 악기를 관리해야 한다는 것이다.
▶ 주절의 주격보어인 명사절을 유도해야 하는데, they are not toys가 문장 필수 성분의 결핍이 없는 완전한 문장이다. 따라서 관계대명사 what이 아닌 접속사 that을 써야 한다.

13 정확한 연주는 가장 적절한 음질을 찾고 오랜 시간 동안 잘 다루면서 연주할 수 있도록 가장 편안한 연주 자세를 찾으려는 열망에서 나온다.
▶ 앞에 있는 the desire를 수식하는 형용사적 용법의 to부정사(to find)와 병렬 구조로 이어지므로 to가 생략된 find를 써야 한다.

14 어떤 냄새를 맡을 수 있는 능력이나 그것이 얼마나 좋은 느낌을 주는지와 관련된 개체 간의 차이 또한 존재한다.
▶ the ability를 수식하는 형용사적 용법의 to부정사를 써야 한다.

15 미취학 아동들은 그들의 부모가 그들에게 하는 말을 매우 뜻깊게 여긴다.
▶ believe의 목적어가 필요한 문장이다. what이 tell의 직접목적어이자 believe의 목적어로, 명사절을 이끄는 what을 believe 바로 뒤에 쓰고 그 뒤에 their parents tell them이 나오면 된다.

16 어떤 종도 그것이 살고 있는 환경에 존재하는 모든 분자를 감지할 수는 없는데, 즉 우리는 맡을 수가 없지만 몇몇 다른 동물들은 맡을 수 있는 몇 가지 냄새가 있고, 그 반대의 경우도 있다.
▶ 앞에 제시된 전치사 in의 목적어로 명사구인 the environment가 쓰이고, 이를 in which it lives의 관계절이 수식하는 구조로 써야 한다. 이때, the environment which it lives in의 형태도 가능하다.

01 adapting　　**02** to come　　**03** to develop

04 it　　**05** found　　**06** is　　**07** appear

08 to treat　　**09** risk　　**10** rejected　　**11** them

12 using　　**13** when

14 where individuals are at greatest threat

15 Not only did it turn

01 광고주들은 그들이 홍보하는 상품의 시장 지위에 맞게 그들의 주장을 조절하는 상당한 능력을 자주 보여 주었다.
　▶ 전치사 in의 목적어가 되어야 하므로, 동명사 adapting을 써야 한다. 그 뒤의 their claims는 adapting의 목적어이다.

02 Fleischmann의 효모의 생산자는 판매를 촉진하기 위해서 다른 마케팅 전략을 고안하도록 J. Walter Thompson 광고 대행사를 고용했다.
　▶ '~을 …하도록 고용하다'라는 의미가 되도록 「hire+목적어+목적격보어(to부정사)」의 형태로 써야 하므로 목적격보어 to come으로 써야 한다.

03 이로 인해 기업은 구매자 및 고객과 더 긴밀한 관계를 발전시켜야 했고, 이것은 결과적으로 기업이 합리적인 가격에 양질의 제품을 생산하는 것만으로는 충분하지 않다는 것을 깨닫게 했다.
　▶ force는 「force+목적어+목적격보어」의 5형식 문장으로 쓸 수 있는데, 이때 목적격보어로 to부정사를 쓰므로 to develop로 써야 한다.

04 사실, 고객이 실제로 원하는 제품을 내놓는 것은 마찬가지로 매우 중요했다.
　▶ 뒤에 있는 to deliver products that customers actually wanted가 진주어이므로 가주어 it을 써야 한다.

05 식물의 성장은 식물의 줄기와 뿌리의 끝에서 발견되는 옥신이라고 불리는 호르몬 그룹에 의해 조절된다.
　▶ '식물의 줄기와 뿌리의 끝에서 발견되는' 옥신이라는 내용이 되어야 하므로, 현재분사가 아니라 과거분사 found를 써야 한다.

06 줄기의 끝에서 생산된 옥신은 그늘진 곳에 있는 줄기의 옆면에 축적되는 경향이 있다.
　▶ 주격 관계대명사절의 동사를 판단하는 문제이다. that이 the stem을 받으므로, 동사는 단수 동사 is를 써야 한다.

07 이 현상은 줄기가 휘어지게 하고 빛을 향하여 성장하고 있는 것처럼 보이게 한다.
　▶ 「cause+목적어+목적격보어(to부정사)」의 형태이며, to 뒤에 동사원형이 and로 묶인 병렬구조이다. 따라서 and 뒤에는 동사원형 appear를 써야 한다.

08 기대를 없애는 첫 단계는 자신을 친절하게 대하는 것이다.
　▶ 주어는 The first step이고, 문맥상 '주어는 무엇이다'라는 의미가 되어야 하므로 be동사 is 뒤에는 주격보어로 to부정사의 명사적 용법인 to treat를 써야 한다.

09 많은 사람에게 그것(거절)은 너무 고통스럽기 때문에 그들은 요청하고 거절당할 위험을 무릅쓰기보다는 아예 무언가를 요청하지 않는 것이 나을 것이다.
　▶ 「would rather A than B」 구문으로 than 뒤의 ask와 병렬 연결된 구조이므로 risk를 써야 한다.

10 의도적으로 스스로를 거절당할 상황에 놓이게 함으로써 여러분은 더 둔감해지고, 인생에서 훨씬 더 많은 것을 떠맡을 수 있게 되며, 따라서 그것은 호의적이지 않은 상황에 더 성공적으로 대처하게 해 줄 것이다.
　▶ 「get+목적어+목적격보어」 구문으로 목적격보어 reject가 목적어인 yourself와 수동의 관계이므로 과거분사 rejected를 써야 한다.

11 강을 직선화하고 규칙적인 횡단면으로 만들고자 하는 시도는 아마도 이러한 형태-기능 관계의 가장 피해가 막심한 사례일 것이다.
　▶ 앞에 나온 rivers를 가리키는 대명사이므로 복수형 them을 써야 한다.

12 그 가격이면, 여러분은 비용을 의식할 것이고 책을 읽으려고 인공조명을 이용하기 전에 다시 한번 생각할 것이다.
　▶ 전치사 before의 목적어이므로, 동명사 using을 써야 한다.

13 약 1만 년 전, 개의 역할이 대부분 인간 사회에서 확고하게 정해졌을 때, 인간의 뇌도 약 10퍼센트 줄어들었다.
　▶ 시간을 나타내는 어구 About 10,000 years ago를 부연 설명하는 관계사절로 이어지는 문장이 완전한 문장이므로 관계부사 when을 써야 한다.

14 이것은 개체가 특정한 생애 주기 동안에 가장 큰 위협에 놓여 있는 상황에서 가장 성공적이다.
　▶ situations를 꾸며 주는 관계부사절이 필요하므로 「where+주어+동사」의 어순으로 써야 한다.

15 그것은 밤을 낮으로 바꾸었을 뿐 아니라, 자연광이 들어올 수 없는 큰 건물에서 우리가 살고 일할 수 있게 해 주었다.
　▶ 부정어인 Not only가 문두에 왔으므로, 뒤에 「조동사 do+주어+동사원형」의 어순으로 도치되어야 한다.

13강 　빈칸 추론 1 (31~32번)　　　　　　　　　본문 p. 72

01 have　　**02** did　　**03** emerges　　**04** is

05 that　　**06** restricting　　**07** humanize　　**08** is

09 are　　**10** learned　　**11** whatever　　**12** achieve

13 how long things are going to take

14 enabling people to work for

15 Not only does memory underlie

01 자신의 직업에서 높은 수준으로 수행하는 사람들은 흔히 다른 사람들의 즉각적인 신뢰를 얻는다.

▶ who perform at a high level in their profession이 Individuals를 꾸며 주는 관계대명사절로, 이 문장의 주어는 Individuals이다. 그러므로 동사는 복수 동사 have를 써야 한다.

02 그는 그가 농구를 하면서 그간 벌었던 것보다 광고로부터 더 많은 돈을 벌었다.
▶ 비교의 than 뒤에는 앞의 made money에 상응하는 동사를 써야 하므로 대동사로 be동사가 아닌 do의 과거형 did를 써야 한다.

03 뇌와 도시 안에서, 모든 것은, 모든 규모에서, 근거리에서든 원거리에서든, 거주자들 간의 상호 작용으로부터 나타난다.
▶ 주어 everything은 단수 취급하므로 emerges를 써야 한다.

04 일반적으로 동쪽으로 비행하여 여러분의 하루를 단축하는 것보다는 서쪽으로 비행하여 여러분의 하루를 연장하는 것이 더 쉽다.
▶ 접속사 than 뒤에는 앞의 is easier에 상응하는 is (easy)를 써야 한다. 반복되는 형용사 easy가 생략되어 is만 남아 있는 형태이다.

05 46,000 경기가 넘는 메이저 리그 야구 경기에 대한 더 최근의 연구에 의해 동쪽으로 이동하는 것이 서쪽으로 이동하는 것보다 더 힘들다는 추가적인 증거가 발견되었다.
▶ that 이하는 additional evidence와 동격이므로, 동격을 나타내는 that을 써야 한다.

06 Ariely는, 교수에 의해서든 혹은 일을 미루는 자신의 성향을 인식한 학생들에 의해서든, 자유를 제한하는 것이 자기 통제와 성과를 향상시킨다고 결론짓는다.
▶ 동사 concludes의 목적어절의 주어가 되어야 하므로 동사원형이 아니라 동명사 restricting으로 써야 한다. 목적어절의 주어가 동명사, 즉 3인칭 단수이므로 동사는 improves가 된다.

07 글을 인간미 있게 하는 구체적인 사례가 없는 일반화는 청자와 독자에게 지루하다.
▶ examples를 수식하는 주격 관계대명사 that의 동사가 필요하므로 humanize를 써야 한다.

08 사람들이 선택을 하는 데 있어 어려움을 겪는 이유는 자신들이 원하는 것이 자신들이 해야 할 일과 관련이 없다고 믿기 때문이다.
▶ 주어의 핵이 The reason이고 내용상 일반 진술에 해당하므로, 현재 시제 is를 써야 한다.

09 연구에 의하면 운동선수는 운동선수가 아닌 사람들보다 용납할 수 없는 행동을 덜 하는 것 같다고 한다.
▶ are likely to participate in unacceptable behavior를 대신하므로 are를 써야 한다.

10 인성은 학습되는 행동이며, 코치들이 그러한 교훈을 체계적으로 가르치려고 계획할 때만 정정당당한 시합 정신이 발달한다.
▶ 뒤에 있는 명사 behavior를 수식하는 형태가 되어야 하는데, 이때 learn과 behavior는 의미상 수동의 관계이다. 따라서 과거분사 learned를 써야 한다.

11 이것은 그들(아이들)이 느끼고 있는 감정으로부터 그들의 주의를 돌리는 역할을 하고, 그들에게 손과 입으로 할 수 있는 어떤 것을 제공하며, 자신들을 화나게 하는 것이 무엇이든 그것으로부터 그들의 주의를 옮겨 가게 한다.
▶ from의 목적어절을 이끌며, 관계사절에서 주어 역할을 하므로 복합관계대명사 whatever를 써야 한다.

12 그렇게 하면서 그것은 공동체를 성장시키고, 일자리를 창출하고, 경제를 강화하고, 사회와 상업 네트워크를 확장하고, 시간과 에너지를 절약해 주며 수백만 명의 사람들이 더 나은 삶을 누릴 수 있도록 돕는다.
▶ help의 목적격보어이므로 동사원형인 achieve를 써야 한다.

13 만약 매일 하고자 착수하는 일을 성취함으로써 얻게 되는 자신감을 원한다면, 과제가 얼마나 시간이 걸릴지 아는 것이 중요하다.
▶ understand의 목적어절로, 과제가 얼마나 시간이 걸릴지 알아야 한다는 의미가 되어야 하므로 how long을 먼저 쓰고 그 뒤에 주어(things)와 동사(are going to take)를 써야 한다.

14 혁신이 우리의 삶을 바꾸는 최고의 방법은 사람들이 서로를 위해 일할 수 있도록 함으로써이다.
▶ 「enable+목적어+목적격보어(to부정사)」의 형태로 써야 하며 '서로를 위해서'라는 표현이 되기 위해서 마지막에 work for의 순서로 써야 한다.

15 기억이 어쨌든 생각하는 우리의 능력의 기저가 될 뿐만 아니라 우리의 경험의 내용과 앞으로 몇 년 간 우리가 그것을 보존하는 방식을 규정한다.
▶ 부정어인 Not only가 문두에 나오는 구문으로 「Not only+조동사(does)+주어+동사원형」의 어순으로 도치되어야 한다.

14강 **빈칸 추론 2** (33~34번)　　　　본문 p. 74

01 Strange　　**02** that　　**03** delete
04 intellectually　　**05** to use　　**06** being
07 that　　**08** did　　**09** allowed　　**10** to become
11 little　　**12** other　　**13** was it held
14 how the future will be
15 seem to have developed the ability

01 이상하게 들릴지 모르지만, 이 이론은 감정이 우리 신체에서 발생한다고 말한다.
▶ 「(as)+형용사+as+주어+동사」는 '~하지만'이라는 양보의 의미를 갖는 표현으로, 앞에 as는 생략된 형태이다. 동사 sound는 보어로 형용사를 쓰며, 의미상 though it may sound strange이므로 부사가 아닌 형용사 Strange를 써야 한다.

02 그들은 달리고 또 달리지만, 그러다가 Alice는 자신들이 출발했던 그 같은 나무 아래에 여전히 있음을 발견한다.

▶ 선행사 the same tree를 수식하는 관계사절이 이어지는 형태로, 관계사절 안에 전치사 from이 있으며, 그 뒤에 목적어가 없는 불완전한 절이므로 목적격 관계대명사 that을 써야 한다.

03 예를 들어, 만약 여러분이 휴대전화를 멀리하고 여러분의 일에 집중하고 싶다면, 여러분의 주의를 산만하게 하는 앱들을 삭제하거나 친구에게 여러분의 비밀 번호를 바꿔 달라고 요청하라!

▶ 뒤에 있는 or ask에서 알 수 있듯이, 조건 부사절 뒤에 주절로 명령문이 쓰인 문장이다. 따라서 콤마 뒤에는 명령문을 만드는 동사원형 delete를 써야 한다.

04 한 그룹은 글루타민산염 수용체에 대한 유전자를 변형함으로써 지적으로 우월하게 만들어져 있었다.

▶ 「make+목적어+목적격보어」의 수동태 구문으로 목적격보어에 해당하는 형용사 superior를 꾸며 주는 부사 intellectually를 써야 한다.

05 이 기억 저장소는 그들이 자신의 뇌의 신경 회로 내에서 소리 패턴의 빈도를 추적하고 소리 패턴의 의미에 대한 예측을 하기 위해 이 지식을 사용하도록 해 준다.

▶ allows의 목적격보어인 to track과 and로 병렬 연결되어 있으므로 to use를 써야 한다.

06 음악 배급자의 제한된 컬렉션에 국한되지 않고, 또한 최신 히트곡의 '사전 선택자'로서 지역 라디오 프로그램의 안내를 받지 않고, 개인은 적극적으로 자신의 음악적 선호를 선택하고 결정해야 한다.

▶ being ~ music-distributors와 nor로 대등하게 연결되어 전치사 Without의 목적어 역할을 하므로, 동명사 being을 써야 한다.

07 그러나 사회 문화적 관점에서 볼 때, 창작 행위는 제2의 입장, 다시 말해 관객이 부재한 상황에서는 결코 '완전'하지 않다.

▶ the absence of a second position과 동격인 명사구로 반복되는 명사 the absence를 대신하여 단수 대명사 that을 써야 한다.

08 물고기 같은 조상이 그랬던 것처럼, 개구리 역시 물속에 알을 낳아야 한다.

▶ 문맥상 laid their eggs in water를 대신하므로 대동사 did를 써야 한다.

09 그러나 그렇게 하는 것이 허용되더라도, 물리적으로 그렇게 할 수 없기 때문에, 그것이 그들의 '실질적' 자유를 증가시키지는 않을 것이다.

▶ 양보의 부사절에서 「대명사 주어+be동사」가 생략된 구조로, 문맥상 '그들이 허락받는 것'이라는 의미가 되어야 하므로 they are가 생략된 과거분사 allowed를 써야 한다.

10 하지만 현실 세계에서, 대부분의 사람에게는 자신이 되도록 허용된 모든 것이 될 가능성이 없고, 할 수 있는 모든 것을 저지당해야 할 가능성도 없을 것이다.

▶ the opportunity를 수식하며 뒤에 to need ~와 or로 대등하게 연결되어 있으므로 to부정사인 to become을 써야 한다.

11 현대 곤충 군집들은 열대 우림 지역에서 매우 다양하지만, 최근 화석 기록은 그 다양성을 거의 담아내지 않는다.

▶ 추상명사인 that diversity의 극히 일부분을 나타내므로, 셀 수 없는 명사를 받는 대명사 little을 써야 한다.

12 때때로 여러분은 과거에 대한 매우 명확한 그림을 가지지만, 다른 때에는 큰 공백들이 존재하고, 여러분은 그것들이 무엇인지를 인지할 필요가 있다.

▶ 복수 명사인 times를 수식하므로 other를 써야 하고, 이 문장은 「sometimes ~, other times ....」의 구조가 된다.

13 그것은 주장된 데이터에 의존하지 않았고, 소비자들이 다르게 행동할지도 모르는 실험실에서 이루어진 것도 아니었다.

▶ 부정어 nor가 앞으로 도치된 구문이므로, it was held에서 was를 주어 앞에 써서 was it held로 써야 한다.

14 우리는 미래가 어떨지에 대한 아이디어로 시작한다.

▶ 전치사 about의 목적어절이므로, 의문사 how를 먼저 쓴다. 뒤이어 간접의문문의 어순으로 주어(the future)와 동사(will be)를 써야 한다.

15 야외(에 사는) 상대방에 비해 먹이를 잡아먹을 더 적은 기회를 가지는 일부 실내 곤충은 먹이가 제한적일 때 생존할 수 있는 능력을 발달시켜 온 것으로 보인다.

▶ Some indoor insects가 주어이고, 그 뒤의 which ~ counterparts는 그 주어를 추가 설명하는 관계대명사절이다. 이 뒤에 동사가 이어져야 하는데, '능력을 발달시켜 온 것으로 보인다'라는 의미가 되어야 하므로 seem to를 먼저 쓰고, 과거에서부터 현재까지 발달시켜 왔다는 have developed를 쓴 다음 developed의 목적어 the ability를 써야 한다.

15강 무관한 문장 찾기   본문 p. 76

01 requires   **02** it   **03** and   **04** highly

05 it   **06** make   **07** agree with   **08** Creating

09 where   **10** general   **11** stop them from doing

12 Whose story it is   **13** are the days of musicians

14 to ask for permission to build a fanbase

01 또한 새로운 기술을 도입하는 것은 생산 공정에 변화를 야기하거나 직원들에게 새로운 시스템을 배우도록 요구할 때 생산에 부정적인 영향을 미칠 수 있다.

▶ 시간의 부사절 when it causes ~의 causes와 or로 병렬 구조를 이루는 동사이므로 requires를 써야 한다.

02 간단히 말해서, 만약 여러분이 시에게 그렇게 할 기회를 준다면, 시는 제공할 많은 것을 가지고 있다.

▶ 「give+간접목적어(~에게)+직접목적어(~을)」의 구조로 give의 간접목적어는 앞에 나온 poetry이므로 대명사 it을 써야 한다.

03 그리고 취향과 관심에 따라 옷을 입을 때, 우리는 자기 존중과 타인의 즐거움에 대한 관심을 둘 다 보여 준다.

▶ 앞에 both가 나와 「both A and B」 구문을 이루어야 하므로 and를 써야 한다.

04 비록 패션 산업이 유럽과 미국에서 먼저 발전했지만, 오늘날 그것은 국제적이고 매우 세계화된 산업이다.
▶ 문맥상 '매우 세계화된 산업'이라는 의미가 되어야 하므로 highly를 써야 한다. high는 '높은; 높게'라는 뜻이다.

05 실제로 만약 여러분이 자극제를 너무 많이 섭취하면, 신경이 과민해지고 잠을 자기 어려워지며 여러분의 기억 수행이 악화될 것이다.
▶ 「find+가목적어+목적격보어+진목적어(to부정사)」 구문이므로 가목적어에 해당하는 it을 써야 한다.

06 차, 커피 또는 탄산음료에서 흔히 발견되는 가벼운 자극제는 여러분을 더 주의 깊게 해 주고, 따라서 더 잘 기억할 수 있게 한다.
▶ 문장의 주어는 Mild stimulants이고 commonly found ~ sodas는 주어를 수식하는 과거분사구이므로 술어동사가 필요하다. 따라서 동사인 make를 써야 한다.

07 우리는 우리 자신의 주위에 이른바 '필터 버블'을 설치하는데, 그곳에서 우리는 우리가 동의하는 그 자료에만 끊임없이 노출된다.
▶ 목적격 관계대명사 that이 이끄는 절의 동사인 agree는 자동사이므로 목적어를 취하려면 전치사가 필요하다. 따라서 agree with를 써야 한다.

08 다른 사람이 갖고 있지 않은 차이를 만들어 내는 것이 자신의 분야에서 성공하는 방법이며, 혁신의 창조를 이끈다.
▶ a difference 뒤에 오는 that others don't have는 목적격 관계대명사절이고, 문장의 동사는 is이므로, 주어 역할을 하는 동명사 Creating을 써야 한다.

09 인간의 심리는 우리가 개인적인 차원에서 동일시할 수 있는 것을 믿고, 나머지에 대해서는 상상으로 공백을 채우면서 정보가 반드시 존재하지는 않는 경우에 서조차도 그 정보를 찾고 싶게 한다.
▶ it ~ exist가 완전한 절이므로 관계대명사 which가 불가능하며, 문맥상 '~ 상황[곳]에서'의 의미를 나타내므로 접속사로 쓰이는 where를 써야 한다.

10 바넘 효과는 어떤 사람이 매우 일반적인 것을 읽거나 듣지만 그것이 그들에게 적용된다고 믿는 현상이다.
▶ something을 뒤에서 수식하고 있으므로 형용사 general을 써야 한다.

11 이것은 그들이 일을 하는 것을 방해하고 그들의 생산성을 떨어뜨리게 할 수 있다.
▶ stop과 from을 이용한 '~가 …하는 것을 막다'라는 표현은 「stop+목적어+from+동명사」의 순서로 써야 한다.

12 누구의 이야기인지가 무슨 이야기인지에 영향을 미친다.
▶ 소유격 의문대명사 whose는 「whose+명사」의 순서로 써서 뒤의 명사를 수식한다. 그리고 문장의 동사 affects 앞에 주어인 명사절로 써야 하므로 「의문사(구)+평서문」의 어순으로 써야 한다.

13 뮤지션들은 자신들이 주목받을 만하다고 음반사나 TV 프로그램의 문지기(권력을 쥐고 사람들이 들어가는 것을 막는 사람)들이 말해 주기를 기다리던 시대는 지났다.
▶ 보어인 Gone이 문장 앞으로 나와서 강조되고 있으므로 「be동사+주어」의 어순으로 도치되어야 한다. 핵심 주어는 the days이므로, are the days of musicians로 써야 한다.

14 오늘날의 음악 사업에서는 팬층을 만들기 위해 허락을 요청할 필요가 없으며, 더 이상 그렇게 하려고 회사에 수천 달러를 지불할 필요도 없다.
▶ need의 목적어로 to부정사구 to ask for permission이 이어지고, 그 다음에 '~하기 위하여'의 부사적 용법의 to부정사구 to build a fanbase가 연결되어야 한다.

16강 글의 순서   본문 p.78

01 to carry   **02** themselves   **03** move
04 unrealistic   **05** more   **06** built   **07** that
08 to understand   **09** telling   **10** themselves
11 are   **12** starting   **13** gets   **14** that
15 whoever is running short gets help
16 Depending on when they were written

01 예를 들어, 성직자들은 언제 종교적인 의식을 수행해야 하는지 알고 싶었다.
▶ when carrying ~(~을 수행할 때)이라고 하면, 분사구문으로 부사의 역할이다. 하지만 이 문장에서 when 이하는 동사 know의 목적어(명사)가 되어야 하므로 when to carry ~(언제 ~을 수행해야 하는지)를 써야 한다.

02 공동체 생활이 사람들로 하여금 스스로를 더 효율적으로 조직할 수 있게 했다.
▶ 사람들이 스스로를 더 효율적으로 조직할 수 있게 했다는 내용으로 organize하는 주어와 목적어가 동일하므로 재귀대명사 themselves를 써야 한다.

03 마그마가 식으면서, 마그마의 원자는 열에너지를 잃고, 서로 더 가까이 이동해, 화합물로 결합하기 시작한다.
▶ 주어 its atoms 뒤에 동사 lose ~가 있고, 마지막에 , and begin ~이 있는 것을 보아, 동사 lose, move, begin이 'A, B, and C'로 연결되어 있는 구조임을 알아야 한다. 그러므로 현재형 move를 써야 한다.

04 그 숫자들이 약간 비현실적으로 보인다고 말할지 모르지만, 그 위협은 현실이다.
▶ seem은 보어를 취하는 동사이며 보어 자리에는 부사를 쓸 수 없으므로 형용사 unrealistic을 써야 한다.

05 과거의 양식은 사람들이 그들의 집에서 필요했던 것보다는 허세와 더 관계가 있었다.

▶ 비교 대상 앞에 than이 있으므로 비교급 more를 써야 한다.

06 그 재료는 지역적이었고 단순하게 사용되었는데, 이러한 방식으로 건축된 집들은 실내가 평범한 나무 바닥과 회반죽을 칠한 벽으로 되어 있었다.

▶ 주어 houses의 동사는 had이므로, houses를 수식하는 과거분사구가 되도록 built를 써야 한다.

07 여기서 이 거장이 말하고 있는 것은 좋은 음악과 나쁜 음악이 있다는 것이다.

▶ 동사 is의 보어로 쓰인 완전한 문장을 이끄는 명사절 접속사가 필요하므로 that을 써야 한다.

08 연주자의 기본 임무는 음악의 의미를 이해하려고 노력하고, 그러고 나서 그것을 다른 사람들에게 정직하게 전달하는 것이다.

▶ 문맥상 '~하려고 노력하다'라는 의미가 되어야 하므로, try의 목적어로 to understand를 써야 한다.

09 하지만 작품의 보여 주기 대 말하기의 비율이 어떻든지 간에 독자가 해석해야 하는 무언가가 항상 존재한다.

▶ 문맥상 '작품의 A 대 B의 비율'이라는 의미로 전치사 to 뒤에는 앞에 오는 동명사 showing과 동일한 형태의 telling을 써야 한다. a work's는 동명사 showing과 telling의 의미상의 주어이다.

10 인간은 멀리서 또는 어둠 속에서 얼굴을 알아볼 수 있음으로써 누군가가 다가오는지 알 수 있었고, 가능한 위험으로부터 자신들을 보호할 수 있었다.

▶ protect의 목적어가 주어인 humans와 동일하므로 재귀대명사 themselves를 써야 한다.

11 2016년 Stanford 대학의 잘 알려진 한 연구는 젊은이들이 특히 소셜 미디어 채널을 통해 잘못된 정보에 쉽게 속는다는 것을 보여 주었다.

▶ youth는 집합적으로 '젊은이들'이라는 복수 명사로 쓰이므로 복수 동사 are를 써야 한다.

12 경기의 규칙들은 항상 공의 크기와 무게부터 시작하여 허용되는 공의 유형에 대한 규칙들을 포함하고 있다.

▶ 문맥상 의미상 주어인 the rules와 start가 능동의 관계이므로 현재분사 starting을 써야 한다.

13 이 현상은 플래시에서 나오는 빛이 동공을 통해 눈을 통과한 뒤, 많은 양의 피가 있는 눈 뒤쪽에서 카메라로 반사되기 때문에 발생한다.

▶ the light from the flash를 주어로 하는 술어동사이며 penetrates와 and로 대등하게 연결되어 있으므로 gets를 써야 한다.

14 이런 이유로, 연구자들이 독립 변인과 종속 변인의 관계에 대한 인과 관계를 주장하려고 시도할 때 그들은 허위 관계를 만들어 낼 수도 있는 다른 변인들을 통제하거나 배제해야 한다.

▶ other variables를 선행사로 취해 이를 수식하는 관계절을 유도하므로 관계대명사 that을 써야 한다.

15 풍부한 당을 가진 쪽이 누구든 간에 일부를 건네주고, 부족해지는 쪽이 누구든 간에 도움을 받는다.

▶ 앞에 나와 있는 절로 보아, 당이 많으면 나누어 주고, 부족해지면 도움을 받게 된다는 내용임을 짐작해야 한다. 그러므로 앞의 절과 비슷한 구조로 whoever를 먼저 쓰고 이를 설명하는 is running short를 쓴 다음, 동사와 목적어(gets help)를 써야 한다.

16 그것들이 언제 그리고 누구에 의해 쓰였는지에 따라 문학 작품들은 많은 양의 직접적 말하기와 더 적은 양의 암시와 함축을 포함할 수도 있다.

▶ 문맥상 '그것들이 언제 쓰여졌는지에 따라'라는 의미가 되어야 하므로 '~에 따라'라는 의미의 depending on 다음에 간접의문문이 와야 한다. 따라서 「Depending on+의문사+주어+동사」의 어순으로 써야 한다.

<table>
<tr><td colspan="2">17강</td><td>주어진 문장 넣기</td><td>본문 p. 80</td></tr>
</table>

01 far	**02** are	**03** from which	**04** were told
05 fundamental	**06** would	**07** slipping	
08 using	**09** to keep	**10** will	**11** unchanged
12 Whether	**13** when	**14** reasonably	
15 The rougher the surface is			
16 that could have been avoided			

01 때때로 변화의 속도는 훨씬 더 느리다.

▶ '훨씬 더 ~한'과 같이 비교급 slower를 강조할 수 있는 말은 far, much, still, even, a lot 등이 있다. very, too, so는 원급을 강조할 때 사용하며 비교급을 강조할 땐 쓰지 않는다. 따라서 far를 써야 한다.

02 그러한 믿음을 가능하게 하는 신경 경로는 더 빠르고 자동적으로 이루어지게 되고 반면에, 아이가 주기적으로 사용하지 않는 경로는 제거된다.

▶ while절의 주어는 the ones(= the neural pathways)이고 그 뒤에 있는 that the child doesn't use regularly는 주어를 설명하는 목적격 관계대명사절이다. 그러므로 이어 나올 동사로는 복수 주어에 맞는 are를 써야 한다.

03 그것의 구조는 복잡하지 않기 때문에, 그것은 분해되기 쉽고 그것이 만들어지는 당 외에 몸을 위한 영양소를 거의 가지고 있지 않다.

▶ 선행사 the sugars를 수식하는 관계사절이 they are made from과 같이 from을 포함하고 있다면 관계대명사 that이나 which를 쓸 수 있지만, 이 관계사절 안에는 from이 없는 완전한 문장이므로 from which를 써야 한다.

04 학생들의 절반은 '따뜻하다'라는 단어가 포함된 설명을 들었고, 나머지 절반은 그 강사가 '차갑다'는 말을 들었다.

▶ 앞에 나온 절의 동사 received로 보아 과거가 되어야 하고, 말한 것이 아니라 들은 것이므로 were told를 써야 한다.

05 그러나 현대 인지 과학은 언어가 인간에게 매우 중요한 사고의 한 측면일 뿐 모든 종류의 사고에 근본적이지는 않다고 당연히 판단한다.

▶ 동사 is의 보어로 just one aspect와 not fundamental이 and로 연결되는 병렬 구조의 문장이다. 부사는 보어로 올 수 없으므로, fundamental을 써야 한다.

06 만약 우리가 마법처럼 그 유리잔들을 없앨 수 있다면, 우리는 두 액체가 잘 섞이지 않는다는 것을 알게 될 것이다.

▶ 현재 사실에 반대되는 것을 가정(만일 ~한다면, ~할 텐데)하는 가정법 과거 시제로, if절에는 「if+주어+과거형 동사」로 쓰고, 주절에는 「주어+조동사의 과거형+동사원형」으로 쓰므로 would를 써야 한다.

07 마찰력은 우리가 걸을 때 신발이 바닥에서 미끄러지는 것을 막아 주고 자동차 타이어가 도로에서 미끄러지는 것을 막아 주므로 유용한 힘이 될 수 있다.

▶ 동사 prevents의 목적어는 문맥상 '신발이 미끄러지는 것'이고, our shoes가 의미상의 주어이므로 동명사 slipping을 써야 한다.

08 정상 시력을 가진 사람들은 형태, 조명 그리고 색의 시각적 기억을 사용하여 친한 친구에 대해 꿈을 꿀 것이다.

▶ 문장의 주어와 동사는 A person과 will dream이고, '~하면서'라는 의미로 주절에 대한 부대 상황을 나타내는 분사구문이 필요하다. 따라서 using을 써야 한다.

09 실용적인 수준에서, 밤하늘은 과거 세대들이 시간을 기록하고 달력을 만드는 것을 도와주었는데, 이는 농업과 계절에 따른 수확의 보조 도구로서 사회를 발전시키는 데 필수적이었다.

▶ 동사 helped의 목적격보어가 필요하므로 to keep을 써야 한다.

10 우리는 이것들이 우리에게 더 많은 에너지를 주고 우리가 겨울에 감기에 걸리는 것을 막아 주거나 혹은 우리의 피부와 모발을 개선해 주기를 바란다.

▶ 문맥상 동사 hope은 앞으로의 일에 대한 소망을 나타내므로 목적어절의 동사는 미래 시제 또는 현재 시제로 나타낸다. 따라서 will을 써야 한다.

11 총에너지가 변하지 않는 채로 있는 반면, 총에너지의 운동과 위치 에너지 비율은 항상 변할 수 있다.

▶ 동사 remains의 보어이고, 주어인 the total energy와 수동의 관계에 있으므로 과거분사 unchanged를 써야 한다.

12 그것이 체중을 줄이는 것이든, 선수권을 얻는 것이든, 또는 다른 어떤 목표를 달성하는 것이든 간에, 모든 사람이 이야기하게 될 세상을 떠들썩하게 할 만한 향상을 이루도록 우리는 스스로에게 부담을 준다.

▶ 문맥상 「Whether A, B or C ....」 구문을 써서 'A이든, B이든, C이든'의 의미를 나타내는 것이 적절하므로 Whether를 써야 한다.

13 햇빛은 비록 (그것이) 있을 때는 중요하고 우선되는 신호지만, 햇빛이 뇌가 생체 시계 재설정을 목적으로 사용할 수 있는 유일한 신호는 아니다.

▶ 보어로 쓰인 형용사 present만 남아 있으므로, 시간의 부사절에서 「대명사 주어+be동사」가 생략된 구조로 보아 접속사 when을 써야 한다.

14 주로, 사람들은 꽤 안정적인 식량 공급을 얻게 될 것을 바라며 여러 지역에 다양한 작물을 심었다.

▶ 형용사 stable을 수식하므로 부사 reasonably를 써야 한다.

15 표면이 거칠수록 더 많은 마찰력이 발생한다.

▶ '더 ~할수록, 더 …하다'라는 의미의 비교급 구문이므로 「The+비교급+주어+동사」의 어순으로 써야 한다.

16 이는 매우 중요한데, 대부분의 생존 상황이 피할 수도 있었던 일련의 사건의 결과로 발생하기 때문에 그러하다.

▶ events를 선행사로 하는 관계대명사 that이 쓰이고, 이하에 조동사가 사용된 현재완료 수동태가 적절하므로 that could have been avoided로 써야 한다.

18강 요약문 완성   본문 p.82

01 stays	**02** has	**03** To help	**04** ones
05 facing	**06** do	**07** another	**08** to have
09 which	**10** how	**11** whose	
12 all they had to do		**13** didn't pick it up	
14 asking people not to remove			

01 또는 프라이드치킨을 가끔 먹지만, 그렇지 않은 경우에는 튀긴 음식을 멀리하는 십 대의 경우를 예로 들어 보자.

▶ 선행사 the teenager는 3인칭 단수로, 이를 수식하는 who 관계사절의 동사를 eats로 썼다. 따라서 but으로 병렬 구조를 갖는 stay도 주어와 일치시켜 stays로 써야 한다.

02 하지만 채소나 과일을 거의 먹지 않으면서 매일 튀긴 음식을 먹고, 간식으로 초대형 탄산음료, 사탕, 그리고 감자 칩으로 배를 가득 채우는 사람은 나쁜 식단을 가지고 있는 것이다.

▶ 이 문장의 주어는 the person으로 3인칭 단수이고, 주어 뒤의 who eats ~ for snacks는 주격 관계대명사절로 주어 the person을 수식하고 있다. 따라서 이 문장의 동사는 have가 아니라 has로 써야 한다.

03 무엇이 위험하고 무엇이 안전한지, 누가 신뢰할 수 있고 누가 신뢰할 수 없는지를 결정하는 것을 돕기 위해, 우리는 '사회적 증거'를 찾는다.

▶ 문장의 주절은 we look for social evidence로 주절 앞에는 부사구나 부사절이 되어야 한다. 따라서 '~하기 위해'라는 의미의 to부정사 To help를 써야 한다.

04 3주 후에, 자신의 가치에 관해 썼던 학생들은 좋은 것에만 초점을 맞췄던 학생들보다 더 행복하고, 더 건강하고, 스트레스를 다루는 자신의 능력에 대해 더 자신 있었다.

▶ 자신의 가치에 관해 썼던 학생들과 좋은 것에만 초점을 맞췄던 학생들을 비교하는 문장이므로, 앞의 the students를 받는 the ones를 써야 한다.

05 이 연구는, 어려움에 직면했을 때, 권위가 있는 양육 방식에 노출된 청소년들이 덜 수동적이고, 덜 무기력하며, 실패를 덜 두려워한다고 보고한다.

▶ 동사 reports의 목적어인 that절의 주어와 동사는 adolescents와 are (less likely to be ~)이다. 부사어구인 「접속사+분사구」의 의미상의 주어는 adolescents이고, 주어와 능동의 관계에 있으므로 facing을 써야 한다.

06 마지막으로, 권위가 있는 부모들은 다른 부모들에 비해 학문적 탁월함과 근면함의 중요성을 더 많이 칭찬한다.

▶ 비교 대상을 나타내는 「than+주어+대동사」의 시제는 authoritative parents praise와 일치해야 하므로 do를 써야 한다.

07 common blackberry(Rubus allegheniensis)는 뿌리를 이용하여 토양의 한 층에서 다른 층으로 망가니즈를 옮기는 놀라운 능력이 있다.

▶ 문맥상 one layer와 대구를 이루는 '또 다른 하나'라는 의미의 부정대명사가 와야 하므로 another를 써야 한다.

08 이것은 식물이 가지기에는 기이한 재능처럼 보일 수도 있지만, 그것이 근처의 식물에 미치는 영향을 깨닫고 나면 전부 명확해진다.

▶ 명사 talent를 수식하는 어구가 필요하므로, for a plant가 의미상의 주어인 to부정사의 형용사적 용법이 적절하다. 따라서 to have를 써야 한다.

09 과학의 영역에는 흔히 많은 불확실성이 존재하는데, 일반 대중은 그것을 불편하다고 느낀다.

▶ 주절 전체를 선행사로 취하는 관계대명사가 필요하므로 which를 써야 한다.

10 이에 대한 완벽한 하나의 예시는 어떤 음식이 '좋은지' 그리고 '나쁜지'에 관해 사람들이 확정적인 답변을 원하는 방식이다.

▶ 동사 is를 뒤따르는 절이 '~하는 방식'이라는 의미의 보어 역할을 해야 하므로, the way가 생략된 형태의 관계부사 how를 써야 한다.

11 Kinzler와 그녀의 팀은 가족들이 영어만을 말하는 5개월 된 아이들 한 무리를 뽑아 두 개의 영상을 보여 주었다.

▶ a bunch of five-month-olds를 수식하는 관계절을 유도하며 families를 수식해야 하므로 소유격 관계대명사 whose를 써야 한다.

12 그리고 그들이 했어야 할 모든 일은 그들의 경험을 개인적인 가치로 긍정적으로 재구성하면서 그것에 대해 돌아보고 쓰는 것이었다.

▶ was 앞에는 주어인 명사가 필요하므로 they로 시작하는 절을 쓸 수 없다. 따라서 '그들이 했어야 할 모든 것'의 의미로 「all+(관계대명사)+주어+동사」의 순서로 써야 한다. 여기서는 관계대명사가 생략되어 있다.

13 메시지를 확인하려고 그것(휴대전화)을 집어 들지 않았기 때문에 자기 자신이 잘했다고 느꼈을지도 모르지만, 여러분이 확인하지 않은 메시지는 여전히 맞은편에 앉아 있는 사람과의 관계를 해치고 있었다.

▶ didn't 뒤에 구동사 pick up의 목적어로 대명사 it이 쓰이고 있으므로 구동사 사이에 위치하여 didn't pick it up으로 써야 한다.

14 행동 변화에 대한 한 연구 논문을 읽은 후, Rhonda는 한 곳의 화장실에 사람들에게 화장실 화장지는 함께 쓰는 물건이므로 가져가지 말라는 쪽지를 두었다.

▶ a note를 부연 설명하는 분사구로 이어져야 하며, ask는 to부정사를 목적격보어로 취하는 동사로 부정일 경우는 not이 to부정사 앞에 오므로, asking people not to remove로 써야 한다.

19강 장문의 이해 본문 p. 84

01 it	**02** making	**03** puzzled	**04** their
05 was	**06** were	**07** doing	**08** but
09 for	**10** easily	**11** whether	
12 unless	**13** are		

14 how to see was more difficult than he'd anticipated

15 This is not to say that

---

01 그 대가로, 비농민들은 농업 인구에게 리더십과 안보를 제공하여, 그들이 식량/에너지 생산량을 지속적으로 늘리고 항상 더 많은 잉여를 제공할 수 있게 하였다.

▶ 「enable+목적어+목적격보어(to부정사)」는 '~가 …할 수 있게 하다'라는 의미이다. 여기서는 목적격보어(to continue to increase)의 주체(enabling의 목적어)를 묻는 문제로 의미상 farmers로 생각할 수 있겠지만, 문장에 있는 farming population이 사실상의 주체이므로 대명사 it을 써야 한다.

02 숙련된 발레 무용수가 경험이 적은 무용수보다 더 긴 연속 스텝을 반복할 수 있고, 무작위로 배열된 스텝보다 정해진 춤 동작을 이루는 연속 스텝을 더 잘 반복할 수 있다.

▶ 명사구 a sequence of steps가 a routine을 '이루는(make up)' 주체이므로 능동의 의미인 현재분사 making을 써야 한다.

03 그가 만지는 것과 냄새를 통해 자신의 가족을 알아보는 것을 배운 후에는, 그는 자신의 눈으로 자신의 아이들을 알아볼 수 없다는 것을 알게 되었고, 이것은 그를 혼란스러운 상태로 남겨 두었다.

▶ 「leave+목적어+목적격보어」의 형태로 목적격보어로 분사 또는 형용사를 취할 수 있는데 목적어 him이 '혼란스러운'이라는 수동의 의미이므로 과거분사 puzzled를 써야 한다.

04 그 자원자들은 7일간 특별한 시계를 착용해야만 했고 그래서 그 연구원들은 그들의 수면과 기상 시간에 대한 데이터를 수집할 수 있었다.

▶ 관계대명사 whose 앞에는 선행사가 나와야 하고, 관계사절 내에서 whose가 수식하는 명사 뒤에는 주어와 동사가 뒤따른다. 전치사 on의 목적어 sleeping and waking times 앞에는 소유격 대명사 their를 써야 한다.

05 그는 우리의 몸이 아침 빛에 맞추어 깨어나는 것이 중요하고, 잠자리에 드는 가장 나쁜 시간이 자정 이후인데 그것은 우리의 체내 시계를 재설정하는 아침 빛을 볼 가능성을 줄일 수도 있기 때문이라고 말했다.

▶ 「He said that 명사절, and that 명사절」 구문으로 that 명사절의 시제는 주절의 동사 said의 시제에 일치하여 was를 써야 한다.

06 만일 우리를 가로막는 모든 것을 우리가 사랑할 수 있다면 어떻게 될까?
▶ 「what if+가정법 과거」 구문으로 가정법 과거는 가상의 현실, 추측, 의견 등을 표현한다. 따라서 were를 써야 한다.

07 우리를 비참하게 만드는 모든 사람은 우리와 같다. 그들은 아마도 분명히 최선을 다하고 있으며 부모로부터 깊이 사랑받는 인간, 자녀 또는 친구일 것이다.
▶ a human being 뒤에 현재분사구(most likely doing)와 과거분사구(deeply loved by ~)가 연결된 구문으로 doing을 써야 한다. 「계속적 용법의 관계대명사 who+is」가 생략된 형태이다.

08 우리는 단지 (유전) 암호화의 표현이 아니라 우리의 통제 내부와 외부 모두에 있는 놀랍도록 다양한 상호 작용의 산물이다.
▶ 「not merely A but B」 구문이므로 but을 써야 한다.

09 여러분을 노출할 필요가 있는 사교적 상황이 여러분이 그것들을 원할 때 형성되지 않을 수 있고, 또는 그것들이 상황에 통제 가능하다고 감지할 만큼 잘 진행되지 않을지도 모른다.
▶ 「enough+to부정사」는 '~가 …하기에 충분한'의 의미를 나타내며, 이때 이 to부정사의 의미상의 주어는 「for+목적격」으로 나타내므로 전치사 for를 써야 한다.

10 그것은 여러분이 그 새로운 피드백 기술을 더 여러 차례 사용해 볼수록, 여러분이 그것을 필요로 할 때 그것이 더 쉽게 여러분에게 다가올 것을 의미한다.
▶ 문맥상 more와 함께 동사구 will come을 수식하므로 부사 easily를 써야 한다.

11 그러나 어른으로 살면서 새로운 것을 시도해 볼 때 우리는 대개 단 한 번만 시도해 보고 나서 그것이 잘되었는지 판단하려 한다.
▶ judging의 목적어인 명사절을 유도하며, '~인지'의 뜻을 나타내는 whether를 써야 한다.

12 이러한 것들이 대화가 이해해야 할 것들의 목록 중 맨 위에 놓이지 않는 한, 인간 언어의 기원이 효과적으로 논의될 수 없는 몇 가지 이유이다.
▶ 문맥상 '~하지 않으면'의 뜻을 나타내야 하므로, 접속사 unless를 써야 한다.

13 언어의 다른 요소들, 즉 문법과 이야기 같은 것은 대화에 부차적인 것이다.
▶ 주어 Other components of language에 연결되는 동사이며, 문맥상 일반적인 사실에 대한 진술이므로 복수 동사 현재형 are를 써야 한다.

14 그리고 May의 뇌의 다른 영역들이 주로 그의 다른 감각을 통해 정보를 처리하는 것에 적응해 왔기 때문에, 보는 방법을 배우는 과정은 그가 예상했던 것보다 더 어려웠다.
▶ learning의 목적어로 how to see가 제일 먼저 나오고, 그 뒤에 더 어려웠다는 서술어구 was more difficult 다음에 비교의 대상 than he'd anticipated를 써야 한다.

15 이것은 사람을 사귈 때 여러분의 두려움을 직면하는 것이 의미가 없다고 말하는 것은 아니다.
▶ '이것은 ~라고 말하는 것은 아니다'의 의미를 나타내므로 「This is not to say that ~」을 써야 한다.

20강 **복합 문단의 이해** 본문 p.86

01 standing	**02** so	**03** doing
04 have appeared	**05** looking	**06** him
07 working	**08** was	**09** what	**10** where
11 make	**12** thinking	**13** if

14 was told what happened

15 would offer them whatever he was given

01 심장병 때문에 극심한 고통을 겪고 있어서, 그는 제복을 입은 젊은 군인이 그의 옆에 서 있는 것을 간신히 보았다.
▶ 지각동사 see는 뒤에 목적어와 목적격보어를 취할 수 있는데, 이때 목적어와 목적격보어의 관계가 능동일 때는 원형부정사나 현재분사가 올 수 있으므로 standing을 써야 한다.

02 그 괴물이 너무 추하고 냄새가 나서 경비병들은 충격으로 얼어붙었다.
▶ '매우[너무] ~해서 …하다'라는 의미를 만드는 such는 형용사의 수식을 받는 명사를 강조하는 말로 「such+형용사+명사+that」의 형태로 쓰며, so는 형용사나 부사를 강조하여 「so+형용사/부사+that」의 형태로 쓴다. 따라서 뒤의 형용사를 강조하는 so를 써야 한다.

03 그 종업원은 자기는 이전에 자신의 가족을 위해 그런 일을 해 준 어떤 사람도 가진 적이 없었다고 말했다.
▶ 대명사 anyone을 수식하는 분사가 필요하며, 수식받는 대명사 anyone과 능동 관계를 이루어 '~해 준'이라는 의미가 되어야 하므로 현재분사 doing으로 써야 한다.

04 그것은 다른 이들에게는 평범한 시계로 보였을지도 모르지만 그것은 그에게 어린 시절의 많은 행복한 기억을 가져다주었다.
▶ 문맥상 과거에 있었던 일에 대한 추측을 나타내고 있으므로 「may have+과거분사」 형태가 되어야 하므로 have appeared를 써야 한다.

05 시계를 찾는 아이들의 숫자가 천천히 줄어들었고 지친 아이들 몇 명만이 남았다.
▶ 문장의 주어와 동사는 The number와 decreased이고, children 뒤에는 수식어구가 와야 하므로 능동 의미의 현재분사 looking을 써야 한다.

06 농부가 막 헛간 문을 닫고 있었을 때 한 어린 소년이 그에게 다가와서 자신에게 또 한 번의 기회를 달라고 요청했다.
▶ to give의 의미상의 주어는 the farmer이고, 간접목적어는 a little boy로 두 대상이 다르므로 재귀대명사를 쓸 수 없다. a little boy를 받는 목적격 대명사 him을 써야 한다.

07 그는 걷다가 들판에서 일하는 한 수도승을 발견했다.
▶ 지각동사 noticed의 목적격보어로는 원형부정사 또는 현재분사가 온다. 따라서 working을 써야 한다.

08 나는 마치 그 마을의 가족의 일원인 것처럼 느꼈다.

▶ 「as if+가정법 과거」는 '마치 ~인 것처럼'의 뜻으로 사실이 아닌 일을 의미하므로 were 또는 was를 써야 한다.

09 저는 산속의 마을로부터 골짜기의 마을로 여행을 가고 있는데 당신이 골짜기의 마을은 어떤지 아시는지 궁금합니다.
▶ 동사 knew의 목적어절을 이끄는 접속사 역할과 뒤따르는 전치사 (it is) like의 목적어 역할을 하는 의문사 what을 써야 한다.

10 그를 자랑스럽게 여기면서 나는 놀라워했고 1920년에 법으로 흑인과 백인을 여전히 분리시켰던 최남부 지역에서, 그렇게 어리고 백인이었던 그가 어떻게 그것(연설)을 할 용기가 있었는지 궁금했다.
▶ 장소를 나타내는 the deep South를 부연 설명하는 절을 이끌고 the law ~ white가 완전한 문장이므로 관계부사 where를 써야 한다.

11 이 북을 만드는 데 사용된 사슴가죽은 그녀(암사슴)의 짝, 우리가 작년에 사냥한 그 사슴입니다.
▶ '~하기 위해'의 의미를 나타내야 하므로 to부정사가 되어야 한다. 따라서 make를 써야 한다.

12 모두가 그것이 농담이라고 생각하며 웃음을 터뜨리기 시작했다.
▶ 부대상황(~하면서)을 나타내는 분사구문으로, Everyone과 think가 문맥상 능동 관계이므로 현재분사 thinking을 써야 한다.

13 지도자는 어느 날 James가 레슬링 선수로서 자신의 기술을 보여 줄 것임을 알렸고, 사람들에게 상금을 위해 그에게 도전할 사람이 있는지 물었다.
▶ asked의 목적어로 쓰인 명사절을 이끌며 '~인지'의 의미를 나타내도록 접속사 if를 써야 한다.

14 그녀가 무슨 일이 있었는지 들은 후, 그녀는 그와 함께 병실로 돌아갔다.
▶ 4형식 「주어+tell+간접목적어+직접목적어」를 수동태로 쓴 문장으로, 간접목적어를 주어(she)로 쓰고, 그 뒤에 동사를 수동태 was told로 쓰고, 그 뒤에 직접목적어(what happened)의 순서로 써야 한다.

15 그는 그들에게 자신이 받은 것은 무엇이든지 권하고 그들은 그것을 함께 먹곤 했다.
▶ 「offer+간접목적어+직접목적어」의 어순으로 써야 한다. 동사 offer 앞에 '~하곤 했다'라는 의미로 조동사 would가 오고, 직접목적어는 '자신이 받은 것은 무엇이든지'의 의미가 되도록 「복합관계대명사+주어+was+given」을 써야 한다.

MEMO

MEMO

양기영	다니엘어학원	김신	와이(Y) 아카데미	심경아
우지아	종로엠스쿨	김영연	전문과외	심유진

양기영 다니엘어학원　김신 와이(Y) 아카데미　심경아 Shim's English　이수미 이수미어학원　이순실 종로엠스쿨(하단분원)

우지아 종로엠스쿨　김영연 전문과외　심유진 대구유신학원　이영란 일인주의 학원　이윤호 메트로 영어

윤지연 에이프릴어학원　김원경 전문과외　엄재경 하이엔드영어학원　이원성 파스칼베스티안학원　이재우 무한꿈터

이근호 레이첼 잉글리쉬　김유경 프라임아카데미　오다인 헬렌영어 프리미어 1관,2관　이재근 이재근영어수학학원　이지현 Serena영어

이수길 명성학원　김유희 김유희 영어학원　원현지 원쌤영어교습소　이홍원 홍T영어　이혜정 로엠학원

이아현 다름학원　김윤희 수프림 영어공부방　위은령 브릿지영어　임혜지 마이더스 손 영어학원　임정연 침팬지영어학원 마린시티점

이연홍 Rhee's English Class　김인화 김인화영어학원　유지연 에스피영어학원　장유리 테스영어　장민지 탑클래스영어학원

이원평 코치클래스 영어학원　나혜영 윤선생우리집앞영어교실　윤이강 윤이강 영어　정동혁 대성외국어　정승덕 성균관 영어

이인아 인잉글리쉬　문장엽 엠제이영어수학전문학원　이근성 헬렌영어학원　정라라 영어문화원 정라라 영어교습소　정영훈 J&C영어전문학원(제이엔씨)

이지훈 엠베스트SE학원 신진주 캠퍼스　박주형 봉선동 한수위 영어학원　이동현 쌤마스터입시학원　정예슬 유레카학원　조정훈 입시영어전문 THOUGHT

임나영 삼성영어셀레나 남양영어교습소　봉병주 철수와영수　이미경 전문과외　정윤희 Alex's English　채지영 리드앤톡영어도서관학원

임진희 진해쎔영어학원　신지수 온에어영어학원　이수희 EAON 영어학원　정혜수 쌜리영어　최승빈 다온학원

장은정 케이트어학원　양신애 윤학당오름국어영어학원　이승민 KEREC　조재형 에듀플렉스　최우성 초이English&Pass

장재훈 ASK 배움학원　오승리 이지스터디　이승현 학문당입시학원　조현 퍼스트학원　최이내 전문과외

장지영 잉글리시아이 명동사랑채점　오평안 상무 지산한길어학원　이지민 아이플러스 수학　채송은 위캔영어학원　최효선 해피트리어학원

정상락 비상잉글리시아이 대운점영어교습소　우진일 블루페스 영어학원　이지현 대구 지니영어교습소　최성호 에이스영어교습소　탁아진 에이블영어.국어학원

정수정 지탑영어　유현주 유즈영어교습소　이진영 전문과외　최현우 파스칼베스티안학원　한영희 미래탐구 해운대

최승관 창선고등학교　윤상혁 하이엔드 영어 학원　이현욱 이현욱 영어학원　한왕호 김태현영어학원

최지영 시퀀스영수학원　이남주 장원학원　임지민 헬렌영어학원　한형식 서대전여자고등학교　**서울**

최환준 Jun English　이민정 롱맨학원　임형주 사범대단과학원　황지현 공부자존감영어입시학원　kimhyerim 아르테에비뉴

최효정 인에이블영수학원　이현창 진월유앤아이어학원　장지연 이지영어　　가혜림 벨쌤.com

하동권 네오시스템영어학원　임지상 외대학원　장현희 고려대EIE어학원(현풍)　**부산**　강민정 네오 과학학원

한지용 성민국영수학원　전솔 서강고등학교　전윤애 올링글리쉬　강민주 전문과외　강보경 크라센어학원

허민정 허달영어　정지선 이지스터디　전윤영 뮤엠영어 경동초점　강하늘 뉴스터디종합학원　강성호 대원고등학교

황다영 헤럴드어학원　채성문 마하나임 영수학원　전지민 헬렌영어학원　고경원 JS 영수학원　강정훈 더(the)상승학원

황은영 에이블어학원　한기석 이(E)영어교습소　정대운 유신학원　김도담 도담한영어교실　강준수 전문과외

경북　한방엽 베스트영수학원　정소영 씨즈더데이월암어학원　김도윤 코어영어 교습소　강현숙 토피아어학원 중계캠퍼스

Kailey Pak 케일리 영어　　정연주 대한민국 입시학원　김동혁 코어영어수학전문학원　공리아 리더스 잠실

강민표 현일고등학교　**대구**　정용희 에스피영어　김동휘 장정호 영어전문학원　구나현 플러스잉글리쉬영어교습소

강유진 지니쌤영어　강정임 CanTalk English　정은경 전문과외　김미혜 더멘토영어　구대만 잇올 스파르타 독재학원

강은석 미래인재학원　고은진 헬렌영어　조혜연 연쌤영어수학학원　김병택 탑으로가는 영어 교습소　구민모 키움학원

강혜성 EiE 고려대 어학원　곽민경 조성애세움영어수학학원　진보라 메이킹어학원　김서영 대치명인학원(해운대)　구지은 DYB최선Mate 본사

계지숙 Happy Helen English　권보현 씨즈더데이어학원　최정임 컬럼비아 영어학원　김성미 다올영어　권혜령 전문과외

김광현 그린빌　권오길 공부를 디자인하다　최현희 다온수학학원　김소림 엘라영어학원　김경수 탑킨입시앤영어

김도량 다이너마이트잉글리쉬　권익재 제이슨영어교습소　최효진 너를 위한 영어　김소연 전문과외　김나결 레이쌤영어교습소

김도영 김도영영어학원　권하련 아너스이엠에스학원　한정아 능인고등학교　김수정 리더스학원　김남철 마이티마우스학원

김상호 전문과외　김근아 블루힐영어학원　황윤슬 사적인영어　김연주 링구아어학원　김명열 대치명인학원

김주훈 아너스영어　김기목 목샘영어교습소　　김은숙 강동초등학교　김미은 오늘도맑음 영어교습소

김지훈 알앤비　김나래 더베스트영어학원　**대전**　김재경 부산진구 탑클래스 영어학원　김미정 전문과외

김혜지 스카이 프라임 에듀　김다영 헬렌영어학원　Tony Park 전문과외　김지애 김지애영어연구소　김병준 iLO ENGLISH

문상헌 안동 에이원영어　김미나 메이쌤 영어　강은혜 노마드국어영어학원　김진규 의문을열다　김보경 클라우드캐슬영어교습소

박경애 포항 대성초이스학원　김민재 열공열강 영수학원　고우리 영어의 꿈　김효은 김효은 영어전문학원　김빛나 뮤엠영어피닉스영어교습소

박계민 영광중학교　김병호 LU영어　권현이 디디쌤영어　남재호 제니스학원　김상희 스카이플러스학원

박규정 베네치아 영어 교습소　김상완 YEP영어학원　길민주 전문과외　류미향 류미향입시영어　김선경 대치마크영어

박지은 능률주니어랩꿈터학원　김연정 유니티영어　김경미 영어서당학원　박미진 MJ영어학원　김성근 배움자리학원

배세왕 BK영수전문학원　김예지 헬렌 영어　김근범 딱쌤학원　박수진 제이엔씨 영어학원　김성연 대치열린영어

변민준 한솔플러스영수학원 약목점　김유환 잉글리쉬한글　김기형 상승학원　박영주 전문과외　김소정 브로든 영어

손누리 이든샘영수학원　김정혜 제니퍼영어　김영철 빅뱅잉글리시캠퍼스　박지우 영어를 ON하다　김승환 Arnold English Class

유진욱 공부의힘 영어수학전문학원　김종석 에이블영수학원　김유진 굿티처강남학원　박지은 박지은영어전문과외방　김연아 올리비아 영어교습소

윤재호 이상렬 일등단과학원　김준석 크누KNU입시학원　김주리 위드제이영어　박창현 오늘도,영어그리고수학　김영삼 YS영어공부방

이강정 이룸단과학원　김지영 김지영 영어　김하나 위드유학원　배찬빈 에이플러스 영어교습소　김은영 루시아 잉글리시

이상원 필즈학원　김진호 강성영어　나규성 비전21학원　변혜련 전문과외　김은정 전문과외

이지연 전문과외　김철우 합격 영어　남영종 엠베스트SE 대전 전민점　성장우 전문과외　김은진 에이스영어교습소

이지은 Izzy English　김하나 하나로운영어　노현서 앨리잉글리쉬아카데미　손지안 정관 아슬란학원　김정민 더블유 영어학원

장가은 앨리스영어학원　김희정 이선생영어학원　민지원 민쌤영어교습소　송석준 비상아이비츠 해랑학원　김정수 토즈 스터디센터

장미 잉글리시아이 원리학원　노태경 전문과외　박난정 제일학원　송초롱 과정최상위영어　김종헌 김종헌영어

전영아 N&K영어학원　문창숙 지앤비(GnB)스페셜입시학원　박성희 청담프라임학원　심혜정 명품수학　김지헌 다원교육 목동

정보경 울진고등학교　민승규 민승규영어학원　박효진 박효진 영어　안영실 개금국제학원　김태흥 이투스247학원 송파점

정선린 포항항도중학교　박고은 스테듀입시학원　박효춘 수잔스튜터링　안정희 GnB어학원양성캠퍼스　김하은 전문과외

최동희 전문과외　박라율 열공열강영어수학학원　심효령 삼부가람학원　양희주 링구아학원 해운대　김현영 대치웰영어학원

최미선 영천영어전문과외　박소현 공터영어 테크노폴리스센터　안수정 궁극의 사고　오세창 범천반석단과학원　김현정 진심영어

광주　박연희 좀다른영어　오봉주 새미래영수학원　오정안 쏘트　김현지 전문과외

김도엽 스카이영어전문학원　박예빈 영재키움영어수학전문학원　유수민 제일학원　오지은 이루다영어　김혜림 대치 청담 어학원

김동익 이룸교육원　박지환 전문과외　윤영숙 전문과외　윤경은 쌤드루　김혜영 스터디원

김병남 위즈덤 영어　방성모 방성모영어학원　이고은 고은영어　윤지영 잉글리쉬무무영어교습소　김희정 스터디 코치

김상연 공감영어어학원　배정연 이앤하이공부방　이길형 빌드업영어　윤진희 전문과외　나선아 전문과외

김서허 디엔영어　백재민 에소테리카 영어학원　이대희 청명대입학원　이기연 미네르바국제아카데미　노은경 이은재어학원

김수인 광주 모조잉글리쉬　서정인 서울입시학원　이보배 비비영어　이미정 탑에듀영어교습소　노종주 전문과외

　신혜경 전문과외　이성구 청명대입학원　이상석 상석영어　노진숙 최선어학원

이름	소속
노현희	전문과외
노혜정	최강학원
도선혜	중계동 영어 공부방
류하영	전문과외
맹혜선	휘경여자고등학교
명가은	명가은영어학원
문명기	문명기 영어학원
문민아	탄탄대로 입시컨설팅
문지현	반포헨리학원
박광운	영어교습소
박기철	한진연 입시전략연구소
박남규	알짜영어교습소
박미애	명문지혜학원
박미정	위드멘토학원
박병석	주영학원
박선경	씨투엠학원
박소영	JOY English
박소하	전문과외
박솔이	SOLE English
박수정	YBM잉글루 박수정 영어학원
박숭규	이지수능교육
박은경	서영영어
박은경	오늘영어교습소
박정미	드림영어하이수학학원
박정효	성북메가스터디
박준용	은평 G1230 학원
박지연	영어공부연구소
박진경	JAYz ENGLISH
박찬경	펜타곤영어학원
박현정	1등급학원
반향진	세레나영어수학
배수현	남다른이해
배현경	전문과외
변지예	북두칠성학원
서예은	스터디브릭스학원 내신관
서은조	방배중학교
손종민	미즈원어학원
신경훈	탑앤탑 수학영어 학원
신연우	목동 씨앤씨학원
신정애	당산점 와와학습코칭학원
신지혜	비욘드 어드밴스트
신호현	아로새김학원
신희경	신쌤 영어
심나현	성북메가스터디
안미영	스카이플러스학원
안웅희	이엔엠국영수전문학원
양세희	양세희수능영어 학원
양하나	목동 씨앤씨 바이올렛T
어홍주	이-베스트 영어학원
엄태열	대치차오름학원
오남숙	헬리오 오쌤 영어
오은경	전문과외
용혜영	SWEET ENGLISH 영어전문 공부방
우승희	우승희영어학원
유경미	무무&치(천광학원)
윤성	대치동 새움학원
윤은미	CnT 영어학원
윤지인	반포잉글리쉬튜터링
이계훈	이지영어학원
이광희	가온에듀 2관
이국재	공감학원
이남규	신정송현학원
이명순	Top Class English
이미나	위드미영어교습소
이미영	티엠하버드영어학원
이상수	넥서스학원
이석원	숭실중학교
이석호	한샘영재학원
이성택	엠아이씨영어학원
이수정	영샘영어
이승미	금천정상어학원
이아진	AJ INSTITUTE
이연주	Real_YJ English
이윤형	아만다영어학원
이은선	드림영어하이수학학원
이은영	DNA영어학원
이은정	전문과외
이은주	대치써미트영어학원
이자임	자몽영어교습소
이정인	프레임 학원
이정혜	수시이룸교육
이주희	윌링어학원
이지민	대치명인학원 은평캠퍼스
이지연	석률학원
이철웅	비상하는 또또학원
이혜숙	사당대성보습학원
이혜정	이루리학원
이희영	이샘영어 아카데미 교습소
이희진	목동씨앤씨
임서은	형설학원
임소례	윤선생영어교실 신내키움
임은희	전문과외
장서희	전문과외
장소당	최선어학원
전계령	신촌 메가스터디학원
전수진	절대영어학원
전지영	탑클래스영수학원
정가람	촘촘영어
정경록	미즈원어학원
정민혜	정민혜밀착영어학원
정성준	팁탑영어
정유하	YNS 열정과신념 영어학원
정재욱	씨알학원
정지희	대치하이영어전문학원
정해림	서울숭의초등학교 영어전담
조미영	튼튼영어 마스터클럽 구로학원
조민석	더원영수학원
조민재	정성학원
조봉현	조셉영어국어학원
조연아	연쌤 영어
조용수	EMC이승환영어전문학원
조용현	바른스터디학원
조은성	종로학원
조인희	가디언 어학원(본원)
진영민	브로든영어학원
채상우	클레영어
채에스더	문래중학교
천수진	메리트영어
천예은	폴티스 영어학원
최가은	지엔영어
최민주	전문과외
최수린	목동 CNC 국제관
최안나	영어의완성 영어교습소
최유송	목동 씨앤씨학원(CNC)
최유정	강북청솔학원
최정문	한성학원
최형미	전문과외
최희재	SA어학원
편선경	IGSE Academy
표호진	전문과외
하다님	연세마스터스 학원
하제원	더블랙에듀
한인혜	레나잉글리쉬
한혜주	박홍학원
함규민	클레어영어교실
허미영	삼성영어 창일교실 학원

이름	소속
현승준	강남종로학원 교대점
홍대균	홍대균 영어
홍영민	성북상상학원
홍희진	이티영어학원
황상희	어나더레벨 영어전문학원
황선애	앤스영어학원
황혜진	이루다 영어

세종

김보경	더시에나
방종영	세움학원
백승희	백승희영어
손대령	강한영어학원
송지원	베이 교육컨설팅
안성주	더타임학원
안초롱	21세기학원
이지현	OEC 올리비아 영어 교습소
이현지	전문과외
허욱	전문과외

울산

강상배	전문과외
김경수	핀포인트영어학원
김경현	에린영어
김광규	EIE 온양어학원
김주희	하이디 영어교습소
김한중	스마트영어전문학원
서예원	해법멘토영어수학학원
송회철	꿈꾸는고래
양혜정	양혜정영어
엄여은	준쌤영어교습소
윤주이	인생영어학원
이서경	이서경영어
이수현	제이엘영어교습소
이윤미	제이앤에스 영어수학
임재희	임재희영어전문학원
정은선	한국esl어학원
조충일	YBM잉글루 울산안양 제1캠퍼스
최나비	더오름high-end학원
한건수	한스영어
허부배	비즈다과학원
황희정	장검 앵커영어학원

인천

강재민	스터디위드제이쌤
고미경	쎄리영어학원
김갑헌	카일쌤영어학원
김미경	전문과외
김선나	태풍영어학원
김영태	에듀터학원
김영호	조주석수학&영어클리닉학원
김옥경	잉글리쉬 베이
김지연	송도탑영어학원
김지이	Jenna's English
김현미	송도탑영어학원
김현민	에이플러스원영어수학학원
나일지	두드림하이학원
남미경	뮤엠구월서초영어교습소
문지현	고대어학원
박민아	하이영어
박소연	링컨 영어
박정우	영수원칙학원
박주현	Ashley's English Corner
박진영	인천외국어고등학교
배이슬	비상영수학원
서유화	K&C American School
성하용	타이탄 영어
송현민	Kathy's Class
신나리	이루다교육학원
신은주	명문학원

이름	소속
신현경	전문과외
심현정	전문과외
오희정	엠베스트SE논현캐슬
원정연	공탑학원
윤선	밀턴 영어학원
윤효주	프렌잉글리시청라레이크블루
윤희영	세실영어
이가희	S&U영어
이동규	인천상아초등학교
이미선	고품격EM EDU
이수진	전문과외
이윤주	Triple One
이은정	인천 논현 고등학교
이주연	레이첼영어
이진희	이진희 영어
이한아	선한영수
장승혁	지엘학원
전혜원	제일고등학교
정도영	대신학원
정춘기	정상어학원 남동분원
조슈아	와이즈에듀학원
조윤정	원당중학교
최민지	빅뱅영어
최수련	업앤업영어교습소
최지유	J(제이)영수전문학원
최창영	학산에듀
한은경	호크마학원
황성현	인천외국어고등학교

전남

강용문	JK영수
강유미	정상어학원 목포남악분원
고경희	에이블 잉글리쉬
곽혜진	H&J ENGLISH
김미선	여수개인교습
김아름	전문과외
김은정	BestnBest
류성준	타임영어학원
박동규	정상학원
박민지	벨라영어
박현아	정상상어학원 목포남악분원
서창현	목포백련초등학교
손빛나	프렌잉글리시 여수웅천학원
손성호	아름다운 11월학원
양명승	엠에스어학원
오은주	순천금당고등학교
이상호	스카이입시학원
이영주	재키리 영어학원
임동묵	문향고등학교
조소을	수잉글리쉬
차형진	상아탑학원
황상윤	K&H 중고등 영어 전문학원

전북

길지만	비상잉글리시아이영어학원
김대환	엠베스트SE 전주점
김설아	전주 에듀캠프학원
김수정	베이스탑영어
김예진	카일리영어학원
김주원	애플영어학원
박도희	전문과외
서명원	전북 군산 한림학원
안지은	안지은영어학원
유영목	유영목영어전문학원
은장원	의치약한수 학원
이경훈	리더스영수전문학원
이미정	토마토영어학원
이수정	씨에이엔 영어학원
이지원	탄탄영어수학학원
이진주	전문과외

이름	소속
이한결	DNA영어학원
이현준	준영어교습소
이효상	에임하이영수학원
임마지	조아잉글리쉬어학원
조예진	전문과외
조형진	대니아빠앤디영어교습소
최석원	전주에듀캠프학원
한주훈	알파스터디영어수학전문학원
한찬미	찬미쌤영수교실

제주

고보경	제주여자고등학교
고승용	제주알앤케이학원
김민정	제주낭만고등어학원
김평호	서이현 아카데미
김현정	유비고 영어학원
박시연	에임하이학원
배동환	뿌리와샘
이재철	함성소리학원
이호민	대정탑클래스학원
임정열	엑셀영어
정승현	J's English

충남

강유안	전문과외
고유미	고유미영어
권선교	합덕토킹스타학원
김인영	더오름영어
김일환	김일환어학원
김창현	타임영어학원
김현우	프렌잉글리시로엘입시전문학원
남궁선	공부의 맵 학원
박서현	EiE고려대어학원 논산캠퍼스
박재영	로제타스톤 영어교실
박태혁	인디고학원
박희진	박쌤영어 과외
백일선	명사특강
설재윤	마스터입시교육원
우승직	제니스 영어 공부방
윤현미	비비안의 잉글리쉬 클래스
이규현	글로벌학원
이수진	이수진영어
이종화	오름에듀
이호영	이플러스 학원
장성은	상승기류
장완기	장완기학원
장진아	종로엠스쿨 부여점
정래	(주)탑씨크리트교육
조남진	표선생영어학원
최용원	서일고등학교
허지수	전문과외

충북

마종수	새움다움학원
박광수	폴인어학원
박수열	팍스잉글리쉬학원
신유정	비타민어클리닉
연수지	탑클랜영수학학원
우선규	우선규영어교습소
윤홍석	대학가는길 학원
이경수	더에스에이티 영수단과 학원
이재욱	대학가는 길 학원
이재은	파머스영어와이즈톡학원
이혜인	위즈영어학원
임원용	KGI 의대학원
조현국	업클래스학원
최철우	최쌤영어
하선빈	어썸영어수학학원
홍병찬	서울학원

기출의 바이블

고1 영어

특별부록 | 기출 EXTRACT

특별
부록

1권

2권

기출 EXTRACT

- **Part 1** | 듣기편
- **Part 2** | 독해편

정답 및 해설

· 기출 독해 어휘 리스트
· 기출 문법 드릴 문항 제공

Part 1 · 최신 3개년 전국연합 학력평가 듣기 모의고사 12회 수록
· 전 회차 Dictation 제공

Part 2 · 최신 연도순 유형별 20강 수록
· 오답률 BEST 문항 표기

· 정답 근거, 핵심 문장, 주제문 표시
· 구문 분석과 중요 숙어 표현 표시
· 선택지 완벽 분석과 자세한 해설
· 필수 어휘 정리

가르치기 쉽고 빠르게 배울 수 있는 **이투스북**

www.etoosbook.com

○ **도서 내용 문의**
홈페이지 > 이투스북 고객센터 > 1:1 문의

○ **도서 정답 및 해설**
홈페이지 > 도서자료실 > 정답/해설

○ **도서 정오표**
홈페이지 > 도서자료실 > 정오표

○ **선생님을 위한 강의 지원 서비스 T폴더**
홈페이지 > 교강사 T폴더

고 1

영어

기출의

바이블

Bible of English

1권

Part 1 듣기편 | 회차별 최신 기출순 수록 |

Part 2 독해편 | 유형별 최신 기출순 수록 |

이투스북

기출의
바이블

STAFF

발행인 정선욱

퍼블리싱 총괄 남형주

개발 김태원 김한길 박하영 조은정 양소현

기획·디자인·마케팅 조비호 김정인 이연수

유통·제작 서준성 신성철

기출의 바이블 | 고1 영어 202310 제3판 1쇄

펴낸곳 이투스에듀㈜ 서울시 서초구 남부순환로 2547

고객센터 1599-3225 **등록번호** 제2007-000035호 **ISBN** 979-11-389-1946-3 [53740]

고1 ― 영어

기출의
바이블
Bible of English

1권

Part 1 듣기편

Part 2 독해편

이 책의
구성과 특징

1권 Part 1. 듣기편

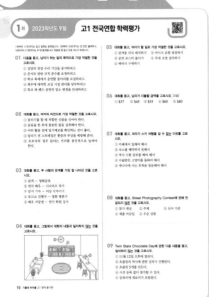

회차별 듣기 모의고사

최신 3개년 전국연합 학력평가 듣기 영역의 전 문항을 수록하였습니다. 모든 회차마다 수록된 QR코드로 편리하게 듣기 음원 파일을 들을 수 있도록 하였습니다.

Dictation

문제 풀이 후 듣기 문항 음원을 다시 듣고 빈칸을 채우면서 정답의 근거와 핵심 어구를 파악하고 학습할 수 있도록 구성하였습니다.

1권 Part 2. 독해편

유형별 독해 모의고사

최신 3개년 전국연합 학력평가 독해 영역의 문항을 유형별로 분류하여 최신 연도순으로 수록하였습니다.

오답률 BEST 문항

각 유형별 오답률이 높은 문항을 표기하여 고난도 문항을 구분하여 학습할 수 있도록 하였습니다.

2권 정답 및 해설편

정답 및 해설

정답 및 해설

듣기편 자세한 해설

모든 스크립트를 완벽히 이해할 수 있도록 해석 및 필수 어휘를 제공하며, 정답률이 낮은 문항은 꼼꼼한 해설을 달아 정확한 문제 풀이가 가능하도록 하였습니다.

독해편 꼼꼼한 지문 해설

모든 지문에 대해 정답률, 정답 단서, 주제문, 핵심 문장, 구문 분석, 중요 숙어 표현을 표기하여 지문의 내용과 구조를 한눈에 파악할 수 있도록 하였습니다.

선택지 완벽 분석

각 선택지에 대한 해석 및 설명과 함께 선택률이 높은 함정 오답 선택지에 대해 완벽 분석하여 올바른 풀이를 할 수 있도록 하였습니다.

특별부록 기출 EXTRACT

WORD EXTRACT 최신 3개년 고1 기출 어휘 리스트

GRAMMAR EXTRACT 1강 글의 목적 파악

WORD EXTRACT

고1 기출 독해 문항의 필수 어휘를 정리한 어휘 리스트를 제공하여 암기할 수 있도록 하였습니다.

GRAMMAR EXTRACT

고1 기출 독해 지문에서 추출한 문장으로 문법 드릴 문항을 구성하여 중요 문법 사항을 학습할 수 있도록 하였습니다.

이 책의
차례 및 학습계획표 Part 1. 듣기편

학습계획표 활용법

❶ 매일 듣기 모의고사 한 회분을 풀고 학습일과 맞은 개수를 기록해 보세요.

❷ 각자의 속도에 맞게 계획을 세우고 실행하여 12일 완성 학습계획표를 채워 보세요.

회차	문제 쪽수	Dictation 쪽수	DAY	맞은 개수	학습일
7회 2022학년도 3월 전국연합 학력평가	46	48	DAY 07	/ 17개	월 일
8회 2021학년도 11월 전국연합 학력평가	52	54	DAY 08	/ 17개	월 일
9회 2021학년도 9월 전국연합 학력평가	58	60	DAY 09	/ 17개	월 일
10회 2021학년도 6월 전국연합 학력평가	64	66	DAY 10	/ 17개	월 일
11회 2021학년도 3월 전국연합 학력평가	70	72	DAY 11	/ 17개	월 일
12회 2020학년도 11월 전국연합 학력평가	76	78	DAY 12	/ 17개	월 일

이 책의 차례 및 학습계획표 Part 2. 독해편

강명	쪽수	DAY	맞은 개수	학습일	
11강 어법	133	DAY 11	/ 12개	월	일
12강 어휘	136	DAY 12	/ 12개	월	일
13강 빈칸 추론 1 (31~32번)	140	DAY 13	/ 24개	월	일
14강 빈칸 추론 2 (33~34번)	148	DAY 14	/ 24개	월	일
15강 무관한 문장 찾기	156	DAY 15	/ 12개	월	일
16강 글의 순서	159	DAY 16	/ 24개	월	일
17강 주어진 문장 넣기	171	DAY 17	/ 24개	월	일
18강 요약문 완성	179	DAY 18	/ 12개	월	일
19강 장문의 이해	185	DAY 19	/ 24개	월	일
20강 복합 문단의 이해	197	DAY 20	/ 36개	월	일

기출의 바이블
고1 영어

Part 1

듣기편

고1 전국연합 학력평가

1번부터 17번까지는 듣고 답하는 문제입니다. 1번부터 15번까지는 한 번만 들려주고, 16번부터 17번까지는 두 번 들려줍니다. 방송을 잘 듣고 답을 하시기 바랍니다.

01 다음을 듣고, 남자가 하는 말의 목적으로 가장 적절한 것을 고르시오.

① 강당의 천장 수리 기간을 공지하려고
② 콘서트 관람 규칙 준수를 요청하려고
③ 학교 축제에서 공연할 동아리를 모집하려고
④ 폭우에 대비한 교실 시설 관리를 당부하려고
⑤ 학교 록 밴드 공연의 장소 변경을 안내하려고

02 대화를 듣고, 여자의 의견으로 가장 적절한 것을 고르시오.

① 달리기를 할 때 적합한 신발을 신어야 한다.
② 운동을 한 후에 충분한 물을 섭취해야 한다.
③ 야외 활동 전에 일기예보를 확인하는 것이 좋다.
④ 달리기 전 스트레칭은 통증과 부상을 예방해 준다.
⑤ 초보자의 경우 달리는 거리를 점진적으로 늘려야 한다.

03 대화를 듣고, 두 사람의 관계를 가장 잘 나타낸 것을 고르시오.

① 관객 – 영화감독
② 연극 배우 – 시나리오 작가
③ 잡지 기자 – 의상 디자이너
④ 토크쇼 진행자 – 영화 평론가
⑤ 배우 지망생 – 연기 학원 강사

04 대화를 듣고, 그림에서 대화의 내용과 일치하지 않는 것을 고르시오.

05 대화를 듣고, 여자가 할 일로 가장 적절한 것을 고르시오.

① 관객용 의자 배치하기   ② 마이크 음향 점검하기
③ 공연 포스터 붙이기   ④ 무대 조명 설치하기
⑤ 배터리 구매하기

06 대화를 듣고, 남자가 지불할 금액을 고르시오. [3점]

① $37   ② $45   ③ $55   ④ $60   ⑤ $80

07 대화를 듣고, 여자가 스키 여행을 갈 수 없는 이유를 고르시오.

① 카페에서 일해야 해서
② 숙소를 예약하지 못해서
③ 역사 시험 공부를 해야 해서
④ 수술받은 고양이를 돌봐야 해서
⑤ 캐나다에 사는 친척을 방문해야 해서

08 대화를 듣고, Street Photography Contest에 관해 언급되지 않은 것을 고르시오.

① 참가 대상   ② 주제   ③ 심사 기준
④ 제출 마감일   ⑤ 우승 상품

09 Twin Stars Chocolate Day에 관한 다음 내용을 듣고, 일치하지 않는 것을 고르시오.

① 11월 12일 오후에 열린다.
② 초콜릿의 역사에 관한 강의가 진행된다.
③ 초콜릿 5개를 만든다.
④ 사전 등록 없이 참가할 수 있다.
⑤ 등록비에 재료비가 포함된다.

10 다음 표를 보면서 대화를 듣고, 두 사람이 주문할 실내 사이클링 자전거를 고르시오.

Indoor Cycling Bikes

	Model	Price	Color	Foldable	Customer Rating
①	A	$100	White	×	★★★★
②	B	$150	Black	×	★★★
③	C	$190	Black	○	★★★★
④	D	$250	Black	○	★★★★★
⑤	E	$320	White	×	★★★★★

11 대화를 듣고, 여자의 마지막 말에 대한 남자의 응답으로 가장 적절한 것을 고르시오.

① Sure. I'll send you a link to the website.
② It would look better in a different color.
③ Sorry. I forgot to bring your sweater.
④ You need your receipt to return it.
⑤ My brother bought it on sale, too.

12 대화를 듣고, 남자의 마지막 말에 대한 여자의 응답으로 가장 적절한 것을 고르시오.

① Let's take the leftovers home.
② I prefer fried chicken over pizza.
③ I don't want to go out for lunch today.
④ I'll call the restaurant and check our order.
⑤ The letter was delivered to the wrong address.

13 대화를 듣고, 여자의 마지막 말에 대한 남자의 응답으로 가장 적절한 것을 고르시오.

Man: _____

① You're right. I won't skip meals anymore.
② Thank you for the lunch you prepared for me.
③ You need to check when the cafeteria is open.
④ Trust me. I can teach you good table manners.
⑤ No problem. We'll finish the science project on time.

14 대화를 듣고, 남자의 마지막 말에 대한 여자의 응답으로 가장 적절한 것을 고르시오. [3점]

Woman: _____

① No. It isn't difficult for me to learn Spanish.
② I'm glad you finally passed the vocabulary test.
③ Exactly. Learning a language starts with repetition.
④ It's very helpful to use a dictionary while writing.
⑤ You should turn in your homework by this afternoon.

15 다음 상황 설명을 듣고, Brian이 Melissa에게 할 말로 가장 적절한 것을 고르시오. [3점]

Brian: _____

① Let's clean the classroom after art class.
② Did you remove the stickers from the board?
③ Please turn off the heater when you leave the room.
④ When is the final date to sign up for the design class?
⑤ Will you design stickers that encourage energy saving?

[16~17] 다음을 듣고, 물음에 답하시오.

16 남자가 하는 말의 주제로 가장 적절한 것은?

① advantages of renting houses in cities
② reasons tourists prefer visiting old cities
③ ways cities deal with overtourism problems
④ correlation between cities' sizes and overtourism
⑤ how cities face their aging transportation systems

17 언급된 도시가 <u>아닌</u> 것은?

① Barcelona   ② Amsterdam   ③ London
④ Venice   ⑤ Paris

Dictation

녹음 내용을 다시 듣고, 빈칸을 채워 넣으세요.

01

M Attention, Fargo High School students. This is your music teacher, Mr. Nelson. Our school rock band was supposed to hold its concert _____ _____ _____ today. I'm sure you've been looking forward to the concert. Unfortunately, the rain yesterday caused a leak in the ceiling of the auditorium. The ceiling _____ _____ _____ _____, so we decided to _____ _____ _____ of the concert. The rock band will now perform in the school theater. The time for the concert _____ _____. I hope you'll enjoy the performance.

02

W Simon, are you doing anything after school?

M Nothing special. What about you?

W I'm planning to go for a run in the park. It's a five-kilometer route.

M The weather is perfect for running. Can I go with you?

W Why not? [Pause] Wait! You're _____ _____. Those aren't good for running.

M It's okay. I can run in slippers.

W No way. Slippers aren't designed for running. You can _____ _____ if you run in them.

M You mean I need to _____ _____ _____?

W You got it. You need to _____ _____ _____ _____ for running.

M All right. I'll go home and change.

03

M Good morning, Ms. Clapton. It's nice to meet you.

W Nice to meet you, too. I'm a _____ _____ _____ _____.

M You won many awards at the film festival this year. Congratulations!

W Thank you. I was lucky to work with a great director and talented actors.

M The _____ _____ _____ in the movie are impressive. How do you start your costume designs?

W I read the script to fully understand the characters. Then I research the characters' backgrounds.

M That sounds like a lot of work. Which of the _____ _____ _____ _____ is your favorite?

W It's hard to pick just one because I love all of my designs.

M I totally understand. Thank you for sharing your story with the _____ _____ _____ _____.

W It was my pleasure.

04

W Come look at the new reading room in the library.

M Wow! It's much better than I thought.

W Same here. I like the rug in the center of the room.

M The _____ _____ of the rug makes the room feel warm.

W I agree. I think putting the sofa _____ _____ _____ was a good idea.

M Right. We can sit there and read for hours.

W There's a _____ _____ on the wall.

M I have the same clock at home. Oh, the _____ _____ _____ _____ is full of books.

W We can read the books at the long table.

M Yeah, it looks like a good place to read. The _____ _____ _____ _____ will make it easy to focus.

W Good lighting is important for reading.

M I can't wait to start using the reading room.

05

M Kelly, the school musical is tomorrow. Shall we go over the final checklist together?

W Let's do it. What's first? *[Pause]* Oh, the posters. We _____ _____ _____ around school last week.

M Right. Do we have _____ _____ for the wireless microphones?

W Yeah. I bought them yesterday. We should check that the microphones _____ _____ _____ the sound system.

M I did that this morning. They sound terrific.

W How about the _____ _____?

M They work perfectly. I think everyone will love the lighting design you made.

W Really? Thanks. It looks like we've finished everything.

M No, wait. The _____ _____ _____ _____ haven't been arranged yet.

W You're right! I'll go take care of that now.

M The musical is going to be fantastic.

06

W Welcome to Libby's Flowers. How can I help you?

M I'd like to order a rose basket for my parents' wedding anniversary.

W All right. Our rose baskets come in two sizes.

M What are the options?

W The regular size is 30 dollars, and the _____ _____ is 50 dollars.

M Hmm... I think the _____ _____ _____.

W Good choice. So, you'll get one rose basket in the large size. By the way, we're giving a _____ _____ on all purchases this week.

M Excellent! When will my order be ready?

W It'll be ready around 11 a.m. If you can't pick it up, we offer a _____ _____. It's 10 dollars.

M Oh, great. I'd like it to be delivered. Here's my credit card.

07

M You seem busy this morning, Olivia.

W I am. I had to see Professor Martin about my history test.

M Oh, I see. Do you remember that our club's ski trip is this weekend?

W Yeah. I heard that a nice ski resort has _____ _____ for the trip.

M I didn't know that. I'm so excited to go skiing at a nice resort.

W I bet it'll be great, but I don't think I can go this time.

M Why? You don't work at the cafe _____ _____ _____, do you?

W No, I don't. But I need to _____ _____ _____ _____ _____. She's recovering _____ _____.

M Isn't there anyone else who can look after your cat?

W No one but me. My _____ _____ _____ _____ in Canada. They won't be back for two weeks.

M I'm sorry that you can't join us.

W Me, too. Have fun this weekend.

08

W What are you doing, Tim?

M I'm looking at the Street Photography Contest website.

W I've heard about that. It's a contest for college students, right?

M Actually, it's _____ _____ high school students, too. Why don't you try it?

W Really? Maybe I will. Does the contest have a theme?

M Sure. _____ _____ _____ is Daily Life.

W That sounds interesting. When is the deadline?

M You _____ _____ _____ your photographs by September 15.

W That's sooner than I expected.

M You should hurry and choose your photos. The winner will receive a _____ _____ _____ _____.

W Okay! Wish me luck.

09

M Hello, listeners. I'm Charlie Anderson from the Twin Stars Chocolate Museum. I'm happy to introduce the Twin Stars Chocolate Day, a special opportunity to create your own delicious chocolates. It'll be _____ _____ _____ _____ from 1 p.m. to 4 p.m. First, you'll listen to a lecture about the _____ _____ _____. Then you'll have a chance to taste our most popular flavors. At the end of the event, you'll _____ _____ _____ yourself. If you want to take part in the event, you must _____ _____ _____. You can sign up on our website until November 1. The registration fee is 20 dollars, which _____ _____ _____ of ingredients. Don't miss this sweet opportunity!

10

M Honey, what are you looking at?

W I'm looking at indoor cycling bikes. Would you like to choose one together?

M Sure, let me see. *[Pause]* The price differs by model.

W I don't want to _____ _____ _____ 300 dollars. That's too expensive.

M I agree. Which color do you like?

W I prefer a _____ _____ because it goes well with our living room.

M Okay. Then we shouldn't get a white one. What do you think about the _____ _____?

W We definitely need that. It'll take up less storage space.

M We have just two options left. Which one should we get?

W I think we should go with the one with a _____ _____ _____. The reviews are based on actual customers' experiences.

M Sounds good. Let's order this one.

11

W Jason, is that a new sweater? It _____ _____ _____ you.

M Thanks. I _____ _____ _____. It was on sale.

W I'd love to buy the same one for my brother. Can you tell me _____ _____ _____ _____?

M ▓▓▓▓▓▓▓▓▓▓▓▓▓▓▓▓▓▓▓▓▓▓▓▓

12

M Becky, did you _____ _____ _____ for dinner?

W Yes. I _____ _____ about an hour ago.

M An hour ago? Delivery usually takes _____ _____ 40 minutes.

W ▓▓▓▓▓▓▓▓▓▓▓▓▓▓▓▓▓▓▓▓▓▓▓▓

13

W I _____ _____ _____ in the cafeteria this week. Where have you been?

M I've been in the library working on my science project.

W Does that mean you've been _____ _____?

M Yeah. This project is really important for my grade.

W You shouldn't do that. It's _____ _____ _____ your health.

M Don't worry. I always have a big dinner when I get home.

W That's the problem. Skipping meals _____ _____ _____ later.

M I hadn't thought of that. Then what should I do?

W It's simple. You should _____ _____ to stay healthy.

M ▓▓▓▓▓▓▓▓▓▓▓▓▓▓▓▓▓▓▓▓

14

M Excuse me, Ms. Lopez. Can I ask you something?

W Sure, Tony. What can I do for you?

M I want to do _____ _____ _____, but I don't know how to improve.

W You seem to do well during class. Do you study when you're at home?

M I do all my homework and try to learn 20 new words every day.

W That's a good start. Do you also practice _____ _____ _____ repeatedly?

M Do I need to do that? That sounds like it'll take a lot of time.

W It does. But since you're still a beginner, you have to put in more effort to _____ _____ _____ _____ _____.

M I see. So are you suggesting that I practice them _____ _____ _____?

W ▨▨▨▨▨▨▨▨▨▨▨▨▨▨▨▨▨▨▨▨▨

15

W Brian is a class leader. He is passionate about _____ _____ and saving energy. Recently, he's noticed that his classmates don't _____ _____ _____ _____ when they leave the classroom. Brian thinks this is very careless. He wants to make stickers that remind his classmates to _____ _____ by turning off the lights. He tells this idea to his classmate Melissa, and she agrees it's a good idea. Brian knows Melissa is a great artist, so he wants to _____ _____ _____ _____ _____ that encourage their classmates to save energy. In this situation, what would Brian most likely say to Melissa?

Brian ▨▨▨▨▨▨▨▨▨▨▨▨▨▨▨▨▨▨▨▨▨

16~17

M Good afternoon, everyone. Last time, we learned that overtourism happens when there are too many visitors to a particular destination. Today, we'll learn _____ _____ _____ _____ the problems caused by overtourism. First, _____ _____ _____ the number of hotels so there are fewer places for visitors to stay. In Barcelona, building new hotels is not allowed in the city center. Second, other cities promote _____ _____ _____ popular sites. For instance, Amsterdam encourages tourists to visit less-crowded areas. Third, many cities have tried to limit access. For example, Venice has tried to _____ _____ _____ by stopping large cruise ships from docking on the island. Similarly, Paris has focused on reducing tourism to certain parts of the city by having _____ _____. Now, let's watch some video clips.

1번부터 17번까지는 듣고 답하는 문제입니다. 1번부터 15번까지는 한 번만 들려주고, 16번부터 17번까지는 두 번 들려줍니다. 방송을 잘 듣고 답을 하시기 바랍니다.

01 다음을 듣고, 여자가 하는 말의 목적으로 가장 적절한 것을 고르시오.
① 체육대회 종목을 소개하려고
② 대회 자원봉사자를 모집하려고
③ 학생 회장 선거 일정을 공지하려고
④ 경기 관람 규칙 준수를 당부하려고
⑤ 학교 홈페이지 주소 변경을 안내하려고

02 대화를 듣고, 남자의 의견으로 가장 적절한 것을 고르시오.
① 산책은 창의적인 생각을 할 수 있게 돕는다.
② 식사 후 과격한 운동은 소화를 방해한다.
③ 지나친 스트레스는 집중력을 감소시킨다.
④ 독서를 통해 창의력을 증진할 수 있다.
⑤ 꾸준한 운동은 기초체력을 향상시킨다.

03 대화를 듣고, 두 사람의 관계를 가장 잘 나타낸 것을 고르시오.
① 고객 – 우체국 직원
② 투숙객 – 호텔 지배인
③ 여행객 – 여행 가이드
④ 아파트 주민 – 경비원
⑤ 손님 – 옷가게 주인

04 대화를 듣고, 그림에서 대화의 내용과 일치하지 않는 것을 고르시오.

05 대화를 듣고, 남자가 할 일로 가장 적절한 것을 고르시오.
① 초대장 보내기
② 피자 주문하기
③ 거실 청소하기
④ 꽃다발 준비하기
⑤ 스마트폰 사러 가기

06 대화를 듣고, 여자가 지불할 금액을 고르시오. [3점]
① $54 ② $60 ③ $72 ④ $76 ⑤ $80

07 대화를 듣고, 남자가 록 콘서트에 갈 수 없는 이유를 고르시오.
① 일을 하러 가야 해서
② 피아노 연습을 해야 해서
③ 할머니를 뵈러 가야 해서
④ 친구의 개를 돌봐야 해서
⑤ 과제를 아직 끝내지 못해서

08 대화를 듣고, Eco Day에 관해 언급되지 않은 것을 고르시오.
① 행사 시간
② 행사 장소
③ 참가비
④ 준비물
⑤ 등록 방법

09 Eastville Dance Contest에 관한 다음 내용을 듣고, 일치하지 않는 것을 고르시오.
① 처음으로 개최되는 경연이다.
② 모든 종류의 춤이 허용된다.
③ 춤 영상을 8월 15일까지 업로드 해야 한다.
④ 학생들은 가장 좋아하는 영상에 투표할 수 있다.
⑤ 우승팀은 상으로 상품권을 받게 될 것이다.

10 다음 표를 보면서 대화를 듣고, 두 사람이 구입할 정수기를 고르시오.

Water Purifiers

	Model	Price	Water Tank Capacity (liters)	Power-saving Mode	Warranty
①	A	$570	4	×	1 year
②	B	$650	5	○	1 year
③	C	$680	5	×	3 years
④	D	$740	5	○	3 years
⑤	E	$830	6	○	3 years

11 대화를 듣고, 남자의 마지막 말에 대한 여자의 응답으로 가장 적절한 것을 고르시오.

① Great. We don't have to wait in line.
② All right. We can come back later.
③ Good job. Let's buy the tickets.
④ No worries. I will stand in line.
⑤ Too bad. I can't buy that car.

12 대화를 듣고, 여자의 마지막 말에 대한 남자의 응답으로 가장 적절한 것을 고르시오.

① Yes. You can register online.
② Sorry. I can't see you next week.
③ Right. I should go to his office now.
④ Fantastic! I'll take the test tomorrow.
⑤ Of course. I can help him if he needs my help.

13 대화를 듣고, 여자의 마지막 말에 대한 남자의 응답으로 가장 적절한 것을 고르시오. [3점]

Man: _____

① I agree. You can save a lot by buying secondhand.
② Great idea! Our message would make others smile.
③ Sorry. I forgot to write a message in the book.
④ Exactly. Taking notes during class is important.
⑤ Okay. We can arrive on time if we leave now.

14 대화를 듣고, 남자의 마지막 말에 대한 여자의 응답으로 가장 적절한 것을 고르시오. [3점]

Woman: _____

① Why not? I can bring some food when we go camping.
② I'm sorry. That fishing equipment is not for sale.
③ I don't think so. The price is most important.
④ Really? I'd love to meet your family.
⑤ No problem. You can use my equipment.

15 다음 상황 설명을 듣고, Violet이 Peter에게 할 말로 가장 적절한 것을 고르시오.

Violet: _____

① Will you join the science club together?
② Is it okay to use a card to pay for the drinks?
③ Why don't we donate our books to the library?
④ How about going to the cafeteria to have lunch?
⑤ Can you borrow the books for me with your card?

[16~17] 다음을 듣고, 물음에 답하시오.

16 남자가 하는 말의 주제로 가장 적절한 것은?

① different causes of sleep disorders
② various ways to keep foods fresh
③ foods to improve quality of sleep
④ reasons for organic foods' popularity
⑤ origins of popular foods around the world

17 언급된 음식이 아닌 것은?

① kiwi fruits ② milk ③ nuts
④ tomatoes ⑤ honey

녹음 내용을 다시 듣고, 빈칸을 채워 넣으세요.

01

W Good afternoon, everybody. This is your student council president, Monica Brown. Our school's annual e-sports competition _____ _____ _____ _____ the last day of the semester. For the competition, we _____ _____ _____ to help set up computers. If you're interested in helping us make the competition successful, please fill out the _____ _____ _____ and email it to me. For more information, please visit our school website. I hope many of you will join us. Thank you for listening.

02

M Hannah, how's your design project going?

W Hey, Aiden. I'm still working on it, but I'm not making much progress.

M Can you tell me what the problem is?

W Hmm... [Pause] It's hard to _____ _____ _____ _____. I feel like I'm wasting my time.

M I understand. Why don't you _____ _____ _____?

W How can that help me to _____ _____ _____?

M It will actually make your brain more active. Then you'll see things differently.

W But I don't have time for that.

M You don't need a lot of time. Even a _____ _____ _____ _____ you to come up with creative ideas.

W Then I'll try it. Thanks for the tip.

03

W Excuse me. Could you please tell me where I can put this box?

M Right here on this counter. How can I help you today?

W _____ _____ _____ _____ _____ to Jeju Island.

M Sure. Are there _____ _____ _____ in the box?

W No, there are only clothes in it.

M Then, there should be no problem.

W I see. What's the fastest way to send it?

M You can send the package _____ _____ _____, but there's an extra charge.

W That's okay. I want it _____ _____ _____ as soon as possible. When will it arrive in Jeju if it goes out today?

M If you send it today, it will be there by this Friday.

W Oh, Friday will be great. I'll do the express mail.

04

M Kayla, I heard you went busking on the street last weekend.

W It was amazing! I've got a picture here. Look!

M Oh, you're _____ _____ _____ I gave you.

W Yeah, I really like it.

M Looks great. This boy _____ _____ _____ next to you must be your brother Kevin.

W You're right. He played while I sang.

M Cool. Why did you _____ _____ _____ _____?

W That's for the audience. If they like our performance, they give us some money.

M Oh, and you set up _____ _____!

W I did. I recently bought them.

M I see. And did you design _____ _____ _____ _____ _____?

W Yeah. My brother and I worked on it together.

M It sounds like you really had a lot of fun!

05

W Honey, are we _____ _____ Jake's birthday party tomorrow?

M I sent the invitation cards last week. What about other things?

W I'm not sure. Let's check.

M We are expecting a lot of guests. How about the dinner menu?

W I haven't decided yet.

M We won't have much time to cook, so let's just order pizza.

W Okay. I'll do it tomorrow. What about the present?

M Oh, you mean _____ _____? I forgot to get it!

W That's alright. Can you _____ _____ _____ _____ _____ and buy it now?

M No problem. I'll do it right away.

W Good. Then, I'll clean up the living room while _____ _____.

06

M Good morning! How can I help you?

W Hi. I'm looking for a blanket and some cushions for my sofa.

M Okay. We've got some on sale. Would you like to have a look?

W Yes. _____ _____ _____ this green blanket?

M That's $40.

W Oh, I love the color green. Can you also show me some cushions that go well with this blanket?

M Sure! How about these?

W They look good. I need _____ _____ _____. How much are they?

M The cushions are $20 _____.

W Okay. I'll take one green blanket and two cushions. Can I use this coupon?

M Sure. It will give you 10% _____ _____ _____.

W Thanks! Here's my credit card.

07

W Hello, Justin. What are you doing?

M Hi, Ellie. I'm doing my project for art class.

W Can you _____ _____ _____ _____ _____ with me this Saturday? My sister gave me two tickets!

M I'd love to! *[Pause]* But _____ _____ _____ _____.

W Do you have to work that day?

M No, I don't work on Saturdays.

W Then, why not? I thought you really like rock music.

M Of course I do. But I have to _____ _____ _____ my friend's dog this Saturday.

W Oh, really? Is your friend going somewhere?

M He's visiting his grandmother that day.

W Okay, no problem. I'm sure I can find someone else to go with me.

08

W Scott, did you see this Eco Day poster?

M No, not yet. Let me see. *[Pause]* It's an event for _____ _____ _____ while walking around a park.

W Why don't we do it together? It's _____ _____ from 10 a.m. to 5 p.m.

M Sounds good. I've been thinking a lot about the environment lately.

W Me, too. Also, the event will _____ _____ _____ Eastside Park. You know, we often used to go there.

M That's great. Oh, look at this. We _____ _____ _____ our own gloves and small bags for the trash.

W No problem. I have extra. I can bring some for you as well.

M Okay, thanks. Do we have to _____ _____ _____ the event?

W Yes. The poster says we can do it online.

M Let's do it right now. I'm looking forward to it.

09

M Hello, Eastville High School students. This is your P.E. teacher, Mr. Wilson. I'm pleased to let you know that we're hosting _____ _____ Eastville Dance Contest. Any Eastville students who love dancing can participate in the contest as a team. _____ _____ _____ dance are allowed. If you'd like to participate, _____ _____ your team's dance video to our school website by August 15th. Students _____ _____ for their favorite video from August 16th to 20th. The winning team will _____ _____ _____ as a prize. Don't miss this great opportunity to show off your talents!

10

M Honey, we need a water purifier for our new house.

W You're right. Let's order one online.

M Good idea. *[Clicking Sound]* Look! These are the five bestsellers.

W I see. What's our budget?

M Well, I _____ _____ _____ _____ more than 800 dollars.

W Okay, how about the water tank capacity?

M I think the five-liter tank would _____ _____ for us.

W I think so, too. And I like the ones with a power-saving mode.

M Okay, then we can _____ _____. Now, there are just two options left.

W Let's look at the warranties. _____ _____, _____ _____.

M I agree. We should order this model.

11

M Let's get inside. I'm so excited to see this auto show.

W Look over there. So many people are already _____ _____ _____ to buy tickets.

M Fortunately, I _____ _____ _____ in advance.

W ▨▨▨▨▨▨▨▨▨▨▨▨▨▨▨▨▨▨▨▨

12

W Hi, Chris. Did you _____ _____ _____ for the history test we took last week?

M Yes. But I think there's _____ _____ with my grade.

W Don't you think you _____ _____ _____ Mr. Morgan about it?

M ▨▨▨▨▨▨▨▨▨▨▨▨▨▨▨▨▨▨▨▨

13

M Mom, did you write this note?

W What's that?

M I found this in the book you gave me.

W Oh, the one I bought for you at the secondhand bookstore last week?

M Yes. At first I thought it was a bookmark, but it wasn't. It's a note _____ _____ _____!

W What does it say?

M It says, "I hope you enjoy this book."

W How sweet! That really _____ _____ _____ to my face.

M Yeah, mom. I love this message so much.

W Well, then, why don't we _____ _____ _____ if we resell this book later?

M ▨▨▨▨▨▨▨▨▨▨▨▨▨▨▨▨▨▨▨▨

14

M Do you have any plans for this weekend, Sandy?

W Hey, Evan. I'm planning to _____ _____ with my family.

M I've never gone before. Do you go camping often?

W Yes. Two or three times a month at least.

M That's cool. Why do you like it so much?

W I like spending time in nature with my family. It _____ _____ _____ _____ to them.

M I understand. It's like a family hobby, right?

W Yes, you're right. Camping helps me _____ _____ _____ _____, too.

M Sounds interesting. I'd love to try it.

W If you go camping with your family, you'll see what I mean.

M I wish I could, but I don't _____ _____ _____ for it.

W ▨▨▨▨▨▨▨▨▨▨▨▨▨▨▨▨▨▨▨▨▨

15

W Violet and Peter are classmates. They're doing their science group assignment together. On Saturday morning, they meet at the public library. They decide to _____ _____ _____ they need in different sections of the library. Violet finds two useful books and tries to check them out. Unfortunately, she suddenly realizes that she didn't bring _____ _____ _____. At that moment, Peter walks up to Violet. So, Violet wants to ask Peter to _____ _____ _____ _____ for her because she knows he has _____ _____ _____. In this situation, what would Violet most likely say to Peter?

Violet ▨▨▨▨▨▨▨▨▨▨▨▨▨▨▨▨▨▨▨▨▨

16~17

M Hello, everyone. I'm Shawn Collins, a doctor at Collins Sleep Clinic. Sleep is one of the most essential parts of our daily lives. So today, I'm going to introduce the best foods for _____ _____ _____ _____. First, kiwi fruits _____ _____ _____ _____ of hormones that help you fall asleep more quickly, sleep longer, and wake up less during the night. Second, milk is _____ _____ vitamin D and it calms the mind and nerves. If you drink a cup of milk before you go to bed, it will definitely help you get a good night's sleep. Third, _____ _____ _____ to produce the hormone that controls your internal body clock and sends signals for the body to sleep at the right time. The last one is honey. _____ _____ _____ _____ _____ because it reduces the hormone that keeps the brain awake! Now, I'll show you some delicious diet plans using these foods.

1번부터 17번까지는 듣고 답하는 문제입니다. 1번부터 15번까지는 한 번만 들려주고, 16번부터 17번까지는 두 번 들려줍니다. 방송을 잘 듣고 답을 하시기 바랍니다.

01 다음을 듣고, 남자가 하는 말의 목적으로 가장 적절한 것을 고르시오.

① 아이스하키부의 우승을 알리려고
② 아이스하키부 훈련 일정을 공지하려고
③ 아이스하키부 신임 감독을 소개하려고
④ 아이스하키부 선수 모집을 안내하려고
⑤ 아이스하키부 경기의 관람을 독려하려고

02 대화를 듣고, 여자의 의견으로 가장 적절한 것을 고르시오.

① 과다한 항생제 복용을 자제해야 한다.
② 오래된 약을 함부로 폐기해서는 안 된다.
③ 약을 복용할 때는 정해진 시간을 지켜야 한다.
④ 진료 전에 자신의 증상을 정확히 확인해야 한다.
⑤ 다른 사람에게 처방된 약을 복용해서는 안 된다.

03 대화를 듣고, 두 사람의 관계를 가장 잘 나타낸 것을 고르시오.

① 관람객 – 박물관 관장   ② 세입자 – 건물 관리인
③ 화가 – 미술관 직원   ④ 고객 – 전기 기사
⑤ 의뢰인 – 건축사

04 대화를 듣고, 그림에서 대화의 내용과 일치하지 않는 것을 고르시오.

05 대화를 듣고, 남자가 할 일로 가장 적절한 것을 고르시오.

① 티켓 디자인하기   ② 포스터 게시하기
③ 블로그 개설하기   ④ 밴드부원 모집하기
⑤ 콘서트 장소 대여하기

06 대화를 듣고, 여자가 지불할 금액을 고르시오. [3점]

① $70   ② $90   ③ $100   ④ $110   ⑤ $120

07 대화를 듣고, 남자가 지갑을 구매하지 못한 이유를 고르시오.

① 해당 상품이 다 팔려서
② 브랜드명을 잊어버려서
③ 계산대의 줄이 길어서
④ 공항에 늦게 도착해서
⑤ 면세점이 문을 닫아서

08 대화를 듣고, Youth Choir Audition에 관해 언급되지 않은 것을 고르시오.

① 지원 가능 연령   ② 날짜
③ 심사 기준   ④ 참가비
⑤ 지원 방법

09 2023 Career Week에 관한 다음 내용을 듣고, 일치하지 않는 것을 고르시오.

① 5일 동안 열릴 것이다.
② 미래 직업 탐색을 돕는 프로그램이 있을 것이다.
③ 프로그램 참가 인원에 제한이 있다.
④ 특별 강연이 마지막 날에 있을 것이다.
⑤ 등록은 5월 10일에 시작된다.

10 다음 표를 보면서 대화를 듣고, 여자가 구입할 프라이팬을 고르시오.

Frying Pans

	Model	Price	Size (inches)	Material	Lid
①	A	$30	8	Aluminum	○
②	B	$32	9.5	Aluminum	○
③	C	$35	10	Stainless Steel	×
④	D	$40	11	Aluminum	×
⑤	E	$70	12.5	Stainless Steel	○

11 대화를 듣고, 남자의 마지막 말에 대한 여자의 응답으로 가장 적절한 것을 고르시오.

① I don't think I can finish editing it by then.
② I learned it by myself through books.
③ This short movie is very interesting.
④ You should make another video clip.
⑤ I got an A⁺ on the team project.

12 대화를 듣고, 여자의 마지막 말에 대한 남자의 응답으로 가장 적절한 것을 고르시오.

① All right. I'll come pick you up now.
② I'm sorry. The library is closed today.
③ No problem. You can borrow my book.
④ Thank you so much. I'll drop you off now.
⑤ Right. I've changed the interior of my office.

13 대화를 듣고, 남자의 마지막 말에 대한 여자의 응답으로 가장 적절한 것을 고르시오.

Woman: _____

① Try these tomatoes and cucumbers.
② I didn't know peppers are good for skin.
③ Just wear comfortable clothes and shoes.
④ You can pick tomatoes when they are red.
⑤ I'll help you grow vegetables on your farm.

14 대화를 듣고, 여자의 마지막 말에 대한 남자의 응답으로 가장 적절한 것을 고르시오. [3점]

Man: _____

① You're right. I'll meet her and apologize.
② I agree with you. That's why I did it.
③ Thank you. I appreciate your apology.
④ Don't worry. I don't think it's your fault.
⑤ Too bad. I hope the two of you get along.

15 다음 상황 설명을 듣고, John이 Ted에게 할 말로 가장 적절한 것을 고르시오. [3점]

John: _____

① How can we find the best sunrise spot?
② Why do you go mountain climbing so often?
③ What time should we get up tomorrow morning?
④ When should we come down from the mountain top?
⑤ Where do we have to stay in the mountain at night?

[16~17] 다음을 듣고, 물음에 답하시오.

16 여자가 하는 말의 주제로 가장 적절한 것은?

① indoor sports good for the elderly
② importance of learning rules in sports
③ best sports for families to enjoy together
④ useful tips for winning a sports game
⑤ history of traditional family sports

17 언급된 스포츠가 아닌 것은?

① badminton
② basketball
③ table tennis
④ soccer
⑤ bowling

녹음 내용을 다시 듣고, 빈칸을 채워 넣으세요.

01

M Hello, Villeford High School students. This is principal Aaron Clark. As a big fan of the Villeford ice hockey team, I'm very excited about the upcoming National High School Ice Hockey League. As you all know, the first game _____ _____ _____ _____ the Central Rink at 6 p.m. this Saturday. I want as many of you as possible to _____ _____ _____ our team to victory. I've seen them put in an incredible amount of effort to win the league. It will _____ _____ _____ _____ just to see you there cheering for them. I really hope to see you at the rink. Thank you.

02

W Honey, are you okay?

M I'm afraid I've caught a cold. I've got _____ _____ _____.

W Why don't you go see a doctor?

M Well, I don't think it's necessary. I've found some medicine in the cabinet. I'll take it.

W You _____ _____ _____ _____. That's what I got prescribed last week.

M My symptoms are similar to yours.

W Honey, you shouldn't take medicine prescribed for others.

M It's just a cold. I'll get better if I take your medicine.

W It _____ _____ _____ to take someone else's prescription.

M Okay. Then I'll go see a doctor this afternoon.

03

W Hi, Mr. Thomson. How are your preparations going?

M You arrived at the right time. I have something to tell you.

W Okay. What is it?

M Well, I'm afraid that we have to _____ _____ _____ _____ for your paintings.

W May I ask why?

M Sure. We have _____ _____ _____ there.

W I see. Then where are you going to exhibit my works?

M Our gallery is going to exhibit your paintings _____ _____ _____ _____.

W Okay. Can I see the hall now?

M Sure. Come with me.

04

M Hi, Grace. What are you looking at on your phone?

W Hi, James. It's a photo I took when I did some volunteer work. We painted pictures on a street wall.

M Let me see. Wow, I like the whale _____ _____ _____ _____.

W I like it, too. How do you like the house under the whale?

M It's beautiful. What are these two chairs for?

W You can _____ _____ _____ sitting there. The painting becomes the background.

M Oh, I see. Look at this tree! It has _____ _____.

W That's right. We named it the Love Tree.

M _____ _____ on the tree branch is lovely, too.

W I hope a lot of people enjoy the painting.

05

M Hi, Stella. How are you doing these days?

W Hi, Ryan. I've been busy helping my granddad with his concert. He made a rock band with his friends.

M There must be _____ _____ _____ _____ to do.

W Yeah. I reserved a place for the concert yesterday.

M What about posters and tickets?

W Well, I've just finished _____ _____ _____.

M Then I think I can help you.

W Really? How?

M Actually, I have a music blog. I think I can _____ _____ _____ there.

W That's great!

M Just send the poster to me, and I'll _____ _____ _____.

W Thanks a lot.

06

M Good morning. How may I help you?

W Hi. I want to buy _____ _____ _____.

M Okay. You can choose from these coffee pots.

W I like this one. How much is it?

M It was originally $60, but it's now _____ _____ _____ $50.

W Okay, I'll buy it. I'd also like to buy this red tumbler.

M Actually, it comes _____ _____ _____.
This smaller one is $20 and a bigger one is $30.

W The smaller one would be easier to carry around. I'll buy _____ _____ _____.

M All right. Is there anything else you need?

W No, that's all. Thank you.

M Okay. How would you like to pay?

W I'll pay by credit card. Here you are.

07

[Cell phone rings.]

W Hi, Brian.

M Hi, Mom. I'm in line to get on the plane.

W Okay. By the way, did you _____ _____ _____ _____ _____ _____ in the airport?

M Yes, but I _____ _____ _____ _____ you asked me to buy.

W Did you forget the brand name?

M No. I remembered that. I took a memo.

W Then did you arrive late at the airport?

M No, I had enough time to shop.

W Then why couldn't you buy the wallet?

M Actually, because they were _____ _____ _____.

W Oh, really?

M Yeah. The wallet must be _____ _____.

W Okay. Thanks for checking anyway.

08

M Lucy, look at this.

W Wow. It's about the Youth Choir Audition.

M Yes. It's _____ _____ _____ aged 13 to 18.

W I'm interested in joining the choir. When is it?

M _____ _____, from 9 a.m. to 5 p.m.

W The place for the audition is the Youth Training Center. It's really _____ _____ _____.

M I think you should leave early in the morning.

W That's no problem. Is there an entry fee?

M No, _____ _____.

W Good. I'll apply for the audition.

M Then you should _____ _____ _____ _____ form on this website.

W All right. Thanks.

09

W Hello, Rosehill High School students! I'm your school counselor, Ms. Lee. I'm so happy to announce a special event, the 2023 Career Week. It'll be held from May 22nd _____ _____ _____. There will be many programs to help you _____ _____ _____ _____. Please kindly note that the number of participants for each program is _____ _____ _____. A special lecture on future career choices will be presented _____ _____ _____ _____. Registration begins _____ _____ _____. For more information, please visit our school website. I hope you can come and enjoy the 2023 Career Week!

10

M Jessica, what are you doing?

W I'm trying to buy one of these five frying pans.

M Let me see. This frying pan seems pretty expensive.

W Yeah. I _____ _____ _____ _____ more than $50.

M Okay. And I think 9 to 12-inch frying pans will _____ _____ most of your cooking.

W I think so, too. An 8-inch frying pan seems too small for me.

M What about the material? Stainless steel pans are good for fast cooking.

W I know, but they are heavier. I'll _____ _____ _____ _____.

M Then you have two options left. Do you need a lid?

W Of course. A lid keeps _____ _____ _____ _____. I'll buy this one.

M Good choice.

11

M _____ _____ _____ your team's short-movie project?

W Not yet. I'm still editing the video clip.

M Oh, you edit? _____ _____ _____ _____ to do that?

W ▨▨▨▨▨▨▨▨▨▨▨▨▨▨▨▨▨▨▨

12

[Cell phone rings.]

W Daddy, are you still working now?

M No, Emma. I'm _____ _____ _____ _____ my car and drive home.

W Great. Can you _____ _____ _____ _____? I'm at the City Library near your office.

M ▨▨▨▨▨▨▨▨▨▨▨▨▨▨▨▨▨▨▨

13

M Claire, how's _____ _____ _____?

W Great! I harvested some cherry tomatoes and cucumbers last weekend. Do you want some?

M Of course. I'd like some very much.

W Okay. I'll bring you some tomorrow.

M Thanks. Are you going to the farm this weekend too?

W Yes. The peppers are almost ready to be picked.

M Can I go with you? I'd like to look around your farm and _____ _____ _____ _____ _____.

W Sure. It would be fun to work on the farm together.

M Sounds nice. Is there anything I _____ _____ _____?

W ▨▨▨▨▨▨▨▨▨▨▨▨▨▨▨▨▨▨▨

14

W Daniel, what's wrong?

M Hi, Leila. I _____ _____ _____ with Olivia.

W Was it serious?

M I'm not sure, but I think I _____ _____ _____.

W So that's why you have a long face.

M Yeah. I want to get along with her, but she's still angry at me.

W Did you say you're sorry to her?

M Well, I texted her saying that I'm sorry.

W I don't think it's a good idea to express your apology _____ _____ _____ _____.

M Do you think so? Now I know why I haven't received any response from her yet.

W I think it'd be best to go and _____ _____ _____ _____ _____.

M ▨▨▨▨▨▨▨▨▨▨▨▨▨▨▨▨▨▨▨▨▨▨

15

M Ted and John are college freshmen. They are climbing Green Diamond Mountain together. Now they have reached the campsite near the mountain top. After climbing the mountain all day, they _____ _____ _____ _____ at the campsite. While drinking coffee, Ted suggests to John that they _____ _____ _____ at the mountain top the next morning. John thinks it's a good idea. So, now John wants to ask Ted _____ _____ they should _____ _____ to see the sunrise. In this situation, what would John most likely say to Ted?

John ▨▨▨▨▨▨▨▨▨▨▨▨▨▨▨▨▨▨▨▨▨▨

16~17

W Good morning, everyone. Do you _____ _____ _____ _____ _____ with your family? One of the best ways to spend time with your family is to _____ _____ _____. Today, I will share some of the best sports that families can play together. The first one is badminton. The whole family can enjoy the sport _____ _____ _____. The second one is basketball. You can easily find a basketball court near your house. The third one is table tennis. It can be played indoors anytime. The last one is bowling. Many families _____ _____ _____ _____ playing it together. When you go home today, how about playing one of these sports with your family?

4회 **2022학년도 11월** **고1 전국연합 학력평가**

1번부터 17번까지는 듣고 답하는 문제입니다. 1번부터 15번까지는 한 번만 들려주고, 16번부터 17번까지는 두 번 들려줍니다. 방송을 잘 듣고 답을 하시기 바랍니다.

01 다음을 듣고, 남자가 하는 말의 목적으로 가장 적절한 것을 고르시오.

① 얼음으로 덮인 일부 등산로 폐쇄를 공지하려고
② 등산객에게 야간 산행의 위험성을 경고하려고
③ 겨울 산행을 위한 안전 장비를 안내하려고
④ 긴급 제설에 필요한 작업자를 모집하려고
⑤ 일출 명소인 전망대를 소개하려고

02 대화를 듣고, 남자의 의견으로 가장 적절한 것을 고르시오.

① 조리법을 있는 그대로 따를 필요는 없다.
② 요리 도구를 정기적으로 소독해야 한다.
③ 설탕 섭취는 단기 기억력을 향상시킨다.
④ 열량이 높은 음식은 건강에 좋지 않다.
⑤ 신선한 재료는 요리의 풍미를 높인다.

03 대화를 듣고, 두 사람의 관계를 가장 잘 나타낸 것을 고르시오.

① 음악 평론가 – 방송 연출가
② 작곡가 – 게임 제작자
③ 독자 – 웹툰 작가
④ 삽화가 – 소설가
⑤ 영화감독 – 배우

04 대화를 듣고, 그림에서 대화의 내용과 일치하지 <u>않는</u> 것을 고르시오.

05 대화를 듣고, 남자가 할 일로 가장 적절한 것을 고르시오.

① 음료 구매하기   ② 연필 준비하기
③ 의자 설치하기   ④ 마이크 점검하기
⑤ 스케치북 가져오기

06 대화를 듣고, 여자가 지불할 금액을 고르시오. [3점]

① $17   ② $22   ③ $35   ④ $37   ⑤ $39

07 대화를 듣고, 남자가 얼음낚시를 갈 수 <u>없는</u> 이유를 고르시오.

① 손목을 다쳐서
② 병원에 입원해야 해서
③ 직장에 출근해야 해서
④ 기상 여건이 나빠져서
⑤ 친구와 농구를 해야 해서

08 대화를 듣고, Kids' Pottery Class에 관해 언급되지 <u>않은</u> 것을 고르시오.

① 날짜   ② 장소   ③ 수강 인원
④ 수강료   ⑤ 등록 방법

09 2022 Online Whistling Championship에 관한 다음 내용을 듣고, 일치하지 <u>않는</u> 것을 고르시오.

① 좋아하는 어떤 노래든 선택할 수 있다.
② 12월 4일까지 동영상을 업로드 해야 한다.
③ 녹음 시 마이크의 에코 효과를 반드시 꺼야 한다.
④ 운영진의 심사에 의해 수상자들이 결정될 것이다.
⑤ 결과는 웹사이트에 발표될 것이다.

10 다음 표를 보면서 대화를 듣고, 두 사람이 선택할 커튼을 고르시오.

Curtains

	Product	Price	Care Instruction	Blackout	Color
①	A	$70	machine washable	×	navy
②	B	$80	machine washable	○	brown
③	C	$90	dry cleaning only	○	ivory
④	D	$95	machine washable	○	gray
⑤	E	$110	dry cleaning only	×	white

11 대화를 듣고, 남자의 마지막 말에 대한 여자의 응답으로 가장 적절한 것을 고르시오.

① I've been waiting for 30 minutes.
② I've enjoyed this ride very much.
③ You're standing in the correct line.
④ I have enough time to wait for you.
⑤ You may end the construction in a year.

12 대화를 듣고, 여자의 마지막 말에 대한 남자의 응답으로 가장 적절한 것을 고르시오.

① No way. I don't know who's lost.
② Okay. Let's see if he needs our help.
③ Exactly. Just stop crying like a child.
④ Sure. He loves walking around the park.
⑤ Thanks. We were worried about our son.

13 대화를 듣고, 남자의 마지막 말에 대한 여자의 응답으로 가장 적절한 것을 고르시오. [3점]

Woman: _____

① Great. I believe my previous offer will benefit your company.
② I'm sorry. Your interview has been delayed to next Wednesday.
③ Good. Your effort will give a good impression on the interviewer.
④ Excellent. The second candidate's work experience caught my eye.
⑤ No worries. You can purchase nice clothes for the upcoming party.

14 대화를 듣고, 여자의 마지막 말에 대한 남자의 응답으로 가장 적절한 것을 고르시오.

Man: _____

① Please wait. I'll be back with the shoes in a minute.
② Hurry up. You don't have enough time to do this.
③ Of course. You can get a refund for these shoes.
④ Don't worry. The color doesn't matter to me.
⑤ Sorry. The red ones are already sold out.

15 다음 상황 설명을 듣고, Amelia가 Jacob 교수에게 할 말로 가장 적절한 것을 고르시오. [3점]

Amelia: _____

① Could you extend the deadline for the assignment?
② Would it be possible to change our appointment?
③ Why don't you join my final psychology project?
④ Do you want to meet at the information center?
⑤ How about visiting the doctor for a checkup?

[16~17] 다음을 듣고, 물음에 답하시오.

16 여자가 하는 말의 주제로 가장 적절한 것은?

① ways to stop the spread of false information
② methods of delivering messages in the past
③ modes of communication in modern times
④ types of speeches according to purposes
⑤ means to survive in prehistoric times

17 언급된 수단이 <u>아닌</u> 것은?

① drum ② smoke ③ pigeon
④ flag ⑤ horse

Dictation

01

[Chime bell rings.]

M Good morning. This is Ethan Cooper from the Reindeer Mountain maintenance office. Last night, we had 20 cm of _____ _____. Most of the snow melted away with the sun out in the morning, but some of it froze in the shade. For hikers' safety, we've _____ _____ _____ _____ _____ covered with ice. At this moment, Sunrise Trail and Lakeview Trail are _____ _____ _____. I'll make an announcement later when the trails are ready to be reopened. Until then, keep in mind that Sunrise Trail and Lakeview Trail _____ _____. Thank you.

02

M Honey, what are you doing?

W I'm looking for the measuring spoons. Do you know where they are?

M They're in the first drawer. Why do you need them?

W The recipe says four teaspoons of sugar.

M Dear, you _____ _____ _____ _____ the recipe as it is.

W What do you mean?

M A recipe is just an example. You _____ _____ _____ _____ the same amount of ingredients as stated in the recipe.

W Hmm. Right. Sometimes the food is too sweet when I cook based on the recipe instructions.

M See? You _____ _____ _____ _____ to the recipe.

W Okay. I'll remember that.

03

[Door knocks.]

W Can I come in?

M Yes. Oh, Ms. Smith. Did you read the email I sent?

W I did. I liked _____ _____ _____. The characters exploring space were very mysterious. How did you create the characters?

M Actually, old science fiction movies inspired me to design those characters.

W Interesting. Now, could you describe the main character more specifically? It'll be helpful when I compose _____ _____ _____ for the character.

M Well, he's a thrill seeker. So, a strong, bold, and rhythmic sound would suit him.

W Okay. Do you need anything else?

M I also want you to make some _____ _____.

W Of course. When do you need them?

M By December 21st. I'd like to start _____ _____ _____ _____ the game by then.

W All right. Then I'll talk to you later.

04

M Hi, Chelsea. Did you finish your art assignment?

W Oh, my dream room drawing? Yes. Here's the picture.

M Wow, it's so creative. There is _____ _____ _____ _____ the door.

W Yes. I've always dreamed of a room with two floors. Look at the _____ _____ _____ above the staircase.

M They look very stylish. And I like _____ _____ _____ above the sofa. It'll bring warmth to your room.

W Thanks. Check out the _____ _____ on the floor.

M It goes well with this place. Oh, there is _____ _____ _____ _____ _____.

W You're right. I want to keep my favorite books nearby.

M That's a good idea.

05

W Jamie, is the cartoon artist on her way?

M Yes. She'll arrive at our studio in an hour.

W Perfect. Let's check if we _____ _____ _____ for our talk show.

M Okay. I set up a chair for our guest yesterday.

W Great. And I bought a drink and put it on the table.

M Good. Did you prepare a pencil? The artist said she'll draw caricatures of us during the live show.

W Oh, she told me that she'll bring her own pencil.

M She did? Then we don't need it.

W Yeah. By the way, _____ _____ _____?

M Oops. I left it in my car. I'll _____ _____ _____ right now.

W Fine. Then I'll _____ _____ _____.

M Thanks.

06

M Welcome to Crispy Fried Chicken. What would you like to order?

W What kind of chicken do you have?

M We only have two kinds. Fried chicken is $15 and barbecue chicken is $20.

W I'll have _____ _____ _____ _____ _____ chicken.

M Okay. Would you like some potato chips with your order? They're our _____ _____ _____ _____.

W How much are they?

M One basket of potato chips is $2.

W Then I'll _____ _____ _____.

M Will that be all?

W Yes. And can I use this coupon for a free soda?

M Of course. You can grab any soda from the fridge.

W Great. Here's my credit card.

07

[Cell phone rings.]

W Leo, I'm sorry I missed your call. What's up?

M Well, I just called to tell you that I _____ _____ _____ _____ with you this weekend.

W Oh, no. I heard the weather will be perfect this weekend.

M I'm sorry. I really wish I could go.

W Didn't you say you're off from work this weekend?

M I am. It's not because of work. Actually, I _____ _____ _____.

W That's terrible. Are you okay?

M Don't worry. I'll be fine.

W How did you get injured?

M I was playing basketball with a friend and _____ _____ _____.

W Did you go to the hospital?

M I did. The doctor told me that it'll be better in a month.

W That's good. I hope you feel better soon.

08

M Honey, look at this flyer about Kids' Pottery Class.

W Okay. Let's take a look.

M I think our little Austin would love to make his own cereal bowl.

W I think so, too. It says that the class is held on October 8th. We can take him there on that day.

M Great. And it's held _____ _____ _____. It's a 10-minute drive from our home.

W That's so close. And check out the price. The class _____ _____ $15.

M That's reasonable. We should sign up. How can we register for the class?

W It says you can simply scan the QR code to _____ _____.

M Okay. Let's do it right away.

4회

22년 11월

09

W Hello, listeners. The most interesting music competition is back! You can now sign up for the 2022 Online Whistling Championship. You can _____ _____ _____ that you like, but note that the length of your whistling video is _____ _____ _____ _____. To enter the competition, you must upload your video on our website by December 4th. When recording your whistling, be sure to _____ _____ _____ _____ _____ on the microphone. Winners will be decided by _____ _____ _____. The result will _____ _____ _____ our website. We look forward to your enthusiastic participation.

10

M Honey, I'm looking at a shopping site to choose curtains for our bedroom. But there are too many options to consider.

W Okay. Let's pick one together.

M I don't think we should spend _____ _____ $100.

W I agree. Let's drop this one. And some of them are _____ _____ at home.

M Fantastic. We won't have to pay for dry cleaning all the time.

W Good for us. Let's cross out this one then. What about a blackout option?

M We definitely need it. It'll completely _____ _____, so we won't be disturbed. And which color do you like?

W I don't mind any color _____ _____ _____.

M Okay. Then we narrowed it down to one.

W Well then, let's choose this one.

11

M Excuse me. Is this really the line for the rollercoaster?

W Yes. This is _____ _____ _____ _____ _____.

M Oh, no. I can't believe it. There are so many people standing in line. _____ _____ _____ _____ _____ waiting here?

W ▓▓▓▓▓▓▓▓▓▓▓▓▓▓▓▓

12

W Chris, what are you looking at?

M A little boy is _____ _____ _____ around the park. He's all by himself.

W Oh, I see him, too. We should ask him _____ _____ _____.

M ▓▓▓▓▓▓▓▓▓▓▓▓▓▓▓▓

13

M Hi, Ava.

W Hi, Samuel. Are you all set for _____ _____ _____?

M I'm still working on it. I've come up with a list of questions the interviewer might ask.

W Good job. Preparing answers to those questions will help you for the interview.

M But I think I'm not ready.

W Hmm. Have you thought about how you'll _____ _____ _____ _____ _____?

M Could you be more specific?

W You know a smile makes you look confident. Also, people usually dress up to give a favorable impression.

M That's a good point.

W I believe you'll _____ _____ _____ _____ _____ with a proper presentation of yourself.

M Okay. Then I'm going to practice smiling and look for my best suit.

W ▓▓▓▓▓▓▓▓▓▓▓▓▓▓▓▓

14

W Excuse me.

M Yes, ma'am. How can I help you?

W How much are those shoes?

M They're $60. But today only, we're offering a 30% discount.

W That's a good price. Do you have a size six?

M Sure. Here they are. Take a seat here and try them on.

W Thank you. *[Pause]* Well, these shoes are _____ _____ _____ for me. Can I get a size six and a half?

M I'm sorry. That size in this color is _____ _____.

W Do you have these shoes _____ _____ _____ _____?

M Let me check. *[Typing sounds]* We have red and green in storage.

W A green pair sounds good. I want to _____ _____ _____.

M ▢▢▢▢▢▢▢▢▢▢▢▢▢▢▢▢▢▢▢▢

15

M Amelia is a high school student. She is working on a psychology project. She thinks that an interview with an expert in the field will _____ _____ _____ _____ _____. She emails Professor Jacob, who is a renowned psychology professor. Even though he's busy, she _____ _____ _____ _____ an interview with him. Unfortunately, on that morning, she eats a sandwich and feels sick. She knows this interview is important, and difficult to set up again. But she can't go meet him because of _____ _____ _____. So she wants to ask him if he can _____ _____ _____. In this situation, what would Amelia most likely say to Professor Jacob?

Amelia ▢▢▢▢▢▢▢▢▢▢▢▢▢▢▢▢

16~17

W Good morning, students. These days we can easily _____ _____ to each other using phones or computers. However, communication has not always been as simple as it is today. Here are a few ways people in the past used to carry their messages. First, some tribes _____ _____ _____ _____. They were able to send warnings or important information by varying the pitch or beat. Next, other people used _____ _____ _____ _____ over long distances. For example, our ancestors used smoke to signal attacks from enemies. Third, a pigeon was _____ _____ _____ of communication. It always found its way home with messages attached to its legs. Finally, a horse was one of the most efficient ways to communicate.

_____ _____ _____ _____ _____ on its back delivered mail more quickly than runners. Now you may understand the ways of sending messages back in the old days. Then let's take a look in detail at each communication method.

1번부터 17번까지는 듣고 답하는 문제입니다. 1번부터 15번까지는 한 번만 들려주고, 16번부터 17번까지는 두 번 들려줍니다. 방송을 잘 듣고 답을 하시기 바랍니다.

01 다음을 듣고, 여자가 하는 말의 목적으로 가장 적절한 것을 고르시오.

① 도서관 확장 이전을 공지하려고
② 도서관 이용 안내 영상을 소개하려고
③ 독서 습관 형성 프로그램을 홍보하려고
④ 독해력 향상 방안에 대한 의견을 구하려고
⑤ 독서 프로그램 만족도 조사 참여를 요청하려고

02 대화를 듣고, 남자의 의견으로 가장 적절한 것을 고르시오.

① 중고품은 직접 만나서 거래해야 한다.
② 물품 구매 시 여러 제품을 비교해야 한다.
③ 계획적으로 예산을 세워 물품을 구매해야 한다.
④ 온라인 거래 시 개인 정보 유출에 유의해야 한다.
⑤ 중고품 구매 시 세부 사항을 꼼꼼히 확인해야 한다.

03 대화를 듣고, 두 사람의 관계를 가장 잘 나타낸 것을 고르시오.

① 의사 – 간호사
② 안경사 – 고객
③ 보건 교사 – 학부모
④ 사진사 – 모델
⑤ 앱 개발자 – 의뢰인

04 대화를 듣고, 그림에서 대화의 내용과 일치하지 않는 것을 고르시오.

05 대화를 듣고, 여자가 할 일로 가장 적절한 것을 고르시오.

① 식료품 주문하기
② 자동차 수리 맡기기
③ 보고서 제출하기
④ 고객 센터에 전화하기
⑤ 냉장고에 식료품 넣기

06 대화를 듣고, 남자가 지불할 금액을 고르시오. [3점]

① $27 ② $30 ③ $36 ④ $40 ⑤ $45

07 대화를 듣고, 여자가 가방을 구입한 이유를 고르시오.

① 유명 연예인들이 착용해서
② 재활용 소재를 사용해서
③ 많은 친구들이 추천해서
④ 디자인이 독특해서
⑤ 가격이 저렴해서

08 대화를 듣고, Youth Street Dance Contest에 관해 언급되지 않은 것을 고르시오.

① 신청 마감일
② 심사 기준
③ 우승 상금액
④ 참가 부문
⑤ 신청 방법

09 Lakewoods Plogging에 관한 다음 내용을 듣고, 일치하지 않는 것을 고르시오.

① 참가자는 운동복과 운동화를 착용해야 한다.
② 쓰레기를 담을 봉투가 배부된다.
③ 10월 1일 오전 7시부터 진행될 것이다.
④ 학교 웹사이트에서 신청할 수 있다.
⑤ 참가자 모두 스포츠 양말을 받을 것이다.

10 다음 표를 보면서 대화를 듣고, 두 사람이 주문할 휴대용 캠핑히터를 고르시오.

Portable Camping Heater

	Model	Weight (kg)	Price	Energy Source	Customer Rating
①	A	4.2	$85	Oil	★★★
②	B	3.6	$90	Oil	★★★★
③	C	3.4	$92	Electricity	★★★★★
④	D	3.2	$95	Electricity	★★★★
⑤	E	2.8	$115	Electricity	★★★★★

11 대화를 듣고, 여자의 마지막 말에 대한 남자의 응답으로 가장 적절한 것을 고르시오.

① You can join the tour, too.
② The bike wasn't that expensive.
③ I haven't decided the place, yet.
④ I'm going to rent a bike in the park.
⑤ Autumn is the best season for the tour.

12 대화를 듣고, 남자의 마지막 말에 대한 여자의 응답으로 가장 적절한 것을 고르시오.

① Great. I'll be there at that time.
② Okay. I'll change my toothbrush.
③ Too bad. I hope you get well soon.
④ No worries. Your painkillers work well.
⑤ Sure. Let me know when he's available.

13 대화를 듣고, 여자의 마지막 말에 대한 남자의 응답으로 가장 적절한 것을 고르시오.

Man: _____

① Fantastic! We'll be a really good team.
② Sorry. I don't understand why you like it.
③ Good idea! I'll find another partner for you.
④ No problem. I can use my racket to practice.
⑤ I know. Everyone loves watching sports competitions.

14 대화를 듣고, 남자의 마지막 말에 대한 여자의 응답으로 가장 적절한 것을 고르시오. [3점]

Woman: _____

① Nice! I'm curious about what you'll ask.
② Sure. You should study hard for the quiz.
③ Okay. I'll make some questions right away.
④ All right. I'll see if I can add more pictures.
⑤ Don't worry. It won't take too long to answer.

15 다음 상황 설명을 듣고, Ms. Olson이 Steven에게 할 말로 가장 적절한 것을 고르시오. [3점]

Ms. Olson: _____

① You can come see me any time you want.
② I'm happy to hear that you've met the CEO.
③ Why do you want to run a gaming company?
④ How about going to your role model's book-signing?
⑤ You should buy more books written by your role model.

[16~17] 다음을 듣고, 물음에 답하시오.

16 남자가 하는 말의 주제로 가장 적절한 것은?

① tips for caring for musical instruments
② ways to choose a good musical instrument
③ effects of the weather on musical instruments
④ benefits of learning musical instruments as a child
⑤ difficulties of making your own musical instruments

17 언급된 악기가 <u>아닌</u> 것은?

① flutes   ② trumpets   ③ pianos
④ drums   ⑤ guitars

5회

22년 9월

01

W　Good evening, Vermont citizens. I'm Elizabeth Bowen, the Director of the Vermont City Library. I'd like to tell you about our online 15-Minute Book Reading program. This program _____ _____ _____ _____ your children form good reading habits at home. Every day, individual tutoring is provided for 15 minutes. It's completely personalized to your child's reading level! Don't _____ _____ _____ _____ your children for this amazing opportunity _____ _____ _____ _____ _____! For more information, please visit the Vermont City Library. Thank you.

02

M　Clara, why the long face?

W　Aw, Dad, I bought this hair dryer, but the cool air mode doesn't work.

M　Where did you get it?

W　I bought it second-hand online.

M　Did you _____ _____ _____ before you ordered it?

W　I did, but I missed the seller's note that said the cool air mode doesn't work.

M　Oh dear. It's important to check all the details when you buy second-hand items.

W　You're right. I was just so excited because it was _____ _____ _____ _____ other hair dryers.

M　Some second-hand items are almost like new, but others are not. So, you should read _____ _____ _____ _____ _____ carefully.

W　Thanks, Dad. I'll keep that in mind.

03

M　Hello, Ms. Adams! It's been a while since you were here.

W　Last time I came, you told me I should _____ _____ _____ every year.

M　That's right. When did you last visit us?

W　I guess I came here last October.

M　Okay. Then, let me check your vision. Please sit here. [Pause] Hmm... your eyesight got a little worse.

W　Yeah, maybe it's because I've been working on a computer for too long.

M　Actually, the blue light from computers and smartphones _____ _____ _____ _____.

W　Really? Is there a lens that blocks the light?

M　Sure. You can wear these blue light blocking lenses.

W　That sounds perfect. But I'd like to use this frame again.

M　No problem, you can just change the lenses. You can come _____ _____ _____ in a week.

W　Okay, thank you so much. See you then.

04

W　Carl, what are you looking at?

M　Oh, hi, Amy. Come take a look. It's a picture of my grandparents' house. I was there last weekend.

W　What a beautiful house! There's even a pond under the tree!

M　Yes, my grandfather _____ _____ _____. And how about that flower-patterned tablecloth?

W　I love it. It makes the table look cozy.

M　Did you see _____ _____ _____ _____ _____ on the door?

W　Oh! Did you paint that?

M　Yeah, I did it when I was 8 years old.

W　It's cute. And _____ _____ _____ _____ on the roof.

M　Right, we get a lot of sunlight through the windows.

W　I like that! And can you still _____ _____ _____ next to the house?

M　Of course. That's the best spot to see the sunset.

W　Wow, your grandparents' house looks like a nice place!

05

M Honey, there's a box in the doorway. What is it?

W I ordered some groceries online. Would you bring it in?

M Sure. Is this for the house-warming party today?

W Yeah. Since I had to _____ _____ _____ _____, I couldn't go shopping yesterday.

M Sorry, I should've taken you to the market.

W That's okay. You worked late to meet the deadline for your report. Would you open the box for me?

M Sure. *[Pause]* Oh no, some eggs are broken! Have a look.

W Ah... that's _____ _____ _____.

M Why don't we call the customer center about it?

W Okay. I'll _____ _____ _____ _____.

M While you do that, I'll put the other food _____ _____ _____.

W Thanks.

06

W Hello, welcome to Kelly's Bake Shop. How can I help you?

M Hi, I'd like to order a carrot cake.

W Okay, we have two sizes. A small one is $25 and a large one is $35. Which one would you like?

M Well, we're four people, so a large one _____ _____ _____.

W Great. Do you need candles?

M No thanks, but can you write on the cake?

W We can. It costs $5. What would you like the message to say?

M Please write "Thank You Mom" on it.

W Sure. It takes about _____ _____ _____. Is that okay?

M No problem. Can I use this 10% off coupon?

W Certainly. You get 10% _____ _____ _____.

M Thanks. Here's my credit card.

07

M Anna, I haven't seen you use this bag before. Did you buy a new one?

W Hi, Jason. Yeah, I bought it online last week.

M I saw some celebrities posting about it on their social media.

W Really? I didn't know that, but this bag _____ _____ _____ _____.

M It does, but its design isn't that unique. It's too plain.

W Yeah, and it's _____ _____ _____ compared to other bags.

M Well, then why did you buy it?

W I bought it because it's _____ _____ _____ _____.

M Oh, you're a responsible consumer.

W Exactly. So, I'm recommending it to all my friends.

M Good idea. I'll check the website for more information.

08

W Jimmy, what are you doing with your smartphone?

M I'm looking at a poster about the Youth Street Dance Contest.

W Oh, isn't it a street dance contest for high school students?

M Yeah. Why don't you enter? I know _____ _____ _____ _____.

W Hmm... when is it?

M The competition is October 22nd, but _____ _____ _____ _____ is September 30th.

W Okay, good. I have a few months to practice.

M And look! The winner gets $2,000!

W That's amazing! What types of dancing are there?

M It says participants should choose one of these three types: hip-hop, locking, and breakdancing.

W I'm really into breakdancing lately, so I'll enter with that. How do I apply?

M You just download the application form from the website and _____ _____ _____ _____.

W Okay! It'll be a great experience for me to try out.

09

M Hello, Lakewoods High School students! I'm Lawrence Cho, president of the student council. I'm happy to announce a special new event to reduce waste around our school: Lakewoods Plogging! Since plogging is the activity of _____ _____ _____ _____ _____, all participants should wear workout clothes and sneakers. We provide eco-friendly bags for the trash, so you _____ _____ _____ _____ any. The event _____ _____ _____ _____ October 1st from 7 a.m. to 9 a.m. You can sign up for the event on the school website starting tomorrow. The first 30 participants will get _____ _____ _____ _____ _____. For more information, please visit our school website. Don't miss this fun opportunity!

10

M Honey, what are you doing?

W I'm looking at a website _____ _____ _____ _____ _____ for winter camping. Would you like to choose one together?

M Sure, let me see.

W We should be able to carry it easily, so its weight is important. I think we should get one of these under 4kg.

M Good point. Oh, this one is pretty expensive.

W I know. Let's choose _____ _____ _____ _____ less than $100.

M Okay. And I think an electric heater would be good. What do you think?

W I agree. It's safer to use.

M Now we have these two models left.

W I'd like _____ _____ _____ _____ _____ customer rating.

M All right. Let's order this one.

11

W Kevin, _____ _____ _____ yours?

M Yes, I bought it for my bike tour.

W Really? Where are you _____ _____ _____?

M ▓▓▓▓▓▓▓▓▓▓▓▓▓▓▓▓▓▓▓▓▓

12

[Telephone rings.]

M Hello, this is Ashley's Dental Clinic. How may I help you?

W Hello, this is Emily Gibson. Can I _____ _____ _____ today? I have a terrible toothache.

M Just a second. Let me check. *[Pause]* He's _____ _____ 4:30 this afternoon.

W ▓▓▓▓▓▓▓▓▓▓▓▓▓▓▓▓▓▓▓▓▓

13

W Hey, Justin. Do you know where those students are going?

M They're probably going to the gym _____ _____ _____.

W Why are so many students practicing badminton?

M Haven't you heard about the School Badminton Tournament? Many of the students have already _____ _____ _____ _____.

W Really? Why is it so popular?

M The winners will get a big scholarship and there are lots of other prizes as well.

W That's nice! Why don't you sign up for it, too?

M I'd like to, but only doubles can participate. And I haven't found a partner, yet.

W Actually, I used to be a badminton player in my elementary school.

M Wow! I have a top expert right here! How about _____ _____ _____?

W Sure. Not an expert, but I can try.

M ▓▓▓▓▓▓▓▓▓▓▓▓▓▓▓▓▓▓▓▓▓

14

M Hey, Natalie. What are you doing on your computer?

W Hi, Dave. I'm working on my presentation for social studies class. It's about traditional games in Asia.

M Sounds interesting. Can I see it?

W Sure. I'll introduce some games with these pictures.

M That's a great idea, but I think you have too many words on the slides.

W You're right. I'm worried it might be boring.

M Then, how about shortening your explanation and _____ _____ _____? It would make your presentation more interesting.

W Great idea! What do you think about True-or-False questions?

M That's good. Your audience will be able to focus on your presentation _____ _____ _____ the answers.

W But... what if they don't know the answers?

M It doesn't matter. They'll have fun _____ _____ _____.

W ▨▨▨▨▨▨▨▨▨▨▨▨▨▨▨▨▨▨▨

15

W Steven is a high school student and Ms. Olson is a career counselor at his school. Steven has much interest in the video game industry. A few days ago, Ms. Olson _____ _____ _____ written by a CEO who runs a famous gaming company. After reading the book, Steven told her that the CEO is his role model. This morning, Ms. Olson hears the news that the CEO is going to _____ _____ _____ at a bookstore nearby. She thinks Steven _____ _____ _____ _____ his role model in person. So, Ms. Olson wants to tell Steven that he should go see the CEO at the event. In this situation, what would Ms. Olson most likely say to Steven?

Ms. Olson ▨▨▨▨▨▨▨▨▨▨▨▨▨▨▨▨▨

16~17

M Hello, students. Last class, we took a brief look at how to tune your musical instruments. Today, we're going to talk a bit about how to take care of and maintain your instruments. First, let's take flutes. They may have moisture from the air _____ _____ _____, so you should clean and wipe the mouth piece before and after playing. Next are trumpets. They can _____ _____ _____, so you should air dry the parts in a cool dry place, away from direct sunlight. And as for pianos, they don't need everyday care, but it's essential to protect the keys by covering them with a protective pad _____ _____ _____ _____. The last ones are string instruments like guitars. Their strings need replacement. When you replace the strings, it's good to do it gradually, _____ _____ _____ _____. Proper care can lengthen the lifespan of your musical instruments. I hope this lesson _____ _____ _____ _____ your musical instruments safe from damage.

1번부터 17번까지는 듣고 답하는 문제입니다. 1번부터 15번까지는 한 번만 들려주고, 16번부터 17번까지는 두 번 들려줍니다. 방송을 잘 듣고 답을 하시기 바랍니다.

01 다음을 듣고, 남자가 하는 말의 목적으로 가장 적절한 것을 고르시오.
① 사생활 보호의 중요성을 강조하려고
② 건물 벽 페인트 작업을 공지하려고
③ 회사 근무시간 변경을 안내하려고
④ 새로운 직원 채용을 공고하려고
⑤ 친환경 제품 출시를 홍보하려고

02 대화를 듣고, 여자의 의견으로 가장 적절한 것을 고르시오.
① 운전자는 제한 속도를 지켜야 한다.
② 교통경찰을 더 많이 배치해야 한다.
③ 보행자의 부주의가 교통사고를 유발한다.
④ 교통사고를 목격하면 즉시 신고해야 한다.
⑤ 대중교통을 이용하면 이동시간을 줄일 수 있다.

03 대화를 듣고, 두 사람의 관계를 가장 잘 나타낸 것을 고르시오.
① 작가 – 출판사 직원
② 관람객 – 박물관 해설사
③ 손님 – 주방장
④ 탑승객 – 항공 승무원
⑤ 학생 – 사서

04 대화를 듣고, 그림에서 대화의 내용과 일치하지 않는 것을 고르시오.

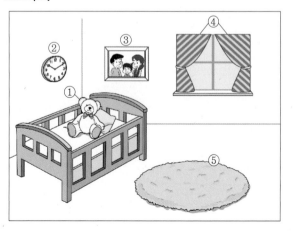

05 대화를 듣고, 남자가 할 일로 가장 적절한 것을 고르시오.
① 보고서 제출하기　　② 티켓 예매하기
③ 자전거 수리하기　　④ 축구 연습하기
⑤ 팝콘 구입하기

06 대화를 듣고, 여자가 지불할 금액을 고르시오. [3점]
① $40　② $60　③ $80　④ $100　⑤ $120

07 대화를 듣고, 남자가 음식 부스에 갈 수 없는 이유로 가장 적절한 것을 고르시오.
① 밴드 오디션 연습을 해야 해서
② 보드게임 부스를 설치해야 해서
③ 영어 프로젝트를 끝내야 해서
④ 샌드위치를 준비해야 해서
⑤ 친구를 만나러 가야 해서

08 대화를 듣고, Spanish culture class에 관해 언급되지 않은 것을 고르시오.
① 강사　　② 활동 종류　　③ 수업 요일
④ 준비물　　⑤ 수강료

09 Summer Flea Market에 관한 다음 내용을 듣고, 일치하지 않는 것을 고르시오. [3점]
① 일주일 동안 진행된다.
② 학교 주차장에서 열린다.
③ 장난감, 양초와 같은 물품을 살 수 있다.
④ 상태가 좋은 중고 물품을 판매할 수 있다.
⑤ 첫날 방문하면 할인 쿠폰을 선물로 받는다.

10 다음 표를 보면서 대화를 듣고, 여자가 구입할 운동화를 고르시오.

Sneakers

	Model	Price	Style	Waterproof	Color
①	A	$50	casual	×	black
②	B	$60	active	×	white
③	C	$65	casual	○	black
④	D	$70	casual	○	white
⑤	E	$85	active	○	white

11 대화를 듣고, 여자의 마지막 말에 대한 남자의 응답으로 가장 적절한 것을 고르시오.

① All children's books are 20% off.
② It takes time to write a good article.
③ I like to read action adventure books.
④ There are too many advertisements on TV.
⑤ The store has been closed since last month.

12 대화를 듣고, 남자의 마지막 말에 대한 여자의 응답으로 가장 적절한 것을 고르시오.

① You're welcome. I'm happy to help you.
② That's not true. I made it with your help.
③ Okay. Good food always makes me feel better.
④ Really? You should definitely visit the theater later.
⑤ Never mind. You'll do better on the next presentation.

13 대화를 듣고, 여자의 마지막 말에 대한 남자의 응답으로 가장 적절한 것을 고르시오.

Man: _____

① I'm excited to buy a new guitar.
② Summer vacation starts on Friday.
③ You can find it on the school website.
④ Let's go to the school festival together.
⑤ You can get some rest during the vacation.

14 대화를 듣고, 남자의 마지막 말에 대한 여자의 응답으로 가장 적절한 것을 고르시오.

Woman: _____

① I agree. There are many benefits of exercising at the gym.
② You're right. Not all exercise is helpful for your brain.
③ Don't worry. It's not too difficult for me to exercise.
④ That sounds great. Can I join the course, too?
⑤ That's too bad. I hope you get well soon.

15 다음 상황 설명을 듣고, Ted가 Monica에게 할 말로 가장 적절한 것을 고르시오. [3점]

Ted: _____

① Can I draw your club members on the poster?
② Are you interested in joining my drawing club?
③ Could you tell me how to vote in the election?
④ Can you help me make posters for the election?
⑤ Would you run in the next school president election?

[16~17] 다음을 듣고, 물음에 답하시오.

16 여자가 하는 말의 주제로 가장 적절한 것은?

① downsides of fatty food
② healthy foods for breakfast
③ ways to avoid eating snacks
④ easy foods to cook in 5 minutes
⑤ the importance of a balanced diet

17 언급된 음식이 <u>아닌</u> 것은?

① eggs　　② cheese　　③ potatoes
④ yogurt　　⑤ berries

녹음 내용을 다시 듣고, 빈칸을 채워 넣으세요.

01

M Good afternoon, this is the building manager, Richard Carson. We are planning to _____ _____ _____ _____ on our building next week. The working hours will be from 9 a.m. to 6 p.m. Don't be surprised to see workers outside your windows. Please _____ _____ _____ _____ while they are painting. There might be some smell from the paint. But don't worry. It is totally _____ _____ _____. Sorry for any inconvenience and thank you for your cooperation.

02

M Hello, Veronica.

W Hi, Jason. I heard that you are trying to _____ _____ _____ _____ these days. How is it going?

M You know what? I already got it. Look!

W Oh, good for you! How was the driving test?

M Well, while taking the driving test, I _____ _____ _____ because some people were driving so fast.

W But there are _____ _____ _____ everywhere.

M Right, there are. But so many drivers ignore speed limits these days.

W That's terrible. Those drivers could cause _____ _____ _____.

M That's true. Driving too fast can be dangerous for everybody.

W Exactly. In my opinion, all drivers should follow the speed limits.

M I totally agree with you.

03

W Excuse me. Can you help me find some books for my homework?

M Sure. What is your homework about?

W It's for my history class. The topic is _____ _____ _____ France and Germany.

M What about this world history book?

W _____ _____ _____. Do you have any other books?

M I can also recommend this European history book.

W Great. How many books can I borrow at a time?

M You can _____ _____ _____ _____ _____ for three weeks each.

W Okay. I'll take these two books, then.

M All right. *[Beep sound]* Don't _____ _____ _____ them on time.

04

M Honey, come to Lucy's room. Look at _____ _____ _____ for her.

W It looks great. Is that a toy bear on the bed?

M Yes. That's right. She can sleep with the toy bear.

W It's cute. Oh, and I like the round clock on the wall.

M The round clock _____ _____ _____ the room, doesn't it? How do you like the family picture next to the window?

W That's so sweet. I also love the striped curtains on the window.

M I'm happy you like them. _____ _____ _____ _____ the star-shaped rug on the floor?

W It is lovely. Lucy will feel safe and warm on the rug.

M Looks like everything's prepared.

W Thanks, honey. You've _____ _____ _____ _____.

05

W David, did you fix your bicycle yesterday?

M Yes. Luckily, I _____ _____ _____ _____ it by myself. How was your soccer practice, Christine?

W A new coach came to our soccer club and we practiced very hard.

M You _____ _____ _____ _____. Do you still want to see a movie this afternoon?

W Of course, I booked the tickets two weeks ago.

M All right. Let's get going.

W Wait, did you email your science report to Mr. Smith? _____ _____ _____.

M *[Pause]* Oh, no! I finished it but forgot to send it. What should I do?

W Why don't you send it before meeting me at the movie theater?

M Good idea. _____ _____ _____ _____ and send the report, but can you buy some popcorn for me before I get there?

W No problem. See you there.

06

M Good morning. Welcome to Happy Land.

W Hello. I'd like to buy some tickets. How much are they?

M $20 for the amusement park and $10 for the water park. _____ _____ _____ do you need?

W We're five people in total, and we only want to go to the amusement park.

M Okay. Do you have _____ _____ _____?

W I printed out a birthday coupon from your website. It's my birthday today.

M It's your birthday? Just let me check your ID, please.

W Here you are.

M Oh, happy birthday! With your birthday coupon, _____ _____ _____ _____.

W That's great. Please give me five tickets including my ticket.

M Let me see. That'll be four people _____ _____ _____ _____, and one person with a birthday coupon.

W Right. Here is my credit card.

07

W Hi, Alex. How is it going?

M I'm good. Thanks. I've just finished my English project. How about you, Tracy?

W I'm _____ _____ _____ _____ for my food booth.

M A food booth? What for?

W My school festival is next Tuesday. I'm running a food booth that day.

M That is so cool. What is _____ _____ _____?

W We're making sandwiches. You should come.

M I'd love to, but I can't.

W You can't? I was really _____ _____ _____ _____ you at my school.

M I'm terribly sorry. I have to practice for a band audition.

W Oh, I see. Well, _____ _____ _____ your audition.

M Thank you.

08

[Telephone rings.]

W Hello, this is the World Culture Center. How can I help you?

M Hi, I'm calling about a Spanish culture class for my teenage son.

W Okay. We have _____ _____ _____ for teenagers.

M Great. Who teaches it?

W A Korean teacher and a native speaker teach it together.

M _____ _____ _____ _____ are there in the class?

W Students can cook traditional foods, learn new words, and _____ _____ _____ _____.

M On what day is the class?

W It's on Wednesday and Friday afternoons.

M I see. Is there anything my son should prepare before the class?

W He just _____ _____ _____ a pen and a notebook. The center provides all the other class materials.

M Perfect. Thanks for the information.

09

W Good afternoon, residents. This is the head of the Pineville Community Center. We're holding the Summer Flea Market for one week. _____ _____ _____ in the parking lot of Pineville Middle School. You can get many different kinds of items such as toys and candles _____ _____ _____. You can also sell any of your own used items if they are _____ _____ _____.
On the first day, every resident visiting the market will _____ _____ _____ _____ as a gift. For more information, please check out the community center's website.

10

W Kyle, I'm looking for some sneakers. Can you help me find some good ones?

M Of course. Let me see... *[Pause]* Look. These are the _____ _____ _____.

W Wow, they all look so cool. It's hard to choose among them.

M Well, _____ _____ _____?

W I don't want to spend more than 80 dollars.

M All right. Which style do you want, active or casual?

W I prefer casual ones. I think they match my clothes better.

M Good. And I'd like to recommend waterproof shoes for rainy days.

W Okay, I will _____ _____ _____.

M So you have two options left. Which color do you prefer?

W Most of my shoes are black, so I'll buy white ones this time.

M You _____ _____ _____ _____.

11

W Justin, what are you reading?

M An advertisement. _____ _____ _____ _____ at Will's Bookstore downtown.

W _____ _____ _____ event is it?

M ▨▨▨▨▨▨▨▨▨▨▨▨▨▨▨▨▨▨▨▨▨▨▨▨▨▨

12

M You _____ _____ _____. What's wrong, Liz?

W I didn't do well on my presentation yesterday.

M Sorry about that. To help take your mind off of it, _____ _____ _____ a nice meal?

W ▨▨▨▨▨▨▨▨▨▨▨▨▨▨▨▨▨▨▨▨▨▨▨▨▨▨

13

M Jenny, what class do you want to take this summer vacation?

W Well, *[Pause]* _____ _____ _____ the guitar class.

M Cool! I'm interested in playing the guitar, too.

W Really? It _____ _____ _____ if we took the class together.

M I know, but I am thinking of taking a math class instead. I didn't do well _____ _____ _____ _____.

W Oh, there is a math class? I didn't know that.

M Yes. Mrs. Kim said she is offering a math class for first graders.

W That _____ _____ _____ _____ to improve my skills, too. Where can I check the schedule for the math class?

M ▨▨▨▨▨▨▨▨▨▨▨▨▨▨▨▨▨▨▨▨▨▨▨▨▨▨

14

M Hi, Claire! How are you doing?

W I'm good. You're looking great!

M Thanks. _____ _____ _____ _____ these days.

W I need to start working out, too. What kind of exercise do you do?

M I _____ _____ and some stretching at home.

W At home? Do you exercise alone?

M Yes and no. I _____ _____ with other people.

W Exercising online with others? What do you mean by that?

M I'm taking an online fitness course. We _____ _____ _____ on the Internet every evening at 7.

W ▨▨▨▨▨▨▨▨▨▨▨▨▨▨▨▨▨▨▨▨▨▨▨

15

M Ted is a high school student. He is planning to _____ _____ _____ _____ this year. He really wants to win the election. He thinks using posters is an effective way to _____ _____ _____ _____ on his schoolmates. But he is not good at drawing. His friend, Monica, is a member of a drawing club and she _____ _____ _____ _____. So, he wants to ask her to help him draw posters. In this situation, what would Ted most likely say to Monica?

Ted ▨▨▨▨▨▨▨▨▨▨▨▨▨▨▨▨▨▨▨▨▨▨▨

16~17

W Good morning, listeners. This is your host Rachel at the Morning Radio Show. What do you eat for breakfast? Today I will introduce a healthy breakfast food list. Eggs are _____ _____ _____ because they are high in protein. High-protein foods such as eggs provide energy for the brain. Cheese is another good option. It _____ _____ so it supports weight loss. Yogurt is also great to eat in the morning. It contains probiotics that _____ _____ _____. Eating berries such as blueberries or strawberries is another perfect way to start the morning. They are _____ _____ _____ than most other fruits, but _____ _____ _____. Add them to yogurt for a tasty breakfast. Start every day with a healthy meal. Thank you.

1번부터 17번까지는 듣고 답하는 문제입니다. 1번부터 15번까지는 한 번만 들려주고, 16번부터 17번까지는 두 번 들려줍니다. 방송을 잘 듣고 답을 하시기 바랍니다.

01 다음을 듣고, 남자가 하는 말의 목적으로 가장 적절한 것을 고르시오.
① 농구 리그 참가 등록 방법의 변경을 알리려고
② 확정된 농구 리그 시합 일정을 발표하려고
③ 농구 리그의 심판을 추가 모집하려고
④ 농구 리그 경기 관람을 권장하려고
⑤ 농구 리그 우승 상품을 안내하려고

02 대화를 듣고, 여자의 의견으로 가장 적절한 것을 고르시오.
① 평소에 피부 상태를 잘 관찰할 필요가 있다.
② 여드름을 치료하려면 피부과 병원에 가야 한다.
③ 얼굴을 손으로 만지는 것은 얼굴 피부에 해롭다.
④ 지성 피부를 가진 사람은 자주 세수를 해야 한다.
⑤ 손을 자주 씻는 것은 감염병 예방에 도움이 된다.

03 대화를 듣고, 두 사람의 관계를 가장 잘 나타낸 것을 고르시오.
① 방송 작가 – 연출자
② 만화가 – 환경 운동가
③ 촬영 감독 – 동화 작가
④ 토크쇼 진행자 – 기후학자
⑤ 제품 디자이너 – 영업 사원

04 대화를 듣고, 그림에서 대화의 내용과 일치하지 <u>않는</u> 것을 고르시오.

05 대화를 듣고, 여자가 남자에게 부탁한 일로 가장 적절한 것을 고르시오.
① 장난감 사 오기   ② 풍선 달기
③ 케이크 가져오기   ④ 탁자 옮기기
⑤ 아이들 데려오기

06 대화를 듣고, 남자가 지불할 금액을 고르시오. [3점]
① $14   ② $16   ③ $18   ④ $20   ⑤ $22

07 대화를 듣고, 두 사람이 오늘 실험을 할 수 <u>없는</u> 이유를 고르시오.
① 실험용 키트가 배달되지 않아서
② 실험 주제를 변경해야 해서
③ 과학실을 예약하지 못해서
④ 보고서를 작성해야 해서
⑤ 남자가 감기에 걸려서

08 대화를 듣고, Stanville Free-cycle에 관해 언급되지 <u>않은</u> 것을 고르시오.
① 참가 대상   ② 행사 장소   ③ 주차 가능 여부
④ 행사 시작일   ⑤ 금지 품목

09 River Valley Music Camp에 관한 다음 내용을 듣고, 일치하지 <u>않는</u> 것을 고르시오.
① 4월 11일부터 5일 동안 진행된다.
② 학교 오케스트라 단원이 아니어도 참가할 수 있다.
③ 자신의 악기를 가져오거나 학교에서 빌릴 수 있다.
④ 마지막 날에 공연을 촬영한다.
⑤ 참가 인원에는 제한이 없다.

10 다음 표를 보면서 대화를 듣고, 여자가 주문할 소형 진공 청소기를 고르시오.

Handheld Vacuum Cleaners

	Model	Price	Working Time	Weight	Washable Filter
①	A	$50	8 minutes	2.5 kg	×
②	B	$80	12 minutes	2.0 kg	○
③	C	$100	15 minutes	1.8 kg	○
④	D	$120	20 minutes	1.8 kg	×
⑤	E	$150	25 minutes	1.6 kg	○

11 대화를 듣고, 남자의 마지막 말에 대한 여자의 응답으로 가장 적절한 것을 고르시오.

① Why don't you rinse your eyes with clean water?
② Can you explain more about the air pollution?
③ I need to get myself a new pair of glasses.
④ I agree that fine dust is a serious problem.
⑤ We should go outside and take a walk.

12 대화를 듣고, 여자의 마지막 말에 대한 남자의 응답으로 가장 적절한 것을 고르시오.

① That's not fair. I booked this seat first.
② Thank you. My friend will be glad to know it.
③ You're welcome. Feel free to ask me anything.
④ Not at all. I don't mind changing seats with you.
⑤ That's okay. I think the seat next to it is available.

13 대화를 듣고, 남자의 마지막 말에 대한 여자의 응답으로 가장 적절한 것을 고르시오.

Woman: _____

① Smells good. Can I try the pizza?
② Great. I'll bring chips and popcorn.
③ No problem. I'll cancel the tickets.
④ Sorry. I don't like watching baseball.
⑤ Sure. Here's the hammer I borrowed.

14 대화를 듣고, 여자의 마지막 말에 대한 남자의 응답으로 가장 적절한 것을 고르시오. [3점]

Man: _____

① Exactly. This is a best-selling novel.
② Sounds cool. I'll join a book club, too.
③ Not really. Books make good presents.
④ New year's resolutions are hard to keep.
⑤ Let's buy some books for your book club.

15 다음 상황 설명을 듣고, Brian이 Sally에게 할 말로 가장 적절한 것을 고르시오. [3점]

Brian: _____

① You shouldn't touch a guide dog without permission.
② The dog would be happy if we give it some food.
③ I'm sure it's smart enough to be a guide dog.
④ I suggest that you walk your dog every day.
⑤ I'm afraid that dogs are not allowed in here.

[16~17] 다음을 듣고, 물음에 답하시오.

16 여자가 하는 말의 주제로 가장 적절한 것은?

① activities that help build muscles
② ways to control stress in daily life
③ types of joint problems in elderly people
④ low-impact exercises for people with bad joints
⑤ importance of daily exercise for controlling weight

17 언급된 운동이 <u>아닌</u> 것은?

① swimming   ② cycling
③ horseback riding   ④ bowling
⑤ walking

01

M Good afternoon, everybody. This is Student President Sam Wilson. As you know, the lunch basketball league will begin soon. Many students _____ _____ _____ joining the league and waiting for the sign-up sheet to be handed out at the gym. For easier access, _____ _____ _____ _____ the registration method. Instead of going to the gym to register, simply log into the school website and _____ _____ the registration form online. Thank you for listening and let's have a good league.

02

W Daniel, what are you doing in front of the mirror?

M I have skin problems these days. I'm trying to pop these pimples on my face.

W Pimples are _____ _____, but I wouldn't do that.

M Why not?

W When you pop them with your hands, you're touching your face.

M Are you saying that I shouldn't touch my face?

W Exactly. You know our hands _____ _____ _____ bacteria, right?

M So?

W You'll be spreading bacteria all over your face with your hands. _____ _____ _____ your skin problems.

M Oh, I didn't know that.

W Touching your face with your hands is bad for your skin.

M Okay, _____ _____ _____.

03

M Excuse me. You're Chloe Jones, aren't you?

W Yes, I am. Have we met before?

M No, but I'm _____ _____ _____ _____ yours. I've watched your speeches on climate change, and they're very inspiring.

W Thank you. I'm so glad to hear that.

M And, I also think your _____ _____ _____ has been very successful.

W As an environmental activist, that means a lot to me.

M May I make a suggestion? I thought it'd be nice if more children could hear your ideas.

W That's _____ _____ _____ _____. Do you have any good ideas?

M Actually, I'm a cartoonist. Perhaps I can make comic books _____ _____ _____ _____.

W That is a wonderful idea. Can I contact you later to discuss it more?

M Sure. By the way, my name is Jack Perse. Here's my business card.

04

W Yesterday, I decorated my fish tank like a beach.

M I'd like to see it. Do you have a picture?

W Sure. Here. *[Pause]* Do you recognize the boat in the bottom left corner?

M Yes. It's the one I gave you, isn't it?

W Right. _____ _____ _____ in the fish tank, doesn't it?

M It does. I love the beach chair in the center.

W Yeah. I like it, too.

M I see a starfish _____ _____ _____.

W Isn't it cute? And do you see these two surf boards on the right side of the picture?

M Yeah. I like how you put both of them _____ _____ _____.

W I thought that'd look cool.

M Your fish in _____ _____ _____ _____ looks happy with its new home.

W I hope so.

05

[Cell phone rings.]

M Hello, honey. I'm on the way home. How's setting up Mike's birthday party going?

W Good, but I still _____ _____ _____ _____. Mike and his friends will get here soon.

M Should I pick up the birthday cake?

W No, that's okay. I already did that.

M Then, do you want me to put up the balloons around the doorway when I get there?

W I'll _____ _____ _____ it. Can you take the table out to the front yard?

M Sure. Are we having the party outside?

W Yes. The weather is beautiful so I made _____ _____ _____ _____.

M Great. The kids can play with water guns in the front yard.

W Good idea. I'll go to the garage and _____ _____ _____ _____.

06

W Welcome to Green Eco Shop. How can I help you?

M Hi, do you sell _____ _____?

W Yes, we have a few types over here. Which do you like?

M Hmm.... How much are these?

W They're $2 each. They are made from bamboo.

M All right. I'll take four of them.

W _____ _____. Anything else?

M I also need bath sponges.

W They're _____ _____ _____. They're plastic-free and only $3 each.

M Okay. I'll also take four of them. That'll be all.

W If you have a store membership, you can get a 10% discount _____ _____ _____ _____.

M Great. I'm a member. Here are my credit and membership cards.

07

[Cell phone rings.]

M Hey, Suji. Where are you?

W I'm in the library _____ _____ _____. I'll be heading out to the science lab for our experiment in a couple of minutes.

M I guess you haven't checked my message yet. We can't do the experiment today.

W Really? Isn't _____ _____ _____ today?

M Yes, it is, but I canceled our reservation.

W Why? Are you still _____ _____ _____ _____?

M No, I'm fine now.

W That's good. Then why aren't we doing the experiment today? We need to hand in the science report by next Monday.

M Unfortunately, the experiment kit _____ _____ _____ yet. It'll arrive tomorrow.

W Oh, well. The experiment has to wait one more day, then.

08

W Honey, did you see the poster about the Stanville Free-cycle?

M Free-cycle? What is that?

W It's another way of recycling. You _____ _____ _____ you don't need and anybody can take them for free.

M Oh, it's like one man's garbage is another man's treasure. Who can participate?

W It's open to everyone living in Stanville.

M Great. Where _____ _____ _____ _____?

W At Rose Park on Second Street.

M When does the event start?

W It starts on April 12 and _____ _____ _____ _____.

M Let's see what we can free-cycle, starting from the cupboard.

W Okay. But breakable items like glass dishes or cups won't be accepted.

M I see. I'll _____ _____ _____ _____.

09

M Hello, River Valley High School students. This is your music teacher, Mr. Stailor. Starting on April 11, we _____ _____ _____ have the River Valley Music Camp for five days. You don't need to be a member of the school orchestra to join the camp. You may _____ _____ _____ _____ or you can borrow one from the school. On the last day of camp, we are going to _____ _____ _____ and play it on screen at the school summer festival. Please keep in mind the camp _____ _____ _____ 50 students. Sign-ups start this Friday, on a first-come-first-served basis. Come and make music together!

10

W Ben, do you have a minute?

M Sure. What is it?

W I'm trying to buy a handheld vacuum cleaner among these five models. Could you _____ _____ _____ _____?

M Okay. How much are you willing to spend?

W No more than $130.

M Then we can cross this one out. What about the working time?

W I think it should _____ _____ _____ 10 minutes.

M Then that narrows it down to these three.

W Should I go with one of the lighter ones?

M Yes. Lighter ones _____ _____ _____ _____ while cleaning.

W All right. What about the filter?

M The one with a washable filter would be _____ _____ _____.

W I got it. Then I'll order this one.

11

M _____ _____ _____ _____ today.

W Too bad. Maybe _____ _____ _____ in your eyes.

M You're probably right. What should I do?

W ▨▨▨▨▨▨▨▨▨▨▨▨▨▨▨▨▨▨▨

12

W Excuse me. Would you mind if I sit here?

M I'm sorry, but it's my friend's seat. He'll be _____ _____ _____ _____.

W Oh, I didn't know that. _____ _____ _____ you.

M ▨▨▨▨▨▨▨▨▨▨▨▨▨▨▨▨▨▨▨

13

M Hey, Jasmine.

W Hi, Kurt. Are you going to be at home tomorrow afternoon?

M Yeah, I'm going to watch the baseball game with my friends at home.

W Good. Can I _____ _____ _____ _____ and give you back the hammer I borrowed?

M Sure. Come over any time. By the way, _____ _____ _____ join us and watch the game?

W I'd love to. Which teams are playing?

M Green Thunders and Black Dragons.

W _____ _____ _____. What time should I come?

M Come at five. We'll have pizza before the game.

W Perfect. Do you want me to bring anything?

M Maybe some snacks to eat _____ _____ _____ _____.

W ▨▨▨▨▨▨▨▨▨▨▨▨▨▨▨▨▨▨▨

14

W Hi, Tom.

M Hi, Jane. What are you reading?

W It's a novel by Charles Dickens. I'm going to talk about it with my book club members this weekend.

M Oh, you're _____ _____ _____ _____?

W Yes. I joined it a few months ago. And now I read much more than before.

M Really? Actually one of my _____ _____ _____ is to read more books.

W Then, joining a book club will surely help.

M Hmm.... _____ _____ _____ can I get if I join one?

W You can also share your reading experiences with others.

M That'd be nice.

W Yeah, it really _____ _____ _____ . I really recommend you to join a book club.

M

15

M Brian and Sally are walking down the street together. A blind man and his guide dog are walking towards them. Sally likes dogs very much, so she _____ _____ _____ _____ the guide dog. Brian doesn't think that Sally should do that. The guide dog needs to _____ _____ _____ the blind person. If someone touches the dog, the dog can lose its focus. So Brian wants to tell Sally not to touch the guide dog _____ _____ _____ of the dog owner. In this situation, what would Brian most likely say to Sally?

Brian

16~17

W Hello, everybody. Welcome to the health workshop. I'm Alanna Reyes, the head trainer from Eastwood Fitness Center. As you know, joints are body parts that link bones together. And doing certain physical activities _____ _____ _____ the joints. But the good news is that people with bad joints can still do certain exercises. They have _____ _____ _____ on the joints. Here are some examples. The first is swimming. While swimming, the water supports your body weight. The second is cycling. You put almost no stress _____ _____ _____ _____ when you pedal smoothly. Horseback riding is another exercise that puts very little stress on your knees. Lastly, walking is great because it's low-impact, unlike running. If you have bad joints, don't give up exercising. Instead, _____ _____ and _____ _____!

1번부터 17번까지는 듣고 답하는 문제입니다. 1번부터 15번까지는 한 번만 들려주고, 16번부터 17번까지는 두 번 들려줍니다. 방송을 잘 듣고 답을 하시기 바랍니다.

01 다음을 듣고, 남자가 하는 말의 목적으로 가장 적절한 것을 고르시오.

① 지하철 앱 출시를 홍보하려고
② 지하철 연장 운행을 안내하려고
③ 지하철 운행 지연에 대해 사과하려고
④ 지하철 시설 보수 공사 일정을 공지하려고
⑤ 지하철 내 영화 촬영에 대한 양해를 구하려고

02 대화를 듣고, 여자의 의견으로 가장 적절한 것을 고르시오.

① 날씨가 더울수록 수분 보충이 중요하다.
② 적당한 준비 운동이 부상 위험을 줄인다.
③ 흐린 날에도 자외선 차단제를 발라야 한다.
④ 햇빛이 강한 날에는 야외 활동을 자제해야 한다.
⑤ 화상을 입었을 때 신속하게 응급 처치를 해야 한다.

03 대화를 듣고, 두 사람의 관계를 가장 잘 나타낸 것을 고르시오.

① 세차장 직원 – 고객
② 청소 업체 직원 – 집주인
③ 중고차 판매원 – 구매자
④ 분실물 센터 직원 – 방문자
⑤ 액세서리 디자이너 – 의뢰인

04 대화를 듣고, 그림에서 대화의 내용과 일치하지 않는 것을 고르시오.

05 대화를 듣고, 남자가 할 일로 가장 적절한 것을 고르시오.

① 가방 준비하기
② 배지 가져오기
③ 스크린 점검하기
④ 동영상 편집하기
⑤ 포스터 업로드하기

06 대화를 듣고, 여자가 지불할 금액을 고르시오. [3점]

① $45 ② $50 ③ $54 ④ $55 ⑤ $60

07 대화를 듣고, 남자가 London Walking Tour에 참여하지 못한 이유를 고르시오.

① 발목에 통증이 있어서
② 뮤지컬을 관람해야 해서
③ 투어 예약을 하지 못해서
④ 기념품을 사러 가야 해서
⑤ 날씨로 인해 투어가 취소되어서

08 대화를 듣고, Winter Lake Festival에 관해 언급되지 않은 것을 고르시오.

① 기간
② 장소
③ 입장료
④ 기념품
⑤ 활동 종류

09 Mascot Design Contest에 관한 다음 내용을 듣고, 일치하지 않는 것을 고르시오.

① 팀을 사랑하는 누구든 참여할 수 있다.
② 디자인은 팀 슬로건과 관련되어야 한다.
③ 수상작은 팬 투표로 선정될 것이다.
④ 수상자는 상으로 시즌 티켓을 받게 될 것이다.
⑤ 참가 희망자는 디자인을 이메일로 보내야 한다.

10 다음 표를 보면서 대화를 듣고, 두 사람이 예약할 캠핑장을 고르시오.

2021 Best Campsites

	Campsite	Location	Price (per night)	Type	Kids' Playground
①	A	Seaside	$65	tent	✕
②	B	Jungle Hut	$70	tent	○
③	C	Rose Valley	$85	camping car	○
④	D	Blue Forest	$90	camping car	✕
⑤	E	Pine Island	$110	camping car	○

11 대화를 듣고, 남자의 마지막 말에 대한 여자의 응답으로 가장 적절한 것을 고르시오.

① It takes an hour by bus.
② It's bigger than your office.
③ You should've left home earlier.
④ The company moved last month.
⑤ I had a hard time getting the job.

12 대화를 듣고, 여자의 마지막 말에 대한 남자의 응답으로 가장 적절한 것을 고르시오.

① Okay. I'll order a shrimp pizza.
② Thanks. You're good at cooking.
③ No. The pizza isn't delivered yet.
④ Sure. You can come over anytime.
⑤ Yes. Skipping meals is bad for your health.

13 대화를 듣고, 남자의 마지막 말에 대한 여자의 응답으로 가장 적절한 것을 고르시오.

Woman: _____

① Too late. The meeting is already over.
② Sure. There are lots of French cookbooks.
③ I agree. You spend too much time reading.
④ No. We're not allowed to eat in the library.
⑤ You're right. I'll change the reservation now.

14 대화를 듣고, 여자의 마지막 말에 대한 남자의 응답으로 가장 적절한 것을 고르시오. [3점]

Man: _____

① Sorry. I forgot to bring my laptop.
② Then, I'd like to replace the battery.
③ Well, the screen still doesn't work well.
④ Good. A new repair shop opened yesterday.
⑤ Actually, I don't have a receipt for a refund.

15 다음 상황 설명을 듣고, Amy가 Terry에게 할 말로 가장 적절한 것을 고르시오. [3점]

Amy: _____

① How about using a colorful font on the poster?
② You'd better inform your friends of the concert.
③ Can you make the letter size bigger on the poster?
④ Why don't we hold a concert in the school festival?
⑤ You should put important information on the poster.

[16~17] 다음을 듣고, 물음에 답하시오.

16 여자가 하는 말의 주제로 가장 적절한 것은?

① ways to prevent plant diseases
② factors that affect plant growth
③ benefits of growing plants at home
④ plants that can grow in shaded areas
⑤ materials that help plants grow in shade

17 언급된 식물이 아닌 것은?

① lemon balm   ② ivy
③ mint   ④ camellia
⑤ lavender

Dictation

녹음 내용을 다시 듣고, 빈칸을 채워 넣으세요.

01

[Chime bell rings.]

M Hello, passengers. I'm James Walker from the Greenville Subway System. As you know, the international film festival will be held in our city next month. Throughout the festival, some movies will run _____ _____ _____ _____. So, for our citizens' convenience, the Greenville City Council has decided to provide longer subway service hours during the festival. All Greenville subway lines will _____ _____ _____ while the festival is going on. You can easily check the extended service schedules using the Greenville Subway App. I hope you can _____ _____ _____ _____ the festival experience with our services. Thank you.

02

W Good morning, Jason. It's sports day today. Do you have everything you need?

M Yes, Mom. I put a water bottle, some snacks, and a towel in my bag. Is there anything I forgot?

W What about sunblock? Did you _____ _____ _____?

M Sunblock? It's not sunny outside.

W Jason, you _____ _____ _____ even on a cloudy day.

M But I don't feel the sun in weather like this.

W Even if you don't feel the sun on your skin, the harmful light from the sun can _____ _____ _____ because the clouds don't block it.

M Really? You mean I can still get a sunburn even on a cloudy day?

W Yes. That's why you shouldn't _____ _____ _____ sunblock even if it's not sunny outside.

M I didn't know that. I'll put it on now.

03

M Hello, Ms. Green. You came _____ _____ _____.

W Really? I thought I was early.

M No. Your car is over there. Follow me, please.

W Wow. All the dirt is gone. It looks like a new car.

M Yeah. But some stains were difficult to remove. It's better to _____ _____ _____ _____ right after it gets dirty.

W I _____ _____ _____ _____ _____ for a month, so I didn't have time. I'll keep that in mind.

M Anyway, while cleaning the inside, we found this earring under the driver's seat.

W Really? I thought I had lost that. Thank you.

M You're welcome. Would you like to pay _____ _____ _____ or _____ _____?

W I'll pay in cash. Here you are.

M Okay. [Pause] Here is your receipt. And this is a discount coupon for our car wash center. You can use it on your next visit.

W That's nice. Thank you.

04

W Hi, Harry. Congratulations on your wedding. Did you _____ _____ the new house?

M I just finished the living room. Look at this picture, Linda.

W Wow. I love the striped curtains on the window.

M Thanks. Do you see those two cushions on the sofa? My sister made them _____ _____ _____.

W That's lovely. Oh, you put a round table on the rug.

M Yeah. We _____ _____ _____ _____ around the table. What do you think of the clock on the bookshelf?

W It looks good in that room. By the way, is that a plant under the calendar?

M Yes. I placed it there because the plant _____ _____ _____ _____ _____.

W You decorated your house really well.

M Thanks. I'll invite you over when we have the housewarming party.

05

M Jane, the Stop Using Plastic campaign starts tomorrow. Let's do _____ _____ _____.

W Okay, Robin. I just finished editing a video clip about plastic waste.

M Then, I'm going to check the screen that we'll use for the video.

W No worries. I've already done it, and _____ _____ _____.

M That's nice. I uploaded a campaign poster on our organization's website.

W Yeah. Some of my friends saw it and texted me they're coming.

M My friends, too. They _____ _____ _____ _____ in the reusable bag decorating activity. The bags are ready in that box.

W Good. By the way, where are the badges you ordered for visitors?

M Oh, I left the badges in my car. I'll bring them right away.

W Great. _____ _____ _____ everything is prepared.

06

M Welcome to Kids Clothing Club. How may I help you?

W I'm looking for a muffler for my son. He's 5 years old.

M Okay. Follow me. *[Pause]* This red muffler is one of _____ _____ _____ in our shop.

W I love the color. How much is it?

M It's $50. This one is popular because of the cartoon character here.

W Oh, that's my son's favorite character. I'll buy one red muffler, then.

M Great. _____ _____?

W How much are these winter socks?

M A pair of socks is $5.

W All right. I'll buy two pairs.

M So, one red muffler and _____ _____ _____ winter socks, right?

W Yes. Can I use this discount coupon?

M Of course. With that coupon, you can _____ _____ _____ the total price.

W Good. Here's my credit card.

07

W Hi, Jeremy. How was your trip to London?

M It was fantastic, Julia. I watched the musical _____ _____.

W Good. What about the London Walking Tour? Did you enjoy it?

M Unfortunately, I couldn't join the tour.

W Why? Didn't you say you booked it?

M Yes. I _____ _____ _____ for the tour in advance.

W Oh, was the tour canceled because of the weather?

M No. The weather was no problem at all.

W Then, why couldn't you join the tour?

M Actually, I fell down the day before the tour, so I had some pain in my ankle. That's why _____ _____ _____ _____.

W I'm sorry to hear that. Is it okay, now?

M Yes. It's completely fine now. Oh, I _____ _____ _____ the souvenir I bought for you. I'll bring it tomorrow.

W That's so sweet. Thanks.

08

M What are you doing, Laura?

W Hi, Tim. I'm looking for winter festivals to visit _____ _____.

M Is there anything good?

W Yes, look at this. There is a new local event called the Winter Lake Festival.

M Awesome. When does it start?

W December 18th and it'll be held for two weeks.

M Cool. Oh, _____ _____ _____ in Stevenson Park.

W Great. It's near our school. If you don't have any plans during vacation, let's go together.

M Of course. Is there _____ _____ _____?

W Yes. Here, it says $3. It's not expensive.

M Good. Look! There are so _____ _____ _____ _____ to enjoy.

W Yeah, there is ice skating, ice fishing, and a snowball fight.

M They all sound exciting. Let's have fun there.

09

W Hello, supporters! I'm Christine Miller, manager of Western Football Club. This year, we're holding a Mascot Design Contest to celebrate our team's 1st championship. Anyone who loves our team can _____ _____ this contest. The mascot design should _____ _____ _____ our team's slogan "One team, one spirit." The winning design will be chosen through a fan vote. And the winner will receive a team uniform _____ _____ _____. People who want to participate should send their design by email by December 5th. _____ _____ _____ and love for our team through active participation. For more information, please visit our website. Thank you.

10

W Honey, what are you looking at?

M This is a list of the best campsites in 2021. _____ _____ _____ to one of them next month?

W Sounds great. Let me see. [Pause] There are five different campsites.

M Yeah. Since we went to Seaside campsite last time, _____ _____ _____ the other four.

W Good. Hmm, I don't want to spend more than $100 per night. It's too expensive.

M I agree with that. What do you think of staying in a camping car?

W Oh, I want to try it. It'll _____ _____ _____ _____.

M Then, we can choose between these two.

W What about going to this campsite? Since this has a kids' playground, our children can have more fun.

M Cool! I'll _____ _____ _____ for this campsite.

11

M Kate, I heard your company moved to a new office. How is it?

W It's all good _____ _____ _____. It's far from my house.

M Oh, really? _____ _____ _____ _____ _____ to get there?

W ▓▓▓▓▓▓▓▓▓▓▓▓▓▓▓▓▓▓▓▓▓▓▓

12

W Honey, you know my nephew _____ _____ _____ this evening. How about ordering pizza for dinner?

M Sure. Which topping _____ _____ _____, grilled beef or shrimp?

W Oh, he doesn't like beef. He loves seafood.

M ▓▓▓▓▓▓▓▓▓▓▓▓▓▓▓▓▓▓▓▓▓▓▓

13

M Honey, did you read this leaflet on the table?

W Not yet. What's it about?

M It says the local children's library _____ _____ _____ _____ some events to celebrate their reopening.

W Is there anything good?

M Let me see. [Pause] There will be a Meet-the-Author event. Rebecca Moore is coming.

W Oh, she's one of our son's favorite writers.

M Yes. He'll be excited if he can _____ _____ _____ _____.

W Let's take him to that event. When is it?

M It's next Saturday, 1 p.m.

W But we have a lunch reservation at the French restaurant at that time.

M Oh, I forgot. Then _____ _____ _____ lunch? It's a rare chance to meet the author.

W ▓▓▓▓▓▓▓▓▓▓▓▓▓▓▓▓▓▓▓▓▓▓▓

14

[Cell phone rings.]

W This is Fairview Laptop Repair. How may I help you?

M Hello, this is David Brown. I _____ _____ _____ this morning.

W Oh, Mr. Brown. You requested the screen repair yesterday, right?

M Yes. Is there any problem?

W The screen is all repaired. But we found another problem with your laptop. You _____ _____ _____ the battery.

M Oh, I didn't know that. How bad is it?

W Even when the battery is fully charged, it _____ _____ _____ than an hour.

M Really? How much does it cost to change the battery?

W It's $70. _____ _____ _____ now.

M That sounds great. But, I'm worried it'll delay the laptop pick-up time, 5 p.m. today.

W Don't worry. You can still pick it up at that time.

M ▨▨▨▨▨▨▨▨▨▨▨▨▨▨▨▨▨▨▨▨

15

M Amy is the leader of a high school band and Terry is one of the band members. The band is going to hold a mini concert in the school festival, and Terry is _____ _____ _____ _____ a concert poster. When he completes the poster, he shows it to the band members. Even though the poster has _____ _____ _____ _____, it's hard to read it because the size of the letters is too small. Amy thinks if Terry changes the font size to a larger one, it could be easier to notice. So, Amy wants to suggest that Terry _____ _____ _____ of the letters on the poster. In this situation, what would Amy most likely say to Terry?

Amy ▨▨▨▨▨▨▨▨▨▨▨▨▨▨▨▨▨▨▨▨

16~17

W Hello, students. Previously, we discussed why gardening is a great hobby. But not everyone has a sunny front yard. So, today we'll learn about plants that _____ _____ _____ _____. First, lemon balm survives in full shade. So if your place is sunless, it's the plant you should choose. Next, ivy is the ultimate shade-loving plant. Its ability to grow in shade _____ _____ _____ under trees where most plants can't. Also, there's mint. It lives well under low-light conditions, so you can grow it in a small pot indoors. Lastly, camellia grows better in _____ _____. Especially when it's a young plant, it _____ _____ _____ the sun. Many plants like these can live even in the shade. Isn't it fascinating? Now, let's watch a video clip about how to grow these plants.

1번부터 17번까지는 듣고 답하는 문제입니다. 1번부터 15번까지는 한 번만 들려주고, 16번부터 17번까지는 두 번 들려줍니다. 방송을 잘 듣고 답을 하시기 바랍니다.

01 다음을 듣고, 남자가 하는 말의 목적으로 가장 적절한 것을 고르시오.

① 시민 자율 방범 단원을 모집하려고
② 어린이 안전 교육 장소를 안내하려고
③ 초등학교 개교 기념행사를 홍보하려고
④ 학교 주변 제한 속도 준수를 독려하려고
⑤ 시청에서 열리는 공청회 일정을 공지하려고

02 대화를 듣고, 남자의 의견으로 가장 적절한 것을 고르시오.

① 고민이 있을 때는 가족이나 친구와 대화해야 한다.
② 가까운 사람일수록 말을 신중하게 하는 것이 좋다.
③ 사과를 받아들일 수 있는 넓은 마음이 필요하다.
④ 일어나지 않은 일을 미리 걱정할 필요는 없다.
⑤ 가족이라도 개인 공간을 존중해야 한다.

03 대화를 듣고, 두 사람의 관계를 가장 잘 나타낸 것을 고르시오.

① 교사 – 학생
② 방송 작가 – 배우
③ 라디오 진행자 – 청취자
④ 이벤트 업체 직원 – 고객
⑤ 설문 조사원 – 설문 응답자

04 대화를 듣고, 그림에서 대화의 내용과 일치하지 않는 것을 고르시오.

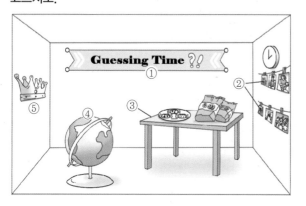

05 대화를 듣고, 남자가 할 일로 가장 적절한 것을 고르시오.

① 생일 카드 쓰기
② 스웨터 구매하기
③ 거실 장식하기
④ 케이크 찾아오기
⑤ 샌드위치 재료 주문하기

06 대화를 듣고, 여자가 지불할 금액을 고르시오. [3점]

① $16 ② $20 ③ $21 ④ $23 ⑤ $26

07 대화를 듣고, 남자가 헬스장 회원권을 연장하지 않은 이유를 고르시오.

① 어깨 부상이 회복되지 않아서
② 운동에 흥미를 잃어서
③ 샤워 시설이 낡고 좁아서
④ 가격이 인상되어서
⑤ 방과후 수업에 참여해야 해서

08 대화를 듣고, Tour of Liberty University에 관해 언급되지 않은 것을 고르시오.

① 날짜
② 활동 내용
③ 참가 가능 인원수
④ 기념품
⑤ 신청 방법

09 Green Action Photo Contest에 관한 다음 내용을 듣고, 일치하지 않는 것을 고르시오.

① 9월 한 달간 사진을 업로드 할 수 있다.
② 정해진 해시태그를 붙이면 자동으로 참가하게 된다.
③ 사진은 5장까지 올릴 수 있다.
④ 우승 상품은 10월 11일까지 직접 찾아가야 한다.
⑤ 우승 사진은 연말까지 마을 웹 사이트에 게시된다.

10 다음 표를 보면서 대화를 듣고, 여자가 주문할 Rolling Cart를 고르시오.

Rolling Cart

	Model	Material	Number of Shelf	Lockable Wheel	Price
①	A	Metal	2	○	$80
②	B	Metal	3	○	$95
③	C	Wood	3	○	$105
④	D	Wood	4	×	$110
⑤	E	Plastic	4	×	$75

11 대화를 듣고, 여자의 마지막 말에 대한 남자의 응답으로 가장 적절한 것을 고르시오.

① Okay. Then let's ask them if they lost their dog.
② Take it easy. This dog is not dangerous at all.
③ Sorry. I tried my best, but I couldn't find it.
④ What a relief! I thought I had lost my dog forever.
⑤ Right! Dog owners must walk their pets twice a day.

12 대화를 듣고, 남자의 마지막 말에 대한 여자의 응답으로 가장 적절한 것을 고르시오.

① We're open from 11 o'clock in the morning.
② Sorry, but all the tables are full right now.
③ Our special for today is barbecue chicken.
④ Thank you for visiting our restaurant.
⑤ I don't have enough time to cook.

13 대화를 듣고, 여자의 마지막 말에 대한 남자의 응답으로 가장 적절한 것을 고르시오. [3점]

Man: _____

① Don't worry. You can book another hotel.
② That's right. You have already paid your bill.
③ Yes. But you don't have to pay for a full day.
④ Sorry. You should have cancelled your reservation.
⑤ Of course. You can stay in the lobby till the afternoon.

14 대화를 듣고, 남자의 마지막 말에 대한 여자의 응답으로 가장 적절한 것을 고르시오. [3점]

Woman: _____

① Oh, no! I can come over today to help you clear it out.
② Never mind. Everyone needs time to make a decision.
③ Okay. We can go to the basement if we're in danger.
④ Yes. Why don't you water your trees more often?
⑤ Sorry. I don't know how to change a light bulb.

15 다음 상황 설명을 듣고, Emily가 Chris에게 할 말로 가장 적절한 것을 고르시오.

Emily: _____

① Luckily, I have finished my homework.
② May I watch the movie with my brother?
③ Thanks, and I'll gratefully enjoy your cookies.
④ I'm sorry, but I need to take care of my brother.
⑤ Will you watch over my brother for just a minute?

[16~17] 다음을 듣고, 물음에 답하시오.

16 여자가 하는 말의 주제로 가장 적절한 것은?

① different animals that are popular in different cultures
② unique sleeping habits that animals use for survival
③ wild animals that are becoming endangered species
④ how animals have changed their ways of eating
⑤ animals that bring people good luck

17 언급된 동물이 <u>아닌</u> 것은?

① bats　　② ducks　　③ chimpanzees
④ giraffes　　⑤ dolphins

Dictation

01

M Hello, citizens of Portland. This is Jerry Wilson, your Mayor. As you know, Port Elementary School has opened, and it is so nice to hear the kids playing. _____ _____ _____ _____ of the students at the school, we've been communicating with the New Jersey State Police and requested that they _____ _____ _____ in the area around the school. This is in response to the many complaints City Hall has received _____ _____ _____, especially in front of the school. Please _____ speed limits for the safety of the kids and your fellow citizens. Thank you for your cooperation. Stay safe and healthy.

02

M Lily, what's wrong? Are you all right?

W Oh, it's nothing.

M Are you sure? You look pretty worried.

W Actually, I _____ _____ _____ to my sister and I feel really bad about it.

M What did you say to her?

W I said she's the worst sister because she wore my favorite jacket again!

M Jeez! She _____ _____ _____ _____ _____ by that.

W Yeah, but I told her not to wear my jacket a million times. She never listens.

M Still, you _____ _____ _____ _____ when you talk to _____ _____ _____ _____.

W I know, but I was so angry.

M People get hurt more easily when someone close to them says mean things.

W Yeah, you're right. I'll apologize to her when I get home.

03

W Hi, listeners! Now we have _____ _____ _____ _____ _____. He has something special to share with us. Hello, you're on the air!

M Hello. Wow! I'm surprised that I _____ _____ _____ you. Thank you for taking my call.

W Sure. Please introduce yourself.

M I'm Jin, a high school student. I'm a big fan of the show.

W Thank you, Jin. By the way, you left a message on our website, didn't you?

M Yes. Today is my parents' 20th wedding anniversary. I wanted to honor them on the show.

W I see. Are your parents listening now?

M Yes, they _____ _____ _____ _____ every day.

W That's great. What is your message to your parents?

M Hmm... Mom and Dad, you're amazing parents. Happy Anniversary to you both!

W What a lovely message! Thank you for calling us today, Jin.

M Thanks again for taking my call.

04

W Hi, Tim. How's everything going with the festival?

M Hey, Julie! It's going great. This is a picture of what our booth will look like.

W What will people do at your booth?

M They'll be asked to answer questions and be given snacks if they _____ _____.

W Okay, that sounds good. I like the banner that says 'Guessing Time' in the center.

M Thanks. What do you think about the photos that are under the clock?

W Great idea! What are you using the _____ _____ for?

M We're going to put the snacks on it.

W That makes sense. Then, what about the _____ _____ _____ _____?

M It's for choosing countries. We're going to ask people geography questions.

W That should be interesting. What's that crown on the left side?

M That's a _____ _____ _____ _____ _____.

W Cool. I can't wait for this year's festival!

05

M Kasey, how's everything coming along for grandma's birthday this Sunday?

W Hey, dad. I wrote a card for her and _____ _____ _____ yesterday.

M That's good!

W Have you gotten anything for her yet?

M I already bought a sweater. Can I help with decorating the living room for the party?

W Clara will take care of that. Also, _____ _____ _____ a birthday cake.

M Awesome! Your grandma will be so happy because you guys are going to make her birthday so special.

W I hope so. What about food? What can we make for her?

M How about grilled salmon sandwiches? She loves those!

W Good idea, but I _____ _____ _____ _____ that on my own.

M Then, I'll order salmon and vegetables online today.

W Thanks, dad! That's a big help.

06

M Hello. How can I help you?

W Hi, how much is the ice cream?

M It _____ _____ _____ _____. The small cup is $5, the medium is $10, and the large is $15. What size would you like?

W I'll take _____ _____ _____ _____ _____.

M Okay. What flavor would you like?

W I'll take chocolate for all three cups.

M Sounds good. Do you want any toppings on your ice cream? We have chocolate chips and crunchy nuts. Toppings cost $1 each.

W Oh, yes. I'll have _____ _____ _____ _____ _____ _____ and nothing on the small cups.

M Good choice. Do you need anything else?

W No, that's it.

M How would you like to pay? Cash or credit?

W I'll pay with my credit card.

07

M Mom, I'm home.

W Hi. Did you go to the gym?

M Yes. My _____ _____ today, but I didn't renew it.

W Why? Does your shoulder still hurt?

M No, my shoulder feels completely fine.

W So, what's the problem? I thought you were enjoying exercising.

M I was. It's actually been fun.

W Then why didn't you renew your membership?

M Well, the _____ _____ at the gym are too old, and there's _____ _____ _____ in the shower stalls.

W I see. Why don't you check out the new health club nearby? It may be more expensive, but the facilities are probably a lot better.

M Okay. Maybe I should visit there tomorrow on my way home after school.

W That sounds like a good plan!

08

W Hey, Bruce! I'm going to take a tour of Liberty University. Do you want to come?

M Absolutely! That's one of the schools that I'm interested in. When is the tour?

W There's one on October 3rd and another one on October 10th. They're both Saturdays. _____ _____ _____ _____ for you?

M October 10th is better for me. What will we do during the tour?

W We'll get to see the campus in the morning and then we'll _____ _____ _____ _____ _____ in the afternoon. You can ask them questions about the admissions process when we see them.

M Okay, then I should make a list of questions. I have a lot of things to ask them.

W That's a good idea. Also, everyone who goes on the tour will get a free Liberty University T-shirt _____ _____ _____ _____.

M Really? That's cool. So how do I _____ _____ _____ the tour?

W You can sign up on their website.

M Okay, I will do that. Thank you so much for telling me about it.

09

W Are you taking actions to help the environment? Then, why don't you join our Green Action Photo Contest? As long as you are a resident of our town, you can be the winner! From September 1st until September 30th, 2021, you can upload photos of you participating in _____ _____ on social media. _____ _____ _____ _____ with the hash tag #GreenAction, you can automatically participate in our contest. The _____ _____ of photos you can post is five. The winner will be announced on October 4th. The prize for the winner _____ _____ _____ by October 11th. The winning photos will be posted on the town's website until the end of this year. Show us your green actions. No action is too small!

10

M Hey, Jessica. What are you working on?

W Hey! I'm trying to order a new rolling cart for our school's library. Do you want to help me?

M Sure. Let's see. Hmm... How about this plastic one? It looks like it's easy to use.

W Well, the cart we have now is plastic and it's not strong enough, so, I'd prefer to buy one that's _____ _____ _____ _____ _____.

M That makes sense. Then, let's get one that's made of metal or wood. What about the number of shelves?

W I think it would be nice to have a cart that has _____ _____ _____ shelves.

M That's a good idea. I would also recommend one that _____ _____ _____ because that makes it easier to control.

W You're right! The one we have now doesn't have lockable wheels, so it's really hard to control.

M I understand. That leaves us with these two options.

W Well, we _____ _____ _____ _____ in our budget. I can't spend more than $100.

M All right. Then, this one would be the best choice.

W Okay, then I'll order this one. Thanks for your help.

11

W Hey, Sean! Is this your dog? _____ _____!

M He's actually not my dog. I think he's lost, but I don't know what to do.

W Oh, really? [Pause] Look at the couple over there! It seems like they're _____ _____ _____.

M

12

M Hi, we just wanted to see if we could still sit and order dinner.

W Umm... I'm sorry but the kitchen closes in five minutes, so we _____ _____ _____ _____ _____ you.

M That's disappointing. _____ _____ _____ _____ _____ tomorrow?

W

13

M Good morning, ma'am. May I help you?

W Yes, please. I just heard that _____ _____ _____ _____ _____ for six hours.

M Oh, I'm sorry to hear that. Is there anything I can do for you?

W Well, I know I have to check out of my room by 11, but that means I would be waiting at the airport for almost eight hours.

M I understand. That's a long time to sit around and wait.

W Is it _____ _____ _____ _____ _____ in my room for a couple more hours until I leave this afternoon?

M Let me check to see if the room is available. *[Pause]* Luckily, ma'am, the room _____ _____ _____ for today.

W Okay, then if I stay for a couple more hours, do I have to _____ _____ _____ _____?

M ▨▨▨▨▨▨▨▨▨▨▨▨▨▨▨▨▨▨▨▨▨▨▨▨▨▨

14

W Hi, James. Is everything okay? I heard there was a huge storm in your area last night.

M Yeah, we had some really _____ _____ throughout the night. There was some damage.

W Did anyone get hurt?

M Thankfully, no, but there were a lot of fallen trees, and the roads were blocked.

W Oh, my! That must have been scary!

M Yeah, it was. Then the _____ _____ _____ while the roads were being cleared.

W So you didn't have any power last night?

M No, I couldn't turn on any lights or use any _____ _____, but it's okay now.

W That must have been so frustrating. Is there anything you need help with?

M Well, _____ _____ _____ _____ _____. The water is up to my knees and all of my stuff down there is wet.

W ▨▨▨▨▨▨▨▨▨▨▨▨▨▨▨▨▨▨▨▨▨▨▨▨▨▨

15

M Emily and Chris are classmates. Emily is making cookies when she gets a call from Chris. He says he is going to see a movie with his friends and _____ _____ _____ _____ _____. She says that she would love to, but she can't go because her parents aren't home and she has to watch her younger brother. Chris suggests that Emily _____ _____ _____ with her to the movie. Emily explains to Chris that her little brother has _____ _____ _____, so he can't go either. She wants to tell Chris that she _____ _____ _____ _____ her brother. In this situation, what would Emily most likely say to Chris?

Emily ▨▨▨▨▨▨▨▨▨▨▨▨▨▨▨▨▨▨▨▨▨▨▨▨▨▨

16~17

W Everyone loves a good night's sleep, but for wild animals, finding the right time and place can be difficult. Whether it's staying safe, keeping warm, or remembering to breathe, animals have a lot to consider before they go to bed. As a result, they've come up with some _____ _____ _____ _____. To start with, bats sleep in caves while _____ _____ _____. Doing that not only keeps them away from enemies but also means they are in the perfect position to fly away if necessary. Meanwhile, ducks sleep side by side in rows. The ducks on the outside of the rows sleep with one eye open _____ _____ _____ _____, while the ducks on the inside sleep with both eyes closed. Giraffes require little rest, sleeping for only five minutes at a time or as little as 30 minutes a day. They sleep _____ _____ _____, sometimes sitting down or even standing up, so that they're ready to run. Finally, dolphins have to _____ _____ in order to breathe, even when they're sleeping. They only let part of their brain relax and keep one eye open as they sleep.

10회 2021학년도 6월 고1 전국연합 학력평가

1번부터 17번까지는 듣고 답하는 문제입니다. 1번부터 15번까지는 한 번만 들려주고, 16번부터 17번까지는 두 번 들려줍니다. 방송을 잘 듣고 답을 하시기 바랍니다.

01 다음을 듣고, 남자가 하는 말의 목적으로 가장 적절한 것을 고르시오.

① 건강 검진 일정을 공지하려고
② 독감 예방 접종을 권장하려고
③ 개인 위생 관리를 당부하려고
④ 보건소 운영 기간을 안내하려고
⑤ 독감 예방 접종 부작용을 경고하려고

02 대화를 듣고, 여자의 의견으로 가장 적절한 것을 고르시오.

① 독서 습관을 기르자.
② 지역 서점을 이용하자.
③ 지역 특산품을 애용하자.
④ 중고 서점을 활성화시키자.
⑤ 온라인을 통한 도서 구입을 늘리자.

03 대화를 듣고, 두 사람의 관계를 가장 잘 나타낸 것을 고르시오.

① 호텔 직원 – 투숙객
② 열쇠 수리공 – 집주인
③ 경비원 – 입주민
④ 은행원 – 고객
⑤ 치과의사 – 환자

04 대화를 듣고, 그림에서 대화의 내용과 일치하지 않는 것을 고르시오.

05 대화를 듣고, 남자가 여자를 위해 할 일로 가장 적절한 것을 고르시오. [3점]

① 부엌 청소하기
② 점심 준비하기
③ 카메라 구매하기
④ 딸 데리러 가기
⑤ 요리법 검색하기

06 대화를 듣고, 여자가 지불할 금액을 고르시오.

① $30 　 ② $50 　 ③ $63 　 ④ $65 　 ⑤ $70

07 대화를 듣고, 남자가 공연장에 갈 수 없는 이유로 가장 적절한 것을 고르시오.

① 출장을 가야 해서
② 숙제를 끝내야 해서
③ 조카를 돌봐야 해서
④ 이사 준비를 해야 해서
⑤ 친구와 만날 약속을 해서

08 대화를 듣고, 강아지 키우기에 관해 언급되지 않은 것을 고르시오.

① 산책시키기
② 먹이 주기
③ 목욕시키기
④ 배변 훈련시키기
⑤ 소변 패드 치우기

09 Sharing Friday Movement에 관한 다음 내용을 듣고, 일치하지 않는 것을 고르시오. [3점]

① 매주 금요일에 2달러씩 기부하는 운동이다.
② 2001년 핀란드에서 시작되었다.
③ 기부금은 가난한 지역에 깨끗한 물을 공급하는 데 쓰인다.
④ 올해 20명의 학생에게 장학금을 지급했다.
⑤ 추가 정보는 홈페이지를 통해 얻을 수 있다.

10 다음 표를 보면서 대화를 듣고, 여자가 구입할 모델을 고르시오.

Selfie Sticks

	Model	Weight	Maximum Length	Bluetooth Remote Control	Price
①	A	150g	60cm	×	$10
②	B	150g	80cm	○	$30
③	C	180g	80cm	○	$20
④	D	180g	100cm	×	$15
⑤	E	230g	100cm	○	$25

11 대화를 듣고, 남자의 마지막 말에 대한 여자의 응답으로 가장 적절한 것을 고르시오.

① Again? You've lost your bag twice.
② You're right. I'll take a warm jacket.
③ Why? I know you prefer cold weather.
④ What? I finished packing a present for you.
⑤ Sorry. But you can't join the trip at this point.

12 대화를 듣고, 여자의 마지막 말에 대한 남자의 응답으로 가장 적절한 것을 고르시오.

① No thank you. I've had enough.
② Great. I'll book for five people at six.
③ That's a good choice. The food is wonderful.
④ Okay. I'll set a place and time for the meeting.
⑤ Sorry to hear that. I'll cancel the reservation now.

13 대화를 듣고, 남자의 마지막 말에 대한 여자의 응답으로 가장 적절한 것을 고르시오.

Woman: _____

① I'm in charge of giving the presentation.
② I think you're the right person for that role.
③ It's important to choose your team carefully.
④ The assignment is due the day after tomorrow.
⑤ I hope we don't stay up late to finish the project.

14 대화를 듣고, 여자의 마지막 말에 대한 남자의 응답으로 가장 적절한 것을 고르시오.

Man: _____

① I'm good at public speaking.
② I'm sorry for forgetting my assignment.
③ Unfortunately, my alarm doesn't wake me up.
④ The speech contest is just around the corner.
⑤ It helps me keep deadlines to complete specific tasks.

15 다음 상황 설명을 듣고, Harold가 Kate에게 할 말로 가장 적절한 것을 고르시오. [3점]

Harold: _____

① Okay. You'd better put your best effort into the match.
② I see. You should play the match instead of her.
③ Take it easy. Take good care of yourself first.
④ You deserve it. Practice makes perfect.
⑤ Don't worry. You'll win this match.

[16~17] 다음을 듣고, 물음에 답하시오.

16 여자가 하는 말의 주제로 가장 적절한 것은?

① problems with illegal hunting
② characteristics of migrating animals
③ effects of light pollution on wild animals
④ various ways to save endangered animals
⑤ animal habitat change due to water pollution

17 언급된 동물이 <u>아닌</u> 것은?

① sea turtles ② fireflies ③ salmon
④ honey bees ⑤ tree frogs

10회 | 21년 6월

01

M Hello, students. This is Allan, your school nurse. Many students _____ _____ with seasonal influenza. Some cases can lead to serious pain or even hospitalization. I _____ _____ you to get a flu vaccine. A flu shot can keep you from getting sick. Also, since flu viruses keep changing, flu vaccines are updated to protect against such viruses. Please _____ _____ _____ _____ offered in doctors' offices or health departments by the end of this month. Thank you.

02

M Irene, where are you heading?

W Hello, Mason. I'm going to the bookstore to buy some books.

M The bookstore? Isn't it more convenient to order books online?

W Yes, but I like to _____ _____ the pages at bookstores.

M Yeah, but buying books online is cheaper.

W Right. But we can _____ _____ _____ when we buy books from them.

M I guess you're right. The bookstore near my house _____ _____ last month.

W It's a pity to see local bookstores going out of business nowadays.

M I agree. Next time I need a book, I'll try to _____ _____ _____ _____ _____.

03

[Telephone rings.]

M Hello. This is G-Solution. How may I help you?

W Hello. _____ _____ _____ _____ my home. The keypad on my door isn't responding.

M It might be an electric problem. It's probably a simple fix and it _____ _____ much.

W How much is it?

M It's 30 dollars including the service charge. But you'll have to pay extra if there're any additional problems.

W I got it. Can you _____ _____ right away?

M I'm afraid not. I'm doing a job at the Capital Bank.

W How long will it _____ _____ _____ _____?

M Just one hour. I'll call you as soon as I'm done. Address, please?

W 705 Cozy Street near Lee's Dental Clinic.

M Okay. See you soon.

04

M Grace, let me show you my newly designed room.

W Wow, Jake! It's so cool.

M Look at the monitor _____ _____ _____. I changed my old monitor for this new one.

W Looks nice. But isn't your desk _____ _____ _____ _____ your electric keyboard on it?

M It's fine with me. I find it convenient there.

W Is that a microphone _____ _____ _____? Do you sing?

M Yes. Singing is my all-time favorite hobby.

W What's that _____ _____ on the wall? Where did you get it?

M I won that medal at a guitar contest with my dad.

W Incredible! Do you often _____ _____ _____ with your dad?

M Sure. That's why there're two guitars in the room.

05

W Smells nice, Daniel. What did you _____ _____ _____?

M Creamy pasta. I found the recipe online.

W Fantastic. But don't you think the kitchen is _____ _____ _____ _____?

M Sorry. I'll clean it up later.

W You promise?

M Yes. Let's have lunch. *[Pause]* By the way, do you remember you have to pick up our daughter from the library this afternoon?

W Oh, my! I _____ _____. What should I do? My friend Amy is coming in an hour.

M Don't worry. I planned to go camera shopping, but _____ _____ _____ Betty, instead.

W Thanks. How sweet of you! Then I'll clean the kitchen.

06

M Good afternoon. May I help you?

W Yes, please. I want to buy a bag for my laptop. Can you recommend one?

M How about this one? It's only 30 dollars _____ _____. The original price was 65 dollars.

W Wow, more than 50% off?

M It's a very good deal.

W I like the design and color, but it's _____ _____ _____.

M If you want something bigger, how about this one? It has a USB charging port, too.

W I like it, but it looks expensive.

M It's 70 dollars. But I can give you a 10% discount.

W Well... It's still _____ _____ _____. Let me look at the first one again.

M Here it is. 30 dollars _____ _____ _____.

W Okay. I'll take it.

07

W Hi, Chris. How was your business trip?

M It went fine. By the way, I heard Emma _____ _____ _____ this Saturday.

W You're right. She's very busy preparing to move. So she gave me two tickets for a musical because she can't go.

M Good for you. What's the name of the musical?

W It's "Heroes."

M Really? I heard it's popular. Who are you _____ _____?

W No one, yet. My sister _____ _____ _____ because she has to finish her homework.

M Well, can I go with you instead?

W Sure. Why not? The show is at 8 p.m. this Friday.

M Friday? Oh, no! I promised to _____ _____ _____ _____ _____ at that time.

W No problem. I'll ask Susan to go with me then.

08

W Dad, I want to have a puppy just like my friend, Julie.

M Why not? But do you know how hard it is to _____ _____ _____?

W Yes, but I'm ready. I think I will name my puppy Toby.

M Okay. But _____ _____ _____ Toby every day?

W That'll be easy.

M Also, you'll _____ _____ _____ Toby three times a day.

W No big deal. Anything else?

M You'll have to toilet train Toby, too.

W Really?

M Of course. Plus, you'll need to _____ _____ the dog's pee pads.

W Hmm... Dad, you'll help me, right?

M Sometimes. But remember having a dog takes responsibility.

10회 **67**

09

W Good afternoon, listeners. Why don't you join the Sharing Friday Movement and _____ _____ _____ to our fund every Friday? This movement started in 2001 in Finland as an idea to encourage people _____ _____ _____. Since then, this idea has grown into a global movement. Most of the donations go to poor areas across the world and help people _____ _____ _____. This year, _____ _____ _____ to 100 students in these areas to celebrate our 20th anniversary. Please join us, and help make a difference. If you want to get more information, visit our homepage.

10

W Kevin, I'm looking for a selfie stick. Can you help me?

M Sure, mom. You can buy one on your smart phone. *[Pause]* What kind of selfie stick do you want?

W I'd prefer a light one.

M Then _____ _____ _____ a selfie stick over 200 grams. How about the length?

W I have no idea. What's your opinion?

M Hmm... It _____ _____ up to 80cm at least.

W Okay. I also want a bluetooth remote control. I heard they're _____ _____ _____.

M Then you have two options left. Which one do you want?

W I'll buy this _____ _____.

M Great choice.

11

M Have you finished _____ _____ _____ for your trip to Mount Jiri?

W I think so. Look! What else do I need?

M You'd better _____ _____ the cold weather at night.

W ▨▨▨▨▨▨▨▨▨▨▨▨▨▨▨▨▨▨▨▨▨

12

W Honey, we _____ _____ _____ tomorrow evening.

M Why not? I've already _____ _____ _____ at the restaurant.

W I'm sorry. I have an important business meeting at that time.

M ▨▨▨▨▨▨▨▨▨▨▨▨▨▨▨▨▨▨▨▨▨

13

M Why do you look so busy?

W I'm _____ _____ a team project.

M What's it about?

W It's about 'Climate Change.'

M Sounds interesting. Who's _____ _____ _____?

W You know Chris? He's the leader.

M I know him very well. He's responsible and smart.

W Jenny is _____ _____ _____ and Alex is making the slides.

M What a nice team! Then _____ _____ _____?

W ▨▨▨▨▨▨▨▨▨▨▨▨▨▨▨▨▨▨▨▨▨

14

M Hi, Diana. You look down. What's the problem?

W Hi, Peter. I _____ _____ _____ for the speech contest. It was yesterday.

M No way. You'd been waiting for it for a long time.

W Yeah. It totally slipped my mind. I'm so forgetful.

M Why don't you _____ _____ to remember things?

W I've tried, but it doesn't work. I even forget _____ _____ _____ the notes.

M How about using a time management application like me?

W Well... _____ _____ _____ your app?

M ▨▨▨▨▨▨▨▨▨▨▨▨▨▨▨▨▨▨▨▨▨

15

M Harold is a tennis coach. He's been teaching Kate, a _____ _____ _____ player, for years. While practicing for an upcoming match, Kate injured her elbow badly. Her doctor strongly recommends she stop playing tennis for a month. However, Kate _____ _____ playing the match. Harold knows how heart-broken she would be to _____ _____ _____. But he's concerned about her tennis career if her elbow doesn't recover. So he wants to persuade her _____ _____ _____ and focus on her recovery. In this situation, what would Harold most likely say to Kate?

Harold ▨▨▨▨▨▨▨▨▨▨▨▨▨▨▨▨▨▨▨▨▨

16~17

W This is Linda from "Life and Science." Did you know _____ _____ from bright lights at night can drive wildlife to death? For example, sea turtles lay eggs on beaches and their babies _____ _____ _____ to the sea with the help of moonlight. But artificial lights can confuse them and cause them not to reach the sea and die. Fireflies have been disappearing across the globe. Male fireflies _____ _____ by artificial lights when they try to attract mates. This means less fireflies are born. Also, salmon migrate randomly when exposed to artificial lights at night. This threatens their _____ _____ _____. Lastly, light pollution interrupts the mating calls of tree frogs at night. As male frogs reduce the number of their mating calls, the females don't reproduce. So light pollution can be a matter of life and death for some animals.

1번부터 17번까지는 듣고 답하는 문제입니다. 1번부터 15번까지는 한 번만 들려주고, 16번부터 17번까지는 두 번 들려줍니다. 방송을 잘 듣고 답을 하시기 바랍니다.

01 다음을 듣고, 남자가 하는 말의 목적으로 가장 적절한 것을 고르시오.

① 교내 청소 일정을 공지하려고
② 학교 시설 공사의 지연에 대해 사과하려고
③ 하교 시 교실 창문을 닫을 것을 요청하려고
④ 교내의 젖은 바닥을 걸을 때 조심하도록 당부하려고
⑤ 깨끗한 교실 환경 조성을 위한 아이디어를 공모하려고

02 대화를 듣고, 여자의 의견으로 가장 적절한 것을 고르시오.

① 짧은 낮잠은 업무 효율을 높인다.
② 야식은 숙면에 방해가 될 수 있다.
③ 사람마다 최적의 수면 시간이 다르다.
④ 베개를 바꾸면 숙면에 도움이 될 수 있다.
⑤ 숙면을 위해 침실을 서늘하게 하는 것이 좋다.

03 대화를 듣고, 두 사람의 관계를 가장 잘 나타낸 것을 고르시오.

① 파티 주최자 – 요리사
② 슈퍼마켓 점원 – 손님
③ 배달 기사 – 음식점 주인
④ 영양학자 – 식품 제조업자
⑤ 인테리어 디자이너 – 의뢰인

04 대화를 듣고, 그림에서 대화의 내용과 일치하지 않는 것을 고르시오.

05 대화를 듣고, 남자가 할 일로 가장 적절한 것을 고르시오.

① 영화 예매하기
② 지갑 가져오기
③ 시간표 출력하기
④ 학생증 재발급받기
⑤ 영화 감상문 제출하기

06 대화를 듣고, 여자가 지불할 금액을 고르시오. [3점]

① $72   ② $80   ③ $90   ④ $100   ⑤ $110

07 대화를 듣고, 남자가 보고서를 완성하지 못한 이유를 고르시오.

① 실험을 다시 해서
② 제출일을 착각해서
③ 주제가 변경되어서
④ 컴퓨터가 고장 나서
⑤ 심한 감기에 걸려서

08 대화를 듣고, Spring Virtual Run에 관해 언급되지 않은 것을 고르시오.

① 달리는 거리   ② 참가 인원   ③ 달리는 장소
④ 참가비   ⑤ 기념품

09 Family Night at the Museum에 관한 다음 내용을 듣고, 일치하지 않는 것을 고르시오.

① 박물관 정규 운영 시간 종료 후에 열린다.
② 행성과 별 모형 아래에서 잠을 잔다.
③ 참가자들에게 침낭이 제공된다.
④ 6세부터 13세까지를 위한 프로그램이다.
⑤ 사전 등록 없이 현장에서 참가할 수 있다.

10 다음 표를 보면서 대화를 듣고, 여자가 구매할 스마트 워치를 고르시오.

Smart Watches

	Model	Waterproof	Warranty	Price
①	A	×	2 years	$90
②	B	○	3 years	$110
③	C	○	1 year	$115
④	D	×	2 years	$120
⑤	E	○	4 years	$125

11 대화를 듣고, 여자의 마지막 말에 대한 남자의 응답으로 가장 적절한 것을 고르시오.

① Oh, I should get it exchanged.
② Sure. I'll order a shirt for you.
③ Well, it's too expensive for me.
④ No. Please find me a smaller size.
⑤ Sorry, but this shirt is not on sale.

12 대화를 듣고, 남자의 마지막 말에 대한 여자의 응답으로 가장 적절한 것을 고르시오.

① Good. Let's meet around six.
② That's okay. I don't like donuts.
③ I want to open my own donut shop.
④ Don't worry. I can do that by myself.
⑤ Thanks for sharing your donut recipe.

13 대화를 듣고, 여자의 마지막 말에 대한 남자의 응답으로 가장 적절한 것을 고르시오. [3점]

Man: _____

① This coffee place is very popular.
② You can stop using plastic straws.
③ I'll order drinks when you're ready.
④ Your drink will be ready in a minute.
⑤ The cups come in various colors and shapes.

14 대화를 듣고, 남자의 마지막 말에 대한 여자의 응답으로 가장 적절한 것을 고르시오. [3점]

Woman: _____

① Luckily, I didn't get hurt in the accident.
② I have enough money to get a new bike.
③ You really need one for your own safety.
④ You may feel sleepy after biking to school.
⑤ We can put our bikes in the school parking lot.

15 다음 상황 설명을 듣고, Jasper가 Mary에게 할 말로 가장 적절한 것을 고르시오.

Jasper: _____

① Where is the audition being held?
② How about writing your own song?
③ Let's play a different song this time.
④ I think you should be our lead singer.
⑤ Don't you think we need more practice?

[16~17] 다음을 듣고, 물음에 답하시오.

16 남자가 하는 말의 주제로 가장 적절한 것은?

① eco-friendly toys for pets
② roles of toys in pets' well-being
③ types of pets' unusual behaviors
④ foods that are dangerous to pets
⑤ difficulties in raising children with pets

17 언급된 동물이 아닌 것은?

① cat   ② hamster   ③ dog
④ turtle   ⑤ parrot

01

M Good morning, students. This is Mr. Lewis from the school administration office. Last night there was a heavy rainstorm. The pouring rain left some of the school's hallways _____ _____ _____. The first floor hallway and the central stairway are especially dangerous to walk on. Please _____ _____ _____ when you walk through these areas. You could get seriously hurt if you _____ _____ _____ _____ _____. We're doing our best to take care of the situation. Thank you.

02

W Mike, you look very tired today.

M I am. I'm _____ _____ _____ at night these days.

W What's the matter?

M I don't know. I just can't fall asleep until late at night.

W I feel bad for you.

M I need to find a way to sleep better.

W Can I share _____ _____ _____ my sleeping problem?

M Sure.

W After I changed my pillow, I was able to sleep much better. _____ _____ _____ can help you with your sleeping problem.

M Thanks for the tip. I hope that works for me, too.

03

M Hi, I'm Daniel Jones. I'm glad to finally meet you.

W Welcome. Mr. Harvey told me you're coming.

M He told me nice things about you.

W Thanks. I hear that you're _____ _____ _____ at your house in two weeks.

M That's right. I'm hoping you could _____ _____ _____ the food for my party.

W Sure. You can always _____ _____ _____ _____ _____ _____.

M Great. Is there anything I need to prepare for you?

W No need. I'll be taking care of the party food _____ _____ _____ _____.

M Sounds fantastic.

W Now let's talk about the menu.

04

W Is that the photo of our school's new studio?

M Yes. We can shoot online lectures here.

W Can I have a look?

M Sure. Do you see that camera _____ _____ _____? It's the latest model.

W I see. What is that ring on the stand next to the camera?

M That's the lighting. It's to brighten the teacher's face.

W Hmm.... _____ _____ _____ on the wall looks simple and modern.

M Teachers can check the time on the clock while shooting.

W The microphone on the table _____ _____ _____.

M It really does. Also, I like the tree in the corner. It _____ _____ _____ the studio.

05

M Hi, Jamie. You remember we're going to the movies later today, right?

W Of course. I'll see you after class.

M Didn't you say there's a _____ _____ on the movie ticket?

W Yes, I did. Don't forget to bring your student ID card.

M But I've lost my ID. Is there any other way to get the discount?

W Probably not. Why don't you go _____ _____ _____ _____ _____ from the school office?

M Do you know _____ _____ _____ _____?

W Yes. It's on the first floor.

M Okay. I'll go there right away.

06

W Hi, I'm looking for camping chairs. Can you recommend one?

M Good morning. This is our bestselling chair. They're _____ _____.

W That sounds good. I'll take it.

M How many do you need?

W I need _____ _____.

M Okay. Is there anything else you need?

W I also need a camping knife.

M How about this one? It's $20.

W That _____ _____. I'll buy one. Do you offer any discounts?

M Yes. Since your total purchase is over $80, we'll give you a _____ _____ on the total amount.

W That sounds nice. I'll pay with my credit card.

07

M Hi, Rebecca. What's up?

W Hey, Tom. Can I borrow your laptop today?

M Yes, but I have to finish my science report first.

W Really? Wasn't the science report _____ _____ _____?

M Yes, it was. But I couldn't finish it.

W What happened? I thought your experiment _____ _____.

M Actually, it didn't. I made a mistake in the _____ _____.

W Oh, no. Did you have to do the experiment _____ _____ _____?

M Yes, it took a lot of time. So I haven't finished my report yet.

W I see. Let me know when you're done.

08

W Hi, Asher. What are you doing on the computer?

M I'm _____ _____ _____ an event called the Spring Virtual Run.

W The Spring Virtual... Run?

M It's a race. Participants upload their record after running either a three-mile race or a ten-mile race.

W Can you run _____ _____ _____?

M Yes. I can choose any place in the city.

W That sounds interesting. I want to participate, too.

M Then you should sign up online and pay the _____ _____. It's twenty dollars.

W Twenty dollars? That's pretty expensive.

M But _____ _____ _____ in the fee. All participants will get a T-shirt and a water bottle.

W That's reasonable. I'll sign up.

09

W Do your children love adventures? Here's a great adventure for you and your children. The Museum of Natural History is starting a special program — Family Night at the Museum. When the regular museum hours _____ _____, you and your children get to walk around the museum with a flashlight. After your adventure is complete, you will sleep under the amazing models of planets and stars. Sleeping bags, snacks, and water _____ _____ _____. This program is for children ages 6 to 13. All _____ _____ want to join must register in advance. On-site registration _____ _____ _____. Why not call today and sign up?

10

M Hi, how can I help you today?

W Hi, I'm looking for a smart watch.

M Sure. We have these five models.

W Hmm.... I want to wear it when I swim.

M Then you're looking for one that's _____.

W That's right. Do you think a _____ _____ is too short?

M Yes. I recommend one that has a warranty longer than one year.

W Okay. I'll _____ _____ _____.

M That leaves you with these two options. I'd get the cheaper one because it's _____ _____ _____ the other one.

W I see. Then I'll go with the cheaper one.

M Good choice.

11

W Liam, _____ _____ _____ _____ _____?

M It was good, Mom. I got this shirt at a good price.

W It looks nice. Wait! It's _____ _____ _____.

M ▨▨▨▨▨▨▨▨▨▨▨▨▨▨▨▨▨▨

12

M Alicia, these donuts are delicious. Can you tell me _____ _____ _____ them?

W They're from a new donut shop. I can _____ _____ _____ if you want.

M That'd be nice. How's today _____ _____?

W ▨▨▨▨▨▨▨▨▨▨▨▨▨▨▨▨▨▨

13

W Brandon, I'm sorry I'm late.

M That's okay. Let's order our drinks. I'll get my coffee in my personal cup.

W Oh, you brought _____ _____ _____?

M Yes, it is a reusable cup. I'm trying to reduce my plastic footprint.

W What is plastic footprint?

M It is the total amount of plastic a person uses and _____ _____.

W You care a lot about the environment.

M I do. Plastic waste is a huge _____ _____.

W I should use a reusable cup, too. _____ _____ _____ _____ _____ to reduce my plastic footprint?

M ▨▨▨▨▨▨▨▨▨▨▨▨▨▨▨▨▨▨

14

M Good morning, Kathy. That's a cool helmet.

W Hi, Alex. It's for biking. I _____ _____ _____ to school.

M How often do you ride your bike to school?

W I try to do it every day. It's very _____.

M Sounds nice. I'm _____ _____ _____ to school, too.

W Good! We should ride together.

M Let's do that, but I'm not very good at biking.

W It's okay. We can go slowly. Also, _____ _____ _____ your helmet.

M But I don't have a helmet yet.

W ▨▨▨▨▨▨▨▨▨▨▨▨▨▨▨▨▨▨▨▨▨

15

W Jasper and Mary are _____ _____ _____ a rock band for the school band competition. Mary plays the guitar, and Jasper is the drummer. They pick a keyboard player _____ _____ _____. Now, they need a lead singer. Although the band is not completely formed, they begin their first practice today. Since they don't have a lead singer yet, Mary sings while playing the guitar. _____ _____ _____, the other members are amazed. Mary has the perfect voice for rock music! So Jasper wants to tell Mary _____ _____ _____ _____ _____ for their band. In this situation, what would Jasper most likely say to Mary?

Jasper ▨▨▨▨▨▨▨▨▨▨▨▨▨▨▨▨▨▨

16~17

M Good afternoon, everybody. Today, we'll talk about what our animal companions love: Toys. _____ _____ _____ _____ our pets? First, toys play a very important role in keeping your pet happy. A toy like a scratcher helps to reduce your cat's stress. Second, toys are _____ _____ _____ for a pet to get exercise. For example, a hamster loves to run on a wheel toy. Third, toys _____ _____ _____ between you and your pet. Playing with a small soft ball will give you and your dog a joyful experience. Lastly, toys help keep your pet entertained. A small hiding tent will make your parrot _____ _____ _____ when you are not around. Now let's watch a video of pets playing with their toys.

1번부터 17번까지는 듣고 답하는 문제입니다. 1번부터 15번까지는 한 번만 들려주고, 16번부터 17번까지는 두 번 들려줍니다. 방송을 잘 듣고 답을 하시기 바랍니다.

01 다음을 듣고, 남자가 하는 말의 목적으로 가장 적절한 것을 고르시오.

① 교통사고 발생 시 대처 요령을 안내하려고
② 자전거 투어 시 안전 규칙을 설명하려고
③ 자전거 전용 도로 확충을 요청하려고
④ 단체 관광 일정 변경을 공지하려고
⑤ 자전거 대회 참가를 독려하려고

02 대화를 듣고, 여자의 의견으로 가장 적절한 것을 고르시오.

① 잠들기 직전의 운동은 수면을 방해할 수 있다.
② 운동은 규칙적으로 하는 것이 효과적이다.
③ 과격한 운동은 심장에 무리를 줄 수 있다.
④ 충분한 수면은 건강 관리에 도움이 된다.
⑤ 지나친 스트레스는 건강을 해친다.

03 대화를 듣고, 두 사람의 관계를 가장 잘 나타낸 것을 고르시오.

① 구급 대원 – 간호사　　② 피부과 의사 – 환자
③ 화장품 판매원 – 손님　　④ 제약 회사 직원 – 약사
⑤ 물리 치료사 – 운동선수

04 대화를 듣고, 그림에서 대화의 내용과 일치하지 않는 것을 고르시오.

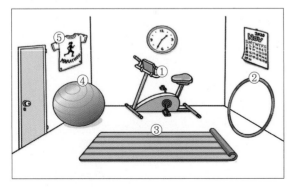

05 대화를 듣고, 여자가 할 일로 가장 적절한 것을 고르시오.

① 모금함 만들기　　② 물품 배치하기
③ 가격표 붙이기　　④ 스피커 점검하기
⑤ 동영상 제작하기

06 대화를 듣고, 남자가 지불할 금액을 고르시오. [3점]

① $41　② $45　③ $46　④ $50　⑤ $54

07 대화를 듣고, 남자가 학생 패션쇼에 갈 수 없는 이유를 고르시오.

① 친구 생일 선물을 사야 해서
② 가족과 식사를 하기로 해서
③ 집수리를 도와줘야 해서
④ 회의에 참석해야 해서
⑤ 콘서트에 가기로 해서

08 대화를 듣고, World Dinosaur Exhibition에 관해 언급되지 않은 것을 고르시오.

① 장소　　② 프로그램　　③ 운영 시간
④ 입장료　　⑤ 교통편

09 Greenville Animation Film Festival에 관한 다음 내용을 듣고, 일치하지 않는 것을 고르시오.

① 1995년에 시작된 행사이다.
② 일주일 동안 열린다.
③ 올해의 주제는 우정이다.
④ 영화 스케줄은 웹사이트에 게시될 것이다.
⑤ 근처에 주차장이 있다.

10 다음 표를 보면서 대화를 듣고, 여자가 등록할 그리기 강좌를 고르시오.

One-day Drawing Lessons

	Class	Material	Lesson Type	Day	Time
①	A	Oil paint	Group	Monday	11 a.m.
②	B	Acrylic paint	Private	Wednesday	11 a.m.
③	C	Crayon	Group	Wednesday	6 p.m.
④	D	Colored pencil	Group	Friday	11 a.m.
⑤	E	Pastel	Private	Friday	6 p.m.

11 대화를 듣고, 남자의 마지막 말에 대한 여자의 응답으로 가장 적절한 것을 고르시오.

① *Bulgogi* is already sold out.
② You can choose what to eat.
③ We'll meet at the restaurant.
④ I'll order the food for tomorrow.
⑤ I got the recipe from the Internet.

12 대화를 듣고, 여자의 마지막 말에 대한 남자의 응답으로 가장 적절한 것을 고르시오.

① No problem. Your car is repaired.
② Sorry. I can't go camping with you.
③ Of course. You can borrow my tent.
④ Okay. I'll bring you the speakers now.
⑤ Don't worry. I already turned them off.

13 대화를 듣고, 남자의 마지막 말에 대한 여자의 응답으로 가장 적절한 것을 고르시오.

Woman: _____

① Then, you should sell the items using this app.
② Good. Let's buy a sweater in the marketplace.
③ All right. It's easy to order this bag online.
④ No worries. I'll lend you some money.
⑤ Well, you'd better buy new clothes.

14 대화를 듣고, 여자의 마지막 말에 대한 남자의 응답으로 가장 적절한 것을 고르시오. [3점]

Man: _____

① Don't worry. I'll send you a notice by email.
② Great. Let me know how to use your services.
③ I don't agree. You can get a refund without a receipt.
④ Good. I'm looking forward to watching a movie tonight.
⑤ Okay. I'll call customer service to cancel the membership.

15 다음 상황 설명을 듣고, Ms. Brown이 Chris에게 할 말로 가장 적절한 것을 고르시오. [3점]

Ms. Brown: _____

① You should stop worrying about your major.
② You'd better read an English book every day.
③ Why don't you start writing a diary in English?
④ I think you need to learn a lot of English words.
⑤ How about having conversations with foreigners?

[16~17] 다음을 듣고, 물음에 답하시오.

16 여자가 하는 말의 주제로 가장 적절한 것은?

① positive effects of raising animals
② useful tips for recording animal behavior
③ common characteristics sea animals have
④ different ways animals use to communicate
⑤ importance of protecting endangered species

17 언급된 동물이 아닌 것은?

① 개   ② 돌고래   ③ 고릴라
④ 코끼리   ⑤ 기린

12회

20년 11월

01

M Hello, welcome to Fun Bike Touring. I'm Harry Wilson, your tour guide. Before starting the tour, let me tell you the _____ _____. First, always keep your helmet on. Wearing a helmet _____ _____ _____ serious injuries in case of an accident. Second, you should use bicycle-only lanes. If you ride _____ _____ _____ _____, there is a chance that you could be hit by a car. Lastly, don't use your cell phone while riding. Taking pictures or talking on the phone _____ _____ can be really dangerous to you and others. Now, are you ready to start? Let's go!

02

M Good morning, Rosa.

W Hi, Tony. You look tired. Are you all right?

M Yeah, I'm okay. I'm just having a hard time _____ _____ these days.

W Why? Are you worried about something?

M No. Since I started _____ _____ _____ _____, it's been hard to fall asleep.

W What time do you exercise?

M I usually go to the gym around 10 p.m. When I come back, it's almost midnight.

W Hmm, I think _____ _____ you can't sleep well.

M Really?

W As far as I know, when you exercise, your heart rate and temperature go up, which makes you stay awake. These can _____ _____ _____.

M Oh, that makes sense.

W So, it's not a good idea to exercise right before going to bed.

M I'll keep that in mind. Thanks for your advice.

03

[Door knocks.]

W Hello, Mr. Cooper. Come on in. Have a seat, please.

M Thank you.

W You came here last week _____ _____ _____ _____. How are the symptoms now?

M Much better.

W Great. Let me look at the sunburn. *[Pause]* The redness is almost gone.

M Yeah. The cream _____ _____ was really helpful.

W Good. Do you still have any pain?

M Not anymore.

W I'm glad to hear that. If you put the cream on for a few days more, your skin will completely recover.

M Okay. But I don't have any more cream. Could you _____ _____ _____ _____?

W Sure. *[Typing sound]* If you have any problems, please come back.

M Thank you.

04

M Hi, Claire. What did you do yesterday?

W Hi, Henry. I set up an exercise room in my house. Look at this picture.

M Cool! The _____ _____ under the clock looks nice.

W Thanks. I bought the bike a few days ago.

M Good. Is that a hula-hoop _____ _____ _____?

W Yes. I exercise with it for 30 minutes every day. What do you think of the mat _____ _____ _____ _____ on the floor?

M I love it. By the way, what's the big ball next to the door?

W It's a gym ball. I use it for _____ _____.

M Good. Oh, I know that T-shirt on the wall.

W Yeah. It's from the marathon we ran together.

M Great. It _____ _____ _____ your room.

W Thanks. Next time, come over and we'll exercise together.

05

W Simon, I think we're ready for the _____ _____.

M Right. Let's do one last check.

W Okay. We're going to play a short video clip for the event. Is the screen working?

M Yes. I _____ _____ _____ and there's no problem at all.

W Great. What about the speakers?

M I already tried using them, and they worked fine. Did you bring the _____ _____?

W Yes. Look. I made it by myself.

M Wow! It looks nice.

W Thanks. All the items we're going to sell are nicely set up on the table.

M Okay. The only thing left is to put _____ _____ _____ _____. I'll do that later because I have to go to my part-time job now.

W Oh, don't worry. I'll put the price tags on.

M Really? Thanks.

06

M Good afternoon.

W Hello. Welcome to Happy Pet World. How can I help you?

M I'm looking for a cushion for my dog.

W Okay, _____ _____ _____? These are the most popular models.

M The pink one looks cute. How much is it?

W Originally, it was $40. But due to a special promotion, you can get a 10 percent discount _____ _____.

M Great. I'll buy one cushion, then.

W Sure. Anything else?

M Do you have dog biscuits?

W Of course. They're right over here. Each box of biscuits is $5.

M I'll buy _____ _____ _____ biscuits. Do I get a discount on the biscuits, too?

W I'm sorry. We _____ _____ a discount on biscuits.

M Okay, then. Here's my credit card.

07

[Cell phone rings.]

W Hello.

M Hi, Linda. Did you call me earlier? I was in my book club meeting. What's up?

W I called you to make sure you can come to the student fashion show. The schedule _____ _____.

M Really? When is the show now?

W It has changed to 6 p.m. next Friday. The place we were going to use _____ _____ _____ this week.

M I see. I'm afraid I can't go then.

W Oh, didn't you say you're going to a concert next Friday?

M No, that's next Saturday.

W Then, why _____ _____ _____?

M It's my mom's birthday. So, I'm going to _____ _____ _____ my family.

W Oh, I understand. Have a good time.

M Thanks.

08

M Honey, what are you reading?

W Look at this article. There will be a World Dinosaur Exhibition this Saturday. _____ _____ _____ bring the kids?

M That sounds great! Where's the exhibition held?

W At the Redstone Science Museum.

M Good. I know where that is.

W There are _____ _____ _____ _____ like making dinosaur toys and watching a 3D dinosaur movie.

M Our kids will love them. What time shall we go?

W Since _____ _____ _____ from 10 a.m. to 5 p.m., how about going there in the afternoon?

M Okay. How much is _____ _____ _____?

W It's $10 for an adult and $5 for a child and if we register online, we can get a discount.

M Really? Let's register now.

W Okay.

09

W Hello, listeners! Are you excited for the Greenville Animation Film Festival? This festival, one of Greenville's largest events, began in 1995. This year, it'll start on December 5th and continue _____ _____ _____. The theme for this year is friendship. Throughout the festival, visitors can watch different animation movies related to the theme every night. The movie schedule _____ _____ _____ on our website. Remember, there's _____ _____ _____ nearby. So, please use public transportation. For more information, visit www.GAFF.com. Thank you.

10

M Jane, what are you doing?

W Dad, I'm searching for a one-day drawing lesson, but it's not easy to choose one. Can you help me?

M Sure. Is there any particular drawing material you want to use?

W I've done pastel drawing before. So, this time _____ _____ _____ _____ a new material, not pastel.

M Okay. Do you want to have a private lesson?

W No, I want to learn _____ _____ _____.

M Okay. You have piano lessons Monday mornings, right?

W Yes. So I should choose a lesson on _____ _____ _____.

M That leaves you two choices.

W Let me think. *[Pause]* I'd rather take a lesson _____ _____ _____.

M There's only one left then.

W Yes. I'll register for that lesson. Thank you, dad.

11

M Emma, it smells good in here. What's that _____ _____?

W I cooked some *Bulgogi*. Try some.

M Okay. Wow, it's really delicious. _____ _____ _____ _____ the recipe?

W ▨▨▨▨▨▨▨▨▨▨▨▨▨▨▨▨

12

W Honey, _____ _____ _____ _____ we used when we went camping?

M Oh, I just left them in my car.

W Really? I _____ _____ _____ _____ tomorrow.

M ▨▨▨▨▨▨▨▨▨▨▨▨▨▨▨▨

13

M Kelly, what are you doing?

W Hey, Paul. I'm _____ _____ _____ my old sweater using the Local Market app.

M Local Market app? What's that?

W It's a kind of online marketplace for used items. I can buy or sell items _____ _____ _____.

M Interesting! How do you use it?

W If I upload pictures of my sweater, somebody who needs a sweater will see and buy it.

M That's great. Have you ever bought anything using the app?

W Sure. Look at this bag. I bought it for only $5.

M Wow, that's a good deal! I also have _____ _____ _____ _____ to sell.

W ▨▨▨▨▨▨▨▨▨▨▨▨▨▨▨▨

14

W Honey, look at this bill. Have you been using a movie streaming service?

M No. But a few months ago, I used a one-month free trial.

W Look. A $15 _____ _____ has been charged for three months.

M Oh, no! There must be something wrong.

W Did you get any notice about that?

M Well, I did, but I didn't pay much attention to it when I _____ _____ _____ it.

W Let's check it now.

M Wait. *[Clicking sound]* Hmm, it says the membership fee _____ _____ _____ if I don't cancel it after the free trial.

W Well, one of my friends was in the same situation and she tried to get a refund but she couldn't.

M Then, what should I do?

W Hmm, the only thing you can do is _____ _____ _____ _____.

M ▨▨▨▨▨▨▨▨▨▨▨▨▨▨▨▨▨▨▨▨▨▨▨▨▨▨▨

15

M Ms. Brown teaches English in high school. Chris is one of the students who takes her class. Since he wants to _____ _____ English Literature at university, he thinks _____ _____ _____ are important. To get advice, Chris visits Ms. Brown and asks _____ _____ _____ his English writing skills. Ms. Brown thinks that writing in English regularly is important. So she wants to suggest that Chris _____ _____ _____ for his English writing skills. In this situation, what would Ms. Brown most likely say to Chris?

Ms. Brown ▨▨▨▨▨▨▨▨▨▨▨▨▨▨▨▨▨▨▨▨▨▨▨

16~17

W Hello, everyone. I'm Monica Dale from Blue River Animal Center. Today, let's talk about the different _____ _____ _____. First, smell is probably the most basic type of animal communication. For example, dogs _____ _____ _____ with their smell to send a clear message to others to stay away. Second, when animals make sounds, those usually _____ _____ _____. For instance, dolphins get the attention of others in the area by using various sounds. Sometimes, they sing to their mates. Third, visual signals are widely used by many animals. Gorillas _____ _____ their tongues to show anger. Lastly, many animals make use of touch to communicate their feelings to others. Giraffes press their necks together when _____ _____ _____ each other. Now, let's take a look at a video clip that contains interesting animal communication.

기출의 바이블

고1 영어

Part 2

독해편

01

202309 18번

다음 글의 목적으로 가장 적절한 것은?

Dear Professor Sanchez,

My name is Ellis Wight, and I'm the director of the Alexandria Science Museum. We are holding a Chemistry Fair for local middle school students on Saturday, October 28. The goal of the fair is to encourage them to be interested in science through guided experiments. We are looking for college students who can help with the experiments during the event. I am contacting you to ask you to recommend some students from the chemistry department at your college who you think are qualified for this job. With their help, I'm sure the participants will have a great experience. I look forward to hearing from you soon.

Sincerely,
Ellis Wight

① 과학 박물관 내 시설 이용 제한을 안내하려고
② 화학 박람회 일정이 변경된 이유를 설명하려고
③ 중학생을 위한 화학 실험 특별 강연을 부탁하려고
④ 중학교 과학 수업용 실험 교재 집필을 의뢰하려고
⑤ 화학 박람회에서 실험을 도울 대학생 추천을 요청하려고

02

202306 18번

다음 글의 목적으로 가장 적절한 것은?

ACC Travel Agency Customers:

Have you ever wanted to enjoy a holiday in nature? This summer is the best time to turn your dream into reality. We have a perfect travel package for you. This travel package includes special trips to Lake Madison as well as massage and meditation to help you relax. Also, we provide yoga lessons taught by experienced instructors. If you book this package, you will enjoy all this at a reasonable price. We are sure that it will be an unforgettable experience for you. If you call us, we will be happy to give you more details.

① 여행 일정 변경을 안내하려고
② 패키지 여행 상품을 홍보하려고
③ 여행 상품 불만족에 대해 사과하려고
④ 여행 만족도 조사 참여를 부탁하려고
⑤ 패키지 여행 업무 담당자를 모집하려고

03

202303 18번

다음 글의 목적으로 가장 적절한 것은?

To whom it may concern,

I am a resident of the Blue Sky Apartment. Recently I observed that the kid zone is in need of repairs. I want you to pay attention to the poor condition of the playground equipment in the zone. The swings are damaged, the paint is falling off, and some of the bolts on the slide are missing. The facilities have been in this terrible condition since we moved here. They are dangerous to the children playing there. Would you please have them repaired? I would appreciate your immediate attention to solve this matter.

Yours sincerely,
Nina Davis

① 아파트의 첨단 보안 설비를 홍보하려고
② 아파트 놀이터의 임시 폐쇄를 공지하려고
③ 아파트 놀이터 시설의 수리를 요청하려고
④ 아파트 놀이터 사고의 피해 보상을 촉구하려고
⑤ 아파트 공용 시설 사용 시 유의 사항을 안내하려고

04 오답률 BEST

다음 글의 목적으로 가장 적절한 것은?

Dear Mr. Krull,

I have greatly enjoyed working at Trincom Enterprises as a sales manager. Since I joined in 2015, I have been a loyal and essential member of this company, and have developed innovative ways to contribute to the company. Moreover, in the last year alone, I have brought in two new major clients to the company, increasing the company's total sales by 5%. Also, I have voluntarily trained 5 new members of staff, totaling 35 hours. I would therefore request your consideration in raising my salary, which I believe reflects my performance as well as the industry average. I look forward to speaking with you soon.

Kimberly Morss

① 부서 이동을 신청하려고
② 급여 인상을 요청하려고
③ 근무 시간 조정을 요구하려고
④ 기업 혁신 방안을 제안하려고
⑤ 신입 사원 연수에 대해 문의하려고

05

다음 글의 목적으로 가장 적절한 것은?

Dear Parents/Guardians,

Class parties will be held on the afternoon of Friday, December 16th, 2022. Children may bring in sweets, crisps, biscuits, cakes, and drinks. We are requesting that children do not bring in home-cooked or prepared food. All food should arrive in a sealed packet with the ingredients clearly listed. Fruit and vegetables are welcomed if they are pre-packed in a sealed packet from the shop. Please DO NOT send any food into school containing nuts as we have many children with severe nut allergies. Please check the ingredients of all food your children bring carefully. Thank you for your continued support and cooperation.

Yours sincerely,
Lisa Brown, Headteacher

① 학급 파티 일정 변경을 공지하려고
② 학교 식당의 새로운 메뉴를 소개하려고
③ 학생의 특정 음식 알레르기 여부를 조사하려고
④ 학부모의 적극적인 학급 파티 참여를 독려하려고
⑤ 학급 파티에 가져올 음식에 대한 유의 사항을 안내하려고

06

다음 글의 목적으로 가장 적절한 것은?

Dear Boat Tour Manager,

On March 15, my family was on one of your Glass Bottom Boat Tours. When we returned to our hotel, I discovered that I left behind my cell phone case. The case must have fallen off my lap and onto the floor when I took it off my phone to clean it. I would like to ask you to check if it is on your boat. Its color is black and it has my name on the inside. If you find the case, I would appreciate it if you would let me know.

Sincerely,
Sam Roberts

① 제품의 고장 원인을 문의하려고
② 분실물 발견 시 연락을 부탁하려고
③ 시설물의 철저한 관리를 당부하려고
④ 여행자 보험 가입 절차를 확인하려고
⑤ 분실물 센터 확장의 필요성을 건의하려고

07

다음 글의 목적으로 가장 적절한 것은?

Dear Ms. Robinson,

The Warblers Choir is happy to announce that we are invited to compete in the International Young Choir Competition. The competition takes place in London on May 20. Though we wish to participate in the event, we do not have the necessary funds to travel to London. So we are kindly asking you to support us by coming to our fundraising concert. It will be held on March 26. In this concert, we shall be able to show you how big our passion for music is. Thank you in advance for your kind support and help.

Sincerely,
Arnold Reynolds

① 합창 대회 결과를 공지하려고
② 모금 음악회 참석을 요청하려고
③ 음악회 개최 장소를 예약하려고
④ 합창곡 선정에 조언을 구하려고
⑤ 기부금 사용 내역을 보고하려고

08

다음 글의 목적으로 가장 적절한 것은?

To the school librarian,

I am Kyle Thomas, the president of the school's English writing club. I have planned activities that will increase the writing skills of our club members. One of the aims of these activities is to make us aware of various types of news media and the language used in printed newspaper articles. However, some old newspapers are not easy to access online. It is, therefore, my humble request to you to allow us to use old newspapers that have been stored in the school library. I would really appreciate it if you grant us permission.

Yours truly,
Kyle Thomas

① 도서관 이용 시간 연장을 건의하려고
② 신청한 도서의 대출 가능 여부를 문의하려고
③ 도서관에 보관 중인 자료 현황을 조사하려고
④ 글쓰기 동아리 신문의 도서관 비치를 부탁하려고
⑤ 도서관에 있는 오래된 신문의 사용 허락을 요청하려고

09

다음 글의 목적으로 가장 적절한 것은?

Dear Mr. Dennis Brown,

We at G&D Restaurant are honored and delighted to invite you to our annual Fall Dinner. The annual event will be held on October 1st, 2021 at our restaurant. At the event, we will be introducing new wonderful dishes that our restaurant will be offering soon. These delicious dishes will showcase the amazing talents of our gifted chefs. Also, our chefs will be providing cooking tips, ideas on what to buy for your kitchen, and special recipes. We at G&D Restaurant would be more than grateful if you can make it to this special occasion and be part of our celebration. We look forward to seeing you. Thank you so much.

Regards,
Marcus Lee, Owner – G&D Restaurant

① 식당 개업을 홍보하려고
② 식당의 연례행사에 초대하려고
③ 신입 요리사 채용을 공고하려고
④ 매장 직원의 실수를 사과하려고
⑤ 식당 만족도 조사 참여를 부탁하려고

10

202106 18번

다음 글의 목적으로 가장 적절한 것은?

Dear Mr. Jones,

I am James Arkady, PR Director of KHJ Corporation. We are planning to redesign our brand identity and launch a new logo to celebrate our 10th anniversary. We request you to create a logo that best suits our company's core vision, 'To inspire humanity.' I hope the new logo will convey our brand message and capture the values of KHJ. Please send us your logo design proposal once you are done with it. Thank you.

Best regards,
James Arkady

① 회사 로고 제작을 의뢰하려고
② 변경된 회사 로고를 홍보하려고
③ 회사 비전에 대한 컨설팅을 요청하려고
④ 회사 창립 10주년 기념품을 주문하려고
⑤ 회사 로고 제작 일정 변경을 공지하려고

11

202103 18번

다음 글의 목적으로 가장 적절한 것은?

Dear members of Eastwood Library,

Thanks to the Friends of Literature group, we've successfully raised enough money to remodel the library building. John Baker, our local builder, has volunteered to help us with the remodelling but he needs assistance. By grabbing a hammer or a paint brush and donating your time, you can help with the construction. Join Mr. Baker in his volunteering team and become a part of making Eastwood Library a better

place! Please call 541-567-1234 for more information.

Sincerely,
Mark Anderson

① 도서관 임시 휴관의 이유를 설명하려고
② 도서관 자원봉사자 교육 일정을 안내하려고
③ 도서관 보수를 위한 모금 행사를 제안하려고
④ 도서관 공사에 참여할 자원봉사자를 모집하려고
⑤ 도서관에서 개최하는 글쓰기 대회를 홍보하려고

12 오답률 BEST

202011 18번

다음 글의 목적으로 가장 적절한 것은?

To whom it may concern:

I was born and raised in the city of Boulder and have enjoyed our scenic natural spaces for my whole life. The land through which the proposed Pine Hill walking trail would cut is home to a variety of species. Wildlife faces pressure from development, and these animals need space where they can hide from human activity. Although trails serve as a wonderful source for us to access the natural world and appreciate the wildlife within it, if we continue to destroy habitats with excess trails, the wildlife will stop using these areas. Please reconsider whether the proposed trail is absolutely necessary.

Sincerely,
Tyler Stuart

① 환경 보호 캠페인 참여를 부탁하려고
② 지역 관광 프로그램에 대해 문의하려고
③ 산책로 조성 계획의 재고를 요청하려고
④ 보행자 안전을 위해 인도 설치를 건의하려고
⑤ 야생 동물 보호구역 관리의 문제점을 지적하려고

01 오답률 BEST

📄 202309 19번

다음 글에 나타난 'I'의 심경 변화로 가장 적절한 것은?

Gregg and I had been rock climbing since sunrise and had had no problems. So we took a risk. "Look, the first bolt is right there. I can definitely climb out to it. Piece of cake," I persuaded Gregg, minutes before I found myself pinned. It wasn't a piece of cake. The rock was deceptively barren of handholds. I clumsily moved back and forth across the cliff face and ended up with nowhere to go...but down. The bolt that would save my life, if I could get to it, was about two feet above my reach. My arms trembled from exhaustion. I looked at Gregg. My body froze with fright from my neck down to my toes. Our rope was tied between us. If I fell, he would fall with me.

＊barren of: ~이 없는

① joyful → bored
② confident → fearful
③ nervous → relieved
④ regretful → pleased
⑤ grateful → annoyed

02

📄 202306 19번

다음 글에 드러난 'I'의 심경 변화로 가장 적절한 것은?

When I woke up in our hotel room, it was almost midnight. I didn't see my husband nor daughter. I called them, but I heard their phones ringing in the room. Feeling worried, I went outside and walked down the street, but they were nowhere to be found. When I decided I should ask someone for help, a crowd nearby caught my attention. I approached, hoping to find my husband and daughter, and suddenly I saw two familiar faces. I smiled, feeling calm. Just then, my daughter saw me and called, "Mom!" They were watching the magic show. Finally, I felt all my worries disappear.

① anxious → relieved
② delighted → unhappy
③ indifferent → excited
④ relaxed → upset
⑤ embarrassed → proud

03

📄 202303 19번

다음 글에 드러난 'I'의 심경 변화로 가장 적절한 것은?

On a two-week trip in the Rocky Mountains, I saw a grizzly bear in its native habitat. At first, I felt joy as I watched the bear walk across the land. He stopped every once in a while to turn his head about, sniffing deeply. He was following the scent of something, and slowly I began to realize that this giant animal was smelling me! I froze. This was no longer a wonderful experience; it was now an issue of survival. The bear's motivation was to find meat to eat, and I was clearly on his menu.

＊scent: 냄새

① sad → angry
② delighted → scared
③ satisfied → jealous
④ worried → relieved
⑤ frustrated → excited

04

📄 202211 19번

다음 글에 드러난 'I'의 심경 변화로 가장 적절한 것은?

On one beautiful spring day, I was fully enjoying my day off. I arrived at the nail salon, and muted my cellphone so that I would be disconnected for the hour and feel calm and peaceful. I was so comfortable while I got a manicure. As I left the place, I checked my cellphone and saw four missed calls from a strange number. I knew immediately that something bad was coming, and I called back. A young woman answered and said that my father had fallen over a stone and was injured, now seated on a bench. I was really concerned since he had just recovered from his knee surgery. I rushed getting into my car to go see him.

① nervous → confident
② relaxed → worried
③ excited → indifferent
④ pleased → jealous
⑤ annoyed → grateful

05

다음 글에 나타난 'I'의 심경 변화로 가장 적절한 것은?

It was two hours before the submission deadline and I still hadn't finished my news article. I sat at the desk, but suddenly, the typewriter didn't work. No matter how hard I tapped the keys, the levers wouldn't move to strike the paper. I started to realize that I would not be able to finish the article on time. Desperately, I rested the typewriter on my lap and started hitting each key with as much force as I could manage. Nothing happened. Thinking something might have happened inside of it, I opened the cover, lifted up the keys, and found the problem — a paper clip. The keys had no room to move. After picking it out, I pressed and pulled some parts. The keys moved smoothly again. I breathed deeply and smiled. Now I knew that I could finish my article on time.

① confident → nervous ② frustrated → relieved
③ bored → amazed ④ indifferent → curious
⑤ excited → disappointed

06

다음 글에 드러난 Matthew의 심경 변화로 가장 적절한 것은?

One Saturday morning, Matthew's mother told Matthew that she was going to take him to the park. A big smile came across his face. As he loved to play outside, he ate his breakfast and got dressed quickly so they could go. When they got to the park, Matthew ran all the way over to the swing set. That was his favorite thing to do at the park. But the swings were all being used. His mother explained that he could use the slide until a swing became available, but it was broken. Suddenly, his mother got a phone call and she told Matthew they had to leave. His heart sank.

① embarrassed → indifferent
② excited → disappointed
③ cheerful → ashamed
④ nervous → touched
⑤ scared → relaxed

07

다음 글에 드러난 Zoe의 심경 변화로 가장 적절한 것은?

The principal stepped on stage. "Now, I present this year's top academic award to the student who has achieved the highest placing." He smiled at the row of seats where twelve finalists had gathered. Zoe wiped a sweaty hand on her handkerchief and glanced at the other finalists. They all looked as pale and uneasy as herself. Zoe and one of the other finalists had won first placing in four subjects so it came down to how teachers ranked their hard work and confidence. "The Trophy for General Excellence is awarded to Miss Zoe Perry," the principal declared. "Could Zoe step this way, please?" Zoe felt as if she were in heaven. She walked into the thunder of applause with a big smile.

① hopeful → disappointed ② guilty → confident
③ nervous → delighted ④ angry → calm
⑤ relaxed → proud

08

다음 글에 드러난 "I"의 심경 변화로 가장 적절한 것은?

When my mom came home from the mall with a special present for me I was pretty sure I knew what it was. I was absolutely thrilled because I would soon communicate with a new cell phone! I was daydreaming about all of the cool apps and games I was going to download. But my mom smiled really big and handed me a book. I flipped through the pages, figuring that maybe she had hidden my new phone inside. But I slowly realized that my mom had not got me a phone and my present was just a little book, which was so different from what I had wanted.

① worried → furious
② surprised → relieved
③ ashamed → confident
④ anticipating → satisfied
⑤ excited → disappointed

09

📋 202109 19번

다음 글의 상황에 나타난 분위기로 가장 적절한 것은?

In the middle of the night, Matt suddenly awakened. He glanced at his clock. It was 3:23. For just an instant he wondered what had wakened him. Then he remembered. He had heard someone come into his room. Matt sat up in bed, rubbed his eyes, and looked around the small room. "Mom?" he said quietly, hoping he would hear his mother's voice assuring him that everything was all right. But there was no answer. Matt tried to tell himself that he was just hearing things. But he knew he wasn't. There was someone in his room. He could hear rhythmic, scratchy breathing and it wasn't his own. He lay awake for the rest of the night.

① humorous and fun   ② boring and dull
③ calm and peaceful   ④ noisy and exciting
⑤ mysterious and frightening

10

📋 202106 19번

다음 글에 드러난 Cindy의 심경 변화로 가장 적절한 것은?

One day, Cindy happened to sit next to a famous artist in a café, and she was thrilled to see him in person. He was drawing on a used napkin over coffee. She was looking on in awe. After a few moments, the man finished his coffee and was about to throw away the napkin as he left. Cindy stopped him. "Can I have that napkin you drew on?", she asked. "Sure," he replied. "Twenty thousand dollars." She said, with her eyes wide-open, "What? It took you like two minutes to draw that." "No," he said. "It took me over sixty years to draw this." Being at a loss, she stood still rooted to the ground.

① relieved → worried
② indifferent → embarrassed
③ excited → surprised
④ disappointed → satisfied
⑤ jealous → confident

11

📋 202103 19번

다음 글에 드러난 Shirley의 심경으로 가장 적절한 것은?

On the way home, Shirley noticed a truck parked in front of the house across the street. New neighbors! Shirley was dying to know about them. "Do you know anything about the new neighbors?" she asked Pa at dinner. He said, "Yes, and there's one thing that may be interesting to you." Shirley had a billion more questions. Pa said joyfully, "They have a girl just your age. Maybe she wants to be your playmate." Shirley nearly dropped her fork on the floor. How many times had she prayed for a friend? Finally, her prayers were answered! She and the new girl could go to school together, play together, and become best friends.

① curious and excited   ② sorry and upset
③ jealous and annoyed   ④ calm and relaxed
⑤ disappointed and unhappy

★12 오답률 BEST

📋 202011 19번

다음 글에 드러난 'I'의 심경 변화로 가장 적절한 것은?

On my seventh birthday, my mom surprised me with a puppy waiting on a leash. It had beautiful golden fur and an adorable tail. It was exactly what I had always dreamed of. I took the dog everywhere and slept with it every night. A few months later, the dog got out of the backyard and was lost. I sat on my bed and cried for hours while my mother watched me silently from the doorway of my room. I finally fell asleep, exhausted from my grief. My mother never said a word to me about my loss, but I knew she felt the same as I did.

① delighted → sorrowful
② relaxed → annoyed
③ embarrassed → worried
④ excited → horrified
⑤ disappointed → satisfied

01

📄 202309 20번

다음 글에서 필자가 주장하는 바로 가장 적절한 것은?

We are always teaching our children something by our words and our actions. They learn from seeing. They learn from hearing and from *overhearing*. Children share the values of their parents about the most important things in life. Our priorities and principles and our examples of good behavior can teach our children to take the high road when other roads look tempting. Remember that children do not learn the values that make up strong character simply by being *told* about them. They learn by seeing the people around them *act* on and *uphold* those values in their daily lives. Therefore show your child good examples of life by your action. In our daily lives, we can show our children that we respect others. We can show them our compassion and concern when others are suffering, and our own self-discipline, courage and honesty as we make difficult decisions.

① 자녀를 타인과 비교하는 말을 삼가야 한다.
② 자녀에게 행동으로 삶의 모범을 보여야 한다.
③ 칭찬을 통해 자녀의 바람직한 행동을 강화해야 한다.
④ 훈육을 하기 전에 자녀 스스로 생각할 시간을 주어야 한다.
⑤ 자녀가 새로운 것에 도전할 때 인내심을 가지고 지켜봐야 한다.

02 오답률 BEST

📄 202306 20번

다음 글에서 필자가 주장하는 바로 가장 적절한 것은?

Research shows that people who work have two calendars: one for work and one for their personal lives. Although it may seem sensible, having two separate calendars for work and personal life can lead to distractions. To check if something is missing, you will find yourself checking your to-do lists multiple times. Instead, organize all of your tasks in one place. It doesn't matter if you use digital or paper media. It's okay to keep your professional and personal tasks in one place. This will give you a good idea of how time is divided between work and home. This will allow you to make informed decisions about which tasks are most important.

① 결정한 것은 반드시 실행하도록 노력하라.
② 자신이 담당한 업무에 관한 전문성을 확보하라.
③ 업무 집중도를 높이기 위해 책상 위를 정돈하라.
④ 좋은 아이디어를 메모하는 습관을 길러라.
⑤ 업무와 개인 용무를 한 곳에 정리하라.

03

📄 202303 20번

다음 글에서 필자가 주장하는 바로 가장 적절한 것은?

It is difficult for any of us to maintain a constant level of attention throughout our working day. We all have body rhythms characterised by peaks and valleys of energy and alertness. You will achieve more, and feel confident as a benefit, if you schedule your most demanding tasks at times when you are best able to cope with them. If you haven't thought about energy peaks before, take a few days to observe yourself. Try to note the times when you are at your best. We are all different. For some, the peak will come first thing in the morning, but for others it may take a while to warm up.

＊ alertness: 기민함

① 부정적인 감정에 에너지를 낭비하지 말라.
② 자신의 신체 능력에 맞게 운동량을 조절하라.
③ 자기 성찰을 위한 아침 명상 시간을 확보하라.
④ 생산적인 하루를 보내려면 일을 균등하게 배분하라.
⑤ 자신의 에너지가 가장 높은 시간을 파악하여 활용하라.

04

다음 글에서 필자가 주장하는 바로 가장 적절한 것은?

You already have a business and you're about to launch your blog so that you can sell your product. Unfortunately, here is where a 'business mind' can be a bad thing. Most people believe that to have a successful business blog promoting a product, they have to stay strictly 'on the topic.' If all you're doing is shamelessly promoting your product, then who is going to want to read the latest thing you're writing about? Instead, you need to give some useful or entertaining information away for free so that people have a reason to keep coming back. Only by doing this can you create an interested audience that you will then be able to sell to. So, the best way to be successful with a business blog is to write about things that your audience will be interested in.

① 인터넷 게시물에 대한 윤리적 기준을 세워야 한다.
② 블로그를 전문적으로 관리할 인력을 마련해야 한다.
③ 신제품 개발을 위해 상업용 블로그를 적극 활용해야 한다.
④ 상품에 대한 고객들의 반응을 정기적으로 분석할 필요가 있다.
⑤ 상업용 블로그는 사람들이 흥미 있어 할 정보를 제공해야 한다.

05 오답률 BEST

다음 글에서 필자가 주장하는 바로 가장 적절한 것은?

Experts on writing say, "Get rid of as many words as possible." Each word must do something important. If it doesn't, get rid of it. Well, this doesn't work for speaking. It takes more words to introduce, express, and adequately elaborate an idea in speech than it takes in writing. Why is this so? While the reader can reread, the listener cannot rehear. Speakers do not come equipped with a replay button. Because listeners are easily distracted, they will miss many pieces of what a speaker says. If they miss the crucial sentence, they may never catch up. This makes it necessary for speakers to talk *longer* about their points, using more words on them than would be used to express the same idea in writing.

① 연설 시 중요한 정보는 천천히 말해야 한다.
② 좋은 글을 쓰려면 간결한 문장을 사용해야 한다.
③ 말하기 전에 신중히 생각하는 습관을 길러야 한다.
④ 글을 쓸 때보다 말할 때 더 많은 단어를 사용해야 한다.
⑤ 청중의 이해를 돕기 위해 미리 연설문을 제공해야 한다.

06

다음 글에서 필자가 주장하는 바로 가장 적절한 것은?

Meetings encourage creative thinking and can give you ideas that you may never have thought of on your own. However, on average, meeting participants consider about one third of meeting time to be unproductive. But you can make your meetings more productive and more useful by preparing well in advance. You should create a list of items to be discussed and share your list with other participants before a meeting. It allows them to know what to expect in your meeting and prepare to participate.

① 회의 결과는 빠짐없이 작성해서 공개해야 한다.
② 중요한 정보는 공식 회의를 통해 전달해야 한다.
③ 생산성 향상을 위해 정기적인 평가회가 필요하다.
④ 모든 참석자의 동의를 받아서 회의를 열어야 한다.
⑤ 회의에서 다룰 사항은 미리 작성해서 공유해야 한다.

07

다음 글에서 필자가 주장하는 바로 가장 적절한 것은?

When I was in the army, my instructors would show up in my barracks room, and the first thing they would inspect was our bed. It was a simple task, but every morning we were required to make our bed to perfection. It seemed a little ridiculous at the time, but the wisdom of this simple act has been proven to me many times over. If you make your bed every morning, you will have accomplished the first task of the day. It will give you a small sense of pride and it will encourage you to do another task and another. By the end of the day, that one task completed will have turned into many tasks completed. If you can't do little things right, you will never do the big things right.

* barracks room: (병영의) 생활관 ** accomplish: 성취하다

① 숙면을 위해서는 침대를 깔끔하게 관리해야 한다.
② 일의 효율성을 높이려면 협동심을 발휘해야 한다.
③ 올바른 습관을 기르려면 정해진 규칙을 따라야 한다.
④ 건강을 유지하기 위해서는 기상 시간이 일정해야 한다.
⑤ 큰일을 잘 이루려면 작은 일부터 제대로 수행해야 한다.

08

다음 글에서 필자가 주장하는 바로 가장 적절한 것은?

Some experts estimate that as much as half of what we communicate is done through the way we move our bodies. Paying attention to the nonverbal messages you send can make a significant difference in your relationship with students. In general, most students are often closely tuned in to their teacher's body language. For example, when your students first enter the classroom, their initial action is to look for their teacher. Think about how encouraging and empowering it is for a student when that teacher has a friendly greeting and a welcoming smile. Smiling at students — to let them know that you are glad to see them — does not require a great deal of time or effort, but it can make a significant difference in the classroom climate right from the start of class.

① 교사는 학생 간의 상호 작용을 주의 깊게 관찰해야 한다.
② 수업 시 교사는 학생의 수준에 맞는 언어를 사용해야 한다.
③ 학생과의 관계에서 교사는 비언어적 표현에 유의해야 한다.
④ 학교는 학생에게 다양한 역할 경험의 기회를 제공해야 한다.
⑤ 교사는 학생 안전을 위해 교실의 물리적 환경을 개선해야 한다.

09

다음 글에서 필자가 주장하는 바로 가장 적절한 것은?

As you set about to write, it is worth reminding yourself that while you ought to have a point of view, you should avoid telling your readers what to think. Try to hang a question mark over it all. This way you allow your readers to think for themselves about the points and arguments you're making. As a result, they will feel more involved, finding themselves just as committed to the arguments you've made and the insights you've exposed as you are. You will have written an essay that not only avoids passivity in the reader, but is interesting and gets people to think.

① 저자의 독창적인 견해를 드러내야 한다.
② 다양한 표현으로 독자에게 감동을 주어야 한다.
③ 독자가 능동적으로 사고할 수 있도록 글을 써야 한다.
④ 독자에게 가치판단의 기준점을 명확히 제시해야 한다.
⑤ 주관적 관점을 배제하고 사실을 바탕으로 글을 써야 한다.

◆ 정답 및 해설(2권) p.75

10

202106 20번

다음 글에서 필자가 주장하는 바로 가장 적절한 것은?

Sometimes, you feel the need to avoid something that will lead to success out of discomfort. Maybe you are avoiding extra work because you are tired. You are actively shutting out success because you want to avoid being uncomfortable. Therefore, overcoming your instinct to avoid uncomfortable things at first is essential. Try doing new things outside of your comfort zone. Change is always uncomfortable, but it is key to doing things differently in order to find that magical formula for success.

① 불편할지라도 성공하기 위해서는 새로운 것을 시도해야 한다.
② 일과 생활의 균형을 맞추는 성공적인 삶을 추구해야 한다.
③ 갈등 해소를 위해 불편함의 원인을 찾아 개선해야 한다.
④ 단계별 목표를 설정하여 익숙한 것부터 도전해야 한다.
⑤ 변화에 적응하기 위해 직관적으로 문제를 해결해야 한다.

11

202103 20번

다음 글에서 필자가 주장하는 바로 가장 적절한 것은?

At a publishing house and at a newspaper you learn the following: *It's not a mistake if it doesn't end up in print.* It's the same for email. Nothing bad can happen if you haven't hit the Send key. What you've written can have misspellings, errors of fact, rude comments, obvious lies, but it doesn't matter. If you haven't sent it, you still have time to fix it. You can correct any mistake and nobody will ever know the difference. This is easier said than done, of course.

Send is your computer's most attractive command. But before you hit the Send key, make sure that you read your document carefully one last time.

① 중요한 이메일은 출력하여 보관해야 한다.
② 글을 쓸 때에는 개요 작성부터 시작해야 한다.
③ 이메일을 전송하기 전에 반드시 검토해야 한다.
④ 업무와 관련된 컴퓨터 기능을 우선 익혀야 한다.
⑤ 업무상 중요한 내용은 이메일보다는 직접 전달해야 한다.

12

202011 20번

다음 글에서 필자가 주장하는 바로 가장 적절한 것은?

When I was in high school, we had students who could study in the coffee shop and not get distracted by the noise or everything happening around them. We also had students who could not study if the library was not super quiet. The latter students suffered because even in the library, it was impossible to get the type of complete silence they sought. These students were victims of distractions who found it very difficult to study anywhere except in their private bedrooms. In today's world, it is impossible to run away from distractions. Distractions are everywhere, but if you want to achieve your goals, you must learn how to tackle distractions. You cannot eliminate distractions, but you can learn to live with them in a way that ensures they do not limit you.

① 자신에게 적합한 시간 관리법을 찾아야 한다.
② 집중을 방해하는 요인에 대처할 줄 알아야 한다.
③ 학습 공간과 휴식 공간을 명확하게 분리해야 한다.
④ 집중력 향상을 위해 정돈된 학습환경을 유지해야 한다.
⑤ 공공장소에서 타인에게 피해를 주는 행동을 삼가야 한다.

01 오답률 BEST

202309 21번

밑줄 친 fall silently in the woods가 다음 글에서 의미하는 바로 가장 적절한 것은? [3점]

Most people have no doubt heard this question: If a tree falls in the forest and there is no one there to hear it fall, does it make a sound? The correct answer is no. Sound is more than pressure waves, and indeed there can be no sound without a hearer. And similarly, scientific communication is a two-way process. Just as a signal of any kind is useless unless it is perceived, a published scientific paper (signal) is useless unless it is both received *and* understood by its intended audience. Thus we can restate the axiom of science as follows: A scientific experiment is not complete until the results have been published *and understood*. Publication is no more than pressure waves unless the published paper is understood. Too many scientific papers fall silently in the woods.

＊ axiom: 자명한 이치

① fail to include the previous study
② end up being considered completely false
③ become useless because they are not published
④ focus on communication to meet public demands
⑤ are published yet readers don't understand them

02

202306 21번

밑줄 친 become unpaid ambassadors가 다음 글에서 의미하는 바로 가장 적절한 것은?

Why do you care how a customer reacts to a purchase? Good question. By understanding post-purchase behavior, you can understand the influence and the likelihood of whether a buyer will repurchase the product (and whether she will keep it or return it). You'll also determine whether the buyer will encourage others to purchase the product from you. Satisfied customers can become unpaid ambassadors for your business, so customer satisfaction should be on the top of your to-do list. People tend to believe the opinions of people they know. People trust friends over advertisements any day. They know that advertisements are paid to tell the "good side" and that they're used to persuade them to purchase products and services. By continually monitoring your customer's satisfaction after the sale, you have the ability to avoid negative word-of-mouth advertising.

① recommend products to others for no gain
② offer manufacturers feedback on products
③ become people who don't trust others' words
④ get rewards for advertising products overseas
⑤ buy products without worrying about the price

03

202303 21번

밑줄 친 The divorce of the hands from the head가 다음 글에서 의미하는 바로 가장 적절한 것은? [3점]

If we adopt technology, we need to pay its costs. Thousands of traditional livelihoods have been pushed aside by progress, and the lifestyles around those jobs removed. Hundreds of millions of humans today work at jobs they hate, producing things they have no love for. Sometimes these jobs cause physical pain, disability, or chronic disease. Technology creates many new jobs that are certainly dangerous. At the same time, mass education and media train humans to avoid low-tech physical work, to seek jobs working in the digital world. The divorce of the hands from the head puts a stress on the human mind. Indeed, the sedentary nature of the best-paying jobs is a health risk — for body and mind.

＊ chronic: 만성의 ＊＊ sedentary: 주로 앉아서 하는

① ignorance of modern technology
② endless competition in the labor market
③ not getting along well with our coworkers
④ working without any realistic goals for our career
⑤ our increasing use of high technology in the workplace

04

202211 21번

밑줄 친 challenge this sacred cow가 다음 글에서 의미하는 바로 가장 적절한 것은? [3점]

Our language helps to reveal our deeper assumptions. Think of these revealing phrases: When we accomplish something important, we say it took "blood, sweat, and tears." We say important achievements are "hard-earned." We recommend a "hard day's work" when "day's work" would be enough. When we talk of "easy money," we are implying it was obtained through illegal or questionable means. We use the phrase "That's easy for you to say" as a criticism, usually when we are seeking to invalidate someone's opinion. It's like we all automatically accept that the "right" way is, inevitably, the harder one. In my experience this is hardly ever questioned. What would happen if you do challenge this sacred cow? We don't even pause to consider that something important and valuable could be made easy. What if the biggest thing keeping us from doing what matters is the false assumption that it has to take huge effort?

＊invalidate: 틀렸음을 입증하다

① resist the tendency to avoid any hardship
② escape from the pressure of using formal language
③ doubt the solid belief that only hard work is worthy
④ abandon the old notion that money always comes first
⑤ break the superstition that holy animals bring good luck

05

202209 21번

밑줄 친 fire a customer가 다음 글에서 의미하는 바로 가장 적절한 것은?

Is the customer *always* right? When customers return a broken product to a famous company, which makes kitchen and bathroom fixtures, the company nearly always offers a replacement to maintain good customer relations. Still, "there are times you've got to say 'no,'" explains the warranty expert of the company, such as when a product is undamaged or has been abused. Entrepreneur Lauren Thorp, who owns an e-commerce company, says, "While the customer is 'always' right, sometimes you just have to fire a customer." When Thorp has tried everything to resolve a complaint and realizes that the customer will be dissatisfied no matter what, she returns her attention to the rest of her customers, who she says are "the reason for my success."

① deal with a customer's emergency
② delete a customer's purchasing record
③ reject a customer's unreasonable demand
④ uncover the hidden intention of a customer
⑤ rely on the power of an influential customer

06

202206 21번

밑줄 친 put the glass down이 다음 글에서 의미하는 바로 가장 적절한 것은? [3점]

A psychology professor raised a glass of water while teaching stress management principles to her students, and asked them, "How heavy is this glass of water I'm holding?" Students shouted out various answers. The professor replied, "The absolute weight of this glass doesn't matter. It depends on how long I hold it. If I hold it for a minute, it's quite light. But, if I hold it for a day straight, it will cause severe pain in my arm, forcing me to drop the glass to the floor. In each case, the weight of the glass is the same, but the longer I hold it, the heavier it feels to me." As the class nodded their heads in agreement, she continued, "Your stresses in life are like this glass of water. If you still feel the weight of yesterday's stress, it's a strong sign that it's time to put the glass down."

① pour more water into the glass
② set a plan not to make mistakes
③ let go of the stress in your mind
④ think about the cause of your stress
⑤ learn to accept the opinions of others

07

밑줄 친 Leave those activities to the rest of the sheep 이 다음 글에서 의미하는 바로 가장 적절한 것은? [3점]

A job search is not a passive task. When you are searching, you are not browsing, nor are you "just looking". Browsing is not an effective way to reach a goal you claim to want to reach. If you are acting with purpose, if you are serious about anything you chose to do, then you need to be direct, focused and whenever possible, clever. Everyone else searching for a job has the same goal, competing for the same jobs. You must do more than the rest of the herd. Regardless of how long it may take you to find and get the job you want, being proactive will logically get you results faster than if you rely only on browsing online job boards and emailing an occasional resume. Leave those activities to the rest of the sheep.

① Try to understand other job-seekers' feelings.
② Keep calm and stick to your present position.
③ Don't be scared of the job-seeking competition.
④ Send occasional emails to your future employers.
⑤ Be more active to stand out from other job-seekers.

08

밑줄 친 a slap in our own face가 다음 글에서 의미하는 바로 가장 적절한 것은? [3점]

When it comes to climate change, many blame the fossil fuel industry for pumping greenhouse gases, the agricultural sector for burning rainforests, or the fashion industry for producing excessive clothes. But wait, what drives these industrial activities? Our consumption. Climate change is a summed product of each person's behavior. For example, the fossil fuel industry is a popular scapegoat in the climate crisis. But why do they drill and burn fossil fuels? We provide them strong financial incentives: some people regularly travel on airplanes and cars that burn fossil fuels. Some people waste electricity generated by burning fuel in power plants. Some people use and throw away plastic products derived from crude oil every day. Blaming the fossil fuel industry while engaging in these behaviors is a slap in our own face.

* scapegoat: 희생양

① giving the future generation room for change
② warning ourselves about the lack of natural resources
③ refusing to admit the benefits of fossil fuel production
④ failing to recognize our responsibility for climate change
⑤ starting to deal with environmental problems individually

09 오답률 BEST

밑줄 친 "matter out of place"가 다음 글에서 의미하는 바로 가장 적절한 것은?

Nothing is trash by nature. Anthropologist Mary Douglas brings back and analyzes the common saying that dirt is "matter out of place." Dirt is relative, she emphasizes. "Shoes are not dirty in themselves, but it is dirty to place them on the dining-table; food is not dirty in itself, but it is dirty to leave pots and pans in the bedroom, or food all over clothing; similarly, bathroom items in the living room; clothing lying on chairs; outdoor things placed indoors; upstairs things downstairs, and so on." Sorting the dirty from the clean — removing the shoes from the table, putting the dirty clothing in the washing machine — involves systematic ordering and classifying. Eliminating dirt is thus a positive process.

① something that is completely broken
② a tiny dust that nobody notices
③ a dirty but renewable material
④ what can be easily replaced
⑤ a thing that is not in order

10

📰 202106 21번

밑줄 친 <u>want to use a hammer</u>가 다음 글에서 의미하는 바로 가장 적절한 것은? [3점]

We have a tendency to interpret events selectively. If we want things to be "this way" or "that way" we can most certainly select, stack, or arrange evidence in a way that supports such a viewpoint. Selective perception is based on what seems to us to stand out. However, what seems to us to be standing out may very well be related to our goals, interests, expectations, past experiences, or current demands of the situation — "with a hammer in hand, everything looks like a nail." This quote highlights the phenomenon of selective perception. If we <u>want to use a hammer</u>, then the world around us may begin to look as though it is full of nails!

① are unwilling to stand out
② make our effort meaningless
③ intend to do something in a certain way
④ hope others have a viewpoint similar to ours
⑤ have a way of thinking that is accepted by others

11

📰 202103 21번

밑줄 친 <u>translate it from the past tense to the future tense</u>가 다음 글에서 의미하는 바로 가장 적절한 것은? [3점]

Get past the 'I wish I hadn't done that!' reaction. If the disappointment you're feeling is linked to an exam you didn't pass because you didn't study for it, or a job you didn't get because you said silly things at the interview, or a person you didn't impress because you took entirely the wrong approach, accept that it's *happened* now. The only value of 'I wish I hadn't done that!' is that you'll know better what to do next time. The learning pay-off is useful and significant. This 'if only I ...' agenda is virtual. Once you have worked that out, it's time to <u>translate it from the past tense to the future tense</u>: 'Next time I'm in this situation, I'm going to try to ...'.

* agenda: 의제 ** tense: 시제

① look for a job linked to your interest
② get over regrets and plan for next time
③ surround yourself with supportive people
④ study grammar and write clear sentences
⑤ examine your way of speaking and apologize

12 오답률 BEST

📰 202011 21번

밑줄 친 <u>popped out of the box</u>가 다음 글에서 의미하는 바로 가장 적절한 것은?

With the Internet, everything changed. Product problems, overpromises, the lack of customer support, differential pricing — all of the issues that customers actually experienced from a marketing organization suddenly <u>popped out of the box</u>. No longer were there any controlled communications or even business systems. Consumers could generally learn through the Web whatever they wanted to know about a company, its products, its competitors, its distribution systems, and, most of all, its truthfulness when talking about its products and services. Just as important, the Internet opened up a forum for customers to compare products, experiences, and values with other customers easily and quickly. Now the customer had a way to talk back to the marketer and to do so through public forums instantly.

* differential pricing: 가격 차등

① could not be kept secret anymore
② might disappear from public attention
③ were no longer available to marketers
④ became too complicated to understand
⑤ began to improve companies' reputations

01

다음 글의 요지로 가장 적절한 것은?

We all negotiate every day, whether we realise it or not. Yet few people ever learn *how* to negotiate. Those who do usually learn the traditional, win-lose negotiating style rather than an approach that is likely to result in a win-win agreement. This old-school, adversarial approach may be useful in a one-off negotiation where you will probably not deal with that person again. However, such transactions are becoming increasingly rare, because most of us deal with the same people repeatedly — our spouses and children, our friends and colleagues, our customers and clients. In view of this, it's essential to achieve successful results for ourselves and maintain a healthy relationship with our negotiating partners at the same time. In today's interdependent world of business partnerships and long-term relationships, a win-win outcome is fast becoming the *only* acceptable result.

* adversarial: 적대적인

① 협상 상대의 단점뿐 아니라 장점을 철저히 분석해야 한다.
② 의사소통 과정에서 서로의 의도를 확인하는 것이 바람직하다.
③ 성공적인 협상을 위해 다양한 대안을 준비하는 것이 중요하다.
④ 양측에 유리한 협상을 통해 상대와 좋은 관계를 유지해야 한다.
⑤ 원만한 인간관계를 위해 상호독립성을 인정하는 것이 필요하다.

02 오답률 BEST

다음 글의 요지로 가장 적절한 것은?

The promise of a computerized society, we were told, was that it would pass to machines all of the repetitive drudgery of work, allowing us humans to pursue higher purposes and to have more leisure time. It didn't work out this way. Instead of more time, most of us have less. Companies large and small have off-loaded work onto the backs of consumers. Things that used to be done for us, as part of the value-added service of working with a company, we are now expected to do ourselves. With air travel, we're now expected to complete our own reservations and check-in, jobs that used to be done by airline employees or travel agents. At the grocery store, we're expected to bag our own groceries and, in some supermarkets, to scan our own purchases.

* drudgery: 고된 일

① 컴퓨터 기반 사회에서는 여가 시간이 더 늘어난다.
② 회사 업무의 전산화는 업무 능률을 향상시킨다.
③ 컴퓨터화된 사회에서 소비자는 더 많은 일을 하게 된다.
④ 온라인 거래가 모든 소비자들을 만족시키기에는 한계가 있다.
⑤ 산업의 발전으로 인해 기계가 인간의 일자리를 대신하고 있다.

03

다음 글의 요지로 가장 적절한 것은?

When students are starting their college life, they may approach every course, test, or learning task the same way, using what we like to call "the rubber-stamp approach." Think about it this way: Would you wear a tuxedo to a baseball game? A colorful dress to a funeral? A bathing suit to religious services? Probably not. You know there's appropriate dress for different occasions and settings. Skillful learners know that "putting on the same clothes" won't work for every class. They are flexible learners. They have different strategies and know when to use them. They know that you study for multiple-choice tests differently than you study for essay tests. And they not only know what to do, but they also know how to do it.

① 숙련된 학습자는 상황에 맞는 학습 전략을 사용할 줄 안다.
② 선다형 시험과 논술 시험은 평가의 형태와 목적이 다르다.
③ 문화마다 특정 행사와 상황에 맞는 복장 규정이 있다.
④ 학습의 양보다는 학습의 질이 학업 성과를 좌우한다.
⑤ 학습 목표가 명확할수록 성취 수준이 높아진다.

04

다음 글의 요지로 가장 적절한 것은?

The old saying is that "knowledge is power," but when it comes to scary, threatening news, research suggests the exact opposite. Frightening news can actually rob people of their inner sense of control, making them less likely to take care of themselves and other people. Public health research shows that when the news presents health-related information in a pessimistic way, people are actually less likely to take steps to protect themselves from illness as a result. A news article that's intended to warn people about increasing cancer rates, for example, can result in fewer people choosing to get screened for the disease because they're so terrified of what they might find. This is also true for issues such as climate change. When a news story is all doom and gloom, people feel depressed and become less interested in taking small, personal steps to fight ecological collapse.

① 두려움을 주는 뉴스는 사람들이 문제에 덜 대처하게 할 수 있다.
② 정보를 전달하는 시기에 따라 뉴스의 영향력이 달라질 수 있다.
③ 지속적인 환경 문제 보도가 사람들의 인식 변화를 가져온다.
④ 정보 제공의 지연은 정확한 문제 인식에 방해가 될 수 있다.
⑤ 출처가 불분명한 건강 정보는 사람들에게 유익하지 않다.

05

다음 글의 요지로 가장 적절한 것은?

A recent study from Carnegie Mellon University in Pittsburgh, called "When Too Much of a Good Thing May Be Bad," indicates that classrooms with too much decoration are a source of distraction for young children and directly affect their cognitive performance. Being visually overstimulated, the children have a great deal of difficulty concentrating and end up with worse academic results. On the other hand, if there is not much decoration on the classroom walls, the children are less distracted, spend more time on their activities, and learn more. So it's our job, in order to support their attention, to find the right balance between excessive decoration and the complete absence of it.

① 아이들의 집중을 돕기 위해 과도한 교실 장식을 지양할 필요가 있다.
② 아이들의 인성과 인지 능력을 균형 있게 발달시키는 것이 중요하다.
③ 아이들이 직접 교실을 장식하는 것은 창의력 발달에 도움이 된다.
④ 다양한 교실 활동은 아이들의 수업 참여도를 증진시킨다.
⑤ 풍부한 시각 자료는 아이들의 학습 동기를 높인다.

06

다음 글의 요지로 가장 적절한 것은?

Your emotions deserve attention and give you important pieces of information. However, they can also sometimes be an unreliable, inaccurate source of information. You may feel a certain way, but that does not mean those feelings are reflections of the truth. You may feel sad and conclude that your friend is angry with you when her behavior simply reflects that she's having a bad day. You may feel depressed and decide that you did poorly in an interview when you did just fine. Your feelings can mislead you into thinking things that are not supported by facts.

① 자신의 감정으로 인해 상황을 오해할 수 있다.
② 자신의 생각을 타인에게 강요해서는 안 된다.
③ 인간관계가 우리의 감정에 영향을 미친다.
④ 타인의 감정에 공감하는 자세가 필요하다.
⑤ 공동체를 위한 선택에는 보상이 따른다.

07

다음 글의 요지로 가장 적절한 것은?

Many people view sleep as merely a "down time" when their brain shuts off and their body rests. In a rush to meet work, school, family, or household responsibilities, people cut back on their sleep, thinking it won't be a problem, because all of these other activities seem much more important. But research reveals that a number of vital tasks carried out during sleep help to maintain good health and enable people to function at their best. While you sleep, your brain is hard at work forming the pathways necessary for learning and creating memories and new insights. Without enough sleep, you can't focus and pay attention or respond quickly. A lack of sleep may even cause mood problems. In addition, growing evidence shows that a continuous lack of sleep increases the risk for developing serious diseases.

* vital: 매우 중요한

① 수면은 건강 유지와 최상의 기능 발휘에 도움이 된다.
② 업무량이 증가하면 필요한 수면 시간도 증가한다.
③ 균형 잡힌 식단을 유지하면 뇌 기능이 향상된다.
④ 불면증은 주위 사람들에게 부정적인 영향을 미친다.
⑤ 꿈의 내용은 깨어 있는 시간 동안의 경험을 반영한다.

08

다음 글의 요지로 가장 적절한 것은?

Information is worthless if you never actually use it. Far too often, companies collect valuable customer information that ends up buried and never used. They must ensure their data is accessible for use at the appropriate times. For a hotel, one appropriate time for data usage is check-in at the front desk. I often check in at a hotel I've visited frequently, only for the people at the front desk to give no indication that they recognize me as a customer. The hotel must have stored a record of my visits, but they don't make that information accessible to the front desk clerks. They are missing a prime opportunity to utilize data to create a better experience focused on customer loyalty. Whether they have ten customers, ten thousand, or even ten million, the goal is the same: create a delightful customer experience that encourages loyalty.

① 기업 정보의 투명한 공개는 고객 만족도를 향상시킨다.
② 목표 고객층에 대한 분석은 기업의 이익 창출로 이어진다.
③ 고객 충성도를 높이기 위해 고객 정보가 활용될 필요가 있다.
④ 일관성 있는 호텔 서비스 제공을 통해 단골 고객을 확보할 수 있다.
⑤ 사생활 침해에 대한 우려로 고객 정보를 보관하는 데 어려움이 있다.

09 오답률 BEST

다음 글의 요지로 가장 적절한 것은?

It's important that you think independently and fight for what you believe in, but there comes a time when it's wiser to stop fighting for your view and move on to accepting what a trustworthy group of people think is best. This can be extremely difficult. But it's smarter, and ultimately better for you to be open-minded and have faith that the conclusions of a trustworthy group of people are better than whatever you think. If you can't understand their view, you're probably just blind to their way of thinking. If you continue doing what you think is best when all the evidence and trustworthy people are against you, you're being dangerously confident. The truth is that while most people can become incredibly open-minded, some can't, even after they have repeatedly encountered lots of pain from betting that they were right when they were not.

① 대부분의 사람들은 진리에 도달하지 못하고 고통을 받는다.
② 맹목적으로 다른 사람의 의견을 받아들이는 것은 위험하다.
③ 남을 설득하기 위해서는 타당한 증거로 주장을 뒷받침해야 한다.
④ 믿을만한 사람이 누구인지 판단하려면 열린 마음을 가져야 한다.
⑤ 자신의 의견이 최선이 아닐 수 있다는 것을 인정하는 것이 필요하다.

◆ 정답 및 해설(2권) p.85

10

202106 22번

다음 글의 요지로 가장 적절한 것은?

Rather than attempting to punish students with a low grade or mark in the hope it will encourage them to give greater effort in the future, teachers can better motivate students by considering their work as incomplete and then requiring additional effort. Teachers at Beachwood Middle School in Beachwood, Ohio, record students' grades as *A*, *B*, *C*, or *I* (Incomplete). Students who receive an *I* grade are required to do additional work in order to bring their performance up to an acceptable level. This policy is based on the belief that students perform at a failure level or submit failing work in large part because teachers accept it. The Beachwood teachers reason that if they no longer accept substandard work, students will not submit it. And with appropriate support, they believe students will continue to work until their performance is satisfactory.

① 학생에게 평가 결과를 공개하는 것은 학습 동기를 떨어뜨린다.
② 학생에게 추가 과제를 부여하는 것은 학업 부담을 가중시킨다.
③ 지속적인 보상은 학업 성취도에 장기적으로 부정적인 영향을 준다.
④ 학생의 자기주도적 학습 능력은 정서적으로 안정된 학습 환경에서 향상된다.
⑤ 학생의 과제가 일정 수준에 도달하도록 개선 기회를 주면 동기 부여에 도움이 된다.

11

202103 22번

다음 글의 요지로 가장 적절한 것은?

If you care deeply about something, you may place greater value on your ability to succeed in that area of concern. The internal pressure you place on yourself to achieve or do well socially is normal and useful, but when you doubt your ability to succeed in areas that are important to you, your self-worth suffers. Situations are uniquely stressful for each of us based on whether or not they activate our doubt. It's not the pressure to perform that creates your stress. Rather, it's the self-doubt that bothers you. Doubt causes you to see positive, neutral, and even genuinely negative experiences more negatively and as a reflection of your own shortcomings. When you see situations and your strengths more objectively, you are less likely to have doubt as the source of your distress.

* distress: 괴로움

① 비판적인 시각은 객관적인 문제 분석에 도움이 된다.
② 성취 욕구는 스트레스를 이겨 낼 원동력이 될 수 있다.
③ 적절한 수준의 스트레스는 과제 수행의 효율을 높인다.
④ 실패의 경험은 자존감을 낮추고, 타인에 의존하게 한다.
⑤ 자기 의심은 스트레스를 유발하고, 객관적 판단을 흐린다.

12 오답률 BEST

202011 22번

다음 글의 요지로 가장 적절한 것은?

FOBO, or Fear of a Better Option, is the anxiety that something better will come along, which makes it undesirable to commit to existing choices when making a decision. It's an affliction of abundance that drives you to keep all of your options open and to avoid risks. Rather than assessing your options, choosing one, and moving on with your day, you delay the inevitable. It's not unlike hitting the snooze button on your alarm clock only to pull the covers over your head and fall back asleep. As you probably found out the hard way, if you hit snooze enough times, you'll end up being late and racing for the office, your day and mood ruined. While pressing snooze feels so good at the moment, it ultimately demands a price.

* affliction: 고통

① 적당한 수준의 불안감은 업무 수행에 도움이 된다.
② 성급한 의사 결정은 의도하지 않은 결과를 초래한다.
③ 반복되는 실수를 줄이기 위해서는 신중함이 요구된다.
④ 더 나은 선택을 위해 결정을 미루는 것은 결국 해가 된다.
⑤ 규칙적인 생활 습관은 직장에서의 성공 가능성을 높인다.

01 오답률 BEST

📋 202309 23번

다음 글의 주제로 가장 적절한 것은?

The interaction of workers from different cultural backgrounds with the host population might increase productivity due to positive externalities like knowledge spillovers. This is only an advantage up to a certain degree. When the variety of backgrounds is too large, fractionalization may cause excessive transaction costs for communication, which may lower productivity. Diversity not only impacts the labour market, but may also affect the quality of life in a location. A tolerant native population may value a multicultural city or region because of an increase in the range of available goods and services. On the other hand, diversity could be perceived as an unattractive feature if natives perceive it as a distortion of what they consider to be their national identity. They might even discriminate against other ethnic groups and they might fear that social conflicts between different foreign nationalities are imported into their own neighbourhood.

＊externality: 외부 효과 ＊＊fractionalization: 분열

① roles of culture in ethnic groups
② contrastive aspects of cultural diversity
③ negative perspectives of national identity
④ factors of productivity differences across countries
⑤ policies to protect minorities and prevent discrimination

02

📋 202306 23번

다음 글의 주제로 가장 적절한 것은?

We tend to believe that we possess a host of socially desirable characteristics, and that we are free of most of those that are socially undesirable. For example, a large majority of the general public thinks that they are more intelligent, more fair-minded, less prejudiced, and more skilled behind the wheel of an automobile than the average person. This phenomenon is so reliable and ubiquitous that it has come to be known as the "Lake Wobegon effect," after Garrison Keillor's fictional community where "the women are strong, the men are good-looking, and all the children are above average." A survey of one million high school seniors found that 70% thought they were above average in leadership ability, and only 2% thought they were below average. In terms of ability to get along with others, *all* students thought they were above average, 60% thought they were in the top 10%, and 25% thought they were in the top 1%!

＊ubiquitous: 도처에 있는

① importance of having a positive self-image as a leader
② our common belief that we are better than average
③ our tendency to think others are superior to us
④ reasons why we always try to be above average
⑤ danger of prejudice in building healthy social networks

03 오답률 BEST

📋 202303 23번

다음 글의 주제로 가장 적절한 것은?

As the social and economic situation of countries got better, wage levels and working conditions improved. Gradually people were given more time off. At the same time, forms of transport improved and it became faster and cheaper to get to places. England's industrial revolution led to many of these changes. Railways, in the nineteenth century, opened up now famous seaside resorts such as Blackpool and Brighton. With the railways came many large hotels. In Canada, for example, the new coast-to-coast railway system made possible the building of such famous hotels as Banff Springs and Chateau Lake Louise in the Rockies. Later, the arrival of air transport opened up more of the world and led to tourism growth.

① factors that caused tourism expansion
② discomfort at a popular tourist destination
③ importance of tourism in society and economy
④ negative impacts of tourism on the environment
⑤ various types of tourism and their characteristics

04

202211 23번

다음 글의 주제로 가장 적절한 것은?

The most remarkable and unbelievable consequence of melting ice and rising seas is that together they are a kind of time machine, so real that they are altering the duration of our day. It works like this: As the glaciers melt and the seas rise, gravity forces more water toward the equator. This changes the shape of the Earth ever so slightly, making it fatter around the middle, which in turns slows the rotation of the planet similarly to the way a ballet dancer slows her spin by spreading out her arms. The slowdown isn't much, just a few thousandths of a second each year, but like the barely noticeable jump of rising seas every year, it adds up. When dinosaurs lived on the Earth, a day lasted only about twenty-three hours.

① cause of rising temperatures on the Earth
② principles of planets maintaining their shapes
③ implications of melting ice on marine biodiversity
④ way to keep track of time without using any device
⑤ impact of melting ice and rising seas on the length of a day

05 오답률 BEST

202209 23번

다음 글의 주제로 가장 적절한 것은?

For creatures like us, evolution smiled upon those with a strong need to belong. Survival and reproduction are the criteria of success by natural selection, and forming relationships with other people can be useful for both survival and reproduction. Groups can share resources, care for sick members, scare off predators, fight together against enemies, divide tasks so as to improve efficiency, and contribute to survival in many other ways. In particular, if an individual and a group want

the same resource, the group will generally prevail, so competition for resources would especially favor a need to belong. Belongingness will likewise promote reproduction, such as by bringing potential mates into contact with each other, and in particular by keeping parents together to care for their children, who are much more likely to survive if they have more than one caregiver.

① skills for the weak to survive modern life
② usefulness of belonging for human evolution
③ ways to avoid competition among social groups
④ roles of social relationships in children's education
⑤ differences between two major evolutionary theories

06

202206 23번

다음 글의 주제로 가장 적절한 것은?

Every day, children explore and construct relationships among objects. Frequently, these relationships focus on how much or how many of something exists. Thus, children count — "One cookie, two shoes, three candles on the birthday cake, four children in the sandbox." Children compare — "Which has more? Which has fewer? Will there be enough?" Children calculate — "How many will fit? Now, I have five. I need one more." In all of these instances, children are developing a notion of quantity. Children reveal and investigate mathematical concepts through their own activities or experiences, such as figuring out how many crackers to take at snack time or sorting shells into piles.

① difficulties of children in learning how to count
② how children build mathematical understanding
③ why fingers are used in counting objects
④ importance of early childhood education
⑤ advantages of singing number songs

07

202203 23번

다음 글의 주제로 가장 적절한 것은? [3점]

The whole of human society operates on knowing the future weather. For example, farmers in India know when the monsoon rains will come next year and so they know when to plant the crops. Farmers in Indonesia know there are two monsoon rains each year, so next year they can have two harvests. This is based on their knowledge of the past, as the monsoons have always come at about the same time each year in living memory. But the need to predict goes deeper than this; it influences every part of our lives. Our houses, roads, railways, airports, offices, and so on are all designed for the local climate. For example, in England all the houses have central heating, as the outside temperature is usually below 20°C, but no air-conditioning, as temperatures rarely go beyond 26°C, while in Australia the opposite is true: most houses have air-conditioning but rarely central heating.

① new technologies dealing with climate change
② difficulties in predicting the weather correctly
③ weather patterns influenced by rising temperatures
④ knowledge of the climate widely affecting our lives
⑤ traditional wisdom helping our survival in harsh climates

08

202111 23번

다음 글의 주제로 가장 적절한 것은?

We used to think that the brain never changed, but according to the neuroscientist Richard Davidson, we now know that this is not true — specific brain circuits grow stronger through regular practice. He explains, "Well-being is fundamentally no different than learning to play the cello. If one practices the skills of well-being, one will get better at it." What this means is that you can actually train your brain to become more grateful, relaxed, or confident, by repeating experiences that evoke gratitude, relaxation, or confidence. Your brain is shaped by the thoughts you repeat. The more neurons fire as they are activated by repeated thoughts and activities, the faster they develop into neural pathways, which cause lasting changes in the brain. Or in the words of Donald Hebb, "Neurons that fire together wire together." This is such an encouraging premise: bottom line — we can intentionally create the habits for the brain to be happier.

* evoke: (감정을) 불러일으키다 ** premise: 전제

① possibility of forming brain habits for well-being
② role of brain circuits in improving body movements
③ importance of practice in playing musical instruments
④ effect of taking a break on enhancing memory capacity
⑤ difficulty of discovering how neurons in the brain work

09

202109 23번

다음 글의 주제로 가장 적절한 것은?

Vegetarian eating is moving into the mainstream as more and more young adults say no to meat, poultry, and fish. According to the American Dietetic Association, "approximately planned vegetarian diets are healthful, are nutritionally adequate, and provide health benefits in the prevention and treatment of certain diseases." But health concerns are not the only reason that young adults give for changing their diets. Some make the choice out of concern for animal rights. When faced with the statistics that show the majority of animals raised as food live in confinement, many teens give up meat to protest those conditions. Others turn to vegetarianism to support the environment. Meat production uses vast amounts of water, land, grain, and energy and creates problems with animal waste and resulting pollution.

* poultry: 가금류(닭 · 오리 · 거위 등)

① reasons why young people go for vegetarian diets
② ways to build healthy eating habits for teenagers
③ vegetables that help lower your risk of cancer
④ importance of maintaining a balanced diet
⑤ disadvantages of plant-based diets

◆ 정답 및 해설(2권) p. 90

10
202106 23번

다음 글의 주제로 가장 적절한 것은?

Curiosity makes us much more likely to view a tough problem as an interesting challenge to take on. A stressful meeting with our boss becomes an opportunity to learn. A nervous first date becomes an exciting night out with a new person. A colander becomes a hat. In general, curiosity motivates us to view stressful situations as challenges rather than threats, to talk about difficulties more openly, and to try new approaches to solving problems. In fact, curiosity is associated with a less defensive reaction to stress and, as a result, less aggression when we respond to irritation.

* colander: (음식 재료의 물을 빼는 데 쓰는) 체

① importance of defensive reactions in a tough situation
② curiosity as the hidden force of positive reframes
③ difficulties of coping with stress at work
④ potential threats caused by curiosity
⑤ factors that reduce human curiosity

11
202103 23번

다음 글의 주제로 가장 적절한 것은?

When two people are involved in an honest and open conversation, there is a back and forth flow of information. It is a smooth exchange. Since each one is drawing on their past personal experiences, the pace of the exchange is as fast as memory. When one person lies, their responses will come more slowly because the brain needs more time to process the details of a new invention than to recall stored facts. As they say, "Timing is everything." You will notice the time lag when you are having a conversation with someone who is making things up as they go. Don't forget that the other person may be reading your body language as well, and if you seem to be disbelieving their story, they will have to pause to process that information, too.

* lag: 지연

① delayed responses as a sign of lying
② ways listeners encourage the speaker
③ difficulties in finding useful information
④ necessity of white lies in social settings
⑤ shared experiences as conversation topics

12
202011 23번

다음 글의 주제로 가장 적절한 것은?

The use of renewable sources of energy to produce electricity has increasingly been encouraged as a way to harmonize the need to secure electricity supply with environmental protection objectives. But the use of renewable sources also comes with its own consequences, which require consideration. Renewable sources of energy include a variety of sources such as hydropower and ocean-based technologies. Additionally, solar, wind, geothermal and biomass renewable sources also have their own impact on the environment. Hydropower dams, for example, have an impact on aquatic ecosystems and, more recently, have been identified as significant sources of greenhouse emissions. Wind, solar, and biomass also cause negative environmental impacts, such as visual pollution, intensive land occupation and negative effects on bird populations.

* geothermal: 지열의 ** biomass: 에너지로 사용 가능한 생물체

① environmental side effects of using renewable energy sources
② practical methods to meet increasing demand for electricity
③ negative impacts of the use of traditional energy sources
④ numerous ways to obtain renewable sources of energy
⑤ effective procedures to reduce greenhouse emissions

01

202309 24번

다음 글의 제목으로 가장 적절한 것은?

We think we are shaping our buildings. But really, our buildings and development are also shaping us. One of the best examples of this is the oldest-known construction: the ornately carved rings of standing stones at Göbekli Tepe in Turkey. Before these ancestors got the idea to erect standing stones some 12,000 years ago, they were hunter-gatherers. It appears that the erection of the multiple rings of megalithic stones took so long, and so many successive generations, that these innovators were forced to settle down to complete the construction works. In the process, they became the first farming society on Earth. This is an early example of a society constructing something that ends up radically remaking the society itself. Things are not so different in our own time.

＊ornately: 화려하게 ＊＊megalithic: 거석의

① Buildings Transform How We Live!
② Why Do We Build More Than We Need?
③ Copying Ancient Buildings for Creativity
④ Was Life Better in Hunter-gatherer Times?
⑤ Innovate Your Farm with New Constructions

02

202306 24번

다음 글의 제목으로 가장 적절한 것은?

Few people will be surprised to hear that poverty tends to create stress: a 2006 study published in the American journal *Psychosomatic Medicine*, for example, noted that a lower socioeconomic status was associated with higher levels of stress hormones in the body. However, richer economies have their own distinct stresses. The key issue is time pressure. A 1999 study of 31 countries by American psychologist Robert Levine and Canadian psychologist Ara Norenzayan found that wealthier, more industrialized nations had a faster pace of life — which led to a higher standard of living, but at the same time left the population feeling a constant sense of urgency, as well as being more prone to heart disease. In effect, fast-paced productivity creates wealth, but it also leads people to feel time-poor when they lack the time to relax and enjoy themselves.

＊ prone: 걸리기 쉬운

① Why Are Even Wealthy Countries Not Free from Stress?
② In Search of the Path to Escaping the Poverty Trap
③ Time Management: Everything You Need to Know
④ How Does Stress Affect Human Bodies?
⑤ Sound Mind Wins the Game of Life!

03

202303 24번

다음 글의 제목으로 가장 적절한 것은?

Success can lead you off your intended path and into a comfortable rut. If you are good at something and are well rewarded for doing it, you may want to keep doing it even if you stop enjoying it. The danger is that one day you look around and realize you're so deep in this comfortable rut that you can no longer see the sun or breathe fresh air; the sides of the rut have become so slippery that it would take a superhuman effort to climb out; and, effectively, you're stuck. And it's a situation that many working people worry they're in now. The poor employment market has left them feeling locked in what may be a secure, or even well-paying — but ultimately unsatisfying — job.

＊ rut: 틀에 박힌 생활

① Don't Compete with Yourself
② A Trap of a Successful Career
③ Create More Jobs for Young People
④ What Difficult Jobs Have in Common
⑤ A Road Map for an Influential Employer

04 오답률 BEST 📄 202211 24번

다음 글의 제목으로 가장 적절한 것은?

Have you ever brought up an idea or suggestion to someone and heard them immediately say "No, that won't work."? You may have thought, "He/she didn't even give it a chance. How do they know it won't work?" When you are right about something, you close off the possibility of another viewpoint or opportunity. Being right about something means that "it is the way it is, period." You may be correct. Your particular way of seeing it may be true with the facts. However, considering the other option or the other person's point of view can be beneficial. If you see their side, you will see something new or, at worse, learn something about how the other person looks at life. Why would you think everyone sees and experiences life the way you do? Besides how boring that would be, it would eliminate all new opportunities, ideas, invention, and creativity.

① The Value of Being Honest
② Filter Out Negative Points of View
③ Keeping Your Word: A Road to Success
④ Being Right Can Block New Possibilities
⑤ Look Back When Everyone Looks Forward

05 📄 202209 24번

다음 글의 제목으로 가장 적절한 것은?

Many people make a mistake of only operating along the safe zones, and in the process they miss the opportunity to achieve greater things. They do so because of a fear of the unknown and a fear of treading the unknown paths of life. Those that are brave enough to take those roads less travelled are able to get great returns and derive major satisfaction out of their courageous moves. Being overcautious will mean that you will miss attaining the greatest levels of your potential. You must learn to take those chances that many people around you will not take, because your success will flow from those bold decisions that you will take along the way.

* tread: 밟다

① More Courage Brings More Opportunities
② Travel: The Best Way to Make Friends
③ How to Turn Mistakes into Success
④ Satisfying Life? Share with Others
⑤ Why Is Overcoming Fear So Hard?

06 📄 202206 24번

다음 글의 제목으로 가장 적절한 것은?

Only a generation or two ago, mentioning the word *algorithms* would have drawn a blank from most people. Today, algorithms appear in every part of civilization. They are connected to everyday life. They're not just in your cell phone or your laptop but in your car, your house, your appliances, and your toys. Your bank is a huge web of algorithms, with humans turning the switches here and there. Algorithms schedule flights and then fly the airplanes. Algorithms run factories, trade goods, and keep records. If every algorithm suddenly stopped working, it would be the end of the world as we know it.

① We Live in an Age of Algorithms
② Mysteries of Ancient Civilizations
③ Dangers of Online Banking Algorithms
④ How Algorithms Decrease Human Creativity
⑤ Transportation: A Driving Force of Industry

07

다음 글의 제목으로 가장 적절한 것은?

Our ability to accurately recognize and label emotions is often referred to as *emotional granularity*. In the words of Harvard psychologist Susan David, "Learning to label emotions with a more nuanced vocabulary can be absolutely transformative." David explains that if we don't have a rich emotional vocabulary, it is difficult to communicate our needs and to get the support that we need from others. But those who are able to distinguish between a range of various emotions "do much, much better at managing the ups and downs of ordinary existence than those who see everything in black and white." In fact, research shows that the process of labeling emotional experience is related to greater emotion regulation and psychosocial well-being.

＊nuanced: 미묘한 차이가 있는

① True Friendship Endures Emotional Arguments
② Detailed Labeling of Emotions Is Beneficial
③ Labeling Emotions: Easier Said Than Done
④ Categorize and Label Tasks for Efficiency
⑤ Be Brave and Communicate Your Needs

08 오답률 BEST

다음 글의 제목으로 가장 적절한 것은?

In modern times, society became more dynamic. Social mobility increased, and people began to exercise a higher degree of choice regarding, for instance, their profession, their marriage, or their religion. This posed a challenge to traditional roles in society. It was less evident that one needed to commit to the roles one was born into when alternatives could be realized. Increasing control over one's life choices became not only possible but desired. Identity then became a problem. It was no longer almost ready-made at birth but something to be discovered. Traditional role identities prescribed by society began to appear as masks imposed on people whose real self was to be found somewhere underneath.

＊impose: 부여하다

① What Makes Our Modern Society So Competitive?
② How Modern Society Drives Us to Discover Our Identities
③ Social Masks: A Means to Build Trustworthy Relationships
④ The More Social Roles We Have, the Less Choice We Have
⑤ Increasing Social Mobility Leads Us to a More Equal Society

09 오답률 BEST

다음 글의 제목으로 가장 적절한 것은?

Diversity, challenge, and conflict help us maintain our imagination. Most people assume that conflict is bad and that being in one's "comfort zone" is good. That is not exactly true. Of course, we don't want to find ourselves without a job or medical insurance or in a fight with our partner, family, boss, or coworkers. One bad experience can be sufficient to last us a lifetime. But small disagreements with family and friends, trouble with technology or finances, or challenges at work and at home can help us think through our own capabilities. Problems that need solutions force us to use our brains in order to develop creative answers. Navigating landscapes that are varied, that offer trials and occasional conflicts, is more helpful to creativity than hanging out in landscapes that pose no challenge to our senses and our minds. Our two million-year history is packed with challenges and conflicts.

① Technology: A Lens to the Future
② Diversity: A Key to Social Unification
③ Simple Ways to Avoid Conflicts with Others
④ Creativity Doesn't Come from Playing It Safe
⑤ There Are No Challenges That Can't Be Overcome

10

다음 글의 제목으로 가장 적절한 것은?

When people think about the development of cities, rarely do they consider the critical role of vertical transportation. In fact, each day, more than 7 billion elevator journeys are taken in tall buildings all over the world. Efficient vertical transportation can expand our ability to build taller and taller skyscrapers. Antony Wood, a Professor of Architecture at the Illinois Institute of Technology, explains that advances in elevators over the past 20 years are probably the greatest advances we have seen in tall buildings. For example, elevators in the Jeddah Tower in Jeddah, Saudi Arabia, under construction, will reach a height record of 660m.

① Elevators Bring Buildings Closer to the Sky
② The Higher You Climb, the Better the View
③ How to Construct an Elevator Cheap and Fast
④ The Function of the Ancient and the Modern City
⑤ The Evolution of Architecture: Solutions for Overpopulation

11

다음 글의 제목으로 가장 적절한 것은?

Think, for a moment, about something you bought that you never ended up using. An item of clothing you never ended up wearing? A book you never read? Some piece of electronic equipment that never even made it out of the box? It is estimated that Australians alone spend on average $10.8 billion AUD (approximately $9.99 billion USD) every year on goods they do not use — more than the total government spending on universities and roads. That is an average of $1,250 AUD (approximately $1,156 USD) for each household. All the things we buy that then just sit there gathering dust are waste — a waste of money, a waste of time, and waste in the sense of pure rubbish. As the author Clive Hamilton observes, 'The difference between the stuff we buy and what we use is waste.'

① Spending Enables the Economy
② Money Management: Dos and Don'ts
③ Too Much Shopping: A Sign of Loneliness
④ 3R's of Waste: Reduce, Reuse, and Recycle
⑤ What You Buy Is Waste Unless You Use It

12

다음 글의 제목으로 가장 적절한 것은?

Chewing leads to smaller particles for swallowing, and more exposed surface area for digestive enzymes to act on. In other words, it means the extraction of more fuel and raw materials from a mouthful of food. This is especially important for mammals because they heat their bodies from within. Chewing gives mammals the energy needed to be active not only during the day but also the cool night, and to live in colder climates or places with changing temperatures. It allows them to sustain higher levels of activity and travel speeds to cover larger distances, avoid predators, capture prey, and make and care for their young. Mammals are able to live in an incredible variety of habitats, from Arctic tundra to Antarctic pack ice, deep open waters to high-altitude mountaintops, and rainforests to deserts, in no small measure because of their teeth.

＊enzyme: 효소

① Chewing: A Way to Ease Indigestion
② Boost Your Energy by Chewing More!
③ How Chewing Helps Mammals Survive
④ Different Types and Functions of Teeth
⑤ A Harsh Climate Makes Mammals Stronger

01

다음 도표의 내용과 일치하지 <u>않는</u> 것은?

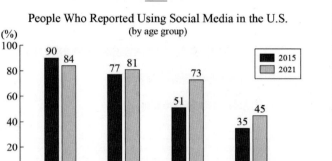

People Who Reported Using Social Media in the U.S.
(by age group)

The graph above shows the percentages of people in different age groups who reported using social media in the United States in 2015 and 2021. ① In each of the given years, the 18–29 group had the highest percentage of people who said they used social media. ② In 2015, the percentage of people who reported using social media in the 30–49 group was more than twice that in the 65 and older group. ③ The percentage of people who said they used social media in the 50–64 group in 2021 was 22 percentage points higher than that in 2015. ④ In 2021, except for the 65 and older group, more than four-fifths of people in each age group reported using social media. ⑤ Among all the age groups, only the 18–29 group showed a decrease in the percentage of people who reported using social media from 2015 to 2021.

02

다음 도표의 내용과 일치하지 <u>않는</u> 것은?

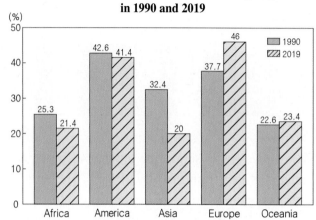

**Share of Forest Area in Total Land Area by Region
in 1990 and 2019**

The above graph shows the share of forest area in total land area by region in 1990 and 2019. ① Africa's share of forest area in total land area was over 20% in both 1990 and 2019. ② The share of forest area in America was 42.6% in 1990, which was larger than that in 2019. ③ The share of forest area in Asia declined from 1990 to 2019 by more than 10 percentage points. ④ In 2019, the share of forest area in Europe was the largest among the five regions, more than three times that in Asia in the same year. ⑤ Oceania showed the smallest gap between 1990 and 2019 in terms of the share of forest area in total land area.

03

📄 202303 25번

다음 도표의 내용과 일치하지 <u>않는</u> 것은?

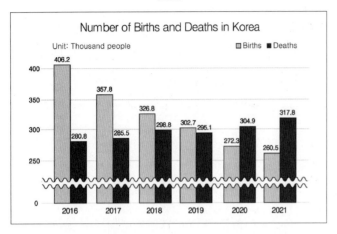

The above graph shows the number of births and deaths in Korea from 2016 to 2021. ① The number of births continued to decrease throughout the whole period. ② The gap between the number of births and deaths was the largest in 2016. ③ In 2019, the gap between the number of births and deaths was the smallest, with the number of births slightly larger than that of deaths. ④ The number of deaths increased steadily during the whole period, except the period from 2018 to 2019. ⑤ In 2021, the number of deaths was larger than that of births for the first time.

04

📄 202211 25번

다음 도표의 내용과 일치하지 <u>않는</u> 것은?

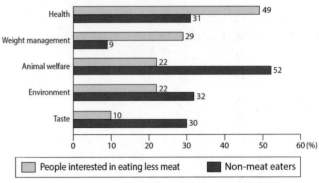

The graph above shows the survey results on reasons for people interested in eating less meat and those eating no meat in the UK in 2018. ① For the group of people who are interested in eating less meat, health is the strongest motivator for doing so. ② For the group of non-meat eaters, animal welfare accounts for the largest percentage among all reasons, followed by environment, health, and taste. ③ The largest percentage point difference between the two groups is in animal welfare, whereas the smallest difference is in environment. ④ The percentage of non-meat eaters citing taste is four times higher than that of people interested in reducing their meat consumption citing taste. ⑤ Weight management ranks the lowest for people who don't eat meat, with less than 10 percent.

05

다음 도표의 내용과 일치하지 <u>않는</u> 것은?

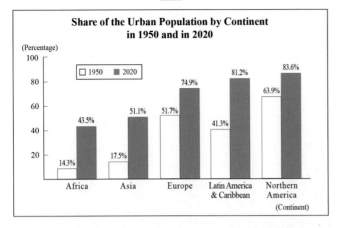

The graph above shows the share of the urban population by continent in 1950 and in 2020. ① For each continent, the share of the urban population in 2020 was larger than that in 1950. ② From 1950 to 2020, the share of the urban population in Africa increased from 14.3% to 43.5%. ③ The share of the urban population in Asia was the second lowest in 1950 but not in 2020. ④ In 1950, the share of the urban population in Europe was larger than that in Latin America and the Caribbean, whereas the reverse was true in 2020. ⑤ Among the five continents, Northern America was ranked in the first position for the share of the urban population in both 1950 and 2020.

06

다음 도표의 내용과 일치하지 <u>않는</u> 것은?

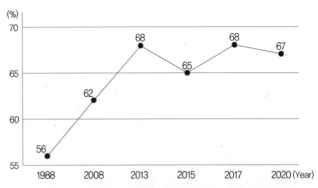

The graph above shows the percent of households with pets in the United States (U.S.) from 1988 to 2020. ① In 1988, more than half of U.S. households owned pets, and more than 6 out of 10 U.S. households owned pets from 2008 to 2020. ② In the period between 1988 and 2008, pet ownership increased among U.S. households by 6 percentage points. ③ From 2008 to 2013, pet ownership rose an additional 6 percentage points. ④ The percent of U.S. households with pets in 2013 was the same as that in 2017, which was 68 percent. ⑤ In 2015, the rate of U.S. households with pets was 3 percentage points lower than in 2020.

07 오답률 BEST

다음 도표의 내용과 일치하지 <u>않는</u> 것은?

**Percentage of UK People
Who Used Online Course and Online Learning Material
(in 2020, by age group)**

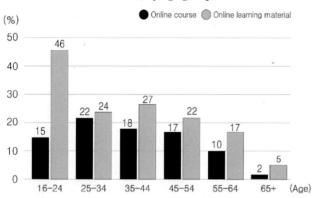

The above graph shows the percentage of people in the UK who used online courses and online learning materials, by age group in 2020. ① In each age group, the percentage of people who used online learning materials was higher than that of people who used online courses. ② The 25–34 age group had the highest percentage of people who used online courses in all the age groups. ③ Those aged 65 and older were the least likely to use online courses among the six age groups. ④ Among the six age groups, the gap between the percentage of people who used online courses and that of people who used online learning materials was the greatest in the 16–24 age group. ⑤ In each of the 35–44, 45–54, and 55–64 age groups, more than one in five people used online learning materials.

08

다음 도표의 내용과 일치하지 <u>않는</u> 것은?

Percentage of U.S. Students Participating in Cultural Activities (2016)

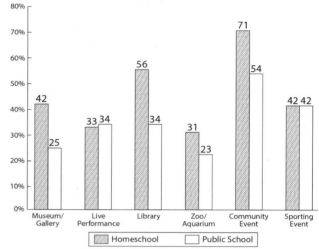

The graph above shows the percentage of U.S. homeschooled and public school students participating in cultural activities in 2016. ① With the exception of live performances and sporting events, the percentage of homeschooled students participating in cultural activities was higher than that of public school students. ② For each group of students, community events accounted for the largest percentage among all cultural activities. ③ The percentage point difference between homeschooled students and their public school peers was largest in visiting libraries. ④ The percentage of homeschooled students visiting museums or galleries was more than twice that of public school students. ⑤ Going to zoos or aquariums ranked the lowest for both groups of students, with 31 and 23 percent respectively.

09

다음 도표의 내용과 일치하지 <u>않는</u> 것은?

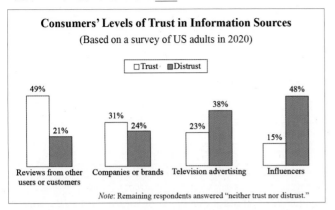

The graph above shows the consumers' levels of trust in four different types of information sources, based on a survey of US adults in 2020. ① About half of US adults say they trust the information they receive from reviews from other users or customers. ② This is more than double those who say they hold distrust for reviews from other users or customers. ③ The smallest gap between the levels of trust and distrust among the four different types of information sources is shown in the companies or brands' graph. ④ Fewer than one-fifth of adults say they trust information from television advertising, outweighed by the share who distrust such information. ⑤ Only 15% of adults say they trust the information provided by influencers, while more than three times as many adults say they distrust the same source of information.

10

다음 도표의 내용과 일치하지 <u>않는</u> 것은?

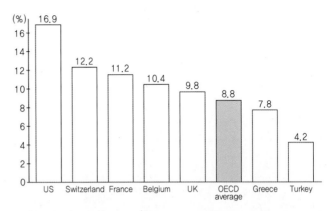

The above graph shows health spending as a share of GDP for selected OECD countries in 2018. ① On average, OECD countries were estimated to have spent 8.8 percent of their GDP on health care. ② Among the given countries above, the US had the highest share, with 16.9 percent, followed by Switzerland at 12.2 percent. ③ France spent more than 11 percent of its GDP, while Turkey spent less than 5 percent of its GDP on health care. ④ Belgium's health spending as a share of GDP sat between that of France and the UK. ⑤ There was a 3 percentage point difference in the share of GDP spent on health care between the UK and Greece.

8강

도표의 이해

◆ 정답 및 해설(2권) p. 101

11
📄 202103 25번

다음 도표의 내용과 일치하지 <u>않는</u> 것은?

Devices Students Used to Access Digital Content

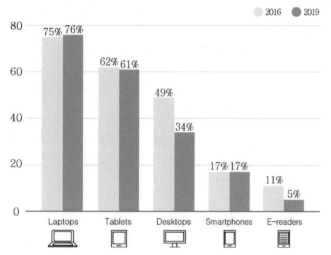

The above graph shows the percentage of students from kindergarten to 12th grade who used devices to access digital educational content in 2016 and in 2019. ① Laptops were the most used device for students to access digital content in both years. ② Both in 2016 and in 2019, more than 6 out of 10 students used tablets. ③ More than half the students used desktops to access digital content in 2016, and more than a third used desktops in 2019. ④ The percentage of smartphones in 2016 was the same as that in 2019. ⑤ E-readers ranked the lowest in both years, with 11 percent in 2016 and 5 percent in 2019.

12
📄 202011 25번

다음 표의 내용과 일치하지 <u>않는</u> 것은?

Age Children Quit Regularly Playing a Sport

Sport	Average Age of Last Regular Participation	Average Length in Years of Participation
Soccer	9.1	3.0
Ice Hockey	10.9	3.1
Tennis	10.9	1.9
Basketball	11.2	3.2
Field Hockey	11.4	5.1
Golf	11.8	2.8
Skateboarding	12.0	2.8
Track and Field	13.0	2.0

The above table shows the average age of last regular participation of children in a sport and the average length of participation based on a 2019 survey. ① Among the eight sports above, soccer was the only sport that children quit at an average age of younger than 10. ② Children quit playing ice hockey and tennis at the same age on average, but the average length of participation in tennis was shorter than that in ice hockey. ③ Basketball, field hockey, and golf were sports which children quit playing on average before they turned 12, but golf had the shortest average participation length among the three sports. ④ Skateboarding was a sport children quit at the average age of 12, and the average length of participation was the same as golf. ⑤ Meanwhile, children quit participating in track and field at the average age of 13, but the average length of participation was the shortest among the eight sports.

01

202309 26번

Bill Evans에 관한 다음 글의 내용과 일치하지 <u>않는</u> 것은?

American jazz pianist Bill Evans was born in New Jersey in 1929. His early training was in classical music. At the age of six, he began receiving piano lessons, later adding flute and violin. He earned bachelor's degrees in piano and music education from Southeastern Louisiana College in 1950. He went on to serve in the army from 1951 to 1954 and played flute in the Fifth Army Band. After serving in the military, he studied composition at the Mannes School of Music in New York. Composer George Russell admired his playing and hired Evans to record and perform his compositions. Evans became famous for recordings made from the late-1950s through the 1960s. He won his first Grammy Award in 1964 for his album *Conversations with Myself*. Evans' expressive piano works and his unique harmonic approach inspired a whole generation of musicians.

① 6세에 피아노 수업을 받기 시작했다.
② Southeastern Louisiana 대학에서 학위를 취득했다.
③ 군 복무 이후 뉴욕에서 작곡을 공부했다.
④ 작곡가 George Russell을 고용했다.
⑤ 1964년에 자신의 첫 번째 그래미상을 수상했다.

02

202306 26번

Gary Becker에 관한 다음 글의 내용과 일치하지 <u>않는</u> 것은?

Gary Becker was born in Pottsville, Pennsylvania in 1930 and grew up in Brooklyn, New York City. His father, who was not well educated, had a deep interest in financial and political issues. After graduating from high school, Becker went to Princeton University, where he majored in economics. He was dissatisfied with his economic education at Princeton University because "it didn't seem to be handling real problems." He

earned a doctor's degree in economics from the University of Chicago in 1955. His doctoral paper on the economics of discrimination was mentioned by the Nobel Prize Committee as an important contribution to economics. Since 1985, Becker had written a regular economics column in *Business Week*, explaining economic analysis and ideas to the general public. In 1992, he was awarded the Nobel Prize in economic science.

* discrimination: 차별

① New York City의 Brooklyn에서 자랐다.
② 아버지는 금융과 정치 문제에 깊은 관심이 있었다.
③ Princeton University에서의 경제학 교육에 만족했다.
④ 1955년에 경제학 박사 학위를 취득했다.
⑤ *Business Week*에 경제학 칼럼을 기고했다.

03

202303 26번

Lilian Bland에 관한 다음 글의 내용과 일치하지 <u>않는</u> 것은?

Lilian Bland was born in Kent, England in 1878. Unlike most other girls at the time she wore trousers and spent her time enjoying adventurous activities like horse riding and hunting. Lilian began her career as a sports and wildlife photographer for British newspapers. In 1910 she became the first woman to design, build, and fly her own airplane. In order to persuade her to try a slightly safer activity, Lilian's dad bought her a car. Soon Lilian was a master driver and ended up working as a car dealer. She never went back to flying but lived a long and exciting life nonetheless. She married, moved to Canada, and had a kid. Eventually, she moved back to England, and lived there for the rest of her life.

① 승마와 사냥 같은 모험적인 활동을 즐겼다.
② 스포츠와 야생 동물 사진작가로 경력을 시작했다.
③ 자신의 비행기를 설계하고 제작했다.
④ 자동차 판매원으로 일하기도 했다.
⑤ 캐나다에서 생의 마지막 기간을 보냈다.

04

202211 26번

Margaret Knight에 관한 다음 글의 내용과 일치하지 <u>않는</u> 것은?

Margaret Knight was an exceptionally prolific inventor in the late 19th century; journalists occasionally compared her to Thomas Edison by nicknaming her "a woman Edison." From a young age, she built toys for her older brothers. After her father died, Knight's family moved to Manchester. Knight left school in 1850, at age 12, to earn money for her family at a nearby textile factory, where she witnessed a fellow worker injured by faulty equipment. That led her to create her first invention, a safety device for textile equipment, but she never earned money from the invention. She also invented a machine that cut, folded and glued flat-bottomed paper bags and was awarded her first patent in 1871 for it. It eliminated the need for workers to assemble them slowly by hand. Knight received 27 patents in her lifetime and entered the National Inventors Hall of Fame in 2006.

* prolific: 다작(多作)의 ** patent: 특허

① 기자들이 '여자 Edison'이라는 별명을 지어 주었다.
② 가족을 위해 돈을 벌려고 학교를 그만두었다.
③ 직물 장비에 쓰이는 안전장치를 발명하여 많은 돈을 벌었다.
④ 밑이 평평한 종이 가방을 자르고 접고 붙이는 기계를 발명했다.
⑤ 2006년에 국립 발명가 명예의 전당에 입성했다.

05

202209 26번

Wilbur Smith에 관한 다음 글의 내용과 일치하지 <u>않는</u> 것은?

Wilbur Smith was a South African novelist specialising in historical fiction. Smith wanted to become a journalist, writing about social conditions in South Africa, but his father was never supportive of his writing and forced him to get a real job. Smith studied further and became a tax accountant, but he finally turned back to his love of writing. He wrote his first novel, *The Gods First Make Mad*, and had received 20 rejections by 1962. In 1964, Smith published another novel, *When the Lion Feeds*, and it went on to be successful, selling around the world. A famous actor and film producer bought the film rights for *When the Lion Feeds*, although no movie resulted. By the time of his death in 2021 he had published 49 novels, selling more than 140 million copies worldwide.

① 역사 소설을 전문으로 하는 소설가였다.
② 아버지는 그가 글 쓰는 것을 지지하지 않았다.
③ 첫 번째 소설은 1962년까지 20번 거절당했다.
④ 소설 *When the Lion Feeds*는 영화화되었다.
⑤ 죽기 전까지 49편의 소설을 출간했다.

06

202206 26번

Claude Bolling에 관한 다음 글의 내용과 일치하지 <u>않는</u> 것은?

Pianist, composer, and big band leader, Claude Bolling, was born on April 10, 1930, in Cannes, France, but spent most of his life in Paris. He began studying classical music as a youth. He was introduced to the world of jazz by a schoolmate. Later, Bolling became interested in the music of Fats Waller, one of the most excellent jazz musicians. Bolling became famous as a teenager by winning the Best Piano Player prize at an amateur contest in France. He was also a successful film music composer, writing the music for more than one hundred films. In 1975, he collaborated with flutist Rampal and published *Suite for Flute and Jazz Piano Trio*, which he became most well-known for. He died in 2020, leaving two sons, David and Alexandre.

① 1930년에 프랑스에서 태어났다.
② 학교 친구를 통해 재즈를 소개받았다.
③ 20대에 Best Piano Player 상을 받았다.
④ 성공적인 영화 음악 작곡가였다.
⑤ 1975년에 플루트 연주자와 협업했다.

07

202203 26번

Antonie van Leeuwenhoek에 관한 다음 글의 내용과 일치하지 <u>않는</u> 것은?

Antonie van Leeuwenhoek was a scientist well known for his cell research. He was born in Delft, the Netherlands, on October 24, 1632. At the age of 16, he began to learn job skills in Amsterdam. At the age of 22, Leeuwenhoek returned to Delft. It wasn't easy for Leeuwenhoek to become a scientist. He knew only one language — Dutch — which was quite unusual for scientists of his time. But his curiosity was endless, and he worked hard. He had an important skill. He knew how to make things out of glass. This skill came in handy when he made lenses for his simple microscope. He saw tiny veins with blood flowing through them. He also saw living bacteria in pond water. He paid close attention to the things he saw and wrote down his observations. Since he couldn't draw well, he hired an artist to draw pictures of what he described.

* cell: 세포 ** vein: 혈관

① 세포 연구로 잘 알려진 과학자였다.
② 22살에 Delft로 돌아왔다.
③ 여러 개의 언어를 알았다.
④ 유리로 물건을 만드는 방법을 알고 있었다.
⑤ 화가를 고용하여 설명하는 것을 그리게 했다.

08

202111 26번

Bessie Coleman에 관한 다음 글의 내용과 일치하지 <u>않는</u> 것은?

Bessie Coleman was born in Texas in 1892. When she was eleven, she was told that the Wright brothers had flown their first plane. Since that moment, she dreamed about the day she would soar through the sky. At the age of 23, Coleman moved to Chicago, where she worked at a restaurant to save money for flying lessons. However, she had to travel to Paris to take flying lessons because American flight schools at the time admitted neither women nor Black people. In 1921, she finally became the first Black woman to earn an international pilot's license. She also studied flying acrobatics in Europe and made her first appearance in an airshow in New York in 1922. As a female pioneer of flight, she inspired the next generation to pursue their dreams of flying.

* flying acrobatics: 곡예 비행

① 11살 때 Wright 형제의 첫 비행 소식을 들었다.
② 비행 수업을 듣기 위해 파리로 가야 했다.
③ 국제 조종사 면허를 딴 최초의 흑인 여성이 되었다.
④ 유럽에서 에어쇼에 첫 출현을 했다.
⑤ 다음 세대가 비행의 꿈을 추구하도록 영감을 주었다.

09 오답률 BEST

202109 26번

Paul Laurence Dunbar에 관한 다음 글의 내용과 일치하지 <u>않는</u> 것은?

Paul Laurence Dunbar, an African-American poet, was born on June 27, 1872. By the age of fourteen, Dunbar had poems published in the *Dayton Herald*. While in high school he edited his high school newspaper. Despite being a fine student, Dunbar was financially unable to attend college and took a job as an elevator operator. In 1893, Dunbar published his first book, *Oak and Ivy*, at his own expense. In 1895, he published the second book, *Majors and Minors*, which brought him national and international recognition. The poems written in standard English were called "majors," and those in dialect were termed "minors." Although the "major" poems in standard English outnumber those written in dialect, it was the dialect poems that brought Dunbar the most attention.

① 14세쯤에 *Dayton Herald*에 시를 발표했다.
② 고등학교 재학 시 학교 신문을 편집했다.
③ 재정상의 이유로 대학에 진학하지 못했다.
④ 두 번째 출판한 책으로 국내외에서 인정받게 되었다.
⑤ 표준 영어로 쓴 시들로 가장 큰 주목을 받았다.

◆ 정답 및 해설(2권) p. 107

10 오답률 BEST　　　　　📄 202106 26번

Lithops에 관한 다음 글의 내용과 일치하지 <u>않는</u> 것은?

　Lithops are plants that are often called 'living stones' on account of their unique rock-like appearance. They are native to the deserts of South Africa but commonly sold in garden centers and nurseries. Lithops grow well in compacted, sandy soil with little water and extreme hot temperatures. Lithops are small plants, rarely getting more than an inch above the soil surface and usually with only two leaves. The thick leaves resemble the cleft in an animal's foot or just a pair of grayish brown stones gathered together. The plants have no true stem and much of the plant is underground. Their appearance has the effect of conserving moisture.

＊ cleft: 갈라진 틈

① 살아있는 돌로 불리는 식물이다.
② 원산지는 남아프리카 사막 지역이다.
③ 토양의 표면 위로 대개 1인치 이상 자란다.
④ 줄기가 없으며 땅속에 대부분 묻혀 있다.
⑤ 겉모양은 수분 보존 효과를 갖고 있다.

11　　　　　📄 202103 26번

Elizabeth Catlett에 관한 다음 글의 내용과 일치하지 <u>않는</u> 것은?

　Elizabeth Catlett was born in Washington, D.C. in 1915. As a granddaughter of slaves, Catlett heard the stories of slaves from her grandmother. After being disallowed entrance from the Carnegie Institute of Technology because she was black, Catlett studied design and drawing at Howard University. She became one of the first three students to earn a master's degree in fine arts at the University of Iowa. Throughout her life, she created art representing the voices of people suffering from social injustice. She was recognized with many prizes and honors both in the United States and in Mexico. She spent over fifty years in Mexico, and she took Mexican citizenship in 1962. Catlett died in 2012 at her home in Mexico.

① 할머니로부터 노예 이야기를 들었다.
② Carnegie Institute of Technology로부터 입학을 거절당했다.
③ University of Iowa에서 석사 학위를 취득했다.
④ 미국과 멕시코에서 많은 상을 받았다.
⑤ 멕시코 시민권을 결국 받지 못했다.

12　　　　　📄 202011 26번

Sarah Breedlove에 관한 다음 글의 내용과 일치하지 <u>않는</u> 것은?

　Born in 1867, Sarah Breedlove was an American businesswoman and social activist. Orphaned at the age of seven, her early life was marked by hardship. In 1888, she moved to St. Louis, where she worked as a washerwoman for more than a decade, earning barely more than a dollar a day. During this time, long hours of backbreaking labor and a poor diet caused her hair to fall out. She tried everything that was available but had no success. After working as a maid for a chemist, she invented a successful hair care product and sold it across the country. Not only did she sell, she also recruited and trained lots of women as sales agents for a share of the profits. In the process she became America's first self-made female millionaire and she gave Black women everywhere an opportunity for financial independence.

① 미국인 사업가이자 사회 운동가였다.
② St. Louis에서 10년 넘게 세탁부로 일했다.
③ 장시간의 노동과 열악한 식사로 머리카락이 빠졌다.
④ 모발 관리 제품을 수입하여 전국에 판매했다.
⑤ 흑인 여성들에게 재정적 독립의 기회를 주었다.

01

Silversmithing Class에 관한 다음 안내문의 내용과 일치하지 <u>않는</u> 것은?

Silversmithing Class

Kingston Club is offering a fine jewelry making class. Don't miss this great chance to make your own jewelry!

When & Where
· Saturday, October 21, 2023 (2 p.m. to 4 p.m.)
· Kingston Club studio

Registration
· Available only online
· Dates: October 1 – 14, 2023
· Fee: $40 (This includes all tools and materials.)
· Registration is limited to 6 people.

Note
· Participants must be at least 16 years old.
· No refund for cancellation on the day of the class

---

① 두 시간 동안 진행된다.
② 10월 1일부터 등록할 수 있다.
③ 등록 인원은 6명으로 제한된다.
④ 참가 연령에 제한이 없다.
⑤ 수업 당일 취소 시 환불이 불가하다.

02

2023 Ocean Awareness Film Contest에 관한 다음 안내문의 내용과 일치하는 것은?

2023 Ocean Awareness Film Contest

Join our 7th annual film contest and show your knowledge of marine conservation.

□ **Theme**
– Ocean Wildlife / Ocean Pollution
  (Choose one of the above.)

□ **Guidelines**
– Participants: High school students
– Submission deadline: September 22, 2023
– The video must be between 10 and 15 minutes.
– All entries must be uploaded to our website.
– Only one entry per person

□ **Prizes**
· 1st place: $100
· 2nd place: $70
· 3rd place: $50
  (Winners will be announced on our website.)

For more information, please visit www.oceanawareFC.com.

---

① 세 가지 주제 중 하나를 선택해야 한다.
② 중학생이 참가할 수 있다.
③ 영상은 10분을 넘길 수 없다.
④ 1인당 두 개까지 출품할 수 있다.
⑤ 수상자는 웹사이트에 공지될 것이다.

03

2023 Drone Racing Championship에 관한 다음 안내문의 내용과 일치하지 <u>않는</u> 것은?

2023 Drone Racing Championship

Are you the best drone racer? Then take the opportunity to prove you are the one!

When & Where
· 6 p.m. – 8 p.m., Sunday, July 9
· Lakeside Community Center

Requirements
· Participants: High school students only
· Bring your own drone for the race.

Prize
· $500 and a medal will be awarded to the winner.

Note
· The first 10 participants will get souvenirs.

For more details, please visit www.droneracing. com or call 313-6745-1189.

---

① 7월 9일 일요일에 개최된다.
② 고등학생만 참가할 수 있다.
③ 자신의 드론을 가져와야 한다.
④ 상금과 메달이 우승자에게 수여될 것이다.
⑤ 20명의 참가자가 기념품을 받을 것이다.

04

Summer Scuba Diving One-day Class에 관한 다음 안내문의 내용과 일치하는 것은?

Summer Scuba Diving One-day Class

Join our summer scuba diving lesson for beginners, and become an underwater explorer!

Schedule
· 10:00 – 12:00 Learning the basics
· 13:00 – 16:00 Practicing diving skills in a pool

Price
· Private lesson: $150
· Group lesson (up to 3 people): $100 per person
· Participants can rent our diving equipment for free.

Notice
· Participants must be 10 years old or over.
· Participants must register at least 5 days before the class begins.

For more information, please go to www. ssdiver.com.

---

① 오후 시간에 바다에서 다이빙 기술을 연습한다.
② 그룹 수업의 최대 정원은 4명이다.
③ 다이빙 장비를 유료로 대여할 수 있다.
④ 연령에 관계없이 참가할 수 있다.
⑤ 적어도 수업 시작 5일 전까지 등록해야 한다.

05

Call for Articles에 관한 다음 안내문의 내용과 일치하지 <u>않는</u> 것은?

Call for Articles

Do you want to get your stories published? *New Dream Magazine* is looking for future writers! This event is open to anyone aged 13 to 18.

Articles
· Length of writing: 300 – 325 words
· Articles should also include high-quality color photos.

Rewards
· Five cents per word
· Five dollars per photo

Notes
· You should send us your phone number together with your writing.
· Please email your writing to us at article@ndmag.com.

---

① 13세에서 18세까지의 누구나 참여할 수 있다.
② 기사는 고화질 컬러 사진을 포함해야 한다.
③ 사진 한 장에 5센트씩 지급한다.
④ 전화번호를 원고와 함께 보내야 한다.
⑤ 원고를 이메일로 제출해야 한다.

06

Greenhill Roller Skating에 관한 다음 안내문의 내용과 일치하는 것은?

Greenhill Roller Skating

Join us for your chance to enjoy roller skating!

· Place: Greenhill Park, 351 Cypress Avenue
· Dates: Friday, April 7 – Sunday, April 9
· Time: 9 a.m. – 6 p.m.
· Fee: $8 per person for a 50-minute session

Details
– Admission will be on a first-come, first-served basis with no reservations.
– Children under the age of 10 must be accompanied by an adult.
– We will lend you our roller skates for free.

Contact the Community Center for more information at 013-234-6114.

---

① 오전 9시부터 오후 9시까지 운영한다.
② 이용료는 시간 제한 없이 1인당 8달러이다.
③ 입장하려면 예약이 필요하다.
④ 10세 미만 어린이는 어른과 동행해야 한다.
⑤ 추가 요금을 내면 롤러스케이트를 빌려준다.

07

E-Waste Recycling Day에 관한 다음 안내문의 내용과 일치하지 <u>않는</u> 것은?

E-Waste Recycling Day

E-Waste Recycling Day is an annual event in our city. Bring your used electronics such as cell phones, tablets, and laptops to recycle. Go green!

When
Saturday, December 17, 2022
8:00 a.m. – 11:00 a.m.

Where
Lincoln Sports Center

Notes
· Items NOT accepted: light bulbs, batteries, and microwaves
· All personal data on the devices must be wiped out in advance.
· This event is free but open only to local residents.

Please contact us at 986–571–0204 for more information.

① 3시간 동안 진행된다.
② Lincoln 스포츠 센터에서 열린다.
③ 전자레인지는 허용되지 않는 품목이다.
④ 기기 속 모든 개인 정보는 미리 삭제되어야 한다.
⑤ 거주 지역에 상관없이 참가할 수 있다.

08

Undersea Walking Activity에 관한 다음 안내문의 내용과 일치하는 것은?

Undersea Walking Activity

Enjoy a fascinating underwater walk on the ocean floor. Witness wonderful marine life on foot!

Age Requirement
10 years or older

Operating Hours
from Tuesday to Sunday
9:00 a.m. – 4:00 p.m.

Price
$30 (insurance fee included)

What to Bring
swim suit and towel

Notes
· Experienced lifeguards accompany you throughout the activity.
· With a special underwater helmet, you can wear glasses during the activity.
· Reservations can be made on-site or online at www.seawalkwonder.com.

① 연중무휴로 운영된다.
② 가격에 보험료는 포함되어 있지 않다.
③ 숙련된 안전 요원이 활동 내내 동행한다.
④ 특수 수중 헬멧 착용 시 안경을 쓸 수 없다.
⑤ 현장 예약은 불가능하다.

09

2022 Springfield Park Yoga Class에 관한 다음 안내문의 내용과 일치하지 <u>않는</u> 것은?

2022 Springfield Park Yoga Class

The popular yoga class in Springfield Park returns! Enjoy yoga hosted on the park lawn. If you can't make it to the park, join us online on our social media platforms!

◈ **When**: Saturdays, 2 p.m. to 3 p.m., September

◈ **Registration**: At least TWO hours before each class starts, `sign up here`.

◈ **Notes**
- For online classes: find a quiet space with enough room for you to stretch out.
- For classes in the park: mats are not provided, so bring your own!

※ The class will be canceled if the weather is unfavorable.

For more information, `click here`.

---

① 온라인으로도 참여할 수 있다.
② 9월 중 토요일마다 진행된다.
③ 수업 시작 2시간 전까지 등록해야 한다.
④ 매트가 제공된다.
⑤ 날씨가 좋지 않으면 취소될 것이다.

10

Kenner High School's Water Challenge에 관한 다음 안내문의 내용과 일치하는 것은?

Kenner High School's Water Challenge

Kenner High School's Water Challenge is a new contest to propose measures against water pollution. Please share your ideas for dealing with water pollution!

Submission
- How: Submit your proposal by email to admin@khswater.edu.
- When: September 5, 2022 to September 23, 2022

Details
- Participants must enter in teams of four and can only join one team.
- Submission is limited to one proposal per team.
- Participants must use the proposal form provided on the website.

Prizes
- 1st: $50 gift certificate
- 2nd: $30 gift certificate
- 3rd: $10 gift certificate

Please visit www.khswater.edu to learn more about the challenge.

---

① 제안서는 직접 방문하여 제출해야 한다.
② 9월 23일부터 제안서를 제출할 수 있다.
③ 제안서는 한 팀당 4개까지 제출할 수 있다.
④ 제공된 제안서 양식을 사용해야 한다.
⑤ 2등은 10달러의 상품권을 받는다.

11

Kids Taekwondo Program에 관한 다음 안내문의 내용과 일치하지 <u>않는</u> 것은?

Kids Taekwondo Program

Enjoy our taekwondo program this summer vacation.

☐ **Schedule**
- Dates: August 8th – August 10th
- Time: 9:00 a.m. – 11:00 a.m.

☐ **Participants**
- Any child aged 5 and up

☐ **Activities**
- Self-defense training
- Team building games to develop social skills

☐ **Participation Fee**
- $50 per child (includes snacks)

☐ **Notice**
- What to bring: water bottle, towel
- What not to bring: chewing gum, expensive items

① 8월 8일부터 3일간 운영한다.
② 5세 이상의 어린이가 참가할 수 있다.
③ 자기 방어 훈련 활동을 한다.
④ 참가비에 간식비는 포함되지 않는다.
⑤ 물병과 수건을 가져와야 한다.

12

Moonlight Chocolate Factory Tour에 관한 다음 안내문의 내용과 일치하는 것은?

Moonlight Chocolate Factory Tour

Take this special tour and have a chance to enjoy our most popular chocolate bars.

☐ **Operating Hours**
- Monday – Friday, 2:00 p.m. – 5:00 p.m.

☐ **Activities**
- Watching our chocolate-making process
- Tasting 3 types of chocolate (dark, milk, and mint chocolate)

☐ **Notice**
- Ticket price: $30
- Wearing a face mask is required.
- Taking pictures is not allowed inside the factory.

① 주말 오후 시간에 운영한다.
② 초콜릿 제조 과정을 볼 수 있다.
③ 네 가지 종류의 초콜릿을 시식한다.
④ 마스크 착용은 참여자의 선택 사항이다.
⑤ 공장 내부에서 사진 촬영이 가능하다.

13

Rachel's Flower Class에 관한 다음 안내문의 내용과 일치하지 <u>않는</u> 것은?

Rachel's Flower Class

Make Your Life More Beautiful!

Class Schedule (Every Monday to Friday)

Flower Arrangement	11 a.m. – 12 p.m.
Flower Box Making	1 p.m. – 2 p.m.

Price

- $50 for each class (flowers and other materials included)
- Bring your own scissors and a bag.

Other Info.
- You can sign up for classes either online or by phone.
- No refund for cancellations on the day of your class

To contact, visit www.rfclass.com or call 03-221-2131.

---

① 플라워 박스 만들기 수업은 오후 1시에 시작된다.
② 수강료에 꽃값과 다른 재료비가 포함된다.
③ 수강생은 가위와 가방을 가져와야 한다.
④ 수업 등록은 전화로만 할 수 있다.
⑤ 수업 당일 취소 시 환불을 받을 수 없다.

14

Nighttime Palace Tour에 관한 다음 안내문의 내용과 일치하는 것은?

Nighttime Palace Tour

Date: Friday, April 29 – Sunday, May 15

Time

Friday	7 p.m. – 8:30 p.m.
Saturday & Sunday	6 p.m. – 7:30 p.m.
	8 p.m. – 9:30 p.m.

Tickets & Booking
- $15 per person (free for kids under 8)
- Bookings will be accepted up to 2 hours before the tour starts.

Program Activities
- Group tour with a tour guide (1 hour)
- Trying traditional foods and drinks (30 minutes)

※ You can try on traditional clothes with no extra charge.
※ For more information, please visit our website, www.palacenighttour.com.

---

① 금요일에는 하루에 두 번 투어가 운영된다.
② 8세 미만 어린이의 티켓은 5달러이다.
③ 예약은 투어 하루 전까지만 가능하다.
④ 투어 가이드의 안내 없이 궁궐을 둘러본다.
⑤ 추가 비용 없이 전통 의상을 입어 볼 수 있다.

15 오답률 BEST   📄 202111 27번

2021 Camptonville Nature Photo Contest에 관한 다음 안내문의 내용과 일치하지 <u>않는</u> 것은?

2021 Camptonville Nature Photo Contest

This is the fourth year of the annual Camptonville Nature Photo Contest. You can show the beauty of nature in Camptonville by sharing your most amazing photos!

Submission
– Upload a maximum of 20 photos onto our website www.camptonvillephotocontest.org.
– Deadline is December 1.

Prizes
• 1st Place: $500 • 2nd Place: $200 • 3rd Place: $100 (Winners will be posted on our website on December 31.)

Details
– All winning photos will be exhibited at City Hall.
– Please contact us at 122-861-3971 for further information.

---

① 매년 열리는 대회이며 올해가 네 번째이다.
② 최대 20장의 사진을 이메일로 제출해야 한다.
③ 제출 마감 기한은 12월 1일이다.
④ 수상자는 웹 사이트에 게시될 것이다.
⑤ 모든 수상작은 시청에 전시될 것이다.

---

16   📄 202111 28번

Willow Valley Hot Air Balloon Ride에 관한 다음 안내문의 내용과 일치하는 것은?

Willow Valley Hot Air Balloon Ride

Enjoy the best views of Willow Valley from the sky with our hot air balloon ride!

• **Capacity**: up to 8 people including a pilot

• **Time Schedule**

Spring & Summer (from April to September)	5:00 a.m. – 7:00 a.m.
Autumn & Winter (from October to March)	6:00 a.m. – 8:00 a.m.

＊ Duration of Flight: about 1 hour

• **Fee**: $150 per person (insurance not included)

• **Note**
– Reservations are required and must be made online.
– You can get a full refund up to 24 hours in advance.
– Visit www.willowvalleyballoon.com for more information.

---

① 조종사를 제외하고 8인까지 탈 수 있다.
② 여름에는 오전 6시에 시작한다.
③ 요금에 보험이 포함되어 있다.
④ 예약은 온라인으로 해야 한다.
⑤ 환불은 예외 없이 불가능하다.

17

Premier Reading Challenge에 관한 다음 안내문의 내용과 일치하지 <u>않는</u> 것은?

Premier Reading Challenge

This is not a competition, but rather a challenge to inspire students with the love of reading.

- **Participants**
  – Students from 6th grade to 9th grade

- **Dates**
  – From June 1st to December 31st

- **Challenge**
  – Each student in 6th and 7th grade must read 15 books.
  – Each student in 8th and 9th grade must read 20 books.

- **Prize**
  – A bookmark for every participant
  – A Certificate of Achievement for students who complete the challenge

- **Registration**
  – Online only — www.edu.prc.com

∗ For more information, see the school librarian or visit the website above.

---

① 6학년부터 9학년까지의 학생들을 대상으로 한다.
② 6월부터 5개월간 진행되는 행사이다.
③ 7학년의 도전과제는 15권의 책을 읽는 것이다.
④ 모든 참가자는 책갈피를 받는다.
⑤ 온라인으로만 등록할 수 있다.

18

Wolf Howls in Algonquin Park에 관한 다음 안내문의 내용과 일치하는 것은?

Wolf Howls in Algonquin Park

Wolf Howls in Algonquin Park is offering you a once-in-a-lifetime experience tonight! Don't miss the chance to hear the wolves communicate with our staff.

When & Where
- 8 p.m. Wednesday, August 25th, 2021 (Only if the weather permits and a wolf pack is nearby.)
- Meet our staff at the outdoor theater and travel with them to the wolf howling location.

Fee
- $18.00 per person (Free for Ontario residents 65 and older)

Note
- Dress warmly for this special program which will last longer than three hours.
- No dogs are allowed during the event.
- If there are less than 5 people for the event, it will be cancelled.

∗ Visit our website at www.algonquinpark.on for more information.

---

① 날씨에 상관없이 진행된다.
② Ontario 거주자 모두에게 무료이다.
③ 소요 시간은 3시간 미만이다.
④ 행사 내내 반려견을 동반할 수 있다.
⑤ 참가자 수에 따라 취소될 수 있다.

19

"Go Green" Writing Contest에 관한 다음 안내문의 내용과 일치하지 <u>않는</u> 것은?

"Go Green" Writing Contest

Share your talents & conserve the environment

□ **Main Topic**:
Save the Environment

□ **Writing Categories**
• Slogan   • Poem   • Essay

□ **Requirements**:
• Participants: High school students
• Participate in one of the above categories
(only one entry per participant)

□ **Deadline**: July 5th, 2021
• Email your work to apply@gogreen.com.

□ **Prize for Each Category**
• 1st place: $80   • 2nd place: $60
• 3rd place: $40

□ The winners will be announced only on the website on July 15th, 2021. No personal contact will be made.

□ For more information, visit www.gogreen.com.

---

① 대회 주제는 환경 보호이다.
② 참가자는 한 부문에만 참가해야 한다.
③ 마감 기한은 7월 5일이다.
④ 작품은 이메일로 제출해야 한다.
⑤ 수상자는 개별적으로 연락받는다.

20

Virtual Idea Exchange에 관한 다음 안내문의 내용과 일치하는 것은?

Virtual Idea Exchange

Connect in real time and have discussions about the upcoming school festival.

□ **Goal**
• Plan the school festival and share ideas for it.

□ **Participants**: Club leaders only

□ **What to Discuss**
• Themes   • Ticket sales   • Budget

□ **Date & Time**: 5 to 7 p.m. on Friday, June 25th, 2021

□ **Notes**
• Get the access link by text message 10 minutes before the meeting and click it.
• Type your real name when you enter the chatroom.

---

① 동아리 회원이라면 누구나 참여 가능하다.
② 티켓 판매는 논의 대상에서 제외된다.
③ 회의는 3시간 동안 열린다.
④ 접속 링크를 문자로 받는다.
⑤ 채팅방 입장 시 동아리명으로 참여해야 한다.

21

Spring Farm Camp에 관한 다음 안내문의 내용과 일치하지 않는 것은?

Spring Farm Camp

Our one-day spring farm camp gives your kids true, hands-on farm experience.

When: Monday, April 19 – Friday, May 14

Time: 9 a.m. – 4 p.m.

Ages: 6 – 10

Participation Fee: $70 per person
(lunch and snacks included)

Activities:
- making cheese from goat's milk
- picking strawberries
- making strawberry jam to take home

We are open rain or shine.
For more information, go to www.b_orchard.com.

① 6세 ~ 10세 어린이가 참가할 수 있다.
② 참가비에 점심과 간식이 포함되어 있다.
③ 염소젖으로 치즈를 만드는 활동을 한다.
④ 딸기잼을 만들어 집으로 가져갈 수 있다.
⑤ 비가 오면 운영하지 않는다.

22

Great Aquarium에 관한 다음 안내문의 내용과 일치하는 것은?

Great Aquarium

Opening Hours:
10 a.m. – 6 p.m., daily
Last entry is at 5 p.m.

Events

| Fish Feeding | 10 a.m. – 11 a.m. |
| Penguin Feeding | 1 p.m. – 2 p.m. |

Ticket Prices

Age	Price
Kids (12 and under)	$25
Adults (20 – 59)	$33
Teens (13 – 19) Seniors (60 and above)	$30

＊ Ticket holders will receive a free drink coupon.

Booking Tickets
- ALL visitors are required to book online.
- Booking will be accepted up to 1 hour before entry.

① 마지막 입장 시간은 오후 6시이다.
② 물고기 먹이 주기는 오후 1시에 시작한다.
③ 60세 이상의 티켓 가격은 33달러이다.
④ 티켓 소지자는 무료 음료 쿠폰을 받는다.
⑤ 예약은 입장 30분 전까지 가능하다.

23

2020 Student Building Block Competition에 관한 다음 안내문의 내용과 일치하지 <u>않는</u> 것은?

2020 Student Building Block Competition

Students in every grade will compete to build the most creative and livable structure made out of blocks!

When & Where
- 2 p.m. – 4 p.m. Saturday, November 21
- Green Valley Elementary School Gym

Rules
- All building projects must be completed on site with supplied blocks only.
- Participants are not allowed to receive outside assistance.

Gifts & Prizes
- All the participants receive a T-shirt.
- One winner from each grade group wins $100 and a medal.

Sign up
- Participation is FREE!
- Email jeremywilson@greenvalley.org by November 15.
  (Registration on site is not available.)

---

① 초등학교 체육관에서 열린다.
② 제공되는 블록을 사용해야 한다.
③ 외부의 도움 없이 작품을 완성해야 한다.
④ 우승자에게 상금과 메달을 준다.
⑤ 현장에서 등록하는 것이 가능하다.

24

Crystal Castle Fireworks에 관한 다음 안내문의 내용과 일치하는 것은?

Crystal Castle Fireworks

Come and enjoy the biggest fireworks display in the South West of England!

Dates: 5th & 6th December, 2020

Location: Crystal Castle, 132 Oak Street

Time: 15:00 – 16:00 Live Music Show
16:30 – 17:30 Maze Garden
18:00 – 18:30 Fireworks Display

Parking: Free car park opens at 13:00.

Note:
Any child aged 12 or under must be accompanied by an adult.
All tickets must be reserved beforehand on our website www.crystalcastle.com.

---

① 영국의 북부 지역에서 가장 큰 불꽃놀이이다.
② 라이브 음악 쇼가 불꽃놀이 이후에 진행된다.
③ 불꽃놀이는 1시간 동안 진행된다.
④ 주차장은 오후 1시부터 유료로 이용 가능하다.
⑤ 12세 이하의 아동은 성인과 동행해야 한다.

01 오답률 BEST
202309 29번

다음 글의 밑줄 친 부분 중, 어법상 틀린 것은?

There is a reason the title "Monday Morning Quarterback" exists. Just read the comments on social media from fans discussing the weekend's games, and you quickly see how many people believe they could play, coach, and manage sport teams more ① successfully than those on the field. This goes for the boardroom as well. Students and professionals with years of training and specialized degrees in sport business may also find themselves ② being given advice on how to do their jobs from friends, family, or even total strangers without any expertise. Executives in sport management ③ have decades of knowledge and experience in their respective fields. However, many of them face criticism from fans and community members telling ④ themselves how to run their business. Very few people tell their doctor how to perform surgery or their accountant how to prepare their taxes, but many people provide feedback on ⑤ how sport organizations should be managed.

＊boardroom: 이사회실

02
202306 29번

다음 글의 밑줄 친 부분 중, 어법상 틀린 것은? [3점]

Although praise is one of the most powerful tools available for improving young children's behavior, it is equally powerful for improving your child's self-esteem. Preschoolers believe what their parents tell ① them in a very profound way. They do not yet have the cognitive sophistication to reason ② analytically and reject false information. If a preschool boy consistently hears from his mother ③ that he is smart and a good helper, he is likely to incorporate that information into his self-image. Thinking of himself as a boy who is smart and knows how to do things ④ being likely to make him endure longer in problem-solving efforts and increase his confidence in trying new and difficult tasks. Similarly, thinking of himself as the kind of boy who is a good helper will make him more likely to volunteer ⑤ to help with tasks at home and at preschool.

＊profound: 뜻 깊은 ＊＊sophistication: 정교화(함)

03
202303 29번

다음 글의 밑줄 친 부분 중, 어법상 틀린 것은? [3점]

The most noticeable human characteristic projected onto animals is ① that they can talk in human language. Physically, animal cartoon characters and toys ② made after animals are also most often deformed in such a way as to resemble humans. This is achieved by ③ showing them with humanlike facial features and deformed front legs to resemble human hands. In more recent animated movies the trend has been to show the animals in a more "natural" way. However, they still use their front legs ④ like human hands (for example, lions can pick up and lift small objects with one paw), and they still talk with an appropriate facial expression. A general strategy that is used to make the animal characters more emotionally appealing, both to children and adults, ⑤ are to give them enlarged and deformed childlike features.

＊deform: 변형하다 ＊＊paw: (동물의) 발

04 오답률 BEST
202211 29번

다음 글의 밑줄 친 부분 중, 어법상 틀린 것은? [3점]

You may have seen headlines in the news about some of the things machines powered by artificial intelligence can do. However, if you were to consider all the tasks ① that AI-powered machines could actually perform, it would be quite mind-blowing! One of the key features of artificial intelligence ② is that it enables machines to learn new things, rather than requiring programming specific to new tasks. Therefore, the core difference between computers of the future and ③ those of the past is that future computers will be able to learn and self-improve. In the near future, smart virtual assistants will know more about you than your closest friends and family members ④ are. Can you imagine how that might change our lives? These kinds of changes are exactly why it is so important ⑤ to recognize the implications that new technologies will have for our world.

05

202209 29번

다음 글의 밑줄 친 부분 중, 어법상 틀린 것은? [3점]

The human brain, it turns out, has shrunk in mass by about 10 percent since it ① peaked in size 15,000–30,000 years ago. One possible reason is that many thousands of years ago humans lived in a world of dangerous predators ② where they had to have their wits about them at all times to avoid being killed. Today, we have effectively domesticated ourselves and many of the tasks of survival — from avoiding immediate death to building shelters to obtaining food — ③ has been outsourced to the wider society. We are smaller than our ancestors too, and it is a characteristic of domestic animals ④ that they are generally smaller than their wild cousins. None of this may mean we are dumber — brain size is not necessarily an indicator of human intelligence — but it may mean that our brains today are wired up differently, and perhaps more efficiently, than ⑤ those of our ancestors.

06

202206 29번

다음 글의 밑줄 친 부분 중, 어법상 틀린 것은?

Despite all the high-tech devices that seem to deny the need for paper, paper use in the United States ① has nearly doubled recently. We now consume more paper than ever: 400 million tons globally and growing. Paper is not the only resource ② that we are using more of. Technological advances often come with the promise of ③ using fewer materials. However, the reality is that they have historically caused more materials use, making us ④ dependently on more natural resources. The world now consumes far more "stuff" than it ever has. We use twenty-seven times more industrial minerals, such as gold, copper, and rare metals, than we ⑤ did just over a century ago. We also each individually use more resources. Much of that is due to our high-tech lifestyle.

* copper: 구리

07

202203 29번

다음 글의 밑줄 친 부분 중, 어법상 틀린 것은?

We usually get along best with people who we think are like us. In fact, we seek them out. It's why places like Little Italy, Chinatown, and Koreatown ① exist. But I'm not just talking about race, skin color, or religion. I'm talking about people who share our values and look at the world the same way we ② do. As the saying goes, birds of a feather flock together. This is a very common human tendency ③ what is rooted in how our species developed. Imagine you are walking out in a forest. You would be conditioned to avoid something unfamiliar or foreign because there is a high likelihood that ④ it would be interested in killing you. Similarities make us ⑤ relate better to other people because we think they'll understand us on a deeper level than other people.

* species: 종(생물 분류의 기초 단위)

08

202111 29번

다음 글의 밑줄 친 부분 중, 어법상 틀린 것은? [3점]

The reduction of minerals in our food is the result of using pesticides and fertilizers ① that kill off beneficial bacteria, earthworms, and bugs in the soil that create many of the essential nutrients in the first place and prevent the uptake of nutrients into the plant. Fertilizing crops with nitrogen and potassium ② has led to declines in magnesium, zinc, iron and iodine. For example, there has been on average about a 30% decline in the magnesium content of wheat. This is partly due to potassium ③ being a blocker against magnesium absorption by plants. Lower magnesium levels in soil also ④ occurring with acidic soils and around 70% of the farmland on earth is now acidic. Thus, the overall characteristics of soil determine the accumulation of minerals in plants. Indeed, nowadays our soil is less healthy and so are the plants ⑤ grown on it.

* pesticide: 살충제

09 오답률 BEST   📋 202109 29번

다음 글의 밑줄 친 부분 중, 어법상 틀린 것은? [3점]

An economic theory of Say's Law holds that everything that's made will get sold. The money from anything that's produced is used to ① buy something else. There can never be a situation ② which a firm finds that it can't sell its goods and so has to dismiss workers and close its factories. Therefore, recessions and unemployment are impossible. Picture the level of spending like the level of water in a bath. Say's Law applies ③ because people use all their earnings to buy things. But what happens if people don't spend all their money, saving some of ④ it instead? Savings are a 'leakage' of spending from the economy. You're probably imagining the water level now falling, so there's less spending in the economy. That would mean firms producing less and ⑤ dismissing some of their workers.

＊recession: 경기 후퇴

10   📋 202106 29번

다음 글의 밑줄 친 부분 중, 어법상 틀린 것은? [3점]

There have been occasions ① in which you have observed a smile and you could sense it was not genuine. The most obvious way of identifying a genuine smile from an insincere ② one is that a fake smile primarily only affects the lower half of the face, mainly with the mouth alone. The eyes don't really get involved. Take the opportunity to look in the mirror and manufacture a smile ③ using the lower half your face only. When you do this, judge ④ how happy your face really looks — is it genuine? A genuine smile will impact on the muscles and wrinkles around the eyes and less noticeably, the skin between the eyebrow and upper eyelid ⑤ are lowered slightly with true enjoyment. The genuine smile can impact on the entire face.

11   📋 202103 29번

다음 글의 밑줄 친 부분 중, 어법상 틀린 것은? [3점]

Although there is usually a correct way of holding and playing musical instruments, the most important instruction to begin with is ① that they are not toys and that they must be looked after. ② Allow children time to explore ways of handling and playing the instruments for themselves before showing them. Finding different ways to produce sounds ③ are an important stage of musical exploration. Correct playing comes from the desire ④ to find the most appropriate sound quality and find the most comfortable playing position so that one can play with control over time. As instruments and music become more complex, learning appropriate playing techniques becomes ⑤ increasingly relevant.

12   📋 202011 29번

다음 글의 밑줄 친 부분 중, 어법상 틀린 것은? [3점]

Each species of animals can detect a different range of odours. No species can detect all the molecules that are present in the environment ① in which it lives — there are some things that we cannot smell but which some other animals can, and vice versa. There are also differences between individuals, relating to the ability to smell an odour, or how ② pleasantly it seems. For example, some people like the taste of coriander — known as cilantro in the USA — while others find ③ it soapy and unpleasant. This effect has an underlying genetic component due to differences in the genes ④ controlling our sense of smell. Ultimately, the selection of scents detected by a given species, and how that odour is perceived, will depend upon the animal's ecology. The response profile of each species will enable it ⑤ to locate sources of smell that are relevant to it and to respond accordingly.

＊coriander: 고수

01

202309 30번

다음 글의 밑줄 친 부분 중, 문맥상 낱말의 쓰임이 적절하지 않은 것은? [3점]

While moving is difficult for everyone, it is particularly stressful for children. They lose their sense of security and may feel disoriented when their routine is disrupted and all that is ① familiar is taken away. Young children, ages 3–6, are particularly affected by a move. Their understanding at this stage is quite literal, and it is ② easy for them to imagine beforehand a new home and their new room. Young children may have worries such as "Will I still be me in the new place?" and "Will my toys and bed come with us?" It is important to establish a balance between validating children's past experiences and focusing on helping them ③ adjust to the new place. Children need to have opportunities to share their backgrounds in a way that ④ respects their past as an important part of who they are. This contributes to building a sense of community, which is essential for all children, especially those in ⑤ transition.

02

202306 30번

다음 글의 밑줄 친 부분 중, 문맥상 낱말의 쓰임이 적절하지 않은 것은?

Advertisers often displayed considerable facility in ① adapting their claims to the market status of the goods they promoted. Fleischmann's yeast, for instance, was used as an ingredient for cooking homemade bread. Yet more and more people in the early 20th century were buying their bread from stores or bakeries, so consumer demand for yeast ② increased. The producer of Fleischmann's yeast hired the J. Walter Thompson advertising agency to come up with a different marketing strategy to ③ boost sales. No longer the "Soul of Bread," the Thompson agency first turned yeast into an important source of vitamins with significant health ④ benefits. Shortly thereafter, the advertising agency transformed yeast into a natural laxative. ⑤ Repositioning yeast helped increase sales.

＊laxative: 완하제(배변을 쉽게 하는 약·음식·음료)

03 오답률 BEST

202303 30번

다음 글의 밑줄 친 부분 중, 문맥상 낱말의 쓰임이 적절하지 않은 것은? [3점]

The major philosophical shift in the idea of selling came when industrial societies became more affluent, more competitive, and more geographically spread out during the 1940s and 1950s. This forced business to develop ① closer relations with buyers and clients, which in turn made business realize that it was not enough to produce a quality product at a reasonable price. In fact, it was equally ② essential to deliver products that customers actually wanted. Henry Ford produced his best-selling T-model Ford in one color only (black) in 1908, but in modern societies this was no longer ③ possible. The modernization of society led to a marketing revolution that ④ strengthened the view that production would create its own demand. Customers, and the desire to ⑤ meet their diverse and often complex needs, became the focus of business.

＊affluent: 부유한

04

다음 글의 밑줄 친 부분 중, 문맥상 낱말의 쓰임이 적절하지 <u>않은</u> 것은? [3점]

Plant growth is controlled by a group of hormones called auxins found at the tips of stems and roots of plants. Auxins produced at the tips of stems tend to accumulate on the side of the stem that is in the shade. Accordingly, the auxins ① <u>stimulate</u> growth on the shaded side of the plant. Therefore, the shaded side grows faster than the side facing the sunlight. This phenomenon causes the stem to bend and appear to be growing ② <u>towards</u> the light. Auxins have the ③ <u>opposite</u> effect on the roots of plants. Auxins in the tips of roots tend to limit growth. If a root is horizontal in the soil, the auxins will accumulate on the lower side and interfere with its development. Therefore, the lower side of the root will grow ④ <u>faster</u> than the upper side. This will, in turn, cause the root to bend ⑤ <u>downwards</u>, with the tip of the root growing in that direction.

05

다음 글의 밑줄 친 부분 중, 문맥상 낱말의 쓰임이 적절하지 <u>않은</u> 것은? [3점]

It is widely believed that certain herbs somehow magically improve the work of certain organs, and "cure" specific diseases as a result. Such statements are unscientific and groundless. Sometimes herbs appear to work, since they tend to ① <u>increase</u> your blood circulation in an aggressive attempt by your body to eliminate them from your system. That can create a ② <u>temporary</u> feeling of a high, which makes it seem as if your health condition has improved.

Also, herbs can have a placebo effect, just like any other method, thus helping you feel better. Whatever the case, it is your body that has the intelligence to ③ <u>regain</u> health, and not the herbs. How can herbs have the intelligence needed to direct your body into getting healthier? That is impossible. Try to imagine how herbs might come into your body and intelligently ④ <u>fix</u> your problems. If you try to do that, you will see how impossible it seems. Otherwise, it would mean that herbs are ⑤ <u>less</u> intelligent than the human body, which is truly hard to believe.

＊ placebo effect: 위약 효과

06

다음 글의 밑줄 친 부분 중, 문맥상 낱말의 쓰임이 적절하지 <u>않은</u> 것은? [3점]

Do you sometimes feel like you don't love your life? Like, deep inside, something is missing? That's because we are living someone else's life. We allow other people to ① <u>influence</u> our choices. We are trying to meet their expectations. Social pressure is deceiving — we are all impacted without noticing it. Before we realize we are losing ownership of our lives, we end up ② <u>ignoring</u> how other people live. Then, we can only see the greener grass — ours is never good enough. To regain that passion for the life you want, you must ③ <u>recover</u> control of your choices. No one but yourself can choose how you live. But, how? The first step to getting rid of expectations is to treat yourself ④ <u>kindly</u>. You can't truly love other people if you don't love yourself first. When we accept who we are, there's no room for other's ⑤ <u>expectations</u>.

07

다음 글의 밑줄 친 부분 중, 문맥상 낱말의 쓰임이 적절하지 <u>않은</u> 것은? [3점]

Rejection is an everyday part of our lives, yet most people can't handle it well. For many, it's so painful that they'd rather not ask for something at all than ask and ① <u>risk</u> rejection. Yet, as the old saying goes, if you don't ask, the answer is always no. Avoiding rejection ② <u>negatively</u> affects many aspects of your life. All of that happens only because you're not ③ <u>tough</u> enough to handle it. For this reason, consider rejection therapy. Come up with a ④ <u>request</u> or an activity that usually results in a rejection. Working in sales is one such example. Asking for discounts at the stores will also work. By deliberately getting yourself ⑤ <u>welcomed</u> you'll grow a thicker skin that will allow you to take on much more in life, thus making you more successful at dealing with unfavorable circumstances.

* deliberately: 의도적으로

08 오답률 BEST

다음 글의 밑줄 친 부분 중, 문맥상 낱말의 쓰임이 적절하지 <u>않은</u> 것은?

For species approaching extinction, zoos can act as a last chance for survival. ① <u>Recovery</u> programs are established to coordinate the efforts of field conservationists and wildlife authorities. As populations of those species ② <u>diminish</u> it is not unusual for zoos to start captive breeding programs. Captive breeding acts to protect against extinction. In some cases captive-bred individuals may be released back into the wild, supplementing wild populations. This is most successful in situations where individuals are at greatest threat during a ③ <u>particular</u> life stage. For example, turtle eggs may be removed from high-risk locations until after they hatch. This may ④ <u>increase</u> the number of turtles that survive to adulthood. Crocodile programs have also been successful in protecting eggs and hatchlings, ⑤ <u>capturing</u> hatchlings once they are better equipped to protect themselves.

* captive breeding: 포획 사육 ** hatch: 부화하다

09

다음 글의 밑줄 친 부분 중, 문맥상 낱말의 쓰임이 적절하지 <u>않은</u> 것은? [3점]

Hunting can explain how humans developed *reciprocal altruism* and *social exchange*. Humans seem to be unique among primates in showing extensive reciprocal relationships that can last years, decades, or a lifetime. Meat from a large game animal comes in quantities that ① <u>exceed</u> what a single hunter and his immediate family could possibly consume. Furthermore, hunting success is highly ② <u>variable</u>; a hunter who is successful one week might fail the next. These conditions ③ <u>encourage</u> food sharing from hunting. The costs to a hunter of giving away meat he cannot eat immediately are ④ <u>high</u> because he cannot consume all the meat himself and leftovers will soon spoil. The benefits can be large, however, when those who are given his food return the generous favor later on when he has failed to get food for himself. In essence, hunters can ⑤ <u>store</u> extra meat in the bodies of their friends and neighbors.

* reciprocal altruism: 상호 이타주의 ** primates: 영장류

10 오답률 BEST

다음 글의 밑줄 친 부분 중, 문맥상 낱말의 쓰임이 적절하지 <u>않은</u> 것은? [3점]

Detailed study over the past two or three decades is showing that the complex forms of natural systems are essential to their functioning. The attempt to ① <u>straighten</u> rivers and give them regular cross-sections is perhaps the most disastrous example of this form-and-function relationship. The natural river has a very ② <u>irregular</u> form: it curves a lot, spills across floodplains, and leaks into wetlands, giving it an ever-changing and incredibly complex shoreline. This allows the river to ③ <u>prevent</u> variations in water level and speed. Pushing the river into tidy geometry ④ <u>destroys</u> functional capacity and results in disasters like the Mississippi floods of 1927 and 1993 and, more recently, the unnatural disaster of Hurricane Katrina. A $50 billion plan to "let the river loose" in Louisiana recognizes that the ⑤ <u>controlled</u> Mississippi is washing away twenty-four square miles of that state annually.

* geometry: 기하학 ** capacity: 수용능력

11

다음 글의 밑줄 친 부분 중, 문맥상 낱말의 쓰임이 적절하지 <u>않은</u> 것은? [3점]

When the price of something fundamental drops greatly, the whole world can change. Consider light. Chances are you are reading this sentence under some kind of artificial light. Moreover, you probably never thought about whether using artificial light for reading was worth it. Light is so ① <u>cheap</u> that you use it without thinking. But in the early 1800s, it would have cost you four hundred times what you are paying now for the same amount of light. At that price, you would ② <u>notice</u> the cost and would think twice before using artificial light to read a book. The ③ <u>increase</u> in the price of light lit up the world. Not only did it turn night into day, but it allowed us to live and work in big buildings that ④ <u>natural</u> light could not enter. Nearly nothing we have today would be ⑤ <u>possible</u> if the cost of artificial light had not dropped to almost nothing.

* artificial: 인공의

12

(A), (B), (C)의 각 네모 안에서 문맥에 맞는 낱말로 가장 적절한 것은? [3점]

Recent research suggests that evolving humans' relationship with dogs changed the structure of both species' brains. One of the various (A) physical / psychological changes caused by domestication is a reduction in the size of the brain: 16 percent for horses, 34 percent for pigs, and 10 to 30 percent for dogs. This is because once humans started to take care of these animals, they no longer needed various brain functions in order to survive. Animals who were fed and protected by humans did not need many of the skills required by their wild ancestors and (B) developed / lost the parts of the brain related to those capacities. A similar process occurred for humans, who seem to have been domesticated by wolves. About 10,000 years ago, when the role of dogs was firmly established in most human societies, the human brain also (C) expanded / shrank by about 10 percent.

	(A)	(B)	(C)
①	physical	developed	expanded
②	physical	lost	expanded
③	physical	lost	shrank
④	psychological	developed	shrank
⑤	psychological	lost	shrank

01

202309 31번

다음 빈칸에 들어갈 말로 가장 적절한 것을 고르시오.

Many people are terrified to fly in airplanes. Often, this fear stems from a lack of control. The pilot is in control, not the passengers, and this lack of control instills fear. Many potential passengers are so afraid they choose to drive great distances to get to a destination instead of flying. But their decision to drive is based solely on emotion, not logic. Logic says that statistically, the odds of dying in a car crash are around 1 in 5,000, while the odds of dying in a plane crash are closer to 1 in 11 million. If you're going to take a risk, especially one that could possibly involve your well-being, wouldn't you want the odds in your favor? However, most people choose the option that will cause them the least amount of _____. Pay attention to the thoughts you have about taking the risk and make sure you're basing your decision on facts, not just feelings.

*instill: 스며들게 하다

① anxiety
② boredom
③ confidence
④ satisfaction
⑤ responsibility

02 오답률 BEST

202309 32번

다음 빈칸에 들어갈 말로 가장 적절한 것을 고르시오. [3점]

The famous primatologist Frans de Waal, of Emory University, says humans downplay similarities between us and other animals as a way of maintaining our spot at the top of our imaginary ladder. Scientists, de Waal points out, can be some of the worst offenders — employing technical language to _____. They call "kissing" in chimps "mouth-to-mouth contact"; they call "friends" between primates "favorite affiliation partners"; they interpret evidence showing that crows and chimps can make tools as being somehow qualitatively different from the kind of toolmaking said to define humanity. If an animal can beat us at a cognitive task — like how certain bird species can remember the precise locations of thousands of seeds — they write it off as instinct, not intelligence. This and so many more tricks of language are what de Waal has termed "linguistic castration." The way we use our tongues to disempower animals, the way we invent words to maintain our spot at the top.

* primatologist: 영장류학자 ** affiliation: 제휴

① define human instincts
② overestimate chimps' intelligence
③ distance the other animals from us
④ identify animals' negative emotions
⑤ correct our misconceptions about nature

03

202306 31번

다음 빈칸에 들어갈 말로 가장 적절한 것을 고르시오.

Individuals who perform at a high level in their profession often have instant credibility with others. People admire them, they want to be like them, and they feel connected to them. When they speak, others listen — even if the area of their skill has nothing to do with the advice they give. Think about a world-famous basketball player. He has made more money from endorsements than he ever did playing basketball. Is it because of his knowledge of the products he endorses? No. It's because of what he can do with a basketball. The same can be said of an Olympic medalist swimmer. People listen to him because of what he can do in the pool. And when an actor tells us we should drive a certain car, we don't listen because of his expertise on engines. We listen because we admire his talent. _____ connects. If you possess a high level of ability in an area, others may desire to connect with you because of it.

* endorsement: (유명인의 텔레비전 등에서의 상품) 보증 선전

① Patience
② Sacrifice
③ Honesty
④ Excellence
⑤ Creativity

04

다음 빈칸에 들어갈 말로 가장 적절한 것을 고르시오. [3점]

Think of the brain as a city. If you were to look out over a city and ask "where is the economy located?" you'd see there's no good answer to the question. Instead, the economy emerges from the interaction of all the elements — from the stores and the banks to the merchants and the customers. And so it is with the brain's operation: it doesn't happen in one spot. Just as in a city, no neighborhood of the brain _____. In brains and in cities, everything emerges from the interaction between residents, at all scales, locally and distantly. Just as trains bring materials and textiles into a city, which become processed into the economy, so the raw electrochemical signals from sensory organs are transported along superhighways of neurons. There the signals undergo processing and transformation into our conscious reality.

* electrochemical: 전기화학의

① operates in isolation
② suffers from rapid changes
③ resembles economic elements
④ works in a systematic way
⑤ interacts with another

05

다음 빈칸에 들어갈 말로 가장 적절한 것을 고르시오.

People differ in how quickly they can reset their biological clocks to overcome jet lag, and the speed of recovery depends on the _____ of travel. Generally, it's easier to fly westward and lengthen your day than it is to fly eastward and shorten it. This east-west difference in jet lag is sizable enough to have an impact on the performance of sports teams. Studies have found that teams flying westward perform significantly better than teams flying eastward in professional baseball and college football. A more recent study of more than 46,000 Major League Baseball games found additional evidence that eastward travel is tougher than westward travel.

* jet lag: 시차로 인한 피로감

① direction   ② purpose
③ season   ④ length
⑤ cost

06

다음 빈칸에 들어갈 말로 가장 적절한 것을 고르시오.

If you want the confidence that comes from achieving what you set out to do each day, then it's important to understand _____. Over-optimism about what can be achieved within a certain time frame is a problem. So work on it. Make a practice of estimating the amount of time needed alongside items on your 'things to do' list, and learn by experience when tasks take a greater or lesser time than expected. Give attention also to fitting the task to the available time. There are some tasks that you can only set about if you have a significant amount of time available. There is no point in trying to gear up for such a task when you only have a short period available. So schedule the time you need for the longer tasks and put the short tasks into the spare moments in between.

* gear up: 준비를 갖추다, 대비하다

① what benefits you can get
② how practical your tasks are
③ how long things are going to take
④ why failures are meaningful in life
⑤ why your leisure time should come first

07

다음 빈칸에 들어갈 말로 가장 적절한 것을 고르시오.

To demonstrate how best to defeat the habit of delaying, Dan Ariely, a professor of psychology and behavioral economics, performed an experiment on students in three of his classes at MIT. He assigned all classes three reports over the course of the semester. The first class had to choose three due dates for themselves, up to and including the last day of class. The second had no deadlines — all three papers just had to be submitted by the last day of class. In his third class, he gave students three set deadlines over the course of the semester. At the end of the semester, he found that students with set deadlines received the best grades, the students with no deadlines had the worst, and those who could choose their own deadlines fell somewhere in the middle. Ariely concludes that _____ — whether by the professor or by students who recognize their own tendencies to delay things — improves self-control and performance.

① offering rewards
② removing obstacles
③ restricting freedom
④ increasing assignments
⑤ encouraging competition

08 오답률 BEST

다음 빈칸에 들어갈 말로 가장 적절한 것을 고르시오. [3점]

The best way in which innovation changes our lives is by _____. The main theme of human history is that we become steadily more specialized in what we produce, and steadily more diversified in what we consume: we move away from unstable self-sufficiency to safer mutual interdependence. By concentrating on serving other people's needs for forty hours a week — which we call a job — you can spend the other seventy-two hours (not counting fifty-six hours in bed) relying on the services provided to you by other people. Innovation has made it possible to work for a fraction of a second in order to be able to afford to turn on an electric lamp for an hour, providing the quantity of light that would have required a whole day's work if you had to make it yourself by collecting and refining sesame oil or lamb fat to burn in a simple lamp, as much of humanity did in the not so distant past.

* a fraction of a second: 아주 짧은 시간 ** refine: 정제하다

① respecting the values of the old days
② enabling people to work for each other
③ providing opportunities to think creatively
④ satisfying customers with personalized services
⑤ introducing and commercializing unusual products

09

다음 빈칸에 들어갈 말로 가장 적절한 것을 고르시오. [3점]

We worry that the robots are taking our jobs, but just as common a problem is that the robots are taking our _____. In the large warehouses so common behind the scenes of today's economy, human 'pickers' hurry around grabbing products off shelves and moving them to where they can be packed and dispatched. In their ears are headpieces: the voice of 'Jennifer', a piece of software, tells them where to go and what to do, controlling the smallest details of their movements. Jennifer breaks down instructions into tiny chunks, to minimise error and maximise productivity — for example, rather than picking eighteen copies of a book off a shelf, the human worker would be politely instructed to pick five. Then another five. Then yet another five. Then another three. Working in such conditions reduces people to machines made of flesh. Rather than asking us to think or adapt, the Jennifer unit takes over the thought process and treats workers as an inexpensive source of some visual processing and a pair of opposable thumbs.

* dispatch: 발송하다 ** chunk: 덩어리

① reliability   ② judgment
③ endurance   ④ sociability
⑤ cooperation

10

다음 빈칸에 들어갈 말로 가장 적절한 것을 고르시오.

The prevailing view among developmental scientists is that people are active contributors to their own development. People are influenced by the physical and social contexts in which they live, but they also play a role in influencing their development by interacting with, and changing, those contexts. Even infants influence the world around them and construct their own development through their interactions. Consider an infant who smiles at each adult he sees; he influences his world because adults are likely to smile, use "baby talk," and play with him in response. The infant brings adults into close contact, making one-on-one interactions and creating opportunities for learning. By engaging the world around them, thinking, being curious, and interacting with people, objects, and the world around them, individuals of all ages are "_____."

① mirrors of their generation
② shields against social conflicts
③ explorers in their own career path
④ followers of their childhood dreams
⑤ manufacturers of their own development

11

다음 빈칸에 들어갈 말로 가장 적절한 것을 고르시오.

One of the big questions faced this past year was how to keep innovation rolling when people were working entirely virtually. But experts say that digital work didn't have a negative effect on innovation and creativity. Working within limits pushes us to solve problems. Overall, virtual meeting platforms put more constraints on communication and collaboration than face-to-face settings. For instance, with the press of a button, virtual meeting hosts can control the size of breakout groups and enforce time constraints; only one person can speak at a time; nonverbal signals, particularly those below the shoulders, are diminished; "seating arrangements" are assigned by the platform, not by individuals; and visual access to others may be limited by the size of each participant's screen. Such _____ are likely to stretch participants beyond their usual ways of thinking, boosting creativity.

① restrictions   ② responsibilities
③ memories   ④ coincidences
⑤ traditions

12

다음 빈칸에 들어갈 말로 가장 적절한 것을 고르시오. [3점]

The law of demand is that the demand for goods and services increases as prices fall, and the demand falls as prices increase. *Giffen goods* are special types of products for which the traditional law of demand does not apply. Instead of switching to cheaper replacements, consumers demand more of giffen goods when the price increases and less of them when the price decreases. Taking an example, rice in China is a giffen good because people tend to purchase less of it when the price falls. The reason for this is, when the price of rice falls, people have more money to spend on other types of products such as meat and dairy and, therefore, change their spending pattern. On the other hand, as rice prices increase, people _____.

① order more meat   ② consume more rice
③ try to get new jobs   ④ increase their savings
⑤ start to invest overseas

13 오답률 BEST

202203 31번

다음 빈칸에 들어갈 말로 가장 적절한 것을 고르시오.

Generalization without specific examples that humanize writing is boring to the listener and to the reader. Who wants to read platitudes all day? Who wants to hear the words great, greater, best, smartest, finest, humanitarian, on and on and on without specific examples? Instead of using these 'nothing words,' leave them out completely and just describe the _____. There is nothing worse than reading a scene in a novel in which a main character is described up front as heroic or brave or tragic or funny, while thereafter, the writer quickly moves on to something else. That's no good, no good at all. You have to use less one word descriptions and more detailed, engaging descriptions if you want to make something real.

* platitude: 상투적인 말

① similarities   ② particulars
③ fantasies   ④ boredom
⑤ wisdom

14

202203 32번

다음 빈칸에 들어갈 말로 가장 적절한 것을 고르시오.

Face-to-face interaction is a uniquely powerful — and sometimes the only — way to share many kinds of knowledge, from the simplest to the most complex. It is one of the best ways to stimulate new thinking and ideas, too. Most of us would have had difficulty learning how to tie a shoelace only from pictures, or how to do arithmetic from a book. Psychologist Mihàly Csikszentmihàlyi found, while studying high achievers, that a large number of Nobel Prize winners were the students

of previous winners: they had access to the same literature as everyone else, but _____ made a crucial difference to their creativity. Within organisations this makes conversation both a crucial factor for high-level professional skills and the most important way of sharing everyday information.

* arithmetic: 계산 ** literature: (연구) 문헌

① natural talent   ② regular practice
③ personal contact   ④ complex knowledge
⑤ powerful motivation

15

202111 31번

다음 빈칸에 들어갈 말로 가장 적절한 것을 고르시오.

We don't send telegraphs to communicate anymore, but it's a great metaphor for giving advance notice. Sometimes, you must inform those close to you of upcoming change by conveying important information well in advance. There's a huge difference between saying, "From now on, we will do things differently," which doesn't give people enough time to understand and accept the change, and saying something like, "Starting next month, we're going to approach things differently." Telegraphing empowers people to _____. Telegraphing involves the art of seeing an upcoming event or circumstance and giving others enough time to process and accept the change. Telegraph anything that will take people out of what is familiar and comfortable to them. This will allow processing time for them to accept the circumstances and make the most of what's happening.

① unite   ② adapt
③ object   ④ compete
⑤ recover

16

다음 빈칸에 들어갈 말로 가장 적절한 것을 고르시오.

Not only does memory underlie our ability to think at all, it defines the content of our experiences and how we preserve them for years to come. Memory _____. If I were to suffer from heart failure and depend upon an artificial heart, I would be no less myself. If I lost an arm in an accident and had it replaced with an artificial arm, I would still be essentially *me*. As long as my mind and memories remain intact, I will continue to be the same person, no matter which part of my body (other than the brain) is replaced. On the other hand, when someone suffers from advanced Alzheimer's disease and his memories fade, people often say that he "is not himself anymore," or that it is as if the person "is no longer there," though his body remains unchanged.

* intact: 손상되지 않은

① makes us who we are
② has to do with our body
③ reflects what we expect
④ lets us understand others
⑤ helps us learn from the past

17

다음 빈칸에 들어갈 말로 가장 적절한 것을 고르시오.

Sometimes it is the _____ that gives a business a competitive advantage. Until recently, bicycles had to have many gears, often 15 or 20, for them to be considered high-end. But fixed-gear bikes with minimal features have become more popular, as those who buy them are happy to pay more for much less. The overall profitability of these bikes is much higher than the more complex ones because they do a single thing really well without the cost of added complexity. Companies should be careful of getting into a war over adding more features with their competitors, as this will increase cost and almost certainly reduce profitability because of competitive pressure on price.

* high-end: 최고급의

① simpler product
② affordable price
③ consumer loyalty
④ customized design
⑤ eco-friendly technology

18

다음 빈칸에 들어갈 말로 가장 적절한 것을 고르시오.

Many evolutionary biologists argue that humans _____. We needed to trade, and we needed to establish trust in order to trade. Language is very handy when you are trying to conduct business with someone. Two early humans could not only agree to trade three wooden bowls for six bunches of bananas but establish rules as well. What wood was used for the bowls? Where did you get the bananas? That business deal would have been nearly impossible using only gestures and confusing noises, and carrying it out according to terms agreed upon creates a bond of trust. Language allows us to be specific, and this is where conversation plays a key role.

① used body language to communicate
② instinctively knew who to depend on
③ often changed rules for their own needs
④ lived independently for their own survival
⑤ developed language for economic reasons

19 오답률 BEST   📄 202106 31번

다음 빈칸에 들어갈 말로 가장 적절한 것을 고르시오.

In a culture where there is a belief that you can have anything you truly want, there is no problem in choosing. Many cultures, however, do not maintain this belief. In fact, many people do not believe that life is about getting what you want. Life is about doing what you are *supposed* to do. The reason they have trouble making choices is they believe that what they may want is not related to what they are supposed to do. The weight of outside considerations is greater than their _____. When this is an issue in a group, we discuss what makes for good decisions. If a person can be unburdened from their cares and duties and, just for a moment, consider what appeals to them, they get the chance to sort out what is important to them. Then they can consider and negotiate with their external pressures.

① desires   ② merits
③ abilities   ④ limitations
⑤ worries

20 오답률 BEST   📄 202106 32번

다음 빈칸에 들어갈 말로 가장 적절한 것을 고르시오.

Research has confirmed that athletes are less likely to participate in unacceptable behavior than are non-athletes. However, moral reasoning and good sporting behavior seem to decline as athletes progress to higher competitive levels, in part because of the increased emphasis on winning. Thus winning can be _____ in teaching character development. Some athletes may want to win so much that they lie, cheat, and break team rules. They may develop undesirable character traits that can enhance their ability to win in the short term. However, when athletes resist the temptation to win in a dishonest way, they can develop positive character traits that last a lifetime. Character is a learned behavior, and a sense of fair play develops only if coaches plan to teach those lessons systematically.

* trait: 특성

① a piece of cake
② a one-way street
③ a bird in the hand
④ a fish out of water
⑤ a double-edged sword

21   📄 202103 31번

다음 빈칸에 들어갈 말로 가장 적절한 것을 고르시오.

One of the most important aspects of providing good care is making sure that an animal's needs are being met consistently and predictably. Like humans, animals need a sense of control. So an animal who may get enough food but doesn't know when the food will appear and can see no consistent schedule may experience distress. We can provide a sense of control by ensuring that our animal's environment is _____: there is always water available and always in the same place. There is always food when we get up in the morning and after our evening walk. There will always be a time and place to eliminate, without having to hold things in to the point of discomfort. Human companions can display consistent emotional support, rather than providing love one moment and withholding love the next. When animals know what to expect, they can feel more confident and calm.

* eliminate: 배설하다

① silent   ② natural
③ isolated   ④ dynamic
⑤ predictable

22

다음 빈칸에 들어갈 말로 가장 적절한 것을 고르시오.

When a child is upset, the easiest and quickest way to calm them down is to give them food. This acts as a distraction from the feelings they are having, gives them something to do with their hands and mouth and shifts their attention from whatever was upsetting them. If the food chosen is also seen as a treat such as sweets or a biscuit, then the child will feel 'treated' and happier. In the shorter term using food like this is effective. But in the longer term it can be harmful as we quickly learn that food is a good way to _____. Then as we go through life, whenever we feel annoyed, anxious or even just bored, we turn to food to make ourselves feel better.

① make friends
② learn etiquettes
③ improve memory
④ manage emotions
⑤ celebrate achievements

23

다음 빈칸에 들어갈 말로 가장 적절한 것을 고르시오.

There is nothing more fundamental to the human spirit than the need to be _____. It is the intuitive force that sparks our imaginations and opens pathways to life-changing opportunities. It is the catalyst for progress and personal freedom. Public transportation has been vital to that progress and freedom for more than two centuries. The transportation industry has always done more than carry travelers from one destination to another. It connects people, places, and possibilities. It provides access to what people need, what they love, and what they aspire to become. In so doing, it grows communities, creates jobs, strengthens the economy,

expands social and commercial networks, saves time and energy, and helps millions of people achieve a better life.

＊catalyst: 촉매, 기폭제

① secure
② mobile
③ exceptional
④ competitive
⑤ independent

24

다음 빈칸에 들어갈 말로 가장 적절한 것을 고르시오. [3점]

Business consultant Frans Johansson describes the *Medici effect* as the emergence of new ideas and creative solutions when different backgrounds and disciplines come together. The term is derived from the 15th-century Medici family, who helped usher in the Renaissance by bringing together artists, writers, and other creatives from all over the world. Arguably, the Renaissance was a result of the exchange of ideas between these different groups in close contact with each other. Sound familiar? If you are unable to diversify your own talent and skill, then _____ might very well just do the trick. Believing that all new ideas come from combining existing notions in creative ways, Johansson recommends utilizing a mix of backgrounds, experiences, and expertise in staffing to bring about the best possible solutions, perspectives, and innovations in business.

＊usher in: ~이 시작되게 하다

① having others around you to compensate
② taking some time to reflect on yourself
③ correcting the mistakes of the past
④ maximizing your own strength
⑤ setting a specific objective

01

다음 빈칸에 들어갈 말로 가장 적절한 것을 고르시오.

A key to engagement and achievement is providing students with _____. My scholarly work and my teaching have been deeply influenced by the work of Rosalie Fink. She interviewed twelve adults who were highly successful in their work, including a physicist, a biochemist, and a company CEO. All of them had dyslexia and had had significant problems with reading throughout their school years. While she expected to find that they had avoided reading and discovered ways to bypass it or compensate with other strategies for learning, she found the opposite. "To my surprise, I found that these dyslexics were enthusiastic readers...they rarely avoided reading. On the contrary, they sought out books." The pattern Fink discovered was that all of her subjects had been passionate in some personal interest. The areas of interest included religion, math, business, science, history, and biography. What mattered was that they read voraciously to find out more.

＊dyslexia: 난독증　＊＊voraciously: 탐욕스럽게

① examples from official textbooks
② relevant texts they will be interested in
③ enough chances to exchange information
④ different genres for different age groups
⑤ early reading experience to develop logic skills

02 오답률 BEST

다음 빈칸에 들어갈 말로 가장 적절한 것을 고르시오. [3점]

For many people, *ability* refers to intellectual competence, so they want everything they do to reflect how smart they are — writing a brilliant legal brief, getting the highest grade on a test, writing elegant computer code, saying something exceptionally wise or witty in a conversation. You could also define ability in terms of a particular skill or talent, such as how well one plays the piano, learns a language, or serves a tennis ball. Some people focus on their ability to be attractive, entertaining, up on the latest trends, or to have the newest gadgets. However ability may be defined, a problem occurs when _____. The performance becomes the *only* measure of the person; nothing else is taken into account. An outstanding performance means an outstanding person; an average performance means an average person. Period.

① it is the sole determinant of one's self-worth
② you are distracted by others' achievements
③ there is too much competition in one field
④ you ignore feedback about a performance
⑤ it is not accompanied by effort

03

다음 빈칸에 들어갈 말로 가장 적절한 것을 고르시오. [3점]

Someone else's body language affects our own body, which then creates an emotional echo that makes us feel accordingly. As Louis Armstrong sang, "When you're smiling, the whole world smiles with you." If copying another's smile makes us feel happy, the emotion of the smiler has been transmitted via our body. Strange as it may sound, this theory states that _____. For example, our mood can be improved by simply lifting up the corners of our mouth. If people are asked to bite down on a pencil lengthwise, taking care not to let the pencil touch their lips (thus forcing the mouth into a smile-like shape), they judge cartoons funnier than if they have been asked to frown. The primacy of the body is sometimes summarized in the phrase "I must be afraid, because I'm running."

＊lengthwise: 길게　＊＊frown: 얼굴을 찡그리다

① language guides our actions
② emotions arise from our bodies
③ body language hides our feelings
④ what others say affects our mood
⑤ negative emotions easily disappear

04

다음 빈칸에 들어갈 말로 가장 적절한 것을 고르시오. [3점]

_____ boosts sales. Brian Wansink, Professor of Marketing at Cornell University, investigated the effectiveness of this tactic in 1998. He persuaded three supermarkets in Sioux City, Iowa, to offer Campbell's soup at a small discount: 79 cents rather than 89 cents. The discounted soup was sold in one of three conditions: a control, where there was no limit on the volume of purchases, or two tests, where customers were limited to either four or twelve cans. In the unlimited condition shoppers bought 3.3 cans on average, whereas in the scarce condition, when there was a limit, they bought 5.3 on average. This suggests scarcity encourages sales. The findings are particularly strong because the test took place in a supermarket with genuine shoppers. It didn't rely on claimed data, nor was it held in a laboratory where consumers might behave differently.

* tactic: 전략

① Promoting products through social media
② Reducing the risk of producing poor quality items
③ Restricting the number of items customers can buy
④ Offering several options that customers find attractive
⑤ Emphasizing the safety of products with research data

05

다음 빈칸에 들어갈 말로 가장 적절한 것을 고르시오. [3점]

In Lewis Carroll's *Through the Looking-Glass*, the Red Queen takes Alice on a race through the countryside. They run and they run, but then Alice discovers that they're still under the same tree that they started from. The Red Queen explains to Alice: "*here*, you see, it takes all the running you can do, to keep in the same place." Biologists sometimes use this Red Queen Effect to explain an evolutionary principle. If foxes evolve to run faster so they can catch more rabbits, then only the fastest rabbits will live long enough to make a new generation of bunnies that run even faster — in which case, of course, only the fastest foxes will catch enough rabbits to thrive and pass on their genes. Even though they might run, the two species _____.

* thrive: 번성하다

① just stay in place
② end up walking slowly
③ never run into each other
④ won't be able to adapt to changes
⑤ cannot run faster than their parents

06

다음 빈칸에 들어갈 말로 가장 적절한 것을 고르시오. [3점]

Everything in the world around us was finished in the mind of its creator before it was started. The houses we live in, the cars we drive, and our clothing — all of these began with an idea. Each idea was then studied, refined and perfected before the first nail was driven or the first piece of cloth was cut. Long before the idea was turned into a physical reality, the mind had clearly pictured the finished product. The human being designs his or her own future through much the same process. We begin with an idea about how the future will be. Over a period of time we refine and perfect the vision. Before long, our every thought, decision and activity are all working in harmony to bring into existence what we _____.

* refine: 다듬다

① didn't even have the potential to accomplish
② have mentally concluded about the future
③ haven't been able to picture in our mind
④ considered careless and irresponsible
⑤ have observed in some professionals

07

다음 빈칸에 들어갈 말로 가장 적절한 것을 고르시오.

If you've ever made a poor choice, you might be interested in learning how to break that habit. One great way to trick your brain into doing so is to sign a "Ulysses Contract." The name of this life tip comes from the Greek myth about Ulysses, a captain whose ship sailed past the island of the Sirens, a tribe of dangerous women who lured victims to their death with their irresistible songs. Knowing that he would otherwise be unable to resist, Ulysses instructed his crew to stuff their ears with cotton and tie him to the ship's mast to prevent him from turning their ship towards the Sirens. It worked for him and you can do the same thing by _____. For example, if you want to stay off your cellphone and concentrate on your work, delete the apps that distract you or ask a friend to change your password!

* lure: 유혹하다 ** mast: 돛대

① letting go of all-or-nothing mindset
② finding reasons why you want to change
③ locking yourself out of your temptations
④ building a plan and tracking your progress
⑤ focusing on breaking one bad habit at a time

08

다음 빈칸에 들어갈 말로 가장 적절한 것을 고르시오. [3점]

Our homes aren't just ecosystems, they're unique ones, hosting species that are adapted to indoor environments and pushing evolution in new directions. Indoor microbes, insects, and rats have all evolved the ability to survive our chemical attacks, developing resistance to antibacterials, insecticides, and poisons. German cockroaches are known to have developed a distaste for glucose, which is commonly used as bait in roach traps. Some indoor insects, which have fewer opportunities to feed than their outdoor counterparts, seem to have developed the ability to survive when food is limited. Dunn and other ecologists have suggested that as the planet becomes more developed and more urban, more species will _____. Over a long enough time period, indoor living could drive our evolution, too. Perhaps my indoorsy self represents the future of humanity.

* glucose: 포도당 ** bait: 미끼

① produce chemicals to protect themselves
② become extinct with the destroyed habitats
③ evolve the traits they need to thrive indoors
④ compete with outside organisms to find their prey
⑤ break the boundaries between wildlife and humans

09

다음 빈칸에 들어갈 말로 가장 적절한 것을 고르시오. [3점]

The demand for freshness can _____. While freshness is now being used as a term in food marketing as part of a return to nature, the demand for year-round supplies of fresh produce such as soft fruit and exotic vegetables has led to the widespread use of hot houses in cold climates and increasing reliance on total quality control — management by temperature control, use of pesticides and computer/satellite-based logistics. The demand for freshness has also contributed to concerns about food wastage. Use of 'best before', 'sell by' and 'eat by' labels has legally allowed institutional waste. Campaigners have exposed the scandal of over-production and waste. Tristram Stuart, one of the global band of anti-waste campaigners, argues that, with freshly made sandwiches, over-ordering is standard practice across the retail sector to avoid the appearance of empty shelf space, leading to high volumes of waste when supply regularly exceeds demand.

* pesticide: 살충제 ** logistics: 물류, 유통

① have hidden environmental costs
② worsen the global hunger problem
③ bring about technological advances
④ improve nutrition and quality of food
⑤ diversify the diet of a local community

10

다음 빈칸에 들어갈 말로 가장 적절한 것을 고르시오. [3점]

In the studies of Colin Cherry at the Massachusetts Institute for Technology back in the 1950s, his participants listened to voices in one ear at a time and then through both ears in an effort to determine whether we can listen to two people talk at the same time. One ear always contained a message that the listener had to repeat back (called "shadowing") while the other ear included people speaking. The trick was to see if you could totally focus on the main message and also hear someone talking in your other ear. Cleverly, Cherry found it was impossible for his participants to know whether the message in the other ear was spoken by a man or woman, in English or another language, or was even comprised of real words at all! In other words, people could not _____.

① decide what they should do in the moment
② remember a message with too many words
③ analyze which information was more accurate
④ speak their own ideas while listening to others
⑤ process two pieces of information at the same time

11

다음 빈칸에 들어갈 말로 가장 적절한 것을 고르시오. [3점]

In a study at Princeton University in 1992, research scientists looked at two different groups of mice. One group was made intellectually superior by modifying the gene for the glutamate receptor. Glutamate is a brain chemical that is necessary in learning. The other group was genetically manipulated to be intellectually inferior, also done by modifying the gene for the glutamate receptor. The smart mice were then raised in standard cages, while the inferior mice were raised in large cages with toys and exercise wheels and with lots of social interaction. At the end of the study, although the intellectually inferior mice were genetically handicapped, they were able to perform just as well as their genetic superiors. This was a real triumph for nurture over nature. Genes are turned on or off _____.

* glutamate: 글루타민산염 ** manipulate: 조작하다

① by themselves for survival
② free from social interaction
③ based on what is around you
④ depending on genetic superiority
⑤ so as to keep ourselves entertained

12

다음 빈칸에 들어갈 말로 가장 적절한 것을 고르시오. [3점]

Researchers are working on a project that asks coastal towns how they are preparing for rising sea levels. Some towns have risk assessments; some towns even have a plan. But it's a rare town that is actually carrying out a plan. One reason we've failed to act on climate change is the common belief that _____. For decades, climate change was a prediction about the future, so scientists talked about it in the future tense. This became a habit — so that even today many scientists still use the future tense, even though we know that a climate crisis is ongoing. Scientists also often focus on regions most affected by the crisis, such as Bangladesh or the West Antarctic Ice Sheet, which for most Americans are physically remote.

① it is not related to science
② it is far away in time and space
③ energy efficiency matters the most
④ careful planning can fix the problem
⑤ it is too late to prevent it from happening

13

202203 33번

다음 빈칸에 들어갈 말로 가장 적절한 것을 고르시오. [3점]

Most times a foreign language is spoken in film, subtitles are used to translate the dialogue for the viewer. However, there are occasions when foreign dialogue is left unsubtitled (and thus incomprehensible to most of the target audience). This is often done if the movie is seen mainly from the viewpoint of a particular character who does not speak the language. Such absence of subtitles allows the audience to feel a similar sense of incomprehension and alienation that the character feels. An example of this is seen in *Not Without My Daughter*. The Persian language dialogue spoken by the Iranian characters is not subtitled because the main character Betty Mahmoody does not speak Persian and the audience is _____.

* subtitle: 자막(을 넣다) ** incomprehensible: 이해할 수 없는
***alienation: 소외

① seeing the film from her viewpoint
② impressed by her language skills
③ attracted to her beautiful voice
④ participating in a heated debate
⑤ learning the language used in the film

14 오답률 BEST

202203 34번

다음 빈칸에 들어갈 말로 가장 적절한 것을 고르시오. [3점]

One dynamic that can change dramatically in sport is the concept of the home-field advantage, in which perceived demands and resources seem to play a role. Under normal circumstances, the home ground would appear to provide greater perceived resources (fans, home field, and so on). However, researchers Roy Baumeister and Andrew Steinhilber were among the first to point out that these competitive factors can change; for example, the success percentage for home teams in the final games of a playoff or World Series seems to drop. Fans can become part of the perceived demands rather than resources under those circumstances. This change in perception can also explain why a team that's struggling at the start of the year will _____ to reduce perceived demands and pressures.

* perceive: 인식하다 **playoff: 우승 결정전

① often welcome a road trip
② avoid international matches
③ focus on increasing ticket sales
④ want to have an eco-friendly stadium
⑤ try to advertise their upcoming games

15

202111 33번

다음 빈칸에 들어갈 말로 가장 적절한 것을 고르시오. [3점]

Over time, babies construct expectations about what sounds they will hear when. They hold in memory the sound patterns that occur on a regular basis. They make hypotheses like, "If I hear *this* sound first, it probably will be followed by *that* sound." Scientists conclude that much of babies' skill in learning language is due to their _____. For babies, this means that they appear to pay close attention to the patterns that repeat in language. They remember, in a systematic way, how often sounds occur, in what order, with what intervals, and with what changes of pitch. This memory store allows them to track, within the neural circuits of their brains, the frequency of sound patterns and to use this knowledge to make predictions about the meaning in patterns of sounds.

① lack of social pressures
② ability to calculate statistics
③ desire to interact with others
④ preference for simpler sounds
⑤ tendency to imitate caregivers

16

다음 빈칸에 들어갈 말로 가장 적절한 것을 고르시오. [3점]

Some deep-sea organisms are known to use bioluminescence as a lure, to attract prey with a little glow imitating the movements of their favorite fish, or like fireflies, as a sexual attractant to find mates. While there are many possible evolutionary theories for the survival value of bioluminescence, one of the most fascinating is to _____. The color of almost all bioluminescent molecules is blue-green, the same color as the ocean above. By self-glowing blue-green, the creatures no longer cast a shadow or create a silhouette, especially when viewed from below against the brighter waters above. Rather, by glowing themselves, they can blend into the sparkles, reflections, and scattered blue-green glow of sunlight or moonlight. Thus, they are most likely making their own light not to see, but to be un-seen.

＊bioluminescence: 생물 발광 ＊＊lure: 가짜 미끼

① send a signal for help
② threaten enemies nearby
③ lift the veil of hidden prey
④ create a cloak of invisibility
⑤ serve as a navigation system

17

다음 빈칸에 들어갈 말로 가장 적절한 것을 고르시오.

One big difference between science and stage magic is that while magicians hide their mistakes from the audience, in science you make your mistakes in public. You show them off so that everybody can learn from them. This way, you get the advantage of everybody else's experience, and not just your own idiosyncratic path through the space of mistakes. This, by the way, is another reason why we humans are so much smarter than every other species. It is not that our brains are bigger or more powerful, or even that we have the ability to reflect on our own past errors, but that we _____ that our individual brains have earned from their individual histories of trial and error.

＊idiosyncratic: (개인에게) 특유한

① share the benefits
② overlook the insights
③ develop creative skills
④ exaggerate the achievements
⑤ underestimate the knowledge

18

다음 빈칸에 들어갈 말로 가장 적절한 것을 고르시오. [3점]

The last two decades of research on the science of learning have shown conclusively that we remember things better, and longer, if _____. This is the teaching method practiced by physics professor Eric Mazur. He doesn't lecture in his classes at Harvard. Instead, he asks students difficult questions, based on their homework reading, that require them to pull together sources of information to solve a problem. Mazur doesn't give them the answer; instead, he asks the students to break off into small groups and discuss the problem among themselves. Eventually, nearly everyone in the class gets the answer right, and the concepts stick with them because they had to find their own way to the answer.

① they are taught repeatedly in class
② we fully focus on them without any distractions
③ equal opportunities are given to complete tasks
④ there's no right or wrong way to learn about a topic
⑤ we discover them ourselves rather than being told them

19 오답률 BEST

다음 빈칸에 들어갈 말로 가장 적절한 것을 고르시오. [3점]

Due to technological innovations, music can now be experienced by more people, for more of the time than ever before. Mass availability has given individuals unheard-of control over their own sound-environment. However, it has also confronted them with the simultaneous availability of countless genres of music, in which they have to orient themselves. People start filtering out and organizing their digital libraries like they used to do with their physical music collections. However, there is the difference that the choice lies in their own hands. Without being restricted to the limited collection of music-distributors, nor being guided by the local radio program as a 'preselector' of the latest hits, the individual actively has to _____. The search for the right song is thus associated with considerable effort.

＊ simultaneous: 동시의

① choose and determine his or her musical preferences
② understand the technical aspects of recording sessions
③ share unique and inspiring playlists on social media
④ interpret lyrics with background knowledge of the songs
⑤ seek the advice of a voice specialist for better performances

20

다음 빈칸에 들어갈 말로 가장 적절한 것을 고르시오. [3점]

It is common to assume that creativity concerns primarily the relation between actor(creator) and artifact(creation). However, from a sociocultural standpoint, the creative act is never "complete" in the absence of a second position — that of an audience. While the actor or creator him/herself is the first audience of the artifact being produced, this kind of distantiation can only be achieved by _____. This means that, in order to be an audience to your own creation, a history of interaction with others is needed. We exist in a social world that constantly confronts us with the "view of the other." It is the view we include and blend into our own activity, including creative activity. This outside perspective is essential for creativity because it gives new meaning and value to the creative act and its product.

＊ artifact: 창작물

① exploring the absolute truth in existence
② following a series of precise and logical steps
③ looking outside and drawing inspiration from nature
④ internalizing the perspective of others on one's work
⑤ pushing the audience to the limits of its endurance

21

다음 빈칸에 들어갈 말로 가장 적절한 것을 고르시오. [3점]

Scientists believe that the frogs' ancestors were water-dwelling, fishlike animals. The first frogs and their relatives gained the ability to come out on land and enjoy the opportunities for food and shelter there. But they _____. A frog's lungs do not work very well, and it gets part of its oxygen by breathing through its skin. But for this kind of "breathing" to work properly, the frog's skin must stay moist. And so the frog must remain near the water where it can take a dip every now and then to keep from drying out. Frogs must also lay their eggs in water, as their fishlike ancestors did. And eggs laid in the water must develop into water creatures, if they are to survive. For frogs, metamorphosis thus provides the bridge between the water-dwelling young forms and the land-dwelling adults.

＊ metamorphosis: 탈바꿈

① still kept many ties to the water
② had almost all the necessary organs
③ had to develop an appetite for new foods
④ often competed with land-dwelling species
⑤ suffered from rapid changes in temperature

22 오답률 BEST

202103 34번

다음 빈칸에 들어갈 말로 가장 적절한 것을 고르시오. [3점]

It is important to distinguish between being legally allowed to do something, and actually being able to go and do it. A law could be passed allowing everyone, if they so wish, to run a mile in two minutes. That would not, however, increase their *effective* freedom, because, although allowed to do so, they are physically incapable of it. Having a minimum of restrictions and a maximum of possibilities is fine. But in the real world most people will never have the opportunity either to become all that they are allowed to become, or to need to be restrained from doing everything that is possible for them to do. Their effective freedom depends on actually _____.

* restriction: 제약 ** restrain: 저지하다

① respecting others' rights to freedom
② protecting and providing for the needy
③ learning what socially acceptable behaviors are
④ determining how much they can expect from others
⑤ having the means and ability to do what they choose

23

202011 33번

다음 빈칸에 들어갈 말로 가장 적절한 것을 고르시오. [3점]

As much as we can learn by examining fossils, it is important to remember that they seldom _____. Things only fossilize under certain sets of conditions. Modern insect communities are highly diverse in tropical forests, but the recent fossil record captures little of that diversity. Many creatures are consumed entirely or decompose rapidly when they die, so there may be no fossil record at all for important groups. It's a bit similar to a family photo album. Maybe when you were born your parents took lots of pictures, but over the years they took photographs occasionally, and sometimes they got busy and forgot to take pictures at all. Very few of us have a complete photo record of our life. Fossils are just like that. Sometimes you get very clear pictures of the past, while at other times there are big gaps, and you need to notice what they are.

* decompose: 부패하다

① tell the entire story
② require further study
③ teach us a wrong lesson
④ change their original traits
⑤ make room for imagination

24 오답률 BEST

202011 34번

다음 빈칸에 들어갈 말로 가장 적절한 것을 고르시오. [3점]

Back in 1996, an American airline was faced with an interesting problem. At a time when most other airlines were losing money or going under, over 100 cities were begging the company to service their locations. However, that's not the interesting part. What's interesting is that the company turned down over 95 percent of those offers and began serving only four new locations. It turned down tremendous growth because _____. Sure, its executives wanted to grow each year, but they didn't want to grow too much. Unlike other famous companies, they wanted to set their own pace, one that could be sustained in the long term. By doing this, they established a safety margin for growth that helped them continue to thrive at a time when the other airlines were flailing.

* flail: 마구 흔들리다

① it was being faced with serious financial crises
② there was no specific long-term plan on marketing
③ company leadership had set an upper limit for growth
④ its executives worried about the competing airlines' future
⑤ the company had emphasized moral duties more than profits

01 오답률 BEST

202309 35번

다음 글에서 전체 흐름과 관계 <u>없는</u> 문장은? [3점]

Sensory nerves have specialized endings in the tissues that pick up a particular sensation. If, for example, you step on a sharp object such as a pin, nerve endings in the skin will transmit the pain sensation up your leg, up and along the spinal cord to the brain. ① While the pain itself is unpleasant, it is in fact acting as a protective mechanism for the foot. ② That is, you get used to the pain so the capacity with which you can avoid pain decreases. ③ Within the brain, nerves will connect to the area that controls speech, so that you may well shout 'ouch' or something rather less polite. ④ They will also connect to motor nerves that travel back down the spinal cord, and to the muscles in your leg that now contract quickly to lift your foot away from the painful object. ⑤ Sensory and motor nerves control almost all functions in the body — from the beating of the heart to the movement of the gut, sweating and just about everything else.

＊spinal cord: 척수 ＊＊gut: 장

02

202306 35번

다음 글에서 전체 흐름과 관계 <u>없는</u> 문장은?

Although technology has the potential to increase productivity, it can also have a negative impact on productivity. For example, in many office environments workers sit at desks with computers and have access to the internet. ① They are able to check their personal e-mails and use social media whenever they want to. ② This can stop them from doing their work and make them less productive. ③ Introducing new technology can also have a negative impact on production when it causes a change to the production process or requires workers to learn a new system. ④ Using technology can enable businesses to produce more goods and to get more out of the other factors of production. ⑤ Learning to use new technology can be time consuming and stressful for workers and this can cause a decline in productivity.

03

202303 35번

다음 글에서 전체 흐름과 관계 <u>없는</u> 문장은?

Whose story it is affects *what* the story is. Change the main character, and the focus of the story must also change. If we look at the events through another character's eyes, we will interpret them differently. ① We'll place our sympathies with someone new. ② When the conflict arises that is the heart of the story, we will be praying for a different outcome. ③ Consider, for example, how the tale of Cinderella would shift if told from the viewpoint of an evil stepsister. ④ We know Cinderella's kingdom does not exist, but we willingly go there anyway. ⑤ *Gone with the Wind* is Scarlett O'Hara's story, but what if we were shown the same events from the viewpoint of Rhett Butler or Melanie Wilkes?

＊sympathy: 공감

04

202211 35번

다음 글에서 전체 흐름과 관계 <u>없는</u> 문장은?

Developing a personal engagement with poetry brings a number of benefits to you as an individual, in both a personal and a professional capacity. ① Writing poetry has been shown to have physical and mental benefits, with expressive writing found to improve immune system and lung function, diminish psychological distress, and enhance relationships. ② Poetry has long been used to aid different mental health needs, develop empathy, and reconsider our relationship with both natural and built environments. ③ Poetry is also an incredibly effective way of actively targeting the cognitive development period, improving your productivity and scientific creativity in the process. ④ Poetry is considered to be an easy and useful means of expressing emotions, but you fall into frustration when you realize its complexity. ⑤ In short, poetry has a lot to offer, if you give it the opportunity to do so.

＊cognitive: 인지적인

05 오답률 BEST

다음 글에서 전체 흐름과 관계 <u>없는</u> 문장은?

The fast-paced evolution of Information and Communication Technologies (ICTs) has radically transformed the dynamics and business models of the tourism and hospitality industry. ① This leads to new levels/forms of competitiveness among service providers and transforms the customer experience through new services. ② Creating unique experiences and providing convenient services to customers leads to satisfaction and, eventually, customer loyalty to the service provider or brand (i.e., hotels). ③ In particular, the most recent *technological* boost received by the tourism sector is represented by mobile applications. ④ Increasing competitiveness among service providers does not necessarily mean promoting quality of customer services. ⑤ Indeed, empowering tourists with mobile access to services such as hotel reservations, airline ticketing, and recommendations for local attractions generates strong interest and considerable profits.

* hospitality industry: 서비스업(호텔·식당업 등)

06

다음 글에서 전체 흐름과 관계 <u>없는</u> 문장은?

According to Marguerite La Caze, fashion contributes to our lives and provides a medium for us to develop and exhibit important social virtues. ① Fashion may be beautiful, innovative, and useful; we can display creativity and good taste in our fashion choices. ② And in dressing with taste and care, we represent both self-respect and a concern for the pleasure of others. ③ There is no doubt that fashion can be a source of interest and pleasure which links us to each other. ④ Although the fashion industry developed first in Europe and America, today it is an international and highly globalized industry. ⑤ That is, fashion provides a sociable aspect along with opportunities to imagine oneself differently — to try on different identities.

* virtue: 가치

07

다음 글에서 전체 흐름과 관계 <u>없는</u> 문장은?

Who hasn't used a cup of coffee to help themselves stay awake while studying? Mild stimulants commonly found in tea, coffee, or sodas possibly make you more attentive and, thus, better able to remember. ① However, you should know that stimulants are as likely to have negative effects on memory as they are to be beneficial. ② Even if they could improve performance at some level, the ideal doses are currently unknown. ③ If you are wide awake and well-rested, mild stimulation from caffeine can do little to further improve your memory performance. ④ In contrast, many studies have shown that drinking tea is healthier than drinking coffee. ⑤ Indeed, if you have too much of a stimulant, you will become nervous, find it difficult to sleep, and your memory performance will suffer.

* stimulant: 자극제 ** dose: 복용량

08

다음 글에서 전체 흐름과 관계 <u>없는</u> 문장은?

Internet activist Eli Pariser noticed how online search algorithms encourage our human tendency to grab hold of everything that confirms the beliefs we already hold, while quietly ignoring information that doesn't match those beliefs. ① We set up a so-called "filter-bubble" around ourselves, where we are constantly exposed only to that material that we agree with. ② We are never challenged, never giving ourselves the opportunity to acknowledge the existence of diversity and difference. ③ Creating a difference that others don't have is a way to succeed in your field, leading to the creation of innovations. ④ In the best case, we become naive and sheltered, and in the worst, we become radicalized with extreme views, unable to imagine life outside our particular bubble. ⑤ The results are disastrous: intellectual isolation and the real distortion that comes with believing that the little world we create for ourselves is *the* world.

* naive: 세상을 모르는 ** radicalize: 과격하게 만들다 *** distortion: 왜곡

◆ 정답 및 해설(2권) p.158

09

다음 글에서 전체 흐름과 관계 없는 문장은?

The Zeigarnik effect is commonly referred to as the tendency of the subconscious mind to remind you of a task that is incomplete until that task is complete. Bluma Zeigarnik was a Lithuanian psychologist who wrote in the 1920s about the effects of leaving tasks incomplete. ① She noticed the effect while watching waiters serve in a restaurant. ② The waiters would remember an order, however complicated, until the order was complete, but they would later find it difficult to remember the order. ③ Zeigarnik did further studies giving both adults and children puzzles to complete then interrupting them during some of the tasks. ④ They developed cooperation skills after finishing tasks by putting the puzzles together. ⑤ The results showed that both adults and children remembered the tasks that hadn't been completed because of the interruptions better than the ones that had been completed.

10

다음 글에서 전체 흐름과 관계 없는 문장은? [3점]

Health and the spread of disease are very closely linked to how we live and how our cities operate. The good news is that cities are incredibly resilient. Many cities have experienced epidemics in the past and have not only survived, but advanced. ① The nineteenth and early-twentieth centuries saw destructive outbreaks of cholera, typhoid, and influenza in European cities. ② Doctors such as Jon Snow, from England, and Rudolf Virchow, of Germany, saw the connection between poor living conditions, overcrowding, sanitation, and disease. ③ A recognition of this connection led to the replanning and rebuilding of cities to stop the spread of epidemics. ④ In spite of reconstruction efforts, cities declined in many areas and many people started to leave. ⑤ In the mid-nineteenth century, London's pioneering sewer system, which still serves it today, was built as a result of understanding the importance of clean water in stopping the spread of cholera.

* resilient: 회복력이 있는 ** sewer system: 하수 처리 시스템

11

다음 글에서 전체 흐름과 관계 없는 문장은?

Today's music business has allowed musicians to take matters into their own hands. ① Gone are the days of musicians waiting for a gatekeeper (someone who holds power and prevents you from being let in) at a label or TV show to say they are worthy of the spotlight. ② In today's music business, you don't need to ask for permission to build a fanbase and you no longer need to pay thousands of dollars to a company to do it. ③ There are rising concerns over the marketing of child musicians using TV auditions. ④ Every day, musicians are getting their music out to thousands of listeners without any outside help. ⑤ They simply deliver it to the fans directly, without asking for permission or outside help to receive exposure or connect with thousands of listeners.

12

다음 글에서 전체 흐름과 관계 없는 문장은?

The Barnum Effect is the phenomenon where someone reads or hears something very general but believes that it applies to them. ① These statements appear to be very personal on the surface but in fact, they are true for many. ② Human psychology allows us to want to believe things that we can identify with on a personal level and even seek information where it doesn't necessarily exist, filling in the blanks with our imagination for the rest. ③ This is the principle that horoscopes rely on, offering data that appears to be personal but probably makes sense to countless people. ④ Reading daily horoscopes in the morning is beneficial as they provide predictions about the rest of the day. ⑤ Since the people reading them want to believe the information so badly, they will search for meaning in their lives that make it true.

* horoscope: 별자리 운세

01

주어진 글 다음에 이어질 글의 순서로 가장 적절한 것을 고르시오.
[3점]

Maybe you've heard this joke: "How do you eat an elephant?" The answer is "one bite at a time."

(A) Common crystal habits include squares, triangles, and six-sided hexagons. Usually crystals form when liquids cool, such as when you create ice cubes. Many times, crystals form in ways that do not allow for perfect shapes. If conditions are too cold, too hot, or there isn't enough source material, they can form strange, twisted shapes.

(B) So, how do you "build" the Earth? That's simple, too: one atom at a time. Atoms are the basic building blocks of crystals, and since all rocks are made up of crystals, the more you know about atoms, the better. Crystals come in a variety of shapes that scientists call *habits*.

(C) But when conditions are right, we see beautiful displays. Usually, this involves a slow, steady environment where the individual atoms have plenty of time to join and fit perfectly into what's known as the *crystal lattice*. This is the basic structure of atoms that is seen time after time.

① (A) – (C) – (B)　　② (B) – (A) – (C)
③ (B) – (C) – (A)　　④ (C) – (A) – (B)
⑤ (C) – (B) – (A)

02

주어진 글 다음에 이어질 글의 순서로 가장 적절한 것을 고르시오.

When you pluck a guitar string it moves back and forth hundreds of times every second.

(A) The vibration of the wood creates more powerful waves in the air pressure, which travel away from the guitar. When the waves reach your eardrums they flex in and out the same number of times a second as the original string.

(B) Naturally, this movement is so fast that you cannot see it — you just see the blurred outline of the moving string. Strings vibrating in this way on their own make hardly any noise because strings are very thin and don't push much air about.

(C) But if you attach a string to a big hollow box (like a guitar body), then the vibration is amplified and the note is heard loud and clear. The vibration of the string is passed on to the wooden panels of the guitar body, which vibrate back and forth at the same rate as the string.

＊pluck: (현악기를) 뜯다　＊＊amplify: 증폭시키다

① (A) – (C) – (B)　　② (B) – (A) – (C)
③ (B) – (C) – (A)　　④ (C) – (A) – (B)
⑤ (C) – (B) – (A)

03

주어진 글 다음에 이어질 글의 순서로 가장 적절한 것을 고르시오.

[3점]

Up until about 6,000 years ago, most people were farmers. Many lived in different places throughout the year, hunting for food or moving their livestock to areas with enough food.

(A) For example, priests wanted to know when to carry out religious ceremonies. This was when people first invented clocks — devices that show, measure, and keep track of passing time.

(B) There was no need to tell the time because life depended on natural cycles, such as the changing seasons or sunrise and sunset. Gradually more people started to live in larger settlements, and some needed to tell the time.

(C) Clocks have been important ever since. Today, clocks are used for important things such as setting busy airport timetables — if the time is incorrect, aeroplanes might crash into each other when taking off or landing!

① (A) – (C) – (B)　　② (B) – (A) – (C)
③ (B) – (C) – (A)　　④ (C) – (A) – (B)
⑤ (C) – (B) – (A)

04

주어진 글 다음에 이어질 글의 순서로 가장 적절한 것을 고르시오.

Managers are always looking for ways to increase productivity, which is the ratio of costs to output in production. Adam Smith, writing when the manufacturing industry was new, described a way that production could be made more efficient, known as the "division of labor."

(A) Because each worker specializes in one job, he or she can work much faster without changing from one task to another. Now 10 workers can produce thousands of pins in a day — a huge increase in productivity from the 200 they would have produced before.

(B) One worker could do all these tasks, and make 20 pins in a day. But this work can be divided into its separate processes, with a number of workers each performing one task.

(C) Making most manufactured goods involves several different processes using different skills. Smith's example was the manufacture of pins: the wire is straightened, sharpened, a head is put on, and then it is polished.

* ratio: 비율

① (A) – (C) – (B)　　② (B) – (A) – (C)
③ (B) – (C) – (A)　　④ (C) – (A) – (B)
⑤ (C) – (B) – (A)

05

202303 36번

주어진 글 다음에 이어질 글의 순서로 가장 적절한 것을 고르시오.

In the Old Stone Age, small bands of 20 to 60 people wandered from place to place in search of food. Once people began farming, they could settle down near their farms.

(A) While some workers grew crops, others built new houses and made tools. Village dwellers also learned to work together to do a task faster.

(B) For example, toolmakers could share the work of making stone axes and knives. By working together, they could make more tools in the same amount of time.

(C) As a result, towns and villages grew larger. Living in communities allowed people to organize themselves more efficiently. They could divide up the work of producing food and other things they needed.

* dweller: 거주자

① (A) – (C) – (B)　　② (B) – (A) – (C)
③ (B) – (C) – (A)　　④ (C) – (A) – (B)
⑤ (C) – (B) – (A)

06 오답률 BEST

202303 37번

주어진 글 다음에 이어질 글의 순서로 가장 적절한 것을 고르시오.
[3점]

Natural processes form minerals in many ways. For example, hot melted rock material, called magma, cools when it reaches the Earth's surface, or even if it's trapped below the surface. As magma cools, its atoms lose heat energy, move closer together, and begin to combine into compounds.

(A) Also, the size of the crystals that form depends partly on how rapidly the magma cools. When magma cools slowly, the crystals that form are generally large enough to see with the unaided eye.

(B) During this process, atoms of the different compounds arrange themselves into orderly, repeating patterns. The type and amount of elements present in a magma partly determine which minerals will form.

(C) This is because the atoms have enough time to move together and form into larger crystals. When magma cools rapidly, the crystals that form will be small. In such cases, you can't easily see individual mineral crystals.

* compound: 화합물

① (A) – (C) – (B)　　② (B) – (A) – (C)
③ (B) – (C) – (A)　　④ (C) – (A) – (B)
⑤ (C) – (B) – (A)

16강

글의 순서

07

202211 36번

주어진 글 다음에 이어질 글의 순서로 가장 적절한 것을 고르시오.

Things are changing. It has been reported that 42 percent of jobs in Canada are at risk, and 62 percent of jobs in America will be in danger due to advances in automation.

(A) However, what's difficult to automate is the ability to creatively solve problems. Whereas workers in "doing" roles can be replaced by robots, the role of creatively solving problems is more dependent on an irreplaceable individual.

(B) You might say that the numbers seem a bit unrealistic, but the threat is real. One fast food franchise has a robot that can flip a burger in ten seconds. It is just a simple task but the robot could replace an entire crew.

(C) Highly skilled jobs are also at risk. A supercomputer, for instance, can suggest available treatments for specific illnesses in an automated way, drawing on the body of medical research and data on diseases.

① (A) – (C) – (B)　　　② (B) – (A) – (C)
③ (B) – (C) – (A)　　　④ (C) – (A) – (B)
⑤ (C) – (B) – (A)

08

202211 37번

주어진 글 다음에 이어질 글의 순서로 가장 적절한 것을 고르시오.
[3점]

Each beech tree grows in a particular location and soil conditions can vary greatly in just a few yards. The soil can have a great deal of water or almost no water. It can be full of nutrients or not.

(A) This is taking place underground through the roots. Whoever has an abundance of sugar hands some over; whoever is running short gets help. Their network acts as a system to make sure that no trees fall too far behind.

(B) However, the rate is the same. Whether they are thick or thin, all the trees of the same species are using light to produce the same amount of sugar per leaf. Some trees have plenty of sugar and some have less, but the trees equalize this difference between them by transferring sugar.

(C) Accordingly, each tree grows more quickly or more slowly and produces more or less sugar, and thus you would expect every tree to be photosynthesizing at a different rate.

*photosynthesize: 광합성하다

① (A) – (C) – (B)　　　② (B) – (A) – (C)
③ (B) – (C) – (A)　　　④ (C) – (A) – (B)
⑤ (C) – (B) – (A)

09

주어진 글 다음에 이어질 글의 순서로 가장 적절한 것을 고르시오.

> With nearly a billion hungry people in the world, there is obviously no single cause.

(A) The reason people are hungry in those countries is that the products produced there can be sold on the world market for more than the local citizens can afford to pay for them. In the modern age you do not starve because you have no food, you starve because you have no money.

(B) However, far and away the biggest cause is poverty. Seventy-nine percent of the world's hungry live in nations that are net exporters of food. How can this be?

(C) So the problem really is that food is, in the grand scheme of things, too expensive and many people are too poor to buy it. The answer will be in continuing the trend of lowering the cost of food.

* net exporter: 순수출국 **scheme: 체계, 조직

① (A) – (C) – (B)　　② (B) – (A) – (C)
③ (B) – (C) – (A)　　④ (C) – (A) – (B)
⑤ (C) – (B) – (A)

10 오답률 BEST

주어진 글 다음에 이어질 글의 순서로 가장 적절한 것을 고르시오.
[3점]

> Most people have a perfect time of day when they feel they are at their best, whether in the morning, evening, or afternoon.

(A) When your mind and body are less alert than at your "peak" hours, the muse of creativity awakens and is allowed to roam more freely. In other words, when your mental machinery is loose rather than standing at attention, the creativity flows.

(B) However, if the task you face demands creativity and novel ideas, it's best to tackle it at your "worst" time of day! So if you are an early bird, make sure to attack your creative task in the evening, and vice versa for night owls.

(C) Some of us are night owls, some early birds, and others in between may feel most active during the afternoon hours. If you are able to organize your day and divide your work, make it a point to deal with tasks that demand attention at your best time of the day.

* roam: (어슬렁어슬렁) 거닐다

① (A) – (C) – (B)　　② (B) – (A) – (C)
③ (B) – (C) – (A)　　④ (C) – (A) – (B)
⑤ (C) – (B) – (A)

11

주어진 글 다음에 이어질 글의 순서로 가장 적절한 것을 고르시오.

Mrs. Klein told her first graders to draw a picture of something to be thankful for. She thought that most of the class would draw turkeys or Thanksgiving tables. But Douglas drew something different.

(A) The class was so responsive that Mrs. Klein had almost forgotten about Douglas. After she had the others at work on another project, she asked Douglas whose hand it was. He answered softly, "It's yours. Thank you, Mrs. Klein."

(B) Douglas was a boy who usually spent time alone and stayed around her while his classmates went outside together during break time. What the boy drew was a hand. But whose hand? His image immediately attracted the other students' interest.

(C) So, everyone rushed to talk about whose hand it was. "It must be the hand of God that brings us food," said one student. "A farmer's," said a second student, "because they raise the turkeys." "It looks more like a police officer's," added another, "they protect us."

① (A) – (C) – (B)　　　② (B) – (A) – (C)
③ (B) – (C) – (A)　　　④ (C) – (A) – (B)
⑤ (C) – (B) – (A)

12

주어진 글 다음에 이어질 글의 순서로 가장 적절한 것을 고르시오.
[3점]

According to legend, once a vampire bites a person, that person turns into a vampire who seeks the blood of others. A researcher came up with some simple math, which proves that these highly popular creatures can't exist.

(A) In just two-and-a-half years, the original human population would all have become vampires with no humans left. But look around you. Have vampires taken over the world? No, because there's no such thing.

(B) If the first vampire came into existence that day and bit one person a month, there would have been two vampires by February 1st, 1600. A month later there would have been four, the next month eight, then sixteen, and so on.

(C) University of Central Florida physics professor Costas Efthimiou's work breaks down the myth. Suppose that on January 1st, 1600, the human population was just over five hundred million.

① (A) – (C) – (B)　　　② (B) – (A) – (C)
③ (B) – (C) – (A)　　　④ (C) – (A) – (B)
⑤ (C) – (B) – (A)

13

주어진 글 다음에 이어질 글의 순서로 가장 적절한 것을 고르시오.

Toward the end of the 19th century, a new architectural attitude emerged. Industrial architecture, the argument went, was ugly and inhuman; past styles had more to do with pretension than what people needed in their homes.

(A) But they supplied people's needs perfectly and, at their best, had a beauty that came from the craftsman's skill and the rootedness of the house in its locality.

(B) Instead of these approaches, why not look at the way ordinary country builders worked in the past? They developed their craft skills over generations, demonstrating mastery of both tools and materials.

(C) Those materials were local, and used with simplicity — houses built this way had plain wooden floors and whitewashed walls inside.

＊pretension: 허세, 가식

① (A) – (C) – (B)
② (B) – (A) – (C)
③ (B) – (C) – (A)
④ (C) – (A) – (B)
⑤ (C) – (B) – (A)

14

주어진 글 다음에 이어질 글의 순서로 가장 적절한 것을 고르시오.
[3점]

Robert Schumann once said, "The laws of morals are those of art." What the great man is saying here is that there is good music and bad music.

(A) It's the same with performances: a bad performance isn't necessarily the result of incompetence. Some of the worst performances occur when the performers, no matter how accomplished, are thinking more of themselves than of the music they're playing.

(B) The greatest music, even if it's tragic in nature, takes us to a world higher than ours; somehow the beauty uplifts us. Bad music, on the other hand, degrades us.

(C) These doubtful characters aren't really listening to what the composer is saying — they're just showing off, hoping that they'll have a great 'success' with the public. The performer's basic task is to try to understand the meaning of the music, and then to communicate it honestly to others.

＊incompetence: 무능 ＊＊degrade: 격하시키다

① (A) – (C) – (B)
② (B) – (A) – (C)
③ (B) – (C) – (A)
④ (C) – (A) – (B)
⑤ (C) – (B) – (A)

16강

글의 순서

15 오답률 BEST

📄 202111 36번

주어진 글 다음에 이어질 글의 순서로 가장 적절한 것을 고르시오.

Roughly twenty years ago, brick-and-mortar stores began to give way to electronic commerce. For good or bad, the shift fundamentally changed consumers' perception of the shopping experience.

(A) Before long, the e-commerce book market naturally expanded to include additional categories, like CDs and DVDs. E-commerce soon snowballed into the enormous industry it is today, where you can buy everything from toilet paper to cars online.

(B) Nowhere was the shift more obvious than with book sales, which is how online bookstores got their start. Physical bookstores simply could not stock as many titles as a virtual bookstore could. There is only so much space available on a shelf.

(C) In addition to greater variety, online bookstores were also able to offer aggressive discounts thanks to their lower operating costs. The combination of lower prices and greater selection led to the slow, steady rise of online bookstores.

＊brick-and-mortar: 오프라인 거래의

① (A) – (C) – (B)　　② (B) – (A) – (C)
③ (B) – (C) – (A)　　④ (C) – (A) – (B)
⑤ (C) – (B) – (A)

16

📄 202111 37번

주어진 글 다음에 이어질 글의 순서로 가장 적절한 것을 고르시오.
[3점]

Literary works, by their nature, suggest rather than explain; they imply rather than state their claims boldly and directly.

(A) What a text implies is often of great interest to us. And our work of figuring out a text's implications tests our analytical powers. In considering what a text suggests, we gain practice in making sense of texts.

(B) But whatever the proportion of a work's showing to telling, there is always something for readers to interpret. Thus we ask the question "What does the text suggest?" as a way to approach literary interpretation, as a way to begin thinking about a text's implications.

(C) This broad generalization, however, does not mean that works of literature do not include direct statements. Depending on when they were written and by whom, literary works may contain large amounts of direct telling and lesser amounts of suggestion and implication.

① (A) – (C) – (B)　　② (B) – (A) – (C)
③ (B) – (C) – (A)　　④ (C) – (A) – (B)
⑤ (C) – (B) – (A)

17

주어진 글 다음에 이어질 글의 순서로 가장 적절한 것을 고르시오.
[3점]

Understanding how to develop respect for and a knowledge of other cultures begins with reexamining the golden rule: "I treat others in the way I want to be treated."

(A) It can also create a frustrating situation where we believe we are doing what is right, but what we are doing is not being interpreted in the way in which it was meant. This miscommunication can lead to problems.

(B) In a multicultural setting, however, where words, gestures, beliefs, and views may have different meanings, this rule has an unintended result; it can send a message that my culture is better than yours.

(C) This rule makes sense on some level; if we treat others as well as we want to be treated, we will be treated well in return. This rule works well in a monocultural setting, where everyone is working within the same cultural framework.

① (A) – (C) – (B)　　② (B) – (A) – (C)
③ (B) – (C) – (A)　　④ (C) – (A) – (B)
⑤ (C) – (B) – (A)

18 오답률 BEST

주어진 글 다음에 이어질 글의 순서로 가장 적절한 것을 고르시오.
[3점]

In a study, a researcher pretending to be a volunteer surveyed a California neighborhood, asking residents if they would allow a large sign reading "Drive Carefully" to be displayed on their front lawns.

(A) The reason that they agreed was this: two weeks earlier, these residents had been asked by another volunteer to make a small commitment to display a tiny sign that read "Be a Safe Driver" in their windows.

(B) Since it was such a small and simple request, nearly all of them agreed. The astonishing result was that the initial small commitment deeply influenced their willingness to accept the much larger request two weeks later.

(C) To help them understand what it would look like, the volunteer showed his participants a picture of the large sign blocking the view of a beautiful house. Naturally, most people refused, but in one particular group, an incredible 76 percent actually approved.

① (A) – (C) – (B)　　② (B) – (A) – (C)
③ (B) – (C) – (A)　　④ (C) – (A) – (B)
⑤ (C) – (B) – (A)

19

202106 36번

주어진 글 다음에 이어질 글의 순서로 가장 적절한 것을 고르시오.

Starting from birth, babies are immediately attracted to faces. Scientists were able to show this by having babies look at two simple images, one that looks more like a face than the other.

(A) These changes help the organisms to survive, making them alert to enemies. By being able to recognize faces from afar or in the dark, humans were able to know someone was coming and protect themselves from possible danger.

(B) One reason babies might like faces is because of something called evolution. Evolution involves changes to the structures of an organism(such as the brain) that occur over many generations.

(C) By measuring where the babies looked, scientists found that the babies looked at the face-like image more than they looked at the non-face image. Even though babies have poor eyesight, they prefer to look at faces. But why?

① (A) – (C) – (B)　　② (B) – (A) – (C)
③ (B) – (C) – (A)　　④ (C) – (A) – (B)
⑤ (C) – (B) – (A)

20

202106 37번

주어진 글 다음에 이어질 글의 순서로 가장 적절한 것을 고르시오.

People spend much of their time interacting with media, but that does not mean that people have the critical skills to analyze and understand it.

(A) Research from New York University found that people over 65 shared seven times as much misinformation as their younger counterparts. All of this raises a question: What's the solution to the misinformation problem?

(B) One well-known study from Stanford University in 2016 demonstrated that youth are easily fooled by misinformation, especially when it comes through social media channels. This weakness is not found only in youth, however.

(C) Governments and tech platforms certainly have a role to play in blocking misinformation. However, every individual needs to take responsibility for combating this threat by becoming more information literate.

＊counterpart: 상대방

① (A) – (C) – (B)　　② (B) – (A) – (C)
③ (B) – (C) – (A)　　④ (C) – (A) – (B)
⑤ (C) – (B) – (A)

21

📃 202103 36번

주어진 글 다음에 이어질 글의 순서로 가장 적절한 것을 고르시오.

> Almost all major sporting activities are played with a ball.

(A) A ball might have the correct size and weight but if it is made as a hollow ball of steel it will be too stiff and if it is made from light foam rubber with a heavy center it will be too soft.

(B) The rules of the game always include rules about the type of ball that is allowed, starting with the size and weight of the ball. The ball must also have a certain stiffness.

(C) Similarly, along with stiffness, a ball needs to bounce properly. A solid rubber ball would be too bouncy for most sports, and a solid ball made of clay would not bounce at all.

＊ stiffness: 단단함

① (A) – (C) – (B)　　② (B) – (A) – (C)
③ (B) – (C) – (A)　　④ (C) – (A) – (B)
⑤ (C) – (B) – (A)

22

📃 202103 37번

주어진 글 다음에 이어질 글의 순서로 가장 적절한 것을 고르시오.

[3점]

> If you had to write a math equation, you probably wouldn't write, "Twenty-eight plus fourteen equals forty-two." It would take too long to write and it would be hard to read quickly.

(A) For example, the chemical formula for water is H_2O. That tells us that a water molecule is made up of two hydrogen ("H" and "2") atoms and one oxygen ("O") atom.

(B) You would write, "28 + 14 = 42." Chemistry is the same way. Chemists have to write chemical equations all the time, and it would take too long to write and read if they had to spell everything out.

(C) So chemists use symbols, just like we do in math. A chemical formula lists all the elements that form each molecule and uses a small number to the bottom right of an element's symbol to stand for the number of atoms of that element.

＊ chemical formula: 화학식　＊＊ molecule: 분자

① (A) – (C) – (B)　　② (B) – (A) – (C)
③ (B) – (C) – (A)　　④ (C) – (A) – (B)
⑤ (C) – (B) – (A)

16강

글의 순서

◆ 정답 및 해설(2권) p.163

23

202011 36번

주어진 글 다음에 이어질 글의 순서로 가장 적절한 것을 고르시오.

Imagine yourself at a party. It is dark and a group of friends ask you to take a picture of them. You grab your camera, point, and shoot your friends.

(A) This is a common problem called the *red-eye effect*. It is caused because the light from the flash penetrates the eyes through the pupils, and then gets reflected to the camera from the back of the eyes where a large amount of blood is present.

(B) The camera automatically turns on the flash as there is not enough light available to produce a correct exposure. The result is half of your friends appear in the picture with two bright red circles instead of their eyes.

(C) This blood is the reason why the eyes look red in the photograph. This effect is more noticeable when there is not much light in the environment. This is because pupils dilate when it is dark, allowing more light to get inside the eye and producing a larger red-eye effect.

* penetrate: 통과하다 ** pupil: 동공 *** dilate: 확장(팽창)하다

① (A) – (C) – (B) ② (B) – (A) – (C)
③ (B) – (C) – (A) ④ (C) – (A) – (B)
⑤ (C) – (B) – (A)

24

202011 37번

주어진 글 다음에 이어질 글의 순서로 가장 적절한 것을 고르시오.

Even though two variables seem to be related, there may not be a causal relationship.

(A) Does this mean that the size of one's feet (independent variable) causes an improvement in reading skills (dependent variable)? Certainly not. This false relationship is caused by a third factor, age, that is related to shoe size as well as reading ability.

(B) Hence, when researchers attempt to make causal claims about the relationship between an independent and a dependent variable, they must control for — or rule out — other variables that may be creating a spurious relationship.

(C) In fact, the two variables may merely seem to be associated with each other due to the effect of some third variable. Sociologists call such misleading relationships spurious. A classic example is the apparent association between children's shoe size and reading ability. It seems that as shoe size increases, reading ability improves.

* variable: 변인 ** spurious: 허위의, 가짜의

① (A) – (C) – (B) ② (B) – (A) – (C)
③ (B) – (C) – (A) ④ (C) – (A) – (B)
⑤ (C) – (B) – (A)

01 오답률 BEST

202309 38번

글의 흐름으로 보아, 주어진 문장이 들어가기에 가장 적절한 곳을 고르시오. [3점]

> Other individuals prefer integrating work and family roles all day long.

Boundaries between work and home are blurring as portable digital technology makes it increasingly possible to work anywhere, anytime. Individuals differ in how they like to manage their time to meet work and outside responsibilities. (①) Some people prefer to separate or segment roles so that boundary crossings are minimized. (②) For example, these people might keep separate email accounts for work and family and try to conduct work at the workplace and take care of family matters only during breaks and non-work time. (③) We've even noticed more of these "segmenters" carrying two phones — one for work and one for personal use. (④) Flexible schedules work well for these individuals because they enable greater distinction between time at work and time in other roles. (⑤) This might entail constantly trading text messages with children from the office, or monitoring emails at home and on vacation, rather than returning to work to find hundreds of messages in their inbox.

* entail: 수반하다

02

202309 39번

글의 흐름으로 보아, 주어진 문장이 들어가기에 가장 적절한 곳을 고르시오.

> However, do not assume that a product is perfectly complementary, as customers may not be completely locked in to the product.

A "complementary good" is a product that is often consumed alongside another product. (①) For example, popcorn is a complementary good to a movie, while a travel pillow is a complementary good for a long plane journey. (②) When the popularity of one product increases, the sales of its complementary good also increase. (③) By producing goods that complement other products that are already (or about to be) popular, you can ensure a steady stream of demand for your product. (④) Some products enjoy perfect complementary status — they *have* to be consumed together, such as a lamp and a lightbulb. (⑤) For example, although motorists may seem required to purchase gasoline to run their cars, they can switch to electric cars.

03

202306 38번

글의 흐름으로 보아, 주어진 문장이 들어가기에 가장 적절한 곳을 고르시오.

> Yet we know that the face that stares back at us from the glass is not the same, cannot be the same, as it was 10 minutes ago.

Sometimes the pace of change is far slower. (①) The face you saw reflected in your mirror this morning probably appeared no different from the face you saw the day before — or a week or a month ago. (②) The proof is in your photo album: Look at a photograph taken of yourself 5 or 10 years ago and you see clear differences between the face in the snapshot and the face in your mirror. (③) If you lived in a world without mirrors for a year and then saw your reflection, you might be surprised by the change. (④) After an interval of 10 years without seeing yourself, you might not at first recognize the person peering from the mirror. (⑤) Even something as basic as our own face changes from moment to moment.

* peer: 응시하다

04 오답률 BEST 202306 39번

글의 흐름으로 보아, 주어진 문장이 들어가기에 가장 적절한 곳을 고르시오. [3점]

As children absorb more evidence from the world around them, certain possibilities become much more likely and more useful and harden into knowledge or beliefs.

According to educational psychologist Susan Engel, curiosity begins to decrease as young as four years old. By the time we are adults, we have fewer questions and more default settings. As Henry James put it, "Disinterested curiosity is past, the mental grooves and channels set." (①) The decline in curiosity can be traced in the development of the brain through childhood. (②) Though smaller than the adult brain, the infant brain contains millions more neural connections. (③) The wiring, however, is a mess; the lines of communication between infant neurons are far less efficient than between those in the adult brain. (④) The baby's perception of the world is consequently both intensely rich and wildly disordered. (⑤) The neural pathways that enable those beliefs become faster and more automatic, while the ones that the child doesn't use regularly are pruned away.

＊default setting: 기본값 ＊＊groove: 고랑 ＊＊＊prune: 가지치기하다

05 202303 38번

글의 흐름으로 보아, 주어진 문장이 들어가기에 가장 적절한 곳을 고르시오.

Bad carbohydrates, on the other hand, are simple sugars.

All carbohydrates are basically sugars. (①) Complex carbohydrates are the good carbohydrates for your body. (②) These complex sugar compounds are very difficult to break down and can trap other nutrients like vitamins and minerals in their chains. (③) As they slowly break down, the other nutrients are also released into your body, and can provide you with fuel for a number of hours. (④) Because their structure is not complex, they are easy to break down and hold few nutrients for your body other than the sugars from which they are made. (⑤) Your body breaks down these carbohydrates rather quickly and what it cannot use is converted to fat and stored in the body.

＊carbohydrate: 탄수화물 ＊＊convert: 바꾸다

06 202303 39번

글의 흐름으로 보아, 주어진 문장이 들어가기에 가장 적절한 곳을 고르시오. [3점]

It was also found that those students who expected the lecturer to be warm tended to interact with him more.

People commonly make the mistaken assumption that because a person has one type of characteristic, then they automatically have other characteristics which go with it. (①) In one study, university students were given descriptions of a guest lecturer before he spoke to the group. (②) Half the students received a description containing the word 'warm', the other half were told the speaker was 'cold'. (③) The guest lecturer then led a discussion, after which the students were asked to give their impressions of him. (④) As expected, there were large differences between the impressions formed by the students, depending upon their original information of the lecturer. (⑤) This shows that different expectations not only affect the impressions we form but also our behaviour and the relationship which is formed.

07

202211 38번

글의 흐름으로 보아, 주어진 문장이 들어가기에 가장 적절한 곳을 고르시오. [3점]

> Nevertheless, language is enormously important in human life and contributes largely to our ability to cooperate with each other in dealing with the world.

Should we use language to understand mind or mind to understand language? (①) Analytic philosophy historically assumes that language is basic and that mind would make sense if proper use of language was appreciated. (②) Modern cognitive science, however, rightly judges that language is just one aspect of mind of great importance in human beings but not fundamental to all kinds of thinking. (③) Countless species of animals manage to navigate the world, solve problems, and learn without using language, through brain mechanisms that are largely preserved in the minds of humans. (④) There is no reason to assume that language is fundamental to mental operations. (⑤) Our species *homo sapiens* has been astonishingly successful, which depended in part on language, first as an effective contributor to collaborative problem solving and much later, as collective memory through written records.

* appreciate: (제대로) 인식하다

08

202211 39번

글의 흐름으로 보아, 주어진 문장이 들어가기에 가장 적절한 곳을 고르시오.

> If we could magically remove the glasses, we would find the two water bodies would not mix well.

Take two glasses of water. Put a little bit of orange juice into one and a little bit of lemon juice into the other. (①) What you have are essentially two glasses of water but with a completely different chemical makeup. (②) If we take the glass containing orange juice and heat it, we will still have two different glasses of water with different chemical makeups, but now they will also have different temperatures. (③) Perhaps they would mix a little where they met; however, they would remain separate because of their different chemical makeups and temperatures. (④) The warmer water would float on the surface of the cold water because of its lighter weight. (⑤) In the ocean we have bodies of water that differ in temperature and salt content; for this reason, they do not mix.

09

202209 38번

글의 흐름으로 보아, 주어진 문장이 들어가기에 가장 적절한 곳을 고르시오.

> Unfortunately, it is also likely to "crowd out" other activities that produce more sustainable social contributions to our social well-being.

Television is the number one leisure activity in the United States and Europe, consuming more than half of our free time. (①) We generally think of television as a way to relax, tune out, and escape from our troubles for a bit each day. (②) While this is true, there is increasing evidence that we are more motivated to tune in to our favorite shows and characters when we are feeling lonely or have a greater need for social connection. (③) Television watching does satisfy these social needs to some extent, at least in the short run. (④) The more television we watch, the less likely we are to volunteer our time or to spend time with people in our social networks. (⑤) In other words, the more time we make for *Friends*, the less time we have for friends in real life.

* *Friends*: 프렌즈(미국의 한 방송국에서 방영된 시트콤)

10

202209 39번

글의 흐름으로 보아, 주어진 문장이 들어가기에 가장 적절한 곳을 고르시오. [3점]

What we need is a reliable and reproducible method for measuring the relative hotness or coldness of objects rather than the rate of energy transfer.

We often associate the concept of temperature with how hot or cold an object feels when we touch it. In this way, our senses provide us with a qualitative indication of temperature. (①) Our senses, however, are unreliable and often mislead us. (②) For example, if you stand in bare feet with one foot on carpet and the other on a tile floor, the tile feels colder than the carpet *even though both are at the same temperature.* (③) The two objects feel different because tile transfers energy by heat at a higher rate than carpet does. (④) Your skin "measures" the rate of energy transfer by heat rather than the actual temperature. (⑤) Scientists have developed a variety of thermometers for making such quantitative measurements.

＊thermometer: 온도계

11

202206 38번

글의 흐름으로 보아, 주어진 문장이 들어가기에 가장 적절한 곳을 고르시오.

For example, if you rub your hands together quickly, they will get warmer.

Friction is a force between two surfaces that are sliding, or trying to slide, across each other. For example, when you try to push a book along the floor, friction makes this difficult. Friction always works in the direction opposite to the direction in which the object is moving, or trying to move. So, friction always slows a moving object down. (①) The amount of friction depends on the surface materials. (②) The rougher the surface is, the more friction is produced. (③) Friction also produces heat. (④) Friction can be a useful force because it prevents our shoes slipping on the floor when we walk and stops car tires skidding on the road. (⑤) When you walk, friction is caused between the tread on your shoes and the ground, acting to grip the ground and prevent sliding.

＊skid: 미끄러지다 ＊＊tread: 접지면, 바닥

12

202206 39번

글의 흐름으로 보아, 주어진 문장이 들어가기에 가장 적절한 곳을 고르시오.

But, a blind person will associate the same friend with a unique combination of experiences from their non-visual senses that act to represent that friend.

Humans born without sight are not able to collect visual experiences, so they understand the world entirely through their other senses. (①) As a result, people with blindness at birth develop an amazing ability to understand the world through the collection of experiences and memories that come from these non-visual senses. (②) The dreams of a person who has been without sight since birth can be just as vivid and imaginative as those of someone with normal vision. (③) They are unique, however, because their dreams are constructed from the non-visual experiences and memories they have collected. (④) A person with normal vision will dream about a familiar friend using visual memories of shape, lighting, and colour. (⑤) In other words, people blind at birth have similar overall dreaming experiences even though they do not dream in pictures.

13

글의 흐름으로 보아, 주어진 문장이 들어가기에 가장 적절한 곳을 고르시오. [3점]

> But, when there is biodiversity, the effects of a sudden change are not so dramatic.

When an ecosystem is biodiverse, wildlife have more opportunities to obtain food and shelter. Different species react and respond to changes in their environment differently. (①) For example, imagine a forest with only one type of plant in it, which is the only source of food and habitat for the entire forest food web. (②) Now, there is a sudden dry season and this plant dies. (③) Plant-eating animals completely lose their food source and die out, and so do the animals that prey upon them. (④) Different species of plants respond to the drought differently, and many can survive a dry season. (⑤) Many animals have a variety of food sources and don't just rely on one plant; now our forest ecosystem is no longer at the death!

* biodiversity: (생물학적) 종 다양성 ** habitat: 서식지

14 오답률 BEST

글의 흐름으로 보아, 주어진 문장이 들어가기에 가장 적절한 곳을 고르시오.

> Since the dawn of civilization, our ancestors created myths and told legendary stories about the night sky.

We are connected to the night sky in many ways. (①) It has always inspired people to wonder and to imagine. (②) Elements of those narratives became embedded in the social and cultural identities of many generations. (③) On a practical level, the night sky helped past generations to keep track of time and create calendars — essential to developing societies as aids to farming and seasonal gathering. (④) For many centuries, it also provided a useful navigation tool, vital for commerce and for exploring new worlds. (⑤) Even in modern times, many people in remote areas of the planet observe the night sky for such practical purposes.

* embed: 깊이 새겨 두다 ** commerce: 무역

15

글의 흐름으로 보아, 주어진 문장이 들어가기에 가장 적절한 곳을 고르시오.

> Worse, some are contaminated with other substances and contain ingredients not listed on the label.

According to top nutrition experts, most nutrients are better absorbed and used by the body when consumed from a whole food instead of a supplement. (①) However, many people feel the need to take pills, powders, and supplements in an attempt to obtain nutrients and fill the gaps in their diets. (②) We hope these will give us more energy, prevent us from catching a cold in the winter, or improve our skin and hair. (③) But in reality, the large majority of supplements are artificial and may not even be completely absorbed by your body. (④) For example, a recent investigative report found heavy metals in 40 percent of 134 brands of protein powders on the market. (⑤) With little control and regulation, taking supplements is a gamble and often costly.

* contaminate: 오염시키다 ** supplement: 보충제

16 오답률 BEST
📄 202111 39번

글의 흐름으로 보아, 주어진 문장이 들어가기에 가장 적절한 곳을 고르시오. [3점]

> But after this brief moment of rest, the pendulum swings back again and therefore part of the total energy is then given in the form of kinetic energy.

In general, kinetic energy is the energy associated with motion, while potential energy represents the energy which is "stored" in a physical system. Moreover, the total energy is always conserved. (①) But while the total energy remains unchanged, the kinetic and potential parts of the total energy can change all the time. (②) Imagine, for example, a pendulum which swings back and forth. (③) When it swings, it sweeps out an arc and then slows down as it comes closer to its highest point, where the pendulum does not move at all. (④) So at this point, the energy is completely given in terms of potential energy. (⑤) So as the pendulum swings, kinetic and potential energy constantly change into each other.

* pendulum: 추(錘) **arc: 호(弧)

17
📄 202109 38번

글의 흐름으로 보아, 주어진 문장이 들어가기에 가장 적절한 곳을 고르시오.

> However, using caffeine to improve alertness and mental performance doesn't replace getting a good night's sleep.

Studies have consistently shown caffeine to be effective when used together with a pain reliever to treat headaches. (①) The positive correlation between caffeine intake and staying alert throughout the day has also been well established. (②) As little as 60 mg (the amount typically in one cup of tea) can lead to a faster reaction time. (③) One study from 2018 showed that coffee improved reaction times in those with or without poor sleep, but caffeine seemed to increase errors in the group with little sleep. (④) Additionally, this study showed that even with caffeine, the group with little sleep did not score as well as those with adequate sleep. (⑤) It suggests that caffeine does not fully make up for inadequate sleep.

18
📄 202109 39번

글의 흐름으로 보아, 주어진 문장이 들어가기에 가장 적절한 곳을 고르시오.

> The sales director kept an air horn outside his office and would come out and blow the horn every time a salesperson settled a deal.

Rewarding business success doesn't always have to be done in a material way. (①) A software company I once worked for had a great way of recognizing sales success. (②) The noise, of course, interrupted anything and everything happening in the office because it was unbelievably loud. (③) However, it had an amazingly positive impact on everyone. (④) Sometimes rewarding success can be as easy as that, especially when peer recognition is important. (⑤) You should have seen the way the rest of the sales team wanted the air horn blown for them.

* air horn: (압축 공기로 작동하는) 경적

19

글의 흐름으로 보아, 주어진 문장이 들어가기에 가장 적절한 곳을 고르시오.

> As the sticks approach each other, the air immediately in front of them is compressed and energy builds up.

Sound and light travel in waves. An analogy often given for sound is that of throwing a small stone onto the surface of a still pond. Waves radiate outwards from the point of impact, just as sound waves radiate from the sound source. (①) This is due to a disturbance in the air around us. (②) If you bang two sticks together, you will get a sound. (③) When the point of impact occurs, this energy is released as sound waves. (④) If you try the same experiment with two heavy stones, exactly the same thing occurs, but you get a different sound due to the density and surface of the stones, and as they have likely displaced more air, a louder sound. (⑤) And so, a physical disturbance in the atmosphere around us will produce a sound.

* analogy: 비유 ** radiate: 사방으로 퍼지다

20

글의 흐름으로 보아, 주어진 문장이 들어가기에 가장 적절한 곳을 고르시오. [3점]

> It has been observed that at each level of transfer, a large proportion, 80~90 percent, of the potential energy is lost as heat.

Food chain means the transfer of food energy from the source in plants through a series of organisms with the repeated process of eating and being eaten. (①) In a grassland, grass is eaten by rabbits while rabbits in turn are eaten by foxes. (②) This is an example of a simple food chain. (③) This food chain implies the sequence in which food energy is transferred from producer to consumer or higher trophic level. (④) Hence the number of steps or links in a sequence is restricted, usually to four or five. (⑤) The shorter the food chain or the nearer the organism is to the beginning of the chain, the greater the available energy intake is.

* trophic: 영양의

21 오답률 BEST

글의 흐름으로 보아, 주어진 문장이 들어가기에 가장 적절한 곳을 고르시오.

> Meanwhile, improving by 1 percent isn't particularly notable, but it can be far more meaningful in the long run.

It is so easy to overestimate the importance of one defining moment and underestimate the value of making small improvements on a daily basis. Too often, we convince ourselves that massive success requires massive action. (①) Whether it is losing weight, winning a championship, or achieving any other goal, we put pressure on ourselves to make some earthshaking improvement that everyone will talk about. (②) The difference this tiny improvement can make over time is surprising. (③) Here's how the math works out: if you can get 1 percent better each day for one year, you'll end up thirty-seven times better by the time you're done. (④) Conversely, if you get 1 percent worse each day for one year, you'll decline nearly down to zero. (⑤) What starts as a small win or a minor failure adds up to something much more.

22

글의 흐름으로 보아, 주어진 문장이 들어가기에 가장 적절한 곳을 고르시오. [3점]

Before a trip, research how the native inhabitants dress, work, and eat.

The continued survival of the human race can be explained by our ability to adapt to our environment. (①) While we may have lost some of our ancient ancestors' survival skills, we have learned new skills as they have become necessary. (②) Today, the gap between the skills we once had and the skills we now have grows ever wider as we rely more heavily on modern technology. (③) Therefore, when you head off into the wilderness, it is important to fully prepare for the environment. (④) How they have adapted to their way of life will help you to understand the environment and allow you to select the best gear and learn the correct skills. (⑤) This is crucial because most survival situations arise as a result of a series of events that could have been avoided.

＊ inhabitant: 주민

23

글의 흐름으로 보아, 주어진 문장이 들어가기에 가장 적절한 곳을 고르시오.

It is the reason that individuals with certain forms of blindness do not entirely lose their circadian rhythm.

Daylight isn't the only signal that the brain can use for the purpose of biological clock resetting, though it is the principal and preferential signal, when present. (①) So long as they are reliably repeating, the brain can also use other external cues, such as food, exercise, and even regularly timed social interaction. (②) All of these events have the ability to reset the biological clock, allowing it to strike a precise twenty-four-hour note. (③) Despite not receiving light cues due to their blindness, other phenomena act as their resetting triggers. (④) Any signal that the brain uses for the purpose of clock resetting is termed a zeitgeber, from the German "time giver" or "synchronizer." (⑤) Thus, while light is the most reliable and thus the primary zeitgeber, there are many factors that can be used in addition to, or in the absence of, daylight.

＊ circadian rhythm: 24시간 주기 리듬

24

글의 흐름으로 보아, 주어진 문장이 들어가기에 가장 적절한 곳을 고르시오. [3점]

More recently, agriculture has in many places lost its local character, and has become incorporated into the global economy.

Earlier agricultural systems were integrated with and co-evolved with technologies, beliefs, myths and traditions as part of an integrated social system. (①) Generally, people planted a variety of crops in different areas, in the hope of obtaining a reasonably stable food supply. (②) These systems could only be maintained at low population levels, and were relatively non-destructive (but not always). (③) This has led to increased pressure on agricultural land for exchange commodities and export goods. (④) More land is being diverted from local food production to "cash crops" for export and exchange; fewer types of crops are raised, and each crop is raised in much greater quantities than before. (⑤) Thus, ever more land is converted from forest (and other natural systems) for agriculture for export, rather than using land for subsistence crops.

＊ subsistence crop: 자급자족용 작물

01

다음 글의 내용을 한 문장으로 요약하고자 한다. 빈칸 (A), (B)에 들어갈 말로 가장 적절한 것은?

It's not news to anyone that we judge others based on their clothes. In general, studies that investigate these judgments find that people prefer clothing that matches expectations — surgeons in scrubs, little boys in blue — with one notable exception. A series of studies published in an article in June 2014 in the *Journal of Consumer Research* explored observers' reactions to people who broke established norms only slightly. In one scenario, a man at a black-tie affair was viewed as having higher status and competence when wearing a red bow tie. The researchers also found that valuing uniqueness increased audience members' ratings of the status and competence of a professor who wore red sneakers while giving a lecture. The results suggest that people judge these slight deviations from the norm as positive because they suggest that the individual is powerful enough to risk the social costs of such behaviors.

A series of studies show that people view an individual ___(A)___ when the individual only slightly ___(B)___ the norm for what people should wear.

	(A)		(B)
①	positively	……	challenges
②	negatively	……	challenges
③	indifferently	……	neglects
④	negatively	……	meets
⑤	positively	……	meets

02

다음 글의 내용을 한 문장으로 요약하고자 한다. 빈칸 (A), (B)에 들어갈 말로 가장 적절한 것은?

Nearly eight of ten U.S. adults believe there are "good foods" and "bad foods." Unless we're talking about spoiled stew, poison mushrooms, or something similar, however, no foods can be labeled as either good or bad. There are, however, combinations of foods that add up to a healthful or unhealthful diet. Consider the case of an adult who eats only foods thought of as "good" — for example, raw broccoli, apples, orange juice, boiled tofu, and carrots. Although all these foods are nutrient-dense, they do not add up to a healthy diet because they don't supply a wide enough variety of the nutrients we need. Or take the case of the teenager who occasionally eats fried chicken, but otherwise stays away from fried foods. The occasional fried chicken isn't going to knock his or her diet off track. But the person who eats fried foods every day, with few vegetables or fruits, and loads up on supersized soft drinks, candy, and chips for snacks has a bad diet.

Unlike the common belief, defining foods as good or bad is not ___(A)___ ; in fact, a healthy diet is determined largely by what the diet is ___(B)___ .

	(A)		(B)
①	incorrect	……	limited to
②	appropriate	……	composed of
③	wrong	……	aimed at
④	appropriate	……	tested on
⑤	incorrect	……	adjusted to

03

202303 40번

다음 글의 내용을 한 문장으로 요약하고자 한다. 빈칸 (A), (B)에 들어갈 말로 가장 적절한 것은?

To help decide what's risky and what's safe, who's trustworthy and who's not, we look for *social evidence*. From an evolutionary view, following the group is almost always positive for our prospects of survival. "If everyone's doing it, it must be a sensible thing to do," explains famous psychologist and best selling writer of *Influence*, Robert Cialdini. While we can frequently see this today in product reviews, even subtler cues within the environment can signal trustworthiness. Consider this: when you visit a local restaurant, are they busy? Is there a line outside or is it easy to find a seat? It is a hassle to wait, but a line can be a powerful cue that the food's tasty, and these seats are in demand. More often than not, it's good to adopt the practices of those around you.

* subtle: 미묘한 ** hassle: 성가신 일

↓

We tend to feel safe and secure in ___(A)___ when we decide how to act, particularly when faced with ___(B)___ conditions.

	(A)		(B)
①	numbers	……	uncertain
②	numbers	……	unrealistic
③	experiences	……	unrealistic
④	rules	……	uncertain
⑤	rules	……	unpleasant

04

202211 40번

다음 글의 내용을 한 문장으로 요약하고자 한다. 빈칸 (A), (B)에 들어갈 말로 가장 적절한 것은?

One of the most powerful tools to find meaning in our lives is reflective journaling — thinking back on and writing about what has happened to us. In the 1990s, Stanford University researchers asked undergraduate students on spring break to journal about their most important personal values and their daily activities; others were asked to write about only the good things that happened to them in the day. Three weeks later, the students who had written about their values were happier, healthier, and more confident about their ability to handle stress than the ones who had only focused on the good stuff. By reflecting on how their daily activities supported their values, students had gained a new perspective on those activities and choices. Little stresses and hassles were now demonstrations of their values in action. Suddenly, their lives were full of meaningful activities. And all they had to do was reflect and write about it — positively reframing their experiences with their personal values.

* hassle: 귀찮은 일

↓

Journaling about daily activities based on what we believe to be ___(A)___ can make us feel that our life is meaningful by ___(B)___ our experiences in a new way.

	(A)		(B)
①	factual	……	rethinking
②	worthwhile	……	rethinking
③	outdated	……	generalizing
④	objective	……	generalizing
⑤	demanding	……	describing

05 오답률 BEST

다음 글의 내용을 한 문장으로 요약하고자 한다. 빈칸 (A), (B)에 들어갈 말로 가장 적절한 것은?

My colleagues and I ran an experiment testing two different messages meant to convince thousands of resistant alumni to make a donation. One message emphasized the opportunity to do good: donating would benefit students, faculty, and staff. The other emphasized the opportunity to feel good: donors would enjoy the warm glow of giving. The two messages were equally effective: in both cases, 6.5 percent of the unwilling alumni ended up donating. Then we combined them, because two reasons are better than one. Except they weren't. When we put the two reasons together, the giving rate dropped below 3 percent. Each reason alone was more than twice as effective as the two combined. The audience was already skeptical. When we gave them different kinds of reasons to donate, we triggered their awareness that someone was trying to persuade them — and they shielded themselves against it.

* alumni: 졸업생   ** skeptical: 회의적인

In the experiment mentioned above, when the two different reasons to donate were given   (A)   , the audience was less likely to be   (B)   because they could recognize the intention to persuade them.

	(A)		(B)
①	simultaneously	……	convinced
②	separately	……	confused
③	frequently	……	annoyed
④	separately	……	satisfied
⑤	simultaneously	……	offended

06

다음 글의 내용을 한 문장으로 요약하고자 한다. 빈칸 (A), (B)에 들어갈 말로 가장 적절한 것은? [3점]

According to a study of Swedish adolescents, an important factor of adolescents' academic success is how they respond to challenges. The study reports that when facing difficulties, adolescents exposed to an authoritative parenting style are less likely to be passive, helpless, and afraid to fail. Another study of nine high schools in Wisconsin and northern California indicates that children of authoritative parents do well in school, because these parents put a lot of effort into getting involved in their children's school activities. That is, authoritative parents are significantly more likely to help their children with homework, to attend school programs, to watch their children in sports, and to help students select courses. Moreover, these parents are more aware of what their children do and how they perform in school. Finally, authoritative parents praise academic excellence and the importance of working hard more than other parents do.

The studies above show that the children of authoritative parents often succeed academically, since they are more   (A)   to deal with their difficulties and are affected by their parents'   (B)   involvement.

	(A)		(B)
①	likely	……	random
②	willing	……	minimal
③	willing	……	active
④	hesitant	……	unwanted
⑤	hesitant	……	constant

07

다음 글의 내용을 한 문장으로 요약하고자 한다. 빈칸 (A), (B)에 들어갈 말로 가장 적절한 것은?

The common blackberry (*Rubus allegheniensis*) has an amazing ability to move manganese from one layer of soil to another using its roots. This may seem like a funny talent for a plant to have, but it all becomes clear when you realize the effect it has on nearby plants. Manganese can be very harmful to plants, especially at high concentrations. Common blackberry is unaffected by damaging effects of this metal and has evolved two different ways of using manganese to its advantage. First, it redistributes manganese from deeper soil layers to shallow soil layers using its roots as a small pipe. Second, it absorbs manganese as it grows, concentrating the metal in its leaves. When the leaves drop and decay, their concentrated manganese deposits further poison the soil around the plant. For plants that are not immune to the toxic effects of manganese, this is very bad news. Essentially, the common blackberry eliminates competition by poisoning its neighbors with heavy metals.

* manganese: 망가니즈(금속 원소) ** deposit: 축적물

↓

The common blackberry has an ability to (A) the amount of manganese in the surrounding upper soil, which makes the nearby soil quite (B) for other plants.

	(A)		(B)
①	increase	……	deadly
②	increase	……	advantageous
③	indicate	……	nutritious
④	reduce	……	dry
⑤	reduce	……	warm

08

다음 글의 내용을 한 문장으로 요약하고자 한다. 빈칸 (A), (B)에 들어갈 말로 가장 적절한 것은?

There is often a lot of uncertainty in the realm of science, which the general public finds uncomfortable. They don't want "informed guesses," they want certainties that make their lives easier, and science is often unequipped to meet these demands. In particular, the human body is fantastically complex, and some scientific answers can never be provided in black-or-white terms. All this is why the media tends to oversimplify scientific research when presenting it to the public. In their eyes, they're just "giving people what they want" as opposed to offering more accurate but complex information that very few people will read or understand. A perfect example of this is how people want definitive answers as to which foods are "good" and "bad." Scientifically speaking, there are no "good" and "bad" foods; rather, food quality exists on a continuum, meaning that some foods are *better* than others when it comes to general health and well-being.

* continuum: 연속(체)

With regard to general health, science, by its nature, does not (A) the public's demands for certainty, which leads to the media giving less (B) answers to the public.

	(A)		(B)
①	satisfy	……	simple
②	satisfy	……	complicated
③	ignore	……	difficult
④	ignore	……	simple
⑤	reject	……	complicated

09 오답률 BEST

202109 40번

다음 글의 내용을 한 문장으로 요약하고자 한다. 빈칸 (A), (B)에 들어갈 말로 가장 적절한 것은? [3점]

Nancy Lowry and David Johnson conducted an experiment to study a teaching environment where fifth and sixth graders were assigned to interact on a topic. With one group, the discussion was led in a way that built an agreement. With the second group, the discussion was designed to produce disagreements about the right answer. Students who easily reached an agreement were less interested in the topic, studied less, and were less likely to visit the library to get additional information. The most noticeable difference, though, was revealed when teachers showed a special film about the discussion topic — during lunch time! Only 18 percent of the agreement group missed lunch time to see the film, but 45 percent of the students from the disagreement group stayed for the film. The thirst to fill a knowledge gap — to find out who was right within the group — can be more powerful than the thirst for slides and jungle gyms.

↓

According to the experiment above, students' interest in a topic ___(A)___ when they are encouraged to ___(B)___ .

	(A)	(B)
①	increases	differ
②	increases	approve
③	increases	cooperate
④	decreases	participate
⑤	decreases	argue

10

202106 40번

다음 글의 내용을 한 문장으로 요약하고자 한다. 빈칸 (A), (B)에 들어갈 말로 가장 적절한 것은?

A woman named Rhonda who attended the University of California at Berkeley had a problem. She was living near campus with several other people — none of whom knew one another. When the cleaning people came each weekend, they left several rolls of toilet paper in each of the two bathrooms. However, by Monday all the toilet paper would be gone. It was a classic tragedy-of-the-commons situation: because some people took more toilet paper than their fair share, the public resource was destroyed for everyone else. After reading a research paper about behavior change, Rhonda put a note in one of the bathrooms asking people not to remove the toilet paper, as it was a shared item. To her great satisfaction, one roll reappeared in a few hours, and another the next day. In the other note-free bathroom, however, there was no toilet paper until the following weekend, when the cleaning people returned.

↓

A small ___(A)___ brought about a change in the behavior of the people who had taken more of the ___(B)___ goods than they needed.

	(A)	(B)
①	reminder	shared
②	reminder	recycled
③	mistake	stored
④	mistake	borrowed
⑤	fortune	limited

18강

상완문요약

11

다음 글의 내용을 한 문장으로 요약하고자 한다. 빈칸 (A), (B)에 들어갈 말로 가장 적절한 것은?

In one study, researchers asked pairs of strangers to sit down in a room and chat. In half of the rooms, a cell phone was placed on a nearby table; in the other half, no phone was present. After the conversations had ended, the researchers asked the participants what they thought of each other. Here's what they learned: when a cell phone was present in the room, the participants reported the quality of their relationship was worse than those who'd talked in a cell phone-free room. The pairs who talked in the rooms with cell phones thought their partners showed less empathy. Think of all the times you've sat down to have lunch with a friend and set your phone on the table. You might have felt good about yourself because you didn't pick it up to check your messages, but your unchecked messages were still hurting your connection with the person sitting across from you.

＊empathy: 공감

↓

The presence of a cell phone ___(A)___ the connection between people involved in conversations, even when the phone is being ___(B)___ .

	(A)		(B)
①	weakens	⋯⋯	answered
②	weakens	⋯⋯	ignored
③	renews	⋯⋯	answered
④	maintains	⋯⋯	ignored
⑤	maintains	⋯⋯	updated

12

다음 글의 내용을 한 문장으로 요약하고자 한다. 빈칸 (A), (B)에 들어갈 말로 가장 적절한 것은?

In their study in 2007 Katherine Kinzler and her colleagues at Harvard showed that our tendency to identify with an in-group to a large degree begins in infancy and may be innate. Kinzler and her team took a bunch of five-month-olds whose families only spoke English and showed the babies two videos. In one video, a woman was speaking English. In the other, a woman was speaking Spanish. Then they were shown a screen with both women side by side, not speaking. In infant psychology research, the standard measure for affinity or interest is attention — babies will apparently stare longer at the things they like more. In Kinzler's study, the babies stared at the English speakers longer. In other studies, researchers have found that infants are more likely to take a toy offered by someone who speaks the same language as them. Psychologists routinely cite these and other experiments as evidence of our built-in evolutionary preference for "our own kind."

＊affinity: 애착

↓

Infants' more favorable responses to those who use a ___(A)___ language show that there can be a(n) ___(B)___ tendency to prefer in-group members.

	(A)		(B)
①	familiar	⋯⋯	inborn
②	familiar	⋯⋯	acquired
③	foreign	⋯⋯	cultural
④	foreign	⋯⋯	learned
⑤	formal	⋯⋯	innate

[01~02]
다음 글을 읽고, 물음에 답하시오. 📄 202309 41~42번

Claims that local food production cut greenhouse gas emissions by reducing the burning of transportation fuel are usually not well founded. Transport is the source of only 11 percent of greenhouse gas emissions within the food sector, so reducing the distance that food travels after it leaves the farm is far (a) <u>less</u> important than reducing wasteful energy use on the farm. Food coming from a distance can actually be better for the (b) <u>climate</u>, depending on how it was grown. For example, field-grown tomatoes shipped from Mexico in the winter months will have a smaller carbon footprint than (c) <u>local</u> winter tomatoes grown in a greenhouse. In the United Kingdom, lamb meat that travels 11,000 miles from New Zealand generates only one-quarter the carbon emissions per pound compared to British lamb because farmers in the United Kingdom raise their animals on feed (which must be produced using fossil fuels) rather than on clover pastureland.

When food does travel, what matters most is not the (d) <u>distance</u> traveled but the travel mode (surface versus air), and most of all the load size. Bulk loads of food can travel halfway around the world by ocean freight with a smaller carbon footprint, per pound delivered, than foods traveling just a short distance but in much (e) <u>larger</u> loads. For example, 18-wheelers carry much larger loads than pickup trucks so they can move food 100 times as far while burning only one-third as much gas per pound of food delivered.

＊freight: 화물 운송

01

윗글의 제목으로 가장 적절한 것은?

① Shorten the Route, Cut the Cost
② Is Local Food Always Better for the Earth?
③ Why Mass Production Ruins the Environment
④ New Technologies: What Matters in Agriculture
⑤ Reduce Food Waste for a Smaller Carbon Footprint

02 오답률 BEST

밑줄 친 (a) ~ (e) 중에서 문맥상 낱말의 쓰임이 적절하지 **않은** 것은?

① (a)   ② (b)   ③ (c)   ④ (d)   ⑤ (e)

[03~04]

📄 202306 41~42번

다음 글을 읽고, 물음에 답하시오.

Early hunter-gatherer societies had (a) <u>minimal</u> structure. A chief or group of elders usually led the camp or village. Most of these leaders had to hunt and gather along with the other members because the surpluses of food and other vital resources were seldom (b) <u>sufficient</u> to support a full-time chief or village council. The development of agriculture changed work patterns. Early farmers could reap 3–10 kg of grain from each 1 kg of seed planted. Part of this food/energy surplus was returned to the community and (c) <u>limited</u> support for nonfarmers such as chieftains, village councils, men who practice medicine, priests, and warriors. In return, the nonfarmers provided leadership and security for the farming population, enabling it to continue to increase food/energy yields and provide ever larger surpluses.

With improved technology and favorable conditions, agriculture produced consistent surpluses of the basic necessities, and population groups grew in size. These groups concentrated in towns and cities, and human tasks (d) <u>specialized</u> further. Specialists such as carpenters, blacksmiths, merchants, traders, and sailors developed their skills and became more efficient in their use of time and energy. The goods and services they provided brought about an (e) <u>improved</u> quality of life, a higher standard of living, and, for most societies, increased stability.

＊reap: (농작물을) 베어들이다 ＊＊chieftain: 수령, 두목

03

윗글의 제목으로 가장 적절한 것은?

① How Agriculture Transformed Human Society
② The Dark Shadow of Agriculture: Repetition
③ How Can We Share Extra Food with the Poor?
④ Why Were Early Societies Destroyed by Agriculture?
⑤ The Advantages of Large Groups Over Small Groups in Farming

04

밑줄 친 (a) ~ (e) 중에서 문맥상 낱말의 쓰임이 적절하지 <u>않은</u> 것은? [3점]

① (a)   ② (b)   ③ (c)   ④ (d)   ⑤ (e)

[05~06]

다음 글을 읽고, 물음에 답하시오.

202303 41~42번

Chess masters shown a chess board in the middle of a game for 5 seconds with 20 to 30 pieces still in play can immediately reproduce the position of the pieces from memory. Beginners, of course, are able to place only a few. Now take the same pieces and place them on the board randomly and the (a) difference is much reduced. The expert's advantage is only for familiar patterns — those previously stored in memory. Faced with unfamiliar patterns, even when it involves the same familiar domain, the expert's advantage (b) disappears.

The beneficial effects of familiar structure on memory have been observed for many types of expertise, including music. People with musical training can reproduce short sequences of musical notation more accurately than those with no musical training when notes follow (c) unusual sequences, but the advantage is much reduced when the notes are ordered randomly. Expertise also improves memory for sequences of (d) movements. Experienced ballet dancers are able to repeat longer sequences of steps than less experienced dancers, and they can repeat a sequence of steps making up a routine better than steps ordered randomly. In each case, memory range is (e) increased by the ability to recognize familiar sequences and patterns.

* expertise: 전문 지식 ** sequence: 연속, 순서
*** musical notation: 악보

05

윗글의 제목으로 가장 적절한 것은?

① How Can We Build Good Routines?
② Familiar Structures Help Us Remember
③ Intelligence Does Not Guarantee Expertise
④ Does Playing Chess Improve Your Memory?
⑤ Creative Art Performance Starts from Practice

06 오답률 BEST

밑줄 친 (a) ~ (e) 중에서 문맥상 낱말의 쓰임이 적절하지 <u>않은</u> 것은?

① (a)　　② (b)　　③ (c)　　④ (d)　　⑤ (e)

[07~08] 📄202211 41~42번
다음 글을 읽고, 물음에 답하시오.

Mike May lost his sight at the age of three. Because he had spent the majority of his life adapting to being blind — and even cultivating a skiing career in this state — his other senses compensated by growing (a) stronger. However, when his sight was restored through a surgery in his forties, his entire perception of reality was (b) disrupted. Instead of being thrilled that he could see now, as he'd expected, his brain was so overloaded with new visual stimuli that the world became a frightening and overwhelming place. After he'd learned to know his family through touch and smell, he found that he couldn't recognize his children with his eyes, and this left him puzzled. Skiing also became a lot harder as he struggled to adapt to the visual stimulation.

This (c) confusion occurred because his brain hadn't yet learned to see. Though we often tend to assume our eyes function as video cameras which relay information to our brain, advances in neuroscientific research have proven that this is actually not the case. Instead, sight is a collaborative effort between our eyes and our brains, and the way we process (d) visual reality depends on the way these two communicate. If communication between our eyes and our brains is disturbed, our perception of reality is altered accordingly. And because other areas of May's brain had adapted to process information primarily through his other senses, the process of learning how to see was (e) easier than he'd anticipated.

07
윗글의 제목으로 가장 적절한 것은?

① Eyes and Brain Working Together for Sight
② Visualization: A Useful Tool for Learning
③ Collaboration Between Vision and Sound
④ How to Ignore New Visual Stimuli
⑤ You See What You Believe

08
밑줄 친 (a) ~ (e) 중에서 문맥상 낱말의 쓰임이 적절하지 <u>않은</u> 것은?

① (a)　　② (b)　　③ (c)　　④ (d)　　⑤ (e)

[09~10]
다음 글을 읽고, 물음에 답하시오.
202209 41~42번

In a society that rejects the consumption of insects there are some individuals who overcome this rejection, but most will continue with this attitude. It may be very (a) difficult to convince an entire society that insects are totally suitable for consumption. However, there are examples in which this (b) reversal of attitudes about certain foods has happened to an entire society. Several examples in the past 120 years from European-American society are: considering lobster a luxury food instead of a food for servants and prisoners; considering sushi a safe and delicious food; and considering pizza not just a food for the rural poor of Sicily. In Latin American countries, where insects are already consumed, a portion of the population hates their consumption and (c) associates it with poverty. There are also examples of people who have had the habit of consuming them and (d) encouraged that habit due to shame, and because they do not want to be categorized as poor or uncivilized. According to Esther Katz, an anthropologist, if the consumption of insects as a food luxury is to be promoted, there would be more chances that some individuals who do not present this habit overcome ideas under which they were educated. And this could also help to (e) revalue the consumption of insects by those people who already eat them.

09
윗글의 제목으로 가장 적절한 것은?

① The More Variety on the Table, The Healthier You Become
② Edible or Not? Change Your Perspectives on Insects
③ Insects: A Key to Solve the World Food Shortage
④ Don't Let Uniqueness in Food Culture Disappear
⑤ Experiencing Various Cultures by Food

10
밑줄 친 (a) ~ (e) 중에서 문맥상 낱말의 쓰임이 적절하지 않은 것은?

① (a)   ② (b)   ③ (c)   ④ (d)   ⑤ (e)

19강
장문의 이해

[11~12] 202206 41~42번

다음 글을 읽고, 물음에 답하시오.

U.K. researchers say a bedtime of between 10 p.m. and 11 p.m. is best. They say people who go to sleep between these times have a (a) lower risk of heart disease. Six years ago, the researchers collected data on the sleep patterns of 80,000 volunteers. The volunteers had to wear a special watch for seven days so the researchers could collect data on their sleeping and waking times. The scientists then monitored the health of the volunteers. Around 3,000 volunteers later showed heart problems. They went to bed earlier or later than the (b) ideal 10 p.m. to 11 p.m. timeframe.

One of the authors of the study, Dr. David Plans, commented on his research and the (c) effects of bedtimes on the health of our heart. He said the study could not give a certain cause for their results, but it suggests that early or late bedtimes may be more likely to disrupt the body clock, with (d) positive consequences for cardiovascular health. He said that it was important for our body to wake up to the morning light, and that the worst time to go to bed was after midnight because it may (e) reduce the likelihood of seeing morning light which resets the body clock. He added that we risk cardiovascular disease if our body clock is not reset properly.

*disrupt: 혼란케 하다 **cardiovascular: 심장 혈관의

11

윗글의 제목으로 가장 적절한 것은?

① The Best Bedtime for Your Heart
② Late Bedtimes Are a Matter of Age
③ For Sound Sleep: Turn Off the Light
④ Sleeping Patterns Reflect Personalities
⑤ Regular Exercise: A Miracle for Good Sleep

12

밑줄 친 (a) ~ (e) 중에서 문맥상 낱말의 쓰임이 적절하지 않은 것은? [3점]

① (a)　　② (b)　　③ (c)　　④ (d)　　⑤ (e)

[13~14]

202203 41~42번

다음 글을 읽고, 물음에 답하시오.

The longest journey we will make is the eighteen inches between our head and heart. If we take this journey, it can shorten our (a) <u>misery</u> in the world. Impatience, judgment, frustration, and anger reside in our heads. When we live in that place too long, it makes us (b) <u>unhappy</u>. But when we take the journey from our heads to our hearts, something shifts (c) <u>inside</u>. What if we were able to love everything that gets in our way? What if we tried loving the shopper who unknowingly steps in front of us in line, the driver who cuts us off in traffic, the swimmer who splashes us with water during a belly dive, or the reader who pens a bad online review of our writing?

Every person who makes us miserable is (d) <u>like</u> us — a human being, most likely doing the best they can, deeply loved by their parents, a child, or a friend. And how many times have we unknowingly stepped in front of someone in line? Cut someone off in traffic? Splashed someone in a pool? Or made a negative statement about something we've read? It helps to (e) <u>deny</u> that a piece of us resides in every person we meet.

* reside: (어떤 장소에) 있다

13

윗글의 제목으로 가장 적절한 것은?

① Why It Is So Difficult to Forgive Others
② Even Acts of Kindness Can Hurt Somebody
③ Time Is the Best Healer for a Broken Heart
④ Celebrate the Happy Moments in Your Everyday Life
⑤ Understand Others to Save Yourself from Unhappiness

14

밑줄 친 (a) ~ (e) 중에서 문맥상 낱말의 쓰임이 적절하지 <u>않은</u> 것은?

① (a)　　② (b)　　③ (c)　　④ (d)　　⑤ (e)

[15~16] 📄 202111 41~42번

다음 글을 읽고, 물음에 답하시오.

Since the turn of the twentieth century we've believed in genetic causes of diagnoses — a theory called genetic determinism. Under this model, our genes (and subsequent health) are determined at birth. We are "destined" to inherit certain diseases based on the misfortune of our DNA. Genetic determinism doesn't (a) consider the role of family backgrounds, traumas, habits, or anything else within the environment. In this dynamic we are not (b) active participants in our own health and wellness. Why would we be? If something is predetermined, it's not (c) necessary to look at anything beyond our DNA. But the more science has learned about the body and its interaction with the environment around it (in its various forms, from our nutrition to our relationships to our racially oppressive systems), the more (d) simplistic the story becomes. We are not merely expressions of coding but products of a remarkable variety of interactions that are both within and outside of our control. Once we see beyond the narrative that genetics are (e) destiny, we can take ownership of our health. This allows us to see how "choiceless" we once were and empowers us with the ability to create real and lasting change.

＊oppressive: 억압적인

15

윗글의 제목으로 가장 적절한 것은?

① Health Is in Our Hands, Not Only in Our Genes
② Genetics: A Solution to Enhance Human Wellness
③ How Did DNA Dominate Over Environment in Biology?
④ Never Be Confident in Your Health, but Keep Checking!
⑤ Why Scientific Innovation Affects Our Social Interactions

16

밑줄 친 (a) ~ (e) 중에서 문맥상 낱말의 쓰임이 적절하지 않은 것은? [3점]

① (a)   ② (b)   ③ (c)   ④ (d)   ⑤ (e)

[17~18]

202109 41~42번

다음 글을 읽고, 물음에 답하시오.

The market's way of telling a firm about its failures is harsh and brief. Not only are complaints less expensive to handle but they also can cause the seller to (a) improve. The seller may learn something as well. I remember a cosmetics company that received complaints about sticky sunblock lotion. At the time, all such lotions were more or less sticky, so the risk of having customers buy products from a rival company was not (b) great. But this was also an opportunity. The company managed to develop a product that was not sticky and captured 20 percent of the market in its first year. Another company had the (c) opposite problem. Its products were not sticky enough. The company was a Royal Post Office in Europe and the product was a stamp. The problem was that the stamp didn't stick to the envelope. Management contacted the stamp producer who made it clear that if people just moistened the stamps properly, they would stick to any piece of paper. What to do? Management didn't take long to come to the conclusion that it would be (d) less costly to try to educate its customers to wet each stamp rather than to add more glue. The stamp producer was told to add more glue and the problem didn't occur again.

Since it is better for the firm to have buyers complain rather than go elsewhere, it is important to make it (e) easier for dissatisfied customers to complain.

＊ stamp: 우표

17

윗글의 제목으로 가장 적절한 것은?

① Designs That Matter the Most to Customers
② Complaints: Why Firms Should Welcome Them
③ Cheap Prices Don't Necessarily Mean Low Quality
④ More Sticky or Less Sticky: An Unsolved Problem
⑤ Treat Your Competitors Like Friends, Not Enemies

18 오답률 BEST

밑줄 친 (a) ~ (e) 중에서 문맥상 낱말의 쓰임이 적절하지 <u>않은</u> 것은? [3점]

① (a)　　② (b)　　③ (c)　　④ (d)　　⑤ (e)

19강
정답의 이해

[19~20]

다음 글을 읽고, 물음에 답하시오.

📄 202106 41~42번

If you were afraid of standing on balconies, you would start on some lower floors and slowly work your way up to higher ones. It would be easy to face a fear of standing on high balconies in a way that's totally controlled. Socializing is (a) trickier. People aren't like inanimate features of a building that you just have to be around to get used to. You have to interact with them, and their responses can be unpredictable. Your feelings toward them are more complex too. Most people's self-esteem isn't going to be affected that much if they don't like balconies, but your confidence can (b) suffer if you can't socialize effectively.

It's also harder to design a tidy way to gradually face many social fears. The social situations you need to expose yourself to may not be (c) available when you want them, or they may not go well enough for you to sense that things are under control. The progression from one step to the next may not be clear, creating unavoidable large (d) decreases in difficulty from one to the next. People around you aren't robots that you can endlessly experiment with for your own purposes. This is not to say that facing your fears is pointless when socializing. The principles of gradual exposure are still very (e) useful. The process of applying them is just messier, and knowing that before you start is helpful.

19 오답률 BEST

윗글의 제목으로 가장 적절한 것은?

① How to Improve Your Self-Esteem
② Socializing with Someone You Fear: Good or Bad?
③ Relaxation May Lead to Getting Over Social Fears
④ Are Social Exposures Related with Fear of Heights?
⑤ Overcoming Social Anxiety Is Difficult; Try Gradually!

20

밑줄 친 (a) ~ (e) 중에서 문맥상 낱말의 쓰임이 적절하지 않은 것은?

① (a)　　② (b)　　③ (c)　　④ (d)　　⑤ (e)

[21~22]

다음 글을 읽고, 물음에 답하시오.

202103 41~42번

As kids, we worked hard at learning to ride a bike; when we fell off, we got back on again, until it became second nature to us. But when we try something new in our adult lives we'll usually make just one attempt before judging whether it's (a) worked. If we don't succeed the first time, or if it feels a little awkward, we'll tell ourselves it wasn't a success rather than giving it (b) another shot.

That's a shame, because repetition is central to the process of rewiring our brains. Consider the idea that your brain has a network of neurons. They will (c) connect with each other whenever you remember to use a brain-friendly feedback technique. Those connections aren't very (d) reliable at first, which may make your first efforts a little hit-and-miss. You might remember one of the steps involved, and not the others. But scientists have a saying: "neurons that fire together, wire together." In other words, repetition of an action (e) blocks the connections between the neurons involved in that action. That means the more times you try using that new feedback technique, the more easily it will come to you when you need it.

21

윗글의 제목으로 가장 적절한 것은?

① Repeat and You Will Succeed
② Be More Curious, Be Smarter
③ Play Is What Makes Us Human
④ Stop and Think Before You Act
⑤ Growth Is All About Keeping Balance

22

밑줄 친 (a) ~ (e) 중에서 문맥상 낱말의 쓰임이 적절하지 <u>않은</u> 것은?

① (a) ② (b) ③ (c) ④ (d) ⑤ (e)

[23~24]
📄 202011 41~42번

다음 글을 읽고, 물음에 답하시오.

Like all humans, the first *Homo* species to begin the long difficult process of constructing a language from scratch almost certainly never said entirely what was on their minds. At the same time, these primitive hominins would not have simply made (a) random sounds or gestures. Instead, they would have used means to communicate that they believed others would understand. And they also thought their hearers could "fill in the gaps", and connect their knowledge of their culture and the world to interpret what was uttered.

These are some of the reasons why the (b) origins of human language cannot be effectively discussed unless conversation is placed at the top of the list of things to understand. Every aspect of human language has evolved, as have components of the human brain and body, to (c) engage in conversation and social life. Language did not fully begin when the first hominid uttered the first word or sentence. It began in earnest only with the first conversation, which is both the source and the (d) goal of language. Indeed, language changes lives. It builds society and expresses our highest aspirations, our basest thoughts, our emotions and our philosophies of life. But all language is ultimately at the service of human interaction. Other components of language — things like grammar and stories — are (e) crucial to conversation.

＊hominin: 인간의 조상으로 분류되는 종족 ＊＊hominid: 사람과(科)의 동물

23

윗글의 제목으로 가장 적절한 것은?

① Various Communication Strategies of Our Ancestors
② Conversation: The Core of Language Development
③ Ending Conversation Without Offending Others
④ How Language Shapes the Way You Think
⑤ What Makes You a Good Communicator?

24 오답률 BEST

밑줄 친 (a) ~ (e) 중에서 문맥상 낱말의 쓰임이 적절하지 <u>않은</u> 것은? [3점]

① (a)　　② (b)　　③ (c)　　④ (d)　　⑤ (e)

[01~03] 📄202309 43~45번
다음 글을 읽고, 물음에 답하시오.

(A)

Long ago, an old man built a grand temple at the center of his village. People traveled to worship at the temple. So the old man made arrangements for food and accommodation inside the temple itself. He needed someone who could look after the temple, so (a) he put up a notice: Manager needed.

(B)

When that young man left the temple, the old man called him and asked, "Will you take care of this temple?" The young man was surprised by the offer and replied, "I have no experience caring for a temple. I'm not even educated." The old man smiled and said, "I don't want any educated man. I want a qualified person." Confused, the young man asked, "But why do (b) you consider me a qualified person?"

(C)

The old man replied, "I buried a brick on the path to the temple. I watched for many days as people tripped over that brick. No one thought to remove it. But you dug up that brick." The young man said, "I haven't done anything great. It's the duty of every human being to think about others. (c) I only did my duty." The old man smiled and said, "Only people who know their duty and perform it are qualified people."

(D)

Seeing the notice, many people went to the old man. But he returned all the applicants after interviews, telling them, "I need a qualified person for this work." The old man would sit on the roof of (d) his house every morning, watching people go through the temple doors. One day, (e) he saw a young man come to the temple.

01
주어진 글 (A)에 이어질 내용을 순서에 맞게 배열한 것으로 가장 적절한 것은?

① (B) – (D) – (C) 　② (C) – (B) – (D)
③ (C) – (D) – (B) 　④ (D) – (B) – (C)
⑤ (D) – (C) – (B)

02
밑줄 친 (a) ~ (e) 중에서 가리키는 대상이 나머지 넷과 다른 것은?

① (a) 　② (b) 　③ (c) 　④ (d) 　⑤ (e)

03
윗글에 관한 내용으로 적절하지 않은 것은?

① 노인은 마을 중심부에 사원을 지었다.
② 젊은이가 사원을 나설 때 노인이 그를 불렀다.
③ 젊은이는 노인의 제안에 놀랐다.
④ 노인은 사원으로 통하는 길에 묻혀있던 벽돌을 파냈다.
⑤ 공고를 보고 많은 사람들이 노인을 찾아갔다.

[04~06]
다음 글을 읽고, 물음에 답하시오.

202306 43~45번

(A)

A nurse took a tired, anxious soldier to the bedside. "Jack, your son is here," the nurse said to an old man lying on the bed. She had to repeat the words several times before the old man's eyes opened. Suffering from the severe pain because of heart disease, he barely saw the young uniformed soldier standing next to him. (a) He reached out his hand to the soldier.

(B)

Whenever the nurse came into the room, she heard the soldier say a few gentle words. The old man said nothing, only held tightly to (b) him all through the night. Just before dawn, the old man died. The soldier released the old man's hand and left the room to find the nurse. After she was told what happened, she went back to the room with him. The soldier hesitated for a while and asked, "Who was this man?"

(C)

She was surprised and asked, "Wasn't he your father?" "No, he wasn't. I've never met him before," the soldier replied. She asked, "Then why didn't you say something when I took you to (c) him?" He said, "I knew there had been a mistake, but when I realized that he was too sick to tell whether or not I was his son, I could see how much (d) he needed me. So, I stayed."

(D)

The soldier gently wrapped his fingers around the weak hand of the old man. The nurse brought a chair so that the soldier could sit beside the bed. All through the night the young soldier sat there, holding the old man's hand and offering (e) him words of support and comfort. Occasionally, she suggested that the soldier take a rest for a while. He politely said no.

04

주어진 글 (A)에 이어질 내용을 순서에 맞게 배열한 것으로 가장 적절한 것은?

① (B) − (D) − (C) ② (C) − (B) − (D)
③ (C) − (D) − (B) ④ (D) − (B) − (C)
⑤ (D) − (C) − (B)

05 오답률 BEST

밑줄 친 (a) ~ (e) 중에서 가리키는 대상이 나머지 넷과 <u>다른</u> 것은?

① (a) ② (b) ③ (c) ④ (d) ⑤ (e)

06

윗글에 관한 내용으로 적절하지 <u>않은</u> 것은?

① 노인은 심장병으로 극심한 고통을 겪고 있었다.
② 군인은 간호사를 찾기 위해 병실을 나갔다.
③ 군인은 노인과 이전에 만난 적이 있다고 말했다.
④ 간호사는 군인이 앉을 수 있도록 의자를 가져왔다.
⑤ 군인은 잠시 쉬라는 간호사의 제안을 정중히 거절하였다.

[07~09]

다음 글을 읽고, 물음에 답하시오.

📄 202303 43~45번

(A)

Once upon a time, there was a king who lived in a beautiful palace. While the king was away, a monster approached the gates of the palace. The monster was so ugly and smelly that the guards froze in shock. He passed the guards and sat on the king's throne. The guards soon came to their senses, went in, and shouted at the monster, demanding that (a) <u>he</u> get off the throne.

＊ throne: 왕좌

(B)

Eventually the king returned. He was wise and kind and saw what was happening. He knew what to do. He smiled and said to the monster, "Welcome to my palace!" He asked the monster if (b) <u>he</u> wanted a cup of coffee. The monster began to grow smaller as he drank the coffee.

(C)

The king offered (c) <u>him</u> some takeout pizza and fries. The guards immediately called for pizza. The monster continued to get smaller with the king's kind gestures. (d) <u>He</u> then offered the monster a full body massage. As the guards helped with the relaxing massage, the monster became tiny. With another act of kindness to the monster, he just disappeared.

(D)

With each bad word the guards used, the monster grew more ugly and smelly. The guards got even angrier — they began to brandish their swords to scare the monster away from the palace. But (e) <u>he</u> just grew bigger and bigger, eventually taking up the whole room. He grew more ugly and smelly than ever.

＊ brandish: 휘두르다

07

주어진 글 (A)에 이어질 내용을 순서에 맞게 배열한 것으로 가장 적절한 것은?

① (B) – (D) – (C)　　　② (C) – (B) – (D)
③ (C) – (D) – (B)　　　④ (D) – (B) – (C)
⑤ (D) – (C) – (B)

08

밑줄 친 (a) ~ (e) 중에서 가리키는 대상이 나머지 넷과 <u>다른</u> 것은?

① (a)　　② (b)　　③ (c)　　④ (d)　　⑤ (e)

09

윗글에 관한 내용으로 적절하지 <u>않은</u> 것은?

① 왕이 없는 동안 괴물이 궁전 문으로 접근했다.
② 왕은 미소를 지으며 괴물에게 환영한다고 말했다.
③ 왕의 친절한 행동에 괴물의 몸이 계속 더 작아졌다.
④ 경비병들은 괴물을 마사지해 주기를 거부했다.
⑤ 경비병들은 겁을 주어 괴물을 쫓아내려 했다.

20강 2020~2023   **복합 문단의 이해**

[10~12]   202211 43~45번
다음 글을 읽고, 물음에 답하시오.

(A)

On my daughter Marie's 8th birthday, she received a bunch of presents from her friends at school. That evening, with her favorite present, a teddy bear, in her arms, we went to a restaurant to celebrate her birthday. Our server, a friendly woman, noticed my daughter holding the teddy bear and said, "My daughter loves teddy bears, too." Then, we started chatting about (a) <u>her</u> family.

(B)

When Marie came back out, I asked her what she had been doing. She said that she gave her teddy bear to our server so that she could give it to (b) <u>her</u> daughter. I was surprised at her sudden action because I could see how much she loved that bear already. (c) <u>She</u> must have seen the look on my face, because she said, "I can't imagine being stuck in a hospital bed. I just want her to get better soon."

(C)

I felt moved by Marie's words as we walked toward the car. Then, our server ran out to our car and thanked Marie for her generosity. The server said that (d) <u>she</u> had never had anyone doing anything like that for her family before. Later, Marie said it was her best birthday ever. I was so proud of her empathy and warmth, and this was an unforgettable experience for our family.

(D)

The server mentioned during the conversation that her daughter was in the hospital with a broken leg. (e) <u>She</u> also said that Marie looked about the same age as her daughter. She was so kind and attentive all evening, and even gave Marie cookies for free. After we finished our meal, we paid the bill and began to walk to our car when unexpectedly Marie asked me to wait and ran back into the restaurant.

10

주어진 글 (A)에 이어질 내용을 순서에 맞게 배열한 것으로 가장 적절한 것은?

① (B) – (D) – (C)   ② (C) – (B) – (D)
③ (C) – (D) – (B)   ④ (D) – (B) – (C)
⑤ (D) – (C) – (B)

★11 오답률 BEST

밑줄 친 (a) ~ (e) 중에서 가리키는 대상이 나머지 넷과 <u>다른</u> 것은?

① (a)   ② (b)   ③ (c)   ④ (d)   ⑤ (e)

12

윗글에 관한 내용으로 적절하지 <u>않은</u> 것은?

① Marie는 테디 베어를 팔에 안고 식당에 갔다.
② 'I'는 Marie의 갑작스러운 행동에 놀랐다.
③ 종업원은 Marie의 관대함에 고마워했다.
④ 종업원은 자신의 딸이 팔이 부러져서 병원에 있다고 말했다.
⑤ 종업원은 Marie에게 쿠키를 무료로 주었다.

[13~15]

📄 202209 43~45번

다음 글을 읽고, 물음에 답하시오.

(A)

A boy had a place at the best school in town. In the morning, his granddad took him to the school. When (a) he went onto the playground with his grandson, the children surrounded them. "What a funny old man," one boy smirked. A girl with brown hair pointed at the pair and jumped up and down. Suddenly, the bell rang and the children ran off to their first lesson.

* smirk: 히죽히죽 웃다

(B)

In some schools the children completely ignored the old man and in others, they made fun of (b) him. When this happened, he would turn sadly and go home. Finally, he went onto the tiny playground of a very small school, and leant against the fence, exhausted. The bell rang, and the crowd of children ran out onto the playground. "Sir, are you all right? Shall I bring you a glass of water?" a voice said. "We've got a bench in the playground — come and sit down," another voice said. Soon a young teacher came out onto the playground.

(C)

The old man greeted (c) him and said: "Finally, I've found my grandson the best school in town." "You're mistaken, sir. Our school is not the best — it's small and cramped." The old man didn't argue with the teacher. Instead, he made arrangements for his grandson to join the school, and then the old man left. That evening, the boy's mom said to (d) him: "Dad, you can't even read. How do you know you've found the best teacher of all?" "Judge a teacher by his pupils," the old man replied.

* cramped: 비좁은

(D)

The old man took his grandson firmly by the hand, and led him out of the school gate. "Brilliant, I don't have to go to school!" the boy exclaimed. "You do, but not this one," his granddad replied. "I'll find you a school myself." Granddad took his grandson back to his own house, asked grandma to look after him, and went off to look for a teacher (e) himself. Every time he spotted a school, the old man went onto the playground, and waited for the children to come out at break time.

13

주어진 글 (A)에 이어질 내용을 순서에 맞게 배열한 것으로 가장 적절한 것은?

① (B) – (D) – (C)   ② (C) – (B) – (D)
③ (C) – (D) – (B)   ④ (D) – (B) – (C)
⑤ (D) – (C) – (B)

14

밑줄 친 (a) ~ (e) 중에서 가리키는 대상이 나머지 넷과 다른 것은?

① (a)   ② (b)   ③ (c)   ④ (d)   ⑤ (e)

15

윗글에 관한 내용으로 적절하지 않은 것은?

① 갈색 머리 소녀가 노인과 소년을 향해 손가락질했다.
② 노인은 지쳐서 울타리에 기댔다.
③ 노인은 선생님과 논쟁을 벌였다.
④ 노인은 글을 읽을 줄 몰랐다.
⑤ 소년은 학교에 가지 않아도 된다고 소리쳤다.

[16~18] 📄 202206 43~45번

다음 글을 읽고, 물음에 답하시오.

(A)

Once, a farmer lost his precious watch while working in his barn. It may have appeared to be an ordinary watch to others, but it brought a lot of happy childhood memories to him. It was one of the most important things to (a) him. After searching for it for a long time, the old farmer became exhausted.

＊barn: 헛간(곡물·건초 따위를 두는 곳)

(B)

The number of children looking for the watch slowly decreased and only a few tired children were left. The farmer gave up all hope of finding it and called off the search. Just when the farmer was closing the barn door, a little boy came up to him and asked the farmer to give him another chance. The farmer did not want to lose out on any chance of finding the watch so let (b) him in the barn.

(C)

After a little while the boy came out with the farmer's watch in his hand. (c) He was happily surprised and asked how he had succeeded to find the watch while everyone else had failed. He replied "I just sat there and tried listening for the sound of the watch. In silence, it was much easier to hear it and follow the direction of the sound." (d) He was delighted to get his watch back and rewarded the little boy as promised.

(D)

However, the tired farmer did not want to give up on the search for his watch and asked a group of children playing outside to help him. (e) He promised an attractive reward for the person who could find it. After hearing about the reward, the children hurried inside the barn and went through and round the entire pile of hay looking for the watch. After a long time searching for it, some of the children got tired and gave up.

16

주어진 글 (A)에 이어질 내용을 순서에 맞게 배열한 것으로 가장 적절한 것은?

① (B) – (D) – (C)　　② (C) – (B) – (D)
③ (C) – (D) – (B)　　④ (D) – (B) – (C)
⑤ (D) – (C) – (B)

17

밑줄 친 (a) ～ (e) 중에서 가리키는 대상이 나머지 넷과 <u>다른</u> 것은?

① (a)　② (b)　③ (c)　④ (d)　⑤ (e)

18

윗글에 관한 내용으로 적절하지 <u>않은</u> 것은?

① 농부의 시계는 어린 시절의 행복한 기억을 불러일으켰다.
② 한 어린 소년이 농부에게 또 한 번의 기회를 달라고 요청했다.
③ 소년이 한 손에 농부의 시계를 들고 나왔다.
④ 아이들은 시계를 찾기 위해 헛간을 뛰쳐나왔다.
⑤ 아이들 중 일부는 지쳐서 시계 찾기를 포기했다.

[19~21]
📄 202203 43~45번

다음 글을 읽고, 물음에 답하시오.

(A)

One day a young man was walking along a road on his journey from one village to another. As he walked he noticed a monk working in the fields. The young man turned to the monk and said, "Excuse me. Do you mind if I ask (a) you a question?" "Not at all," replied the monk.

＊monk: 수도승

(B)

A while later a middle-aged man journeyed down the same road and came upon the monk. "I am going to the village in the valley," said the man. "Do you know what it is like?" "I do," replied the monk, "but first tell (b) me about the village where you came from." "I've come from the village in the mountains," said the man. "It was a wonderful experience. I felt as though I was a member of the family in the village."

(C)

"I am traveling from the village in the mountains to the village in the valley and I was wondering if (c) you knew what it is like in the village in the valley." "Tell me," said the monk, "what was your experience of the village in the mountains?" "Terrible," replied the young man. "I am glad to be away from there. I found the people most unwelcoming. So tell (d) me, what can I expect in the village in the valley?" "I am sorry to tell you," said the monk, "but I think your experience will be much the same there." The young man lowered his head helplessly and walked on.

(D)

"Why did you feel like that?" asked the monk. "The elders gave me much advice, and people were kind and generous. I am sad to have left there. And what is the village in the valley like?" he asked again. "(e) I think you will find it much the same," replied the monk. "I'm glad to hear that," the middle-aged man said smiling and journeyed on.

★19 오답률 BEST

주어진 글 (A)에 이어질 내용을 순서에 맞게 배열한 것으로 가장 적절한 것은?

① (B) – (D) – (C) ② (C) – (B) – (D)
③ (C) – (D) – (B) ④ (D) – (B) – (C)
⑤ (D) – (C) – (B)

★20 오답률 BEST

밑줄 친 (a) ~ (e) 중에서 가리키는 대상이 나머지 넷과 다른 것은?

① (a)   ② (b)   ③ (c)   ④ (d)   ⑤ (e)

21

윗글에 관한 내용으로 적절하지 않은 것은?

① 한 수도승이 들판에서 일하고 있었다.
② 중년 남자는 골짜기에 있는 마을로 가는 중이었다.
③ 수도승은 골짜기에 있는 마을에 대해 질문 받았다.
④ 수도승의 말을 듣고 젊은이는 고개를 숙였다.
⑤ 중년 남자는 산속에 있는 마을을 떠나서 기쁘다고 말했다.

20강
복합 문단의 이해

[22~24] 📄 202111 43~45번

다음 글을 읽고, 물음에 답하시오.

(A)

One day a poor man brought a bunch of grapes to a prince as a gift. He was very excited to be able to bring a gift for (a) him because he was too poor to afford more. He placed the grapes beside the prince and said, "Oh, Prince, please accept this small gift from me." His face beamed with happiness as he offered his small gift.

(B)

If the prince had offered the grapes to them, they might have made funny faces and shown their distaste for the grapes. That would have hurt the feelings of that poor man. He thought to himself that it would be better to eat all of them cheerfully and please (b) him. He did not want to hurt the feelings of that poor man. Everyone around him was moved by his thoughtfulness.

(C)

The prince thanked him politely. As the man looked at him expectantly, the prince ate one grape. Then (c) he ate another one. Slowly the prince finished the whole bunch of grapes by himself. He did not offer grapes to anyone near him. The man who brought those grapes to (d) him was very pleased and left. The close friends of the prince who were around him were very surprised.

(D)

Usually the prince shared whatever he had with others. He would offer them whatever he was given and they would eat it together. This time was different. Without offering it to anyone, (e) he finished the bunch of grapes by himself. One of the friends asked, "Prince! How come you ate all the grapes by yourself and did not offer them to any one of us?" He smiled and said that he ate all the grapes by himself because the grapes were too sour.

22

주어진 글 (A)에 이어질 내용을 순서에 맞게 배열한 것으로 가장 적절한 것은?

① (B) – (D) – (C) ② (C) – (B) – (D)
③ (C) – (D) – (B) ④ (D) – (B) – (C)
⑤ (D) – (C) – (B)

23

밑줄 친 (a) ~ (e) 중에서 가리키는 대상이 나머지 넷과 다른 것은?

① (a) ② (b) ③ (c) ④ (d) ⑤ (e)

24

윗글의 왕자에 관한 내용으로 적절하지 않은 것은?

① 가난한 남자에게 포도 한 송이를 선물로 받았다.
② 가난한 남자의 감정을 상하게 하고 싶지 않았다.
③ 곁에 있던 어떤 이에게도 포도를 권하지 않았다.
④ 가지고 있는 어떤 것이든 평소에 다른 사람들과 나눴다.
⑤ 포도가 너무 시어서 혼자 다 먹지 못했다.

[25~27]

202109 43~45번

다음 글을 읽고, 물음에 답하시오.

(A)

A rich merchant lived alone in his house. Knowing that he was the only person living in the house, he was always prepared in case thieves came to his house. So, one day, when a thief entered his home, he remained calm and cool. Although he was awake, the merchant pretended to be in a deep sleep. He lay in bed and watched the thief in action. The thief had brought a new white sheet with (a) him to carry away the stolen goods.

(B)

(b) He then lay down and pretended to be asleep. When the thief had finished collecting as many valuables as he could, he hurriedly tied a knot in the white sheet which he thought was his. The merchant meanwhile ran out into the garden and yelled — "Thief! Thief!" with all the air in his lungs. The thief got nervous and quickly lifted the sheet. To (c) his surprise, the thin white sheet, filled with stolen goods, was torn apart.

(C)

All the stolen goods fell down on the floor creating a very loud and unpleasant noise. Seeing many people run towards him, the thief had to give up on all of the stolen goods. Leaving the goods behind in the house, he ran away in a hurry saying under his breath: "This man is such a skillful merchant; he is a businessman to the core. He has not only managed to save his valuables but has also taken away (d) my new sheet. He has stolen from a thief!" As he said that to himself, he ran away from the house.

(D)

He spread it out on the floor with the idea of putting all the stolen valuables into it, tying it, and carrying it away. While (e) he was busy gathering expensive-looking items from the merchant's luxurious house, the merchant quickly got out of the bed. Then he replaced the new white sheet with a similar looking white sheet, which was much weaker and much cheaper than the thief's one.

25

주어진 글 (A)에 이어질 내용을 순서에 맞게 배열한 것으로 가장 적절한 것은?

① (B) – (D) – (C) ② (C) – (B) – (D)
③ (C) – (D) – (B) ④ (D) – (B) – (C)
⑤ (D) – (C) – (B)

26 오답률 BEST

밑줄 친 (a) ~ (e) 중에서 가리키는 대상이 나머지 넷과 다른 것은?

① (a) ② (b) ③ (c) ④ (d) ⑤ (e)

27

윗글에 관한 내용으로 적절하지 않은 것은?

① 상인은 도둑이 드는 상황에 항상 대비하고 있었다.
② 상인은 정원으로 뛰어나가 크게 소리쳤다.
③ 도둑이 훔친 물건들이 바닥에 떨어졌다.
④ 도둑은 상인의 물건들을 집밖으로 가지고 달아났다.
⑤ 상인의 보자기는 도둑의 보자기보다 값싼 것이었다.

[28~30]

📄 202106 43~45번

다음 글을 읽고, 물음에 답하시오.

(A)

When I was 17, I discovered a wonderful thing. My father and I were sitting on the floor of his study. We were organizing his old papers. Across the carpet I saw a fat paper clip. Its rust dusted the cover sheet of a report of some kind. I picked it up. I started to read. Then I started to cry.

(B)

"Daddy," I said, handing him the pages, "this speech — how did you ever get permission to give it? And weren't you scared?" "Well, honey," he said, "I didn't ask for permission. I just asked myself, 'What is the most important challenge facing my generation?' I knew immediately. Then (a) I asked myself, 'And if I weren't afraid, what would I say about it in this speech?'"

(C)

It was a speech he had written in 1920, in Tennessee. Then only 17 himself and graduating from high school, he had called for equality for African Americans. (b) I marvelled, proud of him, and wondered how, in 1920, so young, so white, and in the deep South, where the law still separated black from white, (c) he had had the courage to deliver it. I asked him about it.

(D)

"I wrote it. And I delivered it. About half way through I looked out to see the entire audience of teachers, students, and parents stand up — and walk out. Left alone on the stage, (d) I thought to myself, 'Well, I guess I need to be sure to do only two things with my life: keep thinking for myself, and not get killed.'" He handed the speech back to me, and smiled. "(e) You seem to have done both," I said.

28

주어진 글 (A)에 이어질 내용을 순서에 맞게 배열한 것으로 가장 적절한 것은?

① (B) – (D) – (C) ② (C) – (B) – (D)
③ (C) – (D) – (B) ④ (D) – (B) – (C)
⑤ (D) – (C) – (B)

29 오답률 BEST

밑줄 친 (a) ~ (e) 중에서 가리키는 대상이 나머지 넷과 다른 것은?

① (a) ② (b) ③ (c) ④ (d) ⑤ (e)

30

윗글에 관한 내용으로 적절하지 않은 것은?

① 아버지와 나는 서류를 정리하고 있었다.
② 나는 서재에서 발견한 것을 읽고 나서 울기 시작했다.
③ 아버지는 연설을 하기 위한 허락을 구하지 않았다.
④ 아버지가 연설문을 썼을 당시 17세였다.
⑤ 교사, 학생, 학부모 모두 아버지의 연설을 끝까지 들었다.

[31~33]

📄 202103 43~45번

다음 글을 읽고, 물음에 답하시오.

(A)

Once upon a time, there lived a young king who had a great passion for hunting. His kingdom was located at the foot of the Himalayas. Once every year, he would go hunting in the nearby forests. (a) He would make all the necessary preparations, and then set out for his hunting trip.

(B)

Seasons changed. A year passed by. And it was time to go hunting once again. The king went to the same forest as the previous year. (b) He used his beautiful deerskin drum to round up animals. But none came. All the animals ran for safety, except one doe. She came closer and closer to the drummer. Suddenly, she started fearlessly licking the deerskin drum.

* round up: ~을 몰다 ** doe: 암사슴

(C)

Like all other years, the hunting season had arrived. Preparations began in the palace and the king got ready for (c) his hunting trip. Deep in the forest, he spotted a beautiful wild deer. It was a large stag. His aim was perfect. When he killed the deer with just one shot of his arrow, the king was filled with pride. (d) The proud hunter ordered a hunting drum to be made out of the skin of the deer.

* stag: 수사슴

(D)

The king was surprised by this sight. An old servant had an answer to this strange behavior. "The deerskin used to make this drum belonged to her mate, the deer who we hunted last year. This doe is mourning the death of her mate," (e) the man said. Upon hearing this, the king had a change of heart. He had never realized that an animal, too, felt the pain of loss. He made a promise, from that day on, to never again hunt wild animals.

* mourn: 애도하다

31

주어진 글 (A)에 이어질 내용을 순서에 맞게 배열한 것으로 가장 적절한 것은?

① (B) – (D) – (C) ② (C) – (B) – (D)
③ (C) – (D) – (B) ④ (D) – (B) – (C)
⑤ (D) – (C) – (B)

32

밑줄 친 (a) ~ (e) 중에서 가리키는 대상이 나머지 넷과 다른 것은?

① (a) ② (b) ③ (c) ④ (d) ⑤ (e)

33

윗글에 관한 내용으로 적절하지 않은 것은?

① 왕은 매년 근처의 숲으로 사냥 여행을 갔다.
② 암사슴은 북 치는 사람으로부터 도망갔다.
③ 왕은 화살로 단번에 수사슴을 맞혔다.
④ 한 나이 든 신하가 암사슴의 행동의 이유를 알고 있었다.
⑤ 왕은 다시는 야생 동물을 사냥하지 않겠다고 약속했다.

◆ 정답 및 해설(2권) p. 199

[34~36]
202011 43~45번
다음 글을 읽고, 물음에 답하시오.

(A)

James Walker was a renowned wrestler and he made his living through wrestling. In his town, there was a tradition in which the leader of the town chose a day when James demonstrated his skills. The leader announced one day that James would exhibit his skills as a wrestler and asked the people if there was anyone to challenge (a) him for the prize money.

(B)

When James saw the old man, he was speechless. Like everyone else, he thought that the old man had a death wish. The old man asked James to come closer since (b) he wanted to say something to him. James moved closer and the old man whispered, "I know it is impossible for me to win but my children are starving at home. Can you lose this competition to me so I can feed them with the prize money?"

(C)

Everyone was looking around in the crowd when an old man stood up and said with a shaking voice, "I will enter the contest against (c) him." Everyone burst out laughing thinking that it was a joke. James would crush him in a minute. According to the law, the leader could not stop someone who of his own free will entered the competition, so he allowed the old man to challenge the wrestler.

(D)

James thought he had an excellent opportunity to help a man in distress. (d) He did a couple of moves so that no one would suspect that the competition was fixed. However, he did not use his full strength and allowed the old man to win. The old man was overjoyed when he received the prize money. That night James felt the most victorious (e) he had ever felt.

34

주어진 글 (A)에 이어질 내용을 순서에 맞게 배열한 것으로 가장 적절한 것은?

① (B) – (D) – (C) ② (C) – (B) – (D)
③ (C) – (D) – (B) ④ (D) – (B) – (C)
⑤ (D) – (C) – (B)

35

밑줄 친 (a) ~ (e) 중에서 가리키는 대상이 나머지 넷과 다른 것은?

① (a) ② (b) ③ (c) ④ (d) ⑤ (e)

36

윗글에 관한 내용으로 적절하지 않은 것은?

① James는 레슬링으로 생계를 유지했다.
② James는 노인을 보고 말문이 막혔다.
③ 노인의 아이들은 집에서 굶주리고 있었다.
④ 지도자는 노인이 James와 겨루는 것을 말렸다.
⑤ James는 노인과의 시합에서 전력을 다하지 않았다.

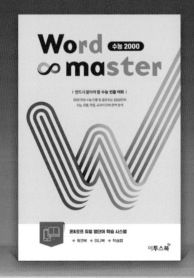

회차	문항 번호와 정답									
1회	01 ⑤	02 ①	03 ③	04 ⑤	05 ①	06 ③	07 ④	08 ③	09 ④	10 ④
	11 ①	12 ④	13 ①	14 ③	15 ⑤	16 ③	17 ③			
2회	01 ②	02 ①	03 ①	04 ④	05 ⑤	06 ③	07 ④	08 ③	09 ⑤	10 ④
	11 ①	12 ③	13 ②	14 ⑤	15 ⑤	16 ③	17 ④			
3회	01 ⑤	02 ⑤	03 ③	04 ⑤	05 ②	06 ②	07 ①	08 ③	09 ④	10 ②
	11 ②	12 ①	13 ③	14 ①	15 ③	16 ③	17 ④			
4회	01 ①	02 ①	03 ②	04 ④	05 ⑤	06 ④	07 ①	08 ③	09 ④	10 ②
	11 ①	12 ②	13 ③	14 ①	15 ②	16 ②	17 ④			
5회	01 ③	02 ⑤	03 ②	04 ④	05 ④	06 ③	07 ②	08 ②	09 ⑤	10 ③
	11 ③	12 ①	13 ①	14 ③	15 ④	16 ①	17 ④			
6회	01 ②	02 ①	03 ⑤	04 ⑤	05 ①	06 ③	07 ①	08 ⑤	09 ⑤	10 ④
	11 ①	12 ③	13 ③	14 ④	15 ④	16 ②	17 ③			
7회	01 ①	02 ③	03 ②	04 ④	05 ④	06 ③	07 ①	08 ③	09 ⑤	10 ③
	11 ①	12 ⑤	13 ②	14 ②	15 ①	16 ④	17 ④			
8회	01 ②	02 ③	03 ①	04 ⑤	05 ②	06 ③	07 ①	08 ④	09 ④	10 ③
	11 ①	12 ①	13 ⑤	14 ②	15 ③	16 ④	17 ⑤			
9회	01 ④	02 ②	03 ③	04 ③	05 ⑤	06 ③	07 ②	08 ③	09 ④	10 ②
	11 ①	12 ①	13 ③	14 ①	15 ④	16 ②	17 ③			
10회	01 ②	02 ②	03 ②	04 ④	05 ④	06 ①	07 ③	08 ③	09 ④	10 ③
	11 ②	12 ⑤	13 ①	14 ⑤	15 ③	16 ③	17 ④			
11회	01 ④	02 ④	03 ①	04 ③	05 ④	06 ③	07 ①	08 ②	09 ⑤	10 ②
	11 ①	12 ①	13 ②	14 ③	15 ④	16 ②	17 ④			
12회	01 ②	02 ①	03 ②	04 ③	05 ③	06 ③	07 ②	08 ⑤	09 ⑤	10 ④
	11 ⑤	12 ④	13 ①	14 ⑤	15 ③	16 ④	17 ④			

강	문항 번호와 정답											
1강	01 ⑤	02 ②	03 ③	04 ②	05 ⑤	06 ②	07 ②	08 ⑤	09 ②	10 ①	11 ④	12 ③
2강	01 ②	02 ①	03 ②	04 ②	05 ②	06 ②	07 ③	08 ⑤	09 ⑤	10 ③	11 ①	12 ①
3강	01 ②	02 ⑤	03 ⑤	04 ⑤	05 ④	06 ⑤	07 ⑤	08 ③	09 ③	10 ①	11 ③	12 ②
4강	01 ⑤	02 ①	03 ⑤	04 ③	05 ③	06 ③	07 ⑤	08 ④	09 ⑤	10 ①	11 ①	12 ①
5강	01 ④	02 ③	03 ①	04 ①	05 ①	06 ①	07 ①	08 ③	09 ⑤	10 ⑤	11 ⑤	12 ④
6강	01 ②	02 ②	03 ①	04 ⑤	05 ②	06 ②	07 ④	08 ①	09 ①	10 ②	11 ①	12 ①
7강	01 ①	02 ①	03 ②	04 ④	05 ①	06 ①	07 ②	08 ②	09 ④	10 ①	11 ①	12 ③
8강	01 ④	02 ④	03 ⑤	04 ④	05 ③	06 ⑤	07 ⑤	08 ④	09 ④	10 ⑤	11 ③	12 ⑤
9강	01 ④	02 ③	03 ⑤	04 ③	05 ④	06 ③	07 ③	08 ④	09 ⑤	10 ③	11 ⑤	12 ④
10강	01 ④	02 ⑤	03 ⑤	04 ⑤	05 ③	06 ④	07 ⑤	08 ③	09 ④	10 ④	11 ④	12 ④
	13 ④	14 ⑤	15 ②	16 ④	17 ②	18 ⑤	19 ⑤	20 ④	21 ⑤	22 ④	23 ⑤	24 ⑤
11강	01 ④	02 ④	03 ⑤	04 ④	05 ③	06 ④	07 ③	08 ④	09 ②	10 ④	11 ③	12 ④
12강	01 ②	02 ②	03 ④	04 ④	05 ②	06 ②	07 ⑤	08 ⑤	09 ④	10 ③	11 ③	12 ③
13강	01 ①	02 ③	03 ④	04 ①	05 ②	06 ③	07 ③	08 ②	09 ②	10 ⑤	11 ③	12 ②
	13 ②	14 ③	15 ②	16 ①	17 ①	18 ⑤	19 ①	20 ⑤	21 ⑤	22 ④	23 ②	24 ①
14강	01 ②	02 ①	03 ③	04 ③	05 ①	06 ③	07 ③	08 ③	09 ①	10 ④	11 ③	12 ②
	13 ①	14 ①	15 ②	16 ④	17 ①	18 ⑤	19 ①	20 ④	21 ①	22 ⑤	23 ①	24 ③
15강	01 ②	02 ④	03 ④	04 ④	05 ④	06 ②	07 ④	08 ③	09 ④	10 ④	11 ③	12 ④
16강	01 ②	02 ③	03 ②	04 ⑤	05 ④	06 ②	07 ③	08 ⑤	09 ②	10 ⑤	11 ③	12 ⑤
	13 ③	14 ②	15 ③	16 ⑤	17 ⑤	18 ④	19 ⑤	20 ②	21 ②	22 ③	23 ②	24 ④
17강	01 ⑤	02 ⑤	03 ②	04 ⑤	05 ④	06 ⑤	07 ⑤	08 ③	09 ④	10 ⑤	11 ④	12 ⑤
	13 ④	14 ②	15 ④	16 ⑤	17 ③	18 ②	19 ②	20 ④	21 ②	22 ④	23 ③	24 ③
18강	01 ①	02 ②	03 ①	04 ②	05 ①	06 ③	07 ①	08 ②	09 ①	10 ①	11 ③	12 ①
19강	01 ②	02 ⑤	03 ①	04 ③	05 ②	06 ③	07 ①	08 ⑤	09 ②	10 ④	11 ①	12 ④
	13 ⑤	14 ⑤	15 ①	16 ④	17 ②	18 ④	19 ⑤	20 ④	21 ①	22 ⑤	23 ②	24 ⑤
20강	01 ④	02 ③	03 ④	04 ④	05 ⑤	06 ③	07 ④	08 ④	09 ④	10 ④	11 ③	12 ④
	13 ④	14 ③	15 ③	16 ④	17 ②	18 ④	19 ③	20 ④	21 ⑤	22 ③	23 ②	24 ⑤
	25 ④	26 ②	27 ④	28 ②	29 ②	30 ⑤	31 ②	32 ⑤	33 ②	34 ②	35 ②	36 ④

기출의 바이블

고1 영어

1권 │ 듣기편 + 독해편

특별부록

기출 EXTRACT

· 기출 독해 어휘 리스트
· 기출 문법 드릴 문항 제공

1권

◆ **Part 1** │ 듣기편
◆ **Part 2** │ 독해편

Part 1 · 최신 3개년 전국연합 학력평가 듣기 모의고사 12회 수록
· 전 회차 Dictation 제공

Part 2 · 최신 연도순 유형별 20강 수록
· 오답률 BEST 문항 표기

2권

정답 및 해설

· 정답 근거, 핵심 문장, 주제문 표시
· 구문 분석과 중요 숙어 표현 표시
· 선택지 완벽 분석과 자세한 해설
· 필수 어휘 정리

가르치기 쉽고 빠르게 배울 수 있는 **이투스북**

www.etoosbook.com

○ **도서 내용 문의**
홈페이지 > 이투스북 고객센터 > 1:1 문의

○ **도서 정답 및 해설**
홈페이지 > 도서자료실 > 정답/해설

○ **도서 정오표**
홈페이지 > 도서자료실 > 정오표

○ **선생님을 위한 강의 지원 서비스 T폴더**
홈페이지 > 교강사 T폴더

기출의 바이블

Bible of English

2권 **정답 및 해설**

| 선택지 완벽 분석과 자세한 해설 |

이투스북

기출의 바이블

고1 영어

정답 및 해설

듣기편

정답 및 해설

1회 **2023학년도 9월** | **고1 전국연합 학력평가** | 1권 p. 10

01 ⑤	02 ①	03 ③	04 ⑤	05 ①	06 ③
07 ④	08 ③	09 ④	10 ④	11 ①	12 ④
13 ①	14 ③	15 ⑤	16 ③	17 ③	

01 정답 ⑤

정답률 94%

M Attention, Fargo High School students. This is your music teacher, Mr. Nelson. Our school rock band was supposed to hold its concert in the auditorium today. I'm sure you've been looking forward to the concert. Unfortunately, the rain yesterday caused a leak in the ceiling of the auditorium. The ceiling needs to be fixed, so we decided to change the location of the concert. The rock band will now perform in the school theater. The time for the concert hasn't changed. I hope you'll enjoy the performance.

해석

남 Fargo 고등학교 학생 여러분, 주목하세요. 음악 선생님 Nelson입니다. 오늘 저희 학교 록 밴드가 강당에서 콘서트를 열기로 되어 있었습니다. 공연을 기대하셨을 거예요. 안타깝게도, 어제 내린 비로 인해 강당 천장에 누수가 발생했습니다. 천장을 수리해야 해서 공연 장소를 변경하기로 결정했습니다. 록 밴드는 학교 극장에서 공연을 하게 되었습니다. 공연 시간은 바뀌지 않았습니다. 공연을 즐겨 주시기를 바랍니다.

어휘

attention 주목 be supposed to ~하기로 되어 있다 hold 열다, 개최하다 auditorium 강당 look forward to ~하기를 고대하다 leak 누수, 새는 곳 perform 공연하다, 연주하다

02 정답 ①

정답률 98%

W Simon, are you doing anything after school?
M Nothing special. What about you?
W I'm planning to go for a run in the park. It's a five-kilometer route.
M The weather is perfect for running. Can I go with you?
W Why not? *[Pause]* Wait! You're wearing slippers. Those aren't good for running.
M It's okay. I can run in slippers.
W No way. Slippers aren't designed for running. You can get hurt if you run in them.
M You mean I need to put on running shoes?
W You got it. You need to wear the right shoes for running.
M All right. I'll go home and change.

해석

여 Simon, 방과 후에 뭐 할 거야?
남 특별한 건 없어. 너는 어때?

여 공원에서 달리기를 할 계획이야. 5킬로미터 경로야.
남 달리기에 딱 좋은 날씨네. 같이 가도 될까?
여 왜 안 되겠어? *[잠시 후]* 너 슬리퍼 신었네. 달리기에 안 좋은 신발이잖아.
남 괜찮아. 슬리퍼 신고 달릴 수 있어.
여 말도 안 돼. 슬리퍼는 달리기 위한 것이 아니야. 그걸 신고 달리면 다칠 수도 있어.
남 운동화를 신어야 한다는 의미야?
여 맞아. 달리기에 알맞은 신발을 신어야 해.
남 알겠어. 집에 가서 갈아 신고 올게.

어휘

route 길, 경로, 루트 get hurt 다치다

03 정답 ③

정답률 92%

M Good morning, Ms. Clapton. It's nice to meet you.
W Nice to meet you, too. I'm a fan of your articles.
M You won many awards at the film festival this year. Congratulations!
W Thank you. I was lucky to work with a great director and talented actors.
M The clothes and accessories in the movie are impressive. How do you start your costume designs?
W I read the script to fully understand the characters. Then I research the characters' backgrounds.
M That sounds like a lot of work. Which of the costumes from this film is your favorite?
W It's hard to pick just one because I love all of my designs.
M I totally understand. Thank you for sharing your story with the readers of our magazine.
W It was my pleasure.

해석

남 좋은 아침이에요, Clapton 씨. 만나서 반갑습니다.
여 저도 만나서 반갑습니다. 당신 기사의 팬이에요.
남 당신은 올해 영화제에서 많은 상을 수상하셨네요. 축하드려요!
여 감사합니다. 좋은 감독님과 재능 있는 배우들과 함께 작업할 수 있어서 행운이었습니다.
남 영화 속 의상과 액세서리가 인상적이에요. 의상 디자인은 어떻게 시작하나요?
여 등장인물들을 충분히 이해하기 위해 대본을 읽죠. 그런 다음 등장인물들의 배경을 조사해요.
남 작업량이 많을 것 같네요. 이 영화에서 어떤 의상이 가장 좋은가요?
여 제가 제 디자인을 모두 다 좋아해서 하나만 고르기는 어려워요.
남 완전히 이해해요. 저희 잡지의 독자들과 이야기를 공유해 주셔서 감사합니다.
여 저도 즐거웠어요.

어휘

article 기사 win an award 상을 받다 talented 재능 있는 impressive 인상적인 costume 의상 script 대본 character 등장인물 research 조사하다 share 공유하다, 나누다

04 정답 ⑤

정답률 87%

W Come look at the new reading room in the library.
M Wow! It's much better than I thought.
W Same here. I like the rug in the center of the room.
M The striped pattern of the rug makes the room feel warm.
W I agree. I think putting the sofa between two plants was a good idea.
M Right. We can sit there and read for hours.
W There's a round clock on the wall.
M I have the same clock at home. Oh, the bookshelf under the clock is full of books.
W We can read the books at the long table.
M Yeah, it looks like a good place to read. The two lamps on the table will make it easy to focus.
W Good lighting is important for reading.
M I can't wait to start using the reading room.

해석

여 도서관에 새로 생긴 열람실을 구경하러 오세요.
남 와! 생각보다 훨씬 더 좋은데요.
여 저도 마찬가지입니다. 방 중앙에 있는 러그가 마음에 들어요.
남 러그의 줄무늬 패턴이 그 방을 따뜻하게 만들어 주네요.
여 동의해요. 두 식물 사이에 소파를 두는 것도 좋은 생각이었던 것 같아요.
남 맞아요. 거기 앉아서 몇 시간 동안 책을 읽을 수 있어요.
여 벽에 둥근 시계가 있네요.
남 저도 집에 똑같은 시계가 있어요. 오, 시계 밑에 있는 책장이 책으로 가득하네요.
여 긴 탁자에서 책을 읽을 수 있어요.
남 네, 책 읽기 좋은 곳 같아요. 탁자 위에 있는 램프 두 개가 집중하기 쉽게 해 줄 거예요.
여 좋은 조명은 독서에 중요하죠.
남 독서실을 이용하는 것을 빨리 시작하고 싶네요.

어휘

rug 러그, 깔개 striped pattern 줄무늬 be full of ~으로 가득하다
focus 집중하다 lightning 조명

05 정답 ①

정답률 90%

M Kelly, the school musical is tomorrow. Shall we go over the final checklist together?
W Let's do it. What's first? [Pause] Oh, the posters. We put them up around school last week.
M Right. Do we have extra batteries for the wireless microphones?
W Yeah. I bought them yesterday. We should check that the microphones work well with the sound system.
M I did that this morning. They sound terrific.
W How about the stage lights?
M They work perfectly. I think everyone will love the lighting design you made.
W Really? Thanks. It looks like we've finished everything.

M No, wait. The chairs for the audience haven't been arranged yet.
W You're right! I'll go take care of that now.
M The musical is going to be fantastic.

해석

남 Kelly, 학교 뮤지컬이 내일이야. 최종 체크리스트를 같이 검토해 볼까?
여 그러자. 첫 번째가 뭘까? [잠시 후] 아, 포스터. 지난주에 학교 근처에 붙였어.
남 맞아. 무선 마이크에 쓸 여분의 배터리가 있나?
여 응. 어제 샀어. 마이크가 음향 시스템과 잘 맞는지 확인해 봐야 해.
남 오늘 아침에 해 봤어. 소리가 정말 좋아.
여 무대 조명은 어때?
남 완벽하게 작동해. 네가 만든 조명 디자인을 모두가 좋아할 것 같아.
여 정말? 고마워. 다 끝낸 것 같네.
남 아니, 잠시만. 아직 관객용 의자가 마련되지 않았어.
여 네 말이 맞아! 내가 지금 가서 처리할게.
남 뮤지컬은 정말 환상적일 거야.

어휘

go over 점검하다, 살피다 wireless microphone 무선 마이크
terrific 아주 좋은, 엄청난 audience 청중, 관객 be arranged 준비되다, 마련되다
take care of ~을 처리하다 fantastic 환상적인

06 정답 ③

정답률 84%

W Welcome to Libby's Flowers. How can I help you?
M I'd like to order a rose basket for my parents' wedding anniversary.
W All right. Our rose baskets come in two sizes.
M What are the options?
W The regular size is 30 dollars, and the large size is 50 dollars.
M Hmm... I think the bigger one is better.
W Good choice. So, you'll get one rose basket in the large size. By the way, we're giving a 10-percent discount on all purchases this week.
M Excellent! When will my order be ready?
W It'll be ready around 11 a.m. If you can't pick it up, we offer a delivery service. It's 10 dollars.
M Oh, great. I'd like it to be delivered. Here's my credit card.

해석

여 Libby의 꽃집에 오신 것을 환영합니다. 어떻게 도와드릴까요?
남 부모님 결혼기념일에 장미꽃 바구니를 주문하고 싶어요.
여 알겠습니다. 저희 장미 바구니는 두 가지 사이즈가 있습니다.
남 어떤 옵션이 있나요?
여 일반 사이즈는 30달러이고, 라지 사이즈는 50달러예요.
남 음… 더 큰 게 더 좋은 것 같아요.
여 좋은 선택이에요. 그래서 장미 바구니를 라지 사이즈로 하나 가져가실 거고요. 그런데 이번 주에는 모든 구매에 대해 10% 할인을 해 드리고 있어요.
남 좋네요! 주문한 것은 언제쯤 준비될까요?
여 오전 11시쯤에 준비될 거예요. 가져가실 수 없으면, 배달 서비스를 해 드려요. 10달러입니다.
남 오, 잘됐네요. 배달되면 좋겠어요. 여기 제 신용 카드요.

해설

남자는 부모님 결혼기념일 선물로 50달러인 장미 바구니 라지 사이즈를 구매했다. 10% 할인으로 45달러를 지불해야 하는데, 더불어 10달러인 배달 서비스를 요청했

으로, 남자가 지불해야 할 총 금액은 ③ '$55'(55달러)이다.

어휘

order 주문하다; 주문   anniversary 기념일   regular 정기적인, 일반적인
discount 할인   purchase 구매   delivery service 배달 서비스

07 정답 ④

M You seem busy this morning, Olivia.
W I am. I had to see Professor Martin about my history test.
M Oh, I see. Do you remember that our club's ski trip is this weekend?
W Yeah. I heard that a nice ski resort has been booked for the trip.
M I didn't know that. I'm so excited to go skiing at a nice resort.
W I bet it'll be great, but I don't think I can go this time.
M Why? You don't work at the cafe on the weekends, do you?
W No, I don't. But I need to take care of my cat. She's recovering from surgery.
M Isn't there anyone else who can look after your cat?
W No one but me. My parents are visiting relatives in Canada. They won't be back for two weeks.
M I'm sorry that you can't join us.
W Me, too. Have fun this weekend.

해석

남 오늘 아침에 바빠 보이네, Olivia.
여 그래. 역사 시험 때문에 Martin 교수님을 뵈어야 했거든.
남 아, 그렇구나. 우리 동아리 스키 여행이 이번 주말인 거 기억하지?
여 응. 이번 여행에 좋은 스키장이 예약되었다고 들었어.
남 나는 그건 몰랐네. 좋은 리조트에서 스키를 타다니 너무 신나.
여 분명 좋을 것 같은데, 나는 이번에는 못 갈 것 같아.
남 왜? 주말에는 카페에서 일하지 않잖아, 그렇지?
여 아니, 안 해. 하지만 고양이를 돌봐야 하거든. 고양이가 수술을 받고 회복 중이야.
남 고양이를 돌봐 줄 다른 누군가가 없어?
여 나 말고는 아무도 없어. 부모님께서 캐나다에 계신 친척들을 방문하실 거거든. 2주 동안은 안 오실 거야.
남 우리와 함께하지 못한다니 아쉬워.
여 나도. 이번 주말 재미있게 보내.

어휘

be booked 예약되다   recover 회복하다   surgery 수술   look after ~을 돌보다
relative 친척

08 정답 ③

W What are you doing, Tim?
M I'm looking at the Street Photography Contest website.
W I've heard about that. It's a contest for college students, right?
M Actually, it's open to high school students, too. Why don't you try it?

W Really? Maybe I will. Does the contest have a theme?
M Sure. This year's theme is Daily Life.
W That sounds interesting. When is the deadline?
M You have to submit your photographs by September 15.
W That's sooner than I expected.
M You should hurry and choose your photos. The winner will receive a laptop as a prize.
W Okay! Wish me luck.

해석

여 뭐 하고 있어, Tim?
남 길거리 사진 공모전 웹사이트를 보고 있어.
여 그것에 대한 얘기 들었어. 대학생을 위한 대회 맞지?
남 사실 고등학생들에게도 열려 있어. 한번 해 보는 게 어때?
여 정말? 그럴 수도. 대회 주제가 있니?
남 물론이지. 올해의 주제는 '일상생활'이야.
여 흥미롭네. 마감일이 언제야?
남 9월 15일까지 사진을 제출해야 해.
여 기대했던 것보다 더 빠르네.
남 사진을 서둘러 골라야 해. 우승자는 상품으로 노트북 컴퓨터를 받을 거야.
여 좋아! 행운을 빌어 줘.

어휘

college 대학   theme 주제   deadline 마감 기한   submit 제출하다
laptop 노트북 컴퓨터

09 정답 ④

M Hello, listeners. I'm Charlie Anderson from the Twin Stars Chocolate Museum. I'm happy to introduce the Twin Stars Chocolate Day, a special opportunity to create your own delicious chocolates. It'll be held on November 12 from 1 p.m. to 4 p.m. First, you'll listen to a lecture about the history of chocolate. Then you'll have a chance to taste our most popular flavors. At the end of the event, you'll make five chocolates yourself. If you want to take part in the event, you must register in advance. You can sign up on our website until November 1. The registration fee is 20 dollars, which includes the cost of ingredients. Don't miss this sweet opportunity!

해석

남 안녕하세요, 청취자 여러분. 저는 Twin Stars 초콜릿 박물관의 Charlie Anderson입니다. 여러분만의 맛있는 초콜릿을 만들 수 있는 특별한 기회인 Twin Stars Chocolate Day를 소개하게 되어 기쁩니다. 11월 12일 오후 1시부터 4시까지 열릴 것입니다. 먼저, 초콜릿의 역사에 대한 강의를 들을 것입니다. 그리고 나서 우리의 가장 인기 있는 맛을 맛볼 기회가 있을 것입니다. 행사의 마지막에는, 5개의 초콜릿을 직접 만들 것입니다. 만약 행사에 참여하고 싶다면, 사전에 등록하셔야 합니다. 11월 1일까지 우리의 웹사이트에서 등록할 수 있습니다. 등록비는 20달러인데, 재료비가 포함된 가격입니다. 이 달콤한 기회를 놓치지 마세요!

어휘

opportunity 기회   flavor 맛, 풍미   take part in ~에 참여하다
in advance 사전에, 미리   sign up 등록하다   registration fee 등록비, 참가비
include 포함하다   ingredient (요리 등의) 재료

10 정답 ④

정답률 92%

M Honey, what are you looking at?

W I'm looking at indoor cycling bikes. Would you like to choose one together?

M Sure, let me see. *[Pause]* The price differs by model.

W I don't want to pay more than 300 dollars. That's too expensive.

M I agree. Which color do you like?

W I prefer a dark color because it goes well with our living room.

M Okay. Then we shouldn't get a white one. What do you think about the foldable one?

W We definitely need that. It'll take up less storage space.

M We have just two options left. Which one should we get?

W I think we should go with the one with a higher customer rating. The reviews are based on actual customers' experiences.

M Sounds good. Let's order this one.

해석

남 여보, 뭘 보고 있나요?

여 실내 자전거를 보고 있어요. 같이 고를래요?

남 물론이죠, 어디 한번 볼게요. *[잠시 후]* 모델별로 가격이 다르네요.

여 300달러 이상은 지불하고 싶지 않아요. 그건 너무 비싸요.

남 동의해요. 어떤 색이 좋아요?

여 우리 거실과 잘 어울려서 어두운 색이 더 좋네요.

남 좋아요. 그럼 흰색은 구매하지 않아야겠어요. 접을 수 있는 건 어때요?

여 우리는 그것이 꼭 필요해요. 그것은 저장 공간을 덜 차지할 거예요.

남 이제 두 가지 옵션만 남았네요. 어떤 걸로 살까요?

여 고객 등급이 더 높은 걸로 해야 할 것 같아요. 그 후기들은 실제 고객의 경험을 바탕으로 한 거예요.

남 좋아요. 이걸로 주문하죠.

어휘

prefer 더 좋아하다, 선호하다   foldable 접을 수 있는   take up 차지하다
storage space 저장 공간   customer rating 고객 등급

11 정답 ①

정답률 93%

W Jason, is that a new sweater? It looks good on you.

M Thanks. I bought it online. It was on sale.

W I'd love to buy the same one for my brother. Can you tell me where you got it?

M Sure. I'll send you a link to the website.

해석

여 Jason, 새 스웨터네? 너한테 잘 어울려.

남 고마워. 인터넷으로 구매했어. 할인 중이었거든.

여 오빠한테 똑같은 거 사 주고 싶어. 어디에서 샀는지 말해 줄 수 있어?

남 물론. 홈페이지 링크를 보내 줄게.

② 다른 색이 더 좋아 보여.

③ 미안해. 네 스웨터를 가져오는 걸 깜빡했어.

④ 반품하려면 영수증이 필요해.

⑤ 오빠도 할인해서 그걸 샀어.

어휘

look good on ~에게 어울리다   on sale 할인 중인

12 정답 ④

정답률 83%

M Becky, did you order our food for dinner?

W Yes. I ordered pizza about an hour ago.

M An hour ago? Delivery usually takes less than 40 minutes.

W I'll call the restaurant and check our order.

해석

남 Becky, 저녁 식사 주문했어?

여 응. 한 시간 전쯤에 피자를 주문했어.

남 한 시간 전? 배달은 보통 40분이 안 걸리는데.

여 식당에 전화해서 주문을 확인해 볼게.

① 남은 음식은 집으로 가져가자.

② 나는 피자보다 프라이드치킨이 더 좋아.

③ 오늘은 점심 먹으러 나가고 싶지 않아.

⑤ 편지가 잘못된 주소로 배달되었어.

어휘

delivery 배달   less than ~보다 적게

13 정답 ①

정답률 89%

W I haven't seen you in the cafeteria this week. Where have you been?

M I've been in the library working on my science project.

W Does that mean you've been skipping lunch?

M Yeah. This project is really important for my grade.

W You shouldn't do that. It's not good for your health.

M Don't worry. I always have a big dinner when I get home.

W That's the problem. Skipping meals makes you overeat later.

M I hadn't thought of that. Then what should I do?

W It's simple. You should eat regularly to stay healthy.

M You're right. I won't skip meals anymore.

해석

여 이번 주에는 구내식당에서 너를 못 봤네. 어디 갔다 왔어?

남 도서관에서 과학 프로젝트를 하고 있거든.

여 그럼 점심을 거르고 있다는 거야?

남 응. 이 프로젝트는 내 성적에 정말 중요해.

여 그러면 안 돼. 건강에 좋지 않아.

남 걱정하지 마. 집에 가면 항상 저녁을 많이 먹으니까.

여 그게 문제야. 식사를 거르면 나중에 과식하게 되잖아.

남 그런 생각을 못 했네. 그럼 어떻게 해야 하지?

여 간단해. 건강하기 위해서는 규칙적으로 먹어야 해.

남 맞아. 더 이상 식사를 거르지 않을게.

② 나를 위해 준비해 준 점심 잘 먹었어.

③ 구내식당이 언제 문을 여는지 확인할 필요가 있어.

④ 나를 믿어. 내가 좋은 식사 예절을 가르쳐 줄 수 있어.

⑤ 문제없어. 우리는 과학 프로젝트를 제시간에 끝낼 거야.

어휘

cafeteria 구내식당   skip 거르다, 빼먹다   overeat 과식하다, 많이 먹다

14 정답 ③

- **M** Excuse me, Ms. Lopez. Can I ask you something?
- **W** Sure, Tony. What can I do for you?
- **M** I want to do better in Spanish, but I don't know how to improve.
- **W** You seem to do well during class. Do you study when you're at home?
- **M** I do all my homework and try to learn 20 new words every day.
- **W** That's a good start. Do you also practice saying those words repeatedly?
- **M** Do I need to do that? That sounds like it'll take a lot of time.
- **W** It does. But since you're still a beginner, you have to put in more effort to get used to new words.
- **M** I see. So are you suggesting that I practice them over and over?
- **W** Exactly. Learning a language starts with repetition.

해석

- **남** 실례합니다, Lopez 선생님. 뭐 좀 물어봐도 될까요?
- **여** 그럼요, Tony. 뭘 도와줄까요?
- **남** 스페인어를 더 잘하고 싶은데, 향상시키는 방법을 모르겠어요.
- **여** 수업 시간에 잘하고 있는 것 같아요. 집에 있을 때는 공부를 하나요?
- **남** 숙제를 다 하고 매일 20개의 새로운 단어를 배우려고 하고 있어요.
- **여** 좋은 출발이네요. 그 단어들을 반복해서 말하는 연습도 하나요?
- **남** 그렇게 할 필요가 있나요? 시간이 많이 걸릴 것 같아요.
- **여** 그래요. 하지만 아직 초보자이기 때문에, 새로운 단어에 익숙해지기 위해서는 더 많은 노력을 해야 해요.
- **남** 알겠습니다. 그러니까 여러 번 되풀이해서 연습해야 한다고 제안하시는 거죠?
- **여** 정확해요. 언어를 배우는 것은 반복으로 시작되거든요.

① 아니요. 저는 스페인어를 배우는 것이 어렵지 않아요.
② 당신이 결국 어휘 시험에 합격했다니 기쁘네요.
④ 글을 쓸 때는 사전을 이용하는 것이 매우 도움이 돼요.
⑤ 당신은 오늘 오후까지 숙제를 제출해야 해요.

해설

남자는 스페인어를 더 잘할 수 있는 방법을 여자에게 묻고 있고, 여자는 반복해서 말하는 연습을 하라고 조언하고 있다. 그러므로, 반복해서 연습하라는 말이냐는 남자의 마지막 말에 대한 여자의 응답으로 가장 적절한 것은 ③ '정확해요. 언어를 배우는 것은 반복으로 시작되거든요.'이다.

어휘

Spanish 스페인어 improve 향상시키다 repeatedly 반복해서
put in effort to ~에 노력을 기울이다 get used to ~에 익숙해지다
suggest 제안하다 over and over 여러 번 되풀이해서, 반복해서

15 정답 ⑤

- **W** Brian is a class leader. He is passionate about environmental issues and saving energy. Recently, he's noticed that his classmates don't turn the lights off when they leave the classroom. Brian thinks this is very careless. He wants to make stickers that remind his classmates to save energy by turning off the lights. He tells this idea to his classmate Melissa, and she agrees it's a good idea. Brian knows Melissa is a great artist, so he wants to ask her to design stickers that encourage their classmates to save energy.

In this situation, what would Brian most likely say to Melissa?

Brian Will you design stickers that encourage energy saving?

해석

- **여** Brian은 반장이다. 그는 환경 문제와 에너지 절약에 대해 열정적이다. 최근에, 그는 반 친구들이 교실을 떠날 때 불을 끄지 않는 것을 알게 되었다. Brian은 이것이 매우 부주의하다고 생각한다. 그는 불을 꺼서 에너지를 절약하도록 반 친구들에게 상기시키는 스티커를 만들고 싶어 한다. 그는 이 생각을 반 친구 Melissa에게 말하고, 그녀는 그것이 좋은 생각이라는 것에 동의한다. Brian은 Melissa가 훌륭한 예술가라는 것을 알고 있어서, 그는 그녀에게 반 친구들이 에너지를 절약하도록 격려하는 스티커를 디자인해 달라고 요청하고 싶어 한다. 이런 상황에서, Brian은 Melissa에게 뭐라고 말할 것 같은가?

Brian 에너지 절약을 장려하는 스티커를 디자인해 줄래?

① 미술 시간 이후에 교실을 청소하자.
② 네가 보드에서 스티커를 제거했니?
③ 방에서 나갈 때 히터를 꺼 줘.
④ 디자인 수업을 신청하는 최종 날짜가 언제니?

어휘

passionate 열정적인 environmental issue 환경 문제 recently 최근에
notice 알아채다. 알게 되다 careless 부주의한 remind 상기시키다. 생각나게 하다
encourage 격려하다, 장려하다

16 정답 ③ 　　## 17 정답 ③

- **M** Good afternoon, everyone. Last time, we learned that overtourism happens when there are too many visitors to a particular destination. Today, we'll learn how cities deal with the problems caused by overtourism. First, some cities limit the number of hotels so there are fewer places for visitors to stay. In Barcelona, building new hotels is not allowed in the city center. Second, other cities promote areas away from popular sites. For instance, Amsterdam encourages tourists to visit less-crowded areas. Third, many cities have tried to limit access. For example, Venice has tried to reduce tourism overall by stopping large cruise ships from docking on the island. Similarly, Paris has focused on reducing tourism to certain parts of the city by having car-restricted areas. Now, let's watch some video clips.

해석

- **남** 안녕하세요, 여러분. 지난 시간에, 우리는 특정한 목적지에 방문하는 사람들이 너무 많을 때 과잉 관광이 일어난다는 것을 배웠습니다. 오늘은 과잉 관광으로 인한 문제를 도시들이 어떻게 다루는지 배울 것입니다. 첫째, 일부 도시들은 호텔의 수를 제한해서 방문객들이 머무를 수 있는 장소가 더 적어집니다. 바르셀로나에서는, 도심에 새로운 호텔을 짓는 것이 허용되지 않습니다. 둘째, 다른 도시들은 인기 있는 장소들로부터 떨어진 지역을 홍보합니다. 예를 들어, 암스테르담은 관광객들로 하여금 좀 덜 붐비는 지역을 방문하도록 장려합니다. 셋째, 많은 도시들은 접근을 제한하려고 노력합니다. 예를 들어, 베니스는 대형 유람선들이 섬에 정박하는 것을 막음으로써 전반적으로 관광을 줄이려고 노력합니다. 비슷하게, 파리는 자동차 제한 구역을 둠으로써 도시의 특정 지역으로의 관광을 줄이는 데 집중해 왔습니다. 이제, 몇 개의 비디오 영상을 봅시다.

16
① 도시에서 주택을 임대하는 것의 장점들
② 관광객들이 오래된 도시를 방문하는 것을 선호하는 이유들
③ 도시들이 과잉 관광 문제들을 다루는 방법들
④ 도시 규모와 과잉 관광 사이의 상관관계
⑤ 도시들이 노후화된 교통 시스템에 직면하는 방법

17
① 바르셀로나 ② 암스테르담 ③ 런던 ④ 베니스 ⑤ 파리

---

01 ②	02 ①	03 ①	04 ④	05 ⑤	06 ③
07 ④	08 ③	09 ⑤	10 ④	11 ①	12 ③
13 ②	14 ⑤	15 ⑤	16 ③	17 ④	

2회

23년 6월

01 정답 ②

정답률 94%

W Good afternoon, everybody. This is your student council president, Monica Brown. Our school's annual e-sports competition will be held on the last day of the semester. For the competition, we need some volunteers to help set up computers. If you're interested in helping us make the competition successful, please fill out the volunteer application form and email it to me. For more information, please visit our school website. I hope many of you will join us. Thank you for listening.

해석

여 모두들, 안녕하세요. 학생 회장 Monica Brown입니다. 우리 학교의 연례 e스포츠 대회는 학기 마지막 날에 열릴 것입니다. 대회를 위해, 우리는 컴퓨터 설치를 도와줄 자원봉사자들이 필요합니다. 대회를 성공적으로 개최할 수 있도록 도와주는 데 관심이 있으시면 자원봉사 신청서를 작성하여 저에게 이메일로 보내 주시기 바랍니다. 더 많은 정보를 위해서는, 우리 학교 웹사이트를 방문해 주세요. 많은 분들이 함께 해 주시면 좋겠습니다. 들어주셔서 감사합니다.

어휘

student council president 학생 회장 annual 연례의 competition 대회
be held on ~에 열리다 semester 학기 volunteer 자원봉사자
set up ~을 설치하다 fill out (서식을) 작성하다 application form 신청서

02 정답 ①

정답률 92%

M Hannah, how's your design project going?
W Hey, Aiden. I'm still working on it, but I'm not making much progress.
M Can you tell me what the problem is?
W Hmm... *[Pause]* It's hard to think of creative ideas. I feel like I'm wasting my time.
M I understand. Why don't you take a walk?
W How can that help me to improve my creativity?
M It will actually make your brain more active. Then you'll see things differently.
W But I don't have time for that.
M You don't need a lot of time. Even a short walk will help you to come up with creative ideas.
W Then I'll try it. Thanks for the tip.

해석

남 Hannah, 디자인 프로젝트는 잘 진행되고 있어?
여 안녕, Aiden. 나는 아직도 공들이고 있지만, 별로 진전이 없어.
남 뭐가 문제인지 말해 줄래?

여 음… *[잠시 후]* 창의적인 아이디어를 생각하는 것은 어려워. 시간을 낭비하고 있는 것 같아.

남 이해해. 산책하는 게 어때?

여 그게 내 창의력을 향상시키는 데 어떻게 도움이 될까?

남 그것은 실제로 뇌를 더 활동적으로 만들어 줄 거야. 그러면 상황을 다르게 보게 될 것이고.

여 하지만 그럴 시간이 없어.

남 시간이 많이 필요하지는 않아. 조금만 걸어도 창의적인 아이디어를 내는 데 도움이 될 거야.

여 그럼 해 볼게. 조언 고마워.

어휘

make progress 진행하다, 전진하다 creative 창의적인 take a walk 산책하다
improve 향상시키다 creativity 창의성 actually 실제로, 사실은
active 활동적인 come up with ~을 생각해 내다

03 정답 ①

W Excuse me. Could you please tell me where I can put this box?

M Right here on this counter. How can I help you today?

W I'd like to send this to Jeju Island.

M Sure. Are there any breakable items in the box?

W No, there are only clothes in it.

M Then, there should be no problem.

W I see. What's the fastest way to send it?

M You can send the package by express mail, but there's an extra charge.

W That's okay. I want it to be delivered as soon as possible. When will it arrive in Jeju if it goes out today?

M If you send it today, it will be there by this Friday.

W Oh, Friday will be great. I'll do the express mail.

해석

여 실례합니다. 제가 이 상자를 어디에 둘 수 있는지 말씀해 주시겠어요?

남 바로 여기 이 카운터 위예요. 오늘 제가 어떻게 도와드릴까요?

여 이걸 제주도로 보내고 싶은데요.

남 물론이죠. 상자 안에 깨지기 쉬운 물건이 있나요?

여 아니요, 그 안에는 옷밖에 없어요.

남 그러면, 아무 문제없을 거예요.

여 그렇군요. 가장 빨리 보내는 방법이 무엇인가요?

남 소포를 속달로 보낼 수 있지만, 추가 요금이 있어요.

여 괜찮아요. 그것이 가능한 한 빨리 배달되기를 원하거든요. 오늘 나가면 제주에 언제 도착할까요?

남 오늘 보내면 이번 주 금요일까지는 도착할 거예요.

여 오, 금요일 좋네요. 속달 우편으로 할게요.

어휘

breakable 깨질 수 있는 clothes 옷, 의류 package 소포, 포장물
express mail 속달 우편, 급행 우편 extra charge 추가 요금
be delivered 배달되다 as soon as possible 가능한 한 빨리
by this Friday 이번 주 금요일까지

04 정답 ④

M Kayla, I heard you went busking on the street last weekend.

W It was amazing! I've got a picture here. Look!

M Oh, you're wearing the hat I gave you.

W Yeah, I really like it.

M Looks great. This boy playing the guitar next to you must be your brother Kevin.

W You're right. He played while I sang.

M Cool. Why did you leave the guitar case open?

W That's for the audience. If they like our performance, they give us some money.

M Oh, and you set up two speakers!

W I did. I recently bought them.

M I see. And did you design that poster on the wall?

W Yeah. My brother and I worked on it together.

M It sounds like you really had a lot of fun!

해석

남 Kayla, 네가 지난 주말에 길거리에서 버스킹을 했다고 들었어.

여 정말 놀라웠어! 내가 사진을 가져왔거든. 봐봐!

남 오, 내가 준 모자를 쓰고 있네.

여 응, 그게 정말 맘에 들거든.

남 좋아 보이네. 네 옆에서 기타를 치고 있는 이 소년은 틀림없이 네 남동생 Kevin일 거야.

여 네 말이 맞아. 내가 노래하는 동안 그가 연주했거든.

남 멋있네. 왜 기타 케이스를 열어 두었어?

여 그건 관객들을 위한 거야. 우리의 공연이 좋으면, 그들은 우리에게 약간의 돈을 주거든.

남 아, 그리고 스피커를 두 개 설치했구나!

여 그랬지. 최근에 그것들을 샀거든.

남 그렇구나. 그리고 벽에 있는 포스터는 네가 디자인한 거야?

여 응. 동생과 내가 함께 그것을 작업했어.

남 정말 재미있었겠네!

어휘

go busking 버스킹을 하다 leave ~ open ~을 열어 두다 audience 청중, 관객
performance 공연 recently 최근에

05 정답 ⑤

W Honey, are we ready for Jake's birthday party tomorrow?

M I sent the invitation cards last week. What about other things?

W I'm not sure. Let's check.

M We are expecting a lot of guests. How about the dinner menu?

W I haven't decided yet.

M We won't have much time to cook, so let's just order pizza.

W Okay. I'll do it tomorrow. What about the present?

M Oh, you mean the smartphone? I forgot to get it!

W That's alright. Can you go to the electronics store and buy it now?

M No problem. I'll do it right away.

W Good. Then, I'll clean up the living room while you're out.

해석

여 여보, 우리 내일 Jake 생일 파티 준비 다 되었을까요?

남 초대장을 지난주에 보냈어요. 다른 것들은 어때요?

여 잘 모르겠어요. 같이 확인해 봐요.
남 손님이 많이 올 거예요. 저녁 메뉴는 어때요?
여 아직 결정하지 못했어요.
남 요리할 시간이 별로 없을 테니까 피자를 주문하자고요.
여 좋아요. 내일 할게요. 선물은요?
남 아, 스마트폰 말하는 거죠? 깜빡했네요!
여 괜찮아요. 당신이 지금 전자제품 가게에 가서 그것을 살 수 있나요?
남 문제없죠. 바로 갈게요.
여 좋아요. 그럼, 당신이 외출해 있는 동안 제가 거실을 청소할게요.

어휘
be ready for ~을 위해 준비되다 expect 기대하다 decide 결정하다
order 주문하다 present 선물 electronics store 전자제품 가게
clean up 청소하다

06 정답 ③

정답률 84%

M Good morning! How can I help you?
W Hi. I'm looking for a blanket and some cushions for my sofa.
M Okay. We've got some on sale. Would you like to have a look?
W Yes. How much is this green blanket?
M That's $40.
W Oh, I love the color green. Can you also show me some cushions that go well with this blanket?
M Sure! How about these?
W They look good. I need two of them. How much are they?
M The cushions are $20 each.
W Okay. I'll take one green blanket and two cushions. Can I use this coupon?
M Sure. It will give you 10% off the total.
W Thanks! Here's my credit card.

해석
남 좋은 아침이에요! 무엇을 도와드릴까요?
여 안녕하세요. 소파에 놓을 담요와 쿠션을 찾고 있어요.
남 알겠어요. 할인 중인 것도 있어요. 한번 보시겠어요?
여 네. 이 초록색 담요는 얼마인가요?
남 40달러입니다.
여 오, 초록색이 정말 좋네요. 이 담요와 잘 어울리는 쿠션도 보여 주실 수 있나요?
남 물론이죠! 이것들은 어떠세요?
여 좋아 보이네요. 두 개가 필요해요. 얼마예요?
남 쿠션은 한 개에 20달러예요.
여 네. 저는 녹색 담요 한 장과 쿠션 두 개를 가져갈게요. 이 쿠폰을 사용할 수 있나요?
남 물론이죠. 총 10%를 할인받으실 거예요.
여 고마워요! 여기 제 신용 카드입니다.

해설
여자는 40달러짜리 녹색 담요 하나와 20달러짜리 쿠션 2개를 구매하기로 했다. 10% 할인 쿠폰을 사용할 수 있다고 했으므로, 여자가 지불할 금액은 총 ③ '$72'(72달러)이다.

어휘
blanket 담요 on sale 할인 중인 have a look 한번 보다
go well with ~과 잘 어울리다 10% off the total 총 10% 할인의

07 정답 ④

정답률 94%

W Hello, Justin. What are you doing?
M Hi, Ellie. I'm doing my project for art class.
W Can you go to a rock concert with me this Saturday? My sister gave me two tickets!
M I'd love to! [Pause] But I'm afraid I can't.
W Do you have to work that day?
M No, I don't work on Saturdays.
W Then, why not? I thought you really like rock music.
M Of course I do. But I have to take care of my friend's dog this Saturday.
W Oh, really? Is your friend going somewhere?
M He's visiting his grandmother that day.
W Okay, no problem. I'm sure I can find someone else to go with me.

해석
여 안녕, Justin. 뭐 하고 있어?
남 안녕, Ellie. 나는 미술 수업을 위한 프로젝트를 하고 있어.
여 이번 주 토요일에 나와 함께 록 콘서트에 갈 수 있어? 언니가 티켓 두 장을 줬거든!
남 그러고 싶어! [잠시 후] 하지만 안 될 것 같아.
여 그날 일해야 해?
남 아니, 토요일에는 일하지 않아.
여 그럼, 왜 안 돼? 나는 네가 록 음악을 정말 좋아하는 줄 알았어.
남 물론 그래. 하지만 나는 이번 토요일에 친구의 강아지를 돌봐야 해.
여 아, 정말? 네 친구는 어딘가를 가니?
남 그는 그날 그의 할머니를 방문할 거야.
여 알았어, 괜찮아. 나와 함께 갈 다른 사람을 찾을 수 있을 거야.

어휘
art class 미술 수업 take care of ~을 돌보다 someone else 다른 누군가

08 정답 ③

정답률 94%

W Scott, did you see this Eco Day poster?
M No, not yet. Let me see. [Pause] It's an event for picking up trash while walking around a park.
W Why don't we do it together? It's next Sunday from 10 a.m. to 5 p.m.
M Sounds good. I've been thinking a lot about the environment lately.
W Me, too. Also, the event will be held in Eastside Park. You know, we often used to go there.
M That's great. Oh, look at this. We have to bring our own gloves and small bags for the trash.
W No problem. I have extra. I can bring some for you as well.
M Okay, thanks. Do we have to sign up for the event?
W Yes. The poster says we can do it online.
M Let's do it right now. I'm looking forward to it.

해석
여 Scott, 이 Eco Day 포스터 봤어?
남 아니, 아직. 어디 보자. [잠시 후] 공원을 걸어 다니면서 쓰레기를 줍는 이벤

트네.

여 같이 하는 게 어때? 다음 일요일 오전 10시부터 오후 5시까지야.

남 좋을 것 같아. 나 최근에 환경에 대해 생각을 많이 하고 있거든.

여 나도 그래. 또한, 이 행사는 Eastside Park에서 열릴 거야. 너도 알다시피, 우리는 종종 그곳에 가곤 했잖아.

남 잘됐네. 오, 이것 좀 봐. 우리는 쓰레기를 위해 우리만의 장갑과 작은 가방을 가져와야 해.

여 문제없어. 여분이 있어. 너를 위한 것도 몇 개 가져올 수 있어.

남 좋아, 고마워. 그 행사에 등록해야 해?

여 응. 포스터에 온라인으로 할 수 있다고 쓰여 있어.

남 지금 당장 하자. 기대가 되네.

어휘

pick up 줍다   trash 쓰레기   environment 환경   lately 최근에
used to ~하곤 했다   extra 여분, 추가   as well 또한
sign up for ~을 등록하다   look forward to ~을 기대하다

09 정답 ⑤
정답률 84%

M Hello, Eastville High School students. This is your P.E. teacher, Mr. Wilson. I'm pleased to let you know that we're hosting the first Eastville Dance Contest. Any Eastville students who love dancing can participate in the contest as a team. All kinds of dance are allowed. If you'd like to participate, please upload your team's dance video to our school website by August 15th. Students can vote for their favorite video from August 16th to 20th. The winning team will receive a trophy as a prize. Don't miss this great opportunity to show off your talents!

해석

남 안녕하세요, Eastville 고등학교 학생 여러분. 저는 체육 선생님 Wilson입니다. 첫 번째 Eastville 댄스 경연대회를 개최하여 여러분에게 소개하게 되어 기쁩니다. 댄스를 사랑하는 Eastville 학생들은 누구나 한 팀으로 이 대회에 참가할 수 있습니다. 모든 종류의 춤이 허용됩니다. 참가하실 분들은 8월 15일까지 학교 홈페이지에 팀의 댄스 영상을 업로드 해 주세요. 학생들은 8월 16일부터 20일까지 가장 좋아하는 비디오에 투표할 수 있습니다. 우승한 팀은 상품으로 트로피를 받을 것입니다. 여러분의 재능을 뽐낼 수 있는 이 좋은 기회를 놓치지 마세요!

어휘

P.E. teacher 체육 선생님   host 개최하다   participate in ~에 참가하다
all kinds of dance 모든 종류의 춤   allow 허락하다   vote 투표하다
receive 받다   miss 놓치다   opportunity 기회   show off ~을 자랑하다

10 정답 ④
정답률 90%

M Honey, we need a water purifier for our new house.

W You're right. Let's order one online.

M Good idea. [Clicking Sound] Look! These are the five bestsellers.

W I see. What's our budget?

M Well, I don't want to spend more than 800 dollars.

W Okay, how about the water tank capacity?

M I think the five-liter tank would be perfect for us.

W I think so, too. And I like the ones with a power-saving mode.

M Okay, then we can save electricity. Now, there are just two options left.

W Let's look at the warranties. The longer, the better.

M I agree. We should order this model.

해석

남 여보, 우리 새 집에 정수기가 필요해요.

여 당신 말이 맞아요. 온라인으로 하나 주문해요.

남 좋은 생각이에요. [클릭하는 소리] 보세요! 이것들이 베스트셀러 5가지예요.

여 그렇군요. 예산이 얼마나 되죠?

남 음, 800달러 이상은 쓰고 싶지 않아요.

여 좋아요, 물탱크 용량은 어때요?

남 5리터 탱크가 우리에게 딱 좋을 것 같아요.

여 저도 그렇게 생각해요. 그리고 절전 모드가 있는 것들이 좋을 것 같아요.

남 좋아요, 그러면 전기를 절약할 수 있어요. 이제 두 가지 선택지만 남았어요.

여 보증 내용을 살펴보자고요. 길수록 좋죠.

남 동의해요. 우리는 이 모델을 주문해야겠어요.

어휘

water purifier 정수기   budget 예산   capacity 용량, 수용력
perfect 딱 맞는, 완벽한   power-saving mode 절전 모드   electricity 전기
option 선택지   warranty 보증

11 정답 ①
정답률 77%

M Let's get inside. I'm so excited to see this auto show.

W Look over there. So many people are already standing in line to buy tickets.

M Fortunately, I bought our tickets in advance.

W Great. We don't have to wait in line.

해석

남 안으로 들어가자. 나는 이 자동차 전시회를 볼 수 있어서 너무 신이 나.

여 저기 좀 봐. 너무 많은 사람들이 이미 표를 사기 위해 줄을 서 있어.

남 다행히도, 나는 우리 표를 미리 샀어.

여 훌륭해. 우리는 줄을 설 필요가 없네.

② 맞아. 나중에 돌아갈 수 있어.

③ 잘했어. 표를 사자.

④ 걱정하지 마. 내가 줄을 설게.

⑤ 너무 아쉬워. 저 차를 살 수 없어.

해설

여자와 남자는 자동차 전시회를 보러 갔는데, 이미 많은 사람들이 표를 사려고 줄을 서 있는 상황이다. 이미 표를 사 두었다는 남자의 말에 대한 여자의 응답으로 가장 적절한 것은 ① '훌륭해. 우리는 줄을 설 필요가 없네.'이다.

어휘

get inside 안으로 들어가다   stand in line 줄을 서다   fortunately 다행히도
in advance 미리

12 정답 ③
정답률 76%

W Hi, Chris. Did you check your grade for the history test we took last week?

M Yes. But I think there's something wrong with my grade.

W Don't you think you should go ask Mr. Morgan about it?

M Right. I should go to his office now.

여 안녕, Chris. 지난주에 본 역사 시험 성적 확인했어?

남 응. 하지만 내 성적에 뭔가 문제가 있는 것 같아.

여 Morgan 선생님한테 가서 물어봐야 하지 않을까?

남 맞아. 지금 그의 사무실로 가 봐야겠어.

① 응. 온라인으로 등록할 수 있어.

② 미안. 다음 주에 너를 만날 수 없어.

④ 멋진데! 내일 시험을 볼 거야.

⑤ 물론이지. 그가 내 도움을 필요로 한다면, 그를 도울 수 있어.

어휘

grade 성적   something wrong 잘못된 무언가

13 정답 ②

정답률 83%

M Mom, did you write this note?

W What's that?

M I found this in the book you gave me.

W Oh, the one I bought for you at the secondhand bookstore last week?

M Yes. At first I thought it was a bookmark, but it wasn't. It's a note with a message!

W What does it say?

M It says, "I hope you enjoy this book."

W How sweet! That really brings a smile to my face.

M Yeah, mom. I love this message so much.

W Well, then, why don't we leave a note if we resell this book later?

M Great idea! Our message would make others smile.

해석

남 엄마, 이 노트 엄마가 쓰신 거예요?

여 그게 뭔데?

남 엄마가 주신 책에서 이걸 찾았어요.

여 아, 내가 지난주에 헌책방에서 사다 준 거 말이니?

남 네. 처음에는 책갈피인 줄 알았는데 아니었어요. 메시지가 있는 쪽지예요!

여 뭐라고 쓰여 있는데?

남 "이 책을 재미있게 읽으시길 바랍니다."라고 쓰여 있어요.

여 정말 다정하네! 그것은 정말 내 얼굴에 미소를 짓게 하는구나.

남 네, 엄마. 이 메시지가 너무 좋아요.

여 음, 그럼, 나중에 이 책을 재판매하게 되면 메모를 남기는 게 어떨까?

남 좋은 생각이에요! 우리의 메시지가 다른 사람들을 미소 짓게 만들 거예요.

① 동의해요. 중고품을 사면 많이 절약할 수 있어요.

③ 죄송해요. 그 책에 메시지를 쓰는 것을 깜빡했어요.

④ 정확해요. 수업 중에 필기를 하는 것은 중요해요.

⑤ 알겠어요. 지금 출발하면 제시간에 도착할 수 있어요.

어휘

secondhand bookstore 헌책방, 중고 서점   bookmark 책갈피
leave a note 메모를 남기다   resell 재판매하다, 다시 팔다   later 나중에

14 정답 ⑤

정답률 89%

M Do you have any plans for this weekend, Sandy?

W Hey, Evan. I'm planning to go camping with my family.

M I've never gone before. Do you go camping often?

W Yes. Two or three times a month at least.

M That's cool. Why do you like it so much?

W I like spending time in nature with my family. It makes me feel closer to them.

M I understand. It's like a family hobby, right?

W Yes, you're right. Camping helps me relieve all my stress, too.

M Sounds interesting. I'd love to try it.

W If you go camping with your family, you'll see what I mean.

M I wish I could, but I don't have any equipment for it.

W No problem. You can use my equipment.

해석

남 Sandy, 이번 주말에 무슨 계획 있어요?

여 안녕, Evan. 나는 가족과 함께 캠핑을 갈 계획이에요.

남 나는 한 번도 가 본 적이 없어요. 캠핑을 자주 가나요?

여 네. 적어도 한 달에 두세 번은요.

남 멋지네요. 그게 왜 그렇게 좋아요?

여 가족과 함께 자연에서 시간을 보내는 게 좋아요. 그들과 더 가깝게 느끼게 만들어 주거든요.

남 이해해요. 가족 취미 같은 거죠, 그렇죠?

여 네, 맞아요. 캠핑은 모든 스트레스를 푸는 데도 도움이 돼요.

남 흥미롭게 들리네요. 해 보고 싶네요.

여 가족과 함께 캠핑을 가면, 내가 무슨 말을 하는지 알 수 있을 거예요.

남 나도 그러고 싶지만, 나는 장비가 없네요.

여 문제없어요. 제 장비를 사용하셔도 돼요.

① 왜 안 되겠어요? 우리가 캠핑을 갈 때 내가 약간의 음식을 가져갈 수 있어요.

② 죄송합니다. 그 낚시 장비는 비매품이에요.

③ 그렇게 생각하지 않아요. 가격이 가장 중요하죠.

④ 정말요? 당신의 가족을 만나고 싶어요.

어휘

go camping 캠핑을 가다   two or three times a month 한 달에 두세 번
at least 적어도   relieve (스트레스 등을) 없애 주다   equipment 장비

15 정답 ⑤

정답률 93%

W Violet and Peter are classmates. They're doing their science group assignment together. On Saturday morning, they meet at the public library. They decide to find the books they need in different sections of the library. Violet finds two useful books and tries to check them out. Unfortunately, she suddenly realizes that she didn't bring her library card. At that moment, Peter walks up to Violet. So, Violet wants to ask Peter to check out the books for her because she knows he has his library card. In this situation, what would Violet most likely say to Peter?

Violet Can you borrow the books for me with your card?

해석

여 Violet과 Peter는 반 친구이다. 그들은 과학 그룹 과제를 함께 하고 있다. 토요일 아침에, 그들은 공공 도서관에서 만난다. 그들은 도서관의 서로 다른 구역에서 그들이 필요한 책들을 찾아보기로 결정한다. Violet은 두 권

의 유용한 책을 찾아서 빌리려고 한다. 불행하게도, 그녀는 갑자기 도서관 카드를 가져오지 않았다는 것을 깨닫는다. 그 순간, Peter가 Violet을 향해 걸어온다. 그래서 Violet은 Peter가 도서관 카드를 가지고 있다는 것을 알기 때문에 Peter에게 책을 빌려달라고 부탁하고 싶어 한다. 이런 상황에서 Violet은 Peter에게 뭐라고 말할 것 같은가?

Violet 나를 위해 네 카드로 책을 빌려줄 수 있어?

① 과학 동아리에 함께 가입할래?
② 음료를 결제할 때 카드를 사용해도 괜찮아?
③ 도서관에 우리 책을 기부하는 게 어때?
④ 점심 먹으러 구내식당에 가는 게 어때?

Violet과 Peter는 과학 과제를 위해 도서관에 있고, Violet이 필요한 책을 찾아서 빌리려고 하는데 도서관 카드를 가져오지 않은 상황이다. Peter의 카드로 책을 빌리고 싶어 하는 상황이므로, Violet이 할 말로 가장 적절한 것은 ⑤ '나를 위해 네 카드로 책을 빌려줄 수 있어?'이다.

group assignment 그룹 과제 decide to ~하기로 결정하다
check out 빌리다, 대출하다 unfortunately 불행하게도 suddenly 갑자기
realize 깨닫다 at that moment 그 순간

---

16 정답 ③ 정답률 95%   **17** 정답 ④ 정답률 94%

M Hello, everyone. I'm Shawn Collins, a doctor at Collins Sleep Clinic. Sleep is one of the most essential parts of our daily lives. So today, I'm going to introduce the best foods for helping you sleep better. First, kiwi fruits contain a high level of hormones that help you fall asleep more quickly, sleep longer, and wake up less during the night. Second, milk is rich in vitamin D and it calms the mind and nerves. If you drink a cup of milk before you go to bed, it will definitely help you get a good night's sleep. Third, nuts can help to produce the hormone that controls your internal body clock and sends signals for the body to sleep at the right time. The last one is honey. Honey helps you sleep well because it reduces the hormone that keeps the brain awake! Now, I'll show you some delicious diet plans using these foods.

남 안녕하세요, 여러분. 저는 Collins 수면 클리닉의 Shawn Collins입니다. 잠은 우리의 일상생활에서 가장 필수적인 부분 중 하나입니다. 그래서 저는 오늘 여러분이 더 잘 잘 수 있도록 도와주는 최고의 음식을 소개하려고 합니다. 첫째로, 키위 과일은 여러분이 더 빨리 잠들고, 더 오래 자고, 밤에 덜 깨어나도록 돕는 높은 수준의 호르몬을 포함하고 있습니다. 둘째, 우유는 비타민 D가 풍부하고 마음과 신경을 진정시켜 줍니다. 만약 여러분이 잠들기 전에 우유 한 잔을 마신다면, 그것은 분명히 여러분이 숙면을 취하는 데 도움을 줄 것입니다. 셋째, 견과류는 체내 시계를 조절하고 신체가 적절한 시간에 잠을 잘 수 있도록 신호를 보내는 호르몬을 생산하는 것을 도울 수 있습니다. 마지막은 꿀입니다. 꿀은 뇌를 깨어 있게 하는 호르몬을 감소시키기 때문에 여러분이 잠을 잘 잘 수 있도록 도와줍니다! 이제, 이 음식들을 이용한 맛있는 식단을 보여 드리겠습니다.

16
① 수면 장애의 다른 원인들
② 음식을 신선하게 유지하는 다양한 방법
③ 수면의 질을 향상시키는 음식
④ 유기농 식품이 인기 있는 이유
⑤ 세계적으로 인기 있는 음식의 기원

17
① 키위 과일   ② 우유   ③ 견과류   ④ 토마토   ⑤ 꿀

essential 필수적인, 아주 중요한 contain 함유하다
a high level of 높은 수치의 ~ fall asleep 잠들다 wake up 깨다, 일어나다
rich 풍부한 nerve 신경 produce 생산하다 internal body clock 체내 시계
signal 신호 reduce 감소시키다 keep ~ awake ~을 계속 깨어 있게 하다

01 ⑤	02 ⑤	03 ③	04 ⑤	05 ②	06 ②
07 ①	08 ③	09 ④	10 ②	11 ②	12 ①
13 ③	14 ①	15 ③	16 ③	17 ④	

01 정답 ⑤

정답률 87%

M Hello, Villeford High School students. This is principal Aaron Clark. As a big fan of the Villeford ice hockey team, I'm very excited about the upcoming National High School Ice Hockey League. As you all know, the first game will be held in the Central Rink at 6 p.m. this Saturday. I want as many of you as possible to come and cheer our team to victory. I've seen them put in an incredible amount of effort to win the league. It will help them play better just to see you there cheering for them. I really hope to see you at the rink. Thank you.

해석

남 안녕하세요, Villeford 고등학교 학생 여러분. 저는 교장 Aaron Clark입니다. Villeford 아이스하키 팀의 열렬한 팬으로서, 저는 다가오는 전국 고등학교 아이스하키 리그에 대해 매우 흥분됩니다. 다들 아시다시피, 이번 주 토요일 오후 6시에 Central Rink에서 첫 경기가 열릴 것입니다. 가능한 한 많은 분들이 오셔서 우리 팀의 승리를 응원해 주시기 바랍니다. 저는 그들이 리그 우승을 위해 엄청난 노력을 기울이는 것을 봐 왔습니다. 그곳에서 그들을 응원하는 여러분을 보는 것만으로도 그들이 더 잘 경기하는 데 도움이 될 것입니다. 링크에서 여러분을 꼭 보게 되기를 바랍니다. 감사합니다.

어휘

principal 교장   upcoming 다가오는   be held 개최되다   victory 승리
incredible 엄청난, 믿을 수 없는

02 정답 ⑤

정답률 91%

W Honey, are you okay?

M I'm afraid I've caught a cold. I've got a sore throat.

W Why don't you go see a doctor?

M Well, I don't think it's necessary. I've found some medicine in the cabinet. I'll take it.

W You shouldn't take that medicine. That's what I got prescribed last week.

M My symptoms are similar to yours.

W Honey, you shouldn't take medicine prescribed for others.

M It's just a cold. I'll get better if I take your medicine.

W It could be dangerous to take someone else's prescription.

M Okay. Then I'll go see a doctor this afternoon.

해석

여 여보, 괜찮아요?

남 감기에 걸린 것 같아요. 목이 아파요.

여 병원에 가 보는 게 어때요?

남 음, 그럴 필요는 없을 것 같아요. 캐비닛에서 약을 좀 찾았어요. 그걸 먹을게요.

여 그 약을 먹으면 안 돼요. 그건 내가 지난주에 처방받은 거예요.

남 내 증상이 당신의 증상과 비슷해요.

여 여보, 다른 사람들에게 처방된 약을 먹으면 안 돼요.

남 그냥 감기인 걸요. 당신의 약을 먹으면 좋아질 거예요.

여 다른 사람의 처방약을 먹는 것은 위험할 수 있어요.

남 알았어요. 그럼 오늘 오후에 병원에 가 볼게요.

어휘

catch a cold 감기 걸리다(catch-caught-caught)   sore 아픈   throat 목
necessary 필요한   take the medicine 약을 먹다   prescribe 처방하다
symptom 증상   prescription 처방(약)

03 정답 ③

정답률 87%

W Hi, Mr. Thomson. How are your preparations going?

M You arrived at the right time. I have something to tell you.

W Okay. What is it?

M Well, I'm afraid that we have to change the exhibition room for your paintings.

W May I ask why?

M Sure. We have some electrical problems there.

W I see. Then where are you going to exhibit my works?

M Our gallery is going to exhibit your paintings in the main hall.

W Okay. Can I see the hall now?

M Sure. Come with me.

해석

여 안녕하세요, Thomson 씨. 준비는 어떻게 되고 있나요?

남 제시간에 도착하셨군요. 당신에게 얘기할 게 있어요.

여 네. 뭔가요?

남 음, 유감스럽게도 당신의 그림 전시실을 바꿔야 할 것 같아요.

여 이유를 물어봐도 될까요?

남 물론이죠. 그곳에 전기적인 문제가 좀 있어요.

여 그렇군요. 그럼 제 작품은 어디서 전시하게 되나요?

남 우리 갤러리는 메인 홀에 당신의 그림을 전시할 거예요.

여 네. 지금 그 전시실을 볼 수 있나요?

남 물론이죠. 저와 함께 가시죠.

어휘

preparation 준비   exhibition 전시   electrical 전기의

04 정답 ⑤

정답률 89%

M Hi, Grace. What are you looking at on your phone?

W Hi, James. It's a photo I took when I did some volunteer work. We painted pictures on a street wall.

M Let me see. Wow, I like the whale with the flower pattern.

W I like it, too. How do you like the house under the whale?

M It's beautiful. What are these two chairs for?

W You can take a picture sitting there. The painting becomes the background.

M Oh, I see. Look at this tree! It has heart-shaped leaves.

W That's right. We named it the Love Tree.

정답 및 해설 **13**

M The butterfly on the tree branch is lovely, too.

W I hope a lot of people enjoy the painting.

남 안녕, Grace. 휴대전화에서 무엇을 보고 있어?

여 안녕, James. 이건 내가 봉사활동을 할 때 찍은 사진이야. 우리가 거리의 벽에 그림을 그렸거든.

남 한번 보자. 와, 꽃무늬가 있는 고래가 마음에 들어.

여 나도 맘에 들어. 고래 밑에 있는 집은 어떠니?

남 아름다워. 이 두 개의 의자는 무엇을 위한 거야?

여 거기 앉아서 사진 찍을 수 있어. 그림이 배경이 되는 거지.

남 아, 그렇구나. 이 나무를 봐! 그것은 하트 모양의 잎을 가지고 있어.

여 맞아. 우리는 그것을 사랑의 나무라고 이름 지었어.

남 나뭇가지에 있는 나비도 사랑스러워.

여 많은 사람들이 그 그림을 즐기기를 바라고 있어.

어휘

volunteer work 자원봉사   take a picture 사진을 찍다
heart-shaped 하트 모양의   leaf 잎, 나뭇잎(*pl.* leaves)

05 정답 ②

정답률 91%

M Hi, Stella. How are you doing these days?

W Hi, Ryan. I've been busy helping my granddad with his concert. He made a rock band with his friends.

M There must be a lot of things to do.

W Yeah. I reserved a place for the concert yesterday.

M What about posters and tickets?

W Well, I've just finished designing a poster.

M Then I think I can help you.

W Really? How?

M Actually, I have a music blog. I think I can upload the poster there.

W That's great!

M Just send the poster to me, and I'll post it online.

W Thanks a lot.

해석

남 안녕, Stella. 요즘 어떻게 지내?

여 안녕, Ryan. 나는 할아버지의 콘서트를 돕느라 바빴어. 할아버지가 친구들과 록 밴드를 만들었거든.

남 할 일이 많겠네.

여 응. 어제는 콘서트 장소를 예약했어.

남 포스터랑 티켓은 어때?

여 음, 방금 포스터 디자인을 끝냈어.

남 그럼 내가 도와줄 수 있을 것 같아.

여 정말? 어떻게?

남 사실, 나는 음악 블로그를 가지고 있거든. 거기에 포스터를 올릴 수 있을 것 같아.

여 잘됐네!

남 포스터만 보내 주면, 온라인으로 게시할게.

여 고마워.

어휘

reserve 예약하다   upload 업로드하다   post 게시하다

06 정답 ②

정답률 81%

M Good morning. How may I help you?

W Hi. I want to buy a coffee pot.

M Okay. You can choose from these coffee pots.

W I like this one. How much is it?

M It was originally $60, but it's now on sale for $50.

W Okay, I'll buy it. I'd also like to buy this red tumbler.

M Actually, it comes in two sizes. This smaller one is $20 and a bigger one is $30.

W The smaller one would be easier to carry around. I'll buy two smaller ones.

M All right. Is there anything else you need?

W No, that's all. Thank you.

M Okay. How would you like to pay?

W I'll pay by credit card. Here you are.

해석

남 좋은 아침입니다. 무엇을 도와드릴까요?

여 안녕하세요. 커피포트를 사고 싶은데요.

남 알겠어요. 이 커피포트들 중에서 고르실 수 있어요.

여 이게 맘에 드네요. 얼마인가요?

남 원래는 60달러였는데, 지금은 50달러로 할인하고 있어요.

여 좋아요, 그걸 살게요. 저는 이 빨간 텀블러도 사고 싶어요.

남 사실, 두 가지 사이즈가 있어요. 이 작은 것은 20달러이고 큰 것은 30달러입니다.

여 작은 것이 휴대하기 더 쉽겠네요. 작은 것 두 개를 살게요.

남 좋아요. 그 밖에 더 필요한 건 없으세요?

여 아니, 그게 다입니다. 감사합니다.

남 알겠습니다. 계산은 어떻게 하시겠어요?

여 신용 카드로 계산할게요. 여기 있습니다.

해설

원래 60달러짜리였던 커피포트를 50달러에 하나 구매하고, 20달러짜리 작은 텀블러를 2개 구매하고 있으므로, 여자가 지불할 금액은 총 ② '$90'(90달러)이다.

어휘

coffee pot 커피포트   originally 원래   on sale 할인 중인
carry around 가지고 다니다, 휴대하다

07 정답 ①

정답률 93%

[Cell phone rings.]

W Hi, Brian.

M Hi, Mom. I'm in line to get on the plane.

W Okay. By the way, did you drop by the duty free shop in the airport?

M Yes, but I couldn't buy the wallet you asked me to buy.

W Did you forget the brand name?

M No. I remembered that. I took a memo.

W Then did you arrive late at the airport?

M No, I had enough time to shop.

W Then why couldn't you buy the wallet?

M Actually, because they were all sold out.

W Oh, really?

M Yeah. The wallet must be very popular.

W Okay. Thanks for checking anyway.

해석

[휴대전화가 울린다.]

여 안녕, Brian.

남 안녕하세요, 엄마. 저는 비행기를 타려고 줄을 서 있어요.

여 그래. 그런데, 공항에 있는 면세점에는 들렀니?

남 네, 그런데 엄마가 사 달라고 하신 지갑을 사지 못했어요.

여 상표 이름을 잊어버렸어?

남 아니요. 그건 기억했어요. 메모를 해 두었거든요.

여 그럼 공항에 늦게 도착했니?

남 아니요, 쇼핑할 시간은 충분했어요.

여 그럼 왜 그 지갑을 못 산 거야?

남 사실, 다 팔렸대요.

여 아, 그래?

남 네. 그 지갑은 틀림없이 매우 인기가 많나 봐요.

여 그래. 어쨌든 확인해 줘서 고마워.

어휘

be in line 줄을 서 있다   drop by ~에 잠시 들르다   duty free shop 면세점
wallet 지갑   be all sold out 다 팔리다. 품절되다

---

08 정답 ③

정답률 **88%**

M Lucy, look at this.

W Wow. It's about the Youth Choir Audition.

M Yes. It's open to anyone aged 13 to 18.

W I'm interested in joining the choir. When is it?

M April 2nd, from 9 a.m. to 5 p.m.

W The place for the audition is the Youth Training Center. It's really far from here.

M I think you should leave early in the morning.

W That's no problem. Is there an entry fee?

M No, it's free.

W Good. I'll apply for the audition.

M Then you should fill out an application form on this website.

W All right. Thanks.

해석

남 Lucy, 이것 좀 봐.

여 와. 청소년 합창 오디션에 관한 거네.

남 응. 13세에서 18세까지 누구에게나 열려 있대.

여 합창단에 들어가는 데 관심이 있어. 그게 언제야?

남 4월 2일 오전 9시부터 오후 5시까지야.

여 오디션 장소는 청소년 수련원이야. 여기서 정말 멀어.

남 너는 아침 일찍 출발해야겠네.

여 그건 문제없어. 참가비가 있니?

남 아니, 무료야.

여 좋아. 나는 오디션에 지원할 거야.

남 그럼 이 웹사이트에서 신청서를 작성해야 해.

여 좋아. 고마워.

어휘

choir 합창단   far from here 여기서 먼   entry fee 참가비   free 무료의
apply for ~에 지원하다   fill out ~을 작성하다   application form 지원서

---

09 정답 ④

정답률 **90%**

W Hello, Rosehill High School students! I'm your school counselor, Ms. Lee. I'm so happy to announce a special event, the 2023 Career Week. It'll be held from May 22nd for five days. There will be many programs to help you explore various future jobs. Please kindly note that the number of participants for each program is limited to 20. A special lecture on future career choices will be presented on the first day. Registration begins on May 10th. For more information, please visit our school website. I hope you can come and enjoy the 2023 Career Week!

해석

여 안녕하세요, Rosehill 고등학교 학생 여러분! 저는 여러분의 학교 상담사인 이 선생님입니다. 저는 특별한 행사인 2023 Career Week를 알려 드리게 되어 매우 기쁩니다. 5월 22일부터 5일간 개최될 것입니다. 다양한 미래 직업을 탐색할 수 있도록 많은 프로그램이 있을 예정이에요. 각 프로그램의 참가 인원은 20명으로 제한되어 있으니 참고 부탁드립니다. 첫날에는 미래 진로 선택 특강이 진행될 것입니다. 등록은 5월 10일에 시작합니다. 더 많은 정보를 원하시면, 우리 학교 웹사이트를 방문해 주세요. 여러분이 2023 Career Week에 와서 즐길 수 있기를 바랍니다!

어휘

counselor 상담사   announce 알리다, 발표하다   explore 탐색하다, 탐험하다
note 주의하다   participant 참가자   be limited to ~으로 제한되다
registration 등록

---

10 정답 ②

정답률 **92%**

M Jessica, what are you doing?

W I'm trying to buy one of these five frying pans.

M Let me see. This frying pan seems pretty expensive.

W Yeah. I don't want to spend more than $50.

M Okay. And I think 9 to 12-inch frying pans will work for most of your cooking.

W I think so, too. An 8-inch frying pan seems too small for me.

M What about the material? Stainless steel pans are good for fast cooking.

W I know, but they are heavier. I'll buy an aluminum pan.

M Then you have two options left. Do you need a lid?

W Of course. A lid keeps the oil from splashing. I'll buy this one.

M Good choice.

해석

남 Jessica, 뭐 하고 있어요?

여 이 다섯 개의 프라이팬 중 하나를 사려고 해요.

남 어디 봐요. 이 프라이팬은 꽤 비싼 것 같네요.

여 네. 나는 50달러 이상을 쓰고 싶지는 않아요.

남 좋아요. 그리고 나는 9인치에서 12인치의 프라이팬이 대부분의 요리에 맞을 거라고 생각돼요.

여 저도 그렇게 생각해요. 8인치 프라이팬은 저에게 너무 작을 것 같아요.

남 소재는 어때요? 스테인리스 냄비는 빠른 요리에 좋아요.

여 알아요, 하지만 더 무겁죠. 저는 알루미늄 팬을 살 거예요.

남 그럼 두 가지 선택지가 남았군요. 뚜껑이 필요해요?

여 물론이죠. 뚜껑은 기름이 튀는 것을 막아줘요. 저는 이걸로 살래요.

남 좋은 선택이에요.

11 정답 ②

M Have you finished your team's short-movie project?
W Not yet. I'm still editing the video clip.
M Oh, you edit? How did you learn to do that?
W I learned it by myself through books.

해석

남 너희 팀의 단편 영화 프로젝트는 다 끝냈어?
여 아직이야. 내가 비디오 클립을 아직 편집 중이거든.
남 오, 네가 편집해? 어떻게 그런 걸 배웠어?
여 책으로 독학했어.

① 그때까지 편집하는 것을 끝낼 수 있을 것 같지 않아.
③ 이 단편 영화는 매우 흥미로워.
④ 너는 또 다른 비디오 클립을 만들어야겠네.
⑤ 나는 팀 프로젝트에서 A⁺를 받았어.

어휘
edit 편집하다

12 정답 ①

[Cell phone rings.]
W Daddy, are you still working now?
M No, Emma. I'm about to get in my car and drive home.
W Great. Can you give me a ride? I'm at the City Library near your office.
M All right. I'll come pick you up now.

해석

[휴대전화가 울린다.]
여 아빠, 지금도 일하는 중이세요?
남 아니, Emma. 차를 타고 집으로 가려던 참이란다.
여 좋아요. 저 좀 태워 주실 수 있나요? 저는 아빠 사무실 근처에 있는 시립 도서관에 있어요.
남 좋지. 지금 데리러 갈게.

② 미안하구나. 오늘 도서관은 닫혔어.
③ 문제없어. 너는 내 책을 빌릴 수 있어.
④ 정말 고마워. 지금 너를 차에서 내려 줄게.
⑤ 맞아. 사무실의 인테리어를 바꿨거든.

어휘
be about to 막 ~하려던 참이다   give ~ a ride ~을 차에 태워 주다

13 정답 ③

M Claire, how's your farm doing?
W Great! I harvested some cherry tomatoes and cucumbers last weekend. Do you want some?
M Of course. I'd like some very much.
W Okay. I'll bring you some tomorrow.
M Thanks. Are you going to the farm this weekend too?
W Yes. The peppers are almost ready to be picked.
M Can I go with you? I'd like to look around your farm and help you pick the peppers.
W Sure. It would be fun to work on the farm together.
M Sounds nice. Is there anything I need to prepare?
W Just wear comfortable clothes and shoes.

해석

남 Claire, 농장은 어때요?
여 좋아요! 지난 주말에는 방울토마토와 오이를 좀 수확했어요. 좀 드릴까요?
남 물론이죠. 너무나 먹어 보고 싶어요.
여 네. 내일 좀 가져다드릴게요.
남 감사합니다. 이번 주말에도 농장에 갈 건가요?
여 네. 고추는 거의 딸 준비가 되어 있거든요.
남 같이 가도 될까요? 나는 당신의 농장을 둘러보고 고추를 따는 것을 돕고 싶어요.
여 물론이죠. 농장에서 같이 일하면 재미있을 거예요.
남 좋네요. 제가 준비해야 할 것이 있나요?
여 그냥 편한 옷과 신발을 신고 오면 돼요.

① 이 토마토와 오이를 좀 드셔 보세요.
② 고추가 피부에 좋다는 건 몰랐어요.
④ 토마토가 빨간색이면 따도 돼요.
⑤ 당신의 농장에서 채소들이 자라도록 도울게요.

어휘
harvest 수확하다   cucumber 오이   pepper 고추
be ready to ~할 준비가 되다   look around ~을 둘러보다   prepare 준비하다

14 정답 ①

W Daniel, what's wrong?
M Hi, Leila. I had an argument with Olivia.
W Was it serious?
M I'm not sure, but I think I made a mistake.
W So that's why you have a long face.
M Yeah. I want to get along with her, but she's still angry at me.
W Did you say you're sorry to her?
M Well, I texted her saying that I'm sorry.
W I don't think it's a good idea to express your apology through a text message.
M Do you think so? Now I know why I haven't received any response from her yet.
W I think it'd be best to go and talk to her in person.
M You're right. I'll meet her and apologize.

해석

여 Daniel, 무슨 일이야?
남 안녕, Leila. Olivia와 말다툼을 했어.
여 심각한 일이었어?
남 확실하지는 않지만, 내가 실수를 한 것 같아.
여 그래서 네가 우울한 거구나.

남 응. 나는 그녀와 잘 지내고 싶지만, 그녀는 여전히 나에게 화가 나 있어.

여 그녀에게 미안하다고 말했어?

남 음, 미안하다고 문자 보냈어.

여 나는 문자 메시지로 사과를 표현하는 것은 좋은 생각이 아니라고 생각해.

남 그렇게 생각해? 왜 아직까지 그녀에게서 아무런 답장을 받지 못했는지 이제야 알겠네.

여 직접 가서 얘기하는 게 가장 좋을 것 같아.

남 네가 옳아. 그녀를 만나서 사과할게.

② 너에게 동의해. 그게 내가 그걸 한 이유야.

③ 고마워. 너의 사과 감사해.

④ 걱정하지 마. 네 잘못이라고 생각하지 않아.

⑤ 너무 안됐다. 너희 둘이 잘 지내길 바랄게.

15 정답 ③

정답률 82%

M Ted and John are college freshmen. They are climbing Green Diamond Mountain together. Now they have reached the campsite near the mountain top. After climbing the mountain all day, they have a relaxing time at the campsite. While drinking coffee, Ted suggests to John that they watch the sunrise at the mountain top the next morning. John thinks it's a good idea. So, now John wants to ask Ted how early they should wake up to see the sunrise. In this situation, what would John most likely say to Ted?

John What time should we get up tomorrow morning?

해석

남 Ted와 John은 대학 신입생이다. 그들은 함께 Green Diamond 산을 오르고 있다. 이제 그들은 산 정상 근처의 야영지에 도착했다. 하루 종일 산에 오른 후, 그들은 캠핑장에서 편안한 시간을 보낸다. 커피를 마시는 동안, Ted는 John에게 다음날 아침 산 정상에서 일출을 볼 것을 제안한다. John은 그것이 좋은 생각이라고 생각한다. 그래서, 이제 John은 Ted에게 일출을 보기 위해 얼마나 일찍 일어나야 하는지 묻고 싶어 한다. 이 상황에서 John은 Ted에게 뭐라고 말할 것 같은가?

John 내일 아침에 우리는 몇 시에 일어나야 할까?

① 가장 좋은 일출 장소를 어떻게 찾을 수 있을까?

② 너는 왜 그렇게 자주 산에 오르는 거야?

④ 언제 산 정상에서 내려가야 할까?

⑤ 밤에 산에서 우리는 어디에 묵어야 하지?

해설

Ted와 John은 함께 Green Diamond 산을 올라, 산 정상 근처의 야영지에서 좀 쉬고 있다. 다음날 아침 산 정상에서 일출을 보자는 Ted의 제안에, John은 일출을 보려면 몇 시에 일어나야 하는지 물어보고 싶어 하는 상황이므로, John이 할 말로 가장 적절한 것은 ③ '내일 아침에 우리는 몇 시에 일어나야 할까?'이다.

16 정답 ③   정답률 95%   17 정답 ④   정답률 95%

W Good morning, everyone. Do you spend a lot of time with your family? One of the best ways to spend time with your family is to enjoy sports together. Today, I will share some of the best sports that families can play together. The first one is badminton. The whole family can enjoy the sport with minimal equipment. The second one is basketball. You can easily find a basketball court near your house. The third one is table tennis. It can be played indoors anytime. The last one is bowling. Many families have a great time playing it together. When you go home today, how about playing one of these sports with your family?

해석

여 모두들 좋은 아침이에요. 가족과 많은 시간을 보내시나요? 가족과 함께 시간을 보내는 가장 좋은 방법 중 하나는 함께 스포츠를 즐기는 것입니다. 오늘은 가족들이 함께 할 수 있는 최고의 스포츠들 중 몇 가지를 공유하겠습니다. 첫 번째는 배드민턴입니다. 온 가족이 최소한의 장비로 그 스포츠를 즐길 수 있습니다. 두 번째는 농구입니다. 여러분은 집 근처에서 농구장을 쉽게 찾을 수 있습니다. 세 번째는 탁구입니다. 그것은 실내에서 언제든지 할 수 있습니다. 마지막은 볼링입니다. 많은 가족들이 함께 스포츠를 하면서 즐거운 시간을 보냅니다. 오늘 집에 가서, 가족들과 함께 이런 스포츠를 하는 건 어떨까요?

16

① 노인분들에게 좋은 실내 스포츠

② 스포츠에서 규칙을 배우는 것의 중요성

③ 가족이 함께 즐길 수 있는 최고의 스포츠

④ 스포츠 경기에서 이기기 위한 유용한 조언들

⑤ 전통적인 가족 스포츠의 역사

17

① 배드민턴   ② 농구   ③ 탁구   ④ 축구   ⑤ 볼링

3회

23년 3월

01 ①	02 ①	03 ②	04 ④	05 ⑤	06 ④
07 ①	08 ③	09 ④	10 ②	11 ①	12 ②
13 ③	14 ①	15 ②	16 ②	17 ④	

01 정답 ①

정답률 91%

[Chime bell rings.]

M Good morning. This is Ethan Cooper from the Reindeer Mountain maintenance office. Last night, we had 20 cm of heavy snow. Most of the snow melted away with the sun out in the morning, but some of it froze in the shade. For hikers' safety, we've closed some of the trails covered with ice. At this moment, Sunrise Trail and Lakeview Trail are unavailable for hikers. I'll make an announcement later when the trails are ready to be reopened. Until then, keep in mind that Sunrise Trail and Lakeview Trail are closed. Thank you.

해석

[차임벨이 울린다.]

남 좋은 아침입니다. 저는 Reindeer산 관리 사무소의 Ethan Cooper입니다. 어젯밤에는 20cm의 폭설이 내렸습니다. 아침 햇살이 내리쬐면서 대부분의 눈이 녹았지만, 일부는 그늘에서 얼어붙었습니다. 등산객들의 안전을 위해, 얼음으로 뒤덮인 등산로 일부를 폐쇄했습니다. 현재 Sunrise Trail과 Lakeview Trail은 등산객들이 이용할 수 없습니다. 산책로가 다시 열릴 준비가 되면 나중에 알려 드리겠습니다. 그 전까지는, Sunrise Trail과 Lakeview Trail이 폐쇄된다는 점을 명심해 주세요. 감사합니다.

어휘

maintenance office 관리 사무소   melt away 녹아서 사라지다
freeze 얼다(-froze-frozen)   shade 그늘   trail 등산로, 산길
covered with ~으로 뒤덮인   at this moment 지금, 현재
unavailable 이용 불가능한   make an announcement 발표하다, 공표하다
keep in mind 명심하다

02 정답 ①

정답률 97%

M Honey, what are you doing?

W I'm looking for the measuring spoons. Do you know where they are?

M They're in the first drawer. Why do you need them?

W The recipe says four teaspoons of sugar.

M Dear, you don't have to follow the recipe as it is.

W What do you mean?

M A recipe is just an example. You don't need to add the same amount of ingredients as stated in the recipe.

W Hmm. Right. Sometimes the food is too sweet when I cook based on the recipe instructions.

M See? You don't need to stick to the recipe.

W Okay. I'll remember that.

해석

남 여보, 뭐 하는 거예요?

여 계량스푼을 찾고 있어요. 어디에 있는지 아나요?

남 첫 번째 서랍에 있어요. 당신은 왜 그것들이 필요한가요?

여 요리법에 설탕 4티스푼이라고 되어 있어서요.

남 여보, 요리법을 그대로 따를 필요는 없어요.

여 무슨 말이에요?

남 요리법은 단지 예시일 뿐이에요. 요리법에 명시된 것과 같은 똑같은 양의 재료를 넣을 필요는 없거든요.

여 음, 맞아요. 조리법에 따라 요리하면 가끔은 음식이 너무 달더라고요.

남 그렇죠? 요리법을 고집할 필요는 없어요.

여 좋아요. 기억하고 있을게요.

어휘

measuring spoon 계량스푼   drawer 서랍
don't have to ~할 필요는 없다(= don't need to)   add 더하다, 첨가하다
same amount 같은 양   ingredient (음식의) 재료   based on ~에 근거하여
recipe instruction 요리법 지시   stick to ~을 지키다, ~을 고수하다

03 정답 ②

정답률 93%

[Door knocks.]

W Can I come in?

M Yes. Oh, Ms. Smith. Did you read the email I sent?

W I did. I liked your game scenario. The characters exploring space were very mysterious. How did you create the characters?

M Actually, old science fiction movies inspired me to design those characters.

W Interesting. Now, could you describe the main character more specifically? It'll be helpful when I compose the theme song for the character.

M Well, he's a thrill seeker. So, a strong, bold, and rhythmic sound would suit him.

W Okay. Do you need anything else?

M I also want you to make some background music.

W Of course. When do you need them?

M By December 21st. I'd like to start putting the music into the game by then.

W All right. Then I'll talk to you later.

해석

[문을 두드린다.]

여 들어가도 될까요?

남 네. 아, Smith 씨. 제가 보낸 이메일을 읽었나요?

여 읽었죠. 당신의 게임 시나리오가 좋더라고요. 우주를 탐험하는 캐릭터들이 매우 신비롭더군요. 어떻게 캐릭터를 만들었나요?

남 사실, 오래된 공상 과학 영화들이 제가 그 캐릭터들을 디자인하도록 영감을 주었어요.

여 흥미롭네요. 이제, 주인공에 대해 좀 더 구체적으로 설명해 주시겠어요? 제가 캐릭터 주제곡을 작곡할 때 도움이 될 것 같아요.

남 음, 그는 스릴을 추구하는 사람이에요. 그래서, 강하고, 대담하고, 리드미컬한 소리가 그에게 어울릴 거예요.

여 좋아요. 그 밖에 또 필요한 것이 있나요?

남 저는 당신이 배경 음악 또한 만들기를 원해요.

여 물론이에요. 언제 필요하세요?

남 12월 21일까지요. 그때까지 게임에 음악을 입히는 걸 시작하고 싶어요.

여 좋습니다. 그럼 나중에 다시 얘기해요.

4회
22년 11월

어휘
scenario 시나리오, 각본   character 캐릭터   explore 탐험하다
mysterious 신비한   science fiction movie 공상 과학 영화   inspire 영감을 주다
describe 묘사하다   thrill seeker 스릴을 추구하는 사람   suit 어울리다, 적절하다

04 정답 ④

정답률 88%

M Hi, Chelsea. Did you finish your art assignment?
W Oh, my dream room drawing? Yes. Here's the picture.
M Wow, it's so creative. There is a staircase next to the door.
W Yes. I've always dreamed of a room with two floors. Look at the three light bulbs above the staircase.
M They look very stylish. And I like the flower picture above the sofa. It'll bring warmth to your room.
W Thanks. Check out the square-shaped rug on the floor.
M It goes well with this place. Oh, there is a bookshelf by the sofa.
W You're right. I want to keep my favorite books nearby.
M That's a good idea.

해석
남 안녕, Chelsea. 미술 숙제는 다 했어?
여 오, 내 꿈의 방 그림? 응. 여기 그림이 있어.
남 와, 정말 창의적이네. 문 옆에 계단이 있네.
여 응. 나는 항상 2층짜리 방을 꿈꿔 왔어. 계단 위에 있는 전구 세 개를 봐.
남 그것들은 매우 스타일리시해 보여. 그리고 소파 위에 있는 꽃 그림이 마음에 들어. 그게 네 방에 따뜻함을 가져다줄 거야.
여 고마워. 바닥에 있는 정사각형 모양의 깔개도 봐봐.
남 이 장소랑 잘 어울리네. 아, 소파 옆에 책장이 있구나.
여 맞아. 나는 좋아하는 책을 근처에 두고 싶거든.
남 좋은 생각이야.

어휘
assignment 과제, 숙제   staircase 계단   light bulb 전구
warmth 따뜻함   square-shaped rug 정사각형 모양의 깔개
go well with ~와 잘 어울리다

05 정답 ⑤

정답률 96%

W Jamie, is the cartoon artist on her way?
M Yes. She'll arrive at our studio in an hour.
W Perfect. Let's check if we have everything ready for our talk show.
M Okay. I set up a chair for our guest yesterday.
W Great. And I bought a drink and put it on the table.
M Good. Did you prepare a pencil? The artist said she'll draw caricatures of us during the live show.
W Oh, she told me that she'll bring her own pencil.
M She did? Then we don't need it.
W Yeah. By the way, where's the sketchbook?
M Oops. I left it in my car. I'll go get it right now.
W Fine. Then I'll check the microphones.
M Thanks.

해석
여 Jamie, 그 만화가가 오고 있나요?
남 네. 그녀는 한 시간 후에 우리 스튜디오에 도착할 거예요.
여 완벽하군요. 토크쇼 준비가 다 되었는지 확인해 보자고요.
남 네. 나는 어제 우리 손님을 위해 의자를 준비해 두었어요.
여 훌륭해요. 그리고 저는 음료수를 사서 테이블 위에 놓았어요.
남 좋아요. 연필을 준비했나요? 그 예술가가 라이브 쇼가 진행되는 동안 우리 캐리커처를 그려 준다고 하셨어요.
여 아, 그녀가 직접 자기 연필을 가져오겠다고 했어요.
남 그랬어요? 그럼 필요 없겠네요.
여 네. 그런데, 스케치북은 어디에 있나요?
남 이런. 제 차에 두고 왔어요. 지금 바로 가져올게요.
여 좋아요. 그럼 제가 마이크를 확인해 볼게요.
남 고마워요.

어휘
cartoon artist 만화가   perfect 완벽한   prepare 준비하다   caricature 캐리커처
own 자신의   microphone 마이크

06 정답 ④

정답률 70%

M Welcome to Crispy Fried Chicken. What would you like to order?
W What kind of chicken do you have?
M We only have two kinds. Fried chicken is $15 and barbecue chicken is $20.
W I'll have one fried and one barbecue chicken.
M Okay. Would you like some potato chips with your order? They're our most popular side dish.
W How much are they?
M One basket of potato chips is $2.
W Then I'll get one basket.
M Will that be all?
W Yes. And can I use this coupon for a free soda?
M Of course. You can grab any soda from the fridge.
W Great. Here's my credit card.

해석
남 Crispy Fried Chicken에 오신 것을 환영합니다. 무엇을 주문하시겠습니까?
여 어떤 종류의 치킨이 있나요?
남 두 가지 종류가 있어요. 프라이드 치킨은 15달러, 바비큐 치킨은 20달러입니다.
여 프라이드 치킨 하나와 바비큐 치킨 하나 주세요.
남 네. 주문하신 것과 함께 감자칩을 드시겠습니까? 그게 가장 인기 있는 곁들임 음식이에요.
여 얼마예요?
남 포테이토 칩 한 바구니에 2달러입니다.
여 그럼 바구니 하나 주세요.
남 그게 다인가요?
여 네. 그리고 이 쿠폰을 탄산음료 무료로 사용할 수 있나요?
남 물론이에요. 냉장고에서 탄산음료 하나를 가져갈 수 있어요.
여 좋습니다. 여기 제 신용 카드입니다.

해설
여자는 15달러인 프라이드 치킨, 20달러인 바비큐 치킨, 그리고 2달러인 포테이토

칩 하나를 주문하고 있다. 음료는 무료 쿠폰으로 이용 가능하다고 했으므로, 여자가 지불할 금액은 ④ '$37'(37달러)이다.

어휘

order 주문하다   kind 종류   side dish 곁들임 요리   grab 붙잡다, 가져가다
fridge 냉장고

07 정답 ①

[Cell phone rings.]

W Leo, I'm sorry I missed your call. What's up?

M Well, I just called to tell you that I can't go ice fishing with you this weekend.

W Oh, no. I heard the weather will be perfect this weekend.

M I'm sorry. I really wish I could go.

W Didn't you say you're off from work this weekend?

M I am. It's not because of work. Actually, I hurt my wrist.

W That's terrible. Are you okay?

M Don't worry. I'll be fine.

W How did you get injured?

M I was playing basketball with a friend and sprained my wrist.

W Did you go to the hospital?

M I did. The doctor told me that it'll be better in a month.

W That's good. I hope you feel better soon.

해석

[휴대전화가 울린다.]

여 Leo, 전화 못 받아서 미안해요. 무슨 일이에요?

남 음, 이번 주말에 당신과 얼음낚시하러 갈 수 없다고 말하려고 전화했어요.

여 오, 안 돼요. 이번 주말에 날씨가 완벽할 거라고 들었는데요.

남 미안해요. 정말 갈 수 있으면 좋겠지만요.

여 이번 주말에 일을 쉰다고 하지 않았나요?

남 그래요. 일 때문이 아니에요. 사실, 제가 손목을 다쳤거든요.

여 끔찍하군요. 괜찮아요?

남 걱정하지 마세요. 난 괜찮을 거예요.

여 어떻게 다쳤어요?

남 친구와 농구를 하다가 손목을 삐었어요.

여 병원에 갔나요?

남 다녀왔어요. 의사가 한 달 지나면 나을 거라고 하더군요.

여 다행이에요. 빨리 회복되길 바랄게요.

어휘

miss 놓치다   go ice fishing 얼음낚시하러 가다
off from work 일을 하지 않는, 쉬는   wrist 손목   get injured 다치다
sprain (손목, 발목을) 삐다, 접지르다

08 정답 ③

M Honey, look at this flyer about Kids' Pottery Class.

W Okay. Let's take a look.

M I think our little Austin would love to make his own cereal bowl.

W I think so, too. It says that the class is held on October 8th. We can take him there on that day.

M Great. And it's held in Pottery Village. It's a 10-minute drive from our home.

W That's so close. And check out the price. The class costs only $15.

M That's reasonable. We should sign up. How can we register for the class?

W It says you can simply scan the QR code to register online.

M Okay. Let's do it right away.

해석

남 여보, 어린이 도자기 교실에 관한 이 전단지를 보세요.

여 네. 어디 한번 봅시다.

남 제 생각에 우리의 어린 Austin이 자기만의 시리얼 그릇을 만들고 싶어 할 것 같아요.

여 나도 그렇게 생각해요. 수업이 10월 8일에 진행된다고 하네요. 우리는 그 날 아이를 그곳으로 데려갈 수 있어요.

남 좋아요. 그리고 그건 도자기 마을에서 열려요. 우리 집에서 차로 10분 거리예요.

여 많이 가깝네요. 그리고 가격을 확인해 보세요. 그 수업은 15달러에 불과해요.

남 적절한 가격이네요. 가입해야겠어요. 어떻게 그 수업에 등록할 수 있죠?

여 간단하게 QR 코드를 스캔해서 온라인으로 등록하면 된다고 하네요.

남 네. 지금 바로 해요.

어휘

flyer 전단지   pottery 도자기   own 자기 자신의
be held on ~에 열리다[개최되다]   a 10-minute drive 10분 운전 거리
reasonable 적정한, 타당한, 합당한   sign up 가입하다, 참가하다
register for ~에 등록하다

09 정답 ④

W Hello, listeners. The most interesting music competition is back! You can now sign up for the 2022 Online Whistling Championship. You can select any song that you like, but note that the length of your whistling video is limited to three minutes. To enter the competition, you must upload your video on our website by December 4th. When recording your whistling, be sure to turn off the echo effect on the microphone. Winners will be decided by public online voting. The result will be announced on our website. We look forward to your enthusiastic participation.

해석

여 안녕하세요, 청취자 여러분. 가장 흥미로운 음악 경연대회가 돌아왔습니다! 지금 2022년 온라인 휘파람 챔피언십에 가입하실 수 있습니다. 좋아하는 노래를 선택할 수 있지만 휘파람 비디오의 길이는 3분으로 제한되어 있다는 점을 주목해 주세요. 대회에 참가하기 위해서는, 12월 4일까지 우리 웹사이트에 당신의 동영상을 업로드 해야 합니다. 휘파람 소리를 녹음할 때는 마이크의 에코 효과를 꺼야 합니다. 우승자는 공개 온라인 투표로 결정될 것입니다. 결과는 우리 웹사이트에 발표될 것입니다. 여러분의 열정적인 참여를 기대합니다.

어휘

competition 경쟁, 대회   sign up for ~에 가입하다   select 선별하다, 고르다
note 주목하다, 주의하다   length 길이   be limited to ~으로 제한되다
turn off ~을 끄다   public online voting 공개 온라인 투표
announce 발표하다, 공표하다   enthusiastic 열렬한, 열정적인
participation 참여

10 정답 ②

M Honey, I'm looking at a shopping site to choose curtains for our bedroom. But there are too many options to consider.

W Okay. Let's pick one together.

M I don't think we should spend more than $100.

W I agree. Let's drop this one. And some of them are machine washable at home.

M Fantastic. We won't have to pay for dry cleaning all the time.

W Good for us. Let's cross out this one then. What about a blackout option?

M We definitely need it. It'll completely block sunlight, so we won't be disturbed. And which color do you like?

W I don't mind any color except for gray.

M Okay. Then we narrowed it down to one.

W Well then, let's choose this one.

해석

남 여보, 침실을 위한 커튼을 고르기 위해 쇼핑 사이트를 보고 있어요. 하지만 고려해야 할 선택지가 너무 많네요.

여 네, 같이 골라요.

남 나는 우리가 100달러 이상 쓰는 건 아니라고 생각해요.

여 동의해요. 이건 내려놓죠. 그리고 그것들 중 일부는 집에서 세탁기로 세탁할 수 있네요.

남 너무 좋네요. 항상 드라이클리닝 비용을 지불할 필요가 없을 거예요.

여 잘됐네요. 그럼 이것도 삭제하죠. 암막 옵션은 어때요?

남 우리는 그것이 꼭 필요해요. 햇빛을 완전히 차단해서 방해받지 않을 거예요. 그리고 어떤 색이 좋으세요?

여 회색 말고는 어떤 색이든 상관없어요.

남 알았어요. 그러면 우리는 하나로 좁혀졌네요.

여 그럼, 이걸로 선택하죠.

해설

두 사람은 침실을 위한 커튼을 고르고 있다. 100달러 이하, 집의 세탁기로 세탁 가능, 햇빛 완전 차단, 회색이 아닌 색의 커튼을 고르고 있으므로, 두 사람이 선택할 커튼으로 가장 적절한 것은 ②이다.

어휘

consider 고려하다   machine washable 세탁기로 세탁할 수 있는
cross out 지우다, 삭제하다   blackout option 암막 옵션   definitely 분명히, 꼭
block 차단하다   be disturbed 방해받다   except for ~를 제외하고
narrow down 좁히다

11 정답 ①

M Excuse me. Is this really the line for the rollercoaster?

W Yes. This is the line for the ride.

M Oh, no. I can't believe it. There are so many people standing in line. How long have you been waiting here?

W I've been waiting for 30 minutes.

해석

남 실례합니다. 이게 정말 롤러코스터 줄인가요?

여 네, 여기가 놀이기구 타는 줄이에요.

남 오, 안 돼. 믿을 수가 없군요. 줄 서 있는 사람들이 너무 많아요. 여기서 얼마나 기다렸나요?

여 저는 30분 동안 기다리고 있는 중이에요.

② 이 놀이기구 아주 많이 즐거웠어요.

③ 당신은 올바른 줄에 서 계신 거예요.

④ 나는 당신을 기다릴 수 있는 충분한 시간이 있어요.

⑤ 일 년 후면 공사를 마칠 거예요.

어휘

line 줄, 선   ride 탈 것, 놀이기구   stand in line 줄을 서다

12 정답 ②

W Chris, what are you looking at?

M A little boy is crying and wandering around the park. He's all by himself.

W Oh, I see him, too. We should ask him if he's lost.

M Okay. Let's see if he needs our help.

해석

여 Chris, 뭘 보고 있어?

남 한 어린 소년이 울면서 공원 주변을 배회하고 있어. 그 아이는 완전 혼자야.

여 오, 나도 봤어. 길을 잃었는지 물어봐야겠어.

남 좋아. 우리 도움이 필요한지 알아보자.

① 안 돼. 누가 길을 잃었는지 모르겠어.

③ 정확해. 아이처럼 그만 울라고.

④ 물론이지. 그는 공원 주위를 걷는 걸 아주 좋아하거든.

⑤ 고마워. 우리는 아들에 대해 걱정했잖아.

어휘

wander around ~ 주위를 헤매다[배회하다]   all by oneself 완전 혼자인
lost 길을 잃은

13 정답 ③

M Hi, Ava.

W Hi, Samuel. Are you all set for the job interview?

M I'm still working on it. I've come up with a list of questions the interviewer might ask.

W Good job. Preparing answers to those questions will help you for the interview.

M But I think I'm not ready.

W Hmm. Have you thought about how you'll make a good first impression?

M Could you be more specific?

W You know a smile makes you look confident. Also, people usually dress up to give a favorable impression.

M That's a good point.

W I believe you'll get a good interview result with a proper presentation of yourself.

M Okay. Then I'm going to practice smiling and look for my best

4회
22년 11월

suit.

W Good. Your effort will give a good impression on the interviewer.

해석

남 안녕, Ava.

여 안녕, Samuel. 취업 면접 준비는 다 되었어?

남 아직도 작업 중이야. 면접관이 물어볼 수 있는 질문들의 목록을 생각해 냈어.

여 잘했네. 그 질문들에 대한 답을 준비하는 것이 면접에 도움이 될 거야.

남 하지만 난 준비가 안 된 것 같아.

여 흠. 어떻게 좋은 첫인상을 남길지 생각해 봤어?

남 좀 더 구체적으로 말해 줄래?

여 미소가 자신감 있게 보이게 한다는 것을 알잖아. 또한, 사람들은 보통 호의적인 인상을 주기 위해 옷을 차려입고.

남 좋은 지적이야.

여 나는 네가 자신에 대한 적절한 발표를 하면 좋은 면접 결과를 얻을 수 있을 거라고 믿어.

남 알았어. 그럼 나는 웃는 연습을 하고 나의 가장 좋은 양복을 찾아볼게.

여 좋아. 너의 노력이 면접관에게 좋은 인상을 줄 거야.

① 훌륭해. 나의 이전 제안이 너희 회사에 이익이 될 거라고 믿어.

② 미안해. 너의 면접은 다음 수요일로 연기되었어.

④ 훌륭한데, 두 번째 후보자의 직업 경력이 내 눈을 사로잡았어.

⑤ 걱정 마. 너는 다가오는 파티를 위해 좋은 옷을 구매할 수 있을 거야.

어휘

come up with ~을 생각해 내다 prepare 준비하다
make a good first impression 좋은 첫인상을 주다 specific 구체적인
confident 자신감 있는, 확신 있는 dress up 옷을 차려입다
proper 적절한 presentation 발표 suit 양복, 의복

14 정답 ①

정답률 **91%**

W Excuse me.

M Yes, ma'am. How can I help you?

W How much are those shoes?

M They're $60. But today only, we're offering a 30% discount.

W That's a good price. Do you have a size six?

M Sure. Here they are. Take a seat here and try them on.

W Thank you. *[Pause]* Well, these shoes are a little tight for me. Can I get a size six and a half?

M I'm sorry. That size in this color is sold out.

W Do you have these shoes in a different color?

M Let me check. *[Typing sounds]* We have red and green in storage.

W A green pair sounds good. I want to try them on.

M Please wait. I'll be back with the shoes in a minute.

해석

여 실례합니다.

남 네, 부인. 무엇을 도와드릴까요?

여 그 신발은 얼마인가요?

남 60달러예요. 하지만 오늘만 30% 할인해 드립니다.

여 좋은 가격이네요. 6사이즈 있나요?

남 물론이죠. 여기 있어요. 여기 앉아서 신어 보세요.

여 감사합니다. *[잠시 후]* 음, 이 신발은 제게 좀 꽉 끼네요. 6사이즈 반으로 줄 수 있나요?

남 미안해요. 이 색상의 그 사이즈는 다 팔렸거든요.

여 이 신발의 다른 색은 있나요?

남 확인해 보겠습니다. *[타이핑 소리]* 빨간색과 초록색이 창고에 있네요.

여 초록색이 좋을 것 같네요. 그걸로 신어 보고 싶어요.

남 잠깐만 기다려 주세요. 잠시 후에 그 신발을 가지고 돌아오겠습니다.

② 서두르세요. 이걸 할 시간이 충분하지 않아요.

③ 물론이죠. 이 신발에 대한 환불을 받을 수 있어요.

④ 걱정하지 마세요. 색깔은 저에게 중요하지 않아요.

⑤ 미안해요. 빨간 신발은 이미 다 팔렸거든요.

어휘

discount 할인 take a seat 자리에 앉다 try ~ on ~을 신어 보다
tight 꽉 끼는 be sold out 다 팔리다 storage 창고

15 정답 ②

정답률 **78%**

M Amelia is a high school student. She is working on a psychology project. She thinks that an interview with an expert in the field will make her project even better. She emails Professor Jacob, who is a renowned psychology professor. Even though he's busy, she manages to set up an interview with him. Unfortunately, on that morning, she eats a sandwich and feels sick. She knows this interview is important, and difficult to set up again. But she can't go meet him because of a severe stomachache. So she wants to ask him if he can reschedule their meeting. In this situation, what would Amelia most likely say to Professor Jacob?

Amelia Would it be possible to change our appointment?

해석

남 Amelia는 고등학생이다. 그녀는 심리학 프로젝트를 하고 있다. 그녀는 그 분야의 전문가와의 인터뷰가 그녀의 프로젝트를 훨씬 더 좋게 만들어 줄 것이라고 생각한다. 그녀는 Jacob 교수에게 이메일을 보내는데, 그는 유명한 심리학 교수이다. 그는 바쁘지만, 그녀는 간신히 그와의 인터뷰를 마련한다. 불행하게도, 그날 아침, 그녀는 샌드위치를 먹고 속이 좋지 않다. 그녀는 이 인터뷰가 중요하고, 다시 마련하기는 어렵다는 것을 알고 있다. 하지만 그녀는 심한 복통 때문에 그를 만나러 갈 수 없다. 그래서 그녀는 그에게 회의 일정을 다시 잡을 수 있는지 묻고 싶다. 이 상황에서 Amelia는 Jacob 교수에게 뭐라고 말할 것 같은가?

Amelia 우리 약속을 변경하는 게 가능할까요?

① 과제 기한을 연장해 주실 수 있나요?

③ 나의 마지막 심리학 프로젝트를 함께 하는 게 어때요?

④ 안내 센터에서 만나기를 원하나요?

⑤ 건강검진을 위해 의사를 방문하는 게 어떨까요?

어휘

psychology 심리학 expert 전문가 field 분야 professor 교수
renowned 유명한, 명성 있는 manage to 간신히 ~하다
set up 주선하다, 마련하다 severe 심한 stomachache 복통, 배아픔
reschedule 일정을 다시 잡다

16 정답 ②
정답률 **90%**

17 정답 ④
정답률 **93%**

W Good morning, students. These days we can easily send

messages to each other using phones or computers. However, communication has not always been as simple as it is today. Here are a few ways people in the past used to carry their messages. First, some tribes used a special drum. They were able to send warnings or important information by varying the pitch or beat. Next, other people used smoke to send messages over long distances. For example, our ancestors used smoke to signal attacks from enemies. Third, a pigeon was a reliable means of communication. It always found its way home with messages attached to its legs. Finally, a horse was one of the most efficient ways to communicate. The horse with a messenger on its back delivered mail more quickly than runners. Now you may understand the ways of sending messages back in the old days. Then let's take a look in detail at each communication method.

해석

여 학생 여러분, 좋은 아침입니다. 요즘 우리는 전화기나 컴퓨터를 사용하여 서로에게 메시지를 쉽게 보낼 수 있습니다. 하지만, 의사소통이 항상 오늘날처럼 간단하지는 않았습니다. 여기 과거 사람들이 메시지를 전달하곤 했던 몇 가지 방법들이 있습니다. 먼저, 어떤 부족들은 특별한 북을 사용했습니다. 그들은 음의 고저나 박자를 변화시킴으로써 경고나 중요한 정보를 보낼 수 있었습니다. 다음으로, 다른 사람들은 장거리에서 메시지를 보내기 위해 연기를 사용했습니다. 예를 들어, 우리의 조상들은 적들의 공격을 알리기 위해 연기를 사용했습니다. 셋째, 비둘기는 믿을 만한 의사소통 수단이었습니다. 비둘기는 다리에 부착된 메시지와 함께 집으로 가는 길을 항상 찾았습니다. 마지막으로, 말은 의사소통을 하는 가장 효율적인 방법 중 하나였습니다. 메신저를 등에 업은 말은 달리기 선수들보다 우편물을 더 빨리 배달했습니다. 이제 여러분은 예전에 메시지를 보내는 방법을 이해할 수 있을 것입니다. 그럼 각 의사소통 방법을 자세히 살펴보도록 하겠습니다.

16

① 거짓 정보 전파를 막기 위한 방법들
② 과거에 메시지를 전달했던 방법들
③ 현대 시대의 의사소통의 방식들
④ 목적에 따른 연설의 형태들
⑤ 선사 시대에 살아남기 위한 수단

17

① 북 ② 연기 ③ 비둘기 ④ 깃발 ⑤ 말

어휘

in the past 과거에 used to ~하곤 했다 tribe 부족 warning 경고
vary 달리하다, 변화를 주다 pitch (음의) 고저, 피치 beat 박자, 비트
over long distances 장거리에 걸쳐 ancestor 조상
signal 신호를 보내다, 알리다 attack 공격 enemy 적, 적군 pigeon 비둘기
reliable 믿을 만한 means 수단 attached to ~에 부착된
efficient 효율적인 in detail 자세히, 상세히 method 방법

5회 2022학년도 9월 고1 전국연합 학력평가

1권 p. 34

01 ③	02 ⑤	03 ②	04 ④	05 ④	06 ③
07 ②	08 ②	09 ⑤	10 ③	11 ③	12 ①
13 ①	14 ③	15 ④	16 ①	17 ④	

01 정답 ③

정답률 94%

W Good evening, Vermont citizens. I'm Elizabeth Bowen, the Director of the Vermont City Library. I'd like to tell you about our online 15-Minute Book Reading program. This program is designed to help your children form good reading habits at home. Every day, individual tutoring is provided for 15 minutes. It's completely personalized to your child's reading level! Don't hesitate to sign up your children for this amazing opportunity to build their reading habits! For more information, please visit the Vermont City Library. Thank you.

해석

여 안녕하세요, Vermont 시민 여러분. 저는 Vermont 시 도서관 관장 Elizabeth Bowen입니다. 저는 여러분께 저희의 온라인 15분 독서 프로그램에 관하여 말씀드리고 싶습니다. 이 프로그램은 여러분의 자녀들이 집에서 좋은 독서 습관을 형성하게 도와주기 위해 고안되었습니다. 매일 15분 간 개별적인 교습이 제공됩니다. 이것은 여러분의 자녀의 독서 수준에 완벽하게 개별화된 것입니다! 여러분의 자녀들이 그들의 독서 습관을 형성하기 위한 이 놀라운 기회에 등록하는 것을 주저하지 마세요! 더 많은 정보를 원하시면 Vermont 시 도서관을 방문해 주세요. 감사합니다.

어휘

individual 개별적인, 개인의 tutoring 교습, 지도 provide 제공하다
personalized 개별화된, 개인에 맞춰진 hesitate 주저하다 opportunity 기회

02 정답 ⑤

정답률 94%

M Clara, why the long face?
W Aw, Dad, I bought this hair dryer, but the cool air mode doesn't work.
M Where did you get it?
W I bought it second-hand online.
M Did you check the condition before you ordered it?
W I did, but I missed the seller's note that said the cool air mode doesn't work.
M Oh dear. It's important to check all the details when you buy second-hand items.
W You're right. I was just so excited because it was much cheaper than other hair dryers.
M Some second-hand items are almost like new, but others are not. So, you should read every detail of the item carefully.
W Thanks, Dad. I'll keep that in mind.

해석

남 Clara, 왜 우울하니?
여 에이, 아빠, 제가 이 헤어 드라이를 샀는데 냉풍 기능이 작동하지 않아요.
남 그것을 어디서 샀어?

여　온라인 중고품 시장에서 샀어요.

남　그것을 주문하기 전에 상태를 확인해 봤어?

여　네, 했어요. 하지만 판매자가 냉풍 기능이 작동하지 않는다고 적어 놓은 메모를 놓쳤어요.

남　오, 얘야. 중고품을 살 때는 모든 세부 사항들을 확인하는 것이 중요해.

여　맞아요. 그것이 다른 헤어 드라이보다 훨씬 쌌기 때문에 제가 너무 흥분했어요.

남　몇몇 중고품들은 거의 새것과 같은데 다른 것들은 그렇지 않아. 그러니까 그 물품에 관한 모든 세부 내용들을 주의 깊게 읽어 봐야 해.

여　고마워요, 아빠. 명심할게요.

어휘
long face 우울한 얼굴　second-hand 중고의　detail 세부 사항
keep in mind 명심하다

03　정답 ②

정답률 95%

M　Hello, Ms. Adams! It's been a while since you were here.

W　Last time I came, you told me I should get a checkup every year.

M　That's right. When did you last visit us?

W　I guess I came here last October.

M　Okay. Then, let me check your vision. Please sit here. *[Pause]* Hmm... your eyesight got a little worse.

W　Yeah, maybe it's because I've been working on a computer for too long.

M　Actually, the blue light from computers and smartphones makes your eyes tired.

W　Really? Is there a lens that blocks the light?

M　Sure. You can wear these blue light blocking lenses.

W　That sounds perfect. But I'd like to use this frame again.

M　No problem, you can just change the lenses. You can come pick them up in a week.

W　Okay, thank you so much. See you then.

해석

남　안녕하세요, Adams 씨! 당신이 여기 온 이후로 오랜만이네요.

여　지난번에 제가 왔을 때 당신이 매년 검진을 받아야 한다고 말씀하셨죠.

남　맞아요. 마지막으로 언제 저희를 방문하셨죠?

여　지난 10월에 여기 왔던 것 같아요.

남　좋아요. 그러면 시력을 확인해 볼게요. 여기 앉으세요. *[잠시 후]* 음… 당신 시력이 약간 더 나빠졌네요.

여　네, 아마도 제가 너무 오랫동안 컴퓨터로 일을 해왔기 때문일 거예요.

남　사실 컴퓨터와 스마트폰에서 나오는 블루 라이트가 당신의 눈을 피곤하게 만들어요.

여　정말요? 그 빛을 차단해 주는 렌즈가 있나요?

남　물론이죠. 이 블루 라이트 차단 렌즈를 착용하실 수 있습니다.

여　그거 괜찮을 것 같아요. 하지만 저는 이 안경테를 다시 사용하고 싶어요.

남　문제없어요, 렌즈만 교환할 수 있어요. 일주일 후에 그것들을 찾아 가실 수 있습니다.

여　좋아요, 감사합니다. 그 때 봬요.

어휘
checkup 검진　vision 시력　eyesight 시력　frame 안경테, 프레임

04　정답 ④

정답률 95%

W　Carl, what are you looking at?

M　Oh, hi, Amy. Come take a look. It's a picture of my grandparents' house. I was there last weekend.

W　What a beautiful house! There's even a pond under the tree!

M　Yes, my grandfather dug it himself. And how about that flower-patterned tablecloth?

W　I love it. It makes the table look cozy.

M　Did you see the painting of a bear on the door?

W　Oh! Did you paint that?

M　Yeah, I did it when I was 8 years old.

W　It's cute. And there are two windows on the roof.

M　Right, we get a lot of sunlight through the windows.

W　I like that! And can you still ride the swings next to the house?

M　Of course. That's the best spot to see the sunset.

W　Wow, your grandparents' house looks like a nice place!

해석

여　Carl, 무엇을 보고 있니?

남　오, 안녕, Amy. 와서 봐. 우리 조부모님의 집 사진이야. 나는 지난 주말에 그곳에 있었어.

여　참 아름다운 집이구나! 나무 밑에 연못도 있어.

남　응, 우리 할아버지가 직접 그것을 파셨어. 그리고 저 꽃무늬의 식탁보는 어때?

여　마음에 들어. 그것이 식탁을 아늑하게 보이게 만들어.

남　너 문에 곰 그림을 봤니?

여　오! 네가 그것을 그렸어?

남　응, 내가 8살 때 그것을 그렸어.

여　귀여워. 그리고 지붕에 두 개의 창문이 있네.

남　맞아, 우리는 그 창문을 통해서 많은 햇빛을 받았어.

여　난 그게 좋아! 그리고 집 옆에 있는 그네를 아직도 탈 수 있니?

남　당연하지. 그곳이 일몰을 보는 가장 좋은 장소야.

여　와, 너희 조부모님의 집은 멋진 장소처럼 보여!

어휘
dig (땅을) 파다　cozy 아늑한　swing 그네

05　정답 ④

정답률 77%

M　Honey, there's a box in the doorway. What is it?

W　I ordered some groceries online. Would you bring it in?

M　Sure. Is this for the house-warming party today?

W　Yeah. Since I had to have my car repaired, I couldn't go shopping yesterday.

M　Sorry, I should've taken you to the market.

W　That's okay. You worked late to meet the deadline for your report. Would you open the box for me?

M　Sure. *[Pause]* Oh no, some eggs are broken! Have a look.

W　Ah... that's never happened before.

M　Why don't we call the customer center about it?

W　Okay. I'll do it right now.

M　While you do that, I'll put the other food in the fridge.

W　Thanks.

남 여보, 현관 앞에 상자가 하나 있어요. 그게 뭐예요?

여 온라인으로 식료품을 몇 가지 주문했어요. 그것을 안으로 가져다줄래요?

남 물론이죠. 이것이 오늘 집들이 파티를 위한 거예요?

여 네. 제 차를 수리 맡겨야 했기 때문에 어제 쇼핑을 하러 갈 수 없었어요.

남 미안해요. 내가 시장에 당신을 데려갔어야 했는데요.

여 괜찮아요. 당신은 보고서를 기한에 맞추기 위해 늦게까지 일했잖아요. 상자를 좀 열어 줄래요?

남 물론이죠. *[잠시 후]* 오 이런, 계란이 몇 개 깨졌어요! 한번 봐요.

여 아… 전에는 이런 일이 일어난 적이 없었는데요.

남 고객 센터에 그 일에 관해서 전화해 보는 게 어때요?

여 좋아요. 즉시 그렇게 할게요.

남 당신이 전화하는 동안 내가 다른 음식을 냉장고에 넣을게요.

여 고마워요.

해설

대화의 끝부분에서 남자가 고객 센터에 전화해 보는 게 어떠냐고 제안하자 여자가 즉시 그렇게 하겠다고 응답하였으므로, 여자가 할 일로 가장 적절한 것은 ④ '고객 센터에 전화하기'이다. 냉장고에 식료품을 넣는 것은 남자가 하기로 한 일임에 유의한다.

어휘

doorway 현관, 출입구   house-warming party 집들이 파티   fridge 냉장고

06 정답 ③

정답률 **86%**

W Hello, welcome to Kelly's Bake Shop. How can I help you?

M Hi, I'd like to order a carrot cake.

W Okay, we have two sizes. A small one is $25 and a large one is $35. Which one would you like?

M Well, we're four people, so a large one would be good.

W Great. Do you need candles?

M No thanks, but can you write on the cake?

W We can. It costs $5. What would you like the message to say?

M Please write "Thank You Mom" on it.

W Sure. It takes about half an hour. Is that okay?

M No problem. Can I use this 10% off coupon?

W Certainly. You get 10% off the total.

M Thanks. Here's my credit card.

해석

여 안녕하세요, Kelly's Bake Shop에 오신 것을 환영합니다. 어떻게 도와드릴까요?

남 안녕하세요, 당근 케이크를 주문하고 싶어요.

여 알겠습니다. 두 가지 크기가 있어요. 작은 것은 25달러이고 큰 것은 35달러입니다. 어느 것을 원하세요?

남 음, 저희가 4명이어서 큰 것이 좋을 것 같아요.

여 좋습니다. 초가 필요하세요?

남 아니 괜찮아요, 하지만 케이크 위에 글자를 써 주실 수 있나요?

여 네, 그것은 5달러예요. 어떤 메시지를 쓰고 싶으세요?

남 '엄마 감사해요'라고 써 주세요.

여 알겠습니다. 30분 정도 걸립니다. 괜찮으세요?

남 문제없습니다. 이 10% 할인 쿠폰을 사용할 수 있나요?

여 물론이죠. 총액에서 10% 할인을 받을 수 있습니다.

남 감사합니다. 여기 제 신용 카드요.

해설

남자는 35달러인 큰 크기의 당근 케이크를 사면서 케이크 위에 문구를 써 달라고 요구하고 있다. 문구를 쓰는 것이 추가로 5달러가 들고, 총액에서 10% 할인을 받을 수 있는 쿠폰을 사용하고 있으므로, 남자가 지불할 금액은 ③ '$36'(36달러)이다.

어휘

half an hour 30분   Certainly. 물론이죠.

07 정답 ②

정답률 **96%**

M Anna, I haven't seen you use this bag before. Did you buy a new one?

W Hi, Jason. Yeah, I bought it online last week.

M I saw some celebrities posting about it on their social media.

W Really? I didn't know that, but this bag seems to be popular.

M It does, but its design isn't that unique. It's too plain.

W Yeah, and it's a little expensive compared to other bags.

M Well, then why did you buy it?

W I bought it because it's made from recycled materials.

M Oh, you're a responsible consumer.

W Exactly. So, I'm recommending it to all my friends.

M Good idea. I'll check the website for more information.

해석

남 Anna, 나는 네가 이 가방을 전에 사용하는 것을 본 적이 없네. 새 것을 하나 샀니?

여 안녕, Jason. 그래, 지난주에 온라인으로 그것을 샀어.

남 나는 몇 명의 유명 인사들이 그들의 소셜 미디어에 그것에 관해서 포스팅한 것을 보았어.

여 정말? 나는 그것을 몰랐어, 하지만 이 가방이 인기 있는 것 같아.

남 그래, 하지만 그것의 디자인은 그리 독특하지 않아. 너무 단순해.

여 응, 그리고 다른 가방들에 비해서 약간 비싸.

남 음, 그러면 너는 왜 그것을 샀어?

여 나는 그것이 재활용된 재료들로 만들어져 있기 때문에 샀지.

남 오, 넌 현명한 소비자구나.

여 바로 그거야. 그래서 나는 그것을 내 모든 친구들에게 추천하고 있어.

남 좋은 생각이야. 더 많은 정보를 위해서 웹사이트를 확인해 볼게.

어휘

celebrity 유명 인사   unique 독특한, 특이한   plain 단순한, 평이한
compare to ~와 비교하다   recycled 재활용된   material 재료
responsible 현명한, 책임감 있는   consumer 소비자   recommend 추천하다

08 정답 ②

정답률 **94%**

W Jimmy, what are you doing with your smartphone?

M I'm looking at a poster about the Youth Street Dance Contest.

W Oh, isn't it a street dance contest for high school students?

M Yeah. Why don't you enter? I know you're good at dancing.

W Hmm... when is it?

M The competition is October 22nd, but the deadline for entry is September 30th.

W Okay, good. I have a few months to practice.

M And look! The winner gets $2,000!

W That's amazing! What types of dancing are there?

M It says participants should choose one of these three types: hip-hop, locking, and breakdancing.

W I'm really into breakdancing lately, so I'll enter with that. How do I apply?

M You just download the application form from the website and submit it by email.

W Okay! It'll be a great experience for me to try out.

해석
여 Jimmy, 너 스마트폰으로 무엇을 하고 있니?

남 청소년 거리 댄스 경연대회에 관한 포스터를 보고 있어.

여 오, 그것은 고등학생들을 위한 거리 댄스 경연대회 아냐?

남 응. 너 참가해 보지 그래? 네가 춤을 잘 춘다는 거 알아.

여 음… 그게 언제야?

남 경연은 10월 22일인데, 참가 마감은 9월 30일이야.

여 알았어, 좋아. 연습할 시간이 몇 개월 정도 있구나.

남 그리고 봐! 우승자는 2,000달러를 받아!

여 놀랍다! 어떤 종류의 춤이 있어?

남 참가자는 힙합, 로킹, 그리고 브레이크댄싱 이 세 가지 유형 중에서 하나를 선택해야 한다고 써 있어.

여 난 최근에 브레이크댄싱에 정말로 관심이 있어. 그래서 거기에 참가할래. 어떻게 신청해?

남 웹사이트에서 신청서 양식을 다운 받아서 이메일로 제출해.

여 좋아! 그것은 내가 시도해 볼 훌륭한 경험이 될 거야.

어휘
youth 청소년 be good at -ing ~을 잘하다 entry 참가, 가입
participant 참가자 be into ~에 관심이 있다 lately 최근에
apply 신청하다 application form 신청서 양식 submit 제출하다

09 정답 ⑤

M Hello, Lakewoods High School students! I'm Lawrence Cho, president of the student council. I'm happy to announce a special new event to reduce waste around our school: Lakewoods Plogging! Since plogging is the activity of picking up trash while running, all participants should wear workout clothes and sneakers. We provide eco-friendly bags for the trash, so you don't need to bring any. The event will be held on October 1st from 7 a.m. to 9 a.m. You can sign up for the event on the school website starting tomorrow. The first 30 participants will get a pair of sports socks. For more information, please visit our school website. Don't miss this fun opportunity!

해석
남 안녕하세요, Lakewoods 고등학교 학생 여러분! 저는 학생회장 Lawrence Cho입니다. 저는 우리 학교 주변의 쓰레기를 줄일 수 있는 새로운 특별 행사인 Lakewoods 플로깅에 대해 안내하게 되어 행복합니다! 플로깅은 달리기를 하면서 쓰레기를 줍는 활동이기 때문에, 모든 참가자들은 운동복과 운동화를 착용해야 합니다. 우리는 쓰레기를 담을 친환경 봉투를 제공하며, 그래서 여러분은 아무것도 가져올 필요가 없습니다. 그 행사는 10월 1일 오전 7시부터 오전 9시까지 열릴 것입니다. 여러분은 내일부터 학교 웹사이트에서 그 행사에 등록하실 수 있습니다. 최초 30명의 참가자들은 스포츠 양말 한 켤레를 받을 것입니다. 더 많은 정보를 원하시면 우리 학교 웹사이트를 방문해 주세요. 이 재미있는 기회를 놓치지 마세요!

해설
최초로 신청한 30명의 학생들에게만 양말을 준다고 언급되어 있으므로, 내용과 일치하지 않는 것은 ⑤ '참가자 모두 스포츠 양말을 받을 것이다.'이다.

어휘
student council 학생회 workout clothes 운동복 opportunity 기회

10 정답 ③

M Honey, what are you doing?

W I'm looking at a website to order a portable heater for winter camping. Would you like to choose one together?

M Sure, let me see.

W We should be able to carry it easily, so its weight is important. I think we should get one of these under 4kg.

M Good point. Oh, this one is pretty expensive.

W I know. Let's choose one of these for less than $100.

M Okay. And I think an electric heater would be good. What do you think?

W I agree. It's safer to use.

M Now we have these two models left.

W I'd like the one with a five-star customer rating.

M All right. Let's order this one.

해석
남 여보, 뭐 하고 있어요?

여 겨울 캠핑을 위해 휴대용 난로를 주문하려고 웹사이트를 살펴보고 있어요. 같이 하나 골라 볼래요?

남 물론이죠, 어디 봐요.

여 우리는 그것을 쉽게 가지고 다닐 수 있어야 해서 그것의 무게가 중요해요. 이 4kg 이하의 것들 중에서 하나 골라야 할 것 같아요.

남 좋은 지적이에요. 오, 이것은 꽤 비싸네요.

여 알아요. 100달러 이하인 것들에서 하나 고릅시다.

남 좋아요. 그리고 내 생각엔 전기 난로가 좋을 것 같아요. 당신은 어떻게 생각해요?

여 동의해요. 그것이 사용하기에 더 안전해요.

남 이제 이 두 가지 모델만 남아요.

여 저는 소비자 평가 등급이 별 다섯 개인 것이 좋아요.

남 좋아요. 이것을 주문해요.

어휘
weight 무게 electric 전기의 customer rating 소비자 평가 등급

11 정답 ③

W Kevin, is this bike yours?

M Yes, I bought it for my bike tour.

W Really? Where are you planning to go?

M I haven't decided the place, yet.

해석
여 Kevin, 이 자전거 네 거야?

남 응, 자전거 여행을 하려고 샀지.

여 정말? 어디로 갈 예정인데?

남 아직 장소를 결정하지 않았어.

① 너도 그 여행에 참여해도 돼.

② 그 자전거는 그리 비싸지 않았어.
④ 나는 공원에서 자전거를 대여할 거야.
⑤ 가을은 여행하기에 가장 좋은 계절이야.

어휘

be planning to ~할 예정이다

12 정답 ①
정답률 91%

[Telephone rings.]

M Hello, this is Ashley's Dental Clinic. How may I help you?
W Hello, this is Emily Gibson. Can I see the dentist today? I have a terrible toothache.
M Just a second. Let me check. [Pause] He's available at 4:30 this afternoon.
W Great. I'll be there at that time.

해석

[전화벨이 울린다.]

남 여보세요, Ashley 치과 병원입니다. 어떻게 도와드릴까요?
여 여보세요, 저는 Emily Gibson인데요. 오늘 치과 진료를 볼 수 있을까요? 심한 치통이 있어서요.
남 잠시만요. 확인해 볼게요. [잠시 후] 오늘 오후 4시 30분에 시간이 있습니다.
여 좋아요. 그 시간에 갈게요.

② 좋습니다. 제 칫솔을 바꿀게요.
③ 안됐군요. 당신이 곧 좋아지길 바라요.
④ 걱정 마세요. 당신의 진통제가 효과가 좋아요.
⑤ 물론이죠. 그가 시간이 있을 때 알려 주세요.

어휘

dental 치과의   see the dentist 치과 진료를 보다
available 시간이 있는, 여유가 되는

13 정답 ①

정답률 82%

W Hey, Justin. Do you know where those students are going?
M They're probably going to the gym to practice badminton.
W Why are so many students practicing badminton?
M Haven't you heard about the School Badminton Tournament? Many of the students have already signed up for it.
W Really? Why is it so popular?
M The winners will get a big scholarship and there are lots of other prizes as well.
W That's nice! Why don't you sign up for it, too?
M I'd like to, but only doubles can participate. And I haven't found a partner, yet.
W Actually, I used to be a badminton player in my elementary school.
M Wow! I have a top expert right here! How about we partner up?
W Sure. Not an expert, but I can try.
M Fantastic! We'll be a really good team.

해석

여 이봐, Justin. 너 저 학생들이 어디 가고 있는지 알아?
남 아마도 그들은 배드민턴을 연습하려고 체육관으로 가고 있을 거야.

여 왜 저렇게 많은 학생들이 배드민턴을 연습하고 있어?
남 학교 배드민턴 토너먼트에 대해 들어본 적 없어? 많은 학생들이 이미 그것에 등록했어.
여 정말? 그게 왜 그렇게 인기가 있어?
남 우승자는 많은 장학금을 받게 될 거고 다른 상들도 많아서 그래.
여 멋지다! 너도 등록하지 그래?
남 그러고 싶지만 복식 경기로만 참가할 수 있어. 그리고 난 아직 파트너를 찾지 못했어.
여 사실, 난 초등학교에서 배드민턴 선수였어.
남 와! 최고의 전문가를 여기서 만나네! 우리 파트너가 되는 게 어때?
여 좋아. 전문가는 아니지만 노력할게.
남 굉장해! 우린 정말로 좋은 팀이 될 거야.

② 미안해. 난 네가 왜 그것을 좋아하는지 이해가 안 돼.
③ 좋은 생각이야! 너를 위해 다른 파트너를 찾아볼게.
④ 문제없어. 난 연습하기 위해 내 라켓을 사용할 수 있어.
⑤ 나도 알아. 모든 사람들이 스포츠 경기를 보는 것을 좋아해.

어휘

probably 아마도   tournament 토너먼트, 선수권 대회   scholarship 장학금
doubles 복식 경기   top expert 최고의 전문가   partner up 파트너가 되다

14 정답 ③

정답률 89%

M Hey, Natalie. What are you doing on your computer?
W Hi, Dave. I'm working on my presentation for social studies class. It's about traditional games in Asia.
M Sounds interesting. Can I see it?
W Sure. I'll introduce some games with these pictures.
M That's a great idea, but I think you have too many words on the slides.
W You're right. I'm worried it might be boring.
M Then, how about shortening your explanation and using some questions? It would make your presentation more interesting.
W Great idea! What do you think about True-or-False questions?
M That's good. Your audience will be able to focus on your presentation while thinking about the answers.
W But... what if they don't know the answers?
M It doesn't matter. They'll have fun just doing it.
W Okay. I'll make some questions right away.

해석

남 안녕, Natalie. 너 컴퓨터로 뭘 하고 있니?
여 안녕, Dave. 나 사회 수업 시간에 발표를 위해 작업하고 있어. 아시아의 전통 경기에 관한 거야.
남 재미있을 것 같은데. 내가 봐도 돼?
여 물론이지. 난 이 사진들을 가지고 몇 가지 경기들을 소개할 거야.
남 좋은 생각이야, 하지만 내 생각엔 슬라이드에 너무 많은 글자가 있는 것 같아.
여 맞아. 나도 그것이 좀 지루할 것 같아서 걱정이야.
남 그러면, 설명을 좀 줄이고 문제를 좀 이용하는 게 어때? 그것이 네 발표를 좀 더 재미있게 만들어 줄 거야.
여 좋은 생각이야! OX 퀴즈는 어때?
남 좋은 생각이야. 청중들이 문제에 대한 답을 생각하면서 네 발표에 집중할 수 있을 거야.
여 하지만⋯ 그들이 답을 모르면 어떻게 하지?
남 그건 중요하지 않아. 그들은 그저 그렇게 하는 것으로도 재미있어 할 거야.
여 좋아. 지금 즉시 문제를 좀 만들게.

① 멋지다! 난 네가 무엇을 물어볼지 궁금해.
② 물론이지. 너는 문제를 위해 열심히 공부해야 해.
④ 좋아. 내가 사진들을 더 첨가할 수 있는지 볼게.
⑤ 걱정하지 마. 대답하는 데 그리 오래 걸리지 않을 거야.

15 정답 ④

정답률 75%

W Steven is a high school student and Ms. Olson is a career counselor at his school. Steven has much interest in the video game industry. A few days ago, Ms. Olson recommended a book written by a CEO who runs a famous gaming company. After reading the book, Steven told her that the CEO is his role model. This morning, Ms. Olson hears the news that the CEO is going to have a book-signing at a bookstore nearby. She thinks Steven would love to meet his role model in person. So, Ms. Olson wants to tell Steven that he should go see the CEO at the event. In this situation, what would Ms. Olson most likely say to Steven?

Ms. Olson How about going to your role model's book-signing?

해석

여 Steven은 고등학교 학생이고 Olson 선생님은 그의 학교 진로 상담 교사이다. Steven은 비디오 게임 산업에 관심이 많다. 며칠 전에 Olson 선생님은 유명한 게임 회사를 경영하는 한 CEO가 쓴 책을 추천했다. 그 책을 읽은 후 Steven은 그녀에게 그 CEO가 자신의 롤모델이라고 말했다. 오늘 아침 Olson 선생님은 그 CEO가 근처 서점에서 책 사인회를 열 것이라는 뉴스를 듣는다. 그녀는 Steven이 자신의 롤모델을 직접 만나고 싶어 할 거라고 생각한다. 그래서 Olson 선생님은 Steven에게 그 행사에 가서 CEO를 만나는 게 좋을 것 같다고 말하고 싶다. 이 상황에서 Olson 선생님은 Steven에게 뭐라고 말할 것 같은가?

Ms. Olson 네 롤모델의 책 사인회에 가는 게 어때?

① 네가 원하는 시간에 언제라도 나를 보러 와도 돼.
② 네가 그 CEO를 만났다는 소식을 들어서 행복해.
③ 왜 너는 게임 회사를 경영하고 싶니?
⑤ 너는 네 롤모델이 쓴 책을 더 많이 사야 해.

해설

steven의 롤모델이자 유명한 게임 회사 CEO가 근처 서점에서 책 사인회를 열 것이라는 소식을 듣고 Steven에게 거기에 참여해 보라고 말해야 하는 상황이므로, Ms. Olson이 할 말로 가장 적절한 것은 ④ '네 롤모델의 책 사인회에 가는 게 어때?'이다.

16 정답 ①

정답률 87%

17 정답 ④

정답률 96%

M Hello, students. Last class, we took a brief look at how to tune your musical instruments. Today, we're going to talk a bit about how to take care of and maintain your instruments. First, let's take flutes. They may have moisture from the air blown through them, so you should clean and wipe the mouth piece before and after playing. Next are trumpets. They can be taken apart, so you should air dry the parts in a cool dry place, away from direct sunlight. And as for pianos, they don't need everyday care, but it's essential to protect the keys by covering them with a protective pad when not in use. The last ones are string instruments like guitars. Their strings need replacement. When you replace the strings, it's good to do it gradually, one at a time. Proper care can lengthen the lifespan of your musical instruments. I hope this lesson helps you to keep your musical instruments safe from damage.

해석

남 안녕하세요, 학생 여러분. 지난 수업에서 우리는 악기를 어떻게 조율하는지 간략하게 살펴봤습니다. 오늘 우리는 어떻게 악기를 관리하고 유지하는지에 관하여 잠깐 이야기해 볼 것입니다. 우선, 플루트를 살펴봅시다. 그것들은 그 안으로 불어 넣어진 공기로부터 수분을 가지고 있을지도 모릅니다. 그러므로, 여러분은 연주하기 전후로 입을 대는 부분을 청소하고 닦아야 합니다. 다음은 트럼펫입니다. 그것들은 분리될 수 있으므로, 여러분은 그 부분들을 직사광선을 피해서 시원하고 건조한 곳에서 자연 건조시켜야 합니다. 그리고 피아노의 경우에는 그것들은 매일 관리할 필요는 없지만, 사용하지 않을 때는 보호 패드로 그것들을 덮어 놓음으로써 건반을 보호해야 하는 것이 필수입니다. 마지막은 기타와 같은 현악기들입니다. 현악기의 줄은 교체할 필요가 있습니다. 줄을 교체할 때는 한번에 하나씩 서서히 하는 것이 좋습니다. 적절한 관리가 여러분의 악기의 수명을 더 연장시킬 수 있습니다. 저는 이 강좌가 여러분의 악기를 손상으로부터 안전하게 유지하는 데 도움이 되기를 바랍니다.

16

① 악기를 관리하는 방법
② 좋은 악기를 선택하는 방법
③ 날씨가 악기에 미치는 영향
④ 아이가 악기를 배우는 것의 이점
⑤ 자신만의 악기를 만드는 것의 어려움

17

① 플루트   ② 트럼펫   ③ 피아노   ④ 드럼   ⑤ 기타

01 ②	02 ①	03 ⑤	04 ⑤	05 ①	06 ③
07 ①	08 ⑤	09 ⑤	10 ④	11 ①	12 ③
13 ③	14 ④	15 ④	16 ②	17 ③	

01 정답 ②
정답률 97%

M Good afternoon, this is the building manager, Richard Carson. We are planning to have the walls painted on our building next week. The working hours will be from 9 a.m. to 6 p.m. Don't be surprised to see workers outside your windows. Please keep your windows closed while they are painting. There might be some smell from the paint. But don't worry. It is totally safe and eco-friendly. Sorry for any inconvenience and thank you for your cooperation.

해석

남 안녕하세요, 저는 건물 관리자 Richard Carson입니다. 우리는 다음 주에 우리 건물 벽에 페인트를 칠할 계획입니다. 작업 시간은 오전 9시부터 오후 6시까지가 될 것입니다. 창문 밖에 있는 작업자분들을 보고 놀라지 마십시오. 그들이 페인트를 칠하는 동안 창문을 닫아 두시기 바랍니다. 페인트에서 나는 약간의 냄새가 있을지도 모릅니다. 하지만 걱정하지 마십시오. 그것은 완전히 안전하며 환경 친화적입니다. 불편을 드려서 죄송하며 여러분의 협조에 감사드립니다.

어휘

paint 페인트를 칠하다   eco-friendly 환경 친화적인   inconvenience 불편
cooperation 협조

02 정답 ①
정답률 97%

M Hello, Veronica.

W Hi, Jason. I heard that you are trying to get a driver's license these days. How is it going?

M You know what? I already got it. Look!

W Oh, good for you! How was the driving test?

M Well, while taking the driving test, I was very nervous because some people were driving so fast.

W But there are speed limit signs everywhere.

M Right, there are. But so many drivers ignore speed limits these days.

W That's terrible. Those drivers could cause serious car accidents.

M That's true. Driving too fast can be dangerous for everybody.

W Exactly. In my opinion, all drivers should follow the speed limits.

M I totally agree with you.

해석

남 안녕, Veronica.

여 안녕, Jason. 나는 네가 요즘 운전면허를 따려고 노력 중이라고 들었어. 어떻게 되어 가니?

남 그거 알아? 나는 이미 그것을 땄어. 봐!

여 오, 잘됐다! 운전면허 시험은 어땠니?

남 음, 운전면허 시험을 치르는 동안 나는 일부 사람들이 너무 빨리 운전을 하고 있어서 매우 긴장됐어.

여 그런데 모든 곳에 제한 속도 표시가 있잖아.

남 맞아, 있어. 하지만 아주 많은 운전자들이 요즘 제한 속도를 무시해.

여 그거 심하네. 그런 운전자들이 심각한 교통사고를 일으킬 수 있어.

남 사실이야. 너무 빨리 운전하는 것은 모든 사람에게 위험할 수 있어.

여 맞아. 내 생각에는 모든 운전자가 제한 속도를 지켜야 해.

남 네 의견에 완전히 동의해.

어휘

driver's license 운전면허(증)   speed limit 제한 속도   follow 지키다, 따르다

03 정답 ⑤
정답률 96%

W Excuse me. Can you help me find some books for my homework?

M Sure. What is your homework about?

W It's for my history class. The topic is the relationship between France and Germany.

M What about this world history book?

W It looks good. Do you have any other books?

M I can also recommend this European history book.

W Great. How many books can I borrow at a time?

M You can borrow up to four books for three weeks each.

W Okay. I'll take these two books, then.

M All right. [Beep sound] Don't forget to return them on time.

해석

여 실례합니다. 제 과제를 위한 책을 좀 찾는 것을 도와주실 수 있나요?

남 물론이죠. 과제가 무엇에 관한 건가요?

여 그것은 제 역사 수업을 위한 거예요. 주제는 프랑스와 독일 간의 관계입니다.

남 이 세계사 책은 어떠세요?

여 괜찮아 보여요. 다른 책들도 있나요?

남 이 유럽 역사책도 추천해 드릴 수 있습니다.

여 좋아요. 한 번에 몇 권을 빌릴 수 있나요?

남 3주 동안 최대 4권의 책을 빌릴 수 있습니다.

여 좋아요. 그럼 이 2권의 책을 가져갈게요.

남 알겠습니다. [삐 소리] 그것들을 시간에 맞춰 반납하는 것을 잊지 마세요.

어휘

recommend 추천하다   at a time 한 번에   return 반납하다
on time 시간에 맞춰, 정각에

04 정답 ⑤
정답률 86%

M Honey, come to Lucy's room. Look at what I did for her.

W It looks great. Is that a toy bear on the bed?

M Yes. That's right. She can sleep with the toy bear.

W It's cute. Oh, and I like the round clock on the wall.

M The round clock goes well with the room, doesn't it? How do you like the family picture next to the window?

W That's so sweet. I also love the striped curtains on the window.

M I'm happy you like them. What do you think of the star-shaped rug on the floor?

W It is lovely. Lucy will feel safe and warm on the rug.

M Looks like everything's prepared.

W Thanks, honey. You've done a great job.

해석

남 여보, Lucy의 방으로 와 봐요. 내가 그녀를 위해 한 것을 봐요.

여 멋지네요. 침대에 있는 저것은 장난감 곰인가요?

남 네, 맞아요. 그녀가 장난감 곰과 잘 수 있어요.

여 귀엽네요. 오, 그리고 나는 벽에 걸린 원형 시계가 마음에 들어요.

남 원형 시계가 방과 잘 어울리죠, 그렇지 않나요? 창문 옆에 있는 가족사진은 어때요?

여 정말 사랑스러워요. 창문에 있는 줄무늬 커튼도 마음에 들어요.

남 그것들이 마음에 든다니 기쁘네요. 바닥에 깔린 별 모양의 러그는 어떻게 생각해요?

여 예뻐요. Lucy가 러그 위에서 안전하고 따뜻하게 느낄 거예요.

남 모든 게 준비된 것 같아요.

여 고마워요, 여보. 정말 잘했어요.

어휘

striped 줄무늬의   star-shaped 별 모양의   rug 러그, 깔개

05 정답 ①

W David, did you fix your bicycle yesterday?

M Yes. Luckily, I was able to fix it by myself. How was your soccer practice, Christine?

W A new coach came to our soccer club and we practiced very hard.

M You must be so tired. Do you still want to see a movie this afternoon?

W Of course, I booked the tickets two weeks ago.

M All right. Let's get going.

W Wait, did you email your science report to Mr. Smith? It's due today.

M [Pause] Oh, no! I finished it but forgot to send it. What should I do?

W Why don't you send it before meeting me at the movie theater?

M Good idea. I'll go home quickly and send the report, but can you buy some popcorn for me before I get there?

W No problem. See you there.

해석

여 David, 어제 자전거를 고쳤니?

남 응. 다행히 나는 혼자 그것을 고칠 수 있었어. Christine, 네 축구 연습은 어땠니?

여 우리 축구 클럽에 새 코치님이 오셔서 우리는 아주 열심히 연습했어.

남 너는 매우 피곤하겠구나. 여전히 오늘 오후에 영화를 보러 가기를 원하니?

여 물론이지, 나는 2주 전에 표를 예매했어.

남 좋아. 가자.

여 잠깐만, Smith 선생님께 과학 보고서를 이메일로 보냈니? 오늘 마감이잖아.

남 [잠시 후] 오, 이런! 나는 그것을 끝내놓고는 보내는 것을 깜빡했어. 어떡하지?

여 영화관에서 나를 만나기 전에 그것을 보내는 게 어때?

남 좋은 생각이야. 빨리 집에 가서 보고서를 보내야겠어. 그런데 내가 거기 도착하기 전에 나를 위해 팝콘을 좀 사 줄 수 있니?

여 문제없어. 거기서 보자.

어휘

practice 연습; 연습하다   book 예매하다, 예약하다   due 마감의, 기한이 된

06 정답 ③

M Good morning. Welcome to Happy Land.

W Hello. I'd like to buy some tickets. How much are they?

M $20 for the amusement park and $10 for the water park. How many tickets do you need?

W We're five people in total, and we only want to go to the amusement park.

M Okay. Do you have any discount coupons?

W I printed out a birthday coupon from your website. It's my birthday today.

M It's your birthday? Just let me check your ID, please.

W Here you are.

M Oh, happy birthday! With your birthday coupon, your ticket is free.

W That's great. Please give me five tickets including my ticket.

M Let me see. That'll be four people at the original price, and one person with a birthday coupon.

W Right. Here is my credit card.

해석

남 안녕하세요. Happy Land에 오신 것을 환영합니다.

여 안녕하세요. 저는 입장권을 몇 장 구입하고 싶어요. 얼마인가요?

남 놀이공원은 20달러이고 워터파크는 10달러입니다. 입장권이 몇 장 필요하세요?

여 저희는 총 5명이고 놀이공원에만 가고 싶어요.

남 알겠습니다. 할인 쿠폰이 있으신가요?

여 웹사이트에서 생일 쿠폰을 출력했어요. 오늘이 제 생일이거든요.

남 오늘이 생일이신가요? 신분증 좀 확인하겠습니다.

여 여기 있습니다.

남 오, 생일 축하드립니다! 생일 쿠폰이 있으면 고객님의 입장권은 무료입니다.

여 잘됐네요. 제 입장권을 포함해서 5장의 입장권을 주세요.

남 확인하겠습니다. 정가로 네 분, 그리고 생일 쿠폰으로 한 분이겠네요.

여 맞아요. 제 신용 카드가 여기 있습니다.

해설

여자는 20달러인 놀이공원 입장권을 총 5장 구입했는데, 4장은 정가로 구입하고 나머지 1장은 생일 쿠폰을 사용하여 무료로 받았으므로, 여자가 지불할 금액은 ③ '$80'(80달러)이다.

어휘

amusement park 놀이공원   print out ~을 출력하다   original price 정가

07 정답 ①

W Hi, Alex. How is it going?

M I'm good. Thanks. I've just finished my English project. How about you, Tracy?

W I'm a little busy preparing for my food booth.

M A food booth? What for?

W My school festival is next Tuesday. I'm running a food booth that day.

M That is so cool. What is on the menu?

W We're making sandwiches. You should come.

M I'd love to, but I can't.

W You can't? I was really looking forward to seeing you at my school.

M I'm terribly sorry. I have to practice for a band audition.

W Oh, I see. Well, good luck with your audition.

M Thank you.

08 정답 ⑤

[Telephone rings.]

W Hello, this is the World Culture Center. How can I help you?

M Hi, I'm calling about a Spanish culture class for my teenage son.

W Okay. We have an interesting class for teenagers.

M Great. Who teaches it?

W A Korean teacher and a native speaker teach it together.

M What kind of activities are there in the class?

W Students can cook traditional foods, learn new words, and try on traditional clothing.

M On what day is the class?

W It's on Wednesday and Friday afternoons.

M I see. Is there anything my son should prepare before the class?

W He just needs to bring a pen and a notebook. The center provides all the other class materials.

M Perfect. Thanks for the information.

09 정답 ⑤

W Good afternoon, residents. This is the head of the Pineville Community Center. We're holding the Summer Flea Market for one week. It'll be held in the parking lot of Pineville Middle School. You can get many different kinds of items such as toys and candles at reasonable prices. You can also sell any of your own used items if they are in good condition. On the first day, every resident visiting the market will get a shopping bag as a gift. For more information, please check out the community center's website.

10 정답 ④

W Kyle, I'm looking for some sneakers. Can you help me find some good ones?

M Of course. Let me see... [Pause] Look. These are the five best-selling ones.

W Wow, they all look so cool. It's hard to choose among them.

M Well, what's your budget?

W I don't want to spend more than 80 dollars.

M All right. Which style do you want, active or casual?

W I prefer casual ones. I think they match my clothes better.

M Good. And I'd like to recommend waterproof shoes for rainy days.

W Okay, I will take your advice.

M So you have two options left. Which color do you prefer?

W Most of my shoes are black, so I'll buy white ones this time.

M You made a good choice.

11 정답 ①

W Justin, what are you reading?

M An advertisement. There's a special event at Will's Bookstore downtown.

W What kind of event is it?

M All children's books are 20% off.

해석

여 Justin, 무엇을 읽고 있니?

남 광고야. 시내에 있는 Will's Bookstore에서 특별 행사가 있어.

여 어떤 종류의 행사니?

남 모든 어린이 도서를 20퍼센트 할인해.

② 좋은 기사를 쓰는 데는 시간이 걸려.

③ 나는 액션 모험 도서를 읽는 것을 좋아해.

④ TV에 너무 많은 광고가 있어.

⑤ 그 가게는 지난달부터 문을 닫았어.

해설

광고를 읽고 있는 남자가 서점에서 특별 행사가 있다고 말하자 여자는 그것이 어떤 종류의 행사인지 물었으므로, 이에 대한 남자의 응답으로 가장 적절한 것은 ①이다.

어휘

advertisement 광고   downtown 시내에, 도심지에   article 기사

12 정답 ③

M You look so worried. What's wrong, Liz?

W I didn't do well on my presentation yesterday.

M Sorry about that. To help take your mind off of it, how about having a nice meal?

W Okay. Good food always makes me feel better.

해석

남 너 무척 걱정스러워 보여. Liz, 무슨 일 있니?

여 나는 어제 내 발표를 잘하지 못했어.

남 안타깝구나. 그것을 잊어버리는 데 도움이 되기 위해 맛있는 식사를 하는 게 어때?

여 알겠어. 맛있는 음식은 항상 내 기분을 나아지게 해.

① 천만에. 나는 너를 도와서 기뻐.

② 그건 사실이 아니야. 나는 네 도움으로 그것을 해냈어.

④ 정말? 너는 나중에 극장을 꼭 방문해야 해.

⑤ 신경 쓰지 마. 너는 다음번 발표에서 더 잘할 거야.

어휘

presentation 발표   take one's mind off ~을 잊어버리다

13 정답 ③

M Jenny, what class do you want to take this summer vacation?

W Well, *[Pause]* I'm thinking of the guitar class.

M Cool! I'm interested in playing the guitar, too.

W Really? It would be exciting if we took the class together.

M I know, but I am thinking of taking a math class instead. I didn't do well on the final exam.

W Oh, there is a math class? I didn't know that.

M Yes. Mrs. Kim said she is offering a math class for first graders.

W That might be a good chance to improve my skills, too. Where can I check the schedule for the math class?

M You can find it on the school website.

해석

남 Jenny, 이번 여름 방학에 무슨 수업을 듣고 싶니?

여 음, *[잠시 후]* 나는 기타 수업을 생각 중이야.

남 멋지다! 나도 기타 연주에 관심이 있어.

여 정말? 우리가 수업을 함께 들으면 재미있겠다.

남 알긴 하지만 나는 대신 수학 수업을 들을 생각이야. 기말 고사를 잘 보지 못했거든.

여 아, 수학 수업이 있니? 나는 그것을 몰랐어.

남 응. Kim 선생님께서 1학년을 위해 수학 수업을 제공할 거라고 말씀하셨어.

여 내 실력도 향상시킬 좋은 기회일 수도 있겠다. 어디에서 수학 수업 일정을 확인할 수 있니?

남 학교 웹사이트에서 그것을 찾을 수 있어.

① 나는 새 기타를 사서 신이 나.

② 여름 방학은 금요일에 시작해.

④ 학교 축제에 같이 가자.

⑤ 너는 방학 동안 휴식을 좀 취할 수 있어.

어휘

final exam 기말 고사   offer 제공하다   first grader 1학년 학생
improve 향상시키다, 개선하다

14 정답 ④

M Hi, Claire! How are you doing?

W I'm good. You're looking great!

M Thanks. I've been working out these days.

W I need to start working out, too. What kind of exercise do you do?

M I do yoga and some stretching at home.

W At home? Do you exercise alone?

M Yes and no. I exercise online with other people.

W Exercising online with others? What do you mean by that?

M I'm taking an online fitness course. We work out together on the Internet every evening at 7.

W That sounds great. Can I join the course, too?

해석

남 안녕, Claire! 어떻게 지내니?

여 잘 지내. 너는 좋아 보인다!

남 고마워. 나는 요즘 운동을 하고 있어.

여 나도 운동을 시작할 필요가 있어. 너는 어떤 종류의 운동을 하니?

남 집에서 요가와 약간의 스트레칭을 해.

여 집에서? 혼자 운동을 하니?

남 그러기도 하고 아니기도 해. 나는 온라인에서 다른 사람들과 운동을 하거든.

여 온라인으로 다른 사람들과 운동한다고? 그게 무슨 말이니?

남 나는 온라인 피트니스 강좌를 듣고 있어. 우리는 매일 저녁 7시에 인터넷에서 함께 운동을 해.

여 그거 멋지다. 나도 그 강좌에 참가할 수 있니?

① 동의해. 체육관에서 운동하는 것의 많은 이점이 있어.
② 맞아. 모든 운동이 네 두뇌에 도움이 되는 것은 아니야.
③ 걱정하지 마. 내가 운동하는 것이 너무 어렵지는 않아.
⑤ 안타깝구나. 빨리 회복하길 바랄게.

work out 운동하다   course 강좌, 강의

15 정답 ④
정답률 85%

M Ted is a high school student. He is planning to run for school president this year. He really wants to win the election. He thinks using posters is an effective way to make a strong impression on his schoolmates. But he is not good at drawing. His friend, Monica, is a member of a drawing club and she is good at drawing. So, he wants to ask her to help him draw posters. In this situation, what would Ted most likely say to Monica?

Ted Can you help me make posters for the election?

해석

남 Ted는 고등학생이다. 그는 올해 학생회장에 출마할 계획 중이다. 그는 정말 선거에서 이기고 싶다. 그는 포스터를 이용하는 것이 학교 친구들에게 강렬한 인상을 주는 효과적인 방법이라고 생각한다. 하지만 그는 그림을 잘 그리지 못한다. 그의 친구 Monica는 그림 동아리 회원이고 그녀는 그림을 잘 그린다. 그래서 그는 그녀에게 그가 포스터를 그리는 것을 도와달라고 부탁하고 싶다. 이 상황에서 Ted는 Monica에게 뭐라고 말하겠는가?

Ted 내가 선거용 포스터를 만드는 것을 도와줄 수 있니?

① 내가 포스터에 너희 동아리 회원들을 그려도 되니?
② 너는 우리 그림 동아리에 가입하는 데 관심이 있니?
③ 선거에서 투표하는 방법을 나한테 말해 줄 수 있니?
⑤ 너는 다음번 학생회장 선거에 출마할 거니?

어휘

run for ~에 출마하다   school president 학생회장   election 선거
effective 효과적인   make an impression ~에게 인상을 주다

16 정답 ②
정답률 97%

17 정답 ③
정답률 94%

W Good morning, listeners. This is your host Rachel at the Morning Radio Show. What do you eat for breakfast? Today I will introduce a healthy breakfast food list. Eggs are an excellent choice because they are high in protein. High-protein foods such as eggs provide energy for the brain. Cheese is another good option. It reduces hunger so it supports weight loss. Yogurt is also great to eat in the morning. It contains probiotics that can improve digestion. Eating berries such as blueberries or strawberries is another perfect way to start the morning. They are lower in sugar than most other fruits, but higher in fiber. Add them to yogurt for a tasty breakfast. Start every day with a healthy meal. Thank you.

해석

여 청취자 여러분, 안녕하세요. Morning Radio Show의 진행자 Rachel입니다. 여러분은 아침으로 무엇을 드시나요? 오늘 저는 건강한 아침 음식 리스트를 소개하겠습니다. 계란은 단백질이 풍부하기 때문에 훌륭한 선택입니다. 계란 같은 고단백 음식은 두뇌에 에너지를 제공합니다. 치즈는 또 다

른 좋은 선택입니다. 그것은 배고픔을 줄여서 체중 감량을 도와줍니다. 요거트 또한 아침에 먹으면 정말 좋습니다. 그것은 소화를 개선할 수 있는 활생균을 함유하고 있습니다. 블루베리나 딸기 같은 산딸기류 열매를 먹는 것은 아침을 시작하는 또 다른 완벽한 방법입니다. 그것은 대부분의 다른 과일보다 설탕은 더 적지만 섬유질이 더 많습니다. 맛있는 아침 식사를 위해 요거트에 그것을 추가하세요. 매일을 건강한 식사로 시작하세요. 감사합니다.

16
① 지방이 많은 식품의 단점
② 아침 식사를 위한 건강한 음식
③ 간식 먹는 것을 피하는 방법
④ 5분 내로 조리하는 손쉬운 음식
⑤ 균형 잡힌 식단의 중요성

17
① 계란   ② 치즈   ③ 감자   ④ 요거트   ⑤ 산딸기류 열매

어휘

protein 단백질   high-protein 고단백의   hunger 배고픔
probiotics 활생균, 프로바이오틱스   digestion 소화   tasty 맛있는

01 ①	02 ③	03 ②	04 ④	05 ④	06 ③
07 ①	08 ③	09 ⑤	10 ③	11 ①	12 ⑤
13 ②	14 ②	15 ①	16 ④	17 ④	

01 정답 ①

정답률 87%

M Good afternoon, everybody. This is Student President Sam Wilson. As you know, the lunch basketball league will begin soon. Many students are interested in joining the league and waiting for the sign-up sheet to be handed out at the gym. For easier access, we've decided to change the registration method. Instead of going to the gym to register, simply log into the school website and fill out the registration form online. Thank you for listening and let's have a good league.

해석

남 여러분, 안녕하세요. 저는 학생회장 Sam Wilson입니다. 알다시피, 점심 농구 리그가 곧 시작될 예정입니다. 많은 학생들이 리그 참가에 관심이 있으며 체육관에서 참가 신청서가 배부되기를 기다리고 있습니다. 더 쉬운 접근을 위해 저희는 등록 방법을 변경하기로 결정했습니다. 체육관에 가서 등록하는 대신 그저 학교 웹사이트에 접속하여 온라인에서 등록 양식을 작성하세요. 들어주셔서 감사드리며 즐거운 리그를 보냅시다.

어휘

sign-up sheet 참가 신청서 gym 체육관 log into ~에 접속하다
fill out ~을 작성하다, 기입하다 registration 등록

02 정답 ③

정답률 96%

W Daniel, what are you doing in front of the mirror?

M I have skin problems these days. I'm trying to pop these pimples on my face.

W Pimples are really annoying, but I wouldn't do that.

M Why not?

W When you pop them with your hands, you're touching your face.

M Are you saying that I shouldn't touch my face?

W Exactly. You know our hands are covered with bacteria, right?

M So?

W You'll be spreading bacteria all over your face with your hands. It could worsen your skin problems.

M Oh, I didn't know that.

W Touching your face with your hands is bad for your skin.

M Okay, I got it.

해석

여 Daniel, 거울 앞에서 뭘 하고 있니?

남 요즘 나는 피부 문제가 있어. 내 얼굴에 있는 이 여드름들을 짜려고 노력 중이야.

여 여드름이 신경에 거슬리기는 하지만 나는 그것을 하지 않을 거야.

남 왜 안 해?

여 네가 손으로 여드름을 짜면 너는 네 얼굴을 만지고 있는 거잖아.

남 내 얼굴을 만지면 안 된다고 말하는 거니?

여 맞아. 우리 손은 세균으로 뒤덮여 있다는 것을 알잖아, 그렇지?

남 그런데?

여 너는 손으로 얼굴 전체에 세균을 퍼뜨리게 될 거야. 그건 네 피부 문제를 악화시킬 수도 있어.

남 아, 나는 그것을 몰랐어.

여 손으로 얼굴을 만지는 것은 피부에 해로워.

남 그래, 알겠어.

어휘

pop 터뜨리다 pimple 여드름 annoying 신경에 거슬리는 bacteria 박테리아
spread 퍼뜨리다 worsen 악화시키다

03 정답 ②

정답률 90%

M Excuse me. You're Chloe Jones, aren't you?

W Yes, I am. Have we met before?

M No, but I'm a big fan of yours. I've watched your speeches on climate change, and they're very inspiring.

W Thank you. I'm so glad to hear that.

M And, I also think your campaign about plastic pollution has been very successful.

W As an environmental activist, that means a lot to me.

M May I make a suggestion? I thought it'd be nice if more children could hear your ideas.

W That's what I was thinking. Do you have any good ideas?

M Actually, I'm a cartoonist. Perhaps I can make comic books based on your work.

W That is a wonderful idea. Can I contact you later to discuss it more?

M Sure. By the way, my name is Jack Perse. Here's my business card.

해석

남 실례합니다. Chloe Jones 씨 아니신가요?

여 네, 맞아요. 우리 전에 만난 적이 있나요?

남 아니요, 하지만 저는 당신의 열혈 팬이에요. 기후 변화에 관한 당신의 연설을 봤는데 그것은 정말 용기를 줘요.

여 고맙습니다. 그 말을 들으니 매우 기쁘네요.

남 그리고 저는 또한 플라스틱 오염에 대한 당신의 캠페인이 아주 성공적이었다고 생각해요.

여 환경 운동가로서 그것은 제게 많은 것을 의미해요.

남 제안을 하나 드려도 될까요? 더 많은 아이들이 당신의 생각을 들을 수 있다면 좋을 거라고 생각했어요.

여 그게 바로 제가 생각하고 있던 바입니다. 어떤 좋은 아이디어가 있나요?

남 사실 저는 만화가예요. 어쩌면 제가 당신의 작업에 바탕을 둔 만화책을 만들 수 있을 거예요.

여 아주 멋진 아이디어네요. 그것을 더 논의하기 위해 나중에 연락드려도 될까요?

남 그럼요. 그런데 제 이름은 Jack Perse입니다. 제 명함이 여기 있습니다.

어휘

climate change 기후 변화 inspiring 용기를 주는, 고무적인 campaign 캠페인
environmental activist 환경 운동가 suggestion 제안 comic book 만화책
business card 명함

04 정답 ④

정답률 76%

W Yesterday, I decorated my fish tank like a beach.

M I'd like to see it. Do you have a picture?

W Sure. Here. *[Pause]* Do you recognize the boat in the bottom left corner?

M Yes. It's the one I gave you, isn't it?

W Right. It looks good in the fish tank, doesn't it?

M It does. I love the beach chair in the center.

W Yeah. I like it, too.

M I see a starfish next to the chair.

W Isn't it cute? And do you see these two surf boards on the right side of the picture?

M Yeah. I like how you put both of them side by side.

W I thought that'd look cool.

M Your fish in the top left corner looks happy with its new home.

W I hope so.

해석

여 어제 나는 어항을 해변처럼 장식했어.

남 그것을 보고 싶어. 사진이 있니?

여 물론이지. 여기 있어. *[잠시 후]* 왼쪽 하단에 있는 보트가 보이니?

남 응. 그것은 내가 너에게 준 거 맞지?

여 맞아. 어항에 잘 어울리지, 그렇지 않니?

남 그래. 나는 중앙에 있는 해변 의자가 마음에 들어.

여 응, 나도 그것이 마음에 들어.

남 의자 옆에는 불가사리가 보이네.

여 귀엽지 않니? 그리고 사진 우측에 있는 이 두 개의 서핑보드가 보이니?

남 응. 나는 그 두 개를 나란히 둔 게 좋아.

여 그것이 멋져 보일 거라고 생각했어.

남 왼쪽 상단에 있는 네 물고기가 새로운 집에서 행복해 보이는구나.

여 그러면 좋겠어.

해설

대화에서는 우측에 두 개의 서핑보드가 있다고 했는데 그림에서는 서핑보드가 한 개 있으므로, 그림에서 대화의 내용과 일치하지 않는 것은 ④이다.

어휘

decorate 장식하다 fish tank 어항 recognize 알아차리다 starfish 불가사리 side by side 나란히

---

05 정답 ④　　　　　　　　정답률 91%

[Cell phone rings.]

M Hello, honey. I'm on the way home. How's setting up Mike's birthday party going?

W Good, but I still have stuff to do. Mike and his friends will get here soon.

M Should I pick up the birthday cake?

W No, that's okay. I already did that.

M Then, do you want me to put up the balloons around the doorway when I get there?

W I'll take care of it. Can you take the table out to the front yard?

M Sure. Are we having the party outside?

W Yes. The weather is beautiful so I made a last minute change.

M Great. The kids can play with water guns in the front yard.

W Good idea. I'll go to the garage and grab the water guns.

해석

[휴대전화가 울린다.]

남 안녕, 여보. 나는 집에 가는 길이에요. Mike의 생일 파티 준비는 어떻게 되어 가고 있어요?

여 잘되긴 하지만 아직도 할 일이 있어요. Mike와 그의 친구들이 곧 여기에 도착할 거예요.

남 내가 생일 케이크를 찾아가야 할까요?

여 아니요, 괜찮아요. 내가 이미 그것을 했어요.

남 그럼 내가 거기 도착하면 현관 주위에 풍선을 설치할까요?

여 그것은 내가 할게요. 테이블을 앞마당으로 꺼내 줄 수 있어요?

남 물론이죠. 밖에서 파티를 할 건가요?

여 네. 날씨가 너무 좋아서 막판에 변경했어요.

남 좋아요. 아이들이 앞마당에서 물총 놀이를 할 수 있어요.

여 좋은 생각이에요. 차고에 가서 물총을 가져올게요.

어휘

doorway 현관 last minute 막판의, 막바지의 garage 차고 grab 가져오다, 잡다

---

06 정답 ③　　　　　　　　정답률 87%

W Welcome to Green Eco Shop. How can I help you?

M Hi, do you sell eco-friendly toothbrushes?

W Yes, we have a few types over here. Which do you like?

M Hmm.... How much are these?

W They're $2 each. They are made from bamboo.

M All right. I'll take four of them.

W Excellent choice. Anything else?

M I also need bath sponges.

W They're right behind you. They're plastic-free and only $3 each.

M Okay. I'll also take four of them. That'll be all.

W If you have a store membership, you can get a 10% discount off the total price.

M Great. I'm a member. Here are my credit and membership cards.

해석

여 Green Eco Shop에 오신 것을 환영합니다. 무엇을 도와드릴까요?

남 안녕하세요, 친환경 칫솔을 판매하시나요?

여 네, 여기에 몇 가지 종류가 있습니다. 어떤 것을 원하시나요?

남 음… 이것들은 얼마인가요?

여 각각 2달러입니다. 그것들은 대나무로 만들어졌어요.

남 좋아요. 그것을 4개 살게요.

여 훌륭한 선택입니다. 또 필요한 게 있으신가요?

남 저는 목욕용 스펀지도 필요해요.

여 그것은 고객님 바로 뒤에 있습니다. 그것은 플라스틱이 없고 개당 3달러밖에 안 합니다.

남 좋아요. 그것도 4개 살게요. 그게 전부겠네요.

여 매장 회원이시면 총 금액에서 10퍼센트 할인을 받으실 수 있습니다.

남 좋아요. 저는 회원입니다. 제 신용 카드와 회원 카드가 여기 있습니다.

어휘

eco-friendly 친환경적인, 환경 친화적인 toothbrush 칫솔 bamboo 대나무 plastic-free 플라스틱이 없는 membership 회원 (자격·신분)

---

07 정답 ①　　　　　　　　정답률 94%

[Cell phone rings.]

M Hey, Suji. Where are you?

W I'm in the library checking out books. I'll be heading out to the science lab for our experiment in a couple of minutes.

M I guess you haven't checked my message yet. We can't do the experiment today.

W Really? Isn't the lab available today?

M Yes, it is, but I canceled our reservation.

W Why? Are you still suffering from your cold?

M No, I'm fine now.

W That's good. Then why aren't we doing the experiment today? We need to hand in the science report by next Monday.

M Unfortunately, the experiment kit hasn't been delivered yet. It'll arrive tomorrow.

W Oh, well. The experiment has to wait one more day, then.

해석

[휴대전화가 울린다.]

남 수지야, 안녕. 어디에 있니?

여 나는 도서관에서 책을 대출하고 있어. 몇 분 후에 우리 실험을 위해 과학실로 출발할 거야.

남 아직 내 메시지를 확인하지 못한 것 같구나. 우리는 오늘 실험을 할 수 없어.

여 정말? 오늘 실험실이 사용 가능하지 않은 거니?

남 아니, 사용할 수 있지만 내가 우리의 예약을 취소했어.

여 왜? 아직도 감기로 고생 중이니?

남 아니, 지금은 괜찮아.

여 다행이다. 그럼 오늘 왜 우리가 실험을 하지 않니? 우리는 다음 주 월요일까지 과학 보고서를 제출해야 하잖아.

남 안타깝게도 실험용 키트가 아직 배송되지 않았어. 내일 도착할 거야.

여 아, 그래. 그럼 실험은 하루 더 기다려야지.

어휘

check out (책을) 대출하다   lab 실험실   experiment 실험
available 사용 가능한   reservation 예약   suffer from ~로 고생하다

08 정답 ③

W Honey, did you see the poster about the Stanville Free-cycle?

M Free-cycle? What is that?

W It's another way of recycling. You give away items you don't need and anybody can take them for free.

M Oh, it's like one man's garbage is another man's treasure. Who can participate?

W It's open to everyone living in Stanville.

M Great. Where is it taking place?

W At Rose Park on Second Street.

M When does the event start?

W It starts on April 12 and runs for a week.

M Let's see what we can free-cycle, starting from the cupboard.

W Okay. But breakable items like glass dishes or cups won't be accepted.

M I see. I'll keep that in mind.

해석

여 여보, Stanville Free-cycle에 관한 포스터를 봤어요?

남 free-cycle(무료 재활용)이요? 그게 뭐죠?

여 재활용을 하는 또 다른 방법이에요. 필요하지 않은 물건을 기부하면 누군가가 무료로 그것을 가져갈 수 있어요.

남 오, 누군가의 쓰레기가 다른 사람의 보물이 되는 것 같군요. 누가 참가할 수 있나요?

여 Stanville에 사는 모든 사람이 참가할 수 있어요.

남 좋네요. 어디서 열릴 예정인가요?

여 2번가에 있는 Rose 공원에서요.

남 그 행사는 언제 시작해요?

여 4월 12일에 시작해서 일주일간 운영해요.

남 찬장부터 시작해서 우리가 무료 재활용할 수 있는 것을 살펴보죠.

여 좋아요. 그런데 유리 접시나 컵처럼 깨지기 쉬운 물건은 받지 않을 거예요.

남 그렇군요. 그것을 명심할게요.

어휘

give away 기부하다, 나누어 주다   participate 참가하다   run 운영하다
cupboard 찬장   breakable 깨지기 쉬운

09 정답 ⑤

M Hello, River Valley High School students. This is your music teacher, Mr. Stailor. Starting on April 11, we are going to have the River Valley Music Camp for five days. You don't need to be a member of the school orchestra to join the camp. You may bring your own instrument or you can borrow one from the school. On the last day of camp, we are going to film our performance and play it on screen at the school summer festival. Please keep in mind the camp is limited to 50 students. Sign-ups start this Friday, on a first-come-first-served basis. Come and make music together!

해석

남 River Valley 고등학교 학생 여러분, 안녕하세요. 저는 음악 교사 Stailor 선생님입니다. 4월 11일부터 5일 동안 우리는 River Valley 음악 캠프를 진행할 것입니다. 캠프에 참가하기 위해서 여러분이 학교 오케스트라 단원일 필요는 없습니다. 여러분은 자신의 악기를 가져와도 되고 아니면 학교에서 악기를 빌릴 수도 있습니다. 캠프 마지막 날에는 우리의 공연을 촬영하여 교내 여름 축제에서 그것을 스크린에 상영할 것입니다. 캠프는 50명의 학생들로 제한된다는 것을 명심해 주세요. 등록은 선착순으로 이번 주 금요일에 시작됩니다. 오셔서 함께 음악을 만드세요!

어휘

orchestra 오케스트라   instrument 악기   performance 공연   limit 제한하다
sign-up 등록, 가입   on a first-come-first-served basis 선착순으로

10 정답 ③

W Ben, do you have a minute?

M Sure. What is it?

W I'm trying to buy a handheld vacuum cleaner among these five models. Could you help me choose one?

M Okay. How much are you willing to spend?

W No more than $130.

M Then we can cross this one out. What about the working time?

W I think it should be longer than 10 minutes.

M Then that narrows it down to these three.

W Should I go with one of the lighter ones?

M Yes. Lighter ones are easier to handle while cleaning.

W All right. What about the filter?

M The one with a washable filter would be a better choice.

W I got it. Then I'll order this one.

해석

여 Ben, 시간 좀 있니?

남 그럼. 무슨 일이니?

여 나는 이 5개의 모델 중에서 소형 진공청소기를 사려고 하는 중이야. 내가 하나 고르는 것을 도와줄 수 있니?

남 좋아. 얼마를 쓸 생각이니?

여 130달러는 넘지 않으려고 해.

남 그럼 이것은 지워도 되겠다. 작동 시간은 어때?

여 10분은 넘어야 할 것 같아.

남 그럼 이 3개로 좁혀지네.

여 내가 더 가벼운 것 중 하나를 선택해야 할까?

남 응. 더 가벼운 것이 청소하는 동안 다루기 더 쉬워.

여 좋아. 필터는 어때?

남 세척 가능한 필터가 있는 것이 더 좋은 선택이 될 거야.

여 알겠어. 그럼 이것을 주문할게.

어휘
handheld 소형의, 손에 들고 쓰는   vacuum cleaner 진공청소기
cross ~ out 줄을 그어 ~을 지우다   narrow 좁히다   washable 세척 가능한
order 주문하다

11 정답 ①

정답률 81%

M My eyes are sore today.

W Too bad. Maybe some dust got in your eyes.

M You're probably right. What should I do?

W Why don't you rinse your eyes with clean water?

해석

남 오늘 내 눈이 아파.

여 안타깝네. 아마 네 눈에 먼지가 좀 들어갔을지도 몰라.

남 네 말이 아마 맞을 거야. 어떻게 하지?

여 깨끗한 물로 눈을 씻는 게 어때?

② 대기 오염에 대해 더 설명해 줄 수 있니?
③ 나는 새 안경을 하나 살 필요가 있어.
④ 나는 미세 먼지가 심각한 문제라는 것에 동의해.
⑤ 우리는 밖에 나가서 산책을 해야 해.

어휘

sore 아픈   dust 먼지   rinse 씻다   pollution 오염   fine dust 미세 먼지

12 정답 ⑤

정답률 80%

W Excuse me. Would you mind if I sit here?

M I'm sorry, but it's my friend's seat. He'll be back in a minute.

W Oh, I didn't know that. Sorry for bothering you.

M That's okay. I think the seat next to it is available.

해석

여 실례합니다. 제가 여기 앉아도 될까요?

남 죄송하지만 제 친구 자리입니다. 그가 곧 돌아올 거예요.

여 아, 그것을 몰랐어요. 귀찮게 해드려서 죄송합니다.

남 괜찮습니다. 그 옆에 있는 자리가 비어 있는 것 같아요.

① 그것은 공정하지 않아요. 제가 이 자리를 먼저 예약했어요.
② 감사합니다. 제 친구가 그것을 알면 기뻐할 거예요.
③ 천만에요. 무엇이든 저에게 편히 물어보세요.
④ 전혀 아닙니다. 당신과 자리를 바꿔도 괜찮습니다.

어휘

in a minute 곧   bother 귀찮게 하다   available 비어 있는, 이용 가능한

13 정답 ②

정답률 93%

M Hey, Jasmine.

W Hi, Kurt. Are you going to be at home tomorrow afternoon?

M Yeah, I'm going to watch the baseball game with my friends at home.

W Good. Can I drop by your house and give you back the hammer I borrowed?

M Sure. Come over any time. By the way, why don't you join us and watch the game?

W I'd love to. Which teams are playing?

M Green Thunders and Black Dragons.

W That'll be exciting. What time should I come?

M Come at five. We'll have pizza before the game.

W Perfect. Do you want me to bring anything?

M Maybe some snacks to eat while watching the game.

W Great. I'll bring chips and popcorn.

해석

남 안녕, Jasmine.

여 안녕, Kurt. 내일 오후에 집에 있을 거니?

남 응, 나는 집에서 친구들과 야구 경기를 시청할 거야.

여 잘됐다. 내가 너희 집에 잠깐 들러서 내가 빌린 망치를 돌려줘도 될까?

남 물론이지. 언제든 들러. 그런데 우리와 함께 경기를 보는 게 어때?

여 그러고 싶어. 어떤 팀들이 경기를 할 예정이니?

남 Green Thunders와 Black Dragons야.

여 그거 재미있겠다. 몇 시에 가야 하니?

남 5시에 와. 우리는 경기 전에 피자를 먹을 거야.

여 좋아. 내가 뭘 가져갈까?

남 혹시 경기를 보면서 먹을 간식을 좀 가져와.

여 좋아. 감자칩과 팝콘을 가져갈게.

① 맛있는 냄새가 나. 내가 피자를 먹어 봐도 될까?
③ 문제없어. 내가 표를 취소할게.
④ 미안해. 나는 야구 보는 것을 좋아하지 않아.
⑤ 물론이지. 내가 빌린 망치가 여기 있어.

어휘

drop by 잠깐 들르다   hammer 망치   borrow 빌리다   come over 들르다

14 정답 ②

정답률 93%

W Hi, Tom.

M Hi, Jane. What are you reading?

W It's a novel by Charles Dickens. I'm going to talk about it with my book club members this weekend.

M Oh, you're in a book club?

W Yes. I joined it a few months ago. And now I read much more than before.

M Really? Actually one of my new year's resolutions is to read more books.

W Then, joining a book club will surely help.

M Hmm.... What other benefits can I get if I join one?

W You can also share your reading experiences with others.

M That'd be nice.

W Yeah, it really broadens your mind. I really recommend you to join a book club.

M Sounds cool. I'll join a book club, too.

해석

여 안녕, Tom.

남 안녕, Jane. 무엇을 읽고 있니?

여 Charles Dickens가 쓴 소설이야. 이번 주말에 독서 동호회 회원들과 그것에 관해 이야기를 나눌 거야.

남 오, 너는 독서 동호회에 들었니?

여 응. 몇 달 전에 그것에 가입했어. 그리고 지금 전보다 훨씬 더 많이 독서를 해.

남 정말? 사실 내 새해 다짐 중 하나가 독서를 더 많이 하는 거야.

여 그러면 독서 동호회에 가입하는 것이 확실히 도움이 될 거야.

남 음… 가입하면 어떤 다른 혜택을 얻을 수 있니?

여 너는 다른 사람들과 독서 경험을 나눌 수도 있어.

남 그거 좋겠다.

여 응, 정말 네 사고를 넓혀 줘. 나는 네가 독서 동호회에 가입하는 것을 정말 추천해.

남 멋진 것 같아. 나도 독서 동호회에 가입할래.

① 바로 그거야. 이것은 소설 베스트셀러야.

③ 그렇지는 않아. 책은 좋은 선물이야.

④ 새해 다짐은 지키기 힘들어.

⑤ 네 독서 동호회를 위해 몇 권의 책을 사자.

어휘

novel 소설 new year's resolution 새해 다짐, 새해 결심 benefit 혜택, 이점 broaden 넓히다 recommend 추천하다

15 정답 ①

정답률 90%

M Brian and Sally are walking down the street together. A blind man and his guide dog are walking towards them. Sally likes dogs very much, so she reaches out to touch the guide dog. Brian doesn't think that Sally should do that. The guide dog needs to concentrate on guiding the blind person. If someone touches the dog, the dog can lose its focus. So Brian wants to tell Sally not to touch the guide dog without the permission of the dog owner. In this situation, what would Brian most likely say to Sally?

Brian You shouldn't touch a guide dog without permission.

해석

남 Brian과 Sally는 함께 길을 걷고 있다. 한 시각 장애인과 그의 안내견이 그들을 향해 걸어오고 있다. Sally는 개를 대단히 좋아해서 그녀는 그 안내견을 만지려고 손을 뻗는다. Brian은 Sally가 그러지 말아야 한다고 생각한다. 그 안내견은 시각 장애인을 안내하는 것에 집중할 필요가 있다. 만약 누군가가 개를 만진다면, 그 개는 집중력을 잃을 수 있다. 그래서 Brian은 Sally에게 개 주인의 허락 없는 그 안내견을 만지지 말라고 말하고 싶다. 이 상황에서 Brian은 Sally에게 뭐라고 말하겠는가?

Brian 너는 허락 없이 안내견을 만지면 안 돼.

② 우리가 개에게 약간의 음식을 주면 그 개는 행복할 거야.

③ 나는 그것이 안내견이 되기에 충분히 똑똑하다고 확신해.

④ 나는 네가 매일 너의 개를 산책시키는 것을 제안해.

⑤ 여기에서는 개가 허용되지 않는 것 같아.

어휘

guide dog 안내견 reach out (손 등을) 뻗다 concentrate 집중하다 permission 허락

16 정답 ④

정답률 77%

17 정답 ④

정답률 92%

W Hello, everybody. Welcome to the health workshop. I'm Alanna Reyes, the head trainer from Eastwood Fitness Center. As you know, joints are body parts that link bones together. And doing certain physical activities puts stress on the joints. But the good news is that people with bad joints can still do certain exercises. They have relatively low impact on the joints. Here are some examples. The first is swimming. While swimming, the water supports your body weight. The second is cycling. You put almost no stress on the knee joints when you pedal smoothly. Horseback riding is another exercise that puts very little stress on your knees. Lastly, walking is great because it's low-impact, unlike running. If you have bad joints, don't give up exercising. Instead, stay active and stay healthy!

해석

여 여러분, 안녕하세요. 건강 워크숍에 오신 것을 환영합니다. 저는 Eastwood 피트니스 센터의 총괄 트레이너 Alanna Reyes입니다. 아시다시피 관절은 뼈를 연결하는 신체 부위입니다. 그리고 특정 신체 활동을 하는 것은 관절에 무리를 줍니다. 하지만 좋은 소식은 안 좋은 관절을 지닌 사람들도 여전히 어떤 운동을 할 수 있다는 것입니다. 그것들은 관절에 비교적 적은 충격을 줍니다. 여기 몇 가지 예가 있습니다. 첫 번째는 수영입니다. 수영을 하는 동안 물은 여러분의 체중을 지탱합니다. 두 번째는 자전거 타기입니다. 여러분이 부드럽게 페달을 밟을 때 무릎 관절에 거의 아무런 무리를 주지 않습니다. 승마는 여러분의 무릎에 거의 무리를 주지 않는 또 다른 운동입니다. 마지막으로, 걷기는 달리기와 달리 충격이 적기 때문에 훌륭한 운동입니다. 만약 관절이 안 좋다면, 운동하는 것을 포기하지 마세요. 대신 활동적으로 지내면서 건강을 유지하세요!

해설

여자는 관절이 안 좋은 사람들도 운동을 할 수 있다고 말하면서 관절에 무리를 주지 않고 적은 충격을 주는 운동을 소개하고 있으므로, 여자가 하는 말의 주제로 가장 적절한 것은 ④이다.

16

① 근육을 만드는 데 도움이 되는 활동

② 일상생활에서 스트레스를 조절하는 방법

③ 노인들의 관절 문제 유형

④ 관절이 안 좋은 사람들에게 충격이 적은 운동

⑤ 체중 조절을 위해 매일 운동하는 것의 중요성

17

① 수영 ② 자전거 타기 ③ 승마 ④ 볼링 ⑤ 걷기

어휘

joint 관절 relatively 비교적 impact 충격, 영향 body weight 체중 pedal 페달을 밟다 give up 포기하다

01 ②	02 ③	03 ①	04 ⑤	05 ②	06 ③
07 ①	08 ④	09 ④	10 ③	11 ①	12 ①
13 ⑤	14 ②	15 ③	16 ④	17 ⑤	

01 정답 ②

정답률 68%

[Chime bell rings.]

M Hello, passengers. I'm James Walker from the Greenville Subway System. As you know, the international film festival will be held in our city next month. Throughout the festival, some movies will run till late at night. So, for our citizens' convenience, the Greenville City Council has decided to provide longer subway service hours during the festival. All Greenville subway lines will run extra hours while the festival is going on. You can easily check the extended service schedules using the Greenville Subway App. I hope you can make the most of the festival experience with our services. Thank you.

해석

[차임벨이 울린다.]

남 승객 여러분, 안녕하세요. 저는 Greenville Subway System의 James Walker입니다. 여러분도 아시다시피, 국제 영화제가 다음 달에 우리 시에서 열릴 것입니다. 축제 내내 일부 영화가 밤늦게까지 상영될 예정입니다. 따라서 우리 시민들의 편의를 위해 Greenville 시 의회는 축제 동안 지하철 운행 시간을 연장하기로 결정했습니다. 모든 Greenville 지하철 노선은 축제가 진행되는 동안 시간을 추가하여 운행할 것입니다. 여러분은 Greenville 지하철 앱을 이용하여 연장된 운행 일정을 쉽게 확인할 수 있습니다. 여러분께서 저희 서비스로 축제 경험을 최대한 즐길 수 있기를 바랍니다. 감사합니다.

해설

남자는 승객들에게 다음 달에 열리는 국제 영화제 기간 동안 지하철 운행을 연장할 예정임을 안내하고 있으므로, 남자가 하는 말의 목적으로 가장 적절한 것은 ②이다.

어휘

passenger 승객 run (연극·영화 등을) 상영[상연]하다; (버스·기차 등을 특정 노선으로) 운행하다 citizen 시민 convenience 편의 extra 추가의 extend 연장하다

02 정답 ③

정답률 98%

W Good morning, Jason. It's sports day today. Do you have everything you need?

M Yes, Mom. I put a water bottle, some snacks, and a towel in my bag. Is there anything I forgot?

W What about sunblock? Did you put it on?

M Sunblock? It's not sunny outside.

W Jason, you should wear sunblock even on a cloudy day.

M But I don't feel the sun in weather like this.

W Even if you don't feel the sun on your skin, the harmful light from the sun can damage your skin because the clouds don't block it.

M Really? You mean I can still get a sunburn even on a cloudy day?

W Yes. That's why you shouldn't forget to wear sunblock even if it's not sunny outside.

M I didn't know that. I'll put it on now.

해석

여 안녕, Jason. 오늘은 운동회 날이구나. 필요한 것을 전부 갖고 있니?

남 네, 엄마. 저는 가방에 물병, 약간의 간식, 그리고 수건을 넣었어요. 제가 잊은 게 있나요?

여 자외선 차단제는? 그것을 발랐니?

남 자외선 차단제요? 밖이 화창하지 않은데요.

여 Jason, 흐린 날에도 자외선 차단제를 발라야 해.

남 하지만 이런 날씨에는 햇빛이 느껴지지 않아요.

여 피부에 햇빛이 느껴지지 않더라도 구름이 그것을 차단하지는 않기 때문에 태양에서 나오는 해로운 빛이 네 피부를 손상시킬 수 있어.

남 정말요? 제가 흐린 날에도 여전히 햇볕에 탈 수 있다는 말인가요?

여 그래. 그래서 밖이 화창하지 않더라도 자외선 차단제를 바르는 것을 잊지 말아야 해.

남 그것을 몰랐어요. 지금 그것을 바를게요.

어휘

sunblock 자외선 차단제 harmful 해로운 damage 손상시키다 block 차단하다, 막다 sunburn 햇볕에 탐

03 정답 ①

정답률 91%

M Hello, Ms. Green. You came just on time.

W Really? I thought I was early.

M No. Your car is over there. Follow me, please.

W Wow. All the dirt is gone. It looks like a new car.

M Yeah. But some stains were difficult to remove. It's better to have your car washed right after it gets dirty.

W I went on a business trip for a month, so I didn't have time. I'll keep that in mind.

M Anyway, while cleaning the inside, we found this earring under the driver's seat.

W Really? I thought I had lost that. Thank you.

M You're welcome. Would you like to pay by credit card or in cash?

W I'll pay in cash. Here you are.

M Okay. [Pause] Here is your receipt. And this is a discount coupon for our car wash center. You can use it on your next visit.

W That's nice. Thank you.

해석

남 Green 씨, 안녕하세요. 시간에 딱 맞춰 오셨군요.

여 정말요? 저는 일찍 왔다고 생각했어요.

남 아닙니다. 고객님의 차가 저쪽에 있습니다. 저를 따라오세요.

여 와. 모든 먼지가 사라졌네요. 새 차처럼 보여요.

남 네. 그런데 일부 얼룩은 없애기 힘들었어요. 더러워진 직후에 세차하는 게 더 좋습니다.

여 제가 한 달간 출장을 가서 시간이 없었어요. 그것을 명심할게요.

남 그건 그렇고, 내부를 청소하는 동안 저희는 운전석 밑에서 이 귀걸이를 발견했습니다.

여 그래요? 그것을 잃어버린 줄 알았어요. 고맙습니다.

남 천만에요. 신용 카드로 결제하시겠어요, 아니면 현금으로 결제하시겠어요?

여 현금으로 결제할게요. 여기 있습니다.

남 알겠습니다. [잠시 후] 여기 영수증입니다. 그리고 이것은 저희 세차장 할인 쿠폰입니다. 다음 방문 시 그것을 사용하실 수 있습니다.

여 좋아요. 감사합니다.

어휘

on time 시간에 맞춰, 정각에 stain 얼룩 remove 없애다, 제거하다 go on a business trip 출장을 가다 keep ~ in mind ~을 명심하다 receipt 영수증

04 정답 ⑤

정답률 88%

W Hi, Harry. Congratulations on your wedding. Did you finish decorating the new house?

M I just finished the living room. Look at this picture, Linda.

W Wow. I love the striped curtains on the window.

M Thanks. Do you see those two cushions on the sofa? My sister made them as wedding gifts.

W That's lovely. Oh, you put a round table on the rug.

M Yeah. We spend time reading books around the table. What do you think of the clock on the bookshelf?

W It looks good in that room. By the way, is that a plant under the calendar?

M Yes. I placed it there because the plant helps to clean the air.

W You decorated your house really well.

M Thanks. I'll invite you over when we have the housewarming party.

해석

여 안녕, Harry. 결혼 축하해. 새집 꾸미기는 마쳤니?

남 방금 거실을 끝냈어. 이 사진을 봐, Linda.

여 와. 창문에 있는 줄무늬 커튼이 마음에 들어.

남 고마워. 소파에 있는 쿠션 두 개가 보이니? 내 여동생이 결혼 선물로 그것을 만들어 줬어.

여 예쁘구나. 아, 러그에 원형 테이블을 놓았구나.

남 응. 우리는 테이블에서 독서를 하며 시간을 보내거든. 책장 위에 있는 시계는 어때?

여 그 방에 잘 어울린다. 그런데 달력 밑에 있는 저것은 식물이니?

남 응. 식물이 공기를 정화하는 데 도움이 되기 때문에 그것을 두었어.

여 너는 집을 정말 잘 꾸몄구나.

남 고마워. 우리가 집들이를 하면 너를 초대할게.

어휘

decorate 꾸미다, 장식하다   striped 줄무늬의   rug 러그, 깔개   bookshelf 책장
housewarming party 집들이

05 정답 ②

정답률 90%

M Jane, the Stop Using Plastic campaign starts tomorrow. Let's do a final check.

W Okay, Robin. I just finished editing a video clip about plastic waste.

M Then, I'm going to check the screen that we'll use for the video.

W No worries. I've already done it, and it works well.

M That's nice. I uploaded a campaign poster on our organization's website.

W Yeah. Some of my friends saw it and texted me they're coming.

M My friends, too. They showed a huge interest in the reusable bag decorating activity. The bags are ready in that box.

W Good. By the way, where are the badges you ordered for visitors?

M Oh, I left the badges in my car. I'll bring them right away.

W Great. It seems that everything is prepared.

해석

남 Jane, '플라스틱 사용 멈추기' 캠페인이 내일 시작돼. 최종 점검을 하자.

여 좋아, Robin. 나는 플라스틱 쓰레기에 관한 동영상 편집을 방금 끝냈어.

남 그럼 나는 우리가 동영상을 위해 사용할 스크린을 점검할게.

여 걱정할 필요 없어. 내가 이미 그것을 했는데 잘 작동해.

남 잘됐다. 나는 우리 단체의 웹사이트에 캠페인 포스터를 업로드했어.

여 응. 내 친구 몇 명이 그것을 보고 나서 나한테 올 거라고 문자를 보냈어.

남 내 친구들도. 그들은 재사용 봉투 꾸미기 활동에 엄청난 관심을 보였어. 봉투는 저 상자에 준비되어 있어.

여 잘됐다. 그런데 방문객을 위해 네가 주문한 배지들은 어디 있니?

남 아, 내 차에 배지들을 두고 왔어. 당장 그것들을 가져올게.

여 좋아. 모든 게 다 준비된 것 같아.

어휘

edit 편집하다   video clip 동영상   organization 단체, 조직   text 문자를 보내다
reusable 재사용할 수 있는   badge 배지

06 정답 ③

정답률 88%

M Welcome to Kids Clothing Club. How may I help you?

W I'm looking for a muffler for my son. He's 5 years old.

M Okay. Follow me. [Pause] This red muffler is one of the best sellers in our shop.

W I love the color. How much is it?

M It's $50. This one is popular because of the cartoon character here.

W Oh, that's my son's favorite character. I'll buy one red muffler, then.

M Great. Anything else?

W How much are these winter socks?

M A pair of socks is $5.

W All right. I'll buy two pairs.

M So, one red muffler and two pairs of winter socks, right?

W Yes. Can I use this discount coupon?

M Of course. With that coupon, you can get 10% off the total price.

W Good. Here's my credit card.

해석

남 Kids Clothing Club에 오신 것을 환영합니다. 무엇을 도와드릴까요?

여 저는 아들에게 줄 목도리를 찾고 있어요. 아이는 5살이에요.

남 알겠습니다. 저를 따라오세요. [잠시 후] 이 빨간 목도리가 저희 가게 베스트셀러 중 하나입니다.

여 색상이 마음에 들어요. 얼마인가요?

남 50달러입니다. 이 목도리는 여기 있는 만화 캐릭터 때문에 인기가 있어요.

여 오, 그건 저희 아들이 가장 좋아하는 캐릭터예요. 그럼 빨간 목도리를 하나 살게요.

남 좋습니다. 또 필요한 게 있으신가요?

여 이 겨울 양말은 얼마죠?

남 양말 한 켤레는 5달러입니다.

여 좋아요. 두 켤레를 살게요.

남 그럼 빨간 목도리 한 개와 겨울 양말 두 켤레가 맞나요?

여 네. 이 할인 쿠폰을 사용할 수 있나요?

남 물론이죠. 이 쿠폰으로 총 금액에서 10퍼센트 할인을 받으실 수 있습니다.

여 잘됐네요. 신용 카드가 여기 있습니다.

해설

여자는 50달러짜리 빨간 목도리 한 개와 5달러짜리 양말 두 켤레를 구입하고 총 금액 60달러에서 할인 쿠폰으로 10퍼센트(6달러) 할인을 받았으므로, 여자가 지불할 금액은 ③ '$54'(54달러)이다.

어휘

muffler 목도리, 머플러   best seller 베스트셀러, 잘 팔리는 상품   cartoon 만화
discount 할인

07 정답 ①

8회 21년 11월

정답률 90%

W Hi, Jeremy. How was your trip to London?

M It was fantastic, Julia. I watched the musical you recommended.

W Good. What about the London Walking Tour? Did you enjoy it?

M Unfortunately, I couldn't join the tour.

W Why? Didn't you say you booked it?

M Yes. I made a reservation for the tour in advance.

W Oh, was the tour canceled because of the weather?

M No. The weather was no problem at all.

W Then, why couldn't you join the tour?

M Actually, I fell down the day before the tour, so I had some pain in my ankle. That's why I couldn't make it.

W I'm sorry to hear that. Is it okay, now?

M Yes. It's completely fine now. Oh, I forgot to bring the souvenir I bought for you. I'll bring it tomorrow.

W That's so sweet. Thanks.

해석

여 안녕, Jeremy. 런던 여행은 어땠니?

남 환상적이었어, Julia. 나는 네가 추천해 준 뮤지컬을 관람했어.

여 잘했네. '런던 도보 투어'는 어땠어? 그것을 즐겼니?

남 아쉽게도 나는 그 투어에 참여하지 못했어.

여 왜? 그것을 예약했다고 말하지 않았니?

남 맞아. 나는 미리 그 투어를 예약했어.

여 아, 날씨 때문에 투어가 취소됐니?

남 아니. 날씨는 전혀 문제가 없었어.

여 그럼 왜 투어에 참여하지 못했니?

남 실은 투어 전날 내가 넘어져서 발목에 통증이 좀 있었어. 그래서 참여하지 못했어.

여 유감이구나. 지금은 괜찮니?

남 응. 지금은 완전히 괜찮아. 아, 너를 위해 구입한 기념품을 가져오는 것을 깜빡했어. 내일 그것을 가져올게.

여 너무 좋아. 고마워.

어휘

book 예약하다   make a reservation 예약하다   in advance 미리
fall down 넘어지다   make it 참여하다, 해내다   souvenir 기념품

08 정답 ④

정답률 96%

M What are you doing, Laura?

W Hi, Tim. I'm looking for winter festivals to visit during vacation.

M Is there anything good?

W Yes, look at this. There is a new local event called the Winter Lake Festival.

M Awesome. When does it start?

W December 18th and it'll be held for two weeks.

M Cool. Oh, it'll take place in Stevenson Park.

W Great. It's near our school. If you don't have any plans during vacation, let's go together.

M Of course. Is there an entrance fee?

W Yes. Here, it says $3. It's not expensive.

M Good. Look! There are so many kinds of activities to enjoy.

W Yeah, there is ice skating, ice fishing, and a snowball fight.

M They all sound exciting. Let's have fun there.

해석

남 Laura, 무엇을 하고 있니?

여 안녕, Tim. 나는 방학 중에 방문할 겨울 축제를 찾는 중이야.

남 괜찮은 게 있니?

여 응, 이것을 봐. '겨울 호수 축제'라고 불리는 새로운 지역 행사가 있어.

남 멋지다. 언제 시작하니?

여 12월 18일에 시작하고 2주간 열릴 거야.

남 멋지다. 오, Stevenson Park에서 개최될 예정이구나.

여 잘됐다. 그곳은 우리 학교 근처야. 방학 중에 계획이 없으면 같이 가자.

남 물론이지. 입장료가 있니?

여 응. 여기에 3달러라고 되어 있어. 비싸지 않아.

남 좋아. 봐! 즐길 만한 아주 많은 종류의 활동이 있어.

여 응, 빙상 스케이팅, 얼음 낚시, 그리고 눈싸움이 있어.

남 다 재미있을 것 같아. 거기서 재미있게 놀자.

어휘

local 지역의   awesome 멋진, 굉장한   entrance fee 입장료
snowball fight 눈싸움

09 정답 ④

정답률 91%

W Hello, supporters! I'm Christine Miller, manager of Western Football Club. This year, we're holding a Mascot Design Contest to celebrate our team's 1st championship. Anyone who loves our team can participate in this contest. The mascot design should be related to our team's slogan "One team, one spirit." The winning design will be chosen through a fan vote. And the winner will receive a team uniform as a prize. People who want to participate should send their design by email by December 5th. Show your creativity and love for our team through active participation. For more information, please visit our website. Thank you.

해석

여 서포터 여러분, 안녕하세요! 저는 Western Football Club의 관리자 Christine Miller입니다. 올해 저희는 우리 팀의 첫 번째 우승을 축하하기 위해 '마스코트 디자인 대회'를 개최할 것입니다. 우리 팀을 사랑하는 누구든 이 대회에 참가할 수 있습니다. 마스코트 디자인은 우리 팀의 슬로건 '하나의 팀, 하나의 정신'과 관련되어야 합니다. 수상 디자인은 팬 투표를 통해 선정될 것입니다. 그리고 수상자는 상으로 팀 유니폼을 받을 것입니다. 참가를 원하는 사람들은 12월 5일까지 자신의 디자인을 이메일로 보내야 합니다. 적극적인 참가를 통해 우리 팀에 대한 여러분의 창의성과 애정을 보여 주세요. 더 많은 정보에 대해서는 우리 웹사이트를 방문해 주십시오. 감사합니다.

어휘

supporter (스포츠 팀·선수의) 서포터   celebrate 축하하다, 기념하다
championship 우승, 선수권   be related to ~와 관계가 있다   creativity 창의성

10 정답 ③

정답률 93%

W Honey, what are you looking at?

M This is a list of the best campsites in 2021. How about going to one of them next month?

W Sounds great. Let me see. [Pause] There are five different campsites.

M Yeah. Since we went to Seaside campsite last time, let's choose among the other four.

W Good. Hmm, I don't want to spend more than $100 per night. It's too expensive.

M I agree with that. What do you think of staying in a camping car?

W Oh, I want to try it. It'll be a special experience.

M Then, we can choose between these two.

W What about going to this campsite? Since this has a kids' playground, our children can have more fun.

M Cool! I'll make a reservation for this campsite.

해석

여 여보, 무엇을 보고 있어요?

남 이것은 2021년 최고의 캠핑장 목록이에요. 다음 달에 그중 한 곳에 가는 게 어때요?

여 좋아요. 어디 봐요. [잠시 후] 5개의 다른 캠핑장이 있군요.

남 네. 우리가 지난번에 Seaside 캠핑장에 갔으니까 다른 네 곳 중에 골라요.

여 좋아요. 음, 나는 1박에 100달러 넘게 쓰고 싶지는 않아요. 그것은 너무 비싸요.

남 그것에 동의해요. 캠핑카에서 지내는 것은 어떻게 생각해요?

여 오, 그것을 해 보고 싶어요. 특별한 경험이 되겠네요.

남 그럼 이 둘 중에서 고르면 돼요.

여 이 캠핑장에 가는 게 어때요? 어린이 운동장이 있으니까 우리 아이들이 더 재밌게 놀 수 있어요.

남 좋아요! 이 캠핑장을 예약할게요.

어휘

campsite 캠핑장 choose 고르다, 선택하다 per night 1박에, 하룻밤에

11 정답 ①

정답률 91%

M Kate, I heard your company moved to a new office. How is it?

W It's all good except one thing. It's far from my house.

M Oh, really? How long does it take to get there?

W It takes an hour by bus.

해석

남 Kate, 너희 회사가 새로운 사무실로 이전했다고 들었어. 그곳은 어때?

여 한 가지 빼고는 다 좋아. 그곳은 우리 집에서 멀어.

남 아, 그래? 거기 도착하는 데 얼마나 걸리니?

여 버스로 한 시간이 걸려.

② 그곳은 네 사무실보다 더 커.

③ 너는 더 일찍 집을 나섰어야 했어.

④ 그 회사는 지난달에 이전했어.

⑤ 나는 취직하는 데 힘든 시간을 보냈어.

어휘

move 옮기다, 이전하다 except ~ 외에는

12 정답 ①

정답률 95%

W Honey, you know my nephew is coming over this evening. How about ordering pizza for dinner?

M Sure. Which topping does he prefer, grilled beef or shrimp?

W Oh, he doesn't like beef. He loves seafood.

M Okay. I'll order a shrimp pizza.

해석

여 여보, 알다시피 내 조카가 오늘 저녁에 들를 거예요. 저녁으로 피자를 주문하는 게 어때요?

남 좋아요. 조카가 구운 쇠고기 또는 새우 중에서 어떤 토핑을 선호해요?

여 아, 개는 쇠고기를 좋아하지 않아요. 해산물을 정말 좋아해요.

남 알겠어요. 새우 피자를 주문할게요.

② 고마워요. 당신은 요리를 잘해요.

③ 아니요. 피자가 아직 배달되지 않았어요.

④ 그럼요. 당신은 언제든지 들러도 돼요.

⑤ 네. 식사를 거르는 것은 당신의 건강에 해로워요.

어휘

come over 들르다 topping 토핑, 고명 grilled 구운 seafood 해산물

13 정답 ⑤

정답률 87%

M Honey, did you read this leaflet on the table?

W Not yet. What's it about?

M It says the local children's library is going to hold some events to celebrate their reopening.

W Is there anything good?

M Let me see. [Pause] There will be a Meet-the-Author event. Rebecca Moore is coming.

W Oh, she's one of our son's favorite writers.

M Yes. He'll be excited if he can meet her in person.

W Let's take him to that event. When is it?

M It's next Saturday, 1 p.m.

W But we have a lunch reservation at the French restaurant at that time.

M Oh, I forgot. Then how about rescheduling lunch? It's a rare chance to meet the author.

W You're right. I'll change the reservation now.

해석

남 여보, 테이블에 있는 이 전단지 읽었어요?

여 아직 안 읽었어요. 무엇에 관한 거예요?

남 지역 어린이 도서관에서 재개관을 축하하는 몇 가지 행사를 개최할 거라고 해요.

여 괜찮은 것이 있나요?

남 한번 볼게요. [잠시 후] 지역 어린이 도서관이 '저자와의 만남' 행사를 개최할 예정이네요. Rebecca Moore가 올 거예요.

여 오, 그녀는 우리 아들이 가장 좋아하는 작가 중 한 명이에요.

남 그래요. 개가 그녀를 직접 만날 수 있다면 신이 날 거예요.

여 개를 그 행사에 데려가요. 언제인가요?

남 다음 주 토요일 오후 1시예요.

여 그런데 우리는 그때 프랑스 식당에서 점심 예약이 있어요.

남 아, 깜빡했어요. 그럼 점심 일정을 변경하는 게 어때요? 저자를 만날 드문 기회잖아요.

여 당신 말이 맞아요. 지금 예약을 변경할게요.

① 너무 늦었어요. 회의가 이미 끝났어요.

② 물론이죠. 많은 프랑스 요리책이 있어요.

③ 동의해요. 당신은 독서에 너무 많은 시간을 보내요.

④ 아니요. 우리는 도서관에서 먹는 것이 허용되지 않아요.

어휘

leaflet 전단지 author 저자 in person 직접 reschedule 일정을 변경하다
rare 드문

14 정답 ②

[Cell phone rings.]

W This is Fairview Laptop Repair. How may I help you?

M Hello, this is David Brown. I missed your call this morning.

W Oh, Mr. Brown. You requested the screen repair yesterday, right?

M Yes. Is there any problem?

W The screen is all repaired. But we found another problem with your laptop. You need to replace the battery.

M Oh, I didn't know that. How bad is it?

W Even when the battery is fully charged, it won't last longer than an hour.

M Really? How much does it cost to change the battery?

W It's $70. It's on sale now.

M That sounds great. But, I'm worried it'll delay the laptop pick-up time, 5 p.m. today.

W Don't worry. You can still pick it up at that time.

M Then, I'd like to replace the battery.

해석

[휴대전화가 울린다.]

여 Fairview Laptop Repair입니다. 무엇을 도와드릴까요?

남 안녕하세요, 저는 David Brown입니다. 오늘 아침에 당신의 전화를 놓쳤어요.

여 오, Brown 씨. 어제 화면 수리를 요청하신 거 맞죠?

남 네. 무슨 문제가 있나요?

여 화면은 모두 수리되어 있습니다. 그런데 고객님의 노트북에서 다른 문제를 발견했어요. 배터리를 교체하셔야 합니다.

남 아, 그것은 몰랐어요. 얼마나 상태가 안 좋나요?

여 배터리가 완전히 충전된 경우에도 한 시간 넘게 지속되지 못할 거예요.

남 정말요? 배터리를 교체하는 비용은 얼마인가요?

여 70달러입니다. 지금 할인 중입니다.

남 잘됐네요. 그런데 그것 때문에 오늘 오후 5시인 노트북 픽업 시간이 지연될까 봐 걱정이에요.

여 걱정하지 마세요. 그때 찾아가실 수 있습니다.

남 그럼 배터리를 교체하고 싶어요.

① 죄송해요. 제 노트북을 가져오는 것을 깜빡했어요.
③ 음, 화면이 아직도 잘 작동하지 않아요.
④ 좋아요. 새로운 수리점이 어제 문을 열었어요.
⑤ 사실 저는 환불을 위한 영수증을 갖고 있지 않아요.

어휘

laptop 노트북, 휴대용 컴퓨터 replace 교체하다 charge 충전하다 last 지속되다
on sale 할인 중인 delay 지연시키다

15 정답 ③

M Amy is the leader of a high school band and Terry is one of the band members. The band is going to hold a mini concert in the school festival, and Terry is in charge of making a concert poster. When he completes the poster, he shows it to the band members. Even though the poster has all the necessary information, it's hard to read it because the size of the letters is too small. Amy thinks if Terry changes the font size to a larger one, it could be easier to notice. So, Amy wants to suggest that Terry increase the size of the letters on the poster. In this situation, what would Amy most likely say to Terry?

Amy Can you make the letter size bigger on the poster?

해석

남 Amy는 고등학교 밴드의 리더이고 Terry는 밴드 멤버 중 한 명이다. 그 밴드는 학교 축제에서 미니콘서트를 개최할 예정이고, Terry는 콘서트 포스터를 만드는 것을 담당하고 있다. 그는 포스터를 완성하자 그것을 밴드 멤버들에게 보여 준다. 포스터에 필요한 모든 정보가 있음에도 글자 크기가 너무 작아서 그것을 읽기가 힘들다. Amy는 Terry가 서체 크기를 더 큰 것으로 바꾸면 더 알아차리기 쉬워질 수 있다고 생각한다. 그래서 Amy는 Terry가 포스터에 있는 글자 크기를 늘려야 한다고 제안하고 싶어 한다. 이 상황에서 Amy는 Terry에게 뭐라고 말할 것 같은가?

Amy 포스터의 글자 크기를 더 크게 해 줄 수 있니?

① 포스터에 알록달록한 서체를 사용하는 게 어때?
② 네 친구들에게 콘서트에 대해 알려 주는 게 낫겠다.
④ 학교 축제에서 콘서트를 개최하는 게 어때?
⑤ 포스터에 중요한 정보를 넣어야 해.

어휘

in charge of ~을 담당하고 있는 complete 완성하다 font 서체
notice 알아차리다 increase 늘리다, 증가시키다

16 정답 ④

17 정답 ⑤

W Hello, students. Previously, we discussed why gardening is a great hobby. But not everyone has a sunny front yard. So, today we'll learn about plants that grow even in shade. First, lemon balm survives in full shade. So if your place is sunless, it's the plant you should choose. Next, ivy is the ultimate shade-loving plant. Its ability to grow in shade makes it survive under trees where most plants can't. Also, there's mint. It lives well under low-light conditions, so you can grow it in a small pot indoors. Lastly, camellia grows better in partial shade. Especially when it's a young plant, it needs protection from the sun. Many plants like these can live even in the shade. Isn't it fascinating? Now, let's watch a video clip about how to grow these plants.

해석

여 학생 여러분, 안녕하세요. 이전에 우리는 정원 가꾸기가 왜 훌륭한 취미인지를 논의했습니다. 하지만 모든 사람이 햇빛이 잘 드는 앞마당을 갖고 있는 것은 아닙니다. 따라서 오늘 우리는 그늘에서도 자라는 식물들에 대해 배울 것입니다. 첫 번째로, 레몬밤은 완전한 그늘에서 살아남습니다. 그래서 여러분의 장소에 햇빛이 들지 않는다면 여러분이 선택해야 하는 것은 바로 그 식물입니다. 다음으로, 담쟁이덩굴은 그늘을 사랑하는 최상의 식물입니다. 그늘에서 자라는 그것의 능력이 대부분의 식물은 생존할 수 없는 나무 밑에서 그것이 생존하도록 해 줍니다. 또한, 박하가 있습니다. 그것은 낮은 밝기 상태에서 잘 살아가므로 여러분은 실내에서 작은 화분에 그것을 키울 수 있습니다. 마지막으로, 동백나무는 부분적인 그늘에서 더 잘 자랍니다. 특히 어린 식물일 때 그것은 햇빛으로부터 보호할 필요가 있습니다. 이처럼 많은 식물들은 그늘에서도 잘 살아갈 수 있습니다. 대단히 흥미롭지 않나요? 이제 이러한 식물들을 기르는 법에 관한 동영상을 시청하시죠.

16

① 식물의 질병을 예방하는 방법
② 식물의 성장에 영향을 주는 요인
③ 가정에서 식물을 기르는 것의 이점
④ 그늘진 장소에서 자랄 수 있는 식물
⑤ 식물이 그늘에서 자라는 것을 도와주는 물질

17

① 레몬밤 　② 담쟁이덩굴 　③ 박하 　④ 동백나무 　⑤ 라벤더

어휘

front yard 앞마당 　grow 자라다; 키우다 　survive 살아남다, 생존하다
sunless 햇빛이 안 드는 　ultimate 최고의, 최상의 　partial 부분적인
protection 보호 　fascinating 대단히 흥미로운, 매력적인

01 ④	02 ②	03 ③	04 ③	05 ⑤	06 ③
07 ③	08 ③	09 ④	10 ②	11 ①	12 ①
13 ③	14 ①	15 ④	16 ②	17 ③	

01 정답 ④

정답률 82%

M Hello, citizens of Portland. This is Jerry Wilson, your Mayor. As you know, Port Elementary School has opened, and it is so nice to hear the kids playing. To ensure the safety of the students at the school, we've been communicating with the New Jersey State Police and requested that they enforce speed limits in the area around the school. This is in response to the many complaints City Hall has received regarding excessive speeding, especially in front of the school. Please obey speed limits for the safety of the kids and your fellow citizens. Thank you for your cooperation. Stay safe and healthy.

해석

남 안녕하세요, Portland 시민 여러분. 저는 시장 Jerry Wilson입니다. 여러분도 아시다시피, Port 초등학교가 개교했고, 아이들이 노는 소리를 듣는 것이 너무 좋습니다. 학교에서의 학생들의 안전을 보장하기 위해, 저희는 뉴저지 주 경찰과 연락을 취해 오고 있으며 학교 주변 지역에서 속도 제한을 시행해 줄 것을 요청했습니다. 이는 시청이 특히, 학교 앞에서의 과도한 과속에 대해 받은 많은 불만들에 따른 것입니다. 어린이와 시민들의 안전을 위해 제한 속도를 지켜 주세요. 협조해 주셔서 감사합니다. 안전하고 건강하게 지내십시오.

어휘

ensure 보장하다, 반드시 ~하게 하다 　request 요청하다 　enforce 집행하다
in response to ~에 응하여 　regarding ~에 관하여 　excessive 과도한
cooperation 협조

02 정답 ②

정답률 89%

M Lily, what's wrong? Are you all right?

W Oh, it's nothing.

M Are you sure? You look pretty worried.

W Actually, I said something mean to my sister and I feel really bad about it.

M What did you say to her?

W I said she's the worst sister because she wore my favorite jacket again!

M Jeez! She must have been really hurt by that.

W Yeah, but I told her not to wear my jacket a million times. She never listens.

M Still, you should be more careful when you talk to someone close to you.

W I know, but I was so angry.

M People get hurt more easily when someone close to them says mean things.

W Yeah, you're right. I'll apologize to her when I get home.

해석

남 Lily, 무슨 일이야? 너 괜찮아?

여 아, 별거 아니야.

남 확실해? 너 꽤 걱정스러워 보여.

여 사실, 나는 내 여동생에게 못된 말을 했는데, 정말 기분이 안 좋아.

남 너 뭐라고 말했니?

여 그녀가 내가 가장 좋아하는 재킷을 또 입어서 그녀에게 최악의 동생이라고 했어.

남 저런! 그녀는 그것으로 정말 상처받았음이 틀림없어.

여 응, 하지만 나는 그녀에게 내 재킷을 입지 말라고 수차례 말했어. 그녀는 절대 듣지 않아.

남 그래도 너와 가까운 사람들과 이야기할 때는 더 조심해야 해.

여 알아, 하지만 나는 너무 화가 났어.

남 사람들은 가까운 사람이 안 좋은 말을 하면 더 쉽게 상처받아.

여 응, 네 말이 맞아. 나는 집에 가면 그녀에게 사과할 거야.

어휘

mean 못된, 심술궂은   must have p.p. ~했음에 틀림없다
hurt 감정을 상하게 하다(-hurt-hurt)   apologize 사과하다

03 정답 ③

정답률 **95%**

W Hi, listeners! Now we have one person on the line. He has something special to share with us. Hello, you're on the air!

M Hello. Wow! I'm surprised that I got through to you. Thank you for taking my call.

W Sure. Please introduce yourself.

M I'm Jin, a high school student. I'm a big fan of the show.

W Thank you, Jin. By the way, you left a message on our website, didn't you?

M Yes. Today is my parents' 20th wedding anniversary. I wanted to honor them on the show.

W I see. Are your parents listening now?

M Yes, they listen to your show every day.

W That's great. What is your message to your parents?

M Hmm… Mom and Dad, you're amazing parents. Happy Anniversary to you both!

W What a lovely message! Thank you for calling us today, Jin.

M Thanks again for taking my call.

해석

여 안녕하세요, 청취자 여러분! 지금 저희는 한 분과 전화 연결 중입니다. 그는 우리와 나눌 특별한 것이 있습니다. 안녕하세요, 당신은 방송에 연결되셨어요!

남 안녕하세요, 와우! 당신과 통화하다니 놀라워요. 제 전화를 받아 주셔서 감사합니다.

여 네. 자기소개 부탁드립니다.

남 저는 고등학생 Jin입니다. 저는 쇼의 열혈 팬입니다.

여 고맙습니다, Jin. 그나저나, 당신이 우리 홈페이지에 메시지를 남기셨잖아요, 그렇지 않나요?

남 네, 오늘이 저희 부모님의 20주년 결혼기념일입니다. 저는 쇼에서 그 분들께 존경을 표하고 싶어요.

여 그렇군요. 당신의 부모님이 지금 듣고 계신가요?

남 네, 그분들은 당신의 쇼를 매일 들으세요.

여 잘됐네요. 부모님께 드리는 당신의 메시지는 무엇인가요?

남 흠… 엄마 아빠, 당신들은 멋진 부모님이세요! 두 분 모두 행복한 기념일 되세요!

여 정말 사랑스러운 메시지네요! 오늘 전화 주셔서 감사합니다, Jin.

남 제 전화를 받아 주셔서 다시 한 번 감사드립니다.

어휘

be on the air 방송 중이다   get through to ~에 전화가 통하다
honor 존경하다, 영광을 주다

04 정답 ③

정답률 **71%**

W Hi, Tim. How's everything going with the festival?

M Hey, Julie! It's going great. This is a picture of what our booth will look like.

W What will people do at your booth?

M They'll be asked to answer questions and be given snacks if they answer correctly.

W Okay, that sounds good. I like the banner that says 'Guessing Time' in the center.

M Thanks. What do you think about the photos that are under the clock?

W Great idea! What are you using the round table for?

M We're going to put the snacks on it.

W That makes sense. Then, what about the globe on the floor?

M It's for choosing countries. We're going to ask people geography questions.

W That should be interesting. What's that crown on the left side?

M That's a photo zone for all participants.

W Cool. I can't wait for this year's festival!

해석

여 안녕, Tim. 축제는 어떻게 되어 가니?

남 안녕, Julie! 잘되어 가고 있어. 이것은 우리 부스가 어떤 모습일지에 관한 사진이야.

여 사람들이 너희 부스에서 무엇을 하게 되니?

남 그들은 질문들에 답을 하도록 요청을 받고, 정답을 맞히면 간식을 받게 될 거야.

여 그렇구나, 좋은 것 같아. 나는 중앙에 있는 'Guessing Time'이라고 적힌 현수막이 마음에 들어.

남 고마워. 시계 아래에 있는 사진들은 어떻게 생각하니?

여 좋은 아이디어 같아! 둥근 탁자는 어디에 쓸 거니?

남 우리는 탁자 위에 간식들을 둘 거야.

여 그거 좋겠다. 그러면, 바닥에 있는 지구본은?

남 그것은 국가를 선택하기 위한 거야. 우리는 사람들에게 지리 문제를 낼 거야.

여 재미있겠다. 왼쪽에 있는 왕관은 무엇이니?

남 그것은 모든 참가자들을 위한 포토존이야.

여 멋지다. 나는 올해의 축제가 너무 기다려져!

해설

여자는 What are you using the round table for?에서 둥근 탁자의 쓰임에 대해 질문하였으나 그림에서는 사각형 탁자로 표현되어 있으므로, 그림에서 대화의 내용과 일치하지 않는 것은 ③이다.

어휘

correctly 바르게   banner 현수막, 플래카드   make sense 타당하다
geography 지리

05 정답 ⑤

정답률 **93%**

M Kasey, how's everything coming along for grandma's birthday this Sunday?

W Hey, dad. I wrote a card for her and got some decorations yesterday.

M That's good!

W Have you gotten anything for her yet?

M I already bought a sweater. Can I help with decorating the living room for the party?

W Clara will take care of that. Also, she's picking up a birthday cake.

M Awesome! Your grandma will be so happy because you guys are going to make her birthday so special.

W I hope so. What about food? What can we make for her?

M How about grilled salmon sandwiches? She loves those!

W Good idea, but I won't have time to handle that on my own.

M Then, I'll order salmon and vegetables online today.

W Thanks, dad! That's a big help.

해석

남 Kasey, 이번 주 일요일 할머니 생신 어떻게 되어 가고 있니?

여 아, 아빠. 할머니께 드릴 카드를 썼고, 어제 장식품들을 좀 받았어요.

남 잘했구나.

여 할머니께 드릴 것을 아직 마련하지 못하셨어요?

남 나는 이미 스웨터를 샀단다. 내가 파티를 위해 거실을 장식하는 것을 도와주어도 될까?

여 Clara가 그것을 맡을 거예요. 그리고 그녀가 생일 케이크를 찾아올 거예요.

남 멋지구나! 너희가 할머니의 생신을 아주 특별하게 만들어 드리게 되어 할머니께서 무척 행복해하시겠구나.

여 저도 그러길 바라요. 음식은요? 저희가 할머니를 위해 무엇을 만들 수 있을까요?

남 구운 연어 샌드위치 어떠니? 할머니께서 그걸 좋아하시거든!

여 좋은 생각이지만, 저 혼자서 그것을 처리할 시간이 없을 것 같아요.

남 그러면, 내가 오늘 연어와 야채들을 온라인으로 주문할게.

여 감사해요, 아빠! 정말 큰 도움이 돼요.

어휘

decoration 장식, 장식품   grilled 구운   handle 처리하다, 다루다
on one's own 혼자서

06 정답 ③

정답률 **90%**

M Hello. How can I help you?

W Hi, how much is the ice cream?

M It depends on the size. The small cup is $5, the medium is $10, and the large is $15. What size would you like?

W I'll take two smalls and one medium.

M Okay. What flavor would you like?

W I'll take chocolate for all three cups.

M Sounds good. Do you want any toppings on your ice cream? We have chocolate chips and crunchy nuts. Toppings cost $1 each.

W Oh, yes. I'll have crunchy nuts only on the medium and nothing on the small cups.

M Good choice. Do you need anything else?

W No, that's it.

M How would you like to pay? Cash or credit?

W I'll pay with my credit card.

해석

남 안녕하세요. 어떻게 도와드릴까요?

여 안녕하세요, 아이스크림은 얼마인가요?

남 그것은 크기에 따라 다릅니다. 작은 컵은 5달러, 중간 컵은 10달러, 그리고 큰 컵은 15달러입니다. 어떤 크기로 드릴까요?

여 작은 컵 두 개와 중간 컵 하나로 선택할게요.

남 알겠습니다. 어떤 맛으로 드릴까요?

여 세 컵 모두 초콜릿으로 할게요.

남 좋습니다. 아이스크림에 토핑을 넣으실 건가요? 초콜릿 칩과 바삭바삭한 견과류가 있습니다. 토핑은 각각 1달러입니다.

여 오, 네. 바삭바삭한 견과류는 중간 컵에만 주시고, 작은 컵에는 아무것도 넣지 말아 주세요.

남 좋은 선택입니다. 그밖에 또 필요한 것이 있으신가요?

여 아니요, 그게 다입니다.

남 결제는 어떻게 하시겠습니까? 현금으로 하시겠어요 아니면 신용 카드로 하시겠어요?

여 신용 카드로 계산할게요.

어휘

flavor 맛, 향   crunchy 바삭바삭한

07 정답 ③

정답률 **96%**

M Mom, I'm home.

W Hi. Did you go to the gym?

M Yes. My membership ended today, but I didn't renew it.

W Why? Does your shoulder still hurt?

M No, my shoulder feels completely fine.

W So, what's the problem? I thought you were enjoying exercising.

M I was. It's actually been fun.

W Then why didn't you renew your membership?

M Well, the shower facilities at the gym are too old, and there's not enough space in the shower stalls.

W I see. Why don't you check out the new health club nearby? It may be more expensive, but the facilities are probably a lot better.

M Okay. Maybe I should visit there tomorrow on my way home after school.

W That sounds like a good plan!

해석

남 엄마, 저 왔어요.

여 안녕. 너 체육관에 갔었니?

남 네. 제 회원권이 오늘 끝나는데, 그것을 갱신하지 않았어요.

여 왜? 네 어깨가 아직 아프니?

남 아니요. 어깨는 완전히 괜찮아요.

여 그럼, 무엇이 문제이니? 나는 네가 운동하는 것을 즐기고 있다고 생각했어.

남 그랬어요. 사실 그것은 정말 재미있었어요.

여 그러면 왜 회원권을 갱신하지 않았니?

남 음, 체육관의 샤워 시설이 너무 낡았고, 샤워 칸막이의 공간이 충분하지 않아요.

여 그렇구나. 근처에 새로 생긴 헬스클럽을 확인해 보는 게 어때? 그곳은 좀 더 비쌀지도 모르지만, 시설은 아마 훨씬 더 나을 것 같아.

남 알았어요. 내일 학교 끝나고 집에 오는 길에 그곳을 방문해야 할 것 같아요.

여 좋은 계획인 것 같아!

어휘

membership 회원권   renew 갱신하다   facilities 시설

shower stall 샤워 칸막이   check out ~을 확인하다
nearby 가까운 곳의; 가까운 곳에

08 정답 ③

정답률 94%

W Hey, Bruce! I'm going to take a tour of Liberty University. Do you want to come?

M Absolutely! That's one of the schools that I'm interested in. When is the tour?

W There's one on October 3rd and another one on October 10th. They're both Saturdays. Which date is better for you?

M October 10th is better for me. What will we do during the tour?

W We'll get to see the campus in the morning and then we'll meet with an admissions counselor in the afternoon. You can ask them questions about the admissions process when we see them.

M Okay, then I should make a list of questions. I have a lot of things to ask them.

W That's a good idea. Also, everyone who goes on the tour will get a free Liberty University T-shirt as a souvenir.

M Really? That's cool. So how do I sign up for the tour?

W You can sign up on their website.

M Okay, I will do that. Thank you so much for telling me about it.

해석

여 이봐, Bruce! 나는 Liberty 대학교 투어를 할 거야. 너도 올래?

남 물론이지! 그것은 내가 관심 있는 학교들 중 하나야. 투어가 언제이니?

여 10월 3일에 하나가 있고 10월 10일에 또 하나가 있어. 둘 다 토요일이야. 너는 어떤 날짜가 더 좋아?

남 나는 10월 10일이 더 좋아. 우리는 투어 동안 무엇을 하게 되니?

여 우리는 아침에 캠퍼스를 구경하고 그러고 나서 오후에 입학 상담사를 만날 거야. 우리는 그들을 만나서 입학 절차에 대해 그들에게 질문할 수 있어.

남 좋아, 그러면 나는 질문 목록을 작성해야겠어. 나는 그들에게 물어보고 싶은 것이 많아.

여 좋은 생각이야. 또한, 투어에 참가하는 모든 사람은 기념품으로 Liberty 대학교 티셔츠를 무료로 받게 돼.

남 정말? 그거 멋지다. 그럼 투어를 어떻게 신청하니?

여 너는 그들의 웹 사이트에서 신청할 수 있어.

남 알았어, 그것을 할게. 그것에 대해 말해 줘서 정말 고마워.

어휘

admission 입학   counselor 상담사   process 절차, 과정   souvenir 기념품
sign up (for) (~에) 신청하다, 등록하다

09 정답 ④

정답률 76%

W Are you taking actions to help the environment? Then, why don't you join our Green Action Photo Contest? As long as you are a resident of our town, you can be the winner! From September 1st until September 30th, 2021, you can upload photos of you participating in eco-friendly activities on social media. By tagging your photos with the hash tag #GreenAction, you can automatically participate in our contest. The maximum number of photos you can post is five. The winner will be announced on October 4th. The prize for the winner will be delivered by October 11th. The winning photos will be posted on the town's website until the end of this year. Show us your green actions. No action is too small!

해석

여 환경에 도움이 되기 위한 행동들을 취하고 있나요? 그럼, 저희의 Green Action Photo Contest(환경 보호 활동 사진 콘테스트)에 참가해 보는 게 어떠세요? 당신이 우리 마을의 주민이라면, 승자가 될 수 있습니다! 2021년 9월 1일부터 9월 30일까지, 소셜 네트워크에 당신이 친환경 활동에 참여하는 사진을 올릴 수 있답니다. #GreenAction이라는 해시태그로 사진을 태그하시면, 자동으로 우리의 콘테스트에 참여하실 수 있습니다. 게시할 수 있는 사진의 최대 개수는 5장입니다. 수상자는 10월 4일에 발표될 예정입니다. 수상자에게는 10월 11일까지 상품이 전달될 예정입니다. 수상 사진은 연말까지 마을의 웹 사이트에 게시될 예정입니다. 당신의 친환경 활동들을 보여주세요! 아주 작은 행동은 없습니다!

어휘

as long as ~하기만 하면   resident 주민, 거주자   tag 태그를 붙이다
automatically 자동적으로   announce 발표하다, 알리다   post 게시하다

10 정답 ②

정답률 92%

M Hey, Jessica. What are you working on?

W Hey! I'm trying to order a new rolling cart for our school's library. Do you want to help me?

M Sure. Let's see. Hmm... How about this plastic one? It looks like it's easy to use.

W Well, the cart we have now is plastic and it's not strong enough, so, I'd prefer to buy one that's made of metal or wood.

M That makes sense. Then, let's get one that's made of metal or wood. What about the number of shelves?

W I think it would be nice to have a cart that has at least three shelves.

M That's a good idea. I would also recommend one that has lockable wheels because that makes it easier to control.

W You're right! The one we have now doesn't have lockable wheels, so it's really hard to control.

M I understand. That leaves us with these two options.

W Well, we don't have much left in our budget. I can't spend more than $100.

M All right. Then, this one would be the best choice.

W Okay, then I'll order this one. Thanks for your help.

해석

남 안녕, Jessica. 너 지금 무슨 일을 하고 있니?

여 안녕! 나는 우리 학교 도서관에서 사용할 새 롤링 카트를 주문하려고 해. 나를 좀 도와줄래?

남 물론이지. 어디 보자. 흠… 이 플라스틱으로 된 것은 어때? 그것은 사용하기 쉬워 보여.

여 음, 우리가 지금 가지고 있는 카트가 플라스틱으로 된 것이고 충분히 튼튼하지가 않아서 나는 금속이나 나무로 만든 카트를 구입하고 싶어.

남 일리가 있네. 그럼, 금속이나 나무로 된 것을 사자. 선반의 개수는?

여 내 생각에는 적어도 세 개의 선반이 있는 카트가 좋을 것 같아.

남 좋은 생각이야. 나는 제어하기 더 쉬우니까 잠글 수 있는 바퀴가 있는 것을 추천하고 싶어.

여 네 말이 맞아! 우리가 지금 가지고 있는 건 바퀴가 잠기지 않아 제어하기가 정말 힘들어.

남 이해해. 그러면 이 두 가지 선택이 남네.

여 음, 우리는 예산이 많이 남지 않았어. 나는 100달러 넘게 쓸 수 없어.

남 알았어. 그럼, 이게 제일 좋은 선택인 것 같아.
여 좋아, 그럼 나는 이걸로 주문할게. 도와줘서 고마워.

어휘
prefer ~을 더 좋아하다 metal 금속 shelf 선반(*pl.* shelves)
lockable 잠글 수 있는 budget 예산

11 정답 ①
정답률 82%

W Hey, Sean! Is this your dog? He's adorable!

M He's actually not my dog. I think he's lost, but I don't know what to do.

W Oh, really? *[Pause]* Look at the couple over there! It seems like they're looking for something.

M Okay. Then let's ask them if they lost their dog.

해석
여 이봐, Sean! 이것이 너의 개니? 사랑스럽다!
남 그는 사실 나의 개가 아니야. 길을 잃은 것 같은데, 나는 어떻게 해야 할지 모르겠어.
여 오, 그래? *[잠시 후]* 저기 커플 좀 봐! 그들이 무엇을 찾고 있는 것 같아.
남 알았어. 그럼 그들에게 개를 잃어버렸는지 물어보자.

② 진정해. 이 개는 전혀 위험하지 않아.
③ 미안해. 나는 최선을 다했지만, 그것을 찾을 수 없었어.
④ 정말 다행이다! 나는 강아지를 영영 잃어버린 줄 알았어.
⑤ 맞아! 개를 기르는 사람들은 자신의 애완견을 하루에 두 번 산책시켜야 해.

어휘
adorable 사랑스러운 actually 사실은, 실제로 relief 안심, 안도

12 정답 ①
정답률 94%

M Hi, we just wanted to see if we could still sit and order dinner.

W Umm... I'm sorry but the kitchen closes in five minutes, so we won't be able to serve you.

M That's disappointing. What time do you open tomorrow?

W We're open from 11 o'clock in the morning.

해석
남 안녕하세요, 아직 앉아서 주문을 할 수 있는지 궁금해요.
여 음… 죄송하지만 주방이 5분 뒤에 마감해서, 식사 제공이 어렵습니다.
남 유감이네요. 내일 몇 시에 문을 여시나요?
여 오전 11시부터 엽니다.

② 죄송합니다만, 지금 모든 테이블이 꽉 찼습니다.
③ 오늘의 특선 요리는 바비큐 치킨입니다.
④ 저희 식당을 방문해 주셔서 감사합니다.
⑤ 저는 요리할 충분한 시간이 없습니다.

어휘
serve (음식을) 제공하다 disappointing 실망스러운

13 정답 ③
정답률 73%

M Good morning, ma'am. May I help you?

W Yes, please. I just heard that my flight will be delayed for six hours.

M Oh, I'm sorry to hear that. Is there anything I can do for you?

W Well, I know I have to check out of my room by 11, but that means I would be waiting at the airport for almost eight hours.

M I understand. That's a long time to sit around and wait.

W Is it possible for me to stay in my room for a couple more hours until I leave this afternoon?

M Let me check to see if the room is available. *[Pause]* Luckily, ma'am, the room hasn't been booked for today.

W Okay, then if I stay for a couple more hours, do I have to pay an additional charge?

M Yes. But you don't have to pay for a full day.

해석
남 안녕하세요, 손님. 도와드릴까요?
여 네. 저는 방금 제 항공편이 6시간 지연될 거라고 들었어요.
남 오, 유감이네요. 제가 도와드릴 일이 있나요?
여 음, 제가 11시까지 체크아웃을 해야 하는 걸 알고 있지만, 그것은 제가 공항에서 거의 8시간을 기다려야 한다는 걸 의미해요.
남 이해합니다. 앉아서 기다리기에는 긴 시간이죠.
여 제가 오늘 오후에 떠날 때까지 몇 시간을 더 방에서 머무는 게 가능할까요?
남 그 방이 이용 가능한지 확인해 보겠습니다. *[잠시 후]* 다행히, 손님, 그 방이 오늘 예약이 되어 있지 않습니다.
여 좋네요, 그럼 제가 몇 시간 더 머무르게 되면, 추가 요금을 내야 하나요?
남 네. 하지만 하루 전체에 해당하는 비용을 내실 필요는 없습니다.

① 걱정 마세요. 당신은 다른 호텔을 예약할 수 있습니다.
② 맞습니다. 당신은 이미 요금을 지불했습니다.
④ 죄송합니다. 당신은 예약을 취소하셨어야 했습니다.
⑤ 물론입니다. 당신은 오후까지 로비에 계셔도 됩니다.

어휘
delay 지연시키다 available 이용 가능한 additional 추가적인 charge 요금
don't have to ~할 필요가 없다

14 정답 ①
정답률 74%

W Hi, James. Is everything okay? I heard there was a huge storm in your area last night.

M Yeah, we had some really intense thunderstorms throughout the night. There was some damage.

W Did anyone get hurt?

M Thankfully, no, but there were a lot of fallen trees, and the roads were blocked.

W Oh, my! That must have been scary!

M Yeah, it was. Then the electricity went out while the roads were being cleared.

W So you didn't have any power last night?

M No, I couldn't turn on any lights or use any electronic devices, but it's okay now.

W That must have been so frustrating. Is there anything you need help with?

M Well, my basement is a mess. The water is up to my knees and all of my stuff down there is wet.

W Oh, no! I can come over today to help you clear it out.

해석
여 안녕, James. 별일 없니? 나는 어젯밤에 너의 지역에 큰 폭풍이 있었다고 들었어.

남 응, 밤새 정말 심한 뇌우가 있었어. 피해도 좀 있었지.

여 다친 사람이 있니?

남 감사하게도, 없어, 하지만 쓰러진 나무들이 많이 있었고, 도로가 차단됐어.

여 오, 세상에! 정말 무서웠겠다!

남 응, 그랬어. 그러더니 도로가 정리되고 있는 동안 전기가 나갔어.

여 그래서 어제 전기가 전혀 안 들어왔어?

남 응, 나는 불을 켤 수 없거나 전자기기를 전혀 사용할 수 없었지만, 지금은 괜찮아.

여 정말 답답했겠다. 도와줄 거 없니?

남 음, 내 지하실이 엉망이야. 물이 내 무릎까지 차고 그 아래에 있는 내 물건들이 다 젖었어.

여 오, 안 돼! 내가 오늘 들러서 네가 그것을 정리하는 것을 도울 수 있어.

② 신경 쓰지 마. 모든 사람들은 결정을 하기 위해서 시간을 필요로 해.

③ 좋아. 위험하면 우리는 지하실로 내려갈 수 있어.

④ 응. 너 나무에 물을 좀 더 자주 주는 게 어때?

⑤ 미안해. 나는 전구를 어떻게 갈아야 할지 몰라.

어휘

intense 심한, 강렬한 thunderstorm 뇌우 throughout 내내, 줄곧
block 차단하다 electricity 전기 electronic 전자의 device 기기, 장치
frustrating 답답하게 하는, 좌절감을 주는

15 정답 ④

정답률 67%

M Emily and Chris are classmates. Emily is making cookies when she gets a call from Chris. He says he is going to see a movie with his friends and asks if she can join them. She says that she would love to, but she can't go because her parents aren't home and she has to watch her younger brother. Chris suggests that Emily bring her brother with her to the movie. Emily explains to Chris that her little brother has homework to finish, so he can't go either. She wants to tell Chris that she has to look after her brother. In this situation, what would Emily most likely say to Chris?

Emily I'm sorry, but I need to take care of my brother.

해석

남 Emily와 Chris는 반 친구이다. Emily는 Chris에게 전화를 받을 때 쿠키를 만드는 중이다. 그는 자신의 친구들과 영화를 보러 갈 예정이라고 말하며 그녀가 함께 할 수 있는지 묻는다. 그녀는 그러고 싶지만, 그녀의 부모님이 집에 계시지 않아서 그녀가 남동생을 돌보아야 한다. Chris는 Emily에게 영화관에 그녀의 동생을 데리고 오라고 제안한다. Emily는 자신의 남동생이 끝내야 할 숙제가 있어서, 그도 갈 수 없다고 Chris에게 설명한다. 그녀는 Chris에게 자신이 그녀의 남동생을 돌보아야 한다고 말하고 싶다. 이러한 상황에서, Emily는 Chris에게 무엇이라고 말하겠는가?

Emily 미안하지만, 나는 내 남동생을 돌봐야 해.

① 다행히도, 나는 숙제를 끝냈어.

② 내가 내 남동생과 영화를 봐도 될까?

③ 고마워, 그리고 네 쿠키 고맙게 잘 먹을게.

⑤ 네가 잠시만 내 동생을 좀 돌봐 줄래?

해설

영화를 보러가자고 하는 Chris에게 Emily는 부모님이 계시지 않아 남동생을 돌봐야 한다고 한다. 이에 Chris는 남동생을 영화관에 데리고 오라고 제안하지만, Emily는 남동생에게 끝내야 할 숙제가 있어 갈 수 없다고 설명한다. 이러한 상황에서 Emily는 Chris에게 자신이 남동생을 돌보아야 한다고 말하고 싶어 하므로, Emily가 Chris에게 할 말로 가장 적절한 것은 ④ '미안하지만, 나는 내 남동생을 돌봐야 해.'이다.

어휘

get a call 전화를 받다 watch 봐주다, 지켜보다 explain 설명하다
luckily 다행히도 gratefully 고맙게, 감사히 watch over ～을 보살피다

16 정답 ②

정답률 96%

17 정답 ③

정답률 95%

W Everyone loves a good night's sleep, but for wild animals, finding the right time and place can be difficult. Whether it's staying safe, keeping warm, or remembering to breathe, animals have a lot to consider before they go to bed. As a result, they've come up with some clever and interesting solutions. To start with, bats sleep in caves while hanging upside down. Doing that not only keeps them away from enemies but also means they are in the perfect position to fly away if necessary. Meanwhile, ducks sleep side by side in rows. The ducks on the outside of the rows sleep with one eye open to watch for danger, while the ducks on the inside sleep with both eyes closed. Giraffes require little rest, sleeping for only five minutes at a time or as little as 30 minutes a day. They sleep in short intervals, sometimes sitting down or even standing up, so that they're ready to run. Finally, dolphins have to consciously think in order to breathe, even when they're sleeping. They only let part of their brain relax and keep one eye open as they sleep.

해석

여 누구나 밤에 숙면을 취하는 것을 좋아하지만, 야생 동물의 경우, 적당한 시간과 장소를 찾는 것이 어려울 수 있습니다. 그것이 안전하게 지내는 것이든, 따뜻하게 지내는 것이든, 또는 숨을 쉬는 것을 기억하는 것이든 동물들은 잠자리에 들기 전에 고려해야 할 것이 많습니다. 그 결과, 그들은 영리하고 흥미로운 해결책을 생각해 냈습니다. 우선, 박쥐는 동굴에서 거꾸로 매달려 잡니다. 그렇게 하는 것은, 그들이 적들로부터 멀리 떨어져 있게 할 뿐만 아니라 필요하다면 날아갈 수 있는 완벽한 위치에 있다는 것을 의미합니다. 한편, 오리들은 줄지어 나란히 잠을 잡니다. 줄의 바깥쪽에 있는 오리들은 위험을 경계하기 위해 한쪽 눈을 뜬 채 잠을 자고, 안쪽에 있는 오리들은 양쪽 눈을 감은 채 잠을 잡니다. 기린들은 휴식을 거의 필요로 하지 않는데, 한 번에 5분 동안만 또는 하루에 30분 정도 잠을 잡니다. 그들은 짧은 간격으로 잠을 자며, 때때로 앉아서 자거나 심지어 서서 자기도 하는데, 그래서 그들은 달릴 준비가 되어 있습니다. 마지막으로, 돌고래들은 잠을 잘 때에도 숨을 쉬기 위해 의식적으로 생각해야 합니다. 그들은 잠을 잘 때, 뇌의 일부만 쉬게 하고 한쪽 눈을 뜨고 있습니다.

16

① 다른 문화권에서 인기 있는 다양한 동물들

② 동물들이 생존을 위해 사용하는 특이한 잠버릇

③ 멸종 위기종이 되어가고 있는 야생 동물들

④ 동물들이 자신들의 식사법을 바꾼 방법

⑤ 사람들에게 행운을 가져다주는 동물들

17

① 박쥐   ② 오리   ③ 침팬지   ④ 기린   ⑤ 돌고래

어휘

consider 고려하다 as a result 그 결과 to start with 우선, 첫째로
upside down 거꾸로 require 요구하다, 필요로 하다 interval 간격
so that 그래서 ～하다 consciously 의식적으로

01 ②	02 ②	03 ②	04 ④	05 ④	06 ①
07 ③	08 ③	09 ④	10 ③	11 ②	12 ⑤
13 ①	14 ⑤	15 ③	16 ③	17 ④	

01 정답 ②

정답률 91%

M Hello, students. This is Allan, your school nurse. Many students get sick with seasonal influenza. Some cases can lead to serious pain or even hospitalization. I would recommend you to get a flu vaccine. A flu shot can keep you from getting sick. Also, since flu viruses keep changing, flu vaccines are updated to protect against such viruses. Please get a flu shot offered in doctors' offices or health departments by the end of this month. Thank you.

해석

남 안녕하세요, 학생 여러분. 여러분의 보건 선생님 Allan입니다. 많은 학생들이 계절성 독감에 걸립니다. 몇 가지 경우들은 심각한 통증이나 심지어 입원으로 이어질 수도 있습니다. 저는 여러분이 독감 예방 접종을 받을 것을 추천하고 싶습니다. 독감 예방 접종은 여러분이 아프지 않게 해 줄 수 있습니다. 또한 독감 바이러스는 계속 변하기 때문에 독감 백신은 그러한 바이러스를 예방하기 위해 업데이트됩니다. 이번 달 말까지 병원이나 보건소에서 제공되는 독감 예방 접종을 받으세요. 감사합니다.

어휘

get sick 병에 걸리다, 병이 나다   seasonal influenza 계절성 독감
hospitalization 입원   keep ~ from -ing ~가 …하지 않게 하다
health department 보건소

02 정답 ②

정답률 90%

M Irene, where are you heading?

W Hello, Mason. I'm going to the bookstore to buy some books.

M The bookstore? Isn't it more convenient to order books online?

W Yes, but I like to flip through the pages at bookstores.

M Yeah, but buying books online is cheaper.

W Right. But we can help bookstore owners when we buy books from them.

M I guess you're right. The bookstore near my house shut down last month.

W It's a pity to see local bookstores going out of business nowadays.

M I agree. Next time I need a book, I'll try to go to a local bookstore.

해석

남 Irene, 너 어디에 가는 중이니?

여 안녕, Mason. 나는 책을 좀 사려고 서점에 가고 있어.

남 서점? 온라인으로 책을 주문하는 게 더 편리하지 않아?

여 그렇지, 하지만 나는 서점에서 책장을 넘기며 훑어보는 것을 좋아해.

남 응, 하지만 온라인으로 책을 사는 게 더 싸.

여 맞아, 하지만 서점에서 책을 사면 서점 주인들을 도울 수 있잖아.

남 네 말이 맞는 것 같아. 우리 집 근처에 있는 서점이 지난달에 폐업했잖아.

여 요즘 지역 서점들이 폐업하는 것을 보니 안타까워.

남 동감이야. 다음에 책이 필요하면, 나도 지역 서점에 가도록 노력할게.

어휘

head 가다, 향하다   convenient 편리한   flip through 훑어보다, 휙 넘겨보다
shut down 폐업하다, 문을 닫다   go out of business 폐업하다

03 정답 ②

정답률 90%

[Telephone rings.]

M Hello. This is G-Solution. How may I help you?

W Hello. I'm locked out of my home. The keypad on my door isn't responding.

M It might be an electric problem. It's probably a simple fix and it won't cost much.

W How much is it?

M It's 30 dollars including the service charge. But you'll have to pay extra if there're any additional problems.

W I got it. Can you come over right away?

M I'm afraid not. I'm doing a job at the Capital Bank.

W How long will it take you to finish?

M Just one hour. I'll call you as soon as I'm done. Address, please?

W 705 Cozy Street near Lee's Dental Clinic.

M Okay. See you soon.

해석

[전화벨이 울린다.]

남 여보세요. G-Solution입니다. 어떻게 도와드릴까요?

여 안녕하세요. 제가 문이 잠겨서 집에 못 들어가고 있어요. 문에 있는 키패드가 반응을 하지 않아요.

남 전기의 문제일 수 있어요. 간단한 수리일 것 같고 비용도 많이 들지 않을 거예요.

여 얼마인가요?

남 서비스 비용을 포함해서 30달러입니다. 하지만 다른 추가적인 문제가 있으면 추가 비용을 지불해야 할 수도 있습니다.

여 알겠습니다. 바로 오실 수 있나요?

남 죄송하지만 그럴 수 없어요. 저는 Capital 은행에서 작업 중이거든요.

여 마치는 데 얼마나 걸릴까요?

남 한 시간이면 됩니다. 끝나는 즉시 전화 드릴게요. 주소가 어떻게 되나요?

여 Lee 치과 병원 근처의 Cozy가 705번지예요.

남 알겠습니다. 곧 뵙겠습니다.

어휘

be locked out of 문이 잠겨서 ~에 들어가지 못하다   respond 반응하다
service charge 봉사료, 서비스료   pay extra 별도로 돈을 치르다
additional 추가의, 부가의

04 정답 ④

정답률 69%

M Grace, let me show you my newly designed room.

W Wow, Jake! It's so cool.

M Look at the monitor between the speakers. I changed my old monitor for this new one.

W Looks nice. But isn't your desk too crowded to put your electric keyboard on it?

M It's fine with me. I find it convenient there.

W Is that a microphone in the corner? Do you sing?

M Yes. Singing is my all-time favorite hobby.

W What's that star-shaped medal on the wall? Where did you get it?

M I won that medal at a guitar contest with my dad.

W Incredible! Do you often practice the guitar with your dad?

M Sure. That's why there're two guitars in the room.

남 Grace, 너에게 새롭게 디자인된 내 방을 보여 줄게.

여 와, Jake! 너무 멋지다.

남 스피커 사이에 있는 모니터를 좀 봐. 내 낡은 모니터를 이 새것으로 바꿨어.

여 멋져 보여. 하지만 전자 키보드를 놓기에 책상이 너무 복잡하지 않니?

남 나한테는 괜찮아. 거기 있으니 편리한 것 같아.

여 모퉁이에 있는 것이 마이크야? 너 노래해?

남 응. 노래하기는 내가 늘 좋아하는 취미지.

여 벽에 있는 저 별 모양의 메달은 무엇이니? 너 그거 어디서 얻은 거야?

남 나는 아빠와 기타 경연 대회에 나가서 그 메달을 땄어.

여 믿을 수 없는데! 너는 아빠랑 기타를 자주 연습하니?

남 당연하지. 그래서 방 안에 기타가 두 개 있잖아.

여자가 벽에 걸려 있는 별 모양의 메달에 대해 질문했으나 둥근 모양으로 표현되어 있으므로, 그림에서 대화의 내용과 일치하지 않는 것은 ④이다.

too ~ to ... …하기에 너무 ~한   incredible 믿을 수 없는
That's why 그래서 ~하다

05 정답 ④

정답률 80%

W Smells nice, Daniel. What did you make for lunch?

M Creamy pasta. I found the recipe online.

W Fantastic. But don't you think the kitchen is a little bit messy?

M Sorry. I'll clean it up later.

W You promise?

M Yes. Let's have lunch. [Pause] By the way, do you remember you have to pick up our daughter from the library this afternoon?

W Oh, my! I totally forgot. What should I do? My friend Amy is coming in an hour.

M Don't worry. I planned to go camera shopping, but I'll pick up Betty, instead.

W Thanks. How sweet of you! Then I'll clean the kitchen.

여 좋은 냄새가 나요, Daniel. 점심으로 무엇을 만들었어요?

남 크림 파스타예요. 온라인에서 요리법을 찾았어요.

여 멋져요. 그런데 부엌이 좀 지저분한 것 같지 않아요?

남 미안해요. 내가 나중에 치울게요.

여 당신 약속하는 거죠?

남 네. 점심 먹읍시다. [잠시 후] 그런데 당신 오늘 오후에 우리 딸을 도서관에서 데려와야 하는 거 기억하죠?

여 오, 안 돼! 완전히 잊어버렸어요. 어떡하죠? 내 친구 Amy가 한 시간 후에 올 거예요.

남 걱정 마요. 카메라 쇼핑을 갈 계획이었는데, 대신 내가 Betty를 데려올게요.

여 고마워요. 당신은 참 친절해요! 그럼 제가 부엌을 치울게요.

a little bit 약간, 다소   messy 지저분한, 어질러진   clean ~ up ~을 깨끗이 치우다
promise 약속하다

06 정답 ①

정답률 87%

M Good afternoon. May I help you?

W Yes, please. I want to buy a bag for my laptop. Can you recommend one?

M How about this one? It's only 30 dollars on sale. The original price was 65 dollars.

W Wow, more than 50% off?

M It's a very good deal.

W I like the design and color, but it's not big enough.

M If you want something bigger, how about this one? It has a USB charging port, too.

W I like it, but it looks expensive.

M It's 70 dollars. But I can give you a 10% discount.

W Well... It's still beyond my budget. Let me look at the first one again.

M Here it is. 30 dollars is a bargain.

W Okay. I'll take it.

남 안녕하세요. 도와드릴까요?

여 네, 부탁드려요. 노트북 컴퓨터용 가방을 하나 사고 싶어요. 하나 추천해 주시겠어요?

남 이거 어떠세요? 할인해서 겨우 30달러예요. 정가는 65달러이고요.

여 와, 50퍼센트 이상 세일하네요?

남 정말 좋은 가격이죠.

여 저는 디자인과 색깔이 마음에 들어요. 하지만 크기가 충분하지 않네요.

남 더 큰 것을 원하시면 이것은 어떠세요? USB 충전 포트도 있어요.

여 마음에 들지만, 좀 비싼 것 같아요.

남 그것은 70달러입니다. 하지만, 제가 10퍼센트를 할인해 드릴게요.

여 음… 여전히 제 예산을 넘어요. 처음 것을 다시 볼게요.

남 여기 있습니다. 30달러는 저렴한 가격이에요.

여 좋아요. 이걸 살게요.

여자는 먼저 정가가 65달러이지만 할인해서 30달러인 가방을 보았으나, 크기가 충분하지 않아 후에 좀 더 큰 가방을 보았다. 그러나 그것의 가격이 자신의 예산을 넘어선다고 하며 처음에 본 가방을 사겠다고 했으므로, 여자가 지불할 금액은 ① '$30'(30달러)이다.

original price 정가   It's a very good deal. 꽤 괜찮은 거래이다.
USB charging port USB 충전 포트   give a discount 할인을 해 주다
beyond one's budget ~의 예산을 넘어서는   bargain 싼 가격, 싼 물건

07 정답 ③

정답률 81%

W Hi, Chris. How was your business trip?

M It went fine. By the way, I heard Emma is moving out this Saturday.

W You're right. She's very busy preparing to move. So she gave me two tickets for a musical because she can't go.

M Good for you. What's the name of the musical?

W It's "Heroes."

M Really? I heard it's popular. Who are you going with?

W No one, yet. My sister turned me down because she has to finish her homework.

M Well, can I go with you instead?

W Sure. Why not? The show is at 8 p.m. this Friday.

M Friday? Oh, no! I promised to take care of my niece at that time.

W No problem. I'll ask Susan to go with me then.

여 안녕, Chris. 너 출장 어땠어?

남 괜찮았어. 그런데, Emma가 이번 토요일에 이사를 간다고 들었어.

여 네 말이 맞아. 그녀는 이사 준비를 하느라 매우 바빠. 그래서 못 간다고 그녀가 뮤지컬 티켓 두 장을 나에게 주었어.

남 잘 됐네. 뮤지컬 제목이 뭐야?

여 〈Heroes〉야.

남 정말? 그거 인기 있다고 들었어. 너 누구랑 갈 거야?

여 아직, 아무도 없어. 내 여동생은 숙제를 끝마쳐야 해서 거절했어.

남 음, 그럼 내가 같이 가도 될까?

여 물론이지. 되고 말고. 그 공연은 이번 금요일 오후 8시야.

남 금요일? 오, 안 돼! 그 시간에 조카를 돌봐 주기로 약속했어.

여 괜찮아. 그럼 Susan에게 같이 가자고 해 볼게.

어휘

business trip 출장   move out 이사를 가다   be busy -ing ~하느라 바쁘다
turn down 거절하다   Why not? 되고 말고., 왜 안 되겠니?

08 정답 ③

정답률 78%

W Dad, I want to have a puppy just like my friend, Julie.

M Why not? But do you know how hard it is to raise a dog?

W Yes, but I'm ready. I think I will name my puppy Toby.

M Okay. But will you walk Toby every day?

W That'll be easy.

M Also, you'll have to feed Toby three times a day.

W No big deal. Anything else?

M You'll have to toilet train Toby, too.

W Really?

M Of course. Plus, you'll need to clean up the dog's pee pads.

W Hmm... Dad, you'll help me, right?

M Sometimes. But remember having a dog takes responsibility.

해석

여 아빠, 저도 제 친구 Julie처럼 강아지를 한 마리 키우고 싶어요.

남 왜 안 되겠니? 하지만 너 개를 기르는 게 얼마나 힘든 건지 알아?

여 알아요. 하지만 저는 준비됐어요. 저는 제 강아지의 이름을 Toby라고 지을 거라고 생각해 놨어요.

남 좋아. 그런데 너 Toby를 매일 산책시킬 거니?

여 그건 쉬울 거예요.

남 또 하루에 세 번씩 Toby에게 먹이도 줘야 할 거야.

여 그리 힘든 일은 아니네요. 또 다른 것은요?

남 Toby에게 배변 훈련도 시켜야 할 거야.

여 정말이요?

남 당연하지. 게다가, 너는 강아지 소변 패드도 청소해야 할 거야.

여 음… 아빠, 저를 도와주실 거죠, 그렇죠?

남 가끔씩. 하지만 개를 기르는 것은 책임이 따르는 일이라는 것을 기억해.

어휘

raise 기르다   No big deal. 별일 아니다.   toilet train 배변 훈련을 시키다
dog's pee pad 강아지 소변 패드   responsibility 책임감

09 정답 ④

정답률 91%

W Good afternoon, listeners. Why don't you join the Sharing Friday Movement and donate two dollars to our fund every Friday? This movement started in 2001 in Finland as an idea to encourage people to do good. Since then, this idea has grown into a global movement. Most of the donations go to poor areas across the world and help people get clean water. This year, scholarships were given to 100 students in these areas to celebrate our 20th anniversary. Please join us, and help make a difference. If you want to get more information, visit our homepage.

해석

여 안녕하세요, 청취자 여러분. Sharing Friday 운동에 참여해서 매주 금요일마다 저희 기금에 2달러씩 기부하는 것이 어떠세요? 이 운동은 사람들에게 선행을 하도록 장려하기 위한 아이디어로서 2001년 핀란드에서 시작되었습니다. 그 이후로, 이 아이디어는 전 세계적인 운동으로 성장했습니다. 대부분의 기부금은 전 세계의 가난한 지역으로 가서 사람들이 깨끗한 물을 얻을 수 있게 도와줍니다. 올해, 저희의 20주년을 기념하기 위해 해당 지역의 100명의 학생들에게 장학금이 주어졌습니다. 동참하셔서 변화를 이룰 수 있도록 도와주세요. 더 많은 정보를 원하시면, 저희 홈페이지를 방문해 주세요.

어휘

movement 운동, 캠페인   donate 기부하다
encourage ~ to ... ~가 …하도록 격려하다   grow into ~으로 성장하다, ~이 되다
scholarship 장학금   celebrate 기념하다   anniversary 기념일
make a difference 변화를 가져오다

10 정답 ③

정답률 92%

W Kevin, I'm looking for a selfie stick. Can you help me?

M Sure, mom. You can buy one on your smart phone. *[Pause]* What kind of selfie stick do you want?

W I'd prefer a light one.

M Then I don't recommend a selfie stick over 200 grams. How about the length?

W I have no idea. What's your opinion?

M Hmm... It should extend up to 80cm at least.

W Okay. I also want a bluetooth remote control. I heard they're convenient to use.

M Then you have two options left. Which one do you want?

W I'll buy this cheaper one.

M Great choice.

해석

여 Kevin, 나는 셀카봉을 하나 찾고 있어. 나를 좀 도와줄래?

남 물론이죠, 엄마. 엄마 스마트폰으로 하나 살 수 있어요. *[잠시 후]* 어떤 종류의 셀카봉을 원하세요?

여 나는 가벼운 게 더 좋을 것 같아.

남 그러면 저는 200그램이 넘는 셀카봉은 추천하지 않아요. 길이는요?

여 잘 모르겠구나. 네 의견은 어때?

남 음… 적어도 80센티미터까지는 늘어나야 해요.

여 좋아. 나는 블루투스 리모컨도 있으면 좋겠어. 그것들은 사용하기 편리하다고 들었거든.

남 그럼 두 가지 선택이 남아요. 어떤 것이 더 좋으세요?

여 나는 이 더 싼 것을 살게.

남 훌륭한 선택이에요.

어휘

selfie stick 셀카봉   length 길이   opinion 의견, 생각   extend 늘어나다
up to ~까지   at least 적어도, 최소한   remote control 리모컨
convenient 편리한

11 정답 ②

정답률 87%

M Have you finished packing your bags for your trip to Mount Jiri?

W I think so. Look! What else do I need?

M You'd better prepare for the cold weather at night.

W You're right. I'll take a warm jacket.

해석

남 너 지리산 여행을 위한 가방은 다 쌌니?

여 그런 것 같아. 봐! 뭐가 더 필요할까?

남 너는 밤에 추운 날씨에 대비하는 게 좋을 것 같아.

여 네 말이 맞아. 따뜻한 재킷을 하나 가져갈게.

① 또? 너는 가방을 두 번이나 잃어버렸어.

③ 왜? 난 네가 추운 날씨를 더 좋아하는 것을 알아.

④ 뭐라고? 너에게 줄 선물을 포장하는 것을 다 끝냈어.

⑤ 미안해. 하지만 너는 지금으로서는 그 여행에 합류할 수 없어.

어휘

pack (짐을) 싸다　prepare for ~을 위해 준비하다
at this point 현 시점에서는, 현재는

12 정답 ⑤

정답률 74%

W Honey, we can't eat out tomorrow evening.

M Why not? I've already booked a table at the restaurant.

W I'm sorry. I have an important business meeting at that time.

M Sorry to hear that. I'll cancel the reservation now.

해석

여 여보, 우리는 내일 저녁에 외식할 수 없어요.

남 왜 못해요? 내가 식당에 자리를 이미 예약해 놨는데요.

여 미안해요. 나는 그 시간에 중요한 사업상 회의가 있어요.

남 그렇다니 유감이에요. 내가 지금 예약을 취소할게요.

① 아니 됐어요. 나는 충분히 먹었어요.

② 좋아요. 내가 6시에 다섯 명의 자리를 예약할게요.

③ 좋은 선택이에요. 음식이 훌륭해요.

④ 좋아요. 내가 회의 장소와 시간을 정할게요.

어휘

eat out 외식하다　book a table 자리를 예약하다　set a place 장소를 정하다
cancel 취소하다

13 정답 ①

정답률 85%

M Why do you look so busy?

W I'm working on a team project.

M What's it about?

W It's about 'Climate Change.'

M Sounds interesting. Who's on your team?

W You know Chris? He's the leader.

M I know him very well. He's responsible and smart.

W Jenny is doing the research and Alex is making the slides.

M What a nice team! Then what's your role?

W I'm in charge of giving the presentation.

해석

남 너 왜 그렇게 바빠 보이니?

여 나는 팀 과제를 준비하고 있어.

남 무엇에 관한 건데?

여 '기후 변화'에 관한 거야.

남 재미있겠다. 누가 너희 팀이야?

여 너 Chris 알아? 그 애가 리더야.

남 그 애는 내가 잘 알지. 그는 책임감 있고 똑똑해.

여 Jenny가 조사를 하고 Alex가 슬라이드를 만들 거야.

남 정말 멋진 팀이네! 그러면 너가 맡은 일은 무엇이니?

여 나는 발표를 담당하고 있어.

② 내 생각에 네가 그 역할에 딱 맞는 것 같아.

③ 팀을 주의 깊게 선택하는 것이 중요해.

④ 그 과제는 모레까지야.

⑤ 나는 우리가 그 과제를 끝내기 위해 늦게까지 깨어 있지 않기를 바라.

어휘

work on ~을 착수하다, ~에 공을 들이다　responsible 책임감 있는
do the research 조사하다　be in charge of -ing ~을 담당하다, ~을 맡다
assignment 과제, 숙제　the day after tomorrow 모레
stay up late 늦게까지 자지 않고 깨어 있다

14 정답 ⑤

정답률 83%

M Hi, Diana. You look down. What's the problem?

W Hi, Peter. I missed the deadline for the speech contest. It was yesterday.

M No way. You'd been waiting for it for a long time.

W Yeah. It totally slipped my mind. I'm so forgetful.

M Why don't you write notes to remember things?

W I've tried, but it doesn't work. I even forget where I put the notes.

M How about using a time management application like me?

W Well... What's good about your app?

M It helps me keep deadlines to complete specific tasks.

해석

남 안녕, Diana. 너 우울해 보여. 무슨 일이야?

여 안녕, Peter. 나는 말하기 대회 마감 날짜를 놓쳤어. 어제까지였어.

남 안 돼. 너 오랫동안 그것을 기다려 왔잖아.

여 그래. 그것을 깜빡 잊어버렸어. 나는 잘 잊어버려.

남 기억하기 위해 메모를 하는 게 어때?

여 해 봤지만 효과가 없어. 나는 심지어 그 메모를 어디 뒀는지도 잊어버려.

남 나처럼 시간 관리 앱을 사용해 보는 건 어때?

여 음… 너의 앱은 어떤 점이 좋아?

남 그것은 내가 특정한 일을 완수하도록 마감일을 지킬 수 있게 도와줘.

① 나는 대중 연설을 잘해.

② 과제를 깜빡해서 미안해.

③ 불행하게도 내 자명종이 나를 깨우지 않아.

④ 말하기 대회가 바로 코앞으로 다가왔어.

어휘

look down 우울해 보이다　slip one's mind 까먹다, 잊어버리다
forgetful 잘 잊어버리는, 건망증이 있는　management 관리
be just around the corner 바로 코앞으로 다가오다, 바로 목전에 와 있다
complete 완수하다　specific 특정한, 구체적인

15 정답 ③

정답률 72%

M Harold is a tennis coach. He's been teaching Kate, a talented and passionate player, for years. While practicing for an upcoming match, Kate injured her elbow badly. Her doctor strongly recommends she stop playing tennis for a month. However, Kate insists on playing the match. Harold knows how heart-broken she would be to miss the match. But he's concerned about her tennis career if her elbow doesn't recover. So he wants to persuade her to calm down and focus on her recovery. In this situation, what would Harold most likely say to Kate?

Harold Take it easy. Take good care of yourself first.

해석

남 Harold는 테니스 코치이다. 그는 재능 있고 열정적인 선수인 Kate를 수년 간 지도해 오고 있다. 다가오는 경기를 위해 연습하던 중, Kate는 팔꿈치를 심하게 다쳤다. 그녀의 담당 의사는 한 달 동안 테니스를 하지 말라고 강력 하게 권고한다. 그러나, Kate는 경기를 고집한다. Harold는 그녀가 경기 에 참가를 못하면 얼마나 가슴 아파할지 알고 있다. 그러나 그는 그녀의 팔 꿈치가 회복되지 않을 경우 그녀의 테니스 경력을 우려하고 있다. 그래서 그는 그녀에게 진정하고 회복에만 집중하라고 설득하고 싶다. 이 상황에서 Harold는 Kate에게 뭐라고 말할 것 같은가?

Harold 진정해. 우선 네 자신을 잘 보살펴.

① 좋아. 너는 경기하는 데 최선을 다하는 게 좋겠어.
② 알아. 너는 그녀 대신에 경기를 해야 해.
④ 넌 그럴 자격이 있어. 연습이 완벽을 만들어.
⑤ 걱정하지 마. 너는 이 경기에서 이길 거야.

어휘

talented 재능 있는   passionate 열정적인, 열의가 있는   insist 고집하다, 주장하다
heart-broken 상심한, 비통해하는
be concerned about ~을 염려하다, ~을 걱정하다   persuade 설득하다
recovery 회복   put one's best effort into ~에 최선의 노력을 쏟다
deserve ~을 받을 만하다

리의 짝짓기 신호를 방해합니다. 수컷 개구리가 짝짓기 신호를 보내는 횟수 를 줄이기 때문에 암컷 개구리가 번식하지 않습니다. 그러므로 빛 공해는 어떤 동물들에게는 삶과 죽음의 문제가 될 수 있습니다.

16
① 밀렵으로 인한 문제점들
② 이동하는 동물들의 특징들
③ 빛 공해가 야생 동물들에게 미치는 영향들
④ 멸종 위기에 처한 동물들을 구하는 다양한 방법들
⑤ 수질 오염으로 인한 동물 서식지 변화

17
① 바다거북   ② 반딧불이   ③ 연어   ④ 꿀벌   ⑤ 청개구리

어휘

light pollution 빛 공해   drive 몰다, 몰아가다   artificial 인공적인
cause ~ to … ~로 하여금 …하게 하다   across the globe 전 세계에서
get disturbed 방해받다   migrate 이동하다, 이주하다
randomly 무작위로, 아무렇게나   interrupt 방해하다   reproduce 번식하다
illegal hunting 밀렵, 불법 사냥   habitat 서식지

---

16 정답 ③   정답률 81%   **17** 정답 ④   정답률 93%

W This is Linda from "Life and Science." Did you know light pollution from bright lights at night can drive wildlife to death? For example, sea turtles lay eggs on beaches and their babies find their way to the sea with the help of moonlight. But artificial lights can confuse them and cause them not to reach the sea and die. Fireflies have been disappearing across the globe. Male fireflies get disturbed by artificial lights when they try to attract mates. This means less fireflies are born. Also, salmon migrate randomly when exposed to artificial lights at night. This threatens their chances of survival. Lastly, light pollution interrupts the mating calls of tree frogs at night. As male frogs reduce the number of their mating calls, the females don't reproduce. So light pollution can be a matter of life and death for some animals.

해석

여 '생활과 과학'의 Linda입니다. 여러분은 밤에 밝은 빛으로 인한 빛 공해가 야생 생물들을 죽음으로 내몰 수 있다는 것을 알고 있나요? 예를 들어, 바 다거북은 해변에 알을 낳고 새끼 거북들은 달빛의 도움을 받아 바다로 가는 길을 찾습니다. 하지만 인공 빛들이 새끼 바다거북을 혼란스럽게 하고 그들 이 바다에 이르지 못하게 해 죽게 할 수 있습니다. 반딧불이는 전 세계에서 사라지고 있습니다. 수컷 반딧불이는 짝을 유혹하려고 할 때 인공 빛에 의 해 방해받게 됩니다. 이것은 반딧불이 새끼들이 적게 태어난다는 것을 의미 합니다. 또한 연어는 밤에 인공 빛에 노출되면 무작위로 이동을 합니다. 이 것은 그들의 생존 가능성을 위협합니다. 마지막으로 빛 공해는 밤에 청개구

01 ④	02 ④	03 ①	04 ③	05 ④	06 ③
07 ①	08 ②	09 ⑤	10 ②	11 ①	12 ①
13 ②	14 ③	15 ④	16 ②	17 ④	

01 정답 ④

정답률 95%

M Good morning, students. This is Mr. Lewis from the school administration office. Last night there was a heavy rainstorm. The pouring rain left some of the school's hallways wet and slippery. The first floor hallway and the central stairway are especially dangerous to walk on. Please be extra careful when you walk through these areas. You could get seriously hurt if you slip on the wet floor. We're doing our best to take care of the situation. Thank you.

해석

남 안녕하세요, 학생 여러분. 학교 행정실의 Lewis 선생님입니다. 어젯밤에 심한 폭풍우가 있었습니다. 퍼붓는 비에 학교 복도의 일부가 젖어서 매우 미끄럽습니다. 1층 복도와 중앙 계단이 특히 걷기에 위험합니다. 이 구역을 걸어갈 때는 각별한 주의를 부탁드립니다. 젖은 바닥에 미끄러진다면 심각한 부상을 입을 수도 있습니다. 저희는 상황을 잘 관리하기 위해 최선을 다하고 있습니다. 감사합니다.

어휘

administration office 행정실 rainstorm 폭풍우 pour 퍼붓다, 쏟다
hallway 복도 slippery 미끄러운 stairway 계단 especially 특히
extra 특별히 seriously 심하게

02 정답 ④

정답률 94%

W Mike, you look very tired today.

M I am. I'm having trouble sleeping at night these days.

W What's the matter?

M I don't know. I just can't fall asleep until late at night.

W I feel bad for you.

M I need to find a way to sleep better.

W Can I share how I handled my sleeping problem?

M Sure.

W After I changed my pillow, I was able to sleep much better. Changing your pillow can help you with your sleeping problem.

M Thanks for the tip. I hope that works for me, too.

해석

여 Mike, 너 오늘 매우 피곤해 보여.

남 피곤해. 나 요즘 밤에 잠을 자는 게 좀 힘들어.

여 뭐가 문제인데?

남 모르겠어. 그냥 밤늦게까지 잠들 수가 없어.

여 참 안됐구나.

남 나는 잠을 잘 자기 위한 방법을 찾아야 해.

여 내가 어떻게 내 수면 문제를 해결했는지 알려 줄까?

남 물론이지.

여 나는 베개를 바꾼 다음부터 잠을 더 잘 잘 수 있었어. 베개를 바꾸는 것이 네 수면 문제에 도움이 될 수 있어.

남 조언 고마워. 그게 나에게도 효과가 있으면 좋겠다.

어휘

have trouble -ing ~하는 데 어려움이 있다 fall asleep 잠이 들다
handle 다루다, 처리하다 pillow 베개 be able to ~할 수 있다

03 정답 ①

정답률 96%

M Hi, I'm Daniel Jones. I'm glad to finally meet you.

W Welcome. Mr. Harvey told me you're coming.

M He told me nice things about you.

W Thanks. I hear that you're holding a party at your house in two weeks.

M That's right. I'm hoping you could take charge of the food for my party.

W Sure. You can always depend on a chef like me.

M Great. Is there anything I need to prepare for you?

W No need. I'll be taking care of the party food from start to finish.

M Sounds fantastic.

W Now let's talk about the menu.

해석

남 안녕하세요, 저는 Daniel Jones입니다. 드디어 당신을 만나게 되어 기쁩니다.

여 환영합니다. Harvey 씨가 당신이 오실 거라고 말씀하셨어요.

남 그분이 제게 당신에 관해 좋은 말씀을 해 주셨어요.

여 감사합니다. 저는 당신이 2주 후에 댁에서 파티를 열 거라고 들었습니다.

남 맞아요. 저는 당신이 제 파티의 음식을 맡아 주셨으면 합니다.

여 물론이죠. 저와 같은 요리사를 항상 믿으시면 됩니다.

남 잘됐네요. 제가 당신을 위해 준비해야 할 것이 있나요?

여 준비하실 것 없습니다. 시작부터 끝까지 제가 파티 음식을 책임질 겁니다.

남 아주 멋지게 들리네요.

여 이제 메뉴에 대해 이야기하시죠.

어휘

hold a party 파티를 열다 take charge of ~을 떠맡다, ~을 책임지다
depend on ~을 믿다, ~에 의존하다

04 정답 ③

정답률 83%

W Is that the photo of our school's new studio?

M Yes. We can shoot online lectures here.

W Can I have a look?

M Sure. Do you see that camera facing the chair? It's the latest model.

W I see. What is that ring on the stand next to the camera?

M That's the lighting. It's to brighten the teacher's face.

W Hmm.... The round clock on the wall looks simple and modern.

M Teachers can check the time on the clock while shooting.

W The microphone on the table looks very professional.

M It really does. Also, I like the tree in the corner. It goes well with the studio.

해석

여 그것이 우리 학교의 새 스튜디오 사진인가요?

남 네. 우리는 여기서 온라인 강의들을 촬영할 수 있어요.

여 제가 한번 봐도 될까요?

남 물론이죠. 의자를 향해 있는 저 카메라 보이죠? 그것은 최신 모델이에요.

여 그렇군요. 카메라 옆 스탠드 위의 저 둥근 모양의 것은 무엇인가요?

남 그것은 조명이에요. 교사의 얼굴을 밝게 해 주기 위한 거죠.

여 음… 벽에 있는 둥근 시계가 심플하고 현대적으로 보여요.

남 촬영하는 동안 선생님들이 시계를 보며 시간을 확인할 수 있어요.

여 탁자 위에 마이크가 매우 전문적인 것처럼 보이네요.

남 그건 정말 그러네요. 또한 모퉁이에 있는 나무도 마음에 들어요. 스튜디오랑 잘 어울리네요.

05 정답 ④

정답률 91%

M Hi, Jamie. You remember we're going to the movies later today, right?

W Of course. I'll see you after class.

M Didn't you say there's a student discount on the movie ticket?

W Yes, I did. Don't forget to bring your student ID card.

M But I've lost my ID. Is there any other way to get the discount?

W Probably not. Why don't you go get a new ID card from the school office?

M Do you know where the office is?

W Yes. It's on the first floor.

M Okay. I'll go there right away.

해석

남 안녕, Jamie. 너 오늘 이따가 영화 보러 가기로 한 거 기억하지, 그렇지?

여 물론이지. 수업 끝나고 보자.

남 너 영화 티켓에 학생 할인이 있다고 말하지 않았니?

여 응, 그랬지. 학생증 가져오는 거 잊지 마.

남 그런데 나 학생증을 잃어버렸어. 할인 받을 수 있는 다른 방법이 있니?

여 아마도 없을 걸. 학교 행정실에 가서 새로 학생증을 발급받지 그래?

남 너 사무처가 어디 있는지 알아?

여 응. 1층에 있어.

남 알았어. 지금 바로 거기 갈게.

06 정답 ③

정답률 83%

W Hi, I'm looking for camping chairs. Can you recommend one?

M Good morning. This is our bestselling chair. They're $20 each.

W That sounds good. I'll take it.

M How many do you need?

W I need four chairs.

M Okay. Is there anything else you need?

W I also need a camping knife.

M How about this one? It's $20.

W That looks convenient. I'll buy one. Do you offer any discounts?

M Yes. Since your total purchase is over $80, we'll give you a 10% discount on the total amount.

W That sounds nice. I'll pay with my credit card.

해석

여 안녕하세요, 저는 캠핑 의자를 찾고 있습니다. 하나 추천해 주시겠어요?

남 안녕하세요. 이것이 저희의 가장 잘 팔리는 의자입니다. 그것들은 하나에

20달러입니다.

여 좋네요. 제가 그것을 살게요.

남 몇 개가 필요하신가요?

여 저는 4개의 의자가 필요합니다.

남 알겠습니다. 더 필요한 것이 있나요?

여 저는 캠핑용 칼도 필요해요.

남 이거 어떠세요? 20달러입니다.

여 편리해 보이네요. 하나 살게요. 할인을 해 주실 수 있나요?

남 네. 총 구입액이 80달러가 넘어서 총액에서 10퍼센트를 할인해 드릴게요.

여 좋습니다. 신용 카드로 지불할게요.

해설

여자는 20달러짜리 의자 4개를 사고, 20달러짜리 캠핑용 칼을 추가 구매하여 총 금액은 ($20×4)+$20=$100(100달러)이나, 총 구매액이 80달러가 넘어서 10% 할인을 받게 되었으므로, 여자가 지불할 금액은 ③ '$90'(90달러)이다.

07 정답 ①

정답률 76%

M Hi, Rebecca. What's up?

W Hey, Tom. Can I borrow your laptop today?

M Yes, but I have to finish my science report first.

W Really? Wasn't the science report due last week?

M Yes, it was. But I couldn't finish it.

W What happened? I thought your experiment went well.

M Actually, it didn't. I made a mistake in the experimental process.

W Oh, no. Did you have to do the experiment all over again?

M Yes, it took a lot of time. So I haven't finished my report yet.

W I see. Let me know when you're done.

해석

남 안녕, Rebecca. 잘 지내니?

여 안녕, Tom. 내가 오늘 네 노트북 컴퓨터를 좀 빌릴 수 있을까?

남 그래, 그런데 나는 내 과학 보고서를 먼저 끝내야 해.

여 정말? 과학 보고서는 지난주가 기한 아니었어?

남 응, 그랬지. 하지만 끝내지 못했어.

여 무슨 일 있었어? 나는 너의 실험이 잘됐는지 알았어.

남 사실, 그렇지 못했어. 나는 실험 과정에서 실수를 좀 했어.

여 오, 안 돼. 실험을 처음부터 다시 해야 했던 거야?

남 응, 시간이 오래 걸렸지. 그래서 내 보고서를 아직 끝내지 못했어.

여 알았어. 네가 다 끝나면 알려 줘.

해설

대화의 마지막 부분에 남자는 실험 과정에서 실수가 있어서 처음부터 다시 실험을 시작해야 했고 그래서 기한 내에 보고서를 끝낼 수 없었다고 언급하고 있으므로, 남자가 보고서를 완성하지 못한 이유는 ① '실험을 다시 해서'이다.

08 정답 ②

정답률 91%

W Hi, Asher. What are you doing on the computer?

M I'm signing up for an event called the Spring Virtual Run.

W The Spring Virtual... Run?

M It's a race. Participants upload their record after running either a three-mile race or a ten-mile race.

W Can you run at any location?

M Yes. I can choose any place in the city.

W That sounds interesting. I want to participate, too.

M Then you should sign up online and pay the registration fee. It's twenty dollars.

W Twenty dollars? That's pretty expensive.

M But souvenirs are included in the fee. All participants will get a T-shirt and a water bottle.

W That's reasonable. I'll sign up.

해석

여 안녕, Asher. 너 컴퓨터로 무엇을 하고 있니?

남 나는 '춘계 가상 달리기'라고 불리는 행사를 신청하고 있어.

여 춘계 가상… 달리기?

남 달리기 경주야. 참가자들은 3마일 경주나 10마일 경주를 완주한 후에 자신의 기록을 업로드하면 돼.

여 어느 장소에서든 달릴 수 있어?

남 응. 도시 안에서 어느 곳이든 선택할 수 있어.

여 재미있게 들린다. 나도 참가하고 싶어.

남 그러면 온라인으로 신청해서 참가비를 지불해야 해. 20달러야.

여 20달러라고? 꽤 비싸구나.

남 하지만 참가비 안에 기념품이 포함되어 있어. 모든 참가자들은 티셔츠와 물병을 받을 거야.

여 적당한 가격이네. 등록할게.

어휘

sign up (for) (~을) 신청하다, 등록하다 virtual 가상의 participant 참가자 location 장소 participate 참가하다 registration fee 참가비, 등록비 souvenir 기념품 reasonable 적당한

09 정답 ⑤

정답률 83%

W Do your children love adventures? Here's a great adventure for you and your children. The Museum of Natural History is starting a special program — Family Night at the Museum. When the regular museum hours are over, you and your children get to walk around the museum with a flashlight. After your adventure is complete, you will sleep under the amazing models of planets and stars. Sleeping bags, snacks, and water will be provided. This program is for children ages 6 to 13. All those who want to join must register in advance. On-site registration is not accepted. Why not call today and sign up?

해석

여 여러분의 아이들이 모험을 좋아하나요? 여기 당신과 당신 아이를 위한 멋진 모험이 있습니다. 자연사 박물관이 '박물관에서의 가족의 밤'이라는 특별 프로그램을 시작할 것입니다. 박물관의 정규 관람 시간이 끝나면 당신과 당신 아이들은 손전등을 가지고 박물관 주위를 걷기 시작합니다. 모험이 끝난 후, 여러분은 아주 놀라운 행성과 별 모형 아래에서 잠을 자게 될 것입니다. 침낭, 간식 그리고 물이 제공될 것입니다. 이 프로그램은 6세에서 13세까지의 아이들을 위한 것입니다. 참여하기를 원하는 모든 분들은 미리 등록을 해야 합니다. 현장 예약은 불가합니다. 오늘 전화해서 신청하는 게 어떠세요?

어휘

regular 정규의 get to ~하기 시작하다 register 등록하다 in advance 미리 on-site 현장의 accept 받아들이다, 수락하다 Why not ~ ? ~하는 게 어때?

10 정답 ②

정답률 86%

M Hi, how can I help you today?

W Hi, I'm looking for a smart watch.

M Sure. We have these five models.

W Hmm…. I want to wear it when I swim.

M Then you're looking for one that's waterproof.

W That's right. Do you think a one-year warranty is too short?

M Yes. I recommend one that has a warranty longer than one year.

W Okay. I'll take your advice.

M That leaves you with these two options. I'd get the cheaper one because it's as good as the other one.

W I see. Then I'll go with the cheaper one.

M Good choice.

해석

남 안녕하세요, 오늘 어떻게 도와드릴까요?

여 안녕하세요, 저는 스마트 워치를 찾고 있어요.

남 그러시군요. 이 다섯 가지 모델이 있습니다.

여 음… 저는 수영할 때 그것을 착용하고 싶어요.

남 그럼 방수 기능이 있는 것을 찾고 계시는군요.

여 맞아요. 1년 보증 기간은 좀 너무 짧다고 생각하시나요?

남 네. 보증 기간이 1년보다 긴 것을 추천해 드립니다.

여 알았어요. 당신의 조언을 따를게요.

남 그렇다면 이 두 가지 선택이 남네요. 저라면 나머지 것만큼 좋으니 더 싼 것으로 사겠어요.

여 알겠어요. 그러면 저는 더 싼 것으로 할게요.

남 좋은 선택입니다.

어휘

waterproof 방수의 warranty 보증 기간 as ~ as … …만큼 ~한

11 정답 ①

정답률 89%

W Liam, how did your shopping go?

M It was good, Mom. I got this shirt at a good price.

W It looks nice. Wait! It's missing a button.

M Oh, I should get it exchanged.

해석

여 Liam, 쇼핑하러 간 것은 어땠어?

남 좋았어요, 엄마. 좋은 가격에 이 셔츠를 샀어요.

여 멋져 보이는구나. 잠깐만! 그것에 단추가 하나 없어.

남 오, 저는 그것을 교환해야겠어요.

② 물론이죠. 제가 엄마를 위해 셔츠를 하나 주문할게요.

③ 글쎄요, 그것은 저에게는 너무 비싸요.

④ 아니요. 더 작은 사이즈를 찾아 주세요.

⑤ 죄송하지만, 이 셔츠는 할인 판매하지 않아요.

어휘

price 가격 get ~ exchanged ~을 교환하다 be on sale 할인 판매하다

12 정답 ①

정답률 83%

M Alicia, these donuts are delicious. Can you tell me where you bought them?

W They're from a new donut shop. I can take you there if you want.

M That'd be nice. How's today after work?

W Good. Let's meet around six.

남 Alicia, 이 도넛들 맛있네요. 그것들을 어디서 샀는지 말해 줄 수 있어요?

여 그것들은 새로 생긴 도넛 가게에서 산 것들이에요. 원하시면 제가 모셔다 드릴 수 있어요.

남 그래 주시면 좋죠. 오늘 퇴근 후에 어때요?

여 좋아요. 6시 경에 만나요.

② 괜찮아요. 저는 도넛을 좋아하지 않아요.

③ 저는 제 도넛 가게를 열고 싶어요.

④ 걱정하지 마세요. 저 혼자서 할 수 있어요.

⑤ 도넛 요리법을 공유해 줘서 고마워요.

어휘

one's own ~의 소유의 share 공유하다. 나누다

---

13 정답 ②

정답률 83%

W Brandon, I'm sorry I'm late.

M That's okay. Let's order our drinks. I'll get my coffee in my personal cup.

W Oh, you brought your own cup?

M Yes, it is a reusable cup. I'm trying to reduce my plastic footprint.

W What is plastic footprint?

M It is the total amount of plastic a person uses and throws away.

W You care a lot about the environment.

M I do. Plastic waste is a huge environmental problem.

W I should use a reusable cup, too. What else can I do to reduce my plastic footprint?

M You can stop using plastic straws.

해석

여 Brandon, 늦어서 죄송해요.

남 괜찮아요. 음료를 주문합시다. 저는 개인 컵에 커피를 담을게요.

여 오, 당신 컵을 가져오셨어요?

남 네, 재사용 컵이에요. 저는 제 플라스틱 발자국을 줄이려고 노력 중이에요.

여 플라스틱 발자국이 뭐예요?

남 그것은 한 사람이 사용하고 버리는 플라스틱의 총량이에요.

여 당신은 환경에 대해 신경을 많이 쓰시는군요.

남 그렇죠. 플라스틱 쓰레기는 거대한 환경 문제예요.

여 저도 재사용 컵을 사용해야겠어요. 저의 플라스틱 발자국을 줄이기 위해 제가 할 수 있는 일이 또 뭐가 있을까요?

남 플라스틱 빨대 사용을 중단할 수 있어요.

① 이 커피숍은 매우 유명해요.

③ 당신이 준비되면 제가 음료를 주문할게요.

④ 당신의 음료가 곧 준비될 거예요.

⑤ 그 컵들은 다양한 색상과 모양으로 나옵니다.

어휘

personal 개인의 reusable 재사용할 수 있는 footprint 발자국 amount 양
throw away 버리다 environment 환경 in a minute 곧, 잠시 후에
come in ~으로 나오다 various 다양한

---

14 정답 ③

정답률 90%

M Good morning, Kathy. That's a cool helmet.

W Hi, Alex. It's for biking. I rode my bike to school.

M How often do you ride your bike to school?

W I try to do it every day. It's very refreshing.

M Sounds nice. I'm thinking of riding to school, too.

W Good! We should ride together.

M Let's do that, but I'm not very good at biking.

W It's okay. We can go slowly. Also, remember to wear your helmet.

M But I don't have a helmet yet.

W You really need one for your own safety.

해석

남 안녕, Kathy. 참 멋진 헬멧이구나.

여 안녕, Alex. 이거 자전거용이야. 나는 자전거를 타고 학교에 가거든.

남 너는 얼마나 자주 자전거로 학교에 가니?

여 나는 매일 하려고 노력해. 아주 상쾌해.

남 멋지다. 나도 자전거로 학교에 가는 걸 생각 중이야.

여 좋아! 함께 자전거 타면 되겠다.

남 그렇게 하자, 그런데 나 자전거를 별로 잘 못 타.

여 괜찮아. 천천히 가면 돼. 또한, 헬멧 쓰는 것 기억하고.

남 하지만 나는 아직 헬멧이 없어.

여 너는 너의 안전을 위해서 정말로 하나 필요해.

① 운이 좋게도, 나는 그 사고에서 다치지 않았어.

② 나는 새 자전거를 살 돈이 충분히 있어.

④ 자전거를 타고 학교에 가면 너는 졸릴지도 몰라.

⑤ 우리는 학교 주차장에 자전거를 둘 수 있어.

어휘

refreshing 상쾌한 think of ~을 고려하다 be good at ~을 잘하다

---

15 정답 ④

정답률 89%

W Jasper and Mary are trying to form a rock band for the school band competition. Mary plays the guitar, and Jasper is the drummer. They pick a keyboard player through an audition. Now, they need a lead singer. Although the band is not completely formed, they begin their first practice today. Since they don't have a lead singer yet, Mary sings while playing the guitar. Hearing her sing, the other members are amazed. Mary has the perfect voice for rock music! So Jasper wants to tell Mary to be the lead singer for their band. In this situation, what would Jasper most likely say to Mary?

Jasper I think you should be our lead singer.

해석

여 Jasper와 Mary는 학교 밴드 경연 대회를 위해 록밴드를 구성하려고 노력 중이다. Mary는 기타를 연주하고, Jasper는 드럼 연주자이다. 그들은 오디션을 통해 키보드 연주자를 뽑는다. 이제, 그들은 리드싱어가 필요하다. 밴드가 완전히 구성되지 않지만, 그들은 오늘 첫 번째 연습을 시작한다. 아직 리드싱어가 없기 때문에, Mary가 기타를 연주하면서 노래를 한다. 그녀가 노래하는 것을 듣고, 나머지 다른 일원들이 놀란다. Mary가 록 음악을 위한 완벽한 목소리를 가진 것이다! 그래서 Jasper는 Mary에게 그들의 밴드의 리드싱어가 되어 달라고 말하고 싶다. 이 상황에서 Jasper는 Mary에게 뭐라고 말할 것 같은가?

Jasper 나는 네가 우리의 리드싱어가 되어야 한다고 생각해.

① 오디션이 어디에서 열리고 있어?

② 너만의 노래를 써 보는 게 어때?

③ 이번에는 다른 노래를 연주하자.

⑤ 우리가 연습이 더 필요하다고 생각하지 않아?

16 정답 ②   정답률 85%   17 정답 ④   정답률 91%

M Good afternoon, everybody. Today, we'll talk about what our animal companions love: Toys. How do toys help our pets? First, toys play a very important role in keeping your pet happy. A toy like a scratcher helps to reduce your cat's stress. Second, toys are a great tool for a pet to get exercise. For example, a hamster loves to run on a wheel toy. Third, toys build a bond between you and your pet. Playing with a small soft ball will give you and your dog a joyful experience. Lastly, toys help keep your pet entertained. A small hiding tent will make your parrot feel less bored when you are not around. Now let's watch a video of pets playing with their toys.

해석

남 안녕하세요, 여러분. 오늘, 우리는 우리의 반려동물이 좋아하는 것, 즉 장난감에 관해서 이야기해 보겠습니다. 장난감이 우리 반려동물들에게 어떻게 도움이 될까요? 첫 번째로, 장난감은 여러분의 반려동물을 행복하게 하는 데 매우 중요한 역할을 합니다. 발톱으로 긁는 것 같은 장난감은 여러분의 고양이의 스트레스를 줄이는 데 도움이 됩니다. 두 번째로, 장난감은 반려동물이 운동을 할 수 있는 아주 훌륭한 도구입니다. 예를 들어, 햄스터는 장난감 바퀴 위에서 달리는 것을 좋아합니다. 세 번째로, 장난감은 여러분과 애완동물 사이에 유대를 형성합니다. 작고 부드러운 공을 가지고 노는 것은 여러분과 여러분의 반려견에게 즐거운 경험을 제공해 줄 것입니다. 마지막으로 장난감은 여러분의 반려동물을 즐겁게 하는 데 도움을 줍니다. 작은 숨기 위한 텐트는 여러분이 곁에 없을 때 여러분의 앵무새를 덜 지루하게 만들 것입니다. 이제 반려동물이 그들의 장난감을 가지고 놀고 있는 동영상을 시청하시죠.

16
① 반려동물을 위한 친환경 장난감
② 반려동물의 행복에 있어서 장난감의 역할들
③ 반려동물의 특이한 행동 유형들
④ 반려동물에게 위험한 음식들
⑤ 반려동물과 함께 아이를 기르는 데 있어서의 어려움들

17
① 고양이   ② 햄스터   ③ 강아지   ④ 거북이   ⑤ 앵무새

어휘
companion 반려, 친구   scratcher (발톱으로) 긁는 장난감   wheel 바퀴
bond 유대 관계   entertain 즐겁게 해 주다

12회 2020학년도 11월 고1 전국연합 학력평가   1권 p.76

01 ②	02 ①	03 ②	04 ③	05 ③	06 ③
07 ②	08 ⑤	09 ⑤	10 ④	11 ⑤	12 ④
13 ①	14 ⑤	15 ③	16 ④	17 ④	

01 정답 ②   정답률 96%

M Hello, welcome to Fun Bike Touring. I'm Harry Wilson, your tour guide. Before starting the tour, let me tell you the safety rules. First, always keep your helmet on. Wearing a helmet protects you from serious injuries in case of an accident. Second, you should use bicycle-only lanes. If you ride out of the lane, there is a chance that you could be hit by a car. Lastly, don't use your cell phone while riding. Taking pictures or talking on the phone while riding can be really dangerous to you and others. Now, are you ready to start? Let's go!

해석

남 안녕하세요, Fun Bike Touring에 오신 것을 환영합니다. 저는 여러분의 투어 가이드 Harry Wilson입니다. 투어를 시작하기 전에, 제가 여러분께 안전 규칙에 대해 말씀드리겠습니다. 첫째, 항상 헬멧을 착용하셔야 합니다. 헬멧을 착용하는 것은 사고가 날 경우 심각한 부상으로부터 여러분을 보호해 줍니다. 둘째, 자전거 전용 도로만 이용하셔야 합니다. 여러분이 그 전용 도로에서 벗어날 경우, 차에 치일 가능성이 있습니다. 마지막으로, 자전거를 타는 동안 휴대전화를 사용하지 마세요. 자전거를 타는 동안 휴대전화로 사진을 찍거나 통화를 하는 것은 여러분과 다른 사람들에게 매우 위험할 수 있습니다. 자, 출발할 준비가 되셨나요? 어서 갑시다!

어휘
safety rule 안전 규칙   protect A from B A를 B로부터 보호하다
in case of ~일 경우   lane 도로   there is a chance (that) ~할 가능성이 있다

02 정답 ①   정답률 95%

M Good morning, Rosa.

W Hi, Tony. You look tired. Are you all right?

M Yeah, I'm okay. I'm just having a hard time falling asleep these days.

W Why? Are you worried about something?

M No. Since I started exercising late at night, it's been hard to fall asleep.

W What time do you exercise?

M I usually go to the gym around 10 p.m. When I come back, it's almost midnight.

W Hmm, I think that's why you can't sleep well.

M Really?

W As far as I know, when you exercise, your heart rate and temperature go up, which makes you stay awake. These can disturb your sleep.

M Oh, that makes sense.

W So, it's not a good idea to exercise right before going to bed.

M I'll keep that in mind. Thanks for your advice.

해석

남 안녕, Rosa.

여 안녕, Tony. 너 피곤해 보여. 괜찮아?

남 응, 괜찮아. 나는 요즘 잠을 이루기가 좀 어려울 뿐이야.

여 왜? 무슨 걱정이 있니?

남 아니. 내가 밤늦게 운동을 시작한 이후로, 잠들기가 힘이 들어.

여 몇 시에 운동하니?

남 나는 보통 오후 10시쯤 체육관에 가. 집에 돌아오면, 거의 자정이야.

여 흠, 내 생각에 그래서 네가 잠을 잘 잘 수 없는 것 같아.

남 정말?

여 내가 알기로, 운동을 할 때, 심박동수와 체온이 올라가는데, 그것이 너를 깨어 있게 만들어. 이러한 것들이 너의 수면을 방해할 수 있어.

남 오, 일리가 있네.

여 그래서, 자러 가기 바로 전에 운동을 하는 것은 좋은 생각이 아니야.

남 그것을 명심할게. 조언 고마워.

어휘

have a hard time -ing ~하는 데 어려움을 겪다   fall asleep 잠들다
midnight 자정   that's why 그래서 ~하다   heart rate 심박동수
awake 깨어 있는   disturb 방해하다

03 정답 ②

정답률 93%

[Door knocks.]

W Hello, Mr. Cooper. Come on in. Have a seat, please.

M Thank you.

W You came here last week because of a sunburn. How are the symptoms now?

M Much better.

W Great. Let me look at the sunburn. [Pause] The redness is almost gone.

M Yeah. The cream you prescribed was really helpful.

W Good. Do you still have any pain?

M Not anymore.

W I'm glad to hear that. If you put the cream on for a few days more, your skin will completely recover.

M Okay. But I don't have any more cream. Could you write me another prescription?

W Sure. [Typing sound] If you have any problems, please come back.

M Thank you.

해석

[문을 두드린다.]

여 안녕하세요, Cooper 씨. 어서 들어오세요. 앉으세요.

남 고맙습니다.

여 지난주에 햇볕으로 화상을 입으셔서 여기 오셨네요. 지금 증상은 어떤가요?

남 많이 나아졌어요.

여 잘됐네요. 제가 햇볕에 그을린 것을 좀 볼게요. [잠시 후] 붉은 기는 거의 사라졌네요.

남 네. 선생님께서 처방해 주신 크림이 정말 도움이 되었어요.

여 잘됐네요. 아직도 통증이 있으신가요?

남 더 이상은 없습니다.

여 그거 정말 다행이네요. 그 크림을 며칠 더 바르면, 피부가 완전히 회복될 거예요.

남 알겠습니다. 하지만, 제가 크림이 더 없어서요. 처방전을 하나 더 써 주시겠어요?

여 물론이죠. [타자치는 소리] 문제가 있으시면, 다시 오세요.

남 감사합니다.

어휘

sunburn 햇볕으로 인한 화상   symptom 증상   redness 붉은 기, 홍조
prescribe 처방하다   recover 회복하다

04 정답 ③

정답률 86%

M Hi, Claire. What did you do yesterday?

W Hi, Henry. I set up an exercise room in my house. Look at this picture.

M Cool! The indoor bike under the clock looks nice.

W Thanks. I bought the bike a few days ago.

M Good. Is that a hula-hoop under the calendar?

W Yes. I exercise with it for 30 minutes every day. What do you think of the mat with the flower pattern on the floor?

M I love it. By the way, what's the big ball next to the door?

W It's a gym ball. I use it for back stretches.

M Good. Oh, I know that T-shirt on the wall.

W Yeah. It's from the marathon we ran together.

M Great. It matches well with your room.

W Thanks. Next time, come over and we'll exercise together.

해석

남 안녕, Claire. 너 어제 뭐 했니?

여 안녕, Henry. 나는 우리 집에 운동실을 만들었어. 이 사진을 봐.

남 멋지다! 시계 아래에 있는 실내용 자전거가 멋져 보여.

여 고마워. 나는 며칠 전에 그 자전거를 샀어.

남 좋다. 달력 아래에 있는 것이 훌라후프야?

여 응, 나는 매일 30분 동안 그걸로 운동해. 바닥에 있는 꽃무늬가 있는 매트 어떻게 생각해?

남 마음에 들어. 그런데, 문 옆에 있는 커다란 공은 무엇이니?

여 그것은 짐볼이야. 나는 등을 스트레칭할 때 그것을 사용해.

남 좋네. 오, 나 벽에 있는 저 티셔츠 알아.

여 응. 그것은 우리가 함께 달렸던 마라톤에서 받은 거야.

남 훌륭해. 그것은 너의 방과 잘 어울려.

여 고마워. 다음에 와서 우리 함께 운동하자.

어휘

set up 마련하다   indoor bike 실내 자전거   match 어울리다
come over (to) ~에 들르다

05 정답 ③

정답률 92%

W Simon, I think we're ready for the fundraising event.

M Right. Let's do one last check.

W Okay. We're going to play a short video clip for the event. Is the screen working?

M Yes. I checked the screen and there's no problem at all.

W Great. What about the speakers?

M I already tried using them, and they worked fine. Did you bring the donation box?

W Yes. Look. I made it by myself.

M Wow! It looks nice.

W Thanks. All the items we're going to sell are nicely set up on the table.

M Okay. The only thing left is to put the price tags on. I'll do that later because I have to go to my part-time job now.

W Oh, don't worry. I'll put the price tags on.

M Really? Thanks.

해석

여 Simon, 우리 모금 행사에 대한 준비가 다 된 것 같아.

남 좋아. 마지막으로 한 번 더 확인해 보자.

여 좋아. 우리는 행사를 위해 짧은 동영상을 재생할 거야. 스크린이 작동하니?

남 응. 내가 스크린을 확인했고, 전혀 문제가 없어.

여 훌륭해. 스피커는 어때?

남 내가 이미 그것들을 사용해 봤고, 그것들은 잘 작동해. 너 모금함 가져왔어?

여 응. 봐. 내가 직접 그것을 만들었어.

남 와! 멋져 보여.

여 고마워. 우리가 판매할 모든 물건들이 테이블 위에 멋지게 준비되어 있어.

남 좋아. 남은 한 가지 일은 가격표를 붙이는 거야. 내가 지금 아르바이트를 하러 가야 해서 나중에 내가 그것을 할게.

여 오, 걱정 마. 내가 가격표를 붙일게.

남 정말? 고마워.

어휘

fundraising 모금, 자금 조달   donation box 모금함   set up 준비하다, 마련하다
price tag 가격표   part-time job 아르바이트

06 정답 ③

M Good afternoon.

W Hello. Welcome to Happy Pet World. How can I help you?

M I'm looking for a cushion for my dog.

W Okay, how about these? These are the most popular models.

M The pink one looks cute. How much is it?

W Originally, it was $40. But due to a special promotion, you can get a 10 percent discount on cushions.

M Great. I'll buy one cushion, then.

W Sure. Anything else?

M Do you have dog biscuits?

W Of course. They're right over here. Each box of biscuits is $5.

M I'll buy two boxes of biscuits. Do I get a discount on the biscuits, too?

W I'm sorry. We don't offer a discount on biscuits.

M Okay, then. Here's my credit card.

해석

남 안녕하세요.

여 안녕하세요. Happy Pet World에 오신 것을 환영합니다. 어떻게 도와드릴까요?

남 저는 저의 강아지를 위한 쿠션을 찾고 있어요.

여 알겠습니다, 이것들은 어떠세요? 이것들이 가장 인기 있는 모델들입니다.

남 분홍색 쿠션이 귀여워 보이네요. 얼마인가요?

여 원래 그것은 40달러였어요. 하지만 특별 판촉 행사로 쿠션을 10퍼센트 할인받으실 수 있어요.

남 잘됐네요. 그럼, 저는 쿠션 하나 살게요.

여 알겠습니다. 다른 것은요?

남 강아지용 비스킷 있나요?

여 물론이죠. 그것들은 바로 여기 있습니다. 비스킷 한 상자당 5달러입니다.

남 비스킷 두 상자를 살게요. 비스킷도 할인받을 수 있나요?

여 죄송합니다. 저희는 비스킷에 대해서는 할인을 제공하지 않습니다.

남 그럼, 알겠습니다. 제 신용 카드 여기 있습니다.

어휘

look for ~을 찾다   special promotion 특별 판촉 행사   offer 제공하다

07 정답 ②

[Cell phone rings.]

W Hello.

M Hi, Linda. Did you call me earlier? I was in my book club meeting. What's up?

W I called you to make sure you can come to the student fashion show. The schedule has changed.

M Really? When is the show now?

W It has changed to 6 p.m. next Friday. The place we were going to use is being repaired this week.

M I see. I'm afraid I can't go then.

W Oh, didn't you say you're going to a concert next Friday?

M No, that's next Saturday.

W Then, why can't you come?

M It's my mom's birthday. So, I'm going to have dinner with my family.

W Oh, I understand. Have a good time.

M Thanks.

해석

[휴대전화가 울린다.]

여 여보세요.

남 안녕, Linda. 너 아까 나에게 전화했었니? 나는 독서 동아리 모임에 있었어. 무슨 일이야?

여 네가 학생 패션쇼에 올 수 있는지 확인하려고 전화했어. 일정이 변경되었거든.

남 정말? 이제 쇼는 언제니?

여 다음 주 금요일 오후 6시로 변경되었어. 우리가 사용하려고 했던 장소가 이번 주에 수리 중이라서.

남 그렇구나. 그럼 나는 못 갈 것 같아.

여 오, 너 다음 주 금요일에 콘서트 갈 거라고 말했었지?

남 아니, 그것은 다음 주 토요일이야.

여 그럼, 왜 올 수 없는 거야?

남 우리 엄마 생신이거든. 그래서 나는 가족과 저녁 식사를 하러 갈 거야.

여 오, 알았어. 좋은 시간 보내.

남 고마워.

어휘

club 동아리   make sure 확실히 하다   repair 수리하다

12회

20년 11월

08 정답 ⑤

M Honey, what are you reading?

W Look at this article. There will be a World Dinosaur Exhibition this Saturday. Why don't we bring the kids?

M That sounds great! Where's the exhibition held?

W At the Redstone Science Museum.

M Good. I know where that is.

W There are fun programs for children like making dinosaur toys and watching a 3D dinosaur movie.

M Our kids will love them. What time shall we go?

W Since the exhibition runs from 10 a.m. to 5 p.m., how about going there in the afternoon?

M Okay. How much is the admission fee?

W It's $10 for an adult and $5 for a child and if we register online, we can get a discount.

M Really? Let's register now.

W Okay.

해석

남 여보, 당신 무엇을 읽고 있어요?

여 이 기사를 좀 봐요. 이번 주 토요일에 세계 공룡 전시회가 있을 거예요. 우리 아이들을 데려가는 게 어때요?

남 그거 멋지네요! 전시회가 어디에서 열려요?

여 Redstone 과학 박물관에서요.

남 좋네요. 나는 그것이 어디에 있는지 알아요.

여 공룡 장난감 만들기와 3D 공룡 영화와 같은 아이들을 위한 재미있는 프로그램들이 있어요.

남 우리 아이들이 그것들을 좋아할 것 같아요. 우리 언제 갈까요?

여 전시회가 오전 10시부터 오후 5시까지 운영되니까 그곳에 오후에 가는 게 어때요?

남 좋아요. 입장료는 얼마예요?

여 성인은 10달러, 어린이는 5달러이고 우리가 온라인으로 등록하면, 할인을 받을 수 있어요.

남 정말요? 지금 등록합시다.

여 좋아요.

어휘

article 기사   exhibition 전시회   admission fee 입장료   register 등록하다

09 정답 ⑤

정답률 92%

W Hello, listeners! Are you excited for the Greenville Animation Film Festival? This festival, one of Greenville's largest events, began in 1995. This year, it'll start on December 5th and continue for one week. The theme for this year is friendship. Throughout the festival, visitors can watch different animation movies related to the theme every night. The movie schedule will be posted on our website. Remember, there's no parking lot nearby. So, please use public transportation. For more information, visit www.GAFF.com. Thank you.

해석

여 안녕하세요. 청취자 여러분! Greenville 만화 영화 축제를 기대하고 계시죠? Greenville의 가장 큰 행사들 중 하나인 이 축제는 1995년에 시작되었습니다. 올해 그것은 12월 5일에 시작해서 한 주 동안 계속될 것입니다. 올해의 주제는 우정입니다. 축제 동안, 방문객들은 매일 밤 그 주제와 관련된 다양한 만화 영화를 관람할 수 있습니다. 영화 일정은 우리의 웹 사이트에 게재될 것입니다. 근처에 주차장이 없다는 걸 기억하세요. 그러므로, 대중교통을 이용해 주세요. 더 많은 정보를 원하시면, www.GAFF.com을 방문해 주시기 바랍니다. 감사합니다.

어휘

throughout ~ 동안, 내내   related to ~와 관련 있는   post 게시하다
parking lot 주차장   public transportation 대중교통

10 정답 ④

정답률 76%

M Jane, what are you doing?

W Dad, I'm searching for a one-day drawing lesson, but it's not easy to choose one. Can you help me?

M Sure. Is there any particular drawing material you want to use?

W I've done pastel drawing before. So, this time I want to try a new material, not pastel.

M Okay. Do you want to have a private lesson?

W No, I want to learn in a group.

M Okay. You have piano lessons Monday mornings, right?

W Yes. So I should choose a lesson on Wednesday or Friday.

M That leaves you two choices.

W Let me think. *[Pause]* I'd rather take a lesson in the morning.

M There's only one left then.

W Yes. I'll register for that lesson. Thank you, dad.

해석

남 Jane, 무엇을 하고 있니?

여 아빠, 저는 하루짜리 그리기 강좌를 찾고 있는데, 하나 고르는 게 쉽지 않아요. 저를 도와주실 수 있어요?

남 물론이지. 네가 사용하고 싶은 특별한 그리기 재료가 있니?

여 저는 전에 파스텔화를 해 본 적이 있어요. 그래서 이번에는 파스텔이 아닌 새로운 재료를 해 보고 싶어요.

남 알았어. 너는 개인 수업을 받고 싶니?

여 아니요, 저는 그룹으로 배우고 싶어요.

남 알았어. 너는 월요일 아침마다 피아노 수업이 있잖아, 맞지?

여 네. 그래서 저는 수요일이나 금요일에 있는 수업을 선택해야 해요.

남 선택할 수 있는 것이 두 가지 남는구나.

여 생각해 볼게요. *[잠시 후]* 저는 오전에 수업을 받는 것이 좋겠어요.

남 그럼 하나만 남네.

여 네, 저는 그 수업에 등록할 거예요. 감사해요, 아빠.

어휘

drawing 그림, 소묘   material 재료   private 개인의   leave 남기다
register for ~에 등록하다

11 정답 ⑤

정답률 94%

M Emma, it smells good in here. What's that you're cooking?

W I cooked some *Bulgogi*. Try some.

M Okay. Wow, it's really delicious. Where did you get the recipe?

W I got the recipe from the Internet.

해석

남 Emma, 여기 좋은 냄새가 나. 네가 요리하고 있는 게 뭐야?

여 나는 불고기를 요리하고 있어. 좀 먹어 봐.

남 좋아. 와, 정말 맛있다. 너 이 요리법 어디서 구했니?

여 나는 인터넷에서 그 요리법을 찾았어.

① 불고기는 이미 다 팔렸어.

② 너는 무엇을 먹을지 선택할 수 있어.

③ 우리는 그 식당에서 만날 거야.

④ 나는 내일 먹을 음식을 주문할 거야.

어휘

smell 냄새가 나다   recipe 요리법   be sold out 다 팔리다

12 정답 ④

정답률 71%

W Honey, where are the speakers we used when we went camping?

M Oh, I just left them in my car.

W Really? I need to use them tomorrow.

M Okay. I'll bring you the speakers now.

할 것이다. 따라서 여자의 응답으로 가장 적절한 것은 ① '그럼, 너는 이 앱을 이용해서 그 물건들을 팔 수 있을 거야.'이다.

어휘

local 지역의   marketplace 시장, 장터   used item 중고 물품   deal 거래

14 정답 ⑤

정답률 92%

W Honey, look at this bill. Have you been using a movie streaming service?

M No. But a few months ago, I used a one-month free trial.

W Look. A $15 membership fee has been charged for three months.

M Oh, no! There must be something wrong.

W Did you get any notice about that?

M Well, I did, but I didn't pay much attention to it when I signed up for it.

W Let's check it now.

M Wait. [Clicking sound] Hmm, it says the membership fee will be charged if I don't cancel it after the free trial.

W Well, one of my friends was in the same situation and she tried to get a refund but she couldn't.

M Then, what should I do?

W Hmm, the only thing you can do is to end the membership.

M Okay. I'll call customer service to cancel the membership.

해석

여 여보, 이 고지서 좀 보세요. 당신 영화 재생 서비스 사용해 왔어요?

남 아니요. 하지만 몇 달 전에 한 달 무료 체험을 사용했어요.

여 봐요. 세 달 동안 15달러의 회비가 청구되었어요.

남 오, 안 돼! 뭔가 잘못된 것이 틀림없어요.

여 당신 그것에 대해 안내받은 것 있어요?

남 음, 그랬죠, 하지만 내가 그것을 신청할 때 그것에 별로 주의를 기울이지 않았어요.

여 지금 그것을 확인해 봐요.

남 기다려 봐요. [클릭하는 소리] 흠, 무료 체험 이후에 그것을 취소하지 않으면 회비가 청구될 것이라고 되어 있네요.

여 음, 내 친구들 중 한 명이 같은 상황에 있었고 그녀는 환불을 받으려고 했지만 받지 못했어요.

남 그러면, 내가 무엇을 해야 할까요?

여 흠, 당신이 할 수 있는 것은 그 멤버십을 해지하는 것뿐이에요.

남 알았어요. 고객 센터에 전화에서 멤버십을 취소할게요.

① 걱정 말아요. 내가 이메일로 당신에게 안내문을 보낼게요.

② 좋아요. 저에게 당신의 서비스를 이용하는 방법을 알려 주세요.

③ 저는 동의하지 않아요. 당신은 영수증 없이 환불받을 수 있어요.

④ 좋아요. 저는 오늘 밤 영화 볼 것을 고대하고 있어요.

어휘

stream (영상이나 음악 따위를) 다운로드와 동시에 재생하다   trial 시험, 시도

charge (요금을) 부과하다   notice 알림, 통지

pay attention to ~에 주의를 기울이다   sign up for ~을 신청하다

get a refund 환불받다   look forward to ~을 고대하다

15 정답 ③

정답률 83%

M Ms. Brown teaches English in high school. Chris is one of the students who takes her class. Since he wants to major in English Literature at university, he thinks English writing skills are

12회

20년 11월

important. To get advice, Chris visits Ms. Brown and asks how to improve his English writing skills. Ms. Brown thinks that writing in English regularly is important. So she wants to suggest that Chris keep a diary for his English writing skills. In this situation, what would Ms. Brown most likely say to Chris?

Ms. Brown Why don't you start writing a diary in English?

남 Brown 선생님은 고등학교에서 영어를 가르친다. Chris는 그녀의 수업을 듣는 학생들 중 한 명이다. 그는 대학에서 영문학을 전공하고 싶어 하기 때문에 영어 작문 실력이 중요하다고 생각한다. 조언을 얻기 위해, Chris는 Brown 선생님을 방문하여 자신의 영어 작문 실력을 향상시킬 수 있는 방법을 여쭤보려고 한다. Brown 선생님은 규칙적인 영어 글쓰기가 중요하다고 생각한다. 그래서 그녀는 영어 작문 실력을 향상시키기 위해 Chris에게 매일 영어로 일기를 쓰라고 제안하고 싶어 한다. 이 상황에서, Brown 선생님은 Chris에서 뭐라고 말하겠는가?

Ms. Brown 영어로 일기 쓰는 것을 시작해 보는 것이 어떠니?

① 너는 전공에 대해 걱정하는 것을 그만둬야 해.
② 너는 매일 영어책을 읽는 것이 좋겠다.
④ 내 생각에 너는 영어 단어를 많이 공부해야 할 것 같아.
⑤ 외국인들과 대화하는 것이 어떠니?

major in ~을 전공하다 skill 능력, 기술 regularly 규칙적으로, 정기적으로
suggest 제안하다 keep a diary 일기 쓰다
have conversation with ~와 대화하다

16

① 동물들을 기르는 것의 긍정적인 영향들
② 동물 행동을 기록하기 위한 유용한 팁들
③ 바다 동물들이 가지고 있는 일반적인 특징들
④ 의사소통하기 위해 동물들이 사용하는 다양한 방법
⑤ 멸종 위기 종들을 보호하는 것의 중요성

communicate 의사소통하다 type 형태, 유형 mark 표시하다 area 영역
convey 전달하다 various 다양한 widely 널리 stick out 내밀다 touch 촉각
attract 마음을 끌다 contain 포함하다

16 정답 ④ 정답률 95%   ## 17 정답 ④ 정답률 89%

W Hello, everyone. I'm Monica Dale from Blue River Animal Center. Today, let's talk about the different ways animals communicate. First, smell is probably the most basic type of animal communication. For example, dogs mark their areas with their smell to send a clear message to others to stay away. Second, when animals make sounds, those usually convey certain messages. For instance, dolphins get the attention of others in the area by using various sounds. Sometimes, they sing to their mates. Third, visual signals are widely used by many animals. Gorillas stick out their tongues to show anger. Lastly, many animals make use of touch to communicate their feelings to others. Giraffes press their necks together when they're attracted to each other. Now, let's take a look at a video clip that contains interesting animal communication.

여 안녕하세요, 여러분. 저는 Blue River Animal Center의 Monica Dale입니다. 오늘 동물들이 의사소통하는 다양한 방법에 대해 이야기해 봅시다. 첫 번째, 냄새는 아마도 동물의 의사소통에서 가장 기본적인 형태일 것입니다. 예를 들어, 개는 자기 영역에 접근하지 못하도록 다른 개들에게 분명한 메시지를 보내기 위해 냄새로 자신의 영역을 표시합니다. 두 번째, 동물들이 소리를 낼 때, 그러한 소리들은 특정한 메시지를 주로 전달합니다. 예를 들어, 돌고래들은 다양한 소리를 사용함으로써 영역에 있는 다른 돌고래들의 주의를 끕니다. 때때로 그들은 자신들의 짝에게 노래를 부릅니다. 세 번째, 시각 신호는 많은 동물들에게서 널리 사용됩니다. 고릴라는 자신이 화가 났다는 것을 보여 주기 위해 혀를 내밉니다. 마지막으로, 많은 동물들이 자신의 감정을 다른 동물들에게 전달하기 위해 촉각을 사용합니다. 기린은 서로에게 끌릴 때, 목을 함께 누릅니다. 이제, 흥미로운 동물들의 의사소통이 담긴 동영상을 봅시다.

기출의 바이블

고1 영어

정답 및 해설

독해편

1권 p.84

1강 2020~2023 **글의 목적 파악**

01 정답 ⑤

202309 18번 정답률 90%

Dear Professor Sanchez,

My name is Ellis Wight, and I'm the director of the Alexandria Science Museum. 단서1 We are holding a Chemistry Fair for local 화학 박람회를 개최할 예정임 middle school students on Saturday, October 28. ✪ The goal (of the ↗주어 fair) / is [to **encourage** them / to be interested in science (through 주격보어: 명사적 용법의 to부정사↲ 목적격보어(to부정사) guided experiments)]. 단서2 We are looking for college students look for: ~을 찾다 who can help with the experiments during the event. 주제문▶ I am 박람회에서 실험을 도와줄 대학생을 찾고 있음 contacting you to ask you to recommend some students from the chemistry department at your college who you think are qualified be qualified for: for this job. With their help, I'm sure the participants will have a ~에 적격이다 great experience. I look forward to hearing from you soon. look forward to v-ing: ~하기를 기다리다 Sincerely,

Ellis Wight

해석

Sanchez 교수님께,

제 이름은 Ellis Wight이고, Alexandria 과학 박물관 관장입니다. 저희는 10월 28일 토요일에 지역 중학생들을 위한 화학 박람회를 개최합니다. 이 박람회의 목적은 방향을 이끌어 주는 실험을 통해 학생들이 과학에 흥미를 느끼도록 장려하려는 것입니다. 저희는 행사 기간 동안 실험을 도와줄 수 있는 대학생을 모집하고 있습니다. 저는 이 일에 적합하다고 생각되는 귀교의 화학과 학생 몇 명을 추천해 달라는 요청을 드리고자 연락드렸습니다. 저는 그 학생들의 도움으로 참가자들이 훌륭한 경험을 할 것이라 확신합니다. 빠른 시일 내에 소식 들을 수 있기를 기대합니다.

Ellis Wight

정답이 보이는 해설

Alexandria 과학 박물관이 중학생을 위한 화학 박람회를 개최할 예정이며 행사를 도와줄 대학생을 모집하고 있으니 이 일에 적합한 화학과 학생들을 추천해 달라고 요청하고 있으므로, 글의 목적으로 가장 적절한 것은 ⑤이다.

필수 어휘

professor 교수 chemistry 화학 fair 박람회 encourage 장려하다
experiment 실험 recommend 추천하다 department 부서, 학과
participant 참가자 experience 경험

02 정답 ②

202306 18번 정답률 94%

ACC Travel Agency Customers:

Have you ever wanted to enjoy a holiday in nature? This summer is the best time to turn your dream into reality. 주제문 단서1 We turn A into B: A를 B로 바꾸다 완벽한 have a perfect travel package for you. ✪ 단서2 This travel package 패키지 여행 상품이 있음 이 여행 상품이 포함하고 있는 / includes / special trips (to Lake Madison) as well as massage and 것들 B B as well as A: A뿐만 아니라 B도 A meditation (to help you relax). Also, we provide yoga lessons taught by experienced instructors. If you book this package, 단서3 you will

enjoy all this at a reasonable price. We are sure that it will be an 이 모든 것을 합리적인 가격으로 즐길 수 있음 be sure that: ~을 확신하다 unforgettable experience for you. If you call us, we will be happy to give you more details.

해석

ACC 여행사 고객님께,

자연 속에서 휴가를 즐기는 것을 원한 적이 있습니까? 이번 여름이 당신의 꿈을 현실로 바꿀 최고의 시간입니다. 우리에게는 당신을 위한 완벽한 패키지 여행 상품이 있습니다. 이 패키지 여행 상품은 당신이 편히 쉴 수 있도록 돕는 마사지와 명상뿐만 아니라 Lake Madison으로의 특별한 여행을 포함합니다. 또한, 우리는 숙련된 강사의 요가 강의도 제공합니다. 만약 당신이 이 패키지를 예약한다면, 당신은 이 모든 것을 합리적인 가격으로 즐길 것입니다. 우리는 그것이 당신에게 잊지 못할 경험이 될 것을 확신합니다. 우리에게 전화하시면, 더 많은 세부 사항을 기꺼이 알려 드리겠습니다.

정답이 보이는 해설

ACC 여행사가 이번 여름 자연 속에서 휴가를 즐기기를 원하는 고객들을 위해, 합리적인 가격으로 마사지와 명상, Lake Madison으로의 여행, 그리고 숙련된 강사의 요가 강의를 모두 즐길 수 있는 패키지 여행 상품을 홍보하고 있으므로, 글의 목적으로 가장 적절한 것은 ②이다.

필수 어휘

travel agency 여행사 customer 고객 reality 현실 include 포함하다
meditation 명상 relax 쉬다 provide 제공하다 experienced 숙련된
instructor 강사 book 예약하다 reasonable 합리적인
unforgettable 잊지 못할, 잊을 수 없는 detail 세부 사항

03 정답 ③

202303 18번 정답률 93%

To whom it may concern,

I am a resident of the Blue Sky Apartment. 주제문▶ Recently 단서1 I observed that the kid zone is in need of repairs. I want you to pay kid zone에 수리가 필요함을 알게 됨 attention to 단서2 the poor condition of the playground equipment ~에 관심을 기울이다 놀이터 시설의 열악한 상태 in the zone. The swings are damaged, the paint is falling off, and some of the bolts on the slide are missing. ✪ The facilities have 시간의 부사절 (~한 이후로)↲ 현재완료 been in this terrible condition // since we moved here. 단서3 They (계속 ~해 왔다) 과거 아이들에게 are dangerous to the children playing there. Would you please have 위험할 수 있음 have+목적어↲ them repaired? I would appreciate your immediate attention to solve p.p.: ~이 …되게 하다 this matter.

Yours sincerely,

Nina Davis

해석

관계자 분께,

저는 Blue Sky 아파트의 거주자입니다. 최근에 저는 아이들을 위한 구역이 수리가 필요하다는 것을 알게 되었습니다. 저는 귀하께서 그 구역 놀이터 설비의 열악한 상태에 관심을 기울여 주시기를 바랍니다. 그네가 손상되었고, 페인트가 떨어져 나가고 있고, 미끄럼틀의 볼트 몇 개가 빠져 있습니다. (놀이터) 시설은 우리가 이곳으로 이사 온 이후로 이렇게 형편없는 상태였습니다. 그것들은 거기서 노는 아이들에게 위험합니다. 그것을 수리해 주시겠습니까? 이 문제를 해결할 즉각적인 관심을 가져 주시면 감사하겠습니다.

Nina Davis 드림

정답이 보이는 해설

손상된 그네, 떨어진 페인트, 볼트가 빠진 미끄럼틀을 언급하며 놀이터 설비가 열악한 상태라서, 아이들에게 위험하기 때문에 시설을 수리해 줄 것을 요청하고 있으므로, 글의 목적으로 가장 적절한 것은 ③이다.

필수 어휘

concern ~에 관계하다 resident 거주자 recently 최근에
observe 보고 알다, 목격하다 repair 수리; 수리하다 equipment 설비
damage 손상시키다, 훼손하다 fall off 떨어져 나가다 facility 시설
terrible 형편없는 appreciate 감사하다 immediate 즉각적인 matter 문제

04 정답 ②

202211 18번 정답률 87%

Dear Mr. Krull,

I have greatly enjoyed working at Trincom Enterprises as a sales
　　　　　　 enjoy v-ing: ~하는 것을 즐기다
manager. Since I joined in 2015, I have been a loyal and essential

member of this company, and have developed innovative ways to

contribute to the company. ✪ Moreover, / (in the last year alone,)
　　　　　　　 bring in: 도입하다, 유치하다　　 시간의 전치사구
/ I have brought in two new major clients to the company, // 단서1
　　분사구문(= and I have increased ~)
increasing the company's total sales by 5%. Also, I have voluntarily
회사의 매출을 증가시킴
trained 5 new members of staff, totaling 35 hours. 주제문 단서2

I would therefore request your consideration in raising my salary,
급여를 인상하는 것에 대한 고려를 요청하고자 함
which I believe reflects my performance as well as the industry
　　　　　　　　　　　　　　　　 B as well as A: A뿐만 아니라 B도
average. I look forward to speaking with you soon.
　　　　　 look forward to v-ing: ~하기를 고대하다
Kimberly Morss

해석

친애하는 Krull 씨께,

저는 Trincom Enterprises에서 영업 매니저로서 일하는 것을 대단히 즐겨 왔습니다. 2015년에 합류한 이후, 저는 이 회사의 충성스럽고 필수적인 구성원이었고, 회사에 기여할 혁신적인 방법들을 개발해 왔습니다. 더욱이, 저는 작년 한 해에만 두 개의 주요 고객사를 회사에 새로 유치하여, 회사의 총매출을 5% 증가시켰습니다. 또한 저는 신규 직원 5명을 자발적으로 교육해 왔고, 그 합계가 35시간이 되었습니다. 따라서 저는 제 급여를 인상하는 것에 대한 당신의 고려를 요청드리고자 하는데, 저는 이것이 업계 평균뿐만 아니라 제 성과까지 반영한다고 믿습니다. 당신과 곧 이야기 나누기를 기대합니다.

Kimberly Morss 드림

정답이 보이는 해설

자신이 지금까지 회사에 기여해 온 사항들을 언급하면서, 급여 인상을 고려해 달라고 요청하고 있으므로, 글의 목적으로 가장 적절한 것은 ②이다.

필수 어휘

loyal 충실한, 충성스러운 essential 필수적인 develop 개발하다
innovative 혁신적인, 획기적인 contribute 기여하다 major 주요한, 중대한
client 고객 voluntarily 자발적으로 request 요청하다 raise 인상하다
reflect 반영하다 performance 실적, 성과 industry 산업, ~업

05 정답 ⑤

202209 18번 정답률 94%

Dear Parents/Guardians,

Class parties will be held on the afternoon of Friday, December

16th, 2022. Children may bring in sweets, crisps, biscuits, cakes,
　　　　　　　　　　　　　 가져오다

and drinks. We are requesting that 단서1 children do not bring
　　　　　　　　　　　　　　　 파티 음식 유의 사항 1: 조리된 음식
in home-cooked or prepared food. 단서2 All food should arrive
불가　　　　　　　　　　　　　 파티 음식 유의 사항 2: 성분 적힌 밀봉
in a sealed packet with the ingredients clearly listed. Fruit and
꾸러미 포장
vegetables are welcomed if they are pre-packed in a sealed packet
　　　　　　　　　　　　　　　　　　　　　 → 부정 명령문(Don't+동사원형 ~)
from the shop. ✪ Please 단서3 **DO NOT** send any food into school
　　　　　　　　　　　　　　　 파티 음식 유의 사항 3: 견과류 불가
[containing nuts] / **as** we have *many children* (with severe nut
현재분사구　　　 이유의 부사절
allergies). 단서4 **Please check the ingredients of all food your**
　　　　　　 파티 음식 유의 사항 4: 성분 확인
children bring carefully. Thank you for your continued support and

cooperation.

Yours sincerely,

Lisa Brown, Headteacher

해석

부모님들/보호자들께,

학급 파티가 2022년 12월 16일 금요일 오후에 열릴 것입니다. 아이들은 사탕류, 포테이토 칩, 비스킷, 케이크, 그리고 음료를 가지고 올 수 있습니다. 우리는 아이들이 집에서 만들거나 조리된 음식을 가져오지 않기를 요청합니다. 모든 음식은 성분을 명확하게 목록으로 작성하여 밀봉된 꾸러미로 가져와야 합니다. 과일과 채소는 가게에서 밀봉된 꾸러미로 사전 포장된 것이라면 환영합니다. 심각한 견과류 알레르기를 가진 학생들이 많이 있으므로 견과류가 포함된 어떤 음식도 학교로 보내지 마십시오. 아이들이 가져오는 모든 음식의 성분을 주의 깊게 확인해 주십시오. 여러분의 지속적인 지원과 협조에 감사드립니다.

교장 Lisa Brown 드림

정답이 보이는 해설

학급 파티 일정을 알리며 학급 파티에 가져올 음식에 대해 조리 음식 불가, 성분이 명확히 작성될 것, 밀봉된 꾸러미에 포장될 것, 견과류가 포함된 음식 불가 등의 유의 사항을 소개하고 있으므로, 글의 목적으로 가장 적절한 것은 ⑤이다.

필수 어휘

guardian 보호자 hold 열다, 개최하다 sweets 사탕 crisp 포테이토 칩
request 요청하다 prepared 조리된 sealed 밀봉된 packet 꾸러미
ingredient 성분 list 목록을 작성하다 pack 포장하다 contain 포함하다
nut 견과류 severe 심각한 support 지원 cooperation 협조
headteacher 교장

06 정답 ②

202206 18번 정답률 97%

Dear Boat Tour Manager,

On March 15, my family was on one of your Glass Bottom

Boat Tours. When we returned to our hotel, I discovered that I left
　　　　　　　　　　　　　　　　　　　　　 fall off: ~에서 떨어지다
behind my cell phone case. ✪ The case **must have fallen** off my
　　　　　　　　　　　　　　　　　　 must have p.p.: ~했음이 틀림없다
lap and onto the floor // **when** I took it off my phone to clean it.
　　　　　　　　　　　　　　시간의 접속사　= the case　 = the case
단서1 I would like to ask you to check if it is on your boat. Its color
휴대전화 케이스가 보트에 있는지 확인해 줄 것을 요청함
is black and it has my name on the inside. 단서2 If you find the case,
　　　　　　　　　　　　　　　　　　　 케이스를 발견하면 알려 달라고
I would appreciate it if you would let me know.
부탁함
Sincerely,

Sam Roberts

해석

보트 투어 담당자께,

3월 15일에 저희 가족은 귀사의 Glass Bottom 보트 투어 중 하나에 참가했습니

다. 저희가 호텔로 돌아왔을 때, 저는 제 휴대전화 케이스를 놓고 왔다는 것을 발견했습니다. 케이스를 닦으려고 휴대전화에서 분리했을 때 케이스가 제 무릎에서 바닥으로 떨어졌던 게 틀림없습니다. 그것이 보트에 있는지 확인해 주시기를 부탁드립니다. 그것의 색은 검은색이며 안쪽에 제 이름이 있습니다. 만약 케이스를 발견하시면, 저에게 알려 주시면 감사하겠습니다.

Sam Roberts 드림

정답이 보이는 해설

보트 투어 중 분실한 휴대전화 케이스가 보트에 있는지 확인해 달라고 부탁하면서 그것을 발견하면 알려 달라고 했으므로, 글의 목적으로 가장 적절한 것은 ②이다.

필수 어휘

return 돌아오다 lap 무릎 floor 바닥 take off ~을 떼어내다 inside 안쪽, 내부
appreciate 감사히 여기다

---

07 정답 ②

202203 18번 정답률 88%

Dear Ms. Robinson,

　The Warblers Choir is happy to announce that we are invited to compete in the International Young Choir Competition. The competition takes place in London on May 20. **단서1** Though we wish to participate in the event, we do not have the necessary funds to travel to London. **단서2** So we are kindly asking you to support us by coming to our fundraising concert. It will be held on March 26. ✪ In this concert, / we shall be able to show you / how big our passion for music is. Thank you in advance for your kind support and help.

Sincerely,

Arnold Reynolds

해석

Robinson 씨께,
Warblers 합창단이 국제 청년 합창 대회에서 경연하도록 초청받은 것을 알려 드리게 되어 기쁩니다. 대회는 5월 20일에 런던에서 열립니다. 저희는 대회에 참가하기를 바라지만, 런던에 가기 위해 필요한 자금이 없습니다. 그래서 귀하께서 저희 모금 음악회에 오셔서 저희를 후원해 주시기를 정중하게 부탁드립니다. 음악회는 3월 26일에 개최될 예정입니다. 이 음악회에서 저희는 음악에 대한 저희의 열정이 얼마나 큰지 귀하에게 보여 드릴 수 있을 것입니다. 귀하의 친절한 후원과 도움에 미리 감사드립니다.

Arnold Reynolds 드림

정답이 보이는 해설

국제 합창 대회에 참가할 자금을 마련하기 위해 합창단의 모금 음악회에 참석하여 후원해 줄 것을 요청하고 있으므로, 글의 목적으로 가장 적절한 것은 ②이다.

필수 어휘

choir 합창단 announce 알리다, 발표하다 compete 겨루다, 경쟁하다
international 국제적인 competition 대회, 경쟁 participate in ~에 참가하다
necessary 필요한 fund 자금, 기금 support 후원하다; 후원 fundraising 모금
passion 열정

---

08 정답 ⑤

202111 18번 정답률 94%

To the school librarian,

　I am Kyle Thomas, the president of the school's English writing club. I have planned activities that will increase the writing skills of our club members. ✪ One of the aims of these activities / is to make us aware of various types of news media / and *the language* (used in printed newspaper articles). However, some old newspapers are not easy to access online. **단서** It is, therefore, my humble request to you to allow us to use old newspapers that have been stored in the school library. I would really appreciate it if you grant us permission.

Yours truly,

Kyle Thomas

해석

학교 사서 선생님께,
저는 교내 영어 글쓰기 동아리의 회장 Kyle Thomas입니다. 저는 우리 동아리 회원들의 작문 실력을 늘릴 활동들을 계획해 왔습니다. 이 활동들의 목표 가운데 하나는 저희가 언론 매체의 다양한 유형 및 인쇄 신문 기사에 사용된 언어를 알게 하는 것입니다. 하지만 일부 오래된 신문은 온라인으로 이용하는 것이 쉽지 않습니다. 따라서 선생님께 드리는 저의 겸허한 요청은 학교 도서관에 보관되어 온 오래된 신문을 저희가 사용하도록 허락해 달라는 것입니다. 선생님께서 저희에게 허락해 주신다면 정말 감사하겠습니다.

Kyle Thomas 드림

정답이 보이는 해설

도서관에 있는 일부 오래된 신문을 온라인으로 이용하는 것이 쉽지 않다고 하면서 도서관에 있는 오래된 신문을 사용하도록 허락해 줄 것을 요청하고 있으므로, 글의 목적으로 가장 적절한 것은 ⑤이다.

필수 어휘

president 회장 increase 늘리다, 증가시키다 aim 목표
news media 언론 매체 printed newspaper 인쇄 신문
access 이용하다, 접근하다 humble 겸허한, 겸손한 appreciate 고마워하다
grant (허가 등을) 주다, 부여하다 permission 허락

---

09 정답 ②

202109 18번 정답률 91%

Dear Mr. Dennis Brown,

단서1 We at G&D Restaurant are honored and delighted to invite you to our annual Fall Dinner. The annual event will be held on October 1st, 2021 at our restaurant. At the event, we will be introducing new wonderful dishes that our restaurant will be offering soon. These delicious dishes will showcase the amazing talents of our gifted chefs. ✪ Also, our chefs will be providing cooking tips, / ideas (on what to buy for your kitchen), / and special recipes. **단서2** We at G&D Restaurant would be more than grateful if you can make it to this special occasion and be part of our celebration. We look forward to seeing you. Thank you so much.

Regards,

Marcus Lee, Owner – G&D Restaurant

해석

Dennis Brown 씨께,

저희 G&D 식당은 저희의 연례행사인 Fall Dinner에 귀하를 초대하게 되어 영광스럽고 기쁘게 생각합니다. 연례행사는 2021년 10월 1일에 저희 식당에서 열리게 됩니다. 그 행사에서, 저희 식당이 곧 제공할 예정인 새로운 훌륭한 음식들을 소개하려고 합니다. 이 맛있는 음식들은 뛰어난 저희 요리사들의 놀라운 재능을 보여 드릴 것입니다. 또한, 저희 요리사들은 요리 정보 및 여러분의 주방을 위해 사야 할 것들에 대한 의견, 그리고 특별한 요리법을 제공할 것입니다. 저희 G&D 식당은 여러분이 이 특별한 행사에 와서 기념 행사의 일원이 되어 주신다면 정말 감사할 것입니다. 여러분을 만나 뵙게 되기를 고대합니다. 대단히 감사합니다.

G&D 식당 주인, Marcus Lee 드림

정답이 보이는 해설

새롭게 제공할 예정인 요리를 선보이고 특별한 요리법을 알려 주는 식당의 연례행사에 참석해 줄 것을 요청하는 초대장이므로, 글의 목적으로 가장 적절한 것은 ②이다.

필수 어휘

be honored 영광스럽다   be delighted to ~하게 되어 기쁘다
annual 매년의, 연례의   offer 제공하다   showcase 소개하다, 전시하다
gifted 재능 있는   grateful 고마워하는, 감사한   occasion 행사, 때
celebration 기념[축하] 행사

10 정답 ①

Dear Mr. Jones,

I am James Arkady, PR Director of KHJ Corporation. 단서1 **We**
                                                            회사
are planning to redesign our brand identity and launch a new logo to
~할 계획이다
브랜드 정체성을 재설계하고 새로운 로고를 선보일 계획 → 새 로고에 대한 필요성 언급
celebrate our 10th anniversary. ✪ We **request** you to create *a logo*
                                          목적어   목적격보어
/ [that best suits our company's core vision, 'To inspire humanity].'
  주격 관계대명사   동격
I hope the new logo will convey our brand message and capture the
values of KHJ. Please 단서2 **send us your logo design proposal** once
                      새 로고 디자인 제안서를 보내 줄 것을 요청
you are done with it.   → 로고 제작을 의뢰했음을 의미함
       ~을 끝내다
Thank you.

Best regards,

James Arkady

해석

친애하는 Jones 씨께,

저는 James Arkady이고, KHJ Corporation의 홍보부 이사입니다. 저희 회사의 창립 10주년을 기념하기 위해서 당사의 브랜드 정체성을 다시 설계하고 새 로고를 출시할 계획입니다. 당사의 가장 중요한 비전인 '인류애를 고취하자'를 가장 잘 반영한 로고를 제작해 주실 것을 요청합니다. 새 로고가 저희 회사의 브랜드 메시지를 전달하고 KHJ의 가치를 표현했으면 합니다. 완성하시는 대로 귀하의 로고 디자인 제안서를 저희에게 보내 주시기 바랍니다. 감사합니다.

James Arkady 드림

정답이 보이는 해설

새로운 회사 로고를 선보일 계획이라고 언급한 후, We request you to create a logo ~에서 회사 로고 제작을 요청하고 있으므로, 글의 목적으로 가장 적절한 것은 ①이다.

필수 어휘

PR director 홍보부 이사(= Public Relations)   corporation 기업
identity 정체성   launch 새로 시작하다   celebrate 축하하다
anniversary 기념일   request A to B A가 B할 것을 요청[의뢰]하다   suit 잘 맞다
inspire 고무하다, 영감을 주다   humanity 인류(애)   convey 전달하다, 알리다
capture 포착하다   value 가치   proposal 제안서

11 정답 ④

Dear members of Eastwood Library,

   Thanks to the Friends of Literature group, we've successfully
   ~ 덕분에
raised enough money to remodel the library building. John
모금하다
Baker, our local builder, has volunteered 단서1 to help us with the
                                                자원봉사로 리모델링 공사를
remodelling but he needs assistance. 단서2 By grabbing a hammer
해 줄 건설업자에게 도움이 필요함   (개조 공사에 필요한) 망치나 페인트
or a paint brush and donating your time, you can help with the
붓을 잡고 시간을 기부함으로써 그를 도울 수 있음 → 회원들의 참여 요청
construction. ✪ Join Mr. Baker (in his volunteering team) / and
                동사1 (명령문)   접속사
become a part of **making** Eastwood Library a better place! Please
동사2   make+목적어+목적격보어(명사): 목적어를 ~으로 만들다
call 541-567-1234 for more information.

Sincerely,

Mark Anderson

해석

Eastwood 도서관 회원들에게,

Friends of Literature 동호회 덕분에, 우리는 도서관 건물을 개조하기에 충분한 자금을 성공적으로 마련했습니다. 우리 지역의 건설업자인 John Baker 씨가 리모델링을 도와주기로 자원했지만, 그분에게는 도움이 필요합니다. 망치나 페인트 붓을 잡고 여러분의 시간을 기부함으로써, 여러분은 공사를 도울 수 있습니다. Baker 씨의 자원봉사 팀에 함께하셔서 Eastwood 도서관을 더 나은 곳으로 만드는 일원이 되십시오! 더 많은 정보를 원하시면 541-567-1234로 전화해 주시기 바랍니다.

Mark Anderson 드림

정답이 보이는 해설

도서관 건물 리모델링 공사를 자원한 건축업자를 도울 수 있다고 하며 도서관을 더 나은 곳으로 만드는 데 참여하라고 권하고 있으므로, 글의 목적으로 가장 적절한 것은 ④이다.

선택지 완벽 분석

③ 도서관 보수를 위한 모금 행사를 제안하려고
보수를 위해 모금을 한 것은 맞지만, 첫 문장에서 이미 모금 행사로 자금이 마련되었다고 했으므로 글을 쓴 목적이 모금 행사 제안은 아니다.

필수 어휘

successfully 성공적으로   raise (자금 등을) 모으다
remodel 리모델링하다, 개축하다   local 지역의   builder 건축업자
volunteer 자원하다   assistance 도움, 지원   grab 쥐다   donate 기부[기증]하다
construction 공사

12 정답 ③

To whom it may concern:

   I was born and raised in the city of Boulder and have enjoyed
our scenic natural spaces for my whole life. ✪ *The land* / [through
                                                주어   전치사+
which the proposed Pine Hill walking trail would cut] / is home to
관계대명사(= which the proposed ~ would cut through)   동사 보어
a variety of species. 단서1 Wildlife faces pressure from development,
다양한(= various)   산책길이 통과 계획인 지역에 사는 야생 동물에게는 숨을 곳이 필
and these animals need space where they can hide from human
요함 → 개발에 대한 반대 의견 피력
activity. Although trails serve as a wonderful source for us to
                           ~의 역할을 하다
access the natural world and appreciate the wildlife within it, if
we continue to destroy habitats with excess trails, the wildlife will
stop using these areas. 단서2 Please reconsider whether the proposed
stop v-ing: ~하는 것을 멈추다   제안된 산책길이 꼭 필요한지에 대한 재고 요청

trail is absolutely necessary.

Sincerely,

Tyler Stuart

해석

관계자 분께,

저는 Boulder 시에서 태어나고 성장했으며 저의 전 생애 동안 우리의 경치 좋은 자연 공간을 즐겨 왔습니다. 제안된 Pine Hill 산책로가 통과하게 될 그 땅은 다양한 종의 서식지입니다. 야생 동물은 개발 압력에 직면해 있는데, 이 동물들은 사람들의 활동으로부터 숨을 수 있는 곳이 필요합니다. 비록 산책로가 우리가 자연 세계에 접근하고 그 안의 야생 동물을 감상할 수 있는 좋은 원천의 역할을 하지만, 만약 계속해서 우리가 넘쳐나는 산책로로 서식지를 파괴한다면 야생 동물은 이 지역들을 이용하는 것을 멈출 것입니다. 제안된 산책로가 꼭 필요한지 다시 한번 고려해 주시기 바랍니다.

Tyler Stuart 드림

정답이 보이는 해설

새롭게 조성될 예정인 산책로가 야생 동물들에게 필요한 공간임을 피력하면서 산책로 건설이 꼭 필요한지 재고해 달라고 요청하고 있으므로, 글의 목적으로 가장 적절한 것은 ③이다.

선택지 완벽 분석

⑤ 야생 동물 보호구역 관리의 문제점을 지적하려고
함정 산책로가 건설될 곳이 사람들의 활동으로부터 야생 동물이 숨을 수 있는 공간이라서 보호해야 한다는 주장이지만 이곳이 야생 동물 보호구역이라는 언급은 없으므로 정답이 될 수 없다.

필수 어휘

scenic 경치 좋은 proposed 제안된 walking trail 산책길, 산책로
wildlife 야생 동물 face 직면하다, 맞닥뜨리다 pressure 압력
access 접근하다; 접근 appreciate 감상하다 destroy 파괴하다 habitat 서식지
excess 지나친, 과잉의 reconsider 재고하다

2강 2020~2023 심경, 분위기 파악

01 정답 ②

Gregg and I had been rock climbing since sunrise and had had no problems. So we took a risk. "Look, the first bolt is right there.
take a risk: 위험을 무릅쓰다
단서1 I can definitely climb out to it. Piece of cake," I persuaded
바위에 오를 수 있다고 확신함   식은 죽 먹기
Gregg, minutes before I found myself pinned. It wasn't a piece
바위에 붙잡을 곳이 없음
of cake. **단서2** The rock was deceptively barren of handholds. I
end up with: 결국 (원하지 않는 결과를) 얻다
clumsily moved back and forth across the cliff face and ended up
앞뒤로, 왔다갔다
with nowhere to go...but down. ✪ The bolt [that would save my
~에 이르다, 도착하다   주어   주격 관계대명사절
life], / (if I could get to it), / was about two feet above my reach. My
조건의 부사절   = the bolt   동사
arms trembled from exhaustion. I looked at Gregg. **단서3** My body
공포로 온몸이
froze with fright from my neck down to my toes. Our rope was tied
얼어붙음
between us. If I fell, he would fall with me.

해석

Gregg와 나는 일출 이후에 암벽 등반을 해 왔고 아무런 문제가 없었다. 그래서 우리는 위험을 감수했다. 나는 "봐, 첫 번째 볼트가 바로 저기에 있어. 나는 틀림없이 거기까지 올라갈 수 있어. 식은 죽 먹기야."라고 Gregg를 설득했고, 얼마 지나지 않아 내가 꼼짝 못하게 되었다는 걸 알았다. 그건 식은 죽 먹기가 아니었다. 그 바위는 믿을 수 없게도 손으로 잡을 곳이 없었다. 나는 서투르게 절벽 면을 이리저리 가로질러 보았지만 갈 곳이… 결국 아래쪽뿐이었다. 만약 내가 거기까지 갈 수 있다면, 내 목숨을 구해 줄 볼트는 손이 닿는 곳에서 약 2피트 위에 있었다. 내 팔은 극도의 피로로 떨렸다. Gregg를 쳐다보았다. 내 몸은 목에서부터 발끝까지 공포로 얼어붙었다. 우리 사이에 밧줄이 묶여 있었다. 내가 떨어지면, 그도 나와 함께 떨어질 것이다.

정답이 보이는 해설

암벽 등반 초반에는 문제없이 올라갈 수 있다고 자신했지만, 바위에 손으로 잡을 만한 곳이 없었고 극도의 피로로 팔까지 떨리면서 온몸이 공포로 얼어붙었다. 게다가 자신이 추락하면 Gregg까지 같이 떨어지는 상황이므로 'I'의 심경 변화로 가장 적절한 것은 ② '자신 있는 → 두려워하는'이다.

선택지 완벽 분석

① joyful → bored 즐거운 → 지루한
② confident → fearful 자신 있는 → 두려워하는
③ nervous → relieved 초조한 → 안도한
④ regretful → pleased 후회하는 → 기쁜
⑤ grateful → annoyed 감사하는 → 짜증이 난

필수 어휘

definitely 확실히, 틀림없이 persuade 설득하다 pinned 꼼짝 못하는
deceptively 믿을 수 없게도 handhold (손으로) 잡을 수 있는 부분
clumsily 서투르게 cliff 절벽 reach 손이 닿는 거리 tremble 떨리다
exhaustion 극도의 피로 fright 공포 tie 묶다

02 정답 ①

When I woke up in our hotel room, it was almost midnight. I didn't see my husband nor daughter. I called them, but I heard
not A nor B: A도 B도 아니다   분사구문
their phones ringing in the room. ✪ **단서1** Feeling worried, / I went
남편과 딸이 보이지 않아 걱정됨   동사1
outside / and walked down the street, // but they were (nowhere)
동사2   = my husband and daughter

to be found. When I decided I should ask someone for help, a
ask A for B: A에게 B를 요청하다
crowd nearby caught my attention. I approached, hoping to find my
catch one's attention: ~의 관심을 끌다
husband and daughter, and suddenly I saw two familiar faces. **단서2**

I smiled, feeling calm. Just then, my daughter saw me and called,
안도하며 미소 지음
"Mom!" They were watching the magic show. Finally, **단서3** I felt
모든
all my worries disappear.
걱정이 사라짐

해석

내가 호텔 방에서 깨어났을 때는, 거의 자정이었다. 남편도 딸도 보이지 않았다. 나는 그들에게 전화를 걸었지만, 나는 그들의 전화가 방에서 울리는 것을 들었다. 걱정이 되어, 나는 밖으로 나가 거리를 걸어 내려갔지만, 그들은 어디에도 없었다. 내가 누군 가에게 도움을 요청하려고 결심했을 때, 근처에 있던 군중이 내 주의를 끌었다. 나는 남편과 딸을 찾으려는 희망을 안고 다가갔고, 갑자기 낯익은 두 얼굴이 보였다. 나는 안도하며, 웃었다. 바로 그때, 딸이 나를 보고 "엄마"라고 외쳤다. 그들은 마술 쇼를 보고 있는 중이었다. 마침내, 나는 내 모든 걱정이 사라지는 것을 느꼈다.

정답이 보이는 해설

거의 자정이 되어 호텔 방에서 깨어났는데, 남편과 딸이 보이지 않아 걱정이 되어 그들을 찾아다니다가, 마술 쇼를 보던 근처의 군중들 속에서 남편과 딸을 찾아 안도했으므로, 'I'의 심경 변화로 가장 적절한 것은 ① '불안해하는 → 안도하는'이다.

선택지 완벽 분석

① anxious → relieved 불안해하는 → 안도하는
② delighted → unhappy 기쁜 → 행복하지 않은
③ indifferent → excited 무관심한 → 흥분한
④ relaxed → upset 느긋한 → 화난
⑤ embarrassed → proud 황당한 → 자랑스러운
남편과 딸이 보이지 않아 황당했다가, 나중에 아무 일도 없음을 알게 되어 자랑스럽다고는 볼 수 없다.

필수 어휘

midnight 자정 nowhere 어디에도 ~없다 nearby 근처의, 가까이에
approach 다가가다 familiar 친숙한, 익숙한 disappear 사라지다

03 정답 ②

202303 19번 정답률 85%

On a two-week trip in the Rocky Mountains, I saw a grizzly
bear in its native habitat. **단서1** At first, I felt joy as I watched the
처음에는 곰을 보고 즐거워졌음
bear walk across the land. He stopped every once in a while to turn
이따금, 가끔
his head about, sniffing deeply. ✪ He was following the scent (of
= the bear
something), // and (slowly) I began to **단서2** realize [that this giant
realize의 목적어절
animal was smelling me]! I froze. This was no longer a wonderful
곰이 내 냄새를 맡고 있음을 알게 됨 더 이상 ~이 아닌
experience; **단서3** it was now an issue of survival. The bear's
이제 생존 문제가 됨
motivation was to find meat to eat, and I was clearly on his menu.

해석

로키산맥에서 2주간의 여행 중, 나는 자연 서식지에서 회색곰 한 마리를 보았다. 처음에 나는 그 곰이 땅을 가로질러 걸어가는 모습을 보았을 때 즐거움을 느꼈다. 곰은 이따금 멈춰 서서 고개를 돌려 깊게 코를 킁킁거렸다. 곰은 무언가의 냄새를 따라가고 있었고, 나는 서서히 거대한 이 동물이 내 냄새를 맡고 있다는 것을 깨닫기 시작했다! 나는 얼어붙었다. 이것은 더 이상은 멋진 경험이 아니었고, 이제 생존의 문제였다. 그 곰의 동기는 먹을 고기를 찾는 것이었고, 나는 분명히 그의 메뉴에 올라 있었다.

정답이 보이는 해설

로키산맥을 여행하던 중, 이따금 냄새를 맡으며 걸어가는 회색곰을 발견하고 처음에는 즐거웠으나, 그 곰이 자신을 먹이로 생각하여 자신의 냄새를 따라오고 있음을 알

게 되자 얼어붙었고, 이제 생존의 문제가 되었다. 그러므로 'I'의 심경 변화로 가장 적절한 것은 ② '기쁜 → 무서운'이다.

선택지 완벽 분석

① sad → angry 슬픈 → 화난
② delighted → scared 기쁜 → 무서운
③ satisfied → jealous 만족하는 → 질투하는
④ worried → relieved 걱정하는 → 안도하는
글의 내용으로 파악하지 않고, 처음에 우연히 곰을 보게 되어 걱정되었다가 아무 일도 아님을 알게 되어 안도되었다고 잘못 추측하면 안 된다.
⑤ frustrated → excited 좌절하는 → 흥분하는

필수 어휘

grizzly bear 회색곰 habitat 서식지 sniff 코를 킁킁거리다 realize 깨닫다
giant 거대한 freeze 얼어붙다, 등골이 오싹하다 experience 경험 issue 문제
survival 생존 motivation 동기

04 정답 ②

202211 19번 정답률 89%

On one beautiful spring day, I was fully enjoying my day off.
휴가
✪ I arrived at the nail salon, / and muted my cellphone // so that I
동사1   동사2   목적을 나타내는 부사절
would be disconnected for the hour / and feel calm and peaceful.
절의 동사1   절의 동사2(앞에 would 생략)
단서1 I was so comfortable while I got a manicure. As I left the
매니큐어를 받는 동안 편안함 → relaxed(느긋한)
place, I checked my cellphone and saw four missed calls from
a strange number. I knew immediately that something bad was
coming, and I called back. A young woman answered and said that
my father had fallen over a stone and was injured, now seated on
fall over: ~에 걸려 넘어지다
a bench. **단서2** I was really concerned since he had just recovered
무릎 수술을 받으신 아버지가 넘어지신 걸 알게 됨 → worried(걱정되는)
from his knee surgery. I rushed getting into my car to go see him.
go and[to] see에서
and[to] 생략 가능

해석

어느 아름다운 봄날, 나는 휴가를 충분히 즐기고 있었다. 나는 네일샵에 도착해서 그 시간 동안 단절되어 차분하고 평화롭게 느낄 수 있도록 나의 휴대폰의 음을 소거했다. 나는 매니큐어를 받는 동안 아주 편안했다. 나는 그 장소를 떠나면서, 나의 휴대폰을 확인했고 낯선 번호로부터 걸려온 네 통의 부재중 전화를 봤다. 나는 나쁜 어떤 일이 생겼다는 것을 즉시 알았고, 다시 전화했다. 한 젊은 여성이 전화를 받아 나의 아버지가 돌에 걸려 넘어져서 다쳤고, 지금 벤치에 앉아 있다고 말했다. 아버지는 무릎 수술에서 막 회복했기 때문에 나는 정말 걱정되었다. 나는 그를 보러 가기 위해 급히 차에 올랐다.

정답이 보이는 해설

하루 휴가를 내고, 네일샵에서 매니큐어를 받는 동안 편안했으나, 네일샵에서 떠나면서 아버지가 다쳤다는 사실을 알게 되었으므로, 'I'의 심경 변화로 가장 적절한 것은 ② '느긋한 → 걱정되는'이다.

선택지 완벽 분석

① nervous → confident 긴장한 → 확신에 찬
② relaxed → worried 느긋한 → 걱정되는
③ excited → indifferent 흥분한 → 무관심한
④ pleased → jealous 기쁜 → 질투가 나는
⑤ annoyed → grateful 짜증이 난 → 감사하는

필수 어휘

mute 소리를 줄이다, 무음으로 하다 disconnect 접속을 끊다, 연결을 끊다
comfortable 편안한 immediately 즉시, 즉각 injured 다친, 부상을 입은
seat 앉히다 concerned 걱정하는 recover 회복되다 surgery 수술
rush 급히 움직이다

05 정답 ②

단서1 It was two hours before the submission deadline and I still
기사 마감 두 시간 전: 기사 작성 미완성 + 타자기 고장 발견
hadn't finished my news article. I sat at the desk, but suddenly, the
typewriter didn't work. No matter how hard I tapped the keys, the
levers wouldn't move to strike the paper. I started to realize that I
would not be able to finish the article on time. Desperately, I rested
제시간에
the typewriter on my lap and started hitting each key with as much
as ~ as 주어 can: 가능한 한 ~한[하게](= as ~ as possible)
force as I could manage. Nothing happened. ✪ **Thinking** something
= the typewriter   분사구문(동시동작)
might have happened inside of it, // I **opened** the cover, **lifted** up
might have+p.p.: ~했을지도 모른다   동사1   동사2
the keys, and **found** the problem — a paper clip. The keys had no
동사3
room to move. After picking it out, I pressed and pulled some parts.
pick ~ out: ~을 꺼내다
단서2 The keys moved smoothly again. I breathed deeply and
타자기를 고치고 안도함
smiled. Now I knew that I could finish my article on time.

해석

제출 마감 시간 두 시간 전이었고 나는 여전히 나의 뉴스 기사를 끝내지 못했다. 나는 책상에 앉았는데, 갑자기 타자기가 작동하지 않았다. 내가 아무리 세게 키를 두드려도, 레버는 종이를 두드리기 위해 움직이려 하지 않았다. 나는 내가 제시간에 그 기사를 끝낼 수 없으리라는 것을 깨닫기 시작했다. 필사적으로, 나는 타자기를 내 무릎 위에 올려놓고 각각의 키를 내가 할 수 있을 만큼의 많은 힘으로 누르기 시작했다. 아무 일도 일어나지 않았다. 그것의 내부에 무슨 일이 일어났을지도 모른다고 생각하면서, 나는 그 덮개를 열고, 키들을 들어 올려서, 문제점을 발견했는데, 클립이 있었던 것이다. 키들이 움직일 공간이 없었다. 그것을 집어서 꺼낸 후에, 나는 몇 개의 부품들을 누르고 당겼다. 키들이 매끄럽게 다시 움직였다. 나는 깊게 숨을 내쉬고 미소 지었다. 이제 내가 제시간에 기사를 끝낼 수 있다는 것을 알았다.

정답이 보이는 해설

뉴스 기사 제출 마감 두 시간 전인데 아직 기사를 끝내지 못한 상황에서 타자기마저 작동하지 않자 제시간에 기사를 못 쓸 것 같아 좌절했지만, 마침내 타자기 안에 클립이 끼어 있는 것을 발견하고 그것을 꺼내 타자기를 고친 뒤 안도의 숨을 내쉬며 미소 짓고 있으므로, 'I'의 심경 변화로 가장 적절한 것은 ② '좌절한 → 안도한'이다.

선택지 완벽 분석

① confident → nervous 자신만만한 → 불안한
② frustrated → relieved 좌절한 → 안도한
③ bored → amazed 지루한 → 깜짝 놀란
   함정 타자기를 고치는 과정을 지루하다고 볼 수 없으며 타자기를 고치고 나서 안도하는 모습을 깜짝 놀란 것으로 볼 수도 없다.
④ indifferent → curious 무관심한 → 호기심에 찬
⑤ excited → disappointed 흥분한 → 실망한

필수 어휘

submission 제출 deadline 마감 시간 article 기사 typewriter 타자기
work 작동하다 lever 레버 strike 두드리다 desperately 필사적으로 rest 놓다
lap 무릎 manage (무기·도구를) 잘 쓰다[사용하다] paper clip 클립, 종이 집게
press 누르다 pull 당기다 smoothly 매끄럽게 breathe 숨을 내쉬다

06 정답 ②

One Saturday morning, Matthew's mother told Matthew that
she was going to take him to the park. **단서1** A big smile came
                                        공원에 간다는 말에 환한 미소
across his face. As he loved to play outside, he ate his breakfast and
를 지음
got dressed quickly so they could go. When they got to the park,
옷을 입다

Matthew ran all the way over to the swing set. That was his favorite
thing to do at the park. But the swings were all being used. ✪ His
mother explained / [that he could use the slide / **until** a swing became
          explained의 목적어절   접속사(~할 때까지)
available], / but it was broken. Suddenly, his mother got a phone
                = the slide
call and she told Matthew they had to leave. **단서2** His heart sank.
                                            아무것도 타지 못하고 돌아가야
                                            한다는 말에 가슴이 내려앉음

해석

어느 토요일 아침, Matthew의 엄마는 Matthew에게 그를 공원에 데려갈 거라고 말했다. 그의 얼굴에 환한 미소가 떠올랐다. 그는 밖에서 노는 것을 좋아했기 때문에, 나갈 수 있도록 서둘러 아침을 먹고 옷을 입었다. 공원에 도착했을 때, Matthew는 그네를 향해 곧장 뛰어갔다. 그것은 그가 공원에서 가장 좋아하는 것이었다. 하지만 그네는 이미 모두 이용 중이었다. 그의 엄마는 그네를 이용할 수 있을 때까지 미끄럼틀을 탈 수 있다고 설명했지만, 그것은 부서져 있었다. 갑자기 그의 엄마는 전화를 받고 Matthew에게 그들이 떠나야 한다고 말했다. 그는 가슴이 내려앉았다.

정답이 보이는 해설

Matthew는 공원에 간다는 엄마의 말에 신나서 뛰어갔는데 그네가 모두 이용 중이었고 미끄럼틀은 부서져 있었으며 공원을 떠나야 한다는 엄마의 말을 듣고 실망했으므로, Matthew의 심경 변화로 가장 적절한 것은 ② '신난 → 실망한'이다.

선택지 완벽 분석

① embarrassed → indifferent 당황한 → 무관심한
② excited → disappointed 신난 → 실망한
③ cheerful → ashamed 기분 좋은 → 부끄러운
④ nervous → touched 긴장한 → 감동받은
⑤ scared → relaxed 무서운 → 편안한

필수 어휘

quickly 서둘러, 빨리 swing 그네 explain 설명하다 slide 미끄럼틀
available 이용 가능한 broken 부서진 sink 내려앉다, 가라앉다

07 정답 ③

The principal stepped on stage. "Now, I present this year's
top academic award to the student who has achieved the highest
placing." ✪ He smiled at *the row of seats* / [**where** twelve finalists
          ~을 보고 미소 짓다   관계부사
had gathered]. **단서1** Zoe wiped a sweaty hand on her handkerchief
과거완료(had+p.p.)   젖은 손을 손수건에 닦음
and glanced at the other finalists. **단서2** They all looked as pale
                                  다른 최종 후보들도 Zoe만큼 불안해
and uneasy as herself. Zoe and one of the other finalists had won
보임
first placing in four subjects so it came down to how teachers
ranked their hard work and confidence. "The Trophy for General
Excellence is awarded to Miss Zoe Perry," the principal declared.
"Could Zoe step this way, please?" **단서3** Zoe felt as if she were in
                                          천국에 있는 것 같은 기분을 느낌
heaven. She walked into the thunder of applause with a big smile.

해석

교장 선생님이 무대 위로 올라갔다. "이제, 최고 등수를 차지한 학생에게 올해의 학업 최우수상을 수여합니다." 그는 열두 명의 최종 후보들이 모여 있는 좌석의 열을 보고 미소를 지었다. Zoe는 땀에 젖은 손을 손수건에 닦고는 나머지 다른 최종 후보들을 힐끗 보았다. 그들은 모두 그녀만큼 창백하고 불안해 보였다. Zoe와 나머지 다른 최종 후보 중 한 명이 네 과목에서 1위를 차지했으므로, 그들의 노력과 자신감을 선생님들이 어떻게 평가하느냐로 좁혀졌다. "전체 최우수상을 위한 트로피는 Zoe Perry 양에게 수여됩니다."라고 교장 선생님이 공표했다. "Zoe는 이쪽으로 나와 주

겠습니까?" Zoe는 마치 천국에 있는 것처럼 느꼈다. 그녀는 환한 미소를 지으며 우레와 같은 박수갈채를 받으며 걸어갔다.

정답이 보이는 해설

다른 최종 후보들과 함께 학업 최우수상 발표를 기다리고 있는 상황에서 손이 땀에 젖을 정도로 매우 긴장하고 있다가 전체 최우수상 수상자로 호명되자 천국에 있는 것 같은 기분을 느끼고 환한 미소를 지으며 걸어 나갔으므로, Zoe의 심경 변화로 가장 적절한 것은 ③ '긴장한 → 기쁜'이다.

선택지 완벽 분석

① hopeful → disappointed 희망에 찬 → 실망한
② guilty → confident 죄책감이 드는 → 자신감 있는
③ nervous → delighted 긴장한 → 기쁜
④ angry → calm 화난 → 침착한
⑤ relaxed → proud 편안한 → 자랑스러운

필수 어휘

principal 교장 academic 학업의 placing 순위 row 열, 줄
finalist 최종 후보, 결선 진출자 sweaty 땀에 젖은 glance 힐끗 보다
uneasy 불안한 rank 평가하다, 순위를 매기다 confidence 자신감
declare 공표하다 applause 박수갈채

08 정답 ⑤

202111 19번 정답률 92%

When my mom came home from the mall with a special present for me I was pretty sure I knew what it was. **단서1** I was absolutely thrilled because I would soon communicate with a new cell phone! I 각에 완전히 신남
was daydreaming about all of the cool apps and games I was going to download. But my mom smiled really big and handed me a book. ⊙ I flipped through the pages, / figuring [that maybe she had hidden flip through: ~을 훑어보다   분사구문   과거완료(had+p.p.)
my new phone inside]. **단서2** But I slowly realized that my mom had 엄마가 사온 것이 원했던 휴대폰이 아니라 책이라는 것을
not got me a phone and my present was just a little book, which was 알게 됨
so different from what I had wanted.

해석

엄마가 나를 위한 특별한 선물을 가지고 쇼핑몰에서 집에 왔을 때 나는 그것이 무엇인지 알고 있다고 상당히 확신했다. 내가 곧 새로운 휴대폰으로 소통할 것이었기 때문에 나는 완전히 신났다! 나는 내가 다운로드할 모든 멋진 어플과 게임에 대한 공상에 잠겨 있었다. 하지만 엄마는 아주 크게 미소를 지으며 내게 책 한 권을 건넸다. 나는 아마도 엄마가 내 새로운 휴대폰을 안에 숨겨 두었을 것이라 생각하면서 책장을 넘겨보았다. 그러나 나는 엄마가 나에게 휴대폰을 사 주지 않았고 내 선물이 겨우 작은 책이라는 것을 서서히 깨달았는데, 그것은 내가 원했던 것과는 너무 달랐다.

정답이 보이는 해설

엄마가 자신을 위한 선물로 휴대폰을 사 왔을 것이라 생각하고 한껏 신나 있다가 엄마가 사온 것이 휴대폰이 아니라 책이었으며 그것은 자신이 원했던 것과 너무 달랐다는 내용이므로, 필자의 심경 변화로 가장 적절한 것은 ⑤ '신남 → 실망한'이다.

선택지 완벽 분석

① worried → furious 걱정하는 → 격분한
② surprised → relieved 놀란 → 안도한
③ ashamed → confident 부끄러운 → 자신감 있는
④ anticipating → satisfied 기대하는 → 만족한
⑤ excited → disappointed 신난 → 실망한

필수 어휘

absolutely 완전히 thrilled 신이 난, 흥분한 communicate 소통하다
daydream 공상하다 cool 멋진 hand 건네다 hide 숨기다 inside 안에

09 정답 ⑤

202109 19번 정답률 92%

In the middle of the night, Matt suddenly awakened. He glanced ~을 힐끗 보다
at his clock. It was 3:23. For just an instant he wondered what had wakened him. Then he remembered. **단서1** He had heard someone 한밤중에 누군가가 자신의 방에 들어
come into his room. Matt sat up in bed, rubbed his eyes, and looked 오는 소리를 들음   → 분사구문
around the small room. ⊙ "Mom?" he said quietly, / hoping he → 목소리가 '안심시키는' 능동의 의미
would hear his mother's voice / assuring him [that everything was 지각동사   목적어   목적격보어(현재분사) 명사절
all right]. But there was no answer. Matt tried to tell himself that he was just hearing things. But he knew he wasn't. **단서2** There was 자신의 방에 누
someone in his room. He could hear rhythmic, scratchy breathing 군가가 있는 상태에서 알 수 없는 그 존재의 숨소리까지 듣게 된 기이한 상황
and it wasn't his own. He lay awake for the rest of the night. 밤새

해석

한밤중에, Matt는 갑자기 잠을 깼다. 그는 자신의 시계를 힐끗 보았다. 3시 23분이었다. 한순간 그는 그를 깨운 것이 무엇인지 궁금했다. 그때 그는 생각이 났다. 그는 누군가가 자신의 방에 들어오는 소리를 들었던 것이다. Matt는 잠자리에서 일어나 앉아, 자신의 눈을 비비고는, 작은 방을 둘러보았다. "엄마?" 그는 다 괜찮다고 자신을 안심시키는 그의 어머니의 목소리를 자신이 들을 수 있기를 바라면서 침착하게 말했다. 그렇지만 답이 없었다. Matt는 자신이 단지 물건들의 소리를 들은 것뿐이었다고 스스로에게 말하려고 애썼다. 그렇지만 자신이 그렇지 않았다는 것을 그는 알았다. 그의 방에는 누군가가 있었다. 그는 규칙적으로 긁는 듯한 숨소리를 들을 수 있었고, 그것은 그의 것이 아니었다. 그는 밤새 잠이 깬 채 누워 있었다.

정답이 보이는 해설

한밤중에 누군가가 자신의 방에 들어오는 소리를 듣고 잠이 깬 상태로, 자신을 안심시켜 줄 사람이 아무도 없는 방에서 존재를 알 수 없는 누군가의 숨소리를 들으며 밤새 누워 있는 상황이므로, 글의 상황에 나타난 분위기로 가장 적절한 것은 ⑤ '기이하고 무서운'이다.

선택지 완벽 분석

① humorous and fun 유머러스하고 재미있는
② boring and dull 지루하고 따분한
③ calm and peaceful 고요하고 평화로운
고요한 한밤중에 일어나는 일이지만 대상을 알 수 없는 침입자가 자신의 방에 들어온 상황이므로 평화로운 분위기라고 할 수는 없다.
④ noisy and exciting 시끌벅적하고 신이 난
⑤ mysterious and frightening 기이하고 무서운

필수 어휘

awaken 잠에서 깨다; 깨우다 glance 힐끗 쳐다보다 instant 순간, 아주 짧은 동안
wonder 궁금해하다 rub 문지르다 assure 안심시키다
rhythmic 규칙적으로 순환하는, 리드미컬한 scratchy 긁는 듯한 소리가 나는
lie 누워 있다, 눕다(-lay-lain)

10 정답 ③

202106 19번 정답률 80%

One day, Cindy happened to sit next to a famous artist in a café, 우연히 ~하다   → 직접
and **단서1** she was thrilled to see him in person. He was drawing 유명한 화가를 직접 보게 되어 매우 기뻐함 → 신이 난(excited)
on a used napkin over coffee. She was looking on in awe. ⊙ After 시간 부사구
a few moments, / the man finished his coffee / and was about to 주어   동사1   동사2
throw away the napkin // as he left. Cindy stopped him. "Can I have 접속사(~할 때)
that napkin you drew on?", she asked. "Sure," he replied. "Twenty

thousand dollars." She said, with her eyes wide-open, "What? It took you like two minutes to draw that." "No," he said. "It took me over sixty years to draw this." **단서2** Being at a loss, she stood still rooted to the ground.

화가의 말에 (너무 놀라 할 말을 잃고) 그 자리에 가만히 서 있었음 → 놀란(surprised)

해석

어느 날, Cindy는 카페에서 우연히 한 유명한 화가 옆에 앉게 되었는데, 그녀는 그를 직접 보게 되어 매우 기뻤다. 그는 커피를 마시면서 사용한 냅킨에 그림을 그리고 있었다. 그녀는 경외심으로 지켜보고 있었다. 잠시 후, 그 남자는 커피를 다 마신 후 자리를 뜨면서 그 냅킨을 버리려고 했다. Cindy는 그를 막았다. "그림을 그리던 그 냅킨을 제가 가져도 될까요?"라고 그녀가 물었다. "물론이죠."라고 그가 대답했다. "2만 달러입니다." 그녀는 눈을 커다랗게 뜨고 말했다, "뭐라고요? 그것을 그리는 데 2분밖에 안 걸리셨잖아요." "아니요."라고 그가 말했다. "나는 이것을 그리는 데 60년 이상이 걸렸어요." 그녀는 당황해서 그 자리에 가만히 서 있었다.

정답이 보이는 해설

우연히 유명한 화가 옆에 앉게 되어 신이 났지만 그가 냅킨 값으로 2만 달러를 요구하자 당황해서 그 자리에 가만히 서 있었다고 했으므로, Cindy의 심경 변화로 가장 적절한 것은 ③ '신이 난 → 놀란'이다.

선택지 완벽 분석

① relieved → worried 안도하는 → 염려하는
② indifferent → embarrassed 무관심한 → 당황한
Cindy가 좋아하는 화가를 직접 보게 되어 신이 났다고(was thrilled) 했으므로 indifferent(무관심하)는 내용과 맞지 않다. embarrassed만 보고 정답으로 고르지 않도록 유의한다.
③ excited → surprised 신이 난 → 놀란
④ disappointed → satisfied 실망한 → 만족한
⑤ jealous → confident 질투가 난 → 자신만만한

필수 어휘

used 사용된 awe 경외심 throw away 던지다, 버리다 stop 말리다, 멈추다
reply 응답하다 at a loss 어쩔 줄을 모르는 still 가만히

11 정답 ①

202103 19번 정답률 93%

★ On the way home, / Shirley **noticed** a truck parked in front
부사구 　　　　　　　　　지각동사　목적어　목적격보어
of the house (across the street). New neighbors! **단서1** Shirley was
dying to know about them. "Do you know anything about the new
그들에 대해 알고 싶은 생각이 간절함 → 궁금한(curious)
neighbors?" she asked Pa at dinner. He said, "Yes, and there's one thing that may be interesting to you." Shirley had a billion more questions. Pa said joyfully, "They have a girl just your age. Maybe
딱 너 정도의 나이인
she wants to be your playmate." Shirley nearly dropped her fork on the floor. **단서2** How many times had she prayed for a friend?
친구를 달라고 무수히 기도했는데 자신의 기도가 응답을 받은 데 대한 감동
Finally, her prayers were answered! She and the new girl could go
→ 신이 난(excited)
to school together, play together, and become best friends.

해석

집에 오는 길에, Shirley는 길 건너편에 있는 집 앞에 트럭 한 대가 주차되어 있는 것을 알아차렸다. 새로운 이웃이었다! Shirley는 그들에 대해 알고 싶어 견딜 수가 없었다. 저녁 식사 시간에 그녀는 "새 이웃에 대해 뭐 좀 아시나요?"라고 아빠에게 물었다. 그는 "그럼, 그리고 너에게 흥미 있을 만한 것이 하나 있지."라고 말했다. Shirley는 더 묻고 싶은 것이 엄청나게 많았다. 아빠는 "딱 너 정도의 나이인 여자아이가 한 명 있더구나. 아마 그 애가 너의 놀이 친구가 되고 싶어 할지도 몰라."라고 즐겁게 말했다. Shirley는 자신의 포크를 바닥에 떨어뜨릴 뻔했다. 친구를 달라고 그녀가 얼마나 많이 기도했던가? 드디어, 그녀의 기도는 응답을 받은 것이었다! 그녀와

새로 온 여자아이는 함께 학교에 가고, 함께 놀고, 그리고 제일 친한 친구가 될 수 있을지도 모른다.

정답이 보이는 해설

새로운 이웃에 대해 궁금해져서 그들에 대해 질문을 이어 가다가 그 집에 자신의 또래 여자아이가 있다는 말에 너무 놀라 친구를 달라는 자신의 기도가 응답을 받았다고 했으므로, Shirley의 심경으로 가장 적절한 것은 ① '궁금하고 신이 난'이다.

선택지 완벽 분석

① curious and excited 궁금하고 신이 난
② sorry and upset 미안하고 화가 난
③ jealous and annoyed 질투가 나고 짜증이 난
④ calm and relaxed 차분하고 느긋한
⑤ disappointed and unhappy 실망하고 기분이 좋지 않은

필수 어휘

notice 알아차리다 neighbor 이웃 joyfully 기쁘게 playmate 놀이 친구
nearly 거의 drop 떨어뜨리다 pray 기도하다

12 정답 ①

202011 19번 정답률 78%

On my seventh birthday, my mom surprised me with a puppy waiting on a leash. It had beautiful golden fur and an adorable tail. **단서1** It was exactly what I had always dreamed of. I took the dog
늘 꿈꿨던 강아지가 생김 → 기쁜(delighted)
everywhere and slept with it every night. A few months later, the dog got out of the backyard and was lost. ★ I sat on my bed and
　　　　　　　　　　　　　　　　　　　　　　동사1
cried for hours // while my mother watched me (silently from the
동사2　　　　　　　접속사　주어　　동사　목적어
doorway of my room). **단서2** I finally fell asleep, exhausted from my
　　　　　　　　　　　　개를 잃어버린 슬픔에 지쳐 잠이 듦 → 슬픈(sorrowful)
grief. My mother never said a word to me about my loss, but I knew
　　　　　　　　　　　한마디하다
she felt the same as I did.
똑같이 느끼다

해석

나의 일곱 번째 생일에, 목줄을 맨 채 기다리고 있는 강아지 한 마리로 엄마는 나를 놀라게 했다. 그것은 멋진 황금빛 털과 귀여운 꼬리를 가지고 있었다. 그것은 바로 내가 언제나 꿈꿨던 것이었다. 나는 그 개를 어디든 데리고 다녔고 매일 밤 함께 잤다. 몇 달 후, 그 개는 뒷마당을 빠져나가 사라져 버렸다. 엄마가 내 방 입구에서 말없이 나를 바라보는 동안 나는 침대에 앉아 몇 시간 동안 울었다. 나는 마침내 슬픔에 지쳐 잠이 들었다. 엄마는 나의 상실에 대해 내게 한마디도 하지 않았지만, 나는 엄마 역시 나와 똑같이 느꼈다는 것을 알고 있었다.

정답이 보이는 해설

자신이 늘 꿈꿔 왔던 강아지가 생겨 기뻐하다가 몇 달 후 언제나 함께이던 그 개가 뒷마당을 빠져나가 사라져 버리자 울다가 슬픔에 지쳐 잠이 들었다고 했으므로, 'I'의 심경 변화로 가장 적절한 것은 ① '기뻐하는 → 슬퍼하는'이다.

선택지 완벽 분석

① delighted → sorrowful 기뻐하는 → 슬퍼하는
② relaxed → annoyed 느긋한 → 짜증이 난
③ embarrassed → worried 당황한 → 걱정하는
④ excited → horrified 신이 난 → 겁에 질린
글의 후반부는 개를 잃어버린 슬픈 상황이다.
⑤ disappointed → satisfied 실망한 → 만족스러운

필수 어휘

leash (개 등을 매어 두는) 가죽 끈 fur 털 adorable 귀여운, 사랑스러운 tail 꼬리
get out of ~ 밖으로 나가다 backyard 뒤뜰 for hours 몇 시간 동안
exhausted 기진맥진한 grief 슬픔, 비애 loss 상실, 잃음

3강 2020~2023 필자의 주장 파악

01 정답 ②

202309 20번 정답률 95%

We are always teaching our children something by our words and our actions. They learn from seeing. They learn from hearing and from *overhearing*. Children share the values of their parents about the most important things in life. Our priorities and principles and our examples of good behavior can teach our children to take the high road when other roads look tempting. **단서1** ✪ Remember / [that children do not learn the values / [that make up strong character] / (simply by being *told* about them)]. **단서2** They learn by seeing the people around them *act* on and *uphold* those values in their daily lives. **주제문** Therefore show your child good examples of life by your action. In our daily lives, we can show our children that we respect others. We can show them our compassion and concern when others are suffering, and our own self-discipline, courage and honesty as we make difficult decisions.

해석

우리는 항상 우리 자녀에게 말과 행동으로 무언가를 가르치고 있다. 그들은 보는 것에서 배운다. 그들은 듣거나 '우연히 듣는 것'에서 배운다. 아이들은 인생에서 가장 중요한 것에 대해 자신들의 부모의 가치를 공유한다. 우리의 우선순위, 원칙, 좋은 행동에 대한 본보기는 다른 길이 유혹적으로 보일 때 우리 자녀에게 올바른 길을 가라고 가르칠 수 있다. 아이들은 확고한 인격을 구성하는 가치를 단순히 그것에 대해 '들음'으로써 배우지 않는다는 것을 기억하라. 그들은 주변 사람들이 그들의 일상생활에서 그러한 가치를 좇아 '행동'하고 '유지'하는 것을 봄으로써 배운다. 그러므로 여러분의 자녀에게 여러분의 행동으로 삶의 모범을 보여라. 일상생활에서 우리는 자녀에게 타인을 존중하는 것을 보여 줄 수 있다. 우리는 타인이 괴로워할 때 우리의 연민과 걱정을, 그리고 우리가 어려운 결정을 할 때 우리 자신의 자제력, 용기, 정직을 그들에게 보여 줄 수 있다.

정답이 보이는 해설

우리는 말과 행동을 통해 항상 아이들을 가르치고 있으며, 우리의 좋은 본보기가 아이들이 올바른 길을 가게 해 준다고 했다. 그런데 아이들은 가치에 대해 들으면서 배우는 것이 아니라, 주변인들이 가치에 따라 행동하고 가치를 유지하는 것을 보면서 배운다고 했으므로, 필자가 주장하는 바로 가장 적절한 것은 ②이다.

선택지 완벽 분석

③ 칭찬을 통해 자녀의 바람직한 행동을 강화해야 한다.
자녀에게 좋은 행동의 본보기를 보여서 가치를 가르치라는 내용이지, 칭찬으로 바람직한 행동을 강화해야 한다는 내용은 아니다.

필수 어휘

overhear 우연히 듣다　priority 우선순위　principle (도덕적) 원칙, 원리
behavior 행동　tempting 유혹적인, 구미가 당기는　uphold 수호하다, 옹호하다
compassion 연민　concern 걱정　self-discipline 자기 훈련, 자제력

02 정답 ⑤

202306 20번 정답률 82%

Research shows that people who work have two calendars: one for work and one for their personal lives. Although it may seem sensible, **단서1** having two separate calendars for work and personal life can lead to distractions. To check if something is missing, you will find yourself checking your to-do lists multiple times. **주제문** Instead, organize all of your tasks in one place. It doesn't matter if you use digital or paper media. It's okay to **단서2** keep your professional and personal tasks in one place. This will give you a good idea of how time is divided between work and home. ✪ This will **allow** you to make informed decisions (about which tasks are most important).

해석

연구는 일하는 사람들이 두 개의 달력을 가지고 있다는 것을 보여 준다. 하나는 업무를 위한 달력이고 하나는 개인적인 삶을 위한 달력이다. 비록 그것이 현명해 보일지도 모르지만, 업무와 개인적인 삶을 위한 두 개의 별도의 달력을 갖는 것은 주의를 산만하게 할 수 있다. 무언가 누락된 것이 있는지를 확인하기 위해, 자신의 할 일 목록을 여러 번 확인하는 스스로를 보게 될 것이다. 대신, 모든 일들을 한 곳에 정리하라. 디지털 매체를 사용하든 종이 매체를 사용하든 중요하지 않다. 업무와 개인 용무를 한 곳에 두는 것이 좋다. 이것은 당신에게 일과 가정 사이에 시간이 어떻게 쪼개지는지에 대해 잘 알게 해 줄 것이다. 이것은 어떤 일이 가장 중요한지에 대한 정보에 입각한 결정을 내리게 해 줄 것이다.

정답이 보이는 해설

연구에 따르면 일하는 사람들이 업무용과 개인 용도의 두 개의 달력을 별도로 사용하고 있으나, 이는 주의를 산만하게 할 수 있으므로, 업무와 개인 용무를 모두 한 곳에 정리하는 게 더 좋을 것이라는 내용이다. 그래야 시간이 어떻게 나뉘어 쓰이는지, 어떤 일이 가장 중요한지 결정을 내릴 때 도움이 된다고 설명하고 있다. 그러므로, 필자가 주장하는 바로 가장 적절한 것은 ⑤이다.

필수 어휘

sensible 현명한, 분별 있는, 합리적인　separate 분리된, 별도의
distraction 주의 산만, 정신이 흐트러짐　missing 없어진, 빠진[누락된], 실종된
to-do list 해야 할 일 목록　multiple 많은, 다수의　organize 정리하다
matter 중요하다　professional 직업의, 전문적인　divide 나누다

03 정답 ⑤

202303 20번 정답률 84%

It is difficult for any of us to maintain a constant level of attention throughout our working day. **단서1** We all have body rhythms characterised by peaks and valleys of energy and alertness. ✪ **주제문** You will achieve more, / and feel confident as a benefit, // if you schedule your most demanding tasks at times / **when** you are best able to cope with them. If you haven't thought about energy peaks before, take a few days to observe yourself. **단서2** Try to note the times when you are at your best. We are all different. For some, the peak will come first thing in the morning, but for others it may take a while to warm up.

해석

우리 중 누구라도 근무일에 종일 일정한 수준의 주의 집중을 유지하기는 어렵다. 우리는 모두 에너지와 기민함의 정점과 저점을 특징으로 하는 신체 리듬을 가지고 있다. 가장 힘든 작업을 그것을 가장 잘 처리할 수 있는 시간에 하도록 계획을 잡으면, 더 많은 것을 이루고 이익으로 자신감을 느낄 것이다. 만약 이전에 에너지 정점에 관

해 생각해 본 적이 없다면, 며칠 동안 스스로를 관찰하라. 자신이 가장 좋은 상태일 때를 알아차리도록 노력하라. 우리는 모두 다르다. 어떤 사람에게는 정점이 아침에 제일 먼저 오지만, 다른 사람에게는 준비되는 데 얼마간의 시간이 걸릴 수도 있다.

〔 정답이 보이는 해설 〕

우리의 신체 리듬은 사람마다 다른 에너지의 정점과 저점이 있고 에너지가 정점일 때 힘든 일을 하면 더 많은 것을 이룰 수 있으므로, 자신의 에너지가 정점이 되는 시간을 찾아야 한다는 내용의 글이다. 그러므로, 필자가 주장하는 바로 가장 적절한 것은 ⑤이다.

〔 필수 어휘 〕

maintain 유지하다 constant 일정한 attention 주의 (집중) throughout 내내
characterise 특징짓다(= characterize) peak 정점, 최고조 valley 저점, 골짜기
demanding 힘든, 부담이 큰 observe 관찰하다 note 알아차리다, 주의하다

---

04 정답 ⑤

You already have a business and you're about to launch your blog
　　　　　　　　　　　　　be about to: 막 ~하려 하다
so that you can sell your product. Unfortunately, here is where a
~하기 위해서
'business mind' can be a bad thing. Most people believe that to have
a successful business blog promoting a product, they have to stay
strictly 'on the topic.' If all you're doing is shamelessly promoting
your product, then who is going to want to read the latest thing
you're writing about? **〔단서〕** Instead, you need to give some useful or
　　　　　　　　　　　대신, 사람들에게 유용하거나 재미있는 정보를 제공해야 함
entertaining information away for free so that people have a reason
　　　　　　　　　　무료로　　도치: 조동사 + 주어 + 본동사
to keep coming back. ❖ (Only by doing this) / can you create *an*
　　　　　　　　　　　전치사구 강조를 위해 문두에 위치
interested audience [that you will then be able to sell to]. **〔주제문〕** So,
　　　　　　　　　목적격 관계대명사절
the best way to be successful with a business blog is to write about
things that your audience will be interested in.
　　　　　　　　　　　~에 관심을 가지다

〔 해석 〕

여러분은 이미 사업체를 가지고 있고 여러분의 제품을 팔 수 있도록 블로그를 시작하려는 참이다. 유감스럽게도, 여기가 '비즈니스 정신'이 나쁜 것이 될 수 있는 지점이다. 대부분의 사람들은 제품을 홍보하는 성공적인 상업용 블로그를 가지기 위해서 그들이 엄격하게 '그 주제에' 머물러야 한다고 믿는다. 만일 여러분이 하는 일의 모두가 뻔뻔스럽게 여러분의 제품을 홍보하는 것이라면, 그렇다면 누가 여러분이 쓰고 있는 최신의 것을 읽고 싶어 할까? 대신, 사람들이 계속해서 다시 방문할 이유를 가질 수 있도록 여러분은 어떤 유용하거나 재미있는 정보를 무료로 줄 필요가 있다. 이렇게 함으로써 여러분은 여러분이 그 다음에 판매를 할 수 있게 될 관심 있는 독자를 만들어 낼 수 있다. 따라서, 상업용 블로그로 성공하기 위한 가장 좋은 방법은 독자들이 관심을 가질 만한 것들에 대해 쓰는 것이다.

〔 정답이 보이는 해설 〕

제품만을 홍보하는 상업용 블로그는 사람들이 읽고 싶어 하지 않으므로, 독자들이 흥미 있어 할 정보를 무료로 제공해야 한다는 내용이다. 따라서 필자가 주장하는 바로 가장 적절한 것은 ⑤이다.

〔 선택지 완벽 분석 〕

③ 신제품 개발을 위해 상업용 블로그를 적극 활용해야 한다.
　〔함정〕 블로그를 이용하여 홍보를 할 때 바람직한 글에 대한 내용이지, 신제품 개발을 위해 블로그를 활용해야 한다는 내용의 글은 아니다.

〔 필수 어휘 〕

launch 시작하다, 착수하다 product 생산물, 상품, 제품 mind 정신, 마음
promote 홍보하다 strictly 엄격하게 shamelessly 뻔뻔스럽게, 부끄러움 없이
give ~ away ~을 그냥 주다 entertaining 재미있는, 즐거움을 주는

---

05 정답 ④

Experts on writing say, "Get rid of as many words as possible."
　　　　　　　　　　　　　 Get rid of: 삭제하다 as ~ as possible: 가능한 한 ~한[하게]
Each word must do something important. If it doesn't, get rid of it.
Well, this doesn't work for speaking. **〔단서〕** It takes more words to
　　　　　　　　　　　　　　　　　　　　　 말을 할 때 더 많은 단어가 필요함
introduce, express, and adequately elaborate an idea in speech than
it takes in writing. Why is this so? While the reader can reread, the
listener cannot rehear. Speakers do not come equipped with a replay
button. Because listeners are easily distracted, they will miss many
pieces of what a speaker says. If they miss the crucial sentence, they
may never catch up. ❖ This **makes it** necessary for speakers [to talk
　　　　　　따라잡다　　make+가목적어+목적격보어+to부정사 의미상 주어+진목적어(to부정사)
longer about their points, / **using** more words on them] /
비교급+than: 비교구문　　　　　　　　　　분사구문(동시동작)　　 = their points
than would be used to express the same idea in writing.
유사 관계대명사(~보다)　　부사적 용법(목적)
(관계대명사는 아니지만 불완전한문장에서 주격 관계대명사 역할)

〔 해석 〕

글쓰기 전문가들은 "가능한 한 많은 단어를 삭제하라."고 말한다. 각 단어는 무언가 중요한 일을 해야 한다. 만약 그렇지 않다면, 그것을 삭제하라. 자, 이 방법은 말하기에서는 통하지 않는다. 말하기에서는 아이디어를 소개하고, 표현하며, 적절히 부연 설명하는 데 글쓰기에서보다 더 많은 단어들이 필요하다. 이것은 왜 그러한가? 독자는 글을 다시 읽을 수 있는 반면, 청자는 다시 들을 수 없다. 화자는 재생 버튼을 갖추고 있지 않다. 청자들은 쉽게 주의력이 흐려지기 때문에, 화자가 말하는 것 중 많은 부분들을 놓칠 것이다. 만약 그들이 중요한 문장을 놓친다면, 절대 따라잡을 수 없을지도 모른다. 이것은 화자들이 같은 아이디어를 표현하기 위해 글쓰기에서 사용될 단어 수보다 그것(요점)에 대해 더 많은 단어들을 사용하여 그들의 요점에 대해 더 길게 말할 필요가 있게 만든다.

〔 정답이 보이는 해설 〕

글쓰기에서 가능한 한 많은 단어를 삭제해야 하지만 말하기에서는 아이디어를 소개하고, 표현하며, 부연 설명하는 데 글쓰기 때보다 더 많은 단어들이 필요하다고 말하고 있다. 따라서 필자가 주장하는 바로 가장 적절한 것은 ④이다.

〔 선택지 완벽 분석 〕

① 연설 시 중요한 정보는 천천히 말해야 한다.
　〔함정〕 말할 때의 속도보다는 단어 수에 초점을 둔 설명이므로 답이 될 수 없다.
② 좋은 글을 쓰려면 간결한 문장을 사용해야 한다.
　글을 쓸 때 가능한 한 많은 단어를 삭제하라는 단편적인 내용만 보고 답으로 고를 수 있다. 그러나 말을 잘하기 위해서는 많은 단어 수가 요구된다는 것을 설명하기 위해 상대적으로 적은 단어 수를 요구하는 글쓰기를 언급한 것이므로 답이 될 수 없다.

〔 필수 어휘 〕

expert 전문가 adequately 적절하게
elaborate (더) 자세히 말[설명]하다, 상술하다 equipped with ~을 갖춘
distract (마음·주의 등을) 흩뜨리다 crucial 중요한

---

06 정답 ⑤

❖ Meetings encourage creative thinking / and can give you *ideas*
　　　　주어　　　　동사1　　　　　　　　　　동사2
[that you **may** never **have thought** of on your own]. However, on
목적격 관계대명사　 may have p.p.: ~했을지도 모른다　　　　　　평균적으로
average, meeting participants consider about one third of meeting
time to be unproductive. But you can make your meetings more
productive and more useful by preparing well in advance. **〔단서〕** You
　　　　　　　　　　　　　　　　　　　　　미리, 사전에　　　　회의에
should create a list of items to be discussed and share your list with
서 논의할 사항을 작성하고 회의 전에 참석자들과 공유해야 함

other participants before a meeting. It allows them to know what to expect in your meeting and prepare to participate.

해석

회의는 창의적인 사고를 촉진하며 여러분이 혼자서는 결코 떠올리지 못할 수도 있는 아이디어를 여러분에게 제공할 수 있다. 그러나 평균적으로 회의 참석자들은 회의 시간의 대략 3분의 1을 비생산적이라고 여긴다. 하지만 여러분은 사전에 잘 준비함으로써 회의를 더 생산적이고 유용하게 만들 수 있다. 여러분은 논의될 사항들의 목록을 만들고 회의 전에 다른 회의 참석자들과 여러분의 목록을 공유해야 한다. 그것은 참석자들이 회의에서 무엇을 기대하는지를 알고 회의 참석을 준비하도록 해 준다.

정답이 보이는 해설

회의에서 논의할 사항을 사전에 회의 참석자들과 공유함으로써 회의를 더 생산적으로 만들 수 있다는 내용이므로, 필자가 주장하는 바로 가장 적절한 것은 ⑤이다.

필수 어휘

encourage 촉진하다, 장려하다   participant 참석자   consider 여기다, 고려하다
unproductive 비생산적인   participate 참석하다, 참여하다

07 정답 ⑤
202203 20번 정답률 87%

★ When I was in the army, // my instructors would show up in
(접속사(~할 때))   (목적격 관계대명사 that 생략)   (나타나다)
my barracks room, / and *the first thing* (they would inspect) was
                              (주어)   (동사)
our bed. It was a simple task, but every morning we were required
to make our bed to perfection. It seemed a little ridiculous at the
   (침대를 정돈하다)
time, but the wisdom of this simple act has been proven to me many
times over. If you make your bed every morning, you will have
accomplished the first task of the day. 단서1 It will give you a small
                                      (작은 과업의 성취는 자존감을 부여하)
sense of pride and it will encourage you to do another task and
(고 다른 일을 연달아 하도록 장려함)
another. 단서2 By the end of the day, that one task completed will
         (완료된 하나의 과업이 결국 여러 개의 완료된 과업으로 바뀌게 됨)
have turned into many tasks completed. 주제문 If you can't do little
things right, you will never do the big things right.

해석

내가 군대에 있을 때, 교관들은 나의 병영 생활관에 모습을 드러내곤 했는데, 그들이 가장 먼저 검사하곤 했던 것은 우리의 침대였다. 그것은 단순한 일이었지만, 매일 아침 우리는 침대를 완벽하게 정돈하도록 요구되었다. 그 당시에는 약간 우스꽝스러워 보였지만, 이 단순한 행동의 지혜는 여러 번 반복하여 나에게 증명되었다. 여러분이 매일 아침 침대를 정돈한다면, 여러분은 하루의 첫 번째 과업을 성취한 것이 될 것이다. 그것은 여러분에게 작은 자존감을 줄 것이고 또 다른 과업을 연달아 하도록 장려할 것이다. 하루가 끝날 무렵에는 완료된 그 하나의 과업이 여러 개의 완료된 과업으로 변해 있을 것이다. 여러분이 작은 일들을 제대로 할 수 없다면, 여러분은 결코 큰일들을 제대로 하지 못할 것이다.

정답이 보이는 해설

군대에서 매일 아침 침대 정돈을 했던 자신의 경험을 예로 들면서, 작은 과업의 성취는 또 다른 과업을 연이어 하도록 격려하며 작은 일을 제대로 수행하지 못하면 큰일도 잘 해내지 못할 것이라고 했으므로, 필자가 주장하는 바로 가장 적절한 것은 ⑤이다.

필수 어휘

instructor 교관   inspect 검사하다   task 일, 과업   require 요구하다
perfection 완벽   ridiculous 우스꽝스러운   prove 증명하다
accomplish 성취하다, 해내다   pride 자존감   encourage 장려하다, 용기를 주다
complete 완료하다   turn into ~로 변하다

08 정답 ③
202111 20번 정답률 89%

                                              (선행사를 포함한 관계사(~하는 것))
★ Some experts estimate [that as much as half of **what** we
                                              (estimate의 목적어 역할을 하는 명사절)
communicate is done through *the way* (we move our bodies)].

주제문 Paying attention to the nonverbal messages you send can
              (~에 주의를 기울이다)
make a significant difference in your relationship with students.
In general, most students are often closely tuned in to their
                                                    (~에 맞추다)
teacher's body language. For example, when your students first
enter the classroom, their initial action is to look for their teacher.
단서1 Think about how encouraging and empowering it is for a
      (교사의 친근한 미소와 인사가 학생들에게 격려와 힘을 불어넣음)
student when that teacher has a friendly greeting and a welcoming
smile. 단서2 Smiling at students — to let them know that you are
glad to see them — does not require a great deal of time or effort,
but it can make a significant difference in the classroom climate
        (학생들에게 미소를 짓는 것이 수업 분위기에 큰 변화를 가져올 수 있음)
right from the start of class.

해석

일부 전문가들은 우리가 의사소통하는 것의 절반 정도가 우리의 몸을 움직이는 방식을 통해 이루어진다고 추정한다. 여러분이 보내는 비언어적인 메시지에 주목하는 것은 학생들과 여러분의 관계에 상당한 변화를 가져올 수 있다. 일반적으로 대부분의 학생들은 흔히 자신의 선생님의 몸짓 언어에 관심이 면밀하게 맞춰져 있다. 예를 들어, 여러분의 학생들이 처음 교실에 들어가면 그들의 첫 행동은 자신의 선생님을 찾는 것이다. 그 선생님이 친근한 인사를 하고 환영의 미소를 지을 때 그것이 학생에게 얼마나 격려가 되고 힘을 주는지 생각해 보라. 학생들에게 미소 짓는 것, 즉 그들에게 여러분이 그들을 봐서 기쁘다는 것을 알려 주는 것이 많은 시간이나 노력을 요구하는 것은 아니지만, 그것은 수업 시작부터 바로 교실 분위기에 상당한 변화를 가져올 수 있다.

정답이 보이는 해설

교사가 학생에게 보내는 비언어적 메시지에 주목하는 것이 학생과의 관계에 변화를 가져올 수 있다고 설명하면서 그 예로 학생들에게 짓는 미소가 학생들에게 격려와 힘을 줄 수 있다고 했으므로, 필자가 주장하는 바로 가장 적절한 것은 ③이다.

필수 어휘

estimate 추정하다   nonverbal 비언어적인   make a difference 변화를 가져오다
significant 상당한   initial 처음의   empowering 힘을 주는   climate 분위기

09 정답 ③
202109 20번 정답률 84%

As you set about to write, it is worth reminding yourself that
        (~에 착수하다)   (be worth v-ing: ~할 가치가 있다)
while you ought to have a point of view, 단서1 you should avoid
                                          (독자에게 생각할 것을 알)
telling your readers what to think. 단서2 Try to hang a question mark
(려 주지 말아야 함)   (글의 관점에 대해 질문하도록 노력하라 함)
over it all. This way you allow your readers to think for themselves
      (= point of view)
about the points and arguments you're making. ★ As a result, / they
                                                            (= readers)
will feel more involved, / **finding** themselves just as committed /
                            (분사구문(동시 상황))
to *the arguments* [you've made] and *the insights* [you've exposed]
              (목적격 관계대명사 생략)   (목적격 관계대명사 생략)
// as you are. You will have written an essay that not only avoids
                                              (not only A but (also) B: A뿐만 아니라 B도)
passivity in the reader, but is interesting and gets people to think.

해석

글쓰기를 시작할 때, 당신이 관점을 가져야 하는 한편, 독자들에게 무엇을 생각할지 알려 주는 것을 피해야 한다는 것을 자신에게 상기시키는 것은 가치가 있다. 그것(관점) 전체에 물음표를 달려고 노력하라. 이러한 방식으로 당신은 당신이 펼치는 요점

과 주장에 대해 독자들이 스스로 생각하게 만든다. 결과적으로 그들(독자들)은 당신만큼이나 당신이 펼친 주장과 당신이 드러낸 통찰에 열성적인 자신을 발견하면서 더 몰두한 것처럼 느낄 것이다. 당신은 독자의 수동성을 피하는 것뿐만 아니라 재미있고 사람들을 생각하게 하는 글을 쓰게 될 것이다.

글을 쓸 때 고려해야 할 것으로 독자들에게 생각할 것을 알려 주지 말아야 하고, 글의 관점에 대해 물음표가 달리도록 노력하면 독자들은 글의 주장과 관점에 대해 스스로 생각하고, 글에 몰입하게 된다는 내용이다. 따라서 필자의 주장으로 가장 적절한 것은 ③이다.

필수 어휘
remind 상기시키다 a point of view 관점 argument 주장
involved 몰입한, 몰두한 committed 열성적인, 헌신적인
insight 통찰, 간파 expose 드러내다, 노출하다 passivity 수동성, 소극성

10 정답 ①

★ Sometimes, you feel *the need* (to avoid *something* [that will lead to success / out of discomfort]). Maybe you are avoiding extra work because you are tired. You are actively shutting out success because you want to avoid being uncomfortable. Therefore, overcoming your instinct to avoid uncomfortable things at first is essential. 단서1 Try doing new things outside of your comfort zone. 단서2 Change is always uncomfortable, but it is key to doing things differently in order to find that magical formula for success.

해석
때때로, 당신은 불편하기 때문에 성공으로 이끌어 줄 어떤 것을 피할 필요가 있다고 느낀다. 당신은 피곤하기 때문에 추가적인 일을 피하고 있는지도 모른다. 불편한 상태를 피하고 싶어서 당신은 적극적으로 성공을 차단하고 있다. 따라서 처음에는 불편한 것을 피하려는 당신의 본능을 극복하는 것이 필수적이다. 당신에게 편안함을 주는 곳을 벗어나서 새로운 일을 시도하라. 변화는 항상 불편하지만, 성공을 위한 마법의 공식을 찾기 위해 일을 색다르게 하려면 그것이 핵심이다.

정답이 보이는 해설
사람들이 불편함 때문에 성공으로 이끌 일을 피하며, 불편함을 피하려는 본능을 이겨내고 안락함을 벗어나 새로운 일을 시도하라고 서술하는 내용의 글이다. 마지막 문장에서 변화는 불편한 것이지만 성공을 위한 핵심이라고 다시금 강조하고 있으므로, 필자의 주장으로 가장 적절한 것은 ①이다.

필수 어휘
avoid 피하다 discomfort 불편(함) extra 추가의 shut out 차단하다
instinct 본능 essential 필수적인 comfort 안락, 편안 formula 공식, 방식

11 정답 ③

At a publishing house and at a newspaper you learn the following: *It's not a mistake if it doesn't end up in print.* It's the same for email. Nothing bad can happen if you haven't hit the Send key. ★ [**What** you've written] / can have misspellings, errors of fact, rude comments, obvious lies, / but it doesn't matter. If you haven't sent it, you still have time to fix it. You can correct any mistake and nobody will ever know the difference. This is easier said than done, of course. Send is your computer's most attractive command.

단서 But before you hit the Send key, make sure that you read your document carefully one last time.

해석
출판사와 신문사에서 당신은 다음과 같은 내용을 배운다. '결국 인쇄물로 나오지 않는다면 그것은 실수가 아니다.' 이메일에서도 마찬가지이다. '보내기' 키를 누르지 않았다면 어떤 나쁜 일도 일어날 수 없다. 당신이 작성한 내용에 틀린 철자, 사실의 오류, 무례한 지적, 명백한 거짓말이 있을 수 있지만 그것은 중요하지 않다. 당신이 그것을 보내지 않았다면, 아직 그것을 고칠 시간이 있다. 당신은 어떤 실수라도 수정할 수 있고 누구도 그 차이를 알지 못할 것이다. 물론 이것은 말이 행동보다 더 쉽다. '보내기'는 컴퓨터에서 가장 매력적인 명령어이다. 하지만 당신이 '보내기' 키를 누르기 전에 반드시 마지막으로 한 번 문서를 주의 깊게 읽도록 하라.

정답이 보이는 해설
마지막 문장에 필자의 주장이 담겨 있다. 이메일에는 오류 등의 문제가 있을 수 있기 때문에 발송하기 전에 마지막으로 작성한 글을 다시 읽으면서 주의 깊게 확인해 보라고 강조하고 있으므로, 필자의 주장으로 가장 적절한 것은 ③이다.

필수 어휘
publishing house 출판사 end up 결국 ~이 되다 misspelling 틀린 철자
comment 지적, 비판 obvious 명백한 matter 중요하다, 문제되다
attractive 매력적인 command 명령 document 문서, 서류

12 정답 ②

★ When I was in high school, // we had *students* [who could study in the coffee shop / and not get distracted / by the noise or *everything* (happening around them)]. We also had students who could not study if the library was not super quiet. The latter students suffered because even in the library, it was impossible to get the type of complete silence they sought. These students were victims of distractions who found it very difficult to study anywhere except in their private bedrooms. In today's world, it is impossible to run away from distractions. 단서 Distractions are everywhere, but if you want to achieve your goals, you must learn how to tackle distractions. You cannot eliminate distractions, but you can learn to live with them in a way that ensures they do not limit you.

해석
내가 고등학생이었을 때, 커피숍에서 공부하면서 주변의 소음이나 일어나는 모든 일에 방해받지 않을 수 있는 학생들이 있었다. 도서관이 아주 조용하지 않으면 공부를 할 수 없는 학생들도 있었다. 후자의 학생들은 도서관에서도 자신들이 원하는 완전한 고요함을 얻을 수 없었기 때문에 힘들어했다. 이 학생들은 개인 침실을 제외하고 어디에서도 공부하기가 어렵다는 것을 알게 된, 집중에 방해가 되는 것들의 피해자였다. 오늘날의 세상에서는 집중에 방해가 되는 것들에서 벗어나는 것이 불가능하다. 집중에 방해가 되는 것들은 어디에나 있지만, 목표를 달성하려면 집중에 방해되는 것들과 맞붙는 법을 배워야 한다. 집중에 방해되는 것들을 제거할 수 없지만, 그것들이 당신을 제한하지 않도록 보장하는 방식으로 함께 살아가기를 배울 수 있다.

정답이 보이는 해설
어디서든 집중할 수 없는 학생들에 대한 문제점과 해결책을 제시하며, 집중을 방해하는 것들은 어디에나 있기 때문에 목표를 이루려면 방해 요인에 대처하는 법을 배워야 한다고 강조하고 있으므로, 필자의 주장으로 가장 적절한 것은 ②이다.

필수 어휘
distracted (정신이) 산만해진 seek 찾다, 얻다(-sought-sought)
distraction 집중에 방해가 되는 것 tackle 맞붙다, 대결하다 ensure 보장하다

4강 2020~2023 밑줄 함의 추론

01 정답 ⑤

Most people have no doubt heard this question: If a tree falls in the forest and there is no one there to hear it fall, does it make a sound? The correct answer is no. 단서1 Sound is more than pressure waves, and indeed there can be no sound without a hearer. 단서2 And similarly, scientific communication is a two-way process. 주제문 ✪ Just as a signal of any kind is useless / [unless it is perceived], / a published scientific paper (signal) is useless / [unless it is both received *and* understood (by its intended audience)]. Thus we can restate the axiom of science as follows: A scientific experiment is not complete until the results have been published *and understood.* 단서3 Publication is no more than pressure waves unless the published paper is understood. Too many scientific papers **fall silently in the woods**.

해석

대부분의 사람은 틀림없이 이 질문을 들어 봤을 것이다. 만약 숲에서 나무가 쓰러지고 그것이 쓰러지는 것을 들을 사람이 거기에 없다면, 소리가 나는 것일까? 정답은 '아니요'이다. 소리는 압력파 이상이며, 정말로 듣는 사람이 없다면 소리는 있을 수 없다. 마찬가지로, 과학적 커뮤니케이션은 양방향 프로세스이다. 어떠한 종류의 신호든 그것이 감지되지 않으면 쓸모없듯이, 출판된 과학 논문(신호)은 그것이 의도된 독자에 의해 수신되고, '그리고' 이해되지 않으면 쓸모가 없다. 그러므로 우리는 과학의 자명한 이치를 다음과 같이 재진술할 수 있다. 과학 실험은 결과가 출판되고 '그리고 이해될' 때까지 완성되지 않는다. 출판된 논문이 이해되지 않으면 출판은 압력파에 지나지 않는다. 너무 많은 과학 논문이 **숲에서 소리 없이 쓰러진다.**

정답이 보이는 해설

듣는 사람이 없다면 소리가 있을 수 없듯이, 과학 논문도 의도된 독자에 의해 수신되고 이해되어야 쓸모 있다는 내용의 글이다. 숲에서 나무가 쓰러져도 쓰러지는 소리를 듣는 사람이 없다면 소리가 없는 셈인 것처럼, 과학적 커뮤니케이션은 양방향 프로세스이기 때문에 과학 실험은 결과가 출판되고 이해될 때야 완성된다고 했으므로 이해되지 않은 과학 논문은 듣는 사람 없이 숲에서 쓰러지는 나무와 비슷하다고 볼 수 있다. 따라서 밑줄 친 부분이 의미하는 바로 가장 적절한 것은 ⑤ '출판되지만 독자들이 그것들을 이해하지 못한다'이다.

선택지 완벽 분석

① fail to include the previous study 이전 연구에 포함되지 못한다

② end up being considered completely false 결국 완전한 실패로 여겨지는 결과를 얻는다

③ become useless because they are not published 출판되지 않기 때문에 쓸모없어진다
출판되지 않기 때문에 쓸모없는 것이 아니라, 출판되어도 독자들이 이해하지 못하면 쓸모없다는 내용이므로 ③을 답으로 고르면 안 된다.

④ focus on communication to meet public demands 대중의 요구에 부응하기 위해 커뮤니케이션에 집중한다

⑤ are published yet readers don't understand them 출판되지만 독자들이 그것들을 이해하지 못한다

필수 어휘

no doubt 틀림없이 (~일 것이다)   pressure waves 압력파
similarly 비슷하게, 마찬가지로   perceive 감지하다, 인지하다
understand 이해하다(-understood-understood)   intended 의도된, 계획된
audience 청중, 관객   restate 재진술하다, 다시 이야기하다   complete 완성된

02 정답 ①

Why do you care how a customer reacts to a purchase? Good question. By understanding post-purchase behavior, you can understand the influence and the likelihood of whether a buyer will repurchase the product (and whether she will keep it or return it). You'll also determine whether 단서1 the buyer will encourage others to purchase the product from you. 주제문 Satisfied customers can **become unpaid ambassadors** for your business, so customer satisfaction should be on the top of your to-do list. People tend to believe the opinions of people they know. 단서2 People trust friends over advertisements any day. ✪ They know / [that advertisements are paid to tell the "good side"] / and [that they're used to persuade them to purchase products and services]. By continually monitoring your customer's satisfaction after the sale, you have the ability to avoid negative word-of-mouth advertising.

해석

고객이 구매품에 어떻게 반응하는지에 대해 왜 신경 쓰는가? 좋은 질문이다. 구매 후 행동을 이해함으로써, 그 영향력과 구매자가 제품을 재구매할지(그리고 그녀가 제품을 가질지 또는 반품할지)의 가능성을 이해할 수 있다. 당신은 구매자가 다른 사람들에게 당신으로부터 제품을 구매하도록 권장할지의 여부도 또한 알아낼 것이다. 만족한 고객은 당신의 사업을 위한 **보수를 받지 않는 대사가 될** 수 있으므로, 고객 만족이 할 일 목록의 최상단에 있어야 한다. 사람들은 그들이 아는 사람들의 의견을 믿는 경향이 있다. 사람들은 언제든 광고보다 친구를 신뢰한다. 그들은 광고에는 "좋은 면"을 말하기 위해 돈이 쓰이고 그리고 그것들이 제품과 서비스를 구매하도록 그들을 설득하는 데 사용된다는 것을 알고 있다. 판매 후 고객의 만족을 지속적으로 모니터함으로써, 당신은 부정적인 입소문 광고를 피할 수 있는 능력을 가진다.

정답이 보이는 해설

구매 권장에 있어 광고보다 친구의 의견이 더 효과적이기에 구매 후 고객이 만족하도록 꾸준히 모니터해야 한다는 내용의 글이다. 구매 후 행동을 이해함으로써, 구매자가 다른 사람들에게 당신으로부터 제품을 구매하도록 권장할지 여부에 대해 언급된 후, 만족한 고객이 당신의 사업을 위한 '보수를 받지 않는 대사가 될' 수 있다는 것은 '보상을 받지 않고도 다른 이들에게 제품을 구매하도록 권장할 수 있다는 것을 의미한다고 볼 수 있다. 따라서 밑줄 친 부분이 의미하는 바로 가장 적절한 것은 ① '보상을 받지 않고도 다른 이들에게 제품을 구매하도록 권장할'이다.

선택지 완벽 분석

① recommend products to others for no gain 보상을 받지 않고도 다른 이들에게 제품을 구매하도록 권장할

② offer manufacturers feedback on products 제조업체에 제품에 대한 피드백을 제공할
함정 판매 후 고객의 만족을 지속적으로 모니터해서, 그 사람이 재구매할지, 다른 사람에게도 권할지 등을 알아낼 수 있다는 부분에서, 업체에 피드백을 제공할 대사라고 잘못 오해하지 않아야 한다.

③ become people who don't trust others' words 남의 말을 믿지 않는 사람이 될

④ get rewards for advertising products overseas 해외에 상품을 광고한 것에 대한 보상을 받을

⑤ buy products without worrying about the price 가격에 대해 걱정하지 않고 제품을 구매할

필수 어휘

post-purchase 구매 후   influence 영향력   likelihood 가능성
repurchase 재구매하다   determine 알아내다, 밝히다
encourage 장려하다, 권장하다   satisfied 만족한   unpaid 무급의, 무보수의

4강 밑줄 함의 추론

ambassador 대사 to-do list 할 일 목록 continually 계속해서 avoid 피하다
negative 부정적인 word-of-mouth 구두의, 입소문의

03 정답 ⑤

202303 21번 정답률 57%

주제문 If we adopt technology, we need to pay its costs. Thousands
of traditional livelihoods have been pushed aside by progress, and
the lifestyles around those jobs removed. Hundreds of millions of
humans today work at jobs they hate, producing things they have no
love for. 단서1 Sometimes these jobs cause physical pain, disability,
or chronic disease. 단서2 Technology creates many new jobs that are
certainly dangerous. ✪ (At the same time,) // mass education and
media / train / humans / to avoid low-tech physical work, / to seek
jobs (working in the digital world). **The divorce of the hands from
the head** puts a stress on the human mind. Indeed, the sedentary
nature of the best-paying jobs is a health risk — for body and mind.

해석

만약 우리가 기술을 받아들이면, 우리는 그것의 비용을 치러야 한다. 수천 가지의 전
통적인 생계 수단이 발전에 의해 밀려났으며, 그 직업과 관련된 생활 방식이 없어졌
다. 오늘날 수억 명의 사람들이 자기가 싫어하는 일자리에서 일하면서, 자신이 아무
런 애정을 느끼지 못하는 것들을 생산한다. 때때로 이러한 일자리는 육체적 고통, 장
애 또는 만성 질환을 유발한다. 기술은 확실히 위험한 많은 새로운 일자리를 창출한
다. 동시에, 대중 교육과 대중 매체는 낮은 기술의 육체노동을 피하고 디지털 세계에
서 일하는 직업을 찾도록 인간을 훈련시킨다. **머리로부터 손이 단절되는 것**은 인간
의 정신에 부담을 준다. 실제로, 가장 보수가 좋은 직업의 주로 앉아서 하는 특성은
신체와 정신에 건강 위험 요소이다.

정답이 보이는 해설

기술의 발전을 받아들이면, 그것에 대한 대가를 치러야 한다는 내용의 글이다. 기술
의 발전은 새로운 일자리를 창출하는 동시에 육체노동을 피하고 디지털과 관련된 일
을 하도록 훈련시킨다는 내용에 이어지고 있으므로, '머리로부터 손이 단절되는 것'
은 육체노동보다 기술을 강조하는 일을 가리킨다는 것을 알 수 있다. 따라서 밑줄 친
부분이 의미하는 바로 가장 적절한 것은 ⑤ '직장에서의 첨단 기술의 사용 증가'이다.

선택지 완벽 분석

① ignorance of modern technology 현대 기술에 대한 무지

② endless competition in the labor market 노동 시장에서의 끝없는
경쟁

③ not getting along well with our coworkers 동료들과 사이가 좋지
않음

④ working without any realistic goals for our career 우리 경력에 대
한 현실적인 목표 없이 일하는 것
> 함정 많은 사람들이 자기가 싫어하는 일자리에서 일하면서, 아무런 애정을 느끼지 못하는 것들을
생산한다는 내용이 있기는 하지만, 이것이 현실적인 목표 없이 일한다는 것으로 이어지지는
않는다는 데에 유의해야 한다.

⑤ our increasing use of high technology in the workplace 직장에
서의 첨단 기술의 사용 증가

필수 어휘

adopt 받아들이다, 채택하다 livelihood 생계 수단 progress 발전, 전진
remove 없애다 produce 생산하다, 제작하다 physical 육체적, 신체의
pain 고통, 통증 disability 장애 disease 질환, 질병 mass 대중(의)
education 교육 train 훈련시키다 avoid 피하다 seek 찾다, 구하다
divorce 단절, 이혼 stress 부담, 긴장 indeed 실제로, 참으로 risk 위험 (요소)

04 정답 ③

202211 21번 정답률 54%

Our language helps to reveal our deeper assumptions. Think of
these revealing phrases: 단서1 When we accomplish something
important, we say it took "blood, sweat, and tears." We say
important achievements are "hard-earned." We recommend a "hard
day's work" when "day's work" would be enough. 단서2 When
we talk of "easy money," we are implying it was obtained through
illegal or questionable means. We use the phrase "That's easy for
you to say" as a criticism, usually when we are seeking to invalidate
someone's opinion. 단서3 It's like we all automatically accept that
the "right" way is, inevitably, the harder one. In my experience this
is hardly ever questioned. What would happen if you do **challenge
this sacred cow**? ✪ We don't even pause (to consider [that
something (important and valuable) could be made easy]). 주제문
What if the biggest thing keeping us from doing what matters is the
false assumption that it has to take huge effort?

해석

우리의 언어는 우리의 더 깊은 전제를 드러내는 것을 돕는다. 이것을 잘 드러내는 다
음과 같은 어구들을 생각해 보라. 우리가 중요한 무언가를 성취할 때, 우리는 그것이
"피, 땀, 그리고 눈물"을 필요로 했다고 말한다. 우리는 중요한 성과는 "힘들게 얻은"
것이라고 말한다. 우리는 "하루 동안의 일"이라는 말로도 충분할 때 "힘든 하루 동안
의 일"이라는 말을 권한다. 우리가 "쉬운 돈"이라고 말할 때, 우리는 그것이 불법적이
거나 의심스러운 수단을 통해 얻어진 것이라는 점을 넌지시 드러내고 있다. 우리는
보통 누군가의 의견이 틀렸음을 입증하고자 할 때, 우리는 "말은 쉽지"라는 문구를
비판으로 사용한다. 이는 마치 우리 모두가 "올바른" 방법은 반드시 더 어려운 방법
이라는 것을 자동적으로 받아들이는 것과 같다. 나의 경험상, 이것은 거의 의문시되
지 않는다. 만약 여러분이 정말로 이 신성한 소에 도전한다면 무슨 일이 일어나겠는
가? 우리는 중요하고 가치 있는 무언가가 쉽게 만들어질 수 있다고 생각해 보기 위
해 잠시 멈추지도 않는다. 만약 우리가 중요한 일을 하지 못하게 하는 가장 큰 것이
그것이 엄청난 노력을 필요로 한다는 잘못된 전제라면 어떨까?

정답이 보이는 해설

우리는 '중요하고 올바른 일'은 곧 어렵고 힘든 일이며, '쉬운 일'은 불법적이고 의심
스러운 방법으로 이루어진 일이라고 자동적으로 받아들이지만, 힘든 일만이 가치가
있다는 확실한 믿음을 의심해 봐야 한다고 주장하는 글이다. 따라서 밑줄 친 부분이
의미하는 바로 가장 적절한 것은 ③ '어려운 일만이 가치가 있다는 견고한 믿음을 의
심한다'이다.
참고로, sacred cow란 '지나치게 신성시되어 비판이나 의심이 허용되지 않는 관습
이나 제도'를 일컫는다.

선택지 완벽 분석

① resist the tendency to avoid any hardship 어떤 역경이라도 피하려
는 경향을 거부한다
> 함정 힘든 일을 피하는 경향을 거부한다는 내용이 아니라, 힘든 일만이 가치가 있을 거라는 믿음
을 의심해 봐야 한다는 내용이므로 답이 될 수 없다.

② escape from the pressure of using formal language 격식 언어를
사용하려는 압박으로부터 도망간다

③ doubt the solid belief that only hard work is worthy 어려운 일만
이 가치가 있다는 견고한 믿음을 의심한다

④ abandon the old notion that money always comes first 돈이 항
상 최우선이라는 오래된 개념을 버린다

⑤ break the superstition that holy animals bring good luck 신성한
동물이 행운을 가져온다는 미신을 타파한다
> 밑줄 친 scared cow를 '신성한 소'라고 함축적 의미를 무시하고 직역하여 정답을 유추하면 안 된다.

필수 어휘

reveal 드러내다   assumption 전제, 추정, 상정   phrase 구절, 관용구
accomplish 성취하다   tear 눈물   achievement 업적, 성취한 것
earn 얻다   imply 넌지시 나타내다   obtain 얻다   means 수단, 방법
criticism 비판, 비난   inevitably 필연적으로, 반드시   challenge 이의를 제기하다
sacred 신성시되는   pause (잠시) 멈추다   valuable 소중한, 귀중한
effort 노력, 수고

warranty (품질·안정성 등의) 보증(서)   undamaged 멀쩡한, 완전한
abuse 남용하다   entrepreneur 기업가   own 소유하다
e-commerce 전자 상거래   fire 해고하다   resolve 해결하다   complaint 불만
dissatisfy 불만을 느끼게 하다   reason 비결, 이유, 동기

---

05 정답 ③

Is the customer *always* right? When customers return a broken product to a famous company, which makes kitchen and bathroom fixtures, the company nearly always offers a replacement to maintain good customer relations. Still, "there are times you've got to say 'no,'" explains the warranty expert of the company, such as when a product is undamaged or has been abused. Entrepreneur Lauren Thorp, who owns an e-commerce company, says, "While the customer is 'always' right, sometimes you just have to **fire a customer**." ❁ **When** Thorp **has tried** everything to resolve a complaint / and **realizes** [that 단서 the customer will be dissatisfied no matter what], // she returns her attention to *the rest of her customers*, [**who** {she says} are "the reason for my success."]

해석

고객은 '항상' 옳은가? 고객들이 주방과 욕실 설비를 만드는 한 유명한 회사에 고장 난 제품을 반품할 때, 그 회사는 좋은 고객 관계를 유지하기 위해 거의 항상 대체품을 제공한다. 그럼에도, 그 회사의 상품 보증 전문가는 상품이 멀쩡하거나 남용되었을 때와 같이, "'안 돼요.'라고 말을 해야 할 때가 있습니다."라고 설명한다. 전자 상거래 회사를 소유한 기업가 Lauren Thorp는 "고객이 '항상' 옳지만, 때로는 당신이 **고객을 해고해야만 합니다**."라고 말한다. Thorp는 모든 수단을 동원해서 불만을 해결했지만 그 고객이 어떠한 경우에도 만족하지 않을 것이라는 사실을 깨달을 때, 그녀는 자신의 주의를 나머지 다른 고객들에게로 돌리는데, 그들이 '내 성공의 비결'이라고 그녀는 말한다.

정답이 보이는 해설

회사는 고객이 항상 옳다고 생각하고 고객의 불만을 해결하기 위해 최선을 다하지만 그럼에도 고객들의 무리한 요구 때문에 해결될 수 없는 경우가 생기며, 이럴 때는 나머지 다른 고객들에게로 주의를 돌리는 게 낫다는 내용의 글이다. 따라서 밑줄 친 부분이 의미하는 바로 가장 적절한 것은 ③ '고객의 무리한 요구를 거절하다'이다.

🔍 선택지 완벽 분석

① deal with a customer's emergency 고객의 비상 사태를 처리하다
  [함정] 고객의 불만을 해결해 주는 것을 그만두어야 한다는 본문의 의미와 상반되는 내용이므로 답이 될 수 없다.

② delete a customer's purchasing record 고객의 구매 기록을 삭제하다

③ reject a customer's unreasonable demand 고객의 무리한 요구를 거절하다

④ uncover the hidden intention of a customer 고객의 숨은 의도를 밝히다

⑤ rely on the power of an influential customer 영향력 있는 고객의 힘에 의지하다
  [함정] 무리한 요구를 계속하는 고객을 대신할 고객으로 나머지 다른 고객이라고만 언급했지 구체적으로 영향력 있는 고객을 언급하지는 않았으므로 답이 될 수 없다.

필수 어휘

customer 고객   return 반품하다, 돌리다   broken 고장 난   fixture 설비(물)
replacement 대체품   maintain 유지하다   relation 관계

---

06 정답 ③

A psychology professor raised a glass of water while teaching stress management principles to her students, and asked them, "How heavy is this glass of water I'm holding?" Students shouted out various answers. The professor replied, "The absolute weight of this glass doesn't matter. It depends on how long I hold it. If I hold it for a minute, it's quite light. ❁ But, **if** I hold it for a day straight, / it will cause severe pain in my arm, / [forcing me to drop the glass to the floor]. In each case, the weight of the glass is the same, but 단서1 the longer I hold it, the heavier it feels to me." As the class nodded their heads in agreement, she continued, 단서2 "Your stresses in life are like this glass of water. If you still feel the weight of yesterday's stress, it's a strong sign that it's time to **put the glass down**."

해석

한 심리학 교수가 학생들에게 스트레스 관리 원칙을 가르치는 동안 물이 든 유리잔(물 잔)을 들어 올리고 "제가 들고 있는 이 물 잔은 얼마나 무거울까요?"라고 물었다. 학생들은 다양한 대답을 외쳤다. 그 교수는 "이 잔의 절대적인 무게는 중요하지 않습니다. 그것은 제가 이것을 얼마나 오래 들고 있느냐에 달려 있죠. 만약 제가 이것을 1분 동안 들고 있다면, 꽤 가볍습니다. 하지만 만약 제가 이것을 하루 종일 들고 있다면 이것은 제 팔에 심각한 고통을 일으키고 제가 잔을 바닥에 떨어뜨리게 할 것입니다. 각 경우에 잔의 무게는 같지만, 제가 오래 들고 있을수록 그것은 저에게 더 무겁게 느껴집니다."라고 답했다. 학생들은 동의하며 고개를 끄덕였고, 교수는 "여러분이 삶에서 느끼는 스트레스도 이 물 잔과 같습니다. 만약 여러분이 여전히 어제 받은 스트레스의 무게를 느낀다면, 그것은 **잔을 내려놓을** 때라는 강한 신호입니다."라고 이어서 말했다.

정답이 보이는 해설

한 심리학 교수가 삶에서 느끼는 스트레스를 물 잔의 예를 통해 설명하는 내용으로, 우리가 스트레스를 계속 가지고 있을수록 그것은 더 무겁게 느껴지므로 스트레스의 무게를 계속 느낀다면 그것을 내려놓을 때라고 말하고 있다. 따라서 밑줄 친 부분이 의미하는 바로 가장 적절한 것은 ③ '마음에 있는 스트레스를 내보낼'이다.

🔍 선택지 완벽 분석

① pour more water into the glass 잔에 물을 더 많이 부을

② set a plan not to make mistakes 실수를 하지 않기 위해 계획을 세울

③ let go of the stress in your mind 마음에 있는 스트레스를 내보낼

④ think about the cause of your stress 스트레스의 원인에 대해 생각할

⑤ learn to accept the opinions of others 다른 사람들의 의견을 받아들이는 것을 배울

필수 어휘

psychology 심리학   raise 들어 올리다   management 관리   principle 원칙
absolute 절대적인   matter 중요하다   severe 심각한   agreement 동의
sign 신호

07 정답 ⑤

202203 21번 정답률 62%

A job search is not a passive task. When you are searching, you are not browsing, nor are you "just looking". ☻ Browsing is not *an effective way* (to reach *a goal* [you claim to want to reach]). If you are acting with purpose, if you are serious about anything you chose to do, then you need to be direct, focused and whenever possible, clever. 단서1 Everyone else searching for a job has the same goal, competing for the same jobs. You must do more than the rest of the herd. Regardless of how long it may take you to find and get the job you want, 단서2 being proactive will logically get you results faster than if you rely only on browsing online job boards and emailing an occasional resume. **Leave those activities to the rest of the sheep**.

해석

구직 활동은 수동적인 일이 아니다. 일자리를 찾고 있을 때, 여러분은 대강 훑어보는 것이 아니며 '그냥 구경만 하고' 있는 것도 아니다. 대강 훑어보는 것은 여러분이 도달하기를 원한다고 주장하는 목표에 도달할 수 있는 효과적인 방법이 아니다. 만약 여러분이 목적을 가지고 행동하고 있다면, 만약 하고자 선택한 어떤 것에 대해 여러분이 진지하다면, 여러분은 직접적이고 집중해야 하며 가능한 한 영리해야 한다. 일자리를 찾는 다른 모든 사람이 같은 목표를 지니고 있고, 같은 일자리를 얻기 위해 경쟁한다. 여러분은 그 무리의 나머지 사람들보다 더 많은 것을 해야 한다. 원하는 직업을 찾아서 얻는 데에 시간이 얼마나 오래 걸리는지에 상관없이, 온라인 취업 게시판을 대충 훑어보고 가끔 이력서를 이메일로 보내는 것에만 의존하는 것보다는 더 능동적으로 행동하는 것이 논리적으로 여러분에게 더 빨리 결과를 가져다줄 것이다. **그런 활동들은 나머지 양들이 하도록 남겨 두라**.

정답이 보이는 해설

구직 활동에서 더욱 빠른 결과를 얻기 위해서는 같은 목표를 지닌 다른 사람들보다 더 능동적이고 적극적으로 임해야 한다는 내용의 글이다. 밑줄 친 부분은 취업 게시판을 검색하고 가끔 이력서를 이메일로 보내는 것과 같은 활동은 나머지 다른 사람들이 하도록 남겨 두라는 것으로, 즉 다른 구직자들보다 두드러지려면 더 적극적으로 행동해야 한다는 의미로 볼 수 있다. 따라서 밑줄 친 부분이 의미하는 바로 가장 적절한 것은 ⑤ '다른 구직자들로부터 돋보이기 위해 더 적극적이 되어라.'이다.

선택지 완벽 분석

① Try to understand other job-seekers' feelings. 다른 구직자들의 감정을 이해하려고 노력하라.

② Keep calm and stick to your present position. 침착함을 유지하고 여러분의 현재 위치를 고수하라.

③ Don't be scared of the job-seeking competition. 구직 경쟁을 두려워하지 마라.
함정 구직 경쟁에서 더 적극적으로 행동하라는 내용의 글로, 구직 경쟁을 두려워하지 말라는 내용은 언급되지 않았다.

④ Send occasional emails to your future employers. 여러분의 미래 고용주들에게 이따금씩 이메일을 보내라.

⑤ Be more active to stand out from other job-seekers. 다른 구직자들로부터 돋보이기 위해 더 적극적이 되어라.

필수 어휘

job search 구직 활동   passive 수동적인   browse 대강 훑어보다
effective 효과적인   claim 주장하다   purpose 목적   direct 직접적인
focused 집중하는   rest 나머지   herd 무리   proactive 상황을 앞서서 주도하는
logically 논리적으로   occasional 가끔의   resume 이력서
sheep 양, 어리석은 사람

---

08 정답 ④

202111 21번 정답률 60%

blame A for B: B에 대해 A를 비난하다

☻ When it comes to climate change, / many blame the fossil fuel industry for pumping greenhouse gases, the agricultural sector for burning rainforests, **or** the fashion industry for producing excessive clothes. But wait, 단서1 what drives these industrial activities? Our consumption. 단서2 Climate change is a summed product of each person's behavior. For example, the fossil fuel industry is a popular scapegoat in the climate crisis. But why do they drill and burn fossil fuels? 단서3 We provide them strong financial incentives: some people regularly travel on airplanes and cars that burn fossil fuels. Some people waste electricity generated by burning fuel in power plants. Some people use and throw away plastic products derived from crude oil every day. Blaming the fossil fuel industry while engaging in these behaviors is **a slap in our own face**.

해석

기후 변화에 관해서라면 많은 사람들은 온실가스를 배출하는 것에 대해 화석 연료 산업을, 열대 우림을 태우는 것에 대해 농업 분야를, 또는 과도한 의복을 생산하는 것에 대해 패션 산업을 비난한다. 하지만 잠깐만, 무엇이 이러한 산업 활동들을 움직이게 하는가? 우리의 소비이다. 기후 변화는 각 개인의 행동이 합쳐진 산물이다. 예를 들어, 화석 연료 산업은 기후 위기에 있어서 일반적인 희생양이다. 하지만 왜 그들은 화석 연료를 시추하고 태우는가? 우리가 그들에게 강력한 금전적인 동기를 제공한다. 예를 들어, 어떤 사람들은 화석 연료를 태우는 비행기와 자동차를 타고 정기적으로 여행을 한다. 어떤 사람들은 발전소에서 연료를 태움으로써 생산된 전기를 낭비한다. 어떤 사람들은 원유에서 얻은 플라스틱 제품을 매일 사용하고 버린다. 이러한 행동에 관여하면서 화석 연료 산업을 비난하는 것은 **우리 자신의 얼굴 때리기**이다.

정답이 보이는 해설

우리는 기후 변화에 관해서 온실가스를 배출하는 산업들을 비난하지만 정작 우리의 소비가 이러한 산업에 금전적인 동기를 제공하며 우리 스스로가 화석 연료를 태움으로써 기후 변화가 발생하는 행동을 하고 있다고 했으므로, 이러한 행동에 관여하면서 화석 연료 산업을 비난하는 것은 기후 변화에 대한 우리의 책임을 인정하지 못하는 것으로 볼 수 있다. 따라서 밑줄 친 부분이 글에서 의미하는 바로 가장 적절한 것은 ④ '기후 변화에 대한 우리의 책임을 인정하지 못하는 것'이다.

선택지 완벽 분석

① giving the future generation room for change 미래 세대에게 변화를 위한 여지를 주는 것

② warning ourselves about the lack of natural resources 천연 자원의 부족에 대해 우리 자신에게 경고하는 것
함정 이 글은 기후 변화와 화석 연료에 관해 다루고 있으므로 천연 자원의 부족과는 거리가 멀다.

③ refusing to admit the benefits of fossil fuel production 화석 연료 생산의 이점을 인정하기를 거부하는 것

④ failing to recognize our responsibility for climate change 기후 변화에 대한 우리의 책임을 인정하지 못하는 것

⑤ starting to deal with environmental problems individually 환경 문제를 개별적으로 다루기 시작하는 것

필수 어휘

fossil fuel 화석 연료   agricultural 농업의   rainforest 열대 우림
excessive 과도한, 지나친   drive ~하게 만들다, 몰아가다   industrial 산업의
consumption 소비   sum 합계하다   drill (드릴로) 구멍을 뚫다, 시추하다
incentive 동기, 유인   crude oil 원유   slap (손바닥으로) 철썩 때리기

82 기출의 바이블 고1 영어 독해편

09 정답 ⑤

Nothing is trash by nature. Anthropologist Mary Douglas brings back and analyzes the common saying that dirt is "**matter out of place.**" 단서1 Dirt is relative, she emphasizes. "Shoes are not dirty in themselves, but it is dirty to place them on the dining-table; food is not dirty in itself, but it is dirty to leave pots and pans in the bedroom, or food all over clothing; similarly, bathroom items in the living room; clothing lying on chairs; outdoor things placed indoors; upstairs things downstairs, and so on." ✪ 단서2 (Sorting the dirty from the clean) / (— removing the shoes from the table, putting the dirty clothing in the washing machine —) / involves systematic ordering and classifying. Eliminating dirt is thus a positive process.

해석

본래부터 쓰레기인 것은 없다. 인류학자인 Mary Douglas는 더러움이 '**제자리에 있지 않은 상황**'이라는 흔한 말을 상기시키며 해석한다. 더러움은 상대적인 것이라고 그녀는 강조한다. "신발은 그 자체로 더럽지 않지만, 식탁 위에 그것들(신발)이 놓이면 더러운 것이다. 음식 자체는 더럽지 않지만, 침실에 냄비와 팬을 놓아두거나 음식이 옷에 다 묻는다면 더러운 것이다. 마찬가지로 거실에 있는 욕실 물품들, 의자 위에 놓인 옷, 실내에 놓인 실외 용품들, 아래층에 있는 위층 물건들, 기타 등등." 깨끗한 것에서 더러운 것을 분류하는 것, 즉 식탁에서 신발을 치우는 것, 세탁기에 더러운 옷을 넣는 것은 체계적인 순서와 분류를 포함한다. 그러므로 더러움을 제거하는 것은 긍정적인 과정이다.

정답이 보이는 해설

더러움의 상대성에 대한 글로, 더러움이 상황에 따른 상대적인 개념이고 깨끗함과 더러움을 분류하는 것은 정리하는 것을 포함한다. 이를 통해 더러움은 깨끗하지 못한 상태로, 정리와 분류가 되지 않은 것이다. 따라서 밑줄 친 부분의 의미로 가장 적절한 것은 ⑤ '정리되지 않은 어떤 것'이다.

🔍 선택지 완벽 분석

① something that is completely broken 완전히 부서진 어떤 것

② a tiny dust that nobody notices 아무도 알아차리지 못한 아주 작은 먼지

③ a dirty but renewable material 더럽지만 재생 가능한 물질
함정 더러움과 관련하여 재생 가능하다는 내용은 언급되지 않았다.

④ what can be easily replaced 쉽게 교체될 수 있는 것
더러움은 교체되는 대상이 아니고, 정리와 분류가 안 된 것이다.

⑤ a thing that is not in order 정리되지 않은 어떤 것

필수 어휘

by nature 본래부터 anthropologist 인류학자 analyze 해석하다, 분석하다
matter 상황, 문제 relative 상대적인 emphasize 강조하다 sort 분류하다
systematic 체계적인 classify 분류하다 eliminate 제거하다

---

a viewpoint]). Selective perception is based on what seems to us to stand out. 단서1 However, what seems to us to be standing out may very well be related to our goals, interests, expectations, past experiences, or current demands of the situation — "with a hammer in hand, everything looks like a nail." 단서2 This quote highlights the phenomenon of selective perception. If we **want to use a hammer**, then the world around us may begin to look as though it is full of nails!

해석

우리는 선택적으로 사건을 해석하는 경향이 있다. 만약 우리가 일이 '이런 방식' 또는 '저런 방식'이기를 원한다면, 우리는 가장 확실히 그러한 관점을 뒷받침하는 방식으로 증거를 선택하거나 쌓거나 배열할 수 있다. 선택적 지각은 우리에게 두드러져 보이는 것에 기반을 둔다. 그러나 우리에게 두드러져 보이고 있는 것은 우리의 목표, 관심사, 기대, 과거의 경험 또는 상황에 대한 현재의 요구와 매우 관련 있을지도 모른다. 즉, "망치를 손에 들고 있으면, 모든 것이 못처럼 보인다"와 같다. 이 인용문은 선택적 지각의 현상을 강조한다. 만약 우리가 **망치를 사용하기를 원한다**면, 그러면 우리 주변의 세상은 못으로 가득 찬 것처럼 보이기 시작할지도 모른다!

정답이 보이는 해설

우리는 사건을 선택적으로 해석하는 경향이 있고, 선택적인 지각이 우리에게 두드러져 보이는 것은 우리의 경험, 관심사, 기대 등과 관련이 있다는 내용의 글이다. 인용문의 '망치를 든다'는 것은 선택적 지각의 예시이고, 있는 그대로가 아닌 보고 싶은 대로 이해한다는 뜻이므로, 밑줄 친 부분의 의미로 적절한 것은 ③ '특정 방식으로 무언가를 하고자 하다'이다.

🔍 선택지 완벽 분석

① are unwilling to stand out 돋보이는 것을 꺼리다
망치 사용은 우리의 선택적 지각을 내보이는 것이므로 꺼린다고 할 수 없다.

② make our effort meaningless 우리의 노력을 헛되게 만들다

③ intend to do something in a certain way 특정 방식으로 무언가를 하고자 하다

④ hope others have a viewpoint similar to ours 다른 사람들이 우리와 비슷한 관점을 갖기를 바라다
선택적 지각은 다른 사람들의 관점이 아닌 자신만의 관점으로 사고하는 것이다.

⑤ have a way of thinking that is accepted by others 다른 사람들에게 받아들여지는 사고방식을 갖다
선택적 지각은 다른 사람들의 사고방식과 관련이 없다.

필수 어휘

tendency 경향 interpret 해석하다 selectively 선택적으로 stack 쌓다
viewpoint 관점 perception 지각, 인식 stand out 두드러지다, 눈에 띄다
expectation 기대, 예상 current 현재의 quote 인용(문) highlight 강조하다
phenomenon 현상

---

10 정답 ③

We have a tendency to interpret events selectively. ✪ If we want things to be "this way" or "that way" // we can most certainly select, stack, or arrange evidence / (in a way [that supports such

---

11 정답 ②

Get past the 'I wish I hadn't done that!' reaction. ✪ If the disappointment [you're feeling] is linked to an exam [you didn't pass because you didn't study for it], / or a job [you didn't get because you said silly things at the interview], / or a person [you didn't impress

/ because you took entirely the wrong approach], // **accept** [that it's happened now]. 단서1 The only value of 'I wish I hadn't done that!' is that you'll know better what to do next time. The learning pay-off is useful and significant. This 'if only I ...' agenda is virtual. Once you have worked that out, it's time to **translate it from the past tense to the future tense**: 단서2 'Next time I'm in this situation, I'm going to try to ...'.

해석
'내가 그것을 하지 않았으면 좋을 텐데!'라는 반응을 넘어가라. 만약 당신이 느끼는 실망이 당신이 그것을 위해 공부하지 않았기 때문에 통과하지 못한 시험, 또는 면접에서 어리석은 말을 했기 때문에 얻지 못한 일자리, 또는 당신이 완전히 잘못된 접근 방식을 취했기 때문에 인상을 남기지 못한 사람과 관련이 있다면, 지금 일이 '일어났다'는 것을 받아들이라. '내가 그것을 하지 않았으면 좋을 텐데'의 유일한 가치는 다음번에 무엇을 해야 할지 더 잘 알게 된다는 것이다. 학습 보상은 유용하고 중요하다. 이 '내가 …이면 좋을 텐데'라는 의제는 가상이다. 일단 당신이 그것을 해결했다면, **과거 시제에서 미래 시제로 옮길** 시기이다. '다음번에 내가 이 상황에 처한다면, 나는 …을 시도할 것이다.'

정답이 보이는 해설
이 글은 '내가 그것을 하지 않았으면 좋을 텐데!'라는 과거 사실에 반대되는 가정을 두고 일어난 일에 대한 후회가 아닌, 다음번에 무엇을 해야 할지 더 잘 알게 된다는 가치를 배우라는 내용이다. 또한 과거에 대해 후회하지 말고, 미래 상황으로 바꿔 생각하라고 서술하고 있으므로, 밑줄 친 부분의 의미로 가장 적절한 것은 ② '후회를 극복하고 다음번을 계획하다'이다.

선택지 완벽 분석
① look for a job linked to your interest 당신의 관심과 연결된 일자리를 찾다
② get over regrets and plan for next time 후회를 극복하고 다음번을 계획하다
③ surround yourself with supportive people 자신을 지지하는 사람들로 둘러싸다
④ study grammar and write clear sentences 문법을 공부하고 명료한 문장으로 글을 쓰다
'과거 시제'는 과거를 후회하는 가정 표현함, '미래 시제'는 앞으로의 계획을 의미한다.
⑤ examine your way of speaking and apologize 당신의 말하는 방식을 검토하고 사과하다

필수 어휘
reaction 반응 disappointment 실망 impress 인상을 남기다
entirely 전적으로 approach 접근법 pay-off 보상, 이득 significant 중요한
virtual 가상의, 허상의 work out ~을 해결하다

---

the Web) / [**whatever** they wanted to know / (about a company, its products, its competitors, its distribution systems, and, most of all, its truthfulness) // (when talking about its products and services)]. Just as important, 단서2 the Internet opened up a forum for customers to compare products, experiences, and values with other customers easily and quickly. Now the customer had a way to talk back to the marketer and to do so through public forums instantly.

해석
인터넷과 함께 모든 것이 변했다. 제품 문제, 과도한 약속, 고객 지원 부족, 가격 차등과 같이 고객이 마케팅 조직에서 실제로 경험한 모든 문제가 갑자기 **상자 밖으로 튀어나왔다**. 더 이상 통제된 의사소통이나 사업 시스템도 없었다. 제품과 서비스에 대해 이야기할 때 소비자들은 일반적으로 웹을 통해서 그들이 회사, 제품, 경쟁업체, 유통 시스템, 그리고 무엇보다도 회사의 진실성에 대해 알고 싶어 했던 것은 무엇이든지 배울 수 있었다. 그만큼 중요하게도 인터넷은 고객이 제품과 경험, 가치를 다른 고객들과 쉽고 빠르게 비교할 수 있는 토론의 장을 열었다. 이제 고객은 마케팅 담당자에게 다시 이야기하고 공개 포럼을 통해 즉시 그렇게 할 수 있는 방법을 갖게 되었다.

정답이 보이는 해설
인터넷 등장으로 모든 것이 변했고, 고객이 실제로 경험한 문제가 '상자 밖으로 튀어 나왔다'는 것인데, 더 이상 의사소통이 통제되지 않는다는 것과 인터넷으로 고객들이 제품에 대해 다른 고객들과 비교할 수 있는 토론이 가능해져 제품 문제가 외부로 드러났다는 것이다. 따라서 밑줄 친 부분의 의미로 가장 적절한 것은 ① '더 이상 비밀로 유지될 수 없었다'이다.

선택지 완벽 분석
① could not be kept secret anymore 더 이상 비밀로 유지될 수 없었다
② might disappear from public attention 대중의 관심에서 사라질지도 몰랐다
③ were no longer available to marketers 더 이상 마케팅 담당자들에게 이용 가능하지 않았다
함정 고객이 제기한 문제는 마케팅 담당자에게 전해진다는 언급은 있지만 마케팅 담당자가 이용할 수 없다는 내용은 없다.
④ became too complicated to understand 너무 복잡해져서 이해할 수 없었다
⑤ began to improve companies' reputations 회사의 평판을 향상시키기 시작했다
회사의 평판에 대한 언급은 없다.

필수 어휘
lack 부족 issue 문제 organization 조직 pop 튀어나오다
competitor 경쟁자 distribution 유통, 배분 truthfulness 진실성
forum 포럼, 토론회 instantly 즉시, 즉각

---

12 정답 ①
202011 21번 정답률 48%

With the Internet, everything changed. Product problems, overpromises, the lack of customer support, differential pricing — 단서1 all of the issues that customers actually experienced from a marketing organization suddenly **popped out of the box**. No longer were there any controlled communications or even business systems. ✪ Consumers could generally learn (through

5강 2020~2023 요지 추론

01 정답 ④

We all negotiate every day, whether we realise it or not. Yet few
people ever learn *how* to negotiate. ✪ Those [**who** do] / usually
<small>= learn how to negotiate</small>
<small>주격 관계대명사절</small>
learn the traditional, win-lose negotiating style / **rather than**
<small>↳ 비교, 대조되는 내용 ↰　　　～보다는, 대신에</small>
an approach / [**that** is likely to result in a win-win agreement].
<small>주격 관계대명사절　　(결과로) ～을 초래하다</small>
단서1 This old-school, adversarial approach may be useful in a
<small>적대적인 구식 방법은 일회성 협상에서 유용함</small>
one-off negotiation where you will probably not deal with that
<small>～와 거래하다</small>
person again. 단서2 However, such transactions are becoming
<small>동일한 사람을 반복적으로 상대하는 일이 많기 때문에 일회성 거래가</small>
increasingly rare, because most of us deal with the same people
<small>드물어짐</small>
repeatedly — our spouses and children, our friends and colleagues,
our customers and clients. 주제문 In view of this, it's essential to
<small>～의 관점에서</small>
achieve successful results for ourselves and maintain a healthy
relationship with our negotiating partners at the same time.
<small>동시에</small>
단서3 In today's interdependent world of business partnerships and
<small>상호 의존적인 오늘날 세계에서 모두에게 이익이 되는 성과가 중요함</small>
long-term relationships, a win-win outcome is fast becoming the
only acceptable result.

해석

우리가 그것을 인식하든 그렇지 않든 간에 우리 모두는 매일 협상한다. 하지만 이제까지 '어떻게' 협상하는지를 배운 사람은 거의 없다. (협상 방식을) 배우는 사람들은 대개 모두에게 이익이 되는 합의를 도출할 가능성이 있는 접근법보다는 전통적이며 한쪽에만 유리한 협상 방식을 배운다. 이 구식의 적대적인 접근법은 아마도 여러분이 그 사람을 다시 상대하지 않을 일회성 협상에서 유용할지도 모른다. 그러나, 우리 대부분은 배우자와 자녀, 친구와 동료, 고객과 의뢰인 같이 동일한 사람들을 반복적으로 상대하기 때문에, 이러한 거래는 더욱 더 드물어지고 있다. 이러한 관점에서, 우리 자신을 위해 성공적인 결과를 얻어내는 동시에 협상 파트너들과 건전한 관계를 유지하는 것이 중요하다. 오늘날 비즈니스 파트너십과 장기적 관계의 상호 의존적인 세계에서 모두에게 이익이 되는 성과는 급속히 '유일하게' 받아들일 수 있는 결과가 되어 가고 있다.

정답이 보이는 해설

예전의 적대적인 협상법은 한쪽에만 유리했기에 일회성 협상에서 유리했지만, 현실은 동일한 사람을 반복적으로 상대하는 일이 많기 때문에 과거의 협상법보다는 상대와 건전한 관계를 유지하는 동시에 모두에게 이익이 되는 협상법이 중요하다는 내용의 글이다. 따라서 글의 요지로 가장 적절한 것은 ④이다.

선택지 완벽 분석

② 의사소통 과정에서 서로의 의도를 확인하는 것이 바람직하다.

성공적인 협상을 위해 서로에게 이익이 되는 결과가 중요하다는 글이지만, 서로의 의도를 확인하자는 언급은 없으므로 유의해야 한다.

필수 어휘

negotiate 협상하다　realise 인식하다, 알고 있다　traditional 전통적인
approach 접근법　win-win 모두에게 이익이 되는　agreement 합의
old-school 옛 방식의, 구식의　one-off 일회성의　transaction 거래
increasingly 더욱 더　rare 드문, 희귀한　repeatedly 반복해서, 거듭
spouse 배우자　essential 필수적인　successful 성공적인
maintain 유지하다　relationship 관계　interdependent 상호 의존적인
outcome 결과　acceptable 받아들일 수 있는

02 정답 ③

✪ <u>The promise</u> (of a computerized society), (we were told,) /
<small>주어　　　　　　　　　　　　　　　　　　　　삽입절</small>
was [that it would pass to machines all of the repetitive drudgery of
<small>동사　was의 보어절　　　　　　　　목적어　　　↳ 목적격보어1</small>
work], // **allowing** us humans to pursue higher purposes and to have
<small>분사구문(= and it would allow ～)　　　　　　　목적격보어2</small>
more leisure time]. It didn't work out this way. Instead of more
<small>～ 대신에</small>
time, most of us have less. Companies large and small 단서1 have
<small>↳ off-load A onto B: A를 B에게 떠넘기다</small>
off-loaded work onto the backs of consumers. 주제문 Things that
<small>고객의 등에 일을 떠넘김</small>
used to be done for us, as part of the value-added service of working
<small>～하곤 했다</small>
with a company, we are now expected to do ourselves. With air
<small>be expected to: ～하도록 기대되다</small>
travel, 단서2 we're now expected to complete our own reservations
<small>예약이나 체크인을 직접 해야 함</small>
and check-in, jobs that used to be done by airline employees or
travel agents. At the grocery store, 단서3 we're expected to bag
<small>슈퍼마켓에서는 봉투에 물건을 담고</small>
our own groceries and, in some supermarkets, to scan our own
<small>계산도 직접 해야 함</small>
purchases.

해석

컴퓨터화된 사회의 약속은, 우리가 듣기로는, 그것이 모든 반복적인 고된 일을 기계에 넘겨, 우리 인간들이 더 높은 목적을 추구하고 더 많은 여가 시간을 가질 수 있게 해 준다는 것이었다. 그것은 이런 식으로 되지는 않았다. 더 많은 시간 대신에, 우리 대부분은 더 적은 시간을 가지고 있다. 크고 작은 회사들은 일을 소비자들의 등에 떠넘겼다. 회사에 맡겨 해결되던 부가 가치 서비스의 일환으로 우리를 위해 행해지던 것들이, 이제 우리 스스로가 하도록 기대된다. 항공 여행의 경우, 항공사 직원이나 여행사 직원들에 의해 행해지던 일이었던 우리의 예약과 체크인을 이제는 우리가 직접 완수하도록 기대된다. 식료품점에서는, 우리가 우리 자신의 식료품을 직접 봉지에 넣도록, 그리고 일부 슈퍼마켓에서는, 우리 자신이 구매한 물건을 스캔하도록 기대된다.

정답이 보이는 해설

모든 반복적인 고된 일을 기계에 넘겨 사람들이 더 많은 여가 시간을 가질 수 있게 될 것이라는 컴퓨터화된 사회에 대한 전망과 달리, 회사가 부가 가치 서비스의 일환으로 소비자들을 위해 하던 일들을 이제는 소비자들이 직접 행하도록 일이 떠넘겨졌다는 내용의 글이다. 따라서 글의 요지로 가장 적절한 것은 ③이다.

선택지 완벽 분석

⑤ 산업의 발전으로 인해 기계가 인간의 일자리를 대신하고 있다.

함정 컴퓨터화된 사회는 기계가 인간이 해야 할 일을 하게 되어 사람들이 더 많은 여가를 갖게 될 것이라는 전망과는 달리, 실제로는 그렇게 되지 않았다는 내용임에 유의해야 한다.

필수 어휘

repetitive 반복적인　pursue 추구하다　purpose 목적　leisure 여가
consumer 소비자　value-added 부가 가치의　complete 완료하다, 완수하다
reservation 예약　employee 직원　agent 대행사　bag 봉지[가방]에 넣다
purchase 구매

03 정답 ①

✪ When students are starting their college life, // they may
<small>시간의 부사절</small>
approach every course, test, or learning task (the same way), / using
<small>똑같은 방식으로　　　　분사구문</small>
[**what** we like to call "the rubber-stamp approach."] Think about it
<small>using의 목적어절</small>
this way: Would you wear a tuxedo to a baseball game? A colorful
dress to a funeral? A bathing suit to religious services? Probably
not. You know there's appropriate dress for different occasions and

settings. **단서1** Skillful learners know that "putting on the same clothes" won't work for every class. They are flexible learners.
숙련된 학습자는 같은 옷을 입는 것이 모든 수업에 효과가 있지는 않다는 것을 알고 있음
주제문 They have different strategies and know when to use them.

단서2 They know that you study for multiple-choice tests differently
선다형 시험과 논술 시험을 위해 각각 다르게 학습함
than you study for essay tests. And they not only know what to do,
not only A but also B: A뿐만 아니라 B도
but they also know how to do it.

해석

대학 생활을 시작할 때 학생들은 우리가 "고무도장 방식"이라고 부르고 싶은 방법을 이용하여, 모든 과목, 시험, 학습 과제를 똑같은 방식으로 접근할지도 모른다. 그것을 이런 식으로 생각해 보라. 야구 경기에 턱시도를 입고 가겠는가? 장례식에 화려한 드레스를 입고 가겠는가? 종교적인 예식에 수영복을 입고 가겠는가? 아마 아닐 것이다. 다양한 행사와 상황마다 적합한 옷이 있음을 여러분은 알고 있다. 숙련된 학습자는 "같은 옷을 입는 것"이 모든 수업에 효과가 있지는 않다는 것을 알고 있다. 그들은 유연한 학습자이다. 그들은 다양한 전략을 갖고 있으며 그것을 언제 사용해야 하는지 안다. 그들은 선다형 시험은 논술 시험을 위해 학습하는 것과는 다르게 학습해야 한다는 것을 안다. 그리고 그들은 무엇을 해야 하는지 알고 있을 뿐만 아니라, 그것을 어떻게 해야 하는지도 알고 있다.

정답이 보이는 해설

대학 생활을 시작할 때 학생들이 모든 과목, 시험, 학습 과제에 대한 학습을 똑같이 접근할지도 모르는데, 다양한 행사와 상황에 맞는 옷이 있듯이, 숙련된 학습자는 다양한 전략을 지니고 있으며 상황에 따라 각기 다른 학습 전략을 어떻게 사용해야 하는지를 안다는 내용의 글이다. 따라서 글의 요지로 가장 적절한 것은 ①이다.

🔍 **선택지 완벽 분석**

② 선다형 시험과 논술 시험은 평가의 형태와 목적이 다르다.
함정 선다형 시험과 논술 시험을 대비하는 데 차이가 있어야 한다는 내용은 있지만, 이것이 이 글의 요지는 아님에 유의해야 한다.
③ 문화마다 특정 행사와 상황에 맞는 복장 규정이 있다.
특정 행사와 상황에 맞는 복장이 있듯이, 학습에도 적절한 다양한 방법이 있다는 내용이 이 글의 요지이다. 예시로 든 내용과 요지를 혼동해서는 안 된다.

📕 **필수 어휘**

approach 접근하다   rubber-stamp 고무도장   funeral 장례식
bathing suit 수영복   religious 종교적인   service 예식   probably 아마
appropriate 적합한, 알맞은   occasion 행사   setting 상황, 장소
skillful 숙련된, 능숙한   flexible 유연한   strategy 전략
multiple-choice test 선다형 시험   essay test 논술 시험

---

04 정답 ①

202211 22번 정답률 79%

The old saying is that "knowledge is power," but when it comes to scary, threatening news, research suggests the exact opposite.
~에 관한 한
주제문 Frightening news can actually rob people of their inner sense of control, making them less likely to take care of themselves and
덜 ~하게 하는
other people. Public health research shows that **단서1** when the news
건강 관련 뉴스가 비관
presents health-related information in a pessimistic way, people
적이면, 사람들은 이에 조치를 덜 취함
are actually less likely to take steps to protect themselves from
조치를 취하다
illness as a result. ❖ A news article [that's intended to warn people
주어   주격 관계대명사절
about increasing cancer rates], (for example,) can result in fewer
동사   choosing의
people choosing to get screened for the disease // because they're so
의미상 주어   원인의 부사절
terrified of [what they might find]. This is also true for issues such
선행사를 포함한 관계대명사절

---

as climate change. **단서2** When a news story is all doom and gloom,
마찬가지로 환경 관련 뉴스도 비관적이기만 하면, 사람들은 조치를
people feel depressed and become less interested in taking small,
덜 취함
personal steps to fight ecological collapse.

해석

오래된 격언은 "아는 것이 힘이다"라고 하지만, 무섭고 위협적인 뉴스에 관한 한, 연구 결과는 정반대를 시사한다. 두려움을 주는 뉴스는 실제로 사람들로부터 내면의 통제력을 앗아갈 수 있어서, 그들이 스스로와 다른 사람들을 돌볼 가능성을 더 낮게 만든다. 공중 보건 연구는 뉴스가 건강과 관련된 정보를 비관적인 방식으로 제시할 때, 결과적으로 사람들이 질병으로부터 스스로를 보호하기 위한 조치를 취할 가능성이 실제로 더 낮다는 것을 보여 준다. 예를 들어, 증가하는 암 발생률에 대해 사람들에게 경고하려 의도된 뉴스 기사는 그들이 발견할 수도 있을 것에 대해 너무 두려워하기 때문에 더 적은 사람들이 그 병에 대해 검사받는 것을 선택하는 결과를 가져올 수 있다. 이것은 기후 변화와 같은 이슈에도 또한 해당된다. 뉴스 기사가 온통 파멸이고 암울하면, 사람들은 우울하게 느끼고 생태학적 붕괴와 싸우기 위한 작고 개인적인 조치를 취하는 것에 흥미를 덜 느끼게 된다.

정답이 보이는 해설

"아는 것이 힘이다"라는 격언과는 다르게, 두려움을 주는 뉴스는 사람들에게 내면의 통제력을 빼앗아 그들 스스로와 다른 사람들을 덜 돌보게 할 수 있다는 내용의 글이다. 따라서 글의 요지로 가장 적절한 것은 ①이다.

🔍 **선택지 완벽 분석**

⑤ 출처가 불분명한 건강 정보는 사람들에게 유익하지 않다.
그럴 듯한 선택지로 위장되었지만, 출처에 관한 내용은 다루고 있지 않음에 유의한다.

📕 **필수 어휘**

threatening 위협적인   suggest 시사하다, 암시하다   exact 정확한, 정밀한
opposite 반대   rob 빼앗다, 강탈하다   present 제시하다   pessimistic 비관적인
intend 의도하다, 생각하다   rate 비율, ~율   screen 검진하다
terrified 두려워하는   doom 파멸   gloom 암울   depressed 우울한
ecological 생태계의   collapse 붕괴

---

05 정답 ①

202209 22번 정답률 85%

❖ *A recent study* (from Carnegie Mellon University in
주어
Pittsburgh), / (called "When Too Much of a Good Thing May Be
과거분사구(A recent study 부연 설명)
Bad,") indicates / [that **단서1** classrooms with too much decoration
동사   명사절(목적어)   명사절 주어 과도하게 장식된 교실은 아이들을 산만하게 함
are a source of distraction for young children / and directly affect
명사절 동사1   명사절 동사2
their cognitive performance]. **단서2** Being visually overstimulated,
아이들은 시각적으로 지나치게 자극되면 잘 집중
the children have a great deal of difficulty concentrating and
하지 못함   have difficulty -ing: ~하는 데 어려움을 겪다
end up with worse academic results. On the other hand, **단서3** if
(결국) ~하게 되다
there is not much decoration on the classroom walls, the children
are less distracted, spend more time on their activities, and learn
~에 시간을 쓰다
more. **주제문** So it's our job, in order to support their attention,
in order to+동사원형: ~하기 위해(목적)
to find the right balance between excessive decoration and the
between A and B: A와 B 사이에
complete absence of it.

해석

피츠버그 시에 있는 Carnegie Mellon 대학교에서 실시한 "너무 많은 좋은 것이 나쁠 수도 있을 때"라고 불리는 최근의 한 연구는 너무 많은 장식을 한 교실이 어린아이들의 주의 산만의 원인이고 그들의 인지적인 수행에 직접적으로 영향을 미친다는 점을 시사한다. 시각적으로 지나치게 자극되었을 때, 아이들은 집중하는 데 많은 어

려움을 겪고 결국 더 나쁜 학습 결과를 초래한다. 반면에, 교실 벽에 장식이 많지 않으면, 아이들은 덜 산만해지고, 그들의 활동에 더 많은 시간을 쓰고, 더 많이 배운다. 그러므로 그들의 집중을 돕기 위해, 지나친 장식과 장식이 전혀 없는 것 사이의 적절한 균형을 찾는 것이 우리가 할 일이다.

[정답이 보이는 해설]

"너무 많은 좋은 것이 나쁠 수도 있을 때"라고 불리는 Carnegie Mellon 대학교의 한 연구를 일례로 들어, 너무 많은 장식을 한 교실은 아이들의 주의를 산만하게 하니 아이들이 집중할 수 있도록 과도한 교실 장식을 지양해야 할 필요가 있다는 내용의 글이다. 따라서 글의 요지로 가장 적절한 것은 ①이다.

[선택지 완벽 분석]

③ 아이들이 직접 교실을 장식하는 것은 창의력 발달에 도움이 된다.
지나치게 많은 장식을 한 교실은 아이들의 주의를 산만하게 한다고 했으며, 아이들의 창의력에 대한 내용은 글에 언급되어 있지 않다.

[필수 어휘]

indicate 시사하다, 보여 주다   decoration 장식   distraction 주의 산만
directly 직접적으로   cognitive 인지적인   performance 수행, 성과
visually 시각적으로   overstimulate 지나치게[과도하게] 자극시키다
concentrate 집중하다   academic 학업의   distracted 산만해진
attention 집중   excessive 지나친, 과도한   complete 완전한
absence 없는 것, 부재

06 정답 ①

202206 22번 정답률 85%

Your emotions deserve attention and give you important pieces
of information. **[주제문]** However, they can also sometimes be an
unreliable, inaccurate source of information. You may feel a
certain way, but that does not mean those feelings are reflections
of the truth. **[단서1]** You may feel sad and conclude that your friend
is angry with you when her behavior simply reflects that she's
having a bad day. ★ **[단서2]** You may feel depressed / and decide
[that you did poorly in an interview // **when** you did just fine].
Your feelings can mislead you into thinking things that are not
supported by facts.

[해석]

여러분의 감정은 주목할 만하고 여러분에게 중요한 정보를 준다. 하지만 그것은 또한 때때로 신뢰할 수 없고 부정확한 정보의 원천이 될 수 있다. 여러분이 분명하게 느낄 수도 있지만, 그것은 그러한 감정이 사실의 반영이라는 것을 의미하지는 않는다. 여러분은 슬픔을 느껴서 친구의 행동이 단지 그녀가 안 좋은 하루를 보내고 있다는 것을 나타낼 때도 그녀가 여러분에게 화가 났다고 결론을 내릴지도 모른다. 여러분은 기분이 우울해서 면접에서 잘했을 때도 못했다고 판단할지도 모른다. 여러분의 감정은 여러분을 속여 사실에 의해 뒷받침되지 않는 것들을 생각하게 할 수 있다.

[정답이 보이는 해설]

우리의 감정은 때때로 신뢰할 수 없고 부정확하며 우리의 감정 상태에 따라 사실을 다르게 잘못 받아들일 수 있다는 내용이므로, 글의 요지로 가장 적절한 것은 ①이다.

[필수 어휘]

attention 주목, 관심   unreliable 신뢰할 수 없는   inaccurate 부정확한
source 원천   reflection 반영   conclude 결론을 내리다
reflect 나타내다, 반영하다   depressed 우울한   mislead 속이다, 잘못 이끌다
support 뒷받침하다

07 정답 ①

202203 22번 정답률 92%

Many people view sleep as merely a "down time" when their
brain shuts off and their body rests. ★ In a rush **to meet** work,
school, family, or household responsibilities, / people cut back
on their sleep, / [thinking it won't be a problem], / **because** all of
these other activities **seem** much more important. But research
reveals that **[단서]** a number of vital tasks carried out during sleep
help to maintain good health and enable people to function at
their best. While you sleep, your brain is hard at work forming the
pathways necessary for learning and creating memories and new
insights. Without enough sleep, you can't focus and pay attention
or respond quickly. A lack of sleep may even cause mood
problems. In addition, growing evidence shows that a continuous
lack of sleep increases the risk for developing serious diseases.

[해석]

많은 사람들은 수면을 단지 뇌가 멈추고 신체가 쉬는 '작동하지 않는 시간'으로 본다. 일, 학교, 가족, 또는 가정의 책임을 다하기 위해 서두르는 가운데, 사람들은 수면을 줄이고, 그것이 문제가 되지 않을 것으로 생각하는데, 그 이유는 이러한 모든 다른 활동들이 훨씬 더 중요해 보이기 때문이다. 하지만 수면 중에 수행되는 많은 매우 중요한 과업이 건강을 유지하는 것을 도와주고 사람들이 최상의 수준으로 기능할 수 있게 해 준다는 것을 연구는 밝히고 있다. 잠을 자는 동안, 여러분의 뇌는 학습하고 기억과 새로운 통찰력을 만드는 데 필요한 경로를 형성하느라 열심히 일하고 있다. 충분한 수면이 없다면, 여러분은 정신을 집중할 수 없고 주의를 기울이거나 빠르게 반응할 수 없다. 수면이 부족하면 심지어 감정 (조절) 문제를 일으킬 수도 있다. 게다가, 계속되는 수면 부족이 심각한 질병의 발생 위험을 증가시킨다는 것을 점점 더 많은 증거가 보여 준다.

[정답이 보이는 해설]

수면 중에도 우리의 뇌는 계속해서 작동하고 있으며, 수면은 우리가 건강을 유지하고 최상의 기능을 발휘하는 데 도움을 주고, 수면이 부족하면 감정 문제뿐만 아니라 질병의 발생 위험도 증가한다는 내용의 글이다. 따라서 글의 요지로 가장 적절한 것은 ①이다.

[필수 어휘]

down time 가동되지 않는 시간   shut off 멈추다   responsibility 책임
cut back on ~을 줄이다   reveal 밝히다, 드러내다   vital 필수적인
maintain 유지하다   enable 가능하게 하다   evidence 증거

08 정답 ③

202111 22번 정답률 78%

Information is worthless if you never actually use it. Far too
often, companies collect valuable customer information that
ends up buried and never used. **[단서1]** They must ensure their
data is accessible for use at the appropriate times. For a hotel,
one appropriate time for data usage is check-in at the front desk.
★ I often check in at *a hotel* [I've visited frequently], / only for the
people at the front desk to give no indication [that they recognize
me as a customer]. The hotel must have stored a record of my

visits, but they don't make that information accessible to the front desk clerks. **단서2** They are missing a prime opportunity to utilize data to create a better experience focused on customer loyalty.
호텔은 정보를 활용하여 고객 충성도에 중점을 둔 더 나은 경험을 만들어 낼 기회를 놓치고 있음

Whether they have ten customers, ten thousand, or even ten
whether A or B: A든 B든
million, the goal is the same: **단서3** create a delightful customer experience that encourages loyalty.
기업의 목표는 충성도를 높이는 즐거운 고객 경험을 만드는 것임

해석

정보는 여러분이 그것을 결코 실제로 사용하지 않는다면 가치가 없다. 너무나 자주 기업들은 결국 묻히고 결코 사용되지 않는 귀중한 고객 정보를 수집한다. 기업들은 그들의 정보가 적절한 때에 사용을 위해 접근 가능하도록 보장해야 한다. 호텔의 경우 정보 사용을 위한 하나의 적절한 때는 프런트 데스크에서의 체크인이다. 나는 내가 자주 방문해 왔던 호텔에서 흔히 체크인하는데, 결국 프런트 데스크에 있는 사람들이 나를 고객으로 알아본다는 표시를 보여 주지 않는다. 그 호텔은 내 방문 기록을 틀림없이 저장하고 있었겠지만 그들은 그 정보가 프런트 데스크 직원들에게 접근 가능하도록 하지 않는다. 그들은 고객 충성도에 중점을 둔 더 나은 경험을 만들어 내기 위해 정보를 활용할 수 있는 최상의 기회를 놓치고 있는 것이다. 그들이 열 명, 만 명을 가지고 있든 심지어 천만 명의 고객을 가지고 있는 목표는 동일하다. 즉, 그것은 충성도를 북돋우는 즐거운 고객 경험을 만들어 내는 것이다.

정답이 보이는 해설

호텔의 프런트 데스크 직원들이 고객 정보에 접근할 수 없어서 단골 고객을 알아보지 못한다는 예를 제시하면서 고객에게 기분 좋은 경험을 제공하고 충성도를 높이기 위해서는 고객 정보가 적절한 때에 활용되어야 한다는 내용의 글이므로, 글의 요지로 가장 적절한 것은 ③이다.

필수 어휘

worthless 가치가 없는   ensure 보장하다   accessible 접근 가능한
appropriate 적절한   frequently 자주   indication 표시, 암시
recognize 알아보다, 인식하다   prime 최상의, 주요한   utilize 활용하다
loyalty 충성(도)   delightful 즐거운, 유쾌한

09 정답 ⑤

202109 22번 정답률 65%

주제문 ✪ It's important / [that you think independently and
가주어   진주어(명사절)
fight for (what you believe in)], // but there comes *a time* [when
전치사 for의 목적어절   to 생략   ↱ ~으로 옮기다   관계부사절
it's wiser to stop fighting for your view / and move on to accepting
가주어   진주어1(to부정사)   진주어2(to부정사)
[what (a trustworthy group of people think) is best]. This can be
accepting의 목적어절
extremely difficult. **단서** But it's smarter, and ultimately better for
마음을 열고 믿을 만한 집단 사람들의 결론이 여러분의 생각보다
you to be open-minded and have faith that the conclusions of a
낫다고 믿는 것이 현명함
trustworthy group of people are better than whatever you think. If

you can't understand their view, you're probably just blind to their

way of thinking. If you continue doing what you think is best when
사고방식
all the evidence and trustworthy people are against you, you're

being dangerously confident. The truth is that while most people

can become incredibly open-minded, some can't, even after they

have repeatedly encountered lots of pain from betting that they were

right when they were not.

해석

여러분이 독자적으로 생각하고 자신이 믿는 것을 위해 싸우는 것이 중요하지만, 자신의 견해를 위해 싸우는 것을 멈추고 신뢰할 수 있는 집단 사람들이 가장 좋다고 생

각하는 것을 받아들이는 것으로 나아가는 것이 더 현명한 때가 온다. 이것은 매우 어려울 수 있다. 하지만 여러분이 마음을 열고 신뢰할 수 있는 집단 사람들의 결론이 여러분이 생각하는 어떤 것보다 더 좋다는 믿음을 가지는 것이 더 영리하고 궁극적으로 더 좋다. 여러분이 그들의 견해를 이해할 수 없다면, 여러분은 아마도 단지 그들의 사고방식을 보지 못하는 것이다. 모든 증거와 신뢰할 수 있는 사람들이 여러분에게 반대할 때 여러분이 최선이라고 생각하는 것을 계속한다면, 여러분은 위험할 정도로 자신감에 차 있는 것이다. 진실은 대부분의 사람들은 믿을 수 없을 정도로 마음을 열게 되는 반면에, 어떤 사람들은 자신이 옳지 않았을 때 옳았다고 확신함으로써 많은 고통을 계속적으로 겪고 난 후조차 그럴 수 없다는 것이다.

정답이 보이는 해설

자신이 믿는 것을 위해 싸우는 것을 그만두고 마음을 열어 신뢰할 수 있는 집단의 사람들이 가장 좋다고 생각하는 것을 받아들일 필요가 있다는 내용이므로, 글의 요지로 가장 적절한 것은 ⑤이다.

선택지 완벽 분석

④ 믿을만한 사람이 누구인지 판단하려면 열린 마음을 가져야 한다.
함정 믿을 만한 사람들의 의견이 자신보다 낫다는 믿음이 필요하다는 내용이지 믿을 만한 사람이 누구인지 판단하는 기준에 대한 내용은 언급되지 않았다.

필수 어휘

independently 독자적으로   trustworthy 신뢰할 수 있는   extremely 매우, 극히
ultimately 궁극적으로, 결국   conclusion 결론   blind ~을 못 보는, 눈이 먼
evidence 증거   incredibly 믿을 수 없을 정도로   encounter 접하다, 마주치다
bet 틀림없다, 분명하다

10 정답 ⑤

202106 22번 정답률 75%

주제문 Rather than attempting to punish students with a low
~보다
grade or mark in the hope it will encourage them to give greater
~을 바라고   ~에게 …하도록 장려하다
effort in the future, **단서1** teachers can better motivate students by
교사는 학생들에게 추가적인 노력을 요구함으로써 동기 부여를 더 잘할 수 있음
considering their work as incomplete and then requiring additional

effort. Teachers at Beachwood Middle School in Beachwood, Ohio,

record students' grades as *A, B, C,* or *I* (Incomplete). ✪ *Students*
주어
[who receive an *I* grade] / are required to do additional work / (in
동사(수동태): ~하도록 요구되다
order to bring their performance up to an acceptable level). This
= students'
policy is based on the belief that students perform at a failure
~에 근거하다
level or submit failing work in large part because teachers accept

it. The Beachwood teachers reason that if they no longer accept
= students ~ work   더 이상 ~ 아닌
substandard work, students will not submit it. **단서2** And with
학생들은 적절한
appropriate support, they believe students will continue to work
도움을 받아 과제 수행이 만족스러울 때까지 계속 노력할 것임
until their performance is satisfactory.

해석

교사는 학생이 앞으로 더 많은 노력을 기울이게 하고 싶은 바람에서 낮은 등급이나 점수로 학생을 벌주는 시도를 하는 것보다, 그들의 과제가 미완성이라고 생각하고 추가적인 노력을 요구함으로써 학생에게 동기 부여를 더 잘할 수 있다. Ohio 주 Beachwood의 Beachwood 중학교 교사들은 학생의 등급을 'A, B, C' 또는 'I (미완성)'로 기록한다. 'I' 등급을 받은 학생은 자신들의 과제 수행을 받아들일 수 있는 수준까지 끌어올리기 위해서 추가적인 과제를 하도록 요구받는다. 이런 방침은, 학생이 낙제 수준으로 과제를 수행하거나 낙제 과제를 제출하는 것은 교사들이 대부분 그것을 받아들이기 때문이라는 믿음에 근거한다. Beachwood의 교사들은 자신들이 더 이상 기준 이하의 과제를 받아들이지 않는다면, 학생들이 그것을 제출하지 않

을 것이라고 판단한다. 그리고 그들은 학생들이 적절한 도움을 받아 자신의 과제 수행이 만족스러울 때까지 계속 노력할 것이라고 믿는다.

첫 번째 문장이 요지이고, 나머지 문장은 이 요지를 뒷받침하기 위한 한 중학교의 사례이다. 즉, 학생이 과제 수행을 더 잘하도록 동기 부여를 하기 위해서는 그들에게 낮은 등급이나 점수를 주는 것보다는 자신들의 과제가 부족하다는 것을 깨닫게 하고 추가적인 노력을 하도록 요구하는 것이 더 좋다는 내용이므로, 글의 요지로 가장 적절한 것은 ⑤이다.

punish 벌주다   motivate 동기 부여를 하다   additional 추가적인, 추가의
performance (과제) 수행   up to ~까지   acceptable 받아들일 수 있는
policy 방침, 방책   submit 제출하다   reason 판단하다, 생각하다
substandard 수준 미달의, 저질의   appropriate 적절한   satisfactory 만족스러운

pressure 압박, 압력   normal 정상적인, 일반적인   doubt 의심하다; 의심
self-worth 자아 존중감   suffer 상처를 입다, 괴로워하다
uniquely 특유의 방식으로   activate 활성화하다   bother 괴롭히다
neutral 중립적인   genuinely 진짜로, 정말로   reflection 반영
shortcoming 단점   objectively 객관적으로

---

11 정답 ⑤

202103 22번 정답률 69%

If you care deeply about something, you may place greater value on your ability to succeed in that area of concern. The internal pressure you place on yourself to achieve or do well socially is normal and useful, but when you doubt your ability to succeed in areas that are important to you, your self-worth suffers. Situations are uniquely stressful for each of us based on whether or not they activate our doubt. 단서1 It's not the pressure to perform that creates your stress. Rather, it's the self-doubt that bothers you. ✪ Doubt causes you to see / positive, neutral, and even genuinely negative experiences (more negatively) and (as a reflection of your own shortcomings). 단서2 When you see situations and your strengths more objectively, you are less likely to have doubt as the source of your distress.

여러분이 어떤 것에 깊이 관심을 가지면, 여러분은 그 관심 영역에서 성공하기 위한 자신의 능력에 더 큰 가치를 둘지도 모른다. 여러분이 성취하거나 사회적으로 성공하기 위해 스스로에게 가하는 내적인 압박은 정상적이고 도움이 되지만, 여러분이 자신에게 중요한 영역에서 성공하기 위한 여러분 자신의 능력을 의심하면, 여러분의 자아 존중감은 상처를 입는다. 상황이 우리의 의심을 활성화하는지 여부에 따라 그것은 우리 각각에게 특유의 방식으로 스트레스를 준다. 여러분의 스트레스를 야기하는 것은 결코 수행에 대한 압박이 아니다. 오히려, 여러분을 괴롭히는 것은 바로 자기 의심이다. 의심은 긍정적 경험, 중립적 경험, 그리고 진짜로 부정적인 경험조차도 더 부정적으로 보게 하고, (그 경험들을) 여러분 자신의 단점을 반영한 것으로 보게 한다. 상황과 여러분의 강점을 더 객관적으로 바라볼 때, 여러분은 괴로움의 원천인 의심을 품을 가능성이 낮다.

자기 의심은 자아 존중감에 상처를 주고 스트레스를 야기하며, 자신의 강점보다는 단점을 반영하여 상황이나 경험에 대한 객관적 판단을 흐리게 한다는 내용이므로, 글의 요지로 가장 적절한 것은 ⑤이다.

③ 적절한 수준의 스트레스는 과제 수행의 효율을 높인다.
글의 도입 부분에서 언급한 내용이지만 글의 요지로 보기에는 지엽적인 내용이다. 두 번째 문장의 but when you doubt ~부터 글의 요지가 드러나 있다.

---

12 정답 ④

202011 22번 정답률 65%

FOBO, or Fear of a Better Option, is the anxiety that something better will come along, which makes it undesirable to commit to existing choices when making a decision. It's an affliction of abundance that drives you to keep all of your options open and to avoid risks. 단서1 Rather than assessing your options, choosing one, and moving on with your day, you delay the inevitable. ✪ It's not unlike hitting the snooze button (on your alarm clock) / (only to pull the covers over your head and fall back asleep). As you probably found out the hard way, if you hit snooze enough times, you'll end up being late and racing for the office, your day and mood ruined. 단서2 While pressing snooze feels so good at the moment, it ultimately demands a price.

FOBO, 즉 더 나은 선택에 대한 두려움은 더 나은 어떤 것이 생길 것이라는 불안감인데, 이것은 결정할 때 기존의 선택지에 전념하는 것을 달갑지 않게 만든다. 그것은 여러분이 모든 선택지를 열어 두고 위험을 피하게 하는 풍족함의 고통이다. 여러분은 자신의 선택지들을 평가하고, 하나를 선택하고, 여러분의 하루를 살아가기보다, 꼭 해야 할 것을 미룬다. 그것은 알람시계의 스누즈 버튼을 누르고는 결국 이불을 머리 위로 뒤집어쓴 채 다시 잠들어 버리는 것과 다르지 않다. 아마도 여러분이 고생하여 알게 되었듯이, 스누즈 버튼을 반복하여 누르면 결국 늦게 되어 사무실로 달리게 되고, 여러분의 하루와 기분을 망치게 된다. 스누즈 버튼을 누르는 것이 그때는 기분이 아주 좋겠지만, 그것은 결국 대가를 요구한다.

FOBO란 더 나은 선택에 대한 두려움 때문에 꼭 해야 할 것을 미루는 현상으로, 이에 대한 예시로 알람시계의 스누즈 버튼을 반복하여 누름으로써 해야 할 일(일어나는 일)을 미루면 당장은 기분이 좋을지 몰라도 결국 대가(지각)를 치르게 되어 기분을 망치게 된다는 내용의 글이므로, 글의 요지로 가장 적절한 것은 ④이다.

① 적당한 수준의 불안감은 업무 수행에 도움이 된다.
불안감이 업무 수행에 도움이 된다는 내용이 아니라 이로 인해 부정적 결과를 초래한다는 내용의 글이다.

option 선택(지), 선택권   anxiety 불안(감), 염려   undesirable 달갑지 않은
abundance 풍요, 풍부   assess 평가하다   move on ~으로 나아가다[이동하다]
inevitable 꼭 해야 할 것, 필연적인 것
snooze button 스누즈 버튼(아침에 잠이 깬 뒤 조금 더 자기 위해 누르는 알람시계나 라디오의 타이머 버튼)   ruin 망치다   ultimately 결국
demand a price 대가를 요구하다

6강 2020~2023 주제 추론

01 정답 ②

202309 23번 정답률 63%

단서1 The interaction of workers from different cultural
다른 문화에서 온 노동자와 현지 주민의 상호 작용은 생산성 증가로 이어짐
backgrounds with the host population might increase productivity

due to positive externalities like knowledge spillovers. **주제문** This
~ 때문에
is only an advantage up to a certain degree. **단서2** When the variety
~까지
of backgrounds is too large, fractionalization may cause excessive
배경이 지나치게 다양하면 분열에 의해 의사소통 비용이 커짐
transaction costs for communication, which may lower productivity.

단서3 Diversity not only impacts the labour market, but may also
not only A but also B: A뿐만 아니라 B도
affect the quality of life in a location. A tolerant native population
다양성은 노동 시장과 삶의 질에도 영향을 미침
may value a multicultural city or region because of an increase in

the range of available goods and services. ✪ On the other hand, /
반면에, 다른 한편으로는(앞의 내용과 반대되는 내용이 이어짐)
diversity could be perceived as an unattractive feature / **if** natives
주절의 주어   주절의 동사   = natives   조건의 부사절
perceive it / as a distortion of [**what** they consider to be their
= diversity   관계대명사 what이 쓰인 명사절   = natives'
national identity]. They might even discriminate against other ethnic

groups and they might fear that social conflicts between different

foreign nationalities are imported into their own neighbourhood.

해석

다른 문화적 배경에서 온 노동자들과 현지 주민의 상호 작용은 지식 파급과 같은 긍정적인 외부 효과로 인해 생산성을 증가시킬 수 있다. 이것은 어느 정도까지만 장점이다. 배경의 다양성이 지나치게 클 경우, 분열은 의사소통을 위해 과도한 거래 비용을 초래하는데, 이는 생산성을 저하시킬 수 있다. 다양성은 노동 시장에 영향을 줄 뿐만 아니라 한 지역의 삶의 질에도 영향을 미칠 수 있다. 관용적인 원주민은 이용할 수 있는 재화 및 용역의 범위가 증가하기 때문에 다문화 도시나 지역을 가치 있게 여길 수 있다. 반면에, 원주민들이 다양성을 그들의 국가 정체성이라고 여기는 것에 대한 왜곡으로 인식한다면 다양성은 매력적이지 않은 특징으로 인식될 수 있다. 그들은 심지어 다른 민족 집단을 차별할 수도 있고, 다른 외국 국적들 간의 사회적 갈등이 그들 인근으로 유입되는 것을 두려워할 수도 있다.

정답이 보이는 해설

다양한 문화적 배경을 지닌 노동자와 현지 주민의 상호 작용은 긍정적인 영향을 가져오기도 하지만, 높아진 의사소통 비용 때문에 생산성이 떨어지고 지역 내 삶의 질에도 영향을 미칠 수 있다고 했다. 그러면서 지역 주민에게 미치는 긍정적인 영향과 부정적인 영향이 모두 제시되므로 글의 주제로 가장 적절한 것은 ② '문화적 다양성의 대조적인 측면'이다.

선택지 완벽 분석

① roles of culture in ethnic groups 민족 집단에서 문화의 역할

② contrastive aspects of cultural diversity 문화적 다양성의 대조적인 측면

③ negative perspectives of national identity 국가 정체성의 부정적인 관점
(문화적) 다양성과 국가 정체성에 관한 내용은 있으나, 국가 정체성의 부정적인 관점에 관한 내용은 아니다.

④ factors of productivity differences across countries 국가 간 생산성 격차의 요소

⑤ policies to protect minorities and prevent discrimination 소수 민족을 보호하고 차별을 예방하는 정책
원주민이 (문화적) 다양성을 국가 정체성으로 왜곡으로 인식하면 다른 민족을 차별할 수 있다는 내용은 있으나, 소수 민족을 보호하고 차별을 예방하는 정책은 언급되지 않았다.

필수 어휘

spillover 파급   degree 정도, 수준   variety 다양성   excessive 과도한
transaction cost 거래 비용   diversity 다양성   impact 영향을 미치다

affect 영향을 미치다   tolerant 관대한, 아량 있는   region 지역   range 범위
available 이용할 수 있는   perceive 인식하다   unattractive 매력적이지 않은
distortion 왜곡   discriminate 차별하다   ethnic 인종의, 민족의   conflict 갈등
import 유입되다, 수입하다

02 정답 ②

202306 23번 정답률 71%

주제문 We tend to believe that we possess a host of socially
~하는 경향이 있다
desirable characteristics, and that we are free of most of those
~이 없는
that are socially undesirable. For example, a large majority of the
대다수의 ~
general public thinks that **단서1** they are more intelligent, more
보통 사람보다 스스로를 더 낫다고 여김
fair-minded, less prejudiced, and more skilled behind the wheel
운전대 뒤에서
of an automobile than the average person. ✪ This phenomenon
is **so** reliable and ubiquitous // **that** it has come to be known as
so ~ that: 너무 ~해서 ···하다   ~으로 알려지다
the "Lake Wobegon effect," / after *Garrison Keillor's fictional*
community [where "the women are strong, the men are good-
관계부사절
looking, and all the children are above average."] A survey of one
평균 이상의
million high school seniors found that **단서2** 70% thought they were
70%의 학생들이 리더십 능력이
above average in leadership ability, and only 2% thought they were
평균보다 높다고 생각함
below average. In terms of ability to get along with others, **단서3** *all*
평균 이하의   ~와 잘 지내다
students thought they were above average, 60% thought they were
다른 사람들과 잘 지내는 능력은 "모든" 학생들이 평균보다 높다고 생각함
in the top 10%, and 25% thought they were in the top 1%!

해석

우리는 우리가 사회적으로 바람직한 특성들을 많이 지니고 있고, 그리고 우리는 사회적으로 바람직하지 않은 특성들의 대부분은 지니고 있지 않다고 믿는 경향이 있다. 예를 들어, 대다수의 일반 대중들은 자기가 보통 사람보다 더 지적이고, 더 공정하고, 편견을 덜 가지고, 자동차를 운전할 때 더 능숙하다고 생각한다. 이 현상은 너무 신뢰할 수 있고 어디서나 볼 수 있기 때문에 "여성들은 강하고, 남성들은 잘생겼으며, 모든 아이들은 평균 이상"인 Garrison Keillor의 허구적인 공동체의 이름을 따서 "와비건 호수 효과"라고 알려지게 되었다. 고등학교 최고 학년 학생 100만 명을 대상으로 한 설문조사에서 70%는 자신이 리더십 능력에 있어 평균 이상이라고 생각했고, 2%만이 자신이 평균 이하라고 생각했다는 것을 발견했다. 다른 사람들과 잘 지내는 능력에 있어서, "모든" 학생들이 자신이 평균 이상이라고 생각했고, 60%는 자신이 상위 10%에 속한다고 생각했고, 25%는 자신이 상위 1%에 속한다고 생각했다!

정답이 보이는 해설

우리는 자신이 사회적으로 바람직한 특성들을 많이 지니고 있으며 바람직하지 않은 특성들은 지니지 않고 있다고 믿는 경향이 있는데, 이런 경향은 "와비건 호수 효과"로 알려져 있다. 고등학생들을 대상으로 한 설문조사에서도 이러한 경향이 확실히 드러나고 있다는 내용의 글이다. 그러므로, 글의 주제로 가장 적절한 것은 ② '우리가 평균보다 더 낫다는 우리의 일반적인 믿음'이다.

선택지 완벽 분석

① importance of having a positive self-image as a leader 리더로서 긍정적인 자아 이미지를 갖는 것의 중요성

② our common belief that we are better than average 우리가 평균보다 더 낫다는 우리의 일반적인 믿음

③ our tendency to think others are superior to us 타인이 우리보다 우월하다고 생각하는 우리의 경향

④ reasons why we always try to be above average 우리가 항상 평균 이상이 되려고 노력하는 이유
함정 평균 이상이 되려고 노력하는 이유에 관한 글이 아니라, 스스로를 평균 이상이라고 생각한다는 내용임에 유의한다.

⑤ danger of prejudice in building healthy social networks 건강한 소셜 네트워크를 구축하는 데 있어서 편견의 위험

03 정답 ①

202303 23번 정답률 49%

As the social and economic situation of countries got better, wage levels and working conditions improved. Gradually [단서1] people were given more time off. At the same time, [단서2] forms of transport improved and it became faster and cheaper to get to places. England's industrial revolution led to many of these changes. Railways, in the nineteenth century, [단서3] opened up now famous seaside resorts such as Blackpool and Brighton. ✪ (With the railways) / came many large hotels. In Canada, for example, the new coast-to-coast railway system [단서4] made possible the building of such famous hotels as Banff Springs and Chateau Lake Louise in the Rockies. Later, [단서5] the arrival of air transport opened up more of the world and led to tourism growth.

해석

국가들의 사회적·경제적 상황이 더 나아지면서, 임금 수준과 근로 여건이 개선되었다. 점차 사람들은 더 많은 휴가를 받게 되었다. 동시에, 운송 형태가 개선되었고 장소에 도착하는 것이 더 빠르고 더 저렴해졌다. 영국의 산업 혁명이 이러한 변화 중 많은 부분들로 이어졌다. 19세기에, 철도로 인해 Blackpool과 Brighton 같은 현재 유명한 해안가 리조트가 문을 열게 되었다. 철도가 생기면서 많은 대형 호텔이 생겨났다. 예를 들어, 캐나다에서는 새로운 대륙 횡단 철도 시스템이 로키산맥의 Banff Springs와 Chateau Lake Louise 같은 유명한 호텔의 건설을 가능하게 했다. 이후에 항공 운송의 출현은 세계의 더 많은 곳으로 가는 길을 열어 주었고 관광 산업의 성장을 이끌었다.

정답이 보이는 해설

사회적·경제적 상황이 나아지면서 사람들은 더 많은 휴가를 받게 되었고, 운송 형태의 개선으로 더 빠르고 저렴한 이동이 가능해졌으며, 영국의 산업 혁명으로 19세기에는 철도와 함께 해안가 리조트와 대형 호텔이 생겨났고, 이후 항공 운송이 출현하면서 관광 산업이 성장했다는 내용의 글이다. 그러므로, 글의 주제로 가장 적절한 것은 ① '관광 산업 확대를 야기한 요인들'이다.

선택지 완벽 분석

① factors that caused tourism expansion 관광 산업 확대를 야기한 요인들
② discomfort at a popular tourist destination 인기 있는 관광지에서의 불편함
③ importance of tourism in society and economy 사회와 경제에서 관광 산업의 중요성
[함정] 관광 산업이 발달한 여러 요인에 관한 내용이지, 관광 산업의 중요성에 관한 글은 아님에 유의한다.
④ negative impacts of tourism on the environment 관광 산업이 환경에 미치는 부정적인 영향
⑤ various types of tourism and their characteristics 다양한 유형의 관광 산업과 그 특징들
관광 산업의 유형들과 그 특징들에 대한 언급은 없다.

04 정답 ⑤

202211 23번 정답률 79%

주제문 The most remarkable and unbelievable consequence of melting ice and rising seas is that together they are a kind of time machine, so real that they are altering the duration of our day. It works like this: As the glaciers melt and the seas rise, gravity forces more water toward the equator. ✪ This changes the shape of the Earth ever so slightly, // making it fatter around the middle, / [단서] which in turns slows the rotation of the planet (similarly to *the way* [a ballet dancer slows her spin by spreading out her arms]). The slowdown isn't much, just a few thousandths of a second each year, but like the barely noticeable jump of rising seas every year, it adds up. When dinosaurs lived on the Earth, a day lasted only about twenty-three hours.

해석

녹고 있는 얼음과 해수면 상승의 가장 놀랍고 믿을 수 없는 결과는 그것들이 합쳐져 일종의 타임머신이라는 것이고, 이것은 너무나 현실적이어서 그것들이 우리 하루의 기간을 바꾸고 있다는 것이다. 그것은 이와 같이 작동한다. 즉, 빙하가 녹고 바다가 상승하면서 중력이 적도를 향해 더 많은 물을 밀어 넣는다. 이것은 지구의 모양을 아주 약간 변화시켜, 가운데 주변으로 그것을 더 불룩하게 만들고, 이것은 결과적으로 발레 무용수가 양팔을 뻗어서 그녀의 회전을 늦추는 방식과 비슷하게 행성의 회전을 늦춘다. 이 감속이 매년 단지 몇천분의 1초로 크지는 않지만, 해마다 상승하는 해수면의 알아차리기 힘든 증가처럼, 그것은 쌓인다. 공룡들이 지구에 살았을 때, 하루는 불과 약 23시간만 지속되었다.

정답이 보이는 해설

극지방의 얼음이 녹아서 해수면이 상승하고, 그 영향으로 중력이 적도를 좀 더 부풀리고 행성의 회전을 늦추게 되어, 아주 작지만 하루의 기간을 아주 조금씩 길어지게 하고, 그것은 계속 쌓이고 있다는 내용의 글이다. 그러므로, 글의 주제로 가장 적절한 것은 ⑤ '녹고 있는 얼음과 해수면 상승이 하루 길이에 대해 미치는 영향'이다.

선택지 완벽 분석

① cause of rising temperatures on the Earth 지구 기온 상승의 원인
② principles of planets maintaining their shapes 행성이 자신의 모양을 유지하는 원리
③ implications of melting ice on marine biodiversity 녹고 있는 얼음이 해양 생물의 다양성에 미치는 영향
④ way to keep track of time without using any device 어떤 기기도 이용하지 않고 시간을 추적하는 방법
⑤ impact of melting ice and rising seas on the length of a day 녹고 있는 얼음과 해수면 상승이 하루 길이에 대해 미치는 영향

05 정답 ②

202209 23번 정답률 62%

For creatures like us, evolution smiled upon those with a strong need to belong. Survival and reproduction are the criteria of success by natural selection, and [단서1] forming relationships with

other people can be useful for both survival and reproduction.
번식에 유용함　　　　　　　　　　both A and B: A와 B 둘 다
★ Groups can share resources, care for sick members, scare
　주어　　　동사1　　　　동사2 ↳돌보다　　　　　동사3
off predators, fight together against enemies, divide tasks (so as to
↳(겁을 주어) 쫓아버리다 ↳동사4　　　　　　　동사5
improve efficiency), and contribute to survival in many other ways.
동사6(병렬 구조)　　↳~에 기여하다
In particular, if an individual and a group want the same resource,
특히
the group will generally prevail, so 단서2 competition for resources
　　　　　　　　　　　　　　　　자원에 대한 경쟁은 소속하려는 욕구를
would especially favor a need to belong. 단서3 Belongingness will
특히 좋아함　　　　　　　　　　　소속되어 있다는 것은 번식을
likewise promote reproduction, such as by bringing potential mates
촉진시킴　　　　　　　이를테면, ~같은
into contact with each other, and in particular by keeping parents
bring ~ into contact with: ~을 만나게[접촉하게] 하다
together to care for their children, 단서4 who are much more likely
　　　　　　　　　　　아이들은 한 명 이상의 돌보는 사람이 있는
to survive if they have more than one caregiver.
경우 생존 가능성 더 많음

해석
우리와 같은 창조물에게 있어 진화는 소속하려는 강한 욕구를 가진 것들에 미소를 지었다. 생존과 번식은 자연 선택에 의한 성공의 기준이고, 다른 사람들과 관계를 형성하는 것은 생존과 번식 둘 다에 유용할 수 있다. 집단은 자원을 공유하고, 아픈 구성원을 돌보고, 포식자를 쫓아버리고, 적에 맞서서 함께 싸우고, 효율성을 향상시키기 위해 업무를 나누고, 많은 다른 방식에서 생존에 기여한다. 특히, 한 개인과 한 집단이 같은 자원을 원하면, 일반적으로 집단이 승리하고, 따라서 자원에 대한 경쟁은 소속하려는 욕구를 특히 좋아할 것이다. 마찬가지로 소속되어 있다는 것은 번식을 촉진시키는데, 이를테면 잠재적인 짝을 서로 만나게 해 주거나, 특히 부모가 자녀를 돌보기 위해 함께 있도록 함으로써, 자녀들은 한 명보다 많은 돌보는 이가 있으면 훨씬 더 생존할 가능성이 많다.

정답이 보이는 해설
창조물에게 있어 진화는 소속하려는 강한 욕구를 가진 것들을 선호하며, 소속하려는 강한 욕구는 생존과 번식 둘 다에 유용하다는 내용의 글이다. 따라서 글의 주제로 가장 적절한 것은 ② '인류 진화를 위한 소속의 유용성'이다.

선택지 완벽 분석
① skills for the weak to survive modern life 약자들이 현대 생활에서 살아남을 수 있는 기술
현대 생활에서 살아남을 수 있는 기술은 언급되어 있지 않으며, 소속하려는 강한 욕구가 생존과 번식에 유용하다는 내용의 글이다.
② usefulness of belonging for human evolution 인류 진화를 위한 소속의 유용성
③ ways to avoid competition among social groups 사회 집단들 간의 경쟁을 피하는 방법
④ roles of social relationships in children's education 아동 교육에서 사회 관계의 역할
⑤ differences between two major evolutionary theories 두 가지 주요 진화론 간의 차이

필수 어휘
evolution 진화 survival 생존 reproduction 번식
criterion 기준, 규준(pl. criteria) resource 자원 predator 포식자
efficiency 효율성 prevail 승리하다, 이기다 competition 경쟁
likewise 마찬가지로 potential 잠재적인 caregiver (아이나 병자를) 돌보는 사람

06 정답 ②
202206 23번 정답률 81%

Every day, children explore and construct relationships among
objects. 단서1 Frequently, these relationships focus on how much
아이들은 사물 간의 관계를 탐구할 때 사물의 양이나 개수에 초점을 둠
or how many of something exists. Thus, children count — "One
cookie, two shoes, three candles on the birthday cake, four children
in the sandbox." Children compare — "Which has more? Which has

fewer? Will there be enough?" Children calculate — "How many
will fit? Now, I have five. I need one more." In all of these instances,
children are developing a notion of quantity. ★ 단서2 Children
　　　　　　　　　　　　　　　　　　　　　아이들은 자신
reveal and investigate mathematical concepts / through their own
만의 활동이나 경험을 통해 수학적 개념을 연구함　　　전치사(~을 통해)
activities or experiences, / such as figuring out [how many crackers
　　　　　　　　　　　　　　　파악하다　　figuring out의 목적어1
to take at snack time] or [sorting shells into piles].
figuring out의 목적어2

해석
매일 아이들은 사물 사이의 관계들을 탐구하고 구성한다. 자주 이러한 관계들은 무언가가 얼마만큼 또는 몇 개 존재하는지에 초점을 둔다. 따라서 아이들은 "쿠키 하나, 신발 두 개, 생일 케이크 위에 초 세 개, 모래 놀이통에 어린이 네 명."이라고 수를 센다. 아이들은 "무엇이 더 많지? 무엇이 더 적지? 충분할까?"라고 비교한다. 아이들은 "몇 개가 알맞을까? 나는 지금 다섯 개가 있어. 하나 더 필요하네."라고 계산한다. 이 모든 사례에서, 아이들은 양의 개념을 발달시키고 있는 것이다. 아이들은 간식 시간에 몇 개의 크래커를 가져갈지 파악하는 것 또는 조개껍질들을 더미로 분류하는 것과 같은, 자신만의 활동이나 경험을 통해 수학적 개념을 밝히고 연구한다.

정답이 보이는 해설
아이들은 매일 사물 사이의 관계를 탐구하고 구성하는데, 수와 양을 비교하고 계산하는 활동을 통해 자신만의 수학적 개념을 형성한다는 내용이므로, 글의 주제로 가장 적절한 것은 ② '아이들이 수학적 이해를 형성하는 방법'이다.

선택지 완벽 분석
① difficulties of children in learning how to count 아이들이 수를 세는 방법을 배우는 것의 어려움
② how children build mathematical understanding 아이들이 수학적 이해를 형성하는 방법
③ why fingers are used in counting objects 사물을 셀 때 손가락이 사용되는 이유
④ importance of early childhood education 유아기 교육의 중요성
⑤ advantages of singing number songs 숫자 노래를 부르는 것의 이점

필수 어휘
construct 구성하다 object 사물, 물체 calculate 계산하다 fit 알맞다, 적합하다
notion 개념 quantity 양 reveal 밝히다, 드러내다
investigate 조사하다, 연구하다 sort 분류하다

07 정답 ④
202203 23번 정답률 67%

주제문 The whole of human society operates on knowing the
future weather. For example, farmers in India know when the
monsoon rains will come next year and so they know when to plant
the crops. Farmers in Indonesia know there are two monsoon rains
each year, so next year they can have two harvests. This is based on
　　　　　　　　　　　　　　　　　　　　　　　　　　～에 근거하다
their knowledge of the past, as the monsoons have always come at
about the same time each year in living memory. 단서1 But the need
　　　　　　　　　　　　　　　　　　　　　　기후 예측의 필요성이
to predict goes deeper than this; it influences every part of our lives.
커지고 그것은 우리 생활의 모든 부분에 영향을 미침
단서2 Our houses, roads, railways, airports, offices, and so on are all
　　집, 철도, 공항, 사무실 등이 지역 기후에 맞춰 설계됨
designed for the local climate. ★ For example, / in England all the
houses have central heating, / as the outside temperature is usually
　　　　　　　　　　　　　접속사(이유)
below 20°C, / but no air-conditioning, / as temperatures rarely
↳(have)　　　　　　　　　　접속사(이유)
go beyond 26°C, // while in Australia the opposite is true: / most
　　　　　　　접속사(반면에)
houses have air-conditioning but rarely central heating.
↳(have)

인간 사회 전체는 미래의 날씨를 아는 것을 기반으로 운영된다. 예를 들어, 인도의 농부들은 내년에 몬순 장마가 언제 올 것인지 알고, 따라서 그들은 언제 작물을 심어야 하는지 안다. 인도네시아의 농부들은 매년 몬순 장마가 두 번 있다는 것을 알고, 그래서 이듬해에 그들은 수확을 두 번 할 수 있다. 이것은 과거에 대한 그들의 지식에 근거하고 있는데, 살아 있는 기억 속에서 몬순은 매년 항상 거의 같은 시기에 오기 때문이다. 그러나 예측할 필요성은 이것보다 더욱 깊어지고, 그것은 우리 생활의 모든 부분에 영향을 미친다. 우리의 집, 도로, 철도, 공항, 사무실 등은 모두 지역의 기후에 맞추어 설계된다. 예를 들어, 영국에서는 외부의 기온이 대체로 섭씨 20도 미만이기 때문에 모든 집은 중앙난방을 갖추고 있지만, 기온이 섭씨 26도 위로 올라가는 일은 거의 없어서 냉방기는 없는 반면, 호주에서는 그 정반대가 사실인데, 즉 대부분의 집은 냉방기를 갖추고 있지만 중앙난방은 거의 없다.

정답이 보이는 해설

날씨를 예측하여 작물을 심고 수확을 하거나 지역의 기후에 맞춰 건물 등이 설계되는 것처럼 기후에 대한 지식은 우리 생활의 모든 부분에 영향을 미친다는 내용으로 인도, 인도네시아, 영국, 호주의 생활 모습을 그 예로 들고 있다. 따라서 글의 주제로 가장 적절한 것은 ④ '우리의 생활에 광범위하게 영향을 미치는 기후에 대한 지식'이다.

선택지 완벽 분석

① new technologies dealing with climate change 기후 변화를 다루는 새로운 기술
② difficulties in predicting the weather correctly 날씨를 정확하게 예측하는 것의 어려움
③ weather patterns influenced by rising temperatures 상승하는 기온에 영향을 받는 날씨 패턴
④ knowledge of the climate widely affecting our lives 우리의 생활에 광범위하게 영향을 미치는 기후에 대한 지식
⑤ traditional wisdom helping our survival in harsh climates 혹독한 기후에서 우리의 생존을 돕는 전통적 지혜

필수 어휘

operate 운영되다
monsoon 몬순(특히 인도양에서 여름은 남서, 겨울은 북동에서 부는 계절풍)
crop 작물 harvest 수확 predict 예측하다 influence 영향을 미치다
railway 철도 design 설계하다 climate 기후 central heating 중앙난방
temperature 기온 air-conditioning 냉방(기) opposite 정반대

08 정답 ①

202111 23번 정답률 78%

We used to think that the brain never changed, but according to (~에 따르면) the neuroscientist Richard Davidson, we now know that this is not true — 단서1 specific brain circuits grow stronger through regular practice. (특정한 뇌 회로는 규칙적 연습을 통해 더 강해짐) He explains, "Well-being is fundamentally no different than learning to play the cello. If one practices the skills of well-being, one will get better at it." What this means is that 단서2 you can actually train your brain to become more grateful, relaxed, or (더 감사하거나 편안하거나 자신감을 갖도록 뇌를 실제로 훈련시킬 수 있음) confident, by repeating experiences that evoke gratitude, relaxation, or confidence. Your brain is shaped by the thoughts you repeat. ❋ **The more** neurons fire as they are activated by repeated thoughts (the 비교급 ~, the 비교급 …: ~할수록 더욱 …하다) (접속사(~함에 따라)) and activities, / **the faster** they develop into neural pathways, / [which cause lasting changes in the brain]. Or in the words of (계속적 용법의 관계대명사절) Donald Hebb, "Neurons that fire together wire together." This is such an encouraging premise: bottom line — 단서3 we can intentionally create the habits for the brain to be happier. (뇌가 더 행복해지도록 의도적으로 습관을 형성할 수 있음)

우리는 뇌가 절대 변하지 않는다고 생각하곤 했지만, 신경과학자 Richard Davidson에 따르면 우리는 이제 이것이 사실이 아니라는 것을, 즉 특정한 뇌 회로가 규칙적인 연습을 통해 더 강해진다는 것을 알고 있다. 그가 설명하기를 "행복은 첼로를 연주하는 것을 배우는 것과 근본적으로 다르지 않다. 만약 어떤 사람이 행복의 기술을 연습한다면 그 사람은 그것을 더 잘하게 될 것이다." 이것이 의미하는 것은 여러분이 감사, 휴식 또는 자신감을 불러일으키는 경험을 반복함으로써 더 감사하거나, 편안하거나 또는 자신감을 갖게 되도록 여러분의 뇌를 실제로 훈련시킬 수 있다는 것이다. 여러분의 뇌는 여러분이 반복하는 생각에 의해 만들어진다. 뉴런은 그것이 반복된 생각과 활동에 의해 활성화됨에 따라 더 많이 점화할수록, 그것은 신경 경로로 더 빠르게 발달하게 되고, 이것은 뇌에 지속적인 변화를 일으킨다. 또는 Donald Hebb의 말로 나타내면 "함께 점화하는 뉴런은 함께 연결된다." 이는 대단히 고무적인 전제인데, 즉 요점은 뇌가 더 행복해지도록 우리가 습관을 의도적으로 만들어 낼 수 있다는 것이다.

정답이 보이는 해설

우리의 뇌가 규칙적인 연습을 통해 강해지고 우리는 뇌를 실제로 훈련시킬 수 있으며 뇌가 더 행복해지도록 습관을 형성할 수 있다는 내용이므로, 글의 주제로 가장 적절한 것은 ① '행복을 위해 뇌 습관을 형성하는 것의 가능성'이다.

선택지 완벽 분석

① possibility of forming brain habits for well-being 행복을 위해 뇌 습관을 형성하는 것의 가능성
② role of brain circuits in improving body movements 신체 움직임을 개선하는 데 있어 뇌 회로의 역할
③ importance of practice in playing musical instruments 악기를 연주하는 데 있어서 연습의 중요성
④ effect of taking a break on enhancing memory capacity 휴식을 취하는 것이 기억 용량을 향상시키는 데 미치는 영향
⑤ difficulty of discovering how neurons in the brain work 뇌의 뉴런이 작동하는 방식을 발견하는 것의 어려움

필수 어휘

neuroscientist 신경과학자 circuit 회로 fundamentally 근본적으로
gratitude 감사 neuron 뉴런, 신경 세포 activate 활성화시키다
encouraging 고무적인, 용기를 주는 bottom line 요점, 핵심
intentionally 의도적으로

09 정답 ①

202109 23번 정답률 79%

Vegetarian eating is moving into the mainstream as more and more young adults say no to meat, poultry, and fish. According to the American Dietetic Association, "approximately planned vegetarian diets are healthful, are nutritionally adequate, and provide health benefits in the prevention and treatment of certain diseases." 주제문 But health concerns are not the only reason that young adults give for changing their diets. 단서1 Some make the choice (채식 선택 이유 1: 동물 권리에 대한) out of concern for animal rights. ❋ When faced with *the statistics* (관심 때문에) (접속사 that 생략) (they(= many teens) are 생략) [that show *the majority of animals* (raised as food) live in (주격 관계대명사) (주어) (동사) confinement], / many teens give up meat (to protest those (포기하다) (부사적 용법(목적)) conditions). 단서2 Others turn to vegetarianism to support the (채식 선택 이유 2: 환경을 지지하려고) environment. Meat production uses vast amounts of water, land, (막대한 양의 ~) grain, and energy and creates problems with animal waste and resulting pollution.

점점 더 많은 젊은이들이 고기, 가금류, 생선에 반대함에 따라 채식은 주류가 되고 있다. 미국 영양사 협회에 따르면, "거의 정확히 계획된 채식 식단이 건강에 좋고, 영양학적으로도 적당하며, 특정 질병의 예방과 치료에 건강상의 이점을 제공한다." 그러나 건강에 대한 염려가 젊은이들이 그들의 식단을 바꾸려고 하는 유일한 이유는 아니다. 어떤 젊은이들은 동물의 권리에 대한 관심 때문에 선택한다. 음식으로 길러지는 대다수의 동물들이 갇혀서 산다는 것을 보여 주는 통계 자료를 볼 때, 많은 십 대들은 그러한 상황에 저항하기 위해 고기를 포기한다. 다른 젊은이들은 환경을 지지하기 위해 채식주의가 된다. 고기 생산은 거대한 양의 물, 땅, 곡식과 에너지를 사용하고, 가축 배설물과 그에 따른 오염과 같은 문제들을 만들어 낸다.

정답이 보이는 해설

많은 젊은이들이 채식을 선택하는 이유는 단지 건강상의 염려 때문이 아니라 동물의 권리나 환경에 대한 생각 때문이라는 내용의 글이므로, 글의 주제로 가장 적절한 것은 ① '젊은 사람들이 채식을 택하는 이유들'이다.

선택지 완벽 분석

① reasons why young people go for vegetarian diets 젊은 사람들이 채식을 택하는 이유들
② ways to build healthy eating habits for teenagers 십 대들이 건강에 좋은 식습관을 기르는 방법들
③ vegetables that help lower your risk of cancer 암의 위험을 낮추는 것을 돕는 채소
④ importance of maintaining a balanced diet 균형 잡힌 식단을 유지하는 것의 중요성
⑤ disadvantages of plant-based diets 식물 기반 식단의 단점

필수 어휘

vegetarian 채식의 mainstream 주류 approximately 거의 정확하게, 가까이
nutritionally 영양학적으로 adequate 적당한 prevention 예방
treatment 치료 statistics 통계자료 confinement 갇힘, 가둠
vegetarianism 채식주의 animal waste 가축 배설물 resulting 결과로 초래된

10 정답 ②

202106 23번 정답률 65%

주제문 Curiosity makes us much more likely to view a tough problem as an interesting challenge to take on. A stressful meeting with our boss becomes an opportunity to learn. A nervous first date becomes an exciting night out with a new person. A colander becomes a hat. ✪ **단서** In general, / curiosity **motivates** us / to view stressful situations as challenges rather than threats, / to talk about difficulties more openly, / and to try new approaches to solving problems. In fact, curiosity is associated with a less defensive reaction to stress and, as a result, less aggression when we respond to irritation.

해석

호기심은 우리로 하여금 어떤 힘든 문제를 떠맡아야 할 재미난 도전이라고 여기도록 할 가능성을 더 크게 만든다. 상사와의 스트레스 가득한 회의는 배울 수 있는 기회가 된다. 긴장이 되는 첫 데이트는 새로운 사람과의 멋진 밤 외출이 된다. 주방용 체는 모자가 된다. 일반적으로, 호기심은 우리가 스트레스 가득한 상황을 위협보다는 도전으로 여기도록 하고, 좀 더 터놓고 어려움에 대해 말하게 하며, 문제 해결에 대한 새로운 접근법을 시도하도록 동기 부여를 해 준다. 실제로, 호기심은 스트레스에 덜 방어적인 반응을 하고, 그 결과 짜증에 반응할 때 덜 공격적인 것과 관련이 있다.

정답이 보이는 해설

호기심이 생기면 우리는 힘든 문제를 재미난 도전으로 생각하게 되고, 스트레스나 짜증에 덜 방어적이고 덜 공격적인 반응을 보인다는 내용이므로, 글의 주제로 가장 적절한 것은 ② '긍정적인 재구성이라는 숨겨진 힘으로서의 호기심'이다.

선택지 완벽 분석

① importance of defensive reactions in a tough situation 힘든 상황에서 방어적인 반응의 중요성
② curiosity as the hidden force of positive reframes 긍정적인 재구성이라는 숨겨진 힘으로서의 호기심
③ difficulties of coping with stress at work 직장에서 스트레스에 대처하는 것의 어려움
④ potential threats caused by curiosity 호기심에 의해 야기된 잠재적인 위협들
⑤ factors that reduce human curiosity 인간의 호기심을 줄이는 요인들

필수 어휘

motivate 동기를 부여하다 threat 위협 approach 접근법, 접근
defensive 방어적인 aggression 공격성, 공격 irritation 짜증, 화

11 정답 ①

202103 23번 정답률 69%

When two people are involved in an honest and open conversation, there is a back and forth flow of information. It is a smooth exchange. Since each one is drawing on their past personal experiences, the pace of the exchange is as fast as memory. **주제문** When one person lies, their responses will come more slowly because the brain needs more time to process the details of a new invention than to recall stored facts. As they say, "Timing is everything." **단서** You will notice the time lag when you are having a conversation with someone who is making things up as they go. ✪ Don't forget [that the other person may be reading your body language as well], / and [if you seem to be disbelieving their story, / they will have to pause to process that information, too].

해석

두 사람이 솔직하고 허심탄회한 대화를 할 때 정보가 왔다갔다하는 흐름이 있다. 그것은 매끄럽게 이야기를 나누는 것이다. 각자가 자신의 개인적인 과거 경험에서 이야기를 끌어내고 있기 때문에, 이야기를 나누는 속도는 기억만큼 빠르다. 한 사람이 거짓말을 하면, 그들의 반응은 더 느리게 나올 것인데, 왜냐하면 뇌는 저장된 사실을 기억해 내는 데 비해 새로 꾸며낸 이야기의 세부 사항을 처리하는 데 더 많은 시간이 필요하기 때문이다. 사람들 말처럼 "타이밍이 가장 중요하다." 여러분은 말을 하면서 이야기를 꾸며내고 있는 누군가와 이야기를 하고 있을 때, 시간이 지연되는 것을 알아차릴 것이다. 상대방 역시 여러분의 몸짓 언어를 읽고 있을지도 모른다는 것, 그리고 만약 여러분이 그 사람의 이야기를 믿지 않고 있는 것처럼 보이면, 그 사람은 또한 그 정보를 처리하기 위해 잠시 멈춰야 한다는 것을 잊지 말라.

정답이 보이는 해설

대화를 할 때 거짓말을 하게 되면 저장된 사실과 꾸며낸 이야기에 대한 뇌의 처리 속도에 차이가 있어 반응하는 데 시간이 더 걸린다는 내용이므로, 글의 주제로 가장 적절한 것은 ① '거짓말의 표시로서 지연된 반응들'이다.

선택지 완벽 분석

① delayed responses as a sign of lying 거짓말의 표시로서 지연된 반응들
② ways listeners encourage the speaker 듣는 사람이 말하는 사람을 격려하는 방법들
③ difficulties in finding useful information 유용한 정보를 찾는 것의 어려움
④ necessity of white lies in social settings 사회적 상황 속에서 선의의 거짓말의 필요성
⑤ shared experiences as conversation topics 대화 주제로서의 공유 경험들

필수 어휘

flow 흐름 exchange 이야기를 나눔, 대화 response 반응 process 처리하다
invention 꾸며낸 이야기, 창작 recall 기억해 내다 stored 저장된
disbelieve 믿지 않다, 의심하다 pause 잠시 멈추다

12 정답 ①

❖ The use (of renewable sources of energy to produce electricity) / has increasingly been encouraged as a way to harmonize the need (to secure electricity supply) / with environmental protection objectives. But the use of renewable sources also comes with its own consequences, which require consideration. Renewable sources of energy include a variety of sources such as hydropower and ocean-based technologies. 주제문 Additionally, solar, wind, geothermal and biomass renewable sources also have their own impact on the environment. 단서1 Hydropower dams, for example, have an impact on aquatic ecosystems and, more recently, have been identified as significant sources of greenhouse emissions. 단서2 Wind, solar, and biomass also cause negative environmental impacts, such as visual pollution, intensive land occupation and negative effects on bird populations.

해석

전기를 생산하기 위한 재생 가능 에너지원의 사용은 전기 공급 확보의 필요성과 환경 보호의 목적이 조화를 이루는 방법으로 점점 더 장려되어 왔다. 그러나 재생 가능한 자원의 이용은 또한 그것 자체의 결과를 수반하는데, 이는 생각해 볼 필요가 있다. 재생 가능한 에너지원은 수력 발전과 해양 기반 기술처럼 다양한 자원을 포함한다. 게다가, 태양열, 풍력, 지열, 그리고 에너지로 사용 가능한 생물체의 재생 가능한 에너지원 또한 환경에 저마다의 영향을 끼친다. 예를 들어, 수력 발전 댐은 수생 생태계에 영향을 끼치고, 더 최근에는 온실가스 배출의 주요 원인으로 확인되었다. 풍력, 태양열, 그리고 에너지로 사용 가능한 생물체는 또한 시각 공해, 집약적인 토지 점유, 조류 개체군에 미치는 부정적인 영향과 같이 환경에 부정적인 영향을 초래한다.

정답이 보이는 해설

전기 공급 확보와 환경 보호를 목적으로 재생 가능한 에너지 사용을 장려하는 것에 대해 생각해 봐야 한다고 하면서, 재생 가능한 에너지원이 다양한 형태로 환경에 부정적인 영향을 초래한다는 내용이므로, 글의 주제로 가장 적절한 것은 ① '재생 가능한 에너지원을 사용하는 것의 환경적인 부작용들'이다.

선택지 완벽 분석

① environmental side effects of using renewable energy sources 재생 가능한 에너지원을 사용하는 것의 환경적인 부작용들

② practical methods to meet increasing demand for electricity 증가하는 전기 수요를 충족시키기 위한 실용적인 방법들

③ negative impacts of the use of traditional energy sources 전통적인 에너지원 사용의 부정적인 영향들

④ numerous ways to obtain renewable sources of energy 재생 가능한 에너지원을 얻는 다양한 방법들

⑤ effective procedures to reduce greenhouse emissions 온실가스 배출을 줄이기 위한 효율적인 절차들

필수 어휘

renewable 재생 가능한 secure 확보하다 objective 목적 consequence 결과
consideration 생각, 숙고 hydropower 수력 발전 aquatic 수생의
identify 확인하다 significant 주요한, 중요한 intensive 집중적인, 집약적인
occupation 점유 population 개체군

7강 2020~2023 제목 추론

01 정답 ①

We think we are shaping our buildings. 주제문 But really, our buildings and development are also shaping us. One of the best examples of this is the oldest-known construction: the ornately carved rings of standing stones at Göbekli Tepe in Turkey. 단서1 Before these ancestors got the idea to erect standing stones some 12,000 years ago, they were hunter-gatherers. It appears that the erection of the multiple rings of megalithic stones took so long, and so many successive generations, 단서2 that these innovators were forced to settle down to complete the construction works. In the process, 단서3 they became the first farming society on Earth. 단서4 ❖ This is an early example of a society / constructing something / [that ends up radically remaking the society itself]. Things are not so different in our own time.

해석

우리는 우리가 건물을 형성한다고 생각한다. 그러나 실제로는 우리의 건물과 개발 역시 우리를 형성하고 있다. 이것의 가장 좋은 예 중 하나는 가장 오래되었다고 알려진 건축물인 튀르키예의 Göbekli Tepe에 있는 화려하게 조각된 입석의 고리이다. 약 12,000년 전에 이 조상들이 입석을 세우겠다는 아이디어를 내기 전에 그들은 수렵 채집인이었다. 거석으로 된 여러 개의 고리를 세우는 데 오랜 시간이 걸렸고 잇따른 여러 세대를 거쳐야 해서 이 혁신가들은 건설 작업을 완료하기 위해 정착해야만 했던 것으로 보인다. 그 과정에서, 그들은 지구상 최초의 농업 사회가 되었다. 이것은 결국 사회 자체를 완전히 재구성하는 무언가를 건설하는 사회의 초기 예이다. 우리 시대에도 상황이 그렇게 다르지 않다.

정답이 보이는 해설

우리가 건축물을 만들 때 건축물도 우리를 만든다는 내용의 글이다. 12,000년 전 튀르키예 사람들이 거석으로 된 다수의 고리를 만들면서 정착 생활을 시작했고, 이것이 최초의 농업 사회라는 예를 들면서 현재 시대에도 상황이 비슷하다는 내용이 이어진다. 따라서 글의 제목으로 가장 적절한 것은 ① '건물은 우리가 사는 방법을 바꾼다!'이다.

선택지 완벽 분석

① Buildings Transform How We Live! 건물은 우리가 사는 방법을 바꾼다!

② Why Do We Build More Than We Need? 우리는 왜 필요한 것보다 많이 짓는가?

③ Copying Ancient Buildings for Creativity 창의력을 위한 고대 건축물 복제
고대 튀르키예 건축물의 건축 과정을 예로 들고 있으나, 창의력을 위해 이를 복제한다는 내용은 없으므로 이 글의 제목으로 적절하지 않다.

④ Was Life Better in Hunter-gather Times? 수렵 채집인 시기의 삶이 더 나았는가?

⑤ Innovate Your Farm with New Constructions 새로운 건축물로 당신의 농장을 쇄신하라

필수 어휘

development 개발 construction 건축물 carve 조각하다
ancestor 조상, 선조 erect 세우다 erection 건설
successive 연이은, 잇따른 generation 세대 innovator 혁신가
process 과정 radically 완전히, 근본적으로 remake 다시 만들다, 탈바꿈하다

02 정답 ①

202306 24번 정답률 68%

Few people will be surprised to hear that poverty tends to
~해서 놀라다
create stress: a 2006 study published in the American journal
Psychosomatic Medicine, for example, noted that a lower
socioeconomic status was associated with higher levels of stress
be associated with: ~과 관련이 있다
hormones in the body. 주제문 **However, richer economies have**
their own distinct stresses. The key issue is time pressure. A 1999
study of 31 countries by American psychologist Robert Levine
and Canadian psychologist Ara Norenzayan found that 단서1
wealthier, more industrialized nations had a faster pace of life —
더 부유하고, 더 산업화된 국가들이 더 빠른 삶의 속도를 가지고 있음
which led to a higher standard of living, but at the same time 단서2
lead to: ~으로 이어지다   동시에
left the population feeling a constant sense of urgency, as well as
사람들이 지속적인 촉박함을 느끼게 함   ~ 뿐만 아니라
being 단서3 **more prone to heart disease.** ✪ (In effect,) / fast-paced
심장병에 더 걸리기 쉬움   사실
productivity creates wealth, // but 단서4 **it also leads people to feel**
시간이 부족하다고 느끼게 함
time-poor / when they lack *the time* [to relax and enjoy themselves].
시간의 부사절   형용사적 용법

해석

가난이 스트레스를 유발하는 경향이 있다는 것을 듣고 놀랄 사람은 거의 없을 것이
다: 예를 들어, 미국의 저널 'Psychosomatic Medicine'에 발표된 2006년 연구
는 더 낮은 사회 경제적 지위가 체내의 더 높은 수치의 스트레스 호르몬과 관련이 있
다고 언급했다. 하지만, 더 부유한 국가는 그들만의 뚜렷한 스트레스를 가지고 있다.
핵심 쟁점은 시간 압박이다. 미국 심리학자 Robert Levine과 캐나다 심리학자 Ara
Norenzayan이 31개국을 대상으로 한 1999년 연구는 더 부유하고, 더 산업화된
국가들이 더 빠른 삶의 속도를 가지고 있다는 것 — 그리고 이것이 더 높은 생활 수
준으로 이어졌지만, 동시에 사람들에게 지속적인 촉박함을 느끼게 했고 그뿐만 아니
라 심장병에 걸리기 더 쉽게 한다는 것을 알아냈다. 사실, 빠른 속도의 생산력은 부를
창출하지만, 그것은 또한 사람들이 긴장을 풀고 즐겁게 지낼 시간이 모자랄 때 시간
에 쪼들린다고 느끼게 한다.

정답이 보이는 해설

가난이 스트레스를 유발하는 경향이 있으나, 더 부유한 국가조차도 그들만의 스트
레스를 갖고 있으며, 이는 시간 압박으로 인한 것이라는 내용의 글이다. 더 빠른 삶의
속도는 지속적인 촉박감을 느끼게 만들고, 심장병에 걸리기 더 쉽게 만들며, 빠른 속
도의 생산력은 사람들이 긴장을 풀고 즐겁게 지낼 시간이 없다고 느끼게 한다고 설
명하고 있다. 따라서 글의 제목으로 가장 적절한 것은 ① '왜 심지어 부유한 나라들도
스트레스로부터 자유롭지 못하는가?'이다.

🔍 선택지 완벽 분석

① Why Are Even Wealthy Countries Not Free from Stress? 왜 심
지어 부유한 나라들도 스트레스로부터 자유롭지 못하는가?

② In Search of the Path to Escaping the Poverty Trap 빈곤의 덫에
서 탈출하는 길을 찾아서

③ Time Management: Everything You Need to Know 시간 관리: 알
아야 할 모든 것

④ How Does Stress Affect Human Bodies? 스트레스는 인체에 어떤
영향을 미치는가?
함정 부유한 국가의 사람들은 시간의 압박에 의해 촉박감을 느끼고, 심장병에 쉽게 걸릴 수 있다
는 내용이 있지만, 그 부분이 이 글 전체를 나타낸다고 볼 수 없으므로, 이 글의 제목으로 적
절하지 않다.

⑤ Sound Mind Wins the Game of Life! 건전한 정신이 인생이라는 게임
에서 승리한다!

필수 어휘

poverty 가난   journal 저널, 학술지   note 언급하다
socioeconomic 사회 경제적   status 지위   economy (경제 주체로서의) 국가
distinct 뚜렷한   pressure 압박   psychologist 심리학자

---

industrialized 산업화된   standard 수준   constant 지속적인
urgency 촉박, 긴급성   productivity 생산력   lack 부족하다
relax 긴장을 풀다, 쉬다

03 정답 ②

202303 24번 정답률 71%

단서1 **Success can lead you off your intended path and into a**
성공은 틀에 박힌 편안한 생활로 이어질 수 있음
comfortable rut. If you are good at something and are well rewarded
be good at: ~을 잘하다
for doing it, 단서2 **you may want to keep doing it even if you stop**
즐겁지 않아도 그냥 계속하게 됨
enjoying it. ✪ The danger is [that (one day) you look around and
is의 보어절   동사1
realize [you're so deep in this comfortable rut that you can no
동사2   realize의 목적어절1 (that 생략)
longer see the sun or breathe fresh air]; [the sides of the rut have
더 이상 ~이 아닌   realize의 목적어절2
become so slippery that it would take a superhuman effort to
so ~ that: 너무 ~해서 …하다
climb out]; / and, [effectively, you're stuck]]. And it's a situation
realize의 목적어절3
that many working people worry they're in now. 주제문 **The poor**
employment market has left them feeling locked in what may be a
secure, or even well-paying — but ultimately unsatisfying — job.

해석

성공은 여러분이 의도한 길에서 벗어나 틀에 박힌 편안한 생활로 이끌 수 있다. 여
러분이 어떤 일을 잘하고 그것을 하는 것에 대한 보상을 잘 받는다면, 그것을 즐기
지 않게 되더라도 계속 그것을 하고 싶을 수도 있다. 위험한 점은 어느 날 여러분이
주변을 둘러보고, 자신이 틀에 박힌 이 편안한 생활에 너무나 깊이 빠져 있어서 더
는 태양을 보거나 신선한 공기를 호흡할 수 없으며, 그 틀에 박힌 생활의 양쪽 면이
너무 미끄럽게 되어 기어올라 나오려면 초인적인 노력이 필요할 것이고, 실질적으로
자신이 꼼짝할 수 없다는 것을 깨닫게 된다는 것이다. 그리고 그것이 바로 많은 근로
자가 현재 자신이 처해 있다고 걱정하는 상황이다. 열악한 고용 시장이 그들을 안정
적이거나 심지어 보수가 좋을 수도 있지만, 궁극적으로는 만족스럽지 못한 일자리에
갇혀 있다고 느끼게 해 놓았다.

정답이 보이는 해설

어떤 일을 잘해서 보상을 잘 받는다면 즐겁지 않아도 그냥 계속하듯이, 직장 생활에
서의 성공은 틀에 박힌 생활을 하게 만들고, 벗어나고 싶어졌을 때 사실상 꼼짝도 못
한다는 것을 깨닫게 될 수 있다. 즉, 많은 근로자들이 안정적이거나 보수가 좋아도 결
국 만족스럽지 못한 일자리에 갇혀 있다고 느끼게 될 수 있다는 내용의 글이다. 따라
서 글의 제목으로 가장 적절한 것은 ② '성공적인 직장 생활의 함정'이다.

🔍 선택지 완벽 분석

① Don't Compete with Yourself 자기 자신과 경쟁하지 마라

② A Trap of a Successful Career 성공적인 직장 생활의 함정

③ Create More Jobs for Young People 젊은이들을 위한 더 많은 일자리
를 창출하라

④ What Difficult Jobs Have in Common 어려운 직업들이 갖는 공통점
함정 성공적인 직장 생활은 틀에 박힌 일상에 갇혀 있게 만들 수 있다는 내용이지, 어려운 직업에
관한 내용은 아님에 유의해야 한다.

⑤ A Road Map for an Influential Employer 영향력 있는 고용주를 위한
로드맵

필수 어휘

intend 의도하다   path 길   comfortable 편안한   reward 보상을 주다; 보상
realize 깨닫다   breathe 호흡하다, 숨 쉬다   slippery 미끄러운
superhuman 초인적인   effort 노력   effectively 사실상, 실질적으로
situation 상황   employment 고용   locked 갇힌   secure 안정적인
ultimately 궁극적으로

04 정답 ④

202211 24번 정답률 57%

Have you ever brought up an idea or suggestion to someone and
bring up: (화제 등)을 꺼내다
heard them immediately say "No, that won't work."? You may have
thought, "He/she didn't even give it a chance. How do they know it
won't work?" **단서** When you are right about something, you close
옳다고 생각하면, 다른 견해나 기회의 가능성을 차단시킬 수 있음
off the possibility of another viewpoint or opportunity. Being right
~을 차단시키다
about something means that "it is the way it is, period." You may be
correct. Your particular way of seeing it may be true with the facts.
주제문 However, considering the other option or the other person's
point of view can be beneficial. ✪ If you see their side, // you will
견해, 관점   조건의 부사절
see something (new) / or, (at worse,) learn something (about [how
동사1   동사2 (will 생략)   about의
the other person looks at life]). Why would you think everyone
목적어절
sees and experiences life the way you do? Besides how boring that
would be, it would eliminate all new opportunities, ideas, invention,
and creativity.

해석
누군가에게 아이디어나 제안을 내놓고, 그들이 즉시 "아니, 그건 안 될 거야."라고 말하는 것을 들어 본 적이 있는가? 여러분은 아마도 "그 사람은 기회조차 주지 않았어. 어떻게 그들은 그것이 안 될 것이라는 것을 알지?"라고 생각했을지 모른다. 여러분은 어떤 일에 대해 옳다면, 다른 관점이나 기회의 가능성을 닫아 버린다. 어떤 일에 대해 옳다는 것은 "그것은 원래 그런 거야, 끝."이라고 하는 것을 의미한다. 여러분이 맞을 수도 있다. 여러분이 그것을 보는 특정한 방법이 사실에 부합할 수도 있다. 하지만 다른 선택이나 다른 사람의 관점을 고려하는 것이 이로울 수 있다. 만약 여러분이 그들의 관점을 안다면, 여러분은 새로운 무언가를 보게 되거나, 그것보다는 더 안 좋게는 다른 사람이 삶을 바라보는 방식에 대한 무언가를 배우게 될 것이다. 왜 모두가 여러분이 하는 방식대로 삶을 바라보고 경험할 것이라고 생각하는가? 그것이 얼마나 지루할지는 제외하고라도, 그것은 모든 새로운 기회, 아이디어, 발명, 그리고 창의성을 없애게 될 것이다.

정답이 보이는 해설
자기가 옳다고 생각하면, 다른 사람의 관점이나 다른 가능성을 닫아 버리게 되는데, 다른 선택이나 다른 사람이 삶을 보는 방식을 고려하는 것이 이로울 수 있다는 내용의 글이다. 따라서 글의 제목으로 가장 적절한 것은 ④ '옳다는 것은 새로운 가능성을 차단할 수 있다'이다.

선택지 완벽 분석
① The Value of Being Honest 정직함의 가치
② Filter Out Negative Points of View 부정적인 견해를 걸러내라
③ Keeping Your Word: A Road to Success 약속 지키기: 성공으로 가는 길
④ Being Right Can Block New Possibilities 옳다는 것은 새로운 가능성을 차단할 수 있다
⑤ Look Back When Everyone Looks Forward 모두가 앞을 볼 때 뒤를 봐라
  함정 다른 사람의 관점이나 다른 선택지를 고려해 봐야 한다는 내용이므로, 뒤를 돌아보려고 노력하라는 내용과는 무관하다.

필수 어휘
suggestion 제안, 의견 immediately 즉시, 바로 possibility 가능성
viewpoint 관점, 시각 opportunity 기회 period 마침표 particular 특정한
consider 고려하다 option 선택, 선택지 beneficial 이로운, 유익한
experience 경험하다 eliminate 없애다, 제거하다

---

05 정답 ①

202209 24번 정답률 69%

실수를 하다
단서1 Many people make a mistake of only operating along
많은 사람들이 안전 구역에서만 움직이기 때문에 더 큰 일을 할 기회를 놓침
the safe zones, and in the process they miss the opportunity
to achieve greater things. They do so because of a fear of the
unknown and a fear of treading the unknown paths of life.
주어   주격 관계대명사절   「형용사+enough+to부정사」   과거분사구
✪ **단서2** *Those* [that are **brave enough to take** *those roads* (less
다른 사람들이 잘 선택하지 않는 길을 택하는 용감한 사람들은 큰 보상과 만족감을 얻음
travelled)] are able to get great returns and derive major satisfaction
동사   └─── 병렬 구조 ───┘
out of their courageous moves. Being overcautious will mean that you
derive A out of B: B로부터 A를 끌어내다
will miss attaining the greatest levels of your potential. **주제문** You
must learn to take those chances that many people around you will
not take, because your success will flow from those bold decisions
that you will take along the way.
그 과정에서

해석
많은 사람들이 안전 구역에서만 움직이는 실수를 하고, 그 과정에서 더 위대한 일을 성취할 기회를 놓친다. 그들은 미지의 세계에 대한 두려움과 알려지지 않은 삶의 경로를 밟는 것에 대한 두려움 때문에 그렇게 한다. 사람들이 잘 다니지 않는 이런 길을 택할 만큼 충분히 용감한 사람들은 훌륭한 보상을 받을 수 있고 자신들의 용감한 행동으로부터 큰 만족감을 끌어낼 수 있다. 지나치게 조심하는 것은 여러분의 잠재력의 최고 수준을 이루는 것을 놓친다는 것을 의미할 것이다. 여러분은 여러분 주변의 많은 사람들이 선택하지 않을 기회를 선택하는 것을 배워야 하는데, 이는 여러분의 성공은 삶의 과정에서 여러분이 내릴 그러한 용감한 결정에서 나올 것이기 때문이다.

정답이 보이는 해설
많은 사람들이 안전 구역에서만 움직여서 기회를 놓치는데, 미지의 세계에 대한 두려움을 극복하고 다른 사람들이 가지 않는 길을 선택해야 더 많은 성공의 기회를 얻을 수 있다는 것을 설명하는 글이다. 따라서 글의 제목으로 가장 적절한 것은 ① '용감할수록 더 많은 기회가 온다'이다.

선택지 완벽 분석
① More Courage Brings More Opportunities 용감할수록 더 많은 기회가 온다
② Travel: The Best Way to Make Friends 여행: 친구를 사귀는 최고의 방법
  'treading the unknown paths'나 'those roads less travelled'만 보고 여행에 관한 글로 잘못 생각할 수 있으나, 가지 않은 길에 대한 두려움을 비유적으로 설명한 표현이며, 여행과 관련된 내용의 글이 아니다.
③ How to Turn Mistakes into Success 실수를 성공으로 바꾸는 방법
④ Satisfying Life? Share with Others 만족스러운 삶인가? 다른 사람들과 공유하라
⑤ Why Is Overcoming Fear So Hard? 두려움을 극복하는 것이 그렇게 어려운 이유는 무엇인가?
  두려움을 극복하는 것이 어려운 이유를 설명한 글이 아니라 용감하게 두려움을 극복해야 더 많은 기회를 얻을 수 있다는 내용의 글이므로, 글의 제목으로 적절하지 않다.

필수 어휘
operate 움직이다, 가동되다 process 과정 achieve 성취하다, 달성하다
returns 보상, 수익 derive 끌어내다 overcautious 지나치게 조심하는
attain 이루다, 달성하다 potential 잠재력 bold 용감한

7강
제목 추론

Only a generation or two ago, mentioning the word *algorithms* would have drawn a blank from most people. 주제문 Today, algorithms appear in every part of civilization. 단서1 They are connected to everyday life. They're not just in your cell phone or your laptop but in your car, your house, your appliances, and your toys. ★ Your bank is a huge web of algorithms, / with humans turning the switches here and there. Algorithms schedule flights and then fly the airplanes. Algorithms run factories, trade goods, and keep records. 단서2 If every algorithm suddenly stopped working, it would be the end of the world as we know it.

아무 반응을 얻지 못하다 / ~와 연결되어 있다 / 알고리즘은 일상생활과 연결되어 있음 / 분사구문(with+목적어+분사) / 모든 알고리즘의 작동이 멈추면 세상도 멈출 것임

해석
한 세대 내지 두 세대 전만 해도 '알고리즘'이라는 단어를 언급하는 것은 대부분의 사람들로부터 아무 반응을 얻지 못했을 것이다. 오늘날 알고리즘은 문명의 모든 부분에서 등장한다. 그것들은 일상생활과 연결되어 있다. 그것들은 여러분의 휴대전화나 노트북 내부뿐만 아니라 여러분의 자동차, 집, 가전제품, 그리고 장난감 안에도 있다. 여러분의 은행은 인간들이 여기저기서 스위치를 전환하고 있는 알고리즘의 거대한 망이다. 알고리즘은 비행 일정을 잡고 그런 다음 비행기를 운항한다. 알고리즘은 공장을 운영하고, 상품을 거래하며, 기록 문서를 보관한다. 만약 모든 알고리즘이 갑자기 작동을 멈춘다면, 이는 우리가 알고 있듯 세상의 종말이 될 것이다.

정답이 보이는 해설
오늘날 알고리즘은 일상생활과 연결되어 있는 문명의 모든 부분에 등장하고 알고리즘이 작동을 멈추면 세상도 멈출 것이라는 내용이므로, 글의 제목으로 가장 적절한 것은 ① '우리는 알고리즘의 시대에 살고 있다'이다.

🔎 선택지 완벽 분석
① We Live in an Age of Algorithms 우리는 알고리즘의 시대에 살고 있다
② Mysteries of Ancient Civilizations 고대 문명의 수수께끼
③ Dangers of Online Banking Algorithms 온라인 뱅킹 알고리즘의 위험성
④ How Algorithms Decrease Human Creativity 알고리즘이 인간의 창의성을 감소시키는 방법
⑤ Transportation: A Driving Force of Industry 운송: 산업의 원동력

필수 어휘
generation 세대   mention 언급하다   algorithm 알고리즘
draw a blank 아무 반응을 얻지 못하다   civilization 문명
everyday 일상의, 매일의   appliances 가전제품   switch 스위치
trade 거래하다   goods 상품   keep records 기록 문서를 보관하다

Our ability to accurately recognize and label emotions is often referred to as *emotional granularity*. In the words of Harvard psychologist Susan David, "Learning to label emotions with a more nuanced vocabulary can be absolutely transformative." ★ David explains [that if we don't have a rich emotional vocabulary, / it is difficult to communicate our needs and to get *the support* (that we need) from others]. But 단서1 those who are able to distinguish between a range of various emotions "do much, much better at managing the ups and downs of ordinary existence than those who see everything in black and white." In fact, research shows that 단서2 the process of labeling emotional experience is related to greater emotion regulation and psychosocial well-being.

be referred to as: ~로 불리다 / 접속사(조건) / explains의 목적어절 / 가주어 / 진주어1 / 진주어2 / 관계대명사 / 다양한 감정을 구별할 수 있는 사람은 모든 것을 흑백 논리로 보는 사람보다 좋은 일과 나쁜 일을 더 잘 관리함 / 감정에 이름을 붙이는 과정은 감정 조절 능력 및 심리 사회적인 행복과 관련되어 있음

해석
감정을 정확히 인식하고 감정에 이름을 붙일 수 있는 우리의 능력은 흔히 '감정 입자도'라고 불린다. Harvard 대학의 심리학자 Susan David의 말에 따르면, "감정에 더 미묘한 차이가 있는 어휘로 이름을 붙이는 법을 배우는 것은 전적으로 (사람을) 변화시킬 수 있다." David는 우리가 풍부한 감정적인 어휘를 갖고 있지 않으면, 우리의 욕구를 전달하고 우리가 필요로 하는 지지를 다른 사람들로부터 얻는 것이 어렵다고 설명한다. 그러나 광범위한 다양한 감정을 구별할 수 있는 사람들은 "모든 것을 흑백 논리로 보는 사람들보다 평범한 존재로 사는 중에 겪는 좋은 일과 나쁜 일을 관리하는 것을 훨씬, 훨씬 더 잘한다." 사실, 감정적인 경험에 이름을 붙이는 과정은 더 큰 감정 조절 및 심리 사회적인 행복과 관련되어 있다는 것을 연구 결과가 보여 준다.

정답이 보이는 해설
감정을 인식하고 그것에 이름을 붙이는 것은 사람을 변화시킬 수 있으며 감정적인 경험에 이름을 붙이는 것은 살면서 겪는 일들을 훨씬 더 잘 관리하고 심리적인 행복과도 관련이 있다는 내용이므로, 글의 제목으로 가장 적절한 것은 ② '감정에 자세한 이름을 붙이는 것은 유익하다'이다.

🔎 선택지 완벽 분석
① True Friendship Endures Emotional Arguments 진정한 우정은 감정적인 논쟁을 견뎌 낸다
② Detailed Labeling of Emotions Is Beneficial 감정에 자세한 이름을 붙이는 것은 유익하다
③ Labeling Emotions: Easier Said Than Done 감정에 이름 붙이기: 말하기는 쉬워도 행하기는 어렵다
함정 이 글은 감정에 이름을 붙이는 것의 긍정적 측면만을 다루고 있으므로, 그것을 행하기 어렵다는 내용과는 관련이 없다.
④ Categorize and Label Tasks for Efficiency 효율성을 위해 작업을 분류하고 이름을 붙여라
⑤ Be Brave and Communicate Your Needs 용감하게 자신의 요구를 전달하라

필수 어휘
accurately 정확하게   recognize 인식하다   label 이름을 붙이다
psychologist 심리학자   absolutely 전적으로   transformative (사람을) 변화시키는
communicate 전달하다   distinguish 구별하다   a range of 다양한 ~
ups and downs 좋은 일과 나쁜 일   ordinary 평범한   existence 존재
regulation 조절   psychosocial 심리 사회적인   well-being 행복

08 정답 ②

In modern times, society became more dynamic. Social mobility increased, and people began to exercise a higher degree of choice regarding, for instance, their profession, their marriage, or their religion. This posed a challenge to traditional roles in society.

★ It was less evident [that one needed to commit to *the roles* (one
가주어   진주어(that절)   ~에 전념하다
was born into) / **when** alternatives could be realized]. 단서1 Increasing
접속사(~할 때)   삶의 선택에 대한
control over one's life choices became not only possible but desired.
통제력 증가가 가능해졌을 뿐만 아니라 바람직한 것이 됨
Identity then became a problem. 단서2 It was no longer almost
정체성은 더 이상 태어날 때 주어진 것이
ready-made at birth but something to be discovered. Traditional role
아니라 발견되어야 할 것이 됨
identities prescribed by society began to appear as masks imposed on people whose real self was to be found somewhere underneath.

해석

현대에 들어서는 사회가 더욱 역동적이게 되었다. 사회적 유동성이 증가했고 사람들은 가령 자신의 직업, 결혼 또는 종교와 관련하여 더 높은 정도의 선택권을 행사하기 시작했다. 이것은 사회의 전통적인 역할에 도전을 제기했다. 개인은 대안이 실현될 수 있을 때 자신이 타고난 역할에 전념해야 한다는 것이 덜 분명해졌다. 개인의 삶의 선택에 대한 통제력을 늘리는 것이 가능해졌을 뿐만 아니라 바람직한 것이 되었다. 그러자 정체성이 문제가 되었다. 그것은 더 이상 태어날 때 거의 주어진 것이 아니라 발견되어야 할 것이었다. 사회에 의해 규정된 전통적인 역할 정체성은 아래 어딘가에서 자신의 진정한 자아가 발견되어야 할 사람들에게 부여된 가면처럼 나타나기 시작했다.

정답이 보이는 해설

현대 사회에서는 사회적 유동성이 증가하고 개인의 선택권이 많아짐에 따라 사람들은 전통적인 역할에 도전을 하게 되었고, 이에 따라 정체성은 사회에 의해 규정되는 것이 아니라 발견되어야 하는 것이 되었다는 내용의 글이다. 따라서 글의 제목으로 가장 적절한 것은 ② '현대 사회가 우리가 우리의 정체성을 발견하도록 이끄는 방법'이다.

선택지 완벽 분석

① What Makes Our Modern Society So Competitive? 무엇이 우리의 현대 사회를 그토록 경쟁적으로 만드는가?
② How Modern Society Drives Us to Discover Our Identities 현대 사회가 우리를 우리의 정체성을 발견하도록 이끄는 방법
③ Social Masks: A Means to Build Trustworthy Relationships 사회적 가면: 신뢰할 수 있는 관계를 형성하기 위한 수단
④ The More Social Roles We Have, the Less Choice We Have 우리가 더 많은 사회적 역할을 가질수록 우리는 더 적은 선택을 하게 된다
함정 현대 사회에서는 사회적 역할에 대한 선택권이 늘어났다는 내용의 글이므로, 우리가 더 많은 사회적 역할을 갖게 되었다는 것과는 관계가 없다.
⑤ Increasing Social Mobility Leads Us to a More Equal Society 사회적 유동성을 증가시키는 것은 우리를 더욱 평등한 사회로 이끈다

필수 어휘

dynamic 역동적인   mobility 이동성   exercise (권력 등을) 행사하다
regarding ~에 관하여   profession 직업   pose 제기하다   evident 분명한
alternative 대안   desired 바람직한   identity 정체성   ready-made 이미 주어진
prescribe 규정하다   underneath 아래에

09 정답 ④

주제문 Diversity, challenge, and conflict help us maintain our imagination. Most people assume that conflict is bad and that being in one's "comfort zone" is good. That is not exactly true. Of course, we don't want to find ourselves without a job or medical insurance or in a fight with our partner, family, boss, or coworkers. One bad experience can be sufficient to last us a lifetime. But small disagreements with family and friends, trouble with technology or finances, or challenges at work and at home can help us think through our own capabilities. 단서 Problems that need solutions
문제가 창의적인 해답을 찾기 위해 뇌를 사용하
force us to use our brains in order to develop creative answers.
게 함

★ Navigating *landscapes* [**that** are varied], [**that** offer trials and
주어(동명사)   주격 관계대명사1   주격 관계대명사2
occasional conflicts], is more helpful to creativity than hanging
단수 동사   주어 Navigating과 비교
out in *landscapes* [**that** pose no challenge to our senses and our
주격 관계대명사
minds]. Our two million-year history is packed with challenges and
~으로 가득한
conflicts.

해석

다양성, 어려움, 그리고 갈등은 우리의 상상력을 유지하도록 돕는다. 대부분의 사람들은 갈등은 나쁜 것이고 '안락 지대'에 머무는 것이 좋은 것이라고 추정한다. 그것은 정확히는 사실이 아니다. 물론, 우리는 직장이나 의료보험이 없거나, 배우자, 가족, 직장 상사, 혹은 직장 동료들과의 다툼에 빠진 자신을 보고 싶어 하지 않는다. 하나의 나쁜 경험이 우리에게 평생 지속되는 데 충분할 수 있다. 하지만 가족과 친구들과의 작은 의견 충돌, 기술적 또는 재정적 문제, 직장과 가정에서의 어려움은 우리 자신의 능력을 충분히 생각하도록 도울 수 있다. 해결책이 필요한 문제들은 창의적인 해답들을 개발하기 위해 우리의 뇌를 사용하도록 강요한다. 시련과 때때로 갈등을 주는, 변화무쌍한 지형을 운전하는 것은 우리 감각과 마음에 아무런 어려움을 제기하지 않는 지형에서 서성대는 것보다 훨씬 더 창의성에 도움을 준다. 우리의 2백만 년 역사는 어려움과 갈등으로 가득 차 있다.

정답이 보이는 해설

다양성, 어려움, 갈등이 상상력과 창의력을 유지하는 데 도움이 된다는 내용의 글이다. 안락 지대에 머무는 것보다 작은 의견 충돌, 기술적 또는 재정적 문제, 가정과 직장에서의 문제들을 접했을 때 해결책을 찾으며 뇌를 사용하게 되고 이러한 시련과 갈등이 어려움이 없는 곳에 있는 것보다 창의성에 도움을 준다고 했으므로, 글의 제목으로 가장 적절한 것은 ④ '창의성은 안전을 기하는 데서 오지 않는다'이다.

선택지 완벽 분석

① Technology: A Lens to the Future 기술: 미래를 보는 렌즈
② Diversity: A Key to Social Unification 다양성: 사회 통합의 열쇠
③ Simple Ways to Avoid Conflicts with Others 타인과의 갈등을 피하는 간단한 방법
④ Creativity Doesn't Come from Playing It Safe 창의성은 안전을 기하는 데서 오지 않는다
⑤ There Are No Challenges That Can't Be Overcome 극복할 수 없는 어려움은 없다
함정 어려움의 극복에 대한 내용이 아니라 어려움이 창의력에 미치는 이점이 글의 주제이다.

필수 어휘

diversity 다양성   challenge 어려움, 도전   conflict 갈등
comfort zone 안락 지대(편안함을 느끼는 구역)   medical insurance 의료보험
sufficient 충분한   finance 재정   capability 능력, 역량
navigate 운전하다, 항해하다   trial 시련   occasional 가끔의
hang out 서성대다, 시간을 보내다   pose (문제 등을) 제기하다

10 정답 ①

When people think about the development of cities, rarely do they consider the critical role of vertical transportation. In fact, each day, more than 7 billion elevator journeys are taken in tall buildings all over the world. 단서 Efficient vertical transportation can expand our ability to build taller and taller skyscrapers. ✪ Antony Wood, (a Professor of Architecture at the Illinois Institute of Technology), / explains [that advances (in elevators) over the past 20 years / are probably *the greatest advances* (we have seen in tall buildings)].
For example, elevators in the Jeddah Tower in Jeddah, Saudi Arabia, under construction, will reach a height record of 660m.

해석

사람들은 도시 발전에 대해 생각할 때, 좀처럼 수직 운송 수단의 중요한 역할을 고려하지 않는다. 실제로 매일 70억 회 이상의 엘리베이터 이동이 전 세계의 고층 건물에서 일어난다. 효율적인 수직 운송 수단은 점점 더 높은 고층 건물을 지을 수 있는 우리의 능력을 확장시킬 수 있다. Illinois 공과 대학의 건축학과 교수인 Antony Wood는 지난 20년간의 엘리베이터의 발전은 아마도 우리가 높은 건물에서 봐 왔던 가장 큰 발전일 것이라고 설명한다. 예를 들어, 건설 중인 사우디아라비아 Jeddah의 Jeddah Tower에 있는 엘리베이터는 660미터라는 기록적인 높이에 이를 것이다.

정답이 보이는 해설

사람들은 엘리베이터의 중요성에 대해 거의 고려하지 않지만 효율적인 수직 운송 수단이 점점 더 높은 고층 건물을 지을 수 있는 능력을 확장시킬 수 있다는 내용이므로, 글의 제목으로 가장 적절한 것은 ① '엘리베이터는 건물을 하늘에 더 가깝게 한다'이다.

선택지 완벽 분석

① Elevators Bring Buildings Closer to the Sky 엘리베이터는 건물을 하늘에 더 가깝게 한다
② The Higher You Climb, the Better the View 더 높이 올라갈수록 전망이 더 좋다
③ How to Construct an Elevator Cheap and Fast 엘리베이터를 저렴하고 빠르게 건설하는 방법
   엘리베이터가 고층 건물 건설 능력을 확장시켰다는 내용으로 엘리베이터 건설 방법에 대해서는 언급되지 않았다.
④ The Function of the Ancient and the Modern City 고대와 현대 도시의 기능
⑤ The Evolution of Architecture: Solutions for Overpopulation 건축의 진화: 인구 과잉에 대한 해결책

필수 어휘

development 발전 rarely 좀처럼 ~하지 않는 critical 대단히 중요한
vertical 수직의, 종적인 transportation 운송, 수송 journey 이동, 여행
efficient 효율적인 skyscraper 고층 건물, 마천루 architecture 건축
advance 발전, 진전 record 기록

11 정답 ⑤

단서 Think, for a moment, about something you bought that you never ended up using. An item of clothing you never ended up wearing? A book you never read? Some piece of electronic equipment that never even made it out of the box? ✪ It is estimated / [that Australians alone **spend** on average $10.8 billion AUD (approximately $9.99 billion USD) every year **on** *goods* (they do not use)] — more than the total government spending on universities and roads. That is an average of $1,250 AUD (approximately $1,156 USD) for each household. 주제문 All the things we buy that then just sit there gathering dust are waste — a waste of money, a waste of time, and waste in the sense of pure rubbish. As the author Clive Hamilton observes, 'The difference between the stuff we buy and what we use is waste.'

해석

여러분이 사 두고 결국은 한 번도 사용하지 않은 물건에 대해 잠시 동안 생각해 보라. 결국에는 여러분이 한 번도 입지 않은 옷 한 점? 절대 읽지 않은 책 한 권? 심지어 상자에서 꺼내 본 적도 없는 어떤 전자 기기? 사용하지 않는 물건에 호주인들만 따져도 매년 평균 108억 호주 달러(약 99억 9천 미국 달러)를 쓰는 것으로 추산되는데, 이는 대학과 도로에 사용하는 정부 지출 총액을 넘어서는 금액이다. 그 금액은 가구당 평균 1,250 호주 달러(약 1,156 미국 달러)이다. 우리가 구입 후에 단지 그 자리에서 먼지만 모을 뿐인 모든 물건은 낭비인데, 돈 낭비, 시간 낭비, 그리고 순전히 쓸모없는 물건이라는 의미에서 낭비이다. 작가 Clive Hamilton이 말하는 것처럼 "우리가 사는 물건에서 우리가 사용하는 것을 뺀 것은 낭비이다."

정답이 보이는 해설

매년 사 놓고 사용하지 않는 물건을 구입하는 데 많은 돈을 쓰는데, 그것은 돈과 시간의 낭비라는 내용의 글이다. 따라서 글의 제목으로 가장 적절한 것은 ⑤ '사는 것은 그것을 사용하지 않으면 낭비이다'이다.

선택지 완벽 분석

① Spending Enables the Economy 지출이 경제를 가능하게 한다
② Money Management: Dos and Don'ts 자금 관리: 해야 할 것과 하지 말아야 할 것
③ Too Much Shopping: A Sign of Loneliness 지나친 쇼핑: 외로움의 신호
④ 3R's of Waste: Reduce, Reuse, and Recycle 쓰레기의 3R: 줄이라, 재사용하라, 재활용하라
⑤ What You Buy Is Waste Unless You Use It 사는 것은 그것을 사용하지 않으면 낭비이다

필수 어휘

electronic equipment 전자 기기 estimate 추산하다 billion 10억
approximately 약, 대략 goods 물건, 제품, 상품 government 정부
household 가구, 세대 dust 먼지 waste 낭비, 쓰레기 pure 순전한, 순수한
rubbish 쓸모없는 물건, 쓰레기 observe (발언·의견을) 말하다 stuff 물건

12 정답 ③

Chewing leads to smaller particles for swallowing, and more exposed surface area for digestive enzymes to act on. In other words, it means the extraction of more fuel and raw materials from a mouthful of food. 주제문 This is especially important for mammals because they heat their bodies from within. ✪ Chewing gives mammals *the energy* / (needed to be active **not only** during the day **but also** the cool night, / and to live in colder climates or places with changing temperatures). 단서1 It allows them to sustain higher levels of activity and travel speeds to cover larger distances, avoid predators, capture prey, and make and care for their young. 단서2 Mammals are able to live in an incredible variety of habitats, from Arctic tundra to Antarctic pack ice, deep open waters to high-altitude mountaintops, and rainforests to deserts, in no small measure because of their teeth.

해석

씹기는 삼키기를 위한 더 작은 조각들 및 소화 효소가 작용할 수 있는 더 많은 노출된 표면으로 이어진다. 다시 말해서, 그것은 한입의 음식으로부터 더 많은 에너지원과 원료를 추출하는 것을 의미한다. 이것은 그것이 체내에서 그들의 몸을 따뜻하게 하기 때문에 포유류에게 특히 중요하다. 씹기는 포유류에게 낮은 물론 서늘한 밤 동안에도 활동하고, 더 추운 기후나 기온이 변하는 곳에서 사는 데 필요한 에너지를 준다. 그것은 그들로 하여금 더 먼 거리를 가고, 포식자를 피하고, 먹이를 포획하고, 새끼를 낳고 돌볼 수 있게 하는 더 높은 수준의 활동과 이동 속도를 유지하게 한다. 포유류는 어느 정도는 그들의 이빨로 인해 북극 툰드라부터 남극의 유빙까지, 심해부터 고도가 높은 산꼭대기까지, 그리고 열대 우림부터 사막까지 엄청나게 다양한 서식지에서 살 수 있다.

정답이 보이는 해설

씹는 동작이 음식에서 더 많은 에너지원과 원료를 추출하도록 하고, 그것이 포유류가 추운 기후를 견디고 새끼를 낳고 돌보며, 더 먼 거리를 이동하여 다양한 서식지에서 살 수 있는 에너지를 준다는 내용이므로, 글의 제목으로 가장 적절한 것은 ③ '씹는 것이 포유류의 생존을 돕는 방법'이다.

선택지 완벽 분석

① Chewing: A Way to Ease Indigestion 씹기: 소화 불량을 완화하는 방법
② Boost Your Energy by Chewing More! 더 많이 씹어서 기력을 높이라!
③ How Chewing Helps Mammals Survive 씹는 것이 포유류의 생존을 돕는 방법
④ Different Types and Functions of Teeth 치아의 다양한 종류와 기능
⑤ A Harsh Climate Makes Mammals Stronger 혹독한 기후는 포유류를 더 강하게 만든다

필수 어휘

chewing 씹기 exposed 노출된 digestive 소화의 extraction 추출
raw material 원료 mammal 포유류 cover (언급된 거리를) 가다[이동하다]
predator 포식자, 천적 capture 포획하다 prey 먹이
incredible 믿을 수 없는, 엄청난 Arctic 북극의 tundra 툰드라
pack ice 유빙, 총빙 high-altitude 고도가 높은

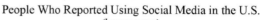

8강 2020~2023 도표의 이해

01 정답 ④

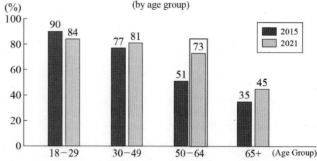

People Who Reported Using Social Media in the U.S.
(by age group)

단서 2021년 50~64세 집단에서 소셜 미디어를 사용한다고 답한 사람은 73%
→ 5분의 4(80%)가 되지 않음

The graph above shows the percentages of people in different age groups who reported using social media in the United States in 2015 and 2021. ① In each of the given years, the 18–29 group had the highest percentage of people who said they used social media. ② In 2015, the percentage of people who reported using social media in the 30–49 group was more than twice that in the 65 and older group. ③ ✪ The percentage of *people* / [**who** said they used social media in the 50–64 group in 2021] / was 22 percentage points higher than / that in 2015. ④ In 2021, except for the 65 and older group, more than four-fifths of people in each age group reported using social media. ⑤ Among all the age groups, only the 18–29 group showed a decrease in the percentage of people who reported using social media from 2015 to 2021.

해석

위 그래프는 2015년과 2021년에 미국에서 소셜 미디어를 사용한다고 보고했던 다양한 연령 집단 속 사람들의 비율을 보여 준다. ① 주어진 각각의 해에서 18~29세 집단에서 소셜 미디어를 사용한다고 말한 사람의 비율이 가장 높았다. ② 2015년에 30~49세 집단에서 소셜 미디어를 사용한다고 보고한 사람의 비율은 65세 이상 집단에서 그것의 두 배 이상이었다. ③ 2021년에 50~64세 집단에서 소셜 미디어를 사용한다고 말한 사람의 비율은 2015년의 그것보다 22퍼센트포인트 더 높았다. ④ 2021년에 65세 이상 집단을 제외한 각 연령 집단에서 5분의 4보다 더 많은 사람들이 소셜 미디어를 사용한다고 보고했다. ⑤ 모든 연령 집단 중에서 18~29세 집단만이 2015년에서 2021년까지 소셜 미디어를 사용한다고 보고한 사람의 비율에서 감소를 보였다.

정답이 보이는 해설

2021년 그래프에서 소셜 미디어를 사용한다고 대답한 사람들의 비율을 살펴보면 18~29세 집단은 84%, 30~49세 집단은 81%, 50~64세 집단은 73%, 65세 이상 집단은 45%이다. 이 중 65세 이상 집단을 제외하고 50~64세 집단에서 소셜 미디어를 사용한다고 대답한 사람은 5분의 4, 즉, 80%가 되지 않으므로, 도표의 내용과 일치하지 않는 것은 ④이다.

필수 어휘

percentage 백분율, 비율 report 보고하다 decrease 감소, 저하

8강
도표의 이해

Share of Forest Area in Total Land Area by Region in 1990 and 2019

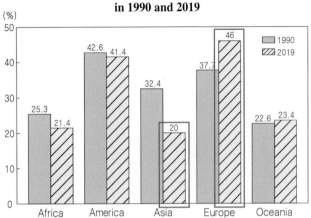

Number of Births and Deaths in Korea

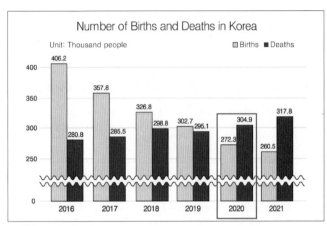

[단서] 2019년 산림 면적 점유율 비교: 유럽(46%) 〉 아시아(20%) → 유럽의 산림 면적 점유율이 아시아의 두 배가 넘음

The above graph shows the share of forest area in total land area by region in 1990 and 2019. ① Africa's share of forest area in total land area was over 20% in both 1990 and 2019. ② ⭐ The share of forest area (in America) was 42.6% (in 1990), / which was larger than that in 2019. ③ The share of forest area in Asia declined from 1990 to 2019 by more than 10 percentage points. ④ In 2019, the share of forest area in Europe was the largest among the five regions, more than three times(→ twice) that in Asia in the same year. ⑤ Oceania showed the smallest gap between 1990 and 2019 in terms of the share of forest area in total land area.

[해석]

위 도표는 1990년과 2019년의 지역별 총 토지 면적에서 산림 면적의 점유율을 보여 준다. ① 아프리카의 전체 토지 면적에서 산림 면적의 점유율이 1990년과 2019년 둘 다 20%를 넘었다. ② 1990년 아메리카의 산림 면적 점유율은 42.6%였고, 이는 2019년의 그것보다 더 컸다. ③ 아시아의 산림 면적 점유율은 1990년부터 2019년까지, 10퍼센트포인트 이상 감소했다. ④ 2019년 유럽의 산림 면적 점유율은 다섯 개 지역 중 가장 컸고, 같은 해 아시아의 그것의 세 배(→ 두 배)가 넘었다. ⑤ 오세아니아는 1990년과 2019년 사이에 총 토지 면적에서 산림 면적의 점유율에 있어 가장 작은 차이를 보였다.

[정답이 보이는 해설]

2019년 유럽의 산림 면적 점유율은 46%로 다섯 개 지역 중 가장 큰 것은 맞지만, 같은 해인 2019년 아시아의 산림 면적 점유율은 20%이므로, 아시아의 점유율의 세 배가 아닌 두 배가 넘는 수치이다. 따라서 도표의 내용과 일치하지 않는 것은 ④이다.

[필수 어휘]

share 점유율 region 지역 decline 감소하다 gap 차이

[단서] 처음으로 사망자 수가 출생자 수보다 더 컸던 해는 2021년이 아니라 2020년임

The above graph shows the number of births and deaths in Korea from 2016 to 2021. ① The number of births continued to decrease throughout the whole period. ② The gap between the number of births and deaths was the largest in 2016. ③ ⭐ In 2019, / the gap (between the number of births and deaths) was the smallest, / with the number of births slightly larger than that of deaths. ④ The number of deaths increased steadily during the whole period, except the period from 2018 to 2019. ⑤ In 2021(→ 2020), the number of deaths was larger than that of births for the first time.

[해석]

위 그래프는 2016년부터 2021년까지 한국에서의 출생자 수와 사망자 수를 보여 준다. ① 출생자 수는 전체 기간 내내 계속 감소했다. ② 출생자 수와 사망자 수 사이의 차이는 2016년에 가장 컸다. ③ 2019년에는 출생자 수와 사망자 수 사이의 차이가 가장 작았는데, 출생자 수가 사망자 수보다 약간 더 컸다. ④ 사망자 수는 2018년과 2019년까지의 기간을 제외하고 전체 기간 동안 꾸준히 증가했다. ⑤ 2021년(→ 2020년)에, 처음으로 사망자 수가 출생자 수보다 더 컸다.

[정답이 보이는 해설]

2016년부터 2021년까지 한국에서의 출생자 수와 사망자 수에 관한 도표이다. 처음으로 사망자 수가 출생자 수보다 더 컸던 해는 2021년이 아니라 2020년이다. 따라서 도표의 내용과 일치하지 않는 것은 ⑤이다.

[필수 어휘]

decrease 감소하다 throughout ～ 동안 쭉, 내내 period 기간 gap 차이
slightly 약간 increase 증가하다 steadily 꾸준히 except ～을 제외하고

04 정답 ④

Reasons for People Interested in Eating Less Meat and Non-meat Eaters in the UK (2018)

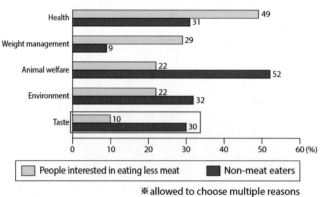

	People interested in eating less meat	Non-meat eaters
Health	49	31
Weight management	29	9
Animal welfare	22	52
Environment	22	32
Taste	10	30

※ allowed to choose multiple reasons

단서 맛(Taste) 영역에서, '고기를 먹지 않는 사람'의 30%는 '고기 섭취를 줄이는 데 관심이 있는 사람'의 비율인 10%의 3배임

❇ The graph above shows the survey results (on reasons for people [interested in eating less meat] and those [eating no meat]) (in the UK in 2018). ① For the group of people who are interested in eating less meat, health is the strongest motivator for doing so. ② For the group of non-meat eaters, animal welfare accounts for the largest percentage among all reasons, followed by environment, health, and taste. ③ The largest percentage point difference between the two groups is in animal welfare, whereas the smallest difference is in environment. ④ The percentage of non-meat eaters citing taste is four times(→ three times) higher than that of people interested in reducing their meat consumption citing taste. ⑤ Weight management ranks the lowest for people who don't eat meat, with less than 10 percent.

(현재분사구 / 과거분사구 / = people / account for: ~을 차지하다 / 뒤이어, 연달아 / = the percentage / ~보다 적은)

해석
위의 그래프는 고기를 덜 먹는 것에 관심 있는 사람들과 고기를 먹지 않는 사람들의 이유에 대한 2018년 영국에서의 조사 결과를 보여 준다. ① 고기를 덜 먹는 것에 관심이 있는 사람들의 집단에게, 건강이 그렇게 하는 가장 강력한 동기이다. ② 고기를 먹지 않는 사람들의 집단의 경우, 모든 이유 중에서 동물 복지가 가장 큰 비율을 차지하고 있고, 환경, 건강, 그리고 맛이 그 뒤를 따른다. ③ 두 집단 사이의 가장 큰 퍼센트 포인트 차이는 동물 복지에 있는 반면, 가장 작은 차이는 환경에 있다. ④ 맛을 언급하면서 고기를 먹지 않는 사람들의 비율은 맛을 언급하면서 고기 섭취를 줄이는 데 관심이 있는 사람들의 비율보다 4배(→ 3배) 높다. ⑤ 체중 관리는 고기를 먹지 않는 사람들에게 10퍼센트 미만으로 가장 낮은 순위를 차지한다.

정답이 보이는 해설
2018년 영국에서 고기를 덜 먹는 것에 관심 있는 사람들과 고기를 먹지 않는 사람들의 이유에 관한 도표이다. 맛을 언급하면서 고기를 먹지 않는 사람들의 비율은 30%이고, 맛을 언급하면서 고기 섭취를 줄이는 데 관심이 있는 사람들의 비율은 10%이므로, 전자가 후자의 비율보다 4배가 아니라 3배 높다. 따라서 도표의 내용과 일치하지 않는 것은 ④이다.

필수 어휘
survey 설문 조사 reason 이유 motivator 동기 (부여 요소) welfare 복지 whereas 반면에, ~임에 반하여 cite 언급하다, 말하다 reduce 줄이다 consumption 섭취, 소비 management 관리

05 정답 ③

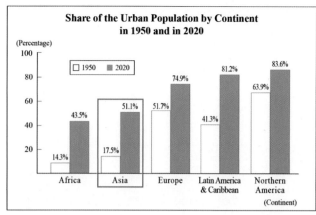

Share of the Urban Population by Continent in 1950 and in 2020

(Continent)	1950	2020
Africa	14.3%	43.5%
Asia	17.5%	51.1%
Europe	51.7%	74.9%
Latin America & Caribbean	41.3%	81.2%
Northern America	63.9%	83.6%

단서 아시아의 도시 인구 점유율은 1950년과 2020년 두 해 모두 두 번째로 낮았음

The graph above shows the share of the urban population by continent in 1950 and in 2020. ① For each continent, the share of the urban population in 2020 was larger than that in 1950. ② From 1950 to 2020, the share of the urban population in Africa increased from 14.3% to 43.5%. ③ The share of the urban population in Asia was the second lowest in 1950 but not in 2020(→ in both 1950 and 2020). ④ ❇ In 1950, the share (of the urban population in Europe) was larger than that in Latin America and the Caribbean, // whereas the reverse was true in 2020. ⑤ Among the five continents, Northern America was ranked in the first position for the share of the urban population in both 1950 and 2020.

(대륙별 / increase from A to B: A에서 B로 증가하다 / 주어 / 동사 / = the share of the urban population / 부사절(대조) 그 반대였다, 역전이 일어났다)

해석
위 그래프는 1950년과 2020년의 대륙별 도시 인구 점유율을 보여 준다. ① 각 대륙에서, 2020년의 도시 인구 점유율이 1950년의 그것보다 더 컸다. ② 1950년부터 2020년까지 아프리카의 도시 인구 점유율은 14.3%에서 43.5%로 증가했다. ③ 아시아의 도시 인구 점유율은 1950년에는 두 번째로 낮았지만, 2020년에는 그렇지 않았다(→ 1950년과 2020년 모두 두 번째로 낮았다). ④ 1950년에는 유럽의 도시 인구 점유율이 라틴 아메리카와 카리브해 지역의 그것보다 더 컸지만, 2020년에는 그 반대였다. ⑤ 다섯 개 대륙 중, 북아메리카는 도시 인구 점유율에서 1950년과 2020년 모두 1위를 차지했다.

정답이 보이는 해설
아시아의 도시 인구 점유율은 1950년에는 17.5%, 2020년에는 51.5%로 두 해 모두 두 번째로 낮았으므로, ③이 도표의 내용과 일치하지 않는다.

필수 어휘
share 점유율, 몫 urban 도시의 continent 대륙 reverse 역전 rank (순위를) 차지하다

06 정답 ⑤

Percent of U.S. Households with Pets

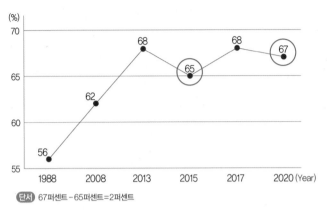

단서 67퍼센트 − 65퍼센트 = 2퍼센트

The graph above shows the percent of households with pets in the United States (U.S.) from 1988 to 2020. ① In 1988, more than [~보다 많이] half of U.S. households owned pets, and more than 6 out of 10 U.S. households owned pets from 2008 to 2020. ② In the period [from A to B: A부터 B까지] between 1988 and 2008, pet ownership increased among U.S. [between A and B: A와 B 사이의] households by 6 percentage points. ③ From 2008 to 2013, pet ownership rose an additional 6 percentage points. ④ ★ The percent [단수 주어] of U.S. households with pets in 2013 / was the same as that in 2017, [단수 동사] [= the percent] / **which** was 68 percent. ⑤ In 2015, the rate of U.S. households with [계속적 용법의 관계대명사(= and it)] pets was 3 percentage(→ 2 percentage) points lower than in 2020.

해석

위 그래프는 1988년부터 2020년까지 미국에서 반려동물을 보유한 가정의 비율을 보여 준다. ① 1988년에는 미국 가정의 절반 이상이 반려동물을 보유했고, 2008년에서 2020년까지 10개 중 6개 이상의 미국 가정이 반려동물을 보유했다. ② 1988년과 2008년 사이의 기간에 반려동물 보유는 미국 가정 사이에서 6퍼센트포인트 증가했다. ③ 2008년과 2013년 사이에 반려동물 보유는 추가로 6퍼센트포인트가 상승했다. ④ 2013년의 반려동물을 보유한 미국 가정의 비율은 2017년의 비율과 같았고, 그것은 68퍼센트였다. ⑤ 2015년에는 반려동물을 보유한 미국 가정의 비율이 2020년보다 3퍼센트포인트(→ 2퍼센트포인트) 더 낮았다.

정답이 보이는 해설

1988년부터 2020년까지 미국에서 반려동물을 보유한 가정의 비율을 나타낸 도표로, 2015년에 반려동물을 보유한 미국 가정의 비율은 65퍼센트로 2020년의 67퍼센트보다 2퍼센트포인트 낮았다. 따라서 도표의 내용과 일치하지 않는 것은 ⑤이다.

필수 어휘

household 가정 ownership 소유 increase 증가하다 additional 추가의 rate 비율

---

07 정답 ⑤

Percentage of UK People
Who Used Online Course and Online Learning Material
(in 2020, by age group)

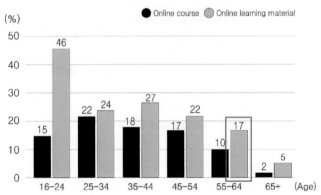

단서 55~64세의 연령 집단에서 온라인 학습 자료를 이용한 사람들의 비율은 17%이므로 1/5에 미치지 않음

The above graph shows the percentage of people in the UK who used online courses and online learning materials, by age group in 2020. ① In each age group, the percentage of people who used online learning materials was higher than that of people who used online courses. ② The 25−34 age group had the highest percentage of people who used online courses in all the age groups. ③ Those aged 65 and older were the least likely to use online courses [be likely to: ~할 가능성이 있다] among the six age groups. ④ ★ **Among** the six age groups, / the [전치사(~ 중에)] [단수 주어] gap **between** the percentage of *people* [who used online courses] [between A and B: A와 B 사이에] **and** that of *people* [who used online learning materials] / was the [= the percentage] [단수 동사] greatest in the 16−24 age group. ⑤ In each of the 35−44, 45−54, and 55−64 age groups, more than one in five people used online learning materials.

해석

위 도표는 2020년에 온라인 강의와 온라인 학습 자료를 이용한 영국 사람들의 비율을 연령 집단별로 보여 준다. ① 각 연령 집단에서 온라인 학습 자료를 이용한 사람들의 비율은 온라인 강의를 이용한 사람들의 비율보다 더 높았다. ② 25~34세 연령 집단은 모든 연령 집단 중에서 온라인 강의를 이용한 사람들의 비율이 가장 높았다. ③ 65세 이상의 사람들은 여섯 개의 연령 집단 중에서 온라인 강의를 이용할 가능성이 가장 낮았다. ④ 6개의 연령 집단 중에서 온라인 강의를 이용한 사람들의 비율과 온라인 학습 자료를 이용한 사람들의 비율 간의 차이는 16~24세 연령 집단에서 가장 컸다. ⑤ 35~44세, 45~54세, 55~64세의 각 연령 집단에서 5명 중 1명이 넘는 비율의 사람들이 온라인 학습 자료를 이용했다.

정답이 보이는 해설

2020년 온라인 강의와 온라인 학습 자료를 이용한 영국 사람들의 비율을 연령 집단별로 나타낸 도표로, 55~64세 연령 집단에서는 온라인 학습 자료를 이용한 사람들의 비율이 17%로 5명 중 1명에 미치지 못하므로, 도표의 내용과 일치하지 않는 것은 ⑤이다.

필수 어휘

course 강의 learning material 학습 자료 age group 연령 집단 graph 도표 aged (나이가) ~살의 gap 차이, 격차

08 정답 ④

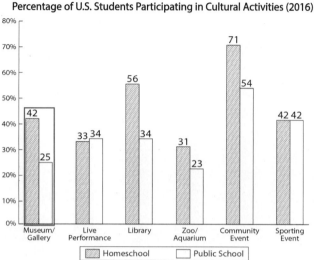

Percentage of U.S. Students Participating in Cultural Activities (2016)

(단서) 25의 두 배는 50〉42

The graph above shows the percentage of U.S. homeschooled and public school students participating in cultural activities in 2016. ① ❂ With the exception of live performances and sporting events, / the percentage of *homeschooled students* (participating in cultural activities) / was higher than that of public school students. ② For each group of students, community events accounted for the largest percentage among all cultural activities. ③ The percentage point difference between homeschooled students and their public school peers was largest in visiting libraries. ④ The percentage of homeschooled students visiting museums or galleries was more(→ less) than twice that of public school students. ⑤ Going to zoos or aquariums ranked the lowest for both groups of students, with 31 and 23 percent respectively.

해석

위 도표는 2016년에 문화 활동에 참여하는 미국의 홈스쿨링을 받는 학생들 및 공립 학교 학생들의 비율을 보여 준다. ① 라이브 공연과 스포츠 경기를 제외하고 문화 활동에 참여하는 홈스쿨링을 받는 학생들의 비율은 공립 학교 학생들의 비율보다 높았다. ② 각 집단의 학생들에게 지역사회 행사는 모든 문화 활동 중에서 가장 큰 비율을 차지했다. ③ 홈스쿨링을 받는 학생들과 그들의 공립 학교 또래 간의 퍼센트포인트 차이는 도서관 방문에서 가장 컸다. ④ 박물관이나 미술관을 방문하는 홈스쿨링을 받는 학생들의 비율은 공립 학교 학생들의 비율의 두 배 이상이었다(→ 두 배보다 적었다). ⑤ 동물원이나 수족관에 가는 것은 두 집단의 학생들에게 가장 낮은 순위를 차지했는데, 각각 31퍼센트와 23퍼센트였다.

정답이 보이는 해설

2016년 문화 활동에 참여하는 미국의 홈스쿨링을 받는 학생들 및 공립 학교 학생들의 비율을 나타낸 도표로, 박물관이나 미술관을 방문하는 홈스쿨링 학생들의 비율은 42%로 공립 학교 학생들의 비율인 25%의 두 배가 넘지 않는다. 따라서 도표의 내용과 일치하지 않는 것은 ④이다.

필수 어휘

homeschool 홈스쿨링을 하다 public school 공립 학교
cultural 문화의 performance 공연 sporting event 스포츠 경기
gallery 미술관 aquarium 수족관 respectively 각각

---

09 정답 ④

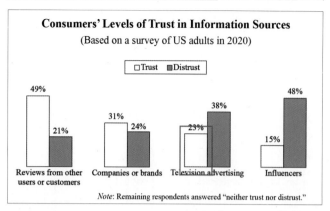

Consumers' Levels of Trust in Information Sources
(Based on a survey of US adults in 2020)

Note: Remaining respondents answered "neither trust nor distrust."

(단서) 5분의 1은 20% 〈 23%

The graph above shows the consumers' levels of trust in four different types of information sources, based on a survey of US adults in 2020. ① About half of US adults say they trust the information they receive from reviews from other users or customers. ② This is more than double those who say they hold distrust for reviews from other users or customers. ③ ❂ The smallest gap (between the levels of trust and distrust) (among the four different types of information sources) / is shown in the companies or brands' graph. ④ Fewer(→ More) than one-fifth of adults say they trust information from television advertising, outweighed by the share who distrust such information. ⑤ Only 15% of adults say they trust the information provided by influencers, while more than three times as many adults say they distrust the same source of information.

해석

위 도표는 2020년 미국 성인들을 대상으로 한 설문 조사에 기반하여 네 가지 다른 종류의 정보 출처들에 대한 소비자의 신뢰 정도를 보여 준다. ① 미국 성인의 절반 정도가 다른 사용자들이나 고객들로부터의 상품평에서 얻은 정보를 믿는다고 말했다. ② 이것은 다른 사용자들이나 고객들로부터의 상품평에 대해 불신을 갖는다고 말한 미국 성인들의 두 배 이상이다. ③ 네 가지 다른 종류의 정보 출처 중에서 신뢰와 불신 정도 사이의 가장 적은 차이는 회사나 상표에서 보인다. ④ (미국) 성인의 5분의 1보다 적은(→ 많은) 수치가 텔레비전 광고로부터의 정보를 신뢰한다고 말했는데, 그러한 정보를 불신하는 쪽의 수치가 이를 능가했다. ⑤ 미국 성인의 15퍼센트만 영향력 있는 사람이 제공하는 정보를 신뢰한다고 말한 반면에, 이보다 세 배 이상 많은 수치의 미국 성인들이 같은 정보 출처를 불신한다고 말했다.

정답이 보이는 해설

2020년 미국 성인들의 네 가지 다른 종류의 정보 출처들에 대한 소비자의 신뢰 정도를 나타낸 도표로, 텔레비전 광고로부터의 정보를 신뢰한다고 말한 사람은 23퍼센트이므로 5분의 1보다 더 많다. 따라서 도표의 내용과 일치하지 않는 것은 ④이다.

필수 어휘

consumer 소비자 trust 신뢰 source 출처, 정보원 distrust 불신
outweigh ~보다 크다[우세하다] influencer 영향력 있는 사람

8강
도표의 이해

202106 25번 정답률 84%

Health Spending as a Share of GDP for Selected OECD Countries (2018)

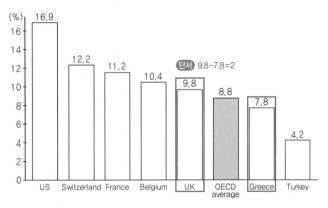

The above graph shows health spending as a share of GDP for selected OECD countries in 2018. ① On average, OECD countries were estimated to have spent 8.8 percent of their GDP on health (평균적으로) care. ② ✪ (Among the given countries above), / the US had the highest share, (with 16.9 percent), / followed by Switzerland at 12.2 percent. ③ France spent more than 11 percent of its GDP, while Turkey spent less than 5 percent of its GDP on health care. ④ Belgium's health spending as a share of GDP sat between that of France and the UK. ⑤ There was a 3 percentage point(→ 2 percentage point) difference in the share of GDP spent on health care between the UK and Greece.

(단서 9.8-7.8=2)

(↦ ~가 뒤를 잇는 / 주어 / 동사)
(주어 the US를 부연 설명하는 분사구문)
(= the health spending as a share of GDP)

해석

위 도표는 선별된 OECD 국가들의 2018년 건강 관련 지출을 GDP 점유율로 보여 준다. ① 평균적으로, OECD 국가들은 건강 관리에 GDP의 8.8퍼센트를 지출한 것으로 추정되었다. ② 위 국가들 중 미국은 (GDP의) 16.9퍼센트로 가장 높은 점유율을 보였고, 스위스가 12.2퍼센트로 그 뒤를 이었다. ③ 프랑스는 GDP의 11퍼센트 이상을 지출한 반면, 터키는 건강 관리에 (GDP의) 5퍼센트 이하를 지출했다. ④ GDP 점유율로서 벨기에의 건강 관련 지출은 프랑스와 영국 사이였다. ⑤ 영국과 그리스 간에는 건강 관리에 지출된 GDP의 점유율에 3퍼센트포인트(→ 2퍼센트포인트) 차이가 있었다.

정답이 보이는 해설

선별된 OECD 국가들의 2018년 건강 관련 지출을 GDP 점유율로 나타낸 도표로, 영국과 그리스의 건강 관련 지출의 GDP 점유율은 각각 9.8%, 7.8%이므로 2퍼센트포인트 차이이다. 따라서 도표의 내용과 일치하지 않는 것은 ⑤이다.

필수 어휘

spending 지출, 소비 share 점유율
GDP 국내 총생산(= gross domestic product) select 선별하다, 선택하다
average 평균 estimate 추정하다 difference 차이, 구분

202103 25번 정답률 82%

Devices Students Used to Access Digital Content

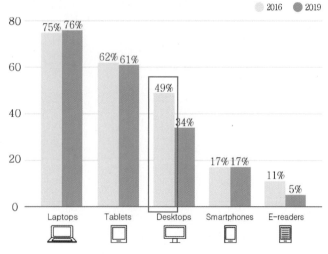

(단서1 49%는 절반에 미치지 못하는 숫자임)

✪ The above graph shows the percentage of *students* (from kindergarten to 12th grade) / [who used devices to access digital educational content / (in 2016 and in 2019)]. ① Laptops were the most used device for students to access digital content in both years. ② Both in 2016 and in 2019, more than 6 out of 10 students used tablets. ③ More(→ Less) than half the students used desktops to access digital content in 2016, and more than a third used desktops in 2019. ④ The percentage of smartphones in 2016 was the same as that in 2019. ⑤ E-readers ranked the lowest in both years, with 11 percent in 2016 and 5 percent in 2019.

(주격 관계대명사 / 부사적 용법(목적))
(Both A and B: A와 B 둘 다)
(= the percentage of smartphones)

해석

위 도표는 2016년과 2019년에 교육용 디지털 콘텐츠에 접속하기 위해 기기를 사용한 유치원에서 12학년까지의 학생들의 비율을 보여 준다. ① 두 해 모두 노트북은 디지털 콘텐츠에 접속하기 위해 학생들이 가장 많이 사용한 기기였다. ② 2016년과 2019년 모두 10명 중 6명이 넘는 학생들이 태블릿을 사용했다. ③ 2016년에는 절반이 넘는(→ 안 되는) 학생들이 데스크톱을 사용하여 디지털 콘텐츠에 접속했고, 2019년에는 3분의 1이 넘는 학생들이 데스크톱을 사용했다. ④ 2016년 스마트폰의 비율은 2019년 그것(스마트폰)의 비율과 같았다. ⑤ 전자책 단말기는 두 해 모두 가장 낮은 순위를 차지했는데, 2016년에는 11퍼센트였고 2019년에는 5퍼센트였다.

정답이 보이는 해설

2016년과 2019년에 교육용 디지털 콘텐츠에 접속하기 위해 기기를 사용한 유치원에서 12학년까지의 학생들의 비율을 나타낸 도표로, 데스크톱 사용 비율은 2016년에 49퍼센트이므로 절반에 미치지 못한다. 따라서 도표의 내용과 일치하지 않는 것은 ③이다.

필수 어휘

device 기기, 장치 access 접속하다, 접근하다 laptop 노트북 (컴퓨터)
e-reader 전자책 단말기 kindergarten 유치원 a third 3분의 1
rank 순위를 차지하다

12 정답 ⑤

202011 25번 정답률 85%

Age Children Quit Regularly Playing a Sport

Sport	Average Age of Last Regular Participation	Average Length in Years of Participation
Soccer	9.1	3.0
Ice Hockey	10.9	3.1
Tennis	10.9	1.9
Basketball	11.2	3.2
Field Hockey	11.4	5.1
Golf	11.8	2.8
Skateboarding	12.0	2.8
Track and Field	13.0	2.0

단서1 참여 기간이 가장 짧았던 것은 1.9인 테니스임

The above table shows the average age of last regular participation of children in a sport and the average length of participation based on a 2019 survey. ① Among the eight sports above, soccer was the only sport that children quit at an average age of younger than 10. ② Children quit playing ice hockey and tennis at the same age on average, but the average length of participation in tennis was shorter than that in ice hockey. ③ ✪ Basketball, field hockey, and golf were
= the average length of participation
sports / [**which** children quit playing on average (before they turned
목적격 관계대명사   quit + 동명사: ~하기를 그만두다   시간 부사절
12)], // but golf had the shortest average participation length (among the three sports). ④ Skateboarding was a sport children quit at the average age of 12, and the average length of participation was the same as golf. ⑤ Meanwhile, children quit participating in track and field at the average age of 13, but the average length of participation was the shortest(→ the second shortest) among the eight sports.

해석

위 표는 2019년에 실시한 조사에 근거하여 어린이들이 마지막으로 스포츠에 정기적으로 참여한 평균 연령과 평균 참여 기간을 보여 준다. ① 위 여덟 개의 스포츠 중에서 축구는 어린이들이 평균 10세보다 어린 나이에 중단한 유일한 스포츠였다. ② 어린이들은 아이스하키와 테니스를 평균적으로 같은 연령에 중단했지만, 테니스에 참여한 평균 기간은 아이스하키에 참여한 평균 기간보다 짧았다. ③ 야구, 필드하키 그리고 골프는 어린이들이 평균적으로 12세가 되기 전에 중단한 스포츠였지만, 골프는 이 세 개의 스포츠 중에서 평균 참여 기간이 가장 짧았다. ④ 스케이트보드는 어린이들이 평균 12세에 중단한 스포츠였고, 그 평균 참여 기간은 골프와 같았다. ⑤ 한편, 어린이들은 육상 경기 참여를 평균 13세에 중단했으나, 평균 참여 기간은 여덟 개의 스포츠 중에서 가장(→ 두 번째로) 짧았다.

정답이 보이는 해설

어린이들이 마지막으로 스포츠에 정기적으로 참여한 평균 연령과 평균 참여 기간을 나타낸 표로, 육상 경기(2.0)는 여덟 개의 스포츠 중에서 테니스(1.9) 다음으로 평균 참여 기간이 짧다. 따라서 표의 내용과 일치하지 않는 것은 ⑤이다.

필수 어휘

quit 중단하다 regularly 정기적으로 participation 참여 survey (설문) 조사
meanwhile 한편, 반면

9강 2020~2023 내용 일치 파악

01 정답 ④

202309 26번 정답률 85%

American jazz pianist Bill Evans was born in New Jersey in
be born in: ~에서 태어나다
1929. His early training was in classical music. At the age of six,
~의 나이에
he began receiving piano lessons, later adding flute and violin.

He earned bachelor's degrees in piano and music education from
earn a degree: 학위를 받다
Southeastern Louisiana College in 1950. He went on to serve in the
go on to: 이어서 ~을 하기 시작하다 ↵
army from 1951 to 1954 and played flute in the Fifth Army Band.
↳ serve in the military: 군에서 복무하다(= serve in the army)
✪ After serving in the military, / he studied composition (at the
시간 접속사: After를 생략하지 않은 분사구문(= After he served ~)
Mannes School of Music) (in New York). **단서** Composer George
Russell admired his playing and hired Evans to record and perform
작곡가 George Russell이 Evans를 고용함
his compositions. Evans became famous for recordings made from
the late-1950s through the 1960s. He won his first Grammy Award
win an award: 상을 타다
in 1964 for his album *Conversations with Myself*. Evans' expressive piano works and his unique harmonic approach inspired a whole generation of musicians.

해석

미국의 재즈 피아니스트 Bill Evans는 뉴저지에서 1929년에 태어났다. 그의 초기 교육은 클래식 음악이었다. 6세에 피아노 수업을 받기 시작해서, 나중에 플루트와 바이올린을 더했다. 그는 1950년에 Southeastern Louisiana 대학에서 피아노와 음악 교육으로 학사 학위를 받았다. 이어서 1951년에서 1954년까지는 군에서 복무하며 제5군악대에서 플루트를 연주했다. 군 복무 이후에는 뉴욕에 있는 Mannes School of Music에서 작곡을 공부했다. 작곡가 George Russell은 그의 연주에 감탄했고, 자신의 곡을 녹음하고 연주하기 위해 Evans를 고용했다. Evans는 1950년대 후반부터 1960년대에 만들어진 음반으로 유명해졌다. 그는 자신의 앨범 'Conversations with Myself'로 1964년에 첫 번째 그래미상을 수상했다. Evans의 표현력이 뛰어난 피아노 작품과 그의 독특한 화성적 접근은 전 세대의 음악가에게 영감을 주었다.

정답이 보이는 해설

Evans의 연주에 감탄한 작곡가 George Russell이 Evans를 고용했다는 내용이 있다. 따라서 글의 내용과 일치하지 않는 것은 ④이다.

필수 어휘

classical music 클래식 음악 bachelor 학사 학위 소지자 education 교육
composition 작곡, 작품 composer 작곡가 admire 감탄하다, 높이 평가하다
hire 고용하다 expressive 표현력이 뛰어난 harmonic 화성의, 화음의
inspire 영감을 주다 generation 세대

02 정답 ③

202306 26번 정답률 89%

Gary Becker was born in Pottsville, Pennsylvania in 1930 and
be born in: ~에서 태어나다
grew up in Brooklyn, New York City. His father, who was not well educated, had a deep interest in financial and political issues. After graduating from high school, Becker went to Princeton University,
graduate from: ~에서 졸업하다   be dissatisfied with: ~에 불만족하다
where he majored in economics. **단서** He was dissatisfied with
major in: ~을 전공하다   대학에서의 경제학 교육에 불만족함
his economic education at Princeton University because "it didn't

---

9강

내용 일치 파악

seem to be handling real problems." He earned a doctor's degree in economics from the University of Chicago in 1955. His doctoral paper on the economics of discrimination was mentioned by the
be mentioned by: ~에 의해 언급되다
Nobel Prize Committee as an important contribution to economics.

⭐ **Since** 1985, / Becker **had written** a regular economics column
전치사구 / since 1985부터 계속 써 옴: 완료
(in *Business Week*), / explaining economic analysis and ideas (to
분사구문
the general public). In 1992, he was awarded the Nobel Prize in
be awarded: 상을 받다
economic science.

해석

Gary Becker는 1930년 Pennsylvania 주 Pottsville에서 태어났고 New York City의 Brooklyn에서 자랐다. 교육을 제대로 받지 못한 그의 아버지는 금융과 정치 문제에 깊은 관심이 있었다. 고등학교를 졸업한 후, Becker는 Princeton University로 진학했고, 거기서 그는 경제학을 전공했다. Princeton University에서의 경제학 교육이 "현실적인 문제를 다루고 있는 것처럼 보이지 않았기" 때문에 그는 그것에 불만족했다. 그는 1955년에 University of Chicago에서 경제학 박사 학위를 취득했다. 차별의 경제학에 대한 그의 박사 논문은 노벨상 위원회에 의해 경제학에 대한 중요한 기여로 언급되었다. 1985년 이후, Becker는 경제학적 분석과 아이디어를 일반 대중에게 설명하며 'Business Week'에 경제학 칼럼을 정기적으로 기고했다. 1992년에, 그는 노벨경제학상을 수상했다.

정답이 보이는 해설

Princeton University에서의 경제학 교육은 "현실적인 문제를 다루고 있는 것처럼 보이지 않았기" 때문에, 그는 불만족했다고 한다. 따라서 글의 내용과 일치하지 않는 것은 ③이다.

필수 어휘

educated 교육을 받은, 교양 있는 financial 금융의, 재정의 political 정치의
economics 경제학 handle 다루다 degree 학위 doctoral 박사학위의
committee 위원회 contribution 기여 regular 정기적인, 정규의 analysis 분석
economic science 경제학

03 정답 ⑤

202303 26번 정답률 92%

Lilian Bland was born in Kent, England in 1878. Unlike most other girls at the time she wore trousers and spent her time enjoying
spend+시간+v-ing: 시간을 ~하는 데 쓰다
adventurous activities like horse riding and hunting. Lilian began her career as a sports and wildlife photographer for British newspapers. In 1910 she became the first woman to design, build,
persuade A to-v: A를 ~하도록 설득하다
and fly her own airplane. ⭐ (In order to **persuade** her **to** try a
목적을 나타내는 to부정사
slightly safer activity,) / Lilian's dad **bought** her a car. Soon Lilian
간접목적어 / 직접목적어
was a master driver and ended up working as a car dealer. She never
end up v-ing: 결국 ~하게 되다
went back to flying but lived a long and exciting life nonetheless.

She married, moved to Canada, and had a kid. **단서** Eventually, she
잉글랜드로 돌아와 나머지
moved back to England, and lived there for the rest of her life.
인생을 살았음

해석

Lilian Bland는 1878년 잉글랜드 Kent에서 태어났다. 그 당시 대부분의 다른 여자아이와 달리 그녀는 바지를 입고, 승마와 사냥 같은 모험적인 활동을 즐기며 시간을 보냈다. Lilian은 영국 신문사의 스포츠와 야생 동물 사진작가로 자신의 경력을 시작했다. 1910년에 그녀는 자신의 비행기를 설계하고, 제작하고, 비행한 최초의 여성이 되었다. 약간이라도 더 안전한 활동을 하도록 그녀를 설득하기 위해, Lilian

---

의 아버지는 그녀에게 자동차를 사 주었다. 곧 Lilian은 뛰어난 운전자가 되었고 결국 자동차 판매원으로 일하게 되었다. 그녀는 결코 비행을 다시 시작하지 않았지만, 그렇더라도 오랫동안 흥미진진한 삶을 살았다. 그녀는 결혼하여 캐나다로 이주했고, 아이를 하나 가졌다. 결국 그녀는 잉글랜드로 돌아와, 거기서 생의 나머지 기간을 보냈다.

정답이 보이는 해설

Lilian Bland는 결국 잉글랜드로 돌아와, 거기서 생의 나머지 기간을 보냈다고 한다. 따라서 글의 내용과 일치하지 않는 것은 ⑤이다.

필수 어휘

trousers 바지 adventurous 모험적인 career 경력 photographer 사진작가
airplane 비행기 persuade 설득하다 slightly 약간 car dealer 자동차 판매원
nonetheless 그렇더라도

04 정답 ③

202211 26번 정답률 89%

Margaret Knight was an exceptionally prolific inventor in the late 19th century; journalists occasionally compared her to Thomas
compare A to B: A와 B를 비교하다
Edison by nicknaming her "a woman Edison." From a young age, she built toys for her older brothers. After her father died, Knight's family moved to Manchester. ⭐ Knight left school (in 1850, at
leave school: 학교를 그만두다
age 12), / to earn money for her family at a nearby textile factory, /
to부정사(목적)
[where she **witnessed** a fellow worker injured by faulty equipment].
관계부사절 동사 목적어 목적격보어
That led her to create her first invention, a safety device for textile
lead A to-v: A가 ~하도록 이끌다
equipment, **단서** but she never earned money from the invention.
직물 장비의 안전장치를 발명한 것으로는 돈을 전혀 벌지 못함
She also invented a machine that cut, folded and glued flat-bottomed paper bags and was awarded her first patent in 1871 for it. It eliminated the need for workers to assemble them slowly by hand.
손으로
Knight received 27 patents in her lifetime and entered the National Inventors Hall of Fame in 2006.

해석

Margaret Knight는 19세기 후반에 특출나게 다작한 발명가였는데, 기자들은 가끔 그녀에게 "여자 Edison"이라는 별명을 지어 주어 Thomas Edison과 비교했다. 어린 나이일 때부터, 그녀는 오빠들을 위해 장난감을 만들었다. 그녀의 아버지가 돌아가신 후, Knight의 가족은 Manchester로 이사했다. Knight는 1850년 12세의 나이에 학교를 그만두었는데, 근처에 있는 직물 공장에서 가족을 위해 돈을 벌기 위해서였고, 그곳에서 그녀는 동료 노동자가 결함이 있는 장비에 의해 부상을 당하는 것을 목격했다. 그것은 그녀가 자신의 첫 번째 발명품, 즉 직물 장비에 쓰이는 안전장치를 만들도록 이끌었지만, 그녀는 그 발명품으로 전혀 돈을 벌지는 못했다. 그녀는 또한 밑이 평평한 종이 가방을 자르고, 접고, 붙이는 기계를 발명했고 1871년에 그것으로 자신의 첫 특허를 받았다. 그것은 작업자들이 손으로 그것들을 천천히 조립할 필요를 없앴다. Knight는 자신의 일생 동안 27개의 특허를 받았고, 2006년에 국립 발명가 명예의 전당에 입성했다.

정답이 보이는 해설

Margaret Knight는 그녀의 첫 발명품인 직물 장비에 쓰이는 안전장치의 발명으로는 전혀 돈을 벌지 못했다고 한다. 따라서 글의 내용과 일치하지 않는 것은 ③이다.

필수 어휘

exceptionally 특별히, 유난히 journalist 기자, 언론인
occasionally 이따금, 가끔 witness 목격하다 faulty 결함이 있는
equipment 장비 invention 발명품 fold 접다 glue (접착제로) 붙이다
flat-bottomed 바닥이 평평한 eliminate 제거하다 assemble 조립하다, 모으다

05 정답 ④

202209 26번 정답률 85%

Wilbur Smith was a South African novelist specialising in
_{~을 전문으로 하다}
historical fiction. ✪ Smith wanted to become a journalist, /
(writing about social conditions in South Africa), // but his father
_{Smith를 의미상 주어로 하는 분사구문}
was never supportive of his writing and forced him to get a real job.
_{동사1 　　　　　　　　　　　　　　　　　　　동사2　목적어　목적격보어}
Smith studied further and became a tax accountant, but he finally
turned back to his love of writing. He wrote his first novel, *The*
_{되돌아오다}
Gods First Make Mad, and had received 20 rejections by 1962. In
1964, Smith published another novel, *When the Lion Feeds*, and it
went on to be successful, selling around the world. 단서 A famous
_{배우이자 영화}
actor and film producer bought the film rights for *When the Lion*
_{제작자가 Smith의 소설에 대한 영화 판권을 샀지만 영화화되지는 않음}
Feeds, although no movie resulted. By the time of his death in 2021
he had published 49 novels, selling more than 140 million copies
worldwide.

해석
Wilbur Smith는 역사 소설을 전문으로 하는 남아프리카 소설가였다. Smith는 남아프리카의 사회적 환경에 관해 글을 쓰면서 언론인이 되기를 원했지만, 그의 아버지는 그가 글을 쓰는 것을 결코 지지하지 않았고 그가 실질적인 직업을 얻도록 강요했다. Smith는 더 공부하여 세무사가 되었지만, 결국 자신이 사랑하는 글 쓰는 일로 되돌아왔다. 그는 첫 번째 소설 'The Gods First Make Mad'를 썼는데 1962년까지 20번의 거절을 당했다. 1964년에 Smith는 또 다른 소설 'When the Lion Feeds'를 출간했고, 그것은 전 세계에 팔리면서 계속해서 성공을 거두었다. 한 유명한 배우이자 영화 제작자가 'When the Lion Feeds'에 대한 영화 판권을 구입했지만, 영화화되지는 않았다. 2021년에 죽기 전까지 그는 49편의 소설을 출간했으며, 전 세계적으로 1억 4천만 부 이상을 판매했다.

정답이 보이는 해설
한 유명한 배우이자 영화 제작자가 Smith의 소설 'When the Lion Feeds'에 대한 영화 판권을 구입했지만 영화화되지는 않았다(no movie resulted)고 한다. 따라서 글의 내용과 일치하지 않는 것은 ④이다.

선택지 완벽 분석
③ 첫 번째 소설은 1962년까지 20번 거절당했다.
　Smith가 쓴 첫 번째 소설이 1962년까지 20번의 거절을 당했다(He wrote his first novel ~ had received 20 rejections by 1962.)고 했으므로 글의 내용과 일치한다.

필수 어휘
journalist 언론인　supportive of ~을 지지하는
force A to B A가 B하도록 강요하다　tax accountant 세무사　rejection 거절
publish 출간하다　producer 제작자　film right 영화 판권
result (결과로서) 생기다, 발생하다　worldwide 전 세계적으로

06 정답 ③

202206 26번 정답률 94%

Pianist, composer, and big band leader, Claude Bolling, was
born on April 10, 1930, in Cannes, France, but spent most of his
life in Paris. He began studying classical music as a youth. He was
introduced to the world of jazz by a schoolmate. Later, Bolling
became interested in the music of Fats Waller, one of the most
excellent jazz musicians. 단서 Bolling became famous as a teenager
_{Bolling은 십 대 때 Best Piano Player 상을 받음}
by winning the Best Piano Player prize at an amateur contest in
_{win a prize: 상을 받다}
France. He was also a successful film music composer, writing the
music for more than one hundred films. ✪ In 1975, / he collaborated
_{동사1}
with flutist Rampal / and published *Suite for Flute and Jazz Piano*
_{동사2}
Trio, / [which he became most well-known for]. He died in 2020,
_{계속적 용법의 목적격 관계대명사(= and he became most well-known for it)}
leaving two sons, David and Alexandre.

해석
피아니스트, 작곡가, 그리고 빅 밴드 리더였던 Claude Bolling은 1930년 4월 10일에 프랑스 칸에서 태어났지만, 그의 삶의 대부분을 파리에서 보냈다. 그는 젊었을 때 클래식 음악을 공부하기 시작했다. 그는 학교 친구에 의해 재즈의 세계를 소개받았다. 나중에 Bolling은 가장 훌륭한 재즈 음악가 중 한 명인 Fats Waller의 음악에 관심을 갖게 되었다. 그는 십 대 때 프랑스의 아마추어 대회에서 Best Piano Player 상을 수상하면서 유명해졌다. 그는 또한 성공적인 영화 음악 작곡가였고, 100편이 넘는 영화를 위한 음악을 작곡했다. 1975년에 그는 플루트 연주자 Rampal과 협업했고, 'Suite for Flute and Jazz Piano Trio'를 발매했으며, 그것으로 가장 잘 알려지게 되었다. 그는 두 아들 David와 Alexandre를 남기고 2020년에 사망했다.

정답이 보이는 해설
십 대 때 Best Piano Player 상을 받았다(Bolling became famous as a teenager by winning the Best Piano Player prize ~.)고 한다. 따라서 글의 내용과 일치하지 않는 것은 ③이다.

필수 어휘
composer 작곡가　classical music 클래식 음악　excellent 훌륭한
win 수상하다　prize 상　amateur 아마추어　successful 성공적인
collaborate 협업하다　publish 발매하다　well-known 잘 알려진

07 정답 ③

202203 26번 정답률 92%

Antonie van Leeuwenhoek was a scientist well known for his cell
_{~으로 알려진}
research. He was born in Delft, the Netherlands, on October 24,
1632. At the age of 16, he began to learn job skills in Amsterdam.
At the age of 22, Leeuwenhoek returned to Delft. It wasn't easy
for Leeuwenhoek to become a scientist. 단서 He knew only one
_{네덜란드어 하나만 알고 있었음}
language — Dutch — which was quite unusual for scientists of his
time. But his curiosity was endless, and he worked hard. He had an
important skill. He knew how to make things out of glass. This skill
came in handy when he made lenses for his simple microscope. He
_{도움이 되다}
saw tiny veins with blood flowing through them. He also saw living
_{세심한 주의를 기울이다　관계대명사 that 생략}
bacteria in pond water. ✪ He paid close attention to *the things* (he
_{동사1}
saw) / and wrote down his observations. Since he couldn't draw
_{동사2}
well, he hired an artist to draw pictures of what he described.

해석
Antonie van Leeuwenhoek은 세포 연구로 잘 알려진 과학자였다. 그는 1632년 10월 24일 네덜란드 Delft에서 태어났다. 그는 16살에 Amsterdam에서 직업 기술을 배우기 시작했다. Leeuwenhoek은 22살에 Delft로 돌아왔다. Leeuwenhoek이 과학자가 되기는 쉽지 않았다. 그는 오직 한 가지 언어, 즉 네덜란드어만을 알고 있었는데, 그것은 그 당시 과학자들에게는 상당히 드문 것이었다. 하지만 그의 호기심은 끝이 없었고, 그는 열심히 노력했다. 그에게는 중요한 기술이

9강
내용 일치 파악

있었다. 그는 유리로 물건을 만드는 방법을 알고 있었다. 이 기술은 그가 자신의 간단한 현미경에 쓰일 렌즈를 만들 때 도움이 되었다. 그는 피가 흐르고 있는 아주 작은 혈관을 보았다. 그는 또한 연못 물속에서 살아 있는 박테리아를 보았다. 그는 자신이 본 것들에 세심한 주의를 기울였고 관찰한 것을 기록했다. 그는 그림을 잘 그릴 수 없었기 때문에, 화가를 고용하여 자신이 설명하는 것을 그림으로 그리게 했다.

정답이 보이는 해설
Antonie van Leeuwenhoek은 네덜란드어 한 가지만 알고 있었다고 한다. 따라서 글의 내용과 일치하지 않는 것은 ③이다.

필수 어휘
Dutch 네덜란드어 unusual 드문 endless 끝없는 come in handy 도움이 되다
microscope 현미경 tiny 아주 작은

08 정답 ④

201111 26번 정답률 88%

Bessie Coleman was born in Texas in 1892. When she was eleven, she was told that the Wright brothers had flown their first plane. Since that moment, she dreamed about the day she would soar through the sky. At the age of 23, Coleman moved to Chicago, where she worked at a restaurant to save money for flying lessons. However, she had to travel to Paris to take flying lessons because
수업을 받다
American flight schools at the time admitted neither women nor
neither A nor B: A도 B도 아닌
Black people. In 1921, she finally became the first Black woman to earn an international pilot's license. She also studied flying acrobatics in Europe and 단서 made her first appearance in an
뉴욕의 에어쇼에 첫 출현을 함
airshow in New York in 1922. ✪ As a female pioneer of flight, / she
전치사(~로서)
inspired the next generation to pursue their dreams of flying.
inspire+목적어+목적격보어(to부정사): ~가 …하도록 영감을 주다

해석
Bessie Coleman은 1892년에 텍사스에서 태어났다. 그녀는 11살이었을 때 Wright 형제가 그들의 첫 비행을 했다는 것을 들었다. 그 순간부터 그녀는 자신이 하늘을 높이 날아오를 그날을 꿈꿨다. 23살의 나이에 Coleman은 시카고로 이사했고, 거기서 그녀는 비행 수업을 위한 돈을 모으기 위해 한 식당에서 일했다. 하지만 그 당시 미국 비행 학교들은 여성이나 흑인을 받아들이지 않았기 때문에 그녀는 비행 수업을 듣기 위해 파리로 가야 했다. 1921년에 그녀는 마침내 국제 조종사 면허를 딴 최초의 흑인 여성이 되었다. 그녀는 또한 유럽에서 곡예 비행을 공부했으며 1922년에 뉴욕의 에어쇼에 첫 출현을 했다. 여성 비행의 개척자로서 그녀는 다음 세대가 그들의 비행의 꿈을 추구하도록 영감을 주었다.

정답이 보이는 해설
Bessie Coleman은 뉴욕의 에어쇼에 첫 출현을 했다고 한다. 따라서 글의 내용과 일치하지 않는 것은 ④이다.

필수 어휘
soar 날아오르다 save (돈을) 모으다 flight 비행
admit (단체·학교 등에서) 받아들이다, 입학을 허락하다 international 국제적인
license 면허 appearance 출현, 나타남 pioneer 개척자 inspire 영감을 주다
generation 세대 pursue 추구하다

09 정답 ⑤

201109 26번 정답률 70%

Paul Laurence Dunbar, an African-American poet, was born

on June 27, 1872. By the age of fourteen, Dunbar had poems published in the *Dayton Herald*. While in high school he edited his high school newspaper. Despite being a fine student, Dunbar was financially unable to attend college and took a job as an
be unable to: ~할 수 없다
elevator operator. In 1893, Dunbar published his first book, *Oak and Ivy*, at his own expense. In 1895, he published the second book,
at one's own expense: 자비로, 사비로
Majors and Minors, which brought him national and international recognition. The poems written in standard English were called "majors," and those in dialect were termed "minors." ✪ Although
= the poems
the "major" poems (in standard English) / outnumber those (written
┌→ it is[was] ~ that 강조 구문   = the poems
in dialect), // 단서 **it was** the dialect poems / **that** brought Dunbar
방언으로 쓴 시들이 가장 주목을 받았음
the most attention.

해석
아프리카계 미국 시인인 Paul Laurence Dunbar는 1872년 6월 27일에 태어났다. 14세가 되자 Dunbar는 'Dayton Herald'에 시를 발표했다. 고등학교에 다니는 동안 그는 학교 신문을 편집했다. 훌륭한 학생이었음에도 불구하고 Dunbar는 재정상 대학에 다닐 수 없어서 엘리베이터 기사로 취직을 했다. 1893년에 Dunbar는 그의 첫 번째 책인 '떡갈나무와 담쟁이덩굴'을 자비로 출간했다. 1895년에 그는 두 번째 책인 '장조와 단조'를 출간했고, 그것은 그에게 국내외적 인정을 가져왔다. 표준 영어로 쓰인 시는 '장조'로 불렸고, 방언으로 쓴 시는 '단조'라고 불리었다. 비록 표준 영어의 '장조' 시들이 방언으로 쓰인 시들보다 많지만, Dunbar에게 가장 큰 주목을 가져온 것은 방언의 시들이었다.

정답이 보이는 해설
마지막 문장에서 Dunbar가 표준 영어로 쓴 시들이 방언으로 쓴 시들보다 많았지만, 가장 큰 주목을 받은 것은 방언으로 쓴 시들이었다(it was the dialect poems that brought Dunbar the most attention)고 한다. 따라서 글의 내용과 일치하지 않는 것은 ⑤이다.

필수 어휘
publish 발표하다 fine 훌륭한 financially 재정적으로
operator (기계) 기사, 조작자 expense 비용 recognition 인정, 인식
dialect 방언, 사투리 outnumber ~보다 많다 attention 주목, 관심

10 정답 ③

201106 26번 정답률 66%

Lithops are plants that are often called 'living stones' on
~ 때문에
account of their unique rock-like appearance. They are native to
= Lithops   ~가 원산지인
the deserts of South Africa but commonly sold in garden centers and nurseries. Lithops grow well in compacted, sandy soil with little water and extreme hot temperatures. 단서 Lithops are small
작은 식물로 지표면 위로
plants, rarely getting more than an inch above the soil surface and
1인치 이상 거의 자라지 않음
usually with only two leaves. ✪ The thick leaves resemble the
주어   동사
cleft / (in an animal's foot) / or just a pair of grayish brown *stones*
목적어1   목적어2
/ (gathered together). The plants have no true stem and much of the
└ 「주격 관계대명사+be동사」 생략
plant is underground. Their appearance has the effect of conserving moisture.

10강 2020~2023 안내문의 이해

01 정답 ④

202309 27번 정답률 96%

Silversmithing Class

Kingston Club is offering a fine jewelry making class.

⭐ Don't miss this great chance / (to make your own jewelry)!
명령문의 동사 to부정사의 형용사적 용법

When & Where

• Saturday, October 21, 2023 (2 p.m. to 4 p.m.)

• Kingston Club studio

Registration

• Available only online

• Dates: October 1 – 14, 2023

• Fee: $40 (This includes all tools and materials.)

• Registration is limited to 6 people.
be limited to: ~으로 제한되다

Note

최소한, 적어도
• 단서 Participants must be at least 16 years old.
참가자는 16세 이상이어야 함
• No refund for cancellation on the day of the class

해석

Silversmithing Class

Kingston Club이 정교한 보석 만들기 수업을 제공합니다. 여러분만의 보석을 만들이 좋은 기회를 놓치지 마세요!

시간과 장소
• 2023년 10월 21일 토요일 (오후 2시부터 오후 4시까지)
• Kingston Club 스튜디오

등록
• 온라인으로만 가능
• 날짜: 2023년 10월 1일~14일
• 비용: 40달러 (이것이 모든 도구와 재료를 포함합니다.)
• 등록은 6명으로 제한됩니다.

유의 사항
• 참가자는 최소 16살이어야 합니다.
• 수업 당일 취소 시 환불 불가

정답이 보이는 해설

보석 만들기 수업을 알리는 안내문이다. Note의 첫 번째 사항을 보면 참가자는 최소 16살이어야(Participants must be at least 16 years old.) 한다. 따라서 안내문의 내용과 일치하지 않는 것은 ④이다.

필수 어휘

offer 제공하다 fine 정교한, 우아한 registration 등록
available 이용할 수 있는, 효력이 있는 fee 비용, 요금 include 포함하다
tool 도구 material 재료 participant 참가자 refund 환불
cancellation 취소

02 정답 ⑤

202309 28번 정답률 94%

2023 Ocean Awareness Film Contest

Join our 7th annual film contest and show your knowledge of marine conservation.

□ **Theme**

– Ocean Wildlife / Ocean Pollution

(Choose one of the above.)

□ **Guidelines**

– Participants: High school students

– Submission deadline: September 22, 2023

– The video must be between 10 and 15 minutes.

– ⭐ All entries must be uploaded (to our website).
조동사가 있는 수동태: must+be+p.p.
– Only one entry per person
1인당

□ **Prizes**

• 1st place: $100

• 2nd place: $70

• 3rd place: $50

단서 (Winners will be announced on our website.)
수상자는 웹사이트에 발표될 것임
For more information, please visit www.oceanawareFC.com.

해석

2023 Ocean Awareness Film Contest

우리의 일곱 번째 연례 영상 대회에 참여하여 해양 보존에 관한 여러분의 지식을 보여 주세요.

□ **주제**
– 해양 야생 생물 / 해양 오염
(위에서 하나를 선택하세요.)

□ **지침**
– 참가자: 고등학생
– 제출 기한: 2023년 9월 22일
– 영상은 10분에서 15분 사이여야 합니다.
– 모든 출품작은 우리 웹사이트에 업로드되어야 합니다.
– 1인당 오직 출품작 하나

□ **상금**
• 1등: 100달러
• 2등: 70달러
• 3등: 50달러
(수상자는 우리 웹사이트에 발표될 것입니다.)
더 많은 정보는 www.oceanawareFC.com을 방문해 주세요.

정답이 보이는 해설

해양 보존 영상 대회에 관한 안내문이다. 수상자는 웹사이트에 발표될 것(Winners will be announced on our website.)이라고 한다. 따라서 안내문의 내용과 일치하는 것은 ⑤이다.

선택지 완벽 분석

① 세 가지 주제 중 하나를 선택해야 한다.
두 가지 주제 중에서 하나를 선택하라(Ocean Wildlife / Ocean Pollution (Choose one of the above.))고 한다.
② 중학생이 참가할 수 있다.
참가자는 고등학생이라고(Participants: High school students) 되어 있다.
③ 영상은 10분을 넘길 수 없다.
영상은 10~15분 사이여야 한다(The video must be between 10 and 15 minutes.)고 한다.
④ 1인당 두 개까지 출품할 수 있다.
1인당 출품작은 오직 하나라고(Only one entry per person) 되어 있다.

필수 어휘

annual 연례의 knowledge 지식 marine 해양의, 바다에 사는
conservation 보호, 보존 theme 주제 pollution 오염 participant 참가자
submission 제출 entry 출품작, 응모작 announce 발표하다

03 정답 ⑤

2023 Drone Racing Championship

Are you the best drone racer? ❁ Then / take *the opportunity* (**to prove** [you are the one])!

When & Where

• 6 p.m. – 8 p.m., Sunday, July 9

• Lakeside Community Center

Requirements

• Participants: High school students only

• Bring your own drone for the race.

Prize

• $500 and a medal will be awarded to the winner.

Note

• 단서 The first 10 participants will get souvenirs.
  For more details, please visit www.droneracing.com or call 313-6745-1189.

해석

2023년 드론 레이싱 선수권 대회

당신은 최고의 드론 레이서인가요? 그렇다면 여러분이 바로 그 사람이라는 것을 증명할 기회를 잡으세요!

언제 & 어디서

• 7월 9일 일요일, 오후 6시부터 오후 8시까지

• Lakeside Community Center

필요조건

• 참가자: 고등학생만

• 레이스를 위한 자신의 드론을 가지고 오세요.

상

• 500달러와 메달이 우승자에게 수여될 것입니다.

참고 사항

• 선착순 10명의 참가자들은 기념품을 받게 될 것입니다.
  더 많은 세부 정보를 원하시면, www.droneracing.com을 방문하거나 313-6745-1189로 전화하세요.

정답이 보이는 해설

드론 레이싱 선수권 대회에 관한 안내문이다. Note에 해당하는 부분에 선착순 10명의 참가자들이 기념품을 받게 될 것이라고(The first 10 participants will get souvenirs.) 한다. 따라서 안내문의 내용과 일치하지 않는 것은 ⑤이다.

필수 어휘

opportunity 기회 prove 증명하다 requirement 필요조건 award 수여하다
participant 참가자 souvenir 기념품 detail 세부 사항

04 정답 ⑤

Summer Scuba Diving One-day Class

❁ Join our summer scuba diving lesson (for beginners), / and become an underwater explorer!

Schedule

• 10:00 – 12:00 Learning the basics

• 13:00 – 16:00 Practicing diving skills in a pool

Price

• Private lesson: $150

• Group lesson (up to 3 people): $100 per person

• Participants can rent our diving equipment for free.

Notice

• Participants must be 10 years old or over.

• 단서 Participants must register at least 5 days before the class begins.

For more information, please go to www.ssdiver.com.

해석

여름 스쿠버 다이빙 일일 수업

초보자를 위한 우리의 여름 스쿠버 다이빙 수업에 참여하여, 수중 탐험가가 되세요!

일정

• 10시 – 12시 기초 배우기

• 13시 – 16시 수영장에서 다이빙 기술 연습하기

가격

• 개인 수업: $150

• 그룹 수업 (최대 3명): 1인당 $100

• 참가자는 다이빙 장비를 무료로 대여할 수 있습니다.

알림

• 참가자는 10세 이상이어야 합니다.

• 참가자는 적어도 수업 시작 5일 전까지 등록해야 합니다.
  더 많은 정보를 원하시면, www.ssdiver.com을 방문하세요.

정답이 보이는 해설

여름 스쿠버 다이빙 수업에 관한 안내문이다. 적어도 수업 시작 5일 전까지 등록해야 한다(Participants must register at least 5 days before the class begins.)고 한다. 따라서 안내문의 내용과 일치하는 것은 ⑤이다.

선택지 완벽 분석

① 오후 시간에 바다에서 다이빙 기술을 연습한다.
  오후에는 수영장에서 다이빙 기술을 연습한다(13:00-16:00 Practicing diving skills in a pool)고 했다.

② 그룹 수업의 최대 정원은 4명이다.
  그룹 수업은 최대 3명(Group lesson (up to 3 people))이다.

③ 다이빙 장비를 유료로 대여할 수 있다.
  다이빙 장비를 무료로 대여할 수 있다(Participants can rent our diving equipment for free.)고 했다.

④ 연령에 관계없이 참가할 수 있다.
  참가자는 10세 이상이어야 한다(Participants must be 10 years old or over.)고 했다.

필수 어휘

beginner 초보자 underwater 수중의 explorer 탐험가 rent 빌리다
equipment 장비 register 등록하다

05 정답 ③

Call for Articles

Do you want to get your stories published? *New Dream Magazine* is looking for future writers! This event is open to anyone aged 13 to 18.

Articles

• Length of writing: 300 – 325 words

- Articles should also include high-quality color photos.

Rewards

- Five cents per word
- 단서 **Five dollars per photo**
  사진 하나당 5달러

Notes

- ✪ You **should send** us your phone number (together with your writing).
  동사　간접목적어　직접목적어
- Please email your writing to us at article@ndmag.com.

해석

기사 모집

여러분의 이야기가 출간되기를 원하시나요? 'New Dream Magazine'은 미래의 작가를 찾고 있습니다! 이 행사는 13세에서 18세까지 누구나 참여할 수 있습니다.

기사

- 원고 길이: 300~325단어
- 기사에는 또한 고화질 컬러 사진이 포함되어야 합니다.

사례금

- 단어당 5센트
- 사진당 5달러

주의 사항

- 원고와 함께 여러분의 전화번호를 보내야 합니다.
- 원고를 이메일 article@ndmag.com으로 보내 주세요.

정답이 보이는 해설

한 잡지사에서 기사를 모집하는 안내문이다. 사진당 5센트가 아니라 5달러(Five dollars per photo)라고 한다. 따라서 안내문의 내용과 일치하지 않는 것은 ③이다.

필수 어휘

article 기사　publish 출간하다　include 포함하다　high-quality 고화질의
per ~당

06 정답 ④

202303 28번 정답률 90%

Greenhill Roller Skating

Join us for your chance to enjoy roller skating!

- Place: Greenhill Park, 351 Cypress Avenue
- Dates: Friday, April 7 – Sunday, April 9
- Time: 9 a.m. – 6 p.m.
- Fee: $8 per person for a 50-minute session
  1인당

Details

- ✪ Admission / will be / on a first-come, first-served basis (with no reservations).
  주어　　동사　　보어
- 단서 Children under the age of 10 must be accompanied by an adult.
  10세 미만의 어린이는 어른과 함께 동행해야 함
- We will lend you our roller skates for free.
  무료로

Contact the Community Center for more information at 013-234-6114.

해석

Greenhill 롤러스케이팅

롤러스케이팅을 즐길 기회를 함께 해요!

- 장소: Greenhill Park, 351 Cypress Avenue
- 일자: 4월 7일 금요일 – 4월 9일 일요일
- 시간: 오전 9시 – 오후 6시
- 요금: 50분간 1인당 8달러

세부 사항

- 입장은 예약 없이 선착순입니다.
- 10세 미만의 어린이는 어른과 동행해야 합니다.
- 롤러스케이트는 무료로 빌려줍니다.

더 많은 정보를 위해서 커뮤니티 센터 013-234-6114로 연락하세요.

정답이 보이는 해설

Greenhill 롤러스케이팅에 관한 안내문이다. 10세 미만의 어린이는 어른과 동행해야 한다(Children under the age of 10 must be accompanied by an adult.)고 한다. 따라서 안내문의 내용과 일치하는 것은 ④이다.

🔍 선택지 완벽 분석

① 오전 9시부터 오후 9시까지 운영한다.
오전 9시부터 오후 6시까지(9 a.m. - 6 p.m.)이다.

② 이용료는 시간 제한 없이 1인당 8달러이다.
이용료는 50분간 1인당 8달러($8 per person for a 50-minute session)이다.

③ 입장하려면 예약이 필요하다.
입장은 예약 없이 선착순(Admission will be on a first-come, first-served basis with no reservations)이다.

⑤ 추가 요금을 내면 롤러스케이트를 빌려준다.
롤러스케이트는 무료로 빌려준다(We will lend you our roller skates for free.)고 했다.

필수 어휘

fee 요금　session 기간, 시간　admission 입장
first-come, first-served 선착순　reservation 예약　accompany 동행하다
adult 어른, 성인　contact 연락하다

07 정답 ⑤

202211 27번 정답률 92%

E-Waste Recycling Day

E-Waste Recycling Day is an annual event in our city. Bring your used electronics such as cell phones, tablets, and laptops to recycle.
　　　　　　　　~와 같은
Go green!
친환경적이 되다

When

Saturday, December 17, 2022

8:00 a.m. - 11:00 a.m.

Where

Lincoln Sports Center

Notes

- Items NOT accepted: light bulbs, batteries, and microwaves
- ✪ All personal data (on the devices) / must be wiped out (in advance).
  　　주어　　　　　　　　　　동사(수동태)
  미리, 사전에
- This event is free 단서 but open only to local residents.
  　　　　　　　　　　　지역 주민들에게만 개방됨

Please contact us at 986-571-0204 for more information.

해석

전자 폐기물 재활용의 날

전자 폐기물 재활용의 날은 우리 시의 연례행사입니다. 휴대전화, 태블릿, 그리고 노트북과 같이 재활용할 중고 전자 제품을 가져오세요. 친환경적이 되세요!

언제

2022년 12월 17일 토요일

오전 8시부터 오전 11시까지

어디서

Lincoln 스포츠 센터

주의 사항

• 허용되지 않는 품목들: 전구, 건전지, 전자레인지

• 기기 속 모든 개인 정보는 미리 삭제되어야 합니다.

• 이 행사는 무료이지만 지역 주민에게만 개방됩니다.

더 많은 정보를 위해서는 986-571-0204로 연락주세요.

┌─ **정답이 보이는 해설** ─┐

전자 폐기물 재활용의 날에 관한 안내문이다. 이 행사는 무료이지만, 지역 주민에게 만 개방된다(but open only to local residents)고 한다. 따라서 안내문의 내용과 일치하지 않는 것은 ⑤이다.

┌─ **필수 어휘** ─┐

annual 연례의, 연간의   electronics 전자 제품   accept 허용하다   light bulb 전구 microwave 전자레인지   wipe out 삭제하다   resident 주민, 거주자

08 정답 ③

202211 28번 정답률 87%

Undersea Walking Activity

Enjoy a fascinating underwater walk on the ocean floor. Witness wonderful marine life on foot!
(걸어서, 도보로)

Age Requirement

10 years or older

Operating Hours

from Tuesday to Sunday

9:00 a.m. – 4:00 p.m.

Price

$30 (insurance fee included)

❂ What to Bring
(what + to부정사: 무엇을 ~할지, ~할 것)
swim suit and towel

Notes

• 단서 Experienced lifeguards accompany you throughout the
(숙련된 안전 요원이 활동 내내 동행함)
activity.

• With a special underwater helmet, you can wear glasses during the activity.

• Reservations can be made on-site or online at www.seawalkwonder.com.

┌─ **해석** ─┐

해저 걷기 활동

해양 바닥에서 매력적인 수중 걷기를 즐기세요. 걸어 다니며 멋진 바다 생물을 직접 보세요!

연령 요건

10세 이상

영업시간

화요일부터 일요일까지

오전 9시부터 오후 4시까지

가격

30달러 (보험료 포함)

가져와야 하는 것

수영복과 수건

주의 사항

• 숙련된 안전 요원이 활동 내내 여러분과 동행합니다.

• 특수 수중 헬멧 착용 시, 여러분은 활동 중에 안경을 쓸 수 있습니다.

• 예약은 현장 또는 www.seawalkwonder.com에서 온라인으로 할 수 있습니다.

┌─ **정답이 보이는 해설** ─┐

해저 걷기 활동에 관한 안내문이다. 숙련된 안전 요원이 활동 내내 여러분과 동행한 다(Experienced lifeguards accompany you throughout the activity.)고 한다. 따라서 안내문의 내용과 일치하는 것은 ③이다.

┌─ 🔍 **선택지 완벽 분석** ─┐

① 연중무휴로 운영된다.
화요일에서 일요일까지(from Tuesday to Sunday) 운영된다.

② 가격에 보험료는 포함되어 있지 않다.
가격은 30달러이고 보험료가 포함된 가격($30 (insurance fee included))이다.

④ 특수 수중 헬멧 착용 시 안경을 쓸 수 없다.
특수 수중 헬멧 착용 시, 활동 중에 안경을 쓸 수 있다(With a special underwater helmet, you can wear glasses during the activity.)고 했다.

⑤ 현장 예약은 불가능하다.
예약은 현장 또는 온라인으로 할 수 있다(Reservations can be made on-site or online) 고 했다.

┌─ **필수 어휘** ─┐

fascinating 매력적인, 매혹적인   witness 보다, 목격하다   marine 해양의 requirement 요건, 조건   insurance fee 보험료   experienced 숙련된, 능숙한 accompany 동행하다, 동반하다   reservation 예약   on-site 현장의, 현지의

09 정답 ④

202209 27번 정답률 96%

2022 Springfield Park Yoga Class

The popular yoga class in Springfield Park returns! Enjoy yoga hosted on the park lawn. If you can't make it to the park, join us
(가다, 참석하다)
online on our social media platforms!

◆ **When**: Saturdays, 2 p.m. to 3 p.m., September

◆ **Registration**: At least TWO hours before each class starts,
(적어도)
sign up here .

◆ **Notes**
(to부정사의 의미상 주어)
• ❂ For online classes: find a quiet space with enough room [for you to stretch out].
(형용사적 용법)
• For classes in the park: 단서 mats are not provided, so bring your
(매트는 제공되지 않으므로 자기 것을 가져와야 함)
own!

※ The class will be canceled if the weather is unfavorable.

For more information, click here .

┌─ **해석** ─┐

2022 Springfield 공원 요가 수업

Springfield 공원에서의 인기 있는 요가 수업이 돌아옵니다! 공원 잔디밭에서 열리 는 요가를 즐기세요. 만약 여러분이 공원에 갈 수 없다면, 우리의 소셜 미디어 플랫폼 에서 온라인으로 우리와 함께하세요!

◆ **언제**: 9월, 토요일마다, 오후 2시부터 오후 3시까지

◆ **등록**: 각 수업이 시작하기 적어도 두 시간 전까지, 여기에서 등록하세요.

◆ **주의 사항**

• 온라인 수업 대상: 여러분이 스트레칭을 할 수 있는 충분한 공간을 가진 조용한 장 소를 찾으세요.

• 공원에서의 수업 대상: 매트는 제공되지 않으므로, 자신의 것을 가져오세요!

※ 만약 날씨가 좋지 않으면 수업은 취소될 것입니다.

10강
영어영역 이해

더 많은 정보를 위해서는, 여기를 클릭하세요.

10 정답 ④

Kenner High School's Water Challenge

Kenner High School's Water Challenge is a new contest to propose measures against water pollution. Please share your ideas for dealing with water pollution!
~에 대한 대책[조치]
~에 대처하다

Submission

– How: Submit your proposal by email to admin@khswater.edu.

– When: September 5, 2022 to September 23, 2022

Details

– Participants must enter in teams of four and can only join one team.

– Submission is limited to one proposal per team.

– ✪ 단서 Participants must use *the proposal form* [provided on the website].
참가자들은 웹사이트에 제공된 양식을 사용해야 함   the proposal form을 수식하는 과거분사구

Prizes

– 1st: $50 gift certificate

– 2nd: $30 gift certificate

– 3rd: $10 gift certificate

Please visit www.khswater.edu to learn more about the challenge.

┌─ 해석 ─┐

Kenner High School's Water Challenge

Kenner High School's Water Challenge는 수질 오염에 대한 대책을 제안하는 새로운 대회입니다. 수질 오염에 대처하기 위한 여러분의 아이디어를 공유해 주세요!
제출
– 어떻게: 여러분의 제안서를 admin@khswater.edu로 이메일로 제출해 주세요.
– 언제: 2022년 9월 5일부터 2022년 9월 23일까지
세부 사항
– 참가자들은 4인으로 구성된 팀으로 참가해야 하며 오직 한 팀에만 참여할 수 있습니다.
– 한 팀당 1개의 제안서만 제출할 수 있습니다.
– 참가자들은 웹사이트에 제공된 제안서 양식을 사용해야 합니다.
상품
– 1등: 50달러 상품권
– 2등: 30달러 상품권
– 3등: 10달러 상품권
그 대회에 대해 더 알아보려면 www.khswater.edu를 방문해 주세요.

---

11 정답 ④

Kids Taekwondo Program

Enjoy our taekwondo program this summer vacation.

☐ **Schedule**

• Dates: August 8th – August 10th

• Time: 9:00 a.m. – 11:00 a.m.

☐ **Participants**

• Any child aged 5 and up

☐ **Activities**

• Self-defense training

• Team building games to develop social skills

☐ **Participation Fee**

• 단서 $50 per child (includes snacks)
  어린이당 50달러의 참가비에 간식이 포함됨

☐ **Notice**

• ✪ **What to bring**: water bottle, towel
  what+to부정사: 무엇을 ~할지, ~할 것
• What not to bring: chewing gum, expensive items

┌─ 해석 ─┐

Kids Taekwondo Program

이번 여름 방학에 우리의 태권도 프로그램을 즐기세요.
☐ 일정
• 날짜: 8월 8일 ~ 8월 10일
• 시간: 오전 9시 ~ 오전 11시
☐ 참가자
• 5세 이상 어린이 누구나
☐ 활동
• 자기 방어 훈련
• 사교 능력 개발을 위한 팀 만들기 게임
☐ 참가비
• 어린이당 50달러(간식 포함)
☐ 공지
• 가져올 것: 물병, 수건
• 가져오지 말아야 할 것: 껌, 비싼 물건

12 정답 ②

Moonlight Chocolate Factory Tour

Take this special tour and have a chance to enjoy our most popular chocolate bars.

□ **Operating Hours**

• Monday – Friday, 2:00 p.m. – 5:00 p.m.

□ **Activities**

• 단서 Watching our chocolate-making process
  초콜릿 제조 과정을 볼 수 있음
• Tasting 3 types of chocolate (dark, milk, and mint chocolate)

□ **Notice**

• Ticket price: $30

• Wearing a face mask is required.

• ✪ Taking pictures is not allowed inside the factory.
  동명사 주어   단수 동사

해석

Moonlight 초콜릿 공장 투어

이 특별한 투어에 참여하여 우리의 가장 인기 있는 초콜릿 바를 즐길 기회를 가지세요.
□ 운영 시간
• 월요일 ～ 금요일, 오후 2시 ～ 오후 5시
□ 활동
• 초콜릿 제조 과정 관람
• 3가지 종류의 초콜릿 시식(다크, 밀크, 민트 초콜릿)
□ 공지
• 티켓 가격: 30달러
• 마스크 착용은 필수입니다.
• 공장 내부에서 사진 촬영은 허용되지 않습니다.

정답이 보이는 해설

초콜릿 공장 투어에 관한 안내문이다. 안내문의 활동(Activities)에서 초콜릿 제조 과정을 볼 수 있다(Watching our chocolate-making process)고 한다. 따라서 안내문의 내용과 일치하는 것은 ②이다.

선택지 완벽 분석

① 주말 오후 시간에 운영한다.
월요일 ～ 금요일 오후 2시 ～ 5시(Monday — Friday, 2:00 p.m. — 5:00 p.m.)에 운영한다.
③ 네 가지 종류의 초콜릿을 시식한다.
세 가지 종류(Tasting 3 types of chocolate)의 초콜릿을 시식한다고 했다.
④ 마스크 착용은 참여자의 선택 사항이다.
마스크 착용은 필수적이라(Wearing a face mask is required.)고 했다.
⑤ 공장 내부에서 사진 촬영이 가능하다.
사진 촬영이 허용되지 않는다(Taking pictures is not allowed inside the factory.)고 했다.

13 정답 ④

Rachel's Flower Class

Make Your Life More Beautiful!

Class Schedule (Every Monday to Friday)

Flower Arrangement	11 a.m. – 12 p.m.
Flower Box Making	1 p.m. – 2 p.m.

Price

• $50 for each class (flowers and other materials included)

• Bring your own scissors and a bag.

Other Info.

• ✪ 단서 You can sign up for classes / **either** online **or** by phone.
  온라인이나 전화로 수업을 등록할 수 있음   either A or B: A 또는 B 둘 중 하나
• No refund for cancellations on the day of your class

To contact, visit www.rfclass.com or call 03-221-2131.

해석

Rachel의 꽃 교실
여러분의 인생을 더 아름답게 만드세요!
수업 일정 (매주 월요일부터 금요일까지)

꽃꽂이	오전 11시 ～ 정오
플라워 박스 만들기	오후 1시 ～ 오후 2시

가격
• 각 수업당 50달러 (꽃값과 다른 재료비 포함)
• 자신의 가위와 가방을 가져오세요.
기타 정보
• 온라인이나 전화로 수업을 등록할 수 있습니다.
• 수업 당일 취소 시 환불 불가
연락하시려면 www.rfclass.com을 방문하시거나 03-221-2131로 전화주세요.

정답이 보이는 해설

꽃 교실에 관한 안내문이다. 기타 정보(Other Info.)에서 수업 등록은 온라인이나 전화로 할 수 있다(You can sign up for classes either online or by phone.)고 한다. 따라서 안내문의 내용과 일치하지 않는 것은 ④이다.

14 정답 ⑤

Nighttime Palace Tour

Date: Friday, April 29 – Sunday, May 15

Time

Friday	7 p.m. – 8:30 p.m.
Saturday & Sunday	6 p.m. – 7:30 p.m.
	8 p.m. – 9:30 p.m.

Tickets & Booking

• $15 per person (free for kids under 8)

• ✪ Bookings will be accepted up to 2 hours / **before** the tour starts.
  미래시제 수동태(will be+p.p.)   접속사(～하기 전에)
                                  최대 ～까지

Program Activities

• Group tour with a tour guide (1 hour)

• Trying traditional foods and drinks (30 minutes)

※ 단서 You can try on traditional clothes with no extra charge.
  추가 비용 없이 전통 의상을 입어 볼 수 있음
※ For more information, please visit our website,

www.palacenighttour.com.

야간 궁궐 투어

날짜: 4월 29일 금요일~5월 15일 일요일

시간

금요일	오후 7시~오후 8시 30분
토요일과 일요일	오후 6시~오후 7시 30분
	오후 8시~오후 9시 30분

티켓 및 예약
- 1인당 15달러 (8세 미만 어린이는 무료)
- 예약은 투어가 시작하기 최대 2시간 전까지 접수될 예정입니다.

프로그램 활동
- 투어 가이드와 단체 투어 (1시간)
- 전통 음식 시식 및 음료 시음 (30분)
※ 추가 비용 없이 전통 의상을 입어 볼 수 있습니다.
※ 더 많은 정보를 원하시면, 저희 웹사이트 www.palacenighttour.com을 방문하세요.

야간 궁궐 투어에 관한 안내문이다. 안내문 후반에 추가 비용 없이 전통 의상을 입어 볼 수 있다(You can try on traditional clothes with no extra charge.)고 한다. 따라서 안내문의 내용과 일치하는 것은 ⑤이다.

① 금요일에는 하루에 두 번 투어가 운영된다.
   금요일에는 오후 7시~오후 8시 30분에 한 번 투어가 운영된다고 했다.
② 8세 미만 어린이의 티켓은 5달러이다.
   8세 미만의 어린이는 티켓이 공짜(free for kids under 8)라고 했다.
③ 예약은 투어 하루 전까지만 가능하다.
   예약은 투어 시작하기 2시간 전까지 접수될 것(Booking will be accepted up to 2 hours before the tour starts.)이라고 했다.
④ 투어 가이드의 안내 없이 궁궐을 둘러본다.
   투어 가이드가 안내하는 단체 투어(Group tour with a tour guide)라고 했다.

palace 궁궐 booking 예약 traditional 전통의, 전통적인
extra charge 추가 비용

15 정답 ②

202111 27번 정답률 83%

2021 Camptonville Nature Photo Contest

This is the fourth year of the annual Camptonville Nature Photo Contest. ✿ You can show the beauty of nature in Camptonville / by sharing your most amazing photos!
by -ing: ~함으로써   놀라운(cf. amazed: 놀란)

Submission

– 단서 Upload a maximum of 20 photos onto our website www.
   최대 20장의 사진을 웹사이트에 업로드해야 함
camptonvillephotocontest.org.

– Deadline is December 1.

Prizes

• 1st Place: $500   •2nd Place: $200   •3rd Place: $100

(Winners will be posted on our website on December 31.)
                     post on: ~에 게시하다

Details

– All winning photos will be exhibited at City Hall.

– Please contact us at 122-861-3971 for further information.

2021 Camptonville 자연 사진 대회

이번이 매년 열리는 Camptonville 자연 사진 대회의 네 번째 해입니다. 여러분은 여러분의 가장 놀라운 사진을 공유함으로써 Camptonville의 자연의 아름다움을 보여 줄 수 있습니다!

제출
- 최대 20장의 사진을 우리 웹 사이트 www.camptonvillephotocontest.org 에 업로드하십시오.
- 마감 기한은 12월 1일입니다.

상
- 1위: 500달러 •2위: 200달러 •3위: 100달러
  (수상자는 12월 31일에 우리 웹 사이트에 게시될 것입니다.)

세부 사항
- 모든 수상 사진은 시청에 전시될 것입니다.
- 추가 정보를 위해서는 122-861-3971로 우리에게 연락 주십시오.

자연 사진 대회에 관한 안내문이다. 제출(Submission)에서 최대 20장의 사진을 웹 사이트에 업로드하라고 한다. 따라서 안내문의 내용과 일치하지 않는 것은 ②이다.

amazing 놀라운, 멋진 maximum 최대 deadline 마감 기한
winner 수상작, 수상자 post 게시하다 exhibit 전시하다
further 추가의, 더 이상의

16 정답 ④

202111 28번 정답률 92%

Willow Valley Hot Air Balloon Ride

Enjoy the best views of Willow Valley from the sky with our hot air balloon ride!

• ✿ **Capacity**: up to 8 people including a pilot
              최대 ~까지   전치사(~을 포함하여)
• **Time Schedule**

Spring & Summer (from April to September)	5:00 a.m. – 7:00 a.m.
Autumn & Winter (from October to March)	6:00 a.m. – 8:00 a.m.

※ Duration of Flight: about 1 hour

• **Fee**: $150 per person (insurance not included)
                  1인당
• **Note**

– 단서 Reservations are required and must be made online.
      예약은 필수이며 온라인으로 해야 함
– You can get a full refund up to 24 hours in advance.
           전액을 환불받다   사전에, 미리
– Visit www.willowvalleyballoon.com for more information.

Willow Valley 열기구 탑승

우리의 열기구를 타고 하늘에서 Willow Valley의 최고의 풍경을 즐기세요!
• **수용 인원**: 조종사 포함 최대 8인
• **시간 일정표**

봄 & 여름 (4월부터 9월까지)	오전 5시 ~ 오전 7시
가을 & 겨울 (10월부터 3월까지)	오전 6시 ~ 오전 8시

• 요금: 인당 150달러 (보험은 포함되지 않음)
• 공지 사항
  – 예약이 요구되며 온라인으로 이루어져야 합니다.
  – 24시간 전까지는 전액 환불을 받을 수 있습니다.
  – 더 많은 정보를 위해서는 www.willowvalleyballoon.com을 방문해 주십시오.

[정답이 보이는 해설]

열기구 탑승에 관한 안내문이다. 공지 사항(Note)에서 예약은 온라인으로 이루어져야 한다고 한다. 따라서 안내문의 내용과 일치하는 것은 ④이다.

[선택지 완벽 분석]

① 조종사를 제외하고 8인까지 탈 수 있다.
조종사를 포함한 8인(up to 8 people including a pilot)이라고 했다.
② 여름에는 오전 6시에 시작한다.
봄과 여름에는 오전 5시에 시작하고, 가을과 겨울에 6시에 시작한다고 했다.
③ 요금에 보험이 포함되어 있다.
요금에 보험이 포함되지 않는다(insurance not included)고 했다.
⑤ 환불은 예외 없이 불가능하다.
24시간 전까지는 전액 환불 가능하다(You can get a full refund up to 24 hours in advance.)고 했다.

[필수 어휘]

hot air balloon 열기구 ride 놀이 기구 capacity 수용 인원
duration 지속 시간 insurance 보험 reservation 예약 full refund 전액 환불
in advance 사전에, 미리

17 정답 ②
202109 27번 정답률 92%

Premier Reading Challenge

❋ This is **not** a competition, / **but** rather a challenge /
not A but B: A가 아니라 B
(to inspire students with the love of reading).
부사적 용법(목적)   inspire A with B: A에게 B를 불어넣다

• **Participants**

  – Students from 6th grade to 9th grade
from A to B: A부터 B까지

• **Dates**

  – 단서 From June 1st to December 31st
6월부터 12월까지 7개월 동안 진행됨

• **Challenge**

  – Each student in 6th and 7th grade must read 15 books.

  – Each student in 8th and 9th grade must read 20 books.

• **Prize**

  – A bookmark for every participant

  – A Certificate of Achievement for students who complete the challenge

• **Registration**

  – Online only — www.edu.prc.com

＊ For more information, see the school librarian or visit the website above.

[해석]

최고의 읽기 도전
이 행사는 (경쟁) 시합이 아니라, 학생들에게 책 읽기 사랑을 불어넣는 도전입니다.
• 참가자들
  – 6학년부터 9학년까지의 학생들

• 날짜
  – 6월 1일부터 12월 31일까지
• 도전 (과제)
  – 6학년과 7학년의 개별 학생은 15권의 책을 읽어야 합니다.
  – 8학년과 9학년의 개별 학생은 20권의 책을 읽어야 합니다.
• 상품
  – 모든 참가자들에게 책갈피
  – 도전 과제를 완료한 학생들에게 '성취 증명서'
• 등록
  – 온라인으로만 — www.edu.prc.com
※ 더 많은 정보를 원하시면, 학교 사서 교사를 만나거나 위의 웹 사이트를 방문하세요.

[정답이 보이는 해설]

책 읽기 도전 행사에 관한 안내문이다. 날짜(Dates)가 6월 1일부터 12월 31일까지 (From June 1st to December 31st)이므로, 7개월 동안 진행된다. 따라서 안내문의 내용과 일치하지 않는 것은 ②이다.

[필수 어휘]

premier 최고의, 제1의 inspire 불어넣다, 격려하다 bookmark 책갈피

18 정답 ⑤
202109 28번 정답률 85%

Wolf Howls in Algonquin Park

Wolf Howls in Algonquin Park is offering you a once-in-a-lifetime experience tonight! Don't miss the chance to hear the wolves communicate with our staff.

When & Where

• 8 p.m. Wednesday, August 25th, 2021

  (Only if the weather permits and a wolf pack is nearby.)

• Meet our staff at the outdoor theater and travel with them to the wolf howling location.

Fee

• $18.00 per person (Free for Ontario residents 65 and older)

Note

• ❋ Dress warmly / (for *this special program*) / [**which** will last
동사(명령문)   주격 관계대명사
longer than three hours].

• No dogs are allowed during the event.

• 단서 If there are less than 5 people for the event, it will be
  ~ 미만
참여 인원이 5명 미만이면 행사는 취소됨
cancelled.

＊ Visit our website at www.algonquinpark.on for more information.

[해석]

Algonquin 공원의 늑대 울음소리
'Algonquin 공원의 늑대 울음소리'는 오늘 밤 여러분에게 평생에 한 번밖에 없는 경험을 제공합니다! 늑대들이 직원들과 소통하는 소리를 들을 수 있는 기회를 놓치지 마세요!

시간과 장소
• 2021년 8월 25일 수요일 오후 8시
  (날씨가 좋고 늑대 무리가 근처에 있는 경우에만.)
• 야외극장에서 직원과 만나 늑대 울음 장소까지 그들과 함께 가세요.
요금

10강
베이스듣기운

- 1인당 18달러 (65세 이상의 Ontario 거주자는 무료)

주의 사항

- 3시간 이상 지속될 이 특별 프로그램을 위해 옷을 따뜻하게 입으세요.
- 반려견은 행사에 허용되지 않습니다.
- 행사에 5명 미만이 신청한다면, 행사는 취소될 것입니다.

※ 더 많은 정보를 원하시면 www.algonquinpark.on의 웹 사이트를 방문하세요.

19 정답 ⑤

"Go Green" Writing Contest

Share your talents & conserve the environment

□ **Main Topic**: Save the Environment

□ **Writing Categories**

- Slogan   • Poem   • Essay

□ **Requirements**:

- Participants: High school students

- Participate in one of the above categories
  (only one entry per participant)

□ **Deadline**: July 5th, 2021

- Email your work to apply@gogreen.com.

□ **Prize for Each Category**

- 1st place: $80   • 2nd place: $60   • 3rd place: $40

□ ✪ The winners will be announced / (only on the website) (on July 15th, 2021). **단서** No personal contact will be made.

□ For more information, visit www.gogreen.com.

해석

'Go Green' 글쓰기 대회
여러분의 재능을 나누세요 & 환경을 보존하세요

□ **주제**: 환경을 지켜라

□ **글쓰기 부문**
   • 슬로건   • 시   • 에세이

□ **필요 요건**:
   • 참가자: 고등학생

- 위 글쓰기 부문 중 하나에 참가하세요.
  (참가자 일인당 한 작품만)

□ **마감 기한**: 2021년 7월 5일
   • apply@gogreen.com으로 작품을 보내세요.

□ **부문별 상금**
   • 1등: 80달러   • 2등: 60달러   • 3등: 40달러

□ 수상자는 2021년 7월 15일에 웹 사이트에서만 공지될 것입니다. 개별 연락은 없을 것입니다.

□ 추가 정보를 원한다면, www.gogreen.com을 방문하세요.

20 정답 ④

Virtual Idea Exchange

Connect in real time and have discussions about the upcoming school festival.

□ **Goal**

- Plan the school festival and share ideas for it.

□ **Participants**: Club leaders only

□ **What to Discuss**

- Themes   • Ticket sales   • Budget

□ **Date & Time**: 5 to 7 p.m. on Friday, June 25th, 2021

□ **Notes**

- ✪ **단서** Get the access link by text message (10 minutes before the meeting) / and click it.
- Type your real name when you enter the chatroom.

해석

가상의 아이디어 교환

실시간으로 접속하여 다가오는 학교 축제에 대해 토론하세요.

□ **목표**
- 학교 축제를 계획하고 그것(축제)에 대한 아이디어를 공유하세요.

□ **참가자**: 동아리 대표들만

□ **토론할 내용**
   • 주제   • 티켓 판매   • 예산

□ **날짜 & 시간**: 2021년 6월 25일 금요일 오후 5시 ~ 7시

□ **주의 사항**
- 회의 10분 전에 문자 메시지로 접속 링크를 받아 클릭하세요.
- 채팅방에 들어올 때 실명을 입력하세요.

필수 어휘

virtual (컴퓨터를 이용한) 가상의 connect 접속하다 upcoming 다가오는
theme 테마, 주제 budget 예산 access 입장, 접근

---

21 정답 ⑤
202103 27번 정답률 94%

Spring Farm Camp

✪ Our one-day spring farm camp / gives your kids
true, hands-on farm experience.

When: Monday, April 19 – Friday, May 14

Time: 9 a.m. – 4 p.m.

Ages: 6 – 10

Participation Fee: $70 per person

(lunch and snacks included)

Activities:

- making cheese from goat's milk
- picking strawberries
- making strawberry jam to take home

We are open rain or shine.

For more information, go to www.b_orchard.com.

해석

봄 농장 캠프
우리의 일일 봄 농장 캠프는 여러분의 자녀에게
진짜로 직접 해 보는 농장 체험을 제공합니다.
기간: 4월 19일 월요일~5월 14일 금요일
시간: 오전 9시~오후 4시
나이: 6세~10세
참가비: 개인당 70달러
(점심과 간식 포함)
활동:
• 염소젖으로 치즈 만들기
• 딸기 따기
• 집으로 가져갈 딸기잼 만들기
우리는 비가 오든 날이 개든 운영합니다.
더 많은 정보를 원하시면 www.b_orchard.com에 접속하세요.

정답이 보이는 해설

봄 농장 캠프에 관한 안내문이다. 안내문 하단에 날씨와 관계없이 운영한다(We are open rain or shine.)고 한다. 따라서 안내문의 내용과 일치하지 않는 것은 ⑤이다.

필수 어휘

hands-on 직접 해 보는 participation 참가, 참여

Great Aquarium

Opening Hours: 10 a.m. – 6 p.m., daily

Last entry is at 5 p.m.

Events

Fish Feeding	10 a.m. – 11 a.m.
Penguin Feeding	1 p.m. – 2 p.m.

Ticket Prices

Age	Price
Kids (12 and under)	$25
Adults (20 – 59)	$33
Teens (13 – 19) Seniors (60 and above)	$30

* Ticket holders will receive a free drink coupon.

Booking Tickets

- ✪ ALL visitors **are required** to book online.
- Booking will be accepted up to 1 hour before entry.

해석

Great 수족관

관람 시간: 매일 오전 10시 ~ 오후 6시
마지막 입장은 오후 5시입니다.

행사

물고기 먹이 주기	오전 10시~오전 11시
펭귄 먹이 주기	오후 1시~오후 2시

티켓 가격

나이	가격
어린이 (12세 이하)	25달러
성인 (20세~59세)	33달러
청소년 (13세~19세) 어르신 (60세 이상)	30달러

* 티켓 소지자는 무료 음료 쿠폰을 받을 것입니다.

티켓 예매

• '모든' 방문객은 온라인으로 예약해야 합니다.
• 예약은 입장 한 시간 전까지 받을 것입니다.

정답이 보이는 해설

수족관 관람 정보에 관한 안내문이다. Ticket Prices(티켓 가격) 표 아래에 티켓 소지자는 무료 음료 쿠폰을 받을 것(Ticket holders will receive a free drink coupon.)이라고 한다. 따라서 안내문의 내용과 일치하는 것은 ④이다.

필수 어휘

aquarium 수족관 entry 입장 holder 보유자, 소지자 up to ~까지

10강

내용문의 이해

23 정답 ⑤

2020 Student Building Block Competition

✪ Students in every grade will compete / (to build **the most**
to부정사의 부사적 용법(목적)
creative and livable *structure* (made out of blocks))!
최상급(비교 표현)　　　　과거분사구

When & Where

- 2 p.m. – 4 p.m. Saturday, November 21

- Green Valley Elementary School Gym

Rules

- All building projects must be completed on site with supplied
현장에서
  blocks only.

- Participants are not allowed to receive outside assistance.

Gifts & Prizes

- All the participants receive a T-shirt.

- One winner from each grade group wins $100 and a medal.

Sign up
등록하다
- Participation is FREE!

- Email jeremywilson@greenvalley.org by November 15.

  (단서 Registration on site is not available.)
  현장 등록은 가능하지 않음

해석

2020 학생 블록 쌓기 대회

모든 학년의 학생들은 블록으로 가장 창의적이고 살기 좋은 건축물을 만들기 위해 경쟁할 것입니다!

시간 & 장소
- 11월 21일 토요일 오후 2시~오후 4시
- Green Valley 초등학교 체육관

규칙
- 모든 건축 과제는 제공된 블록만으로 현장에서 완성되어야 합니다.
- 참가자들은 외부의 도움을 받는 것이 허용되지 않습니다.

선물 & 상
- 모든 참가자들은 티셔츠를 받습니다.
- 각 학년 그룹의 우승자는 100달러와 메달을 받습니다.

등록
- 참가는 '무료'입니다!
- 11월 15일까지 jeremywilson@greenvalley.org로 이메일을 보내세요.
  (현장 등록은 가능하지 않습니다.)

정답이 보이는 해설

블록 쌓기 대회에 관한 안내문이다. 안내문의 마지막에서 현장 등록이 가능하지 않다(Registration on site is not available.)고 한다. 따라서 안내문의 내용과 일치하지 않는 것은 ⑤이다.

필수 어휘

competition 대회, 경기　compete 경쟁하다　livable 살기에 좋은
on site 현장의　assistance 도움　sign up 등록하다　registration 등록

---

24 정답 ⑤

Crystal Castle Fireworks

Come and enjoy the biggest fireworks display in the South West of England!

Dates: 5th & 6th December, 2020

Location: Crystal Castle, 132 Oak Street

Time: 15:00 – 16:00 Live Music Show

16:30 – 17:30 Maze Garden

18:00 – 18:30 Fireworks Display

Parking: Free car park opens at 13:00.

Note:

　　　　　　　　　　　→「주격 관계대명사+be동사」 생략
✪ 단서 *Any child* (aged 12 or under) **must** be accompanied by **an**
12세 이하 아동은 성인과 동행해야 함　　　　　　　~와 동행하다
adult.

All tickets must be reserved beforehand on our website www.
사전에
crystalcastle.com.

해석

Crystal Castle 불꽃놀이

영국의 남서부에서 가장 큰 불꽃놀이에 와서 즐기세요!

날짜: 2020년 12월 5일 & 6일
장소: Crystal Castle, Oak 가 132
시간: 15:00~16:00 라이브 음악 쇼
16:30~17:30 미로 정원
18:00~18:30 불꽃놀이
주차: 무료 주차장이 13시에 개방됩니다.
주의 사항:
12세 이하의 모든 아동은 성인과 동행해야 합니다.
모든 티켓은 저희 웹 사이트 www.crystalcastle.com에서 사전에 예매되어야 합니다.

정답이 보이는 해설

영국에서 열리는 Crystal Castle 불꽃놀이에 관한 안내문이다. Note(주의 사항) 항목에 12세 이하의 아동은 성인과 동행해야 한다(Any child aged 12 or under must be accompanied by an adult.)고 한다. 따라서 안내문의 내용과 일치하는 것은 ⑤이다.

선택지 완벽 분석

① 영국의 북부 지역에서 가장 큰 불꽃놀이이다.
　영국의 남서부(the South West of England)에서 가장 큰 불꽃놀이이다.
② 라이브 음악 쇼가 불꽃놀이 이후에 진행된다.
　라이브 음악 쇼는 15시~16시에, 불꽃놀이는 18시~18시 30분에 진행된다.
③ 불꽃놀이는 1시간 동안 진행된다.
　불꽃놀이는 30분 동안(18:00~18:30) 진행된다.
④ 주차장은 오후 1시부터 유료로 이용 가능하다.
　무료 주차장(Free car park)이다.

필수 어휘

fireworks 불꽃놀이　display 전시, 보여 주는 것　location 위치, 장소
maze 미로　accompany 동행하다　reserve 예약하다
beforehand 사전에, ~ 전에 미리

11강 2020~2023 어법

01 정답 ④

202309 29번 정답률 37%

There is a reason the title "Monday Morning Quarterback" exists. ☀ Just read the comments (on social media) / (from fans discussing the weekend's games), / and you quickly see / [how many people believe / they could play, coach, and manage sport teams more ① successfully than / those on the field]. This goes for the boardroom as well. Students and professionals with years of training and specialized degrees in sport business may also find themselves ② being given advice on how to do their jobs from friends, family, or even total strangers without any expertise. Executives in sport management ③ have decades of knowledge and experience in their respective fields. However, many of them face criticism from fans and community members telling ④ themselves(→ them) how to run their business. Very few people tell their doctor how to perform surgery or their accountant how to prepare their taxes, but many people provide feedback on ⑤ how sport organizations should be managed.

해석

'Monday Morning Quarterback'이라는 호칭이 존재하는 이유가 있다. 주말 경기를 두고 토론하는 팬들의 소셜 미디어의 댓글만 읽어 봐도 여러분은 경기장에 있는 사람들보다 자신이 더 성공적으로 경기를 펼치고, 감독하고, 스포츠 팀을 관리할 수 있다고 얼마나 많은 사람이 믿는지 금방 알 수 있다. 이것은 이사회실에도 들어맞는다. 스포츠 사업에서 수년간 훈련받고 전문적인 학위를 가진 학생들과 전문가들 또한 친구들, 가족, 혹은 전문 지식이 전혀 없는 심지어 완전히 낯선 이로부터 일을 어떻게 해야 하는지에 대한 충고를 듣고 있는 자신을 발견할지도 모른다. 스포츠 경영 임원진들은 자신의 각 분야에서 수십 년의 지식과 경험을 가지고 있다. 하지만, 그들 중 다수가 그들에게 사업 운영 방식을 알려 주는 팬들과 지역 사회 구성원들의 비난에 직면한다. 자신의 의사에게 수술하는 방법을 알려 주거나 자신의 회계사에게 자신의 세금을 준비하는 방법을 알려 주는 사람은 거의 없지만, 많은 사람이 스포츠 조직이 어떻게 관리되어야 하는지에 대한 피드백은 제공한다.

정답이 보이는 해설

④ 재귀대명사 themselves를 쓰면 말하는 주체인 fans and communities members를 뜻하는데, 여기서 듣는 대상은 executives in sport management이므로 이들을 의미하도록 themselves를 them으로 고쳐야 한다. 참고로, Monday Morning Quarterback이란 게임의 결과를 본 후, 어떻게 경기를 해야만 했는지 자세히 의견을 개진하는 풋볼 팬을 가리킨다.

선택지 완벽 분석

① 동사구 could play, coach, and manage sport teams를 수식하면서 more와 than으로 비교급을 만들어야 하므로 부사 successfully는 어법상 적절하다.

② 훈련받고 전문적인 학위가 있는 학생과 전문가조차 다른 사람들로부터 어떻게 일해야 하는지에 관한 충고를 받는다는 내용으로, 현재분사 수동태 being given은 어법상 적절하다.

③ 복수 주어 Executives의 동사이므로 복수 동사 have는 어법상 적절하다.

⑤ 많은 사람이 스포츠 조직이 어떻게 관리되어야 하는지에 대한 피드백을 준다는 내용으로 명사절을 이끌 수 있는 how는 어법상 적절하다.

필수 어휘

exist 존재하다 discuss 토론하다 field 경기장; 분야, 영역
professional 전문가 specialized 전문의, 전문화된 degree 학위
expertise 전문 지식 executive 중역 decade 10년
experience 경험 respective 각각의, 각자의 face 직면하다
criticism 비판, 비난 accountant 회계사 tax 세금 organization 조직

02 정답 ④

202306 29번 정답률 58%

주제문 Although praise is one of the most powerful tools available for improving young children's behavior, it is equally powerful for improving your child's self-esteem. Preschoolers believe what their parents tell ① them in a very profound way. They do not yet have the cognitive sophistication to reason ② analytically and reject false information. If a preschool boy consistently hears from his mother ③ that he is smart and a good helper, he is likely to incorporate that information into his self-image. ☀ Thinking of himself as a boy [who is smart and knows how to do things] / ④ being(→ is) likely to make him endure longer (in problem-solving efforts) and increase his confidence (in trying new and difficult tasks). Similarly, thinking of himself as the kind of boy who is a good helper will make him more likely to volunteer ⑤ to help with tasks at home and at preschool.

해석

칭찬은 어린 아이들의 행동을 개선하는 데 사용할 수 있는 가장 강력한 도구 중 하나이지만, 그것은 아이의 자존감을 향상시키는 데에도 똑같이 강력하다. 미취학 아동들은 그들의 부모가 그들에게 하는 말을 매우 뜻깊게 여긴다. 그들은 분석적으로 추론하고 잘못된 정보를 거부할 수 있는 인지적 정교함을 아직 가지고 있지 않다. 만약 미취학 소년이 그의 어머니로부터 그가 똑똑하고 좋은 조력자라는 것을 지속적으로 듣는다면, 그는 그 정보를 그의 자아상으로 통합시킬 가능성이 높다. 스스로를 똑똑하고 일을 어떻게 하는지 아는 소년으로 생각하는 것은 그가 문제 해결 노력에 있어 더 오래 지속하도록 하고 새롭고 어려운 일을 시도하는 것에 있어 그의 자신감을 높여 줄 가능성이 크다. 마찬가지로, 자신을 좋은 조력자인 그런 부류의 소년으로 생각하는 것은 그가 집에서와 유치원에서 일을 자발적으로 돕게 할 가능성을 더 크게 만들 것이다.

정답이 보이는 해설

④ 동명사 Thinking이 이끄는 주어부 Thinking of himself as a boy who is smart and knows how to do things(스스로를 똑똑하고 일을 어떻게 하는지 아는 소년으로 생각하는 것은)의 동사가 필요하며, 동명사구 주어는 단수로 취급하므로 준동사에 해당하는 being을 단수 동사 is로 고쳐야 한다.

선택지 완벽 분석

① 미취학 아동들은 그들의 부모가 그들에게 말하는 것을 믿는다는 내용이므로, tell의 간접목적어로 쓰인 them은 어법상 적절하다.

② 분석적으로 추론하고 잘못된 정보를 거부할 수 있는 인지적 정교함을 가지고 있지 않다는 내용으로, 여기서 reason은 '추론하다'라는 동사이고, 그 동사를 수식하는 부사 analytically(분석적으로)는 어법상 적절하다.

함정 to reason ② analytically와 (to) reject false information이 the cognitive sophistication을 수식하는 구조로, reason은 명사가 아니라 동사로 쓰였음을 이해해야 한다.

③ 엄마로부터 that 이하의 말을 계속 듣는다는 내용으로, 동사 hears의 목적어절을 이끄는 that은 어법상 적절하다.

⑤ volunteer의 목적어로 to부정사가 온 것이므로, to help는 어법상 적절하다.

03 정답 ⑤

202303 29번 정답률 66%

The most noticeable human characteristic projected onto animals **단서** is ① that they can talk in human language. Physically, animal cartoon characters and **단서** toys ② made after animals are also most often deformed in such a way as to resemble humans. **단서** This is achieved by ③ showing them with humanlike facial features and deformed front legs to resemble human hands. In more recent animated movies the trend has been to show the animals in a more "natural" way. However, **단서** they still use their front legs ④ like human hands (for example, lions can pick up and lift small objects with one paw), and they still talk with an appropriate facial expression. **단서** ✪ A general strategy [that is used to make the animal characters more emotionally appealing, both to children and adults,] / ⑤ are(→ is) / to give them (enlarged and deformed) childlike features.

해석

동물에게 투영되는 가장 눈에 띄는 인간적 특징은 동물이 인간의 언어로 대화할 수 있다는 점이다. 신체적으로도, 동물 만화 캐릭터들과 동물을 본떠 만든 장난감들 또한 인간을 닮게 하는 방식으로 변형되는 경우가 아주 많다. 이것은 인간과 같은 얼굴 특징과 사람의 손을 닮게 변형된 앞다리를 가지고 있는 것으로 그것들을 보여 줌으로써 달성된다. 더 최근의 만화 영화에서 추세는 동물을 더 "자연스러운" 방식으로 보여 주는 것이었다. 그러나 그것들은 (예를 들어 사자가 한 발로 작은 물체를 집어서 들어 올릴 수 있는 것처럼) 여전히 사람의 손처럼 앞다리를 사용하고, 여전히 적절한 얼굴 표정을 지으며 이야기한다. 동물 캐릭터를 아이와 어른 모두에게 더 감정적으로 매력적이게 만들기 위해 이용하는 일반적인 전략은 그것들에 확대되고 변형된 어린이 같은 특징을 부여하는 것이다.

정답이 보이는 해설

⑤ 문장의 주어가 A general strategy [that is used to make the animal characters more emotionally appealing, both to children and adults,]이고, 주어부의 핵인 strategy가 단수 명사이므로 문장의 동사 are는 단수 동사 is로 고쳐야 한다.

선택지 완벽 분석

① 명사절 접속사 that은 be동사 is의 보어절로, 어법상 적절하다.
[함정] that 뒤에는 완전한 절이 이어지고 있으므로, what이 아니라 that이 와야 함을 이해해야 한다.

② made after animals가 앞의 명사 toys를 꾸며 준다. 주어가 '만들어진' 대상이므로 과거분사 made가 쓰인 것은 어법상 적절하다. made 앞에 that[which] are가 생략되어 있다고 볼 수 있다.

③ by -ing는 '~함으로써'의 의미로, by 뒤에 동명사 showing은 어법상 적절하다.

④ 그것들(동물 만화 캐릭터들)은 앞다리를 여전히 사람의 '손'처럼 사용한다는 내용이므로, like는 어법상 적절하다.

04 정답 ④

202211 29번 정답률 51%

You may have seen headlines in the news about some of the things machines powered by artificial intelligence can do. However, if you were to consider **단서** all the tasks ① that AI-powered machines could actually perform, it would be quite mind-blowing! **단서** One of the key features of artificial intelligence ② is that it enables machines to learn new things, rather than requiring programming specific to new tasks. ✪ Therefore, / the core difference (between **단서** computers of the future and ③ those of the past) / is [that future computers will be able to learn and self-improve]. In the near future, smart virtual assistants **단서** will know more about you than your closest friends and family members ④ are(→ do). Can you imagine how that might change our lives? These kinds of changes are exactly why **단서** it is so important ⑤ to recognize the implications that new technologies will have for our world.

have implications for: ~에 영향을 미치다

해석

여러분은 인공 지능으로 구동되는 기계가 할 수 있는 몇 가지 일에 대한 헤드라인들을 뉴스에서 본 적이 있을 것이다. 하지만, AI로 구동되는 기계가 실제로 수행할 수 있는 모든 작업을 고려한다면, 그것은 꽤 놀라울 것이다! 인공 지능의 핵심 특징들 중 하나는 그것이 새로운 작업에 특화된 프로그래밍을 필요로 하기보다는 기계들로 하여금 새로운 것을 학습할 수 있게 한다는 것이다. 그러므로, 미래의 컴퓨터들과 과거의 그것들 사이의 핵심적인 차이점은 미래의 컴퓨터는 학습할 수 있고 스스로 개선할 수 있을 것이라는 점이다. 가까운 미래에, 스마트 가상 비서는 여러분의 가장 가까운 친구나 가족이 아는 것보다 여러분에 대해 더 많이 알게 될 것이다. 그것이 우리의 삶을 어떻게 변화시킬지 상상할 수 있는가? 이러한 종류의 변화들은 새로운 기술들이 우리 세계에 미칠 영향을 인식하는 것이 왜 그렇게 중요한가에 대한 정확한 이유이다.

정답이 보이는 해설

④ 스마트 가상 비서가 여러분에 대해 더 많이 알게 될(will know) 것인데, 그게 가장 가까운 친구나 가족이 아는(know) 것보다 더 많이 그럴 것이라는 내용으로, 일반 동사 know 대신 쓰인 대동사이므로 be동사 are는 do로 고쳐야 한다.

선택지 완벽 분석

① that절은 앞의 명사구 all the tasks를 수식하는 관계대명사절이므로 목적격 관계대명사 that은 어법상 적절하다.

② One of the key features of artificial intelligence가 주어이고, 주어의 핵은 One이므로 단수 동사 is는 어법상 적절하다.

③ those는 앞의 복수 명사 computers를 대신하고 있는 대명사이므로 어법상 적절하다.
[함정] between A and B 구문에서 A가 computers of the future, B가 computers of the past임을 이해해야 한다.

⑤ why가 이끄는 보어절에서 it(가주어) ~ to부정사(진주어) 구문에 해당하므로 진주어인 to부정사 to recognize는 어법상 적절하다.

quite 꽤 mind-blowing 놀라운, 경이로운 feature 특징 require 필요로 하다
specific to ～에게 특화된, 고유한 core 핵심의, 가장 중요한
self-improve 스스로 개선하다 virtual 가상의 assistant 비서, 조수
exactly 정확히 recognize 인식하다 implication 영향, 결과

05 정답 ③

202209 29번 정답률 70%

The human brain, it turns out, has shrunk in mass by about 10
percent since it ① peaked in size 단서 15,000–30,000 years ago. ✪ One
possible reason is [**that** many thousands of years ago / humans
lived in 단서 a world of dangerous predators {② where they had
to have their wits about them at all times to avoid being killed}].
Today, we have effectively domesticated ourselves and 단서 **many of**
the tasks of survival — from avoiding immediate death to building
shelters to obtaining food — ③ **has(→ have)** been outsourced to the
wider society. We are smaller than our ancestors too, and 단서 **it** is a
characteristic of domestic animals ④ that they are generally smaller
than their wild cousins. None of this may mean we are dumber —
brain size is not necessarily an indicator of human intelligence —
but it may mean that our brains today are wired up differently, and
perhaps more efficiently, than ⑤ those of our ancestors.

해석
인간의 뇌는 15,000~30,000년 전에 크기가 절정에 달한 이후 부피가 10퍼센트 정도 줄어든 것으로 드러났다. 한 가지 가능한 이유는 수천 년 전에 인간은 죽임을 당하는 것을 피하기 위해 항상 그들(위험한 포식자)에 대한 자신들의 기지를 발휘해야 하는 위험한 포식자의 세계에서 살았다는 것이다. 오늘날 우리는 우리 스스로를 효율적으로 길들여 왔고 생존의 많은 과업이, 즉각적인 죽음을 피하는 것부터 은신처를 짓는 것과 음식을 얻는 것까지, 더 넓은 사회로 위탁되어 왔다. 우리는 우리의 조상보다 더 작기도 한데, 가축이 그들의 야생 사촌보다 일반적으로 더 작다는 것은 가축의 한 특징이다. 이것의 어떤 것도 우리가 더 어리석다는 것을 의미하지는 않는데, 뇌 크기가 반드시 인간 지능의 지표는 아니기 때문이다. 그러나 그것은 오늘날 우리의 뇌가 다르게, 그리고 아마도 우리 조상들의 뇌보다 더 효율적으로 타고났다는 것을 의미할지도 모른다.

정답이 보이는 해설
③ 주어의 핵이 대명사 many이므로, has는 복수 동사 have로 고쳐야 한다.

선택지 완벽 분석
① 과거를 나타내는 부사구(15,000-30,000 years ago)가 쓰였으므로 과거형 peaked는 어법상 직절하다.
② 장소의 선행사 a world of dangerous predators를 수식하는 관계부사 where는 어법상 직절하다.
④ It(가주어) ~ that(진주어) 구문에 해당하므로 진주어를 이끄는 접속사 that은 어법상 직절하다.
⑤ 앞에 언급된 brains를 가리키고 있으므로 복수형 지시대명사 those는 어법상 직절하다.

필수 어휘
shrink 줄어들다 peak 절정에 달하다 predator 포식자 wit 기지, 재치
domesticate 길들이다 immediate 즉각적인 shelter 은신처
outsource 외부에 위탁하다 characteristic 특징 domestic animal 가축
dumb 멍청한, 어리석은 indicator 지표

06 정답 ④

202206 29번 정답률 62%

Despite all the high-tech devices that seem to deny the need
for paper, 단서 **paper use** in the United States ① has nearly doubled
recently. We now consume more paper than ever: 400 million tons
globally and growing. Paper is not 단서 the only resource ② that
we are using more of. Technological advances often come with the
promise 단서 of ③ using fewer materials. ✪ However, / the reality is
[**that** they have historically caused more materials use], / 단서 **making**
us ④ **dependently(→ dependent)** on more natural resources. The
world now consumes far more "stuff" than it ever has. We use
twenty-seven times more industrial minerals, such as gold, copper,
and rare metals, than we ⑤ did just over a century ago. We also each
individually use more resources. Much of that is due to our high-
tech lifestyle.

해석
종이의 필요성을 부정하는 것처럼 보이는 모든 첨단 기기에도 불구하고, 미국에서 종이 사용은 최근에 거의 두 배가 되었다. 우리는 그 어느 때보다도 더 많은 종이를 소비하고 있는데, 전 세계적으로 4억 톤을 소비하고 있고 증가하고 있다. 종이는 우리가 더 많이 사용하고 있는 유일한 자원이 아니다. 기술의 발전은 흔히 더 적은 재료의 사용 가능성과 함께 온다. 하지만 현실은 그것이 역사적으로 더 많은 재료 사용을 야기하여 우리가 더 많은 천연자원 사용에 의존하게 만든다. 세계는 이제 그 어느 때보다도 훨씬 더 많은 '것'을 소비한다. 우리는 금, 구리, 희귀 금속과 같은 산업 광물을 1세기 이전에 우리가 사용했던 것보다 27배 더 많이 사용한다. 우리는 또한 각자 개인적으로 더 많은 자원을 사용한다. 그중 많은 부분은 우리의 첨단 생활 방식 때문이다.

정답이 보이는 해설
④ make의 목적격보어 자리에는 형용사가 오므로 dependently는 형용사 dependent로 고쳐야 한다.

선택지 완벽 분석
① 주어의 핵이 paper use이므로 단수 동사 has는 어법상 적절하다.
② the only resource를 수식하는 관계대명사절이므로 목적격 관계대명사 that은 어법상 적절하다.
③ 전치사 of의 목적어로 쓰였으므로 동명사 using은 어법상 적절하다.
⑤ 문맥상 used를 대신하고 있으므로 대동사 did는 어법상 적절하다.
　확인 a century ago라는 과거 부사구가 있으므로 대동사 do가 아니라 과거형 did를 써야 한다.

필수 어휘
high-tech 첨단 기술의 double 두 배가 되다 consume 소비하다
globally 전 세계적으로 resource 자원 advance 발전, 진보
promise 가능성, 약속 material 재료 industrial 산업의 mineral 광물
rare metal 희귀 금속 individually 개인적으로

07 정답 ③

202203 29번 정답률 65%

주제문 We usually get along best with people who we think are
like us. In fact, we seek them out. It's why 단서 places like Little
Italy, Chinatown, and Koreatown ① exist. But I'm not just talking
about race, skin color, or religion. I'm talking about people who

share our values and look at the world the same way we ② do. As
the saying goes, birds of a feather flock together. This is (단서) a very
common human tendency ③ what(→ that) is rooted in how our
species developed. Imagine you are walking out in a forest. ★ You
would be conditioned to avoid something unfamiliar or foreign /
because there is a high likelihood [that ④ it would be interested
in killing you]. Similarities (단서) make us ⑤ relate better to other
people because we think they'll understand us on a deeper level
than other people.

해석

우리는 대개 우리와 같다고 생각하는 사람들과 가장 잘 지낸다. 사실, 우리는 그들을
찾아낸다. 그것이 리틀 이탈리아, 차이나타운, 코리아타운 같은 장소들이 존재하는
이유이다. 그러나 나는 인종이나 피부색, 또는 종교에 대해서만 말하는 것이 아니다.
나는 우리의 가치관을 공유하고 우리와 같은 방식으로 세상을 바라보는 사람들에 대
해 말하는 것이다. 속담에도 있듯이, 같은 깃털을 가진 새가 함께 무리 짓는다. 이것
은 우리 종이 발전한 방식에 깊게 뿌리박혀 있는 매우 흔한 인간의 성향이다. 여러분
이 숲에 나가 걷고 있다고 상상해 보라. 익숙하지 않거나 낯선 것은 여러분을 죽이는
데 관심이 있을 가능성이 높기 때문에 여러분은 그런 것을 피하도록 조건화되어 있
을 것이다. 유사성은 우리가 다른 사람들과 마음이 더 잘 통하게 해 주는데, 그들이
우리를 다른 사람들보다 더 깊은 수준으로 이해할 거라고 생각하기 때문이다.

정답이 보이는 해설

③ 관계대명사절의 선행사 a very common human tendency를 수식해야 하므
로 관계대명사 what을 that으로 고쳐야 한다. what은 선행사를 포함하는 관계대명
사이므로 앞에 선행사가 오지 않는다.

선택지 완벽 분석

① 의문사절 내에서 주어 places에 대한 동사 자리이므로 복수 동사 exist는 어법
상 적절하다.

② 앞에 나온 look at the world를 대신하므로 대동사 do는 어법상 적절하다.

④ something unfamiliar or foreign을 가리키므로 대명사 it은 어법상 적절
하다.
    something, anything, nothing과 같이 -thing으로 끝나는 말은 it으로 받는다는 것에
    유의한다.

⑤ 사역동사 make는 목적격보어로 동사원형이 오므로 relate는 어법상 적절하다.

필수 어휘

seek ~ out (특히 많은 노력을 기울여) ~을 찾아내다   religion 종교   value 가치관
feather 깃털   flock 모이다, 무리 짓다   tendency 성향, 경향
be conditioned to ~에 조건화되어 있다   unfamiliar 익숙하지 않은
foreign 낯선   likelihood 가능성   similarity 유사성
relate 마음이 통하다, 잘 어울리다

08 정답 ④

202111 29번 정답률 51%

★ The reduction of minerals in our food is the result of using
(단서) *pesticides and fertilizers* / ① [that kill off *beneficial bacteria,
earthworms, and bugs* in the soil (that create many of the essential
nutrients in the first place), and prevent the uptake of nutrients into
the plant]. (단서) Fertilizing crops with nitrogen and potassium ② has
led to declines in magnesium, zinc, iron and iodine. For example,
there has been on average about a 30% decline in the magnesium
content of wheat. This is partly due (단서) to potassium ③ being

a blocker against magnesium absorption by plants. (단서) Lower
magnesium levels in soil also ④ occurring(→ occur) with acidic
soils and around 70% of the farmland on earth is now acidic. Thus,
the overall characteristics of soil determine the accumulation of
minerals in plants. Indeed, nowadays our soil is less healthy and so
are (단서) the plants ⑤ grown on it.

해석

우리의 식품 속 미네랄의 감소는 우선적으로 많은 필수 영양소를 만들어 내는 토양
의 이로운 박테리아, 지렁이, 그리고 벌레를 죽이고 식물로의 영양소 흡수를 막는 살
충제와 비료를 사용하는 것의 결과이다. 농작물에 질소와 포타슘으로 비료를 주는
것은 마그네슘, 아연, 철, 그리고 요오드의 감소로 이어져 왔다. 예를 들어 밀의 마그
네슘 함량에서는 평균적으로 약 30%의 감소가 있었다. 이는 부분적으로 포타슘이
식물에 의한 마그네슘 흡수에 방해물이 되기 때문이다. 토양의 더 낮은 마그네슘 수
치는 산성 토양에서도 나타나는데, 지구상에 있는 농지의 약 70%가 현재 산성이다.
따라서 토양의 전반적인 특징은 식물 속 미네랄의 축적을 결정한다. 실제로 오늘날
우리의 토양은 덜 건강하고 그 위에서 길러진 식물도 그러하다.

정답이 보이는 해설

④ Lower magnesium levels를 주어로 하는 동사가 나와야 하므로, occurring
은 occur로 고쳐야 한다.

선택지 완벽 분석

① pesticides and fertilizers를 수식하는 절을 이끄는 관계대명사 that은 어
법상 적절하다.

② 주어의 핵은 Fertilizing으로 동명사 주어는 단수 취급하므로 단수 동사 has는
어법상 적절하다.
    주어가 Fertilizing crops가 아니라 동명사 주어 Fertilizing이라는 것에 유의해야 한다.

③ 전치사의 목적어로 의미상 주어 potassium 뒤에 나온 동명사 being은 어법
상 적절하다.

⑤ 식물이 '길러진' 수동 관계이므로 the plants를 수식하는 과거분사 grown은
어법상 적절하다.

필수 어휘

reduction 감소   fertilizer 비료   beneficial 이로운   essential 필수의
nutrient 영양소   in the first place 우선, 첫째로   uptake 흡수
fertilize 비료를 주다   decline 감소   on average 평균적으로
acidic 산성의   overall 전반적인   characteristic 특징   accumulation 축적

09 정답 ②

202109 29번 정답률 50%

An economic theory of Say's Law holds that everything that's
made will get sold. The money from anything that's produced (단서) is
used to ① buy something else. ★ There can never be *a situation* /
② which(→ in which) (단서) a firm finds [that it can't sell its goods
and so has to dismiss workers and close its factories]. Therefore,
recessions and unemployment are impossible. Picture the level
of spending like the level of water in a bath. Say's Law applies
③ because (단서) people use all their earnings to buy things. But
what happens if people don't spend all their (단서) money, saving
some of ④ it instead? Savings are a 'leakage' of spending from the
economy. You're probably imagining the water level now falling,
so there's less spending in the economy. That would mean firms

단서 producing less and ⑤dismissing some of their workers.
and로 연결된 병렬 구조

해석

경제 이론인 Say의 법칙은 만들어진 모든 것은 판매가 이루어질 것이라고 주장한다. 생산된 어떤 것으로부터 얻어지는 돈은 다른 어떤 것을 구입하는 데 사용된다. 어떤 회사가 물품을 판매할 수 없게 되고 그에 따라 자사의 직원들을 해고하고 공장의 문을 닫아야 하는 상황은 절대 있을 수 없다. 따라서, 불황과 실업은 불가능하다. 지출의 수준을 욕조 안의 물 높이로 상상해 보라. Say의 법칙은 사람들이 자신들의 전체 수입을 물품을 사는 데 사용하기 때문에 적용된다. 하지만 만약 사람들이 자신들의 돈을 모두 사용하는 대신, 그것의 일부를 저축한다면 어떤 일이 일어날 것인가? 경제에서 저축은 지출의 '누수'이다. 여러분은 아마 지금 물의 높이가 낮아지고 있는 것, 다시 말해 경제에서 지출이 줄어드는 것을 상상하고 있을 것이다. 그것은 회사들이 더 적게 생산하고 일부 직원들을 해고하는 것을 의미할 것이다.

정답이 보이는 해설

② 선행사가 a situation이고 뒤에 주어와 동사, 목적어가 있는 완전한 절이 이어지고 있으므로 which를 「전치사+관계대명사」 형태의 in which나 where로 고쳐야 한다.

선택지 완벽 분석

① '구입하기 위해'라는 의미의 목적을 나타내는 to부정사의 부사적 용법으로 쓰였으므로 buy는 어법상 적절하다.
함정 앞에 있는 is used to를 보고 '~하는 데 익숙해지다'라는 의미의 「be used to+-ing」 구문으로 생각하지 않도록 유의한다.

③ 주어와 동사로 이루어진 절이 이어지고 있으므로 접속사 because는 어법상 적절하다.

④ 불가산 명사인 money는 단수 취급하므로 대명사 it을 쓴 것은 어법상 적절하다
함정 all their money의 all만 보고 복수 대명사 them을 써야 한다고 생각해서 정답으로 고르지 않도록 한다.

⑤ 접속사 and에 의해 producing과 병렬 연결된 구조이므로 dismissing은 어법상 적절하다.
함정 문장의 주어는 That이고 would mean이 동사이다. firms는 동명사 producing과 dismissing의 의미상 주어라는 것을 파악해야 한다.

필수 어휘

economic 경제의   theory 이론   produce 생산하다   firm 회사
dismiss 해고하다   factory 공장   recession 경기 후퇴, 불경기
unemployment 실업, 실업 상태   earnings 소득, 수입   leakage 누수, 누출

---

10 정답 ⑤

202106 29번 정답률 67%

There have been occasions ①in which **단서** you have observed a
주어   동사
smile and you could sense it was not genuine. ★ The most obvious
목적어 → 완전한 절   주어
way / (of identifying a genuine smile (from an insincere ②one)) / is
= smile   동사
[that a fake smile primarily only affects the lower half of the face],
명사절 접속사 that절 주어   that절 동사
(mainly with the mouth alone). The eyes don't really get involved.
부사구   관여하다
단서 Take the opportunity to look in the mirror and manufacture
주어 you가 생략된 명령문 → you가 직접 '사용하는' 능동의 의미
a smile ③using the lower half your face only. When you do this,

judge ④how happy your face really looks — is it genuine? A

genuine smile will impact on the muscles and wrinkles around the
                        ~에 영향을 주다
eyes and less noticeably, the **단서** skin between the eyebrow and
                              단수 명사(주어의 핵) → 단수 동사를 써야 함
upper eyelid ⑤are(→ is) lowered slightly with true enjoyment.

주제문 The genuine smile can impact on the entire face.

해석

여러분이 관찰한 미소가 진짜가 아니라고 느낄 수 있는 경우가 있다. 참된 미소와 진실되지 못한 미소를 알아보는 가장 확실한 방법은 가짜 미소는 얼굴의 절반 아래쪽 부분, 주로 입에만 영향을 미친다는 것이다. 눈은 사실상 관련이 없다. 거울을 볼 기회를 이용해서 여러분의 얼굴 아랫부분만을 사용해서 미소를 지어 보라. 여러분이 이렇게 할 때, 여러분의 얼굴이 실제로 얼마나 기분 좋아 보이는지를 판단해 보라. 그것이 진짜인가? 참된 미소는 눈가 근육과 주름에 영향을 주며, 티가 덜 나게 눈썹과 윗눈꺼풀 사이의 피부가 진정한 즐거움으로 살짝 내려오는 것이다. 참된 미소는 전체 얼굴에 영향을 줄 수 있다.

정답이 보이는 해설

⑤ 주어가 the skin between the eyebrow and upper eyelid이며 주어의 핵이 단수 명사 skin이므로 are를 단수 동사 is로 고쳐야 한다.

선택지 완벽 분석

① 뒤에 주어와 동사가 있는 완전한 절을 이루므로 관계부사 where에 해당하는 「전치사+관계대명사」인 in which는 어법상 적절하다.

② 단수 명사 a smile을 대신하는 부정대명사 one은 어법상 적절하다.

③ 주어인 you가 '사용하는' 능동의 의미이므로 현재분사 using은 어법상 적절하다.
함정 앞에 and가 없으므로 명령문의 형태인 use를 쓰는 자리가 아니며, 또한 '사용된'이라는 수동의 의미로 과거분사 used를 써야 한다고 생각해서 정답으로 고르지 않도록 유의한다.

④ 동사 judge의 목적어절로 형용사 happy를 꾸며 주는 의문부사 how는 어법상 적절하다.

필수 어휘

occasion 경우, 기회   observe 관찰하다   genuine 진짜의, 참된
obvious 분명한, 명백한   insincere 진실되지 못한   fake 가짜의   primarily 주로
involved 관련이 있는   manufacture 짓다, 제조하다   noticeably 눈에 띄게
slightly 살짝, 약간

---

11 정답 ③

202103 29번 정답률 64%

★ Although there is usually *a correct way* / (of holding and
접속사 (양보 부사절)   부사절의 동사   부사절의 주어   전치사 of의 목적어
playing musical instruments), // the most important instruction
                                                          주어
(to begin with) / is ①[that they are not toys / and that they must
                동사   접속사1= musical instruments   접속사2
be looked after]. ②Allow children **단서** time (to explore ways of
                  동사   간접목적어   직접목적어
handling and playing the instruments for themselves) before showing

them. **단서** Finding different ways to produce sounds ③are(→ is) an
        동명사구 주어 → 단수 취급   단수 동사
important stage of musical exploration. Correct playing comes from

단서 the desire ④to find the most appropriate sound quality and find
           명사를 수식하는 to부정사
the most comfortable playing position so that one can play with
                                                  ~하기 위해
control over time. As instruments and music become more complex,
      오랜 시간 동안
learning appropriate playing techniques becomes ⑤increasingly
                                                  부사 → 형용사 수식
단서 relevant.

해석

대개 악기를 잡고 연주하는 정확한 방법이 있다고 해도, 무엇보다 가장 중요한 가르침은 악기가 장난감이 아니라는 것과 악기를 관리해야 한다는 것이다. 아이들에게 직접 악기를 다루고 연주하는 방법을 알려 주기 전에 그렇게 하는 방법을 탐구할 시간을 허용하라. 소리를 만들어 내는 여러 가지 방법을 찾는 것은 음악적 탐구의 중요한 단계이다. 정확한 연주는 가장 적절한 음질을 찾고 오랜 시간 동안 잘 다루면서 연주할 수 있도록 가장 편안한 연주 자세를 찾으려는 열망에서 나온다. 악기와 음악이 더 복잡해짐에 따라, 적절한 연주법을 알게 되는 것은 더욱 의미가 있어지게 된다.

정답이 보이는 해설

③ Finding different ways to produce sounds가 문장의 주어이고 동명사구 주어는 단수 취급하므로 are를 단수 동사 is로 고쳐야 한다.

① 뒤에 이어지는 문장이 주어와 동사가 있는 완전한 절이므로 접속사 that은 어법상 적절하다.

② children과 time ~ them이 각각 간접목적어, 직접목적어인 명령문이므로 동사원형 Allow는 어법상 적절하다.

④ the desire를 수식하는 to부정사 to find는 어법상 적절하다.

⑤ 형용사 relevant를 수식하는 부사 increasingly는 어법상 적절하다.

필수 어휘

instruction 가르침, 지도 look after ~을 관리하다, ~을 돌보다
explore 탐구하다, 탐험하다 handle 다루다 produce 만들어 내다, 생산하다
stage 단계 desire 욕구, 욕망 appropriate 알맞은 quality 질, 품질
comfortable 편안한 complex 복잡한 relevant 유의미한, 관련된

12 정답 ②

Each species of animals can detect a different range of odours. No species can detect all the molecules that are present in the environment ① in which it 단서 lives — there are some things

(live in: ~에 살다 (선행사: the environment))

that we cannot smell but which some other animals can, and vice versa.

(역으로, 반대로)

There are also differences between individuals, relating to the ability to smell an odour, or how ② pleasantly(→ pleasant) it 단서 seems.

(형용사를 보어로 취하는 동사)

For example, some people like the taste of 단서 coriander — known as cilantro in the USA — while others find ③ it soapy

(~로 알려진) _(= coriander)_

and unpleasant. This effect has an underlying genetic component due to differences in the genes ④ controlling our sense of smell.

★ Ultimately, / the selection of _scents_ (detected by a given species),

_(주어1)_ _(과거분사구)_

/ and (how that odour is perceived), / will depend upon the animal's

(접속사) _(주어2 (간접의문문, 명사절))_ _(동사)_

ecology. The response profile of each species will 단서 enable it

(enable A to-v: A가 ~하게 하다)

⑤ to locate sources of smell that are relevant to it and to respond accordingly.

해석

각각의 동물 종들은 서로 다른 범주의 냄새를 감지할 수 있다. 어떤 종도 그것이 살고 있는 환경에 존재하는 모든 분자를 감지할 수는 없는데, 즉 우리는 맡을 수가 없지만 몇몇 다른 동물들은 맡을 수 있는 몇 가지 냄새가 있고, 그 반대의 경우도 있다. 어떤 냄새를 맡을 수 있는 능력이나 그것이 얼마나 좋은 느낌을 주는지와 관련된 개체 간의 차이 또한 존재한다. 예를 들어, 어떤 사람들은 미국에서는 고수(cilantro)라고 알려진 고수(coriander)의 맛을 좋아하는 반면, 다른 사람들은 그것이 비누 같고 불쾌하다고 생각한다. 이러한 결과에는 우리의 후각을 조절하는 유전자 차이로 인한 내재된 유전적 요소가 있다. 결국, 특정 종에 의해 감지된 냄새들의 집합, 그리고 그 냄새가 어떻게 인식되는가 하는 것은 그 동물의 생태에 달려 있을 것이다. 각각의 종의 반응 도표는 그 종이 자신과 관련된 냄새의 원천을 찾아서 그에 따라 반응할 수 있게 해 줄 것이다.

정답이 보이는 해설

② seems의 보어 자리이므로 형용사 pleasant가 와야 한다. the ability to smell an odour와 how pleasant it seems가 or에 의해 relating to에 연결된 병렬 구조이다.

① 뒤에 it lives로 주어와 동사가 있는 완전한 절이 이어지고 the environment which it lives in의 의미이므로 관계부사 where에 해당하는 「전치사+관계대명사」인 in which는 어법상 적절하다.

③ 「주어+find+목적어+목적격보어」의 구문에서 목적어에 해당하여 coriander를 가리키는 대명사 it은 어법상 적절하다. 이때 find는 '~라고 생각하다'라는 의미이다.

함정 find 다음의 대명사가 가리키는 것이 some people이라고 생각하고 답으로 고르지 않도록 유의한다.

④ controlling ~ smell이 바로 앞의 명사구 the genes를 꾸며 주는 형용사구이므로 현재분사 controlling은 어법상 적절하다.

함정 due to 다음에 절이 올 수 없으므로 control이 the genes의 동사 자리가 아닌 것에 유의한다. controlling은 which[that] are controlling에서 「주격 관계대명사+be동사」가 생략된 형태로 볼 수 있다.

⑤ 'A가 ~하는 것을 가능하게 하다'라는 의미의 「enable A to-v」 구문이므로 to locate는 어법상 적절하다.

필수 어휘

species 종 detect 감지하다 odour[odor] 냄새, 향기 molecule 분자
present 존재하는 soapy 비누 냄새가 나는 unpleasant 유쾌하지 않은
underlying 내재하는 component 구성 성분 perceive 감지하다
depend upon[on] ~에 의지[의존]하다 ecology 생태(학)

12강 2020~2023 어휘

establish 형성하다, 확립하다　balance 균형　validate 헤아리다, 존중하다
past 과거(의)　opportunity 기회　background 배경　respect 존중하다

01 정답 ②

주제문 단서1 While moving is difficult for everyone, it is
이사는 특히 아이들에게 힘든 일임
particularly stressful for children. They lose their sense of security
and may feel disoriented when their routine is disrupted and all
that is ① familiar is taken away. Young children, ages 3–6, are
take away: ~을 빼앗다, 없애다
particularly affected by a move. 단서2 Their understanding at
아이들의 이해력은 고지식함
this stage is quite literal, and it is ② easy(→ difficult) for them
이 단계에서
to imagine beforehand a new home and their new room. Young
children may have worries such as "Will I still be me in the
~와 같은
new place?" and "Will my toys and bed come with us?" ✪ It is
진주어: to부정사의 명사적 용법　가주어
important / [to establish a balance / (**between** validating children's
focus on: ~에 집중하다　　　　　　　　　~에 적응하다
past experiences / **and** focusing on **helping** them ③ adjust to the
help의 목적어 = children　목적격 보어
new place)]. Children need to have opportunities to share their
backgrounds in a way that ④ respects their past as an important part
of who they are. This contributes to building a sense of community,
contribute to: ~에 기여하다
which is essential for all children, especially those in ⑤ transition.
in transition: 변화 중인, 과도기[전환기]에 있는

해석

이사는 모두에게 힘들지만, 아이들에게 특히 스트레스가 많은 일이다. 그들은 안도감을 잃고 그들의 일상이 방해받고 ① 익숙한 모든 것을 빼앗길 때 혼란스럽다고 느낄 수도 있다. 3세에서 6세 사이의 어린아이들이 특히 이사에 영향을 받는다. 이 시기에 그들의 이해력은 꽤 고지식해서 새로운 집과 자신의 새로운 방을 미리 상상하는 것은 ② 쉽다(→ 어렵다). 어린아이들은 '새로운 곳에서도 내가 여전히 나일까?'와 '내 장난감과 침대가 우리와 함께 갈까?'와 같은 걱정들을 가질지도 모른다. 아이들의 과거 경험을 헤아리는 것과 그들이 새로운 곳에 ③ 적응하도록 돕는 데 집중하는 것 사이에 균형을 잡는 것이 중요하다. 아이들은 자신이 누구인지에 대한 중요한 부분으로서 자신의 과거를 ④ 존중하는 방식으로 자신의 배경을 공유할 기회를 가질 필요가 있다. 이것은 공동체 의식을 형성하는 데 기여하고, 모든 아이들, 특히 ⑤ 변화를 겪는 아이들에게 중요하다.

정답이 보이는 해설

이사가 아이들에게 힘든 일이라는 글로서, 특히 3세에서 6세 사이의 아이들은 이해력이 고지식하다고 했으므로 이 아이들에게 새로운 집과 새로운 방을 상상하는 일은 쉽지 않을 것이다. 따라서 ②의 easy는 difficult, hard와 같은 낱말로 바꾸어야 한다.

선택지 완벽 분석

① 이사는 특히 아이들에게 힘든 일인데, 일상이 방해받고 '익숙한' 것을 뺏길 때 혼란을 느낄 수 있다는 흐름은 문맥상 옳다.

③ 이사의 어려움을 다룬 글에서 아이들의 과거 경험을 헤아리는 것과 아이들이 새로운 곳에 '적응하도록' 돕는 데 집중하는 것 사이에서 균형을 잡는다는 흐름은 문맥상 옳다.

④ 바로 앞에 아이들의 과거 경험을 헤아리면서 새로운 곳에 적응하도록 도와야 한다는 내용이 있으므로, 아이들의 과거를 '존중하는' 방식으로 배경을 공유한다는 흐름은 문맥상 옳다.

⑤ 아이들이 이사 때문에 힘들 수 있다는 내용이 반복되므로 '변화, 전환, 이행'을 의미하는 transition과 함께 '변화를 겪는 아이들'이라는 흐름은 문맥상 옳다.

필수 어휘

particularly 특히　security 안도(감)　disoriented 갈피를 못 잡는, 혼란스러운
disrupt 방해하다, 지장을 주다　affect 영향을 미치다
literal 고지식한, 상상력이 부족한　beforehand 미리, 사전에

02 정답 ②

✪ 주제문 Advertisers / (often) displayed / considerable facility
주어　　　　　　　　　　　　　동사　　　　　　목적어
(in ① adapting their claims to the market status of *the goods* [they
전치사구　　　　　　　　　　　　　　　　　　　　　that 생략: 목적격 관계대명사절
promoted]). 단서1 Fleischmann's yeast, for instance, was used as
효모는 빵의 재료였음　　　　　　　be used as: ~로 사용되다
an ingredient for cooking homemade bread. 단서2 Yet more and
more people in the early 20th century were buying their bread from
20세기 초에 많은 사람들이 가게나 빵집에서 빵을 샀음
stores or bakeries, so consumer demand for yeast ② increased(→
declined). The producer of Fleischmann's yeast hired the J. Walter
~을 생각해 내다
Thompson advertising agency 단서3 to come up with a different
판매를 촉진하기 위해 광고 대행사를 고용함
marketing strategy to ③ boost sales. No longer the "Soul of Bread,"
the Thompson agency first turned yeast into an important source
turn A into B: A를 B로 바꾸다
of vitamins with significant health ④ benefits. Shortly thereafter,
직후에
the advertising agency transformed yeast into a natural laxative.
transform A into B: A를 B로 변형시키다
⑤ Repositioning yeast helped increase sales.

해석

광고주들은 그들이 홍보하는 상품의 시장 지위에 맞게 그들의 주장을 ① 조절하는 상당한 능력을 자주 보여 주었다. 예를 들어, Fleischmann의 효모는 집에서 만드는 빵을 요리하는 재료로 사용되었다. 하지만 20세기 초에 점점 더 많은 사람들이 가게나 빵집에서 빵을 사고 있었고, 그래서 효모에 대한 소비자 수요가 ② 증가했다(→감소했다). Fleischmann의 효모의 생산자는 판매를 ③ 촉진하기 위해서 다른 마케팅 전략을 고안하라고 J. Walter Thompson 광고 대행사를 고용했다. Thompson 광고 대행사는 먼저 효모를 더 이상 "Soul of Bread"가 아니라 상당한 건강상의 ④ 이점이 있는 비타민의 중요한 공급원으로 바꾸었다. 그 직후, 광고 대행사는 효모를 천연 완하제로 바꾸었다. 효모의 ⑤ 이미지 전환을 꾀하는 것은 매출을 증가시키는 것을 도왔다.

정답이 보이는 해설

가정용 빵의 재료였던 Fleischmann의 효모가 20세기 초에 점점 더 많은 사람들이 가게나 빵집에서 사서 가정에서 빵을 굽지 않게 되면서 효모에 대한 소비자 수요가 감소했을 것이다. 따라서 ② increased는 declined와 같은 낱말로 바꾸어야 한다.

선택지 완벽 분석

① 이어지는 예시에서 가정용 빵의 재료였던 효모의 수요가 감소하자, 비타민 공급원으로 이후 천연 완하제로 이미지를 바꾸었으므로, 광고주들은 홍보하는 상품의 시장 지위에 맞게 그들의 주장을 '바꾸는' 상당한 능력을 자주 보여 주었다는 흐름은 문맥상 옳다.

③ Fleischmann의 효모의 생산자가 다른 마케팅 전략을 고안하도록 Thompson 광고 대행사를 고용한 목적은 판매를 '촉진하기' 위한 것이므로 문맥상 옳다.

④ Thompson 광고 대행사는 효모를 건강상으로 상당한 '이점들'이 있는 비타민의 중요한 공급원으로 바꾸었다는 흐름은 문맥상 옳다.

⑤ 광고 대행사는 먼저 효모를 더 이상 "Soul of Bread"가 아니라 건강상의 상당한 이점이 있는 비타민의 중요한 공급원으로, 그리고 그 직후에는 천연 완하제로 바꾸었으므로, 효모의 '이미지 전환을 꾀한 것'이라는 흐름은 문맥상 옳다.

필수 어휘

display 보여 주다　considerable 상당한　facility 능력
adapt A to B A를 B에 맞게 바꾸다　ingredient 재료　consumer 소비자
demand 수요　decline 감소하다　hire 고용하다　agency 대행사

strategy 전략   boost 촉진하다   soul 정수, 핵심   significant 상당한
benefit 혜택   reposition (제품의) 이미지 전환을 꾀하다

필수 어휘

philosophical 철학적인   shift 변화   competitive 경쟁적인
geographically 지리적으로   spread out 퍼져 나가다   relation 관계
quality 양질의, 질 좋은   reasonable 합리적인   equally 마찬가지로
essential 매우 중요한   modernization 현대화   revolution 혁명   demand 수요
meet 충족시키다   diverse 다양한   complex 복잡한   focus 초점, 중점

03 정답 ④

202303 30번 정답률 41%

The major philosophical shift in the idea of selling came when industrial societies became more affluent, more competitive, and more geographically spread out during the 1940s and 1950s. ✪
force A to-v: A가 ~하게 강요하다
This **forced** business to develop ① closer relations with buyers
동사　　목적어　　　목적격보어　　　　　realize의 목적어절
and clients, / which in turn **made** business realize [that **it** was not
결과적으로　동사　목적어　목적격보어　　가주어
enough **to produce** a quality product at a reasonable price]. In fact,
진주어　　　　　　합리적인 가격에
it was equally ② essential to deliver products that customers actually
wanted. 단서1 Henry Ford produced his best-selling T-model Ford
Henry Ford는 Ford 차량을 검은 색으로만 생산했는데, 지금은 불가능한 일임
in one color only (black) in 1908, but in modern societies this
was no longer ③ possible. The modernization of society led to a
더 이상 ~이 아닌
marketing revolution that ④ **strengthened(→ destroyed)** the view
that production would create its own demand. 단서2 Customers, and
고객의 다양하고 복잡한
the desire to ⑤ meet their diverse and often complex needs, became
욕구를 충족하고자 하는 것이 기업의 초점이 됨
the focus of business.

해석

산업 사회가 1940년대와 1950년대 동안 더 부유하고, 더 경쟁적이고, 더 지리적으로 퍼져 나가게 되면서, 판매 개념에 주요한 철학적 변화가 일어났다. 이로 인해 기업은 구매자 및 고객과 ① 더 긴밀한 관계를 발전시켜야 했고, 이것은 결과적으로 기업이 합리적인 가격에 양질의 제품을 생산하는 것만으로는 충분하지 않다는 것을 깨닫게 했다. 사실, 고객이 실제로 원하는 제품을 내놓는 것은 마찬가지로 ② 매우 중요했다. 1908년에 Henry Ford는 자신의 가장 많이 팔렸던 T모델 Ford를 단 하나의 색상(검은색)으로만 생산했지만, 현대 사회에서는 이것이 더 이상 ③ 가능하지 않았다. 사회의 현대화는 생산이 그 자체의 수요를 창출할 것이라는 견해를 ④ 강화하는 (→ 파괴하는) 마케팅 혁명으로 이어졌다. 고객과 그들의 다양하고 흔히 복잡한 욕구를 ⑤ 충족하고자 하는 욕망이 기업의 초점이 되었다.

정답이 보이는 해설

산업 사회가 더 경쟁적이게 되면서 기업은 고객과 더 긴밀한 관계를 발전시켜야 했고, 고객들의 복잡하고 다양한 욕구를 충족시키는 것이 기업의 초점이 되었다는 내용의 글이다. 그러므로 사회의 현대화가 불러온 마케팅 혁명은 생산이 그 자체의 수요를 창출할 것이라는 견해가 파괴되었다는 내용으로 이어져야 한다. 따라서 ④ strengthened는 destroyed와 같은 낱말로 바꿔야 한다.

선택지 완벽 분석

① 산업 사회가 더 경쟁적이게 되면서 판매 개념에 주요 변화가 일어났고, 기업이 합리적인 가격에 양질의 제품을 생산하는 것으로는 충분하지 않다는 것을 깨닫게 되었다는 내용이 이어지고 있고, 기업은 구매자와의 '더 긴밀한' 관계를 발전시켜야 했다는 흐름이므로 문맥상 옳다.

② 기업은 합리적인 가격에 양질의 제품을 생산하는 것만으로 충분하지 않다는 것을 깨달았다는 앞 내용에 이어, 새로운 사실을 덧붙이는 In fact(사실)로 시작하여 고객이 실제 원하는 제품을 내놓는 것이 마찬가지로 '매우 중요했다'는 내용은 문맥상 옳다.

③ 고객이 실제로 원하는 제품을 내놓는 것이 매우 중요했다는 앞 문장에서 예시로 Henry Ford가 가장 많이 팔렸던 모델을 한 가지 색상으로만 생산하는 것이 현대 사회에서는 더 이상 '가능하지' 않았다는 흐름은 문맥상 옳다.

⑤ 기업의 초점이 고객과 그들의 다양하고 복잡한 욕구를 '충족하고자' 하는 욕망에 맞춰지게 되었다는 흐름은 문맥상 옳다.

04 정답 ④

202211 30번 정답률 53%

✪ Plant growth / is controlled / by a group of *hormones* [called
주어　　　　　동사　　　　　　　　　　　　　　　　　　과거분사구
auxins] [found at the tips (of stems and roots of plants)]. Auxins
과거분사구
produced at the tips of stems tend to accumulate on the side of
~하는 경향이 있다
the stem that is in the shade. Accordingly, the auxins ① stimulate
growth on the shaded side of the plant. Therefore, the shaded side
grows faster than the side facing the sunlight. This phenomenon
causes the stem to bend and appear to be growing ② towards
cause A to-v: A가 ~하게 하다
the light. 단서1 Auxins have the ③ opposite effect on the roots of
옥신은 식물의 뿌리에서는 반대의 효과를 가짐
plants. Auxins in the tips of roots tend to limit growth. If a root is
horizontal in the soil, 단서2 the auxins will accumulate on the lower
옥신은 아래쪽에 축적되어 그것의 발달을 방해함
side and interfere with its development. Therefore, the lower side
of the root will grow ④ **faster(→ slower)** than the upper side. This
will, in turn, cause the root to bend ⑤ downwards, with the tip of
결과적으로
the root growing in that direction.

해석

식물의 성장은 식물의 줄기와 뿌리의 끝에서 발견되는 옥신이라고 불리는 호르몬 그룹에 의해 조절된다. 줄기의 끝에서 생산된 옥신은 그늘진 곳에 있는 줄기의 옆면에 축적되는 경향이 있다. 따라서, 옥신은 식물의 그늘진 면에서 성장을 ① 자극한다. 그러므로 그늘진 면은 햇빛을 마주하는 면보다 더 빠르게 자란다. 이 현상은 줄기가 휘어지게 하고 빛을 ② 향하여 성장하고 있는 것처럼 보이게 한다. 옥신은 식물의 뿌리에서는 ③ 반대의 효과를 가진다. 뿌리 끝에 있는 옥신은 성장을 억제하는 경향이 있다. 만약 하나의 뿌리가 토양 속에서 수평이라면, 옥신은 아래쪽에 축적되어 그것의 발달을 방해할 것이다. 그러므로 뿌리의 아래쪽은 위쪽보다 ④ 더 빠르게(→ 더 느리게) 자라게 된다. 이것은 결과적으로 뿌리를 ⑤ 아래로 휘어지게 하고, 뿌리의 끝부분은 그 방향으로 자란다.

정답이 보이는 해설

뿌리 끝의 옥신은 성장을 억제하는 경향이 있고, 아래쪽에 축적되어 발달을 방해하므로 뿌리의 아래쪽은 위쪽보다 더 느리게 자라게 될 것이다. 따라서 ④ faster는 slower와 같은 낱말로 바꾸어야 한다.

선택지 완벽 분석

① 줄기 끝에서 생산된 옥신은 그늘진 곳에 있는 줄기의 옆면에 축적되는 경향이 있고, 따라서, 옥신은 식물의 그늘진 면에서의 성장을 '자극할' 것이기 때문에 문맥상 옳다.

② 그늘진 면은 햇빛을 마주하는 면보다 더 빠르게 자라서, 줄기를 휘어지게 하고 빛을 '향하여' 성장하고 있는 것처럼 보이게 할 것이므로 문맥상 옳다.

③ 뒤의 문장 '뿌리 끝에 있는 옥신은 성장을 억제하는 경향이 있다'라는 내용으로 보아, 옥신은 식물의 뿌리에서는 '반대의' 효과를 가진다는 것은 문맥상 옳다.

⑤ 뿌리의 아래쪽은 위쪽보다 더 느리게 자라게 되어, 결과적으로 뿌리를 '아래로' 휘어지게 한다는 것이므로 문맥상 옳다.

필수 어휘

tip 끝   stem 줄기   root 뿌리   accumulate 축적되다   accordingly 따라서

shade 그늘, 그늘지게 하다 face ~을 마주하다 phenomenon 현상
appear to ~하게 보이다 opposite 반대의, 상반하는 horizontal 수평의
interfere 방해하다 development 발달 lower 아래의 upper 위쪽의
downwards 아래로

필수 어휘
somehow 어떻게든 magically 마법처럼, 마법으로 organ 기관, 장기
specific 특정한 groundless 근거 없는 circulation 순환 aggressive 공격적인
eliminate 제거하다 temporary 일시적인 intelligence 지능, 지성
intelligently 영리하게, 총명하게 fix 고치다, 해결하다

05 정답 ⑤

202209 30번 정답률 61%

It is widely believed that certain herbs somehow magically improve the work of certain organs, and "cure" specific diseases as a result. Such statements are unscientific and groundless.
결과적으로
Sometimes herbs appear to work, since they tend to ① increase your blood circulation in an aggressive attempt by your body to eliminate them from your system. That can create a ② temporary feeling of a high, which makes it seem as if your health condition has improved. Also, herbs can have a placebo effect, just like any other method, thus helping you feel better. ✪ **Whatever** the case, / **it** is your body
whatever S +V: 어떤 ~이든   is 생략   강조 대상
[**that** has the intelligence to ③ regain health, and not the herbs].
it is ~ that 강조구문
How can herbs have the intelligence needed to direct your body into getting healthier? That is impossible. 단서1 Try to imagine
허브가 어떻게 우리 몸으로
how herbs might come into your body and intelligently ④ fix your
들어가서 우리의 문제를 영리하게 고칠 수 있는지 상상해 볼 것을 제안함
problems. 단서2 If you try to do that, you will see how impossible
그렇게 하려고 한다면 그것이 얼마나 불가능해 보이는지 알게 될 것임
it seems. Otherwise, it would mean that herbs are ⑤ **less(→ more)** intelligent than the human body, which is truly hard to believe.

해석
어떤 허브는 어떻게든 특정 기관의 기능을 마법처럼 개선시키고, 결과적으로 특정한 질병을 '고친다'고 널리 알려져 있다. 그러한 진술은 비과학적이고 근거가 없다. 때때로 허브는 효과가 있는 것처럼 보이는데, 그 이유는 당신의 신체로부터 그것들을 제거하려는 당신 몸의 적극적인 시도 속에서 그것들이 혈액 순환을 ① 증가시키는 경향이 있기 때문이다. 그것은 ② 일시적인 좋은 기분을 만들어 줄 수 있는데, 이것은 마치 당신의 건강 상태가 호전된 것처럼 보이게 만든다. 또한 허브는 어느 다른 방법과 마찬가지로 위약 효과를 가질 수 있으며, 따라서 당신이 더 나아졌다고 느끼도록 도와준다. 어떤 경우든, 건강을 ③ 되찾게 하는 지능을 가진 것은 허브가 아니라 바로 당신의 몸이다. 허브가 어떻게 당신의 몸을 더 건강해지는 방향으로 안내하기 위해 필요한 지능을 가질 수 있겠는가? 그것은 불가능하다. 어떻게 허브가 당신의 몸으로 들어가서 영리하게 당신의 문제를 ④ 고칠 수 있는지를 상상해 보라. 만약 당신이 그렇게 하려고 한다면, 당신은 그것이 얼마나 불가능해 보이는지 알게 될 것이다. 그렇지 않으면, 그것은 허브가 인간의 몸보다 ⑤ 덜(→ 더) 지적이라는 것을 의미할 것인데, 이는 정말로 믿기 어렵다.

정답이 보이는 해설
허브가 우리 몸으로 들어가서 영리하게 우리의 건강 문제를 고치는 것은 불가능하다고 했으므로, 만약 그것이 가능하다면 허브가 인간의 몸보다 더 지적이라는 것을 의미하게 될 것이다. 따라서 ⑤ less는 more와 같은 낱말로 바꿔야 한다.

선택지 완벽 분석
① 허브가 질병을 고치는 데 효과가 있는 것처럼 보이는 이유는 그것이 혈액 순환을 '증가시키기' 때문일 것이므로 문맥상 옳다.
② 마치 건강 상태가 향상된 것처럼 보이게 해 준다고 했으므로 '일시적으로' 좋은 기분을 만들어 준다는 내용은 문맥상 옳다.
③ 앞 문장에서 우리가 더 건강이 나아졌다고 느끼게 해 준다고 했으므로, 건강을 '되찾는다'는 것은 문맥상 옳다.
④ 몸을 더 건강해지는 방향으로 안내한다는 것은 우리 몸 안의 문제를 '고치는' 것이므로 문맥상 옳다.

06 정답 ②

202206 30번 정답률 64%

Do you sometimes feel like you don't love your life? Like, deep inside, something is missing? That's because we are living someone else's life. We allow other people to ① influence our choices. We are trying to meet their expectations. 단서1 Social pressure is deceiving
사회적 압력은 우리를 현혹시켜서 우리는
— we are all impacted without noticing it. ✪ **Before** we realize
알지도 못한 채 영향을 받음   접속사(~하기 전에)
we are losing ownership of our lives, / we end up ② **ignoring(→**
                                        end up -ing: 결국 ~하게 되다
envying) [how other people live]. 단서2 Then, we can only see the
envying의 목적어절   우리는 타인의 더 좋아 보이는 삶만 보게
greener grass — ours is never good enough. To regain that passion
되고 우리의 삶은 결코 좋지 않은 것이 됨
for the life you want, you must ③ recover control of your choices.
No one but yourself can choose how you live. But, how? The first step to getting rid of expectations is to treat yourself ④ kindly. You
         ~을 없애다
can't truly love other people if you don't love yourself first. When we accept who we are, there's no room for other's ⑤ expectations.

해석
여러분은 때로 자신의 삶을 사랑하지 않는다고 느끼는가? 마치, 마음속 깊은 곳에서 무언가가 빠진 것처럼? 그것은 우리가 다른 누군가의 삶을 살고 있기 때문이다. 우리는 다른 사람들이 우리의 선택에 ① 영향을 미치는 것을 허용한다. 우리는 그들의 기대를 만족시키기 위해 노력하고 있다. 사회적 압력은 (우리를) 현혹시킨다. 우리는 모두 그것을 알아차리지 못한 채 영향을 받는다. 우리의 삶에 대한 소유권을 잃고 있다는 것을 깨닫기도 전에, 우리는 결국 다른 사람들이 어떻게 사는지를 ② **무시하게 된다(→ 부러워하게 된다)**. 그러면 우리는 더 푸른 잔디(타인의 삶이 더 좋아 보이는 것)만 볼 수 있게 된다. 우리의 잔디(삶)는 결코 충분히 좋지 않다. 여러분이 원하는 삶에 대한 열정을 되찾기 위해서는 여러분의 선택에 대한 통제력을 ③ 회복해야 한다. 여러분 자신을 제외한 그 누구도 여러분이 어떻게 사는지를 선택할 수 없다. 하지만 어떻게 해야 할까? 기대를 없애는 첫 단계는 자신을 ④ 친절하게 대하는 것이다. 자신을 먼저 사랑하지 않으면 다른 사람들을 진정으로 사랑할 수 없다. 우리가 있는 그대로의 우리 모습을 받아들일 때, 다른 사람들의 ⑤ 기대를 위한 여지는 남아 있지 않다.

정답이 보이는 해설
우리가 삶에 대한 소유권을 잃고 다른 사람들의 더 좋은 삶만 보게 된다고 했으므로 다른 사람들이 어떻게 사는지를 무시하게 되는 것이 아니라 부러워하게 될 것이다. 따라서 ② ignoring은 envying과 같은 낱말로 바꾸어야 한다.

선택지 완벽 분석
① 우리가 다른 사람들의 기대를 만족시키기 위해 노력하는 것은 다른 사람들이 우리의 선택에 '영향을 미치는' 것을 허용하는 것이므로 문맥상 옳다.
③ 우리가 원하는 삶에 대한 열정을 되찾으려면 우리가 스스로 선택할 수 있는 통제력을 '회복해야' 할 것이므로 문맥상 옳다.
④ 자신을 사랑하는 것, 즉 자신을 '친절하게' 대하는 것이 기대를 없애는 첫 단계일 것이므로 문맥상 옳다.
⑤ 우리 모습을 있는 그대로 받아들일 때 다른 사람들의 '기대'를 없애게 될 것이므로 문맥상 옳다.

필수 어휘
influence 영향을 미치다 expectation 기대 social pressure 사회적 압력
deceiving 현혹시키는, 속이는 impact 영향을 주다 notice 알아차리다

ownership 소유권　end up 결국 ~하게 되다　regain 되찾다　passion 열정
recover 회복하다　room 여지

07 정답 ⑤

202203 30번 정답률 45%

Rejection is an everyday part of our lives, yet most people can't
handle it well. ✪ For many, / it's **so** painful **that** they'**d rather** not
（would rather A than B: B하느니 차라리 A하는 게 낫겠다）
（so ~ that ...: 너무 ~해서 ...하다）
ask for something at all / **than** ask and ① risk rejection. Yet, as the
old saying goes, if you don't ask, the answer is always no. Avoiding
rejection ② negatively affects many aspects of your life. All of
that happens only because you're not ③ tough enough to handle
it. For this reason, consider rejection therapy. 단서 Come up with a
（~을 생각해 내다）
（거절을 유발하는 요청이나）
④ request or an activity that usually results in a rejection. Working
（활동을 생각해 낼 것을 제안함）
in sales is one such example. Asking for discounts at the stores
will also work. By deliberately getting yourself ⑤ **welcomed(→**
rejected) you'll grow a thicker skin that will allow you to take on
（~을 떠맡다）
much more in life, thus making you more successful at dealing with
unfavorable circumstances.

해석

거절은 우리 삶의 일상적인 부분이지만, 대부분의 사람들은 그것을 잘 감당하지 못
한다. 많은 사람들에게 거절은 너무 고통스러워서 그들은 요청하고 거절의 ① 위험
을 무릅쓰기보다는 차라리 무언가를 요청하지 않는 것이 나을 것이다. 하지만 옛말
처럼, 요청하지 않으면 대답은 항상 '아니요'이다. 거절을 피하는 것은 여러분의 삶
의 많은 측면에 ② 부정적으로 영향을 미친다. 이 모든 것은 여러분이 단지 거절을
감당할 만큼 ③ 강하지 않기 때문에 일어난다. 이러한 이유로 거절 요법을 고려해 보
라. 일반적으로 거절을 유발하는 ④ 요청이나 활동을 생각해 내라. 판매 분야에서 일
하는 것이 그러한 사례 중 하나이다. 매장에서 할인을 요청하는 것 또한 효과가 있을
것이다. 의도적으로 스스로를 ⑤ 환영받을(→ 거절당할) 상황에 놓이게 함으로써 여
러분은 더 둔감해지고, 인생에서 훨씬 더 많은 것을 떠맡을 수 있게 되며, 따라서 그
것은 호의적이지 않은 상황을 더 성공적으로 대처하게 해 줄 것이다.

정답이 보이는 해설

거절을 유발하는 요청이나 활동을 생각해 내서 이를 실천하라는 내용이 앞에 언급되
어 있으므로, ⑤ welcomed는 rejected와 같은 낱말로 바꾸어야 한다.

선택지 완벽 분석

① 거절은 고통스럽기 때문에 거절의 '위험을 무릅쓰지' 않고 아예 무언가를 요청하
　지 않는다는 것은 문맥상 옳다.
② 요청하지 않으면 대답이 항상 '아니요'일 것이므로 거절을 피하는 것이 삶에 '부
　정적으로' 영향을 미친다는 것은 문맥상 옳다.
③ 거절을 피하는 이유는 거절을 감당할 만큼 '강하지' 않기 때문일 것이므로 문맥상 옳다.
④ 바로 뒤에서 판매 분야에서 일하거나 매장에서 할인을 요청하는 활동이 언급되
　어 있으므로 거절을 당하게 되는 '요청'을 생각해 내라는 것은 문맥상 옳다.

필수 어휘

rejection 거절　handle 감당하다, 다루다　painful 고통스러운
risk 위험을 무릅쓰다　affect 영향을 미치다　aspect 측면　tough 강한
therapy 요법, 치료　discount 할인　unfavorable 호의적이지 않은
circumstance 상황

08 정답 ⑤

202111 30번 정답률 25%

For species approaching extinction, zoos can act as a last chance
（~의 역할을 하다）
for survival. ① Recovery programs are established to coordinate
the efforts of field conservationists and wildlife authorities.
✪ **As** populations of those species ② diminish / it is not unusual
（접속사(~함에 따라)）　　　　　　　　　　（가주어）
for zoos [to start captive breeding programs]. Captive breeding
（의미상 주어）　　（진주어）
acts to protect against extinction. In some cases 단서1 captive-bred
（포획 사육된 개체가）
individuals may be released back into the wild, supplementing wild
（다시 야생으로 방생되어 야생 개체 수를 보충할 수 있음）
populations. This is most successful in situations where individuals
are at greatest threat during a ③ particular life stage. For example,
turtle eggs may be removed from high-risk locations until after
they hatch. This may ④ increase the number of turtles that survive
to adulthood. 단서2 Crocodile programs have also been successful
（악어 프로그램도 알과 부화한 유생을 보호하는 데 성공적이었음）
in protecting eggs and hatchlings, ⑤ **capturing(→ releasing)**
hatchlings once they are better equipped to protect themselves.
（~할 준비를 갖추다）

해석

멸종에 이르고 있는 종에게 동물원은 생존을 위한 마지막 기회로서 역할을 할 수 있
다. 현장 환경 보호 활동가와 야생 동물 당국의 노력을 통합하기 위해 ① 회복 프로그
램이 수립된다. 그러한 종의 개체 수가 ② 감소함에 따라 동물원이 포획 사육 프로그
램을 시작하는 것은 드물지 않다. 포획 사육은 멸종을 막기 위해 역할을 한다. 어떤 경
우에는 포획 사육된 개체가 다시 야생으로 방생되어 야생 개체 수를 보충할 수도 있
다. 이것은 개체가 ③ 특정한 생애 주기 동안에 가장 큰 위협에 놓여 있는 상황에서 가
장 성공적이다. 예를 들어 거북이 알은 그것이 부화한 이후까지 고위험 위치로부터 제
거될 수도 있다. 이는 성체까지 생존하는 거북이 수를 ④ 증가시킬 수 있다. 악어 프로
그램 또한 알과 부화한 유생을 보호하는 데 있어서 성공적이었으며, 일단 그것이 스스
로를 보호하도록 더 잘 준비가 갖추어지면 부화한 유생을 ⑤ 포획한다(→ 방생한다).

정답이 보이는 해설

포획 사육된 개체가 다시 야생으로 방생되어 야생 개체 수를 보충할 수 있으며 이
것이 특정 생애 주기 동안 위협에 처한 상황에서 가장 성공적이라고 설명하면서 악
어의 경우에도 알과 부화한 유생을 보호하는 데 있어서 성공적이었다고 했으므로,
스스로를 더 잘 보호하도록 준비가 되면 부화한 유생을 방생할 것이다. 따라서 ⑤
capturing은 releasing과 같은 낱말로 바꾸어야 한다.

선택지 완벽 분석

① 멸종에 이르는 동물의 생존을 위한 것이므로 '회복' 프로그램은 문맥상 옳다.
② 포획 사육은 멸종을 막는 역할을 하므로 종의 개체 수가 '감소함'에 따라 포획 사
　육 프로그램을 시작한다는 것은 문맥상 옳다.
③ 바로 뒤에서 거북이의 '특정한' 생애 주기 동안 성공적이었으므로 문맥상 옳다.
④ 포획 사육된 개체가 다시 야생으로 방생되어 야생 개체 수를 보충할 수 있다고
　했으므로 성체까지 생존하는 거북이 수를 '증가시키는' 것은 문맥상 옳다.

필수 어휘

establish 수립하다　coordinate 통합하다　conservationist 환경 보호 활동가
authorities 당국　diminish 감소하다　extinction 멸종　release 풀어 주다
supplement 보충하다　population 개체 수　adulthood 성년
capture 포획하다　hatchling 부화한 유생

09 정답 ④

202109 30번 정답률 54%

Hunting can explain how humans developed *reciprocal altruism*
and *social exchange*. Humans seem to be unique among primates
（~에서 유일무이한）

in showing extensive reciprocal relationships that can last years, decades, or a lifetime. ✪ *Meat* (from a large game animal) comes in *quantities* [that ① exceed what a single hunter and his immediate family could possibly consume]. Furthermore, hunting success is highly ② variable; a hunter who is successful one week might fail the next. These conditions ③ encourage food sharing from hunting. The costs to a hunter of giving away meat he cannot eat immediately are ④ **high(→ low)** because he cannot consume all the meat himself and leftovers will soon spoil. 단서 The benefits can be large, however, when those who are given his food return the generous favor later on when he has failed to get food for himself. In essence, hunters can ⑤ store extra meat in the bodies of their friends and neighbors.

해석

사냥은 인간이 어떻게 '상호 이타주의'와 '사회적 교류'를 발전시켰는지를 설명할 수 있다. 인간은 몇 년, 수십 년, 혹은 평생 지속될 수 있는 광범위한 상호 관계를 보여 준다는 점에서 영장류 중에서 유일무이한 것 같다. 큰 사냥감의 고기는 사냥꾼 한 명과 그의 직계 가족이 소비할 수 있을 만큼 ① 초과하는 양에 이른다. 게다가, 사냥의 성공은 매우 ② 가변적이다. 한 주에는 성공한 사냥꾼이 다음 주에는 실패할 수도 있다. 이러한 조건들은 사냥으로 인한 음식 공유를 ③ 장려한다. 사냥꾼은 혼자서 고기를 다 먹을 수 없고 남은 고기는 곧 상하기 때문에 그가 당장 먹을 수 없는 고기를 나눠주는 데는 비용이 ④ 많이(→ 적게) 든다. 그러나 그 사람이 나중에 스스로 음식을 얻지 못했을 때, 그 사람의 음식을 받은 다른 사람들이 관대한 호의에 보답하면 그 혜택은 클 수 있다. 본질적으로 사냥꾼들은 그들의 친구와 이웃의 몸에 여분의 고기를 ⑤ 저장할 수 있다.

정답이 보이는 해설

사냥의 성공은 매우 가변적이며, 사냥꾼은 자신이 사냥한 고기를 혼자서 다 먹을 수 없고 남은 고기는 곧 상하므로 당장 먹을 수 없는 고기를 나눠주는 데는 적은 비용이 든다고 할 수 있다. 따라서 ④ high는 low와 같은 낱말로 바꾸어야 한다.

필수 어휘

primates 영장류 extensive 광범위한 decade 10년 game 사냥감
exceed 초과하다 immediate family 직계 가족 consume 소비하다, 먹다
variable 가변적인 leftover 남은 음식 spoil 상하다 return 보답하다, 갚다
generous 관대한 extra 여분의, 추가의

---

like the Mississippi floods of 1927 and 1993 and, more recently, the unnatural disaster of Hurricane Katrina. ✪ *A $50 billion plan* (to "**let** the river loose**" in Louisiana) / recognizes [that the ⑤ (controlled) Mississippi is washing away twenty-four square miles (of that state) annually].

해석

지난 20년 혹은 30년 동안의 상세한 연구는 자연계의 복잡한 형태가 그것의 기능에 필수적이라는 것을 보여 주고 있다. 강을 ① 직선화하고 규칙적인 횡단면으로 만들고자 하는 시도는 아마도 이러한 형태-기능 관계의 가장 피해가 막심한 사례일 것이다. 자연 발생적인 강은 매우 ② 불규칙한 형태를 가지고 있다. 그것은 많이 굽이치고, 범람원을 가로질러 넘쳐 흐르고, 습지로 스며들어, 끊임없이 변화하여 엄청나게 복잡한 강가를 만든다. 이것은 강이 수위와 속도 변화를 ③ 막을(→ 조절할) 수 있도록 한다. 강을 질서정연한 기하학적 형태에 맞춰 넣는 것은 기능적 수용 능력을 ④ 파괴하고 1927년과 1993년의 Mississippi강의 홍수, 그리고 더 최근에는, 허리케인 Katrina와 같은 비정상적인 재난으로 이어지게 된다. Louisiana에서 '강을 자유롭게 흐르도록 두기' 위한 500억 달러 계획은 ⑤ 통제된 Mississippi강이 매년 그 주의 24제곱마일을 유실시키고 있다는 것을 인정한 것이다.

정답이 보이는 해설

자연계의 복잡한 형태는 본질적으로 그것의 기능에 필수적이므로 자연 발생적인 강은 불규칙한 형태가 기능에 필수적인데, 그것을 인위적으로 직선화하거나 기하학적 형태로 만들면 강의 기능적 수용 능력이 파괴된다고 했다. 강의 구불구불한 형태가 강의 수위와 속도 변화를 조절하는 것을 가능하게 하는 것이므로 ③ prevent는 accommodate와 같은 낱말로 바꾸어야 한다.

선택지 완벽 분석

① 자연계는 복잡한 형태 그대로 두는 것이 기능에 필수적인데 강을 '직선화하려고' 시도했기 때문에 큰 피해를 가져온 것이므로 문맥상 옳다.
② 자연 발생적인 강은 복잡한 형태, 즉 '불규칙한' 형태를 가지고 있으므로 문맥상 옳다.
④ 강을 질서정연한 기하학에 맞추는 것이 기능적인 측면에서 볼 때 '파괴하는' 좋지 않은 결과를 가져왔으므로 문맥상 옳다.
⑤ Mississippi강을 '통제한' 결과가 땅의 유실을 야기하는 부정적인 결과를 유발한 것이므로 문맥상 옳다.

필수 어휘

decade 10년 straighten 직선으로 하다, 곧게 하다 cross-section 횡단면
disastrous 재앙의, 비참한 spill 넘치다 floodplain 범람원 leak 새다
wetland 습지 ever-changing 늘 변화하는 shoreline 강가
square mile 제곱마일

---

10 정답 ③

202106 30번 정답률 37%

수제분 Detailed study over the past two or three decades is showing that the complex forms of natural systems are essential to their functioning. The attempt to ① straighten rivers and give them regular cross-sections is perhaps the most disastrous example of this form-and-function relationship. The natural river has a very ② irregular form: it curves a lot, spills across floodplains, and leaks into wetlands, giving it an ever-changing and incredibly complex shoreline. This allows the river to ③ **prevent(→ accommodate)** variations in water level and speed. 단서 Pushing the river into tidy geometry ④ destroys functional capacity and results in disasters

---

11 정답 ③

202103 30번 정답률 61%

수제분 When the price of something fundamental drops greatly, the whole world can change. Consider light. Chances are you are reading this sentence under some kind of artificial light. Moreover, you probably never thought about whether using artificial light for reading was worth it. Light is so ① cheap that you use it without thinking. But in the early 1800s, it would have cost you four hundred times what you are paying now for the same amount of light. At that price, you would ② notice the cost and would think twice before using artificial light to read a book. The ③ **increase(→ drop)** in the price of light lit up the world. ✪ **Not only** did it turn

night into day, / but it **allowed** us to live and work in *big buildings* /
not only A but (also) B: A뿐만 아니라 B도   목적격보어1   목적격보어2
[that ④ natural light could not enter]. 단서 Nearly nothing we have
관계대명사   인공조명 비용의 하락이 현재의 삶을
today would be ⑤ possible if the cost of artificial light had not
가능하게 함
dropped to almost nothing.

해석

기본적인 어떤 것의 가격이 크게 하락할 때, 세상 전체가 바뀔 수 있다. 조명을 생각해 보자. 아마 여러분은 어떤 유형의 인공조명 아래에서 이 문장을 읽고 있을 것이다. 게다가, 여러분은 독서를 위해 인공조명을 이용하는 것이 그럴 만한 가치가 있는지에 대해 아마 생각해 본 적이 없을 것이다. 조명은 너무 ① 값이 싸서 여러분은 생각 없이 그것을 이용한다. 하지만 1800년대 초반에는, 같은 양의 조명에 대해 오늘날 지불하고 있는 것의 400배만큼의 비용이 들었을 것이다. 그 가격이면, 여러분은 비용을 ② 의식할 것이고 책을 읽으려고 인공조명을 이용하기 전에 다시 한번 생각할 것이다. 조명 가격의 ③ 인상(→ 하락)은 세상을 밝혔다. 그것은 밤을 낮으로 바꾸었을 뿐 아니라, ④ 자연광이 들어올 수 없는 큰 건물에서 우리가 살고 일할 수 있게 해 주었다. 만약 인공조명의 비용이 거의 공짜 수준으로 하락하지 않았더라면 우리가 오늘날 누리는 것 중에 ⑤ 가능한 것은 거의 없을 것이다.

정답이 보이는 해설

첫 문장이 주제문으로 기본적인 어떤 것의 가격이 크게 하락할 때, 세상 전체가 바뀔 수 있다는 것을 인공조명을 예로 들어 설명한 글이다. 과거의 인공조명은 현재의 400배만큼의 비용이 들었을 것이라고 했고 인공조명의 가격이 싼 덕분에, 밤을 낮으로 바꾸고 자연광이 들어올 수 없는 큰 건물에서 살고 일할 수 있다고 했으므로 ③ increase는 drop과 같은 낱말로 바꾸어야 한다.

🔍 선택지 완벽 분석

① 조명 값이 너무 '싸서' 인공조명을 이용하는 것이 가치가 있는지 생각해 본 적이 없을 것이라고 했으므로 문맥상 옳다.

② 조명 값이 거의 400배만큼의 비용이 든다면 비용을 '의식하게' 될 것이므로 문맥상 옳다.

④ 인공조명의 비용이 싼 덕분에 '자연'광이 들어올 수 없는 큰 건물에서 살고 일할 수 있게 된 것이므로 문맥상 옳다.

⑤ 인공조명의 비용이 거의 공짜 수준으로 하락해서 오늘날 우리가 많은 것을 누리는 것이 '가능한' 것이므로 문맥상 옳다.

필수 어휘

fundamental 기본적인   drop 하락하다   consider 생각하다, 고려하다
artificial light 인공조명   cost ~의 비용이 들다; 비용   amount 양
light up (빛 등으로) ~을 환하게 만들다   turn A into B A를 B로 바꾸다

12 정답 ③

202011 30번 정답률 54%

(A) 단서 Recent research suggests that evolving humans'
인간과 개의 관계가 두 종의 뇌 구조를 변화시킴
relationship with dogs changed the structure of both species' brains.

One of the various (A) physical / psychological changes caused

by domestication is a reduction in the size of the brain: 16 percent

for horses, 34 percent for pigs, and 10 to 30 percent for dogs.

(B) 단서 This is because once humans started to take care of these
인간에게 사육되는 동물은 생존하기 위한 뇌 기능이 불필요해짐   ↑~을 돌보다
animals, they no longer needed various brain functions in order to
                                                        ↑주격 관계대명사
survive. ❂ Animals [who were fed and protected by humans] / did
           주어   수동태1   수동태2   동사1
not need *many of the skills* (required by their wild ancestors) / and

(B) developed / lost the parts of *the brain* (related to those
                동사2
capacities). (C) 단서 A similar process occurred for humans, who
                       늑대에게 길들여진 인간에게도 유사한 과정이 나타남
seem to have been domesticated by wolves. About 10,000 years

ago, when the role of dogs was firmly established in most human

societies, the human brain also (C) expanded / **shrank** by about 10

percent.

해석

최근의 연구는 진화하는 인간과 개와의 관계가 두 종 모두의 뇌 구조를 변화시켰다는 것을 시사한다. 사육으로 야기된 다양한 (A) 신체적 변화 중 하나는 뇌 크기의 감소인데, 말은 16퍼센트, 돼지는 34퍼센트, 그리고 개는 10에서 30퍼센트 감소했다. 이는 일단 인간이 이 동물들을 돌보기 시작하면서 그것들이 생존하기 위해 다양한 뇌 기능을 더는 필요로 하지 않았기 때문이다. 인간이 먹이를 주고 보호해 주는 동물들은 그것들의 야생 조상에게 요구되었던 기술 중 많은 것들을 필요로 하지 않아서 그러한 능력들과 관련된 뇌의 부분들을 (B) 잃어버렸다. 유사한 과정이 늑대에 의해 길들여진 것으로 보이는 인간에게 나타났다. 약 1만 년 전, 개의 역할이 대부분 인간 사회에서 확고하게 정해졌을 때, 인간의 뇌도 약 10퍼센트 (C) 줄어들었다.

정답이 보이는 해설

(A) 뇌 크기의 감소는 '신체적' 변화라고 할 수 있으므로 physical이 적절하다. psychological은 '정신적인, 심리적인'이라는 뜻이다.

(B) 인간에 의해 돌봄을 받게 된 동물들은 그것들의 야생 조상들이 생존하기 위해 요구되었던 기능들을 필요로 하지 않게 되었다고 했으므로 그와 관련된 뇌의 부분들을 '잃어버리게' 되었을 것이다. 따라서 lost가 적절하다. develop은 '발달시키다'라는 뜻이다.

(C) 인간에 의해 사육된 동물들의 뇌 크기가 감소한 것과 유사한 과정이 인간에게도 나타나 인간의 뇌도 '줄어들었을' 것이므로 shrank가 적절하다. expand는 '확대되다'라는 뜻이다.

필수 어휘

evolve 진화하다   relationship 관계   species 종   domestication 사육, 길들이기
reduction 감소   no longer 더 이상 ~ 않다   function 기능   ancestor 조상
firmly 확고하게   establish 확립하다, 규정하다

13강 2020~2023 빈칸 추론 1 (31~32번)

01 정답 ①

Many people are terrified to fly in airplanes. Often, this fear stems from a lack of control. The pilot is in control, not the
stem from: ~에서 비롯되다
passengers, and this lack of control instills fear. ✪ **단서1** Many
많은
potential passengers are **so** afraid [they choose to drive great
　　　　　　　　　　　　　↱(that 생략) 　　　 *「so ~ that ....」 너무 ~해서 …하다*
승객들이 두려워 비행 대신 운전을 선택함
distances (**to get** to a destination) (instead of flying)]. **단서2** But
부사적 용법(목적) 　　　　　 *~하는 대신에*
their decision to drive is based solely on emotion, not logic.
그들의 결정은 논리가 아닌 오로지 감정에 근거함
단서3 Logic says that statistically, the odds of dying in a car crash
통계적으로 비행기 사고로 사망할 확률(1,100만분의 1)이 차 사고로 사망할 확률(5,000분의 1)
are around 1 in 5,000, while the odds of dying in a plane crash are
보다 훨씬 더 적음
closer to 1 in 11 million. If you're going to take a risk, especially one that could possibly involve your well-being, wouldn't you want the odds in your favor? However, most people choose the option
in one's favor: ~에게 유리하도록
that will cause them the least amount of **anxiety**. **주제문** Pay attention
　　　　　　　　　　　　　　　　　　　　　　　　~에 주의를 기울이다
to the thoughts you have about taking the risk and make sure you're basing your decision on facts, not just feelings.

해석

많은 사람들은 비행기를 타는 것을 두려워한다. 종종, 이 두려움은 통제력의 부족에서 비롯된다. 조종사는 통제를 하지만 승객은 그렇지 않으며, 이러한 통제력의 부족은 두려움을 스며들게 한다. 많은 잠재적인 승객들은 너무 두려워서 그들은 비행기를 타는 대신 목적지에 도착하기 위해 먼 거리를 운전하는 것을 선택한다. 그러나 운전을 하기로 한 그들의 결정은 논리가 아닌 오로지 감정에 근거한다. 논리에 따르면 통계적으로 자동차 사고로 사망할 확률은 약 5,000분의 1이고, 반면 비행기 사고로 사망할 확률은 1,100만분의 1에 가깝다고 한다. 만약 여러분이 위험을 감수한다면, 특히 여러분의 안녕을 혹시 포함할 수 있는 위험을 감수한다면, 여러분에게 유리한 확률을 원하지 않겠는가? 그러나 대부분의 사람들은 그들에게 최소한의 **불안감**을 야기할 수 있는 선택을 한다. 위험을 감수하는 것에 대해 여러분이 가지고 있는 생각에 주의를 기울이고 여러분의 결정이 단지 감정이 아닌 사실에 근거하고 있는지 확인하라.

정답이 보이는 해설

대부분의 사람들의 결정은 사실을 기반으로 한 논리가 아닌 감정에 근거한다는 내용이다. 예시로 자신이 통제할 수 없는 비행기를 타는 것이 두려움을 유발하여 먼 거리를 운전하는 것을 선택하지만, 통계적으로 자동차 사고로 사망할 확률이 더 높다고 하였다. 즉, 그들은 논리가 아닌 최소한의 불안감을 유발하는 선택을 한다는 것이므로, 빈칸에 들어갈 말로 가장 적절한 것은 ① '불안감'이다.

선택지 완벽 분석

① anxiety 불안감
② boredom 지루함
③ confidence 자신감
④ satisfaction 만족감
함정 많은 사람들은 감정에 근거한 선택을 하고, 그중에서도 불안감과 같은 부정적인 감정을 최소한으로 야기할 수 있는 선택을 한다는 내용이므로, 만족감과는 거리가 멀다.
⑤ responsibility 책임감

필수 어휘

fear 두려움, 공포　a lack of ~의 부족함　potential 잠재적인
solely 오직, 오로지　statistically 통계적으로　odds 확률　crash 사고, 충돌
involve 포함하다

02 정답 ③

The famous primatologist Frans de Waal, of Emory University, says **단서1** humans downplay similarities between us and other
인간은 우리의 위치를 유지하기 위해 우리와 다른 동물들 사이의 유사성을 경시함
animals as a way of maintaining our spot at the top of our imaginary ladder. Scientists, de Waal points out, can be some of the worst offenders — employing technical language to **distance the other animals from us**. They call "kissing" in chimps "mouth-to-mouth
　　　　　　　　　　　　　　　　　　call A B: A를 B라고 부르다　↳A　　　↳B
contact"; they call "friends" between primates "favorite affiliation
　　　　　　　　　　　　　　　A　　　　　　　　　　　　　　*B*
partners"; they interpret evidence showing that crows and chimps can make tools as being somehow qualitatively different from
　　　　　　　　　　　　　　　　　　　　　　　　　　　　　　　~와는 다른
the kind of toolmaking said to define humanity. If an animal can beat us at a cognitive task — like how certain bird species can remember the precise locations of thousands of seeds — they write
　　　　　　　　　　　　　　　　　　　　　　　　　　　　　　write ~ off:
it off as instinct, not intelligence. ✪ This and so many more tricks
~을 무가치한 것으로 보다, 치부하다　　　　　　　　*주어*
of language are [what de Waal has termed "linguistic castration."]
　　　　　　동사　　　*보어(선행사를 포함한 관계절)*
주제문 **단서2** The way we use our tongues to disempower animals,
이러한 '언어적 거세'는 동물로부터 힘을 뺏고, 우리의 위치를 유지하고자 단어를 만드는
the way we invent words to maintain our spot at the top.
방법임

해석

Emory 대학의 유명한 영장류학자 Frans de Waal은 인간은 상상 속 사다리의 꼭대기에서 우리의 위치를 유지하는 방법으로 우리와 다른 동물들 사이의 유사성을 경시한다고 말한다. de Waal은 과학자들이 **우리와 다른 동물들 사이에 거리를 두기** 위해 기술적인 언어를 사용하는 최악의 죄를 범하는 자들 중 일부일 수 있다고 지적한다. 그들은 침팬지의 '키스'를 '입과 입의 접촉'이라고 부르고, 영장류 사이의 '친구'를 '좋아하는 제휴 파트너'라고 부르며, 그들은 까마귀와 침팬지가 도구를 만들 수 있다는 것을 보여 주는 증거를 인류를 정의한다고 하는 종류의 도구 제작과는 아무래도 질적으로 다르다고 해석한다. 만약 동물이, 특정 종의 새들이 수천 개의 씨앗의 정확한 위치를 기억할 수 있는 방식처럼, 인지적인 과업에서 우리를 이길 수 있다면, 그들은 그것을 지능이 아니라 본능으로 치부한다. 이것과 더 많은 언어적 수법은 de Waal이 '언어적 거세'라고 일컫는 것이다. 우리가 동물로부터 힘을 빼앗기 위해 우리의 언어를 사용하는 방식이며, 우리가 꼭대기에서 우리의 위치를 유지하기 위해 단어들을 만드는 방식이다.

정답이 보이는 해설

영장류학자 de Waal은 인간은 우리와 다른 동물들 사이의 유사성을 경시함으로써 우리의 위치를 유지한다고 하였다. 과학자들은 침팬지의 '키스'를 '입과 입의 접촉'으로, 까마귀와 침팬지가 만드는 도구는 인류가 만든 도구와는 질적으로 다르다고 해석하는 등 여러 기술적인 언어를 사용하여 동물로부터 힘을 빼앗고자 한다고 하였으므로, 빈칸에 들어갈 말로 가장 적절한 것은 ③ '우리와 다른 동물들 사이에 거리를 두기'이다.

선택지 완벽 분석

① define human instincts 인간 본능을 정의하기
함정 새들이 인지적인 과업에서 우리를 이긴다면 그것을 지능이 아닌 본능으로 치부한다고 한 부분에서 '본능'이 언급되었지만, 인간 본능에 관한 내용은 아니므로 답이 될 수 없다.
② overestimate chimps' intelligence 침팬지의 지능을 과대평가하기
③ distance the other animals from us 우리와 다른 동물들 사이에 거리를 두기
④ identify animals' negative emotions 동물의 부정적인 감정을 알아내기
⑤ correct our misconceptions about nature 자연에 관한 오해를 바로잡기

필수 어휘

downplay 경시하다　imaginary 상상의　offender 범죄자, 위반자
employ 쓰다, 이용하다　technical 기술적인, 전문적인　contact 접촉
primates 영장류　qualitatively 질적으로　cognitive 인지의　precise 정확한

term 일컫다, 칭하다; 용어   linguistic 언어의   castration 거세
disempower ~로부터 힘을 빼앗다

area 분야   endorse 보증하다, 선전하다   expertise 전문 지식   talent 재능
excellence 탁월함   connect 관련이 있다   possess 소유하다

03 정답 ④

202306 31번 정답률 58%

단서1 Individuals who perform at a high level in their profession
직업에서 높은 수준으로 수행하면 다른 사람들의 신뢰를 얻음
often have instant credibility with others. People admire them, they
want to be like them, and they feel connected to them. When they
~와 연결되어 있다고 느끼다
speak, others listen — even if the area of their skill has nothing
have nothing to do with: ~과 관련이 없다
to do with the advice they give. Think about a world-famous
basketball player. He has made more money from endorsements
than he ever did playing basketball. Is it because of his knowledge
~ 때문에
of the products he endorses? No. It's **단서2** because of what he can
농구를 잘하기 때문에 돈을 많이 범
do with a basketball. The same can be said of an Olympic medalist
swimmer. People listen to him **단서3** because of what he can do in
수영을 잘하기 때문에 경청함
the pool. ✪ And when an actor **tells** us we should drive a certain
시간의 부사절   동사   간접목적어   직접목적어 (that 생략됨)
car, // we don't listen (because of his expertise (on engines)). We
listen **단서4** because we admire his talent. **Excellence** connects. If
배우의 재능을 존경함
you possess a high level of ability in an area, others may desire to
~하기를 바라다
connect with you because of it.

해석

자신의 직업에서 높은 수준으로 수행하는 사람들은 흔히 다른 사람들의 즉각적인 신
뢰를 얻는다. 사람들은 그들을 존경하고, 그들처럼 되고 싶어 하고, 그들과 연결되어
있다고 느낀다. 그들이 말할 때, 다른 사람들은 비록 그들의 기술 분야가 그들이 해
주는 조언과 전혀 관련이 없을지라도 경청한다. 세계적으로 유명한 농구 선수에 대
해 생각해 보라. 그는 그가 농구를 하면서 그간 벌었던 것보다 광고로부터 더 많은
돈을 벌었다. 그것이 그가 광고하는 제품에 대한 그의 지식 때문일까? 아니다. 그것
은 그가 농구로 할 수 있는 것 때문이다. 올림픽 메달리스트 수영 선수도 마찬가지라
고 말할 수 있다. 사람들은 그가 수영장에서 할 수 있는 것 때문에 그의 말을 경청한
다. 그리고 어떤 배우가 우리에게 특정 자동차를 운전해야 한다고 말할 때, 우리는 엔
진에 대한 그의 전문 지식 때문에 경청하는 것은 아니다. 우리는 그의 재능을 존경하
기 때문에 경청한다. **탁월함**은 연결된다. 만약 당신이 어떤 분야에서 높은 수준의 능
력을 갖고 있다면, 다른 사람들은 그것 때문에 당신과 연결되기를 원할 수도 있다.

정답이 보이는 해설

직업에서 높은 수준으로 수행하는 사람들은 흔히 다른 사람들에게 즉각적인 신뢰를
얻고, 사람들이 그들의 말에 경청한다는 내용의 글이다. 유명한 농구 선수, 올림픽 메
달리스트 수영 선수, 재능 있는 배우가 광고를 하면 경청하는데 그들의 재능을 존경
하기 때문이라고 설명하고 있다. 따라서 빈칸에 들어갈 말로 가장 적절한 것은 ④ '탁
월함'이다.

선택지 완벽 분석

① Patience 인내심
함정 농구 선수나 수영 선수의 예로 보아, 인내하며 운동을 열심히 한다고 생각하여 이것을 답으
로 잘못 고를 수도 있지만, 인내심에 관한 내용은 아님에 유의한다.
② Sacrifice 희생
③ Honesty 정직함
④ Excellence 탁월함
⑤ Creativity 창의성

필수 어휘

perform 수행하다   instant 즉각적인   credibility 신뢰(성)   admire 존경하다

04 정답 ①

202306 32번 정답률 48%

Think of the brain as a city. If you were to look out over a city
think of A as B: A를 B로 생각하다
and ask "where is the economy located?" you'd see there's no good
emerge from: ~에서 나타나다
answer to the question. Instead, **단서1** the economy emerges from
경제는 모든 요소의 상호 작용으로 나타남
the interaction of all the elements — from the stores and the banks
~도 그러하다
to the merchants and the customers. And **단서2** so it is with the
뇌의 작동도 그러해서,
brain's operation; it doesn't happen in one spot. Just as in a city, no
한 지점에서 일어나지 않음
neighborhood of the brain **operates in isolation.** **단서3** In brains and
뇌와 도시 안의 모든
in cities, everything emerges from the interaction between residents,
것은 서로 간의 상호 작용으로 나타남
at all scales, locally and distantly. ✪ **Just as** trains bring *materials*
딱 ~하는 것처럼
and textiles into a city, [which become processed into the economy],
계속적 용법의 관계대명사절(= and they become ~)
// so the raw electrochemical signals (from sensory organs) / are
주어의 핵(복수)   복수 동사
transported (along superhighways of neurons). There the signals
undergo processing and transformation into our conscious reality.

해석

뇌를 도시라고 생각해 보라. 만약 도시를 내다보며 "경제가 어디에 위치해 있나요?"
라고 묻는다면 그 질문에 대한 좋은 답이 없다는 것을 알게 될 것이다. 대신, 경제는
상점과 은행에서 상인과 고객에 이르기까지 모든 요소의 상호 작용으로부터 나타난
다. 그리고 그것은 뇌의 작동도 그러하다: 그것은 한 곳에서 일어나지 않는다. 도시에
서와 마찬가지로, 뇌의 어떤 지역도 **독립적으로 작동하지** 않는다. 뇌와 도시 안에서,
모든 것은, 모든 규모에서, 근거리에서든 원거리에서든, 거주자들 간의 상호 작용으
로부터 나타난다. 기차가 자재와 직물을 도시로 들여오고, 그것이 경제 속으로 처리
되는 것처럼, 그렇게 감각 기관으로부터 오는 가공되지 않은 전기화학적 신호는 뉴
런의 초고속도로를 따라서 전해진다. 거기서 신호는 처리와 우리의 의식적인 현실로
변형을 겪는다.

정답이 보이는 해설

도시에서 경제는 상점과 은행에서 상인과 고객에 이르기까지 모든 요소의 상호 작용
으로부터 나타나며 뇌의 작동도 마찬가지라고 했고, 다음 문장에서 뇌와 도시 안에
서 모든 것은 구성 요소 간의 상호 작용으로부터 나타난다고 했다. 도시에서처럼, 뇌
의 어떤 지역도 구성 요소들의 상호 작용으로 작동한다고 했으므로, 빈칸에 들어갈
말로 가장 적절한 것은 ① '독립적으로 작동하지'이다.

선택지 완벽 분석

① operates in isolation 독립적으로 작동하지
② suffers from rapid changes 급격한 변화에 시달리지
③ resembles economic elements 경제적 요소를 닮지
함정 도시 내에서의 경제와 마찬가지로, 뇌의 작동도 한 지점에서 나타나지 않고 모든 것들의 상호
작용으로 나타난다는 내용으로, 뇌의 작동이 경제와 비슷하다고 설명하는 글임에 유의한다.
④ works in a systematic way 체계적으로 작동하지
⑤ interacts with another 또 다른 것과 상호 작용하지

필수 어휘

interaction 상호 작용   element 요소   merchant 상인   operation 작동
spot 장소   material 재료   process 처리하다   raw 가공되지 않은, 날것의
sensory 감각의   organ 기관   transport 전달하다   superhighway 초고속도로
neuron 뉴런, 신경   undergo 겪다   transformation 변형
conscious 의식적인

05 정답 ①

주제문 People differ in how quickly they can reset their biological
~에 있어서 다르다
clocks to overcome jet lag, and the speed of recovery depends on
~에 달려 있다
the **direction** of travel. Generally, 단서1 it's easier to fly westward
서쪽으로 이동해서 하루를 연장하는 게
and lengthen your day than it is to fly eastward and shorten it. 단서2
더 쉬움
This east-west difference in jet lag is sizable enough to have an
동쪽으로 가느냐 서쪽으로 가느냐에 따라 차이가 큼   ~에 영향을
impact on the performance of sports teams. Studies have found that
미치다
단서3 teams flying westward perform significantly better than teams
서쪽으로 가는 팀이 동쪽으로 가는 팀보다 훨씬 더 잘함
flying eastward in professional baseball and college football. ★ A

more recent study (of more than 46,000 Major League Baseball
             주어
games) / found / additional evidence [that 단서4 eastward travel is
        동사   목적어   └ 동격 ┘   동쪽으로의 이동이 서쪽으로의
tougher than westward travel].
이동보다 더 힘듦

해석

시차로 인한 피로감을 극복하기 위해서 자신의 체내 시계를 얼마나 빨리 재설정할
수 있는지는 사람마다 서로 다르며, 그 회복 속도는 이동 방향에 달려 있다. 일반적으
로 동쪽으로 비행하여 여러분의 하루를 단축하는 것보다는 서쪽으로 비행하여 여러
분의 하루를 연장하는 것이 더 쉽다. 시차로 인한 피로감에서 이러한 동서의 차이는
스포츠 팀의 경기력에 영향을 미칠 만큼 충분히 크다. 연구에 따르면 서쪽으로 비행
하는 팀이 동쪽으로 비행하는 팀보다 프로 야구와 대학 미식축구에서 상당히 더 잘
한다. 46,000 경기가 넘는 메이저 리그 야구 경기에 대한 더 최근의 연구에 의해 동
쪽으로 이동하는 것이 서쪽으로 이동하는 것보다 더 힘들다는 추가적인 증거가 발견
되었다.

정답이 보이는 해설

시차로 인한 피로감 극복은 사람마다 다르지만, 동쪽 비행보다 서쪽 비행이 더 쉬워
서 경기력에도 영향을 주어 서쪽 비행을 하는 팀이 동쪽 비행을 하는 팀보다 더 잘한
다는 내용이다. 즉, 시차로 인한 피로감에서 회복하는 회복 속도는 이동 방향에 달려
있다고 볼 수 있다. 따라서 빈칸에 들어갈 말로 가장 적절한 것은 ① '방향'이다.

선택지 완벽 분석

① direction 방향
② purpose 목적
③ season 계절
④ length 길이
함정 시차로 인한 피로감은 비행 길이와도 상관 있을 듯하지만, 이 글에서는 비행 길이에 관한 내
용은 언급되지 않았다.
⑤ cost 비용

필수 어휘

biological clock 체내 시계 overcome 극복하다 recovery 회복
lengthen 연장하다 shorten 단축하다 sizable 큰 impact 영향
performance 경기력, 성과 perform 행하다, 수행하다 significantly 상당히
professional 프로의, 전문적인 recent 최근의 additional 추가적인
evidence 증거 tough 힘든, 거친

06 정답 ③

★ If you want the confidence [that comes from achieving what
    조건의 부사절   주격 관계대명사절
you set out to do each day], // then it's important **to understand**
                                    가주어   진주어
[how long things are going to take]. Over-optimism about what
how long이 이끄는 understand의 목적어절
can be achieved within a certain time frame is a problem. So

work on it. 단서1 Make a practice of estimating the amount of
개선하기 위해 노력하다   필요한 시간의 양을 추산하는 것을 습관화하라

---

time needed alongside items on your 'things to do' list, and 단서2
learn by experience when tasks take a greater or lesser time than
예상보다 더 많은 시간 또는 더 적은 시간이 걸리는지 알아보라
expected. Give attention also to fitting the task to the available
~에 주의를 기울이다
time. There are some tasks that you can only set about if you have

a significant amount of time available. There is no point in trying to
상당한 양의 ~   ~하는 것은 무의미하다
gear up for such a task when you only have a short period available.

단서3 So schedule the time you need for the longer tasks and put the
시간이 오래 걸리는 과제를 먼저 계획하고, 그 사이의 남는 시간에 짧게 걸리는 과제를 하라
short tasks into the spare moments in between.

해석

만약 매일 하고자 착수하는 일을 성취함으로써 얻게 되는 자신감을 원한다면, 과제
가 얼마나 시간이 걸릴지 아는 것이 중요하다. 어떤 특정 기간 내에 성취될 수 있는
것에 대한 지나친 낙관주의는 문제다. 그러므로 그것을 개선하려고 노력하라. '해야
할 일' 목록에 있는 항목과 함께 필요한 시간의 양을 추산하는 것을 습관화하고, 과제
가 언제 예상보다 더 많은 시간 또는 더 적은 시간이 걸리는지 경험을 통해 배우라.
그 이용 가능한 시간에 과제를 맞추는 것에도 또한 주의를 기울이라. 이용할 수 있는
시간의 양이 상당히 있어야만 시작할 수 있는 과제들도 몇몇 있다. 이용할 수 있는
짧은 시간밖에 없을 때는, 그런 과제를 위해 준비를 갖추려고 애쓰는 것은 무의미하
다. 그러므로 시간이 더 오래 걸리는 과제를 위해 필요한 시간을 계획하고, 그 사이의
남는 시간에 시간이 짧게 걸리는 과제를 배치하라.

정답이 보이는 해설

어떤 특정 기간 내에 성취될 수 있는 것에 대한 지나친 낙관주의가 문제라고 했고,
필요한 시간의 양을 추산하는 것을 습관화하고, 언제 예상보다 더 많은 시간 또는 더
적은 시간이 걸리는지 경험을 통해 배우고, 이용 가능한 시간에 과제를 맞춰야 한다
는 내용이므로, 빈칸에 들어갈 말로 가장 적절한 것은 ③ '과제가 얼마나 시간이 걸릴
지'이다.

선택지 완벽 분석

① what benefits you can get 어떤 혜택을 받을 수 있는지
② how practical your tasks are 과제가 얼마나 실용적인지
과제에 걸리는 시간을 잘 파악해서 계획하라는 내용이지, 과제의 실용성에 따라 시간을 배치하라
는 내용은 아니다.
③ how long things are going to take 과제가 얼마나 시간이 걸릴지
④ why failures are meaningful in life 인생에서 실패가 왜 의미 있는지
⑤ why your leisure time should come first 여가 시간이 왜 우선되어야
   하는지

필수 어휘

confidence 자신감, 확신 achieve 성취하다 set out ~에 착수하다
over-optimism 지나친 낙관주의 make a practice of ~을 습관화하다
estimate 추산하다, 어림잡다 amount 양 expect 기대하다
attention 주의 fit 맞추다 available 이용 가능한 significant 상당한
period 시간, 기간 schedule 일정을 잡다 spare 남는, 여분의

07 정답 ③

부사적 용법(목적)
★ (To demonstrate [**how best to** defeat the habit of delaying],) /
                  목적어(~하기 가장 좋은 방법을)
Dan Ariely, a professor of psychology and behavioral economics,
주어   └ 동격 ┘
performed an experiment (on students in three of his classes at
동사   목적어
MIT). He assigned all classes three reports over the course of
the semester. The first class had to choose three due dates for
themselves, up to and including the last day of class. The second
                  ~까지 포함하여
had no deadlines — all three papers just had to be submitted by

the last day of class. In his third class, he gave students three

set deadlines over the course of the semester. At the end of the
~의 끝에

semester, he found that 단서 students with set deadlines received the
마감일이 정해진 학생들이 최고의 성적을

best grades, the students with no deadlines had the worst, and those
마감일이 없는 학생들은 최하의 성적을 받았으며

who could choose their own deadlines fell somewhere in the middle.
마감일을 직접 선택한 학생들은 그 중간쯤의 위치에 있었음

주제문 Ariely concludes that **restricting freedom** — whether by
whether A or B:

the professor or by students who recognize their own tendencies to
A이든 B이든   tendency to-v:

delay things — improves self-control and performance.
~하려는 경향성

해석

미루는 습관을 가장 잘 무너뜨리는 방법을 설명하기 위해, 심리학 및 행동경제학 교수인 Dan Ariely는 MIT의 자신의 수업 중 세 개 수업에서 학생들을 대상으로 실험을 수행했다. 그는 학기 과정 동안 모든 수업에 세 개의 보고서를 과제로 부여했다. 첫 번째 수업의 학생들은 종강일까지 포함해서 세 개의 마감일을 스스로 선택해야 했다. 두 번째는 마감일이 없었고, 세 개의 보고서 모두 종강일까지 제출되기만 하면 되었다. 그의 세 번째 수업에서, 그는 학기 과정 동안 학생들에게 세 개의 정해진 마감일을 주었다. 학기 말에, 그는 마감일이 정해진 학생들이 최고의 성적을 받았고, 마감일이 없는 학생들은 최하의 성적을 받았으며, 자신의 마감일을 선택할 수 있었던 학생들은 그 중간 어디쯤의 위치에 있었다는 것을 알아냈다. Ariely는, 교수에 의해서든 혹은 일을 미루는 자신의 경향성을 인식한 학생들에 의해서든, **자유를 제한하는 것**이 자기 통제와 성과를 향상시킨다고 결론짓는다.

정답이 보이는 해설

Dan Ariely의 실험에서, 첫 수업은 보고서의 마감일을 선택하게 했고, 두 번째는 마감일이 없었고, 세 번째는 마감일을 정해 주었는데, 세 번째 수업의 학생들이 최고의 성적을 받았고, 두 번째 수업의 학생들이 최하의 성적을 받았다고 했다. 따라서 빈칸에 들어갈 말로 가장 적절한 것은 ③ '자유를 제한하는 것'이다.

선택지 완벽 분석

① offering rewards 보상을 제공하는 것

② removing obstacles 장애물을 제거하는 것

③ restricting freedom 자유를 제한하는 것

④ increasing assignments 과제를 증가시키는 것

⑤ encouraging competition 경쟁을 장려하는 것
과제 마감일만 다르게 정해 주었다는 내용이지 경쟁을 장려하려는 의도는 아니다.

필수 어휘

demonstrate 설명하다, 입증하다   defeat 무너뜨리다, 극복하다
delay 지연시키다   psychology 심리학   behavioral 행동의
economics 경제학   perform 수행하다   assign 할당하다, 과제를 부여하다
semester 학기   due 예정된   for oneself 자신 스스로   submit 제출하다
conclude 결론짓다   recognize 인식하다, 인지하다   improve 향상시키다
self-control 자기 통제   performance 성과

08 정답 ②

202211 32번 정답률 45%

주제문 The best way in which innovation changes our lives is

by **enabling people to work for each other.** The main theme of
enable A to-v: A가 ~할 수 있게 하다

human history is that we become steadily more specialized in what

we produce, and steadily more diversified in what we consume:

단서1 we move away from unstable self-sufficiency to safer mutual
불안정한 자급자족에서 더 안전한 상호의존으로 옮겨감

interdependence. By concentrating on 단서2 serving other people's
일주일에 40시간 일하고

needs for forty hours a week — which we call a job — you can

단서3 spend the other seventy-two hours (not counting fifty-six
72시간을 일하지 않고 보냄

hours in bed) relying on the services provided to you by other
                                                        → 목적격보어

people. ✪ Innovation has made it possible to work (for a fraction of
         주어   동사 가목적어   진목적어

a second) (in order to be able to afford to turn on an electric lamp
                      ~하기 위해서   ~을 켜다

for an hour), // providing *the quantity of light* [that would have
                        분사구문   주격 관계대명사절

required a whole day's work / if you had to make it yourself by
                              가정의 부사절

collecting and refining sesame oil or lamb fat (to burn in a simple
                                              부사적 용법(목적)

lamp), / as much of humanity did (in the not so distant past)].
              부사절   전치사구(시간)

해석

혁신이 우리의 삶을 바꾸는 최고의 방법은 **사람들이 서로를 위해 일할 수 있도록 함**으로써이다. 인류 역사의 주요한 주제는 우리가 생산하는 것에 대해 꾸준히 더 전문화되고 소비하는 것에 대해 꾸준히 더 다양화되는 것이다. 즉, 우리는 불안정한 자급자족에서 더 안전한 서로 간의 상호 의존으로 옮겨간다는 것이다. 일주일에 40시간 동안 다른 사람들의 필요를 충족시키는 것, 즉 우리가 직업이라고 부르는 것에 집중함으로써, 여러분은 다른 사람들에 의해 여러분에게 제공되는 서비스에 의지하여 나머지 72시간(잠자는 56시간은 계산에 넣지 않고)을 보낼 수 있다. 혁신은 전등을 한 시간 동안 켜는 여유를 가질 수 있게 하기 위해 아주 짧은 시간 동안 일하는 것을 가능하게 했고, 그것은 만약 여러분이 그리 멀지 않은 과거에 많은 인류가 했던 것처럼 단순한 등을 켜기 위해 참기름이나 양의 지방을 모으고 정제함으로써 그것을 스스로 만들어야 했다면 하루 종일의 노동을 필요로 했을 빛의 양을 제공했다.

정답이 보이는 해설

우리는 불안정한 자급자족에서 더 안전한 서로 간의 상호 의존으로 옮겨가고 있고, 일주일에 40시간 동안 일함으로써, 나머지 72시간(잠자는 56시간은 계산에 넣지 않고)은 일하지 않고 보낼 수 있다는 내용이다. 따라서 빈칸에 들어갈 말로 가장 적절한 것은 ② '사람들이 서로를 위해 일할 수 있도록 함'이다.

선택지 완벽 분석

① respecting the values of the old days 옛날의 가치를 존중함

② enabling people to work for each other 사람들이 서로를 위해 일할 수 있도록 함

③ providing opportunities to think creatively 창의적으로 생각할 수 있는 기회를 제공함
함정 이 글은 '혁신의 최고 방식: 서로 간의 상호의존'에 관한 글로, 창의적인 생각과는 관련이 없다.

④ satisfying customers with personalized services 개인화된 서비스로 고객을 만족시킴

⑤ introducing and commercializing unusual products 특이한 제품을 소개하고 상품화함

필수 어휘

innovation 혁신   steadily 꾸준히   specialized in ~에 전문화된
diversified 다양화된   consume 소비하다   unstable 불안정한
self-sufficiency 자급자족   mutual 서로 간의   interdependence 상호 의존
concentrate on ~에 집중하다   rely on ~에 의존하다
provide A to B A를 B에 제공하다   afford ~할 여유가 있다
electric 전기의   quantity 양   require 요구하다   sesame 참깨   fat 지방

09 정답 ②

202209 31번 정답률 50%

주제문 We worry that the robots are taking our jobs, but just as

common a problem is that the robots are taking our **judgment.**

✪ In *the large warehouses* [so common behind the scenes of today's
                                    └────── 형용사구

economy], / human 'pickers' hurry around grabbing products
                                                    현재분사1

off shelves and moving them to **where** they can be packed and
                  현재분사2   → 관계부사(~하는 곳)

dispatched. In their ears are headpieces: the voice of 'Jennifer', a

piece of software, tells them where to go and what to do, controlling the smallest details of their movements. Jennifer breaks down
나누다, 분해하다
instructions into tiny chunks, to minimise error and maximise productivity — for example, rather than picking eighteen copies of
~하기보다는
a book off a shelf, the human worker would be politely instructed to pick five. Then another five. Then yet another five. Then another three. 단서1 Working in such conditions reduces people to machines
로봇의 지시에 따라 일하는 것은 사람들을 기계로 격하시킴
made of flesh. 단서2 Rather than asking us to think or adapt, the
로봇 장치는 우리의 생각이나 적응을 요구하지 않고 사고 과정을 가져감
Jennifer unit takes over the thought process and treats workers as an inexpensive source of some visual processing and a pair of opposable thumbs.

해석
우리는 로봇이 우리의 직업을 빼앗고 있다고 걱정하지만, 그만큼 흔한 문제는 로봇이 우리의 판단력을 빼앗고 있다는 것이다. 오늘날의 경제 상황 이면의 아주 흔한 거대한 창고에서, 인간 '집게'는 서둘러서 선반에서 상품을 집어내고 그것들이 포장되고 발송될 수 있는 곳으로 이동시킨다. 그들의 귀에는 헤드폰이 있는데, 한 소프트웨어 프로그램인 'Jennifer'의 목소리가 그들의 움직임의 가장 작은 세부 사항들을 조종하면서, 그들에게 어디로 가야 하고 무엇을 해야 하는지를 알려 준다. Jennifer는 오류를 최소화하고 생산성을 최대화하기 위해 지시 사항을 아주 작은 덩어리로 나눈다. 예를 들어, 인간 작업자는 선반에서 책 18권을 집어내기보다는, 5권을 집어내라고 정중하게 지시받을 것이다. 그런 다음 또 다른 5권을. 그런 다음 다시 또 다른 5권을. 그런 다음 또 다른 3권을. 그러한 조건에서 일하는 것은 사람들을 살로 만들어진 기계로 격하시킨다. 우리에게 생각하거나 적응하라고 요구하기보다는, 그 Jennifer 장치는 사고 과정을 가져가고 작업자들을 약간의 시각적인 처리 과정과 한 쌍의 마주볼 수 있는 엄지손가락을 지닌 값싼 자원으로 취급한다.

정답이 보이는 해설
인간 작업자가 사고 과정 없이 그저 소프트웨어 프로그램의 지시를 받는 대로 행동하는 기계로 취급당한다는 사례를 제시하고 있으므로, 이를 통해 로봇이 우리의 판단과 사고 능력을 빼앗게 된다는 것을 알 수 있다. 따라서 빈칸에 들어갈 말로 가장 적절한 것은 ② '판단력'이다.

선택지 완벽 분석
① reliability 신뢰성
컴퓨터 프로그램의 지시에 따라 행동하는 것은 신뢰성과는 관계가 없다.
② judgment 판단력
③ endurance 인내심
④ sociability 사교성
작업자가 사고 과정 없이 시키는 대로 일한다는 것은 사교성과는 거리가 멀다.
⑤ cooperation 협력

필수 어휘
common 흔한 warehouse 창고 grab 잡다 headpiece 헤드폰
detail 세부 사항 instruction 지시 사항 minimise 최소화하다
maximise 최대화하다 productivity 생산성 flesh 살, 피부 adapt 적응하다
inexpensive 값싼, 비싸지 않은 processing 처리 opposable 마주볼 수 있는

10 정답 ⑤
202209 32번 정답률 57%

주제문 The prevailing view among developmental scientists is that people are active contributors to their own development. People are influenced by the physical and social contexts in which they
~에 영향을 받다
live, but 단서1 they also play a role in influencing their development
역할을 하다
사람들은 주변 환경과 상호 작용하면서 자신의 발달에 영향을 미침

by interacting with, and changing, those contexts. 단서2 Even
유아도
infants influence the world around them and construct their own
주변 세상에 영향을 주고 상호 작용을 통해 자신의 발달을 구성함
development through their interactions. Consider an infant who smiles at each adult he sees; he influences his world because adults are likely to smile, use "baby talk," and play with him in response. The infant brings adults into close contact, making one-on-one
by+-ing: ~함으로써
interactions and creating opportunities for learning. ✪ By engaging
by의 목적어1
the world around them, thinking, being curious, and interacting with
by의 목적어2   by의 목적어3   by의 목적어4
people, objects, and the world around them, / individuals of all ages are "**manufacturers of their own development**."

해석
발달 과학자들 사이에서 지배적인 견해는 사람들이 자신의 발달에 능동적인 기여자라는 것이다. 사람들은 그들이 사는 물리적이고 사회적인 환경에 영향을 받지만, 그들은 또한 그러한 환경과 상호 작용하고 그러한 환경을 변화시킴으로써 그들의 발달에 영향을 주는 역할을 한다. 심지어 유아들도 그들 주변의 세상에 영향을 주고 상호 작용을 통해서 그들 자신의 발달을 구성한다. 그가 바라보는 각각의 어른에게 미소 짓는 유아를 생각해 보라. (그에) 반응하여 어른들이 미소 짓고 '아기 말'을 사용하며 자신과 놀아 줄 것이기 때문에 그는 자신의 세상에 영향을 준다. 그 유아는 어른들을 친밀한 연결로 끌어들여서, 일대일 상호 작용을 하고 학습의 기회를 만든다. 그들 주변 세상의 관심을 끌고, 생각하고, 호기심을 가지고, 그들 주변의 사람들, 사물들, 그리고 세상과 상호 작용함으로써, 모든 연령의 개인들은 "**자신의 발달을 만들어 내는 사람들**"이다.

정답이 보이는 해설
사람들은 자신의 발달에 능동적인 기여자로서 주변 환경과 상호 작용함으로써 자신의 발달에 영향을 미치고, 유아 또한 주변의 세상에 영향을 주며 주변 사람들과 상호 작용하면서 자신의 발달을 구성한다는 내용이므로, 빈칸에 들어갈 말로 가장 적절한 것은 ⑤ '자신의 발달을 만들어 내는 사람들'이다.

선택지 완벽 분석
① mirrors of their generation 그들의 세대의 거울
함정 어른들뿐만 아니라 아이들도 주변 세상과 상호 작용한다는 내용이므로, 자신의 세대를 반영한다는 것과는 거리가 있다.
② shields against social conflicts 사회적 갈등에 대한 방패
③ explorers in their own career path 자신의 진로를 개척하는 사람들
④ followers of their childhood dreams 그들의 어린 시절 꿈을 좇는 사람들
⑤ manufacturers of their own development 자신의 발달을 만들어 내는 사람들

필수 어휘
prevailing 지배적인 developmental 발달의 contributor 기여자, 기부자
influence 영향을 주다 interact with ~와 상호 작용하다 context 환경, 정황
infant 유아 construct 구성하다 interaction 상호 작용
in response 이에 응하여 one-on-one 일대일의 individual 개인
manufacturer 제조자

11 정답 ①
202206 31번 정답률 54%

✪ One of the big questions faced this past year was [how to keep
주어의 핵(단수)   단수 동사 was의 보어(명사구)
innovation rolling] // **when** people were working entirely virtually.
접속사(~할 때)
But experts say that digital work didn't have a negative effect
~에 영향을 미치다
on innovation and creativity. Working within limits pushes us to solve problems. 주제문 Overall, virtual meeting platforms put more

13강

빈칸추론1

constraints on communication and collaboration than face-to-face settings. For instance, with the press of a button, virtual meeting hosts can control the size of breakout groups and enforce time constraints; 단서1 only one person can speak at a time; nonverbal
한 번에 한 사람씩만 말할 수 있고 비언어적 신호는 제한됨
signals, particularly those below the shoulders, are diminished;
단서2 "seating arrangements" are assigned by the platform, not by
좌석은 플랫폼에 의해 배정되고 다른 사람에 대한 시각적 접근이 제한됨
individuals; and visual access to others may be limited by the size of each participant's screen. Such __restrictions__ are likely to stretch
~할 가능성이 있다
participants beyond their usual ways of thinking, boosting creativity.

해석
작년에 직면한 가장 큰 질문 중 하나는 사람들이 완전히 가상으로 작업할 때 어떻게 혁신을 계속 유지할 것인가 하는 것이었다. 그러나 전문가들은 디지털 작업이 혁신과 창의성에 부정적인 영향을 주지 않았다고 말한다. 한계 내에서 일하는 것은 우리에게 문제를 해결하도록 몰아붙인다. 대체로 가상 회의 플랫폼은 대면 환경보다 의사소통과 협업에 더 많은 제약을 가한다. 예를 들어, 버튼을 누르면 가상 회의 진행자는 소모임 그룹의 크기를 제어하고 시간 제한을 강요할 수 있다. 한 번에 한 사람만이 말할 수 있으며, 비언어적 신호, 특히 어깨 아래의 신호는 제한된다. '좌석 배치'는 개인이 아닌 플랫폼에 의해 배정된다. 그리고 다른 사람에 대한 시각적 접근은 각 참가자의 화면 크기에 따라 제한될 수 있다. 그러한 __제한들__은 참가자들을 그들의 일반적인 사고방식 너머까지 확장시켜 창의력을 신장시킬 가능성이 있다.

정답이 보이는 해설
가상 회의 플랫폼은 대면 환경보다 많은 제약을 가한다는 내용으로, 그러한 예로 시간 제한, 한 사람씩 말하기, 비언어적 신호 제한, 플랫폼에 의한 좌석 배정 등이 제시되어 있으므로, 빈칸에 들어갈 말로 가장 적절한 것은 ① '제한들'이다.

🔎 선택지 완벽 분석
① restrictions 제한들
② responsibilities 책임들
함정 가상 회의를 할 때 필요한 책임 관련 내용은 언급되어 있지 않다.
③ memories 기억들
④ coincidences 우연들
함정 제한 사항 중 하나로 좌석이 플랫폼에 의해 배정된다는 언급이 있지만 이는 우연과는 관련이 없다.
⑤ traditions 전통들

필수 어휘
innovation 혁신 entirely 완전히 virtually 가상으로 overall 대체로
constraint 제한 collaboration 협업 setting 환경 enforce 강요하다
nonverbal 비언어적인 arrangement 배정, 배치 assign 배정하다, 할당하다
boost 신장시키다

12 정답 ②
202206 32번 정답률 57%

⭐ The law of demand is [that the demand for goods and services
→ is의 보어절1
increases as prices fall], / and [the demand falls as prices increase].
접속사(= when)   ↳ 접속사 that 생략   접속사(= when)
→ is의 보어절2
Giffen goods are special types of products for which the traditional law of demand does not apply. Instead of switching to cheaper
~ 대신에
replacements, 단서1 consumers demand more of giffen goods when
가격이 상승하면 기펜재의 수요가 늘어나고 가격이 하락하면 기펜재의 수
the price increases and less of them when the price decreases.
요가 감소함
Taking an example, 단서2 rice in China is a giffen good because
중국의 쌀은 가격이 하락하면 사람들이 덜 구매하는 경향이 있
people tend to purchase less of it when the price falls. The reason
으므로 기펜재에 해당함

---

for this is, when the price of rice falls, people have more money to spend on other types of products such as meat and dairy and, therefore, change their spending pattern. On the other hand, as rice
반면에
prices increase, people **consume more rice**.

해석
수요의 법칙은 가격이 하락할 때 상품과 서비스에 대한 수요가 증가하고, 가격이 상승할 때 수요가 감소하는 것이다. '기펜재'는 전통적인 수요 법칙이 적용되지 않는 특별한 유형의 상품이다. 더 저렴한 대체품으로 바꾸는 대신 소비자들은 가격이 상승하면 기펜재를 더 많이, 가격이 하락하면 덜 필요로 한다. 예를 들어 보면, 중국의 쌀은 가격이 하락할 때 사람들이 덜 구매하는 경향이 있기 때문에 기펜재이다. 이것의 이유는, 쌀값이 하락하면 사람들이 고기와 유제품 같은 다른 종류의 상품에 쓸 돈이 많아지고, 따라서 그들의 소비 패턴을 바꾸기 때문이다. 반면에, 쌀값이 상승하면 사람들은 __더 많은 쌀을 소비한다__.

정답이 보이는 해설
전통적인 수요 법칙이 적용되지 않는 기펜재에 관해 설명하는 글로, 소비자는 기펜재의 가격이 상승하면 더 많이 구입하고 가격이 하락하면 덜 구입한다고 했는데, 중국의 쌀은 기펜재에 해당하므로 쌀값이 상승하면 쌀을 더 많이 구입할 것이다. 따라서 빈칸에 들어갈 말로 가장 적절한 것은 ② '더 많은 쌀을 소비한다'이다.

🔎 선택지 완벽 분석
① order more meat 더 많은 고기를 주문한다
② consume more rice 더 많은 쌀을 소비한다
③ try to get new jobs 새로운 직장을 구하려고 노력한다
④ increase their savings 그들의 저축을 늘린다
함정 글에서는 가격이 하락하면 사람들이 다른 종류의 상품에 쓸 돈이 더 많아진다고 했는데, 이는 저축을 늘리는 것과는 차이가 있다.
⑤ start to invest overseas 해외로 투자하기 시작한다

필수 어휘
demand 수요; 필요로 하다
giffen goods 기펜재(가격이 내릴수록 오히려 수요가 적어지는 재화)
traditional 전통적인 apply 적용되다 switch 바꾸다, 전환하다
replacement 대체품 consumer 소비자 tend to ~하는 경향이 있다
purchase 구입하다 dairy 유제품

13 정답 ②
202203 31번 정답률 47%

단서1 Generalization without specific examples that humanize
구체적 사례가 없는 일반화는 청자와 독자 모두에게 지루함
writing is boring to the listener and to the reader. Who wants to read platitudes all day? Who wants to hear the words great, greater, best, smartest, finest, humanitarian, on and on and on without specific examples? Instead of using these 'nothing words,' leave
~ 대신에   ~을 빼다
them out completely and just describe the **particulars**. ⭐ There is nothing worse than reading a scene in *a novel* [in which a main character is described up front as heroic or brave or tragic or funny,
전치사(~로서)
/ **while** thereafter, the writer quickly moves on to something else].
접속사
That's no good, no good at all. 단서2 You have to use less one word
실감 나는 글을 위해서는 세부적인 묘사를 더
descriptions and more detailed, engaging descriptions if you want
많이 사용해야 함
to make something real.

해석
글을 인간미 있게 하는 구체적인 사례가 없는 일반화는 청자와 독자에게 지루하

누가 상투적인 말을 하루 종일 읽고 싶어 하는가? 구체적인 사례가 없이 위대한, 더 위대한, 최고의, 제일 똑똑한, 가장 훌륭한, 인도주의적인, 이런 말들을 누가 계속해서 끊임없이 듣고 싶어 하는가? 이런 '공허한 말들'을 사용하는 대신에, 그것들을 완전히 빼고 **세부 사항들**만 기술하라. 주인공이 대놓고 영웅적이거나 용감하거나 비극적이거나 웃긴 것으로 묘사되고, 그런 다음에 작가가 다른 것으로 빠르게 넘어가는 소설 속의 장면을 읽는 것보다 더 끔찍한 것은 없다. 그것은 좋지 않으며, 전혀 좋지 않다. 어떤 것을 실감 나는 것으로 만들고 싶다면, 한 단어 묘사는 덜 사용하고, 세부적이고 마음을 끄는 묘사를 더 많이 사용해야 한다.

정답이 보이는 해설
구체적 사례가 없이 상투적이고 공허한 말들만 사용하는 것은 독자를 지루하게 만들기 때문에 그것들을 빼고 세부적인 묘사를 더 많이 사용하라는 내용이므로, 빈칸에 들어갈 말로 가장 적절한 것은 ② '세부 사항들'이다.

선택지 완벽 분석
① similarities 유사점들
함정 구체적인 사례 없이 상투적인 말을 사용하는 대신에 구체적인 내용을 기술하라는 것이 핵심 내용이므로 이는 '유사점'을 기술하는 것과는 관계가 없다.
② particulars 세부 사항들
③ fantasies 환상들
④ boredom 따분함
⑤ wisdom 지혜

필수 어휘
generalization 일반화 specific 구체적인 humanize 인간미 있게 하다
finest 가장 훌륭한 humanitarian 인도주의적인 describe 기술하다, 묘사하다
main character 주인공 up front 대놓고 heroic 대담한, 영웅적인
tragic 비극적인 detailed 세부적인, 상세한 engaging 마음을 끄는

14 정답 ③
202203 32번 정답률 53%

주제문 Face-to-face interaction is a uniquely powerful — and sometimes the only — way to share many kinds of knowledge, from the simplest to the most complex. **단서1** It is one of the best ways to stimulate new thinking and ideas, too. ❂ Most of us **would**
어를 자극하는 최고의 방법 중 하나임
have had difficulty learning / [how to tie a shoelace only from
would have p.p.: ~했을 것이다   learning의 목적어1
pictures], / or [how to do arithmetic from a book]. Psychologist
learning의 목적어2
Mihàly Csikszentmihàlyi found, while studying high achievers, that
                              ┌→ 다수의
단서2 a large number of Nobel Prize winners were the students
다수의 노벨상 수상자가 이전 노벨상 수상자의 제자였음
of previous winners: they had access to the same literature as everyone else, but **personal contact** made a crucial difference to their creativity. Within organisations this makes conversation both a crucial factor for high-level professional skills and the most important way of sharing everyday information.

해석
대면 상호 작용은 가장 간단한 것부터 가장 복잡한 것까지 많은 종류의 지식을 공유하는, 유례없이 강력하며, 때로는 유일한 방법이다. 그것은 또한 새로운 생각과 아이디어를 자극하는 최고의 방법 중 하나이다. 우리 대부분이 그림에서만 신발끈 묶는 법을 배웠거나, 아니면 책에서 계산하는 방법을 배웠다면 어려움을 겪었을 것이다. 심리학자 Mihàly Csikszentmihàlyi는 성취도가 높은 사람들을 연구하면서 다수의 노벨상 수상자가 이전 (노벨상) 수상자들의 제자였다는 것을 발견했다. 그들은 다른 사람들과 똑같은 (연구) 문헌에 접근할 수 있었지만, **개인적인 접촉**이 그들의 창의성에 결정적인 차이를 만들었다. 조직 내에서 이것은 대화를 높은 수준의 전문적 기술을 위한 결정적인 요소이자 일상적인 정보를 공유하는 가장 중요한 방식으로 만든다.

정답이 보이는 해설
대면 상호 작용의 중요성을 다루고 있는 글로, 다수의 노벨상 수상자가 이전 수상자들의 제자였다는 사실을 통해 노벨상 수상자들의 창의성에 결정적 차이를 만든 것은 바로 개인적인 상호 작용임을 알 수 있다. 따라서 빈칸에 들어갈 말로 가장 적절한 것은 ③ '개인적인 접촉'이다.

선택지 완벽 분석
① natural talent 천부적인 재능
② regular practice 규칙적인 연습
③ personal contact 개인적인 접촉
④ complex knowledge 복잡한 지식
함정 복잡한 지식을 공유하는 데 대면 상호 작용이 중요하다고 언급되었을 뿐 복잡한 지식이 창의성에 중요하다는 내용과는 거리가 있다.
⑤ powerful motivation 강력한 동기 부여

필수 어휘
face-to-face 대면의 interaction 상호 작용 uniquely 유례없이
complex 복잡한 stimulate 자극하다 shoelace 신발끈
psychologist 심리학자 achiever (~한) 성취도를 보이는 사람 winner 수상자
access 접근 crucial 결정적인, 매우 중요한 professional 전문적인

15 정답 ②
202111 31번 정답률 65%

We don't send telegraphs to communicate anymore, but it's a great metaphor for giving advance notice. Sometimes, you must inform those close to you of upcoming change by conveying
inform A of B: A에게 B를 알리다
important information well in advance. ❂ There's a huge difference
미리
between saying, "From now on, we will do things differently," /
between A and B: A와 B 사이의
which doesn't give people *enough time* (to understand and accept
주격 관계대명사   ┌→to부정사 형용사적 용법
the change), / **and** saying something like, "Starting next month, we're going to approach things differently." Telegraphing empowers people to **adapt**. **단서1** Telegraphing involves the art of seeing an
전보 보내기는 변화를 처리하고 받아들일 충분한 시간을 줌
upcoming event or circumstance and giving others enough time to process and accept the change. Telegraph anything that will take people out of what is familiar and comfortable to them. **단서2** This will allow
전보 보내기는 상황을
processing time for them to accept the circumstances and make the
받아들이고 일어나는 일을 최대한 활용할 수 있는 시간을 허용함   ~을 최대한 활용하다
most of what's happening.

해석
우리는 더 이상 통신하기 위해 전보를 보내지 않지만, 그것은 사전 통보를 하는 것에 대한 훌륭한 비유이다. 때때로 여러분은 중요한 정보를 미리 잘 전달함으로써 다가오는 변화를 여러분과 가까운 사람들에게 알려야 한다. 사람들에게 그 변화를 이해하고 받아들일 충분한 시간을 주지 않는 "지금부터 우리는 일을 다르게 할 것입니다."라고 말하는 것과 "다음 달부터 우리는 일에 다르게 접근할 것입니다."와 같은 말을 하는 것 사이에는 엄청난 차이가 있다. 전보를 보내는 것은 사람들이 **적응할** 수 있도록 해 준다. 전보를 보내는 것은 다가오는 사건이나 상황을 보고 다른 사람들에게 그 변화를 처리하고 받아들일 충분한 시간을 주는 기술을 포함한다. 사람들을 그들에게 익숙하고 편안한 것에서 벗어나게 할 무엇이든 전보로 보내라. 이것은 그들이 그 상황을 받아들이고 일어나고 있는 일을 최대한 활용할 수 있는 처리 시간을 허용해 줄 것이다.

정답이 보이는 해설
사전 통보하는 것을 전보에 비유해 설명하고 있는 글이다. 사람들에게 변화에 대한 정보를 미리 전달하는 것은 사람들이 그 변화를 처리하고 받아들일 충분한 시간을 준다는 내용이므로, 빈칸에 들어갈 말로 가장 적절한 것은 ② '적응할'이다.

🔍 선택지 완벽 분석

① unite 통합할
② adapt 적응할
③ object 반대할
④ compete 경쟁할
⑤ recover 회복할

필수 어휘

telegraph 전보; 전보를 보내다   communicate 통신하다, 연락하다
metaphor 비유   advance notice 사전 통보   inform A of B A에게 B를 알리다
upcoming 다가오는   convey 전달하다   empower ~할 수 있게 하다
circumstance 상황

필수 어휘

underlie ~의 기저가 되다   define 규정하다   preserve 보존하다
suffer from ~을 앓다   heart failure 심부전(心不全)
depend upon ~에 의존하다   replace 교체하다   artificial 인공의
essentially 본질적으로   other than ~을 제외하고
advanced (병의 발달 단계 등이) 후기의, 많이 진행된   fade 희미해지다

---

16 정답 ①

202111 32번 정답률 66%

Not only does memory underlie our ability to think at all, it defines the content of our experiences and how we preserve them for years to come. Memory **makes us who we are**. ✪ If I were to suffer from heart failure and depend upon an artificial heart, / I would be no less myself. If I lost an arm in an accident and had it replaced with an artificial arm, I would still be essentially *me*. 단서1 As long as my mind and memories remain intact, I will continue to be the same person, no matter which part of my body (other than the brain) is replaced. On the other hand, 단서2 when someone suffers from advanced Alzheimer's disease and his memories fade, people often say that he "is not himself anymore," or that it is as if the person "is no longer there," though his body remains unchanged.

해석

기억은 어쨌든 우리의 생각하는 능력의 기저가 될 뿐만 아니라 우리의 경험의 내용과 앞으로 몇 년간 우리가 그것을 보존하는 방식을 규정한다. 기억은 **우리를 우리가 누구인지로 만들어 준다**. 만약 내가 심부전을 앓고 인공 심장에 의존한다고 해도 나는 역시 나일 것이다. 만약 내가 사고로 팔 하나를 잃고 그것을 인공 팔로 교체한다고 해도 나는 여전히 본질적으로 '나'일 것이다. 나의 정신과 기억이 손상되지 않는 한, (뇌를 제외하고) 내 신체의 어떤 부분이 교체되더라도 나는 계속 같은 사람일 것이다. 반면에 어떤 사람이 후기 알츠하이머병을 앓고 그의 기억이 희미해진다면, 비록 그의 신체가 변하지 않은 채로 남아 있긴 하지만 사람들은 흔히 그가 '더 이상 그가 아니라고' 또는 마치 그 사람이 '더 이상 그곳에 없는' 것 같다고 말한다.

정답이 보이는 해설

어떤 사람의 기억이 손상되지 않는 한 신체의 일부가 교체되더라도 여전히 같은 사람인 반면 기억을 잃게 된다면 더 이상 그 사람이 아닐 것이라는 내용이므로 기억은 우리의 본질을 규정한다고 추론할 수 있다. 따라서 빈칸에 들어갈 말로 가장 적절한 것은 ① '우리를 우리가 누구인지로 만들어 준다'이다.

🔍 선택지 완벽 분석

① makes us who we are 우리를 우리가 누구인지로 만들어 준다
② has to do with our body 우리의 신체와 관련이 있다
③ reflects what we expect 우리가 기대하는 것을 반영한다
④ lets us understand others 우리가 다른 사람들을 이해하도록 해 준다
⑤ helps us learn from the past 우리가 과거로부터 배우는 것을 도와준다

---

17 정답 ①

202109 31번 정답률 58%

Sometimes it is the **simpler product** that gives a business a competitive advantage. Until recently, bicycles had to have many gears, often 15 or 20, for them to be considered high-end. 단서 But fixed-gear bikes with minimal features have become more popular, as those who buy them are happy to pay more for much less. ✪ The overall profitability (of these bikes) is much higher / than the more complex ones // because they do a single thing really well / (without the cost of added complexity). Companies should be careful of getting into a war over adding more features with their competitors, as this will increase cost and almost certainly reduce profitability because of competitive pressure on price.

해석

가끔 기업에 경쟁우위를 부여하는 것은 **더 단순한 제품**이다. 최근까지, 자전거는 그것이 최고급으로 여겨지기 위해서는 대개 15개 또는 20개의 많은 기어가 있어야 했다. 그러나 최소한의 특징을 가지는 고정식 기어 자전거가 그것들을 구입하는 사람들이 훨씬 더 적은 것에 대해 기꺼이 더 지불함에 따라 점점 더 인기를 얻게 되었다. 이러한 자전거들의 전반적인 수익성은 더 복잡한 것들보다 훨씬 더 높은데, 그 이유는 그것들이 부가적인 복잡한 특징에 대한 비용 없이 한 가지를 정말로 잘하기 때문이다. 기업들은 더욱 많은 특징을 추가하는 데 있어 자사의 경쟁 업체와 극심한 경쟁을 벌이는 것을 조심해야 하는데, 이것이 가격에 대한 경쟁적인 압박 때문에 비용을 증가시키고 수익성을 거의 확실히 감소시킬 것이기 때문이다.

정답이 보이는 해설

많은 기어가 있는 최고급 사양의 자전거에 비해 최소한의 특징만 가지는 고정식 기어 자전거가 더 인기를 끌고 구매자들이 훨씬 더 적은 것에 기꺼이 더 지불한다는 내용이 이어지고 있으므로, 빈칸에 들어갈 말로 가장 적절한 것은 ① '더 단순한 제품'이다.

🔍 선택지 완벽 분석

① simpler product 더 단순한 제품
② affordable price 적절한 가격
   함정 적은 특징을 가진 제품에 대해 기꺼이 더 지불한다는 언급은 있지만, 이 가격이 적절하기 때문이라는 언급은 없으므로 정답이 될 수 없다.
③ consumer loyalty 소비자 충성도
④ customized design 최적화된 디자인
   함정 구매자들이 최소한의 특징을 가지는 고정식 기어 자전거를 선택하는 이유는 그것이 가지는 기능 때문이지 디자인 때문은 아니다.
⑤ eco-friendly technology 환경친화적인 기술

필수 어휘

competitive 경쟁적인   advantage 이점, 장점   fixed-gear 고정식 기어의
minimal 최소한의, 아주 적은   feature 특징, 특색   profitability 수익성
complexity 복잡함, 복잡성   competitor 경쟁자, 경쟁 업체   pressure 압력, 압박
product 제품, 상품   consumer 소비자   loyalty 충실, 충성심

18 정답 ⑤

Many evolutionary biologists argue that humans **developed language for economic reasons**. We needed to trade, and we needed to establish trust in order to trade. 단서 Language is very handy when you are trying to conduct business with someone. Two early humans could not only agree to trade three wooden bowls for six bunches of bananas but establish rules as well. What wood was used for the bowls? Where did you get the bananas? ❷ That business deal would have been nearly impossible / using only gestures and confusing noises, // and carrying it out (according to *terms* (agreed upon)) creates a bond of trust. 주제문 ▶ Language allows us to be specific, and this is where conversation plays a key role.

해석

많은 진화 생물학자는 인간이 **경제적인 이유로 언어를 발달시켰다**고 주장한다. 우리는 거래를 할 필요가 있었고, 거래하기 위해서는 신뢰를 확고히 해야 했다. 언어는 누군가와 거래할 때 매우 유용하다. 초기 인류 두 사람은 나무로 만든 그릇 세 개를 여섯 다발의 바나나와 거래하기로 합의할 수 있었을 뿐만 아니라 규칙을 정할 수도 있었다. 그 그릇들을 만드는 데 무슨 나무가 사용되었는가? 어디서 그 바나나를 얻게 되었는가? 그 매매 거래는 몸짓, 그리고 헷갈리게 하는 시끄러운 소리만 사용해서는 거의 불가능했을 것이고, 합의가 이루어진 조건에 따라 그것을 실행하는 것은 신뢰라고 하는 유대를 만들어 낸다. 언어는 우리를 구체적이게 해 주며, 이것이 대화가 중요한 역할을 하는 그 지점이다.

정답이 보이는 해설

거래가 이루어지기 위해서는 상호 간에 신뢰가 필요한데, 몸짓과 시끄러운 소리만으로는 필요한 합의와 규칙을 정하는 데 어려움이 있었기 때문에 대화를 통해 이러한 것들이 가능하게 되었다는 내용의 글이며 이러한 거래는 곧 경제를 의미하므로, 빈칸에 들어갈 말로 가장 적절한 것은 ⑤ '경제적인 이유로 언어를 발달시켰다'이다.

선택지 완벽 분석

① used body language to communicate 의사소통을 위해 몸짓 언어를 사용했다
함정 의사소통을 위해 몸짓 언어를 사용했을 것이라는 언급은 있지만, 결국에는 거래상의 신뢰를 위해 유용한 전달 도구인 언어를 발달시켰다는 내용이므로 정답이 될 수 없다.

② instinctively knew who to depend on 누구를 믿을지 본능적으로 알았다

③ often changed rules for their own needs 자신들만의 필요를 위해 종종 규칙을 바꿨다

④ lived independently for their own survival 자신들만의 생존을 위해 독립적으로 살았다

⑤ developed language for economic reasons 경제적인 이유로 언어를 발달시켰다

필수 어휘

evolutionary 진화의   biologist 생물학자   argue 주장하다, 다투다
trade 거래하다; 거래, 교역   deal 거래, (사업상의) 합의   confusing 헷갈리게 하는
term 조건   bond 유대, 결속   specific 구체적인   role 역할

19 정답 ①

In a culture where there is a belief that you can have anything you truly want, there is no problem in choosing. Many cultures, however, do not maintain this belief. In fact, many people do not believe that life is about getting what you want. Life is about doing what you are *supposed* to do. 단서 The reason they have trouble making choices is they believe that what they may want is not related to what they are supposed to do. The weight of outside considerations is greater than their **desires**. When this is an issue in a group, we discuss what makes for good decisions. ❷ If a person can be unburdened / (from their cares and duties) / and, (just for a moment), / consider [what appeals to them], // they get *the chance* / (to sort out [what is important to them]). Then they can consider and negotiate with their external pressures.

해석

자신이 진정으로 원하는 것은 무엇이든지 얻을 수 있다고 믿는 문화에서는 선택이 문제가 되지 않는다. 그러나 많은 문화는 이러한 믿음을 유지하지 못한다. 사실상, 많은 사람이 삶은 여러분이 원하는 것을 얻는 것이라고 믿지 않는다. 인생은 여러분이 하기로 '되어 있는' 것을 하는 것이다. 사람들이 선택을 하는 데 있어 어려움을 겪는 이유는 자신들이 원하는 것이 자신들이 해야 할 일과 관련이 없다고 믿기 때문이다. 외적인 고려 사항의 비중은 그들의 **욕망**보다 더 크다. 이것이 어떤 집단에서 논의 대상이 될 때, 우리는 좋은 결정을 내리기 위해 논의한다. 만약 누군가가 염려와 의무로부터 벗어나 자신들의 마음을 끄는 것이 무엇인지를 잠시 생각해 본다면, 그들은 자신에게 무엇이 중요한지를 구분할 기회를 가지게 될 것이다. 그리고 나서 그들은 외적인 압박을 고려하고 협상할 수 있다.

정답이 보이는 해설

선택을 하는 데 어려움을 겪는 이유는 자신들이 원하는 것과 해야 할 일이 관련이 없기 때문이고, 이것이 논의 대상이 될 경우에는 해야 할 일을 잠시 제외한 후 마음을 끄는 것이 무엇인지 생각해 본다면 진정으로 중요한 것을 가려낼 수 있다는 내용의 글이다. 즉, 도입부에서 선택의 어려움은 외적인 고려 사항의 비중이 자신들의 욕망보다 더 크기 때문임을 시사하고 있으므로, 빈칸에 들어갈 말로 가장 적절한 것은 ① '욕망'이다.

선택지 완벽 분석

① desires 욕망

② merits 장점

③ abilities 능력
함정 선택에 있어 어려움을 겪는 이유가 사람들의 능력과 관련이 있다는 내용은 언급되지 않았다.

④ limitations 제한

⑤ worries 염려

필수 어휘

belief 믿음   truly 진심으로   maintain 유지하다   consideration 고려 사항
unburden 벗어나게 하다   duty 의무   sort out ~을 가려내다
negotiate 협상하다   external 외적인   pressure 부담

20 정답 ⑤

Research has confirmed that athletes are less likely to participate in unacceptable behavior than are non-athletes. However, moral reasoning and good sporting behavior seem to decline as athletes

progress to higher competitive levels, in part because of the increased emphasis on winning. Thus winning can be **a double-edged sword** in teaching character development. 단서1 Some 이기고
athletes may want to win so much that they lie, cheat, and break 싶은 마음이 부정적 인격을 키움
team rules. They may develop undesirable character traits that can enhance their ability to win in the short term. 단서2 However, when 부정직한 방식으로
athletes resist the temptation to win in a dishonest way, they can 이기려는 유혹을 이겨 내면 긍정적인 인성을 발달시킬 수 있음
develop positive character traits that last a lifetime. ✪ Character is 주어1   동사1
a (learned) behavior, // and a sense of fair play develops / only if
└→부사절의 동사   주어2   동사2   ~할 경우에만
coaches plan [to teach those lessons systematically]. (유일한 상황)
부사절의 주어   명사적 용법(목적어)

해석
연구에 의하면 운동선수는 운동선수가 아닌 사람들보다 용납할 수 없는 행동을 덜 하는 것 같다고 한다. 그렇지만 운동선수들은 부분적으로 이기는 것에 대한 강조가 더욱 커지기 때문에, 더 높은 경쟁적 수준까지 올라감에 따라서 도덕적 분별력 및 바람직한 스포츠 행위가 감소하는 것으로 보인다. 따라서 승리는 인성 발달을 가르치는 데 있어 **양날의 검**이 될 수 있다. 어떤 선수는 너무나 이기고 싶은 나머지 거짓말을 하고, 속이며, 팀의 규칙을 위반한다. 그들은 짧은 시간에 이기기 위해 자신의 능력을 강화할 수 있는 바람직하지 못한 인격 특성을 계발할 수도 있다. 그러나 선수가 부정한 방법으로 이기려는 유혹에 저항할 때, 그들은 평생 동안 지속되는 긍정적인 인격 특성을 계발할 수 있다. 인성은 학습되는 행동이며, 코치들이 그러한 교훈을 체계적으로 가르치려고 계획할 때만 정정당당한 시합 정신이 발달한다.

정답이 보이는 해설
운동선수는 승리에 대한 경쟁이 높아질수록 이기기 위해 거짓말을 하는 등 도덕적 분별력 및 스포츠 정신이 감소하고 바람직하지 못한 행위를 발달시킬 수 있다고 서술하면서, 인성 학습을 통해 긍정적 인격 특성을 계발할 수 있다고 주장하는 내용의 글이다. 또한 승리는 받아들여지지 않는 행동을 덜 하는 동시에 바람직하지 않은 행위를 더 하게 될 수 있는 요인이 된다고 했으므로, 빈칸에 들어갈 말로 가장 적절한 것은 ⑤ '양날의 검'이다.

선택지 완벽 분석
① a piece of cake 식은 죽 먹기
함정 승리의 양면성에 대한 내용이며 이기는 것이 인성 발달을 가르치기 쉽다는 것은 언급되지 않았다.
② a one-way street 일방통행
함정 이기는 것과 인성 발달은 서로 밀접한 연관이 있다는 내용이므로 정답이 될 수 없다.
③ a bird in the hand 손 안의 새
'잡은 새'라는 뜻으로 확실한 것을 의미한다.
④ a fish out of water 물 밖의 물고기
물 밖으로 나온 물고기이므로 어울리지 않는 장소 또는 상황에 있는 것을 의미한다.
⑤ a double-edged sword 양날의 검

필수 어휘
research 연구, 조사; 연구하다   confirm 확인하다   participate 참여하다
unacceptable 받아들여질 수 없는   decline 감소하다   progress 진전을 보이다
competitive 경쟁적인   emphasis 강조   resist 저항하다
systematically 체계적으로

21 정답 ⑤
202103 31번 정답률 55%

단서1 One of the most important aspects of providing good care 동물을 보살피는 데 있어 중요한 것 중 한 가지는 일관성과 예측 가능성임
is making sure that an animal's needs are being met consistently and predictably. Like humans, animals need a sense of control.
~의 느낌[감각]

✪ So *an animal* (who may get enough food but doesn't know [when
주어   관계대명사절의 동사1   관계대명사절의 동사2
the food will appear] / and can see no consistent schedule) / may
관계대명사절의 목적어(의문사절)   관계대명사절의 동사3   동사
experience distress. We can provide a sense of control by ensuring
that our animal's environment is **predictable**: 단서2 there is always 항상 이용 가능한 것들이
water available and always in the same place. There is always food 같은 장소에 있다 → '한결같음'을 의미함
when we get up in the morning and after our evening walk. There will always be a time and place to eliminate, without having to hold things in to the point of discomfort. Human companions can display consistent emotional support, rather than providing love one ~하기보다는
moment and withholding love the next. 주제문 When animals know what to expect, they can feel more confident and calm.

해석
좋은 돌봄을 제공하는 것의 가장 중요한 측면 중 한 가지는 반드시 동물의 욕구가 일관적이고 예측 가능하게 충족되도록 하는 것이다. 인간과 마찬가지로, 동물들은 통제감이 필요하다. 따라서 충분한 음식을 받게 되겠지만 그 음식이 언제 나타날지를 알지 못하고 일관된 일정을 알 수 없는 동물은 고통을 받을지 모른다. 우리는 우리의 동물 환경을 **예측 가능하도록** 확실히 함으로써 통제감을 줄 수 있는데, 그것은 마실 수 있는 물이 항상 있고, 그 물이 항상 같은 곳에 있는 것이다. 아침에 일어날 때와 저녁 산책을 한 후에 늘 음식이 있다. 불편할 정도로 참을 필요 없이 배변할 수 있는 시간과 장소가 늘 있을 것이다. 사람 친구가 한순간에는 애정을 주다가 그다음에는 애정을 주지 않는 것보다는 일관된 정서적 지지를 보일 수 있다. 무엇을 기대할 것인지를 알 때, 동물들은 더 많은 자신감과 평온함을 느낄 수 있다.

정답이 보이는 해설
동물에게 좋은 보살핌을 주기 위해서는 동물의 요구를 일관성 있고 예측 가능하게 충족시켜야 한다는 내용의 글이고, 빈칸 다음에 우리가 동물에게 제공할 수 있는 환경의 사례를 들고 있으므로, 빈칸에 들어갈 말로 가장 적절한 것은 ⑤ '예측 가능하도록'이다.

선택지 완벽 분석
① silent 조용하도록
② natural 자연적이도록
함정 동물에게 통제감을 주려면 동물 환경을 자연 그대로의 상태로 만드는 것이라는 설명은 없으므로 정답이 될 수 없다.
③ isolated 고립되도록
④ dynamic 활동적이도록
⑤ predictable 예측 가능하도록

필수 어휘
aspect 측면   make sure 확실히 하다   consistently 일관되게
predictably 예측 가능하게   sense 느낌   distress 고통, 괴로움
ensure ~을 보장하다   get up 일어나다   hold ~ in ~을 참다
discomfort 불편함   companion 친구, 동반자   display 보이다, 나타내다
emotional 정서적인   confident 자신감이 있는, 자신만만한

22 정답 ④
202103 32번 정답률 76%

단서1 When a child is upset, the easiest and quickest way to calm 아이가 화가 났을 때 그것(emotions)을 다스릴(manage) 수 있는 쉽고 빠른 방법에 대해
them down is to give them food. ✪ This acts as a distraction / (from 언급함   주어 동사1   └→ 형용사적 용법
the feelings they are having), / gives them *something* (to do with └ 목적격 관계대명사 that 생략 동사2 간접목적어   직접목적어
their hands and mouth) / and shifts their attention from [whatever 동사3   복합관계대명사

was upsetting them]. If the food chosen is also seen as a treat such as ~와 같은 sweets or a biscuit, then the child will feel 'treated' and happier. In the shorter term using food like this is effective. But in the longer term it can be harmful as we quickly learn that food is a good way to **manage emotions**. 단서2 Then as we go through life, whenever 우리가 감정상의 어려움을 느낄 때마다 그것을 달래기 위해 we feel annoyed, anxious or even just bored, we turn to food to 음식에 의존함 ~에 의존하다 make ourselves feel better.

아이가 화가 났을 때, 그들을 진정시키는 가장 쉽고 빠른 방법은 먹을 것을 주는 것이다. 이것은 아이가 느끼고 있는 감정으로부터 그들의 주의를 돌리는 역할을 하고, 그들에게 손과 입으로 할 수 있는 어떤 것을 제공하며, 자신들을 화나게 하는 것이 무엇이든 그것으로부터 그들의 주의를 옮겨 가게 한다. 또한 선택된 음식이 사탕이나 비스킷 같은 특별한 먹거리로 여겨지면, 그 아이는 '특별한 대접을 받은' 것으로 느끼고 기분이 더 좋아질 것이다. 이처럼 음식을 이용하는 것은 단기적으로는 효과적이다. 그렇지만 음식이 **감정을 다스리는** 좋은 방법이라는 것을 우리가 곧 알게 되기 때문에 그것은 장기적으로는 해가 될 수 있다. 또한 우리가 살아가면서 짜증이 나거나 불안하거나 또는 심지어 그저 지루함을 느낄 때마다, 우리 자신의 기분을 더 좋게 만들기 위해 우리는 음식에 의존한다.

정답이 보이는 해설
감정 조절에 음식을 이용하는 것은 감정을 통제하는 좋은 방법이고 단기적으로는 효과적이지만, 장기적으로 해로울 수 있다는 내용의 글이다. 따라서 빈칸에 들어갈 말로 가장 적절한 것은 ④ '감정을 다스리는'이다.

선택지 완벽 분석
① make friends 친구를 사귀는
② learn etiquettes 예절을 익히는
③ improve memory 기억력을 향상시키는
기억력 향상에 대한 내용은 언급되지 않았다.
④ manage emotions 감정을 다스리는
⑤ celebrate achievements 성과를 축하하는

필수 어휘
calm ~ down ~을 진정시키다 act as ~으로 작용하다
distraction 주의를 돌리는 것 shift 옮기다, 이동시키다 attention 주의
treat 특별한 먹거리; (특별하게) 대접하다 effective 효과적인 harmful 해로운

23 정답 ②
202011 31번 정답률 50%

✪ There is **nothing more** fundamental to the human spirit / **than**
부정어+비교급+than ~: ~가 가장 …하다
the *need* (to be **mobile**). It is the intuitive force that sparks our
형용사적 용법   = the need to be mobile
imaginations and opens pathways to life-changing opportunities.
It is the catalyst for progress and personal freedom. 단서1 Public
대중교통이
transportation has been vital to that progress and freedom for more
그러한 진보와 자유에서 중요한 역할을 해 옴
than two centuries. 단서2 The transportation industry has always
운송 산업은 사람들을 실어나르는 것 이상의 일을 해 옴
done more than carry travelers from one destination to another. It
from A to B: A에서 B까지
connects people, places, and possibilities. It provides access to what
people need, what they love, and what they aspire to become. In so
~하기를 열망하다
doing, it grows communities, creates jobs, strengthens the economy,
expands social and commercial networks, saves time and energy,

and helps millions of people achieve a better life.

인간의 정신에 **이동의** 욕구보다 더 근본적인 것은 없다. 그것은 우리의 상상력을 자극하고 삶을 바꿀 기회로 가는 통로를 열어 주는 직관적인 힘이다. 그것은 진보와 개인의 자유의 촉매이다. 대중교통은 2세기 넘게 그 진보와 자유에 있어 없어서는 안 될 것이었다. 운송 산업은 언제나 한 목적지에서 다른 목적지로 이동하는 사람들을 실어나르는 것 이상의 일을 해 왔다. 그것은 사람, 장소 그리고 가능성을 연결해 준다. 그것은 사람들이 필요로 하는 것, 좋아하는 것, 그리고 그들이 열렬히 되고 싶어 하는 것에 대한 접근성을 제공해 준다. 그렇게 하면서 그것은 공동체를 성장시키고, 일자리를 창출하고, 경제를 강화하고, 사회와 상업 네트워크를 확장하고, 시간과 에너지를 절약해 주며, 수백만 명의 사람들이 더 나은 삶을 누릴 수 있도록 돕는다.

정답이 보이는 해설
인간의 정신에 있어 매우 근본적인 이동의 욕구는 진보와 자유에 있어 촉매제 역할을 하며, 대중교통과 운송 산업이 인간들의 이동에 중요한 역할을 해 왔다는 내용의 글이다. 따라서 빈칸에 들어갈 말로 가장 적절한 것은 ② '이동의'이다.

선택지 완벽 분석
① secure 안전의
② mobile 이동의
③ exceptional 예외적인
④ competitive 경쟁적인
⑤ independent 독립적인

필수 어휘
fundamental 기본적인, 근본적인 human spirit 인간 정신 intuitive 직관적인
spark 촉발시키다, 자극하다 pathway 통로 public transportation 대중교통
progress 진보, 진전 destination 목적지 access 접근 strengthen 강화하다
expand 확대[확장]하다

24 정답 ①
202011 32번 정답률 52%

Business consultant Frans Johansson describes the *Medici effect* as the emergence of new ideas and creative solutions when different backgrounds and disciplines come together. ✪ The term
주어
is derived (from *the 15th-century Medici family*), / [who helped
동사(수동태)   관계대명사의 계속적 용법
usher in the Renaissance / by bringing together *artists, writers, and other creatives* / (from all over the world)]. 단서1 Arguably, the
르네상스 시대는
Renaissance was a result of the exchange of ideas between these
다양한 집단에서 서로 아이디어를 주고받은 결과였음
different groups in close contact with each other. Sound familiar? If you are unable to diversify your own talent and skill, then **having others around you to compensate** might very well just do the
잘하다, 성공하다
trick. Believing that all new ideas come from combining existing notions in creative ways, 단서2 Johansson recommends utilizing a
인력 배치에서 혼합 활용을 권고함 → 상호 보완이 혁신
mix of backgrounds, experiences, and expertise in staffing to bring
에 필수임을 강조한 것
about the best possible solutions, perspectives, and innovations in business.

기업 고문인 Frans Johansson은 '메디치 효과'를 다양한 배경과 학문 분야가 병

합될 때 새로운 아이디어와 창의적인 해결책이 나타나는 것이라고 말한다. 그 용어는 15세기에 전 세계의 예술가, 작가, 그리고 그 밖의 창작자들을 함께 모아서 르네상스 시대가 시작되도록 도운 메디치 가문에서 유래한다. 거의 틀림없이, 르네상스 시대는 밀접하게 가까운 이 다양한 집단 사이에서 서로 아이디어를 주고받은 결과였다. 익숙하게 들리는가? 만약 여러분이 자신의 재능과 기술을 다양화할 수 없다면, 그때는 **여러분의 주위에 보완할 다른 사람들을 두는 것**이 나을 수 있다. 모든 새로운 아이디어는 기존의 개념들을 창의적인 방식으로 병합하는 것에서 나온다고 믿으면서, Johansson은 기업에서 가능한 최고의 해결책, 전망, 그리고 혁신을 유발하기 위해 인력 배치에서 배경과 경험 및 전문 지식을 혼합하여 활용할 것을 권고한다.

정답이 보이는 해설

전 세계의 다양한 사람들이 모여 아이디어를 교환함으로써 르네상스 시대의 도래를 도운 '메디치 효과'를 예로 들며, 혼자만의 기술과 재능을 다양화할 수 없다면 주변에 보완할 사람들을 두는 것이 효율적이라고 서술하는 내용의 글이다. 따라서 빈칸에 들어갈 말로 가장 적절한 것은 ① '여러분의 주위에 보완할 다른 사람들을 두는 것'이다.

선택지 완벽 분석

① having others around you to compensate 여러분의 주위에 보완할 다른 사람들을 두는 것
② taking some time to reflect on yourself 자신에 대해 생각할 시간을 갖는 것
③ correcting the mistakes of the past 과거의 실수를 바로잡는 것
④ maximizing your own strength 자신의 역량을 최대화하는 것
⑤ setting a specific objective 특별한 목표를 설정하는 것

필수 어휘

consultant 고문, 상담가 describe 설명하다 emergence 출현, 발생
discipline 지식 분야, 학과목 be derived from ~에서 유래하다
bring together ~을 함께 모으다 arguably 거의 틀림없이 combine 결합하다
notion 이념, 개념 recommend 권유하다 utilize 활용하다
perspective 관점, 시각 innovation 혁신, 획기적인 것

14강 2020~2023 빈칸 추론 2 (33~34번)

01 정답 ②

주제문 A key to engagement and achievement is providing students with **relevant texts they will be interested in**. My scholarly work and my teaching have been deeply influenced by the work of (be influenced by: ~에 영향을 받다) Rosalie Fink. ✪ She interviewed twelve adults [who were highly (주어 / 동사 / 목적어 / 주격 관계대명사절 (사람, 선행사이므로 who)) successful in their work], / including a physicist, a biochemist, (전치사(~을 포함하여)) and a company CEO. **단서1** All of them had dyslexia and had had (성공한 성인들 모두 난독증으로 인해 읽기에 상당한 문제가 있었음) significant problems with reading throughout their school years. While she expected to find that they had avoided reading and discovered ways to bypass it or compensate with other strategies for learning, **단서2** she found the opposite. "To my surprise, I found (읽기를 피하고 우회하거나 다른 전략들로 보완할 것이라고 예상했으나) that these dyslexics were enthusiastic readers...they rarely avoided (정반대 결과를 찾아냄 / avoid v-ing: ~하는 것을 피하다) reading. On the contrary, they sought out books." The pattern Fink (그와는 반대로) discovered was that **단서3** all of her subjects had been passionate in (결과1: 모두 개인적인 관심사가 있었음) some personal interest. The areas of interest included religion, math, business, science, history, and biography. **단서4** What mattered was (결과2: 그것을 더 많이 알아내고자) that they read voraciously to find out more. (탐욕스럽게 읽었음)

해석

참여와 성취의 핵심은 학생들에게 **그들이 관심 있어 할 적절한 글**을 제공하는 것이다. 나의 학문적인 연구와 나의 수업은 Rosalie Fink의 연구에 깊이 영향을 받아 왔다. 그녀는 물리학자, 생화학자 그리고 회사의 최고 경영자를 포함해 그들의 직업에서 매우 성공한 열두 명의 성인들과 면담했다. 그들 모두가 난독증이 있었고 그들의 학령기 내내 읽기에 상당한 문제를 겪어 왔다. 그녀는 그들이 학습에 있어 읽기를 피했고 그것을 우회하거나 다른 전략들로 상쇄할 방법을 발견했을 것이라고 알아낼 것을 예상했으나, 정반대를 알아냈다. "놀랍게도, 나는 난독증이 있는 이런 사람들이 열성적인 독자인 것을… 그들이 좀처럼 읽기를 피하지 않는다는 것을 알아냈다. 그와는 반대로, 그들은 책을 찾았다." Fink가 발견한 패턴은 그녀의 실험 대상자 모두가 어떤 개인적인 관심사에 열정적이었다는 것이었다. 관심 분야는 종교, 수학, 상업, 과학, 역사 그리고 생물학을 포함했다. 중요한 것은 그들이 더 많이 알아내기 위해 탐욕스럽게 읽었다는 것이다.

정답이 보이는 해설

성공한 성인들을 면담한 결과 그들은 모두 난독증이 있었지만, 읽기를 피하지 않았고 개인적인 관심사에 열정적이어서 그것들을 더 많이 알아내기 위해 책을 찾아 탐욕스럽게 읽었다는 내용이므로, 빈칸에 들어갈 말로 가장 적절한 것은 ② '그들이 관심 있어 할 적절한 글'이다.

선택지 완벽 분석

① examples from official textbooks 공식 교과서로부터의 예시
② relevant texts they will be interested in 그들이 관심 있어 할 적절한 글
③ enough chances to exchange information 정보를 교환하기 위한 충분한 기회
④ different genres for different age groups 다양한 나이대를 위한 다양한 장르
⑤ early reading experience to develop logic skills 논리력을 개발하기 위한 초기 독서 경험
함정 읽기와 관련된 내용의 글은 맞지만, 논리력을 개발하고자 한다는 내용은 언급되지 않았다.

필수 어휘
engagement 참여 scholarly 학문적인 physicist 물리학자
biochemist 생화학자 bypass 우회하다; 우회 도로
compensate 상쇄하다, 보완하다 opposite 정반대
enthusiastic 열성적인, 열렬한 seek out ~을 찾아내다
passionate 열정적인

④ you ignore feedback about a performance 수행에 대한 피드백을
무시할
수행에 대한 피드백에 관한 내용은 언급되지 않았다.
⑤ it is not accompanied by effort 노력이 수반되지 않을

필수 어휘
intellectual 지적의, 지능의 competence 능력 legal 법률의
brief (짧은) 보고서, 발표 elegant 명쾌한, 정연한 exceptionally 비범하게
witty 재치 있는 define 정의하다 gadget 기기 outstanding 뛰어난
average 평균의

02 정답 ①

202309 34번 정답률 39%

For many people, *ability* refers to intellectual competence, so
refer to: ~을 지칭하다, 언급하다
단서1 they want everything they do to reflect how smart they are
사람들은 자신이 얼마나 똑똑한지를(자신의 능력을) 보여 주고 싶어 함
— writing a brilliant legal brief, getting the highest grade on a test,
writing elegant computer code, saying something exceptionally
wise or witty in a conversation. ★ You could also define ability / in
terms of a particular skill or talent, / such as [how well one plays the
~에 관하여, ~ 면에서   간접의문문(how+부사+주어+동사) 동사1
piano, learns a language, or serves a tennis ball]. Some people focus
동사2   동사3(병렬 구조)
on their ability to be attractive, entertaining, up on the latest trends,
or to have the newest gadgets. 주제문 단서2 However ability may
'능력'이 어떻게 정의되든지 어떤
be defined, a problem occurs when **it is the sole determinant of**
경우에는 문제가 생길 수 있음
one's self-worth. 단서3 The performance becomes the *only* measure
수행이 그 사람의 '유일한' 척도가 되어 다른 것은 고려하지 않음
of the person; nothing else is taken into account. An outstanding
take into account: ~을 고려하다
performance means an outstanding person; an average
performance means an average person. Period.

해석
많은 사람들에게 '능력'은 지적 능력을 의미하기 때문에 그들은 자신이 하는 모든 것
이 자신이 얼마나 똑똑한지를 보여 주기를 원한다. 예컨대, 훌륭한 법률 보고서를 작
성하는 것, 시험에서 최고의 성적을 받는 것, 명쾌한 컴퓨터 코드를 작성하는 것, 대
화에서 비범하게 현명하거나 재치 있는 말을 하는 것이다. 여러분은 또한 피아노를
얼마나 잘 치는지, 언어를 얼마나 잘 배우는지, 테니스공을 얼마나 잘 서브하는지와
같은 특정한 기술이나 재능의 관점에서 능력을 정의할 수도 있다. 어떤 사람들은 매
력적이고, 재미있고, 최신 유행에 맞추거나, 최신 기기를 가질 수 있는 그들의 능력에
초점을 맞춘다. 능력이 어떻게 정의되든지, **그것이 자신의 가치를 결정하는 유일한
결정 요소일** 때 문제가 발생한다. 수행이 그 사람의 '유일한' 척도가 되며, 다른 것은
고려되지 않는다. 뛰어난 수행은 뛰어난 사람을 의미하고, 평범한 수행은 평범한 사
람을 의미한다. 끝.

정답이 보이는 해설
사람들은 다양한 방식으로 정의되는 '능력'이 있다는 것을 보여 주기를 원한다는 내
용의 전반부에 이어 빈칸 문장에서 어떤 경우에 문제가 발생한다고 하였는데, 빈칸
의 바로 다음 문장에서 수행이 사람의 유일한 척도가 되어 다른 것은 고려되지 않는
다는 내용의 부연 설명이 이어지고 있으므로, 빈칸에 들어갈 말로 가장 적절한 것은
① '그것이 자신의 가치를 결정하는 유일한 결정 요소일'이다.

선택지 완벽 분석
① it is the sole determinant of one's self-worth 그것이 자신의 가치를
결정하는 유일한 결정 요소일
② you are distracted by others' achievements 다른 사람들의 성취에
주의를 빼앗길
함정 개인이 다른 것은 고려하지 않고, 수행으로만 평가가 된다면 문제가 된다고 하였고, 다른 사
람의 성취로 인해 주의를 빼앗긴다는 내용은 아니다.
③ there is too much competition in one field 한 분야에 너무 많은 경
쟁이 있을

03 정답 ②

202306 33번 정답률 61%

단서1 Someone else's body language affects our own body, which
보디랭귀지는 신체에 영향을 미침
then creates an emotional echo that makes us feel accordingly. As
Louis Armstrong sang, "When you're smiling, the whole world
smiles with you." If copying another's smile makes us feel happy,
단서2 the emotion of the smiler has been transmitted via our body.
감정은 신체를 통해 전달됨
Strange as it may sound, this theory states that **emotions arise**
이상하게 들릴지도 모르지만
from our bodies. For example, 단서3 our mood can be improved by
입꼬리를 올리기만 해도 기분이 좋아질 수 있음
simply lifting up the corners of our mouth. ★ If people are asked to
조건의 부사절 be asked to-v:
bite down on a pencil lengthwise, / taking care not to let the pencil
~하도록 요청받다   분사구문 take care not to-v: ~하지 않도록
touch their lips / (thus forcing the mouth into a smile-like shape), //
조심하다   분사구문
they judge cartoons funnier than / if they have been asked to frown.
주어 동사 목적어   목적격보어
단서4 The primacy of the body is sometimes summarized in the
신체가 우선함
phrase "I must be afraid, because I'm running."

해석
다른 누군가의 보디랭귀지는 우리 자신의 신체에 영향을 미치며, 그것은 그 후 우리
가 그에 따라 느끼도록 하는 감정적인 메아리를 만들어 낸다. Louis Armstrong이
노래했듯이, "당신이 미소 지을 때, 전 세계가 당신과 함께 미소 짓는다." 만약 다른
사람의 미소를 따라하는 것이 우리를 행복하게 만든다면, 그 미소 짓는 사람의 감정
은 우리의 신체를 통해 전달된다. 이상하게 들릴지 모르지만, 이 이론은 **감정이 우리
신체에서 발생한다**고 말한다. 예를 들어, 우리의 기분은 단순히 입꼬리를 올리는 것
으로 좋아질 수 있다. 만약 사람들이 연필을 긴 방향으로 꽉 물라고 요구받으면, 연필
이 그들의 입술에 닿지 않도록 조심하면서 (그리하여 억지로 입을 미소 짓는 것과 같
은 모양이 되도록), 그들은 인상을 찌푸리라고 요구받은 경우보다 만화를 더 재미있
다고 판단한다. 신체가 우선함은 "나는 두려운 것이 분명하다, 왜냐하면 나는 도망치
고 있기 때문이다."라는 구절로 때때로 요약된다.

정답이 보이는 해설
보디랭귀지는 우리 자신의 신체에 영향을 미치는데, 예를 들면 미소 짓는 사람의 감
정이 우리의 신체를 통해 전달되고, 입꼬리를 위로 올리는 것만으로도 기분이 좋아
질 수 있다는 내용의 글이다. 따라서 빈칸에 들어갈 말로 가장 적절한 것은 ② '감정
이 우리 신체에서 발생한다'이다.

선택지 완벽 분석
① language guides our actions 언어가 우리의 행동을 안내한다
언어에 대한 내용이 아니라, 보디랭귀지가 우리의 기분에 영향을 미칠 수 있다는 내용임에 유의
한다.
② emotions arise from our bodies 감정이 우리 신체에서 발생한다
③ body language hides our feelings 보디랭귀지는 우리의 감정을 숨긴다
함정 보디랭귀지로 우리의 기분을 좋게 만들 수 있다는 내용은 있지만, 그것이 우리의 감정을 숨

④ what others say affects our mood 다른 사람들이 말하는 것이 우리의
기분에 영향을 미친다

⑤ negative emotions easily disappear 부정적인 감정은 쉽게 사라진다

04 정답 ③

주제문 **Restricting the number of items customers can buy**

boosts sales. Brian Wansink, Professor of Marketing at Cornell

University, investigated the effectiveness of this tactic in 1998.

He persuaded three supermarkets in Sioux City, Iowa, to offer
persuade A to-v: A에게 ~하라고 설득하다
Campbell's soup at a small discount: 79 cents rather than 89 cents.
A rather than B: B보다 오히려 A
The discounted soup was sold in one of three conditions: a control,

where there was no limit on the volume of purchases, or two tests,

where customers were limited to either four or twelve cans. 단서1
either A or B: A 또는 B 둘 중 하나
In the unlimited condition shoppers bought 3.3 cans on average,
무제한 조건에서는 평균 3.3캔을 구매함
whereas in the scarce condition, when there was a limit, they bought
제한이 있는 희소 조건에서는 평균 5.3캔을 구입함
5.3 on average. 단서2 This suggests scarcity encourages sales. The
평균적으로   희소성이 판매를 장려함
findings are particularly strong because the test took place in a
take place: 발생하다
supermarket with genuine shoppers. ✪ It did**n't** rely on claimed
부정어 (도치)   not A nor B: A도 B도 아닌
data, / **nor** was it held in a laboratory [where consumers might
동사 주어   관계부사절
behave differently].

해석

고객이 구입할 수 있는 품목의 개수를 제한하는 것은 매출을 증가시킨다. Cornell
대학의 마케팅 교수인 Brian Wansink는 1998년에 이 전략의 효과를 조사했다.
그는 Iowa 주(州) Sioux City에 있는 세 개의 슈퍼마켓이 Campbell의 수프를 약
간 할인하여 제공하도록 설득했다: 89센트가 아닌 79센트로. 할인된 수프는 세 가
지 조건 중 하나의 조건으로 판매되었다: 구매량에 제한이 없는 하나의 대조군, 또는
고객이 4개나 12개의 캔으로 제한되는 두 개의 실험군. 무제한 조건에서 구매자들
은 평균 3.3캔을 구입했던 반면, 제한이 있던 희소 조건에서는, 평균 5.3캔을 구입
했다. 이것은 희소성이 판매를 장려한다는 것을 시사한다. 이 실험은 진짜 구매자들
이 있는 슈퍼마켓에서 진행되었기 때문에 그 결과는 특별히 강력하다. 그것은 주장
된 데이터에 의존하지 않았고, 소비자들이 다르게 행동할지도 모르는 실험실에서 이
루어진 것도 아니었다.

정답이 보이는 해설

뒤의 실험 내용을 보면, 구매량에 제한이 없는 경우에는 평균 3.3캔을, 제한이 있는
경우에는 평균 5.3캔이 판매되었다. 이 시험 결과는 희소성이 판매를 장려한다는 것
을 보여 주는 것이다. 따라서 빈칸에 들어갈 말로 가장 적절한 것은 ③ '고객이 구입
할 수 있는 품목의 개수를 제한하는 것'이다.

선택지 완벽 분석

① Promoting products through social media 소셜 미디어를 통해 제품
을 홍보하는 것

② Reducing the risk of producing poor quality items 불량품을 생산
하는 위험을 감소시키는 것

③ Restricting the number of items customers can buy 고객이 구

매할 수 있는 품목의 개수를 제한하는 것

④ Offering several options that customers find attractive 고객이 매
력적이라고 생각하는 몇 가지 옵션을 제공하는 것

함정 수프의 가격을 약간 더 내리고, 구매 개수를 제한하지 않는 군, 4개만 살 수 있는 군, 12개
까지 살 수 있는 군으로 나누어 실험한 것으로, 고객이 매력적이라고 생각할 몇 가지 옵션을
제공한 것은 아님에 유의한다.

⑤ Emphasizing the safety of products with research data 연구 자
료로 제품의 안전성을 강조하는 것

05 정답 ①

In Lewis Carroll's *Through the Looking-Glass*, the Red Queen

takes Alice on a race through the countryside. They run and they

run, but then Alice discovers that 단서1 they're still under the same
아무리 달려도, 출발했던 그 자리에 계속 있음
tree that they started from. The Red Queen explains to Alice: 단서2

"*here*, you see, it takes all the running you can do, to keep in the
같은 자리에 있으려면, 계속 달려야 함
same place." Biologists sometimes use this Red Queen Effect to

단서3 explain an evolutionary principle. ✪ If foxes evolve to run
진화의 원리를 설명하는 데 이용됨   조건의 부사절
faster **so** they can catch more rabbits, / then only the fastest rabbits
목적의 부사절
will live long enough **to make** a new generation of bunnies that run
부사적 용법(결과)
even faster // — in which case, of course, / only the fastest foxes
~을 물려주다
will catch enough rabbits **to thrive** and pass on their genes. Even
부사적 용법(결과)   ~할지라도
though they might run, the two species **just stay in place.**

해석

Lewis Carroll의 'Through the Looking-Glass'에서 붉은 여왕은 Alice를 시골
을 통과하는 한 경주에 데리고 간다. 그들은 달리고 또 달리지만, 그러다가 Alice는
자신들이 출발했던 그 같은 나무 아래에 여전히 있음을 발견한다. 붉은 여왕은 Alice
에게 "'여기서는' 보다시피 같은 장소에 머물러 있으려면 네가 할 수 있는 모든 뜀박
질을 해야 한다."라고 설명한다. 생물학자들은 때때로 이 '붉은 여왕 효과'를 사용
해 진화 원리를 설명한다. 만약 여우가 더 많은 토끼를 잡기 위해 더 빨리 달리도록
진화한다면, 그러면 오직 가장 빠른 토끼만이 충분히 오래 살아 훨씬 더 빨리 달리는
새로운 세대의 토끼를 낳을 텐데, 물론 이 경우 가장 빠른 여우만이 충분한 토끼를
잡아 번성하여 자신들의 유전자를 물려줄 것이다. 그 두 종이 달린다 해도 그것들은
제자리에 머무를 뿐이다.

정답이 보이는 해설

붉은 여왕과 Alice는 계속 달리지만 출발점에 있을 뿐이고, 제자리에 있으려면 가능
한 모든 뜀박질을 해야 한다는 '붉은 여왕 효과'를 가지고 생물학자들이 진화의 원리
를 설명한다. 여우가 토끼를 잡기 위해 더 빨리 달리도록 진화하면, 가장 빠른 토끼만
생존해 번식하고, 다시 가장 빠른 여우만 번식하므로, 결국 두 종이 진화 경쟁을 한
결과가 빈칸에 들어가야 한다. 따라서 빈칸에 들어갈 말로 가장 적절한 것은 ① '그냥
제자리에 머물 뿐이다'이다.

선택지 완벽 분석

① just stay in place 그냥 제자리에 머물 뿐이다

② end up walking slowly 결국 천천히 걷게 된다

③ never run into each other 결코 서로 마주치지 않는다

④ won't be able to adapt to changes 변화에 적응할 수 없을 것이다

함정 여우도 토끼도 계속 더 빠르게 달려야 살아남을 수 있어서 결국은 같은 상태에 남게 된다는 내용으로, 변화에 적응할 수 없다는 내용은 아님에 유의한다.

⑤ cannot run faster than their parents 그들의 부모보다 더 빨리 달릴 수 없다

함정 진화하면서, 계속해서 더 빠르게 달리게 되므로 부모보다 더 빠르게 달리게 될 것이므로, 정답이 될 수 없다.

필수 어휘

discover 발견하다 still 여전히 biologist 생물학자 effect 효과, 영향, 결과
evolutionary 진화의 principle 원리 evolve 진화하다 generation 세대
bunny 토끼 gene 유전자 species 종

06 정답 ②

주제문 **단서1** Everything in the world around us was finished in
세상의 모든 것은 시작되기 전에 마음속에서 완성됨
the mind of its creator before it was started. The houses we live in,
the cars we drive, and our clothing — all of these began with an
아이디어로 시작하다
idea. Each idea was then studied, refined and perfected before the
first nail was driven or the first piece of cloth was cut. **단서2** Long
be turned into: ~으로 변하다   아이디어가
before the idea was turned into a physical reality, the mind had
실체로 바뀌기 훨씬 전에 마음은 완제품을 분명하게 그림
clearly pictured the finished product. The human being designs his
or her own future through much the same process. We begin with an
idea about how the future will be. Over a period of time we refine
머지않아
and perfect the vision. ✪ (Before long,) our every thought, decision
조화롭게   주어
and activity / are all working (in harmony) (to bring into existence
동사   부사적 용법(목적) ~을 존재하게 하다
[what we **have mentally concluded about the future**]).
bring의 목적어절

해석
우리 주변 세상의 모든 것은 시작되기 전에 그것을 만들어 낸 사람의 마음속에서 완성되었다. 우리가 사는 집, 우리가 운전하는 자동차, 우리의 옷, 이 모든 것이 아이디어에서 시작했다. 각각의 아이디어는 그런 다음, 첫 번째 못이 박히거나 첫 번째 천 조각이 재단되기 전에, 연구되고 다듬어지고 완성되었다. 그 아이디어가 물리적 실체로 바뀌기 훨씬 전에 마음은 완제품을 분명하게 그렸다. 인간은 거의 같은 과정을 통해 자기 자신의 미래를 설계한다. 우리는 미래가 어떨지에 대한 아이디어로 시작한다. 일정 기간에 걸쳐서 우리는 그 비전을 다듬어 완성한다. 머지않아, 우리의 모든 생각, 결정, 활동은 우리가 **미래에 대해 머릿속에서 완성했던** 것을 생겨나게 하려고 모두 조화롭게 작용하고 있다.

정답이 보이는 해설
모든 사물은 아이디어에서 시작했고, 제작 전에 마음속에서 먼저 완성되었다는 내용에 이어, 우리 자신의 미래도 거의 같은 과정으로 설계된다는 내용이다. 미래는 아이디어에서 시작하여 마음속으로 비전을 다듬어 완성된다고 했으므로, 빈칸에 들어갈 말로 가장 적절한 것은 ② '미래에 대해 머릿속에서 완성했던'이다.

선택지 완벽 분석

① didn't even have the potential to accomplish 성취할 수 있는 잠재력조차 없었던

② have mentally concluded about the future 미래에 대해 머릿속에서 완성했던

③ haven't been able to picture in our mind 우리의 마음속에서 상상할 수 없었던
함정 마음속에 미리 완성된 것을 실제로 생겨나게 하려고 모든 것이 작용한다는 내용으로, 상상할 수 없었던 것을 생겨나게 한다고 하면 완전히 반대의 의미가 된다.

④ considered careless and irresponsible 부주의하고 무책임한 것으로 간주했던

⑤ have observed in some professionals 일부 전문가에게서 관찰한 바 있는

필수 어휘

clothing 옷 perfect 완성하다 nail 못 drive (못·말뚝 등을) 박다
cloth 천, 직물 physical 물리적인 reality 실체 product 제품
process 과정 period 기간 vision 비전 decision 결정 activity 활동

07 정답 ③

If you've ever made a poor choice, you might be interested in
~에 관심이 있다
learning how to break that habit. One great way to trick your brain
버릇을 없애다
into doing so is to sign a "Ulysses Contract." ✪ The name of this
life tip / comes from / the Greek myth (about Ulysses, a captain
come from: ~에서 유래하다   동격
[whose ship sailed past *the island of the Sirens*, a tribe of dangerous
소유격 관계대명사절   동격
women [who lured victims to their death with their irresistible
주격 관계대명사절
songs]]). Knowing that he would otherwise be unable to resist, **단서1**
~할 수 없다
Ulysses instructed his crew to stuff their ears with cotton and tie him
유혹에 넘어가지 않으려고 Ulysses는 선원들의 귀를 막고 스스로를 돛대에 묶음
to the ship's mast to prevent him from turning their ship towards the
prevent A from v-ing: A가 ~하지 못하게 막다
Sirens. **주제문** It worked for him and you can do the same thing by
locking yourself out of your temptations. For example, **단서2** if
you want to stay off your cellphone and concentrate on your work,
휴대전화를 멀리하고 싶으면, 앱을 삭제하거나 비밀번호를 설정해서 아예 휴대전화를 보지 못하게 하라
delete the apps that distract you or ask a friend to change your
password!

해석
한 번이라도 좋지 못한 선택을 한 적이 있다면, 그 습관을 깨는 방법을 배우는 데 관심이 있을지도 모른다. 그렇게 하도록 뇌를 속이는 한 가지 좋은 방법은 "Ulysses 계약"에 서명하는 것이다. 이러한 인생 조언의 이름은 저항할 수 없는 노래로 희생자들을 죽음으로 유혹했던 위험한 여성들 부족인 사이렌의 섬을 자신의 배로 항해해 지나갔던 선장 Ulysses에 관한 그리스 신화에서 유래되었다. 그는 그렇게 하지 않으면 저항할 수 없다는 것을 알고, Ulysses는 그가 배를 사이렌을 향해 돌리는 것을 막기 위해 자신의 선원들에게 그들의 귀를 솜으로 막고 그를 배의 돛대에 묶으라고 지시했다. 그것은 그에게 효과가 있었고 여러분은 **여러분의 유혹으로부터 스스로를 차단함**으로써 같은 일을 할 수 있다. 예를 들어, 만약 여러분이 휴대전화를 멀리하고 여러분의 일에 집중하고 싶다면, 여러분의 주의를 산만하게 하는 앱들을 삭제하거나 친구에게 여러분의 비밀번호를 바꿔 달라고 요청하라!

정답이 보이는 해설
나쁜 습관에서 벗어나고 싶으면, "Ulysses 계약"을 이용해 보라고 했는데, 이는 Ulysses가 사이렌의 섬으로 가지 않기 위해 선원들은 귀를 솜으로 막고 Ulysses 자신은 배의 돛대에 묶게 했던 신화에서 유래된 것이다. 비슷한 방법으로 만약 휴대폰을 멀리하고 일에 집중하고 싶다면, 주의를 산만하게 하는 앱들을 삭제하거나 친구에게 비밀번호를 바꿔 달라고 요청하라는 내용의 글이다. 따라서 빈칸에 들어갈 말로 가장 적절한 것은 ③ '여러분의 유혹으로부터 스스로를 차단함'이다.

선택지 완벽 분석

① letting go of all-or-nothing mindset 전부가 아니면 아무것도 아니라는 사고방식에서 벗어남

② finding reasons why you want to change 변화하고 싶은 이유를 찾음
함정 나쁜 습관에서 벗어날 수 있는 방법으로 유혹을 아예 없애라는 내용이지, 변화하고 싶은 이유를 찾아보라는 글은 아니다.

③ locking yourself out of your temptations 여러분의 유혹으로부터 스스로를 차단함

④ building a plan and tracking your progress 계획을 수립하고 진행 상황을 추적함

⑤ focusing on breaking one bad habit at a time 한 번에 하나의 나쁜 습관을 고치는 데 집중함
함정 한 번에 하나씩 나쁜 습관을 고치라는 조언의 내용은 아님에 유의한다.

08 정답 ③

주제문 Our homes aren't just ecosystems, they're unique ones,
hosting species that are adapted to indoor environments and pushing
be adapted to: ~에 적응되다
evolution in new directions. 단서1 Indoor microbes, insects, and rats
실내 환경에서 사는 종들은 화학적 공격에서 살아남는
have all evolved the ability to survive our chemical attacks, 단서2
능력을 진화시켜 옴
developing resistance to antibacterials, insecticides, and poisons.
독에 대한 내성도 발달시켜 옴
German cockroaches are known to have developed a distaste for
be known to: ~한 것으로 알려지다
glucose, which is commonly used as bait in roach traps. Some
be used as: ~으로 사용되다
indoor insects, which have fewer opportunities to feed than their
outdoor counterparts, 단서3 seem to have developed the ability to
음식이 적을 때도 생존 능력을 발달시켜 옴
survive when food is limited. ✪ Dunn and other ecologists have
↱ 목적어절 안의 부사절
suggested [that / as the planet becomes more developed and more
suggested의 목적어절
urban, / more species will **evolve the traits they need to thrive**
목적어절 안의 주절
indoors]. Over a long enough time period, 단서4 indoor living could
실내 생활은 인간의 진화도
drive our evolution, too. Perhaps my indoorsy self represents the
이끌 수 있었음
future of humanity.

해석

우리의 집은 단순한 생태계가 아니라, 독특한 곳이며, 실내 환경에 적응된 종들을 수용하고 새로운 방향으로 진화를 밀어붙인다. 실내 미생물, 곤충, 그리고 쥐는 모두 항균제, 살충제, 독에 대한 내성을 발달시키면서 우리의 화학적 공격에서 살아남을 수 있는 능력을 진화시켜 왔다. 독일 바퀴벌레는 포도당에 대한 혐오감을 발달시켜 온 것으로 알려져 있는데, 포도당은 바퀴벌레 덫에서 미끼로 흔히 사용되는 것이다. 야외(에 사는) 상대방에 비해 먹이를 잡아먹을 더 적은 기회를 가지는 일부 실내 곤충은 먹이가 제한적일 때 생존할 수 있는 능력을 발달시켜 온 것으로 보인다. Dunn과 다른 생태학자들은 지구가 점점 더 발전되고 도시화되면서, 더 많은 종들이 **실내에서 번성하기 위해 그들이 필요로 하는 특성들을 진화시킬** 것이라고 제시해 왔다. 충분히 긴 기간에 걸쳐, 실내 생활은 또한 우리의 진화를 이끌 수 있었다. 아마도 실내 생활을 좋아하는 나의 모습이 인류의 미래를 대변할 것이다.

정답이 보이는 해설

실내 환경은 적응된 종들을 수용하고 새롭게 진화시키는데, 화학적 공격에 대한 내성, 미끼를 기피하는 바퀴벌레, 먹이 부족을 견디는 실내 곤충 등 일부 종들의 실내 번성에 필요한 특성을 진화시키고, 실내 생활은 인간 또한 진화시킨다는 내용의 글이다. 빈칸은 더 많은 종들이 앞으로 어떻게 될 것인지 예측하는 문장이므로, 문맥상 빈칸에 들어갈 말로 가장 적절한 것은 ③ '실내에서 번성하기 위해 그들이 필요로 하는 특성들을 진화시킬'이다.

선택지 완벽 분석

① produce chemicals to protect themselves 그들 자신을 보호하기 위해 화학물질을 생산할
② become extinct with the destroyed habitats 파괴된 서식지와 함께 멸종될
③ evolve the traits they need to thrive indoors 실내에서 번성하기 위해 그들이 필요로 하는 특성들을 진화시킬
④ compete with outside organisms to find their prey 먹이를 찾기 위해 외부 유기체와 경쟁할

판정 실내에서 번성하는 종들은 비교적 먹이가 적어도 생존할 수 있는 능력을 발달시켜 왔다는 내용이지, 먹이를 두고 외부 유기체와 경쟁할 것이라는 내용은 아니다.
⑤ break the boundaries between wildlife and humans 야생 동물과 인간의 경계를 허물

09 정답 ①

주제문 The demand for freshness can **have hidden environmental
costs**. While freshness is now being used as a term in food
marketing as part of a return to nature, the demand for year-round
supplies of fresh produce such as soft fruit and exotic vegetables
has led to 단서1 the widespread use of hot houses in cold climates
lead to: ~로 이어지다   신선함에 대한 요구는 온실 사용과 살충제 사용 등 전면적인 품질 관리로 이어짐
and increasing reliance on total quality control — management
by temperature control, use of pesticides and computer/satellite-
based logistics. The demand for freshness has also contributed to
~의 원인이 되다
concerns about food wastage. Use of 'best before', 'sell by' and
'eat by' labels has legally allowed institutional waste. Campaigners
have exposed the scandal of over-production and waste. ✪ Tristram
└─동격─┘
Stuart, one of the global band of anti-waste campaigners, argues
/ [that, with freshly made sandwiches, over-ordering is standard
↳ argues의 목적어절
practice across the retail sector / to avoid the appearance of empty
↱ over-ordering을 의미상 주어로 하는 분사구문
shelf space, 단서2 {leading to high volumes of waste when supply
초과 주문으로 인해 공급이 수요를 초과하는 경우 엄청난 양의 폐기물을
regularly exceeds demand}].
발생시킴

해석

신선함에 대한 요구는 **숨겨진 환경적인 대가를 지닐** 수 있다. 자연으로의 회귀의 일부로서 신선함이 현재 식품 마케팅에서 하나의 용어로 사용되고 있는 반면, 부드러운 과일과 외국산 채소 같은 신선한 식품의 연중 공급에 대한 요구는 추운 기후에서의 광범위한 온실 사용과 전면적인 품질 관리, 즉 온도 조절에 의한 관리, 살충제의 사용, 컴퓨터/위성 기반 물류에 대한 의존의 증가로 이어져 왔다. 신선함에 대한 요구는 또한 식량 낭비에 대한 우려의 원인이 되어 왔다. '유통 기한', '판매 기한', 그리고 '섭취 기한' 라벨 사용은 제도적인 폐기물 생산을 법적으로 허용해 왔다. 운동가들은 과잉 생산과 폐기물에 대한 추문을 폭로해 왔다. 폐기물 반대 세계 연대 소속 운동가 중 한 명인 Tristram Stuart는 신선하게 만들어진 샌드위치와 함께, 비어 있는 판매대가 보이는 것을 막기 위한 초과 주문이 소매 산업 분야 전반에 걸쳐 일반적인 관행이며, 이것은 공급이 정기적으로 수요를 초과할 때 엄청난 양의 폐기물로 이어진다고 주장한다.

정답이 보이는 해설

신선함에 대한 요구는 겨울철 광범위한 온실 사용으로 이어지고 식량 낭비의 원인이 될 수 있으며 과잉 생산과 초과 주문으로 인해 엄청난 폐기물을 발생시킨다는 내용이므로, 빈칸에 들어갈 말로 가장 적절한 것은 ① '숨겨진 환경적인 대가를 지닐'이다.

선택지 완벽 분석

① have hidden environmental costs 숨겨진 환경적 대가를 지닐
② worsen the global hunger problem 세계 기아 문제를 악화시킬
식량 낭비에 대한 언급이 있을 뿐 세계 기아 문제에 관해서는 언급되지 않았다.

③ bring about technological advances 기술의 진보를 가져올
④ improve nutrition and quality of food 음식의 영양과 질을 향상시킬
신선함의 요구가 가져오는 부정적 영향만 다루고 있으므로 음식의 영양과 질을 향상시킨다는 것은 글의 내용과는 거리가 멀다.
⑤ diversify the diet of a local community 지역 사회의 식생활을 다양화할

⑤ process two pieces of information at the same time 두 개의 정보를 동시에 처리할

필수 어휘

participant 참가자 determine 알아내다, 밝히다 contain 포함하다
repeat 반복하다 trick 속임수 totally 완전히 cleverly 영리하게
process 처리하다 accurate 정확한

---

10 정답 ⑤

202209 34번 정답률 55%

In the studies of Colin Cherry at the Massachusetts Institute for Technology back in the 1950s, his participants listened to voices in one ear at a time and then through both ears in an effort to determine whether we can listen to two people talk at the same time. 동시에 One ear always contained a message that the listener had to repeat back (called "shadowing") while the other ear included people speaking. ✪ The trick was to see **if** you could [totally focus on the main message] / and also [hear someone talking in your other ear]. ~인지 아닌지(= whether) / could에 이어지는 동사구1 / could에 이어지는 동사구2 Cleverly, Cherry found 단서 it was impossible for his participants to know whether the message in the other ear was spoken by a man or woman, in English or another language, or was even comprised of 다른 쪽 귀로 들은 목소리가 남자인지 여자인지, 영어인지 다른 언어인지, 실제 단어로 구성된 것인지 알아차리는 것이 불가능했음 / be comprised of: ~로 구성되다 real words at all! 주제문 In other words, people could not **process two pieces of information at the same time**.

해석

1950년대 매사추세츠 공과 대학의 Colin Cherry의 연구에서, 우리가 두 사람이 말하는 것을 동시에 들을 수 있는지 알아내기 위한 노력으로 참가자들은 한 번은 한쪽 귀로 목소리를 들었고 그다음엔 양쪽 귀로 들었다. 한쪽 귀로는 듣는 사람이 다시 반복해야 하는('쉐도잉(shadowing)'이라 불리는) 메시지를 계속 들려주었고, 다른 쪽 귀로는 사람들이 말하는 것을 들려주었다. 속임수는 사람들이 주요 메시지에 완전히 집중하면서 또한 다른 쪽 귀로 누군가가 말하는 것을 들을 수 있는지 알아보는 것이었다. 영리하게도, Cherry는 참가자들이 다른 쪽 귀로 들은 메시지가 남자가 말한 것인지 여자가 말한 것인지, 영어인지 다른 언어인지, 심지어 실제 단어로 구성된 것인지조차 알아차리는 것이 불가능하다는 것을 발견했다! 다시 말해서, 사람들은 **두 개의 정보를 동시에 처리할** 수 없었다.

정답이 보이는 해설

우리가 두 사람이 말하는 것을 동시에 들을 수 있는지 알아보기 위한 연구에서 한쪽 귀로는 주요 메시지를 들려주고 다른 쪽 귀로는 사람들이 말하는 것을 들려주었을 때, 참가자들은 다른 쪽 귀로 들은 메시지를 전혀 알아차리지 못했다는 실험 결과가 제시되고 있으므로, 빈칸에 들어갈 말로 가장 적절한 것은 ⑤ '두 개의 정보를 동시에 처리할'이다.

선택지 완벽 분석

① decide what they should do in the moment 그들이 그 순간에 무엇을 해야 할지 결정할
② remember a message with too many words 단어가 너무 많은 메시지를 기억할
③ analyze which information was more accurate 어떤 정보가 더 정확한지 분석할
④ speak their own ideas while listening to others 다른 사람들의 말을 들으면서 자신의 생각을 말할

---

11 정답 ③

202206 33번 정답률 47%

In a study at Princeton University in 1992, research scientists looked at two different groups of mice. One group was made intellectually superior by modifying the gene for the glutamate receptor. ✪ Glutamate is *a brain chemical* [**that** is necessary in learning]. 주격 관계대명사절 The other group was genetically manipulated to be intellectually inferior, also done by modifying the gene for the glutamate receptor. The smart mice were then raised in standard cages, 단서1 while the inferior mice were raised in large cages with 열등한 쥐는 장난감 및 사회적 상호 작용이 많은 커다란 우리에서 길러짐 toys and exercise wheels and with lots of social interaction. At the end of the study, 단서2 although the intellectually inferior mice were 열등한 쥐는 유전적으로는 장애가 있었지만 우월한 쥐만큼 잘 수행한 genetically handicapped, they were able to perform just as well as 것이 관찰됨 their genetic superiors. This was a real triumph for nurture over nature. Genes are turned on or off **based on what is around you**. ~에 근거하여

해석

1992년에 Princeton 대학의 한 연구에서, 연구 과학자들은 두 개의 다른 쥐 그룹을 관찰했다. 한 그룹은 글루타민산염 수용체에 대한 유전자를 변형함으로써 지적으로 우월하도록 만들어져 있었다. 글루타민산염은 학습에서 필수적인 뇌 화학 물질이다. 다른 그룹 또한 글루타민산염 수용체에 대한 유전자를 변형함으로써, 지적으로 열등하도록 유전적으로 조작되었다. 그런 다음 똑똑한 쥐들은 표준 우리에서 길러졌고, 반면에 열등한 쥐들은 장난감과 운동용 쳇바퀴가 있고 많은 사회적 상호 작용이 있는 큰 우리에서 길러졌다. 연구가 끝날 무렵, 비록 지적으로 열등한 쥐들이 유전적으로 장애가 있었지만, 그들은 그들의 유전적 우월군만큼 잘 수행할 수 있었다. 이것은 천성(선천적 성질)에 대한 양육(후천적 환경)의 진정한 승리였다. 유전자는 **여러분 주변에 있는 것에 근거하여** 켜지거나 꺼진다.

정답이 보이는 해설

쥐를 두 그룹으로 나누어 유전자를 변형한 실험에서 사회적 상호 작용이 많은 큰 우리에서 길러진 열등한 쥐들은 비록 유전적으로 장애가 있었지만 지적으로 우월한 쥐들만큼 잘 수행했다는 연구 결과를 제시하고 있으므로, 이를 통해 유전자는 후천적인 주변의 환경에 따라 작동한다는 것을 알 수 있다. 따라서 빈칸에 들어갈 말로 가장 적절한 것은 ③ '여러분 주변에 있는 것에 근거하여'이다.

선택지 완벽 분석

① by themselves for survival 생존을 위해 스스로
② free from social interaction 사회적 상호 작용을 벗어나
③ based on what is around you 여러분 주변에 있는 것에 근거하여
④ depending on genetic superiority 유전적 우월성에 따라
함정 이 글은 타고난 유전적 성질보다는 주변 환경의 중요성을 강조하고 있으므로, 유전적 우월성에 따라 작동한다는 것은 글의 내용과 상반된다.
⑤ so as to keep ourselves entertained 우리 자신을 즐겁게 하기 위해

필수 어휘

intellectually 지적으로 superior 우월한; 상급자 modify 변형하다

receptor 수용체 chemical 화학 물질 genetically 유전적으로 inferior 열등한
standard 표준의 interaction 상호 작용 handicapped 장애가 있는
triumph 승리 nurture 양육 nature 천성

12 정답 ②

202206 34번 정답률 48%

☆ Researchers are working on *a project* (**that** asks coastal towns
　　　　　　　　　　　　　　　　　　　　　ask의 간접목적어
[how they are preparing for rising sea levels]). Some towns have
　ask의 직접목적어(의문사절)
risk assessments; some towns even have a plan. But it's a rare town
that is actually carrying out a plan. 주제문 One reason we've failed
　　　　　　　　　～을 수행하다
to act on climate change is the common belief that **it is far away in**
time and space. 단서1 For decades, climate change was a prediction
　　　　　　　　　　　　수십 년간 기후 변화는 미래에 대한 예측이었으므로 과학자들은 그것을
about the future, so scientists talked about it in the future tense. This
미래 시제로 이야기함
became a habit — so that even today many scientists still use the
future tense, even though we know that a climate crisis is ongoing.
단서2 Scientists also often focus on regions most affected by the
　　　　과학자들은 기후 위기의 영향을 받는 지역으로 물리적으로 멀리 떨어져 있는 지역에 초점을 둠
crisis, such as Bangladesh or the West Antarctic Ice Sheet, which
for most Americans are physically remote.

해석
연구자들은 해안 마을들이 해수면 상승에 어떻게 대비하고 있는지 물어보는 프로젝트를 진행 중이다. 어떤 마을들은 위험 평가를 하고, 어떤 마을들은 심지어 계획을 가지고 있다. 그러나 실제로 계획을 수행하고 있는 마을은 드물다. 우리가 기후 변화에 대처하는 데 실패해 왔던 한 가지 이유는 **그것이 시공간적으로 멀리 떨어져 있다는** 일반적인 믿음 때문이다. 수십 년 동안, 기후 변화는 미래에 대한 예측이었기 때문에 과학자들은 그것에 대해 미래 시제로 이야기했다. 이것이 습관이 되어 우리가 기후 위기가 진행 중이라는 것을 알고 있음에도, 오늘날에도 많은 과학자들이 여전히 미래 시제를 사용한다. 과학자들은 또한 방글라데시나 서남극 빙상처럼 위기의 영향을 가장 많이 받는 지역에 흔히 초점을 맞추고 있는데, 그 지역은 대부분의 미국인에게는 물리적으로 멀리 떨어져 있다.

정답이 보이는 해설
수십 년 동안 기후 변화가 미래에 일어날 것으로 예측했기 때문에 우리는 기후 위기가 진행 중이라는 것을 알고 있음에도 기후 변화에 대비하지 않고 있으며, 과학자들은 여전히 기후 변화를 미래 시제로 이야기하고 또한 물리적으로 멀리 떨어진 지역에 초점을 맞추고 있다는 내용이므로, 빈칸에 들어갈 말로 가장 적절한 것은 ② '그것이 시공간적으로 멀리 떨어져 있다'이다.

선택지 완벽 분석
① it is not related to science 그것이 과학과 관련되어 있지 않다
② it is far away in time and space 그것이 시공간적으로 멀리 떨어져 있다
③ energy efficiency matters the most 에너지 효율이 가장 중요하다
④ careful planning can fix the problem 세심한 계획이 문제를 해결할 수 있다
⑤ it is too late to prevent it from happening 그것이 발생하는 것을 막기에는 너무 늦었다
함정 이 글은 기후 변화 발생을 막기에는 너무 늦었다는 것이 아니라 기후 변화 발생을 알고 있음에도 이에 대비하지 않고 있다는 내용이다.

필수 어휘
coastal 해안의 assessment 평가 climate change 기후 변화
common 일반적인 for decades 수십 년 동안 prediction 예측 tense 시제
crisis 위기 ongoing 진행 중인 region 지역
West Antarctic Ice Sheet 서남극 빙상 physically 물리적으로
remote 멀리 떨어진

13 정답 ①

202203 33번 정답률 62%

　Most times a foreign language is spoken in film, subtitles are used to translate the dialogue for the viewer. However, there are occasions when foreign dialogue is left unsubtitled (and thus incomprehensible to most of the target audience). 단서1 This is
　　　　　　　　　　　　　　　　　　　　　　　　　　영화가 그
often done if the movie is seen mainly from the viewpoint of a
언어를 모르는 특정 등장인물의 관점에서 보여질 때 자막이 사용되지 않음
particular character who does not speak the language. ☆ 단서2 Such
　　　　　　　　　　→ 목적어　　　allow A to-v: A가 ~하게 하다　자막의
absence of subtitles allows the audience to feel *a similar sense*
부재로 등장인물의 몰이해와 소외의 감정을 관객들도 느끼게 됨　목적격보어(to부정사)
of incomprehension and alienation [that the character feels]. An
　　　　　　　　　　　　　　a similar ~ alienation을 수식하는 관계대명사절
example of this is seen in *Not Without My Daughter*. The Persian
language dialogue spoken by the Iranian characters is not subtitled because the main character Betty Mahmoody does not speak Persian and the audience is **seeing the film from her viewpoint**.

해석
영화에서 외국어가 사용되는 대부분의 경우에 관객을 위해 대화를 통역하기 위해 자막이 사용된다. 하지만 외국어 대화가 자막 없이 (그리하여 대부분의 주요 대상 관객이 이해하지 못하게) 처리되는 경우가 있다. 영화가 그 언어를 할 줄 모르는 특정한 등장인물의 관점에서 주로 보여지는 경우에 흔히 이렇게 처리된다. 그러한 자막의 부재는 관객이 그 등장인물이 느끼는 것과 비슷한 몰이해와 소외의 감정을 느끼게 한다. 이것의 한 예는 'Not Without My Daughter'에서 발견된다. 주인공 Betty Mahmoody가 페르시아어를 하지 못하기 때문에 이란인 등장인물들이 하는 페르시아어 대화는 자막이 없으며, 관객은 **그녀의 관점에서 영화를 보고 있는** 것이다.

정답이 보이는 해설
외국어 대화가 자막 없이 나오는 경우가 있는데 이는 영화가 그 언어를 모르는 특정한 등장인물의 관점에서 보여지기 위한 경우이며, 자막의 부재로 인해 등장인물이 느끼는 것과 비슷한 감정을 관객도 느끼게 된다는 내용이므로, 빈칸에 들어갈 말로 가장 적절한 것은 ① '그녀의 관점에서 영화를 보고 있는'이다.

선택지 완벽 분석
① seeing the film from her viewpoint 그녀의 관점에서 영화를 보고 있는
② impressed by her language skills 그녀의 언어 실력에 감동을 받은
③ attracted to her beautiful voice 그녀의 아름다운 목소리에 매료된
④ participating in a heated debate 가열된 논쟁에 참여하고 있는
⑤ learning the language used in the film 그 영화에 사용된 언어를 배우고 있는

필수 어휘
foreign language 외국어 translate 통역하다, 번역하다 viewer 관객, 시청자
occasion 경우 target audience 주요 대상 관객 mainly 주로
viewpoint 관점, 시각 particular 특정한 character 등장인물 absence 부재
incomprehension 몰이해

14 정답 ①

202203 34번 정답률 21%

☆ *One dynamic* [**that** can change dramatically in sport] / is the
　　주어　　　　주격 관계대명사절　　　　　　　　　　　　　동사
concept of the home-field advantage, / [in which perceived demands
　　　　　　　　　　　　　　　　　계속적 용법의 관계대명사절(= and in the concept ~ advantage)
and resources seem to play a role]. Under normal circumstances, the
　　　　　　　　　　　역할을 하다
home ground would appear to provide greater perceived resources (fans, home field, and so on). However, researchers Roy Baumeister

and Andrew Steinhilber were among the first to point out that these
competitive factors can change; for example, 단서1 the success
percentage for home teams in the final games of a playoff or World
Series seems to drop. 단서2 Fans can become part of the perceived
demands rather than resources under those circumstances. This
change in perception can also explain why a team that's struggling
at the start of the year will **often welcome a road trip** to reduce
perceived demands and pressures.

해석

스포츠에서 극적으로 바뀔 수 있는 하나의 역학은 홈구장 이점이라는 개념으로, 이 개념에서는 인식된 부담과 자원이 역할을 하는 것처럼 보인다. 일반적인 상황에서, 홈그라운드는 인식된 자원(팬, 홈 경기장 등)을 더 많이 제공하는 것처럼 보인다. 하지만, 연구원 Roy Baumeister와 Andrew Steinhilber는 이러한 경쟁력 있는 요소들이 바뀔 수도 있다고 처음으로 지적한 사람들에 속했다. 예를 들어, 우승 결정전이나 (미국 프로 야구) 선수권의 마지막 경기에서 홈 팀들의 성공 비율은 떨어지는 것처럼 보인다. 이러한 상황에서 팬들은 자원보다는 인식된 부담의 일부가 될 수 있다. 이러한 인식의 변화는 연초에 고전하는 팀이 인식된 부담과 압박을 줄이기 위해 **흔히 길을 떠나는 것(원정 경기를 가는 것)을 환영하는** 이유 또한 설명할 수 있다.

정답이 보이는 해설

스포츠의 홈 이점이라는 개념에서는 일반적으로 자원(팬, 홈 경기장 등)이 경쟁력 있는 요소가 되지만, 우승 결정전 같은 상황에서는 팬들이 자원이 아닌 부담으로 인식될 수 있으며 고전하는 팀은 이러한 부담과 압박을 줄이기 위해 원정 경기를 반길 것이라는 내용의 글이다. 따라서 빈칸에 들어갈 말로 가장 적절한 것은 ① '흔히 길을 떠나는 것을 환영하는'이다.

선택지 완벽 분석

① often welcome a road trip 흔히 길을 떠나는 것을 환영하는
② avoid international matches 국제 경기를 피하는
함정 부담이 되는 홈구장 경기를 피한다는 것이지 국제 경기를 피하는 것과는 관련이 없다.
③ focus on increasing ticket sales 증가하는 티켓 판매에 집중하는
④ want to have an eco-friendly stadium 친환경 경기장을 갖고 싶어 하는
⑤ try to advertise their upcoming games 곧 있을 경기를 광고하려고 노력하는
함정 팬들의 부담에서 벗어나고자 하는 것이므로 경기를 광고한다는 것은 글의 내용과 상반된다.

필수 어휘

dynamic 역학 dramatically 극적으로 concept 개념
home-field advantage 홈구장 이점 demand 부담, 요구
resource 자원 circumstance 상황 competitive 경쟁력 있는
perception 인식 struggling 고전하는 reduce 줄이다 pressure 압박

15 정답 ②

202111 33번 정답률 44%

Over time, babies construct expectations about what sounds they
will hear when. 단서1 They hold in memory the sound patterns that
occur on a regular basis. They make hypotheses like, "If I hear *this*
sound first, it probably will be followed by *that* sound." Scientists
conclude that much of babies' skill in learning language is due to
their **ability to calculate statistics**. For babies, this means that they
appear to pay close attention to the patterns that repeat in language.
단서2 They remember, in a systematic way, how often sounds
occur, in what order, with what intervals, and with what changes of

pitch. ✪ This memory store **allows** them to track, within the neural
circuits of their brains, the frequency of sound patterns / and to use
this knowledge (**to make** predictions about the meaning in patterns
of sounds).

해석

시간이 지나면서 아기들은 자신이 어떤 소리를 언제 들을지에 대한 기대를 만든다. 그들은 규칙적으로 발생하는 소리 패턴을 기억한다. 그들은 '내가 '이' 소리를 먼저 들으면 아마도 그것에 '저' 소리가 뒤따를 것이다.'와 같은 가설을 세운다. 과학자들은 언어를 배우는 데 있어 아기들의 기술의 많은 부분이 그들의 **통계를 계산하는 능력** 때문이라고 결론을 내린다. 아기들에게 이것은 그들이 언어에서 반복되는 패턴에 세심한 주의를 기울이는 것처럼 보인다는 것을 의미한다. 그들은 소리가 얼마나 자주, 어떤 순서로, 어떤 간격으로, 그리고 어떤 음조의 변화를 가지고 발생하는지를 체계적인 방식으로 기억한다. 이 기억 저장소는 그들이 자신의 뇌의 신경 회로 내에서 소리 패턴의 빈도를 추적하고 소리 패턴의 의미에 대한 예측을 하기 위해 이 지식을 사용하도록 해 준다.

정답이 보이는 해설

아기들은 반복되는 소리 패턴에 주의를 기울이며 소리의 빈도, 순서, 간격, 음조의 변화를 체계적인 방식으로 기억한다는 내용이 빈칸 뒤에 제시되고 있으므로, 빈칸에 들어갈 말로 가장 적절한 것은 ② '통계를 계산하는 능력'이다.

선택지 완벽 분석

① lack of social pressures 사회적 압력의 부족
② ability to calculate statistics 통계를 계산하는 능력
③ desire to interact with others 다른 사람들과 상호 작용하려는 욕망
④ preference for simpler sounds 더 단순한 소리에 대한 선호
함정 아기들이 단순한 소리를 선호한다는 내용은 언급되지 않았다.
⑤ tendency to imitate caregivers 돌보는 사람을 모방하려는 경향

필수 어휘

construct 만들다, 구성하다 hold ~ in memory ~을 기억하다
on a regular basis 규칙적으로, 정기적으로 hypothesis 가설(*pl.* hypotheses)
conclude 결론을 내리다 systematic 체계적인 interval 간격 pitch 음조
store 저장소 neural circuit 신경 회로 frequency 빈도

16 정답 ④

202111 34번 정답률 59%

✪ Some deep-sea organisms are known to use bioluminescence
[**as** a lure, to attract prey with *a little glow* (imitating the movements
of their favorite fish)], / or like fireflies, [**as** a sexual attractant to
find mates]. While there are many possible evolutionary theories
for the survival value of bioluminescence, one of the most
fascinating is to **create a cloak of invisibility**. The color of almost
all bioluminescent molecules is blue-green, the same color as the
ocean above. 단서1 By self-glowing blue-green, the creatures no
longer cast a shadow or create a silhouette, especially when viewed
from below against the brighter waters above. Rather, by glowing
themselves, they can blend into the sparkles, reflections, and
scattered blue-green glow of sunlight or moonlight. Thus, 단서2 they
are most likely making their own light not to see, but to be un-seen.

해석

일부 심해 생물은 그것들이 좋아하는 물고기의 움직임을 모방하는 작은 빛으로 먹이

를 유인하기 위한 가짜 미끼로서, 또는 반딧불이처럼 짝을 찾기 위한 성적 유인 물질로서 생물 발광을 사용하는 것으로 알려져 있다. 생물 발광의 생존가(생체의 특징이 생존·번식에 기여하는 유용성)에 대한 많은 가능한 진화 이론이 있지만, 가장 매력적인 것 중 하나는 **보이지 않는 망토를 만드는** 것이다. 거의 모든 생물 발광 분자의 색은 바다 위층과 같은 색인 청록색이다. 청록색으로 자체 발광함으로써 생물은 특히 위쪽의 더 밝은 물을 배경으로 아래쪽에서 보여질 때 더 이상 그림자를 드리우거나 실루엣을 만들어 내지 않는다. 오히려 스스로 빛을 냄으로써 그것들은 햇빛이나 달빛의 반짝임, 반사, 그리고 분산된 청록색 빛에 섞일 수 있다. 따라서 그것들은 보기 위해서가 아니라 보이지 않기 위해서 자신만의 빛을 분명 만들어 내고 있을 것이다.

정답이 보이는 해설

생물 발광을 사용하는 심해 생물에 관한 글로 그것들은 바다 위쪽과 같은 색으로 자체 발광함으로써 그림자나 실루엣을 생성하지 않고 보이지 않기 위해 자신만의 빛을 만들어 낸다고 했으므로, 빈칸에 들어갈 말로 가장 적절한 것은 이를 비유적으로 표현한 ④ '보이지 않는 망토를 만드는'이다.

선택지 완벽 분석

① send a signal for help 도움을 요청하는 신호를 보내는
② threaten enemies nearby 근처의 적들을 위협하는
③ lift the veil of hidden prey 숨은 먹이의 베일을 벗기는
함정 눈에 띄지 않기 위해 자신만의 빛을 만들어 낸다고 했으므로, 숨은 먹이의 베일을 벗기는 것과는 관계가 없다.
④ create a cloak of invisibility 보이지 않는 망토를 만드는
⑤ serve as a navigation system 항해 체계로서 역할을 하는

필수 어휘

organism 생물 prey 먹이 glow 빛; 빛나다 firefly 반딧불이
attractant 유인 물질 evolutionary 진화의 fascinating 매력적인
molecule 분자 creature 생물 sparkle 반짝거림 reflection 반사
scattered 분산된 invisibility 보이지 않음

17 정답 ①

202109 33번 정답률 42%

One big difference between science and stage magic is that while magicians hide their mistakes from the audience, in science you make your mistakes in public. You show them off so that everybody can learn from them. **This way, you get the advantage of everybody else's experience, and not just your own idiosyncratic path through the space of mistakes.** This, by the way, is another reason why we humans are so much smarter than every other species. It is **not** [that our brains are bigger or more powerful], / or [even that we have the ability to reflect on our own past errors], / **but** [that we **share _the benefits_** (that our individual brains have earned / from their individual histories of trial and error)].

해석

과학과 무대 마술 사이의 한 가지 큰 차이점은 마술사들이 자신들의 실수를 관중에게 숨기는 반면, 과학에서는 공공연히 실수를 한다는 것이다. 여러분은 모두가 실수로부터 배울 수 있도록 실수를 드러내 보여 준다. 이런 식으로, 여러분은 단지 실수라는 영역을 거쳐 온 여러분 자신만의 특유한 길(에서 얻은 이익)뿐만 아니라, 다른 모든 사람들의 경험이라는 이익을 얻는다. 한편, 이는 왜 우리 인간이 모든 다른 종보다 훨씬 더 영리한지에 대한 또 다른 이유이다. 그것은 우리의 뇌가 더 크거나 더 강력해서, 혹은 심지어 우리가 우리 자신의 과거 실수들을 되돌아보는 능력을 가져서가 아니라, 우리 개개인들의 뇌가 그들 개개인들의 시행착오의 역사로부터 얻어 낸 이

익들을 공유해서이다.

정답이 보이는 해설

무대 마술에서는 실수를 관중에게 숨기지만 과학에서는 실수를 드러내 보이며 이를 통해 자신만의 경험에서 얻은 이익뿐만 아니라 다른 모든 사람들의 경험이라는 이익을 얻는다고 했다. 또한 이것이 인간이 왜 다른 종보다 훨씬 더 영리한지에 대한 이유라고 했으므로 빈칸에 들어갈 말로 가장 적절한 것은 ① '이익들을 공유해서'이다.

선택지 완벽 분석

① share the benefits 이익들을 공유해서
② overlook the insights 통찰력을 간과해서
③ develop creative skills 창의적인 기술을 개발해서
함정 실수를 공공연히 드러냄으로써 다른 사람의 실수를 통해 배운다는 내용이므로 창의적인 기술 개발과는 관련성이 없다.
④ exaggerate the achievements 성과를 과장해서
⑤ underestimate the knowledge 지식을 과소평가해서

필수 어휘

hide 숨기다 show off ~을 자랑스럽게 내보이다
reflect on 되돌아보다, 깊게 생각하다 trial and error 시행착오

18 정답 ⑤

202109 34번 정답률 57%

The last two decades of research on the science of learning have shown conclusively that we remember things better, and longer, if **we discover them ourselves rather than being told them**. This is the teaching method practiced by physics professor Eric Mazur. He doesn't lecture in his classes at Harvard. ❂ Instead, he **asks** students _difficult questions_, / (based on their homework reading), / [that **require** them to pull together sources of _information_ / (to solve a problem)]. Mazur doesn't give them the answer; instead, he asks the students to break off into small groups and discuss the problem among themselves. **Eventually, nearly everyone in the class gets the answer right, and the concepts stick with them because they had to find their own way to the answer.**

해석

학습 과학에 관한 지난 20년간의 연구는 만약 **우리가 무언가에 관해서 듣는 것보다 스스로 발견한다면** 우리는 그것들을 더 잘 기억하고, 더 오래 기억한다는 것을 확정적으로 보여 주었다. 이것은 물리학 교수 Eric Mazur에 의해 실천되는 교수법이다. 그는 Harvard에서의 수업에서 (설명식) 강의를 하지 않는다. 대신에, 그는 독서 활동 과제에 기반하여 학생들에게 문제를 해결하기 위해 정보 자료를 모을 수 있게 만드는 어려운 질문을 던진다. Mazur는 그들에게 답을 주지 않는다. 대신에, 그는 학생들을 소그룹으로 나누어 그들 스스로 문제를 토론하도록 요구한다. 결국, 학급의 거의 모든 사람들이 옳게 답을 얻고, 그들이 정답으로 가는 길을 스스로 찾아야 했기 때문에 이러한 개념들은 그들에게 오래 남는다.

정답이 보이는 해설

무언가를 스스로 발견할 때 그것에 관해 듣는 것보다 더 잘, 더 오래 기억한다는 연구 결론을 물리학 교수 Eric Mazur의 교수법을 예로 들어 설명하는 글이다. 단락의 마지막에서 교수에게서 정답을 듣지 않고 정답으로 가는 길을 스스로 찾아야 했을 때 개념들이 오래 남는다고 했으므로 빈칸에 들어갈 말로 가장 적절한 것은 ⑤ '우리가 무언가에 관해서 듣는 것보다 스스로 발견한다'이다.

② understand the technical aspects of recording sessions 녹음 시간의 기술적 측면을 이해해야

③ share unique and inspiring playlists on social media 소셜 미디어에서 독특하고 영감을 주는 재생 목록을 공유해야

함정 소셜 미디어는 기술 혁신이 가져온 변화라고 할 수 있지만 글의 주제는 과거와 달라진 개인의 적극적 음악 선택권이므로 빈칸에 들어갈 말로 알맞지 않다.

④ interpret lyrics with background knowledge of the songs 노래에 대한 배경지식으로 가사를 해석해야

⑤ seek the advice of a voice specialist for better performances 더 나은 공연을 위해 음성 전문가의 조언을 구해야

필수 어휘

technological 기술의 innovation 혁신 availability 이용 가능성
unheard-of 전례가 없는, 아주 유별난 confront 직면하게 하다
countless 셀 수 없이 많은 genre 장르 orient (새로운 상황에) 적응하다[익숙해지다]
filter out ~을 걸러내다 restrict 한정[제한]하다 distributor 배급업자
considerable 상당한

① they are taught repeatedly in class 수업에서 반복적으로 배운다

② we fully focus on them without any distractions 우리가 산만함 없이 그것에 완전히 집중한다

③ equal opportunities are given to complete tasks 과업을 완수할 수 있는 동등한 기회가 주어진다

④ there's no right or wrong way to learn about a topic 주제에 대해 배우는 옳고 그른 방법이 없다

⑤ we discover them ourselves rather than being told them 우리가 무언가에 관해서 듣는 것보다 스스로 발견한다

필수 어휘

conclusively 확정적으로, 결정적으로 teaching method 교수법
physics 물리학 lecture 강의하다 require 요구하다 eventually 결국
concept 개념

19 정답 ①

202106 33번 정답률 41%

Due to technological innovations, music can now be experienced
~ 때문에, ~로 인해
by more people, for more of the time than ever before. Mass availability has given individuals unheard-of control over their own sound-environment. However, it has also confronted them
= mass availability
with the simultaneous availability of countless genres of music, in which they have to orient themselves. People start filtering out and organizing their digital libraries like they used to do with their physical music collections. **단서** However, there is the difference
기술 혁신 이전과 달리 개인이 선택권을 가짐
that the choice lies in their own hands. ✪ Without being restricted
전치사   동명사1
to the limited collection of music-distributors, / nor being guided /
= and not   동명사2
by the local radio program / as a 'preselector' of the latest hits, // the
주어
individual actively has to **choose and determine his or her musical**
동사1   동사2
preferences. The search for the right song is thus associated with
be associated with: ~와 관련되다
considerable effort.

해석

기술 혁신으로 인해, 음악은 이제 그 어느 때보다 더 많은 시간 동안 더 많은 사람에 의해 경험될 수 있다. 대중 이용 가능성은 개인들에게 그들 자신의 음향 환경에 대한 전례가 없는 통제권을 주었다. 하지만 또한 그것(대중 이용 가능성)으로 인해 그들은 무수한 장르의 음악을 동시에 이용할 수 있는 상황에 직면하게 되었고, 그들은 그 상황에 적응해야만 한다. 사람들은 이전에 물리적 형태를 지닌 음악을 수집했던 것처럼 자신들의 디지털 라이브러리를 걸러내고 조합하기 시작한다. 하지만 선택권은 자신이 가진다는 차이가 있다. 음악 배급자의 제한된 컬렉션에 국한되지 않고, 또한 최신 히트곡의 '사전 선택자'로서 지역 라디오 프로그램의 안내를 받지 않고, 개인은 적극적으로 <u>자신의 음악적 선호를 선택하고 결정해야</u> 한다. 따라서 적절한 노래를 찾는 것은 상당한 노력과 관련이 있다.

정답이 보이는 해설

기술 혁신으로 대중 이용 가능성이 증가하여 개인은 자신의 음향 환경에 대해 통제권을 갖게 되었고 이는 과거와 달리 무수히 많은 장르의 음악을 스스로 걸러내고 조합하며 적극적으로 자신의 선호를 선택하고 결정해야 한다는 내용이므로, 빈칸에 들어갈 말로 가장 적절한 것은 ① '자신의 음악적 선호를 선택하고 결정해야'이다.

선택지 완벽 분석

① choose and determine his or her musical preferences 자신의 음악적 선호를 선택하고 결정해야

20 정답 ④

202106 34번 정답률 52%

✪ It is common to assume / [that creativity concerns primarily
가주어   진주어   명사절(assume의 목적어)
the relation (between actor(creator) and artifact(creation))].
between A and B: A와 B 사이
단서1 However, from a sociocultural standpoint, the creative act is
관객이 부재한 창작 행위는 완벽하지 않음
never "complete" in the absence of a second position — that of an
= the absence
audience. While the actor or creator him/herself is the first audience of the artifact being produced, this kind of distantiation can only be achieved by **internalizing the perspective of others on one's**
in order to *do*: ~하기 위해서
work. **단서2** This means that, in order to be an audience to your
다른 사람과 상호 작용함으로써 자신의 창작 활동의 관객이 됨
own creation, a history of interaction with others is needed. We exist in a social world that constantly confronts us with the "view of the other." It is the view we include and blend into our own activity, including creative activity. **주제문** This outside perspective is essential for creativity because it gives new meaning and value to the creative act and its product.

해석

창조성은 주로 행위자(창작자)와 창작물(창작) 사이의 관계와 관련이 있다고 가정하는 것이 일반적이다. 그러나 사회 문화적 관점에서 볼 때, 창작 행위는 제2의 입장, 다시 말해 관객이 부재한 상황에서는 결코 '완전'하지 않다. 행위자나 창작자 자신은 만들어지고 있는 창작물의 첫 번째 관객이지만, 이러한 거리 두기는 <u>다른 사람의 관점을 자신의 작품에 내면화하는</u> 것으로서만 이루어질 수 있다. 이것은 자신의 창작 활동에 관객이 되기 위해서는 다른 사람들과 상호 작용하는 이력이 필요하다는 것을 의미한다. 우리는 '상대방의 관점'을 끊임없이 마주하는 사회에 살고 있다. 그것은 창조적인 행위를 포함해서 우리가 우리 자신의 활동에 포함하고 통합하는 관점이다. 이러한 외부 관점은 창작 행위와 그 결과물에 새로운 의미와 가치를 부여하기 때문에 창조성에는 필수적이다.

정답이 보이는 해설

창조성은 보통 창작자와 창작물 사이의 관계와 관련이 있다고 생각하지만 제2의 입장인 관객이 있어야 완전해진다는 내용의 글이다. 빈칸 다음에서 창작자가 자신의 창작 활동에 관객이 되기 위해서는 다른 사람들과 상호 작용하는 이력이 필요하고 그 상대방의 관점을 자신의 활동에 포함하여 통합하는 것이 창조성에 필수적이라고 했으므로 빈칸에 들어갈 말로 가장 적절한 것은 ④ '다른 사람의 관점을 자신의 작품에 내면화하는 것'이다.

③ had to develop an appetite for new foods 새로운 먹이에 대한 식욕을 키워야 했다

④ often competed with land-dwelling species 종종 육지에 사는 종들과 경쟁했다

⑤ suffered from rapid changes in temperature 급격한 온도 변화에 고통받았다

필수 어휘

ancestor 조상 water-dwelling 물에 사는 relative 동족, 동류
opportunity 기회, 가능성 shelter 거처, 은신처 lung 폐
take a dip (몸을) 잠깐 담그다, 잠깐 수영을 하다 dry out 건조해지다
lay (알을) 낳다 creature 생물 land-dwelling 육지에 사는 adult 성체

선택지 완벽 분석

① exploring the absolute truth in existence 현존하는 절대적 진리를 탐구하는 것

② following a series of precise and logical steps 일련의 정확하고 논리적인 단계를 따르는 것

③ looking outside and drawing inspiration from nature 밖을 바라보며 자연에서 영감을 얻는 것

④ internalizing the perspective of others on one's work 다른 사람의 관점을 자신의 작품에 내면화하는 것

⑤ pushing the audience to the limits of its endurance 청중을 인내의 한계까지 밀어붙이는 것

필수 어휘

assume 가정하다 creativity 창조성 concern 관련되다 relation 관계
sociocultural 사회 문화적 standpoint 관점 distantiation 거리 두기
interaction 상호 작용 confront 마주하다 blend 혼합하다, 섞다
perspective 관점

21 정답 ①

202103 33번 정답률 62%

Scientists believe that the frogs' ancestors were water-dwelling, fishlike animals. The first frogs and their relatives gained the ability to come out on land and enjoy the opportunities for food and shelter there. But they **still kept many ties to the water**. 단서1 A frog's lungs do not work very well, and it gets part of its oxygen by breathing through its skin. 단서2 But for this kind of "breathing" to work properly, the frog's skin must stay moist. ✪ And so the frog must remain near *the water* / [where it can take a dip every now and then **to keep** from drying out]. Frogs must also lay their eggs in water, as their fishlike ancestors did. And eggs laid in the water must develop into water creatures, if they are to survive. 주제문 For frogs, metamorphosis thus provides the bridge between the water-dwelling young forms and the land-dwelling adults.

해석

과학자들은 개구리의 조상이 물에 사는, 물고기 같은 동물이었다고 믿는다. 최초의 개구리와 그들의 동족은 육지로 나와 그곳에서 먹이와 거처에 대한 기회를 누릴 수 있는 능력을 얻었다. 하지만 그들(개구리들)은 여전히 물과의 여러 인연을 유지했다. 개구리의 폐는 그다지 잘 기능하지 않고, 그것(개구리)은 피부를 통해 호흡함으로써 산소를 일부 얻는다. 하지만 이런 종류의 '호흡'이 제대로 이뤄지기 위해서는, 개구리의 피부가 촉촉하게 유지되어야 한다. 그래서 개구리는 건조해지는 것을 막기 위해 이따금 몸을 잠깐 담글 수 있는 물의 근처에 있어야 한다. 물고기 같은 조상이 그랬던 것처럼, 개구리 역시 물속에 알을 낳아야 한다. 그리고 물속에 낳은 알이 살아남으려면, 물에 사는 생물로 발달해야 한다. 따라서, 개구리에게 있어서 탈바꿈은 물에 사는 어린 형체와 육지에 사는 성체를 이어주는 다리를 제공한다.

정답이 보이는 해설

개구리의 탈바꿈에 관한 글로, 물고기 같은 조상에서 시작해 점차 육지에서 사는 능력을 얻었지만 여전히 호흡이나 번식 등의 이유로 물을 필요로 한다는 내용이 빈칸 뒤에 이어지고 있으므로 빈칸에 들어갈 말로 가장 적절한 것은 ① '여전히 물과의 여러 인연을 유지했다'이다.

선택지 완벽 분석

① still kept many ties to the water 여전히 물과의 여러 인연을 유지했다

② had almost all the necessary organs 필요한 기관을 거의 모두 가지고 있었다

---

22 정답 ⑤

202103 34번 정답률 36%

It is important to distinguish between being legally allowed to do something, and actually being able to go and do it. A law could be passed allowing everyone, if they so wish, to run a mile in two minutes. 단서 That would not, however, increase their *effective* freedom, because, although allowed to do so, they are physically incapable of it. Having a minimum of restrictions and a maximum of possibilities is fine. ✪ But (in the real world) / most people will never have *the opportunity* / **either** to become *all* [that they are allowed to become], / **or** to need to be restrained from doing *everything* [that is *possible* for them to do]. 주제문 Their effective freedom depends on actually **having the means and ability to do what they choose.**

해석

어떤 일을 할 수 있도록 법적으로 허용되는 것과 실제로 그것을 해 버릴 수 있는 것을 구별하는 것은 중요하다. 원한다면, 모든 사람이 2분 안에 1마일(1,609미터)을 달릴 수 있도록 허용하는 법이 통과될 수도 있다. 그러나 그렇게 하는 것이 허용되더라도, 물리적으로 그렇게 할 수 없기 때문에, 그것이 그들의 '실질적' 자유를 증가시키지는 않을 것이다. 최소한의 제약과 최대한의 가능성을 두는 것은 괜찮다. 하지만 현실 세계에서, 대부분의 사람에게는 자신이 되도록 허용된 모든 것이 될 가능성이 없고, 할 수 있는 모든 것을 하는 것을 저지당해야 할 가능성도 없을 것이다. 그들의 실질적 자유는 사실 그들이 선택하는 것을 할 수 있는 수단과 능력을 갖추는 것에 달려 있다.

정답이 보이는 해설

법적으로 허용되는 것과 실제로 할 수 있는 것의 차이를 구별하는 것이 중요한데 법이 허용하더라도 물리적으로 할 수 없으면 실질적 자유는 증가하지 않으므로 실질적 자유는 할 수 있는 능력을 가진 것과 비례함을 알 수 있다. 따라서 빈칸에 들어갈 말로 가장 적절한 것은 ⑤ '그들이 선택하는 것을 할 수 있는 수단과 능력을 갖추는 것'이다.

선택지 완벽 분석

① respecting others' rights to freedom 타인의 자유 권리를 존중하는 것
함정 빈칸을 포함한 문장만으로는 의미가 통하지만, 빈칸을 포함한 문장이 주제문이므로 빈칸에는 주제인 실질적 자유에 대한 내용을 완성하는 말이 와야 한다.

② protecting and providing for the needy 도움이 필요한 사람을 보호하고 부양하는 것

③ learning what socially acceptable behaviors are 사회적으로 용인되는 행동이 무엇인지 배우는 것
실질적 자유를 위해서는 용인되는 것을 실제로 할 수 있는 능력이 필요하다고 했으므로 알맞지 않다.

④ determining how much they can expect from others 그들이 다른 사람들에게 얼마나 기대할 수 있는지 결정하는 것

⑤ having the means and ability to do what they choose 그들이 선택하는 것을 할 수 있는 수단과 능력을 갖추는 것

23 정답 ①

202011 33번 정답률 53%

주제문 As much as we can learn by examining fossils, it is important to remember that they seldom **tell the entire story**. Things only fossilize under certain sets of conditions. Modern insect communities are highly diverse in tropical forests, but the recent fossil record captures little of that diversity. Many creatures are consumed entirely or decompose rapidly when they die, so there may be no fossil record at all for important groups. It's a bit similar to a family photo album. ✪ Maybe (when you were born) your parents took lots of pictures, / but over the years / they took photographs occasionally, / and sometimes they got busy and forgot to take pictures at all. **단서** Very few of us have a complete photo record of our life. Fossils are just like that. Sometimes you get very clear pictures of the past, while at other times there are big gaps, and you need to notice what they are.

해석

우리가 화석을 조사하며 알 수 있는 것만큼이나 그것들이 좀처럼 **완전한 이야기를 전달하지** 않는다는 것을 기억하는 것이 중요하다. 생물들은 일련의 특정 조건하에서만 화석화된다. 현대 곤충 군집들은 열대 우림 지역에서 매우 다양하지만, 최근 화석 기록은 그 다양성을 거의 담아내지 않는다. 많은 생명체는 죽을 때 완전히 먹히거나 급속히 부패해서, 중요한 집단에 관한 화석 기록이 전혀 존재하지 않을 수도 있다. 그것은 가족 사진첩과도 약간 비슷하다. 아마도 여러분이 태어났을 때 여러분의 부모님은 사진을 많이 찍었겠지만, 시간이 흐르면서 그들은 가끔 사진을 찍었고, 때로는 바빠져서 사진 찍는 것을 아예 잊었을지도 모른다. 우리 중 우리 인생의 완전한 사진 기록을 가진 사람은 거의 없다. 화석이 바로 그것과 같다. 때때로 여러분은 과거에 대한 매우 명확한 그림을 가지지만, 다른 때에는 큰 공백들이 존재하고, 여러분은 그것들이 무엇인지를 인지할 필요가 있다.

정답이 보이는 해설

화석 연구에서 화석 기록상 공백이 존재함을 기억하는 것이 중요하다는 내용의 글이다. 현대 곤충 집단의 화석이 곤충의 다양성을 담아내지 못하는 것에서 알 수 있듯이 제한된 조건에서만 화석화될 수 있다고 했다. 인생의 완전한 사진 기록을 가진 사람이 없는 것처럼 화석이 과거를 완전히 보여 줄 수 없다고 했으므로 빈칸에 들어갈 말로 가장 적절한 것은 ① '완전한 이야기를 전달하지'이다.

선택지 완벽 분석

① tell the entire story 완전한 이야기를 전달하지
② require further study 추가적인 연구가 필요하지
③ teach us a wrong lesson 우리에게 잘못된 교훈을 가르치지
④ change their original traits 그것들의 원래 특성을 바꾸지
⑤ make room for imagination 상상의 여지를 만들지

24 정답 ③

202011 34번 정답률 35%

Back in 1996, an American airline was faced with an interesting problem. At a time when most other airlines were losing money or going under, over 100 cities were begging the company to service their locations. However, that's not the interesting part. ✪ [What's interesting] is / [that the company turned down over 95 percent (of those offers) / and began serving only four new locations]. It turned down tremendous growth because **company leadership had set an upper limit for growth.** **단서** Sure, its executives wanted to grow each year, but they didn't want to grow too much. Unlike other famous companies, they wanted to set their own pace, one that could be sustained in the long term. By doing this, they established a safety margin for growth that helped them continue to thrive at a time when the other airlines were flailing.

해석

1996년에 한 미국 항공사가 흥미로운 문제에 직면했다. 대부분의 다른 항공사들이 손해를 보거나 도산하던 시기에, 100개가 넘는 도시가 그 회사에 그들의 지역에 취항할 것을 부탁하고 있었다. 하지만, 그것이 흥미로운 부분은 아니다. 흥미로운 것은 회사는 그 제안의 95퍼센트 넘게 거절했고 네 개의 새로운 지역만 취항을 시작했다는 점이다. 그것은 엄청난 성장을 거절했는데 **회사 수뇌부가 성장의 상한치를 설정했기** 때문이다. 물론, 그 경영진들은 매년 성장하기를 원했지만, 너무 많이 성장하는 것을 원하지는 않았다. 다른 유명한 회사들과 달리, 그들은 장기간 지속될 수 있는 것인 자신만의 속도를 정하기를 원했다. 이렇게 함으로써 그들은 다른 항공사들이 몹시 흔들리던 시기에 그들이 계속 번창하도록 도운 성장의 안전 여유를 설정했다.

정답이 보이는 해설

한 항공사의 장기적 성공 방안인 성장의 안전 여유 설정에 관한 글이다. 항공사에 많은 도시가 취항을 요청했지만 대부분 거절한 이유는 너무 많이 성장하기보다 장기간 성장을 지속할 수 있는 자신만의 속도를 정하기를 원했다고 했으므로 빈칸에 들어갈 말로 가장 적절한 것은 ③ '회사 수뇌부가 성장의 상한치를 설정했기'이다.

선택지 완벽 분석

① it was being faced with serious financial crises 심각한 재정 위기에 직면해 있었기
② there was no specific long-term plan on marketing 마케팅에 대한 구체적인 장기 계획이 없었기
③ company leadership had set an upper limit for growth 회사 수뇌부가 성장의 상한치를 설정했기
④ its executives worried about the competing airlines' future 회사 경영진은 경쟁 항공사의 미래에 대해 걱정했기
　함정 빈칸에는 장기간의 성장을 위한 자신만의 속도를 정하기 원했던 항공사의 결정 내용이 와야 한다.
⑤ the company had emphasized moral duties more than profits 회사는 이익보다 도덕적 의무를 강조했기

14강

빈칸 추론 2

15강 2020~2023 무관한 문장 찾기

01 정답 ②

Sensory nerves have specialized endings in the tissues that pick up a particular sensation. If, for example, you step on a sharp object such as a pin, 단서1 nerve endings in the skin will transmit the pain
피부의 신경 말단이 통증 감각을 뇌까지 위로 전달함
sensation up your leg, up and along the spinal cord to the brain.

① 단서2 While the pain itself is unpleasant, it is in fact acting as
통증 자체는 불쾌하지만, 우리를 보호하는 메커니즘임
a protective mechanism for the foot. ② That is, you get used to
즉, 말하자면   ~에 익숙해지다
the pain so the capacity with which you can avoid pain decreases.

③ ★ Within the brain, nerves will connect to *the area* [that controls
~이내에, 안에   ↱ 아마 ~일 것이다   주격 관계대명사절
speech], // **so that** you may well shout 'ouch' or something rather
so that + 주어 + 동사 ~: 그래서 ~
less polite. ④ They will also connect to motor nerves that travel back down the spinal cord, and to the muscles in your leg that now contract quickly to lift your foot away from the painful object.

⑤ 주제문 Sensory and motor nerves control almost all functions in the body — from the beating of the heart to the movement of the
from A to B: A에서 B까지
gut, sweating and just about everything else.

해석

감각 신경은 특정 감각을 포착하는 특화된 말단을 조직에 가지고 있다. 예를 들어, 만약 핀과 같이 날카로운 물체를 밟는다면, 피부의 신경 말단이 통증 감각을 다리 위로, 그리고 척수를 따라 위로 뇌까지 전달할 것이다. 통증 자체는 불쾌하지만, 사실은 발을 보호하는 메커니즘으로 작용하고 있다. (즉, 여러분은 그 통증에 익숙해져 통증을 피할 수 있는 능력이 감소한다.) 뇌 안에서, 신경은 언어를 통제하는 부분에 연결될 것이고, 그래서 여러분은 '아야' 또는 다소 덜 공손한 무언가를 외칠 것이다. 그것들은 또한 척수를 타고 다시 내려오는 운동 신경에 연결될 것이고, 그리고 이제 재빨리 수축하여 고통을 주는 물체로부터 발을 떼어 들어 올리게 하는 여러분의 다리 근육에 연결될 것이다. 감각 신경과 운동 신경은 심장의 박동에서부터 장 운동, 발한과 그 밖에 모든 것에 이르기까지 신체의 거의 모든 기능을 통제한다.

정답이 보이는 해설

우리가 핀과 같은 날카로운 물체를 밟을 때 일어나는 감각 신경의 반응과 기능을 예시로 들고 있는 글이다. 통증 감각이 다리 위로 척수를 따라 뇌까지 전달된다고 설명하고 있다. 그런데 실은 통증은 우리를 보호하는 메커니즘이라는 내용으로, 통증에 익숙해져 통증을 피할 수 있는 능력이 감소한다는 내용의 ②는 글의 흐름과 관계 없는 문장이다.

선택지 완벽 분석

③ 뇌 안에서, 신경은 언어를 통제하는 부분에 연결될 것이고, 그래서 여러분은 '아야' 또는 다소 덜 공손한 무언가를 외칠 것이다.
함정 '언어를 통제하는 신경'은 앞에 나온 통증에 대한 신체의 반응과 다소 거리가 있어 보이지만, 통증이 생겼을 때 우리가 내는 소리에 관한 내용이므로 글의 흐름상 자연스럽다.
⑤ 감각 신경과 운동 신경은 심장의 박동에서부터 장 운동, 발한과 그 밖에 모든 것에 이르기까지 신체의 거의 모든 기능을 통제한다.
함정 위 예시를 통해 알 수 있듯이 감각 신경과 운동 신경은 신체의 모든 기능을 통제하고 있으므로 글의 흐름상 자연스럽다.

필수 어휘

sensory 감각의   nerve 신경   tissue (세포들로 이뤄진) 조직
sensation 감각, 느낌   transmit 전달하다, 보내다   protective 보호하는
capacity 능력   contract 수축하다   function 기능   movement 움직임

02 정답 ④

주제문 Although technology has the potential to increase
↱ ~에 부정적인 영향을 미치다
productivity, 단서1 it can also have a negative impact on
기술은 생산성에 부정적인 영향을 미칠 수 있음
productivity. For example, in many office environments workers sit at desks with computers and have access to the internet. ① They are
~에 접속하다
able to check their personal e-mails and use social media whenever
↱ 인터넷 기술은 일하는 것을 방해하고 생산성을 떨어뜨릴 수 있음
they want to. ② 단서2 This can stop them from doing their work and
그들이 원할 때는 언제든지   ↱ 동명사 주어
make them less productive. ③ ★ 단서3 Introducing new technology
신기술의 도입도 생산에 부정적인 영향을
/ can also have a negative impact on production // when it causes
미칠 수 있음   시간의 부사절 ↱ 절의 동사1
a change to the production process / or requires workers to learn a
↱ 절의 동사2
new system. ④ Using technology can enable businesses to produce
enable A to-v: A가 ~할 수 있게 하다
more goods and to get more out of the other factors of production.

⑤ 단서4 Learning to use new technology can be time consuming and
신기술을 배우는 것은 시간이 걸리고 스트레스를 줄 수 있음
stressful for workers and this can cause a decline in productivity.

해석

기술은 생산성을 높일 수 있는 잠재력을 가지고 있지만, 또한 생산성에 부정적인 영향을 미칠 수 있다. 예를 들어, 많은 사무실 환경에서 직원들은 컴퓨터가 있는 책상에 앉아 인터넷에 접속한다. 그들은 원할 때마다 개인 이메일을 확인하고 소셜 미디어를 사용할 수 있다. 이것은 그들이 일하는 것을 방해하고 그들의 생산성을 떨어뜨리게 할 수 있다. 또한 새로운 기술을 도입하는 것은 생산 공정에 변화를 야기하거나 직원들에게 새로운 시스템을 배우도록 요구할 때 생산에 부정적인 영향을 미칠 수 있다. (기술을 사용하는 것은 기업이 더 많은 제품을 생산하고 다른 생산 요소로부터 더 많은 것을 얻게 할 수 있다.) 새로운 기술을 사용하는 것을 배우는 것은 직원들에게 시간이 많이 걸리고 스트레스를 줄 수 있으며 이것은 생산성 저하를 야기할 수 있다.

정답이 보이는 해설

기술이 생산성을 높일 수도 있지만, 반대로 생산성에 부정적인 영향을 미칠 수 있다는 내용으로, 주로 부정적인 영향에 관한 것들을 언급하고 있다. 따라서 기술의 사용이 더 많은 제품 생산과 다른 생산 요소로부터 더 많은 것을 얻을 수 있다는 ④는 글의 흐름과 관계 없는 문장이다.

선택지 완벽 분석

① 그들은 원할 때마다 개인 이메일을 확인하고 소셜 미디어를 사용할 수 있다.
함정 이 문장은 기술의 좋은 면을 이야기하지만, 그 뒤에, '이것이 일하는 것을 방해하고 생산성을 떨어뜨리게 할 수 있다'는 것을 언급하기 위함이라는 데에 유의한다.

필수 어휘

potential 잠재력   productivity 생산성   environment 환경   personal 개인적인
productive 생산적인   introduce 도입하다   production 생산
process 공정(工程)   require 요구하다   time consuming 시간이 많이 걸리는
decline 감소

03 정답 ④

주제문 단서1 *Whose* story it is affects *what* the story is. 단서2
'누구의' 이야기인지가 '무슨' 이야기인지에 영향을 미침
Change the main character, and the focus of the story must also
주인공이 바뀌면 이야기의 초점도 바뀜
change. If we look at the events through another character's eyes, we will interpret them differently. ① We'll place our sympathies
place one's sympathies with: ~에 공감하다
with someone new. ② ★ When *the conflict* arises [that is the
주격 관계대명사절
heart of the story], // we will be praying for a different outcome.
~을 간절히 바라다

③ Consider, for example, [단서3] how the tale of Cinderella would
_{신데렐라가 아니라 의붓자매가 주인공이라면 어떨까?}
shift if told from the viewpoint of an evil stepsister. ④ We know

Cinderella's kingdom does not exist, but we willingly go there

anyway. ⑤ *Gone with the Wind* is Scarlett O'Hara's story, but [단서4]

what if we were shown the same events from the viewpoint of Rhett
_{'바람과 함께 사라지다'의 주인공이 바뀌면 어떨지?   ~의 관점에서}
Butler or Melanie Wilkes?

해석

'누구의' 이야기인지가 '무슨' 이야기인지에 영향을 미친다. 주인공을 바꿔라, 그러면
이야기의 초점도 틀림없이 바뀐다. 만약 우리가 또 다른 등장인물의 눈을 통해 사건
을 본다면, 우리는 사건을 다르게 해석할 것이다. 우리는 새로운 누군가에게 공감할
것이다. 이야기의 핵심인 갈등이 발생할 때, 우리는 다른 결과를 간절히 바랄 것이다.
예를 들어, 신데렐라 이야기가 사악한 의붓자매의 관점에서 이야기된다면 어떻게 바
뀔지 생각해 보라. (우리는 신데렐라의 왕국이 존재하지 않는다는 것을 알지만, 어쨌
든 기꺼이 그곳에 간다.) 'Gone with the Wind'는 Scarlett O'Hara의 이야기이
지만, 만약 같은 사건이 Rhett Butler나 Melanie Wilkes의 관점에서 우리에게 제
시된다면 어떠할 것인가?

정답이 보이는 해설

이야기의 주인공이 바뀌면 이야기의 초점도 바뀌어 이야기의 해석, 공감, 바라는 결
말이 달라진다는 내용의 글이다. 의붓자매의 관점으로 제시되는 신데렐라 이야기
와 Scarlett O'Hara가 주인공이 아닌 다른 등장인물의 관점으로 제시되는 'Gone
with the Wind'를 그 예로 들고 있다. 따라서 신데렐라의 왕국이 존재하지는 않
지만, 어쨌든 기꺼이 그곳에 간다는 ④는 글의 흐름과 관계 없는 문장이다.

선택지 완벽 분석

⑤ 'Gone with the Wind'는 Scarlett O'Hara의 이야기이지만, 만약 같은 사
건이 Rhett Butler나 Melanie Wilkes의 관점에서 우리에게 제시된다면 어
떠할 것인가?

함정 '바람과 함께 사라지다'의 예는 신데렐라의 예시인 ③ 바로 뒤에 이어지는 것이 글의 흐름상
자연스럽다.

필수 어휘

affect 영향을 미치다   main character 주인공   focus 초점   event 사건
character 등장인물   interpret 해석하다   conflict 갈등   arise 발생하다
outcome 결과   consider 생각해 보다   tale 이야기   shift 바꾸다
viewpoint 관점   evil 사악한   stepsister 의붓자매   kingdom 왕국
exist 존재하다   willingly 기꺼이

04 정답 ④

202211 35번 정답률 71%

주제문 Developing a personal engagement with [단서1] poetry
_{많은, 다수의   시에는 많은}
brings a number of benefits to you as an individual, in both a
_{이점이 있음   both A and B: A와 B 둘 다}
personal and a professional capacity. ① [단서2] Writing poetry has
_{시를 쓰는 것은 신체적, 정신적}
been shown to have physical and mental benefits, with expressive
_{이점이 있음}
writing found to improve immune system and lung function,

diminish psychological distress, and enhance relationships. ② ★
_{부사적 용법(목적) - 3개의 동사가 to에 연결}
Poetry has (long) been used / (to aid different mental health needs,
_{be used to-v: ~하기 위해 사용되다}
/ develop empathy, / and reconsider our relationship with both
_{(to) 생략   (to) 생략}
natural and built environments). ③ Poetry is also an incredibly

effective way of actively targeting [단서3] the cognitive development
_{시는 인지, 생산성, 창의성도 향상시킴}
period, improving your productivity and scientific creativity in the

process. ④ Poetry is considered to be an easy and useful means of
_{be considered to: ~라고 여겨지다}
expressing emotions, but you fall into frustration when you realize

---

its complexity. ⑤ In short, poetry has a lot to offer, if you give it the
_{간단히 말해서}
opportunity to do so.

해석

시와의 개인적 관계를 발전시키는 것은 개인적인 능력과 전문적인 능력 모두에서 한
개인으로서의 여러분에게 많은 이점을 가져다준다. 표현력이 풍부한 글쓰기는 면역
체계와 폐 기능을 향상시키고, 심리적 고통을 줄이고, 관계를 증진시키는 것으로 밝
혀지면서, 시를 쓰는 것은 신체적, 정신적 이점을 지닌 것으로 보여 왔다. 시는 여러
정신 건강에 필요한 것들을 지원하고, 공감 능력을 개발하고, 자연적 환경과 만들어
진 환경 둘 다와의 관계를 재고하기 위해 오랫동안 사용되어 왔다. 시는 또한 인지
발달 시기를 적극적으로 겨냥하는 믿을 수 없을 정도로 효과적인 방법이며, 그 과정
에서 여러분의 생산성과 과학적 창의력을 향상시킨다. (시는 감정을 표현하는 쉽고
유용한 수단으로 여겨지지만, 여러분이 그것의 복잡성을 깨달으면 여러분은 좌절감
에 빠진다.) 간단히 말해서, 만약 여러분이 시에게 그렇게 할 기회를 준다면, 시는 제
공할 많은 것을 가지고 있다.

정답이 보이는 해설

시를 쓰는 것은 한 개인에게 신체적, 정신적 이점을 가져다준다는 내용의 글이다. 시
의 복잡성을 깨달으면 여러분은 좌절감에 빠진다는 부정적인 내용의 ④는 글의 흐름
과 관계 없는 문장이다.

선택지 완벽 분석

⑤ 간단히 말해서, 만약 여러분이 시에게 그렇게 할 기회를 준다면, 시는 제공할 많
은 것을 가지고 있다.

함정 시는 신체적, 정신적 이점을 지니고 있고, 공감 능력을 개발하고, 또한 인지, 생산성과 과학
적 창의력을 향상시킨다는 ①~③ 문장 바로 다음에 위치해야 함에 유의한다.

필수 어휘

engagement 관여, 관계 맺기   individual 개인   capacity 능력
expressive 표현적인   improve 향상시키다   immune 면역의
function 기능   diminish 감소시키다   psychological 심리적인
distress 고통   enhance 강화하다   aid 지원하다   empathy 공감 (능력)
effective 효과적인   development 발달   opportunity 기회

05 정답 ④

202209 35번 정답률 52%

주제문 The fast-paced evolution of Information and

Communication Technologies (ICTs) has radically transformed the

dynamics and business models of the tourism and hospitality industry.

① [단서1] This leads to new levels/forms of competitiveness among
_{서비스 제공자 간 경쟁 → 새로운 서비스 제공}
service providers and transforms the customer experience through

new services. ② ★ [**Creating** unique experiences and **providing**
_{동명사구 주어(단수 취급)   to의 목적어1}
convenient services to customers] **leads** to [단서2] satisfaction and,
_{to의 목적어2   단수 동사   만족감 및 고객 충성도로}
eventually, customer loyalty to the service provider or brand (i.e.,
_{이어짐}
hotels). ③ In particular, the most recent *technological* boost received
_{특히}
by [단서3] the tourism sector is represented by mobile applications.
_{예: 관광업의 모바일 애플리케이션}
④ Increasing competitiveness among service providers does not

necessarily mean promoting quality of customer services. ⑤ Indeed,
_{반드시 ~인 것은 아니다}
[단서4] empowering tourists with mobile access to services such as
_{각종 관광 서비스 관련 모바일 접근 권한 허용 → 고객 흥미 및 수익 창출}
hotel reservations, airline ticketing, and recommendations for local

attractions generates strong interest and considerable profits.

해석

정보와 의사소통 기술(ICTs)의 빠른 속도의 진화는 관광업과 서비스업의 역동성과
비즈니스 모델을 급격하게 변화시켜 왔다. 이것은 서비스 제공자 간의 새로운 수준/
형식의 경쟁으로 이어지고 새로운 서비스를 통해 고객의 경험을 변화시킨다. 독특

한 경험을 만드는 것과 고객에게 편리한 서비스를 제공하는 것은 만족감과, 결국에는, 서비스 제공자나 상품(즉, 호텔)에 대한 고객 충성도로 이어진다. 특히, 관광 분야에서 받아들여진 가장 최근의 '기술적' 상승은 모바일 애플리케이션에 의해 대표된다. (서비스 제공자 간의 경쟁을 증가시키는 것이 반드시 고객 서비스의 질을 증진시키는 것을 의미하는 것은 아니다.) 사실, 관광객들에게 호텔 예약, 항공권 발권, 그리고 지역 관광지 추천과 같은 서비스에 대한 모바일 접근 권한을 주는 것은 강력한 흥미와 상당한 수익을 만들어 낸다.

정답이 보이는 해설

정보와 의사소통 기술(ICTs)의 빠른 속도의 진화가 관광업과 서비스업을 변화시켰다는 내용으로, 새로운 서비스 제공자 간의 경쟁이 새로운 서비스와 기술적 상승을 가져와 결국에는 고객의 흥미와 그에 따른 상당한 수익을 만들어 냈다는 내용의 글이다. 따라서 서비스 제공자 간의 경쟁이 반드시 고객 서비스 질의 향상을 의미하는 것은 아니라는 내용의 ④는 글의 흐름과 관계 없는 문장이다.

선택지 완벽 분석

② 독특한 경험을 만드는 것과 고객에게 편리한 서비스를 제공하는 것은 만족감과, 결국에는, 서비스 제공자나 상품(즉, 호텔)에 대한 고객 충성도로 이어진다.
①의 '변화된 고객의 경험(transforms the customer experience)'이 ②에서 '독특한 경험(unique experiences)'으로 이어지고 있다.
③ 특히, 관광업 분야에서 받아들여진 가장 최근의 '기술적' 상승은 모바일 애플리케이션에 의해 대표된다.
힌트 관광업 분야의 모바일 애플리케이션의 예로 ⑤에서 관광객에게 호텔 예약, 항공권 발권, 지역 관광지 추천 서비스 등에 대한 모바일 접근 권한을 언급하는 내용으로 이어지고 있음에 유의한다.

필수 어휘

fast-paced 빠른 속도의   evolution 진화   radically 급격하게
transform 변화시키다   dynamics 역동성   competitiveness 경쟁
satisfaction 만족감   loyalty 충성도   boost 상승   promote 증진시키다
empower ~에게 권한을 주다   reservation 예약   recommendation 추천
attractions 관광지   generate 만들어 내다   considerable 상당한
profit 수익, 이익

06 정답 ④
202206 35번 정답률 70%

According to Marguerite La Caze, **주제문** fashion contributes ~에 기여하다
to our lives and provides a medium for us to develop and exhibit important social virtues. ① Fashion may be beautiful, innovative, and useful; we can display creativity and good taste in our fashion choices. ② ★ And in dressing with taste and care, / we represent **both** self-respect **and** a concern for the pleasure of others. ③ There is
both A and B: A와 B 둘 다
no doubt that **단서1** fashion can be a source of interest and pleasure
패션은 우리를 서로 연결해 주는 흥미와 즐거움의 원천임
which links us to each other. ④ Although the fashion industry developed first in Europe and America, today it is an international and highly globalized industry. ⑤ That is, **단서2** fashion provides
↳ ~와 더불어   패션은 우리의 정체성을
a sociable aspect along with opportunities to imagine oneself
시도하는 기회와 더불어 사교적인 측면을 제공함
differently — to try on different identities.

해석

Marguerite La Caze에 따르면, 패션은 우리의 삶에 기여하고 우리가 중요한 사회적 미덕을 개발하고 드러내는 매개체를 제공한다. 패션은 아름답고 혁신적이며 유용할 수 있다. 우리는 패션을 선택하는 데 있어서 창의성과 우수한 취향을 보여 줄 수 있다. 그리고 취향과 관심에 따라 옷을 입을 때, 우리는 자기 존중과 타인의 즐거움에 대한 관심을 둘 다 보여 준다. 의심의 여지없이 패션은 우리를 서로 연결해 주는 흥미와 즐거움의 원천이 될 수 있다. (비록 패션 산업이 유럽과 미국에서 먼저 발전했지만, 오늘날 그것은 국제적이고 매우 세계화된 산업이다.) 다시 말해, 패션은 자신을

다르게 상상하는, 즉 다른 정체성을 시도해 보는 기회와 더불어 사교적인 측면을 제공한다.

정답이 보이는 해설

패션이 사회적 측면에서 제공하는 긍정적인 역할에 대해 설명한 글이므로, 패션이 오늘날 세계화된 산업이 되었다는 내용의 ④는 글의 흐름과 관계 없는 문장이다.

필수 어휘

medium 매개체   exhibit 드러내다, 나타내다   virtue 미덕, 덕목
innovative 혁신적인   self-respect 자기 존중   concern 관심   highly 매우
globalize 세계화하다   sociable 사교적인

07 정답 ④
202203 35번 정답률 61%

Who hasn't used a cup of coffee to help themselves stay awake while studying? Mild stimulants commonly found in tea, coffee, or sodas possibly make you more attentive and, thus, better able to remember. ① ★ However, / you should know [that stimulants
↳ know의 목적어절
are as likely to have negative effects on memory / as they are to
have an effect on: ~에 영향을 미치다   (likely) ↲
be beneficial]. ② Even if they could improve performance at some level, the ideal doses are currently unknown. ③ **단서1** If you are
완전히 깨어 있는
wide awake and well-rested, mild stimulation from caffeine can do
경우에는 카페인의 자극이 기억력 향상에 거의 영향을 주지 않음
little to further improve your memory performance. ④ In contrast, many studies have shown that drinking tea is healthier than drinking coffee. ⑤ **단서2** Indeed, if you have too much of a stimulant, you
자극제를 지나치게 섭취하면 오히려 신경이 과민해지고 수면에 방해가 되며
will become nervous, find it difficult to sleep, and your memory
기억력이 저하됨
performance will suffer.

해석

공부하는 동안 깨어 있는 것을 돕기 위해 커피 한 잔을 이용해 보지 않은 사람이 누가 있겠는가? 차, 커피 또는 탄산음료에서 흔히 발견되는 가벼운 자극제는 여러분을 더 주의 깊게 해 주고, 따라서 더 잘 기억할 수 있게 한다. 하지만, 자극제가 기억력에 이로울 수 있는 만큼 부정적인 영향을 미칠 수도 있다는 것을 여러분은 알아야 한다. 비록 그것이 특정 수준에서 수행을 향상할 수 있다고 하더라도, (자극제의) 이상적인 복용량은 현재 알려지지 않았다. 만약 여러분이 완전히 깨어 있고 충분히 쉰다면, 카페인으로부터의 가벼운 자극은 여러분의 기억 수행을 더욱 향상하는 데 거의 영향을 주지 못할 수 있다. (이와는 대조적으로, 많은 연구는 차를 마시는 것이 커피를 마시는 것보다 건강에 더 좋다는 것을 보여 주었다.) 실제로 만약 여러분이 자극제를 너무 많이 섭취하면, 신경이 과민해지고 잠을 자기 어려워지며 여러분의 기억 수행이 악화될 것이다.

정답이 보이는 해설

커피나 탄산음료에 들어 있는 자극제가 우리에게 미치는 부정적인 영향에 관한 글이므로, 차를 마시는 것이 건강에 좋다는 내용의 ④는 글의 흐름과 관계 없는 문장이다.

필수 어휘

stay awake 깨어 있다   mild 가벼운   soda 탄산음료   attentive 주의 깊은
memory 기억력   beneficial 이로운   improve 향상하다   performance 수행
ideal 이상적인   currently 현재   stimulation 자극   indeed 실제로
suffer 악화되다, 더 나빠지다

08 정답 ③
202111 35번 정답률 66%

Internet activist Eli Pariser noticed how online search algorithms

encourage our human tendency to grab hold of everything that
~을 움켜잡다
confirms the beliefs we already hold, while quietly ignoring
information that doesn't match those beliefs. ① We set up a so-
called "filter-bubble" around ourselves, where we are constantly
exposed only to that material that we agree with. ② **단서1** We
우리는
are never challenged, never giving ourselves the opportunity to
결코 이의를 받지 않고 스스로에게 다양성과 차이를 인정할 기회를 주지 않음
acknowledge the existence of diversity and difference. ③ Creating
a difference that others don't have is a way to succeed in your
~에 성공하다
field, leading to the creation of innovations. ④ **단서2** In the best
우리는 세상을
case, we become naive and sheltered, and in the worst, we become
모르고 보호받거나 극단적인 시각을 지닌 채 특정 세상에 갇히게 됨
radicalized with extreme views, unable to imagine life outside
our particular bubble. ⑤ ✪ The results are disastrous: *intellectual*
isolation and the real distortion (that comes with believing [that the
관계대명사절   believing의 목적어절
little world we create for ourselves is *the* world]).
that절의 주어   that절의 동사

해석

인터넷 활동가 Eli Pariser는 온라인 검색 알고리즘이 우리가 이미 갖고 있는 신념
이 사실임을 확인해 주는 모든 것을 움켜잡는 반면, 그러한 신념과 일치하지 않는 정
보는 조용히 무시하는 우리 인간의 성향을 어떻게 조장하는지에 주목했다. 우리는
우리 자신의 주위에 이른바 '필터 버블'을 설치하는데, 그곳에서 우리는 우리가 동의
하는 그 자료에만 끊임없이 노출된다. 우리는 결코 이의를 받지 않으며, 다양성과 차
이의 존재를 인정할 기회를 스스로에게 결코 주지 않는다. (다른 사람이 갖고 있지
않은 차이를 만들어 내는 것이 여러분의 분야에서 성공하는 방법이며, 혁신의 창조
를 이끈다.) 최상의 경우 우리는 세상을 모르고 보호받게 되며, 최악의 경우 우리는
극단적인 시각으로 과격화되고 우리의 특정 버블 밖의 삶을 상상할 수 없게 된다. 그
결과는 처참한데, 예를 들면 지적 고립과 우리가 스스로 만드는 작은 세계가 '전' 세
계라고 믿는 것으로 오는 진정한 왜곡이 있다.

정답이 보이는 해설

우리는 온라인 검색 알고리즘으로 인해 우리의 신념과 일치하는 자료에만 끊임없이
노출되고 다양성과 차이를 인정할 기회를 갖지 못한다는 내용의 글이다. 따라서 다
른 사람에게 없는 차이를 만드는 것이 성공하는 방법이라는 내용의 ③은 글의 흐름
과 관계 없는 문장이다.

필수 어휘

algorithm 알고리즘 tendency 성향, 경향 grab hold of ~을 움켜잡다
confirm (사실임을) 확인해 주다 so-called 이른바 constantly 끊임없이
challenge 이의를 제기하다 acknowledge 인정하다 diversity 다양성
sheltered 보호를 받는 extreme 극단의 disastrous 처참한 isolation 고립

09 정답 ④

202109 35번 정답률 70%

주제문 The Zeigarnik effect is commonly referred to as the
~라고 언급되다[불리다]
tendency of the subconscious mind to remind you of a task that
remind A of B: A에게 B를 상기시키다
is incomplete until that task is complete. Bluma Zeigarnik was a
Lithuanian psychologist who wrote in the 1920s about the effects of
leaving tasks incomplete. ① She noticed the effect while watching
waiters serve in a restaurant. ② ✪ The waiters would remember an
order, (however complicated,) / until the order was complete, // but
복합관계사
they would later find it difficult to remember the order. ③ Zeigarnik
가목적어   진목적어(to부정사)

did further studies **단서1** giving both adults and children puzzles to
연구 내용: 어른과 아이들 모두에게 완성해야 할 퍼즐을 주고
complete then interrupting them during some of the tasks. ④ They
중간에 과업을 방해함
developed cooperation skills after finishing tasks by putting the
put ~ together: ~을 조립하다[만들다]
puzzles together. ⑤ **단서2** The results showed that both adults and
연구 결과: 완수한 과업보다 완수하지 못한 과업을 더 잘 기억함
children remembered the tasks that hadn't been completed because
of the interruptions better than the ones that had been completed.
= tasks

해석

Zeigarnik 효과는 보통 어떤 과업이 끝날 때까지 그것이 끝나지 않은 과업임을 당
신에게 상기시켜 주는 잠재적인 마음의 경향을 말한다. Bluma Zeigarnik는 1920
년대에 과업을 미완성인 채로 남겨 두는 것이 주는 효과에 대해 쓴 리투아니아 심
리학자이다. 그녀는 한 식당에서 웨이터들이 서빙하는 것을 보고 있을 때 그 효과
를 알았다. 그 웨이터들은 주문이 아무리 복잡하더라도 주문이 끝날 때까지 그것
을 기억했는데, 그들은 나중에는 그 주문을 기억하는 것이 어렵다는 것을 알았다.
Zeigarnik는 어른들과 아이들 둘 다에게 완성할 퍼즐을 준 다음 그 과업들 중 몇 개
를 하는 동안 그들을 방해하는 더 깊은 연구를 했다. (그들은 퍼즐을 맞춤으로써 과업들
을 마친 후에 협동 기술을 발달시켰다.) 그 결과들은 어른들과 아이들 둘 다 방해 때문
에 완성되지 못한 과업들을 완성된 것(과업)들보다 더 잘 기억했다는 것을 보여 주었다.

정답이 보이는 해설

Zeigarnik 효과란 어떤 과업이 끝날 때까지 그것이 끝나지 않은 과업임을 상기시
켜 주는 경향을 말하며, 이를 발견한 심리학자 Zeigarnik가 한 실험을 소개하고 있
다. 퍼즐을 완성해야 하는 과업을 주고 과업을 하는 동안 방해를 하는 실험이었는
데, 그 결과 실험 참가자들은 완성된 과업보다 완성되지 못한 과업을 더 잘 기억
했다는 내용의 글이다. 따라서 퍼즐을 맞춤으로써 협동 기술을 발달시켰다는 내용의
④는 글의 흐름과 관계 없는 문장이다.

필수 어휘

be referred to as ~라고 언급되다[불리다] commonly 흔히
tendency 경향, 성향, 기질 subconscious 잠재적인 task 과업, 과제
incomplete 끝나지 않은, 미완성의 psychologist 심리학자
complicated 복잡한 interrupt 방해하다 cooperation 협동

10 정답 ④

202106 35번 정답률 62%

주제문 Health and the spread of disease are very closely linked
~와 밀접하게 관련된
to how we live and how our cities operate. The good news is that
cities are incredibly resilient. ✪ Many cities **have experienced**
not only A but (also) B: A뿐만 아니라 B도   동사1(현재완료)
epidemics in the past / and **have not only survived**, / but **advanced**.
동사2(현재완료)   동사3(현재완료)
① The nineteenth and early-twentieth centuries saw destructive
outbreaks of cholera, typhoid, and influenza in European cities.
② Doctors such as Jon Snow, from England, and Rudolf Virchow,
~와 같이
of Germany, saw the connection between poor living conditions,
overcrowding, sanitation, and disease. ③ **단서1** A recognition of this
이 연관성이 전염병 확산을 막기
connection led to the replanning and rebuilding of cities to stop
위해 도시 재계획과 재건축으로 이어짐
the spread of epidemics. ④ In spite of reconstruction efforts, cities
~에도 불구하고
declined in many areas and many people started to leave. ⑤ In the
mid-nineteenth century, **단서2** London's pioneering sewer system,
런던 하수 처리 시스템은 콜레라 확산을 막기
which still serves it today, was built as a result of understanding the
위해 만들어짐

importance of clean water in stopping the spread of cholera.

해석

건강과 질병 확산은 우리가 어떻게 살고 우리 도시들이 어떻게 기능하는지와 매우 밀접하게 관련되어 있다. 좋은 소식은 도시들이 믿기 힘들 정도로 회복력이 있다는 것이다. 많은 도시들은 과거에 전염병을 경험했고, 살아남았을 뿐만 아니라 발전했다. 19세기와 20세기 초의 유럽 도시들에서는 콜레라, 장티푸스, 그리고 독감의 파괴적인 창궐이 있었다. 영국 출신의 Jon Snow와 독일의 Rudolf Virchow와 같은 의사들은 열악한 생활 환경, 인구 과밀, 위생, 그리고 질병 간의 연결성을 발견했다. 이 연관성에 대한 인식은 전염병 확산을 막기 위하여 도시 재계획과 재건축으로 이어졌다. (재건의 노력에도 불구하고 도시들은 많은 지역에서 쇠퇴하였고 많은 사람들이 떠나기 시작했다.) 19세기 중반에, 오늘날까지도 사용되는 런던의 선구적인 하수 처리 시스템은 콜레라의 확산을 막는 데 있어 깨끗한 물이 중요하다는 이해의 결과로 만들어졌다.

정답이 보이는 해설

건강과 질병 확산은 우리의 생활 환경과 도시 기능이 밀접하게 연관되어 있다는 첫 문장이 주제문이다. 이어지는 문장에서는 많은 도시들이 과거에 전염병에서 살아남았고, 몇몇 의사들이 이런 연관성을 발견했고, 질병 확산을 막기 위해 도시를 재건하는 노력을 해 왔으며, 그 예로 19세기 중반 런던의 하수 처리 시스템이 탄생했다고 언급하고 있다. 따라서 재건의 노력에도 불구하고 도시들이 쇠퇴하고 사람들이 떠나기 시작했다는 내용의 ④는 글의 흐름과 관계 없는 문장이다.

선택지 완벽 분석

②와 ③은 언뜻 보면 글의 흐름에서 벗어나는 것처럼 보이지만, 몇몇 의사들에 의해 질병과 생활 환경과의 연관성이 발견되었고, 이로 인해 도시를 재계획하고 재건하기 시작했다는 내용으로, ⑤의 내용과 이어지는 내용임을 알 수 있다.

필수 어휘

spread 확산, 전파　operate 기능하다, 작동하다　incredibly 믿기 힘들 정도로
epidemic 전염병　advance 발전하다　destructive 파괴적인
outbreak 창궐, 발생　typhoid 장티푸스　overcrowding 인구 과밀
sanitation 위생　recognition 인식, 인정　pioneering 선구적인

11 정답 ③

202103 35번 정답률 67%

주제문 Today's music business has allowed musicians to take matters into their own hands. ① ☆ Gone are *the days* of musicians / waiting for a gatekeeper (*someone* [who holds power and **prevents** you from being let in]) at a label or TV show / to say [they are worthy of the spotlight]. ② In today's music business, **단서1** you don't need to ask for permission to build a fanbase and you no longer need to pay thousands of dollars to a company to do it. ③ There are rising concerns over the marketing of child musicians using TV auditions. ④ Every day, **단서2** musicians are getting their music out to thousands of listeners without any outside help. ⑤ They simply deliver it to the fans directly, without asking for permission or outside help to receive exposure or connect with thousands of listeners.

해석

오늘날의 음악 사업은 뮤지션들이 직접 일을 할 수 있게 해 주었다. 뮤지션들은 자신들이 주목받을 만하다고 음반사나 TV 프로그램의 문지기(권력을 쥐고 사람들이 들어가는 것을 막는 사람)가 말해 주기를 기다리던 시대는 지났다. 오늘날의 음악 사업에서는 팬층을 만들기 위해 허락을 요청할 필요가 없으며, 더 이상 그렇게 하려고 회사에 수천 달러를 지불할 필요도 없다. (TV 오디션을 이용하여 어린이 뮤지션들을

마케팅 하는 것에 대한 우려가 증가하고 있다.) 매일 뮤지션은 어떤 외부의 도움도 없이 자신들의 음악을 수천 명의 청취자들에게 내놓고 있다. 그들은 (언론) 노출을 얻어내거나 수천 명의 청취자와 연결하기 위해 허가나 외부 도움을 요청하지 않고, 그저 자신들의 음악을 팬들에게 직접 전달한다.

정답이 보이는 해설

오늘날의 뮤지션들은 음반사나 언론사 등 외부의 도움 없이 자신들의 음악을 직접 시청자들이나 팬들에게 전달한다는 내용의 글이다. 따라서 어린이 뮤지션을 마케팅 하는 것에 대한 우려가 증가하고 있다는 내용의 ③은 글의 흐름과 관계 없는 문장이다.

필수 어휘

gatekeeper 문지기, 정보 관리[통제]자　label 음반사　spotlight 주목
permission 허락, 허가　fanbase 팬층　concern 우려, 염려
deliver 전달하다, 배달하다　directly 직접, 곧장　exposure (언론) 노출, 매스컴 출연

12 정답 ④

202011 35번 정답률 66%

The Barnum Effect is the phenomenon where someone reads or hears something very general but believes that it applies to them. ① **주제문** These statements appear to be very personal on the surface but in fact, they are true for many. ② ☆ Human psychology **allows** us to want to believe *things* / [that we can identify with on a personal level] and even seek *information* (where it doesn't necessarily exist), / (filling in the blanks with our imagination for the rest). ③ **단서1** This is the principle that horoscopes rely on, offering data that appears to be personal but probably makes sense to countless people. ④ Reading daily horoscopes in the morning is beneficial as they provide predictions about the rest of the day. ⑤ **단서2** Since the people reading them want to believe the information so badly, they will search for meaning in their lives that make it true.

해석

바넘 효과는 어떤 사람이 매우 일반적인 것을 읽거나 듣지만 그것이 그들에게 적용된다고 믿는 현상이다. 이러한 진술들은 표면적으로 매우 개인적인 것처럼 보이지만 사실 그것들은 많은 사람에게 해당된다. 인간의 심리는 우리가 개인적인 차원에서 동일시할 수 있는 것을 믿고, 나머지에 대해서는 상상으로 공백을 채우면서 정보가 반드시 존재하지는 않는 경우에서조차 그 정보를 찾고 싶게 한다. 이것은 개인적인 것처럼 보이지만 수많은 사람들에게 들어맞는 정보를 제공하는 별자리 운세가 의존하는 원리이다. (아침에 하루의 별자리 운세를 읽는 것은 그것이 남은 하루에 대한 예측을 해 주기 때문에 유익하다.) 그것들을 읽는 사람들이 그 정보를 너무도 간절히 믿고 싶어 하기 때문에 그들은 그것을 사실로 만드는 삶에서 의미를 찾을 것이다.

정답이 보이는 해설

바넘 효과란 사람들이 일반적인 내용을 읽거나 듣고 그것이 자신들에게 적용된다고 믿는 현상으로, 이는 별자리 운세처럼 수많은 사람에게 들어맞는 정보를 읽고 사람들이 자신에게 들어맞기를 믿고 싶어 한다는 내용의 글이다. 따라서 하루의 별자리 운세를 읽는 것이 유익하다는 내용의 ④는 글의 흐름과 관계 없는 문장이다.

필수 어휘

phenomenon 현상　apply 적용하다　statement 진술, 서술　seek 찾다
exist 존재하다　imagination 상상　principle 원리
countless 무수한, 셀 수 없이 많은　beneficial 유익한　prediction 예측, 예견

162 기출의 바이블 고1 영어 독해편

1권 p. 159

16강 2020~2023 글의 순서

01 정답 ②

202309 36번 정답률 77%

Maybe you've heard this joke: **단서1** "How do you eat an
코끼리를 어떻게 먹는가?
elephant?" The answer is "one bite at a time." (B) **단서2** So, how
- '한 번에 한 입'   '지구를 어떻게
do you "build" the Earth? That's simple, too: one atom at a time.
건설하는가?' - '한 번에 하나의 원자' (비슷한 질문이 이어짐)
Atoms are the basic building blocks of crystals, and since all rocks

are made up of crystals, the more you know about atoms, the better.
be made up of: ~로 구성되다   「the + 비교급 ~, the + 비교급 …」; ~할수록 더 …하다
단서3 Crystals come in a variety of shapes that scientists call *habits*.
결정은 '습성'이라고 불리는 다양한 모양으로 나옴
(A) **단서4** Common crystal habits include squares, triangles, and
모양: 사각형, 삼각형, 육면의 육각형을 포함
six-sided hexagons. Usually crystals form when liquids cool, such

as when you create ice cubes. Many times, crystals form in ways

that do not allow for perfect shapes. If conditions are too cold,

too hot, or there isn't enough source material, **단서5** they can form
결정 습성은 이상하고
strange, twisted shapes. (C) **단서6** But when conditions are right,
뒤틀린 모습을 형성할 수 있음   하지만 조건이 맞으면 아름다운 배열을 봄
we see beautiful displays. ✪ Usually, this involves a slow, steady
                                    관계부사절   주어   동사   목적어
environment / **where** the individual atoms have plenty of *time* (**to**
              선행사를 포함한 관계대명사   충분한 ~
join and fit perfectly into [**what**'s known as the *crystal lattice*]).
to부정사(형용사적 용법)   be known as: ~로 알려져 있다
This is the basic structure of atoms that is seen time after time.

해석

아마 여러분은 이 농담을 들어 본 적이 있을 것이다. "코끼리를 어떻게 먹는가?" 정답은 '한 번에 한 입'이다. (B) 그렇다면, 여러분은 어떻게 지구를 '건설'하는가? 그것 또한 간단하다. 한 번에 하나의 원자이다. 원자는 결정의 기본 구성 요소이고, 모든 암석은 결정으로 이루어져 있기 때문에, 여러분은 원자에 대해 더 많이 알수록 더 좋다. 결정은 과학자들이 '습성'이라고 부르는 다양한 모양으로 나온다. (A) 일반적인 결정 습성은 사각형, 삼각형, 육면의 육각형을 포함한다. 보통 여러분이 얼음을 만들 때와 같이 액체가 차가워질 때 결정이 형성된다. 많은 경우, 결정은 완벽한 모양을 허용하지 않는 방식으로 형성된다. 조건이 너무 차갑거나, 너무 뜨겁거나, 혹은 원천 물질이 충분하지 않으면 이상하고 뒤틀린 모양을 형성할 수 있다. (C) 하지만 조건이 맞을 때, 우리는 아름다운 배열을 본다. 보통, 이것은 개별적인 원자들이 결합하고 '결정격자'라고 알려진 것에 완벽하게 들어맞는 충분한 시간을 가지는 느리고 변함없는 환경을 포함한다. 이것은 반복하여 보이는 원자의 기본적인 구조이다.

정답이 보이는 해설

주어진 글은 농담이 섞인 질문으로 시작하고 있고, 비슷한 질문으로 이어지는 (B)에서 원자는 결정의 기본 구성 요소이고, 결정은 '습성'이라고 불리는 다양한 모양으로 나온다고 하였다. 구체적인 결정의 모양의 종류와 형성되는 과정을 설명하고, 결정은 이상하고 뒤틀린 모양을 형성할 수 있다는 내용의 (A)가 온 다음, 그렇지만 조건이 맞으면 아름다운 배열을 볼 수 있다는 내용의 (C)로 이어지는 것이 글의 흐름상 가장 자연스럽다.

필수 어휘

atom 원자   block 덩어리, (모양을 만들기 위한) 형   rock 암석
hexagon 육각형   steady 변함없는, 안정적인
crystal lattice 결정격자(결정을 구성하는 원자와 이온의 규칙적인 배열)

02 정답 ③

202309 37번 정답률 68%

When you pluck a guitar string **단서1** it moves back and forth
                                이리저리, 왔다갔다
기타 줄이 매초 수백 번 이리저리 움직임

hundreds of times every second. (B) Naturally, **단서2** this movement
                                                      이 움직임은 너무 빨라서
is so fast that you cannot see it — you just see the blurred outline
기타 줄을 볼 수 없음
of the moving string. Strings vibrating in this way on their own

단서3 make hardly any noise because strings are very thin and don't
진동하는 줄은 소리가 나지 않음
push much air about. (C) **단서4** But if you attach a string to a big
                        그러나 상자에 줄을 달면, 그 진동이 증폭되어 음이 들림
hollow box (like a guitar body), then the vibration is amplified

and the note is heard loud and clear. ✪ **단서5** The vibration (of
                                            그 줄의 진동은 나무판으로 전달됨
the string) is passed on to the wooden panels (of the guitar body),
              be passed on: ~로 전달되다, 전이되다
[which vibrate back and forth / at the same rate as the string]. (A)
the wooden panels를 선행사로 하는 주격 관계대명사(계속적 용법)   ~처럼, 같이
단서6 The vibration of the wood creates more powerful waves in the
       그 나무의 진동은 더 강력한 파동을 만들어 냄
air pressure, which travel away from the guitar. When the waves

reach your eardrums they flex in and out the same number of times
                                    안팎으로, 들락거리는
a second as the original string.

해석

여러분이 기타 줄을 뜯을 때 그것은 매초 수백 번 이리저리 움직인다. (B) 당연히, 이 움직임은 너무 빨라서 여러분이 그것을 볼 수 없다. 여러분은 그저 움직이는 줄의 흐릿한 윤곽만 본다. 이렇게 스스로 진동하는 줄들은 거의 소리가 나지 않는데, 이는 줄이 매우 가늘어 많은 공기를 밀어내지 못하기 때문이다. (C) 하지만 여러분이 (기타 몸통 같은) 커다란 속이 빈 상자에 줄을 달면, 그 진동은 증폭되어 그 음이 크고 선명하게 들린다. 그 줄의 진동은 기타 몸통의 나무판으로 전달되어 줄과 같은 속도로 왔다갔다 떨린다. (A) 그 나무의 진동은 공기의 압력에 더 강력한 파동을 만들어 내어 기타로부터 멀리 퍼진다. 그 파동이 여러분의 고막에 도달할 때 원래의 줄과 초당 동일한 횟수로 굽이쳐 들어가고 나온다.

정답이 보이는 해설

주어진 글은 기타 줄을 뜯으면 그것은 매초 수백 번 이리저리 움직인다는 내용이다. 이러한 움직임이 너무 빨라서 줄의 윤곽만 볼 수 있으며, 줄이 매우 가늘어 많은 공기를 밀어내지 못하기 때문에 거의 소리가 나지 않는다는 (B)가 먼저 오고, 그렇지만 그 줄을 빈 상자에 달면 진동이 증폭되면서 음이 크게 들린다고 하면서 줄의 진동이 기타 몸통의 나무판으로 전달된다는 (C)가 온 다음, 그 나무의 진동은 더 강력한 파동을 만들어 내어 기타로부터 멀리 퍼진다고 설명하는 내용의 (A)로 이어지는 것이 글의 흐름상 가장 자연스럽다.

선택지 완벽 분석

② (A) '그 나무의 진동'은 (C)에 나오는 '기타 몸통의 나무판'에 대한 설명이므로 (A)는 (C) 다음에 와야 한다.

필수 어휘

string 줄, 끈   blur 흐릿해지다   outline 윤곽; 개요   vibrate 진동하다
hardly 거의 ~없다   attach 달다, 붙이다   hollow (속이) 빈   note 음, 음표
wooden 나무로 된, 목재의   panel 판(넓은 직사각형의 합판)   eardrum 고막
flex 구부리다, 굽히다

03 정답 ②

202306 36번 정답률 82%

Up until about 6,000 years ago, most people were farmers. ✪

단서1 Many lived in different places (throughout the year), // hunting
아주 옛날에는 지역을 돌아다니며 살았음   분사구문1
for food / or moving their livestock (to areas with enough food). (B)
                분사구문2
단서2 There was no need to tell the time because life depended on
       시간을 알 필요가 없었음   depend on: ~에 의존하다
natural cycles, such as the changing seasons or sunrise and sunset.

Gradually more people started to live in larger settlements, and

16강 필의순서

단서3 some needed to tell the time. (A) For example, **단서4** priests
누군가는 시간을 알 필요가 있게 됨   성직자들이
wanted to know when to carry out religious ceremonies. This
시간을 알고 싶어 함
was when **단서5** people first invented clocks — devices that show,
시계가 발명됨
measure, and keep track of passing time. (C) Clocks have been
        ~을 추적하다
important ever since. **단서6** Today, clocks are used for important
                   오늘날에는 시계가 중요한 일에 사용됨
things such as setting busy airport timetables — if the time is
incorrect, aeroplanes might crash into each other when taking off or
                              서로 충돌하다   take off: 이륙하다
landing!

해석

약 6,000년 전까지, 대부분의 사람들은 농부였다. 많은 사람들은 일 년 내내 여러 장소에서 살았고, 식량을 찾아다니거나 충분한 먹이가 있는 지역으로 가축을 옮겼다. (B) 변화하는 계절이나 일출과 일몰 같은, 자연적인 주기에 삶이 달려 있었기 때문에 시간을 알 필요가 없었다. 점점 더 많은 사람들이 더 큰 정착지에서 살기 시작했고, 어떤 사람들은 시간을 알 필요가 있었다. (A) 예를 들어, 성직자들은 언제 종교적인 의식을 수행해야 하는지 알고 싶었다. 이때 사람들이 지나가는 시간을 보여 주고, 측정하고, 흐르는 시간을 추적하는 장치인 시계를 처음으로 발명했다. (C) 시계는 그 이후로도 중요했다. 오늘날, 시계는 바쁜 공항 시간표를 설정하는 것과 같은 중요한 일에 사용된다 — 만약 시간이 부정확하다면, 비행기는 이륙하거나 착륙할 때 서로 충돌할 수도 있다!

정답이 보이는 해설

약 6,000년 전에는, 대부분의 사람들은 농부였고 많은 사람들은 일 년 내내 여러 장소로 옮기며 살았다는 주어진 문장 다음에는, 자연적인 삶이었기에 시간을 알 필요가 없었는데, 점차 시간을 알 필요가 있게 되었다는 (B)가 와야 한다. 시간을 알고 싶어 하는 사람들의 예로 성직자를 언급한 후에 시계가 최초로 만들어지게 되었다는 (A)가 온 다음, 마지막으로 오늘날에도 여전히 시계는 중요하다는 내용의 (C)로 이어지는 것이 글의 흐름상 가장 자연스럽다.

선택지 완벽 분석

① (A)에서 For example 뒤에는 성직자들을 예로 들면서, 그들이 시간을 알고 싶어 했다고 하고 있으므로, (A) 앞에는 어떤 사람들은 시간을 알 필요가 있게 되었다는 (B)가 있어야 한다.

필수 어휘

livestock 가축 sunrise 일출 sunset 일몰 gradually 점점
settlement 정착지 priest 성직자 carry out ~을 수행하다 religious 종교적인
ceremony 의식 device 장치 measure 측정하다 incorrect 부정확한
aeroplane 비행기 land 착륙하다

04 정답 ⑤

202306 37번 정답률 62%

Managers are always looking for ways to increase productivity,
               look for: ~을 찾다
which is the ratio of costs to output in production. **주제문** Adam

Smith, writing when the manufacturing industry was new, described

단서1 a way that production could be made more efficient,
"노동 분업"이라는 더 효율적인 생산법을 설명함
known as the "division of labor." (C) Making most manufactured
~으로 알려진
goods involves **단서2** several different processes using different
                여러 기술을 사용하는 여러 다른 과정을 포함함
skills. Smith's example was the manufacture of pins: the wire is

straightened, sharpened, a head is put on, and then it is polished.

(B) **단서3** One worker could do all these tasks, and make 20 pins in
       노동자 한 명이 모든 작업을 할 수도 있음   ┌ ~으로 분리되다
a day. But this work **단서4** can be divided into its separate processes,
                        여러 과정으로 분리될 수도 있음
with a number of workers each performing one task. (A) Because
     많은 ~

each worker specializes in one job, **단서5** he or she can work
                                    분리하면 일의 속도가 훨씬 더 빠름
much faster without changing from one task to another. ✪ Now

10 workers can produce thousands of pins (in a day) / — a huge
                                         추가 설명
increase (in productivity) (from *the 200* [they would have produced
                       목적격 관계대명사 that 생략 ↰
before]).

해석

관리자들은 항상 생산성을 높일 수 있는 방법을 찾고 있는데, 생산성은 생산에서 비용 대비 생산량의 비율이다. 제조 산업이 새로 등장했을 때 저술한 Adam Smith는 "노동 분업"으로 알려진 생산이 더 효율적으로 될 수 있는 방식을 설명했다. (C) 대부분의 공산품을 만드는 것은 다른 기술을 사용하는 여러 가지 다른 과정을 포함한다. Smith의 예는 핀의 제조였다. 철사가 곧게 펴지고, 뾰족해지고, 상부가 놓이고, 그러고 나서 그것이 다듬어진다. (B) 한 명의 노동자가 이 모든 작업들을 할 수 있고, 하루에 20개의 핀을 만들 수도 있다. 그러나 이 일은 많은 노동자가 각각 한 가지 작업을 수행하는 별개의 과정으로 분리될 수 있다. (A) 각 노동자는 한 가지 작업을 전문으로 하기 때문에, 그 또는 그녀는 한 작업에서 다른 작업으로 변경하지 않고도 훨씬 더 빠르게 일할 수 있다. 이제 10명의 노동자가 하루에 수천 개의 핀을 생산할 수 있다. 이는 이전에 그들이 생산했던 200개로부터 생산성 측면에서 크게 증가한 것이다.

정답이 보이는 해설

제조 산업이 새로 등장했을 때 Adam Smith는 "노동 분업"이라는 더 효율적인 생산 방식을 설명했다는 주어진 문장 다음에, (C) Smith가 예를 든 핀의 제조 과정에 대한 내용이 이어지고, 한 명이 모든 과정을 거치면 20개의 핀을 만들 수 있지만, 각각 별개의 과정으로 분리될 수 있다는 (B)가 온 다음, 한 작업에서 다른 작업으로 변경하지 않고 훨씬 더 빠르게 일해서 하루에 수천 개의 핀을 생산할 수 있다는 내용의 (A)로 이어지는 것이 글의 흐름상 가장 자연스럽다.

선택지 완벽 분석

③ (B)에 있는 all these tasks(이 모든 작업들)는 (C)에 열거된 핀을 만드는 제조 과정들을 가리킨다는 데 유의한다.

필수 어휘

productivity 생산성 output 생산량 production 생산
manufacture 제조; 제조하다 industry 산업 describe 설명하다
efficient 효율적인 division of labor 노동 분업 involve 포함하다
process 과정 straighten 곧게 펴다 sharpen 뾰족하게 하다 polish 다듬다
separate 별개의 specialize in ~을 전문으로 하다 huge 거대한

05 정답 ④

202303 36번 정답률 39%

In the Old Stone Age, small bands of 20 to 60 people wandered

from place to place in search of food. Once people began farming,
                        ~을 찾아
단서1 they could settle down near their farms. (C) **단서2** As a result,
      농사를 짓기 시작하면서, 정착하게 됨   결과적으로
towns and villages grew larger. ✪ Living (in communities) **allowed**
정착의 결과 마을이 더 커짐   주어   동사
people to organize themselves (more efficiently). **단서3** They could
목적어   목적격보어
divide up the work of producing food and other things they needed.
더 효율적으로 일할 수 있게 되어서 일을 나눔
(A) **단서4** While some workers grew crops, others built new houses
         어떤 사람은 농작물을 재배하고, 다른 사람은 집을 짓고 도구를 만듦
and made tools. Village dwellers also learned to work together **단서5**

to do a task faster. (B) For example, toolmakers could share the
일하는 속도도 빨라짐
work of making stone axes and knives. By working together, **단서6**

they could make more tools in the same amount of time.
같은 시간에 더 많은 도구를 만들었음   ~의 같은 양으로

해석

구석기 시대에는 20명에서 60명의 작은 무리가 식량을 찾아 이곳저곳을 돌아다녔다. 일단 농사를 짓기 시작하면서, 사람들은 자신들의 농경지 근처에 정착할 수 있었다. (C) 그 결과, 도시와 마을이 더 커졌다. 공동체 생활이 사람들로 하여금 스스로를 더 효율적으로 조직할 수 있게 했다. 그들은 식량과 자신들에게 필요한 다른 것들을 생산하는 일을 나눌 수 있었다. (A) 어떤 노동자들은 농작물을 재배한 반면, 다른 노동자들은 새로운 집을 짓고 도구를 만들었다. 마을 거주자들은 또한 일을 더 빨리 하기 위해 함께 일하는 것도 배웠다. (B) 예를 들어, 도구 제작자들은 돌도끼와 돌칼을 만드는 작업을 함께 할 수 있었다. 함께 일함으로써, 그들은 같은 시간 안에 더 많은 도구를 만들 수 있었다.

정답이 보이는 해설

구석기 시대에 사람들은 음식을 찾아 떠돌다가, 농사를 짓기 시작하면서 정착할 수 있었다는 주어진 문장 다음에는, 농사와 정착의 결과로 도시와 마을이 더 커졌고 일을 나누어 할 수 있었다는 (C)가 와야 한다. 이어서 일을 나눴던 것의 예로 농작물 재배와 집짓기, 도구 만들기 등을 더 빨리 할 수 있게 되었다는 내용인 (A)가 온 다음, 빨라진 일의 예로, 도구 제작자들은 돌도끼와 돌칼을 만드는 작업을 함께 함으로써 같은 시간 안에 더 많은 도구를 만들 수 있었다는 내용의 (B)로 이어지는 것이 글의 흐름상 가장 자연스럽다.

선택지 완벽 분석

⑤ [함정] (B)의 For example로 보아, (B) 앞에는 일을 더 빨리 하는 것을 배우게 되었다는 (A)의 뒤 부분의 내용이 와야 하므로, (B) 앞에 (A)가 먼저 오는 것이 자연스럽다.

필수 어휘

Old Stone Age 구석기 시대   band 무리   wander (걸어서) 돌아다니다
settle down 정착하다   community 공동체   organize 조직하다
efficiently 효율적으로   produce 생산하다   crop 농작물
toolmaker 도구 제작자   share 함께 하다, 공유하다   ax 도끼

06 정답 ②

202303 37번 정답률 45%

[주제문] Natural processes form minerals in many ways. For
　　　　　　　　　　　　　　　　　　　　　　많은 방법으로
example, hot melted rock material, called magma, cools when it
reaches the Earth's surface, or even if it's trapped below the surface.
　　　　　　　　　　　　　　　　　　　~할 때조차
As magma cools, its atoms lose heat energy, move closer together,
and [단서1] begin to combine into compounds. (B) During this
　　　　　　화합물로 결합하기 시작함
process, [단서2] atoms of the different compounds arrange themselves
　　　　　　그 서로 다른 화합물의 원자들이 배열됨
into orderly, repeating patterns. The type and amount of elements
present in a magma partly determine which minerals will form. (A)
[단서3] Also, the size of the crystals that form depends partly on how
　　　형성되는 결정의 크기 관련 내용　　　　　　depend on: ~에 달려 있다
rapidly the magma cools. ✪ [단서4] When magma cools slowly, // the
　　　　　　　　　　　　　　　천천히 식으면 결정이 큼
crystals [that form] / are generally large enough (to see with the
주어　주격 관계대명사절　동사　　　　　　　~할 만큼 충분히 큰　육안[맨눈]으로
unaided eye). (C) This is because [단서5] the atoms have enough time
　　　　　　　　　　　　　　　큰 이유는 시간이 많기 때문임
to move together and form into larger crystals. When magma cools
rapidly, the crystals that form will be small. In such cases, you can't
　　　　　　　　　　　　　　　　　　　　　　그런 경우에는
easily see individual mineral crystals.

해석

자연 과정은 많은 방법으로 광물을 형성한다. 예를 들어, 마그마라고 불리는 뜨거운 용암 물질은 지구의 표면에 도달할 때, 또는 심지어 표면 아래에 갇혔을 때도 식는다. 마그마가 식으면서, 마그마의 원자는 열에너지를 잃고, 서로 더 가까이 이동해, 화합물로 결합하기 시작한다. (B) 이 과정 동안, 서로 다른 화합물의 원자가 질서 있고 반복적인 패턴으로 배열된다. 마그마에 존재하는 원소의 종류와 양이 어떤 광물이 형

성될지를 부분적으로 결정한다. (A) 또한, 형성되는 결정의 크기는 부분적으로는 마그마가 얼마나 빨리 식느냐에 달려 있다. 마그마가 천천히 식으면, 형성되는 결정은 일반적으로 육안으로 볼 수 있을 만큼 충분히 크다. (C) 이것은 원자가 함께 이동해 더 큰 결정을 형성할 충분한 시간을 가지기 때문이다. 마그마가 빠르게 식으면, 형성되는 결정은 작을 것이다. 그런 경우에는 개별 광물 결정을 쉽게 볼 수 없다.

정답이 보이는 해설

주어진 글은 광물을 형성하는 많은 방법 중에 마그마를 예로 들고 있다. 마그마가 식으면서, 마그마의 원자는 열에너지를 잃고, 서로 더 가까이 이동해 화합물로 결합하기 시작한다는 내용 바로 뒤에는, 이 과정 동안, 서로 다른 화합물의 원자가 질서 있고 반복적인 패턴으로 배열되는데, 마그마에 존재하는 원소의 종류와 양이 어떤 광물이 형성될지를 부분적으로 결정한다는 (B)가 먼저 오고, 형성되는 결정의 크기는 부분적으로는 마그마가 얼마나 빨리 식느냐에 달려 있는데, 마그마가 천천히 식으면, 형성되는 결정이 일반적으로 충분히 크다는 (A)가 온 다음, 그 결정이 큰 원인을 설명(원자가 함께 이동해 더 큰 결정을 형성할 충분한 시간이 있기 때문임)하고, 반대로 빠르게 식을 경우를 설명하는 내용의 (C)로 이어지는 것이 글의 흐름상 가장 자연스럽다.

선택지 완벽 분석

③ [함정] 주어진 문장 다음에 어떤 광물이 형성될지에 관한 내용이 와야 하고, 속도에 따라 달라진다는 (A)와 (C)가 연달아 나와야 하는데 결정의 크기에 대한 내용을 제시하는 (A)가 먼저 나오고 이후에 (C)가 이어지는 것에 유의한다.

필수 어휘

mineral 광물   melt 녹이다, 녹다   material 물질   surface 표면   trap 가두다
atom 원자   combine 결합하다   arrange 배열하다   orderly 질서 있는
element 원소   partly 부분적으로   determine 결정하다   crystal 결정, 결정체
rapidly 빨리   individual 개별의

07 정답 ③

202211 36번 정답률 67%

Things are changing. It has been reported that 42 percent of jobs
in Canada are at risk, and 62 percent of jobs in America will be in
　　　　　　　　위기에 처한
danger due to advances in automation. (B) [단서1] You might say that
　　　~으로 인해　　　　　　　　　　　　　　　　앞에 언급된 숫자가
the numbers seem a bit unrealistic, but the threat is real. One fast
비현실적으로 보일지도 모르지만, 현실임
food franchise has a robot that can flip a burger in ten seconds. It
is just a simple task but the robot could replace an entire crew. (C)
[단서2] Highly skilled jobs are also at risk. ✪ A supercomputer, / (for
단순한 일에 이어 고도로 숙련된 일도 위험에 처함　　주어
instance,) / can suggest / available treatments (for specific illnesses
　　　　　　　　동사　　목적어
in an automated way, / drawing on the body of medical research and
　　　　　　　　　　　　　분사구문
data on diseases). (A) [단서3] However, what's difficult to automate
　　　　　　　　　　　　　하지만 창의적으로 문제를 해결하는 능력은 자동화하기 어려움
is the ability to creatively solve problems. [주제문] Whereas workers
in "doing" roles can be replaced by robots, the role of creatively
　　　　　　　　　~에 의해 대체되다
solving problems is more dependent on an irreplaceable individual.
　　　　　　　　　　　~에 의존하는

해석

상황이 변화하고 있다. 캐나다의 일자리 중 42퍼센트가 위기에 처해 있고, 미국의 일자리 중 62퍼센트가 자동화의 발전으로 인해 위기에 처할 것이라고 보도되어 왔다. (B) 그 숫자들이 약간 비현실적으로 보인다고 말할지 모르지만, 그 위험은 현실이다. 한 패스트푸드 체인점은 10초 안에 버거 하나를 뒤집을 수 있는 로봇이 있다. 그것은 단지 단순한 일일 뿐이지만 그 로봇이 전체 직원을 대체할 수도 있다. (C) 고도로 숙련된 직업들 또한 위기에 처해 있다. 예를 들어, 슈퍼컴퓨터는 질병에 대한 방대한 양의 의학 연구와 데이터를 이용하여 특정한 질병들에 대해 이용 가능한 치료법을 자동화된 방식으로 제안할 수 있다. (A) 하지만, 자동화하기 어려운 것은 창의적으로 문제를 해결하는 능력이다. "(기계적인 일을) 하는" 역할의 노동자들은 로봇

들에 의해 대체될 수 있는 반면에, 창의적으로 문제를 해결하는 역할은 대체 불가능한 개인에 더 의존한다.

캐나다와 미국의 일자리 중 많은 부분(각 42%와 62%)이 자동화로 인해 위기에 처해 있다는 주어진 문장 다음에는, 이 숫자들이 비현실적으로 보일지 모르지만 현실이고, 그 예로 버거를 뒤집는 간단한 일은 로봇으로 대체될 수 있다는 내용의 (B)가 이어지고, 또한 치료법 제안이라는 고도로 숙련된 일까지 이에 해당한다는 (C)가 이어진 다음, 하지만, 창의적 문제 해결은 자동화가 어려워 개인에 의존한다는 내용의 (A)로 이어지는 것이 글의 흐름상 가장 자연스럽다.

선택지 완벽 분석

⑤ (C)의 also로 보아, (C)에는 로봇이 대신할 수 있는 또 하나의 다른 예가 추가되는 것이므로, (C) 앞에 (B)가 먼저 오는 것이 자연스럽다.

필수 어휘

be in danger 위험에 처해 있다 advance 진보 automation 자동화
a bit 약간 unrealistic 비현실적인 threat 위협 flip 뒤집다
replace 대체하다 suggest 제안하다 available 이용 가능한
treatment 치료법 draw on ~에 의지하다, ~을 이용하다
the body of 상당한 양의 ~ disease 질병 irreplaceable 대체할 수 없는
individual 개인

08 정답 ⑤

202211 37번 정답률 60%

Each beech tree grows in a particular location and soil conditions can vary greatly in just a few yards. The soil can have a great deal of water or almost no water. It can be full of nutrients or not. (C) **단서1** Accordingly, each tree grows more quickly or more slowly and produces more or less sugar, and thus you would expect every tree to be photosynthesizing at a different rate. (B) **단서2** However, the rate is the same. Whether they are thick or thin, all the trees of the same species are using light to produce the same amount of sugar per leaf. Some trees have plenty of sugar and some have less, but the trees equalize this difference between them by transferring sugar. (A) **단서3** This is taking place underground through the roots. ✪ **Whoever** has an abundance of sugar hands some over; // **whoever** is running short gets help. Their network acts as a system to make sure that no trees fall too far behind.

해석

각각의 너도밤나무는 고유한 장소에서 자라고 토양의 조건들은 단 몇 야드 안에서도 크게 달라질 수 있다. 토양은 다량의 물을 가지거나 거의 물이 없을 수도 있다. 그것은 영양분이 가득할 수도 아닐 수도 있다. (C) 이에 따라, 각 나무는 더 빨리 혹은 더 느리게 자라고 더 많은 혹은 더 적은 당분을 생산하는데, 그래서 여러분은 모든 나무가 다른 정도로 광합성을 할 것이라고 기대할 것이다. (B) 그러나 그 정도는 동일하다. 그들이 굵든 가늘든 간에, 같은 종의 모든 나무들은 빛을 이용하여 이파리 하나당 같은 양의 당을 생산한다. 어떤 나무들은 충분한 당을 지니고 어떤 것들은 더 적게 지니지만, 나무들은 당을 전달함으로써 그들 사이의 이 차이를 균등하게 한다. (A) 이것은 뿌리들을 통해 지하에서 일어나고 있다. 풍부한 당을 가진 나무가 누구든 간에 일부를 건네주고, 부족해지는 나무는 누구든 간에 도움을 받는다. 그들의 연결망은 그 어떤 나무도 너무 뒤처지지 않도록 확실히 하기 위한 시스템으로서 역할을 한다.

정답이 보이는 해설

너도밤나무는 고유한 장소에서 자라고 토양의 조건들은 크게 달라질 수 있다는 주

어진 문장 다음에는, 이 토양의 상태에 따라 각 나무의 자라는 속도와 생산하는 당분의 양이 달라서, 나무에 따라 광합성의 정도가 다를 것이라고 기대할 수 있다는 내용의 (C)가 오고, 그러나 광합성의 정도는 동일하며, 같은 종의 나무들은 이파리 하나당 같은 양의 당을 생산하는데, 당이 다르면 나무들은 당을 전달함으로써 차이를 균등하게 한다는 내용의 (B)로 이어진 다음, 이런 나눔은 뿌리들을 통해 지하에서 일어나며, 나무의 연결망이 그 어떤 나무도 너무 뒤처지지 않도록 확실히 하기 위한 시스템으로서 역할을 한다는 내용의 (A)로 이어지는 것이 글의 흐름상 가장 자연스럽다.

선택지 완벽 분석

③ (B)의 첫 문장에 나오는 the rate가 (C) 마지막에 나오는 at a different rate를 지칭한다는 데 유의해야 한다.

필수 어휘

beech 너도밤나무 particular 특별한 vary 다양하다 nutrient 영양분
accordingly 이에 따라 species (동식물의) 종 per ~당
equalize 균등하게 하다 transfer 전달하다 take place 일어나다
an abundance of 풍부한 ~ hand over 건네주다 run short 부족해지다
fall behind 뒤처지다

09 정답 ②

202209 36번 정답률 66%

With nearly a billion hungry people in the world, there is obviously no single cause. (B) However, **단서1** far and away the biggest cause is poverty. Seventy-nine percent of the world's hungry live in nations that are net exporters of food. How can this be? (A) ✪ **단서2** *The reason* [people are hungry in those countries] is [that *the products* {produced there} **can be sold** on the world market for more than the local citizens can afford to pay for them]. In the modern age you do not starve because you have no food, you starve because you have no money. (C) **단서3** So the problem really is that food is, in the grand scheme of things, too expensive and many people are too poor to buy it. The answer will be in continuing the trend of lowering the cost of food.

해석

전 세계에 거의 10억 명의 굶주린 사람들이 있는데, 분명히 단 한 개의 원인만 있는 것은 아니다. (B) 하지만 단연코 가장 큰 원인은 빈곤이다. 세계의 굶주린 사람들의 79퍼센트가 식량 순 수출국에 살고 있다. 어떻게 이럴 수가 있을까? (A) 그러한 국가에서 사람들이 굶주리는 이유는 그곳에서 생산된 생산물들이 현지 시민들이 그것들에 지불할 수 있는 것보다 더 비싸게 세계 시장에서 팔릴 수 있기 때문이다. 현대에는 여러분이 식량이 없어서 굶주리는 것이 아니라, 돈이 없어서 굶주리는 것이다. (C) 그러므로 문제는 실제로 거대한 체계로 볼 때 식량이 너무 비싸고 많은 사람들이 너무 가난하여 그것을 살 수 없다는 것이다. 해답은 식량의 가격을 낮추는 추세를 지속하는 데 있을 것이다.

정답이 보이는 해설

전 세계에 거의 10억 명의 굶주린 사람들이 있는데, 그 원인이 단 한 개만이 아니라는 주어진 글 다음에는, 그 많은 원인들 중 가장 큰 원인이 빈곤이라는 (B)가 와야 한다. 이어서 (B)의 마지막 문장에서 질문한 세계의 굶주린 사람들이 식량 순 수출국에 살고 있는 이유가 식량이 없어서가 아니라 돈이 없기 때문이라고 설명하는 (A)가 온 후에, 이에 대한 해결책으로 식량의 가격을 낮추어야 할 것이라는 (C)가 마지막에 오는 것이 글의 흐름상 가장 자연스럽다.

필수 어휘

billion 10억 obviously 분명히 poverty 가난 product 생산물, 산물
local 현지의 starve 굶주리다, 굶어 죽다 grand 거대한, 웅장한
trend 추세, 경향 lower 낮추다

10 정답 ⑤

Most people have a perfect time of day when they feel they are at their best, whether in the morning, evening, or afternoon.
at one's best: 최고의 상태인
(C) 단서1 Some of us are night owls, some early birds, and others
어떤 사람들은 밤 올빼미이고, 어떤 사람들은 일찍 일어나는 새임(최적의 시간은 사람에 따라 다름)
in between may feel most active during the afternoon hours.
그 사이에 있는, 중간에 끼어 있는
❂ 단서2 If you are able to organize your day and divide your work, /
조건의 부사절   업무를 나눌 때 집중을 요구하는 과업은 하루 중 최적의 시간에 처리해야 함
make it a point [to deal with *tasks* {that demand attention at your
가목적어   ~에 중점을 두다   진목적어   주격 관계대명사절
best time of the day}]. (B) 단서3 However, if the task you face
창의성과 아이디어를 요구하는 과업은 하루 중
demands creativity and novel ideas, it's best to tackle it at your
최악의 시간에 처리하는 것이 가장 좋음
"worst" time of day! So if you are an early bird, make sure to attack
반드시 ~하다
your creative task in the evening, and vice versa for night owls.
그 반대로, 역으로
(A) 단서4 When your mind and body are less alert than at your "peak"
하루 중 최악의 시간에 창의성의 영감이 깨어남
hours, the muse of creativity awakens and is allowed to roam more freely. In other words, when your mental machinery is loose rather than standing at attention, the creativity flows.

해석

대부분의 사람들은 아침이든 저녁이든 또는 오후든 간에 하루 중 그들이 자신의 최고의 상태에 있다고 느끼는 완벽한 시간을 갖는다. (C) 우리들 중 몇몇은 밤 올빼미이고, 몇몇은 일찍 일어나는 새이며, 그 사이에 있는 누군가는 오후의 시간 동안 가장 활력을 느낄지도 모른다. 여러분이 하루를 계획하고 업무를 나눈다면, 집중을 요구하는 과업을 하루 중 여러분의 최적의 시간에 처리하는 것에 중점을 두어라. (B) 하지만 만약 여러분이 직면한 과업이 창의성과 새로운 아이디어를 요구한다면, 하루 중 여러분의 '최악의' 시간에 그것을 다루는 것이 최선이다! 그래서 만약 여러분이 일찍 일어나는 새라면 반드시 저녁에 창의적인 작업에 착수하고, 밤 올빼미라면 그 반대로 해라. (A) 여러분의 정신과 몸이 여러분의 '정점의' 시간보다 덜 초롱초롱할 때, 창의성의 영감이 깨어나 더 자유롭게 거니는 것이 허용된다. 다시 말해서, 여러분의 정신 기제가 주의력 있게 기립해 있을 때보다 느슨하게 풀려있을 때 창의성이 샘솟는다.

정답이 보이는 해설

대부분의 사람들은 아침이든 저녁이든 오후든 상관없이 하루 중 최고의 상태인 완벽한 시간을 갖는다는 주어진 글 다음에는, 밤 올빼미(저녁형)이든 일찍 일어나는 새(아침형)이든 집중을 요구하는 과업은 하루 중 최적의 시간에 처리하라는 (C)가 와야 한다. 하지만 창의성과 새로운 아이디어를 요구하는 과업은 최악의 시간에 다루라는 (B)가 이어진 후, 그에 대한 이유로 정신과 몸이 덜 초롱초롱할 때 창의성의 영감이 깨어난다고 부연 설명한 (A)가 마지막에 오는 것이 글의 흐름상 가장 자연스럽다.

필수 어휘

owl 올빼미   organize (어떤 일을) 계획하다, 준비하다   divide 나누다
face 직면하다   tackle (힘든 문제를) 다루다, 씨름하다   attack 착수하다, 덤벼들다
alert (정신이) 초롱초롱한, 기민한   peak 정점(의), 한창(인)
muse 영감, (영감을 주는) 뮤즈   awaken 깨다   loose 느슨하게 풀린, 헐거워진

11 정답 ③

Mrs. Klein told her first graders to draw a picture of something to be thankful for. She thought that most of the class would draw
~에 대해 감사히 여기다
turkeys or Thanksgiving tables. 단서1 But Douglas drew something
Douglas는 친구들과는 다른 그림을 그림
different. (B) ❂ Douglas was *a boy* [who usually spent time alone
관계대명사절 동사1
and stayed around her] / while his classmates went outside together
관계대명사절 동사2   접속사(~하는 동안)
/ during break time. 단서2 What the boy drew was a hand. But
전치사(~ 동안)   그 소년이 그린 것은 손이었음
whose hand? His image immediately attracted the other students'
급히 ~하다
interest. (C) 단서3 So, everyone rushed to talk about whose hand
반 친구들은 그것이 누구의 손인지 앞다투어 이야기함
it was. "It must be the hand of God that brings us food," said one student. "A farmer's," said a second student, "because they raise the turkeys." "It looks more like a police officer's," added another, "they protect us." (A) The class was so responsive that Mrs. Klein had almost forgotten about Douglas. After she had the others at work on another project, she asked Douglas whose hand it was. 단서4 He answered softly, "It's yours. Thank you, Mrs. Klein."
Douglas는 그것이 Klein 선생님의 손이라고 말함

해석

Klein 선생님은 1학년 학생들에게 감사히 여기는 것을 그려 보라고 말했다. 그녀는 반 학생들 대부분이 칠면조나 추수감사절 식탁을 그릴 거라고 생각했다. 그러나 Douglas는 다른 것을 그렸다. (B) Douglas는 쉬는 시간에 그의 반 친구들이 함께 밖으로 나가 있는 동안 보통 혼자 시간을 보내고 그녀 주변에 머무는 남학생이었다. 그 남학생이 그린 것은 손이었다. 그런데 누구의 손일까? 그의 그림은 즉시 다른 학생들의 관심을 끌었다. (C) 그래서 다들 그것이 누구의 손인지에 관해 앞다투어 얘기했다. "그것은 우리에게 음식을 가져다주는 신의 손이 틀림없어."라고 한 학생이 말했다. "농부의 손이야, 왜냐하면 그들은 칠면조를 기르잖아."라고 두 번째 학생이 말했다. "그것은 경찰관의 손과 더 비슷해 보여, 그들은 우리를 보호해 주거든."이라고 또 다른 학생이 덧붙였다. (A) 반 학생들의 호응이 너무 좋아서 Klein 선생님은 Douglas에 대해 하마터면 잊을 뻔했다. 그녀는 나머지 학생들에게 다른 과제를 하게 한 후, Douglas에게 그것이 누구의 손인지 물었다. "선생님의 손이에요. 감사합니다, Klein 선생님."이라고 그는 조용히 대답했다.

정답이 보이는 해설

선생님이 학생들에게 감사히 여기는 대상을 그리게 했는데 Douglas가 예상과 다른 것을 그렸다는 내용의 주어진 글 다음에는, Douglas가 그린 것은 손이었으며 다른 학생들이 그 그림에 즉시 관심을 보였다는 내용의 (B)가 오고, 반 학생들이 그림의 손이 누구의 손인지 추측하는 내용의 (C)가 이어진 다음, 선생님이 Douglas에게 누구의 손을 그렸는지 묻자 선생님의 손이라고 답하는 내용의 (A)로 이어지는 것이 글의 흐름상 가장 자연스럽다.

필수 어휘

first grader 1학년 학생   turkey 칠면조   Thanksgiving 추수감사절
softly 조용히, 부드럽게   image 그림, 이미지   immediately 즉시
attract 끌어들이다   protect 보호하다   responsive 호응하는

12 정답 ⑤

According to legend, once a vampire bites a person, that person
~에 따르면
turns into a vampire who seeks the blood of others. ❂ A researcher
~로 변하다   proves의 목적어절
came up with some simple math, / which proves [that these highly
~을 생각해 내다   계속적 용법(= and it(= some simple math))
popular creatures can't exist]. (C) University of Central Florida physics professor Costas Efthimiou's work breaks down the myth.
~을 깨부수다
단서1 Suppose that on January 1st, 1600, the human population was
1600년 1월 1일에 인구가 5억 명이 넘었다고 가정함
just over five hundred million. (B) 단서2 If the first vampire came
그날 흡혈귀가 생겨나서 한 달에 한 명씩
into existence that day and bit one person a month, there would
물었다면 1600년 2월 1일에는 흡혈귀가 둘이 되었을 것임
have been two vampires by February 1st, 1600. A month later there would have been four, the next month eight, then sixteen, and

---

so on. (A) 단서3 **In just two-and-a-half years, the original human**
2년 반 만에 원래의 인구는 모두 흡혈귀가 되어 남아 있지 않았을 것임
population would all have become vampires with no humans left.

But look around you. Have vampires taken over the world? No,
~을 장악하다
because there's no such thing.

해석

전설에 따르면, 흡혈귀가 사람을 물면 그 사람은 다른 사람의 피를 찾는 흡혈귀로 변한다. 한 연구자가 몇 가지 간단한 계산법을 생각해 냈는데, 그것은 이러한 매우 알려진 존재가 실존할 수 없다는 것을 증명한다. (C) Central Florida 대학의 물리학과 교수 Costas Efthimiou의 연구가 그 미신을 깨부순다. 1600년 1월 1일에 인구가 5억 명이 넘었다고 가정해 보자. (B) 그날 최초의 흡혈귀가 생겨나서 한 달에 한 명을 물었다면, 1600년 2월 1일까지 흡혈귀가 둘 있었을 것이다. 한 달 뒤에 넷, 그 다음 달은 여덟, 그리고 열여섯 등으로 계속 늘어났을 것이다. (A) 불과 2년 반 만에, 원래의 인구는 모두 흡혈귀가 되어 더 이상 남아 있지 않았을 것이다. 그러나 주위를 둘러보아라. 흡혈귀가 세상을 장악하였는가? 아니다. 왜냐하면 그런 것은 존재하지 않으니까.

정답이 보이는 해설

한 연구자가 흡혈귀에 대한 계산법을 생각해 냈는데 그것은 잘 알려진 존재가 실존할 수 없음을 증명한다는 내용의 주어진 글 다음에는, 그 교수의 계산법에서 과거 어느 날의 인구를 가정하는 내용의 (C)가 오고, 그날 흡혈귀가 생겨나서 한 달에 한 명씩 문다면 계속해서 매달 두 배씩 늘어났을 것이라는 내용의 (B)가 온 다음, 그랬다면 결국 인류는 모두 흡혈귀가 되어 있었을 것이지만 그런 일은 일어나지 않았기 때문에 흡혈귀는 존재할 수 없다는 내용의 (A)가 마지막에 오는 것이 글의 흐름상 가장 자연스럽다.

필수 어휘

legend 전설 vampire 흡혈귀 prove 증명하다 creature 존재
myth 미신, 사회적 통념 suppose 가정하다
come into existence 생기다, 나타나다 original 원래의 population 인구

---

13 정답 ③

202203 36번 정답률 61%

Toward the end of the 19th century, a new architectural attitude

emerged. ✪ Industrial architecture, (the argument went,) was

ugly and inhuman; / past styles had more to do with pretension
have to do with: ~와 관계가 있다
/ than [**what** people needed in their homes]. (B) 단서1 **Instead**
↳ 선행사를 포함한 관계대명사(~하는 것)   과거의 건축
of these approaches, why not look at the way ordinary country
양식이 허세와 관련이 있었다는 접근 대신 시골 건축업자들이 과거에 일했던 방식을 볼 것을 제안
builders worked in the past? They developed their craft skills over

generations, demonstrating mastery of both tools and materials.

(C) 단서2 **Those materials were local, and used with simplicity —**
공예의 재료는 지역적이고, 단순하게 사용됨
houses built this way had plain wooden floors and whitewashed

walls inside. (A) 단서3 **But they supplied people's needs perfectly**
하지만 그것들은 사람들의 필요를 완벽하게 충족시킴
and, at their best, had a beauty that came from the craftsman's skill
가장 좋은 상태에
and the rootedness of the house in its locality.

해석

19세기 말이 되면서 새로운 건축학적 사고방식이 출현했다. 그 주장에 따르면, 산업 건축은 추하고 비인간적이었으며, 과거의 양식은 사람들이 그들의 집에서 필요했던 것보다는 허세와 더 관계가 있었다. (B) 이러한 접근 대신에 평범한 시골 건축업자들이 과거에 일했던 방식을 살펴보는 것은 어떤가? 그들은 도구와 재료 모두에 숙달한 기술을 보여 주면서, 세대를 거쳐 공예 기술을 발전시켰다. (C) 그 재료는 지역적이고 단순하게 사용되었는데, 이러한 방식으로 건축된 집들은 실내가 평범한 나무 바닥과 회반죽을 칠한 벽으로 되어 있었다. (A) 그러나 그것들은 사람들의 필요를 완

벽하게 충족시켰고, 가장 잘 된 경우에는, 장인의 솜씨와 그 집의 지역에 뿌리내림에서 비롯된 아름다움을 지니고 있었다.

정답이 보이는 해설

19세기 말에 등장한 새로운 건축학적 사고방식에서는 과거의 건축 양식은 사람들이 집에서 필요한 것보다는 허세와 관련이 있었다고 주장했다는 내용의 주어진 글 다음에는, 시골 건축업자들이 과거에 일했던 방식을 살펴볼 것을 제안하면서 그들이 도구와 재료에 숙달된 기술을 갖고 있고 공예 기술을 발전시켰다는 내용의 (B)가 오고, 이러한 방식으로 건축된 집들은 실내가 평범한 재료로 이루어져 있었다는 내용의 (C)가 온 다음, 그럼에도 그것들은 사람들의 필요를 완벽히 충족시켰다는 내용의 (A)가 오는 것이 글의 흐름상 가장 자연스럽다.

필수 어휘

architectural 건축학의 attitude 사고방식 emerge 출현하다, 나타나다
industrial 산업의 argument 주장 inhuman 비인간적인 ordinary 평범한
generation 세대 mastery 숙달한 기술 simplicity 단순함 plain 평범한
supply (필요를) 충족시키다 craftsman 장인 rootedness 뿌리내림
locality 지역

---

14 정답 ②

202203 37번 정답률 61%

Robert Schumann once said, "The laws of morals are those of

art." What the great man is saying here is that there is good music

and bad music. (B) 단서1 **The greatest music, even if it's tragic in**
위대한 음악은 우리의 세계보다 더 높은 세계로 우리를 데려감
nature, takes us to a world higher than ours; somehow the beauty

uplifts us. **Bad music, on the other hand, degrades us.** (A) It's the
반면 나쁜 음악은 우리를 격하시킴
same with performances: a bad performance isn't necessarily the
                                        not necessarily: 반드시 ~인 것은 아니다
result of incompetence. 단서2 **Some of the worst performances**
                               숙련된 연주자라고 해도 연주하는 곡보다 자기를 더 먼저
occur when the performers, no matter how accomplished, **are**
생각하는 경우 최악의 연주
thinking more of themselves than of the music they're playing. (C)

단서3 **These doubtful characters aren't really listening to what the**
       이러한 연주자들은 작곡가가 말하고 있는 것을 진정으로 듣는 것이 아님
composer is saying — they're just showing off, hoping that they'll
                                      show off: 뽐내다
have a great 'success' with the public. ✪ The performer's basic task

is [to try to understand the meaning of the music], / and then [to
      is의 보어1   is의 보어2
communicate it honestly to others].
= the meaning of the music

해석

Robert Schumann은 "도덕의 법칙은 예술의 법칙이다."라고 말한 적이 있다. 여기서 이 거장이 말하고 있는 것은 좋은 음악과 나쁜 음악이 있다는 것이다. (B) 가장 위대한 음악은, 심지어 그것이 사실상 비극적일지라도 우리의 세계보다 더 높은 세계로 우리를 데려간다. 그래서 어떻게든지 아름다움은 우리를 높인다. 반면에 나쁜 음악은 우리를 격하시킨다. (A) 연주도 마찬가지다. 나쁜 연주가 반드시 무능의 결과는 아니다. 최악의 연주 중 일부는 연주자들이 아무리 숙달되었더라도 연주하고 있는 곡보다 자기 자신을 더 생각하고 있을 때 생긴다. (C) 이 미덥지 못한 사람들은 작곡가가 말하는 것을 정말로 듣고 있는 것이 아니다. 그들은 대중들에게 큰 '성공'을 거두기를 바라며 그저 뽐내고 있을 뿐이다. 연주자의 기본 임무는 음악의 의미를 이해하려고 노력하고, 그러고 나서 그것을 다른 사람들에게 정직하게 전달하는 것이다.

정답이 보이는 해설

도덕과 마찬가지로 음악에도 좋은 음악과 나쁜 음악이 있다는 내용의 주어진 글 다음에는, 좋은 음악은 우리를 더 높은 세계로 이끄는 반면 나쁜 음악은 우리를 격하시킨다는 내용의 (B)가 나오고, 연주의 경우에도 연주자가 아무리 숙달되었다 하더라도 연주하는 음악보다 자신을 더 생각하고 있다면 최악의 연주가 된다는 내용의 (A)가 이어진 다음, 이러한 연주자는 음악의 의미를 이해하기보다는 그저 대중적으로

성공하기만을 바라면서 뽐내고 있을 뿐이라는 내용의 (C)가 오는 것이 글의 흐름상 가장 자연스럽다.

필수 어휘

moral 도덕의 tragic 비극적인 in nature 사실상 somehow 어떻게든지
uplift 높이다, (~을) 감정적으로 고양하다 performance 연주
accomplished 숙달된 doubtful 미덥지 못한 composer 작곡가
communicate 전달하다 honestly 정직하게

15 정답 ③

Roughly twenty years ago, brick-and-mortar stores began to give way to electronic commerce. For good or bad, the shift
~로 바뀌다
fundamentally changed consumers' perception of the shopping experience. (B) 단서1 Nowhere was the shift more obvious than
그 변화(오프라인 상점이 전자 상점으로 바뀐 것)로 온라인 서점이 시작됨
with book sales, which is how online bookstores got their start.

✪ Physical bookstores simply could not stock **as many** titles **as** a
as many[much] 명사 as: ~만큼 많은 …
virtual bookstore could. There is only so much space available on
↳ (stock)
a shelf. (C) 단서2 In addition to greater variety, online bookstores
온라인 서점은 다양성뿐만 아니라 많은 할인을 제공함
were also able to offer aggressive discounts thanks to their lower
~ 덕분에
operating costs. The combination of lower prices and greater selection led to the slow, steady rise of online bookstores. (A) Before long, the e-commerce book market naturally expanded to include additional categories, like CDs and DVDs. 단서3
E-commerce soon snowballed into the enormous industry it is today,
전자 상거래는 거대 산업이 되었고 모든 것을 온라인에서 구입할 수 있음
where you can buy everything from toilet paper to cars online.
from A to B: A에서 B에 이르기까지

해석

대략 20년 전에 오프라인 거래 상점이 전자 상거래로 바뀌기 시작했다. 좋든 나쁘든 그 변화는 쇼핑 경험에 대한 소비자의 인식을 근본적으로 바꾸었다. (B) 그 변화가 도서 판매보다 더 분명한 곳은 어디에도 없었는데, 그것은 온라인 서점이 시작된 방식이다. 물리적인 서점은 가상의 서점이 할 수 있는 만큼 많은 서적을 저장할 수 없었다. 책꽂이 위에 이용 가능한 공간 딱 그 정도밖에 없다. (C) 더 많은 다양성에 더하여 온라인 서점은 또한 그들의 더 낮은 운영비 덕분에 공격적인 할인을 제공할 수 있었다. 더 낮은 가격과 더 많은 선택의 결합은 온라인 서점의 느리지만 꾸준한 상승으로 이어졌다. (A) 머지않아 전자 상거래 도서 시장은 CD와 DVD 같은 추가적인 항목을 포함하도록 자연스럽게 확장되었다. 전자 상거래는 곧 오늘날의 거대 산업으로 눈덩이처럼 커졌고, 그곳에서 여러분은 화장실 휴지에서부터 자동차까지 모든 것을 온라인으로 살 수 있다.

정답이 보이는 해설

오프라인 상점이 전자 상거래로 바뀌면서 소비자의 인식을 근본적으로 바꾸었다는 내용의 주어진 글 다음에는, 그 변화로 온라인 서점이 시작되었는데, 물리적인 서점은 가상 서점만큼 많은 책을 저장할 수 없었기 때문에 이로 인해 온라인 서점이 시작되었다는 내용의 (B)가 이어지고, 온라인 서점은 이러한 다양성뿐만 아니라 더 낮은 가격과 더 많은 선택을 제공하여 꾸준히 상승했다는 내용의 (C)가 온 다음, 전자 상거래 도서 시장이 점점 더 확장되어 현재 거대 산업이 되었다는 내용의 (A)가 오는 것이 글의 흐름상 가장 자연스럽다.

🔍 선택지 완벽 분석

② (C)는 (B)에서 언급한 온라인 서점에 대한 추가 장점을 언급하고 있으므로 (B) 다음에는 (C)가 이어져야 한다.

필수 어휘

electronic commerce 전자 상거래 fundamentally 근본적으로
perception 인식 obvious 분명한, 확실한 physical 물리적인 title 서적
virtual 가상의 aggressive 공격적인 operating cost 운영비
combination 결합 snowball 눈덩이처럼 커지다 enormous 거대한

16 정답 ⑤

Literary works, by their nature, suggest rather than explain; they
~하기보다는
imply rather than state their claims boldly and directly. (C) 단서1
This broad generalization, however, does not mean that works of
하지만 이 넓은 일반화는 문학 작품이 직접적인 진술을 포함하지 않는 것은 아님
literature do not include direct statements. Depending on when
~에 따라
they were written and by whom, literary works may contain large amounts of direct telling and lesser amounts of suggestion and implication. (B) 단서2 But whatever the proportion of a work's
문학 작품의 보여 주기 대 말하기의 비율과 상관없이 독자가 해석해야
showing to telling, there is always something for readers to
하는 것이 항상 존재함
interpret. Thus we ask the question "What does the text suggest?" as a way to approach literary interpretation, as a way to begin thinking about a text's implications. (A) 단서3 What a text implies is
텍스트가 함축하는 바를 파악하는
often of great interest to us. ✪ And our work of figuring out a text's
것은 대단히 흥미로움   단수 주어   ~을 파악하다
implications / tests our analytical powers. In considering what a text
단수 동사
suggests, we gain practice in making sense of texts.
~을 이해하다

해석

문학 작품은 그 본질상 설명하기보다는 암시하며, 그것은 자신의 주장을 뚜렷하고 직접적으로 진술하기보다는 함축한다. (C) 하지만 이 넓은 일반화는 문학 작품이 직접적인 진술을 포함하지 않는다는 것을 의미하지는 않는다. 언제 그리고 누구에 의해 쓰였는지에 따라 문학 작품은 많은 양의 직접적 말하기와 더 적은 양의 암시와 함축을 포함할 수도 있다. (B) 그러나 작품의 보여 주기 대 말하기의 비율이 어떻든 간에 독자가 해석해야 하는 무언가가 항상 있다. 따라서 우리는 문학적 해석에 접근하는 방법이자 텍스트의 함축에 대해 생각하기 시작하는 방법으로서 "그 텍스트가 무엇을 암시하는가?"라는 질문을 한다. (A) 텍스트가 무엇을 함축하는지는 흔히 우리에게 대단히 흥미롭다. 그리고 텍스트의 함축을 파악하는 우리의 노력은 우리의 분석적 능력을 시험한다. 텍스트가 무엇을 암시하는지를 고려하는 것에서 우리는 텍스트를 이해하는 기량을 얻게 된다.

정답이 보이는 해설

문학 작품은 직접적으로 설명하기보다는 함축한다는 내용의 주어진 글 다음에는, 문학 작품이 때에 따라 직접적 진술을 포함할 수도 있다는 내용의 (C)가 오고, 그럼에도 문학 작품에는 독자가 해석해야 하는 무언가가 항상 존재하기 때문에 우리는 텍스트가 무엇을 함축하는지 질문을 한다는 내용의 (B)가 나온 다음, 마지막으로 텍스트가 함축하는 것을 파악하는 노력을 통해 텍스트를 이해하는 기량을 얻게 된다는 (A)가 오는 것이 글의 흐름상 가장 자연스럽다.

필수 어휘

literary work 문학 작품 nature 본질 imply 함축하다 generalization 일반화
literature 문학 statement 진술 implication 함축 proportion 비율
interpret 해석하다 analytical 분석적인 practice 기량, 연습

17 정답 ⑤

✪ [Understanding (how to develop respect for and a knowledge
주어(동명사)   의문사+to부정사

of other cultures)] / begins with reexamining the golden rule: // "I
동사(단수)   →수동형 to부정사: to be+p.p.
treat others *in the way* [I want to be treated]." (C) 단서1 **This rule**
= how   이 법칙(황금률)은
makes sense on some level; if we treat others as well as we want to
어느 정도는 타당함 └ make sense: 의미가 통하다, 타당하다
be treated, we will be treated well in return. This rule works well in
work well: 잘 먹히다. 일을 잘하다
a monocultural setting, where everyone is working within the same
cultural framework. (B) 단서2 **In a multicultural setting, however,**
그러나 다문화 환경에서 이 법칙은 의도치 않은 결과를 얻음
where words, gestures, beliefs, and views may have different
meanings, this rule has an unintended result; it can send a message
that my culture is better than yours. (A) 단서3 **It can also create a**
그것(의도치 않은 결과)은 또한
frustrating situation where we believe we are doing what is right,
불만스러운 상황을 야기함
but what we are doing is not being interpreted in the way in which
it was meant. This miscommunication can lead to problems.
~로 이어지다

해석

타문화에 대한 존중과 지식을 발달시키는 방법을 이해하는 것은 황금률을 재점검해 보는 일로 시작된다. 즉, "나는 내가 대접받고 싶은 방식대로 당신을 대접합니다." (C) 이 법칙은 어느 수준에서는 타당하다. 만약 우리가 대접받고 싶은 만큼 다른 사람들을 대접한다면 우리는 보답으로 잘 대접받게 될 것이다. 이 법칙은 모든 사람이 같은 문화적 틀 안에서 일하는 단일 문화 환경에서는 잘 먹힌다. (B) 그러나 단어, 제스처, 신념과 관점이 다른 의미를 지닐지도 모르는 다문화 환경에서는 이 법칙이 의도하지 않은 결과를 얻는다. 즉, 그것은 나의 문화가 너의 문화보다 낫다는 메시지를 보낼 수 있다. (A) 그것은 또한 우리가 옳은 것을 하고 있다고 믿지만, 우리가 하는 것이 의도된 방식으로 해석되지 않고 있는 불만스러운 상황을 만들 수도 있다. 이러한 의사소통 오류는 문제를 야기할 수 있다.

정답이 보이는 해설

타문화에 대한 존중과 지식을 발달시키려면 "내가 대접받고 싶은 방식대로 당신을 대접한다"라는 황금률을 재점검해 보는 일로 시작된다는 주어진 문장 다음에는, 그 법칙이 같은 문화적 틀 안에서는 잘 먹힌다는 내용의 (C)가 이어지고, 그 반대로 다문화 환경에서는 이 법칙이 의도치 않은 결과를 얻을 수도 있다는 내용의 (B)가 이어지며, 나의 문화가 너의 문화보다 낫다는 메시지를 보낼 수 있다는 (B)의 마지막 말에 이어 우리가 의도하는 방식대로 해석되지 않음으로써 의사소통 오류가 생기고 이는 문제를 야기할 수 있다는 내용의 (A)로 이어지는 것이 글의 흐름상 가장 자연스럽다.

선택지 완벽 분석

④ 함정 (A)의 It은 다음에 이어지는 내용으로 보아 (B)의 마지막 문장인 '규칙이 의도치 않은 결과, 즉 나의 문화가 너의 문화보다 낫다는 메시지를 준다'를 가리킨다. 따라서 (B) 다음에 (A)가 와야 글의 흐름이 자연스럽다.

필수 어휘

respect 존중 reexamine 재점검하다 golden rule 황금률 treat 대접하다
monocultural 단일 문화의 framework 틀, 체제 multicultural 다문화의
unintended 의도하지 않은 frustrating 불만스러운 interpret 해석하다
miscommunication 의사소통 오류

18 정답 ④

202109 37번 정답률 40%

★ In a study, / *a researcher* (pretending to be a volunteer)
주어   →~인 체하다
현재분사구
surveyed a California neighborhood, / asking residents [if they
동사   분사구문(부대상황) ask의 목적어(명사절)
would allow a *large sign* (reading ''Drive Carefully'') to be
to부정사의 수동형(큰 표지판이 전시됨)
displayed on their front lawns]. (C) 단서1 **To help them understand**
~처럼 보이다 그것(큰 표지판)이 어떻게 보이는지
what it would look like, the volunteer showed his participants a
이해시키기 위해 집을 가릴 정도로 큰 표지판을 보여 줌

picture of the large sign blocking the view of a beautiful house.
Naturally, most people refused, but 단서2 **in one particular group,**
한 집단에서 놀랍게도 76%의 거주자
an incredible 76 percent actually approved. (A) 단서3 **The reason**
들이 승낙함   그 이유는 2주 전
that they agreed was this: two weeks earlier, these residents had
작은 표지판을 거는 것에 대해 요청받음
been asked by another volunteer to make a small commitment to
display a tiny sign that read "Be a Safe Driver" in their windows.
(B) 단서4 **Since it was such a small and simple request, nearly all**
그것(요청)이 너무 사소한 것이어서 거의 모든 사람들이 허락함
of them agreed. The astonishing result was that the initial small
commitment deeply influenced their willingness to accept the much
larger request two weeks later.

해석

한 연구에서, 자원봉사자로 가장한 한 연구원이 어느 캘리포니아 동네의 주민들에게 그들의 앞마당에 "운전 조심"이라고 쓰인 큰 표지판을 세워 두는 것을 허락할지를 묻는 설문조사를 했다. (C) 그것이 어떻게 보일지에 대한 그들의 이해를 돕기 위해, 그 자원봉사자는 참여자들에게 아름다운 집의 전망을 막는 큰 표지판 사진을 보여 주었다. 당연히, 대부분의 사람들은 거절했지만, 한 특정 그룹에서 놀랍게도 76퍼센트가 실제로 승낙했다. (A) 그들이 동의한 이유는 이것이었는데, 즉 2주 전에, 이 주민들이 다른 자원봉사자로부터 "안전한 운전자가 되세요"라고 쓰인 아주 작은 표지판을 그들의 창문에 놓는다는 작은 약속을 하도록 요청받은 적이 있었기 때문이었다. (B) 그것은 아주 작고 간단한 요청이었기 때문에, 그들 중 거의 모두가 동의했다. 놀라운 결과는, 그들이 한 처음의 작은 약속이 2주 후의 훨씬 더 큰 요청을 기꺼이 받아들이는 데 큰 영향을 끼쳤다는 것이다.

정답이 보이는 해설

자원봉사자로 가장한 한 연구원이 "운전 조심"이라는 큰 표지판을 세워 두는 것을 허락할지에 관한 설문조사를 했다는 주어진 글 다음에는, 그 큰 표지판이 얼마나 큰지를 설명하면서 대부분의 사람들이 거절했지만 특정 그룹에서는 76퍼센트의 놀라운 사람들이 승낙했다는 내용의 (C)가 이어지고, 그 이유에 대해 설명하는 (A)가 이어지며, 설문조사의 놀라운 결과에 대해 설명하는 (B)로 이어지는 것이 글의 흐름상 가장 자연스럽다.

선택지 완벽 분석

② ③ 함정 주어진 문장에서 큰 표지판을 세워 두는 것을 허락할지에 대한 요청이 작고 단순하다고 생각할 수 있어서 (B)로 이어지는 것이 타당해 보이지만, 다음에 이어지는 문장에서 설문조사의 놀라운 결과에 대해 언급하고 있으므로 (B)는 맨 마지막에 오는 것이 타당하다.

필수 어휘

pretend ~인 척하다 survey 설문조사하다 resident 주민 display 전시하다
participant 참가자 naturally 당연히, 물론 incredible 믿을 수 없는
approve 승낙하다 commitment 약속 request 요청 astonishing 놀라운
initial 처음의 willingness 기꺼이 하려는 의향[마음]

19 정답 ⑤

202106 36번 정답률 73%

주제문 Starting from birth, babies are immediately attracted to
~에서부터
faces. 단서1 Scientists were able to show this by having babies look
과학자들이 아기들에게 두 개의 이미지를 보여 줌으로써 이를 증명함
at two simple images, one that looks more like a face than the other.
(C) 단서2 **By measuring where the babies looked, scientists found**
아기들이 보는 곳을 유심히 살핌으로써 과학자들은 아기들이 얼굴 이미지를 더 많이
that the babies looked at the face-like image more than they looked
본다는 것을 발견함
at the non-face image. Even though babies have poor eyesight, they
prefer to look at faces. 단서3 **But why?** (B) 단서4 **One reason babies**
~을 더 좋아하다   왜 아기들이 얼굴 보는 것을 좋아할까? (얼굴을 좋아하는)

might like faces is because of something called evolution. 단서5
한 가지 이유는 진화라고 불리는 것 때문임

Evolution involves changes to the structures of an organism(such
진화는 변화를 수반함

as the brain) that occur over many generations. (A) 단서6 These
이러한

changes help the organisms to survive, making them alert to
변화는 유기체가 생존하도록 도움을 줌

enemies. ✪ **By being** able to recognize faces / from afar or in the
～함으로써(부사구)

dark, / humans **were able to know** / someone was coming / and
(were able to)　　　동사1

protect themselves from possible danger.
동사2　protect oneself from ～: ～로부터 자신을 보호하다

해석

아기들은 태어나면서부터 즉시 얼굴에 끌린다. 과학자들은 아기들에게 간단한 두 개의 이미지, 즉 한 이미지는 다른 이미지에 비해 좀 더 얼굴처럼 보이는 이미지들을 보여 줌으로써 이것을 증명할 수 있었다. (C) 과학자들은 아기들이 보는 곳을 유심히 살피면서, 아기들이 얼굴처럼 보이지 않는 이미지보다는 얼굴처럼 보이는 이미지를 더 많이 본다는 것을 발견했다. 아기들은 시력이 좋지 않음에도 불구하고 얼굴을 보는 것을 더 좋아한다. 왜 그럴까? (B) 아기들이 얼굴을 좋아할 것 같은 한 가지 이유는 진화라고 불리는 것 때문이다. 진화는 많은 세대를 거쳐 발생하는 유기체 구조(뇌와 같은 것)의 변화를 수반한다. (A) 이런 변화들은 적들을 경계하게 해서 유기체가 살아남도록 도와준다. 인간은 멀리서 또는 어둠 속에서 얼굴을 알아볼 수 있음으로써 누군가가 다가오는지 알 수 있었고, 가능한 위험으로부터 자신들을 보호할 수 있었다.

정답이 보이는 해설

아기들이 태어나면서부터 얼굴에 끌리는데, 이를 증명하기 위해 두 개의 이미지를 아이들에게 보여 주는 실험을 했다는 내용의 주어진 글 다음에는, 실험을 어떻게 진행했는지에 대해 언급한 (C)가 오고, 아이들이 왜 얼굴을 좋아하는지에 대한 대답을 제시하고 있는 (B)가 온 다음, 유기체 구조의 변화들은 적들을 경계하여 유기체가 생존하는 데 도움을 준다는 내용의 (A)가 이어지는 것이 글의 흐름상 가장 자연스럽다.

필수 어휘

attract 끌다　measure 측정하다, 판단하다　eyesight 시력　evolution 진화
involve 수반하다, 관련시키다　organism 유기체　generation 세대
alert 경계하는　recognize 알아보다　afar 멀리, 아득히

20 정답 ②

202106 37번 정답률 69%

People spend much of their time interacting with media, but
～와 상호 작용하다

that does not mean that people have the critical skills to analyze

and understand it. (B) One well-known study from Stanford

University in 2016 demonstrated that youth are easily fooled

by misinformation, especially when it comes through social

media channels. 단서1 This weakness is not found only in youth,
이러한 약점은 젊은이에게서만 발견되는 것이 아님

however. (A) ✪ Research (from New York University) found [that
　　　　　　　　　　　　↳배수사+as+형용사/부사의 원급+as: ～보다 ― 배 더 …하게

단서2 people over 65 shared seven times as much misinformation
65세 이상의 사람들이 젊은이들보다 7배나 더 많이 잘못된 정보를 공유함

as their younger counterparts]. All of this raises a question:
　　　　　　　　　　　　　　　　　　　　　　의문을 제기하다

단서3 What's the solution to the misinformation problem? (C) 단서4
잘못된 정보의 문제에 대한 해결책은 무엇인가?

Governments and tech platforms certainly have a role to play in
정부와 기술 플랫폼은 잘못된 정보를 막아 내는 데 해야 할 역할이 있음

blocking misinformation. 주제문 However, every individual needs

to take responsibility for combating this threat by becoming more

information literate.

해석

사람들은 많은 시간을 미디어와 상호 작용하는 데 보내지만, 그것이 사람들이 미디어를 분석하고 이해하는 데 중요한 기술을 가지고 있다는 것을 의미하는 것은 아니다. (B) 2016년 Stanford 대학의 잘 알려진 한 연구는 젊은이들이 특히 소셜 미디어 채널을 통해 잘못된 정보에 쉽게 속는다는 것을 보여 주었다. 그러나 이러한 약점은 젊은이에게서만 발견되는 것은 아니다. (A) New York 대학의 조사는 65세 이상의 사람들이 좀 더 젊은 상대방보다 7배나 더 많이 잘못된 정보를 공유한다는 것을 알았다. 이 모든 것이 의문을 제기하는데, 즉 잘못된 정보 문제에 대한 해결책은 무엇인가? (C) 정부와 기술 플랫폼은 분명히 잘못된 정보를 막아 내는 데 해야 할 역할이 있다. 그러나 모든 개인은 정보를 더 잘 이용할 줄 앎으로써 이러한 위협에 맞서 싸울 책임을 지닐 필요가 있다.

정답이 보이는 해설

사람들은 미디어와 상호 작용하는 데 많은 시간을 보내지만 그것이 미디어 분석과 이해에 중요한 기술을 가지고 있다는 것을 의미하지 않는다는 내용의 주어진 문장 다음에는, 젊은이들이 소셜 미디어 채널을 통해 잘못된 정보에 쉽게 속는다는 연구 결과를 언급한 (B)가 오고, 또 다른 연구 결과로 65세 이상의 사람들이 젊은이보다 7배나 많은 잘못된 정보를 공유한다는 것을 언급한 후, 이에 대한 해결책이 무엇인지 묻고 있는 (A)가 온 다음, 정부와 기술 플랫폼이 잘못된 정보를 막아 내는 역할을 해야 한다는 내용의 (C)가 이어지는 것이 글의 흐름상 가장 자연스럽다.

필수 어휘

interact 상호 작용하다, 소통하다　critical 중요한　analyze 분석하다
demonstrate 보여 주다, 증명하다　weakness 약점　raise 제기하다
certainly 분명히, 확실히　responsibility 책임　combat 싸우다
information literate 정보를 이용할 줄 아는

21 정답 ②

202103 36번 정답률 58%

Almost all major sporting activities are played with a ball. (B)
　　　　　　　　　　　　스포츠 활동

✪ 단서1 The rules of the game always include rules about *the type*
경기 규칙에는 항상 공의 유형에 대한 규칙이 포함됨

of ball [that is allowed], / (starting with the size and weight of
　　　　　관계대명사절　　　　　　　분사구문(부대상황)

the ball). 단서2 The ball must also have a certain stiffness. (A) A
공은 어느 정도의 단단함이 있어야 함

ball might have the correct size and weight but 단서3 if it is made
　　　　　　　　　　　　　　　　　　　　　　　속이 빈 강철 공은

as a hollow ball of steel it will be too stiff and if it is made from
너무 단단하고, 중심부가 무거운 발포 고무로 만들어진 공은 너무 물렁함

light foam rubber with a heavy center it will be too soft. (C) 단서4
　　↳～와 함께

Similarly, along with stiffness, a ball needs to bounce properly. A
마찬가지로 단단함과 함께 공은 적절히 튀어야 함

solid rubber ball would be too bouncy for most sports, and a solid

ball made of clay would not bounce at all.
　　　　　　　　　　　　전혀 ～ 아니다

해석

거의 모든 주요 스포츠 활동은 공으로 한다. (B) 경기의 규칙들은 항상 공의 크기와 무게부터 시작하여 허용되는 공의 유형에 대한 규칙들을 포함하고 있다. 공은 또한 어느 정도 단단함이 있어야 한다. (A) 공이 적절한 크기와 무게를 가질 수 있지만 속이 빈 강철 공으로 만들어지면 그 공은 너무 단단할 것이고, 무거운 중심부를 가진 가벼운 발포 고무로 만들어지면 그 공은 너무 물렁할 것이다. (C) 마찬가지로, 단단함과 더불어 공은 적절히 튀어야 한다. 순전히 고무로만 된 공은 대부분의 스포츠에서 지나치게 잘 튈 것이고, 순전히 점토로만 만든 공은 전혀 튀지 않을 것이다.

정답이 보이는 해설

모든 주요 스포츠 활동이 공으로 이루어진다는 주어진 문장 다음에는, 경기 규칙에 항상 공의 유형에 관한 규칙이 포함되어 있고, 공이 어느 정도 단단해야 한다는 내용의 (B)가 이어지고, 공의 크기와 무게와 더불어 재질에 따라 단단함의 정도가 다르다는 내용의 (A)가 이어지며, 단단함과 더불어 적절히 튀어야 하는데 공의 재질에 따라 튐의 정도가 다르다는 내용의 (C)가 이어지는 것이 글의 흐름상 가장 자연스럽다.

③ **함정** (C)의 Similarly는 다음에 나오는 내용이 재질에 따라 튐의 정도가 다른 내용이므로, (A)에서 언급한 공의 재질에 따라 단단함의 정도가 다르다는 내용에 이어짐을 알 수 있다. 따라서 (C)는 (A) 다음에 와야 글의 흐름이 자연스럽다.

필수 어휘

include 포함하다 certain 어느 정도의 hollow 속이 빈 light 가벼운
foam rubber 발포 고무 bounce 튀다 properly 적절히
solid 순수한(다른 물질이 섞이지 않은), 고체의 rubber 고무 clay 점토

22 정답 ③

202103 37번 정답률 64%

If you had to write a math equation, **단서1** you probably wouldn't
write, "Twenty-eight plus fourteen equals forty-two." ✪ It would
take too long to write / and it would be hard to read quickly. (B)
단서2 You would write, "28＋14 ＝ 42." Chemistry is the same way.
Chemists have to write chemical equations all the time, and **단서3** it
would take too long to write and read if they had to spell everything
out. (C) **단서4** So chemists use symbols, just like we do in math.
A chemical formula lists all the elements that form each molecule
and **단서5** uses a small number to the bottom right of an element's
symbol to stand for the number of atoms of that element. (A) **단서6**
For example, the chemical formula for water is H₂O. That tells us
that a water molecule is made up of two hydrogen ("H" and "2")
atoms and one oxygen ("O") atom.

해석

여러분이 만일 수학 등식을 써야 한다면, 여러분은 아마 '스물여덟 더하기 열넷은 마흔둘과 같다.'라고 쓰지 않을 것이다. 쓰는 데 너무 오래 걸리고 빨리 읽기가 어려울 것이다. (B) 여러분은 '28＋14 ＝ 42'라고 쓸 것이다. 화학도 마찬가지이다. 화학자들은 항상 화학 방정식을 써야 하고, 만약 그들이 모든 것을 상세히 전부 써야 한다면 쓰고 읽는 것이 너무 오래 걸릴 것이다. (C) 그래서 화학자들은 우리가 수학에서 하듯이 기호를 사용한다. 화학식은 각 분자를 구성하는 모든 원소를 나열하고 그 원소의 원자 수를 나타내기 위해 원소 기호의 오른쪽 아래에 작은 숫자를 쓴다. (A) 예를 들어, 물의 화학식은 H₂O이다. 그것은 우리에게 하나의 물 분자는 두 개의 수소('H'와 '2') 원자와 하나의 산소('O') 원자로 이루어져 있다는 것을 알려 준다.

정답이 보이는 해설

우리가 수학 등식을 쓸 때 문장 형태로 쓰지 않는데, 이렇게 쓰면 쓰는 시간도 오래 걸리고 읽기도 어렵기 때문이라는 내용의 주어진 글 다음에는, 간단한 수학식으로 쓴다고 하면서 이런 방식은 화학에서도 마찬가지라는 내용의 (B)가 이어지고, 그 구체적인 내용으로 화학식에 대해 설명하는 내용의 (C)가 이어지며, (C)에서 언급된 화학식의 한 예로 물의 화학식에 대해 설명하는 (A)가 이어지는 것이 글의 흐름상 가장 자연스럽다.

필수 어휘

equation 등식, 방정식 chemistry 화학 chemist 화학자 list 나열하다, 열거하다
element 원소, 요소 form 구성하다, 형성하다 bottom 아래(의)
atom 원자 hydrogen 수소 oxygen 산소

23 정답 ②

202011 36번 정답률 84%

Imagine yourself at a party. It is dark and a group of friends ask
you to take a picture of them. **단서1** You grab your camera, point,
and shoot your friends. (B) **단서2** The camera automatically turns on
the flash as there is not enough light available to produce a correct
exposure. **단서3** The result is half of your friends appear in the
picture with two bright red circles instead of their eyes. (A) **단서4**
This is a common problem called the *red-eye effect*. It is caused
because the light from the flash penetrates the eyes through the
pupils, and then **단서5** gets reflected to the camera from the back
of the eyes where a large amount of blood is present. (C) **단서6**
This blood is the reason why the eyes look red in the photograph.
This effect is more noticeable when there is not much light in the
environment. ✪ This is [because pupils dilate when it is dark, /
(**allowing** more light to get inside the eye and **producing** a larger
red-eye effect)].

해석

자신이 파티에 있다고 상상해 보라. 어두운데 한 무리의 친구들이 여러분에게 사진을 찍어 달라고 요청한다. 여러분은 카메라를 잡고 초점을 맞춰 친구들의 사진을 찍는다. (B) 정확한 노출을 만들어 내기 위해 사용할 수 있는 빛이 충분하지 않기 때문에 카메라는 자동으로 플래시를 켠다. 그 결과 친구들 중 절반이 두 눈 대신 두 개의 밝은 빨간색 원과 함께 사진에 나온다. (A) 이것은 '적목(赤目) 현상'이라고 불리는 흔한 문제이다. 이 현상은 플래시에서 나오는 빛이 동공을 통해 눈을 통과한 뒤, 많은 양의 피가 있는 눈 뒤쪽에서 카메라로 반사되기 때문에 발생한다. (C) 이 피가 사진에서 눈이 붉게 보이는 원인이다. 이 현상은 주변에 빛이 많지 않을 때 더욱 두드러진다. 이는 어두울 때 동공이 확장하여, 더 많은 빛이 눈 안쪽으로 들어오게 하면서 더 큰 적목 현상을 일으키기 때문이다.

정답이 보이는 해설

파티에서 주변이 어두운데 친구들이 사진을 찍어 달라고 요청해서 사진을 찍는다는 내용의 주어진 글 다음에는, 카메라가 충분한 빛을 만들어 내기 위해 자동 플래시를 켠 결과 사진 속의 친구들 중 절반이 빨간 색 눈을 가지게 된다는 내용의 (B)가 이어지고, 이 현상은 '적목 현상'이며 적목 현상이 어떻게 발생하는지를 설명하는 (A)가 이어지며, 적목 현상이 더 심해지는 경우에 대해 설명하는 (C)가 이어지는 것이 글의 흐름상 가장 적절하다.

필수 어휘

grab 잡다, 움켜쥐다 point 초점을 맞추다 shoot 사진을 찍다, 촬영하다
available 이용할 수 있는 exposure 노출 common 흔한 reflect 반사시키다
present 있는, 존재하는 noticeable 두드러진, 현저한

24 정답 ④

202011 37번 정답률 59%

주제문 Even though two variables seem to be related, there may
not be a causal relationship. (C) **단서1** In fact, the two variables may
merely seem to be associated with each other due to the effect of
some third variable. Sociologists call such misleading relationships

spurious. A classic example is the apparent association between children's shoe size and reading ability. 단서2 It seems that as
신발 크기가 증가함에 따라
shoe size increases, reading ability improves. (A) 단서3 Does this
읽기 능력이 증가하는 것처럼 보임　　　　　　이것은 발 크기가
mean that the size of one's feet (independent variable) causes an
(독립 변인)가 읽기 능력(종속 변인) 향상을 야기한다는 것을 의미하는가?
improvement in reading skills (dependent variable)? Certainly not. ✪ This false relationship is caused by *a third factor, age,* /
　　　　　　동사(수동태)
[that is related to shoe size **as well as** reading ability]. (B) 단서4
관계대명사절　　　　A as well as B: B뿐만 아니라 A도 역시
Hence, when researchers attempt to make causal claims about the
두 변인의 인과 관계를 주장할 때 허위 관계를 만들어 낼 가능성이 있는 다른 변인들을 통제하거나 배제해야 함
relationship between an independent and a dependent variable, they must control for — or rule out — other variables that may be
　　　　　　　　　　　　　　배제하다
creating a spurious relationship.

해석

비록 두 변인이 연관된 것처럼 보여도 인과 관계가 없을 수도 있다. (C) 사실, 그 두 변인은 단지 어떤 제3 변인의 영향 때문에 서로 연관된 것처럼 보일지도 모른다. 사회학자들은 그러한 오해의 소지가 있는 관계를 허위라고 부른다. 전형적인 예는 아이들의 신발 크기와 읽기 능력 사이의 명백한 연관성이다. 신발 크기가 커짐에 따라, 읽기 능력이 향상되는 것처럼 보인다. (A) 이것이 발 크기(독립 변인)가 읽기 능력(종속 변인)의 향상을 야기한다는 것을 의미하는가? 분명히 아니다. 이러한 허위 관계는 읽기 능력은 물론 신발 크기와도 연관된 제3 변인인 나이에 의해 야기된다. (B) 이런 이유로, 연구자들이 독립 변인과 종속 변인의 관계에 대한 인과 관계를 주장하려고 시도할 때 그들은 허위 관계를 만들어 낼 수도 있는 다른 변인들을 통제하거나 배제해야 한다.

정답이 보이는 해설

두 변인이 연관된 것처럼 보여도 인과 관계가 없을 수도 있다는 내용의 주어진 문장 다음에는, 두 변인이 제3 변인의 영향 때문에 서로 연관된 것처럼 보이는 허위 관계를 언급하면서 신발 크기와 읽기 능력 사이의 연관성을 예로 언급한 (C)가 이어지고, 이 연관성은 읽기 능력과 신발 크기와 연관된 제3 변인인 나이에 의해 야기된다는 내용의 (A)가 이어지며, 연구자들이 두 변인의 인과 관계를 주장하려고 할 때 허위 관계를 만들어 낼 수 있는 다른 변인을 통제하거나 배제해야 한다는 내용의 (B)가 이어져야 글의 흐름상 가장 자연스럽다.

필수 어휘

causal 인과 관계의 merely 단지 sociologist 사회학자
misleading 오해의 소지가 있는 classic 전형적인 apparent 명백한
association 연관성, 관련성 ability 능력 independent 독립의
improvement 향상, 개선 dependent 종속의 factor 요인
hence 이런 이유로 claim 주장

---

01 정답 ⑤

202309 38번 정답률 29%

주제문 ✪ *Boundaries* (between work and home) are blurring // as
　　　　　　주어　　　　　　　　　　　　　　　동사　　　接속사
portable digital technology makes **it** increasingly possible [**to work**
(~함에 따라)　　　　　　　　　　　　가목적어　　　　　　진목적어(to부정사)
anywhere, anytime]. Individuals differ in how they like to manage their time to meet work and outside responsibilities. Some people prefer to separate or segment roles so that boundary crossings
　　　　　　　　　　　　　　　　so that+주어+동사 ~: ~하기 위해서
are minimized. For example, these people might keep separate email accounts for work and family and try to conduct work at the workplace and take care of family matters only during breaks and nonwork time. We've even noticed more of these "segmenters" carrying two phones — one for work and one for personal use. Flexible schedules work well for these individuals because they enable greater distinction between time at work and time in other roles. Other individuals prefer integrating work and family roles all
　　　　　　　　　　　　　　　　　　　　　　　　　　　　하루 종일
day long. 단서 This might entail constantly trading text messages
　　　　　사무실에서 아이들과 메시지를 주고받거나 집이나 휴가 중에 이메일을
with children from the office, or monitoring emails at home and on
확인하는 것을 수반함
vacation, rather than returning to work to find hundreds of messages in their inbox.

해석

휴대용 디지털 기술이 언제, 어디서나 작업하는 것을 점차 가능하게 함에 따라 직장과 가정의 경계가 흐릿해지고 있다. 개인들은 직장과 외부의 책임을 수행하기 위해 자신의 시간을 관리하기를 바라는 방식에 차이가 있다. 어떤 사람들은 경계 교차 지점이 최소화되도록 역할을 분리하거나 분할하는 것을 선호한다. 예를 들어, 이러한 사람들은 직장과 가정을 위한 별개의 이메일 계정을 유지하고 직장에서 일을 수행하고 휴식 시간과 일을 하지 않는 시간 동안에만 가정사를 처리하려고 할지도 모른다. 우리는 더 많은 이러한 '분할자들'이 심지어 하나는 업무용이고 하나는 개인용인 두 개의 전화기를 가지고 다니고 있음을 알게 되었다. 유연 근로 시간제는 이런 사람들에게 잘 적용되는데, 직장에서의 시간과 다른 역할에서의 시간 간에 더 큰 구별을 가능하게 하기 때문이다. 다른 사람들은 하루 종일 직장과 가정의 역할을 통합하는 것을 선호한다. 이것은 직장으로 돌아가서 받은 수신함에서 수백 개의 메시지를 발견하는 것 대신 사무실에서 아이들과 문자 메시지를 지속적으로 주고받거나 집에서 그리고 휴가 중에 이메일을 확인하는 것을 수반할지도 모른다.

정답이 보이는 해설

주어진 문장은 다른(Other) 사람들은 직장과 가정의 역할을 통합하는 것을 선호한다는 내용이다. 그러므로 이 문장 앞에는 직장과 가정의 역할을 통합하는 것을 선호하지 않는 어떤 사람들에 관한 내용이 나올 수 있다. 글의 전반부에서 직장과 가정의 경계 교차 지점이 분리되거나 분할하는 것을 선호하는 사람들에 대한 내용이 이어지다가 ⑤ 다음에 직장과 가정의 역할을 통합한 예시가 나오고 있으므로, 주어진 문장이 들어가기에 가장 적절한 곳은 ⑤이다.

🔍 선택지 완벽 분석

④ 함정 유연 근로 시간제는 직장에서의 시간과 다른 역할에서의 시간 간에 더 큰 구별을 가능하게 한다는 점에서 직장과 가정의 역할을 분리하거나 분할하고자 하는 사람들에게 잘 적용되는 제도이므로 주어진 문장이 ④에 들어가는 것은 적절하지 않다.

필수 어휘

boundary 경계 portable 휴대용의 differ 다르다
segment 분할하다, 나누다 minimize 최소화하다 account 계정

conduct 수행하다 matter 일, 사안, 문제 flexible 유연한
distinction 구별, 차별 integrate 통합하다 constantly 지속적으로

02 정답 ⑤

202309 39번 정답률 55%

A "complementary good" is a product that is often consumed alongside another product. For example, popcorn is a complementary good to a movie, while a travel pillow is a complementary good for a long plane journey. When the popularity of one product increases, the sales of its complementary good also increase. ✪ By producing goods [that complement other products [that are already (or about to be) popular]], / you can ensure a steady stream of demand (for your product). 단서1 Some products enjoy perfect complementary status — they *have* to be consumed together, such as a lamp and a lightbulb. However, do not assume that a product is perfectly complementary, as customers may not be completely locked in to the product. 단서2 For example, although motorists may seem required to purchase gasoline to run their cars, they can switch to electric cars.

해석

'보완재'는 종종 다른 제품과 함께 소비되는 제품이다. 예를 들어, 팝콘은 영화에 대한 보완재인 한편, 여행 베개는 긴 비행기 여행에 대한 보완재이다. 한 제품의 인기가 높아지면 그것의 보완재 판매량도 증가한다. 여러분은 이미 인기가 있는 (또는 곧 있을) 다른 제품을 보완하는 제품을 생산함으로써 여러분의 제품에 대한 꾸준한 수요 흐름을 보장할 수 있다. 일부 제품들은 완벽한 보완적 상태를 누리고 있고, 그것들은 램프와 전구와 같이 함께 소비'되어야' 한다. 그러나 고객들이 그 제품에 완전히 고정되어 있지 않을 수 있으므로, 어떤 제품이 완벽하게 보완적이라고 가정하지 마라. 예를 들어, 비록 운전자들이 자신의 차를 운전하기 위해 휘발유를 구매할 필요가 있는 것처럼 보일지라도, 그들은 전기 자동차로 바꿀 수 있다.

정답이 보이는 해설

주어진 문장은 However(그러나)로 시작하여 고객들은 제품에 완전히 고정되어 있지 않을 수도 있으니 어떤 제품이 완벽하게 보완적이라고 가정하지 말라는 내용이다. ⑤ 앞에서 일부 제품은 완벽한 보완적 상태를 누리고 있어서 함께 소비되어야 한다고 하고 있지만, 뒤이어 나온 예시는 고객들이 제품을 바꾸어 제품이 보완적이 아니게 된 경우의 예시가 나오고 있으므로 주어진 문장이 들어가기에 가장 적절한 곳은 ⑤이다.

선택지 완벽 분석

④ 일부 제품들은 완벽한 보완적 상태를 누리고 있고, 램프와 전구와 같이 함께 소비되어야 한다는 내용 뒤에 However에 이은 어떤 제품이 완벽하게 보완적이라고 가정하지 말라는 내용이 오는 것이 자연스러우므로 주어진 문장이 ④에 들어가는 것은 글의 흐름상 자연스럽지 않다.

필수 어휘

complementary 보완적인 consume 소비하다, 소모하다
alongside ~와 함께 pillow 베개 produce 생산하다
ensure 보장하다, 반드시 ~하게 하다 stream 흐름 demand 수요
status 상태 purchase 구매하다; 구매

03 정답 ②

202306 38번 정답률 43%

Sometimes the pace of change is far slower. The face you saw reflected in your mirror this morning 단서1 probably appeared no different from the face you saw the day before — or a week or a month ago. 주제문 Yet we know that the face that stares back at us from the glass 단서2 is not the same, cannot be the same, as it was 10 minutes ago. 단서3 The proof is in your photo album: Look at a photograph taken of yourself 5 or 10 years ago and you see clear differences between the face in the snapshot and the face in your mirror. ✪ If you lived in a world without mirrors for a year / and then saw your reflection, // you might be surprised by the change. After an interval of 10 years without seeing yourself, you might not at first recognize the person peering from the mirror. Even something as basic as our 단서4 own face changes from moment to moment.

해석

때때로 변화의 속도는 훨씬 더 느리다. 오늘 아침 거울 속에 비춰진 여러분이 본 얼굴은 아마도 여러분이 그 전날 또는 일주일이나 한 달 전에 본 얼굴과 다르지 않은 것처럼 보였을 것이다. 그러나 우리는 거울로부터 우리를 쳐다보는 얼굴이 10분 전에 그랬던 것과 같지 않고, 같을 수 없다는 것을 안다. 그 증거는 여러분의 사진 앨범에 들어 있다: 5년 또는 10년 전에 찍힌 여러분의 사진을 보면 여러분은 스냅 사진 속의 얼굴과 거울 속 얼굴 사이의 명확한 차이를 알게 될 것이다. 만약 여러분이 일 년간 거울이 없는 세상에 살고 그 이후 (거울에) 비친 여러분의 모습을 본다면, 여러분은 그 변화 때문에 깜짝 놀랄지도 모른다. 자기 자신을 보지 않고 10년의 기간이 지난 후, 당신은 거울에서 응시하고 있는 사람을 처음에는 알아보지 못할지도 모른다. 심지어 우리 자신의 얼굴같이 아주 기본적인 것조차도 순간순간 변한다.

정답이 보이는 해설

주어진 문장은 Yet(하지만)으로 시작하여 '하지만, 우리는 현재 거울 속 얼굴이 10분 전의 얼굴과 같지 않다는 것을 안다'는 내용이다. 그러므로 이 문장 앞에는 현재의 거울 속 얼굴이 얼마 전의 거울 속 얼굴과 같을 것이라고 생각할지도 모른다는 내용이 와야 한다. 이 내용이 ② 앞에 있으므로, 주어진 문장이 들어가기에 가장 적절한 곳은 ②이다.

선택지 완벽 분석

③ ④ 함정 이후의 내용이 모두 얼굴이 변하는 속도는 느리지만, 하루하루 꾸준히 변하고 있다는 증거들이다. 이 증거들이 시작되기 전인 ②에 주어진 문장이 들어가야, 글의 흐름이 자연스러움에 유의한다.

필수 어휘

pace 속도 reflect 비추다 stare 빤히 쳐다보다 proof 증거
snapshot 스냅사진 reflection (거울에 비친) 모습 interval 기간
recognize 알아보다 basic 기본적인

04 정답 ⑤

202306 39번 정답률 33%

According to educational psychologist Susan Engel, curiosity begins to decrease as young as four years old. By the time we are adults, we have fewer questions and more default settings. As Henry James put it, "Disinterested curiosity is past, the mental grooves and channels set." 주제문 The decline in curiosity can be traced in the development of the brain through childhood. Though smaller than the adult brain, the infant brain contains millions more neural connections. The wiring, however, is a mess; the lines of communication between infant neurons are far less efficient than between those in the adult brain. 단서1 The baby's perception of the world is consequently both intensely rich and wildly disordered. As children absorb more evidence from the world around them, certain possibilities become much more likely and more useful and 단서2 harden into knowledge or beliefs. ✪ The neural pathways [that 단서3 enable those beliefs] become faster and more automatic, / while the ones [that the child doesn't use regularly] are pruned away.

해석
교육 심리학자 Susan Engel에 따르면, 호기심은 네 살 정도의 어린 나이에 줄어들기 시작한다. 우리가 어른이 될 무렵, 질문은 더 적어지고 기본값은 더 많아진다. Henry James가 말했듯이, "흥미를 유발하지 않는 호기심은 사라지고, 정신의 고랑과 경로가 자리잡는다." 호기심의 감소는 유년 시절을 통한 뇌의 발달에서 원인을 찾을 수 있다. 비록 성인의 뇌보다는 작지만, 유아의 뇌는 수백만 개 더 많은 신경 연결을 가지고 있다. 그러나 그 연결 상태는 엉망이다; 유아의 뉴런 간의 전달 라인은 성인 뇌의 그것들 간의 전달 라인보다 훨씬 덜 효율적이다. 결과적으로 세상에 대한 아기의 인식은 매우 풍부하면서도 상당히 무질서하다. 아이들이 그들 주변의 세상으로부터 더 많은 증거를 흡수함에 따라, 특정한 가능성들이 훨씬 더 커지게 되고 더 유용하게 되며 지식이나 믿음으로 굳어진다. 그러한 믿음을 가능하게 하는 신경 경로는 더 빠르고 자동적으로 이루어지게 되고 반면에, 아이가 주기적으로 사용하지 않는 경로는 제거된다.

정답이 보이는 해설
아이들이 세상으로부터 더 많은 증거를 흡수함에 따라, 특정한 가능성들이 훨씬 더 커지고 더 유용해지고 지식이나 믿음으로 굳어진다는 주어진 문장은 어릴 때는 호기심이 많지만, 어른이 되면 호기심이 없어지는 과정의 일부이므로 세상에 대한 아기의 인식은 매우 풍부하면서도 상당히 무질서하다는 ⑤ 앞의 내용과 이어진다. 그러므로, 주어진 문장이 들어가기에 가장 적절한 곳은 ⑤이다.

선택지 완벽 분석
④ 함정 마지막 문장 중 those beliefs는 주어진 문장의 굳어진 지식이나 믿음을 지칭하므로, 주어진 문장은 마지막 문장 바로 앞에 와야 한다.

필수 어휘
psychologist 심리학자 decrease 줄다, 줄어들다 disinterested 흥미 없는 decline 감소 trace 추적하다 infant 유아의 contain ~을 가지고 있다 neural 신경의 connection 연결 efficient 효율적인 perception 인식 consequently 결과적으로 intensely 대단히, 매우 disordered 무질서한 absorb 흡수하다 harden 굳어지다 regularly 주기적으로, 정기적으로

05 정답 ④
202303 38번 정답률 61%

All carbohydrates are basically sugars. 단서1 Complex carbohydrates are the good carbohydrates for your body. These complex sugar compounds 단서2 are very difficult to break down and can trap other nutrients like vitamins and minerals in their chains. 단서3 As they slowly break down, the other nutrients are also released into your body, and can provide you with fuel for a number be released into: ~로 방출되다   provide A with B: A에게 B를 공급하다

of hours. 단서4 Bad carbohydrates, on the other hand, are simple sugars. ✪ 단서5 Because their structure is not complex, // they are easy to break down / and hold few nutrients (for your body) other than the sugars [from which they are made]. 단서6 Your body breaks down these carbohydrates rather quickly and what it cannot use is converted to fat and stored in the body.
be converted to: ~으로 전환되다

해석
모든 탄수화물은 기본적으로 당이다. 복합 탄수화물은 몸에 좋은 탄수화물이다. 이러한 복당류 화합물은 분해하기 매우 어렵고 비타민과 미네랄 같은 다른 영양소를 그것의 사슬 안에 가두어 둘 수 있다. 그것들이 천천히 분해되면서, 다른 영양소도 여러분의 몸으로 방출되고, 많은 시간 동안 여러분에게 연료를 공급할 수 있다. 반면에, 나쁜 탄수화물은 단당류이다. 그것의 구조는 복잡하지 않기 때문에, 그것은 분해되기 쉽고 그것이 만들어지는 당 외에 몸을 위한 영양소를 거의 가지고 있지 않다. 여러분의 몸은 이러한 탄수화물을 상당히 빨리 분해하고 그것(몸)이 사용할 수 없는 것은 지방으로 바뀌어 몸에 축적된다.

정답이 보이는 해설
주어진 문장의 on the other hand로 보아, 이 문장의 앞뒤가 서로 반대의 내용이 되어야 한다는 것을 미리 알 수 있다. 또한 주어진 문장이 Bad(나쁜) 탄수화물로 시작되고 있으므로, 이 문장 앞에는 좋은 탄수화물에 대한 내용이, 이 문장 뒤에는 나쁜 탄수화물에 관한 내용이 와야 한다. ④ 앞의 내용이 분해되기 어렵고 천천히 분해되는 좋은 복합 탄수화물에 관한 내용이고, ④ 뒤의 내용이 구조가 복잡하지 않아서 분해되기 쉽고 지방으로 바뀌어 몸에 축적되는 단당류에 관한 내용이므로, 주어진 문장이 들어가기에 가장 적절한 곳은 ④이다.

필수 어휘
complex 복합의, 복잡한 break down ~을 분해하다, 분해되다 trap 가두다 nutrient 영양소 release 방출하다 fuel 연료 a number of 많은 ~ structure 구조 hold 가지고 있다 rather 상당히 store 저장하다

06 정답 ⑤
202303 39번 정답률 51%

주제문 People commonly make the mistaken assumption that because a person has one type of characteristic, then they automatically have other characteristics which go with it. In one study, 단서1 university students were given descriptions of a guest lecturer before he spoke to the group. Half the students received a description containing the word 'warm', the other half were told the speaker was 'cold'. The guest lecturer then led a discussion, 단서2 after which the students were asked to give their impressions of him. 단서3 As expected, there were large differences between the impressions formed by the students, depending upon their original information of the lecturer. ✪ 단서4 It was also found // that those students [who expected the lecturer to be warm] tended to interact with him more. This shows that different expectations not only affect the impressions we form but also our behaviour and the relationship which is formed.

해석
흔히 사람들은 어떤 사람이 한 가지 유형의 특성을 가지고 있기 때문에, 그러면 자동적으로 그것과 어울리는 다른 특성을 가지고 있다는 잘못된 가정을 한다. 한 연구에

17강 주어진 문장 넣기

정답 및 해설 **175**

서, 대학생들은 초청 강사가 그 (대학생) 집단에게 강연을 하기 전에 그 강사에 대한 설명을 들었다. 학생들의 절반은 '따뜻하다'라는 단어가 포함된 설명을 들었고, 나머지 절반은 그 강사가 '차갑다'는 말을 들었다. 그러고 나서 그 초청 강사가 토론을 이끌었고, 그 후에 학생들은 그(강사)에 대한 그들의 인상을 말해 달라고 요청받았다. 예상한 대로, 학생들에 의해 형성된 인상 간에는 그 강사에 대한 학생들의 최초 정보에 따라 큰 차이가 있었다. 또한, 그 강사가 따뜻할 것이라 기대한 학생들은 그와 더 많이 소통하는 경향이 있다는 것이 밝혀졌다. 이것은 서로 다른 기대가 우리가 형성하는 인상뿐만 아니라 우리의 행동 및 형성되는 관계에도 영향을 미친다는 것을 보여 준다.

정답이 보이는 해설

also(또한)가 포함된 주어진 문장은 강사가 따뜻할 것이라 기대한 학생들은 강사와 더 많이 소통하는 경향이 있다는 추가적인 연구 결과이다. 특성에 관한 사람들의 잘못된 가정에 대한 연구에서, 초청 강사에 대해 '따뜻하다, 차갑다'라는 정보를 미리 받은 학생들의 강사에 대한 인상은 최초 정보에 따라 큰 차이가 났다는 내용 뒤에 들어가야 하므로, 주어진 문장이 들어가기에 가장 적절한 곳은 ⑤이다.

선택지 완벽 분석

④ 주어진 문장을 ④에 넣으면 also로 연결될 만한 내용이 앞에 없기 때문에 흐름상 단절이 일어남에 유의한다.

필수 어휘

commonly 흔히 mistaken 잘못된 assumption 가정 characteristic 특성
automatically 자동적으로 description 설명, 묘사 contain 포함하다
impression 인상 original 최초의, 원래의 interact 소통하다, 상호 작용을 하다
expectation 기대 affect 영향을 미치다 form 형성하다 relationship 관계

---

07 정답 ⑤

202211 38번 정답률 50%

Should we use language to understand mind or mind to understand language? Analytic philosophy historically assumes that language is basic and that mind would make sense if proper use of language was appreciated. ★ Modern cognitive science, (however,) rightly judges [that language is just one aspect (of mind of great importance in human beings) / but not fundamental (to all kinds of thinking)]. Countless species of animals manage to navigate the world, solve problems, and learn without using language, through brain mechanisms that are largely preserved in the minds of humans. **[단서1]** There is no reason to assume that language is fundamental to mental operations. Nevertheless, language is enormously important in human life and contributes largely to our ability to cooperate with each other in dealing with the world. Our species *homo sapiens* has been astonishingly successful, **[단서2]** which depended in part on language, first as an effective contributor to collaborative problem solving and much later, as collective memory through written records.

해석

우리는 사고를 이해하기 위해 언어를 사용해야 하는가 아니면 언어를 이해하기 위해 사고를 사용해야 하는가? 분석 철학은 언어가 기본이고 적절한 언어 사용이 제대로 인식된다면 사고가 이치에 맞을 것이라고 역사적으로 가정한다. 그러나 현대 인지 과학은 언어가 인간에게 매우 중요한 사고의 한 측면일 뿐 모든 종류의 사고에 근본적이지는 않다고 당연히 판단한다. 수많은 종의 동물들이, 인간의 사고 속에 대체

로 보존된 두뇌의 메커니즘을 통해 언어를 사용하지 않고 세계를 항해하고, 문제를 해결하고, 학습해 낸다. 언어가 정신 작용의 근본이라고 가정할 이유는 없다. 그럼에도 불구하고, 언어는 인간의 삶에서 매우 중요하며 세계를 다루는 데 있어서 서로 협력하는 우리의 능력에 상당히 기여한다. 우리 종족, '호모 사피엔스'는 놀라운 성공을 거두어 왔는데, 이것은 처음에는 협력적인 문제 해결에 효과적인 기여 요소로서, 그리고 훨씬 나중에는 글로 쓰인 기록을 통한 집단 기억으로서의 언어에 부분적으로 의존했다.

정답이 보이는 해설

주어진 문장은 Nevertheless(그럼에도 불구하고)로 시작하고, 언어는 인간의 삶에서 매우 중요하며 서로 협력하는 우리의 능력에 상당히 기여한다는 내용으로, 이 문장 앞에는 이와 상반되는 내용이 나와야 한다. ⑤의 앞 내용들이 언어가 정신 작용의 근본이라고 가정할 이유는 없다는 것이고, ⑤의 뒤 내용은 언어가 인간의 성공에 어떤 역할을 해 왔는지에 대한 설명이므로, 주어진 문장이 들어가기에 가장 적절한 곳은 ⑤이다.

선택지 완벽 분석

④ 주어진 문장을 ④에 넣으면 ③ 뒤의 문장과 ④ 뒤의 문장이 분리되고, 중간에 다른 의도의 문장이 들어가게 되어 글의 흐름에 문맥상 단절이 일어난다.

필수 어휘

analytic 분석적인 cognitive 인지의 fundamental 근본적인
countless 수많은 navigate 항해하다 preserve 보존하다 assume 가정하다
operation 작용 enormously 매우, 엄청나게, 대단히 contribute 기여하다
astonishingly 놀랍게도 depend on ~에 의존하다 in part 부분적으로
effective 효과적인 contributor 기여 요소 collaborative 협력적인

---

08 정답 ③

202211 39번 정답률 55%

Take two glasses of water. Put a little bit of orange juice into one and a little bit of lemon juice into the other. What you have are essentially two glasses of water but with a completely different chemical makeup. ★ If we take the glass containing orange juice / and heat it, // we will still have two different glasses of water (with different chemical makeups), / but **[단서1]** now they will also have different temperatures. If we could magically remove the glasses, we would find the two water bodies would not mix well. **[단서2]** Perhaps they would mix a little where they met; however, they would remain separate because of their different chemical makeups and temperatures. The warmer water would float on the surface of the cold water because of its lighter weight. In the ocean we have bodies of water that differ in temperature and salt content; for this reason, they do not mix.

해석

물 두 잔을 가져와라. 하나의 잔에는 약간의 오렌지주스를 넣고 다른 잔에는 약간의 레몬주스를 넣어라. 여러분이 가지고 있는 것은 본질적으로 물 두 잔이지만 완전히 다른 화학적 성질을 지닌 것들이다. 만약 우리가 오렌지주스가 든 잔을 가져와 그것을 가열한다면, 우리는 여전히 다른 화학적 성질을 지닌 두 개의 다른 물잔을 가지고 있을 것이지만, 이제 그것들은 또한 다른 온도를 가질 것이다. 만약 우리가 마법처럼 그 유리잔들을 없앨 수 있다면, 우리는 두 액체가 잘 섞이지 않는다는 것을 알게 될 것이다. 어쩌면 그것들은 그것들이 만났던 곳에서 조금 섞일 것이다. 하지만, 그것들의 다른 화학적 성질과 온도 때문에 그것들은 분리된 상태로 남아 있을 것이다. 더 따뜻한 물은 그것의 더 가벼운 무게 때문에 찬물의 표면에 떠 있을 것이다. 바다에는 온도와 염분 함유량이 다른 액체들이 있다. 이러한 이유로, 그것들은 섞이지 않는다.

주어진 문장은 유리잔을 없애면, 두 액체가 잘 섞이지 않는다는 것을 알게 될 것이라는 내용으로, 주어진 문장을 기점으로 글의 내용이 섞기 전과 후로 나뉘어야 할 것이다. ③ 뒤에서 두 액체가 만나는 곳에서 조금은 섞일지도 모르지만, 여전히 분리된 상태로 남아 있을 것이라는 내용이 나오므로 주어진 문장이 들어가기에 가장 적절한 곳은 ③이다.

선택지 완벽 분석

② 오렌지주스와 레몬주스는 화학적 성질이 다르고, 오렌지주스를 가열하면 서로 온도도 달라질 것이라는 내용으로 이어져야 하기 때문에 주어진 문장은 ②에 들어갈 수 없다.

필수 어휘

essentially 본질적으로 completely 완전히 chemical 화학적인 makeup 성질
contain 들어 있다 temperature 온도 remove 없애다 mix 섞이다
perhaps 아마도, 어쩌면 remain 여전히 ~이다, 남다, 남아 있다 separate 분리된
float 떠다니다, 뜨다 surface 표면 salt content 염분

09 정답 ④   202209 38번 정답률 51%

Television is the number one leisure activity in the United States and Europe, consuming more than half of our free time. We generally think of television as a way to relax, tune out, and escape from our troubles for a bit each day. While this is true, there is increasing evidence that we are more motivated to tune in to our favorite shows and characters when we are feeling lonely or have a greater need for social connection. Television watching does satisfy these social needs to some extent, at least in the short run. Unfortunately, it is also likely to "crowd out" other activities that produce more sustainable social contributions to our social well-being. The more television we watch, / the less likely we are to volunteer our time or to spend time with people in our social networks. In other words, the more time we make for *Friends*, the less time we have for friends in real life.

해석

텔레비전은 미국과 유럽에서 제1의 여가활동인데, 우리의 자유시간 중 절반 이상을 소비한다. 우리는 일반적으로 텔레비전을 휴식하고, 관심을 끄고, 매일 잠시 동안 우리의 문제로부터 탈출하는 하나의 방법으로 생각한다. 이것이 사실이긴 하지만, 우리가 외롭다고 느끼고 있거나 사회적 관계를 위한 더 큰 욕구를 가질 때 우리가 가장 좋아하는 쇼와 등장인물을 보려는 동기가 더 부여된다는 증거가 늘어나고 있다. 적어도 단기적으로는, 텔레비전 시청이 어느 정도는 이러한 사회적 욕구를 정말로 만족시킨다. 불행히도, 그것은 또한 우리의 사회적 행복을 위한 더 지속적인 사회적 기여를 만들어 내는 다른 활동들을 '몰아내기' 쉽다. 우리가 텔레비전을 더 많이 시청할수록, 우리는 사회적 관계망 속에서 우리의 시간을 기꺼이 할애하거나 사람들과 함께 시간을 덜 보내기 쉽다. 다시 말해서, 우리가 'Friends'를 위해 더 많은 시간을 낼수록, 실제 친구들을 위해서는 시간을 덜 갖게 된다.

정답이 보이는 해설

주어진 문장은 그것(텔레비전 시청)은 우리의 사회적 행복을 위한 더 지속적인 사회적 기여를 만들어 내는 다른 활동들을 '몰아내기' 쉽다는 내용으로, ④의 뒤 문장에서 텔레비전 시청이 우리가 실제 사회적 관계망 속에서 할애하는 시간을 적게 한다는 것을 부연 설명하고 있으므로, 주어진 문장이 들어가기에 가장 적절한 곳은 ④이다.

필수 어휘

consume 소비하다 evidence 증거 motivate 동기를 부여하다
sustainable 지속적인, 지속 가능한 volunteer 할애하다, (자발적으로) 제공하다

10 정답 ⑤   202209 39번 정답률 46%

We often associate the concept of temperature with how hot or cold an object feels when we touch it. In this way, our senses provide us with a qualitative indication of temperature. Our senses, however, are unreliable and often mislead us. For example, / if you stand in bare feet (**with** one foot on carpet / and the other on a tile floor), / the tile feels colder than the carpet / *even though both are at the same temperature*. The two objects feel different because tile transfers energy by heat at a higher rate than carpet does. Your skin "measures" the rate of energy transfer by heat rather than the actual temperature. What we need is a reliable and reproducible method for measuring the relative hotness or coldness of objects rather than the rate of energy transfer. Scientists have developed a variety of thermometers for making such quantitative measurements.

해석

우리는 종종 온도 개념을 우리가 물건을 만졌을 때 그것이 얼마나 뜨겁게 혹은 차갑게 느껴지는지와 연관 짓는다. 이런 식으로, 우리의 감각은 우리에게 온도의 정성적인 지표를 제공한다. 하지만, 우리의 감각은 신뢰할 수 없으며 종종 우리를 잘못 인도한다. 예를 들어, 여러분이 맨발로 한쪽 발은 카페트 위에, 다른 한쪽 발은 타일 바닥 위에 놓고 서 있다면, '둘 다 같은 온도임에도 불구하고' 카페트보다 타일이 더 차갑게 느껴질 것이다. 타일이 카페트가 전달하는 것보다 더 높은 비율로 에너지를 열의 형태로 전달하기 때문에 그 두 물체는 다르게 느껴진다. 여러분의 피부는 실제 온도보다는 열에너지 전도율을 '측정한다'. 우리가 필요로 하는 것은 에너지 전도율보다는 물체의 상대적인 뜨거움과 차가움을 측정하기 위한 신뢰할 수 있고 재현 가능한 수단이다. 과학자들은 그런 정량적인 측정을 하기 위해 다양한 온도계를 개발해 왔다.

정답이 보이는 해설

주어진 문장은 에너지 전도율보다는 물체의 상대적인 뜨거움과 차가움을 측정하기 위한 신뢰할 수 있고 재현 가능한 수단이 필요하다는 내용으로, 우리에게 필요한 수단의 예로 온도계를 과학자들이 개발해 왔다는 ⑤의 뒤 문장과 연결되는 것이 자연스러운 흐름이 된다. 따라서 주어진 문장이 들어가기에 가장 적절한 곳은 ⑤이다.

필수 어휘

associate 연관 짓다 concept 개념 object 물건, 물체 qualitative 정성적인
indication 지표, 표시 unreliable 신뢰할 수 없는
mislead 잘못 인도하다, 호도하다 transfer 전달, 이동 reliable 신뢰할 수 있는
reproducible 재현 가능한 relative 상대적인 quantitative 정량적인

11 정답 ④   202206 38번 정답률 77%

Friction is a force between two surfaces that are sliding, or trying to slide, across each other. For example, when you try to push a book along the floor, friction makes this difficult. Friction always works in *the direction* (opposite to *the direction* [in which the object is moving, or trying to move]). So, friction always slows a moving object down. The amount of friction depends on the surface materials. The rougher the surface is, the more friction is produced. Friction also produces heat. For example, if you rub

17강 주어진 문장 넣기

your hands together quickly, they will get warmer. Friction can be
예를 들어 손을 빠르게 문지르면 따뜻해짐
a useful force because it prevents our shoes slipping on the floor

when we walk and stops car tires skidding on the road. When you

walk, friction is caused between the tread on your shoes and the

ground, acting to grip the ground and prevent sliding.

해석

마찰력은 서로 엇갈리게 미끄러지고 있거나 미끄러지려고 하는 두 표면 사이의 힘이
다. 예를 들어, 여러분이 바닥 위의 책을 밀려고 할 때, 마찰이 이것을 어렵게 만든다.
마찰은 항상 물체가 움직이거나 움직이려고 하는 방향과 반대편 방향으로 작용한다.
그래서 마찰은 항상 움직이는 물체를 느리게 만든다. 마찰의 양은 표면 물질에 따라
달라진다. 표면이 거칠수록 더 많은 마찰력이 발생한다. 마찰은 또한 열을 발생시킨
다. 예를 들어, 만약 여러분이 두 손을 빠르게 비비면, 손이 더 따뜻해질 것이다. 마찰
력은 우리가 걸을 때 신발이 바닥에서 미끄러지는 것을 막아 주고 자동차 타이어가
도로에서 미끄러지는 것을 막아 주므로 유용한 힘이 될 수 있다. 여러분이 걸을 때
마찰은 여러분의 신발 접지면과 바닥 사이에 일어나며, 이 마찰은 땅을 붙잡아 미끄
러지는 것을 막아 주는 역할을 한다.

정답이 보이는 해설

주어진 문장은 우리가 두 손을 빠르게 비비면 손이 더 따뜻해질 것이라는 내용으로,
마찰이 열을 발생시킨다는 ④의 앞 문장에 대한 예시에 해당한다. 따라서 주어진 문
장이 들어가기에 가장 적절한 곳은 ④이다.

필수 어휘

friction 마찰력   force (물리적으로 나타나는) 힘   surface 표면   slide 미끄러지다
opposite 반대편의   material 물질, 재료   produce 발생시키다   rub 비비다
prevent 막다, 예방하다   grip 붙잡다

12 정답 ⑤

202206 39번 정답률 49%

Humans born without sight are not able to collect visual

experiences, so they understand the world entirely through their

other senses. As a result, people with blindness at birth develop an
                 그 결과   태어났을 때
amazing ability to understand the world through the collection of

experiences and memories that come from these non-visual senses.

❂ The dreams of *a person* [who has been without sight since birth]
        주어의 핵   관계대명사절
can be just as vivid and imaginative as those of someone with
    동사   = the dreams
normal vision. They are unique, however, because their dreams

are constructed from the non-visual experiences and memories

they have collected. 단서 A person with normal vision will dream
                          정상 시력을 가진 사람은 시각적 기억을 사용하여 친구에 대한
about a familiar friend using visual memories of shape, lighting,
꿈을 꿀 것임
and colour. But, a blind person will associate the same friend with

a unique combination of experiences from their non-visual senses

that act to represent that friend. In other words, people blind at birth
                                즉, 다시 말해
have similar overall dreaming experiences even though they do not

dream in pictures.

해석

시각 장애를 가지고 태어난 사람들은 시각적 경험을 수집할 수 없기 때문에, 그들은
전적으로 다른 감각을 통해 세상을 이해한다. 그 결과, 시각 장애를 가지고 태어난 사
람들은 이러한 비시각적 감각에서 오는 경험과 기억의 수집을 통해 세상을 이해하는
놀라운 능력을 개발한다. 태어날 때부터 시각 장애를 가져왔던 사람이 꾸는 꿈은 정

상 시력을 가진 사람의 꿈만큼 생생하고 상상력이 풍부할 수 있다. 하지만 그들의 꿈
은 그들이 수집한 비시각적 경험과 기억으로부터 구성되기 때문에 특별하다. 정상
시력을 가진 사람들은 형태, 조명, 그리고 색의 시각적 기억을 사용하여 친한 친구에
대한 꿈을 꿀 것이다. 하지만, 시각 장애인은 그 친구를 표현하기 위해 작용하는 비시
각적 감각에서 나온 경험의 독특한 조합으로 그 동일한 친구를 연상할 것이다. 다시
말해, 시각 장애를 가지고 태어난 사람들은 시각적으로 꿈을 꾸지는 않지만, 전반적
으로 비슷한 꿈 경험을 가지고 있다.

정답이 보이는 해설

주어진 문장은 But으로 시작하면서 비시각적 경험에서 나온 경험의 독특한 조합으
로 친구를 연상할 것이라는 내용이므로, 이 문장 앞에는 이와 상반되는 내용이 나와
야 한다. 따라서 정상 시력을 가진 사람들이 친구에 대한 꿈을 꾸는 방식을 설명하는
문장 다음인 ⑤에 주어진 문장이 들어가는 것이 가장 적절하다.

선택지 완벽 분석

③ 앞에는 시각 장애를 가진 사람의 꿈도 마찬가지로 생생할 수 있다는 내용으로 주
어진 문장과 비슷한 맥락이므로 But으로 연결될 수 없다.

필수 어휘

sight 시력   visual 시각적인   collection 수집   imaginative 상상력이 풍부한
unique 독특한, 특별한   construct 구성하다   familiar 친한, 친숙한
lighting 조명   associate 연상하다   combination 조합
represent 표현하다, 나타내다   overall 전반적인

13 정답 ④

202203 38번 정답률 55%

When an ecosystem is biodiverse, wildlife have more

opportunities to obtain food and shelter. Different species react and

respond to changes in their environment differently. For example,

imagine a forest with only one type of plant in it, which is the only

source of food and habitat for the entire forest food web. Now,

there is a sudden dry season and this plant dies. ❂ Plant-eating

animals completely lose their food source and die out, / and [so do
                                        주격 관계대명사
the animals (**that** prey upon them)]. But, when there is biodiversity,
도치구문(= the animals that prey upon them lose their food source and die out)
the effects of a sudden change are not so dramatic. 단서 Different
하지만 종이 다양하면 갑작스런 변화의 영향이 극적이지 않음   다양한 종의
species of plants respond to the drought differently, and many can
식물이 가뭄에 다르게 반응하고 많은 식물이 건기에 살아남을 수 있음
survive a dry season. Many animals have a variety of food sources
                                                    다양한
and don't just rely on one plant; now our forest ecosystem is no
          ~에 의존하다
longer at the death!
    종말에 처한

해석

생태계에 생물 종이 다양할 때, 야생 생물들은 먹이와 서식지를 얻을 더 많은 기회를
얻는다. 다양한 종들은 그들의 환경 변화에 다르게 작용하고 반응한다. 예를 들어, 단
한 종류의 식물만 있는 숲을 상상해 보면, 그 식물은 숲의 먹이 그물 전체의 유일한
먹이원이자 서식지이다. 이제, 갑작스러운 건기가 오고 이 식물이 죽는다. 초식 동물
은 그들의 먹이원을 완전히 잃고 죽게 되고, 그들을 먹이로 삼는 동물들도 그렇게 된
다. 하지만 종 다양성이 있으면, 갑작스러운 변화의 영향은 그렇게 극적이지 않다. 다
양한 종의 식물들이 가뭄에 다르게 반응하고, 많은 식물이 건기에 살아남을 수 있다.
많은 동물은 다양한 먹이원을 가지고 있으며 그저 한 식물에 의존하지는 않는다. 그
래서 이제 우리의 숲 생태계는 더는 종말에 처해 있지 않다!

정답이 보이는 해설

주어진 문장은 종 다양성이 있는 경우 갑작스러운 변화가 극적인 변화를 일으키지
않는다는 내용이므로, 종 다양성이 존재하는 경우 변화에 반응하는 예가 제시되고
있는 문장 앞인 ④에 들어가는 것이 가장 적절하다.

① 주어진 문장은 But으로 시작하므로 앞에는 이와 대조적인 내용이 나와야 한다. 하지만 ①의 앞 문장은 종이 다양할 때 생물은 먹이와 서식지를 얻을 더 많은 기회가 있다는 것으로 주어진 문장과 같은 맥락이므로, 주어진 문장이 ①에 들어가게 되면 논리적 모순이 생긴다.

필수 어휘

ecosystem 생태계 wildlife 야생 생물 opportunity 기회 shelter 서식지
react 작용하다 respond 반응하다 completely 완전히 prey 먹이로 삼다
dramatic 극적인 drought 가뭄 survive 살아남다

14 정답 ②

202203 39번 정답률 38%

We are connected to the night sky in many ways. It has always inspired people to wonder and to imagine. Since the dawn of civilization, our ancestors created myths and told legendary stories
문명 시작부터 선조들은 밤하늘에 관한 신화와 전설을 이야기함
about the night sky. **단서** Elements of those narratives became
신화와 전설의 요소들은 여러 세대의 사회적·문화적 정체성에
embedded in the social and cultural identities of many generations.
새겨짐
✪ On a practical level, / the night sky **helped** past generations
└➤ ~을 기록하다   동사   목적어
to keep track of time and create calendars / — essential to
목적격보어   전치사
developing societies **as** aids to farming and seasonal gathering. For
동명사(to의 목적어)   전치사(~로서)
many centuries, it also provided a useful navigation tool, vital for commerce and for exploring new worlds. Even in modern times, many people in remote areas of the planet observe the night sky for such practical purposes.

해석

우리는 여러 방식으로 밤하늘과 연결되어 있다. 그것은 사람들이 궁금해하고 상상하도록 항상 영감을 불어넣어 왔다. 문명의 시작부터, 우리 선조들은 밤하늘에 대해 신화를 만들었고 전설적 이야기를 했다. 그러한 이야기의 요소들은 여러 세대의 사회적이고 문화적인 정체성에 깊이 새겨졌다. 실용적인 수준에서, 밤하늘은 과거 세대들이 시간을 기록하고 달력을 만드는 것을 도와주었는데, 이것은 농업과 계절에 따른 수확의 보조 도구로서 사회를 발전시키는 데 필수적이었다. 수 세기 동안, 그것은 또한 무역과 새로운 세계를 탐험하는 데 필수적인 유용한 항해 도구를 제공했다. 심지어 현대에도 지구의 외딴 지역에 있는 많은 사람들이 그러한 실용적인 목적을 위해 밤하늘을 관찰한다.

정답이 보이는 해설

주어진 문장은 문명의 시작부터 우리 선조들이 밤하늘에 대해 신화를 만들었고 전설적 이야기를 했다는 내용으로, ②의 뒤 문장에서 주어진 문장의 myths, legendary stories를 those narratives로 받고 있으므로, 주어진 문장이 들어가기에 가장 적절한 곳은 ②이다.

③ **함정** 주어진 문장이 ③에 들어가면 ②의 다음 문장의 those narratives가 가리키는 것이 없어지게 되어 ②의 앞뒤에 문맥상 단절이 일어난다.

필수 어휘

inspire 영감을 주다 dawn 시작, 새벽 civilization 문명 ancestor 선조
myth 신화 legendary 전설의 element 요소 identity 정체성
practical 실용적인 aid 보조 도구 seasonal 계절에 따른 gathering 수확
navigation 항해 remote 외딴, 멀리 떨어진

15 정답 ④

202111 38번 정답률 62%

주제문 According to top nutrition experts, most nutrients are

better absorbed and used by the body when consumed from a whole food instead of a supplement. However, many people feel the need
～ 대신에
to take pills, powders, and supplements in an attempt to obtain
～하려는 시도도 that절 동사1 ┐
nutrients and fill the gaps in their diets. ✪ We hope these will give
┌➤ prevent A from B: A가 B하는 것을 막다   ┕ 접속사 that 생략
us more energy, / prevent us from catching a cold in the winter, / or
that절 동사2
improve our skin and hair. **단서1** But in reality, the large majority of
that절 동사3   대다수의 보충제는 인공적이며 체내에 완전히 흡수되지
supplements are artificial and may not even be completely absorbed
않을 수도 있음
by your body. Worse, some are contaminated with other substances
심하게는 다른 물질로 오염되거나 라벨에 없는 성분이 포함됨
and contain ingredients not listed on the label. **단서2** For example, a
판매되고 있는 단백질
recent investigative report found heavy metals in 40 percent of 134
분말 브랜드 134개 중 40퍼센트에서 중금속이 발견됨
brands of protein powders on the market. With little control and regulation, taking supplements is a gamble and often costly.

해석

최고의 영양 전문가들에 따르면 대부분의 영양소는 보충제 대신에 자연식품으로부터 섭취될 때 신체에 의해 더 잘 흡수되고 사용된다. 하지만 많은 사람들이 영양소를 얻고 자신의 식단에서 부족한 부분을 채우려는 시도로 알약, 분말 그리고 보충제를 섭취할 필요성을 느낀다. 우리는 이것들이 우리에게 더 많은 에너지를 주고, 우리가 겨울에 감기에 걸리는 것을 막아 주거나 또는 우리의 피부와 모발을 개선해 주기를 바란다. 그러나 실제로 대다수의 보충제는 인공적이며 여러분의 신체에 의해 완전히 흡수조차 되지 않을 수도 있다. 심하게는 어떤 것들은 다른 물질로 오염되어 있으며 라벨에 실려 있지 않은 성분을 포함한다. 예를 들어, 최근의 한 조사 보고는 시장에 나와 있는 단백질 분말 134개 브랜드 중 40퍼센트에서 중금속을 발견했다. 단속과 규제가 거의 없다면 보충제를 섭취하는 것은 도박이며 흔히 대가가 크다.

정답이 보이는 해설

주어진 문장은 어떤 보충제들은 다른 물질로 오염되어 있고 라벨에 실려 있지 않은 성분을 포함한다는 내용이므로, 이에 대한 예로 단백질 분말 브랜드의 40퍼센트에서 중금속이 발견되었다는 내용이 제시되고 있는 문장 앞인 ④에 들어가는 것이 가장 적절하다.

필수 어휘

nutrition 영양 nutrient 영양분, 영양소 absorb 흡수하다 consume 섭취하다
attempt 시도 artificial 인공적인, 인위적인 completely 완전히 substance 물질
ingredient 성분 investigative 조사의 regulation 규제 costly 대가가 큰

16 정답 ⑤

202111 39번 정답률 35%

In general, kinetic energy is the energy associated with motion,
일반적으로   ～와 관련되다
while potential energy represents the energy which is "stored" in a physical system. Moreover, the total energy is always conserved. But while the total energy remains unchanged, the kinetic and potential parts of the total energy can change all the time.
항상
Imagine, for example, a pendulum which swings back and forth.
앞뒤로
✪ **When** it swings, / it sweeps out an arc and then slows down **as**
접속사(~할 때)   접속사(~함에 따라) ┘
it comes closer to its highest point, / where the pendulum does not
관계부사(= and at the point)
move at all. **단서1** So at this point, the energy is completely given
추가 멈추는 지점에서 에너지는 완전히 위치 에너지로 주어짐
in terms of potential energy. But after this brief moment of rest, the pendulum swings back again and therefore part of the total energy is then given in the form of kinetic energy. **단서2** So as the pendulum
그 추가 흔들리면서 운동 에너

swings, kinetic and potential energy constantly change into each
지와 위치 에너지는 끊임없이 서로 바뀜
other.

해석

일반적으로 운동 에너지는 움직임과 관련된 에너지인 반면, 위치 에너지는 물리계에 '저장된' 에너지를 나타낸다. 게다가 총에너지는 항상 보존된다. 그러나 총에너지가 변하지 않는 채로 있는 동안, 총에너지의 운동과 위치 에너지 비율은 항상 변할 수 있다. 예를 들어 앞으로 흔들리는 추를 상상해 보자. 그것은 흔들릴 때 호 모양으로 쓸어내리듯 움직이다가 그런 다음 그것이 그 최고점에 더 가까워지면서 속도가 줄어드는데, 이 지점에서 그 추는 더 이상 움직이지 않는다. 따라서 이 지점에서 에너지는 완전히 위치 에너지로 주어진다. 그러나 이 짧은 순간의 멈춤 이후에 그 추는 다시 뒤로 흔들리고 따라서 총에너지의 일부가 그때 운동 에너지의 형태로 주어진다. 따라서 그 추가 흔들리면서 운동 에너지와 위치 에너지는 끊임없이 서로 바뀐다.

정답이 보이는 해설

주어진 문장은 But으로 시작하면서 짧은 시간의 멈춤 이후에 추가 다시 뒤로 흔들리고 그때 총에너지의 일부가 운동 에너지 형태로 주어진다는 내용이므로 앞에는 이와 대조적인 내용이 제시되어야 한다. 따라서 추가 멈추는 지점에서 에너지는 완전히 위치 에너지로 주어진다는 내용의 문장 다음인 ⑤에 들어가는 것이 가장 적절하다.

선택지 완벽 분석

④ [함정] 주어진 문장이 ④에 들어갈 경우, 짧은 멈춤 이후에 추가 다시 흔들리고 총에너지의 일부가 운동 에너지로 주어진다는 내용 다음에, 이 지점에서 에너지가 완전히 위치 에너지로 주어진다는 상반된 내용이 와서 앞뒤 문맥에 모순이 생기게 된다.

필수 어휘

kinetic energy 운동 에너지   be associated with ~와 관련되다
potential energy 위치 에너지   conserve 보존하다   swing 흔들리다
back and forth 앞뒤로   sweep 쓸어내리다   slow down 속도가 줄어들다
completely 완전히   brief 짧은   constantly 끊임없이

---

17 정답 ③

202109 38번 정답률 69%

Studies have consistently shown caffeine to be effective when used together with a pain reliever to treat headaches. The positive correlation between caffeine intake and staying alert throughout
하루 종일
the day has also been well established. [단서1] As little as 60 mg (the
60밀리그램만으로도 빠른 반응
amount typically in one cup of tea) can lead to a faster reaction
시간으로 이어짐 → 긍정적인 상관관계   ~로 이어지다
time. However, using caffeine to improve alertness and mental
하지만 카페인이 숙면 취하는 것을 대신하지 않음
performance doesn't replace getting a good night's sleep. ✪ One
                                                        주어
study (from 2018) showed / [that coffee improved reaction times /
        동사   명사절 주어   동사
(in those (with or without poor sleep))], // [단서2] but caffeine seemed
= the people(사람들)   카페인이 실수를 증가시키는 것으로 보임
to increase errors / (in the group with little sleep). Additionally, this
→ 부정적인 상관관계(주어진 문장에서 언급한 숙면에 관한 근거)
study showed that even with caffeine, the group with little sleep
did not score as well as those with adequate sleep. It suggests that
caffeine does not fully make up for inadequate sleep.
                      보충하다

해석

연구들은 카페인이 두통을 치료하기 위해 진통제와 함께 사용될 때 효과적이라는 것을 일관되게 보여 주었다. 카페인 섭취와 하루 종일 각성된 상태로 있는 것 사이의 긍정적인 상관관계 역시 잘 확립되어 있다. 60밀리그램(일반적으로 차 한 잔에 들어 있는 양)만큼의 적은 양으로도 반응 시간이 빨라질 수 있다. 하지만, 각성과 정신적 수행 능력을 향상시키기 위해 카페인을 사용하는 것은 숙면을 취하는 것을 대신하지 않는다. 2018년의 한 연구에 따르면 커피는 수면이 부족한 사람 또는 부족하지 않은 사람에게 반응 시간은 개선시켰지만, 카페인은 수면이 부족한 집단 내에서는 실

수를 증가시키는 것으로 보인다는 것을 보여 주었다. 뿐만 아니라, 이 연구는 카페인을 섭취한다고 해도 수면이 부족한 집단은 적절한 수면을 취한 집단만큼 점수를 잘 받지 못했다는 것을 보여 주었다. 그것은 카페인이 불충분한 수면을 충분히 보충하지 못한다는 것을 시사한다.

정답이 보이는 해설

역접의 연결사 However로 시작하는 주어진 문장은 카페인과 수면의 부정적인 상관관계에 대한 내용이다. ③ 앞에서 카페인의 긍정적인 상관관계, 즉 각성과 두통 치료의 효과에 대해 서술하였고, ③ 다음 문장에서 카페인 섭취의 부정적인 사례를 근거로 제시하고 있으므로 ③에서 흐름의 반전이 일어난다. 따라서 주어진 문장이 들어가기에 가장 적절한 곳은 ③이다.

선택지 완벽 분석

④ Additionally로 시작하는 ④ 다음 문장은 카페인의 부정적 영향에 대한 두 번째 근거를 추가로 이어서 제시하고 있으므로 주어진 문장이 들어갈 수 없다.

필수 어휘

consistently 일관적으로, 일관되게   effective 효율적인   pain reliever 진통제
treat 치료하다   positive 긍정적인   correlation 상관관계   intake 섭취(량)
stay alert 깨어 있는[각성된] 상태로 있다   reaction 반응, 반작용
additionally 추가로   adequate 적절한, 충분한

---

18 정답 ②

202109 39번 정답률 57%

[주제문] Rewarding business success doesn't always have to be
                                        언제나 ~인 것은 아니다
done in a material way. A software company I once worked for
[단서1] had a great way of recognizing sales success. The sales
        판매 성공을 인정해 주는 훌륭한 방법 → 주어진 문장의 경적 울리기를 가리킴
director kept an air horn outside his office and would come out and
판매 부서의 관리자가 사무실 밖에 경적을 두고 거래가 성사될 때마다 경적을 울림
blow the horn every time a salesperson settled a deal. [단서2] The
noise, of course, interrupted anything and everything happening
주어진 문장의 air horn이 내는 소리
in the office because it was unbelievably loud. However, it had
an amazingly positive impact on everyone. Sometimes rewarding
success can be as easy as that, especially when peer recognition is
                아주 간단한데
important. ✪ You should have seen the way / the rest of the sales
                should have p.p.: ~했어야 했다   관계부사 how 생략
team wanted the air horn blown for them.
      동사   목적어   목적격보어(과거분사) → 경적이 '울리는' 수동의 의미

해석

사업에서의 성공을 보상하는 것이 언제나 물질적인 방식으로 이루어져야 하는 것은 아니다. 내가 예전에 근무했던 한 소프트웨어 회사는 판매 성공을 인정해 주는 훌륭한 방법을 가지고 있었다. 판매 부서의 관리자는 자신의 사무실 밖에 경적을 두었고 영업 직원이 거래를 성사할 때마다 나와서 경적을 불곤 했다. 당연히, 그 소리가 믿을 수 없을 정도로 시끄러웠기 때문에, 사무실에서 일어나는 그 어떤 것, 그리고 모든 것을 방해했다. 하지만 그것은 모든 사람에게 놀랄 만큼 긍정적인 영향을 주었다. 성공을 보상하는 것은 가끔 그와 같이 쉬울 수 있는데, 특히 동료의 인정이 중요할 때 그러하다. 여러분은 그 판매 부서의 나머지 직원들이 자신들을 위해 경적이 울리게 되기를 바라는 그 방식을 보았어야 했다.

정답이 보이는 해설

주어진 문장은 사업의 성공을 인정해 주는 방법에 대한 예시로 필자의 경험을 서술한 내용이다. ② 앞 문장에서 자신이 근무했던 회사에 사업 성공을 인정하는 훌륭한 방법이 있었다고 언급했고, ② 다음 문장에서 언급된 The noise가 주어진 문장의 air horn을 울리는 시끄러운 소리를 가리키므로 주어진 문장이 들어가기에 가장 적절한 곳은 ②이다.

선택지 완벽 분석

③ 주어진 문장이 ③에 들어가면 ③ 앞 문장의 The noise가 가리키는 대상이 없어서 내용에 단절이 일어난다.

19 정답 ③

Sound and light travel in waves. An analogy often given for sound is that of throwing a small stone onto the surface of a still pond.
= the analogy
Waves radiate outwards from the point of impact, just as sound waves radiate from the sound source. This is due to a disturbance in the air around us. 단서1 If you bang two sticks together, you will
주어진 문장의 the sticks로 이어짐
get a sound. As the sticks approach each other, the air immediately
막대기가 가까워지면서 공기 축적
in front of them is compressed and energy builds up. 단서2 When the point of impact occurs, this energy is released as sound waves.
(주어진 문장의 '축적된 에너지'를 재언급함
✪ If you try *the same experiment* (with two heavy stones), // exactly
조건의 부사절(만약 ~라면)　　　　　　　　　　　　　　　　～ 때문에
the same thing occurs, / but you get a different sound / (due to
주어1　　동사1　　　　주어2 동사2　　　　　　　　the stones
the density and surface (of the stones)), / and (as they have likely
접속사(~ 때문에)
displaced more air), / a louder sound. And so, a physical disturbance
you get 생략
in the atmosphere around us will produce a sound.

해석
소리와 빛은 파장으로 이동한다. 소리에 대해 종종 사용되는 비유는 작은 돌멩이를 잔잔한 연못의 수면에 던지는 것의 비유이다. 음파가 음원으로부터 사방으로 퍼지는 것처럼 파장은 충격 지점으로부터 바깥쪽으로 퍼져 나간다. 이것은 우리 주변에 있는 공기 중의 교란 작용 때문이다. 만약에 여러분이 쾅 하고 두 개의 막대기를 함께 친다면, 여러분은 소리를 듣게 될 것이다. 막대기들이 서로 가까워질 때, 그것들의 바로 앞에 있는 공기가 압축되고 에너지는 축적된다. 충돌점이 발생하면 이 에너지는 음파로 퍼져 나간다. 같은 실험을 두 개의 무거운 돌로 해 보면 동일한 일이 일어나지만, 돌의 밀도와 표면으로 인해 여러분은 다른 소리를 듣게 되고, 아마 그 돌이 더 많은 공기를 바꿔 놓았기 때문에 (당신은) 더 큰 소리를 (듣게 된다). 따라서 우리 주변 대기 중에서 일어나는 물리적 교란 작용이 소리를 만든다.

정답이 보이는 해설
주어진 문장은 막대기들이 서로 가까워질 때 공기가 압축되어 에너지가 축적된다는 내용이다. ③ 앞 문장의 two sticks가 주어진 문장의 the sticks로 이어지고, ③ 다음 문장에서 주어진 문장의 '축적된 에너지'를 this energy로 받아 서술을 이어가고 있으므로 주어진 문장이 들어가기에 가장 적절한 곳은 ③이다.

20 정답 ④

Food chain means the transfer of food energy from the source in plants through a series of organisms with the repeated process of eating and being eaten. In a grassland, grass is eaten by rabbits while rabbits in turn are eaten by foxes. This is an example of a
결국, 차례대로
simple food chain. 단서1 This food chain implies the sequence
먹이 사슬은 생산자로부터 소비자로 전해지는 연속적 사건을 의미
in which food energy is transferred from producer to consumer

or higher trophic level. It has been observed that at each level of
각 이동 단계에서 열 손실 발생이 관찰됨
transfer, a large proportion, 80–90 percent, of the potential energy is lost as heat. 단서2 Hence the number of steps or links in a sequence
그에 따라(Hence) 그것을 막기 위해 각 단계를 제한함
is restricted, usually to four or five. ✪ **The shorter** the food chain /
비교급 병렬2　　　　　　　　　　　비교급 병렬1
or **the nearer** the organism is to the beginning of the chain, / **the**
the+비교급, the+비교급: ~할수록 더 …하다
greater the available energy intake is.
주어　　　　　　동사

해석
먹이 사슬은 식품 에너지가 식물에 있는 에너지원으로부터 먹고 먹히는 반복되는 과정과 함께 일련의 유기체를 통해 이동하는 것을 의미한다. 초원에서는 풀이 토끼에게 먹히지만 결국 토끼는 여우에게 먹힌다. 이는 단순한 먹이 사슬의 사례이다. 이 먹이 사슬은 식품 에너지가 생산자로부터 소비자 또는 더 높은 영양 수준으로 전달되는 연속적인 사건을 의미한다. 각각의 이동 단계에서 잠재적 에너지의 상당한 부분인 80~90퍼센트가 열로 손실되는 것으로 관찰되어 왔다. 그래서 하나의 순서 안에 있는 단계나 연결의 수는 보통 4~5개로 제한된다. 먹이 사슬이 짧거나 유기체가 하위 영양 단계에 가까울수록 이용 가능한 에너지 섭취량이 더 커진다.

정답이 보이는 해설
주어진 문장은 이동 단계에서 에너지가 손실된다는 내용이다. 그러므로 '이런 이유로'라는 의미의 Hence로 시작하여 에너지 손실을 막기 위해 단계나 연결의 수를 4~5개로 제한한다는 내용인 ④ 앞에 들어가는 것이 문맥상 자연스럽다. 따라서 주어진 문장이 들어가기에 가장 적절한 곳은 ④이다.

21 정답 ②

It is so easy to overestimate the importance of one defining moment and underestimate the value of making small improvements
on a daily basis. Too often, we convince ourselves that massive
매일　　　　　　　　　　　　　　　　　　　= massive success
success requires massive action. ✪ **Whether** it is losing weight, /
양보의 접속사　　　보어1
winning a championship, or achieving any other goal, / 단서1 we put
보어2　　　　　　부사적 용법(목적)　　　보어3
pressure on ourselves / to make *some earthshaking improvement* /
모두가 놀랄 거창한 진전을 이루도록 스스로에게 부담을 줌
[that everyone will talk about]. Meanwhile, improving by 1 percent
그렇지만 1퍼센트의 진전도 의미가 있음
isn't particularly notable, but it can be far more meaningful in the
결국
long run. 단서2 **The difference this tiny improvement can make**
이러한 작은 발전(1퍼센트의 진전)이 이루는 변화도 놀라움
over time is surprising. Here's how the math works out: if you can get 1 percent better each day for one year, you'll end up thirty-seven times better by the time you're done. Conversely, if you get 1 percent worse each day for one year, you'll decline nearly down to zero. 주제문 What starts as a small win or a minor failure adds up to something much more.

해석
결정적인 어떤 순간의 중요성을 과대평가하고 매일매일 작은 진전을 이루는 것의 가치를 과소평가하는 것은 무척 쉽다. 우리는 너무 자주 큰 성공에는 커다란 행동이 필요하다고 확신한다. 그것이 체중을 줄이는 것이든, 선수권을 얻는 것이든, 또는 다른 어떤 목표를 달성하는 것이든 간에, 모든 사람이 이야기하게 될 세상을 떠들썩하게 할 만한 향상을 이루도록 우리는 스스로에게 부담을 준다. 한편, 1퍼센트의 진전이

특별히 눈에 띄지는 않지만, 결국에는 훨씬 더 의미가 있을 수 있다. 시간이 지남에 따라 이러한 아주 작은 발전이 이룰 수 있는 변화는 놀랍다. 그 계산이 어떻게 이루어지는지를 보면, 만약 여러분이 1년 동안 매일 1퍼센트씩 더 나아질 수 있다면, 끝날 때쯤이면 여러분은 결국 서른 일곱 배 더 나아질 것이다. 정반대로, 1년 동안 매일 1퍼센트씩 나빠지면 여러분은 거의 0까지 내려갈 것이다. 작은 승리 또는 사소한 패배로 시작한 것이 쌓이면 훨씬 더 커다란 어떤 것이 된다.

정답이 보이는 해설

주어진 문장은 내용 전환을 나타내는 부사 Meanwhile로 시작하고 1퍼센트의 발전이 눈에 띄지는 않지만 결국에는 의미가 있다는 내용이므로, 이 내용과 대조를 이루는 내용이 앞에 나와야 한다. ② 앞에 세상을 놀라게 할 향상에 대한 부담이 우리에게 있다는 내용이 있고 ② 다음에 시간이 지남에 따라 작은 발전이 이룰 수 있는 변화가 놀랍다고 했으므로, 주어진 문장이 들어가기에 가장 적절한 곳은 ②이다.

선택지 완벽 분석

③ (함정) 주어진 문장이 ③에 들어갈 경우, 거창한 목표 달성이 ② 다음의 this tiny improvement가 가리키는 대상이 되어 내용 연결이 이루어지지 않는다.

④ (함정) 주어진 문장이 내용 전환의 부사 Meanwhile로 시작한다는 것에 유의한다. 주어진 문장이 ④에 들어갈 경우, ④ 앞의 내용과 내용 전환 없이 이어져야 하므로 Meanwhile을 사용할 수 없다.

필수 어휘

overestimate 과대평가하다   defining 결정적인, 정의하는
underestimate 과소평가하다   convince 확신시키다, 굳게 믿게 하다
massive 거대한   championship 선수권, 우승   achieve 달성하다, 성취하다
pressure 압력   earthshaking 세상을 떠들썩하게 하는   meanwhile 한편
notable 눈에 띄는   meaningful 의미 있는   tiny 작은, 사소한
end up 결국 ~하게 되다   conversely 역으로   decline 떨어지다, 하락하다
minor 사소한   failure 패배

22 정답 ④

202103 39번 정답률 55%

The continued survival of the human race can be explained by our ability to adapt to our environment. While we may have lost
　　　　　　　　　　～에 적응하다
some of our ancient ancestors' survival skills, we have learned new skills as they have become necessary. Today, the gap between the skills we once had and the skills we now have grows ever wider as we rely more heavily on modern technology. **단서1** Therefore, when
　～에 의존하다　　　　　　　　　　　미지의 땅으로 갈 때는
you head off into the wilderness, it is important to fully prepare for
그곳의 환경에 대한 준비가 중요함 → (주어진 문장의) 구체적인 서술로 이어짐
the environment. Before a trip, research how the native inhabitants
　　　　　　　　　　　　　　　　　　　　┌→주어(의문사절)
dress, work, and eat. ✪ **단서2** How they have adapted to their way
　　　　　　　　　　　　　　　(여행갈 곳의) 토착민들의 생활 방식을 아는 것이 도움이 됨
of life / will **help** you to understand the environment / and **allow**
　　　　　　　동사　 help+목적어+목적격보어(동사원형/to부정사): ~가 …하는 것을 돕다　will 생략
you to select the best gear / and learn the correct skills. This is
목적어 목적격보어1(to부정사)　　　　　　　to 생략　└목적격보어2
crucial because most survival situations arise as a result of a series of events that could have been avoided.

해석

인류의 지속적인 생존은 우리가 처한 환경에 적응하는 우리의 능력으로 설명될 수 있다. 우리가 고대 조상들의 생존 기술 중 일부를 잃어버렸을지는 모르지만, 우리는 새로운 기술이 필요해짐에 따라 그것을 터득했다. 오늘날 우리가 현대 기술에 좀 더 많이 의존함에 따라, 한때 우리가 가졌던 기술과 현재 우리가 가진 기술 사이의 간극이 점점 더 커진다. 따라서 미지의 땅으로 향할 때에는, 그 환경에 대해 충분히 준비하는 것이 중요하다. 떠나기 전에, 토착민들이 어떻게 옷을 입고, 일하며, 먹는지를 조사하라. 그들이 자신들의 생활 방식에 적응한 방식은 여러분이 그 환경을 이해하도록 도와줄 것이고, 여러분이 최선의 장비를 선별하고 적절한 기술을 배우는 것을 허용할 것이다. 이는 매우 중요한데, 대부분의 생존 상황은 피할 수도 있었던 일련의 사건의 결과로 발생하기 때문에 그러하다.

정답이 보이는 해설

주어진 문장은 여행을 떠나기 전에 그곳 토착민들이 어떻게 입고 일하며 먹는지를 조사하라는 내용이다. 첫 번째 문장에서 인류의 지속적 생존은 환경에 적응하는 우리의 능력이라고 언급했으므로, 주어진 문장 다음에는 토착민들과 관련된 언급이 나와야 한다. 따라서 주어진 문장이 들어가기에 가장 적절한 곳은 ④이다.

필수 어휘

human race 인류   adapt 적응하다   ancient 고대의   ancestor 조상
gap 간극, 격차   rely on ~에 의존하다   heavily 크게, 몹시   modern 현대의
head off ~로 향하다   wilderness 미지의 땅   native 토착의, 지방 고유의
gear 장비   crucial 중요한   arise 발생하다, 일어나다   avoid 피하다

23 정답 ③

202011 38번 정답률 44%

✪ Daylight isn't the *only signal* / [that the brain can use / for the
　　　　　　　　　　　　　　　　　　주어　　동사　　　～할 목적으로
purpose of biological clock resetting], // though it is the principal
　　　　　　　　　　　　　　　　　　양보의 접속사 ＝daylight
and preferential signal, / when present. So long as they are reliably
　　　　　　　　　　　　　　└it is 생략
repeating, the brain can also use other external cues, such as food, exercise, and even regularly timed social interaction. **단서1** All of these events have the ability to reset the biological clock, allowing
생체 시계를 재설정하는 능력이 24시간 음을 치게 함
it to strike a precise twenty-four-hour note. It is the reason that
　　　　　　　　　　　　　　　　　(24시간 주기의) 리듬을 완전히
individuals with certain forms of blindness do not entirely lose
상실하지 않는 이유
their circadian rhythm. **단서2** Despite not receiving light cues due to
　　　　　　　　　　　　　(그렇기 때문에) 시각 상실로 인해 빛을 받지 않아도
their blindness, other phenomena act as their resetting triggers. Any
다른 현상들이 재설정 역할을 함
signal that the brain uses for the purpose of clock resetting is termed a zeitgeber, from the German "time giver" or "synchronizer." Thus, while light is the most reliable and thus the primary zeitgeber, there are many factors that can be used in addition to, or in the absence
　　　　　　　　　　　　　　　　　　　～뿐만 아니라　　　　～이 없을 경우에
of, daylight.

해석

햇빛은 비록 (그것이) 있을 때는 중요하고 우선되는 신호지만, 햇빛이 뇌가 생체 시계 재설정을 목적으로 사용할 수 있는 유일한 신호는 아니다. 확실하게 반복만 된다면, 뇌는 음식과 운동, 그리고 심지어는 정기적인 사회적 상호 작용과 같은 다른 외부적인 신호를 사용할 수도 있다. 이러한 모든 경우는 생체 시계를 재설정하는 능력이 있어서 정확한 24시간 음을 치도록 한다. 그것이 어떤 형태의 시력 상실을 가진 개인도 24시간 주기의 리듬을 완전히 잃어버리지는 않는 이유이다. 그들의 시력 상실로 인해 빛 신호를 받지 않음에도 불구하고, 다른 현상들이 재설정의 유인 역할을 한다. 뇌가 시계 재설정을 목적으로 이용하는 어떤 신호는 '시간 제공자' 또는 '동기화 장치'라는 독일어에서 유래한 자연 시계라고 불린다. 따라서, 빛은 가장 신뢰할 수 있으며 그에 따른 주요한 자연 시계이긴 하지만, 햇빛과 함께 또는 햇빛이 없을 때 사용될 수 있는 많은 요인이 있다.

정답이 보이는 해설

주어진 문장은 그것이 어떤 형태의 시력 상실을 가진 개인도 24시간 주기의 리듬을 완전히 잃어버리지는 않는 이유라는 내용이다. 여기서 It은 '24시간 주기'에 대한 설명을 포함하는 앞 문장을 가리키며, 뒷 문장의 Despite와 연결되어 시력 상실 때문에 일어나는 현상에 대한 설명이 이어진다. 따라서 주어진 문장이 들어가기에 가장 적절한 곳은 ③이다.

선택지 완벽 분석

④ (함정) 주어진 문장이 ④에 들어가면 '시력 상실로 인해 빛 신호를 받지 않음에도 불구하고'라는 의미가 포함되며 Despite로 시작하는 ④ 앞의 문장과 내용상의 단절이 일어난다.

필수 어휘

daylight 햇빛 signal 신호 purpose 목적 biological clock 생체 시계
reset 재설정하다 principal 주요한 preferential 우선하는 external 외부의
cue 신호 precise 정확한 phenomenon 현상(*pl.* phenomena)
zeitgeber 자연 시계(생물 시계의 주기에 영향을 미치는 외적 요소)
synchronizer 동기화 장치

24 정답 ③

202011 39번 정답률 47%

Earlier agricultural systems were integrated with and co-evolved with technologies, beliefs, myths and traditions as part of an integrated social system. Generally, people planted a variety of crops in different areas, in the hope of obtaining a reasonably stable food supply. 단서1 These systems could only be maintained at low population levels, and were relatively non-destructive (but not always). More recently, agriculture has in many places lost its local character, and has become incorporated into the global economy. 단서2 This has led to increased pressure on agricultural land for exchange commodities and export goods. ✪ More land is being diverted / from local food production to "cash crops" / for export and exchange; // fewer types of crops are raised, / and each crop is raised in **much** greater quantities than before. Thus, ever more land is converted from forest (and other natural systems) for agriculture for export, rather than using land for subsistence crops.

해석

초기 농경 시스템은 통합된 사회 시스템의 일부로서 기술, 신념, 신화, 그리고 전통과 통합되고 함께 진화했다. 주로, 사람들은 꽤 안정적인 식량 공급을 얻게 될 것을 바라며 여러 지역에 다양한 작물을 심었다. 이 시스템은 낮은 인구 수준에서만 유지될 수 있었고, (항상 그런 것은 아니지만) 비교적 비파괴적이었다. 최근 들어서는, 많은 곳에서 농업이 그것의 지역적 특성을 잃고 세계 경제에 통합되어 왔다. 이로 인해 교환 상품과 수출 상품을 위한 농경지에 대한 압력이 증가하게 되었다. 더 많은 땅이 수출과 교환을 위해 지역 식량 생산에서 '환금 작물'로 전환되고 있는데, 더 적은 종류의 작물이 재배되고, 각각의 작물은 그 이전보다 훨씬 더 많은 양이 재배된다. 따라서 자급자족용 작물을 위해 땅을 사용하기보다는, 수출용 농업을 위해 어느 때보다 더 많은 토지가 삼림(그리고 다른 자연 시스템)으로부터 전환된다.

정답이 보이는 해설

주어진 문장은 최근에 많은 곳의 농업이 지역적 특성을 잃고 세계 경제에 통합되었다는 내용이므로, 초기 농경 시스템에 대한 설명 다음, 그리고 최근의 농업이 세계 경제로 통합된 것을 This로 받아서 그 결과 어떤 현상이 나타나는지에 대한 설명을 이어 가는 ③에 들어가는 것이 자연스럽다. 따라서 주어진 문장이 들어가기에 가장 적절한 곳은 ③이다.

🔍 선택지 완벽 분석

- ④ 함정 주어진 문장이 ④에 들어갈 경우, 초기 농경 시스템으로 인해 농경지에 대한 압력이 증가하게 되었다는 내용으로 이어져 내용이 연결되지 않는다.
- ⑤ 함정 Thus를 포함하는 ⑤ 다음 문장은 앞 문장에 그것의 원인이 되는 내용이 있어야 하는데, 주어진 문장이 ⑤에 들어가면 내용상 단절이 일어난다.

필수 어휘

agricultural 농업의 integrate 통합하다 co-evolve 함께 진화하다 myth 신화
tradition 전통 crop 농작물 obtain 얻다, 획득하다 stable 안정적인
maintain 유지하다 non-destructive 비파괴적인
incorporate 통합하다, 포함하다 commodity 상품, 물품 divert 전환하다

18강 2020~2023 요약문 완성

01 정답 ①

202309 40번 정답률 54%

It's not news to anyone that we judge others based on their clothes. In general, studies that investigate these judgments find that people prefer clothing that matches expectations — surgeons in scrubs, little boys in blue — with one notable exception. A series of studies published in an article in June 2014 in the *Journal of Consumer Research* 단서1 explored observers' reactions to people who broke established norms only slightly. ✪ In one scenario, *a man* (at a black-tie affair) was viewed / as **having** higher status and competence (when wearing a red bow tie). The researchers also found that valuing uniqueness increased audience members' ratings of the status and competence of a professor who wore red sneakers while giving a lecture. 주제문 단서2 The results suggest that people judge these slight deviations from the norm as positive because they suggest that the individual is powerful enough to risk the social costs of such behaviors.

⬇

A series of studies show that people view an individual (A) **positively** when the individual only slightly (B) **challenges** the norm for what people should wear.

해석

우리가 다른 사람들을 그들의 의복을 보고 판단하는 것은 누구에게도 새로운 일이 아니다. 일반적으로, 이러한 판단을 조사하는 연구는 사람들이 수술복을 입은 외과 의사, 파란 옷을 입은 남자아이와 같이 예상에 맞는 의복이되 하나의 주목할 만한 예외가 있는 것을 선호한다는 것을 발견한다. 'Journal of Consumer Research'의 2014년 6월 기사에 실린 일련의 연구는 확립된 규범을 아주 약간 어긴 사람들에 대한 관찰자들의 반응을 탐구했다. 한 시나리오에서는, 정장 차림의 행사에서 한 남자가 빨간 나비넥타이를 맸을 때 더 높은 지위와 능력을 가진 것으로 보여졌다. 연구자들은 독특함을 중시하는 것이 강의를 하는 동안 빨간 운동화를 신은 교수의 지위와 역량에 대한 청중들의 평가를 높였다는 것을 또한 발견했다. 그 결과들은 사람들이 규범으로부터 이러한 약간의 일탈들을 긍정적으로 판단한다는 것을 시사하는데, 왜냐하면 그것들은 그 사람이 그러한 행동으로 인한 사회적 비용을 감수할 만큼 충분히 강하다는 것을 시사하기 때문이다.

→ 일련의 연구는 사람들이 무엇을 착용해야 하는지에 대한 규범에 한 사람이 아주 약간 **도전할** 때 사람들이 그 사람을 **긍정적으로** 본다는 것을 나타낸다.

정답이 보이는 해설

사람들은 예상에 맞는 의복이되 하나의 예외가 있는 것을 선호하고, 정장 차림의 행사에서 빨간 나비넥타이를 맨 남자나 강의를 하는 빨간 운동화를 신은 교수의 지위와 능력을 더 높게 평가하였다. 즉, 사람들은 그 사람이 그러한 행동으로 인한 비용을 감수할 만큼 강하다고 받아들여 이러한 약간의 일탈을 긍정적으로 판단한다는 내용이다. 따라서 요약문은 규범에 한 사람이 아주 약간 '도전할' 때 사람들이 그 사람을 '긍정적으로' 본다고 하는 것이 적절하다.

🔍 선택지 완벽 분석

- ① positively ······ challenges   긍정적으로 ······ 도전할
- ② negatively ······ challenges   부정적으로 ······ 도전할

③ indifferently ····· neglects　　냉담하게 ····· 등한시할
④ negatively ····· meets　　부정적으로 ····· 충족할
⑤ positively ····· meets　　긍정적으로 ····· 충족할

> **함정** 사람들이 규범으로부터 약간의 일탈들을 긍정적으로 판단한다는 내용이므로, 규범을 약간 충족한다는 것은 글의 내용과 상반된다.

필수 어휘

judge 판단하다　investigate 조사하다　surgeon 외과 의사
scrubs (외과 의사의) 수술복　notable 주목할 만한, 눈에 띄는
exception 예외　observer 관찰자　establish 확립하다　norm 규범
competence 능력　deviation 일탈

---

02 정답 ②

202306 40번 정답률 59%

Nearly eight of ten U.S. adults believe there are "good foods"
10명 중 거의 8명
and "bad foods." Unless we're talking about spoiled stew, poison

mushrooms, or something similar, however, **단서1** no foods can
　　　　　　　　　　~으로 분류되다　　　　　　어떤 음식도
be labeled as either good or bad. **주제문** There are, however, **단서2**
좋고 나쁨으로 분류될 수 없음　　　↗결국 ~이 되다
combinations of foods that add up to a healthful or unhealthful diet.
건강에 좋거나 좋지 않은 식단은 음식들의 조합임
Consider the case of an adult who eats only foods thought of as

"good" — for example, raw broccoli, apples, orange juice, boiled

tofu, and carrots. **단서3** Although all these foods are nutrient-dense,
　　　　　　　　채소 같은 좋은 음식만 먹어도, 건강한 식단이 되지 않음
they do not add up to a healthy diet because they don't supply a

wide enough variety of the nutrients we need. Or take the case of
폭넓게 충분히 다양한 ~
the teenager who occasionally eats fried chicken, but otherwise

stays away from fried foods. The occasional fried chicken isn't
~을 멀리하다　　　　　　　　　　　　주격 관계대명사절↴
going to knock his or her diet off track. ✪ But / the person [who
　　　　　↗절 안의 동사1　　　　　　　　　　　단수 주어
단서4 eats fried foods every day, with few vegetables or fruits, and
튀긴 음식과 단것만 먹으면 나쁜 식단이 됨
loads up on supersized soft drinks, candy, and chips for snacks] has
　　　　　　　　　　　　　　　　　　　　　　　　단수 동사↗
a bad diet.

↓

Unlike the common belief, defining foods as good or bad is not (A)

appropriate; in fact, a healthy diet is determined largely by what
　　　　　　　　　　　　　　be determined by: ~에 의해 결정되다
the diet is (B) **composed of**.

해석

미국 성인 10명 중 거의 8명이 "좋은 음식"과 "나쁜 음식"이 있다고 믿는다. 하지만, 상한 스튜, 독버섯, 또는 이와 유사한 것에 대해 이야기하고 있지 않는 한, 어떤 음식도 좋고 나쁨으로 분류될 수 없다. 하지만, 결국 건강에 좋은 식단이나 건강에 좋지 않은 식단이 되는 음식들의 조합이 있다. "좋은" 음식이라고 생각되는 음식만 먹는 성인의 경우를 생각해 보라 — 예를 들어, 생브로콜리, 사과, 오렌지 주스, 삶은 두부와 당근. 비록 이 음식들은 모두 영양이 풍부하지만, 그것들은 우리가 필요로 하는 충분히 다양한 영양소를 공급하지 않기 때문에 그것들은 결국 건강한 식단이 되지 않는다. 또는 프라이드치킨을 가끔 먹지만, 그렇지 않으면 튀긴 음식을 멀리하는 십 대의 경우를 예로 들어 보자. 가끔 먹는 프라이드치킨은 그나 그녀의 식단을 궤도에서 벗어나게 하지는 않을 것이다. 하지만 채소나 과일을 거의 먹지 않으면서 매일 튀긴 음식을 먹고, 간식으로 초대형 탄산음료, 사탕, 그리고 감자 칩으로 배를 가득 채우는 사람은 나쁜 식단을 가지고 있는 것이다.

→ 일반적인 믿음과 달리, 음식을 좋고 나쁨으로 정의하는 것은 **적절하지** 않다; 사실,

건강에 좋은 식단은 대체로 그 식단이 무엇으로 **구성되는지**에 의해 결정된다.

> **정답이 보이는 해설**

대부분의 사람들이 좋은 음식과 나쁜 음식이 있다고 믿고 있지만 어떤 음식도 좋고 나쁨으로 분류될 수 없는데, 결국 건강에 좋거나 좋지 않은 식단은 음식들의 조합에 달려 있다는 내용의 글이다. 따라서 요약문은 일반적인 믿음과 달리, 음식을 좋고 나쁨으로 정의하는 것은 '적절하지' 않고, 건강에 좋은 식단은 그 식단이 무엇으로 '구성되는지'에 의해 결정된다고 하는 것이 적절하다.

🔍 선택지 완벽 분석

① incorrect ····· limited to　　부정확하지 ····· 제한되는지

> **함정** 빈칸 (A) 앞에 not이 있다는 데 유의해야 하고, 음식이 제한되어야 한다는 내용이 아니라 어떻게 구성되는지에 따라 건강한 식단이 될 수 있다는 내용이다.

② appropriate ····· composed of　　적절하지 ····· 구성되는지
③ wrong ····· aimed at　　틀리지 ····· 겨냥되는지
④ appropriate ····· tested on　　적절하지 ····· 테스트되는지
⑤ incorrect ····· adjusted to　　부정확하지 ····· 조정되는지

필수 어휘

spoiled stew 상한 스튜　poison mushroom 독버섯　combination 조합
raw 날것의　tofu 두부　nutrient-dense 영양이 풍부한　supply 공급하다
nutrient 영양소　occasionally 가끔　otherwise 그렇지 않으면
load up on ~로 배를 가득 채우다　supersized 초대형의

---

03 정답 ①

202303 40번 정답률 52%

주제문 ✪ To help decide [what's risky and what's safe], [who's
　　　　　　↖부사적 용법(목적)　decide의 목적어1　　　　decide의 목적어2
trustworthy and who's not], // we look for *social evidence*. From
　　　　　　　　　　　　　　　~을 찾다
an evolutionary view, **단서1** following the group is almost always
　　　　　　　　　　집단을 따르는 것이 생존 전망에 거의 항상 긍정적임
positive for our prospects of survival. "If everyone's doing it, it

must be a sensible thing to do," explains famous psychologist and

best selling writer of *Influence*, Robert Cialdini. While we can

frequently see this today in product reviews, even subtler cues
　　　　　　　　　　　　　　　　　　　　　훨씬 더 ~한
within the environment can signal trustworthiness. Consider this:

when you visit a local restaurant, are they busy? Is there a line

outside or is it easy to find a seat? It is a hassle to wait, but **단서2** a

line can be a powerful cue that the food's tasty, and these seats are
식당의 줄은 음식이 맛있고 수요가 많다는 강력한 신호임
in demand. More often than not, it's good to adopt the practices of
　　　　　　　자주, 대개　　　　　　　　　관례를 따르다
those around you.

↓

We tend to feel safe and secure in (A) **numbers** when we decide
~하는 경향이 있다
how to act, particularly when faced with (B) **uncertain** conditions.
어떻게 행동할지

해석

무엇이 위험하고 무엇이 안전한지, 누구를 신뢰할 수 있고 누구를 신뢰할 수 없는지를 결정하는 것을 돕기 위해, 우리는 '사회적 증거'를 찾는다. 진화의 관점에서 볼 때, 집단을 따르는 것이 우리의 생존 전망에 거의 항상 긍정적이다. "모든 사람이 그것을 하고 있다면, 그것은 해야 할 분별 있는 일인 것이 틀림없다."라고 유명한 심리학자이자 'Influence'를 쓴 베스트셀러 작가인 Robert Cialdini는 설명한다. 오늘날 상품 평에서 이것을 자주 볼 수 있지만, 환경 내의 훨씬 더 미묘한 신호가 신뢰성을 나타낼 수 있다. 이것을 생각해 보라. 여러분이 어떤 지역의 음식점을 방문할 때, 사람들이 바쁜가? 밖에 줄이 있는가, 아니면 자리를 찾기가 쉬운가? 기다리는 것은 성가신 일이지만, 줄은 음식이 맛있고 이곳의 좌석은 수요가 많다는 강력한 신호일 수 있

다. 대개는 주변에 있는 사람들의 관례를 따르는 것이 좋다.
→ 우리는 어떻게 행동할지 결정할 때 **숫자**에서 안전하고 안심된다고 느끼는 경향이 있는데, 특히 **불확실한** 상황에 직면했을 때 그렇다.

아님...

정답이 보이는 해설
우리는 어떻게 행동할지를 결정할 때 사회적 증거를 찾는데, 진화의 측면에서 우리의 생존 전망을 긍정적이게 하는 것은 집단을 따르는 것인데, 이에 대한 쉬운 예로, 어떤 식당에서의 긴 줄은 그 식당의 음식이 맛있고 수요가 많다는 강력한 신호일 수 있으므로 주변 사람들의 행동을 따르는 것이 대개는 좋다는 내용의 글이다. 따라서 요약문은 우리는 어떻게 행동할지 결정할 때 '숫자'에서 안전하고 안심된다고 느끼는 경향이 있는데, 특히 '불확실한' 상황에 직면했을 때 그렇다고 하는 것이 적절하다.

선택지 완벽 분석
① numbers ······ uncertain　　숫자 ······ 불확실한
② numbers ······ unrealistic　　숫자 ······ 비현실적인
③ experiences ······ unrealistic　　경험 ······ 비현실적인
어떻게 행동할지 결정할 때, 경험을 참고하라는 것이 아니라 어떤 행동을 하고 있는 사람들의 수가 많을수록 안전하다는 내용이다.
④ rules ······ uncertain　　규칙 ······ 불확실한
⑤ rules ······ unpleasant　　규칙 ······ 유쾌하지 않은

필수 어휘
risky 위험한　trustworthy 신뢰할 수 있는　evidence 증거　evolutionary 진화의 positive 긍정적인　prospect 전망　survival 생존　psychologist 심리학자 frequently 자주, 빈번하게　product review 상품 평　cue 신호　signal 나타내다 in demand 수요가 많은　adopt 따르다, 채택하다　practice 행동, 관행

04 정답 ②
202211 40번 정답률 63%

주제문 One of the most powerful tools to find meaning in our lives is reflective journaling — thinking back on and writing about what has happened to us. In the 1990s, Stanford University researchers asked undergraduate students on spring break **단서1** to journal about their most important personal values and their daily activities; others were asked to write about only the good things that happened to them in the day. *(Three weeks later,)* the students [who had written about their values] were happier, healthier, and more confident (about their ability to handle stress) / than the ones [who had only focused on the good stuff]. **단서2** By reflecting on how their daily activities supported their values, students had gained a new perspective on those activities and choices. Little stresses and hassles were now demonstrations of their values in action. Suddenly, their lives were full of meaningful activities. And all they had to do was **단서3** reflect and write about it — positively reframing their experiences with their personal values.

↓

Journaling about daily activities based on what we believe to be (A) **worthwhile** can make us feel that our life is meaningful by (B) **rethinking** our experiences in a new way.

해석
우리의 삶에서 의미를 찾기 위한 가장 강력한 도구들 중 하나는 성찰적 일기 쓰기, 즉 우리에게 일어난 일을 돌아보고 그것에 대해 쓰는 것이다. 1990년대에 Stanford University 연구진들이 봄 방학에 학부생들에게 그들의 가장 중요한 개인적인 가치와 그들의 하루의 활동들에 대해 쓰도록 요청했다. 반면, 다른 사람들은 그날 그들에게 일어난 좋은 일만 쓰도록 요청되었다. 3주 후에, 자신의 가치에 관해 썼던 학생들은 좋은 것에만 초점을 맞췄던 학생들보다 더 행복하고, 더 건강하고, 스트레스를 다루는 자신의 능력에 대해 더 자신 있었다. 그들의 하루의 활동들이 어떻게 그들의 가치를 뒷받침했는지에 대해 성찰함으로써, 학생들은 그 활동들과 선택들에 대해 새로운 관점을 얻었다. 작은 스트레스와 귀찮은 일들은 이제 행동에서 그들의 가치를 보여 주는 것이었다. 갑자기, 그들의 삶은 의미 있는 활동으로 가득했다. 그리고 그들이 했어야 할 모든 일은 그들의 경험을 개인적인 가치로 긍정적으로 재구성하면서 그것에 대해 돌아보고 쓰는 것이었다.
→ 우리가 **가치 있다고** 믿는 것에 근거하여 일상의 활동에 대해 일기를 쓰는 것은 새로운 방식으로 자신의 경험들을 **다시 생각함**으로써 우리로 하여금 우리의 삶이 의미 있다고 느끼게 만들 수 있다.

정답이 보이는 해설
삶에서 의미를 찾기 위한 가장 강력한 도구는 성찰적 일기 쓰기인데, 하루를 돌아보며 자신의 가치를 성찰함으로써, 삶이 의미 있는 활동으로 가득 차게 된다는 내용이다. 따라서 요약문은 '가치 있다고' 믿는 것에 근거하여 일기를 쓰면, 자신의 경험들을 '다시 생각함'으로써 우리의 삶이 의미 있다고 느끼게 만든다고 하는 것이 적절하다.

선택지 완벽 분석
① factual ······ rethinking　　사실적이라고 ······ 다시 생각함
② worthwhile ······ rethinking　　가치 있다고 ······ 다시 생각함
③ outdated ······ generalizing　　구식이라고 ······ 일반화함
④ objective ······ generalizing　　객관적이라고 ······ 일반화함
⑤ demanding ······ describing　　부담스럽다고 ······ 묘사함

필수 어휘
reflective 반성[숙고]하는　journaling 일기 쓰기　think back on ~을 되돌아보다 researcher 연구인　value 가치　undergraduate student 학부생 confident 자신 있는　handle 다루다　reflect on ~을 되돌아보다 support 뒷받침하다　perspective 관점　demonstration 드러냄, 입증 reframe 재구성하다

05 정답 ①
202209 40번 정답률 45%

My colleagues and I ran an experiment testing two different messages meant to convince thousands of resistant alumni to make a donation. One message emphasized the opportunity to do good: donating would benefit students, faculty, and staff. The other emphasized the opportunity to feel good: donors would enjoy the warm glow of giving. **단서1** The two messages were equally effective: in both cases, 6.5 percent of the unwilling alumni ended up donating. Then we combined them, because two reasons are better than one. Except they weren't. **단서2** When we put the two reasons together, the giving rate dropped below 3 percent. Each reason alone was more than twice as effective as the two combined. The audience was already skeptical. **단서3** When we gave them different kinds of *reasons* (to donate), / we triggered their awareness

요약문 완성

정답 및 해설 **185**

[**that** someone was trying to persuade them] — and they shielded
└ 동격절 접속사 that   주어2   동사2
themselves against it.

↓

In the experiment mentioned above, when the two different reasons
to donate were given (A) **simultaneously**, the audience was less
likely to be (B) **convinced** because they could recognize the
intention to persuade them.

해석

나의 동료들과 나는 수천 명의 저항하는 졸업생을 납득시켜 기부하도록 하는 것을
의도한 두 개의 다른 메시지들을 테스트하는 실험을 실시했다. 한 메시지는 선행을
할 기회를 강조했다. 즉, 기부하는 것은 학생들, 교직원, 그리고 직원들에게 이익을
줄 것임을 강조했다. 다른 메시지는 좋은 기분을 느끼는 기회를 강조했다. 기부자들
은 기부의 따뜻한 온기를 즐길 것임을 강조했다. 그 두 개의 메시지들은 똑같이 효과
적이었다. 두 경우 모두에서, 마음이 내키지 않은 6.5%의 졸업생들이 결국에는 기부
를 했다. 그러고 나서 우리는 그것들을 결합했는데, 왜냐하면 두 개의 이유가 한 개보
다 더 낫기 때문이다. 그러나 그렇지 않았다. 우리가 그 두 개의 이유들을 합쳤을 때,
기부율은 3% 아래로 떨어졌다. 각각의 이유가 단독으로는 그 두 개가 합쳐진 것보다
두 배 넘게 더 효과적이었다. 청중은 이미 회의적이었다. 우리가 그들에게 기부해야
할 서로 다른 종류의 이유를 주었을 때, 우리는 누군가가 그들을 설득하려고 하는 중
이라는 인식을 유발했고, 그리고 그들은 그것에 맞서 스스로를 보호했다.
→ 위에서 언급된 실험에서, 기부라는 두 개의 다른 이유가 **동시에** 주어졌을 때, 청
중은 자신들을 설득시키려는 의도를 알아차릴 수 있었기 때문에 **납득될** 가능성이 더
낮았다.

정답이 보이는 해설

기부를 하지 않으려는 수천 명의 졸업생을 납득시켜 기부하도록 한 실험에서, 선행
과 좋은 기분을 따로 강조한 메시지는 똑같이 효과적이었지만, 선행과 좋은 기분을
하나로 합쳤을 때 기부율이 3% 아래로 떨어졌는데, 이는 청중들이 누군가가 자신들
을 설득하려고 한다는 인식을 유발하여 스스로를 설득당하지 않도록 보호했기 때문
이라는 내용의 글이다. 따라서 요약문은 기부할 두 가지 이유가 '동시에' 주어졌을 때
'납득될' 가능성이 더 낮았다고 하는 것이 적절하다.

선택지 완벽 분석

① simultaneously …… convinced   동시에 …… 납득될
② separately …… confused   따로따로 …… 혼란스러울
③ frequently …… annoyed   빈번히 …… 화가 날
④ separately …… satisfied   따로따로 …… 만족할
⑤ simultaneously …… offended   동시에 …… 기분이 상할

필수 어휘

colleague (직장) 동료   experiment 실험   convince 납득시키다, 설득하다
resistant 저항하는   emphasize 강조하다   donate 기부하다
benefit ~에게 이익[이득]이 되다   faculty 교직원   donor 기부자
glow 온기, 만족감   unwilling 마음이 내키지 않는, 마지못해 하는
combine 합치다, 결합하다   drop 떨어지다   trigger 유발하다
awareness 인식, 인지   shield 보호하다

06 정답 ③

202206 40번 정답률 68%

According to a study of Swedish adolescents, an important factor
of adolescents' academic success is how they respond to challenges.
The study reports that **단서1** when facing difficulties, adolescents
어려움에 직면했을 때 권위 있는 부모에게 양육된 청소년이

---

exposed to an authoritative parenting style are less likely to be
덜 수동적이고 덜 무기력하며 덜 실패할 가능성이 있음
passive, helpless, and afraid to fail. Another study of nine high
schools in Wisconsin and northern California indicates that
단서2 children of authoritative parents do well in school, because
권위 있는 부모의 자녀들이 학습을 잘하는데, 그들의 부모가 자녀의 학교 활동 관여에 많은 노력을
these parents put a lot of effort into getting involved in their
기울이기 때문임   ~에 관여하다
children's school activities. ☉ That is, / authoritative parents are
즉, 말하자면
significantly more likely [to help their children with homework], / [to
     likely에 이어지는 병렬1   병렬2
attend school programs], / [to watch their children in sports], / and
     병렬3
[to help students select courses]. Moreover, these parents are more
   병렬4   be aware of: ~을 알고 있다
aware of what their children do and how they perform in school.
Finally, authoritative parents praise academic excellence and the
importance of working hard more than other parents do.

↓

The studies above show that the children of authoritative parents
often succeed academically, since they are more (A) **willing** to deal
     be willing to: 기꺼이 ~하다
with their difficulties and are affected by their parents' (B) **active**
involvement.

해석

스웨덴 청소년들에 대한 연구에 따르면, 청소년들의 학문적 성공의 중요한 요인은
그들이 어려움에 어떻게 반응하는가이다. 이 연구는, 어려움에 직면했을 때 권위가
있는 양육 방식에 노출된 청소년들이 덜 수동적이고, 덜 무기력하며, 실패를 덜 두려
워할 가능성이 있다고 보고한다. Wisconsin과 북부 California의 9개 고등학교에
대한 또 다른 연구는 권위가 있는 부모의 자녀들이 학습을 잘 하는데, 그 이유는 이
러한 부모들이 자녀의 학교 활동에 관여하는 데 많은 노력을 기울이기 때문이라는
것을 보여 준다. 즉, 권위가 있는 부모들은 자녀의 숙제를 도와주고, 학교 프로그램에
참여하며, 스포츠에 참여하는 자녀를 지켜보고, 자녀가 과목을 선택하는 것을 도와줄
가능성이 상당히 더 높다. 게다가, 이러한 부모들은 자녀가 학교에서 하고 있는 일과
수행하는 방식에 대해 더 잘 알고 있다. 마지막으로, 권위가 있는 부모들은 다른 부모
들에 비해 학문적 탁월함과 근면함의 중요성을 더 많이 칭찬한다.
→ 위 연구는 권위가 있는 부모의 자녀들이 흔히 학문적으로 성공한다는 것을 보여
주는데, 그들은 어려움에 더 **기꺼이** 대처**하고** 부모의 **적극적인** 관여에 영향을 받기
때문이다.

정답이 보이는 해설

청소년들이 어려움에 직면했을 때 권위가 있는 부모의 자녀들은 학문적으로 성공할
가능성이 더 높은데, 그 이유는 권위가 있는 부모는 자녀의 학교 활동에 관여하는 데
더 많은 노력을 기울이고 자녀가 학교에서 어떻게 하고 있는지 잘 알고 있으며 자녀
의 학문적 탁월함을 더 많이 칭찬하기 때문이라는 내용이다. 따라서 요약문은 권위
가 있는 부모의 자녀들이 어려움에 더 '기꺼이' 대처하고 부모의 '적극적인' 관여에
영향을 받는다고 하는 것이 적절하다.

선택지 완벽 분석

① likely …… random   ~할 것 같은 …… 무작위의
② willing …… minimal   기꺼이 ~하는 …… 최소한의
③ willing …… active   기꺼이 ~하는 …… 적극적인
④ hesitant …… unwanted   주저하는 …… 원치 않는
⑤ hesitant …… constant   주저하는 …… 지속적인

필수 어휘

adolescent 청소년   academic 학문적인   challenge 어려움, 도전
authoritative 권위가 있는   parenting 양육   helpless 무기력한
involvement 관여, 개입   perform 수행하다   praise 칭찬하다
excellence 탁월함

07 정답 ①

The common blackberry (*Rubus allegheniensis*) has an amazing ability to move manganese from one layer of soil to another using its roots. ✪ This may **seem like** a funny talent for a plant to have, / but it all becomes clear / **when** you realize [the effect it has on nearby plants]. Manganese can be very harmful to plants, especially at high concentrations. Common blackberry is unaffected by damaging effects of this metal and has evolved two different ways of using manganese to its advantage. 단서1 First, it redistributes manganese from deeper soil layers to shallow soil layers using its roots as a small pipe. 단서2 Second, it absorbs manganese as it grows, concentrating the metal in its leaves. 단서3 When the leaves drop and decay, their concentrated manganese deposits further poison the soil around the plant. For plants that are not immune to the toxic effects of manganese, this is very bad news. Essentially, the common blackberry eliminates competition by poisoning its neighbors with heavy metals.

↓

The common blackberry has an ability to (A) **increase** the amount of manganese in the surrounding upper soil, which makes the nearby soil quite (B) **deadly** for other plants.

해석

common blackberry(Rubus allegheniensis)는 뿌리를 이용하여 토양의 한 층에서 다른 층으로 망가니즈를 옮기는 놀라운 능력이 있다. 이것은 식물이 가지기에는 기이한 재능처럼 보일 수도 있지만, 그것이 근처의 식물에 미치는 영향을 깨닫게 되면 전부 명확해진다. 망가니즈는 식물에 매우 해로울 수 있으며, 특히 고농도일 때 그렇다. common blackberry는 이 금속 원소의 해로운 효과에 영향을 받지 않으며, 망가니즈를 자신에게 유리하게 사용하는 두 가지 다른 방법을 발달시켰다. 첫째, 그것은 뿌리를 작은 관으로 사용하여 망가니즈를 깊은 토양층에서 얕은 토양층으로 재분배한다. 둘째, 그것은 성장하면서 망가니즈를 흡수하여 그 금속 원소를 잎에 농축시킨다. 잎이 떨어지고 부패할 때, 그것의 농축된 망가니즈 축적물은 그 식물 주변의 토양을 독성 물질로 더욱 오염시킨다. 망가니즈의 유독한 영향에 면역성이 없는 식물에게 이것은 매우 나쁜 소식이다. 본질적으로, common blackberry는 중금속으로 그것의 이웃을 중독시킴으로써 경쟁자를 제거한다.
→ common blackberry는 주변의 위쪽 토양에 망가니즈의 양을 **증가시키는** 능력이 있는데, 그것은 근처의 토양이 다른 식물에게 **치명적이게** 만든다.

정답이 보이는 해설

common blackberry는 뿌리를 이용하여 토양의 한 층에서 다른 층으로 망가니즈를 옮기는 능력이 있는데, 망가니즈를 깊은 토양에서 위쪽 토양으로 재분배하고, 망가니즈가 잎에 축적되며 그 망가니즈 축적물이 결국 주변 토양을 독성 물질로 오염시켜 다른 식물을 제거한다는 내용의 글이다. 따라서 요약문은 common blackberry는 주변의 위쪽 토양의 망가니즈의 양을 '증가시키는' 능력이 있는데, 그것은 근처의 토양이 다른 식물에게 '치명적이게' 만든다고 하는 것이 적절하다.

선택지 완벽 분석

① increase …… deadly	증가시키는 …… 치명적이게
② increase …… advantageous	증가시키는 …… 유리하게
③ indicate …… nutritious	나타내는 …… 영양가 있게
④ reduce …… dry	줄이는 …… 건조하게
⑤ reduce …… warm	줄이는 …… 따뜻하게

필수 어휘

layer 층 concentration 농도 damaging 해로운 redistribute 재분배하다 shallow 얕은 absorb 흡수하다 concentrate 농축시키다 decay 썩다 poison (독성 물질로) 오염시키다, 중독시키다 immune 면역성이 있는 toxic 유독한 eliminate 제거하다 competition 경쟁자 surrounding 주변의

---

08 정답 ②

There is often a lot of uncertainty in the realm of science, which the general public finds uncomfortable. 단서1 They don't want "informed guesses," they want certainties that make their lives easier, and science is often unequipped to meet these demands. In particular, the human body is fantastically complex, and some scientific answers can never be provided in black-or-white terms. 단서2 All this is why the media tends to oversimplify scientific research when presenting it to the public. ✪ In their eyes, they're just "giving people what they want" as opposed to offering more accurate but complex *information* [that very few people will read or understand]. A perfect example of this is how people want definitive answers as to which foods are "good" and "bad." Scientifically speaking, there are no "good" and "bad" foods; rather, food quality exists on a continuum, meaning that some foods are *better* than others when it comes to general health and well-being.

↓

With regard to general health, science, by its nature, does not (A) **satisfy** the public's demands for certainty, which leads to the media giving less (B) **complicated** answers to the public.

해석

과학의 영역에는 흔히 많은 불확실성이 존재하는데, 일반 대중은 그것을 불편하다고 느낀다. 그들은 '정보에 근거한 추측'을 원하지 않고 자신의 삶을 더 편하게 해 주는 확실성을 원하는데, 과학은 자주 이러한 요구를 만족시킬 준비가 되어 있지 않다. 특히 인간의 신체는 굉장히 복잡하며, 어떤 과학적인 답변은 흑백 양자택일의 말로 결코 제공될 수 없다. 이 모든 것이 미디어가 과학적 연구를 대중에게 제시할 때 그것을 지나치게 단순화하는 경향이 있는 이유이다. 그들의 눈에는 극소수의 사람들만이 읽거나 이해할 더 정확하지만 복잡한 정보를 제공하는 것이 아니라, 그들은 그저 '사람들에게 그들이 원하는 것을 제공하고' 있는 것이다. 이에 대한 완벽한 하나의 예는 어떤 음식이 '좋은지' 그리고 '나쁜지'에 관해 사람들이 확정적인 답변을 원하는 방식이다. 과학적으로 말하자면 '좋은' 그리고 '나쁜' 음식은 없으며, 오히려 음식의 질은 연속체상에 존재하는데, 이것은 어떤 음식들이 다른 음식들보다 일반 건강과 행복에 관해서는 '더 낫다'는 것을 의미한다.
→ 일반 건강과 관련하여 과학은 그 본질상 확실성에 대한 대중의 요구를 **만족시키지** 않는데, 이것은 미디어가 대중에게 덜 **복잡한** 답변을 제공하는 것으로 이어진다.

정답이 보이는 해설

과학에는 불확실성이 존재하지만 대중은 확실성을 원하기 때문에 미디어는 더 정확하고 복잡한 정보를 제공하는 대신 과학적 연구를 지나치게 단순화하고 사람들이 원하는 확정적인 답변을 제공한다는 내용의 글이다. 따라서 요약문은 과학이 본질상 확실성에 대한 대중의 요구를 '만족시키지' 않는데, 이것은 미디어가 대중에게 덜 '복잡한' 답변을 제공하는 것으로 이어진다고 하는 것이 적절하다.

① satisfy ····· simple	만족시키지 ····· 단순한
② satisfy ····· complicated	만족시키지 ····· 복잡한
③ ignore ····· difficult	무시하지 ····· 어려운
④ ignore ····· simple	무시하지 ····· 단순한
⑤ reject ····· complicated	거절하지 ····· 복잡한

필수 어휘

uncertainty 불확실성   realm 영역   informed 정보에 근거한
in particular 특히   fantastically 엄청나게   complex 복잡한
black-or-white 흑백 양자택일의   oversimplify 지나치게 단순화하다
definitive 확정적인

09 정답 ①

Nancy Lowry and David Johnson conducted an experiment to
study a teaching environment where fifth and sixth graders were
assigned to interact on a topic. With one group, the discussion was
led in a way that built an agreement. With the second group, the
discussion was designed to produce disagreements about the right
answer. ⭐ Students [who easily reached an agreement] / were less
interested in the topic, studied less, and were less likely to visit
the library / to get additional information. The most noticeable
difference, though, was revealed when teachers showed a special
film about the discussion topic — during lunch time! 단서 Only 18
percent of the agreement group missed lunch time to see the film,
but 45 percent of the students from the disagreement group stayed
for the film. The thirst to fill a knowledge gap — to find out who
was right within the group — can be more powerful than the thirst
for slides and jungle gyms.

↓

According to the experiment above, students' interest in a topic (A)
increases when they are encouraged to (B) **differ**.

해석

Nancy Lowry와 David Johnson은 5학년과 6학년 학생들이 한 주제에 대해 상호 작용을 하게 하는 교수 환경을 연구하고자 실험을 했다. 한 그룹에서는 합의를 도출하는 방식으로 토론이 유도되었다. 두 번째 그룹에서는 옳은 정답에 대한 불일치가 나오도록 토론이 설계되었다. 합의에 쉽게 도달한 학생들은 주제에 흥미를 덜 보이고 더 적게 공부했으며 부가적인 정보를 얻기 위해 도서관에 가는 경향이 더 적었다. 그러나 가장 뚜렷한 차이는 교사가 점심시간 동안 학생들에게 토론 주제에 관한 영화를 보여 주었을 때 나타났다! 동의한 그룹의 18퍼센트만이 영화를 보기 위해 점심시간을 놓쳤지만 동의하지 않은 그룹 학생들의 45퍼센트는 그 영화를 보기 위해 남았다. 그룹 내에서 누가 옳았는지 알기 위해 지식 차이를 채우려는 열망은 미끄럼틀과 정글짐을 향한 열망보다 더 강했다.
→ 위의 연구에 따르면, 한 주제에 대한 학생들의 흥미는 학생들이 **의견을 달리하도록** 장려될 때 **증가한다**.

정답이 보이는 해설

5학년과 6학년 학생들이 한 주제에 대해 상호 작용을 하게 하는 교수 환경을 연구하

려는 실험에서, 토론을 통한 합의를 도출하도록 유도된 그룹과 토론을 통해 불일치가 나오도록 설계된 그룹 간 학생들의 흥미도를 비교한 결과, 불일치 그룹에 속한 학생들이 합의에 쉽게 도달한 학생들보다 알려는 열망이 더 강했다는 내용의 글이다. 따라서 요약문은 한 주제에 대한 학생들의 흥미는 학생들이 '의견을 달리 하도록' 장려될 때 '증가한다'고 하는 것이 적절하다.

① increases ····· differ	증가한다 ····· 의견을 달리하도록
② increases ····· approve	증가한다 ····· 찬성하도록

의견이 일치한 그룹보다 의견이 불일치한 그룹의 학생들이 주제에 대한 흥미가 더 강했다는 결과이므로 '찬성하도록'이라는 말은 지문의 내용과 정반대의 내용이 된다.

③ increases ····· cooperate	증가한다 ····· 협동하도록

실험의 목적은 '협동하여' 합의에 도달하도록 하는 것이 아니라 두 그룹이 주제에 대한 흥미도에서 어떤 차이를 보였는지를 알아보는 것이다.

④ decreases ····· participate	감소한다 ····· 참여하도록
⑤ decreases ····· argue	감소한다 ····· 주장하도록

필수 어휘

conduct 실시하다, 실행하다   assign 배치하다   interact 상호 작용하다
agreement 합의, 동의   additional 추가적인   noticeable 뚜렷한, 분명한
reveal 나타나다   thirst 갈망, 열망   differ 의견이 다르다

10 정답 ①

⭐ A woman (named Rhonda) [who attended the University of
California at Berkeley] had a problem. She was living near campus
with several other people — none of whom knew one another.
When the cleaning people came each weekend, they left several
rolls of toilet paper in each of the two bathrooms. However, by
Monday all the toilet paper would be gone. It was a classic tragedy-
of-the-commons situation: because some people took more toilet
paper than their fair share, the public resource was destroyed
for everyone else. After reading a research paper about behavior
change, 단서1 Rhonda put a note in one of the bathrooms asking
people not to remove the toilet paper, as it was a shared item. To
her great satisfaction, 단서2 one roll reappeared in a few hours, and
another the next day. In the other note-free bathroom, however,
there was no toilet paper until the following weekend, when the
cleaning people returned.

↓

A small (A) **reminder** brought about a change in the behavior of
the people who had taken more of the (B) **shared** goods than they
needed.

해석

Berkeley의 California 대학에 다니는 Rhonda라는 이름의 여자는 한 가지 문제가 있었다. 그녀는 몇 명의 다른 사람들과 함께 캠퍼스 근처에 살고 있었는데, 그들 중 누구도 서로 알지 못했다. 청소하는 사람들이 주말마다 와서 두 군데의 각 화장실에 두루마리 화장지 몇 개를 두고 갔다. 그러나 월요일 무렵에 모든 화장지가 없어지곤 했다. 그것은 전형적인 공유지의 비극 상황이었다. 즉, 일부 사람들이 자신들이 사용할 몫보다 더 많은 휴지를 가져갔기 때문에 다른 모두가 쓸 공공재가 파괴되었다. 행동 변화에 대한 한 연구 논문을 읽은 후, Rhonda는 한 곳의 화장실에 사람들

에게 화장실 화장지는 함께 쓰는 물건이므로 가져가지 말라는 쪽지를 붙였다. 아주 만족스럽게도, 몇 시간 후에 화장지 한 개가 다시 나타났고, 그 다음날에는 또 하나가 다시 나타났다. 하지만 쪽지가 없는 다른 화장실에서는 청소하는 사람들이 돌아오는 그 다음 주말까지 화장지가 없었다.

→ **상기시켜 주는** 사소한 **것**이 **함께 쓰는** 물건을 자신들이 필요한 것보다 더 많이 가져간 사람들의 행동에 변화를 가져왔다.

주말에 채워진 휴지가 월요일에 모두 없어지는 상황을 개선하려고 두 화장실 중 한 곳에 '함께 쓰는 물건이므로 가져가지 말라'는 쪽지를 붙였더니 그 효과가 즉각 나타났다는 내용의 글이므로, 요약문은 잘못임을 '상기시켜 주는 것'을 화장실에 붙임으로써 '함께 쓰는' 물건을 더 많이 가져간 사람들의 행동에 변화를 가져왔다고 하는 것이 적절하다.

선택지 완벽 분석

① reminder …… shared   상기시켜 주는 것 …… 함께 쓰는
② reminder …… recycled   상기시켜 주는 것 …… 재활용되는
③ mistake …… stored   실수 …… 저장된
오답 화장실 휴지를 가져간 것을 실수할 수 있다고 생각할 수 있지만 요약문의 내용상 실수가 아니라 실수를 깨닫게 해 주는 것(쪽지)이다.
④ mistake …… borrowed   실수 …… 빌린
⑤ fortune …… limited   재산 …… 제한된

필수 어휘

classic 전형적인   tragedy-of-the-commons 공유지의 비극
share 몫, 할당   destroy 파괴시키다   behavior 행동   remove 없애다
share 함께 쓰다, 공유하다   satisfaction 만족   following 다음의

11 정답 ②

202103 40번 정답률 53%

In one study, researchers asked pairs of strangers to sit down in a room and chat. In half of the rooms, a cell phone was placed on a nearby table; in the other half, no phone was present. ✿ **After the** conversations **had ended**, / the researchers **asked** the participants / [what they thought of each other]. Here's what they learned:
접속사(~ 후에)
부사절의 동사(대과거)   주절의 동사(과거)   간접목적어
직접목적어(명사절)

단서1 when a cell phone was present in the room, the participants
방에 휴대전화가 있을 때 참가자들의 관계의 질은 휴대전화가 없는 방에서보다 더 나쁨
reported the quality of their relationship was worse than those who'd talked in a cell phone-free room. The pairs who talked in the rooms with cell phones thought their partners showed less empathy. Think of all the times you've sat down to have lunch with a friend and set your phone on the table. You might have felt good about yourself because you didn't pick it up to check your messages, but
집어 들다. 집다
단서2 your unchecked messages were still hurting your connection
(앞에 놓인 휴대전화의) 확인되지 않은 메시지도 여전히 맞은편에 앉은 사람과의 관계를 해침
with the person sitting across from you.
~의 맞은편에
↓

The presence of a cell phone (A) **weakens** the connection between people involved in conversations, even when the phone is being (B) **ignored**.

해석

한 연구에서, 연구자들은 모르는 사람끼리 짝이 된 쌍들에게 한 방에 앉아서 이야기

하도록 요청했다. 방의 절반에는 근처의 탁자 위에 휴대전화가 놓여 있었고, 나머지 절반의 방에는 휴대전화가 없었다. 대화가 끝나고 나서, 연구자들은 참가자들에게 서로에 대해 어떻게 생각하는지 물었다. 이것이 그들이 알게 된 것이다. 방에 휴대전화가 있을 때 참가자들의 관계의 질은 휴대전화가 없는 방에서 대화한 참가자들보다 더 나빴다고 말했다. 휴대전화가 있는 방에서 대화한 쌍들은 자신의 상대가 공감을 덜 보였다고 생각했다. 친구와 점심을 먹으려고 자리에 앉아서 휴대전화를 탁자 위에 놓았던 모든 순간을 생각해 보라. 메시지를 확인하려 휴대전화를 집어 들지 않았기 때문에 자기 자신이 잘했다고 느꼈을지도 모르지만, 여러분이 확인하지 않은 메시지도 여전히 맞은편에 앉아 있는 사람과의 관계를 해치고 있었다.

→ 휴대전화의 존재는 심지어 휴대전화가 **무시되고** 있을 때조차 대화에 참여하는 사람들의 관계를 **약화시킨다**.

휴대전화가 있는 방과 휴대전화가 없는 방에서 모르는 사람과 짝이 되어 이야기하게 한 실험에서, 휴대전화가 있는 방에서 대화를 한 참가자들이 휴대전화가 없는 방에서 대화를 한 참가자들보다 대화의 질이 더 나빴다고 답한 실험 결과를 통해, 휴대전화의 존재만으로도 마주앉은 사람과의 관계를 해치고 있다는 내용의 글이다. 따라서 요약문은 휴대전화가 '무시되고' 있을 때조차 대화에 참여하는 사람들의 관계를 '약화시킨다'고 하는 것이 적절하다.

선택지 완벽 분석

① weakens …… answered   약화시킨다 …… 응답되고
실험에서는 휴대전화로 통화를 하는 것이 아니라 그냥 탁자에 놓여 있는 것이므로 '응답되고' 있는 것이라고 할 수 없다.
② weakens …… ignored   약화시킨다 …… 무시되고
③ renews …… answered   재개한다 …… 응답되고
④ maintains …… ignored   유지한다 …… 무시되고
⑤ maintains …… updated   유지한다 …… 갱신되고

필수 어휘

nearby 근처의   present 있는, 존재하는   participant 참가자   quality 질
relationship 관계   check 확인하다   hurt 해치다, 상하게 하다
connection 관계, 연결

12 정답 ①

202011 40번 정답률 53%

In their study in 2007 Katherine Kinzler and her colleagues at Harvard showed that 주제문 our tendency to identify with an
~와 동일시하다
in-group to a large degree begins in infancy and may be innate.
대부분   →동사1
✿ 단서1 Kinzler and her team took a bunch of *five-month-olds*
가족들이 영어만 사용하는 5개월 된 아기들을 뽑아 2개의 비디오를 보여 줌
[whose families only spoke English] / and showed the babies two
소유격 관계대명사   동사2
videos. In one video, a woman was speaking English. In the other, a woman was speaking Spanish. Then they were shown a screen with both women side by side, not speaking. In infant psychology
나란히
research, the standard measure for affinity or interest is attention — babies will apparently stare longer at the things they like more.

단서2 In Kinzler's study, the babies stared at the English speakers
그 아기들은 영어를 말하는 사람을 더 오래 쳐다봄
longer. In other studies, researchers have found that 단서3 infants are more likely to take a toy offered by someone who speaks the
유아들은 자신들과 같은 언어를 말하는 사람이 주는 장난감을 받을 가능성이 더 높음
same language as them. Psychologists routinely cite these and other experiments as evidence of our built-in evolutionary preference for "our own kind."

Infants' more favorable responses to those who use a (A) **familiar** language show that there can be a(n) (B) **inborn** tendency to prefer in-group members.

해석

Katherine Kinzler와 그녀의 하버드 동료들은 2007년의 연구에서 우리의 내집단과 동일시하려는 경향이 대부분 유아기에 시작되고 선천적일 수 있다는 것을 보여 주었다. Kinzler와 그녀의 팀은 가족들이 영어만을 말하는 5개월 된 아이들 한 무리를 뽑아 두 개의 영상을 보여 주었다. 한 영상에서는 한 여성이 영어를 말하고 있었다. 다른 영상에서는 한 여성이 스페인어를 말하고 있었다. 그러고 나서 그들은 두 여성 모두 말하지 않고 나란히 있는 화면을 보았다. 유아 심리학 연구에서 애착이나 관심의 표준 척도는 주의집중인데, 아기들은 분명 자신들이 더 좋아하는 것을 더 오래 쳐다볼 것이다. Kinzler의 연구에서 아기들은 영어 사용자들을 더 오래 쳐다보았다. 다른 연구들에서 연구자들은 유아들이 자신들과 같은 언어를 사용하는 사람이 주는 장난감을 받을 가능성이 더 높다는 것을 발견했다. 심리학자들은 '우리와 같은 종류'에 대한 우리의 내재된 진화론적인 선호에 대한 증거로 이것들과 다른 실험들을 일상적으로 인용한다.

→ **친숙한** 언어를 사용하는 사람들에 대한 유아들의 더 호의적인 반응은 내집단 구성원들을 선호하는 **선천적인** 경향이 있을 수 있다는 것을 보여 준다.

정답이 보이는 해설

가족들이 영어만을 말하는 아기들에게 한 여성이 영어를 말하는 영상과 다른 여성이 스페인어를 말하는 영상을 보여 준 다음, 두 여성을 나란히 보여 주었을 때 아기들이 영어를 말한 여성을 더 많이 쳐다보았다는 실험을 통해 아기들에게 '자신들과 같은 종류'에 대해 내재된 선호가 있다는 것을 알 수 있다는 내용의 글이다. 따라서 요약문은 '친숙한' 언어를 사용하는 사람들에 대한 호의적인 반응은 내집단 구성원들을 선호하는 '선천적인' 경향이 있을 수 있다고 하는 것이 적절하다.

선택지 완벽 분석

① familiar …… inborn　　친숙한 …… 선천적인
② familiar …… acquired　친숙한 …… 습득된
　함정 5개월 된 아기를 실험한 것이므로 '습득된' 경향이라기보다 '선천적인' 경향이라고 보는 것이 적절하다
③ foreign …… cultural　　이질적인 …… 문화적인
④ foreign …… learned　　이질적인 …… 학습된
⑤ formal …… innate　　공식적인 …… 선천적인

필수 어휘

colleague 동료　tendency 경향　infancy 유아기　innate 선천적인
measure 척도　attention 주의집중, 주목　apparently 분명히, 명백히
stare 쳐다보다, 응시하다　routinely 일상적으로, 판에 박힌 듯이　cite 인용하다
evidence 증거　evolutionary 진화론적인　favorable 호의적인

19강 **2020~2023** **장문의 이해**

01 정답 ② 02 정답 ⑤

★ Claims [that local food production cut greenhouse gas
주어 └동격절┘　　동격절 주어　　동사　　목적어
emissions / **by reducing** the burning (of transportation fuel)]
by+~ing: ~함으로써
/ are usually not well founded. Transport is the source of only 11
└─ 동사 ─┘
percent of greenhouse gas emissions within the food sector, so
reducing the distance that food travels after it leaves the farm is far
(a) less important than reducing wasteful energy use on the farm.
01번 단서1 Food coming from a distance can actually be better for the
먼 곳에서 오는 식품이 어떻게 재배되었느냐에 따라 기후에 더 좋을 수 있음
(b) climate, depending on how it was grown. For example, **01번 단서2**
~에 따라
field-grown tomatoes shipped from Mexico in the winter months
멕시코에서 온 토마토가 온실에서 재배된 현지 토마토보다 탄소 발자국이 더 적음
will have a smaller carbon footprint than (c) local winter tomatoes
grown in a greenhouse. In the United Kingdom, **01번 단서3** lamb
meat that travels 11,000 miles from New Zealand generates only
영국에서, 뉴질랜드 양고기가 영국의 양고기에 비해 탄소 배출량을 더 적게 발생시킴
one-quarter the carbon emissions per pound compared to British
~와 비교하여
lamb because farmers in the United Kingdom raise their animals
on feed (which must be produced using fossil fuels) rather than on
clover pastureland.

　When food does travel, what matters most is not the (d) distance
가장 중요한 것은
traveled but the travel mode (surface versus air), and most of all the
무엇보다도
load size. **01번 단서4** Bulk loads of food can travel halfway around the
단거리를 이동하면서 적은 적재량의 식품보다 대량의 적재된 식품이 더 적은
world by ocean freight with a smaller carbon footprint, per pound
탄소 발자국으로 세계의 절반을 이동할 수 있음
delivered, than foods traveling just a short distance but in much (e)
larger(→ smaller) loads. **02번 단서** For example, 18-wheelers carry
18륜 대형트럭이 픽업트럭보다 더 많은 적재량을
much larger loads than pickup trucks so they can move food 100
운반하고 더 적은 연료를 연소하면서 더 멀리 이동할 수 있음
times as far while burning only one-third as much gas per pound of
food delivered.

해석

로컬 푸드 생산이 운송 연료의 연소를 줄임으로써 온실가스 배출을 줄였다는 주장들은 대개 근거가 충분하지 않다. 운송은 식품 부문 내에서 온실가스 배출의 11퍼센트만을 차지하는 원천이기에, 식품이 농장을 떠난 후 이동하는 거리를 줄이는 것은 농장에서 낭비되는 에너지 사용을 줄이는 것보다 훨씬 (a) 덜 중요하다. 먼 곳에서 오는 식품은 그것이 어떻게 재배되었느냐에 따라 실제로 (b) 기후에 더 좋을 수 있다. 예를 들어, 겨울에 멕시코로부터 수송된 밭에서 재배된 토마토는 온실에서 재배된 (c) 현지의 겨울 토마토보다 탄소 발자국이 더 적을 것이다. 영국에서는, 영국의 농부들이 클로버 목초지에서가 아닌 (화석 연료를 사용하여 생산되어야 하는) 사료로 자신의 동물들을 기르기 때문에 뉴질랜드에서 11,000마일을 이동하는 양고기는 영국의 양고기에 비해 파운드당 탄소 배출량의 4분의 1만 발생시킨다.
식품이 이동할 때, 가장 중요한 것은 이동 (d) 거리가 아니라 이동 방식(지상 대 공중), 그리고 무엇보다 적재량의 규모이다. 단지 단거리를 이동하지만 훨씬 (e) 더 많은(→ 더 적은) 적재량의 식품에 비해 대량의 적재된 식품은 배달된 파운드당 탄소 발자국이 더 적은 해상 화물 운송으로 세계의 절반을 이동할 수 있다. 예를 들어, 18륜 대형트럭은 픽업트럭보다 훨씬 더 많은 적재량을 운반하기에 배달된 식품 파운드당 3분의 1의 연료만 연소하면서 100배 멀리 식품을 이동시킬 수 있다.

01

로컬 푸드 생산보다 식품의 재배 방식이나 이동 적재량의 규모에 따라 탄소 발자국이 더 적게 발생하여 환경에 더욱 이로울 수 있다는 내용으로 로컬 푸드가 온실가스 배출을 줄여 환경에 더 좋다는 기존의 주장에 대해 의문을 제기하고 있으므로 글의 제목으로 가장 적절한 것은 ②이다.

선택지 완벽 분석

① Shorten the Route, Cut the Cost 경로를 짧게 하고, 비용을 줄여라

② Is Local Food Always Better for the Earth? 로컬 푸드가 항상 지구에 더 좋은가?

③ Why Mass Production Ruins the Environment 대량 생산이 환경을 파괴하는 이유

④ New Technologies: What Matters in Agriculture 신기술: 농업에서 중요한 것

⑤ Reduce Food Waste for a Smaller Carbon Footprint 더 적은 탄소 발자국을 위해 음식물 쓰레기를 줄이다

02

(e) 다음에 이어지는 예시에서 대형트럭은 훨씬 더 많은 적재량을 싣고 픽업트럭보다 더 적은 연료만 연소하면서 더 멀리 식품을 이동시킬 수 있다고 하였으므로, (e)의 larger는 smaller와 같은 단어로 바꾸는 것이 문맥상 자연스러우므로 정답은 ⑤이다.

선택지 완벽 분석

① 운송은 온실가스 배출의 11퍼센트만을 차지하는 원천이라고 하였으므로, 이동하는 거리를 줄이는 것은 농장에서 낭비되는 에너지 사용을 줄이는 것보다 '덜' 중요하므로 less는 문맥상 적절하다.

필수 어휘

claim 주장 production 생산 greenhouse gas 온실가스 emission 배출
fuel 연료 wasteful 낭비되는 field-grown 밭에서 재배된 ship 수송하다
carbon footprint 탄소 발자국(개인 또는 단체가 발생시키는 온실가스의 총량)
generate 발생시키다 one-quarter 4분의 1 pastureland 목초지 bulk 대량의
halfway 절반

03 정답 ① 04 정답 ③

202306 41~42번 정답률 67% / 63%

Early hunter-gatherer societies had (a) <u>minimal</u> structure. A chief or group of elders usually led the camp or village. Most of these leaders had to hunt and gather along with the other members 〜와 함께
because the surpluses of food and other vital resources were seldom (b) <u>sufficient</u> to support a full-time chief or village council. 주제문
The development of agriculture changed work patterns. Early farmers could reap 3–10 kg of grain from each 1 kg of seed planted.

04번 단서1 Part of this food/energy surplus was returned to the
여분의 식량과 에너지는 지역 사회에 환원됨
community and (c) **limited(→ provided)** support for nonfarmers such as chieftains, village councils, men who practice medicine,
A such as B: B와 같은 A
priests, and warriors. ❻ (In return,) / 04번 단서2 the nonfarmers
provide A for B: B에게 A를 제공하다 비농민들은 농업 인구에게
provided leadership and security **for** the farming population, //
리더십과 안보를 제공함
enabling it to continue to increase food/energy yields / and provide
분사구문 = the farming population continue와 provide가 to에 병렬로 연결
ever larger surpluses.

With improved technology and favorable conditions, 03번 단서1

agriculture produced consistent surpluses of the basic necessities,
농업은 지속적인 흑자를 창출함

and population groups grew in size. These groups concentrated in
grow in size: 규모가 커지다
towns and cities, and 03번 단서2 human tasks (d) specialized further.
인간의 업무는 더욱 전문화됨
Specialists such as carpenters, blacksmiths, merchants, traders, and sailors developed their skills and became more efficient in their use of time and energy. The goods and services they provided brought
bring about: ~을 초래하다
about 03번 단서3 an (e) improved quality of life, a higher standard of
삶의 질이 좋아지고, 생활 수준이 높아지고, 안정성이 향상됨
living, and, for most societies, increased stability.

해석

초기 수렵 채집 사회는 (a) 최소한의 구조만 가지고 있었다. 주로 추장이나 장로 그룹이 캠프나 마을을 이끌었다. 대부분의 이러한 지도자들은 다른 구성원들과 함께 사냥과 채집을 해야 했는데, 왜냐하면 식량과 기타 필수 자원의 잉여분이 전임 추장이나 마을 의회를 지원할 만큼 거의 (b) 충분하지 않았기 때문이었다. 농업의 발전은 작업 패턴을 변화시켰다. 초기 농부들은 심은 씨앗 1kg마다 3~10kg의 곡물을 수확할 수 있었다. 이 식량/에너지 잉여분의 일부는 지역 사회에 환원되었고 족장, 마을 의회, 의술가, 사제, 전사와 같은 비농민에 대한 지원을 (c) 제한했다(→ 제공했다). 그 대가로, 비농민들은 농업 인구에게 리더십과 안보를 제공하여, 그들이 식량/에너지 생산량을 지속적으로 늘리고 항상 더 많은 잉여를 제공할 수 있게 하였다. 개선된 기술과 유리한 조건으로, 농업은 기본 생필품의 지속적인 흑자를 창출했고, 인구 집단은 규모가 커졌다. 이러한 집단은 마을과 도시에 집중되었고, 인간의 업무는 더욱 (d) 전문화되었다. 목수, 대장장이, 상인, 무역업자, 선원과 같은 전문가들은 그들의 기술을 발전시키고 자신의 시간과 에너지 사용을 더 효율적으로 하게 되었다. 그들이 제공한 재화와 서비스로 인해 (e) 향상된 삶의 질, 더 높은 생활 수준, 그리고, 대부분의 사회에서, 향상된 안정성을 가져왔다.

03

최소한의 구조만 가지고 있었던 초기 수렵 채집 사회에서 농업 사회로의 발전은 식량과 기본 생필품의 지속적인 생산을 가능하게 하고, 인간의 업무를 전문화되게 하여 생활 수준이 향상되었다는 내용의 글이다. 따라서 글의 제목으로 가장 적절한 것은 ①이다.

선택지 완벽 분석

① How Agriculture Transformed Human Society 농업이 인간 사회를 변화시킨 방법

② The Dark Shadow of Agriculture: Repetition 농업의 어두운 그림자: 반복

③ How Can We Share Extra Food with the Poor? 여분의 음식을 가난한 사람들과 어떻게 나눌 수 있는가?
함정 농업의 발달로 식량과 에너지에 잉여분이 생겨나서 인간의 업무는 더욱 전문화되었고, 그 결과 삶의 질이 향상되었다는 내용의 글이지, 가난한 사람들과 음식을 나누는 것에 관한 이야기는 아니다.

④ Why Were Early Societies Destroyed by Agriculture? 왜 초기 사회는 농업에 의해 파괴되었는가?

⑤ The Advantages of Large Groups Over Small Groups in Farming 대규모 집단이 소규모 집단에 비해 농업에 미치는 이점

04

농업의 발달로 식량과 에너지의 일부 잉여분이 지역 사회에 환원되었다는 내용과 더불어 농민이 아닌 이들에 대한 지원이 가능했다는 내용이다. 따라서 (c)의 limited를 provided와 같은 단어로 바꾸는 것이 문맥상 자연스러우므로 정답은 ③이다.

선택지 완벽 분석

② 지도자들도 다른 사람들과 함께 사냥과 채집을 해야 했던 이유는 음식이나 에너지의 잉여분이 충분하지 않기 때문이었으므로, '충분하지'는 문맥상 적절하다. 앞에 있는 부정어 seldom에 유의한다.

필수 어휘

chief 추장 surplus 잉여, 흑자 vital 필수적인 sufficient 충분한
council 의회 agriculture 농업 grain 곡물 support 지원하다; 지원
practice 개업하다 priest 성직자 warrior 전사 in return 그 대가로

으므로, 기억의 범위는 익숙한 순서와 패턴을 인식하는 능력에 의해 늘어난다는 내용의 글이다. 따라서 글의 제목으로 가장 적절한 것은 ②이다.

05 정답 ②   06 정답 ③

Chess masters shown a chess board in the middle of a game
~의 중간에
for 5 seconds with 20 to 30 pieces still in play can immediately
reproduce the position of the pieces from memory. Beginners, of
course, are able to place only a few. Now take the same pieces and
be able to: ~할 수 있다
06번 단서1 place them on the board randomly and the (a) difference is
무작위로 놓으면, 차이가 줄어듦
much reduced. **05번 단서1** The expert's advantage is only for familiar
전문가의 유리함은 익숙한 패턴에만 있음
patterns — those previously stored in memory. **05번 단서2** Faced
익숙하지
with unfamiliar patterns, even when it involves the same familiar
않은 패턴에 직면하면, 전문가의 유리함은 사라짐
domain, the expert's advantage (b) disappears.

The beneficial effects of familiar structure on memory have been
observed for many types of expertise, including music. ★ People
주어
(with musical training) can reproduce short sequences (of musical
동사   목적어
notation) **more** accurately / **than** those (with no musical training)
부사구
/ when notes follow (c) **unusual**(→ **conventional**) sequences, //
but **06번 단서2** the advantage is much reduced / when the notes are
역접 등위 접속사   음표가 무작위로 배열되면, 유리함이 많이 줄어듦
ordered randomly. Expertise also improves memory for sequences
of (d) movements. Experienced ballet dancers are able to repeat
longer sequences of steps than less experienced dancers, and they
can repeat a sequence of steps making up a routine better than
~을 이루는
steps ordered randomly. **주제문** In each case, memory range is
각각의 경우
(e) increased by the ability to recognize familiar sequences and
patterns.

해석

게임 중간에 20~30개의 말들이 아직 놓여 있는 상태로 체스판을 5초 동안 본 체스의 달인들은 그 말들의 위치를 기억으로부터 즉시 재현할 수 있다. 물론 초보자들은 겨우 몇 개(의 위치)만 기억해 낼 수 있다. 이제 같은 말들을 가져다가 체스판에 무작위로 놓으면 그 (a) 차이는 크게 줄어든다. 전문가의 유리함은 익숙한 패턴, 즉 이전에 기억에 저장된 패턴에 대해서만 있다. 익숙하지 않은 패턴에 직면하면, 같은 익숙한 분야와 관련 있는 경우라도 전문가의 유리함은 (b) 사라진다.
익숙한 구조가 기억에 미치는 유익한 효과는 음악을 포함하여 많은 유형의 전문 지식에서 관찰되어 왔다. 음표가 (c) 특이한(→ 전형적인) 순서를 따를 때는 음악 훈련을 받은 사람이 음악 훈련을 받지 않은 사람보다 짧은 연속된 악보를 더 정확하게 재현할 수 있지만, 음표가 무작위로 배열되면 그 유리함이 훨씬 줄어든다. 전문 지식은 또한 연속 (d) 동작에 대한 기억을 향상시킨다. 숙련된 발레 무용수가 경험이 적은 무용수보다 더 긴 연속 스텝을 반복할 수 있고, 무작위로 배열된 스텝보다 정해진 춤 동작을 이루는 연속 스텝을 더 잘 반복할 수 있다. 각각의 경우, 기억의 범위는 익숙한 순서와 패턴을 인식하는 능력에 의해 (e) 늘어난다.

정답이 보이는 해설

05

체스 달인, 음악 훈련을 받은 사람, 숙련된 발레 무용수는 무작위로 배열되었을 때보다 전문 지식을 바탕으로 한 익숙한 구조에서 초보자보다 더 정확하게 재현할 수 있

선택지 완벽 분석

① How Can We Build Good Routines? 우리는 좋은 루틴을 어떻게 구축할 수 있는가?

② Familiar Structures Help Us Remember 친숙한 구조는 우리가 기억하는 것을 도와준다

③ Intelligence Does Not Guarantee Expertise 지능이 전문 지식을 보장하지는 않는다

④ Does Playing Chess Improve Your Memory? 체스를 두는 것이 기억력을 향상시키는가?
함정 체스에 관한 내용은 친숙한 구조가 기억에 도움이 된다는 하나의 예에 불과하므로, 이 글의 제목으로는 적절하지 않다.

⑤ Creative Art Performance Starts from Practice 창작 예술 공연은 연습에서 출발한다

06

전문가의 유리함은 익숙한 패턴에 대해서만 있다는 글의 내용으로 보아, 음악을 포함한 많은 전문 지식에서도 익숙한 구조가 기억에 유익하다는 내용이 되어야 하므로, 음악 훈련을 받은 사람은 그렇지 않은 사람보다 더 정확하게 재현할 수 있는 음표는 특이한 순서를 따르는 것이 아니라 전형적인 순서를 따르는 흐름이어야 한다. 따라서 (c)의 unusual을 conventional과 같은 단어로 바꾸는 것이 문맥상 자연스러우므로 정답은 ③이다.

선택지 완벽 분석

④ 뒤에 이어지는 문장에서 숙련된 발레 무용수가 그렇지 않은 무용수보다 긴 연속 스텝과 정해진 춤 동작을 이루는 연속 스텝을 더 잘 반복할 수 있다고 했으므로, 전문 지식이 연속 동작에 대한 기억을 향상시킨다는 흐름의 '동작들'은 문맥상 적절하다.

필수 어휘

piece (장기, 체스의) 말, 조각   reproduce 재현하다   position 위치
place 기억해 내다, 놓다   randomly 무작위로   reduce 줄어들다, 줄이다
expert 전문가   advantage 유리함   previously 이전에   face 직면하다
involve ~와 관련 있다   domain 분야   disappear 사라지다   beneficial 유익한
observe 관찰하다   including ~을 포함하여   accurately 정확하게   note 음표
order 배열하다   range 범위   increase 증가하다, 늘어나다   recognize 인식하다

07 정답 ①   08 정답 ⑤

Mike May lost his sight at the age of three. Because he had
lose one's sight: ~의 시력을 잃다
spent the majority of his life adapting to being blind — and
spend+시간/돈+v-ing: 시간/돈을 ~하는 데 쓰다
even cultivating a skiing career in this state — his other senses
compensated by growing (a) stronger. However, when his sight
was restored through a surgery in his forties, his entire perception
of reality was (b) disrupted. Instead of being thrilled that he could
~하는 대신
see now, as he'd expected, **08번 단서1** his brain was so overloaded
그의 뇌는 새로운 시각적 자극으로 과부하가
with new visual stimuli that the world became a frightening
걸려 세상이 무서워짐   so ~ that: 너무 ~해서 …하다
and overwhelming place. After he'd learned to know his family
through touch and smell, he found that he couldn't recognize his
children with his eyes, and this left him puzzled. **08번 단서2** Skiing
비교급 강조
also became a lot harder as he struggled to adapt to the visual
시각적 자극으로 스키도 훨씬 더 어려워짐
stimulation.

This (c) confusion occurred because his brain hadn't yet learned to see. ✪ Though we often tend to assume [our eyes function as *video cameras* [which relay information to our brain]], // advances (in neuroscientific research) have proven [that this is actually not the case]. Instead, 07번 단서1 sight is a collaborative effort between our eyes and our brains, and 07번 단서2 the way we process (d) visual reality depends on the way these two communicate. If communication between our eyes and our brains is disturbed, our perception of reality is altered accordingly. And because other areas of May's brain had adapted to process information primarily through his other senses, the process of learning how to see was (e) **easier(→ more difficult)** than he'd anticipated.

해석

Mike May는 세 살 때 시력을 잃었다. 그는 자신의 인생의 대부분을 보이지 않는 것에 적응하는 데, 그리고 심지어 이 상태에서 스키 경력을 쌓는 데에 보냈기 때문에, 다른 감각들은 (a) 더 강해지는 것을 통해 보충되었다. 그러나 그의 시력이 40대에 수술을 통해 회복되었을 때, 현실에 대한 그의 전반적 인식은 (b) 방해받았다. 그가 예상했던 것처럼 이제 볼 수 있다는 것에 감격하는 대신, 그의 뇌는 새로운 시각적 자극으로 너무 과부하가 걸려 세상은 두렵고 압도적인 장소가 되었다. 그가 만지는 것과 냄새를 통해 자신의 가족을 알아보는 것을 배운 후에는, 그는 자신의 눈으로 자신의 아이들을 알아볼 수 없다는 것을 알게 되었고, 이것은 그를 혼란스러운 상태로 남겨 두었다. 스키 또한 그가 시각적인 자극에 적응하려고 힘쓰면서 훨씬 더 어려워졌다.

이 (c) 혼란은 그의 뇌가 아직 보는 것을 배우지 못했기 때문에 일어났다. 비록 우리는 종종 우리의 눈이 우리의 뇌에 정보를 전달하는 비디오카메라로서 기능한다고 가정하는 경향이 있지만, 신경 과학 연구의 발전은 이것이 실제로 그렇지 않다는 것을 증명했다. 대신, 시각은 우리의 눈과 뇌 사이의 협력적인 노력이며, 우리가 (d) 시각적 현실을 처리하는 방법은 이 두 가지가 소통하는 방식에 달려 있다. 만약 우리의 눈과 뇌 사이의 의사소통이 방해된다면, 현실에 대한 우리의 인식은 그에 따라 바뀐다. 그리고 May의 뇌의 다른 영역들이 주로 그의 다른 감각을 통해 정보를 처리하는 것에 적응해 왔기 때문에, 보는 방법을 배우는 과정은 그가 예상했던 것보다 (e) 더 쉬웠다(→ 더 어려웠다).

정답이 보이는 해설

07

시각은 우리의 눈과 뇌 사이의 협력적인 노력이며, 시각적 현실을 처리하는 방법은 이 두 가지가 소통하는 방식에 달려 있다고 설명하고 있다. 따라서 글의 제목으로 가장 적절한 것은 ①이다.

선택지 완벽 분석

① Eyes and Brain Working Together for Sight 시력을 위해 함께 일하는 눈과 뇌
② Visualization: A Useful Tool for Learning 시각화: 학습을 위한 유용한 도구
③ Collaboration Between Vision and Sound 보이는 것과 들리는 것의 협업
함정 시각과 뇌의 협업에 관한 내용이므로, 청각, 즉 들리는 것에 대한 내용과는 관계가 없다.
④ How to Ignore New Visual Stimuli 새로운 시각적 자극을 무시하는 방법
⑤ You See What You Believe 당신은 당신이 믿는 것을 본다

08

세 살 때 시력을 잃은 Mike May는 인생의 대부분을 보이지 않는 것에 적응해 왔다. 40대에 시력이 회복되었지만, 그의 뇌는 시각적 자극으로 과부하가 걸렸고 혼란이 일어났다는 내용이다. May에게 눈을 통해 보는 방법을 배우는 과정은 그가 예상했던 것보다 더 어려웠을 것이다. 따라서 (e)의 easier를 more difficult와 같은 단어로 바꾸는 것이 문맥상 자연스러우므로 정답은 ⑤이다.

선택지 완벽 분석

① 시력을 잃은 채로 스키 경력을 쌓고 있었기 때문에, 시각 말고 다른 감각들은 점점 더 강해졌을 것이므로 '더 강해지는'은 문맥상 적절하다.

필수 어휘

adapt 적응하다　cultivate 쌓다, 구축하다　compensate 보충되다
restore 회복하다　perception 인식　disrupt 방해하다
overload 과부하가 걸리게 하다　stimuli 자극(stimulus의 복수형)
frightening 무서운　overwhelming 압도적인　stimulation 자극
confusion 혼란　assume 가정하다　neuroscientific 신경 과학의
collaborative 협력적인　disturb 방해하다　alter 바꾸다　primarily 주로
anticipate 예상하다

---

09 정답 ② 10 정답 ④

202209 41~42번 정답률 61% / 59%

In a society that rejects the consumption of insects there are some individuals who overcome this rejection, but most will continue with this attitude. 09번 단서1 It may be very (a) difficult to convince an entire society that insects are totally suitable for consumption. However, there are examples in which this (b) reversal of attitudes about certain foods has happened to an entire society. Several examples in the past 120 years from European-American society are: considering lobster a luxury food instead of a food for servants and prisoners; considering sushi a safe and delicious food; and considering pizza not just a food for the rural poor of Sicily. In Latin American countries, where insects are already consumed, a portion of the population hates their consumption and (c) associates it with poverty. There are also examples of people who have had the habit of consuming them and (d) **encouraged(→ discouraged)** that habit 10번 단서 due to shame, and because they do not want to be categorized as poor or uncivilized. ✪ According to Esther Katz, an anthropologist, 09번 단서2 if the consumption (of insects as a food luxury) is to be promoted, / there would be more **chances** [that *some individuals* {who do not present this habit} overcome *ideas* {under which they were educated}]. And this could also help to (e) revalue the consumption of insects by those people who already eat them.

해석

곤충 섭취를 거부하는 사회에서는 이러한 거부를 극복한 몇몇 개인들이 있지만, 대부분은 이러한 태도를 지속할 것이다. 곤충이 섭취에 완전히 적합하다는 것을 전체 사회에 납득시키는 것은 매우 (a) 어려울지도 모른다. 하지만, 특정 음식에 대한 이러한 태도의 (b) 역전이 전체 사회에 발생해 온 사례들이 있다. 지난 120년간 유럽-아메리카 사회로부터의 몇몇 사례는 다음과 같다. 바닷가재를 하인과 죄수용 음식 대신 고급 음식으로 여기는 것, 초밥을 안전하고 맛있는 음식으로 여기는 것, 그리고 피자를 단지 시칠리아 시골의 가난한 사람용 음식으로 여기지 않는 것이다. 곤충이 이미 섭취되는 라틴 아메리카 국가들에서, 인구의 일부는 그것들의 섭취를 싫어하고 그것을 빈곤과 (c) 연관 짓는다. 그것들을 섭취하는 습관이 있어 왔으나 수치심 때문에, 그리고 그들이 가난하거나 '미개하다'고 분류되고 싶지 않기 때문에 그 습관을

19강
정답의 이해

(d) **장려한**(→ 그만둔) 사람들의 사례들 또한 있다. 인류학자인 Esther Katz에 따르면, 만약 음식 호사로서의 곤충 섭취가 장려된다면, 이러한 습관을 보이지 않은 몇몇 개인들이 그들이 교육받았던 생각들을 극복할 가능성이 더 많을 것이다. 그리고 이것은 또한 이미 그것을 먹고 있는 그 사람들에 의한 곤충 섭취를 (e) 재평가하는 데에도 도움을 줄 수 있다.

[정답이 보이는 해설]

09

곤충 섭취 거부에 대해 특정 음식에 대한 태도와 인식 전환을 통해 극복할 수 있다는 내용의 글이다. 바닷가재, 초밥, 피자를 고급지고 안전한 음식과 연관 짓거나, 곤충 섭취를 빈곤 및 미개함과 연관 짓는 습관이 있는데, 만약 곤충이 호사로운 음식으로 장려된다면 그간의 곤충 섭취에 관한 부정적 생각을 극복하고 재평가할 수 있을 것이라고 설명하고 있다. 따라서 글의 제목으로 가장 적절한 것은 ②이다.

[선택지 완벽 분석]

① The More Variety on the Table, The Healthier You Become 식탁에 더 많은 종류가 있을수록, 여러분은 더 건강해진다

② Edible or Not? Change Your Perspectives on Insects 식용인가 아니면 비식용인가? 곤충에 대한 관점을 바꿔라

③ Insects: A Key to Solve the World Food Shortage 곤충: 세계 식량 부족을 해결할 열쇠
[함정] 곤충 섭취에 대한 부정적 관점을 바꾸라는 내용이지 식량 부족에 대한 해결책으로 언급한 것은 아니므로 답이 될 수 없다.

④ Don't Let Uniqueness in Food Culture Disappear 음식 문화의 독특함이 사라지지 않도록 하라

⑤ Experiencing Various Cultures by Food 음식에 의한 다양한 문화의 체험
[함정] 바닷가재, 초밥, 피자, 곤충 등은 음식을 통한 다양한 문화 체험의 예가 아니라 그 음식이 가진 선입견을 극복한 예로 제시된 것이므로 답이 될 수 없다.

10

일부 사람들은 곤충을 섭취하는 습관이 있었으나 수치심 또는 가난하거나 미개하다고 분류되고 싶지 않기 때문에 그 습관을 그만둘 것이다. 따라서 (d)의 encouraged를 discouraged로 바꾸는 것이 문맥상 자연스러우므로 정답은 ④이다.

[선택지 완벽 분석]

② 역접의 연결사 However를 전후로 곤충 섭취를 납득시키는 것이 어려울지도 모르지만 이러한 태도의 '역전'이 전체 사회에 발생해 온 사례들을 소개하고 있으므로 문맥상 적절하다.

③ 곤충의 섭취를 싫어하는 사람들은 그것을 빈곤과 '연관 지을' 수 있을 것이므로 문맥상 적절하다.

⑤ 곤충 섭취에 관한 관점이 바뀐다면 곤충 섭취를 '재평가하는' 데 도움이 될 것이므로 문맥상 적절하다.

[필수 어휘]

reject 거부하다　consumption 섭취　individual 개개인　overcome 극복하다
rejection 거부　attitude 태도　convince 납득시키다　lobster 바닷가재
luxury 고급진; 호사　servant 하인　prisoner 죄수　rural 시골의
consume 섭취하다　population 인구　poverty 가난　shame 수치심
categorize 분류하다　uncivilized 미개한　anthropologist 인류학자
promote 장려하다　educate 교육하다

11 정답 ①　**12** 정답 ④　[202206 41~42번 정답률 85% / 73%]

U.K. researchers say a bedtime of between 10 p.m. and 11 p.m. is best. They say 〈11번 단서1〉 people who go to sleep between these times
→ 잠들다
밤 10~11시에 잠드는 사람들이 더 낮은 심장 질환 위험을 갖고 있음
have a (a) lower risk of heart disease. Six years ago, the researchers collected data on the sleep patterns of 80,000 volunteers. The volunteers had to wear a special watch for seven days so the researchers could collect data on their sleeping and waking times.

The scientists then monitored the health of the volunteers. Around 3,000 volunteers later showed heart problems. 〈11번 단서2〉 They went to bed earlier or later than the (b) ideal 10 p.m. to 11 p.m.
심장 문제를 가진 사람들은 밤 10~11시보다 더 일찍 또는 더 늦게 잠들었음
timeframe.

One of the authors of the study, Dr. David Plans, commented on his research and the (c) effects of bedtimes on the health of our heart. He said the study could not give a certain cause for their results, but it suggests that 〈12번 단서〉 early or late bedtimes may
→ ~할 가능성이 있다　　이르거나 늦은 취침 시간은 체내 시계를 방해할
be more likely to disrupt the body clock, with (d) **positive**(→
가능성이 높음　　　　　　　　　　　　　　　　　　가주어
negative) consequences for cardiovascular health. ★ He said [that it
said의 목적어절1
was important for our body to wake up to the morning light], / and
to wake up ~의 의미상 주어　　진주어
[that the worst time to go to bed was after midnight] / because it
said의 목적어절2
may (e) reduce the likelihood of seeing *morning light* [**which** resets
주격 관계대명사절
the body clock]. He added that we risk cardiovascular disease if our body clock is not reset properly.

[해석]

영국 연구원들은 밤 10시와 밤 11시 사이의 취침 시간이 가장 좋다고 말한다. 그들은 이 시간대 사이에 잠드는 사람들이 (a) 더 낮은 심장 질환의 위험을 가지고 있다고 말한다. 6년 전, 그 연구원들은 8만 명의 자원자들의 수면 패턴에 대한 데이터를 수집했다. 그 자원자들은 7일간 특별한 시계를 착용해야 했고 그래서 그 연구원들은 그들의 수면과 기상 시간에 대한 데이터를 수집할 수 있었다. 그리고 나서 과학자들은 자원자들의 건강을 추적 관찰했다. 약 3천 명의 자원자들이 이후에 심장 문제를 보였다. 그들은 밤 10시에서 밤 11시 사이의 (b) 이상적인 시간대보다 더 일찍 또는 더 늦게 잠자리에 들었다.

그 연구 저자 중 한 명인 David Plans 박사는 그의 연구와 취침 시간이 우리의 심장 건강에 미치는 (c) 영향에 대해 언급했다. 그는 그 연구가 그들의 결과에 특정한 원인을 제시할 수는 없지만, 이르거나 늦은 취침 시간이 심장 혈관 건강에 (d) 긍정적인(→ 부정적인) 결과와 더불어 체내 시계를 혼란케 할 가능성이 더 높을 수도 있다는 것을 시사한다고 말했다. 그는 우리의 몸이 아침 빛에 맞추어 깨어나는 것이 중요하고, 잠자리에 드는 가장 안 좋은 시간이 자정 이후인데 그것은 우리의 체내 시계를 재설정하는 아침 빛을 볼 가능성을 (e) 줄일 수도 있기 때문이라고 말했다. 만약 우리의 체내 시계가 적절하게 재설정되지 않는다면 우리가 심장 혈관 질환의 위험을 무릅쓰게 된다고 그는 덧붙였다.

[정답이 보이는 해설]

11

취침 시간이 우리의 심장 건강에 영향을 미친다고 설명하는 글로, 이상적인 취침 시간대인 밤 10~11시에 잠드는 사람들은 심장 질환의 위험이 낮으며 그 시간대에서 벗어난 시간에 잠드는 사람들에게 더 많은 심장 문제가 발생했다는 연구 결과를 제시하고 있으므로, 글의 제목으로 가장 적절한 것은 ①이다.

[선택지 완벽 분석]

① The Best Bedtime for Your Heart 심장에 가장 좋은 취침 시간

② Late Bedtimes Are a Matter of Age 늦은 취침 시간은 나이의 문제이다

③ For Sound Sleep: Turn Off the Light 숙면을 위해: 불을 꺼라

④ Sleeping Patterns Reflect Personalities 수면 패턴은 성격을 반영한다

⑤ Regular Exercise: A Miracle for Good Sleep 규칙적인 운동: 양질의 수면을 위한 기적

12

이상적인 시간대보다 이르거나 늦은 취침 시간이 심장 문제를 일으켰고 체내 시계를 혼란시킬 가능성이 높다고 했으므로, 이러한 이르거나 늦은 취침 시간은 심장 혈관 건강에 부정적인 결과를 가져올 것이다. 따라서 (d)의 positive는 negative와 같은

단어로 바꾸는 것이 문맥상 자연스러우므로 정답은 ④이다.

필수 어휘

bedtime 취침 시간　lower 낮추다　heart disease 심장 질환　volunteer 자원자
monitor 추적 관찰하다　ideal 이상적인　comment 언급하다, 논평하다
body clock 체내 시계　consequence 결과　likelihood 가능성
reset 재설정하다　risk 위험을 무릅쓰다　properly 적절하게

13 정답 ⑤　14 정답 ⑤

202203 41~42번 정답률 55% / 59%

The longest journey we will make is the eighteen inches between our head and heart. If we take this journey, it can shorten our (a) misery in the world. **13번 단서1** Impatience, judgment, frustration,
조급함, 비난, 좌절, 분노가 늘 머릿속에 있으며 그곳에
and anger reside in our heads. When we live in that place too long,
너무 오래 머무르면 우리는 불행해짐
it makes us (b) unhappy. But when we take the journey from our heads to our hearts, something shifts (c) inside. **13번 단서2** What if
우리를 가로
we were able to love everything that gets in our way? ✪ What if we
막는 모든 것을 사랑할 수 있다면 어떨까? 　～라면 어떻게 될까?
tried loving [the shopper (who unknowingly steps in front of us in
　　　　　loving의 목적어1 　↳ 주격 관계대명사
line)], / [the driver (who cuts us off in traffic)], / [the swimmer (who
loving의 목적어2 　　　　　loving의 목적어3
splashes us with water during a belly dive)], / or [the reader (who
　　　　　　　　　　　　　　　　loving의 목적어4
pens a bad online review of our writing)]?

14번 단서 Every person who makes us miserable is (d) like us —
우리를 불행하게 만드는 모든 사람은 우리와 같음
a human being, most likely doing the best they can, deeply loved by their parents, a child, or a friend. And how many times have we unknowingly stepped in front of someone in line? Cut someone
　　　　　　　　　　　　　　　　　　cut off: 끼어들다
off in traffic? Splashed someone in a pool? Or made a negative statement about something we've read? It helps to (e) **deny**(→ **remember**) that a piece of us resides in every person we meet.

해석

우리가 갈 가장 긴 여정은 우리의 머리에서 가슴까지의 18인치이다. 우리가 이 여행을 한다면, 그것은 세상에서 우리의 (a) 불행을 줄일 수 있다. 조급함, 비난, 좌절, 그리고 분노가 우리 머릿속에 있다. 우리가 그 장소에서 너무 오래 살면, 그것은 우리를 (b) 불행하게 만든다. 그러나 우리가 머리부터 가슴까지의 여행을 하면, (c) 내면에서 무엇인가 바뀐다. 만약 우리를 가로막는 모든 것을 우리가 사랑할 수 있다면 어떻게 될까? 만일 줄을 서 있는 우리 앞에 무심코 들어온 그 쇼핑객을, 차량 흐름에서 우리 앞에 끼어든 그 운전자를, 배 쪽으로 다이빙하면서 우리에게 물을 튀게 한 수영하는 그 사람을, 우리의 글에 대해 안 좋은 온라인 후기를 쓴 그 독자를 우리가 사랑하려고 해 본다면 어떨까?
우리를 불행하게 만드는 모든 사람은 우리와 (d) 같다. 그들은 아마도 분명히 최선을 다하고 있으며, 부모로부터 깊이 사랑받는 인간, 자녀 또는 친구일 것이다. 그리고 우리는 몇 번이나 무심코 줄을 서 있는 누군가의 앞에 들어갔을까? 차량 흐름에서 누군가에게 끼어든 적은? 수영장에서 누군가에게 물을 튀게 한 적은? 혹은 우리가 읽은 것에 대해 부정적인 진술을 한 적은 몇 번이었을까? 우리가 만나는 모든 사람 속에 우리의 일부가 있다는 것을 (e) 부정하는(→ 기억하는) 것은 도움이 된다.

정답이 보이는 해설

13

조급함, 비난, 좌절, 분노를 머릿속에 머물게 하는 것은 우리를 불행하게 만들고, 살면서 우리를 방해하는 누군가가 또한 자신이 될 수 있기 때문에 그런 사람들을 이해하고 사랑하라는 내용이므로, 글의 제목으로 가장 적절한 것은 ⑤이다.

선택지 완벽 분석

① Why It Is So Difficult to Forgive Others　다른 사람들을 용서하는 것이
　그렇게 어려운 이유
② Even Acts of Kindness Can Hurt Somebody　심지어 친절의 행위도
　누군가를 다치게 할 수 있다
③ Time Is the Best Healer for a Broken Heart　시간은 실연의 상처를
　치유하는 최고의 치료법이다
　자신을 방해하는 누군가에 대한 분노를 다루고 있으므로 실연에 관한 내용과는 관계가 없다.
④ Celebrate the Happy Moments in Your Everyday Life　여러분의
　일상에서 행복한 순간을 기념하라
　일상에서 자신을 화나게 하는 사람들을 이해하라는 것이지 행복한 순간을 기념하라는 것은 아니다.
⑤ Understand Others to Save Yourself from Unhappiness　불행으
　로부터 자신을 구하기 위해 다른 사람들을 이해하라

14

우리를 불행하게 만드는 모든 사람은 우리와 같고 우리 또한 그들처럼 다른 사람을 방해한 적이 있을 것이라고 했으므로, (e)의 deny는 remember와 같은 단어로 바꾸는 것이 문맥상 자연스러우므로 정답은 ⑤이다.

선택지 완벽 분석

④ 우리를 방해한 사람과 마찬가지로 우리도 누군가를 의도치 않게 방해한 적이 있을 것이라는 내용이 이어지고 있으므로, 우리를 불행하게 만드는 모든 사람이 우리와 '같다'는 것은 문맥상 적절하다.

필수 어휘

journey 여정, 여행　shorten 줄이다　misery 불행, 비참함　impatience 조급함
judgment 비난, 비판　frustration 좌절　shift 바뀌다　unknowingly 무심코
in traffic 차량 흐름에서　splash 튀기다, 끼얹다　pen (글을) 쓰다
miserable 비참한　statement 진술　deny 부정하다

15 정답 ①　16 정답 ④

202111 41~42번 정답률 55% / 61%

Since the turn of the twentieth century we've believed in genetic causes of diagnoses — a theory called genetic determinism. Under this model, our genes (and subsequent health) are determined at birth. We are "destined" to inherit certain diseases based on the
　　　　　　　　　　　　　　　　　　　　　　　～에 근거한
misfortune of our DNA. Genetic determinism doesn't (a) consider the role of family backgrounds, traumas, habits, or anything else within the environment. In this dynamic we are not (b) active participants in our own health and wellness. Why would we be? If something is predetermined, it's not (c) necessary to look at anything beyond our DNA. But the more science has learned about
　　　　　　　　　　　　　　　　the＋비교급, the＋비교급: ～할수록 더 …하다
the body and its interaction with the environment around it (in its various forms, from our nutrition to our relationships to our racially oppressive systems), the more (d) **simplistic**(→ **complex**) the story becomes. **15번 단서1, 16번 단서** We are not merely expressions of coding
　　　　　　　　　　　　　우리는 단지 유전자 암호화의 표현이 아니라 엄청나게 다양한 상호
but products of a remarkable variety of interactions that are both
작용의 산물임
within and outside of our control. Once we see beyond the narrative that genetics are (e) destiny, **15번 단서2** we can take ownership of our
　　　　　　　　　　　　　　　　　우리는 자신의 건강에 대한 소유권을 가질 수 있음
health. ✪ This allows us to see [how "choiceless" we once were] /
　　　　　　　동사1　　　목적격보어 ↳ see의 목적어절
and empowers us with the ability (to create real and lasting change).
　동사2　　　　　　　　　　　 ↳형용사적 용법

20세기로 전환된 이래로 우리는 진단의 유전적인 원인, 즉 유전자 결정론이라 불리는 이론을 믿어 왔다. 이 모델 하에서 우리의 유전자는 (그리고 이후의 건강은) 태어날 때 결정된다. 우리는 자신의 DNA의 불운에 근거한 특정 질병을 물려받을 '운명'이다. 유전자 결정론은 가정환경, 정신적 충격, 습관 또는 환경 내의 다른 어떤 것의 역할을 (a) 고려하지 않는다. 이 역학 관계에서 우리는 우리 자신의 건강과 안녕에 있어 (b) 능동적인 참여자가 아니다. 우리는 왜 이러할까? 만약 무언가가 미리 결정되어 있다면 우리의 DNA를 넘어서 어떤 것을 보는 것이 (c) 필요하지 않다. 하지만 과학이 신체와 그것이 그 주변 환경과 (우리의 영양에서부터 우리의 관계, 그리고 우리의 인종적으로 억압적인 시스템에 이르기까지의 다양한 형태로) 상호 작용하는 것에 대해 더 많이 알게 될수록, 그 이야기는 더욱 (d) 단순해진다(→ 복잡해진다). 우리는 단지 (유전) 암호화의 표현이 아니라 우리의 통제 내부와 외부 모두에 있는 놀랄 만한 다양한 상호 작용의 산물이다. 일단 우리가 유전자가 (e) 운명이라는 이야기를 넘어서 보게 된다면, 우리는 자신의 건강에 대한 소유권을 가질 수 있다. 이것은 우리에게 자신이 한때 얼마나 '선택권이 없는' 상태였는지 알 수 있게 해 주며 우리에게 실제적이고 지속적인 변화를 만들어 낼 수 있는 능력을 부여한다.

정답이 보이는 해설

15

우리의 건강은 타고난 유전자에 의해 결정되는 것이 아니라 신체 및 주변 환경과의 다양한 상호 작용의 영향을 받으며 우리는 자신의 건강에 대한 소유권을 가질 수 있다는 내용이므로, 글의 제목으로 가장 적절한 것은 ①이다.

선택지 완벽 분석

① Health Is in Our Hands, Not Only in Our Genes 건강은 우리의 유전자뿐만 아니라 우리 손 안에 놓여 있다
② Genetics: A Solution to Enhance Human Wellness 유전학: 인간의 건강을 향상시키기 위한 해결책
인간의 건강이 태어날 때 결정된다는 유전자 결정론을 반박하는 글이므로, 유전학이 건강을 향상시키는 해결책이라는 제목은 글의 내용과 상반된다.
③ How Did DNA Dominate Over Environment in Biology? DNA가 생물학에서 어떻게 환경을 지배했는가?
④ Never Be Confident in Your Health, but Keep Checking! 결코 건강에 자신하지 말고 계속 점검하라!
⑤ Why Scientific Innovation Affects Our Social Interactions 과학적 혁신이 우리의 사회적 상호 작용에 영향을 미치는 이유

16

전반부에서는 우리의 유전자가 태어날 때 이미 결정되어 있다는 유전자 결정론에 관해 설명하다가, 중반 이후부터는 이러한 이론에 반박하면서 우리는 다양한 상호 작용의 산물이며 유전자의 운명을 넘어서서 자신의 건강에 대한 소유권을 가질 수 있다는 내용이 제시되고 있다. 따라서 (d)의 simplistic은 complex와 같은 단어로 바꾸는 것이 문맥상 자연스러우므로 정답은 ④이다.

선택지 완벽 분석
⑤ 우리가 스스로의 건강에 대한 소유권을 가질 수 있다는 것은 우리가 유전자의 '운명'을 넘어선다는 것이므로 문맥상 적절하다.

필수 어휘

diagnosis 진단(*pl.* diagnoses) genetic determinism 유전자 결정론
subsequent 이후의 destined ~할 운명인 inherit 물려받다 dynamic 역학
predetermine 미리 결정하다 racially 인종적으로 simplistic 지나치게 단순화한
remarkable 놀랄 만한

17 정답 ② 18 정답 ④

202109 41~42번 정답률 61% / 44%

The market's way of telling a firm about its failures is harsh and brief. **17, 18번 단서1** Not only are complaints less expensive to
불평은 비용이 덜 들고 판매자가 향상되도록 만들 수 있음
handle but they also can cause the seller to (a) improve. The seller

may learn something as well. I remember a cosmetics company that received complaints about sticky sunblock lotion. At the time, all such lotions were more or less sticky, so the risk of having customers buy products from a rival company was not (b) great. But this was also an opportunity. The company managed to develop a
가까스로 ~하다
product that was not sticky and captured 20 percent of the market in its first year. Another company had the (c) opposite problem. Its products were not sticky enough. The company was a Royal Post Office in Europe and the product was a stamp. The problem was that the stamp didn't stick to the envelope. Management contacted the stamp producer who made it clear that if people just moistened the stamps properly, they would stick to any piece of paper. What to do? ✪ Management didn't take long to come to the conclusion /
take long+to-v: ~하는 데 시간이 오래 걸리다
[that it would be (d) **less**(→ **more**) costly (to try to **educate**
가주어   진주어1
its customers to wet each stamp) / rather than (to add more glue)].
educate+목적어+목적격보어(to부정사): A가 B하도록 교육하다   진주어2
18번 단서2 The stamp producer was told to add more glue and the
접착제를 추가하는 비용이 덜 드는 방법으로 소비자의 불만을 해결함
problem didn't occur again.

17번 단서2 Since it is better for the firm to have buyers complain
불만스러워하는 고객이 불평하는 것을 쉽게 만드는 것이 중요함
rather than go elsewhere, it is important to make it (e) easier for dissatisfied customers to complain.

회사에 그것의 실패에 대해 알려 주는 시장의 방식은 가혹하면서 간단하다. 불평은 다루기에 비용이 덜 들뿐만 아니라 판매자가 (a) 향상되도록 만들 수도 있다. 판매자는 또한 어떤 교훈을 얻을지도 모른다. 나는 끈적거리는 자외선 차단 로션에 대한 불평을 받은 한 화장품 회사를 기억한다. 그 당시에, 그러한 로션은 모두 다소 끈적거렸고, 그래서 고객들이 경쟁사의 제품을 사게 하는 위험은 (b) 크지 않았다. 하지만 이것은 또한 기회이기도 했다. 그 회사는 끈적거리지 않는 제품을 개발해 냈고 첫해에 시장의 20퍼센트를 점유했다. 또 다른 회사는 (c) 반대의 문제를 가졌다. 그 회사의 상품은 충분히 끈적거리지 않았다. 그 회사는 유럽에 있는 Royal Post Office였고 상품은 우표였다. 문제는 우표가 편지 봉투에 붙지 않는다는 것이었다. 경영진은 우표 제작자에게 연락했는데, 그 사람은 만약 사람들이 우표를 제대로 적시기만 한다면, 우표가 어떤 종이에도 달라붙을 것이라는 점을 명확히 밝혔다. 어떻게 할까? 경영진이, (우표에) 더 많은 접착제를 첨가하는 것보다 고객에게 우표를 적시도록 교육시키려고 하는 것에 비용이 (d) 덜(→ 더) 들 것이라는 결론에 도달하는 데에는 오래 걸리지 않았다. 우표 제작자는 더 많은 접착제를 첨가하라고 지시받았고 그 문제는 더 이상 일어나지 않았다.

구매가가 다른 곳으로 가게 하는 것보다는 불평하게 하는 것이 회사에는 더 나은 일이기 때문에, 불만스러워하는 고객들이 불평하는 것을 (e) 더 쉽게 만드는 것이 중요하다.

정답이 보이는 해설

17

불만스러워하는 고객들의 불평을 통해 판매자가 향상될 수 있으므로 고객들이 불평하는 것을 더 쉽게 만드는 것이 중요하다는 내용으로, 화장품 회사와 우표 회사의 예를 들어 설명하고 있다. 따라서 글의 제목으로 가장 적절한 것은 ②이다.

18

(d) 다음에 이어지는 문장에서 회사에서는 우표 제작자에게 더 많은 접착제를 첨가할 것을 지시했다고 했으므로, 고객에게 우표를 제대로 적시라고 교육하는 것보다 더 많은 접착제를 첨가하는 것이 비용이 덜 드는 방법이었음을 알 수 있다. 따라서 (d)의 less를 more와 같은 단어로 바꾸는 것이 문맥상 자연스러우므로 정답은 ④이다.

필수 어휘

harsh 가혹한 complaint 불평 handle 다루다 cosmetics 화장품
sticky 끈적거리는 sunblock lotion 자외선 차단 로션 risk 위험
capture 점유하다, 차지하다 opposite 반대의 stick 달라붙다 envelope 봉투
moisten 적시다, 축이다 conclusion 결론 wet 적시다 glue 접착제, 풀
occur 일어나다, 발생하다 dissatisfied 불만족스러운

19 정답 ⑤ 20 정답 ④

202106 41~42번 정답률 45% / 59%

If you were afraid of standing on balconies, you would start on
~을 두려워하다
some lower floors and slowly work your way up to higher ones.
work one's way up: 위로 올라가다. 출세하다
❷ It would be easy / to face *a fear* of *standing on high balconies*
가주어   진주어   동격
/ in *a way* [**that**'s totally controlled]. Socializing is (a) trickier.
주격 관계대명사
People aren't like inanimate features of a building that you just have

to be around to get used to. You have to interact with them, and their
~에 익숙해지다
responses can be unpredictable. Your feelings toward them are more

complex too. Most people's self-esteem isn't going to be affected

that much if they don't like balconies, but your confidence can

(b) suffer if you can't socialize effectively.

19번 단서 It's also harder to design a tidy way to gradually face
사교적 두려움을 점차적으로 마주할 수 있는 방법을 설계하는 것은 어려움
many social fears. 20번 단서 The social situations you need to expose
사교적 상황은 예측 가능하지도 않고 통제하기도 어려움
yourself to may not be (c) available when you want them, or they
expose A to B: A를 B에 노출시키다   = the social situations
may not go well enough for you to sense that things are under
통제되는
control. The progression from one step to the next may not be clear,

creating unavoidable large (d) **decreases(→ increases)** in difficulty

from one to the next. People around you aren't robots that you can

endlessly experiment with for your own purposes. This is not to say
~라고 말하는 것은 아니다
that facing your fears is pointless when socializing. The principles

of gradual exposure are still very (e) useful. 주제문 The process of

applying them is just messier, and knowing that before you start is

helpful.

해석

만약 여러분이 발코니에 서 있는 것을 두려워한다면, 여러분은 조금 더 낮은 층에서 시작해서 천천히 더 높은 층으로 올라갈 것이다. 완전히 통제된 방식으로 높은 발코니에 서 있는 두려움을 직면하는 것은 쉬울 것이다. 사람을 사귄다는 것은 더 (a) 까다롭다. 사람은 주변에 있어서 익숙해지는 건물과 같은 무생물이 아니다. 여러분은 그들과 상호 작용을 해야 하며 그들의 반응은 예측할 수 없을 수도 있다. 그들에 대한 여러분의 느낌 또한 더 복잡하다. 대부분의 사람들의 자존감은 그들이 발코니를 좋아하지 않는다고 해도 그렇게 많이 영향을 받지 않을 것이지만, 여러분이 효과적으로 사람들을 사귈 수 없다면 여러분의 자신감은 (b) 상처받을 수 있다.

많은 사교적 두려움을 점차적으로 마주하게 할 잘 정돈된 방법을 설계하는 것 역시 더 어렵다. 여러분을 노출할 필요가 있는 사교적 상황이 여러분이 그것들을 원할 때 형성되지 않을 (c) 수 있고, 또는 그것들이 상황이 통제 가능하다고 감지할 만큼 잘 진행되지 않을지도 모른다. 한 단계에서 다음 단계로의 진행은 분명하지 않을 수 있으며, 한 단계에서 다음 단계로 진행할 때 피할 수 없이 큰 어려움이 (d) 줄어들게(→ 늘어나게) 된다. 여러분 주변의 사람들은 여러분 자신의 목적을 위해서 끊임없이 실험해 볼 수 있는 로봇이 아니다. 이것은 사람을 사귈 때 여러분의 두려움을 직면하는 것이 의미가 없다고 말하는 것은 아니다. 점진적인 노출의 원칙은 여전히 매우 (e) 유용하다. 그것들을 적용하는 과정은 더 복잡하지만, 여러분이 시작하기 전에 그것을 아는 것은 도움이 된다.

정답이 보이는 해설

19

높은 발코니에 오르는 두려움은 낮은 발코니에서 시작하여 단계적으로 올라가며 극복할 수 있지만, 인간관계는 사교적 두려움을 점차적으로 마주할 수 있는 정돈된 방법을 설계하는 것이 어렵다고 했다. 그럼에도 시작하기 전에 그러한 사실을 아는 것은 도움이 된다고 했으므로 글의 제목으로 가장 적절한 것은 ⑤이다.

20

사교적 두려움은 점차적으로 높은 발코니에 오르는 것과 달리 원할 때 형성되지 않거나 통제할 수 없는 상황으로 진행될 수도 있다고 했으므로 한 단계에서 다음 단계로 진행할 때 어려움은 더 늘어날 것이다. 따라서 (d)의 decreases를 increases와 같은 단어로 바꾸는 것이 문맥상 자연스러우므로 정답은 ④이다.

필수 어휘

socializing 사교 tricky 까다로운 inanimate 무생물의
interact 상호 작용을 하다, 소통하다 response 반응
unpredictable 예측할 수 없는 complex 복잡한 self-esteem 자존감
confidence 자신감 tidy 잘 정돈된, 깔끔한 unavoidable 피할 수 없는
experiment 실험하다 pointless 무의미한 exposure 노출
messy 복잡한, 엉망진창인

21 정답 ① 22 정답 ⑤

202103 41~42번 정답률 75% / 64%

As kids, we worked hard at learning to ride a bike; when we fell

off, we got back on again, until it became second nature to us. But
습관이 되다
when we try something new in our adult lives we'll usually make
make an attempt: 시도하다

just one attempt before judging whether it's (a) worked. If we don't succeed the first time, or if it feels a little awkward, we'll tell ourselves it wasn't a success rather than giving it (b) another shot.

give it another shot: 다시 시도해 보다

That's a shame, because repetition is central to the process of
~에 핵심적인
rewiring our brains. Consider the idea that your brain has a network of neurons. They will (c) connect with each other whenever you remember to use a brain-friendly feedback technique. ☆ Those connections aren't very (d) reliable at first, / [which may **make**
앞 절 내용을 선행사로 하는 주격 관계대명사(계속적 용법)
your first efforts a little hit-and-miss]. You might remember one of
make+목적어+목적격보어(형용사): ~을 …한 상태로 만들다
the steps involved, and not the others. **22번 단서** But scientists have
함께 활성화되는 뉴런들은
a saying: "neurons that fire together, wire together." **주제문** In other
함께 연결됨
words, repetition of an action (e) blocks(→ **strengthens**) the connections between the neurons involved in that action. **21번 단서** That means
새로운 피드백
the more times you try using that new feedback technique, the more
기술을 여러 번 반복해 볼수록 필요할 때 더 쉽게 다가옴
easily it will come to you when you need it.

해석

아이였을 때, 우리는 자전거 타는 법을 열심히 배웠다. 넘어지면 우리는 다시 올라탔는데, 그것이 우리에게 습관이 될 때까지 그렇게 했다. 그러나 어른으로 살면서 새로운 것을 시도해 볼 때 우리는 대개 단 한 번만 시도해 보고 나서 그것이 (a) 잘되었는지 판단하려 한다. 만일 우리가 처음에 성공하지 못하거나 혹은 약간 어색한 느낌이 들면, (b) 또 다른 시도를 해 보기보다는 스스로에게 그것이 성공이 아니었다고 말할 것이다.

그것은 애석한 일인데, 반복이 우리 뇌를 재연결하는 과정에 핵심적이기 때문이다. 여러분의 뇌가 뉴런의 연결망을 가지고 있다는 개념을 생각해 보라. 여러분이 뇌 친화적인 피드백 기술을 잊지 않고 사용할 때마다 그것들은 서로 (c) 연결될 것이다. 그 연결은 처음에는 그리 (d) 신뢰할 만하지 않고, 여러분의 첫 번째 시도를 다소 마구잡이가 되도록 할 수도 있다. 여러분은 연관된 단계 중 하나를 기억하고, 다른 것들은 기억하지 못할 수도 있다. 그러나 과학자들은 "함께 활성화되는 뉴런들은 함께 연결된다."라고 말한다. 다시 말하자면, 어떤 행동의 반복은 그 행동에 연관된 뉴런들 사이의 연결을 (e) 차단한다(→ 강화한다). 그것은 여러분이 그 새로운 피드백 기술을 더 여러 차례 사용해 볼수록, 여러분이 그것을 필요로 할 때 그것이 더 쉽게 여러분에게 다가올 것임을 의미한다.

정답이 보이는 해설

21

자전거 타는 법을 배울 때 넘어지면 다시 올라타서 습관이 될 때까지 반복하는 것처럼, 반복이 우리 뇌를 재연결하는 과정에 핵심적이며 어떤 행동의 반복은 그 행동에 연관된 뉴런들 사이의 연결을 강화한다는 내용의 글이다. 따라서 글의 제목으로 가장 적절한 것은 ①이다.

🔍 **선택지 완벽 분석**

① Repeat and You Will Succeed 반복하라, 그러면 여러분은 성공할 것이다
② Be More Curious, Be Smarter 더 호기심을 갖고, 더 영리해져라
③ Play Is What Makes Us Human 놀이는 우리를 인간답게 만든다
④ Stop and Think Before You Act 행동하기 전에 멈추고 생각하라
⑤ Growth Is All About Keeping Balance 성장의 핵심은 균형을 유지하는 것이다

22

우리의 뇌는 뉴런의 연결망을 가지고 있어 뇌 친화적인 피드백 기술을 잊지 않고 사용할 때마다 서로 연결되며, 처음에는 신뢰할 만하지 않을 수도 있지만 함께 활성화되는 뉴런들은 함께 연결된다고 했다. 따라서 (e)의 blocks를 strengthens와 같은 단어로 바꾸는 것이 문맥상 자연스러우므로 정답은 ⑤이다.

🔍 **선택지 완벽 분석**

① 자전거를 배울 때는 반복해서 시도했지만 어른이 되어서는 단 한 번만 시도해 보고 '잘되었는지' 판단한다고 했으므로 worked는 문맥상 적절하다.

③ 반복할 때마다 함께 활성화되는 뉴런들은 함께 '연결된다'고 했으므로 connect는 문맥상 적절하다.

④ 첫 번째 시도에서 다소 마구잡이가 되도록 할 수도 있다고 했고 이는 '신뢰할 만하지' 않을 것이므로 reliable은 문맥상 적절하다.

필수 어휘

fall off 넘어지다 attempt 시도 judge 판단하다, 판정하다 awkward 어색한
shame 애석한 일, 수치 repetition 반복 central 핵심적인
rewire 재연결하다, 전선을 다시 배치하다 neuron 뉴런, 신경 세포
reliable 신뢰할 만한 hit-and-miss 마구잡이의, 되는대로 하는
involve 연관시키다

---

23 정답 ②   24 정답 ⑤

202011 41~42번 정답률 67% / 48%

Like all humans, the first *Homo* species to begin the long difficult process of constructing a language from scratch almost certainly
사전 준비 없이, 맨 처음부터
never said entirely what was on their minds. At the same time, these
동시에
primitive hominins would not have simply made (a) random sounds or gestures. Instead, they would have used means to communicate that they believed others would understand. And they also thought their hearers could "fill in the gaps", and connect their knowledge of their culture and the world to interpret what was uttered.

☆ These are some of *the reasons* / [**why** the (b) origins of human
관계부사(이유)
language cannot be effectively discussed / (**unless** conversation is
조동사+be+p.p.: 조동사 수동태   조건의 부사절(= if ~ not)
placed at the top of the list of *things* to understand)]. **주제문** Every
to부정사 형용사적 용법(명사 수식)
aspect of human language has evolved, as have components of the human brain and body, to (c) engage in conversation and social life. Language did not fully begin when the first hominid uttered the first
→ 본격적으로, 진심으로
word or sentence. **23번 단서** It began in earnest only with the first
언어는 언어의 기원이자 목적인 대화와 함께 본격적으로 시작됨
conversation, which is both the source and the (d) goal of language. Indeed, language changes lives. It builds society and expresses our highest aspirations, our basest thoughts, our emotions and our philosophies of life. **24번 단서** But all language is ultimately at the
모든 언어는 궁극적으로 인간의 상호 작용을 위한 것
service of human interaction. Other components of language — things like grammar and stories — are (e) **crucial**(→ **secondary**) to conversation.

해석

모든 인간처럼, 아무런 사전 준비 없이 언어를 구성하는 길고 힘든 과정을 시작한 최초의 '호모' 종은 거의 틀림없이 자신의 마음에 있는 것을 온전히 말하지 않았다. 동시에, 이 원시 호미닌(인간의 조상으로 분류되는 종족)들은 단순히 (a) 무작위적인 소리를 내거나 몸짓을 하지는 않았을 것이다. 그 대신, 그들은 남들이 이해할 것이라고 믿는 의사소통 수단을 사용했을 것이다. 그리고 그들은 또한 자신의 청자들이 '빈틈을 메울' 수 있고, 발화된 것을 해석하기 위해 그들의 문화와 세계에 대한 지식을 연결할 수 있다고 생각했다.

이러한 것들이 대화가 이해해야 할 것들의 목록 중 맨 위에 놓이지 않는 한, 인간 언

어의 (b) 기원이 효과적으로 논의될 수 없는 몇 가지 이유들이다. 인간의 뇌와 신체의 구성 요소들이 그래 왔던 것처럼, 인간 언어의 모든 측면은 대화와 사회 생활에 (c) 관여하도록 진화해 왔다. 언어는 최초의 호미니드(사람과(科))의 동물이 최초의 단어나 문장을 (입 밖에) 냈을 때 온전히 시작된 것은 아니었다. 그것은 최초의 대화와 함께 본격적으로 시작되었는데, 이는 언어의 근원이자 (d) 목적이다. 실제로, 언어는 삶을 변화시킨다. 그것은 사회를 세우고, 우리의 가장 높은 열망, 가장 기본적인 생각, 감정, 그리고 삶의 철학을 표현한다. 그러나 모든 언어는 궁극적으로 인간의 상호 작용을 위한 것이다. 언어의 다른 요소들, 즉 문법과 이야기 같은 것들은 대화에 (e) **중요한(→ 부차적인)** 것이다.

정답이 보이는 해설

23

언어는 인간의 조상이 최초의 단어나 문장을 발화했을 때 시작된 것이 아니라 최초의 대화와 함께 본격적으로 시작되었다는 것이 글의 주된 내용으로, 인간의 조상이 언어를 구성하는 과정에서 상대가 이해할 것이라고 믿는 의사소통 수단을 사용했을 것이며 상대 또한 이해를 위해 문화와 세계에 대한 지식을 연결할 수 있다고 생각했다고 했으므로 글의 제목으로 가장 적절한 것은 ②이다.

선택지 완벽 분석

① Various Communication Strategies of Our Ancestors 우리 조상들의 다양한 의사소통 전략
② Conversation: The Core of Language Development 대화: 언어 발달의 핵심
③ Ending Conversation Without Offending Others 상대방의 기분을 상하게 하지 않고 대화 끝내기
④ How Language Shapes the Way You Think 언어가 생각하는 방식을 형성하는 방법
⑤ What Makes You a Good Communicator? 무엇이 여러분을 훌륭한 의사 전달자로 만드는가?

24

인간 언어의 기원을 효과적으로 논의하기 위해서는 대화가 목록의 맨 위에 놓여야 하며 언어는 궁극적으로 인간의 상호 작용을 위한 것이라고 했으므로, 문법이나 이야기 같은 언어의 다른 요소들은 대화에 중요한 것이 아니라 부차적인 것이라 할 수 있다. 따라서 (e)의 crucial을 secondary와 같은 단어로 바꾸는 것이 문맥상 자연스러우므로 정답은 ⑤이다.

필수 어휘

primitive 원시 사회의, 원시적 단계의   random 무작위의   interpret 해석하다
utter (입으로 어떤 소리를) 내다, (말을) 하다   component (구성) 요소, 부품
aspiration 열망, 포부, 염원   ultimately 궁극적으로, 결국
crucial 중대한, 결정적인   core 핵심   offend 기분 상하게[불쾌하게] 하다

1권 p. 197

20강 2020~2023 **복합 문단의 이해**

01 정답 ④   **02** 정답 ③   **03** 정답 ④

202309 43~45번 정답률 87% / 87% / 83%

(A) Long ago, an old man built a grand temple at the center of his village. People traveled to worship at the temple. So the old man made arrangements for food and accommodation inside the temple itself. He needed someone who could look after the temple, **01번 단서1** so (a) he put up a notice: Manager needed.
= the old man 그 노인은 관리자를 구한다는 공고를 붙임

(D) **01번 단서2** Seeing the notice, many people went to the old man.
그 공고를 본 사람들이 그에게 찾아옴
But he returned all the applicants after interviews, telling them, "I need a qualified person for this work." ✪ The old man would sit on the roof (of (d) his house) every morning, / (**watching** people go through the temple doors). **01번 단서3** One day, (e) he saw a young man come to the temple.
노인은 한 젊은이가 사원으로 오는 것을 보았음

(B) **01번 단서4** When that young man left the temple, the old man called him and asked, "Will you take care of this temple?" The young man was surprised by the offer and replied, "I have no experience caring for a temple. I'm not even educated." The old man smiled and said, "I don't want any educated man. I want a qualified person." Confused, **01번 단서5** the young man asked, "But why do (b) you consider me a qualified person?"
여기는지 물어봄 = the old man

(C) **01번 단서6** The old man replied, "I buried a brick on the path to the temple. I watched for many days as people tripped over that brick. No one thought to remove it. **03번 단서** But you dug up that brick." The young man said, "I haven't done anything great. It's the duty of every human being to think about others. (c) I only did my duty." The old man smiled and said, "Only people who know their duty and perform it are qualified people."

해석

(A) 옛날, 한 노인이 마을 중심부에 큰 사원을 지었다. 사람들이 사원에서 예배를 드리기 위해 멀리서 왔다. 그래서 노인은 사원 안에 음식과 숙소를 준비했다. 그는 사원을 관리할 수 있는 사람이 필요했고, 그래서 (a) 그는 '관리자 구함'이라는 공고를 붙였다.
(D) 공고를 보고 많은 사람들이 노인을 찾아갔다. 그러나 그는 면접 후에 그들에게 "나는 이 일에 자격을 갖춘 사람이 필요합니다."라고 말하며, 모든 지원자들을 돌려보냈다. 노인은 사람들이 사원의 문을 통과하는 것을 지켜보며 매일 아침 (d) 그의 집 지붕에 앉아 있곤 했다. 어느 날 (e) 그는 한 젊은이가 사원으로 오는 것을 보았다.
(B) 젊은이가 사원을 나설 때, 노인이 그를 불러 "이 사원의 관리를 맡아 주겠소?"라고 질문했다. 젊은이는 그 제안에 놀라서 "저는 사원을 관리한 경험이 없습니다. 심지어 교육도 받지 못했습니다."라고 대답했다. 노인은 웃으며 "나는 교육을 받은 사람이 필요한 게 아니오. 나는 자격 있는 사람을 원하오."라고 말했다. 당황하여, 젊은이는 "그런데 (b) 당신은 왜 저를 자격이 있는 사람이라고 여기시나요?"라고 물었다.
(C) 노인은 대답했다. "나는 사원으로 통하는 길에 벽돌 한 개를 묻었소. 나는 여러 날 동안 사람들이 그 벽돌에 발이 걸려 넘어지는 것을 지켜보았소. 아무도 그것을 치

울 생각을 하지 않았소. 하지만 당신은 그 벽돌을 파냈소." 젊은이는 "저는 대단한 일을 한 것이 아닙니다. 타인을 생각하는 것은 모든 인간의 의무입니다. (c) 저는 제 의무를 다했을 뿐입니다."라고 말했다. 노인은 미소를 지으며 "자신의 의무를 알고 그 의무를 수행하는 사람만이 자격이 있는 사람이오."라고 말했다.

정답이 보이는 해설

01
한 노인이 사원을 지었고, 사원을 관리할 수 있는 사람이 필요하여 관리자를 구한다는 공고를 붙였다는 내용의 (A) 다음에, 그 공고를 보고 찾아온 지원자들을 모두 돌려보냈다는 내용의 (D)가 오는 것이 적절하다. (D)의 마지막 문장에서 그 노인은 한 젊은이가 사원으로 오는 것을 보았고, 이어서 그에게 이 사원의 관리를 맡아 달라고 요청하였고, 당황한 젊은이는 왜 자신을 자격이 있다고 생각하는지 묻는 (B)가 온 다음, 노인은 아무도 치우지 않은 벽돌을 파내는 것을 보았고, 타인을 생각하는 인간의 의무를 수행하였기에 자격이 있다고 대답한 내용의 (C)가 마지막에 와야 한다.

02
(a), (b), (d), (e)는 모두 노인을 가리키지만, (c)는 젊은이를 가리키므로 정답은 ③이다.

03
(C)에서 사원으로 통하는 길에 묻혀있던 벽돌을 파낸 것은 노인이 아닌 젊은이였으므로 ④가 윗글의 내용으로 적절하지 않다.

필수 어휘
grand 큰, 웅장한   temple 사원   worship 예배를 드리러 가다, 예배하다
accommodation 숙소   notice 공고문, 안내문   applicant 지원자
qualified 자격이 있는   offer 제안; 제안하다   educated 교육받은, 학식 있는
confused 당황스러운   bury 묻다   path 길   trip over 발이 걸려 넘어지다
dig up ~을 땅에서 파내다   duty 의무

---

04 정답 ④   05 정답 ②   06 정답 ③
202306 43~45번 정답률 82% / 69% / 79%

(A) A nurse took a tired, anxious soldier to the bedside. "Jack, your son is here," the nurse said to an old man lying on the bed. She had to repeat the words several times before the old man's eyes opened. ✪ Suffering from the severe pain (because of heart disease), / he barely **saw** the young uniformed soldier standing (next to him). **04번 단서1** (a) He reached out his hand to the soldier.
= the old man   노인이 군인에게 손을 뻗음

(D) **04번 단서2** The soldier gently wrapped his fingers around the
군인이 그 손을 잡음
weak hand of the old man. The nurse brought a chair so that the soldier could sit beside the bed. **04번 단서3** All through the night the
밤새 군인이 노인 곁에 머뭄
young soldier sat there, holding the old man's hand and offering (e) him words of support and comfort. Occasionally, she suggested that
= the old man
the soldier take a rest for a while. He politely said no.
휴식을 취하다

(B) Whenever the nurse came into the room, she heard the soldier say a few gentle words. The old man said nothing, only held tightly to (b) him all through the night. **04번 단서4** Just before dawn, the
= the soldier   동트기 전에, 노인이 죽음
old man died. The soldier released the old man's hand and left the room to find the nurse. After she was told what happened, she went back to the room with him. The soldier hesitated for a while and
잠시 동안
04번 단서5 asked, "Who was this man?"
군인이 노인이 누구였는지 물음

(C) She was surprised and asked, "Wasn't he your father?" "No, he wasn't. **06번 단서** I've never met him before," the soldier replied.
군인은 노인을 만난 적이 없다고 말함
She asked, "Then why didn't you say something when I took you to (c) him?" He said, "I knew there had been a mistake, but when I
= the old man
realized that he was too sick to tell whether or not I was his son, I
too ~ to-v: 너무 ~해서 …하지 못하다
could see how much (d) he needed me. So, I stayed."
= the old man

해석
(A) 한 간호사가 피곤하고 불안해하는 군인을 침대 곁으로 데려갔다. "Jack, 당신 아들이 왔어요."라고 간호사가 침대에 누워 있는 노인에게 말했다. 그 노인이 눈을 뜨기 전에 그녀는 그 말을 여러 번 반복해야 했다. 그는 심장병 때문에 극심한 고통을 겪고 있어서, 제복을 입은 젊은 군인이 그의 옆에 서 있는 것을 간신히 보았다. (a) 그는 손을 그 군인에게 뻗었다.

(D) 그 군인은 노인의 병약한 손을 부드럽게 감쌌다. 간호사는 군인이 침대 옆에 앉을 수 있도록 의자를 가져왔다. 밤새 젊은 군인은 거기에 앉아, 노인의 손을 잡고 (e) 그에게 지지와 위로의 말을 건넸다. 가끔, 그녀는 군인에게 잠시 쉬라고 제안했다. 그는 정중하게 거절했다.

(B) 간호사가 병실에 들어올 때마다, 그녀는 그 군인이 부드러운 몇 마디의 말을 하는 것을 들었다. 밤새도록 (b) 그에게 손이 꼭 쥐어진 채로 노인은 아무 말도 하지 않았다. 동트기 직전에, 그 노인은 죽었다. 그 군인은 노인의 손을 놓고 간호사를 찾기 위해 병실을 나갔다. 그녀가 무슨 일이 있었는지 들은 후, 그녀는 그와 함께 병실로 돌아갔다. 군인은 잠시 머뭇거리고는 "이 남자는 누구였나요?"라고 물었다.

(C) 그녀는 깜짝 놀라서 물었다. "그가 당신의 아버지가 아니었나요?" "아니요, 아니었어요. 저는 그를 이전에 만난 적이 없어요."라고 군인이 대답했다. 그녀는 "그러면 내가 당신을 (c) 그에게 데리고 갔을 때 왜 아무 말도 하지 않았나요?"라고 물었다. 그는 "실수가 있었다는 것을 알았지만, 그는 너무 위독해서 제가 그의 아들인지 아닌지 구별할 수 없다는 걸 알게 되었을 때, 저는 (d) 그가 얼마나 저를 필요로 하는지 알 수 있었습니다. 그래서, 저는 머물렀습니다."라고 말했다.

정답이 보이는 해설

04
(A)에서 한 간호사가 불안해하는 한 군인을 많이 아픈 한 노인의 침대로 데려가서, 당신의 아들이 왔다고 전했고, 노인은 군인에게 손을 뻗었다. 이어 그 손을 부드럽게 감싸는 장면인 (D)가 와야 하는데, 그 후 군인은 밤새 노인 곁을 지켰다. 그런 다음, 동트기 직전에, 노인은 죽었고, 군인이 간호사에게 노인이 누구였는지 묻는 (B)가 나와야 한다. 마지막으로, 군인의 아버지가 아니었냐는 간호사의 질문에 대해 군인의 아버지가 아니지만, 노인이 자기를 얼마나 필요로 했는지 알았기에 머물렀다는 대답이 나오는 (C)가 와야 한다.

05
(a), (c), (d), (e)는 모두 아픈 노인을 가리키지만, (b)는 군인을 가리키므로 정답은 ②이다.

06
(C)에서 군인은 노인을 만난 적이 없다(I've never met him before)고 했으므로 ③이 윗글의 내용으로 적절하지 않다.

필수 어휘
anxious 불안해하는   severe 극심한   heart disease 심장병   barely 간신히
wrap (감)싸다   support 지지, 후원   suggest 제안하다   dawn 동틀 녘, 새벽
release 놓아주다   hesitate 머뭇거리다

---

07 정답 ④   08 정답 ④   09 정답 ④
202303 43~45번 정답률 80% / 79% / 86%

(A) Once upon a time, there was a king who lived in a beautiful
옛날 옛적에

palace. While the king was away, a monster approached the gates of the palace. The monster was **so** ugly and smelly **that** the guards
<small>so ~ that: 너무 ~해서 …하다</small>
froze in shock. He passed the guards and sat on the king's throne. ★ The guards soon <u>came</u> to their senses, <u>went</u> in, and <u>shouted</u> at the
<small>come to one's sense: 정신을 차리다</small>
<small>동사1</small> <small>동사2</small> <small>동사3</small>
monster, / demanding [that (a) he get off the throne].
<small>분사구문</small> <small>= the monster</small>

(D) With each bad word the guards used, the monster grew more ugly and smelly. The guards got even angrier — they began to brandish their swords to <u>scare</u> the monster away from the palace.
<small>겁을 주어 ~에서 쫓아내다</small>
But (e) he just grew bigger and bigger, eventually <u>taking up</u> the
<small>= the monster</small> <small>take up: ~을 차지하다</small>
whole room. **07번 단서1** He grew more ugly and smelly than ever.
<small>점점 더 못생겨지고 냄새도 더 남</small>

(B) Eventually the king returned. He was wise and kind and saw what was happening. He knew <u>what to do</u>. He smiled and said to
<small>무엇을 할지</small>
the monster, "Welcome to my palace!" He asked the monster if (b) he wanted a cup of coffee. **07번 단서2** The monster began to grow
<small>= the monster</small> <small>커피를 마시고 더 작아지기 시작함</small>
smaller as he drank the coffee.

(C) The king offered (c) <u>him</u> some takeout pizza and fries. The
<small>= the monster</small>
guards immediately <u>called</u> for pizza. The monster continued to
<small>call for: ~을 시키다</small>
get smaller with the king's kind gestures. (d) He then offered the
monster a full body massage. **09번 단서** As the guards helped with the
<small>= the king</small> <small>경비병들이 마사지를 도움</small>
relaxing massage, the monster became tiny. **07번 단서3** With another
<small>또 다른 친절로,</small>
act of kindness to the monster, he just disappeared.
<small>괴물이 사라짐</small>

해석

(A) 옛날 옛적에, 아름다운 궁전에 사는 한 왕이 있었다. 왕이 없는 동안, 한 괴물이 궁전 문으로 접근했다. 그 괴물이 너무 추하고 냄새가 나서 경비병들은 충격으로 얼어붙었다. 그(괴물)는 경비병들을 지나 왕의 왕좌에 앉았다. 경비병들은 곧 정신을 차리고, 안으로 들어가, 그 괴물을 향해 소리치며, (a) 그에게 왕좌에서 내려올 것을 요구했다.

(D) 경비병들이 사용하는 각 나쁜 말과 함께, 그 괴물은 더 추해졌고 더 냄새가 났다. 경비병들은 한층 더 화가 났다. 그들은 그 괴물을 겁주어 궁전에서 쫓아내려고 검을 휘두르기 시작했다. 하지만 (e) 그는 그저 점점 더 커져서, 결국 방 전체를 차지했다. 그는 그 어느 때보다 더 추해졌고 더 냄새가 났다.

(B) 마침내 왕이 돌아왔다. 그는 현명하고 친절했으며 무슨 일이 일어나고 있는지 알아차렸다. 그는 무엇을 해야 할지 알았다. 그는 미소를 지으며 그 괴물에게 "나의 궁전에 온 것을 환영하오!"라고 말했다. 왕은 그 괴물에게 (b) 그가 커피 한 잔을 원하는지 물었다. 괴물은 그 커피를 마시면서 더 작아지기 시작했다.

(C) 왕은 (c) 그에게 약간의 테이크아웃 피자와 감자튀김을 제안했다. 경비병들은 즉시 피자를 시켰다. 그 괴물은 왕의 친절한 행동에 몸이 계속 더 작아졌다. 그러고 나서 (d) 그는 그 괴물에게 전신 마사지를 제안했다. 경비병들이 긴장을 풀어 주는 마사지를 도와주자 그 괴물은 매우 작아졌다. 그 괴물에게 또 한 번의 친절한 행동을 베풀자, 그는 바로 사라져 버렸다.

정답이 보이는 해설

07

(A)에서 왕이 자리를 비운 사이에, 추하고 냄새 나는 괴물이 와서 왕좌에 앉았고, 경비병들이 쫓아내려고 했다. 이어서 경비병들의 못된 말로 괴물이 더 추하고 냄새 나게 되었다는 (D)가 온다. 그 후에 현명한 왕이 돌아와서 괴물에게 친절을 베풀자 작아지기 시작했다는 (B)에 이어, 마지막으로 더 많은 친절을 베풀자 괴물이 사라졌다는 (C)가 와야 한다.

08

(a), (b), (c), (e)는 모두 괴물을 가리키지만, (d)는 왕을 가리키므로 정답은 ④이다.

09

(C)에서 왕이 전신 마사지를 제안했고, 경비병들이 괴물이 긴장을 풀 수 있도록 마사지를 도와주자(As the guards helped with the relaxing massage) 괴물이 사라졌다고 했으므로, ④가 윗글의 내용으로 적절하지 않다.

필수 어휘

approach 접근하다 guard 경비병 freeze 얼어붙다, 얼다 demand 요구하다
eventually 결국, 마침내 whole 전체(의) return 돌아오다 immediately 즉시
continue 계속하다 gesture 행동 massage 마사지, 안마 relaxing 편안한
tiny 매우 작은 disappear 사라지다

10 정답 ④ **11** 정답 ③ **12** 정답 ④

202211 43~45번 정답률 82% / 71% / 76%

(A) On my daughter Marie's 8th birthday, she received a <u>bunch</u>
<small>많은 ~</small>
of presents from her friends at school. That evening, with her favorite present, a teddy bear, in her arms, we went to a restaurant to celebrate her birthday. Our server, a friendly woman, noticed my daughter holding the teddy bear and said, "My daughter loves teddy bears, too." Then, we started chatting about (a) <u>her</u> family.
<small>= our server</small>

(D) The server mentioned during the conversation that **12번 단서**
her daughter was in the hospital with a broken leg. (e) She also
<small>종업원의 딸은 다리를 다쳐 병원에 있음</small> <small>= our server</small>
said that Marie looked about the same age as her daughter. She was so kind and attentive all evening, and **10번 단서1** even gave Marie
<small>시간의 부사절</small> <small>종업원이 Marie에게 쿠키를</small>
cookies for free. ★ After we finished our meal, / we paid the bill
<small>무료로 줌</small> <small>시간의 부사절</small> <small>동사1</small>
and began to walk to our car // when unexpectedly Marie asked me
<small>동사2</small> <small>부사절 동사2</small> <small>부사절 동사1</small>
to wait and **10번 단서2** ran back into the restaurant.
<small>식사 후 Marie가 다시 식당으로 감</small>

(B) When Marie came back out, I asked her what she had been doing. She said that **10번 단서3** she gave her teddy bear to our server
<small>Marie가 종업원에게 인형을 줌</small>
so that she could give it to (b) <u>her</u> daughter. I was surprised at her
<small>~하기 위해서</small> <small>= our server</small>
sudden action because I could see how much she loved that bear already. (c) <u>She</u> must have seen the look on my face, because she
<small>= Marie</small>
said, "I can't imagine being stuck in a hospital bed. I just want her to get better soon."

(C) I felt moved by Marie's words as we walked toward the car. Then, **10번 단서4** our server ran out to our car and thanked Marie for
<small>종업원이 Marie에게 고마워함</small>
her generosity. The server said that (d) <u>she</u> had never had anyone
<small>= our server</small>
doing anything like that for her family before. Later, Marie said it was her best birthday ever. I was so proud of her empathy and
<small>be proud of: ~을 자랑스러워하다</small>
warmth, and this was an unforgettable experience for our family.

해석

(A) 나의 딸 Marie의 8번째 생일에, 그녀는 학교에서 친구들로부터 많은 선물을 받았다. 그날 저녁, 그녀가 가장 좋아하는 선물인 테디 베어를 팔에 안고, 우리는 그녀

의 생일을 축하하기 위해 식당에 갔다. 다정한 여성인 우리의 종업원은 나의 딸이 테디 베어를 안고 있다는 것을 알아차렸고, "나의 딸도 테디 베어를 좋아해요."라고 말했다. 그리고 나서, 우리는 (a) 그녀의 가족에 대해 담소를 나누기 시작했다.

(D) 그 종업원은 대화 중에 자신의 딸이 다리가 부러져 병원에 있다고 말했다. (e) 그녀는 또한 Marie가 자신의 딸과 나이가 거의 똑같아 보인다고 말했다. 그녀는 저녁 내내 매우 친절하고 세심했고, 심지어 Marie에게 쿠키를 무료로 주었다. 식사를 마친 후, 우리는 요금을 지불하고 우리 차로 걸어가기 시작했는데 그때 갑자기 Marie가 나에게 기다려 달라고 부탁하고 식당으로 다시 뛰어 들어갔다.

(B) Marie가 돌아왔을 때, 나는 그녀에게 무엇을 하고 있었느냐고 물었다. 그녀는 자신의 테디 베어를 우리의 종업원에게 주어서 그녀가 (b) 그녀의 딸에게 그것을 줄 수 있도록 했다고 말했다. 나는 이미 그녀가 그 테디 베어를 얼마나 좋아하는지 알 수 있었기 때문에 그녀의 갑작스러운 행동에 놀랐다. (c) 그녀는 내 얼굴의 표정을 분명히 봤을 것인데, 왜냐하면 그녀가 "저는 병원 침대에 갇혀 있는 것을 상상할 수 없어요. 저는 그저 그녀가 빨리 낫기를 바랄 뿐이에요."라고 말했기 때문이다.

(C) 우리가 차를 향해 걸어갈 때 나는 Marie의 말에 감동받았다. 그때 우리의 종업원이 우리 차로 달려 나와 Marie의 관대함에 고마워했다. 그 종업원은 (d) 그녀는 이전에 자신의 가족을 위해 그런 일을 해 준 어떤 사람도 가진 적이 없었다고 말했다. 나중에, Marie는 그날이 그녀의 최고의 생일이었다고 말했다. 나는 그녀의 공감과 따뜻함이 너무 자랑스러웠고, 이것은 우리 가족에게 잊을 수 없는 경험이었다.

정답이 보이는 해설

10

(A)에서 딸 Marie가 가장 좋아하는 선물인 테디 베어를 안고, 생일 축하를 위해 식당에 갔는데, 테디 베어를 좋아하는 딸을 가진 종업원과 이야기를 나누게 되었다. 이어서 그 종업원의 딸이 병원에 있는 것을 알게 되고, 식사 후에 Marie가 다시 식당으로 뛰어가는 (D)가 온 다음, 그 종업원의 딸에게 자신의 테디 베어를 주고 왔다는 (B)가 온다. 마지막으로 그 종업원이 다시 나와 고마움을 전하고, Marie가 자랑스러웠다는 내용의 (C)가 와야 한다.

11

(a), (b), (d), (e)는 모두 식당의 종업원 그녀를 가리키지만, (c)는 Marie를 가리키므로 정답은 ③이다.

12

(D)에서 종업원은 대화 중에 자신의 딸이 다리가 부러져 병원에 있다(her daughter was in the hospital with a broken leg)고 말했으므로, ④가 윗글의 내용으로 적절하지 않다.

필수 어휘

present 선물   chat 담소를 나누다   mention 언급하다   attentive 세심한
for free 무료로   unexpectedly 갑자기   stuck 갇힌   get better 회복하다, 낫다
moved 감동받은   generosity 관대함   empathy 공감
unforgettable 잊을 수 없는   experience 경험

13 정답 ④ 14 정답 ③ 15 정답 ③

202209 43~45번 정답률 72% / 71% / 75%

(A) A boy had a place at the best school in town. In the morning, his granddad took him to the school. When (a) he went onto the playground with his grandson, the children surrounded them. "What a funny old man," one boy smirked. A girl with brown hair pointed at the pair and jumped up and down. Suddenly, the bell rang and the children ran off to their first lesson.

(D) The old man took his grandson firmly by the hand, and led him out of the school gate. "Brilliant, I don't have to go to school!"

the boy exclaimed. "You do, but not this one," his granddad replied. "I'll find you a school myself." Granddad took his grandson back to his own house, asked grandma to look after him, and 13번 단서1 went off to look for a teacher (e) himself. ✪ Every time [he spotted a school], // the old man went onto the playground, and waited for the children to come out at break time.

(B) In some schools the children completely ignored the old man and in others, they made fun of (b) him. When this happened, he would turn sadly and go home. Finally, he went onto the tiny playground of a very small school, and leant against the fence, exhausted. The bell rang, and the crowd of children ran out onto the playground. 13번 단서2 "Sir, are you all right? Shall I bring you a glass of water?" a voice said. "We've got a bench in the playground — come and sit down," another voice said. Soon a young teacher came out onto the playground.

(C) The old man greeted (c) him and said: "13번 단서3 Finally, I've found my grandson the best school in town." "You're mistaken, sir. Our school is not the best — it's small and cramped." 15번 단서 The old man didn't argue with the teacher. Instead, he made arrangements for his grandson to join the school, and then the old man left. That evening, the boy's mom said to (d) him: "Dad, you can't even read. How do you know you've found the best teacher of all?" "Judge a teacher by his pupils," the old man replied.

해석

(A) 한 소년이 마을에 있는 가장 좋은 학교에 한 자리를 얻었다. 아침에, 그의 할아버지는 그를 학교에 데리고 갔다. (a) 그가 그의 손자와 함께 운동장으로 들어갔을 때, 아이들이 그들을 둘러쌌다. "정말 우스꽝스러운 할아버지다."라며 한 소년이 히죽히죽 웃었다. 갈색 머리 소녀가 그 둘을 향해 손가락질하며 위아래로 뛰었다. 갑자기, 종이 울렸고 아이들은 그들의 첫 수업에 급히 뛰어갔다.

(D) 노인은 손자의 손을 꽉 잡고, 그를 교문 밖으로 데리고 나갔다. "굉장해요, 저는 학교에 가지 않아도 되네요!"라고 소년이 소리쳤다. "가긴 가야지, 그렇지만 이 학교는 아니야."라고 할아버지가 대답했다. "내가 직접 네게 학교를 찾아주마." 할아버지는 손자를 집으로 데리고 돌아가 할머니에게 그를 돌봐달라고 부탁하고, (e) 그 자신이 선생님을 찾아 나섰다. 학교를 발견할 때마다, 그 노인은 운동장으로 들어가서 쉬는 시간에 아이들이 나오기를 기다렸다.

(B) 몇몇 학교에서는 아이들이 노인을 완전히 무시했고, 다른 학교들에서는 아이들이 (b) 그를 놀렸다. 이런 일이 일어났을 때, 그는 슬프게 돌아서서 집으로 가곤 했다. 마침내, 그는 매우 작은 한 학교의 아주 작은 운동장으로 들어갔고, 지쳐서 울타리에 기댔다. 종이 울렸고, 아이들의 무리가 운동장으로 달려 나왔다. "할아버지, 괜찮으세요? 물 한 잔 가져다드릴까요?"라고 누군가가 말했다. "우리 운동장에 벤치가 있어요. 오셔서 앉으세요."라고 또 다른 누군가가 말했다. 곧 한 젊은 선생님이 운동장으로 나왔다.

(C) 노인은 (c) 그에게 인사하면서 이렇게 말했다. "마침내, 제가 제 손자에게 마을 최고의 학교를 찾아주었네요." "잘못 아신 겁니다, 어르신. 우리 학교는 최고가 아니에요. 작고 비좁은걸요." 노인은 선생님과 논쟁을 벌이지 않았다. 대신, 그는 손자가 그 학교에 다닐 수 있도록 준비했고, 그런 다음에 노인은 떠났다. 그날 저녁, 소년의 어머니는 (d) 그에게 말했다. "아버지, 글을 읽을 줄도 모르시잖아요. 최고의 선생님을 찾았다는 것을 어떻게 아세요?" "선생님은 그 제자를 보고 판단해야 해."라고 노인은 대답했다.

정답이 보이는 해설

13

마을에서 가장 좋은 학교에 간 손자와 할아버지를 보고 학교의 아이들이 우스꽝스럽다며 놀렸다는 내용의 (A) 다음에, 할아버지가 손자를 데리고 나와 할머니에게 손자를 맡기고 손자가 다닐 학교를 직접 찾아 나섰다는 내용의 (D)가 오는 것이 적절하다. 어느 날 노인이 매우 작은 한 학교에 지쳐서 들어갔는데 한 무리의 아이들이 달려와 물 한 잔을 가져다주겠다고 말하는 내용의 (B)가 오고, 그 학교의 선생님에게 마침내 좋은 학교를 찾았다며 손자가 그 학교에 다니도록 준비해 주고 선생님은 제자를 보고 판단해야 한다고 말하는 내용의 (C)가 마지막에 와야 한다.

14

(c)는 노인이 인사하면서 말한 대상인 젊은 선생님을 가리키고, 나머지는 모두 소년의 할아버지[노인]를 가리키므로, 정답은 ③이다.

15

노인은 선생님과 논쟁을 벌이지 않았다(The old man didn't argue with the teacher.)고 했으므로 ③은 글의 내용과 일치하지 않는다.

필수 어휘

surround 둘러싸다   pair 한 쌍   firmly 꽉   gate 문   brilliant 광장한, 화려한
exclaim 외치다   spot 발견하다   break time 쉬는 시간   completely 완전히
ignore 무시하다   lean 기대다(-leant-leant)   fence 울타리
exhausted 지친, 기진맥진한   crowd 무리   voice 목소리   greet ~에게 인사하다
mistaken 잘못된   argue 논쟁하다   arrangements 준비
join ~에 들다, ~의 회원이 되다   pupil 학생

---

16 정답 ④   17 정답 ②   18 정답 ④

202206 43~45번 정답률 80% / 77% / 79%

(A) Once, a farmer lost his precious watch while working in his barn. It may have appeared to be an ordinary watch to others, but it brought a lot of happy childhood memories to him. It was one of the most important things to (a) him. **16번 단서1** After searching for it
= the farmer   잃어버린 시계를 오랫동안 찾고
for a long time, the old farmer became exhausted.
나서 농부는 지쳐버림
→ 포기하다
(D) **16번 단서2** However, the tired farmer did not want to give up
하지만 농부는 포기하지 않고 밖에서 노는 아이들에게 도와달라고 요청함
on the search for his watch and asked a group of children playing outside to help him. (e) He promised an attractive reward for the
= the farmer
person who could find it. After hearing about the reward, **18번 단서**
the children hurried inside the barn and went through and round the
아이들은 서둘러 헛간 안으로 들어가서 시계를 찾기 시작함
entire pile of hay looking for the watch. After a long time searching
~을 찾다
for it, some of the children got tired and gave up.
(B) **16번 단서3** The number of children looking for the watch
시계를 찾는 아이들의 수가 서서히 줄어서 몇 명만 남음
slowly decreased and only a few tired children were left. The farmer gave up all hope of finding it and called off the search. Just when
call off: ~을 중지하다
the farmer was closing the barn door, a little boy came up to him and asked the farmer to give him another chance. The farmer did not want to lose out on any chance of finding the watch so let (b) him
= a little boy
in the barn.
(C) **16번 단서4** After a little while the boy came out with the
한 번 더 기회를 요청한 소년이 농부의 시계를 손에 찾아 들고 나옴
farmer's watch in his hand. ✪ (c) He was happily surprised / and
= the farmer

---

asked [how he had succeeded to find the watch] / **while** everyone
ask의 목적어절   부사적 용법(목적)   접속사(~한 반면에)
else had failed. He replied "I just sat there and tried listening for the sound of the watch. In silence, it was much easier to hear it and follow the direction of the sound." (d) He was delighted to get his
= the farmer
watch back and rewarded the little boy as promised.

해석

(A) 어느 날, 한 농부가 헛간에서 일하는 동안 그의 귀중한 시계를 잃어버렸다. 그것은 다른 이들에게는 평범한 시계로 보였을지도 모르지만, 그것은 그에게 어린 시절의 많은 행복한 기억을 가져다주었다. 그것은 (a) 그에게 가장 중요한 것 중 하나였다. 오랫동안 그것을 찾아 헤맨 뒤에 그 나이 든 농부는 지쳐 버렸다.

(D) 하지만 그 지친 농부는 자신의 시계를 찾는 것을 포기하고 싶지 않았고 밖에서 놀던 한 무리의 아이들에게 자신을 도와달라고 부탁했다. (e) 그는 그것을 찾을 수 있는 사람에게 매력적인 보상을 약속했다. 보상에 대해 듣고 난 후, 그 아이들은 헛간 안으로 서둘러 들어갔고 그 시계를 찾으며 전체 건초 더미 사이와 주변으로 걸어갔다. 시계를 찾느라 오랜 시간을 보낸 후, 아이들 중 일부는 지쳐서 포기했다.

(B) 시계를 찾는 아이들의 수가 서서히 줄어들었고 지친 아이들 몇 명만이 남았다. 그 농부는 시계를 찾는다는 모든 희망을 포기하고 찾는 것을 그만두었다. 농부가 막 헛간 문을 닫고 있었을 때 한 어린 소년이 그에게 다가와서 자신에게 또 한 번의 기회를 달라고 농부에게 요청했다. 농부는 시계를 찾을 어떤 가능성도 놓치고 싶지 않았기 때문에 (b) 그를 헛간 안으로 들어오게 해 주었다.

(C) 잠시 후 그 소년이 한 손에 농부의 시계를 들고 나왔다. (c) 그는 행복에 겨워 놀랐고 다른 모두가 실패했던 반면에 소년이 어떻게 시계를 찾는 데 성공했는지 물었다. 그는 "저는 그냥 거기에 앉아서 시계의 소리를 들으려고 했어요. 적막 속에서, 그것을 듣고 소리의 방향을 따라가는 것이 훨씬 더 쉬웠어요."라고 답했다. (d) 그는 시계를 되찾아 기뻤고 그 어린 소년에게 약속했던 대로 보상을 했다.

정답이 보이는 해설

16

(A)에서 한 농부가 헛간에서 어린 시절의 추억이 담겨 있는 귀중한 시계를 잃어버려서 그것을 찾느라 지쳤다는 내용이다. 이어서 농부가 밖에서 놀던 아이들에게 보상을 약속하며 도와달라고 부탁하자 아이들이 시계를 오랜 시간 찾았지만 일부 아이들은 지쳐서 포기했다는 내용의 (D)가 오고, 농부가 시계 찾기를 포기하고 헛간 문을 닫으려고 할 때 한 어린 소년이 한 번 더 기회를 달라고 요청했다는 내용의 (B)가 나온 다음, 결국 시계를 찾은 소년이 어떻게 그것을 찾았는지 말하고 농부는 소년에게 보상을 했다는 내용의 (C)가 마지막에 와야 한다.

17

(a), (c), (d), (e)는 농부를 가리키고, (b)는 어린 소년을 가리키므로 정답은 ②이다.

18

(D)에서 아이들은 시계를 찾기 위해 헛간 안으로 서둘러 들어갔다고 했으므로, ④가 윗글의 내용과 다르다.

필수 어휘

precious 귀중한   ordinary 평범한   exhausted 지친, 기진맥진한
reward 보상; 보상을 하다   hay 건초(마른 풀)   decrease 줄어들다, 감소하다
chance 기회; 가능성   succeed 성공하다   direction 방향   delighted 기뻐하는

---

19 정답 ②   20 정답 ④   21 정답 ⑤

202203 43~45번 정답률 69% / 66% / 74%

(A) One day a young man was walking along a road on his journey from one village to another. ✪ **As** he walked / he noticed
접속사(~할 때)
a monk (working in the fields). The young man turned to the monk
현재분사구
and said, **19번 단서1** "Excuse me. Do you mind if I ask (a) you a
젊은 남자가 질문을 해도 되는지 묻자 수도승이 흔쾌히 수락함 = the monk
question?" "Not at all," replied the monk.

(C) **19번 단서2** "I am traveling from the village in the mountains to the
<u>산속 마을에서 골짜기 마을로 가고 있는 남자가 골짜기 마을이 어떤지 수도승에게</u>
village in the valley and I was wondering if (c) you knew what it is
질문함   = the monk
like in the village in the valley." "Tell me," said the monk, "what was
your experience of the village in the mountains?" **21번 단서1** "Terrible,"
                                             젊은 남자는 산속의
replied the young man. "I am glad to be away from there. I found
마을이 최악이었고 그곳을 떠나서 기쁘다고 말함
the people most unwelcoming. So tell (d) me, what can I expect in
                                              = the young man
the village in the valley?" "I am sorry to tell you," said the monk,
"but I think your experience will be much the same there." The
young man lowered his head helplessly and walked on.

(B) **19번 단서3** A while later a middle-aged man journeyed down
                   잠시 후 중년 남자도 여행 중에 같은 수도승을 만남
the same road and came upon the monk. "I am going to the village
in the valley," said the man. "Do you know what it is like?" "I do,"
replied the monk, "but first tell (b) me about the village where you
                                  = the monk
came from." "I've come from the village in the mountains," said the
                        마치 ~인 것처럼 ←
man. "It was a wonderful experience. **19번 단서4** I felt as though I
                              중년 남자는 산속 마을에서
was a member of the family in the village."
가족의 일원인 것처럼 느낌
(D) **19번 단서5** "Why did you feel like that?" asked the monk. "The
                 그렇게 느낀 이유를 수도승이 중년 남자에게 질문함
elders gave me much advice, and people were kind and generous.

21번 단서2 I am sad to have left there. And what is the village in the
         중년 남자는 산속 마을을 떠나서 슬프다고 말함
valley like?" he asked again. "(e) I think you will find it much the
                       = the monk
same," replied the monk. "I'm glad to hear that," the middle-aged
man said smiling and journeyed on.

해석

(A) 어느 날 한 젊은 남자가 한 마을에서 다른 마을로 여행하는 중에 길을 따라 걷고 있었다. 그는 걷다가 들판에서 일하는 한 수도승을 발견했다. 그 젊은 남자는 그 수도승을 향해 몸을 돌려 "실례합니다. 제가 (a) 스님께 질문을 하나 드려도 되겠습니까?"라고 말했다. "물론입니다."라고 그 수도승은 대답했다.
(C) "저는 산속에 있는 마을에서 골짜기에 있는 마을로 여행을 가고 있는데 (c) 스님께서 골짜기의 마을은 어떤지 아시는지 궁금합니다." 수도승은 "저에게 말해 보십시오. 산속 마을에서의 경험은 어땠습니까?"라고 말했다. "끔찍했습니다."라고 그 젊은 남자는 대답했다. 그곳을 벗어나서 기쁩니다. 그곳 사람들이 정말로 불친절하다고 생각했습니다. 그러니 (d) 저에게 말씀해 주십시오. 제가 골짜기의 마을에서 무엇을 기대할 수 있을까요?" "말씀드리기 유감이지만, 선생님의 경험은 거기서도 거의 같을 것 같습니다."라고 수도승이 말했다. 그 젊은 남자는 힘없이 고개를 숙이고 계속 걸어갔다.
(B) 잠시 후 한 중년 남자가 같은 길을 여행하다가 그 수도승을 만났다. "저는 골짜기의 마을로 가고 있습니다. 그곳이 어떤지 아십니까?"라고 그 남자가 말했다. "알고 있습니다만, 먼저 (b) 저에게 선생님께서 떠나오신 마을에 관해 말해 주십시오."라고 그 수도승은 대답했다. "저는 산속의 마을에서 왔습니다. 그것은 멋진 경험이었습니다. 저는 마치 그 마을의 가족의 구성원인 것처럼 느꼈습니다."라고 그 남자는 말했다.
(D) 그 수도승은 "왜 그렇게 느끼셨습니까?"라고 물었다. "어르신들은 저에게 많은 조언을 해 주셨고, 사람들은 친절하고 너그러웠습니다. 그곳을 떠나서 슬픕니다. 그런데 골짜기의 마을은 어떻습니까?"라고 그는 다시 물었다. "(e) 제 생각에 선생님은 그곳이 (산속의 마을과) 거의 같다고 생각하실 것 같습니다."라고 수도승은 대답했다. "그 말씀을 들으니 기쁩니다."라고 그 중년 남자는 미소를 지으며 말하고는 여행을 계속했다.

정답이 보이는 해설

19

(A)에서 산속 마을에서 골짜기 마을로 가고 있는 한 젊은 남자가 길을 걷다가 한 수

도승을 발견하고서 질문을 해도 되는지 묻는다. 이어서 산속 마을에서의 경험이 어땠는지 먼저 묻는 수도승의 질문에 남자가 그곳에서의 경험이 끔찍했다고 말하자 수도승이 골짜기 마을도 산속 마을과 똑같을 것이라고 답하는 내용의 (C)가 온다. 그다음에는 역시 골짜기 마을로 가고 있는 중년 남자가 수도승을 만나게 되고 산속 마을이 어땠는지 묻는 수도승의 질문에 멋진 경험이었다고 답하는 내용의 (B)가 오고, 마지막으로 골짜기 마을이 어떤지 다시 묻는 중년 남자에게 그곳이 산속 마을과 거의 같을 것이라고 수도승이 답하는 내용의 (D)가 와야 한다.

20

(a), (b), (c), (e)는 모두 수도승을 가리키지만, (d)는 젊은 남자를 가리키므로 정답은 ④이다.

21

(C)에서 산속에 있는 마을을 떠나서 기쁘다고 말한 사람은 중년 남자가 아니라 젊은 남자였으므로, ⑤가 윗글의 내용과 다르다.

필수 어휘

village 마을   notice 알아차리다   field 들판   reply 대답하다   valley 골짜기
unwelcoming 불친절한   lower 내리다, 낮추다   helplessly 힘없이
middle-aged 중년의   come upon ~을 만나다   wonderful 멋진
generous 너그러운

22 정답 ③   **23** 정답 ②   **24** 정답 ⑤

202111 43~45번 정답률 76% / 76% / 83%

(A) One day a poor man brought a bunch of grapes to a prince
                                  한 송이의
as a gift. He was very excited to be able to bring a gift for (a) him
                                            = the prince
because he was too poor to afford more. He placed the grapes
beside the prince and said, "Oh, Prince, please accept this small gift
from me." His face beamed with happiness as he offered his small
gift.

(C) **22번 단서1** The prince thanked him politely. As the man
          왕자는 자신에게 선물을 준 남자에게 감사의 인사를 함
looked at him expectantly, the prince ate one grape. Then (c) he ate
                                           = the prince
another one. Slowly the prince finished the whole bunch of grapes
by himself. He did not offer grapes to anyone near him. The man
혼자, 스스로
who brought those grapes to (d) him was very pleased and left.
                                    = the prince
22번 단서2 The close friends of the prince who were around him were
          왕자 곁에 있던 친구들은 그가 혼자 포도를 다 먹는 것을 보고 놀람
very surprised.

(D) **22번 단서3** Usually the prince shared whatever he had with
          평소에 왕자는 자신이 가진 것을 다른 사람들과 나눠 먹음
others. He would offer them whatever he was given and they
would eat it together. This time was different. Without offering it to
anyone, (e) he finished the bunch of grapes by himself. One of the
          = the prince
friends asked, "Prince! How come you ate all the grapes by yourself
                              어째서
and did not offer them to any one of us?" He smiled and said that
22번 단서4, 24번 단서 he ate all the grapes by himself because the grapes
          그는 포도가 너무 시어서 혼자 포도를 다 먹음
were too sour.

(B) ✪ **22번 단서5** If the prince **had offered** the grapes to them,
가정법 과거완료: If+주어+had p.p., 주어+조동사의 과거형+have p.p.(과거 사실의 반대를 가정)
/ they **might have made** funny faces and shown their distaste
왕자가 친구들에게 포도를 권했다면 그들은 얼굴을 찡그리고 불쾌감을 나타냈을 것임

for the grapes. That would have hurt the feelings of that poor man. He thought to himself that it would be better to eat all of them cheerfully and please (b) him. He did not want to hurt the
= the poor man
feelings of that poor man. Everyone around him was moved by his thoughtfulness.
be moved by: ~에 감명받다

해석

(A) 어느 날 한 가난한 남자가 포도 한 송이를 왕자에게 선물로 가져왔다. 그는 너무 가난해서 그 이상의 여유가 없었기 때문에 (a) 그를 위한 선물을 가져올 수 있어서 매우 흥분했다. 그는 왕자의 옆에 포도를 두고 "오, 왕자님, 저의 이 작은 선물을 부디 받아 주십시오."라고 말했다. 그가 자신의 작은 선물을 바쳤을 때 그의 얼굴은 행복으로 빛났다.

(C) 왕자는 그에게 정중하게 감사를 표했다. 그 남자가 기대하며 그를 바라보았을 때 왕자는 포도 한 알을 먹었다. 그러더니 (c) 그는 또 다른 하나를 먹었다. 천천히 왕자는 혼자서 포도 한 송이를 전부 먹었다. 그는 자신의 곁에 있는 어느 누구에게도 포도를 권하지 않았다. 그 포도를 (d) 그에게 가져온 남자는 매우 기뻐하며 떠났다. 왕자의 주변에 있던 그의 가까운 친구들은 매우 놀랐다.

(D) 평소에 왕자는 자신이 가지고 있는 것은 무엇이든 다른 사람들과 나누었다. 그는 그들에게 자신이 받은 것은 무엇이든 권하고 그들은 그것을 함께 먹곤 했다. 이번에는 달랐다. 아무에게도 그것을 권하지 않고 (e) 그는 포도 한 송이를 혼자 다 먹었다. 그 친구들 중 한 명이 "왕자님! 어째서 포도 한 송이를 혼자서 다 드시고 우리 중 그 누구에게도 그것을 권하지 않으셨습니까?"라고 물었다. 그는 미소를 지으며 그 포도가 너무 시어서 혼자서 포도를 전부 먹었다고 말했다.

(B) 만약 왕자가 그들에게 그 포도를 권했다면 그들은 우스꽝스러운 표정을 지으며 포도에 대한 불쾌감을 드러냈을 것이다. 그것은 그 가난한 남자의 기분을 상하게 했을 것이다. 그는 모든 포도를 기꺼이 먹고 (b) 그를 기쁘게 하는 것이 더 낫겠다고 속으로 생각했다. 그는 그 가난한 남자의 기분을 상하게 하고 싶지 않았다. 그의 주위에 있던 모든 사람들이 그의 사려 깊음에 감명을 받았다.

정답이 보이는 해설

22

(A)에서 한 가난한 남자가 왕자에게 선물로 포도를 가져왔다. 이어서 왕자가 포도 한 송이를 아무에게도 권하지 않고 혼자 다 먹었다는 내용의 (C)가 온 다음, 평소에 자신이 가진 것을 다른 사람들과 나누던 왕자에게 왜 혼자서 포도를 다 먹었는지 친구 중 한 명이 묻자 왕자가 포도가 너무 시어서 혼자 다 먹었다고 답하는 내용의 (D)가 온다. 마지막으로 왕자가 가난한 남자의 기분을 상하게 하고 싶지 않아서 한 행동이었다는 것을 알고 사람들이 감동을 받았다는 내용의 (B)가 와야 한다.

23

(a), (c), (d), (e)는 왕자를 가리키고, (b)는 가난한 남자를 가리키므로 정답은 ②이다.

24

(D)에서 왕자는 포도가 너무 시어서 혼자 다 먹었다고 말했으므로, ⑤가 왕자에 관한 내용과 다르다.

필수 어휘

afford ~할 여유가 있다   beam 빛나다   offer 권하다, 제공하다
expectantly 기대하며   sour (맛이) 신   distaste 불쾌감
cheerfully 기꺼이, 기분 좋게   please 기쁘게 하다   move 감동시키다
thoughtfulness 사려 깊음

25 정답 ④   **26** 정답 ②   **27** 정답 ④

202109 43~45번 정답률 71% / 51% / 73%

(A) A rich merchant lived alone in his house. ✪ Knowing [**that**
명사절(목적어)
분사구문(이유)
he was *the only person* (living in the house)], / he was always
└「주격 관계대명사+be동사」 생략

---

prepared / in case thieves came to his house. So, one day, when a
(~할) 경우에 대비해서
thief entered his home, he remained calm and cool. Although he was awake, the merchant pretended to be in a deep sleep. He lay in bed and watched the thief in action. **25번 단서1** The thief had brought
the thief   도둑이 새 흰색 천을 가져옴
a new white sheet with a (a) him to carry away the stolen goods.
= the new white sheet   운반해 가다
(D) **25번 단서2** He spread it out on the floor with the idea of
도둑이 바닥에 천을 펼침
putting all the stolen valuables into it, tying it, and carrying it away. While (e) he was busy gathering expensive-looking items from the
= the thief   be busy -ing: ~하느라 바쁘다
merchant's luxurious house, the merchant quickly got out of the
= the merchant
bed. **25번 단서3** Then he replaced the new white sheet with a similar
상인이 새 흰색 천을 비슷한 천으로 바꿔침
looking white sheet, which was much weaker and much cheaper than the thief's one.
= the new white sheet
(B) (b) He then lay down and pretended to be asleep. When the
= the merchant
thief had finished collecting as many valuables as he could, he hurriedly tied a knot in the white sheet which he thought was his.
매듭을 짓다
The merchant meanwhile ran out into the garden and yelled — "Thief! Thief!" with all the air in his lungs. The thief got nervous and quickly lifted the sheet. To (c) his surprise, **25번 단서4** the thin
= the thief
white sheet, filled with stolen goods, was torn apart.
훔친 물건이 가득한 얇은 흰색 천이 찢어짐
(C) **25번 단서5** All the stolen goods fell down on the floor
훔친 모든 물건이 바닥에 떨어짐
creating a very loud and unpleasant noise. Seeing many people run towards him, the thief had to give up on all of the stolen goods.
단념하다, 포기하다
27번 단서 Leaving the goods behind in the house, he ran away
도둑은 (훔친) 물건들을 집에 두고 서둘러 도망감
in a hurry saying under his breath: "This man is such a skillful merchant; he is a businessman to the core. He has not only managed to save his valuables but has also taken away (d) my new sheet. He
= the thief
has stolen from a thief!" As he said that to himself, he ran away
say to oneself: 혼잣말하다
from the house.

해석

(A) 한 부유한 상인이 자신의 집에 홀로 살았다. 그가 그 집에 사는 유일한 사람임을 알기에, 그는 집에 도둑이 드는 상황에 항상 대비했다. 그래서 어느 날, 도둑이 그의 집에 들어왔을 때, 그는 차분히 침착하게 행동했다. 상인은 깨어 있었지만 깊이 잠들어 있는 척했다. 그는 침대에 누워 도둑의 행동을 지켜봤다. 그 도둑은 훔친 물건을 운반해 가기 위해 새 흰색 천을 (a) 그와 함께 가져왔다.

(D) 그는 훔친 귀중품들은 모두 그것(천) 안에 넣어 묶어서 운반해 갈 생각으로 바닥에 그것을 펼쳤다. (e) 그가 상인의 호화로운 집에서 비싸 보이는 물건들을 모으느라 바쁜 동안, 상인은 재빨리 침대 밖으로 나왔다. 그리고 나서 그는 (도둑의) 새 흰색 천을 비슷하게 보이는 흰색 천으로 바꿔치기했는데, 그건 도둑의 것보다 훨씬 더 약하고 값이 더 저렴했다.

(B) 그리고 나서 (b) 그는 누워 자는 척했다. 도둑이 가능한 한 많은 귀중품을 모으는 것을 마쳤을 때, 그는 자신의 것이라 생각하는 흰색 천의 매듭을 서둘러 묶었다. 그동안에 상인은 정원으로 뛰어나가, 있는 힘껏 큰 소리로 "도둑이야! 도둑이야!"라고 외쳤다. 도둑은 초조해져서 그 천을 재빨리 들어 올렸다. (c) 그가 놀랍게도 훔친 물건으로 가득했던 얇고 흰 천은 찢어졌다.

(C) 훔친 모든 물건은 바닥에 떨어져 매우 크고 불쾌한 소음을 냈다. 많은 사람이 자신에게 달려드는 것을 본 도둑은 훔친 모든 물건을 포기해야만 했다. 그 집에 물건

을 남겨 두고, 그는 서둘러 도망치며 숨죽여 말했다. "이 남자는 능숙한 상인이다. 그는 뼛속까지 장사꾼이다. 그는 자신의 귀중품들을 지켜냈을 뿐만 아니라 (d) 나의 새로운 천도 가져갔다. 그는 도둑에게서 훔쳤다!" 그는 그렇게 혼잣말하면서 그 집에서 도망쳤다.

정답이 보이는 해설

25

(A)에서 혼자 사는 부유한 상인의 집에 도둑이 들었고, 도둑은 훔친 물건들을 옮기기 위해 새 흰색 천을 가져왔다는 내용이다. 이어서 도둑이 귀중품을 담기 위해 바닥에 가져온 천을 펼치고, 상인이 일어나 도둑 몰래 도둑의 천과 비슷한 얇은 천으로 바꿨다는 (D)가 온 다음, 도둑이 천이 바뀐 걸 모르고 매듭을 묶자 훔친 물건들로 가득한 얇은 천이 찢어졌다는 (B)로 이어져야 한다. 마지막으로 훔친 물건들이 모두 바닥에 떨어지고, 도둑이 자신의 새로운 천까지 뺏긴 채 아무것도 못 챙기고 도망가는 (C)가 와야 한다.

26

(a), (c), (d), (e)는 도둑을 가리키고, (b)는 상인을 가리키므로 정답은 ②이다.

27

(C)에서 도둑은 훔친 물건들을 남겨 두고(Leaving the goods behind in the house) 도망갔다고 했으므로 ④가 윗글의 내용과 다르다.

필수 어휘

merchant 상인 pretend ~인 척하다 goods 물건, 물품 valuable 귀중품
gather 모으다 luxurious 호화로운 replace 바꾸다, 교체하다 lift 들어 올리다
tear apart ~을 찢다 say under one's breath 숨죽이며 말하다
skillful 능숙한 core 속, 중심

---

28 정답 ② 29 정답 ② 30 정답 ⑤

202106 43~45번 정답률 71% / 48% / 72%

(A) When I was 17, I discovered a wonderful thing. My father and I were sitting on the floor of his study. We were organizing his old papers. Across the carpet I saw a fat paper clip. Its rust dusted the cover sheet of a report of some kind. I picked it up. **28번 단서1** I started to read. Then I started to cry.

(C) **28번 단서2** It was a speech he had written in 1920, in Tennessee. Then only 17 himself and graduating from high school, he had called for equality for African Americans. ✪ (b) I **marvelled**, (proud of him,) and / **wondered** [how, (in 1920, so young, so white, and in the deep South, / **where** the law still separated black from white,) / (c) he **had had** the courage (to deliver it)]. **28번 단서3** I asked him about it.

(B) **28번 단서4** "Daddy," I said, handing him the pages, "this speech — how did you ever get permission to give it? And weren't you scared?" "Well, honey," he said, "I didn't ask for permission. I just asked myself, 'What is the most important challenge facing my generation?' I knew immediately. Then (a) I asked myself, 'And if I weren't afraid, what would I say about it in this speech?'"

(D) **28번 단서5** "I wrote it. And I delivered it. **30번 단서** About half

---

way through I looked out to see the entire audience of teachers, students, and parents stand up — and walk out. Left alone on the stage, (d) I thought to myself, 'Well, I guess I need to be sure to do only two things with my life: keep thinking for myself, and not get killed.'" He handed the speech back to me, and smiled. "(e) You seem to have done both," I said.

해석

(A) 내가 17살이었을 때, 나는 놀라운 물건 하나를 발견했다. 아버지와 나는 그의 서재 바닥에 앉아 있었다. 우리는 그의 오래된 서류들을 정리하고 있었다. 나는 카펫 건너에 있는 두꺼운 종이 클립을 보았다. 그것의 녹이 일종의 보고서의 표지 겉장 부분을 더럽혔다. 나는 그것을 집어 들었다. 나는 읽기 시작했다. 그러고 나서 나는 울기 시작했다.

(C) 그것은 아버지가 Tennessee 주에서 1920년에 썼던 연설문이었다. 당시 (아버지는) 겨우 17살에 고등학교를 졸업했을 때인데, 그는 아프리카계 미국인들을 위한 평등을 요구했다. 그를 자랑스럽게 여기면서 (b) 나는 놀라워했고 1920년에 법으로 흑인과 백인을 여전히 분리시켰던 최남부 지역에서, 그렇게 어리고 백인이었던 (c) 그가 어떻게 그것(연설)을 할 용기가 있었는지 궁금했다. 나는 그에게 그것에 대해 물었다.

(B) "아빠," 나는 그에게 연설문을 넘겨주며 말했다. "이 연설문이요, 어떻게 그것(연설)을 할 허락을 받았어요? 그리고 두렵지 않았어요?" "음, 얘야" 그가 말했다. "나는 허락을 구하지 않았어. 나는 그저 나 자신에게 물었어. '우리 세대가 직면한 가장 중요한 도전 과제는 무엇인가?' 나는 바로 알았지. 그러고 나서 (a) 나는 스스로에게 물었어. '내가 두려워하지 않는다면, 내가 이 연설에서 그것에 대해 무엇을 말할까?'"

(D) "나는 그것(연설문)을 썼어. 그리고 연설을 했지. 나는 (연설) 중간쯤 교사, 학생, 학부모인 전체 청중이 일어나서 나가 버리는 것을 바라보았어. 무대에 홀로 남아서 (d) 나는 마음속으로 생각했어, '그럼, 내 인생에서 두 가지만 확실히 하면 되겠어. 계속 스스로를 생각할 것과 죽임을 당하지 않는 것.'" 그는 연설문을 내게 돌려주며 미소 지었다. "(e) 아빠는 그 두 가지를 모두 해낸 것 같아요."라고 나는 말했다.

정답이 보이는 해설

28

(A)에서 17살의 필자와 그의 아버지가 함께 서류 정리를 하다가 필자가 발견한 보고서 같은 것을 읽기 시작한다. 읽고 있는 그것이 아버지가 쓴 연설문임을 알게 되는 (C)가 오고, 아버지가 한 연설에 대해 궁금한 필자가 그것에 대해 질문하는 (B)로 이어진 후, 아버지가 평등을 요구하는 연설에서 무엇을 말할지 고민하고 연설문을 썼다는 (D)가 마지막으로 와야 한다.

29

(a), (c), (d), (e)는 필자의 아버지를 가리키고, (b)는 필자를 가리키므로 정답은 ②이다.

30

(D)의 앞부분에 연설 중간쯤 청중이 일어나 나가 버리는(stand up — and walk out) 것을 보았으므로 ⑤가 윗글의 내용과 다르다.

필수 어휘

organize 정리하다 paper clip 종이 클립[집게] rust 녹; 녹슬다
dust 먼지투성이로 만들다 equality 평등, 균등 marvel 놀라다, 경탄하다
separate 분리하다, 나누다 deliver (연설을) 하다 hand 건네주다
permission 허락, 허가 scared 겁먹은, 무서워하는 face 직면하다, 마주보다
generation 세대, (비슷한 연령의) 사람들 immediately 즉시

---

31 정답 ② 32 정답 ⑤ 33 정답 ②

202103 43~45번 정답률 83% / 82% / 80%

(A) Once upon a time, there lived a young king who had a great passion for hunting. His kingdom was located at the foot of the

Himalayas. Once every year, he would go hunting in the nearby

forests. 【31번 단서1】 (a) He would make all the necessary preparations,
　　　　　　┌─ = the king
　　　　　왕은 준비를 마치고 사냥을 떠나곤 했음
and then set out for his hunting trip.
　　　　　출발하다, (여행을) 시작하다
　　(C) Like all other years, the hunting season had arrived.

【31번 단서2】 Preparations began in the palace and the king got ready
= the king's　　(사냥) 준비를 궁에서 시작하고 사냥 여행을 시작함　　　~을 준비시키다
for (c) his hunting trip. Deep in the forest, he spotted a beautiful

wild deer. It was a large stag. His aim was perfect. When he killed

the deer with just one shot of his arrow, the king was filled with
　　　　　　　　　　　　　　　　　　　　　　　　　　　　　　~로 가득하다
pride. (d) The proud hunter ordered a hunting drum to be made out
　　　　　　　　= the king
of the skin of the deer.

　　(B) 【31번 단서3】 Seasons changed. A year passed by. And it was
　　　　　　계절이 바뀌고 1년이 지나 다시 사냥을 하러 갈 시기가 옴
time to go hunting once again. The king went to the same forest as

the previous year. (b) He used his beautiful deerskin drum to round
　　　　　　　　　= the king
up animals. But none came. All the animals ran for safety, except
　　　　　　　┌─ = the doe
one doe. 【33번 단서】 She came closer and closer to the drummer.
　　　　= the doe ┘　　암사슴이 북 치는 사람에게 가까이 옴
【31번 단서4】 Suddenly, she started fearlessly licking the deerskin drum.
　　　　　　갑자기 암사슴이 사슴 가죽 북을 핥기 시작함
　　(D) 【31번 단서5】 The king was surprised by this sight. An old servant
　　　　　　　　　왕이 이 광경에 놀람
had an answer to this strange behavior. ❂ "The deerskin (used to
　　　　　　　　　　　　　　　　　　　　　　　　　　　　　　과거분사구
make this drum) belonged to her mate, / the deer [who we hunted
　　　　　　　　　　　　　　　　동격의 콤마(her mate = the deer ~)
last year]. This doe is mourning the death of her mate," (e) the man
　　　　　　　　　　　　　　　　　　　　　　　　　　　　　　= the old servant
said. Upon hearing this, the king had a change of heart. He had
　　upon -ing: ~하자마자
never realized that an animal, too, felt the pain of loss. He made a

promise, from that day on, to never again hunt wild animals.

【해석】

(A) 옛날 옛적에 사냥에 대해 엄청난 열정을 가진 젊은 왕이 살았다. 그의 왕국은 히
말라야산맥의 기슭에 위치했다. 해마다 한 번씩 그는 근처의 숲으로 사냥을 하러 가
곤 했다. (a) 그는 필요한 모든 준비를 한 다음 자신의 사냥 여행을 떠나곤 했다.
(C) 다른 모든 해와 같이, 사냥철이 왔다. 궁에서 (사냥 떠날) 준비가 시작되었고 왕
은 (c) 그의 사냥 여행을 준비했다. 숲속 깊은 곳에서, 그는 한 마리의 아름다운 야생
사슴을 발견했다. 그것은 커다란 수사슴이었다. 그의 조준은 완벽했다. 단지 자신의
화살 한 발만으로 그 사슴을 잡았을 때 그 왕은 의기양양했다. (d) 그 의기양양한 사
냥꾼은 그 사슴의 가죽으로 사냥용 북을 만들라고 명령했다.
(B) 계절이 바뀌었다. 1년이 지났다. 그리고 또다시 사냥을 하러 갈 때가 되었다.
왕은 작년과 같은 숲으로 갔다. (b) 그는 동물을 몰기 위해 아름다운 사슴 가죽으로
만든 북을 사용했다. 그러나 아무것도 오지 않았다. 모든 동물이 안전한 곳으로 달아
났는데, 한 마리 암사슴은 예외였다. 그녀(암사슴)는 북을 치는 사람에게 점점 더 가
까이 다가왔다. 갑자기, 암사슴은 두려움 없이 사슴 가죽의 북을 핥기 시작했다.
(D) 왕은 이 광경에 놀랐다. 한 나이 든 신하가 이 이상한 행동의 이유를 알았다. "이
북을 만드는 데 사용된 사슴 가죽은 그녀(암사슴)의 짝, 우리가 작년에 사냥한 그 사
슴입니다. 이 암사슴은 짝의 죽음을 애도하고 있습니다."라고 (e) 그 남자가 말했다.
이 말을 듣자마자, 왕은 마음이 바뀌었다. 그는 동물도 상실의 고통을 느낀다는 것을
전혀 몰랐다. 그는 그날 이후로 다시는 절대로 야생 동물을 사냥하지 않겠다고 약속
했다.

【정답이 보이는 해설】

31

(A)에서 해마다 숲으로 사냥을 가는 왕이 모든 필요한 준비를 한 뒤 사냥 여행을 떠
난다. 이어서 사냥 시즌이 와서 떠난 왕이 숲에서 수사슴 한 마리를 화살로 죽여 그
가죽으로 사냥용 북을 만들었다는 (C)가 오고, 1년 뒤에 왕이 사냥을 또 나갔는데,

암사슴 한 마리가 북 치는 사람에게 다가와 사슴 가죽으로 만든 북을 핥기 시작했다
는 (B)가 오고, 이 광경에 대해 나이 든 신하가 작년에 사냥한 수사슴의 짝이 암사슴
이라고 알려 주자 왕이 마음을 바꿔 야생 동물을 사냥하지 않겠다고 약속하는 (D)가
마지막으로 와야 한다.

32

(a), (b), (c), (d)는 왕을 가리키고, (e)는 나이 든 신하를 가리키므로 정답은 ⑤이다.

33

(B)의 뒷부분에 암사슴이 북 치는 사람에게 더 가까이 다가와 북을 핥았다고 했으므
로 ②가 윗글의 내용과 다르다.

【필수 어휘】

passion 열정　kingdom 왕국　locate 위치시키다　foot ~의 맨 아래 부분
nearby 인근의, 가까운 곳의　preparation 준비　spot 발견하다
pass by 지나가다　deerskin 사슴 가죽　fearlessly 두려움 없이　lick 핥다
servant 부하, 하인　loss 상실, 죽음

---

34 정답 ②　**35** 정답 ②　**36** 정답 ④

┌─────────────────────────────┐
│ 2020.11 43~45번 정답률 78% / 77% / 82% │
└─────────────────────────────┘

　　(A) James Walker was a renowned wrestler and he made his
　　　　　　　　　　　　　　　　　　　　　　　make one's living: 생계를 유지하다
living through wrestling. In his town, there was a tradition in which

the leader of the town chose a day when James demonstrated his

skills. ❂ The leader announced (one day) / [that James would
　　　　　　　　　동사1　　　　　　　목적어(명사절)
exhibit his skills as a wrestler] // and 【34번 단서1】 asked the people / [if
┌─ 직접목적어(명사절)　　　= James Walker　　　　　동사2　 간접목적어
there was anyone (to challenge (a) him for the prize money)].
지도자가 사람들에게 상금을 위해 James에게 도전할지 물음
　　(C) Everyone was looking around in the crowd 【34번 단서2】 when

an old man stood up and said with a shaking voice, "I will
한 노인이 (레슬링) 시합에 참여하겠다고 함
enter the contest against (c) him." Everyone burst out laughing
　　　　　　　　　　= James Walker　　burst out -ing: 갑자기 ~하기 시작하다
thinking that it was a joke. James would crush him in a minute.

【36번 단서】 According to the law, the leader could not stop someone
　　　　　원칙에 따라 지도자는 자발적으로 시합에 참여하는 사람을 막을 수 없었음
who of his own free will entered the competition, so he allowed the
　　　of one's own free will: 자발적으로
old man to challenge the wrestler.

　　(B) 【34번 단서3】 When James saw the old man, he was speechless.
　　　　　　　　James는 그 노인을 보고 말문이 막힘
Like everyone else, he thought that the old man had a death wish.

The old man asked James to come closer since (b) he wanted to say
　　　　　　　　　　　　　　　　　　　　　　　　= the old man
something to him. James moved closer and the old man whispered, "I
　　　　　　= James Walker
know it is impossible for me to win but my children are starving at

home. 【34번 단서4】 Can you lose this competition to me so I can feed
　　　　　　James는 배고픈 아이들을 먹을 수 있게 시합에 져 줄 수 있는지 물음
them with the prize money?"

　　(D) 【34번 단서5】 James thought he had an excellent opportunity to
　　　　　　　어려운 사람을 도울 기회라고 생각함
help a man in distress. (d) He did a couple of moves so that no one
　　　　　곤경에 처한　　= James Walker　　　~하기 위해서
would suspect that the competition was fixed. However, he did not

use his full strength and allowed the old man to win. The old man

was overjoyed when he received the prize money. That night James

felt the most victorious (e) he had ever felt.
　　　　　　　　　　　　= James Walker

(A) James Walker는 유명한 레슬링 선수였고 그는 레슬링으로 생계를 유지했다. 그의 마을에는 마을의 지도자가 하루를 정해 James가 자신의 기술을 보여 주는 전통이 있었다. 지도자는 어느 날 James가 레슬링 선수로서 자신의 기술을 보여 줄 것임을 알렸고, 사람들에게 상금을 위해 (a) 그에게 도전할 사람이 있는지 물었다.

(C) 한 노인이 일어나서 떨리는 목소리로 "내가 (c) 그에게 도전하여 시합에 참가하겠소."라고 말하자, 모두가 군중 속에서 주위를 둘러보았다. 모두가 그것이 농담이라고 생각하며 웃음을 터뜨리기 시작했다. James가 그를 즉시 쓰러뜨릴 것이었다. 원칙에 따라 지도자는 자신의 자유 의지로 경기에 참여한 사람을 막을 수가 없어서, 그 노인이 그 레슬링 선수에게 도전하는 것을 허용했다.

(B) James가 그 노인을 봤을 때, 그는 말문이 막혔다. 다른 모든 사람처럼, 그는 그 노인이 죽기를 바란다고 생각했다. (b) 그 노인은 자신이 그에게 말하고 싶은 것이 있으니 James에게 더 가까이 와 줄 것을 청했다. James가 더 가까이 움직였고 그 노인은 속삭였다. "내가 이기는 게 불가능하다는 것을 알지만, 내 아이들이 집에서 굶고 있어요. 내가 상금으로 그들(아이들)에게 밥을 먹일 수 있게 나에게 이 시합을 져 줄 수 있겠소?"

(D) James는 자신이 곤경에 처한 사람을 도울 아주 좋은 기회를 얻었다고 생각했다. (d) 그는 아무도 그 시합이 조작되었다고 의심하지 않도록 몇 가지 동작을 했다. 하지만 그는 전력을 다하지 않았고 그 노인이 이기도록 했다. 그 노인은 상금을 받고 매우 기뻐했다. 그날 밤 James는 (e) 자신이 지금껏 느껴 본 적 없는 가장 큰 승리감을 느꼈다.

34

(A)에서 마을 지도자가 상금을 위해 레슬링 선수인 James Walker에게 도전할 사람이 있는지를 묻는다. 이어 (C)에서 시합에 참가하겠다고 한 노인이 James에게 상금으로 아이들 밥을 먹일 수 있도록 시합에 져 달라고 요청하는 (B)가 오고, 곤경에 처한 노인을 돕기 위해 James가 시합에 지고 지금껏 느껴 본 적 없는 큰 승리감을 느끼는 (D)가 마지막에 온다.

35

(a), (c), (d), (e)는 James Walker를 가리키고, (b)는 노인을 가리키므로 정답은 ②이다.

36

(C)의 뒷부분에서 원칙에 따라 지도자는 자발적으로 시합에 참가하는 사람을 막을 수 없었다고 했으므로 ④가 윗글의 내용과 다르다.

renowned 유명한 tradition 전통 demonstrate 보여 주다, 설명하다
exhibit 전시하다, 보이다 speechless 말을 못하는
death wish 죽음에 대한 동경 whisper 속삭이다 starve 굶주리다
distress 고통, 괴로움 suspect 의심하다 victorious 승리한

기출의
바이블

Bible of English

기출의 바이블
고1 영어

2권 | 정답 및 해설

특별부록	1권	2권
기출 EXTRACT	◆ **Part 1** 듣기편 ◆ **Part 2** 독해편	**정답 및 해설**

	Part 1 · 최신 3개년 전국연합 학력평가 듣기 모의고사 12회 수록 · 전 회차 Dictation 제공	
· 기출 독해 어휘 리스트 · 기출 문법 드릴 문항 제공	Part 2 · 최신 연도순 유형별 20강 수록 · 오답률 BEST 문항 표기	· 정답 근거, 핵심 문장, 주제문 표시 · 구문 분석과 중요 숙어 표현 표시 · 선택지 완벽 분석과 자세한 해설 · 필수 어휘 정리

가르치기 쉽고 빠르게 배울 수 있는 **이투스북**

www.etoosbook.com

○ **도서 내용 문의**
홈페이지 > 이투스북 고객센터 > 1:1 문의

○ **도서 정답 및 해설**
홈페이지 > 도서자료실 > 정답/해설

○ **도서 정오표**
홈페이지 > 도서자료실 > 정오표

○ **선생님을 위한 강의 지원 서비스 T폴더**
홈페이지 > 교강사 T폴더